W T H D R A W N

W9-ABZ-531

WITHDRAWN

The Causes of Behavior

READINGS IN CHILD DEVELOPMENT
AND EDUCATIONAL PSYCHOLOGY

THIRD EDITION

The Causes of Behavior

READINGS IN CHILD DEVELOPMENT AND EDUCATIONAL PSYCHOLOGY

Edited by

JUDY F. ROSENBLITH, *Professor of Psychology, Wheaton College, and Member, Institute of Life Sciences, Brown University*

WESLEY ALLINSMITH, *Professor of Psychology, University of Cincinnati*

JOANNA P. WILLIAMS, *Associate Professor, Graduate School of Education, University of Pennsylvania*

ALLYN AND BACON, INC., BOSTON

To Sandra, Ronald, Justin, Bryan, Wendy, and Craig

A Note on the Cover Design

Visual acuity of infants was tested with one row of such stripes: $\frac{1}{8}$, $\frac{1}{16}$, $\frac{1}{32}$, and $\frac{1}{64}$ inch wide. Each pattern was displayed with a gray square of equal brightness, placed 10 inches from the infant's eyes. It had been established that infants preferred patterns to solid colors; so, in this test, the finest stripe pattern consistently preferred to gray showed how narrow a stripe the infant could perceive. Infants under a month old responded to the $\frac{1}{8}$-inch stripes and infants six months old to the $\frac{1}{64}$-inch stripes.

From Robert L. Fantz, The origin of form perception, Scientific American, 1961, 204 (5), 66–72 and 204; copyright © 1961 by Scientific American, Inc., all rights reserved; reprinted with abridgement by permission in the first edition of Causes of Behavior.

CONTENTS

    HAVIOR   243

    36. The Effect of Psychological Environment on Childbirth:
        Combined Cross-Cultural and Experimental Approach   244
        Niles Newton

    37. Perceptual Articulation and Task Effectiveness in Several
        Israel Subcultures   248
        Ilana Preale, Yehuda Amir, and Shlomo Sharan (Singer)

    38. A Comparative Analysis of Fantasy Need Achievement
        among High and Low Achieving Male Hawaiian-Americans   253
        *Barbara B. Sloggett, Ronald Gallimore, and Edward S.
        Kubany*

    39. Interpersonal Spacing in Natural Settings   259
        James C. Baxter

    40. Social Class Differences in Some Aspects of the Nonverbal
        Communication between Mother and Preschool Child   266
        Terry Hore

    41. Race, Class, Family, and School Achievement   271
        Steven R. Tulkin

    42. Chaotic Reinforcement: A Socioeconomic Leveler   277
        Jean L. Bresnahan and William L. Blum

    43. A Note on the Relation of Reading Failure to Peer-Group
        Status in Urban Ghettos   280
        William Labov and Clarence Robins

VII. AGE OR DEVELOPMENTAL STAGE AS A DETERMI-
     NANT OF BEHAVIOR   287

    44. A Healthy Personality for Every Child   289
        *White House Conference on Children and Youth, 1951
        (Adapted from the writings of Erik H. Erikson)*

    45. Competence and the Psychosexual Stages of Development   300
        Robert W. White

    46. Learning Capacities of the Human Infant   308
        Lewis P. Lipsitt

    47. Adolescence   317
        Anna Freud

    48. Crises in Normal Personality Development   324
        Gordon W. Allport

    49. Jean Piaget and the World of the Child   329
        Read D. Tuddenham

CROSS-REFERENCE CHART

Section	See Also	Consult in the Index
I. GENERAL INTRODUCTION (Articles 1–6)	III. 13 VII. 45 VII. 48 XI. 73 XI. 78	Attention Behaviorism Continuity Man Naturalism Psychology Relevance Self
II. BIOLOGICAL BASES FOR BEHAVIOR (Articles 7–12)	III. 13 IV. 24 VI. 41 VII. 46 VIII. 52	Animals (Baboons, Birds, Dogs, Monkeys) Constitutional factors Environment Genetics Heredity Heritability Imprinting
III. LEARNING AS A DETERMINANT OF BEHAVIOR (Articles 13–18)	II. 12 IV. 19 IV. 25 IV. 26 IV. 27 V. 31 VI. 41 VI. 42 VI. 43 VII. 46	Aggression Anxiety Drives Dyadic sequences Personality Punishment Reinforcement Reward
IV. INTERPERSONAL EXPERIENCES AS DETERMINANTS OF BEHAVIOR (Articles 19–29)	II. 11 III. 16 III. 18 VI. 37 VI. 39 VI. 40 VI. 43 VII. 47 VII. 48 VIII. 52	Aggression Authority Father Identification Imitation Models Mother Parents Peers Permissiveness Socialization
V. SETTINGS AND SPECIFIC STIMULI AS DETERMINANTS OF BEHAVIOR (Articles 30–35)	III. 14 IV. 27 VI. 43 VII. 48 X. 69 X. 72 XI. 78 XII. 81	Achievement motivation Classroom Conformity Role Social influence, social learning, social power Street groups Teachers
VI. GROUP MEMBERSHIPS AS DETERMINANTS OF BEHAVIOR (Articles 36–43)	I. 6 III. 18 IV. 26 V. 33 V. 34 VIII. 50 VIII. 51 VIII. 53 VIII. 56 IX. 62 XII. 81	Communication Culture Disadvantaged children Peer groups Race Social class Socioeconomic status (SES)

Section	See Also	Consult in the Index
VII. AGE OR DEVELOPMENTAL STAGE AS A DETERMINANT OF BEHAVIOR (Articles 44–49)	II. 8 II. 9 III. 17 IV. 22 IV. 25 V. 32 VI. 39 VIII. 51 IX. 57 XI. 59 XI. 60 XI. 64	Adolescence Biological bases Competence Crises Critical periods Infants Motivation Neonates Psychosexual stages Regression Stability
VIII. SEX AS A DETERMINANT OF BEHAVIOR (Articles 50–56)	II. 8 III. 17 IV. 22 IV. 23 IV. 26 IV. 27 IV. 29 V. 31 VI. 39 VI. 41 VII. 48 IX. 58 IX. 63 XII. 82	Sex Sex differences Sex role Socialization
IX. INTELLIGENCE AS A DETERMINANT OF BEHAVIOR (Articles 57–66)	IV. 22 VI. 43 VII. 49	Geniuses Gifted children Intelligence Intelligence quotient (IQ) Testing Tests
X. MOTIVATIONAL RESULTANTS (Articles 67–72)	VII. 45 VIII. 54 VIII. 55	Achievement Anxiety Apathy Compulsivity Daydreams Defenses Delay Generosity
XI. EDUCATIONAL IMPLICATIONS (Articles 73–80)	V. 33 V. 34 V. 35 VI. 43 VIII. 54 VIII. 55 IX. 58 IX. 61 X. 69 X. 70	Discrimination Fear Motivation Organizers Passivity Reading Schools Teaching machines Testing Textbooks
XII. TEACHERS AND TEACHING (Articles 81–85)	III. 14 III. 15 V. 34 VIII. 55 X. 69 X. 70	Attitudes Classroom Disadvantaged children Education Schools Teacher Teaching

PREFACE

A number of universities and colleges offer courses that combine educational psychology with child and adolescent psychology or human development. The selections in this book were assembled as a result of the editors' experience in teaching such combined courses. A new editor (J. P. W.) was added for this edition in order to strengthen the offerings in educational psychology.

Many of the articles in this volume are also available in our two smaller Allyn and Bacon volumes *(Readings in Child Development: The Causes of Behavior* and *Readings in Educational Psychology: The Causes of Behavior),* intended for courses that focus on only one of the topics. The smaller books contain supplementary articles in addition to the ones reprinted from this main volume.

Each of the three books is organized as follows. The "Orientation to the Book" explains the organization and gives information to help a reader interpret statistics used in some of the articles. Section I, an introductory section, presents a group of selections that conveys the range of outlooks in the field. Sections II through X each deal with one of the explanations of behavior that have been emphasized by important theorists or schools of thought about developmental psychology or human behavior. Articles applicable to educational issues—matters that no student of child development can afford to ignore—are often presented within the framework of one of these broad avenues to the understanding of behavior. Some of these themes are more basic or inclusive than others. A theme that may be derivative of others is assigned a section of its own when the factor it emphasizes is an important determinant of behavior, either in theory or practice. Complexly interwoven behaviors are discussed primarily in Sections IX and X. The emphasis of this book is on various approaches to understanding the behavior of children rather than educational psychology in any narrow sense. The final sections of the book (XI and XII), as well as a number of articles in the earlier sections, deal with research and problems that have specific educational implications.

A book such as this, organized around several explanations of human behavior, is obviously relevant to much of psychology. Its emphases on the development of behavior and on behaviors relevant to the educator make it particularly appropriate for students in developmental psychology, educational psychology, or the combined type of course referred to in the first paragraph.

Our experience indicates that most reading assignments provoke a considerable variety of reactions. The article that some students consider the most valuable of all is one that other students rate as having limited merit. As a result of the diversity of opinion, we recognize that not all students (or all teachers) will necessarily be pleased by every article included. We have attempted to offer a collection that changes pace frequently, ranging widely in topics covered, in techniques of investigation used, in levels of difficulty, and in the views espoused by the authors. In order to show the variety of existing methods and to convey some of the information that exists in areas not yet subjected to precise research, we have included work of investigators who, in opening up new areas of study, have used approaches that lack scientific rigor.

In general, we believe that articles in a collection of readings should be reproduced in their entirety. Nevertheless, we have had to abridge some selections. In certain cases we did this almost entirely to save space, but without sacrificing the crucial points. In other cases we considered portions of a selection too difficult for a typical student to follow. In all instances the author's agreement has been obtained. We have also taken care to indicate all deletions so that the interested student or teacher can check the original source. Congruent with our interest in completeness of content, we have usually included the original references and footnotes (our own footnotes are indicated by "Editor"). The inclusion of references is especially important for those students who are preparing a paper or planning and conducting a study.

When introducing articles we have tried to specify the authors' affiliations to show readers where active research in educational and child psychology is being conducted. We expect that students contemplating graduate study, particularly, will want to know the location of people with whom they might like to work. Readers are also enabled to write an author for details of a study or reports of further investigations.

We wish to express our gratitude to the authors and publishers who have allowed us to use their material in this book. They are credited in footnotes at the beginning of each selection.

We are indebted to Wheaton College and the University of Cincinnati for leaves of absence and support in preparation of the manuscript. We are also grateful to the University of Pennsylvania for aid in preparing the manuscript and obtaining the necessary permissions. Rebecca Anderson Huntington of the Institute of Life Sciences, Brown University, gave sage advice, editorial assistance, and help in assembling the manuscript.

The hundreds of students who have given us the benefit of their reactions often made useful suggestions that went beyond standard questionnaire responses. We acknowledge their generosity, as well as that of many colleagues who have commented on the second edition's merits and lacks. For willing and able assistance we thank Ruth Church of Wheaton College; Christine Bebel, Irving Sears, Cheryl Sopko, and Carol Weiss of the University of Pennsylvania; and Wendy Allinsmith.

Judy F. Rosenblith
Wesley Allinsmith
Joanna P. Williams

PSYCHOLOGY AND THE TEACHER

. . . you make a great, a very great mistake, if you think that psychology, being the science of the mind's laws, is something from which you can deduce definite programs and schemes and methods of instruction for immediate schoolroom use. Psychology is a science, and teaching is an art; and sciences never generate arts directly out of themselves. An intermediary inventive mind must make the application, by using its originality.

The science of logic never made a man reason rightly, and the science of ethics (if there is such a thing) . . . never made a man behave rightly. The most such sciences can do is to help us catch ourselves up and check ourselves more articulately after we have made mistakes. . . .

And so everywhere the teaching must *agree* with the psychology, but need not necessarily be the only kind of teaching that would so agree; for many diverse methods of teaching may equally well agree with psychological laws. . . .

But, if the use of psychological principles thus be negative rather than positive, it does not follow that it may not be a great use, all the same. It certainly narrows the path for experiments and trials. We know in advance, if we are psychologists, that certain methods will be wrong so our psychology saves us from mistakes. It makes us, moreover, more clear as to what we are about.

From William James, *Talks to Teachers on Psychology* (New York: Holt, Rinehart, and Winston Inc., 1920, first published in 1899), pp. 7–11. Reprinted by permission.

[We are grateful to Professor Gordon Hendrickson of the University of Cincinnati for calling this passage to our attention. In our observation, where the word "teacher" is used, one could substitute "parent," and for "teaching," "child-rearing."—EDITOR.]

ORIENTATION TO THE BOOK

In describing the purposes of a pioneering investigation in which a number of factors relevant to the prediction of children's actions were taken simultaneously into account, John W. M. Whiting of Harvard University wrote:

> Various positions have been taken as to the major determinants of a child's behavior. Gesell and Piaget, taking a developmental point of view, say the most important thing to know in order to predict a child's behavior is how old he is; Freud and his followers would insist that the most important determinant of a child's behavior is his life history, especially his relationship with his father and mother; the learning theorists would insist that a knowledge of previous rewards and punishments for the particular behavior in question is what is needed. The Gestalt school, as exemplified by Lewin, Baldwin, and Barker and Wright, would take an ahistorical approach and insist that a knowledge of the situation, that is, the setting and instigation, is the thing to have; and, of course, the anthropologists would insist that if you don't know what society the child is a member of, you can't predict a thing.[1]

Whiting goes on to cite one more factor as possibly having some weight, namely, whether the child is a male or a female. He concludes, "We suspect there is a grain of truth in each of these positions."

We believe that Whiting has put his finger on a key characteristic of the social and behavioral sciences today. Because the determinants of behavior are multiple, *each* theoretical view is more or less "true." Full understanding and precise prediction must wait until we have the formula that can assign a suitable weight to each of the factors. Nevertheless, prior to such a Utopian state of affairs, we can increase our understanding of behavior by studying each of its possible determinants. We have accordingly organized this book into parts, most of which deal with a class of determinant.

We realize that our selection of classes of determinants is not the only selection possible. Also, the classes to which we assign a label, and thus a section, are not mutually exclusive or nonoverlapping. We recognize, furthermore, that some factors to which we have assigned a role as primary determinants are themselves a resultant of other determinants. An example is *intelligence* (an aspect of cognition, Section IX), which may be conceived of as a consequence both of biological factors and of learning experiences. However, intelligence plays an important role in educational psychology and in psychology generally; it is frequently viewed as a determinant and used as an independent variable in research studies. Hence, we have chosen to present it in that context.

In addition to discussing the purpose of every section at its outset, we have written editors' comments to precede each of the articles. If an article's open-

---

[1] These statements are from a paper entitled "The Observation of Children's Behavior—A Cross-Cultural Approach," given by Dr. Whiting at the December 1958 Meeting of the American Association for the Advancement of Science.

ing statement or summary does not say all that we think might be of help to students, we give our description or interpretation of the material to be covered.
We also call attention to overlap with other articles or sections. Additional
readings are listed in the cross-reference chart at the beginning of the book.
They will be of interest to students who lack an adequate background for the topic
under discussion or who may wish to pursue the topic in greater depth.

How to Read Statistics

A number of the articles in this book present numerical findings from psychological research. The reader who has never delved into the research literature
of psychology or education may need some help in reading these data papers.
The data in such articles are accompanied by statistical statements. In this section we present some information about statistical statements that should help
you read and understand the articles even if you do not know statistics.[2]

The statistical tests most frequently used in these articles deal with the question
of what probability exists that random error, or chance,[3] could have led to findings or relationships of the magnitude obtained. Such probability statements
are pivotal concepts in statistics. The lower the probability of obtaining a result
through random error, the more confidence one can have in the finding. For example, an experimental outcome with a probability (p) of $<.05$ (less than five
in a hundred) would have occurred by chance less than one time in twenty. If
the experiment were run a hundred times, results as extreme as those found
would, on the average, occur less than five times out of the hundred if there were
no systematic relation between the variables. To put it another way, even if there
were no relation between the variables, findings with a p of .05 would still occur,
on the average, five times out of a hundred just because of chance.

In psychological and educational research, when a finding is described as
"statistically significant" the author usually means "the probability that the
result is due to chance is .05 or 'better.'" A "better" probability is a lower one;
that is, one which indicates less likelihood of the results having occurred by
chance. Better p's would be .02, .01, or .001, which means that such a result
would be obtained by chance only two times in a hundred, one time in a hundred,
or one time in one thousand.

In psychological writings, the remark that a result is "significant" does not
mean that it is "meaningful" or "important," but that it is *statistically* significant.
Of course, $p = .06$ and $p = .07$ are not much different in probability from $p = .05$.
One can place almost as much confidence in them. Yet, by convention, the term

---

[2] It may help to call attention to the most basic abbreviations used. S is an abbreviation for research subject, Ss for subjects (plural); N is for the number of subjects (N=23 or N23 means there
were 23 subjects or Ss); p stands for probability level; $<$ means less than and $>$ more than; $\overline{X}$ stands
for the mean or average; ANOVA (or sometimes ANVAR) stands for analysis of variance, a tech-
nique discussed below.

We assume that readers are familiar with purely descriptive statistics or that their instructors
will acquaint them with measures of central tendency (mean, median, mode), with measures of dis-
persion (range, standard deviation), and with the basic idea of correlation. The chapters on statistics
in many introductory texts constitute valuable sources for review. For a highly readable, non-math-
ematical account that may aid in better understanding of statistical reasoning, the student is referred
to the chapter on statistical thinking in Donald O. Hebb, *A Textbook of Psychology*, 2d ed. (Saunders,
1966), pp. 165–186.

[3] "Random error," or chance, is a factor in research results just as it is in other matters; if you
shuffle and deal four bridge or poker hands, you may find some rare, unlikely hands (e.g., a full house)
"just by chance." Or, to take one more example, if you flip an unbiased coin ten times, you can get
nine heads "just by chance." In the same way, the psychological experimenter may be "lucky" or
"unlucky." Statistics provide a means of assessing this luck factor.

"significant" is usually applied only to results that have a *p* value of .05 or less. Some authors give no actual probability figures when the *p* is greater than .05, merely labeling the results N.S. for "not significant." Others report probabilities such as .10 or .12 to indicate trends that might have reached a more acceptable "*p* level" if there had been more cases in the sample or if the results obtained had been a little more striking.

Two qualifications about "*p* values" should be understood by all students of psychology. (1) The fact that a result is significant does not rule out the possibility that it is due to chance, or random error. Out of one hundred findings based on the same experiment, five (on the average) might be significant at the .05 level or better even if only chance were operating. (2) The fact that a finding is "significant" does not, as we have said before, mean that it is important. If there were a difference between the average heights of redheads and blondes, and enough women of each coloring were measured, the difference might be statistically significant, that is, greater than is likely to be accounted for by random errors, even though the actual difference in average heights was only .1 inch. Needless to say, it would be futile under such circumstances to use the information that "redheads are taller than blondes" to predict the relative heights of a particular unknown redhead and blonde who are to be matched with a tall and a short man as blind dates.

The findings that are discussed in terms of their significance or probability level are of three major classes:

1. *Significance of Differences.* The differences may be of various types: (a) between two different performances by the same people (e.g., between history achievement and arithmetic achievement); (b) between two groups of people measured on the same performance or characteristic (e.g., heights of blondes and redheads, arithmetic performance of 6- and 8-year-olds); or (c) between the results of two experimental treatments (e.g., arithmetic performance of those taught by method A and those taught by method B).

2. *Relationship (and Degree of Relationship) Between Two Variables.* The second class of findings discussed in terms of significance levels or *p* values is concerned with the existence of a relationship between two variables. Such findings are frequently assessed by methods such as Chi-square (χ^2). The studies that assess the degree of relation between two variables use correlational techniques of which the Pearson product moment correlation (*r*) is used most frequently. Another way to assess degree of relationship is by use of Rho or rank order correlation. Findings assessing relations, like those examining differences, may be significant without indicating a close or important relationship. To illustrate, two indices or variables such as chronological age and score on a given test may correlate .20 with one another ($r = .20$). This may be a significant association ($p < .05$) if the sample on which the correlation was obtained was sufficiently large. However, the capacity to predict the test score from knowing the chronological age (or vice versa) is low indeed. The amount of variability in one factor that is controlled by the other is found by squaring the correlation coefficient (r^2). In the example just given where $r = .20$, $r^2 = .04$, or 4% of the variance. Thus, only 4% of the variability in test scores may be said to be determined by or covary with chronological age.

3. *Interaction among Variables.* In recent years increasing numbers of studies have looked at more than one variable in relation to the behavior being studied. (This trend reflects the growing maturity of our field and the greater ease of doing necessary computations in the computer age.) Therefore, more of the studies we reprint have these more complex statistical analyses. They can still be under-

stood by the student who lacks real statistical training if the basic principles of probability levels are kept in mind.

In such multivariate studies, one is, however, also concerned with "interactions." These are usually assessed by statistical procedures called analysis of variance, which take into account the fact that it often takes two conditions acting together to affect an organism's behavior. Neither condition alone may suffice. If, in a research study, sex of subject has an effect on the results, but only among middle class *S*s, then one says that social class and gender *interact*. For example, middle class girls may act differently from middle class boys and differently from lower class girls and boys. In this case one would say that social class affects behavior, but only among girls. In complex studies, the use of analysis of variance is necessary to establish whether variables are really interacting and which ones are. In addition, the technique yields probability statements about the effects of the main variables.

Let us look at some examples of research strategies and of appropriate and inappropriate conclusions that might be drawn from research findings. A child development researcher wants to determine what effects the age of weaning has on the development of conscience, or on some other characteristic assessed at a later age. There are two research strategies he might adopt. (1) He may look for differences in conscience (or whatever variable he is concerned with) between two (or more) groups that differ in the age at which they were weaned. He would categorize all of his subjects into two or more groups according to the age of weaning (early vs. late, or early, average, and late). He would then measure a later behavior (amount of guilt at age twelve, say) by some specified technique. Then he would compare the amount of guilt shown by his groups and determine whether the difference (or differences) is significant. (2) Instead of looking for differences between groups, he may look for the *degree of relationship* between the variable age of weaning and the variable amount of guilt. Age is, of course, almost automatically quantified. The data on guilt must also be expressed in quantitative form (scores, perhaps). Then the correlation between the two can be determined and the degree of relationship thus assessed. In case 1, the finding might be that there is a significant *difference* between a group weaned early and one weaned late. In case 2, a significant *degree of relationship* between age of weaning and amount of guilt may be found. The actual magnitude (or size) of the difference or relationship may be large or small. If small yet statistically significant, it may be of importance for psychological theory. In such an event, the author of the study should not be misinterpreted as having shown that guilt at age twelve (or whenever) is determined in any close or direct fashion by age of weaning taken by itself. Even if a strong degree of relationship were found between two such variables, it does not necessarily mean that one causes the other. Each might be the result of a third, unstudied factor. An example of a possible finding of this nature follows.

The number of pots and pans in home kitchens might prove to be correlated with the political preferences of the householders, with more utensils in the kitchens of Republicans. Such a finding should not be used to argue that Republicans are fonder of food, are more "oral" in their personality tendencies, or dislike eating in restaurants. It would probably be because, on the average, persons with more money have tended both to buy more pots and pans and to vote for the party with the more conservative monetary policies. Thus, the correlation of both Republicanism and possession of kitchen utensils with a third factor, income, would give rise to the finding. Republicanism per se would not be a cause of utensil purchases! (Or vice versa.)

In addition to calling attention to the fact that significant relationships may be so small as to be of more theoretical than practical importance, we must call attention to the many which are large or important enough to have great practical utility for group prediction, but which are nevertheless not very useful for individual prediction. During World War II, for example, millions of dollars were saved by using psychological tests to screen candidates for pilot training. Predictions of success were far more accurate than those that could be obtained by coin-flipping or other arbitrary procedures. As a group, the trainees chosen by this means were more likely to succeed. Nevertheless, a number of those who underwent training did not succeed. Conversely, there is evidence for believing that many of those rejected for training would have succeeded. In short, the tests were good for group prediction, but imperfect for individual prediction.[4] Readers of psychological literature who understand this distinction between group and individual prediction and who bear in mind the other qualifications cited about the meanings of statistical results will be able to avoid the most common misinterpretations of investigators' findings.

---

[4] For a good elementary discussion related to this point, see Brown and Gilhousen, *College Psychology* (Prentice-Hall, 1950), Chapter 18, "Measuring Individuals," pp. 459–477.

I

GENERAL INTRODUCTION

This section does not deal with a "cause of behavior" or any other specific topic. The articles span a wide variety of issues and viewpoints. We hope that they will serve as stimuli to thinking and give readers perspective on important issues in child and educational psychology. Such perspective should help in organizing students' thoughts so that they are less confused by the heterogeneity they will find in the rest of the book, in modern psychology, and in the behavioral sciences generally.

1

Psychology as a Means of Promoting Human Welfare [1]

GEORGE A. MILLER

As the opening article we present excerpts from George Miller's presidential address to the American Psychological Association. His ideas about the ways in which psychology will be of worth to mankind may be surprising. The speech might have been entitled "How to Give Psychology Away."

After many years at Harvard University as both student and professor, Miller moved to Rockefeller University in 1968. He is currently spending a period of leave at the Institute for Advanced Study in Princeton.

... In my opinion, scientific psychology is potentially one of the most revolutionary intellectual enterprises ever conceived by the mind of man. ...

One reason the psychological revolution is not more obvious may be that we have been looking for it in the wrong place. We have assumed that psychology should provide new technological options, and that a psychological revolution will not occur until someone in authority exercises those options to attain socially desirable goals. One reason for this assumption, perhaps, is that it follows the model we have inherited from previous applications of science to practical problems. An applied scientist is supposed to provide instrumentalities for modifying the environment— instrumentalities that can then, under public regulation, be used by wealthy and powerful interests to achieve certain goals. The psychological revolution, when it comes, may follow a very different course, at least in its initial stages.

. . .

I believe that the real impact of psychology will be felt, not through the technological products it places in the hands of powerful men, but through its effects on the public at large, through a new and different public conception of what is humanly possible and what is humanly desirable.

I believe that any broad and successful application of psychological knowledge to human problems will necessarily entail a change in our conception of ourselves and of how we live and love and work together. Instead of inventing some new technique for modifying the environment, or some new product for society to adapt itself to however it can, we are proposing to tamper with the adaptive process itself. Such an innovation is quite different from a "technological fix." I see little reason to believe that the traditional model for scientific revolutions should be appropriate.

Consider, for example, the effect that Freudian psychology has already had on Western society. It is obvious that its effects, though limited to certain segments of society, have been profound, yet I do not believe that one can argue that those effects were achieved by providing new instrumentalities for achieving goals socially agreed upon. As a method of therapy, psychoanalysis has had limited success even for those who can afford it. It has been more successful as a method of investigation, perhaps, but even there it has been only one of several available methods. The impact of Freud's thought has been due far less to the instrumentalities he provided than to the changed conception of ourselves that he inspired. The wider range of psychological problems that Freud opened up for professional psychologists is only part of his contribution. More important in the scale of history has been his effect on the broader intellectual community and, through it, on the public at

[1] [Excerpts from the] Presidential Address to the American Psychological Association in Washington, D.C., September 1969. It is customary on this occasion to summarize one's own research. Although that would be a more comfortable role, I have decided instead to take this opportunity to express some personal opinions about the current state of our discipline and its potential role in meeting the human problems of our society. This departure from tradition is intended to honor the theme of the 1969 Convention, "Psychology and the Problems of Society." I am indebted to several friends, and especially to J. A. Varela, for critical comments on earlier drafts.

George A. Miller, "Psychology as a means of promoting human welfare," *American Psychologist, 24,* 1969, 1036–1075. Copyright 1969 by the American Psychological Association, and reproduced with abridgement by permission.

large. Today we are much more aware of the irrational components of human nature and much better able to accept the reality of our unconscious impulses. The importance of Freudian psychology derives far less from its scientific validity than from the effects it has had on our shared image of man himself.

I realize that one might argue that changes in man's conception of himself under the impact of advances in scientific knowledge are neither novel nor revolutionary. For example, Darwin's theory changed our conception of ourselves, but not until the past decade has it been possible to mount a truly scientific revolution based on biological science. One might argue that we are now only at the Darwinian stage in psychology, and that the real psychological revolution is still a century or more in the future. I do not find this analogy appropriate, however.

To discover that we are not at the center of the universe, or that our remote ancestors lived in a tree, does indeed change our conception of man and society, but such new conceptions can have little effect on the way we behave in our daily affairs and in our institutional contexts. A new conception of man based on psychology, however, would have immediate implications for the most intimate details of our social and personal lives. This fact is unprecedented in any earlier stage of the Industrial Revolution.

The heart of the psychological revolution will be a new and scientifically based conception of man as an individual and as a social creature. When I say that the psychological revolution is already upon us, what I mean is that we have already begun to change man's self-conception. If we want to further that revolution, not only must we strengthen its scientific base, but we must also try to communicate it to our students and to the public. It is not the industrialist or the politician who should exploit it, but Everyman, every day.

The enrichment of public psychology by scientific psychology constitutes the most direct and important application of our science to the promotion of human welfare. Instead of trying to foresee new psychological products that might disrupt our existing social arrangements, therefore, we should be self-consciously analyzing the general effect that our scientific psychology may have on popular psychology. As I try to perform this analysis for myself, I must confess that I am not altogether pleased with the results.

I would like now to consider briefly some of the effects we are having and where, in my view, our influence is leading at the present time. Let me begin with a thumbnail sketch of one major message that many scientific psychologists are trying to communicate to the public.

CONTROL OF BEHAVIOR

One of the most admired truisms of modern psychology is that some stimuli can serve to reinforce the behavior that produces them. The practical significance of this familiar principle arises from the implication that if you can control the occurrence of these reinforcing stimuli, then you can control the occurrence of adaptive behavior intended to achieve or avoid them. This contingency between behavior and its consequences has been demonstrated in many studies of animal behavior, where environmental conditions can be controlled, or at least specified, and where the results can be measured with some precision.

Something similar holds for the human animal, of course, although it is complicated by man's symbolic proclivities and by the fact that the disparity between experimenter and subject changes when the subject is also a man. Between men, reinforcement is usually a mutual relation and each person controls the other to some extent. This relation of mutual reinforcement, which man's genius for symbols has generalized in terms of money or the promise of money, provides the psychological basis for our economic system of exchange. Psychologists did not create this economic system for controlling behavior, of course. What we have tried to do is to describe its psychological basis and its limits in terms sufficiently general to hold across different species, and to suggest how the technique might be extended to educational, rehabilitative, therapeutic, or even political situations in which economic rewards and punishments would not normally be appropriate. Once a problem of behavior control has been phrased in these terms, we may then try to discover the most effective schedule of reinforcements.

My present concern has nothing to do with the validity of these ideas. I am concerned with their effect on the public at large, for it is there, if I am right, that we are most likely to achieve a psychological revolution.

In the public view, I suspect, all this talk about controlling behavior comes across as unpleasant, if not actually threatening. Freud has already established in the public mind a general belief that all behavior is motivated. The current message says that psychologists now know how to use this motivation to control what people will do. When they hear this, of course, our scientific colleagues are likely to accuse us of pseudoscientific claims; less scientific segments of the public are likely to resent what they perceive as a threat to their personal freedom. Neither reaction is completely just, but neither is completely unjustifiable.

. . .

If the assumption that behavior control is feasible in some precise scientific sense becomes firmly rooted in public psychology, it could have unfortunate consequences, particularly if it is coupled with an assumption that control should be exercised by an industrial or bureaucratic elite. Psychologists must always respect and advocate the principle of *habeas mentem*—the right of a man to his own mind (Sanford, 1955). If we really did have a new scientific way to control human behavior, it would be highly immoral to let it fall into the hands of some small group of men, even if they were psychologists.

. . .

Personally, I believe there is a better way to advertise psychology and to relate it to social problems. Reinforcement is only one of many important ideas that we have to offer. Instead of repeating constantly that reinforcement leads to control, I would prefer to emphasize that reinforcement can lead to satisfaction and competence. And I would prefer to speak of understanding and prediction as our major scientific goals.

In the space remaining, therefore, I want to try to make the case that understanding and prediction are better goals for psychology than is control—better both for psychology and for the promotion of human welfare—because they lead us to think, not in terms of coercion by a powerful elite, but in terms of the diagnosis of problems and the development of programs that can enrich the lives of every citizen.

Public Psychology: Two Paradigms

. . . I have somewhere in the back of my mind two alternative images of what the popular conception of human nature might become under the impact of scientific advances in psychology. One of these images is unfortunate, even threatening; the other is vaguer, but full of promise. Let me try to make these ideas more concrete.

. . .

My two images are not very different from what McGregor (1960) once called Theory X and Theory Y. Theory X is the traditional theory which holds that because people dislike work, they must be coerced, controlled, directed, and threatened with punishment before they will do it. People tolerate being directed, and many even prefer it, because they have little ambition and want to avoid responsibility. McGregor's alternative Theory Y, based on social science, holds that work is as natural as play or rest. External control and threats are not the only means for inspiring people to work. People will exercise self-direction and self-control in the service of objectives to which they are committed; their commitment is a function of the rewards associated with the achievement of their objectives. People can learn not only to accept but to seek responsibility. Imagination, ingenuity, and creativity are widely distributed in the population, although these intellectual potentialities are poorly utilized under the conditions of modern industrial life.

McGregor's Theory X and Theory Y evolved in the context of his studies of industrial management. They are rival theories held by industrial managers about how best to achieve their institutional goals. A somewhat broader view is needed if we are to talk about public psychology generally, and not merely the managerial manifestations of public psychology. So let me amplify McGregor's distinction by referring to the ideas of Varela, a very remarkable engineer in Montevideo, Uruguay, who uses scientific psychology in the solution of a wide range of personal and social problems.

Varela (1970, in press) contrasts two conceptions of the social nature of man. Following Kuhn's (1962) discussion of scientific revolutions, he refers to these two conceptions as "paradigms." The first paradigm is a set of assumptions on which our social institutions are presently based. The second is a contrasting paradigm based on psychological research. Let me outline them for you very briefly.

Our current social paradigm is characterized as follows: All men are created equal. Most behavior is motivated by economic competition, and conflict is inevitable. One truth underlies all controversy, and unreasonableness is best countered by facts and logic. When something goes wrong, someone is to blame, and every effort must be made to establish his guilt so that he can be punished. The guilty person is responsible for his own misbehavior and for his own rehabilitation. His teachers and supervisors are too busy to become experts in social science; their role is to devise solutions and see to it that their students or subordinates do what they are told.

For comparison, Varela offers a paradigm based on psychological research: There are large individual differences among people, both in ability and personality. Human motivation is complex and no one ever acts as he does for any single reason, but, in general, positive incentives are more effective than threats or punishments. Conflict is no more inevitable than disease and can be resolved or, still better, prevented. Time and resources for resolving social problems are strictly limited. When something goes wrong, how a person perceives the situation is more important to him than the "true facts," and he cannot reason about the situation until his irrational feelings have been toned down. Social problems are solved by correcting causes, not symptoms, and this can be done more effectively in groups than individually. Teachers and supervisors must be experts in social science because they are responsible for the cooperation and individual improvement of their students or subordinates.

No doubt other psychologists would draw the picture somewhat differently. Without reviewing the psychological evidence on which such generalizations are based, of course, I cannot argue their validity. But I think most of you will recognize the lines of research on which McGregor's Theory Y and Varela's second paradigm are based. Moreover, these psychologically based paradigms are incompatible in several respects with the prevailing ideology of our society.

Here, then, is the real challenge: How can we foster a social climate in which some such new public conception of man based on psychology can take root and flourish? In my opinion, this is the proper translation of our more familiar question about how psychology might contribute to the promotion of human welfare.

I cannot pretend to have an answer to this question, even in its translated form, but I believe that part of the answer is that psychology must be practiced by nonpsychologists. We are not physicians; the secrets of our trade need not be reserved for highly trained specialists. Psychological facts should be passed out freely to all who need and can use them. And from successful applications of psychological principles the public may gain a better appreciation for the power of the new conception of man that is emerging from our science.

If we take seriously the idea of a peaceful revolution based on a new conception of human nature, our scientific results will have to be instilled in the public consciousness in a practical and usable form so that what we know can be applied by ordinary people. There simply are not enough psychologists, even including nonprofessionals, to meet every need for psychological services. The people at large will have to be their own psychologists, and make their own applications of the principles that we establish.

Of course, everyone practices psychology, just as everyone who cooks is a chemist, everyone who reads a clock is an astronomer, everyone who drives a car is an engineer. I am not suggesting any radical departure when I say that nonpsychologists must practice psychology. I am simply proposing that we should teach them to practice it

better, to make use self-consciously of what we believe to be scientifically valid principles.

Our responsibility is less to assume the role of experts and try to apply psychology ourselves than to give it away to the people who really need it—and that includes everyone. The practice of valid psychology by nonpsychologists will inevitably change people's conception of themselves and what they can do. When we have accomplished that, we will really have caused a psychological revolution.

How to Give Psychology Away

I am keenly aware that giving psychology away will be no simple task. In our society there are depths of resistance to psychological innovations that have to be experienced to be believed (Graziano, 1969).

Solving social problems is generally considered to be more difficult than solving scientific problems. A social problem usually involves many more independent variables, and it cannot be finally solved until society has been persuaded to adopt the solution. Many who have tried to introduce sound psychological practices into schools, clinics, hospitals, prisons, or industries have been forced to retreat in dismay. They complain, and with good reason, that they were unable to buck the "System," and often their reactions are more violent than sensible. The System, they say, refuses to change even when it does not work.

This experience has been so common that in my pessimistic moments I have been led to wonder whether anything less than complete reform is possible.

Deutsch (1969) has made an interesting case that competitive and cooperative social relationships tend to be mutually exclusive. He summarizes the result of considerable research in the following terms:

The strategy of power and the tactics of coercion, threat, and deception result from and also result in a competitive relationship. Similarly, the strategy of mutual problem solving and the tactics of persuasion, openness, and mutual enhancement elicit and also are elicited by a cooperative orientation [p. 4].

Each orientation has its own internal consistency; elements of one are not easily injected into the other.

Perhaps a similar pressure toward internal coherence lies at the root of public resistance to many of our innovative suggestions. It often seems that any one of our ideas taken alone is inadequate. Injected into the existing social paradigm it is either a foreign body, incompatible with the other presuppositions that shape our social institutions, or it is distorted and trivialized to fit the preexisting paradigm.

One of the most basic ideas in all the social sciences is the concept of culture. Social anthropologists have developed a conception of culture as an organic whole, in which each particular value, practice, or assumption must be understood in the context of the total system. They tell terrible tales about the consequences of introducing Western reforms into aboriginal cultures without understanding the social equilibria that would be upset.

Perhaps cultural integrity is not limited to primitive cultures, but applies also to our own society here and now. If so, then our attempts at piecemeal innovation may be doomed either to fail or to be rejected outright.

I label these thoughts pessimistic because they imply a need for drastic changes throughout the whole system, changes that could only be imposed by someone with dangerous power over the lives of others. And that, I have argued, is not the way our psychological revolution should proceed.

In my more optimistic moments, however, I recognize that you do not need complete authority over a social organization in order to reform it. The important thing is not to control the system, but to understand it. Someone who has a valid conception of the system as a whole can often introduce relatively minor changes that have extensive consequences throughout the entire organization. Lacking such a conception, worthwhile innovations may be total failures.

. . .

Diagnosing practical problems and developing detailed plans to deal with them may or may not be more difficult than solving scientific problems, but it is certainly different. Many psychologists, trained in an empiricist, experimental tradition, have tried to serve two masters at once. That is to say, they have tried to solve practical problems and simultaneously to collect data of scientific value on the effects of their interventions. Other fields, however, maintain a more equitable division of labor between scientist and engineer. Scientists are responsible for the validity of the principles; engineers accept them and try to use them to solve practical problems.

Although I recognize the importance of evaluating an engineer's product, in this domain it is no easy thing to do. Assessing social innovations is a whole art in itself, one that we are only beginning to develop. Economic considerations are relevant, of course, but we must also learn to evaluate the subtler psychological and social implications of our new solutions (Bauer, 1966). Technological assessment in this sense will not be achieved by insisting that every reform should resemble a well-designed experiment. In particular, the need for assessment should not be allowed to discourage those who enjoy and have a talent for social engineering.

We are in serious need of many more psychological technologists who can apply our science to the personal and social problems of the general public, for it is through them that the public will eventually discover the new paradigm that psychologists are developing. That is to say, it is through the success of such practical applications that we have our best hope for revolutionizing public psychology.

. . .

In order to get a factory supervisor or a ghetto mother involved, we must give them something they can use. . . . If a ghetto mother is not giving her children sufficient intellectual challenge, perhaps we should teach her how to encourage their motor, perceptual, and linguistic skills. The techniques involved are not some esoteric branch of witchcraft that must be reserved for those with PhD degrees in psychology. When the ideas are made sufficiently concrete and explicit, the scientific foundations of psychology can be grasped by sixth-grade children. . . . Not every personnel decision has to be made by a psychometrician; not every interview has to be conducted by a clinical psychologist. . . . Psychological principles and techniques can be usefully applied by everyone. If our suggestions actually work, people should be eager to learn more. If they do not work, we should improve them. But we should not try to give people something whose value they cannot recognize, then complain when they do not return for a second meeting.

Consider the teaching of reading, for example. Here is an obviously appropriate area for the application of psychological principles. So what do we do? We assemble experts who decide what words children know, and in what order they should learn to read them; then we write stories with those words and teachers make the children read them, or we use them in programmed instruction that exploits the principles of reinforcement. But all too often the children fail to recognize the value of learning these carefully constructed lessons.

Personally, I have been much impressed with the approach of Ashton-Warner (1963), who begins by asking a child what words he wants. Mummy, daddy, kiss, frightened, ghost, their own names—these are the words children ask for, words that are bound up with their own loves and fears. She writes each child's word on a large, tough card and gives it to him. If a child wants words like police, butcher, knife, kill, jail, and bomb, he gets them. And he learns to read them almost immediately. It is *his* word, and each morning he retrieves his own words from the pile collected each night by the teacher. These are not dead words of an expert's choosing, but words that live in a child's own experience. Given this start, children begin to write, using their own words, and from there the teaching of reading follows naturally. Under this regimen, a word is not an imposed task to be learned with reinforcements borrowed from some external source of motivation. Learning the word is itself reinforcing; it gives the child something he wants, a new way to cope with a desire or fear. Each child decides where he wants to start, and each child receives something whose value he can recognize.

Could we generalize this technique discovered by an inspired teacher in a small New Zealand school? In my own thinking I have linked it with something that White (1959) has called competence motivation.* In order to tap this motivational system we must use psychology to give people skills that will satisfy their urge to feel more effective. Feeling effective is a very personal thing, for it must be a feeling of effectiveness in coping with personal problems in one's own life. From that beginning some might want to learn more about the science that helped them increase their competence, and then perhaps we could afford to be more abstract. But in the beginning we must try to diagnose and solve the problems people think they have, not the problems we experts think they ought to have, and we must learn to understand those problems in the social and institutional contexts that define them. With this approach we might do something practical for nurses, policemen, prison guards, salesmen—for people in many different walks of life. That, I believe, is what we should mean when we talk about applying psychology to the promotion of human welfare.

· · ·

The demand for social relevance that we have been voicing as psychologists is only one aspect of a general dissatisfaction with the current state of our society. On every hand we hear complaints about the old paradigm. People are growing increasingly alienated from a society in which a few

* See article by White in Section VII of this book.—EDITOR

wise men behind closed doors decide what is good for everyone. Our system of justice based on punishment and retribution is not working. Even those most blessed by economic rewards are asking for something more satisfying to fill their lives. We desperately need techniques for resolving conflicts, and for preventing them from becoming public confrontations from which reasonable retreat is impossible. Anyone who reads the newspapers must realize that vast social changes are in the making, that they must occur if civilized society is to survive.

Vested interests will oppose these changes, of course, but as someone once said, vested interests, however powerful, cannot withstand the gradual encroachment of new ideas. If we psychologists are ready for it, we may be able to contribute a coherent and workable philosophy, based on the science of psychology, that will make this general agitation less negative, that will make it a positive search for something new.

· · ·

For myself . . . I can imagine nothing we could do that would be more relevant to human welfare, and nothing that could pose a greater challenge to the next generation of psychologists, than to discover how best to give psychology away.

REFERENCES

ASHTON-WARNER, S. *Teacher*. New York: Simon & Schuster, 1963.

BAUER, R. A. (Ed.) *Social indicators*. Cambridge: M.I.T. Press, 1966.

DEUTSCH, M. Socially relevant science: Reflections on some studies of interpersonal conflict, *American Psychologist*, 1969, *24*, 1076–1092.

GRAZIANO, A. M. Clinical innovation and the mental health power structure: A social case history. *American Psychologist*, 1969, *24*, 10–18.

KUHN, T. *The structure of scientific revolutions*. Chicago: University of Chicago Press, 1962.

McGREGOR, D. *The human side of enterprise*. New York: McGraw-Hill, 1960.

SANFORD, F. H. Creative health and the principle of *habeas mentem*. *American Psychologist*, 1955, *10*, 829–835.

VARELA, J. A. *Introduction to social science technology*. New York: Academic Press, 1970, in press.

WHITE, R. W. Motivation reconsidered: The concept of competence. *Psychological Review*, 1959, *66*, 297–333.

2

On the Need for Relativism [1]

JEROME KAGAN

The opening article proposed the adoption of a new attitude toward applying psychological knowledge. In the present article, Jerome Kagan discusses the need for new attitudes among psychologists if psychology is to advance as a basic science. After pointing out certain vital complexities with which a mature science must deal, Kagan calls attention to the concept of "attention," suggesting that it, together with contiguity, may be the key to knowledge of how humans learn.

An author or coauthor of two other articles in these volumes, Kagan spent some years at the Fels Research Institute in Yellow Springs, Ohio. This Institute has long been a major center for longitudinal investigations. Since 1964 Kagan has been a professor of developmental psychology at Harvard University.

The psychology of the first half of this century was absolutistic, outer directed, and intolerant of ambiguity. When a college student carries this unholy trio of traits he is called authoritarian, and

such has been the temperament of the behavioral sciences. But the era of authoritarian psychology may be nearing its dotage, and the decades ahead may nurture a discipline that is relativistic, oriented to internal processes, and accepting of the idea that behavior is necessarily ambiguous.

Like her elder sisters, psychology began her dialogue with nature using a vocabulary of absolutes. Stimulus, response, rejection, affection, emotion, reward, and punishment were labels for classes of phenomena that were believed to have a fixed reality. We believed we could write a definition of these constructs that would fix them permanently and allow us to know them unequivocally at any time in any place.

Less than 75 years ago biology began to drift from the constraints of an absolute view of events and processes when she acknowledged that the fate of a small slice of ectodermal tissue depended on whether it was placed near the area of the eye or the toe. Acceptance of the simple notion that whether an object moves or not depends on where you are standing is a little over a half century old in a science that has 5 centuries of formalization. With physics as the referent in time, one might expect a relativistic attitude to influence psychology by the latter part of the twenty-third century. But philosophical upheavals in one science catalyze change in other disciplines and one can see signs of budding relativism in the intellectual foundations of the social sciences.

The basic theme of this paper turns on the need for more relativistic definitions of selected theoretical constructs. "Relativistic" refers to a definition in which context and the state of the individual are part of the defining statement. Relativism does not preclude the development of operational definitions, but makes that task more difficult. Nineteenth-century physics viewed mass as an absolute value; twentieth-century physics made the definition of mass relative to the speed of light. Similarly, some of psychology's popular constructs have to be defined in relation to the state and belief structure of the organism, rather than in terms of an invariant set of external events. Closely related to this need is the suggestion that some of the energy devoted to a search for absolute, stimulus characteristics of reinforcement be redirected to a search for the determinants of attention in the individual.

It is neither possible nor wise to assign responsibility to one person or event for major changes in conceptual posture, but Helson's recent book on adaptation-level theory (Helson, 1964), Schachter's

[1] Preparation of this paper was supported in part by research Grant MH–8792 from the National Institute of Mental Health, United States Public Health Service. This paper is an abridged version of a lecture presented at the Educational Testing Service, Princeton, New Jersey, January 1966.

(Schachter & Singer, 1962) hypothesis concerning the cognitive basis of affects, and Hernández-Peón's demonstration of the neurophysiological bases of selective attention (Hernández-Peón, Scherrer, & Jouvet, 1956) are contemporary stimulants for a relativistic view of psychological phenomena.

Three messages are implicit in the work of these men.

1. If a stimulus is to be regarded as an event to which a subject responds or is likely to respond then it is impossible to describe a stimulus without describing simultaneously the expectancy, and preparation of the organism for that stimulus. Effective stimuli must be distinct from the person's original adaptation level. Contrast and distinctiveness, which are relative, are part and parcel of the definition of a stimulus.

2. The failure of one individual to respond to an event that is an effective stimulus for a second individual is not always the result of central selection after all the information is in, but can be due to various forms of peripheral inhibition. Some stimuli within inches of the face do not ever reach the interpretive cortex and, therefore, do not exist psychologically.

3. Man reacts less to the objective quality of external stimuli than he does to categorizations of those stimuli.

These new generalizations strip the phrase "physical stimulus" of much of its power and certainty, and transfer the scepter of control—in man, at least—to cognitive interpretations. *Contrast, cognitively interpreted, becomes an important key to understanding the incentives for human behavior.* Since contrast depends so intimately on context and expectancy, it must be defined relativistically.

The issue of relativism can be discussed in many contexts. Many existing constructs are already defined in terms of contextual relations. The concept of authority only has meaning if there are fiefs to rule. The role of father has no meaning without a child. The concept of noun, verb, or adjective is defined by context—by the relation of the word to other constituents. We shall consider in some detail the ways in which a relativistic orientation touches two other issues in psychology: the learning of self-descriptive statements (the hoary idea of the self-concept), and, even more fundamentally, some of the mechanisms that define the learning process.

The Concept of the Self

The development and establishment of a self-concept is often framed in absolute terms. The classic form of the statement assumes that direct social reinforcements and identification models have fixed, invariant effects on the child. Praise and love from valued caretakers are assumed to lead the child to develop positive self-evaluations; whereas, criticism and rejection presumably cause self-derogatory beliefs. The presumed cause-effect sequences imply that there is a something—a definable set of behavior—that can be labeled social rejection, and that the essence of these rejecting acts leads to invariant changes in the self-concept of the child. Let us examine the concept of rejection under higher magnification.

The concept of rejection—peer or parental—has been biased toward an absolute definition. Witness the enormous degree of commonality in conceptualization of this concept by investigators who have studied a mother's behavior with her child (Baldwin, Kalhorn, & Breese, 1945; Becker, 1964; Kagan & Moss, 1962; Schaefer, 1959; Schaefer & Bayley, 1963; Sears, Maccoby, & Levin, 1957). These investigators typically decide that harsh physical punishment and absence of social contact or physical affection are the essential indexes of an attitude called maternal rejection. It would be close to impossible for an American rater to categorize a mother as high on both harsh beating of her child and on a loving attitude. A conventionally trained psychologist observing a mother who did not talk to her child for 5 hours would probably view the mother as rejecting. This may be a high form of provincialism. Alfred Baldwin[2] reports that in the rural areas of northern Norway, where homes are 5 to 10 miles apart, and the population constant for generations, one often sees maternal behaviors which an American observer would regard as pathognomonically rejecting in an American mother. The Norwegian mother sees her 4-year-old sitting in the doorway blocking the passage to the next room. She does not ask him to move, but bends down, silently picks him up and moves him away before she passes into the next room. Our middle-class observer would be tempted to view this indifference as a sign of dislike. However, most mothers in this Arctic outpost behave this way and the children do not behave the way rejected children should by our current theoretical propositions.

An uneducated Negro mother from North Carolina typically slaps her 4-year-old across the face when he does not come to the table on time. The intensity of the mother's act tempts our observer to conclude that the mother hates, or at best, does not like her child. However, during a half-hour conversation the mother says she loves her child and wants to guarantee that he does not grow up

---

[2] Personal communication.

to be a bad boy or a delinquent. And she believes firmly that physical punishment is the most effective way to socialize him. Now her behavior seems to be issued in the service of affection rather than hate. Determination of whether a parent is rejecting or not cannot be answered by focusing primarily on the behaviors of the parents. Rejection is not a fixed, invariant quality of behavior qua behavior. Like pleasure, pain, or beauty, rejection is in the mind of the rejectee. It is a belief held by the child; not an action by a parent.

We must acknowledge, first, a discontinuity in the meaning of an acceptance-rejection dimension before drawing further implications. We must distinguish between the child prior to 30 or 36 months of age, before he symbolically evaluates the actions of others, and the child thereafter.

We require, first, a concept to deal with the child's belief of his value in the eyes of others. The child of 4 or 5 years is conceptually mature enough to have recognized that certain resources parents possess are difficult for the child to obtain. He views these resources as sacrifices and interprets their receipt as signs that the parents value him. The child constructs a tote board of the differential value of parental gifts—be they psychological or material. The value of the gift depends on its scarcity. A $10.00 toy from a busy executive father is not a valued resource; the same toy from a father out of work is much valued. The value depends on the child's personal weightings. This position would lead to solipsism were it not for the fact that most parents are essentially narcissistic and do not readily give the child long periods of uninterrupted companionship. Thus, most children place high premium on this act. Similarly, parents are generally reluctant to proffer unusually expensive gifts to children, and this act acquires value for most youngsters. Finally, the child learns from the public media that physical affection means positive evaluation and he is persuaded to assign premium worth to this set of acts. There is, therefore, some uniformity across children in a culture in the evaluation of parental acts. But the anchor point lies within the child, not with the particular parental behaviors.

This definition of acceptance or rejection is not appropriate during the opening years. The 1-year-old does not place differential symbolic worth on varied parental acts, and their psychological significance derives from the overt responses they elicit and strengthen. A heavy dose of vocalization and smiling to an infant is traditionally regarded as indicative of maternal affection and acceptance. This bias exists because we have accepted the myth that "affection" is the essential nutrient that produces socially adjusted children, adolescents, and adults. The bias maintains itself because we observe a positive association between degree of parental smiling and laughing to the infant and prosocial behavior in the child during the early years. The responses of smiling, laughing, and approaching people are learned in the opening months of life on the basis of standard conditioning principles. This conclusion is supported by the work of Rheingold and Gewirtz (1959) and Brackbill (1958). However, phenotypically similar behaviors in a 10- or 20-year-old may have a different set of antecedents. The argument that different definitions of rejection-acceptance must be written for the pre- and postsymbolic child gains persuasive power from the fact that there are no data indicating that degree of prosocial behavior in the child is stable from 6 months to 16 years. Indeed, the longitudinal material from the Fels Research Institute study of behavior stability (Kagan & Moss, 1962) showed no evidence of any relation between joy or anxiety in the presence of adults during the first 2–3 years of life and phenotypically similar behaviors at 6, 12, or 24 years of age. The child behaviors that are presumed, by theory, to be the consequences of low or high parental rejection do not show stability from infancy through adolescence. This may be because the childhood responses, though phenotypically similar to the adult acts, may be acquired and maintained through different experiences at different periods.

It seems reasonable to suggest, therefore, that different theoretical words are necessary for the following three classes of phenomena: (*a*) an attitude on the part of the parent, (*b*) the quality and frequency of acts of parental care and social stimulation directed toward the infant, and (*c*) a child's assessment of his value in the eyes of another. All three classes are currently viewed as of the same cloth. The latter meaning of "rejection" (i.e., a belief held by a child) is obviously relativistic for it grows out of different experiences in different children.

Self-Descriptive Labels

Let us probe further into the ideas surrounding the learning of self-evaluation statements, beyond the belief, "I am not valued." The notion of a self-concept has a long and spotted history and although it has masqueraded by many names in different theoretical costumes, its intrinsic meaning has changed only a little. A child presumably learns self-descriptive statements whose contents touch the salient attributes of the culture. The mechanisms classically invoked to explain how these attributes are learned have stressed the invariant effects of direct social reinforcement and identification. The girl who is told she is attractive, annoying, or inventive, comes to believe these appellations and to apply these qualifiers to herself. We have assumed that the laws governing the learning of self-descriptive labels resemble the learning of other verbal habits with frequency and contiguity of events being the shapers of the habit. Identification as a source of self-labels involves a different mechanism, but retains an absolutistic frame of reference. The child assumes that he shares attributes with particular models. If the model is viewed as subject to violent rages, the child concludes that he, too, shares this tendency.

Theory and data persuade us to retain some faith in these propositions. But relativistic factors also seem to sculpt the acquisition of self-descriptive labels, for the child evaluates himself on many psychological dimensions by inferring his rank order from a delineated reference group. The 10-year-old does not have absolute measuring rods to help him decide how bright, handsome, or likeable he is. He naturally and spontaneously uses his immediate peer group as the reference for these evaluations. An immediate corollary of this statement is that the child's evaluation is dependent upon the size and psychological quality of the reference group, and cannot be defined absolutely. Specifically, the larger the peer group, the less likely a child will conclude he is high in the rank order, the less likely he will decide he is unusually smart, handsome, or capable of leadership. Consider two boys with IQs of 130 and similar intellectual profiles. One lives in a small town, the other in a large city. It is likely that the former child will be the most competent in his peer group while the latter is likely to regard himself as fifth or sixth best. This difference in perceived rank order has obvious action consequences since we acknowledge that expectancies govern behavior. In sum, aspects of the self-descriptive process appear to develop in relativistic soil.

LEARNING AND ATTENTION

A second issue that touches relativistic definitions deals with a shift from external definitions of reinforcement—that is, reward or pleasure—to definitions that are based more directly on internal processes involving the concept of attention. Failure to understand the nature of learning is one of the major intellectual frustrations for many psychologists. The query, "What is learning?" has the same profound ring as the question, "What is a gene?" had a decade ago. Our biological colleagues have recently had a major insight while psychology is still searching. The murky question, "What is learning?" usually reduces to an attempt to discover

the laws relating stimuli, pain, and pleasure, on the one hand, with habit acquisition and performance, on the other. Pain, pleasure, and reinforcement are usually defined in terms of events that are external to the organism and have an invariant flavor. Miller (1951) suggested that reinforcement was isomorphic with stimulus reduction; Leuba (1955) argued for an optimal level of stimulation, but both implied that there was a level that could be specified and measured. We should like to argue first that sources of pleasure, and therefore of reinforcement, are often relative, and second, that the essence of learning is more dependent on attentional involvement by the learner than on specific qualities of particular external events.

The joint ideas that man is a pleasure seeker and that one can designate specific forms of stimulation as sources of pleasure are central postulates in every man's theory of behavior. Yet we find confusion when we seek a definition of pleasure. The fact that man begins life with a small core set of capacities for experience that he wishes to repeat cannot be disputed. This is a pragmatic view of pleasure and we can add a dash of phenomenology to bolster the intuitive validity of this point of view. A sweet taste and a light touch in selected places are usually pleasant. Recently, we have added an important new source of pleasure. It is better to say we have rediscovered a source of pleasure, for Herbert Spencer was a nineteenth-century progenitor of the idea that *change in stimulation* is a source of pleasure for rats, cats, monkeys, or men. But, change is short-lived, quickly digested, and transformed to monotony. Popping up in front of an infant and saying peek-a-boo is pleasant for a 3-month-old infant for about 15 minutes, for a 10-month-old infant for 3 minutes and for a 30-month-old child, a few seconds. This pleasant experience, like most events that elicit their repetition a few times before dying, is usually conceptualized as a change in stimulation. The source of the pleasure is sought in the environment. Why should change in external stimulation be pleasant? The understanding of pleasure and reinforcement in man is difficult enough without having to worry about infrahuman considerations. Let us restrict the argument to the human. The human is a cognitive creature who is attempting to put structure or create schema for incoming stimulation. A schema is a representation of an external pattern; much as an artist's illustration is a representation of an event. A schema for a visual pattern is a partial and somewhat distorted version of what the photograph would be. Consider the usefulness of the following hypothesis:

The creation of a schema for an event is one major source of pleasure. When one can predict an event perfectly, the schema is formed. As long as prediction is not perfect the schema is not yet formed. The peek-a-boo game works for 15 minutes with a 12-week-old for it takes him that long to be able to predict the event—the "peek-a-boo." Charlesworth (1965) has demonstrated the reinforcing value of "uncertainty" in an experiment in which the peek-a-boo face appeared either in the same locus every trial, alternated between two loci, or appeared randomly in one of two loci. The children persisted in searching for the face for a much longer time under the random condition than under the other two conditions. The random presentation was reinforcing for a longer period of time, not because it possessed a more optimum level of external stimulation than the other reinforcement schedules, but because it took longer for the child to create a schema for the random presentation and the process of creating a schema is a source of pleasure.

Consider another sign of pleasure besides persistence in issuing a particular response. Display of a smile or laugh is a good index of pleasure. Indeed, Tomkins' (1962) scheme for affect demands that pleasure be experienced if these responses appear. Consider two studies that bear on the relation between pleasure and the creation of schema. In our laboratory during the last 2 years, we have seen the same infants at 4, 8, and 13 months of age and have shown them a variety of visual patterns representative of human faces and human forms. In one episode, the 4-month-old infants are shown achromatic slides of a photograph of a regular male face, a schematic outline of a male face, and two disarranged, disordered faces. The frequency of occurrence of smiling to the photograph of the regular face is over *twice* the frequency observed to the regular schematic face—although looking time is identical—and over *four times* the frequency shown to the disordered faces. In another, more realistic episode, the 4-month-old infants see a regular, flesh-colored sculptured face in three dimensions and a distorted version of that face in which the eyes, nose, and mouth are rearranged. At 4 months of age the occurrence of smiling to the regular face is over three times the frequency displayed to the distorted version, but looking time is identical. There are two interpretations of this difference (Kagan, Henker, Hen-Tov, Levine, & Lewis, 1966). One explanation argues that the mother's face has become a secondary reward; the regular face stands for pleasure because it has been associated with care and affection from the mother. As a result, it elicits more smiles. An alternative interpretation is that the smile response has become conditioned to the human face via reciprocal contact between mother and infant. A third interpretation, not necessarily exclusive of these, is that the smile can be elicited when the infant matches stimulus to schema—when he has an "aha" reaction; when he makes a cognitive discovery. The 4-month-old infant is cognitively close to establishing a relatively firm schema of a human face. When a regular representation of a face is presented to him there is a short period during which the stimulus is assimilated to the schema and then after several seconds, a smile may occur. The smile is released following the perceptual recognition of the face, and reflects the assimilation of the stimulus to the infant's schema—a small, but significant act of creation. This hypothesis is supported by the fact that the typical latency between the onset of looking at the regular face (in the 4-month-old) and the onset of smiling is about 3 to 5 seconds. The smile usually does not occur immediately but only after the infant has studied the stimulus. If one sees this phenomenon live, it is difficult to avoid the conclusion that the smile is released following an act of perceptual recognition.

Additional data on these and other children at 8 months of age support this idea. At 8 months, frequency of smiling to both the regular and distorted faces is *reduced dramatically,* indicating that smiling does not covary with the reward value of the face. The face presumably has acquired more reward value by 8 months than it had at 4 months. However, the face is now a much firmer schema and recognition of it is immediate. There is no effortful act of recognition necessary for most infants. As a result, smiling is less likely to occur. Although smiling is much less frequent at 8 than 4 months to all faces, the frequency of smiling to the distorted face now *equals* the frequency displayed to the regular face. We interpret this to mean that the distorted face is sufficiently similar to the child's schema of a regular face that it can be recognized as such.

The pattern of occurrence of cardiac deceleration to the regular and distorted three-dimensional faces furnishes the strongest support for this argument. A cardiac deceleration of about 8 to 10 beats often accompanies attention to selected incoming visual stimuli in adults, school-age children, and infants. Moreover, the deceleration tends to be maximal when the stimuli are not overly familiar or completely novel, but are of intermediate familiarity. One hypothesis maintains that a large deceleration is most likely to occur when an act of perceptual recognition occurs, when the organism has a cognitive surprise. Let us assume that there is one trial for which this type of reaction occurs with maximal magnitude. If one examines the one stimulus presentation (out of a total of 16 trials) that produces the largest cardiac deceleration, a lawful change occurs between 4 and 8 months of age. At 4 months of age more of the infants showed their largest deceleration to the regular face (45% of the group: $n = 52$) than to the scrambled (34%), no eyes (11%), or blank faces (10%). At 8 months, the majority of the infants ($n = 52$) showed their largest deceleration to the scrambled face (50% to scrambled versus 21% to regular face). This difference is interpreted to mean that the scrambled face now assumes a similar position on the assimilation continuum that the regular face did 16 weeks earlier.

At 13 months of age these infants are shown six three-dimensional representations of a male human form and a free form matched for area, coloration, and texture with the human form. The stimuli include a faithful representation of a regular man, that same man with his head placed between his legs, the same man with all limbs and head collaged in an unusual and scrambled pattern, the man's body with a mule's head, and the mule's head on the man's body, the man's body with three identical heads, and a free form. The distribution of smiles to these stimuli is leptokurtic, with over 70% of all the smiles occurring to the animal head on the human body and the three-headed man, forms that were moderate transformations of the regular man, and stimuli that required active assimilation. The free form and the scrambled man rarely elicited smiles from these infants. These stimuli are too difficult to assimilate to the schema of a human form possessed by a 13-month-old infant. It is interesting to note that the regular human form sometimes elicited the verbal response "daddy" or a hand waving from the child. These instrumental social reactions typically did not occur to the transformations. The occurrence of cardiac deceleration to these patterns agrees with this hypothesis. At 13 months of age, the man with his head between his legs, the man with the animal head, or the three-headed man, each elicited the largest cardiac decelerations more frequently than the regular man, the scrambled man, or the free form ($p < .05$ for each comparison). Thus, large cardiac decelerations and smiles were most likely to occur to stimuli that seemed to require tiny, quiet cognitive discoveries—miniaturized versions of Archimedes' "Eureka."

It appears that the act of matching stimulus to schema when the match is close but not yet perfect is a dynamic event. Stimuli that deviate a critical amount from the child's schema for a pattern are capable of eliciting an active process of recognition, and this process behaves as if it were a source of pleasure. Stimuli that are easily assimilable or too difficult to assimilate do not elicit these reactions.

A recent study by Edward Zigler[3] adds important support to the notion that the smile indicates the pleasure of an assimilation. Children in Grades 2, 3, 4, and 5 looked at cartoons that required little or no reading. The children were asked to explain the cartoon while an observer coded the spontaneous occurrence of laughing and smiling while the children were studying the cartoons. It should come as no surprise that verbal comprehension of the cartoons increased in a linear fashion with age. But laughing and smiling increased through Grade 4 and then declined markedly among the fifth-grade children. The fifth graders understood the cartoons too well. There was no gap between stimulus and schema and no smiling. Sixteen-week-old infants and 8-year-old children smile spontaneously at events that seem to have one thing in common—the event is a partial match to an existing schema and an active process of recognitory assimilation must occur.

The fact that a moderate amount of mismatch between event and schema is one source of pleasure demands the conclusion that it is not always possible to say that a specific event will always be a source of pleasure. The organism's state and structure must be in the equation. This conclusion parallels the current interest in complexity and information uncertainty. The psychologist with an information-theory prejudice classifies a stimulus as uncertain and often assumes that he does not have to be too concerned with the attributes of the viewer. This error of the absolute resembles the nineteenth-century error in physics and biology. This is not a titillating or pedantic, philosophical issue. Psychology rests on a motive-reinforcement foundation which regards pleasure and pain as pivotal ideas in the grand theory. These constructs have tended to generate absolute definitions. We have been obsessed with finding a fixed and invariant characterization of pleasure, pain, and reinforcement. Melzack & Wall (1965) point out that although the empirical data do not support the notion of a fixed place in the brain that mediates pain, many scientists resist shedding this comfortable idea. Olds' (1958, 1962) discovery of brain reinforcing areas has generated excitement because many of us want to believe that pleasure has a fixed and absolute locus. The suspicious element in this discovery of pleasure spots is that there is no habituation of responses maintained by electrical stimulation to hypothalamic or septal nuclei, and minimal resistance to extinction of habits acquired via this event. Yet, every source of pleasure known

---

[3] Unpublished paper; personal communication.

to phenomenal man does satiate—for awhile or forever—and habits that lead to pleasant events do persist for a while after the pleasure is gone. These observations are troubling and additional inquiry is necessary if we are to decide whether these cells are indeed the bed where pleasure lies.

We are convinced that contiguity alone does not always lead to learning. Something must ordinarily be added to contiguity in order to produce a new bond. Psychology has chosen to call this extra added mysterious something reinforcement, much like eighteenth-century chemists chose to label their unknown substance phlogiston. If one examines the variety of external events that go by the name of reinforcement it soon becomes clear that this word is infamously inexact. A shock to an animal's paw is a reinforcement, a verbal chastisement is a reinforcement, an examiner's smile is a reinforcement, a pellet of food is a reinforcement, and a sigh indicating tension reduction after watching a killer caught in a Hitchcock movie is a reinforcement. These events have little, if any, phenotypic similarity. What then, do they have in common? For if they have nothing in common it is misleading to call them by the same name. Learning theorists have acknowledged their failure to supply an independent a priori definition of reinforcement and the definition they use is purely pragmatic. A reinforcement is anything that helps learning. And so, we ask: What has to be added to contiguity in order to obtain learning? A good candidate for the missing ingredient is the phrase "attentional involvement." Let us consider again the events called reinforcements: a shock, food, a smile, each of these acts to attract the attention of the organism to some agent or object. They capture the organism's attention and maybe that is why they facilitate learning. Consider the idea that what makes an event reinforcing is the fact that it (a) elicits the organism's attention to the feedback from the response he has just made and to the mosaic of stimuli in the learning situation and (b) acts as an incentive for a subsequent response. The latter quality is what ties the word "reinforcement" to the concepts of motivation and need, but much learning occurs without the obvious presence of motives or needs. Ask any satiated adult to attend carefully and remember the bond syzygy-aardvark. It is likely that learning will occur in one trial. It is not unreasonable to argue that a critical component of events that have historically been called reinforcement is their ability to attract the organism's attention. They have been distinctive cues in a context; they have been events discrepant from the individual's adaptation level. If attention is acknowledged as critical in new mental acquisitions it is appropriate to ask if

attention is also bedded in relativistic soil. The answer appears to be "Yes." The dramatic experiments of Hernández-Peón and his colleagues (1956) are persuasive in indicating that attention investment may not be distributed to many channels at once. One has to know the state of the organism. Knowledge of the organism's distribution of attention in a learning situation may clarify many controversial theoretical polemics that range from imprinting in chickens to emotion in college undergraduates. For example, comparative psychologists quarrel about which set of external conditions allow imprinting to occur with maximal effect. Some say the decoy should move; others argue that the young chick should move; still others urge that the decoy be brightly colored (e.g., Bateson, 1964a, 1964b; Hess, 1959; Klopfer, 1965; Thompson & Dubanoski, 1964). The quarrel centers around the use of phenotypically different observable conditions. Perhaps all these suggestions are valid. Moving the decoy, or active following by the infant chick, or a distinctively colored decoy all maximize the organism's level of attention to the decoy. The genotypic event may remain the same across all of these manipulations.

A similar interpretation can be imposed on Held's (1965) recent hypothesis concerning the development of space and pattern perception. Held controlled the visual experience of pairs of kittens. The only exposure to light was limited to a few hours a day when one kitten was placed in a gondola and moved around by an active, free kitten in an arena whose walls were painted in vertical stripes. After 30 hours of such experience each kitten was tested. The free kitten showed appropriate visual reactions. It blinked when an object approached; it put up its paws to avoid collision when carried near to a surface; it avoided the deep side of a visual cliff. The passive passenger kitten did not show these normal reactions. Why? Held, focusing on the obvious external variable of activity versus no activity, concludes that the sensory feedback accompanying movement is necessary to develop visual-motor control. This conclusion rests on the assumption that the passive kitten sitting in the gondola was attending to the stripes on the wall as intently as the free walking kitten. This assumption may be gratuitous. If the passive kitten were staring blankly—as many human infants do—then one would not expect these animals to develop normal perceptual structures. This interpretation may not be better, but it has a different flavor than the one suggested by Held.

A final example of the central role of attention is seen in Aronfreed's (1964, 1965) recent work on the learning of self-critical comments. Aronfreed states that the learning of a self-critical comment proceeds best if the child is first punished and then hears a social agent speak the self-critical statement. He interprets this result in drive reduction language. However, suppose one asks which sequence is most likely to maximize a child's attention to the adult's comment—Punish first and then speak to the child? Or speak first and then punish? The former sequence should be more effective. The punishment is a violation of what the child expects from a strange adult and recruits the child's attention to the adult. The child is primed to listen to the self-critical commendation and thus more likely to learn it.

DISTINCTIVENESS OF CUES

The above examples suggest that the organism's distribution of attention is a critical process that should guide our search for the bases of many diverse phenomena. One of the critical bases for recruitment of attention pivots on the idea of distinctiveness of the signal. Jakobson and Halle (1956) argue that the chronology of acquisition of phonemes proceeds according to a principle of distinctive elements. Distinctive elements capture the child's attention and give direction to the order of learning.

The importance of *relative distinctiveness of cues* finds an interesting illustration in the concept of affect. The concept of emotion has lived through three distinct eras in modern times. The pre-Jamesian assumed the sequence was: stimulus event—cognition—visceral response. James interchanged events two and three and said that the visceral afferent feedback occurred before the cognition. But Cannon quieted Jamesian ideas until Schachter's ingenious studies and catching explanations suggested that the individual experiences a puzzling set of visceral afferent sensations and integrates them cognitively. The language integration of visceral feelings, cognition, and context is an affect. This imaginative suggestion may be maximally valid for Western adults but perhaps minimally appropriate for children because of a developmental change in the relative distinctiveness of visceral cues.

Let us share a small set of assumptions before we proceed with the argument. Aside from pain and its surrogates, the major psychological elicitors of unpleasant visceral afferent sensations are violations of expectancies (uncertainty); anticipation of receiving or losing a desired goal; anticipation of seeing or losing a nurturant person; blocking of goal attainment; and anticipation of harm to the integrity of the body. Each of these event situations becomes conditioned to visceral afferent feedback early in life. These events—or conditioned

stimuli—are salient and maximally distinctive for children and affect words are attached to the events, not primarily to the visceral afferent sensations. Thus, the 6-year-old says he is mad because mother did not let him watch television; he says he is sad because the cat died; he says he is happy because he just received a prized toy. Affect words are labels for a set of external events. With development, individuals—with the help of social institutions—learn to protect themselves against most of the unpleasant sources of visceral afferent feedback—against the apocalyptic horsemen of uncertainty, loss of nurturance, goal blocking, and bodily harm. Moreover, they erect defenses against recognizing these events. They defend against recognition that they are confused, rejected, unable to attain a goal, or afraid. Thus, when events occur that are, in fact, representations of these situations, the events are not salient or distinctive and are not labeled. However, the conditioned visceral afferent sensations do occur, as they always have in the past. In the adult, the visceral afferent sensations become more distinctive or salient; whereas, for the child, the external events were salient and distinctive. The adult provides us with the situation Schachter and his colleagues have described. The adult often has visceral afferent sensations but cannot decide why he has them or what they mean. So he scans and searches the immediate past and context and decides that he is happy, sad, alienated, uncommitted, or in love. The essence of this argument is that for the child the external event is more distinctive than the visceral afferent sensations and the affect word is applied to external events. In the adult, the visceral afferent sensations are relatively more distinctive and the affect words are more often applied to them.

The personality differences ascribed to children in different ordinal positions are the result, in part, of differences in relative distinctiveness of social agents. For the firstborn, the adult is the distinctive stimulus to whom to attend; for the second born the older sibling has distinctive value and competes for the attention of the younger child. Only children lie alone for long periods of uninterrupted play. A parent who enters the room and speaks to the infant is necessarily a distinctive stimulus. For a fifth born whose four older siblings continually poke, fuss, and vocalize into the crib, the caretaking adult is, of necessity, less distinctive and, as a result, less attention will be paid to the adult. The importance of distinctiveness with respect to adaptation level engages the heated controversy surrounding the role of stimulus enrichment with infants and young children from deprived milieux. The pouring on of visual, auditory, and tactile stimulation willy-nilly should be less effective than a single distinctive stimulus presented in a context of quiet so it will be discrepant from the infant's adaptation level. If one takes this hypothesis seriously, a palpable change in enrichment strategies is implied. The theme of this change involves a shifting from a concern with increasing absolute level of stimulation to focusing on distinctiveness of stimulation. Culturally disadvantaged children are not deprived of stimulation; they are deprived of distinctive stimulation.

The early learning of sex role standards and the dramatic concern of school children with sex differences and their own sex role identity becomes reasonable when one considers that the differences between the sexes are highly distinctive. Voice, size, posture, dress, and usual locus of behavior are distinctive attributes that focus the child's attention on them.

One of the reasons why the relation between tutor and learner is important is that some tutors elicit greater attention than others. They are more distinctive. Those of us who contend that learning will be facilitated if the child is identified with or wants to identify with a tutor believe that one of the bases for the facilitation is the greater attention that is directed at a model with whom the child wishes to identify. A recent experiment touches on this issue.

The hypothesis can be simply stated. An individual will attend more closely to an initial stranger with whom he feels he shares attributes than to a stranger with whom he feels he does not share attributes, other things equal. The former model is more distinctive, for a typical adult ordinarily feels he does not share basic personality traits with most of the strangers that he meets. The subjects in this study were 56 Radcliffe freshmen and sophomores preselected for the following pair of traits. One group, the academics, were rated by four judges—all roommates—as being intensely involved in studies much more than they were in dating, clubs, or social activities. The second group, the social types, were rated as being much more involved in dating and social activities than they were in courses or grades. No subject was admitted into the study unless all four judges agreed that she fit one of these groups.

Each subject was seen individually by a Radcliffe senior, and told that each was participating in a study of creativity. The subject was told that Radcliffe seniors had written poems and that two of the poets were selected by the Harvard faculty as being the best candidates. The faculty could not decide which girl was the more creative and the student was going to be asked to judge the creativity of each of two poems that the girls had written. The subjects were told that creativity is

independent of IQ for bright people and they were told that since the faculty knew the personality traits of the girls, the student would be given that information also. The experimenter then described one of the poets as an academic grind and the other as a social activist. Each subject listened to two different girls recite two different poems on a tape. Order of presentation and voice of the reader were counterbalanced in an appropriate design. After the two poems were read the subject was asked for a verbatim recall of each poem, asked to judge its creativity, and finally, asked which girl she felt most similar to. Incidentally, over 95% of the subjects said they felt more similar to the model that they indeed matched in reality. Results supported the original hypothesis. Recall was best when a girl listened to a communicator with whom she shared personality traits. The academic subjects recalled more of the poem when it was read by the academic model than by the social model; whereas, the social subjects recalled more of the poem when it was read by the social model than the academic model. This study indicates that an individual will pay more attention to a model who possesses similar personality attributes, than to one who is not similar to the subject. Distinctiveness of tutor is enhanced by a perceived relation between learner and tutor.

Myths and superstitions are established around the kinds of experimental manipulations teachers or psychologists should perform in order to maximize the probability that learning will occur. When one focuses on the kind of manipulation—providing a model, giving a reinforcement, labeling the situation, punishing without delay—there is a strong push to establish superstitions about how behavioral change is produced. Recipes are written and adopted. If one believes, on the other hand, that a critical level of attention to incoming information is the essential variable, then one is free to mix up manipulations, to keep the recipe open, as long as one centers the subject's attention on the new material.

The most speculative prediction from this general argument is that behavioral therapy techniques will work for some symptoms—for about 20 years. A violation of an expectancy is a distinctive stimulus that attracts attention. The use of operant shaping techniques to alleviate phobias is a dramatic violation of an expectancy for both child and adult, and attention is magnetized and focussed on the therapeutic agent and his paraphernalia. As a result, learning is facilitated. But each day's use of this strategy may bring its demise closer. In time, a large segment of the populace will have adapted to this event; it will be a surprise no more and its attention getting and therapeutic value will be attenuated. Much of the power of psycho-analytic techniques began to wane when the therapist's secrets became public knowledge. If therapy is accomplished by teaching new responses, and if the learning of new responses is most likely to occur when attention to the teacher is maximal, it is safe to expect that we may need a new strategy of teaching patients new tricks by about 1984.

Let us weave the threads closer in an attempt at final closure. The psychology of the first half of this century was the product of a defensively sudden rupture from philosophy to natural science. The young discipline needed roots, and like a child, attached itself to an absolute description of nature, much as a 5-year-old clings to an absolute conception of morality. We now approach the latency years and can afford to relax and learn something from developments in our sister sciences. The message implicit in the recent work in psychology, biology, and physics contains a directive to abandon absolutism in selected theoretical areas. Conceptual ideas for mental processes must be invented, and this task demands a relativistic orientation. Learning is one of the central problems in psychology and understanding of the mechanisms of learning requires elucidation and measurement of the concept of attention. Existing data indicate that attention is under the control of distinctive stimuli and distinctiveness depends intimately on adaptation level of subject and context, and cannot be designated in absolute terms.

These comments are not to be regarded as a plea to return to undisciplined philosophical introspection. Psychology does possess some beginning clues as to how it might begin to measure elusive, relative concepts like "attention." Autonomic variables such as cardiac and respiratory rate appear to be useful indexes, and careful studies of subtle motor discharge patterns may provide initial operational bases for this construct.

Neurophysiologists have been conceptualizing their data in terms of attention distribution for several years, and they are uncovering some unusually provocative phenomena. For example, amplitude of evoked potentials from the association areas of the cortex are beginning to be regarded as a partial index of attention. Thompson and Shaw (1965) recorded evoked potentials from the association area of the cat's cortex—the middle suprasylvian gyrus—to a click, a light, or a shock to the forepaw. After they established base level response to each of these "standard" stimuli, the investigators presented these standard stimuli when the cat was active or when novel stimuli were introduced. The novel events were a rat in a bell jar, an air jet, or a growling sound. The results were unequivocal. Any one of these novel stimuli or activity by the cat produced reduced cortical evoked responses to the click, light, or shock. The authors suggest that the "amplitude of the evoked responses are inversely proportional to attention to a particular event [p. 338]." Psychology is beginning to develop promising strategies of measurement for the murky concept of attention and should begin to focus its theorizing and burgeoning measurement technology on variables having to do with the state of the organism, not just the quality of the external stimulus. The latter events can be currently objectified with greater elegance, but the former events seem to be of more significance. Mannheim once chastised the social sciences for seeming to be obsessed with studying what they could measure without error, rather than measuring what they thought to be important with the highest precision possible. It is threatening to abandon the security of the doctrine of absolutism of the stimulus event. Such a reorientation demands new measurement procedures, novel strategies of inquiry, and a greater tolerance for ambiguity. But let us direct our inquiry to where the pot of gold seems to shimmer and not fear to venture out from cozy laboratories where well-practiced habits have persuaded us to rationalize a faith in absolute monarchy.

REFERENCES

ARONFREED, J. The origin of self criticism. *Psychological Review,* 1964, *71,* 193–218

ARONFREED, J. Internalized behavioral suppression and the timing of social punishment. *Journal of Personality and Social Psychology,* 1965, *1,* 3–16.

BALDWIN, A. L., KALHORN, J., & BREESE, F. H. Patterns of parent behavior. *Psychological Monographs,* 1945, *58* (3, Whole No. 268).

BATESON, P. P. G. Changes in chicks' responses to novel moving objects over the sensitive period for imprinting. *Animal Behavior,* 1964, *12,* 479–489. (a)

BATESON, P. P. G. Relation between conspicuousness of stimuli and their effectiveness in the imprinting situation. *Journal of Comparative and Physiological Psychology,* 1964, *58,* 407–411. (b)

BECKER, W. C. Consequences of different kinds of parental discipline. In M. L. Hoffman & L. W. Hoffman (Eds.), *Review of child development research.* Vol. 1. New York: Russell Sage Foundation, 1964. Pp. 169–208.

BRACKBILL, Y. Extinction of the smiling response in infants as a function of reinforcement schedule. *Child Development,* 1958, *29,* 115–124.

CHARLESWORTH, W. R. Persistence of orienting and attending behavior in young infants as a function of stimulus uncertainty. Paper read at Society for Research in Child Development, Minneapolis, March 1965.

HELD, R. Plasticity in sensory motor systems. *Scientific American,* 1965, *213* (5), 84–94.

HELSON, H. *Adaptation level theory: An experimental and systematic approach to behavior.* New York: Harper & Row, 1964.

HERNÁNDEZ-PEÓN, R., SCHERRER, H., & JOUVET, M. Modification of electrical activity in cochlear nucleus during attention in unanesthetized cats. *Science,* 1956, *123,* 331–332.

HESS, E. H. Two conditions limiting critical age for imprinting. *Journal of Comparative and Physiological Psychology,* 1959, *52,* 515–518.

JAKOBSON, R., & HALLE, M. *Fundamentals of language.* The Hague: Mouton, 1956.

KAGAN, J., HENKER, B. A., HEN-TOV, A., LEVINE, J., & LEWIS, M. Infants' differential reactions to familiar and distorted faces. *Child Development,* 1966, *37,* 519–532.

KAGAN, J., & MOSS, H. A. *Birth to maturity.* New York: Wiley, 1962.

KLOPFER, P. H. Imprinting: A reassessment. *Science,* 1965, *147,* 301–303.

LEUBA, C. Toward some integration of learning theories: The concept of optimal stimulation. *Psychological Reports,* 1955, *1,* 27–33.

MELZACK, R., & WALL, P. D. Pain mechanisms: A new theory. *Science,* 1955, *150,* 971–979.

MILLER, N. E. Learnable drives and rewards. In S. S. Stevens (Ed.), *Handbook of experimental psychology.* New York: Wiley, 1951. 435–472.

OLDS, J. Self stimulation of the brain. *Science,* 1958, *127,* 315–324.

OLDS, J. Hypothalamic substrates of reward. *Physiological Review,* 1962, *42,* 554–604.

RHEINGOLD, H., GEWIRTZ, J. L., & ROSS, H. Social conditioning of vocalizations in the infant. *Journal of Comparative and Physiological Psychology,* 1959, *52,* 68–73.

SCHACHTER, S., & SINGER, J. E. Cognitive, social and physiological determinants of emotional states. *Psychological Review,* 1962, *69,* 379–399.

SCHAEFER, E. S. A circumplex model for maternal behavior. *Journal of Abnormal and Social Psychology,* 1959, *59,* 226–235.

SCHAEFER, E. S., & BAYLEY, N. Maternal behavior, child behavior and their intercorrelations from infancy through adolescence. *Monographs of the Society for Research in Child Development,* 1963, *28,* No. 87.

SEARS, R. R., MACCOBY, E. E., & LEVIN, H. *Patterns of child rearing.* Row Peterson, 1957.

THOMPSON, R. F., & SHAW, J. A. Behavioral correlates of evoked activity recorded from association areas of the cerebral cortex. *Journal of Comparative and Physiological Psychology,* 1965, *60,* 329–339.

THOMPSON, W. R., & DUBANOSKI, R. A. Imprinting and the law of effort. *Animal Behavior,* 1964, *12,* 213–218.

TOMKINS, S. S. *Affect imagery consciousness.* Vol. 1. *The positive affects.* New York: Springer, 1962.

3

Freud and the Image of Man [1]

JEROME S. BRUNER

Bruner assesses the theoretical and practical impact of Freudian ideas in this paper, which takes cognizance of people's increasing psychological sophistication during the past half century. His 1965 presidential address to the American Psychological Association ("The Growth of Mind") is included in Section XI. Long a professor of psychology at Harvard University and director of its Center for Cognitive Studies, in 1971 he accepted appointment as Watts Professor of Psychology at Oxford University in England.

By the dawn of the sixth century before Christ, the Greek physicist-philosophers had formulated a conception of the physical world as a unitary material phenomenon. The Ionics had set forth a conception of matter as fundamental substance, transformation of which accounted for the myriad forms and substances of the physical world. Anaximander was subtle enough to recognize that matter must be viewed as a generalized substance, free of any particular sensuous properties. Air, iron, water, or bone were only elaborated forms, derived from a more general stuff. Since that time, the phenomena of the physical world have been conceived as continuous and monistic, as governed by the common laws of matter. The view was a bold one, bold in the sense of running counter to the immediate testimony of the senses. It has served as an axiomatic basis of physics for more than two millennia. The bold view eventually became the obvious view, and it gave shape to our common understanding of the physical world. Even the alchemists rested their case upon this doctrine of material continuity and, indeed, had they known about neutron bombardment, they might even have hit upon the proper philosopher's stone.

The good fortune of the physicist—and these matters are always relative, for the material monism of physics may have impeded nineteenth century thinking and delayed insights into the nature of complementarity in modern physical theory—this early good fortune or happy insight has no counterpart in the sciences of man. Lawful continuity between man and the animal kingdom, between dreams and unreason on one side and waking rationality on the other, between madness and sanity, between consciousness and unconsciousness, between the mind of the child and the adult mind, between primitive and civilized man—each of these has been a cherished discontinuity preserved in doctrinal canons. There were voices in each generation, to be sure, urging the exploration of continuities. Anaximander had a passing good approximation to a theory of evolution based on natural selection; Cornelius Agrippa offered a plausible theory of the continuity of mental health and disease in terms of bottled-up sexuality. But Anaximander did not prevail against Greek conceptions of man's creation nor Cornelius Agrippa against the demonopathy of the *Malleus Maleficarum.* Neither in establishing the continuity between the varied states of man nor in pursuing the continuity between man and animal was there conspicuous success until the nineteenth century.

I need not insist upon the social, ethical, and political significance of this image, for it is patent that the view one takes of man affects profoundly one's standard of the humanly possible. And it is in the light of such a standard that we establish our laws, set our aspirations for learning, and judge the fitness of men's acts. It is no surprise, then, that those who govern must perforce be jealous guardians of man's ideas about man, for the structure of government rests upon an uneasy consensus about human nature and human wants. The idea of man is of the order of *res publica,* and by virtue of its public status, it is an idea that is not subject to change without public debate. The behavioral

[1] This article also appeared in the July 1956 *Partisan Review* and was read earlier in the year at the Conference on Science and the Modern World View under the auspices of the American Academy of Arts and Science.

Jerome S. Bruner, "Freud and the image of man," *American Psychologist,* 1956, *11,* 463–466. Reprinted by permission.

scientist, as some nowadays insist on calling him, may propose, but it is the society at large that disposes. Nor is it simply a matter of public concern. For man as individual has a deep and emotional investment in his image of himself. If we have learned anything in the last half-century of psychology, it is that man has powerful and exquisite capacities for defending himself against violations of his cherished self-image. This is not to say that Western man has not persistently asked: "What is man that thou art mindful of him?" It is only that the question, when pressed, brings us to the edge of anxiety where inquiry is no longer free.

Two figures stand out massively as the architects of our present-day conception of man: Darwin and Freud. Freud's was the more daring, the more revolutionary, and in a deep sense, the more poetic insight. But Freud is inconceivable without Darwin. It is both timely and perhaps historically just to center our inquiry on Freud's contribution to the modern image of man. Darwin I shall treat as a necessary condition for Freud and for his success, recognizing, of course, that this is a form of psychological license. Not only is it the centenary of Freud's birth; it is also a year in which the current of popular thought expressed in commemoration of the date quickens one's awareness of Freud's impact on our times.

Rear-guard fundamentalism did not require a Darwin to slay it in an age of technology. He helped, but this contribution was trivial in comparison with another. What Darwin had done was to propose a set of principles unified around the conception that all organic species had their origins and took their form from a common set of circumstances—the requirements of biological survival. All living creatures were on a common footing. When the post-Darwin era of exaggeration had passed and religious literalism had abated into a new nominalism, what remained was a broad, orderly, and unitary conception of organic nature, a vast continuity from the monocellular protozoans to man. Biology had at last found its unifying principle in the doctrine of evolution. Man was not unique but the inheritor of an organic legacy.

As the summit of an evolutionary process, man could still view himself with smug satisfaction, indeed proclaim that God or Nature had shown a persistent wisdom in its effort to produce a final, perfect product. It remained for Freud to present the image of man as the unfinished product of nature: struggling against unreason, impelled by driving inner vicissitudes and urges that had to be contained if man were to live in society, host alike to seeds of madness and majesty, never fully free from an infancy anything but innocent. What Freud

was proposing was that man at best and man at worst is subject to a common set of explanations: good and evil grow from a common process.

Freud was strangely yet appropriately fitted for his role as architect of a new conception of man. We must pause to examine his qualifications, for the image of man that he created was in no small measure founded on his painfully achieved image of himself and of his times. We are concerned not so much with his psychodynamics, but with the intellectual traditions he embodies. A child of his century's materialism, he was wedded to the determinism and the classical physicalism of 19th-century physiology so boldly represented by Helmholtz. Indeed, the young Freud's devotion to the exploration of anatomical structures was a measure of the strength of this inheritance. But at the same time, as both Lionel Trilling and W. H. Auden have recognized with much sensitivity, there was a deep current of romanticism in Freud—a sense of the role of impulse, of the drama of life, of the power of symbolism, of ways of knowing that were more poetic than rational in spirit, of the poet's cultural alienation. It was perhaps this romantic's sense of drama that led to his gullibility about parental seduction and to his generous susceptibility to the fallacy of the dramatic instance.

Freud also embodies two traditions almost as antithetical as romanticism and nineteenth century scientism. He was profoundly a Jew, not in a doctrinal sense but in his conception of morality, in his love of the skeptical play of reason, in his distrust of illusion, in the form of his prophetic talent, even in his conception of mature eroticism. His prophetic talent was antithetic to a Utopianism either of innocence or of social control. Nor did it lead to a counsel of renunciation. Free oneself of illusion, of neurotic infantilism, and "the soft voice of intellect" would prevail. Wisdom for Freud was neither doctrine nor formula, but the achievement of maturity. The patient who is cured is the one who is now free enough of neurosis to decide intelligently about his own destiny. As for his conception of mature love, it has always seemed to me that its blend of tenderness and sensuality combined the uxorious imagery of the Chassidic tradition and the sensual quality of the Song of Songs. And might it not have been Freud rather than a commentator of the Haftorahs who said, "In children, it was taught, God gives humanity a chance to make good its mistakes." For the modern trend of permissiveness toward children is surely a feature of the Freudian legacy. [*In actuality, the respects in which Freudian writers have advocated indulgence of children are balanced by others in which they have urged parental firmness. If Freud-*

ian pronouncements gave rise to excessive leniency it is generally because they were misinterpreted.—Editor]

But for all the Hebraic quality, Freud is also in the classical tradition—combining the Stoics and the great Greek dramatists. For Freud as for the Stoics, there is no possibility of man disobeying the laws of nature. And yet, it is in this lawlessness that for him the human drama inheres. His love for Greek drama and his use of it in his formulation are patent. The sense of the human tragedy, the inevitable working out of the human plight—these are the hallmarks of Freud's case histories. When Freud, the tragic dramatist, becomes a therapist, it is not to intervene as a directive authority. The therapist enters the drama of the patient's life, makes possible a play within a play, the transference,* and when the patient has "worked through" and understood the drama, he has achieved the wisdom necessary for freedom. Again, like the Stoics, it is in the recognition of one's own nature and in the acceptance of the laws that govern it that the good life is to be found.

Freud's contribution lies in the continuities of which he made us aware. The first of these is the continuity of organic lawfulness. Accident in human affairs was no more to be brooked as "explanation" than accident in nature. The basis for accepting such an "obvious" proposition had, of course, been well prepared by a burgeoning 19th-century scientific naturalism. It remained for Freud to extend naturalistic explanation to the heart of human affairs. The *Psychopathology of Everyday Life* is not one of Freud's deeper works, but "the Freudian slip" has contributed more to the common acceptance of lawfulness in human behavior than perhaps any of the more rigorous and academic formulations from Wundt to the present. The forgotten lunch engagement, the slip of the tongue, the barked shin could no longer be dismissed as accident. Why Freud should have succeeded where novelists,

philosophers, and academic psychologists had failed we will consider in a moment.

Freud's extension of Darwinian doctrine beyond Haeckel's theorem that ontogeny recapitulates phylogeny is another contribution to continuity. It is the conception that in the human mind, the primitive, infantile, and archaic exist side by side with the civilized and evolved.

Where animals are concerned we hold the view that the most highly developed have arisen from the lowest. . . . In the realm of mind, on the other hand, the primitive type is so commonly preserved alongside the transformations which have developed out of it that it is superfluous to give instances in proof of it. When this happens, it is usually the result of a bifurcation in development. One quantitative part of an attitude or an impulse has survived unchanged while another has undergone further development. This brings us very close to the more general problem of conservation in the mind. . . . Since the time when we recognized the error of supposing that ordinary forgetting signified destruction or annihilation of the memory-trace, we have been inclined to the opposite view that nothing once formed in the mind could ever perish, that everything survives in some way or other, and is capable under certain conditions of being brought to light again. . . . (Freud, *Civilization and Its Discontents,* pp. 14–15).

What has now come to be common sense is that in everyman there is the potentiality for criminality, and that these are neither accidents nor visitations of degeneracy, but products of a delicate balance of forces that, under different circumstances, might have produced normality or even saintliness. Good and evil, in short, grow from a common root.

Freud's genius was in his resolution of polarities. The distinction of child and adult was one such. It did not suffice to reiterate that the child was father to the man. The theory of infantile sexuality and the stages of psychosexual development were an effort to fill the gap, the latter clumsy, the former elegant. Though the alleged progression of sexual expression from oral, to anal, to phallic, to genital has not found a secure place either in common sense or in general psychology, the developmental continuity of sexuality has been recognized by both. Common sense honors the continuity in the baby-books and in the permissiveness with which young parents of today resolve their doubts. And the research of Beach and others has shown the profound effects of infantile experience on adult sexual behavior—even in lower organisms.

If today people are reluctant to report their dreams with the innocence once attached to such recitals, it is again because Freud brought into

---

* Transference. Misinterpretations of a therapist's statements or actions, or other misperceptions of the therapist on the part of a psychotherapeutic patient, arising from the tendency to react to the therapist as though he were some other person important in the patient's emotional life. The study by therapist and patient of these perceptual distortions is one of the ways in which patients undergoing some kinds of psychotherapy are helped to understand and control their proclivities to perceive certain people inaccurately and to behave inappropriately. The corresponding term "counter-transference" refers to distortions of the therapist about the patient. For instance, a therapist may at times respond emotionally to a female patient as though she were his daughter, sister, or mother. The well-trained therapist has become adept at noticing his own tendencies to distort. As a result, the intrusion of his personal needs upon his professional work can be minimal.—EDITOR.

common question the discontinuity between the rational purposefulness of waking life and the seemingly irrational purposelessness of fantasy and dream. While the crude symbolism of Freud's early efforts at dream interpretation has come increasingly to be abandoned, the conception of the dream as representing disguised wishes and fears has become common coin. And Freud's recognition of deep unconscious processes in the creative act has gone far toward enriching our understanding of the kinship between the artist, the humanist, and the man of science.

It is our heritage from Freud that the all-or-none distinction between mental illness and mental health has been replaced by a more humane conception of the continuity of these states. The view that neurosis is a severe reaction to human trouble is as revolutionary in its implications for social practice as it is daring in formulation. The "bad seed" theories, and nosologies of the 19th century, the demonologies and doctrines of divine punishment—none of these provided a basis for comparison toward human suffering comparable to that of our time.

One may argue, finally, that Freud's sense of the continuity of human conditions, of the likeness of the human plight, has made possible a deeper sense of the brotherhood of man. It has in any case tempered the spirit of punitiveness toward what once we took as evil and what we now see as sick. We have not yet resolved the dilemma posed by these two ways of viewing. Its resolution is one of the great moral challenges of our age.

Why, after such initial resistance, were Freud's views so phenomenally successful in transforming common conceptions of man?

One reason we have already considered: the readiness of the Western World to accept naturalistic explanation of organic phenomena and, concurrently, to be readier for such explanation in the mental sphere. There had been at least four centuries of uninterrupted scientific progress, recently capped by a theory of evolution that brought man into continuity with the rest of the animal kingdom. The rise of naturalism as a way of understanding nature and man saw a corresponding decline in the explanatory aspirations of religion. By the close of the 19th century, religion, to quote Morton White, "too often agreed to accept the role of a non-scientific spiritual grab-bag, or an ideological know-nothing." Elucidation of the human plight has been abandoned by religion and not yet adopted by science.

It was the inspired imagery, the proto-theory of Freud, that was to fill the gap. Success in transforming the common conception of man was not simply its recourse to the "cause-and-effect" discourse of science. Rather it is Freud's imagery, I think, that provides the clue to his ideological power. It is an imagery of necessity, if I may call it that, an imagery that combines the dramatic, the tragic, and the scientific views of necessity. It is here that Freud's intellectual heritage matters so deeply. Freud's is a theory or a proto-theory peopled with actors. The characters are from life: the blind, energic, pleasure-seeking id; the priggish and punitive superego; the ego, battling for its being by diverting the energy of the others to its own use. The drama has an economy and a terseness. The ego develops canny mechanisms for dealing with the threat of id impulses: denial, projection, and the rest. Balances are struck between the actors, and in the balance is character and neurosis. Freud was using the dramatic technique of decomposition, the play whose actors are parts of a single life—a technique that he himself had recognized in phantasies and dreams, one which is honored in his essay, "The Poet and the Daydream."

The imagery of the theory, moreover, has an immediate resonance with the dialectic of experience. True, it is not the stuff of superficial conscious experience. But it fits the human plight, its conflictedness, its private torment, its impulsiveness, its secret and frightening urges, its tragic quality.

In its scientific imagery, it is marked by the necessity of the classical mechanics. At times the imagery is hydraulic: suppress this stream of impulses, and it breaks out in a displacement elsewhere. The system is closed and mechanical, at times electrical, as when cathexes are formed and withdrawn like electrical charges. The way of thought fitted well the common-sense physics of its age.

Finally, the image of man presented was thoroughly secular; its ideal type was the mature man free of infantile neuroticism, capable of finding his own way. This freedom from both Utopianism and asceticism has earned Freud the contempt of ideological totalitarians of the Right and the Left. But the image has found a ready home in the rising, liberal intellectual middle class. For them, the Freudian ideal type has become a rallying point in the struggle against spiritual regimentation.

I have said virtually nothing about Freud's equation of sexuality and impulse. It was surely and still is a stimulus to resistance. But to say that Freud's success lay in forcing a reluctant Victorian world to accept the importance of sexuality is as empty as hailing Darwin for his victory over fundamentalism. Each had a far more profound effect.

Can Freud's contribution to the common understanding of man in the twentieth century be likened to the impact of such great physical and biological theories as Newtonian physics and Darwin's conception of evolution? The question is an empty one. Freud's mode of thought is not a theory in the conventional sense, it is a metaphor, an analogy, a way of conceiving man, a drama. I would propose that Anaximander is the proper parallel: his view of the connectedness of physical nature was also an analogy—and a powerful one. Freud is the ground from which theory will grow, and he has prepared the twentieth century to nurture the growth. But far more important, he has provided an image of man that has made him comprehensible without at the same time making him contemptible.

4

Psychological Models
for Guidance

GORDON W. ALLPORT

*Gordon Allport evaluates three alternative ways
of looking at human behavior. The first of these is
the typical stance of the "experimental" psychologist or "behaviorist" or "learning theorist." The
second is that of most clinical psychologists, especially those who are psychoanalytically oriented
(i.e., influenced heavily by Freud's writings). The
third is just becoming popular. Allport calls it
existential psychology. It is also referred to as
humanistic psychology. Major proponents of this
outlook include Carl Rogers and the late Abraham Maslow. We recommend reading Maslow's
"Toward a Humanistic Biology" (American Psychologist, 1969, 24, 724–735).*

*Allport's article is a commentary not only upon
the Freudian orientation described by Bruner (preceding selection), but also upon many of the articles in this book that reflect the work of behavioristic
laboratories such as that of B. F. Skinner.*

*Until his death in 1967, Allport taught social
psychology and personality at Harvard University. He was president of the American Psychological Association in 1939. In 1963 he received the
Gold Medal of the American Psychological Foundation for his lifelong contributions to psychology.*

However excellent his natural eyesight may be,
a counselor always looks at his client through professional spectacles. It could not be otherwise.
After all, he has invested time and money in his
psychological training. Of what use is it unless it
adds special prisms to his own unaided eyesight?

The lenses we wear are ground to the prescrip-
tion of our textbooks and teachers. Even while
we are undergraduates a certain image of the
nature of man is fitted to our eyes. We grow accustomed to the image and when we become practi-
tioners or teachers we may still take it for granted.

But every so often comes a time for optical re-
examination. Perhaps the image we have is still the
best fit we can get; perhaps it is not. We can tell
only by examining alternative lenses. In particular
I believe that three are worthy of special scrutiny:

1. MAN SEEN AS A REACTIVE BEING. Under this rubric I
   would include outlooks known as naturalism, positivism, behaviorism, operationism, physicalism; these
   are also sometimes called—mistakenly, I think—
   "scientific psychology."

2. MAN SEEN AS A REACTIVE BEING IN DEPTH. Here I
   include what is variously called psychoanalysis, psychodynamics, depth psychology.

3. MAN SEEN AS A BEING-IN-PROCESS-OF-BECOMING.
   This label covers recent trends known as holism,
   orthopsychology, personalistics, existential psychology.

These three images provide a focus not only for
guidance practices, but for all other professional
psychological activity whether it be teaching, research, counseling or therapy.

MAN: A REACTIVE BEING

One hundred years ago in his *Beiträge* Wilhelm
Wundt mapped a program for the newly conceived
science of psychology. His own view of the proper
development of this science was broad and permissive, especially in the field of social psychology.
But what has taken hold in the Anglo-American
tradition is the experimental outlook of his *Physio-
logische Psychologie*. Fusing with Darwinism,
Machian positivism, the quantitative outlook of
Galton and his successors, as well as with techniques invented by Binet, Pavlov, Hull and others
—this experimental outlook prevailed and has
ground the lens that is fitted to the eyes of almost
all undergraduate students of psychology. Many of
us who continue in the profession feel no need for
further correction in this image of man.

Gordon W. Allport, "Psychological models for guidance," *Harvard Educational Review,* 1962, *32* (4), 373–381. Reprinted by permission.

Seen through this lens man is no different in kind from any other living reactor; and therefore, like the paramecium or pigeon, may be studied biologically, behaviorally, mathematically. To be sure a few special concepts need to be devised to take care of the vast complexity of human behavior, but all these concepts—among them habit hierarchy, secondary reinforcement, input and output of information, and the like—are consistent with the postulates of physicalism and naturalism.

If we ask, "What does it mean to be a human being?" this school of thought replies, "Man is one more creature of nature; his behavior though complex is predictable in principle. His present state is determined by his past state. A man's consciousness is unreliable and must be distrusted, preferably disregarded altogether. We seek the general laws of nature, not personal uniqueness. We study man, not men; objective reality, not subjective."

In principle this broad positive tradition, which we all know so well, puts a desirable end to psychological naïveté. It cautions us not to believe every verbal report that comes to our ears; it warns us to be skeptical of our own naked eyesight; and from it we learn to check ourselves for observer reliability. It teaches us to use precise and repeatable methods. Because of its stress on reliable methods this favored tradition in psychology has become known as "scientific psychology." Its methods are indeed scientific; but its primary postulate—that man is simply a reactive organism—is no more scientific than any other postulate.

It is here that the counselor encounters his first difficulty. Trained in tests, statistics, and experimental design, he may think, quite mistakenly, that to employ these useful aids he must also view his client as a reactive being—an exclusive product of stimulus impact, homeostasis, drive-reduction and reinforcement learning. The term "scientific" has spread like a grease spot from method to theory. Just because most of our methods evolved through the positivistic tradition does not mean that the postulates of this tradition concerning the nature of man are the only acceptable postulates for scientific psychology.

A counselor whose theoretical spectacles disclose a merely reactive being, is likely to think of his client in terms of past conditioning and potential re-conditioning; in terms of reinforcements, in terms of environmental determinism. He will assume that his client's basic motives are drive-reduction or second-order conditionings which in some shadowy way are supposed to account for all his adult interests and vocational ambitions.

The vocabulary emanating from this type of postulate is replete with terms like *reaction, re-* *sponse, reinforcement, reflex, respondent, reintegration*—all sorts of *re*-compounds. The reference is backward. What *has* been is more important than what *will* be. Terms such as *proaction, progress, program, production, problem-solving,* or *propriate* are characteristically lacking. One would think that the client seated opposite would *pro*test, for the language of response negates the subject's immediate certainty that his life lies in the future.

The positivistic view of man as a reactor has performed a good service, shaking us out of common sense naïveté, endowing us with useful methods, and correctly informing us that man is, in *some* aspects of his being, a simple respondent to simple pressures. Its postulates are, however, questionable. It sees reality as ordered but not as personal; it sees consciousness as a nuisance; it looks at man as reactive, not proactive.

It is probably true that no counselor fully follows this creed in his daily practice. Indeed he could not do so. It is too impoverished a view of real life. When a convinced positivist attempts to fit his image of man to concrete human situations, as B. F. Skinner has done in *Walden Two,* the result strikes many of us as threadbare, even pitiable.

Probably for this reason many behaviorists (starting even as far back as E. B. Holt in *The Freudian Wish and its Place in Ethics*) attempt to combine stimulus-response with psychoanalysis. Neal Miller and John Dollard in their *Personality and Psychotherapy* offer a good example. Man as a reactive being is combined with man as a reactive being in depth.

MAN: A REACTIVE BEING IN DEPTH

So influential is this image of man that we find it everywhere: dominant in literature, in social work, in guidance, in therapeutic practice, and in the market place. There is no need today to describe this image to any educated, or even semi-educated, American adult. Freudianism, like positivism, is our daily dish.

What I should like to do is to make clear that Freudianism (in spite of its less reliable methods) is a close kin of traditional positivism. The only change in the image of man lies in adding the depth dimension. To the long psychological vocabulary of *re*-compounds, depth psychology adds *repression, regression, resistance, abreaction, reaction formation,* and many others.

Like other simple naturalistic views of man, psychoanalysis puts its chief weight upon the press of pleasure and pain. This pressure produces in the organism a tendency to seek an equilibrium between the force of his drives and the circumstances of reality. The fact that Freud maximizes the role of sex and locates the whole constellation of reactive forces chiefly in the unconscious does not alter the essential similarity.

For Freud causation lies in the past history of the individual just as it does for the conditioned-response theorist. Both have a dismaying disregard for the person's phenomenology of the future, for his sense of personhood and sense of freedom. The ego is a reactive agent, having no energy of its own, but borrowing from the unsocialized Id.

Central to depth psychology, and important for guidance, is the doctrine of *recall* and *recovery* (two more *re*-compounds). Therapy, and presumably guidance, proceeds by disclosing to the client some buried motive, or a troublesome and repressed psychic trauma. The client's salvation, if indeed he has any, lies in this vital recall. A troublesome memory is brought to cognizable form. Presumably the result is helpful to the individual in solving his conflicts. The theory, however, does not allow for any interaction between the person and the recovered memory. Simple re-instatement is itself, as Freud says, the "pure gold" of psychoanalysis. What values a client should live by when once the re-instatement has taken place is not the "pure gold" of psychoanalysis. That all adult values are simply sublimated aim-inhibited wishes, is the central doctrine. Freud never allows for the individual's capacity to disregard his past or to reshape it freely. Indeed, since the structure of the Id never changes, the future can at best be a redirection, never a transformation, of one's purposes. What one becomes is essentially what one is, and what one was.

Among the valid portions of psychoanalysis of special use to all counselors, is the brilliant account given us by Freud and by his daughter Anna, of the defensive mechanisms of the ego. In dealing with our client we do well to follow the advice of psychoanalysis and watch for rationalizations, denials of reality through repression, and displacements of aggression. All these, and other, ego-defenses belong to the nature of man, and therefore must find a place in any theory of human personality.

But what perplexes me is why so many of the ego-processes described by psychoanalysis should be merely protective strategies. Are there no ego-processes that lead to a transformation of what is recovered? To a creative cognition? To a revised sense of personhood and a new phenomenology of the future? To Freud the person seems never to be truly proactive, seldom even active. Almost always he is seen as reactive to early fixations—perhaps to some castration threat that occurred years ago, or to some other unsocialized infant complex, especially to Oedipal fantasies. My difficulty with this image of man is summed up most tersely by the late satirist, Max Beerbohm, who said, "They were a tense and peculiar family—those Oedipuses."

There is, I am well aware, a large group of theories that derive from the psychodynamic tradition but at the same time deviate considerably from the orthodox view of reactivity-in-depth. All these theories, in my judgment, move in a desirable direction. Here I shall mention only some of the relevant authors: Adler, Jung, Hartmann, Horney, Erikson, Fromm. Still more deviant from Freud are Goldstein, Maslow, Rogers, and Robert White. These and other writers offer a type of theory that views man as a being in the process of becoming. Many of them ask the pivotal question differently from the reactivist schools of thought. And it makes a good deal of difference just how a question is asked.

A story is told about two priests. They were arguing whether it was proper to smoke and to pray at the same time. One said "Yes," the other "No." To settle the matter they decided that both should write to the Holy Father for his opinion. Sometime later they met and compared notes. Each claimed that the Holy Father had supported his view. They were perplexed. Finally one asked, "How did you phrase your question?" The other replied: "I asked whether it was proper to smoke while one is praying; and the Pope answered, 'Certainly not, praying is serious business and permits no distractions.' And how did you phrase your question?" "Well," said the other, "I asked if it were proper to pray while smoking, and the Pope answered, 'Certainly, prayer is always in order.'"

Instead of asking Aristotle's question, "What is the place of man in Nature?" many authors today are asking St. Augustine's question, "Who am I?" This question, rephrased in the 20th Century, has opened the floodgates to a new theorizing of the broad type often labeled *existentialist*.

MAN: BEING IN THE PROCESS OF BECOMING

Seelye Bixler, former president of Colby College, tells of a student who recently remarked, "I can't tell you how much satisfaction I take in my existential despair." In some student circles despair has always been popular. To label it "existentialist" makes it doubly attractive, in fact irresistible.

But overlooking the fashionable flavor of existentialism it is surely necessary for the modern counselor to take seriously the present-day anxieties of the younger generation. No longer can youth contemplate its future under the protection of the great social stabilizers of the past. No longer can one counsel within the framework of Victorian decorum, theological certainties, or the Pax Britannica. It is obvious to us all that some sort of shattering transformation is under way. The comfortable stabilities of culture, caste, the gold standard, and military supremacy are no longer ours.

Nor are the comfortable stabilities of traditional psychology adequate. Of what use is it to invoke an impersonal theory of learning, a biological theory of motivation, and a late Victorian formula for the unconscious, when youth's problems today are acutely conscious, intensely personal, and propelling him like an unguided astronaut into an unknown future? A counselor is not equipped for his job unless he can share in some degree the apprehensions of modern youth, and sense the swampy underpinning on which youth treads. Over his desk the counselor might well tack the wisdom of the Spanish writer Unamuno, "Suffering is the life blood that runs through us all and binds us together." While not every youth who comes to the counselor is at that moment a sufferer, it is a safe assumption that he comes for guidance that will fortify him for the inevitable suffering that he will encounter in his course of life.

TENTATIVENESS AND COMMITMENT

From the existential point of view the ideal counselor will strive to develop two attitudes in his client. Taken separately they seem antithetical; but fused into a world-view they provide strength for the future. One attitude is *tentativeness* of outlook. Since certainties are no longer certain, let all dogmas be fearlessly examined, especially those cultural idols that engender a false sense of security: dogmas of race supremacy, of naïve scientism, of unilinear evolutionary progress. Let one face the worst in oneself and in the world around him, so that one may correctly estimate the hazards.

Taken by itself such tentativeness, such insightfulness, might well lead to ontological despair. Yet acceptance of the worst does not prevent us from making the best of the worst. Up to now psychologists have not dealt with the remarkable ability of human beings to blend a tentative outlook with firm commitment to chosen values. The poet Tennyson perceived the point.

> There lives more faith in honest doubt,
> Believe me, than in half the creeds.

A commitment is, as Pascal has said, a wager. One may lose it, but one may also win. Cardinal Newman warned us that our religion can never be a matter of certainty. It is at best a subjective condition of certitude which he defined as "probability supported by faith and love." Yet a mature religion, thus defined, can be infinitely sustaining and heroically motivating. Existentialism, whether theistic or atheistic, makes the same point. We have the freedom to commit ourselves to great causes with courage, even though we lack certainty. We can be at one and the same time half-sure and whole-hearted.

William James, probably America's greatest thinker, tried to teach us this lesson, but fifty years ago we were not ready for it. It is surely noteworthy that, writing as he did in a period of social stability, James saw clearly how ultimately uncertain are our foundations of value. Wealth, he saw was a false god, leading us into a national disease that has recently been called "galloping consumption." The more we build up our material resources, the more we fear poverty. In religion, James knew, there was no certainty; yet, like Cardinal Newman, he recognized the constructive power of a mature religious commitment. Whatever ideal leads to long-range constructive consequences is psychologically sound. It is also pragmatically true. And who is to say that we have a test for truth more absolute than our own commitment in so far as it is validated by fruitful consequences?

Neither positivistic nor psychodynamic schools of thought allow for the fact that our psychological constitution permits both total tentativeness and total commitment. Such a paradox reminds us of the electron that is able to go in two opposite directions at the same time. Taken by itself tentativeness is disintegrative; commitment is integrative. Yet the blend seems to occur in personalities that we admire for their soundness and perspective. Presumably through teaching and guidance we may develop both attitudes in our youth.

Whenever the two attitudes coexist in a life we find important desirable by-products from the fusion. One is a deep sense of compassion for the lot of the human race in general and in each separate social encounter that marks our daily life. The other by-product is likewise graceful; it is the sense of humor. Humor requires the perspective of tentativeness, but also an underlying system of values that prevents laughter from souring into cynicism. As Meredith said, humor is a capacity to laugh at the things you love and still to love them.

RATIONALISM VS. IRRATIONALISM

The chief criticism made of existentialism is that it leads away from reason and exalts irrationalism.

While this charge may apply to certain literary and theological trends in the existential movement I doubt that it jeopardizes the future of scientific psychology. The attitudes of tentativeness and commitment of which I speak are perfectly sound concepts—call them "intervening variables" if you wish. Indeed in so far as they reflect important states in human personality, and thus lead to improvement in understanding, prediction, and direction of human behavior, they are sounder scientific concepts than many of those we have been using.

And just what is rationalism? We venerate the ancient Greeks for their exaltation of human reason; and as psychologists we venerate Aristotle for asking the question, "What is man's place in nature." But Greek rationalism was broader than the limited, method-centered, scientism into which it has degenerated. The Greeks themselves saw a place for tentativeness and commitment within the scope of reason. The case is beautifully stated in an ancient inscription found somewhere on the coast of Greece:

> A shipwrecked sailor buried on this coast
> Bids you set sail.
> Full many a bark, when we were lost,
> Weathered the gale.

The dead sailor urges us to make the wager, take the risk, although we cannot be sure of coming through to our destination.

IMPLICATIONS FOR THEORY

What does all this mean in terms of psychological theory, and in terms of guidance? First of all it means that in order to achieve a more realistic image of man and his potentialities, we need to revise our current theories of learning and growth, of motivation and personality structure. Elsewhere (in *Pattern and Growth in Personality,* 1961) I have discussed some of the needed changes in detail, and so shall say only a few words about each.

The trouble with our current theories of learning is not so much that they are wrong, but that they are partial. They fit best the learning of animals and young children. The concepts of conditioning, reinforcement, identification, seem a bit hollow when the counselor tries to apply them to his work. They are not very helpful, for example, in explaining how a youth may learn both tentativeness of outlook and firmness of commitment. Supplementary theories in terms of organizational, biographical, and propriate learning are needed.

Except in the sense of physical maturation the concept of *growth* scarcely exists in psychology at all. Nor will it have its proper place until we have agreed upon normative standards for the maturity of personality. Up to now normative problems, except in the sense of statistical norms, are much neglected.

As for motivation and personality structure psychologists are in a state of turmoil and disagreement. That the past stages of a life do not fully explain the motivational "go" of the present, I for one am firmly convinced. Therefore we need a concept (*functional autonomy*, I think will do) to represent that portion of a life that is oriented toward the future and not toward the past. Also we need a theory of personal structure (of *personal dispositions*) to represent the important cleavages and foci of a given, concrete personality. Such a theory will, I am convinced, carry us much further than a conception of uniform variables to which every client is forcibly ordered, whether we call these variables factors, needs, dimensions, or common traits.

Most of all we need to surrender the models that would compress human personality into the routine homeostatic situation that we find in quasi-closed systems. Human personality is a wide-open system, responsive to tangible and intangible culture, on the look-out for new ideas, and capable of asking an altogether new type of question—asked by no other creature in nature, viz., "Who am I?"

There are, I am glad to say, many psychologists who feel as strongly as I that these various types of improvement need to be made before the counselor will have a fully fashioned science of psychology to undergird his practice.

IMPLICATIONS FOR GUIDANCE

Guidance is not a matter of gimmicks, nor of rules of thumb. A guide, like a philosopher and friend, is a person who loves wisdom and loves his fellow men. True, he has skills to mark him off from the professional philosopher or the untrained friend. To some extent the counselor's present-day skills are useful. Standard tests and measurements are helpful; so too achievement records and focused interviews. Most of our devices come from researches conducted under the positivistic outlook, or (in the case of projective techniques) under the psychodynamic. While many of them are serviceable I look forward to the invention of new instruments still better suited to the study of the central or propriate aspects of single personalities.

Most important, of course, are the spectacles the counselor wears. The image should no longer be borrowed from the tradition of simple naïve reactivism. Just as centimeters, grams, seconds are outmoded in modern physics so too are simple stimulus-response connections in modern psychology. In psychology, even more than in physics, we need theory capable of dealing with fluid becoming.

The plain fact is that man is more than a reactive being, more even than a reactive being in depth. If he were comfortably fixed at these levels we could with confidence apply a uniform stencil in studying his nature. But the life process is no less paradoxical than the processes of modern physics. How can one deal with space that is both finite and unbounded, with light that is both wave and particle, with electrons that pass from orbit to orbit without traversing the space between? Similarly, a human person is both structure and process, a being both biological and noetic, a being who changes his identity even while he retains it. Small wonder that at the end of his life, the famous physicist, P. W. Bridgman, said, "The structure of nature may eventually be such that our processes of thought do not correspond to it sufficiently to permit us to think about it at all."

We need not, I think, be quite so pessimistic. Our first duty is to affirm a new and wider rationalism; that is to say, to redouble our efforts to find a more adequate image of man to guide us in fashioning a more suitable science of personality.

And what about our personal attitudes as guidance specialists or teachers? Should we not cultivate the same twin virtues that we recommend to client and student: tentativeness and commitment? We can hold our own present image, of man on trial, reviewing our own past psychological training in critical perspective. At the same time we can embrace courageously our task of interpreting the wisdom of the past in such a way as to make it most available to the youthful personality who is facing an uncertain, but not uninviting, future. Tentativeness and commitment are twin ideals for both counselor and client. To my mind they lie at the heart and center of guidance, of teaching, and of living.

5

Continuity and Change in Personality [1]

W ALTER M ISCHEL

Walter Mischel examines the question of the extent to which a person remains "himself" over the years and the extent to which he becomes a "different person" as he adapts to new circumstances. Mischel artfully sifts the sometimes confusing evidence on this topic and draws the implications for personality theories. A professor of psychology at Stanford University, Mischel is the author of Introduction to Personality *(New York: Holt, Rinehart & Winston, 1971).*

The question of continuity and change in personality has enduring importance, and the position that one takes on this topic profoundly influences one's approach to most other issues in personality psychology. Almost no psychologist, myself included, would argue with the basic and widely shared assumption that continuity does exist in personality development (e.g., Kagan, 1969). Indeed, few other phenomena seem to be so intuitively self-evident. The experience of subjective continuity in ourselves—of basic oneness

and durability in the self—is perhaps the most compelling and fundamental feature of personality. This experience of continuity seems to be an intrinsic feature of the mind, and the loss of a sense of felt consistency may be a chief characteristic of personality disorganization.

Clinically, it seems remarkable how each of us generally manages to reconcile his seemingly diverse behaviors into one self-consistent whole. A man may steal on one occasion, lie on another, donate generously to charity on a third, cheat on a fourth, and still construe himself readily as "basically honest and moral." Just like the personality theorist who studies them, our subjects also are skilled at transforming their seemingly discrepant behavior into a constructed continuity, making unified wholes out of almost anything.

It might be interesting to fantasize a situation in which the personality theorist and his subjects sat down together to examine each subject's data on behavioral consistency cross-situationally or over time. Actually it might not even be a bad idea for psychologists to enact such a fantasy. In inspecting these data the theorist would look for genotypic unities that he is sure must be there; his subject would look for genotypic unities and be even more convinced that they exist and would proceed to find his own, often emerging with unities unknown to the theorist. But the consistency data on the IBM sheets, even if they reached statistical significance, probably would account for only a trivial portion of the variance, as Hunt (1965) has pointed out. A correlation of .30 leaves us understanding less than 10% of the relevant variance. [The proportion of variation that is accounted for by a correlation is given by the square of the correlation coefficient: $.30 \times .30 = .09$ or 9% of the variation.— E DITOR] And even correlations of that magnitude are not very common and have come to be considered good in research on the consistency of any noncognitive dimension of personality.

How does one reconcile our shared perception of continuity with the equally impressive evidence that on virtually all of our dispositional measures of personality substantial changes occur in the characteristics of the individual longitudinally over time and, even more dramatically, across seemingly similar settings cross-sectionally? I had the occasion to broadly review the voluminous evidence available on this topic of consistency and specificity (Mischel, 1968). In my appraisal, the overall evidence from many sources (clinical, experimental, developmental, correlational) shows the human

[1] This article is based on a paper presented at the symposium "Behavioral Continuity and Change with Development," held at the meeting of the Society for Research in Child Development, Santa Monica, California, March 27, 1969. Preparation of this paper was facilitated by Grant M-6830, from the National Institutes of Health, United States Public Health Service.

mind to function like an extraordinarily effective reducing valve that creates and maintains the perception of continuity even in the face of perpetual observed changes in actual behavior. Often this cognitive construction of continuity, while not arbitrary, is only very tenuously related to the phenomena that are construed.

To understand continuity properly it is necessary to be more specific and to talk about types of variations and the conditions that regulate them. In this regard it may be useful to distinguish between consistency in various types of human activity.

There is a great deal of evidence that our cognitive constructions about ourselves and the world— our personal theories about ourselves and those around us (both in our roles as persons and as psychologists)—often are extremely stable and highly resistant to change. Data from many sources converge to document this point. Studies of the self-concept, of impression formation in person perception and in clinical judgment, of cognitive sets guiding selective attention—all these phenomena and many more document the consistency and tenacious continuity of many human construction systems (Mischel, 1968). Often these construction systems are built quickly and on the basis of little information (e.g., Bruner, Olver, & Greenfield, 1966). But, once established, these theories, whether generated by our subjects or ourselves, become exceedingly difficult to disconfirm.

An impressive degree of continuity also has been shown for another aspect of cognition: These are the features of problem solving called cognitive styles. Significant continuity often has been demonstrated on many cognitive style dimensions (e.g., Kagan, 1969; Witkin, Goodenough, & Karp, 1967). The current prolific cognitive style explorations on this topic provide excellent evidence of developmental continuity. In this case the research also reveals a welcome continuity in our professional developmental history. Research into consistent individual differences in cognition has had deep roots and a long and distinguished history in experimental psychology. Simple cognitive measures like reaction time and response speed and duration have intrigued psychologists since the earliest laboratory work on mental measurement began more than 70 years ago. Individual differences on specific measures of problem solving, such as speed of reaction time and weight judgments, began to be explored in 1890 by James McKeen Cattell and others. Their studies of responses on specific cognitive and ability measures in the early laboratories were neglected when the development of practical intelligence testing started in this century. At that time, Binet and Henri shifted at-

tention to the measurement of generalized intelligence by studying individual differences in more complex global tasks. Now it is refreshing to witness the reawakened interest in such enduringly important topics as reaction time and "conceptual tempo" and it is good to see sophisticated consistency evidence for it (Kagan, 1969). The generality and stability of behaviors assessed by these cognitive measures often have been found to be among the best available in personality research.

Some puzzling problems may arise, however, from the correlations found between some of the most promising new cognitive style measures and the traditional measures of generalized intelligence such as the performance IQ on the WISC. That is, correlations between measures of generalized intelligence and cognitive style such as Witkin's field dependence raise the question of the degree to which the consistency of cognitive styles may be due to their associations with intellectual abilities. The obtained generality and stability, as well as the external personality correlates, of at least some cognitive style measures thus may rest in part on their sizable correlations with indexes of more generalized intelligence and achievement behavior, as has been found in other studies (e.g., Crandall & Sinkeldam, 1964; Elliott, 1961). To illustrate, the Witkin measures of cognitive style are strongly related to performance IQ ability indexes. Indeed the relationship between the Witkin Embedded Figures Test and the Wechsler Intelligence Block Design subtest is so strong that Witkin (1965) has indicated he is willing to use Block Design scores when available as a substitute for other field-dependence measures. When such cognitive styles as field independence and such coping patterns as "intellectualization" are substantially correlated with IQ then the stability reported for them and their correlates (e.g., by Schimek, 1968) may partly reflect the stability of the IQ.

This issue might also constitute a problem in interpreting such cognitive styles as Kagan's conceptual tempo. To the extent that conceptual tempo involves reaction time, and fast reaction time is a determinant of generalized performance IQ, one would have to be alert to their interrelations, as has been pointed out by Campbell and Fiske (1959). It will be interesting to continue to explore exactly how conceptual tempo and other cognitive styles based on performance indexes such as response speed and accuracy take us beyond generalized ability measurement and into the domain of personality traits. Ultimately research on cognitive styles surely will provide a clearer analysis of intellective behavior. The implications of cognitive styles for the concept of general intelligence (as well as the reverse relation) should then become more explicit than they are now. In the course of these explorations the meaning of inter-correlations among diverse cognitive style measures —such as conceptual tempo, field dependence-independence, leveling-sharpening, and so on—will become clearer. At the same time our understanding of the interactions among cognitive and non-cognitive personality dimensions hopefully will improve.

When we turn away from cognitive and intellective dimensions to the domain of personality and interpersonal behavior, consistency evidence is generally much harder to establish, at least whenever we use conventional tactics and the correlation coefficient (e.g., Maccoby, 1969). On the basis of past literature on this topic, one should no longer be surprised when consistency correlations for social behavior patterns turn out to be quite low. Theoretically, in my view, one should not expect social behavior to be consistent unless the relevant social learning and cognitive conditions are arranged to maintain the behavior cross-situationally. On theoretical as well as on empirical grounds, much of the time there is no reason to expect great consistency in the social behaviors comprising most of our personality dimensions.

It is not possible to even begin to cite here the extensive evidence that I believe supports this point, namely, that noncognitive global personality dispositions are much less global than traditional psychodynamic and trait positions have assumed them to be (Mischel, 1968). A great deal of behavioral specificity has been found regularly on character traits such as rigidity, social conformity, aggression, on attitudes to authority, and on virtually any other nonintellective personality dimension (Mischel, 1968; Peterson, 1968; Vernon, 1964). Some of the data on delay of gratification with young children, emerging from our current studies at Stanford, are illustrative. In an ongoing longitudinal study on this problem we have obtained evidence that delay of gratification has some developmental consistency and increases with age, up to a point.[2] Much more impressive in my view, however, is our finding that within any child there exists tremendous variability on this dimension. Now we are studying how long preschool children will actually sit still alone in a chair waiting for a preferred but delayed outcome before they signal to terminate the waiting period and settle for

a less preferred but immediately available gratification. We are finding that the same $3\frac{1}{2}$-year-old child who on one occasion may terminate his waiting in less than half a minute may be capable of waiting by himself up to an hour on another occasion a few weeks earlier or later, *if* cognitive and attentional conditions are appropriately arranged. Our conclusion is that some significant predictions of length of voluntary delay of gratification certainly can be made from individual differences data; but the most powerful predictions by far come from knowledge of the cognitive and incentive conditions that prevail in the particular situation of interest.

These results are not at all atypical. A tribute to the interaction of person and environment is usually offered at the front of every elementary textbook in the form of Kurt Lewin's famous equation: Behavior is a function of person and environment. In spite of such lip service to the stimulus, most of our personality theories and methods still take no serious account of conditions in the regulation of behavior. Literally thousands of tests exist to measure dispositions, and virtually none is available to measure the psychological environment in which development and change occurs.

Evidence on observed instability and inconsistency in behavior often has been interpreted to reflect the imperfections of our tests and tools and the resulting unreliability and errors of our measurements, as due to the fallibility of the human clinical judge and his ratings, and as due to many other methodological problems. Undoubtedly all these sources contribute real problems. Some of these have been excellently conceptualized by Emmerich (1969). His emphasis on the need for considering rate and mean changes over age if one is to achieve a proper understanding of continuity, growth, and psychological differentiation is especially important. Likewise, his call for longitudinal, multimeasure, and multivariate studies needs to be heeded most seriously.

I am more and more convinced, however, hopefully by data as well as on theoretical grounds, that the observed inconsistency so regularly found in studies of noncognitive personality dimensions often reflects the state of nature and not merely the noise of measurement. Of course, that does not imply a capriciously haphazard world—only one in which personality consistencies seem greater than they are and in which behavioral complexities seem simpler than they are. This would, if true, be extremely functional. After all, if people tried to be radical behaviorists and to describe each other in operational terms they would soon run out of breath and expire. It is essential for the

---

[2] W. Mischel, E. B. Ebbesen, & A. Raskoff. In progress research report, Stanford University, entitled "Determinants of Delay of Gratification and Waiting Behavior in Preschool Children."

mind to be a reducing valve—if it were not it might literally blow itself!

Perhaps the most widely accepted argument for consistency in the face of seeming diversity is the one mentioned so often, the distinction between the phenotypic and the genotypic. Thus most theorizing on continuity seems to have been guided by a model that assumes a set of genotypic personality dispositions that endure, although their overt response forms may change. This model, of course, is the one shared by traditional trait and dynamic dispositional theories of personality. The model was well summarized in the example of how a child at age 12 may substitute excessive obedience to a parent for his earlier phobic reaction as a way of reducing anxiety over parental rejection (Kagan, 1969). At the level of physical analogy Kagan spoke of how the litre of water in the closed system is converted to steam and recondensed to liquid.

This type of hydraulic Freudian-derived personality model, while widely shared by personality theorists, is of course not the only one available and not the only one necessary to deal with phenomena of continuity and change. Indeed, in the opinion of many clinical psychologists the hydraulic phenotypic-genotypic model applied to personality dynamics, psychotherapy, and symptom substitution has turned out to be a conceptual trap leading to some tragic pragmatic mistakes in clinical treatment and diagnosis for the last 50 years (e.g., Mischel, 1968; Peterson, 1968). I am referring, of course, to the unjustified belief that seemingly diverse personality problems must constitute symptoms of an underlying generalized core disorder rather than being relatively discrete problems often under the control of relatively independent causes and maintaining conditions.

The analysis of diverse behaviors as if they were symptomatic surface manifestations of more unitary underlying dispositional forces also is prevalent in our theories of personality development (e.g., Kagan, 1969; Maddi, 1968). But while diverse behaviors often may be in the service of the same motive or disposition, often they are not. In accord with the genotype-phenotype distinction, if a child shows attachment and dependency in some contexts but not in others one would begin a search to separate phenotypes from genotypes. But it is also possible that seeming inconsistencies, rather than serving one underlying motive, actually may be under the control of relatively separate causal variables. The two behavior patterns may not reflect a phenotype in the service of a genotype but rather may reflect discrimination learning in the service of the total organism. Likewise, while a child's fears sometimes may be in the service of an underlying motive, most research on the topic would lead me to predict it is more likely that the fear would involve an organized response system with its own behavioral life, being evoked and maintained by its own set of regulating conditions (e.g., Bandura, 1969; Paul, 1967).

When we observe a woman who seems hostile and fiercely independent some of the time but passive, dependent, and feminine on other occasions, our reducing valve usually makes us choose between the two syndromes. We decide that one pattern is in the service of the other, or that both are in the service of a third motive. She must be a really castrating lady with a facade of passivity—or perhaps she is a warm, passive-dependent woman with a surface defense of aggressiveness. But perhaps nature is bigger than our concepts and it is possible for the lady to be a hostile, fiercely independent, passive, dependent, feminine, aggressive, warm, castrating person all-in-one. Of course which of these she is at any particular moment would not be random and capricious—it would depend on whom she is with, when, how, and much, much more. But each of these aspects of her self may be a quite genuine and real aspect of her total being. (Perhaps we need more adjectives and hyphens in our personality descriptions. That is what is meant, I think, by "moderator variables.")

I am skeptical about the utility of the genotype-phenotype distinction at the present level of behavioral analysis in personality psychology because I fear it grossly oversimplifies the complexity of organized behavior and its often nonlinear causes. The genotype-phenotype oversimplification may mask the complex relations between the behavior and the organism that generates it, the other behaviors available to the organism, the history of the behavior, and the current evoking and maintaining conditions that regulate its occurrence and its generalization.

The question of the nature of the similarity or dissimilarity among the diverse responses emitted by a person is one of the thorniest in psychology. Even when one response pattern is not in the service of another the two of course may still interact. No matter how seemingly separated the various branches of behavior may be, one can always construe some common origins for them and some current interactions. At the very least, all behavior from an organism, no matter how diverse, still has unity because it is all generated from the same source—from the same one person. At the other extreme, incidentally, few response patterns are ever phenotypically or physically identical: Their similarity always has to be grouped on some higher-order dimension of meaning. To make sense of bits of raw behavior one always has to group them into larger common categories. The interesting theoretical issue is just what the bases of these groupings should be. Dispositional theories try to categorize behaviors in terms of the hypothesized historical psychic forces that diverse behaviors supposedly serve; but it is also possible to categorize the behaviors in terms of the unifying evoking and maintaining conditions that they jointly share.

Moreover, few potent response patterns can occur without exerting radical consequences for the other alternatives available to the person. Thus an extremely "fast-tempo" child may be so active that, in addition to fatiguing his parents, he may as Kagan (1969) found, smile less. Perhaps that happens because he is too busy to smile. My comment about how fast-tempo children may be too busy to smile is not really facetious. One of the intriguing features of any strong response syndrome is that it soon prevents all kinds of other intrinsically incompatible behaviors. If a child darts about a lot and is fast there are all sorts of other things he automatically cannot do. His speed in living, his pace, not only automatically influences his other possible behavior, it also soon starts to shape his environment. I now expect my fast-tempo children to be fast tempo, and currently it takes almost no cues from them to convince me I am right about them.

It would have been relatively simple to assess and predict personality if it had turned out to consist mainly of stable highly generalized response patterns that occur regularly in relation to many diverse stimulus constellations. The degree and subtlety of discrimination shown in human behavior, however, is at least as impressive as is the variety and extensiveness of stimulus generalization. What people do in any situation may be altered radically even by seemingly minor variations in prior experiences or slight modifications in stimulus attributes or in the specific characteristics of the evoking situation. From my theoretical perspective this state of affairs—namely, the enormously subtle discriminations that people continuously make, and consequently the flexibility of behavior—is not a cause of gloom. Instead, the relative specificity of behavior, and its dependence on environmental supports, is the expected result of complex discrimination learning and subtle cognitive differentiation. When the eliciting and evoking conditions that maintain behavior change—as they generally do across settings—then behavior surely will change also. While the continuous interplay of person and condition may have been a surprise for faculty and trait psychology it should come as no upset for us now. If one pays more than verbal

tribute to the dependency of behavior on conditions, and to the modification of behavior when situations change, then the so-called negative results of dispositional research on behavioral continuity appear attributable largely to the limitations of the assumptions that have guided the research. From the viewpoint of social behavior theory the findings of behavioral specificity, rather than primarily reflecting measurement errors, are actually congruent with results from experimental research on the determinants and modification of social behavior (Mischel, 1968). When response consequences and valences change so do actions; but when maintaining conditions remain stable so does behavior.

The last decade has seen an exciting growth of research on cognitive styles and many researchers have begun to study the person as an information-processing and problem-solving organism. Generally, however, these processes have been viewed in dimensional and dispositional terms and quickly translated back to fit the consistency assumptions of traditional global trait and psychodynamic theory. Individual differences on dimensions such as conceptual tempo, field dependence, leveling-sharpening, and so on, have been isolated with some promising results. Less progress has been made in applying the concepts and language of information processing and cognitive styles to forming a better theoretical conception of personality structure itself. It has become fashionable to speak of the organism as creating plans, generating rules, and, depending on his needs and situations, devising strategies. These tactics yield payoffs and consequences, and in light of these the person modifies his plans accordingly. But when contingencies change stably, what happens? For example, what happens when the mother-dependent child finds that his preschool peers now consistently have little patience for his whining, attention-getting bids, and instead respect independence and self-confidence? Generally the child's behavior changes in accord with the new contingencies, and if the contingencies shift so does the behavior—if the contingencies remain stable so does the new syndrome that the child now displays. Then what has happened to the child's dependency trait?

One might argue that the basic genotype remained but its manifestation phenotypically has altered. But is this just a "symptom" change leaving unaffected the psyche that generated it and the life space in which it unfolds? A vigorous "No!" to this question comes from much research on behavior change in the last few years (e.g., Bijou, 1965; Fairweather, 1967; Mischel, 1966; Patterson, Ray, & Shaw, 1969).

What would happen conceptually if we treated the organism as truly active and dynamic rather than as the carrier of a stable dispositional reservoir of motives and traits? Might one then more easily think of changes in the developing organism not as phenotypic overlays that mask genotypic unities but as genuinely new strategies in which many of the person's old plans are discarded and replaced by more appropriate ones in the course of development? (Perhaps Gordon Allport's idea of functional autonomy needs to be rethought.) Can the person even become involved in plans to change what he *is* as well as what he does? George Kelly and the existentialists in their search for human nature noted that existence precedes essence. According to that position, to find out what I *am* I need to know what I *do*. And if my actions change do they leave me (the "real me") behind? Or perhaps they just leave some of my discarded psychological genotypes behind?

A search for a personality psychology that has conceptual room for major variability and changes within the individual's dispositions can easily be misinterpreted as undermining the concept of personality itself. That would be an unfortunate misconstruction. Instead, we do need to recognize that discontinuities—real ones and not merely superficial or trivial veneer changes—are part of the genuine phenomena of personality. If one accepts that proposition, an adequate conceptualization of personality will have to go beyond the conventional definition of stable and broad enduring individual differences in behavioral dispositions. We may have to tolerate more dissonance than we like in our personality theory. To be more than nominally dynamic our personality theories will have to have as much room for human discrimination as for generalization, as much place for personality change as for stability, and as much concern for man's self-regulation as for his victimization by either enduring intrapsychic forces or by momentary environmental constraints.

REFERENCES

BANDURA, A. *Principles of behavior modification.* New York: Holt, Rinehart & Winston, 1969.

BIJOU, S. W. Experimental studies of child behavior, normal and deviant. In L. Krasner & L. P. Ullmann (Eds.), *Research in behavior modification.* New York: Holt, Rinehart & Winston, 1965.

BRUNER, J. S., OLVER, R. R., & GREENFIELD, P. M. *Studies in cognitive growth.* New York: Wiley, 1966.

CAMPBELL, D., & FISKE, D. Convergent and discriminant validation by the multitrait-multimethod matrix. *Psychological Bulletin,* 1959, *56,* 81–105.

CRANDALL, V. J., & SINKELDAM, C. Children's dependent and achievement behaviors in social situations and their perceptual field dependence. *Journal of Personality,* 1964, *32,* 1–22.

ELLIOTT, R. Interrelationships among measures of field dependence, ability, and personality traits. *Journal of Abnormal and Social Psychology,* 1961, *63,* 27–36.

EMMERICH, W. Models of continuity and change. Paper presented at the meeting of the Society for Research in Child Development, March 27, 1969, Santa Monica, California.

FAIRWEATHER, G. W. *Methods in experimental social innovation.* New York: Wiley, 1967.

HUNT, J. McV. Traditional personality theory in the light of recent evidence. *American Scientist,* 1965, *53,* 80–96.

KAGAN, J. Continuity in development. Paper presented at the meeting of the Society for Research in Child Development, March 27, 1969, Santa Monica, California.

MACCOBY, E. E. Tracing individuality within age-related change. Paper presented at the meeting of the Society for Research in Child Development, March 27, 1969, Santa Monica, California.

MADDI, S. R. *Personality theories: A comparative analysis.* Homewood, Ill.: Dorsey Press, 1968.

MISCHEL, W. A social learning view of sex differences in behavior. In E. E. Maccoby (ed.), *The development of sex differences.* Stanford: Stanford University Press, 1966.

MISCHEL, W. *Personality and assessment.* New York: Wiley, 1968.

PATTERSON, G. R., RAY, R. S., & SHAW, D. A. Direct intervention in families of deviant children. *Oregon Research Institute Bulletin,* 1969, *8*(9), 1–62.

PAUL, G. L. Insight versus desensitization in psychotherapy two years after termination. *Journal of Consulting Psychology,* 1967, *31,* 333–348.

PETERSON, D. *The clinical study of social behavior.* New York: Appleton-Century-Crofts, 1968.

SCHIMEK, J. G. Cognitive style and defenses: A longitudinal study of intellectualization and field independence. *Journal of Abnormal Psychology,* 1968, *73,* 575–580.

VERNON, P. S. *Personality assessment: A critical survey.* New York: Wiley, 1964.

WITKIN, H. Psychological differentiation and forms of pathology. *Journal of Abnormal Psychology,* 1965, *70,* 317–336.

WITKIN, H. A., GOODENOUGH, D. R., & KARP, S. A. Stability of cognitive style from childhood to young adulthood. *Journal of Personality and Social Psychology,* 1967, *7,* 291–300.

realist. But if we don't change things, we will go down the drain like Greece and Rome and other societies that fall apart.[1]

Dr. Bronfenbrenner has long been a professor at Cornell's Department of Child Development and Family Relations, one of the leading centers for the study of human development. The department is now a part of Cornell's College of Ecology.

6

The Split-level American Family

URIE BRONFENBRENNER

Influences upon children are not the same as they used to be. Urie Bronfenbrenner describes ways in which the lives of most American children today are drastically different from those of most American children of the past. The explanation of these differences is not simply technological changes such as the dishwashing machine and TV set. As Bronfenbrenner summarizes, the "conditions of life have changed."

Because the clock cannot be turned back, cures are needed for what ails the interpersonal environment of the nation's young. In 1970 Bronfenbrenner proposed that business create new work schedules to give men and women more time with their families. The Los Angeles Times *quoted him as follows:*

> *. . . although we like to think of America as a child-oriented society, a hard look at our way of life shows that the priorities of parents lie elsewhere. We put our children last, after everything else. . . . In today's world, parents find themselves at the mercy of a society which imposes pressures and priorities that allow neither time nor place for meaningful activities, and [which imposes] relations between children and adults which down-grade the role of parent and the functions of parenthood, and which prevent the parent from doing the things he wants to do as a guide, friend and companion to his children. . . .*

> *I don't know how long it will take us before we are able to turn this around. I am not a prophet, only a*

Children used to be brought up by their parents.

It may seem presumptuous to put that statement in the past tense. Yet it belongs to the past. Why? Because *de facto* responsibility for upbringing has shifted away from the family to other settings in the society, where the task is not always recognized or accepted. While the family still has the primary moral and legal responsibility for developing character in children, the power or opportunity to do the job is often lacking in the home, primarily because parents and children no longer spend enough time together in those situations in which such training is possible. This is not because parents don't want to spend time with their children. It is simply that conditions of life have changed.

To begin with, families used to be bigger—not in terms of more children so much as more adults—grandparents, uncles, aunts, cousins. Those relatives who didn't live with you lived nearby. You often went to their houses. They came as often to yours, and stayed for dinner. You knew them all—the old folks, the middle-aged, the older cousins. And they knew you. This had its good side and its bad side.

On the good side, some of these relatives were interesting people, or so you thought at the time. Uncle Charlie had been to China. Aunt Sue made the best penuche fudge on the block. Cousin Bill could read people's minds (according to him). And all these relatives gave you Christmas presents.

But there was the other side. You had to give Christmas presents to all your relatives. And they all minded your business throughout the years. They wanted to know where you had been, where you were going, and why. If they didn't like your answers, they said so (particularly if you had told them the truth).

Not just your relatives minded your business. Everybody in the neighborhood did. Again this had its two sides.

If you walked on the railroad trestle, the phone would ring at your house. Your parents would know

---

[1] *Los Angeles Times,* Dec. 13, 1970.

---

what you had done before you got back home. People on the street would tell you to button your jacket, and ask why you weren't in church last Sunday.

But you also had the run of the neighborhood. You were allowed to play in the park. You could go into any store, whether you bought anything or not. They would let you go back of the store to watch them unpack the cartons and to hope that a carton would break. At the lumber yard, they let you pick up good scraps of wood. At the newspaper office, you could punch the linotype and burn your hand on the slugs of hot lead. And at the railroad station (they had railroad stations then), you could press the telegraph key and know that the telegraphers heard your dit-dah-dah all the way to Chicago.

These memories of a gone boyhood have been documented systematically in the research of Professor Herbert Wright and his associates at the University of Kansas. The Midwestern investigators have compared the daily life of children growing up in a small town with the lives of children living in a modern city or suburb. The contrast is sobering. Children in a small town get to know well a substantially greater number of adults in different walks of life and, in contrast to their urban and suburban agemates, are more likely to be active participants in the adult settings that they enter.

As the stable world of the small town has become absorbed into an ever-shifting suburbia, children are growing up in a different kind of environment. Urbanization has reduced the extended family to a nuclear one with only two adults, and the functioning neighborhood—where it has not decayed into an urban or rural slum—has withered to a small circle of friends, most of them accessible only by motor car or telephone. Whereas the world in which the child lived before consisted of a diversity of people in a diversity of settings, now for millions of American children the neighborhood is nothing but row upon row of buildings inhabited by strangers. One house, or apartment, is much like another, and so are the people. They all have about the same income, and the same way of life. And the child doesn't even see much of that, for all the adults in the neighborhood do is come home, have a drink, eat dinner, mow the lawn, watch TV, and sleep. Increasingly often, today's housing projects have no stores, no shops, no services, no adults at work or play. This is the sterile world in which many of our children grow, the "urban renewal" we offer to the families we would rescue from the slums.

Neighborhood experiences available to children are extremely limited nowadays. To do anything at all—go to a movie, get an ice cream cone, go swimming, or play ball—they have to travel by bus or private car. Rarely can a child watch adults working at their trades. Mechanics, tailors, or shopkeepers are either out of sight or unapproachable. A child cannot listen to gossip at the post office as he once did. And there are no abandoned houses, barns, or attics to break into. From a young point of view, it's a dull world.

Hardly any of this really matters, for children aren't home much, anyway. A child leaves the house early in the day, on a schoolbound bus, and it's almost suppertime when he gets back. There may not be anybody home when he gets there. If his mother isn't working, at least part-time (more than a third of all mothers are), she's out a lot—because of social obligations, not just friends—doing things for the community. The child's father leaves home in the morning before the child does. It takes the father an hour and a half to get to work. He's often away weekends, not to mention absences during the week.

If a child is not with his parents or other adults, with whom does he spend his time? With other kids, of course—in school, after school, over weekends, on holidays. In these relationships, he is further restricted to children of his own age and the same socioeconomic background. The pattern was set when the old neighborhood school was abandoned as inefficient. Consolidated schools brought homogeneous grouping by age, and the homogenizing process more recently has been extended to segregate children by levels of ability; consequently, from the preschool years onward the child is dealing principally with replicas of the stamp of his own environment. Whereas social invitations used to be extended to entire families on a neighborhood basis, the cocktail party of nowadays has its segregated equivalent for every age group down to the toddlers.

It doesn't take the children very long to learn the lesson adults teach: Latch onto your peers. But to latch he must contend with a practical problem. He must hitch a ride. Anyone going in the right direction can take him. But if no one is going in that direction just then, the child can't get there.

The child who can't go somewhere else stays home, and does what everybody else does at home. He watches TV. Studies indicate that American youngsters see more TV than children in any other country do. By the late 1950s, the TV-watching figure had risen to two hours a day for the average five-year-old, three hours a day during the watching peak age period of twelve to fourteen years.

In short, whereas American children used to spend much of their time with parents and other grownups, more and more waking hours are now lived in the world of peers and of the television screen.

What do we know about the influence of the peer group, or of television, on the lives of young children? Not much.

The prevailing view in American society (indeed in the West generally) holds that the child's psychological development, to the extent that it is susceptible to environmental influence, is determined almost entirely by the parents and within the first six years of life. Scientific investigators—who are, of course, products of their own culture, imbued with its tacit assumptions about human nature—have acted accordingly. Western studies of influences on personality development in childhood overwhelmingly take the form of research on parent-child relations, with the peer group, or other extraparental influences, scarcely being considered.

In other cultures, this is not always so. A year ago, at the International Congress of Psychology in Moscow, it was my privilege to chair a symposium on "Social Factors in Personality Development." Of a score of papers presented, about half were from the West (mostly American) and half from the Socialist countries (mostly Russian). Virtually without exception, the Western reports dealt with parent-child relationships; those from the Soviet Union and other East European countries focused equally exclusively on the influence of the peer group, or, as they call it, the children's collective.

Some relevant studies have been carried out in our own society. For example, I, with others, have done research on a sample of American adolescents from middle-class families. We have found that children who reported their parents away from home for long periods of time rated significantly lower on such characteristics as responsibility and leadership. Perhaps because it was more pronounced, absence of the father was more critical than that of the mother, particularly in its effect on boys. Similar results have been reported in studies of the effects of father absence among soldiers' families during World War II, in homes of Norwegian sailors and whalers, and in Negro households with missing fathers, both in the West Indies and the United States. In general, father absence contributes to low motivation for achievement, inability to defer immediate for later gratification, low self-esteem, susceptibility to group influence, and juvenile delinquency. All of these effects are much more marked for boys than for girls.

The fact that father-absence increases susceptibility to group influence leads us directly to the question of the impact of the peer group on the child's attitudes and behavior. The first—and as yet the only—comprehensive research on this question was carried out by two University of North Carolina sociologists, Charles Bowerman and John Kinch, in 1959. Working with a sample of several hundred students from the fourth to the tenth grades in the Seattle school system, these investigators studied age trends in the tendency of children to turn to parents versus peers for opinion, advice, or company in various activities. In general, there was a turning point at about the seventh grade. Before that, the majority looked mainly to their parents as models, companions, and guides to behavior; thereafter, the children's peers had equal or greater influence.

Though I can cite no documentation from similar investigations since then, I suspect the shift comes earlier now, and is more pronounced.

In the early 1960s, the power of the peer group was documented even more dramatically by James Coleman in his book *The Adolescent Society*. Coleman investigated the values and behaviors of teenagers in eight large American high schools. He reported that the aspirations and actions of American adolescents were primarily determined by the "leading crowd" in the school society. For boys in this leading crowd, the hallmark of success was glory in athletics; for girls, it was the popular date.

Intellectual achievement was, at best, a secondary value. The most intellectually able students were not those getting the best grades. The classroom wasn't where the action was. The students who did well were "not really those of highest intelligence, but only the ones who were willing to work hard at a relatively unrewarded activity."

The most comprehensive study relevant to the subject of our concern here was completed only a year ago by the same James Coleman. The data were obtained from more than 600,000 children in grades one to twelve in 4,000 schools carefully selected as representative of public education in the United States. An attempt was made to assess the relative contribution to the child's intellectual development (as measured by standardized intelligence and achievement tests) of the following factors: (1) family background (e.g., parents' education, family size, presence in the home of reading materials, records, etc.); (2) school characteristics (e.g., per pupil expenditure, classroom size, laboratory and library facilities, etc.); (3) teacher characteristics (e.g., background, training, years of experience, verbal skills, etc.); and (4) characteristics of other children in the same school (e.g., their background, academic achievement, career plans, etc.).

Of the many findings of the study, two were particularly impressive; the first was entirely expected, the second somewhat surprising. The expected finding was that home background was the most important element in determining how well the child did at school, more important than any of all aspects of the school which the child attended. This generalization, while especially true for Northern whites, applied to a lesser degree to Southern whites and Northern Negroes, and was actually reversed for Southern Negroes, for whom the characteristics of the school were more important than those of the home. The child apparently drew sustenance from wherever sustenance was most available. Where the home had most to offer, the home was the most determining; but where the school could provide more stimulation than the home, the school was the more influential factor.

The second major conclusion concerned the aspects of the school environment which contributed most to the child's intellectual achievement. Surprisingly enough, such items as per pupil expenditure, number of children per class, laboratory space, number of volumes in the school library, and the presence or absence of ability grouping were of negligible significance. Teacher qualifications accounted for some of the child's achievement. But by far the most important factor was the pattern of characteristics of the other children attending the same school. Specifically, if a lower-class child had schoolmates who came from advantaged homes, he did reasonably well; but if all the other children also came from deprived backgrounds, he did poorly.

What about the other side of the story? What happens to a middle-class child in a predominantly lower-class school? Is he pulled down by his classmates? According to Coleman's data, the answer is no; the performance of the advantaged children remains unaffected. It is as though good home background had immunized them against the possibility of contagion.

This is the picture so far as academic achievement is concerned. How about other aspects of psychological development? Specifically, how about social behavior—such qualities as responsibility, consideration for others, or, at the opposite pole, aggressiveness or delinquent behavior? How are these affected by the child's peer group?

The Coleman study obtained no data on this score. Some light has been shed on the problem, however, by an experiment which my Cornell colleagues and I recently carried out with school children in the United States and in the Soviet Union. Working with a sample of more than 150 sixth-graders (from six classrooms) in each country, we placed the children in situations in which we could test their readiness to engage in morally disapproved behavior such as cheating on a test, denying responsibility for property damage, etc. The results indicated that American children were far more ready to take part in such actions.

The effect of the peer group (friends in school) was quite different in the two societies. When told that their friends would know of their actions, American children were even more willing to engage in misconduct. Soviet youngsters showed just the opposite tendency. In their case, the peer group operated to support the values of the adult society, at least at their age level.

We believe these contrasting results are explained in part by the differing role of the peer group in the two societies. In the Soviet Union, *vospitanie,* or character development, is regarded as an integral part of the process of education, and its principal agent—even more important than the family—is the child's collective in school and out. A major goal of the Soviet educational process, beginning in the nursery, is "to forge a healthy, self-sufficient collective" which, in turn, has the task of developing the child into a responsible, altruistic, and loyal member of a socialist society. In contrast, in the United States, the peer group is often an autonomous agent relatively free from adult control and uncommitted—if not outrightly opposed—to the values and codes of conduct approved by society at large. Witness the new phenomenon of American middle-class vandalism and juvenile delinquency, with crime rates increasing rapidly not only for teen-agers but for younger children as well.

How early in life are children susceptible to the effects of contagion? Professor Albert Bandura and his colleagues at Stanford University have conducted some experiments which suggest that the process is well developed at the preschool level. The basic experimental design involves the following elements. The child finds himself in a familiar playroom. As if by chance, in another corner of the room a person is playing with toys. Sometimes this person is an adult (teacher), sometimes another child. This other person behaves very aggressively. He strikes a large Bobo doll (a bouncing inflated figure), throws objects, and mutilates dolls and animal toys, with appropriate language to match. Later on, the experimental subject (*i.e.,* the child who "accidentally" observed the aggressive behavior) is tested by being allowed to play in a room containing a variety of toys, including some similar to those employed by the aggressive model. With no provocation, perfectly normal, well-adjusted preschoolers engage in aggressive acts, not only repeating what they had observed but elaborating on it. Moreover, the words and gestures accompanying the actions leave no doubt that the child is living through an emotional experience of aggressive expression.

It is inconvenient to use a live model every time. Thus it occurred to Bandura to make a film. In fact, he made two, one with a live model and a second film of a cartoon cat that said and did everything the live model had said and done. The films were presented on a TV set left on in a corner of the room, as if by accident. When the children were tested, the TV film turned out to be just as effective as real people. The cat aroused as much aggression as the human model.

As soon as Bandura's work was published, the television industry issued a statement calling his conclusions into question on the interesting ground that the children had been studied "in a highly artificial situation," since no parents were present either when the TV was on or when the aggressive behavior was observed. "What a child will do under normal conditions cannot be projected from his behavior when he is carefully isolated from normal conditions and the influences of society," the statement declared. Bandura was also criticized for using a Bobo doll (which, the TV people said, is "made to be struck") and for failing to follow up his subjects after they left the laboratory. Since then, Bandura has shown that only a ten-minute exposure to an aggressive model still differentiates children in the experimental group from their controls (children not subjected to the experiment) six months later.

Evidence for the relevance of Bandura's laboratory findings to "real life" comes from a subsequent field study by Dr. Leonard Eron, now at the University of Iowa. In a sample of more than 600 third-graders, Dr. Eron found that the children who were rated most aggressive by their classmates were those who watched TV programs involving a high degree of violence.

At what age do people become immune from contagion to violence on the screen? Professor Richard Walters of Waterloo University in Canada, and his associate, Dr. Llewellyn Thomas, showed two movie films to a group of thirty-four-year-old hospital attendants. Half of these adults were shown a knife fight between two teen-agers from the picture, *Rebel Without a Cause;* the other half saw a film depicting adolescents engaged in art work. Subsequently, all the attendants were asked to assist in carrying out an experiment on the effects of punishment in learning.

In the experiment, the attendants gave an unseen subject an electric shock every time the subject made an error. The lever for giving shocks had settings from zero to ten. To be sure the assistant understood what the shocks were like, he was given several, not exceeding the level of four, before the experiment. Since nothing was said about the level of shocks to be administered, each assistant was left to make his own choice. The hospital attendants who had seen the knife-fight film gave significantly more severe shocks than those who had seen the art-work film. The same experiment was repeated with a group of twenty-year-old females. This time the sound track was turned off so that only visual cues were present. But neither the silence nor the difference in sex weakened the effect. The young women who had seen the aggressive film administered more painful shocks.

These results led designers of the experiment to wonder what would happen if no film were shown and no other deliberate incitement were introduced in the immediate setting of the experiment. Would the continuing emotional pressures of the everyday environment of adolescents—who see more movies and more TV and are called on to display virility through aggressive acts in teen-age gangs—provoke latent brutality comparable to that exhibited by the older people under direct stimulation of the movie of the knife fight?

Fifteen-year-old high school boys were used to test the answer to this question. Without the suggestive power of the aggressive film to step up their feelings, they pulled the shock lever to its highest intensities (levels eight to ten). A few of the boys made such remarks as "I bet I made that fellow jump."

Finally, utilizing a similar technique in a variant of what has come to be known as the "Eichmann experiment," Professor Stanley Milgram, then at Yale University, set up a situation in which the level of shock to be administered was determined by the lowest level proposed by any one of three "assistants," two of whom were confederates of Milgram and were instructed to call for increasingly higher shocks. Even though the true subjects (all adult males) could have kept the intensity to a minimum simply by stipulating mild shocks, they responded to the confederates' needling and increased the degree of pain they administered. [A more important criticism of all these studies is to be found in the work on the demand characteristics of experiments (Orne).—EDITOR]

All of these experiments point to one conclusion. At all age levels, pressure from peers to engage in aggressive behavior is extremely difficult to resist, at least in American society.

Now if the peer group can propel its members into antisocial acts, what about the opposite possibility? Can peers also be a force for inducing constructive behavior?

Evidence on this point is not so plentiful, but some relevant data exist. To begin with, experiments on conformity to group pressure have shown that the presence of a single dissenter—for example, one "assistant" who refuses to give a severe shock—can be enough to break the spell so that the subject no longer follows the majority. But the only research explicitly directed at producing moral conduct as a function of group experience is a study conducted by Muzafer Sherif and his colleagues at the University of Oklahoma and known as the "Robber's Cave Experiment." In the words of Elton B. McNeil:

War was declared at Robber's Cave, Oklahoma, in the summer of 1954 (Sherif *et al.,* 1961). Of course, if you have seen one war you have seen them all, but this was an interesting war, as wars go, because only the observers knew what the fighting was about. How, then, did this war differ from any other war? This one was caused, conducted, and concluded by behavioral scientists. After years of religious, political, and economic wars, this was, perhaps, the first scientific war. It wasn't the kind of war that an adventurer could join just for the thrill of it. To be eligible, ideally, you had to be an eleven-year-old, middle-class, American, Protestant, well-adjusted boy who was willing to go to an experimental camp.

Sherif and his associates wanted to demonstrate that within the space of a few weeks they could produce two contrasting patterns of behavior in this group of normal children. First, they could bring the group to a state of intense hostility, and then completely reverse the process by inducing a spirit of warm friendship and active cooperation. The success of their efforts can be gauged by the following two excerpts describing the behavior of the boys after each stage had been reached. After the first experimental treatment of the situation was introduced . . .

good feeling soon evaporated. The members of each group began to call their rivals "stinkers," "sneaks," and "cheaters." They refused to have anything more to do with individuals in the opposing groups. The boys . . . turned against buddies whom they had chosen as "best friends" when they first arrived at the camp. A large proportion of the boys in each group gave negative ratings to all the boys in the other. The rival groups made threatening posters and planned raids, collecting secret hoards of green apples for ammunition. To the Robber's Cave came the Eagles, after a defeat in a tournament game, and burned a banner left behind by the Rattlers; the next morning the Rattlers seized the Eagles' flag when they arrived on the athletic field. From that time on name-calling, scuffles, and raids were the rule of the day.
. . . In the dining-hall line they shoved each other aside, and the group that lost the contest for the head of the line shouted "Ladies first!" at the winner. They threw paper, food, and vile names at each other at the tables. An Eagle bumped by a Rattler was admonished by his fellow Eagles to brush "the dirt" off his clothes.

But after the second experimental treatment . . .

. . . The members of the two groups began to feel more friendly to each other. For example, a Rattler whom the Eagles disliked for his sharp tongue and skill in defeating them became a "good egg." The boys stopped shoving in the meal line. They no longer called each other names, and sat together at the table. New friendships developed between individuals in the two groups.
In the end the groups were actively seeking opportunities to mingle, to entertain and "treat" each other. They decided to hold a joint campfire. They took turns presenting skits and songs. Members of both groups requested that they go home together on the same bus, rather than on the separate buses in which they had come. On the way the bus stopped for refreshments. One group still had $5 which they had won as a prize in a contest. They decided to spend this sum on refreshments. On their own initiative they had invited their former rivals to be their guests for malted milks.

How were each of these effects achieved? Treatment One has a familiar ring:

. . . To produce friction between the groups of boys we arranged a tournament of games: baseball, touch football, a tug-of-war, a treasure hunt, and so on. The tournament started in a spirit of good sportsmanship. But as the play progressed good feeling soon evaporated.

How does one turn hatred into harmony? Before undertaking this task, Sherif wanted to demonstrate that, contrary to the views of some students of human conflict, mere interaction—pleasant social contact between antagonists—would not reduce hostility.

. . . we brought the hostile Rattlers and Eagles together for social events: going to the movies, eating in the same dining room, and so on. But far from reducing conflict, these situations only served as opportunities for the rival groups to berate and attack each other.

How was conflict finally dispelled? By a series of stratagems, of which the following is an example:

. . . Water came to our camp in pipes from a tank about a mile away. We arranged to interrupt it and then called the boys together to inform them of the crisis. Both groups promptly volunteered to search the water line for trouble. They worked together harmoniously, and before the end of the afternoon they had located and corrected the difficulty.

On another occasion, just when everyone was hungry and the camp truck was about to go to town for food, it developed that the engine wouldn't start, and the boys had to pull together to get the vehicle going.

To move from practice to principle, the critical element for achieving harmony in human relations, according to Sherif, is joint activity in behalf of a *superordinate goal.* "Hostility gives way when groups pull together to achieve overriding goals which are real and compelling for all concerned."

Here, then, is the solution for the problems posed by autonomous peer groups and rising rates of juvenile delinquency: Confront the youngsters with some superordinate goals, and everything will turn out fine.

What superordinate goals can we suggest? Washing dishes and emptying wastebaskets? Isn't it true that meaningful opportunities for children no longer exist?

This writer disagrees. Challenging activities for children can still be found; but their discovery requires breaking down the prevailing patterns of segregation identified earlier in this essay—segregation not merely by race (although this is part of the story) but to an almost equal degree by age, class, and ability. I am arguing for greater involvement of adults in the lives of children and, conversely, for greater involvement of children in the problems and tasks of the larger society.

We must begin by desegregating age groups, ability groups, social classes, and once again engaging children and adults in common activities. Here, as in Negro-white relations, integration is not enough. In line with Sherif's findings, contact between children and adults, or between advantaged and disadvantaged, will not of itself reduce hostility and evoke mutual affection and respect. What is needed in addition is involvement in a superordinate goal, common participation in a challenging job to be done.

Where is a job to be found that can involve children and adults across the dividing lines of race, ability, and social class?

Here is one possibility. Urbanization and industrialization have not done away with the need to care for the very young. To be sure, "progress" has brought us to the point where we seem to believe that only a person with a master's degree is truly qualified to care for young children. An exception is made for parents, and for babysitters, but these are concessions to practicality; we all know that professionals could do it better.

It is a strange doctrine. For if present-day knowledge of child development tells us anything at all, it tells us that the child develops psychologically as a function of reciprocal interaction with those who love him. This reciprocal interaction need be only of the most ordinary kind—caresses, looks, sounds, talking, singing, playing, reading stories—the things that parents, and everybody else, have done with children for generation after generation.

Contrary to the impression of many, our task in helping disadvantaged children through such programs as Head Start is not to have a "specialist" working with each child but to enable the child's parents, brothers, sisters, and all those around him to provide the kinds of stimulation which families ordinarily give children but which can fail to develop in the chaotic conditions of life in poverty. It is for this reason that Project Head Start places such heavy emphasis on the involvement of parents, not only in decision-making but in direct interaction with the children themselves, both at the center and (especially) at home. Not only parents but teenagers and older children are viewed as especially significant in work with the very young, for, in certain respects, older siblings can function more effectively than adults. The latter, no matter how warm and helpful they may be, are in an important sense in a world apart; their abilities, skills, and standards are so clearly superior to those of the child as to appear beyond childish grasp.

Here, then, is a context in which adults and children can pursue together a superordinate goal, for there is nothing so "real and compelling to all concerned" as the need of a young child for the care and attention of his elders. The difficulty is that we have not yet provided the opportunities—the institutional settings—which would make possible the recognition and pursuit of this superordinate goal.

The beginnings of such an opportunity structure, however, already exist in our society. As I have indicated, they are to be found in the poverty program, particularly those aspects of it dealing with children: Head Start, which involves parents, older children, and the whole community in the care of the very young; Follow Through, which extends Head Start into the elementary grades, thus breaking down the destructive wall between the school on the one hand and parents in the local community on the other; Parent and Child Centers, which provide a neighborhood center where all generations can meet to engage in common activities in behalf of children, etc.

The need for such programs is not restricted to the nation's poor. So far as alienation of children is concerned, the world of the disadvantaged simply reflects in more severe form a social disease that has infected the entire society. The cure for the society as a whole is the same as that for its sickest segment. Head Start, Follow Through, Parent and Child Centers are all needed by the middle class as much as by the economically less favored. Again, contrary to popular impression, the principal purpose of these programs is not remedial education but the giving to both children and their families of a sense of dignity, purpose, and meaningful activity without which children cannot develop capacities in any sphere of activity, including the intellectual.

Service to the very young is not the only superordinate goal potentially available to children in our society. The very old also need to be saved. In segregating them in their own housing projects and, indeed, in whole communities, we have deprived both them and the younger generations of an essential human experience. We need to find ways in which children once again can assist and comfort old people, and, in return, gain insight to character development that occurs through such experiences. [Swedish communities which earlier built separate accommodations for the elderly, later chose to integrate units for the elderly in general purpose housing.—EDITOR]

Participation in constructive activities on behalf of others will also reduce the growing tendency to aggressive and antisocial behavior in the young, if only by diversion from such actions and from the stimuli that instigate them. But so long as these stimuli continue to dominate the TV screen, those exposed to TV can be expected to react to the influence. Nor, as we have seen, is it likely that the TV industry will be responsive to the findings of research or the arguments of concerned parents and professionals. The only measure that is likely to be effective is pressure where it hurts most. The sponsor must be informed that his product will be boycotted until programing is changed.

My proposals for child rearing in the future may appear to some as a pipedream, but they need not be a dream. For just as autonomy and aggression have their roots in the American tradition, so have neighborliness, civic concern, and devotion to the young. By re-exploring these last, we can rediscover our moral identity as a society and as a nation.

II

BIOLOGICAL BASES FOR BEHAVIOR

The label "biological bases for behavior" avoids old and often sterile dichotomies, for example, heredity versus environment, or nature versus nurture. A more useful distinction is that between learned and non-learned attributes. Non-learned attributes include not only those that are genetically determined but also others such as the effects of disease and injury. Thus, birth injury is not hereditary but acquired, and it is a biological (in this case congenital [1]) and non-learned determinant of behavior.

When the theorist who emphasizes biological determinants of behavior and the unfolding of innate or congenital potentialities seeks to explain behavior, he is likely to ask the following kinds of questions: What species of organism is this? What are the characteristics of the species? Is it a particular strain of the species? Does that strain have particular characteristics? What is the specific genetic inheritance of this individual organism? What environmental events (other than opportunities for learning) have affected the organism?

Over the centuries, psychological thought has gone through periods when the predominant fashion was to consider heredity, constitution, or—more broadly—man's biological makeup as *the* all-important determinant of his behavior. This included his individual behavior, and not just those behaviors characteristic of his species. The swing of the pendulum came, and it became "unfashionable" to consider any influences other than environmental experiences, or individual life history, as important in determining the individual's behavior. These different emphases have not been unrelated to the political thinking of the times. Democracy, after all, de-emphasized hereditary position. It is an optimistic philosophy of government, and it produced men who could see more possibility for change and improvement through control of the environment than through control of biology or heredity. Recent work with such genetic diseases as phenylketonuria has shown that environmental action can alter the effects of some genetic "errors." In such an instance we see that acceptance of genetic determinism does not necessarily rule out optimism regarding the outcome.

At present, it is fair to say that most psychologists would defend some compromise position, not claiming all importance for one or the other side of the old dichotomy. There is general recognition that (in the words of the old song about "love and marriage") "you can't have one without the other." Nevertheless, one or the other set of determinants is emphasized by various workers.

As this edition is being completed, one of the most widely discussed issues in this area is what can only be labeled "the Jensen controversy." In order to cover the complexities of this controversy completely, we would have to print much too much material. We shall, however, try to summarize it and provide the interested reader with some of the basic references.

The Winter 1969 issue of *Harvard Educational Review* (vol. 39, no. 1) con-

---

[1] "Congenital"—acquired during development in the uterus or dating from birth; it is to be distinguished from "hereditary."

tained a 123-page article entitled "How Much Can We Boost IQ and Scholastic Achievement?" by Arthur R. Jensen, a nationally respected professor of educational psychology at the University of California at Berkeley. A substantial portion of this article dealt with the question of the "heritability" of intelligence, or the degree to which IQ is determined genetically. To grasp this aspect of the article you must understand the statistical procedures used to arrive at the estimates of "heritability." The article is, nevertheless, quite readable, and we encourage you to look it up. Another issue raised by Jensen is the effectiveness of compensatory education. Jensen's thesis is that compensatory education has failed, and many psychologists have taken issue with him on this aspect of the paper. Some have criticized his choice of data and his interpretation of those data. Others feel that we have never made a realistic test of compensatory education, thus it cannot be fairly evaluated at present. However, the controversy surrounding this aspect of Jensen's paper is nothing compared to that surrounding the ten or so pages he specifically devoted to race and IQ. (Since much of his discussion of SES and IQ applies equally to race under current circumstances of overlap, ten pages may underestimate his emphasis on race.)

Under the heading "Genetic Aspects of Racial Differences" Jensen states:

> No one, to my knowledge, questions the role of environmental factors, including influences from past history, in determining at least some of the variance between racial groups in standard measures of intelligence, school performance, and occupational status. . . . I recently co-edited a book which is largely concerned with the environmental aspects of disadvantaged minorities (Deutsch, Katz, & Jensen, 1968). But the possible importance of genetic factors in racial behavioral differences has been greatly ignored, almost to the point of being a tabooed subject, just as were the topics of venereal disease and birth control a generation or so ago (pp. 79–80).

Jensen's charge is undoubtedly correct, and relatively few psychologists (though there are some) would argue that one should not be allowed to do research on the topic, or to analyze the existing data. At the same time, however, many psychologists have disputed his conclusions or his methods of arriving at them, and have opposed even more strongly the implications that seem so readily drawn from his presentation, despite his many disclaimers.

The Spring 1969 issue of the *Harvard Educational Review* presented seven solicited responses to his paper. The Summer 1969 issue (vol. 39, no. 3) presented a rebuttal by Jensen and four articles that had been triggered by his original article, including a paper by Deutsch (see above). The journal also devoted about 50 pages of correspondence to the issues raised. A thorough reading and comprehension of those papers and letters would make one a considerable expert in the field. Moreover, the material is instructive in relation to the problems faced by social and even biological science when these fields deal with complex issues that relate to public policies.

Jensen's original paper and the subsequent "Jensen controversy" were picked up by the mass media. As a result, many students may feel that they have sufficient acquaintance with the topic. However, we earnestly suggest that they go to the original sources cited here. In addition to the materials from the *Harvard Educational Review,* we recommend the following: "Intelligence and Race," by Bodmer and Cavalli-Sforza, in the October 1970 issue of *Scientific American* (vol. 223, no. 4), which presents a more popularized response by geneticists; and "Black Genes—White Environment," in the June 1969 issue of *Trans-Action,* which presents a popularized response by the psychologist J. McVicker Hunt.

Readers will want to keep in mind the issues posed in this biological determinants section when they read other parts of the book. The topics of Age or Developmental Stage (Sec. VII), Sex (Sec. VIII), and Cognition (Sec. IX) are all topics in which biological causes play an important role. In addition, biological causes are clearly germane to Group Memberships (Sec. VI), which includes both race and SES. Differences between the sexes in behavior and differences among people in intelligence are products, after all, of both biology and learning. Certain workers who have placed major emphasis on age or developmental stage have assumed the primacy of biological over experiential determinants. Much of the writing that takes its intellectual origin from either Freud or Jean Piaget is of this type. The cross-reference chart at the beginning of this book lists all the articles included that bear on biological determinants.

The student with little or no background in genetics might find it helpful to consult one or more of the following sources:

1. *Heredity and the Nature of Man* (Harcourt, Brace & World, 1964). By the important geneticist Theodosius Dobzhansky, this book is based on a lecture series given in the springs of 1963 and 1964.
2. *Behavior Genetics* (John Wiley and Sons, 1960, reprinted in 1967). This book is by two psychologists, John L. Fuller and William R. Thompson.
3. *The Future Man* (Basic Books, 1959). This book is based on a series of BBC lectures by the British Nobel Laureate geneticist Peter Medawar. Chapters 4 and 6 are of particular interest for the purposes of readers of this book.
4. *The Language of Life: An Introduction to the Science of Genetics* (Doubleday & Co., 1966). This book is by George and Muriel Beadle. He is a Nobel Prize winner in genetics and she is a well known author.* Chapters 13 through 21 and Chapter 24 are perhaps most interesting for the novice.
5. *The Code of Life* (Columbia University Press, 1965). By Ernest Borek, this book is intended for the educated layman. Chapter 23 of the Beadles' book above is also suitable for this level.

In addition to the books listed above, we would like to refer to two articles. "Should We Weaken or Strengthen Our Genetic Heritage?" (Daedalus, 1961, *90*, 432–450) is an abridgement by Hermann J. Muller of a longer and more technical article. He too is a Nobel Laureate. It would be of particular interest to contrast his views with those of Medawar (see above). In addition, some readers may be interested in the genetic code itself. An article on it for educated laymen appeared in *Scientific American* (1962, *207*, 66–74), written by F. H. C. Crick, another British Nobel Laureate in genetics.

Those who do not desire to go into genetics per se but would like to understand the issues raised by Jensen, might want to consult chapter 6 of Donald O. Hebb's *A Textbook of Psychology*. It is entitled "Heredity, Maturation, Early Learning." Those who would like to understand more about the mechanisms that mediate hereditary and environmental effects on behaviors, such as learning, should read Mark R. Rosenzweig's "Effects of Heredity and Environment on Brain Chemistry, Brain Anatomy, and Learning Ability in the Rat," published in *Kansas Studies in Education,* 1964, *14,* 3–15.

---

* Among her works is a book entitled *The Child's Mind: How Children Learn During the Critical Years from Birth to Age 5* (Doubleday & Co., 1970).

7

Constitutional Factors in Behavior

SIDNEY L. BECK
AND JUDY F. ROSENBLITH

This paper was prepared for this volume to take into account the burgeoning amount of work showing the importance of genetic factors and their mechanisms of operation. We had been unable to discover a single article that described a reasonable portion of this literature simply enough for those who are not biology students. While the introduction to this section has cited some of the literature on genetics that is valuable to students of child or educational psychology, a partial survey seemed necessary here.

Dr. Beck is Professor of Biology at Wheaton College, where Judy Rosenblith is also located.

Biological contributions to behavioral parameters are many and varied. They can be classified into major groupings depending upon the period during ontogeny when they manifest themselves. Or, more precisely, one can distinguish between those biological determinants which are inherited in a truly genetic sense, or transmitted through the genome, and those which are congenital, or a consequence of developmental events and not transmitted through the genome. Finally there are those which manifest themselves only after birth but which nevertheless contribute to the biological constitution of the child. The latter may well be familial without being either genetic or congenital in origin.

Considering only the more easily ascertained category of abnormal behavior, genetic causes would include mutations of a single gene and chromosomal abnormalities. Non-genetic congenital defects would include those caused by drugs, bacterial or viral infections, and physical insults during gestation, as well as traumata occasioned by the birth process itself. Finally, post-natal defects may be occasioned by nutritional factors, disease processes, or physical damage.

Although we shall in the remainder of this paper deal primarily with those aspects of the biological endowment which are important in atypical behavior, it must be recognized that the constitution of the individual sets the limits within which all subsequent environmental events act. In a very fundamental sense it is specious to speak of "nature versus nurture." Rather, all behavior, indeed all characteristics, both behavioral and physical, represent a series of interactions between constitutional and environmental agencies. Thus one must always consider the role of nature *and* nurture in shaping the individual.

GENETIC FACTORS

While genetic contribution to normal behavioral attributes has been investigated using twin studies, the attributes studied are almost always controlled by a large number of genes each producing small additive effects. The best that can be determined from this is an estimate of heritability. The method of investigation of heritability involves a comparison of like-sexed dizygotic (DZ) twins and monozygotic (MZ) twins controlled for age, socioeconomic factors, etc. Since MZ twins have an identical genetic makeup, any variation between members of a pair of MZ twins for a given trait can be attributed to environmental factors. Variation between members of DZ twin pairs, on the other hand, includes both genetic and environmental factors. Therefore, if the amount of measurable variation between members of MZ twin-pairs is less than between DZ twin-pairs, the difference is due to differences in genetic factors among the DZ individuals. Such genetic variation (expressed as a fraction of the total variation which can be measured) gives an estimate of *heritability* for that trait. Twin studies do not reveal *how* genes operate, or even *what* genes are operating; only *whether* genetic factors are operating and roughly how much of the total variation observed is genetic in origin.

A number of identifiable genes are known to influence behavior in detectable ways. Some of these genes primarily affect sensory capacities, others physical appearance, physiological characteristics, or intellectual functioning. Behavioral effects may be secondary and socially conditioned. They include various forms of blindness, deafness, deafmutism, cretinism, albinism, chondrodystrophy, muscular dystrophy, Huntington's chorea, and palsy, to name but a few. For a detailed discussion the reader is referred to Stern (1960). Single gene effects on intellectual capacity include amaurotic idiocy (Tay-Sachs disease) and phenylketonuria. The last named is an intriguing example of how nurture can dramatically influence the expression of a severe behavioral disorder which is clearly inherited as a simple recessive gene. Phenylalanine is a normal constituent of most proteins taken in as food. It is made available for the synthesis of other products by digestion. The first step in the normal utilization of phenylalanine is its conversion to a different compound, tyrosine, by an enzyme produced in the liver. In phenylketonurics this enzyme is lacking and phenylalanine builds up to abnormally high concentrations. At these concentrations other pathways of utilization occur and some of the end products will cause severe mental retardation, especially between the ages of 4 months and 4 years. Indeed, in one study it was found that up to 1 percent of all patients in hospitals for the mentally deficient were phenylketonurics (Harris, 1966). One of the end products of phenylalanine metabolism, phenylpyruvic acid, is excreted in the urine of phenylketonurics. It is not excreted to any appreciable extent by normal individuals, and it is easily detected.* Since phenylalanine is an essential amino acid it cannot be completely eliminated from the diet, but it has been possible to prepare diets with a severely restricted phenylalanine content and when these are given to phenylketonurics at any age the blood levels of phenylalanine can be kept at normal levels. If this low-phenylalanine diet is exclusively fed to phenylketonurics up to four years of age, mental retardation can be prevented. After four years of age it appears that it may no longer be necessary to restrict phenylalanine, the sensitive period being then past.† There are other genetically determined metabolic diseases or "inborn errors of metabolism" which are receiving this type of biochemical analysis with its logically associated treatment possibilities (Stanbury et al., 1960). Such studies are still in early stages.

A great deal of excitement has been generated in recent years by improvements in methods of detecting other kinds of genetically determined defects involving abnormalities of larger genetic units, the chromosomes. It is now possible to take specimens from blood or smears from inside the mouth, or cells from sternal puncture and treat the

cells in various ways to accurately separate each of the chromosomes one from another. These spread chromosomes can then be photographed, cut out of the photograph and arranged in order of size for subsequent analysis (Figure 1). This process, called karyotyping, revealed that the true number of chromosomes in man was 46, rather than the previously published number of 48 (Tjio and Levan, 1956). Since the establishment of karyotype analysis, progress in detecting abnormal variations at the chromosome level has been rapid and the information obtained has been so voluminous as to have required the establishment of a committee of investigators in this field to standardize nomenclature (Chicago Conference, 1966). The usefulness of karyotype analysis has been greatly enhanced by the recently developed technique of amniocentesis. In this process samples of the amniotic fluid which surrounds the fetus are taken using a hypodermic syringe. This is relatively free of hazard. The fluid removed contains cells that have been sloughed off by the fetus. Karyotyping of these cells permits detection of an ever growing list of abnormalities early in pregnancy. The advent of the computer has simplified the task of karyotyping considerably, making such determinations feasible for greater numbers of patients.

The normal complement of human chromosomes consists of twenty-two pairs of autosomes and a single pair of sex chromosomes. The sex chromosomes in females are both alike (XX) and in males are morphologically and functionally different (XY). The chromosomes are numbered consecutively according to size. When arranged by size (see Figure 1) they form seven groups. The members of a single group are difficult to distinguish from one another, but each group is clearly different from the others. Currently a technique involving treatment of the chromosomes with a fluorescent dye (quinocrine) (Caspersson et al., 1970) gives promise of allowing all 23 pairs to be unequivocally distinguished from one another.

In addition to size, the chromosomes also differ with respect to the location of the centromere, a structure which gives the chromosome a "waist." The centromere divides the chromosome into arms. Since the chromosomes are taken from dividing cells in which the chromosomes have doubled, each appears with four arms held together by the centromere. The short arm of a chromosome is labelled "p" and the long arm "q." Shortening or absence of an arm or of a chromosome is indicated with a minus sign; increase in length of an arm or the presence of an extra chromosome is indicated with a plus sign.

The first defect in man known to be attributable to a chromosomal abnormality was Mongolism,

---

* Tests immediately after birth are not conclusive, however.

† Currently, new findings have complicated this picture, but until the issues now raised are resolved, we accept this view.

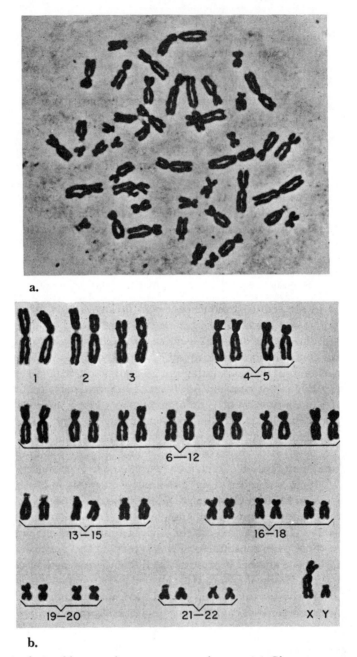

a.

b.

FIGURE 1. *Analysis of human chromosome complement. (a) Chromosome spread from leukocyte culture. (b) Arrangement of chromosomes into standard karyotype. (Furnished by Dr. J. J. Biesele.)* [*From* An Introduction to Human Genetics *by H. Eldon Sutton. Copyright © 1965 by Holt, Rinehart and Winston, Inc. Reprinted by permission of Holt, Rinehart and Winston, Inc.*]

or more properly, Down's syndrome. This disorder is due to the presence of an extra chromosome 21, and the abbreviation of the resultant karyotype is 47,XY,21+ in a male and 47,XX,21+ in a female. The syndrome was originally described by Down in 1866, and its association with an extra chromosome was suggested by Waardenburg in 1932. In 1959, three groups of investigators independently and nearly simultaneously established that the condition was due to the presence of an extra chromosome-21, or trisomy-21. Individuals with Down's syndrome are characterized by the presence of an epicanthic fold on the eyelid which, along with a yellowish cast to the skin, first led Down to apply the term "Mongolism." Other stigmata associated include abnormalities of the face, a somewhat enlarged tongue, the presence of a simian crease on the palmar surface of the hand as well as characteristic patterns of ridges on the fingers and palms, high susceptibility to infection, and a variable degree of mental retardation. This is a fairly common abnormality, with an overall incidence of about 0.15 percent in caucasian populations (Stern, 1960). There is a very striking effect of maternal age on likelihood of occurrence: women who are 35 years or older are 100 times more likely to produce a child with trisomy-21 than those mothers who are under 35. More than one in 40 children born to women over forty years of age will have Down's syndrome. This age-related difference in frequency of occurrence suggests that in the formation of the fertilized ovum the two chromosomes-21 fail to separate (non-disjunction), thus giving rise to the extra chromosome. Various explanations for this phenomenon have been proposed including aging effects on an ovum held so long in the ovary, aging effects on an ovum fertilized longer after its release,* viral infection of the ovum, etc., but the cause is not known. There is a variant form of the disorder, familial mongolism. In these cases there are but 46 chromosomes instead of a 47,XX,21+ or 47,XY,21+. Karyotype analysis reveals that there is indeed extra chromosome-21 material but that it is attached to another chromosome. Translocation of chromosomal material shows no effect due to age of mother, but will likely affect several members of a sibship. A young mother, not herself a carrier of translocation, who had an offspring suffering from trisomy-21 would not be more likely than any other mother to have this disorder occur in subsequent progeny, since primary trisomy-21 is a random non-disjunctional event. Women carrying a translocated chromosome-21 are themselves normal, but their karyotype is 45,XX,21−. About one in five of the progeny of such a carrier will have Down's syndrome; the others will appear and behave normally, but may be carriers of the disorder. Surviving individuals with trisomy of chromosomes 18 or 13 (see Nusbacher and Hirschhorn, 1968 for a review) and trisomies involving the sex chromosomes are also known. In general, however, trisomy is incompatible with life.

If trisomy is a result of non-disjunction of a chromosome during gamete formation, then there should be comparable classes of fetuses which are monosomic as well; that is, which contain only one of a pair of chromosomes. Monosomics are known involving the sex chromosomes (45,XO), but no other viable monosomic chromosome con-

stitutions are known. Indeed, except for those mentioned above, no other aneuploid chromosome patterns (i.e., other than complete sets) appear to be viable. Recent studies (see Inhorn 1967 for review) have shown, however, that chromosomal abnormalities account for a large proportion of "spontaneous" abortions. Some studies have shown that between 20 (Carr, 1967) and 65 percent (Boué et al., 1967) of fetuses aborted in the first trimester have abnormal chromosomal complements. Although trisomy-21 was the first major viable chromosomal abnormality to be studied, the most studied group of abnormal chromosome patterns are those involving the sex chromosomes. The presence of an extra X-chromosome (47,XXX or 47,XXY), an extra Y (47,XYY), or absence of an X (45,XO) are all known and are associated with behavioral derangement of varying degrees. One can easily detect an extra or absent X-chromosome because of the fact that each X-chromosome in excess of one is visible in the nuclei of non-dividing cells as a sex-chromatin mass (Barr and Bertram, 1949). Thus normal females (XX) show a single sex-chromatin mass at the periphery of nearly all of their cells, whereas normal males (XY) do not show this phenomenon. Disorders involving aneuploidy of the sex chromosomes are Turner's and Klinefelter's syndromes. Turner's syndrome affects females; they show reduced stature, poor mammary development, immature external genitalia, and failure to commence menstruation. The ovaries of these individuals are almost entirely absent and have no ova whatever (see McKusick, 1964 for additional details). These individuals have no sex chromatin, and karyotype analysis reveals a 45,XO constitution, or absence of the second X-chromosome. Klinefelter's syndrome affects males; they have immature and small testes, little body hair, and, frequently, female-like breast development. These individuals show sex chromatin and their karyotype is 47,XXY. Klinefelter's occurs with a frequency of one in 400–600 births; Turner's, one in 5,000.

Recently there has been considerable interest in another abnormality of the sex chromosomes, the presence of an extra Y. The 47,XYY karyotype was discovered to be present in a high proportion of males in prison populations and there is the suggestion from subsequent studies that the extra Y-chromosome may be associated with increased stature, an increased tendency towards aggressive and antisocial behavior, and crimes of violence (Marinello et al., 1969). A few examples of 47,XXX females are known, and while they may show some mental deficiency they tend not to be grossly abnormal.

While the presence of even a single extra auto-

---

* This may occur because the older woman is having less frequent intercourse.

some is usually incompatible with life, this does not seem to be the case with the sex chromosomes, and cases of 48,XXXY and 48XXXX are known. Individuals with five X-chromosomes have also been described. They often appear as exaggerated Klinefelter's types if a Y is also present. An explanation for the viability of the four-X and five-X karyotypes comes from the interesting observation that, with an increase in the number of X-chromosomes, there is an increase in the number of sex chromatin masses seen in the cells. This observation, plus the related observations that female humans and mice may be mosaic for a number of traits carried on the X-chromosome, led Mary Lyon (1961, 1966) to propose the theory that all of the X-chromosomes but one are inactivated early in embryonic development in mammals. This theory accounts for the fact that there are no differences in expression of X-linked genes in males and females, since, if the theory is true, only one X-chromosome would in fact be active in both men and women. It would also account for why such great variation in the number of X-chromosomes can be tolerated, whereas aneuploidy for most of the other chromosomes (except 13, 18, and 21) is inviable. That is, no matter how many X-chromosomes are present, only one is active.

Karyotype analysis has also revealed numerous cases of individuals who are mosaics with respect to chromosomal abnormalities. That is, some of their cells may be abnormal while others appear perfectly normal. Thus karyotypes from different cells of the same individual may show 45,XO and 46,XX patterns, or 47,XX,21+ and 46,XX, etc. These individuals are generally less severely affected and may even appear normal but, if the gamete-producing cells are affected as well, they may transmit the abnormality to progeny. The presence of mosaics can be explained by non-disjunction or loss from other causes during embryogenesis.

Not only may entire chromosomes be abnormally represented in an individual, but parts of a chromosome may be duplicated or lost. One striking example of this type of disorder was originally described as the "cri-du-chat" or cry of the cat syndrome (Nusbacher and Hirschhorn, 1968). This syndrome, so-named because afflicted individuals issue a peculiar cat-like cry, invariably involves mental retardation, and other abnormalities in differing proportions of cases. The defect is more common in females and was shown to be a result of reduction or absence of the short arm of chromosome-5 (46,XX,5p— or 46,XY,5p—). Deletions are also known involving chromosome-18. Other bizarre patterns have been reported including duplications, deletions, and formation of ring-shaped chromosomes. Each has its own characteristic pattern of associated abnormalities almost invariably including mental retardation.

In summary, then, we have presented an overview of a variety of easily describable biological factors that influence behavior in predictable and measurable ways. While we have focused on those determinants concerned with abnormalities and abnormal behavioral patterns, it is equally clear that the coefficient of biological determination of any behavioral attribute is measurably greater than zero, and in no case can constitutional factors be ignored.

TERATOLOGICAL FACTORS

Increases in the number of man-made chemicals as a consequence of new technologies and modern medicine, and the changing epidemiological patterns of infectious disease as a consequence of freer travel, are not without hazard to man's biological endowment. Of particular interest in the present context are those birth defects attributable to non-genetic causes which have behavioral ramifications.

The relatively young discipline of teratology, or the study of abnormal development, gained momentum as a result of the production of thousands of malformed babies in parts of Europe and Japan following the introduction of the mild sedative Thalidomide prescribed as a relaxant for anxious pregnant women (Lenz, 1964). The characteristic disturbances associated with Thalidomide teratogenesis are gross malformations of the limbs, especially the arms. Typically the arms are "flipper-like" or almost totally absent. These children clearly pose serious problems to the physician and psychologist. Thalidomide is an example of a chemical teratogen. In the broadest sense, a teratogen is any agent, physical or chemical, which may act directly on the fetus or indirectly through the mother in such a way as to interfere with normal fetal development. Other drugs have been implicated as being teratogenic in man with greater or lesser degrees of certainty. These include the tranquilizer meclazine, the abortifacient aminopterin, the radiomimetic myleran, the steroid cortisone (Lenz, 1964, Smithells, 1966), and the antibiotic tetracycline (Carter and Wilson, 1963). Progestational compounds used to maintain pregnancy in women with histories of recurrent abortions can cause masculinization of female fetuses (Smithells, 1966). There are very clear data in experimental animals (Filippi, 1967) on the severe teratogenic effect of a variety of maternal vitamin deficiencies and antibiotic excesses which will lead to vitamin deficiencies.

Another important class of teratogenic situations

involves maternal viral infection during the first third of pregnancy. The best documented and most serious of these is infection with rubella, the German measles virus. The presence of rubella and other viruses in the fetus following maternal infection can be detected by means of amniocentesis. Rubella periodically reaches epidemic proportions and can cause a broad spectrum of defects in from 10 to more than 50 percent of the fetuses of infected mothers, depending on when during gestation the infection occurs (Desmond et al., 1970). The principal disorders produced are cataracts, deafness, heart defects, and a variety of behavioral disturbances, neuro-motor defects, autistic tendencies, and mental retardation. Other viruses have also been implicated as being teratogenic, and the suggestion has been made (Stoller, 1968) that infectious hepatitis, a presumed viral disease, is in part responsible for Down's syndrome, by being responsible for the maternal non-disjunction of chromosome-21.

X-irradiation has been described as a "universal teratogen" in animals, producing maldevelopment in all organ systems depending upon the time of administration and the dose. Not only are high acute doses damaging, but chronic low doses administered to rats and mice have resulted in reduced fertility and poor performance in a variety of learning situations. Radiation has been implicated in human teratogenesis as well, and is definitely known to cause chromosome breakage with a subsequent loss of parts of broken chromosomes. Data on the possible effects of radiation on behavioral parameters in man are lacking because the obvious physical danger has tended to limit his exposure (Hicks and D'Amato, 1966).

ADDITIONAL CONSIDERATIONS

The contributions of biological determinants to behavior do not cease with birth; culture simply intervenes and becomes a prominent factor. Not only do the constitutional characteristics of the child continue to operate, but new biological factors enter the picture. The effect, for example, of nutritional factors on intelligence is one basic concern about which much heat and little light has been generated. The data are clear in animal studies: malnutrition *in utero* can be teratogenic; malnutrition in early post-natal life can depress learning performance; malnutrition in both periods has the most drastic effects—greater than a simply additive mechanism would account for. The corresponding data for man are less clear. It is clear, however, that nutritional level does contribute to man's constitution and health (Scrimshaw and Gordon, 1968).

Implicit in much of the discussion of the preceding sections is the idea of variability in symptoms. Different individuals who have the same genetic (or constitutional) characteristic show great variation in the severity of their symptoms. This is true both with respect to physical stigmata and intellectual capacity. There is always interaction between environmental and biological factors in determining any behavioral attribute. In addition, there is always a continuum of directness-indirectness in the operation of constitutional factors on behavior. At one extreme, essential physical prerequisites for normal intellectual development may be lacking as a result of severe brain injury or of hereditary metabolic disorders. Here there is a very direct relation to the outcome.

A different level of determinism is shown in a disorder such as deafness. Whether it is due to heredity or to non-hereditary congenital factors (e.g., a result of some intrauterine factor such as rubella), it can lead to handicaps in communication and even retardation. However, these result from interference with language acquisition, poor social interaction, lack of schooling, etc. Adequate special instruction, especially at an early age, may act to reduce or eliminate the handicaps. The importance of starting such training early means that the child deaf at birth due to heredity may have a better chance to minimize the handicaps since he will be suspect and therefore more apt to be detected early and thus receive the appropriate training. Only if the mother is known to have had rubella during pregnancy are the chances of early detection as good for the non-hereditarily congenitally deaf child. This is especially true since we have no good ways of assessing hearing in the newborn period (Hardy, 1970 and Rosenblith, 1970). In summary, the effects of congenital deafness on communication and intelligence are not very direct and depend on the early environment to a very large degree.

A still less direct way in which heredity may influence behavior is through social stereotypes. The physical characteristics that serve to trigger such stereotypes may lead to either special restriction or to special opportunity, to enhanced or to enfeebled self-concept. As one proceeds along the continuum of indirectness which we have tried to indicate in these examples:

". . . the range of variation of possible outcomes of hereditary factors expands rapidly. At each step in the causal chain, there is fresh opportunity for interaction with other hereditary factors as well as with environmental factors. And since each interaction in turn determines the direction of subsequent interactions, there is an ever-widening network of possible outcomes" (Anastasi, p. 46, as reprinted in Rosenblith and Allinsmith, 2nd edition).

Again, as Anastasi (1958) has so clearly stated: "Hereditary influences—as well as environmental factors of an organic nature—vary along a 'continuum of indirectness.' The more indirect their connection with behavior, the wider will be the range of possible outcomes" (pp. 51–52).

It should now be clear that behavior in the psychological domain cannot be predicted from knowledge of genetic factors alone. At the same time there is much excitement over the new knowledge from genetics that helps us understand (and sometimes even treat) clinical syndromes. However, when we attempt to assess the biological contributions to normal behavior or behavior in congenitally normal individuals, the situation is much less clear. Here the environmental influences are easier for the psychologist to assess. Wide diversity of methods of study, psychological functions studied, and subjects studied is necessary if we are to arrive at a better understanding of the ways in which hereditary and environmental influences interact in the development of behavior.

The effects of early experience in relation to genetic variables is one important type of research needed. Recent work indicates that major revisions of research methodology and of interpretation of results may be needed (Henderson, 1968). Henderson's studies indicate that the rate of acquisition, the retention, and the extinction of conditioned fears are all heritable characteristics. However, the evidence points to their being inherited independently of each other. Additional evidence points to genetic independence of other heritable traits that appear to be involved in the effects of early experience. Henderson shows that different genotypes of mice are likely to react quite differently to varied early experiences such as "enrichment." *

Reasonable methods for estimating heritability have existed in agricultural research where the complexity of genotype-environment interactions are analogous to those in the behavioral sciences. These methods are beginning to be applied to behavioral research (Roberts, 1967). After even a cursory examination of the behavior-genetic studies using primarily sub-human animals (see Hirsch, 1967, e.g.), it becomes clear that one cannot generalize responses to identical stimuli across genotypes within a species (rats or mice). Therefore, we must certainly be very modest in our expectations of the ease with which we shall be able to understand the effects of early experience (for example,

enrichment) on children whose individual differences are as great as strain differences in mice.

Perhaps these new emphases on genetics and on other biological factors (including nutrition, viral diseases, drugs, etc., operating *in utero* to determine the constitution of the newborn) and on behavioral genetics may serve to enhance the concern of psychology with individuals or with individuality. Much of the life of psychology has seemingly been devoted to trying to control for individual differences in the hopes of finding general laws of development and behavior. In the process, concern has often been with the average differences between groups which are commonly very small compared to the differences within the groups (individual differences). The time may now be right for increasing concern with individual differences. A recent book written at a popular level by the biochemist Roger J. Williams (1967) is concerned with human individuality. In a chapter devoted to psychology and psychiatry he says: "We can in one sentence summarize the future of psychology and psychiatry in the new and different world where everyone is recognized as having a high degree of inborn individuality. Psychology and psychiatry will expand and become far more useful and expert through centering attention on real individuals. Insofar as psychology's interest has been in the average man, the tail has been wagging the dog. Eventually 'differential psychology' † with all of its ramifications will be the dog, wagging the rest of psychology as an appendage" (p. 177).

REFERENCES

ANASTASI, ANNE (1958). Heredity, environment and the question how. *Psychol. Rev. 65:* 197–208. (Reprinted in Rosenblith and Allinsmith, *The Causes of Behavior,* 2d ed.)

BARR, M. L., & E. G. BERTRAM (1949). A morphological distinction between neurones of the male and female and the behavior of the nucleolar satellite during accelerated nucleoprotein synthesis. *Nature 163:* 676–677.

BOUÉ, J. G., A. BOUÉ, & P. LAZAR (1967). Les aberrations chromosomiques dans les avortements. *Ann. Génétique 10:* 179–187.

CARR, D. H. (1967). Chromosome anomalies as a cause of spontaneous abortion. *Am. J. Obstet. Gynec. 97:* 283–293.

CARTER, M. P., & F. WILSON (1963). Antibiotics and congenital malformations. *Lancet* I, p. 1267.

CASPERSSON, T., L. ZECH, & C. JOHANSSON (1970). Analysis of human metaphase chromosome set by

---

* One should also note that the effects of early experience may vary not only according to genotype, but also according to early experiences of a previous generation (See Section II, Article 11).—EDITOR

---

† Differential psychology is the study of "individual differences," of the variations between people in whatever attributes are being investigated.—EDITOR

aid of DNA-binding fluorescent agents. *Exp. Cell Res. 62:* 490–492.

CHICAGO CONFERENCE (1966). Standardization in Human Cytogenetics. Birth defects, original article series, Vol II, No. 2, The National Foundation. New York.

DESMOND, M. M., G. S. WILSON, W. M. VERNIAUD, J. L. MELNICK, & W. E. RAWLS (1970). The early growth and development of infants with congenital rubella. *Adv. Teratol. 4:* 39–63.

DOWN, J. L. (1866). Observations on an ethnic classification of idiots. *Lond. Hosp. Rep. 3:* 259. (Cited in Penrose, 1966)

FILIPPI, B. (1967). Antibiotics and congenital malformations: Evaluation of the teratogenicity of antibiotics. *Adv. Teratol. 2:* 239–256.

HARDY, JANET B., WILLIAM G. HARDY, & MIRIAM P. HARDY (1970). Some problems in neonatal screening. *Trans. of the American Academy of Ophthalmology and Otolaryngology 74:* 1229–1235.

HARRIS, H. (1966). *Human Biochemical Genetics.* Cambridge University Press, Cambridge, England.

HENDERSON, N. D. (1968). The confounding effects of genetic variables in early experience research: Can we ignore them? *Developmental Psychobiology,* 1(2):146–152.

HICKS, S. P., & CONSTANCE D'AMATO (1966). Effects of ionizing radiations on mammalian development. In *Advances in Teratology,* D. H. M. Woollam, Ed., Academic Press, New York.

HIRSCH, J. (1967). *Behavior-Genetic Analysis.* McGraw-Hill, New York.

INHORN, S. L. (1967). Chromosomal studies of spontaneous human abortions. *Adv. Teratol. 2:* 37–99.

LENZ, W. (1964). Chemicals and malformations in man. in *Proc. II Int. Congress Cong. Malf.,* Int. Med. Congress, New York. pp. 263–276.

LYON, M. F. (1961). Gene action in the X-chromosome of the mouse (*Mus musculus* L.). *Nature 190:* 372–373.

LYON, M. F. (1966). X-chromosome inactivation in mammals. *Adv. Teratol. 1:* 25–54.

MARINELLO, M. J., R. A. BERKSON, J. A. EDWARDS, & R. M. BANNERMAN (1969). A study of the XYY syndrome in tall men and juvenile delinquents. *J. Amer. Med. Assoc. 208:* 321–325.

MCKUSICK, V. A. (1964). *Human Genetics.* Prentice-Hall, New Jersey.

NUSBACHER, J., & K. HIRSCHHORN (1968). Autosomal anomalies in man. *Adv. Teratol. 3:* 11–63.

PENROSE, L. S. (1966). The causes of Down's syndrome. *Adv. Teratol. 1:* 9–24.

ROBERTS, R. C. (1967). Some concepts and methods in quantitative genetics. in *Behavior-Genetic Analysis,* J. Hirsch, Ed., pp. 214–257.

ROSENBLITH, JUDY F. (1970). Our newborn auditory responses prognostic of deafness. *Trans. of the American Academy of Ophthalmology and Otolaryngology 74:* 1215–1228.

SCRIMSHAW, N. S., & I. E. GORDON (1968). *Malnutrition, Learning and Behavior.* MIT Press, Cambridge, Mass.

SMITHELLS, R. W. (1966). Drugs and human malformations. *Adv. Teratol. 1:* 251–278.

STANBURY, J. B., J. B. WYNGAARDEN, & D. S. FREDERICKSON (1960). *The Metabolic Basis of Inherited Disease.* McGraw-Hill, New York.

STERN, C. (1960). *Principles of Human Genetics,* 2nd Ed. Freeman, San Francisco.

STOLLER, A. (1968). Virus-chromosome interaction as a possible cause of cases of Down's syndrome (Mongolism) and other congenital anomalies. *Adv. Teratol. 3:* 97–126.

TJIO, J. H., & A. LEVAN (1956). The chromosome number of man. *Hereditas 42:* 1–6.

WAARDENBURG, P. J. (1932). Das menschliche Auge und seine Erbenlagen. *Nijhoff,* The Hague. (Cited by Penrose, 1966)

WILLIAMS, R. J. (1967). *You Are Extraordinary.* Random House, N. Y.

8

Prediction of Behavior from Birth to Maturity

MARJORIE P. HONZIK

(A Book Review of *Birth to Maturity: A Study in Psychological Development,* by JEROME KAGAN and HOWARD MOSS)

Dr. Marjorie Honzik has long been connected with Berkeley, one of the important centers for longitudinal studies. In this article she reviews a book that is based on data from the longitudinal studies at the Fels Research Institute. The book deals with the stability of behavior from birth to maturity.

The review offers a cogent commentary on longitudinal studies in general, and compares the results of other studies to those presented in the book reviewed. If certain behaviors are indeed stable from birth to maturity, one can present a strong argument for their being biologically determined (without ruling out the effects of interaction with the environment).

Because the actual findings of the book emphasize sex differences, the review could have been placed in Section VIII instead of here.

Other aspects of continuity in behavior (over a shorter span) have been studied by a research group made up of two psychiatrists—Dr. Alexander Thomas and his wife, Dr. Stella Chess—and Dr. Herbert G. Birch, who is both a psychologist and a pediatrician. Their article "The Origin of Personality" (Scientific American, 1970, 223 (2), 102–109) is a highly readable account of their work.

The idea of such continuities in behavior has, of course, been emphasized in earlier work. For example, in 1948 Patricia (Neilon) Naka had

judges match personality sketches written about children who had been studied in their first two years with sketches made when they were seventeen years old.[1] The persons writing the later sketches had no knowledge of the earlier sketches or data. The judges had significant success; however, some individuals appeared to have been much more stable over time than others. There also appeared to be more stability in personality characteristics than in some of the more physical characteristics, for example, height. Thus, we have a precursor of some of the researches in this section. The greater stability of some individuals than of others could, of course, be given either a biological or an environmental interpretation. Unfortunately, Naka did not analyze her data for some of the more obvious changes in the family situations of stable children as compared with less stable children.

From birth to maturity is a long time. It is not surprising, therefore, that longitudinal research covering the entire period of growth has been so slow in yielding its findings. And it is with a feeling of excitement that we approach the analysis of stability and change in certain personality variables for a group of young people who grew to maturity between 1929 and 1958.

Few research centers had elected to study personality development longitudinally around 1930. Notable exceptions were the Fels Research Institute's investigation which Lester Sontag, M.D., initiated in 1929 and has continued to direct for 35 years; the three independent investigations, with differing purposes, launched by the University of California's Institute of Child Welfare between 1928 and 1931—the Berkeley Growth Study, the Guidance Study, and the Oakland Growth Study (Jones, Macfarlane, and Eichorn, 1960); and the two-year investigation of Mary Shirley (1931) at the University of Minnesota's Institute of Child Welfare with the follow-up by Neilon in 1948. The children first described by Escalona and Heider in their study of "Prediction and Outcome" (1959) and later by Lois B. Murphy in "The Widening World of Childhood" (1962) were born in the 1940's. This was also true of the children in the study by Anderson et al. (1960) of the prediction of adjustment of the school children of Nobles County over a seven-year period. More recently an investigation specifically concerned with personality development in early childhood was undertaken in this country (Chess, Thomas, Birch,

---

[1] *J. Genet. Psychol.,* "Shirley's Babies after Fifteen Years," 1948, *73,* 175–186.

Marjorie P. Honzik, "Prediction of behavior from birth to maturity," a book review of *Birth to maturity: a study in psychological development,* by Jerome Kagan and Howard Moss (New York: Wiley, 1962). *Merrill-Palmer Quarterly of Behavior and Development,* 1965, *11* (1), 77–88. Reprinted by permission.

and Hertzig, 1960); and a series of longitudinal growth studies have gotten under way in London (Moore, Hindley, and Falkner, 1954), Western Europe (Skard, 1960), and Africa (Geber, 1962) during the past decade. While this listing covers some of the major projects, it is well to keep in mind that the total number of individuals included in all longitudinal studies of personality development is an infinitesimal sampling of the world's peoples.

Investigations of mental growth have been more numerous than those of personality consistency and change and the results have been more definitive. It is reassuring to note that when the measuring instruments are as reliable as carefully administered intelligence tests, the results from the various centers and universities are remarkably similar (Bayley, 1949; Ebert et al., 1943; Honzik et al., 1948; Sontag et al., 1958). This fact encourages us to believe that if comparable care is used in defining and measuring behavior and personality, we may have in the next decade a verified body of facts leading to more encompassing theories of personality development.

The purpose of the Kagan and Moss investigation was, in their words, to find "the link between child and adult behavior . . . and to discover classes of stable response systems and the developmental periods during which they become manifest." They chose to look for continuity and change in "motive related behaviors, sources of anxiety, defensive behavior and modes of social interaction" rated at different age periods in childhood and in early adulthood. More specifically, they considered the stability of "passivity and dependence, aggression, fear of physical harm, achievement, sex typed activity, and spontaneity." The rationale for the choice of behavior variables was "the emphasis in current theory and research on four classes of variables: (a) behaviors aimed at attainment of culturally salient goals (i.e., motive related behaviors), (b) sources of anxiety and conflict, (c) defensive responses to anxiety arousing situations and conflicts, and (d) modes of interpersonal interaction."

We propose to examine in some detail the methodology, results, and interpretations of the Kagan and Moss investigation and to compare certain of their procedures and findings with those of other longitudinal studies. The reasons for this are twofold. The results are basic to personality theory, and decisions as to sampling of cases and behaviors and the nature of data analysis become magnified many times in importance when personality is considered in a time perspective. A decision to include or not to include certain individuals will color not one but all relationships. The decision to use a certain type of analysis will determine not one

but the many relationships at an age and through time. And, of course, the point of view or theoretical vantage point of the investigators determine not only what they look for, and at, but how the results are interpreted; and once a course of action is taken, it has to be maintained.

Kagan and Moss used a correlational analysis in looking for continuities of behavior. In this type of analysis, the size and nature of the available sample is crucial. Although the method of selecting the Fels longitudinal sample is not described, the parents' education approximates a normal distribution. However, the major difficulty in using the described group in a correlational analysis of consistency of behavior is that "the 89 children came from 63 different families, with 19 families supplying 45 of the children." Further, 44 families had one child in the study, 12 had two children, and 7 families had three children in the group. One of the three-child families had male triplets whose zygosity is not reported. After an initial clear statement of the sample composition, the authors make no further mention of the group other than to report that 71 of the 89 subjects participated in the adult assessment. Since Pearsonian correlation coefficients constitute the sole method of describing stability and change in behavior, the inclusion of siblings of some but not all children presents a major methodological difficulty in assessing the results. If the siblings, and especially the triplets, are more alike in their behaviors than randomly selected children, the correlation coefficients may be remarkably inflated. Not only learning theory but also recent studies of the "heritability of personality dimensions" (Cattell et al., 1957; Gottesman, 1963) support this hypothesis. It would be of considerable interest to know whether the relationships would be changed if only one child from each family were selected for study. A recomputing of these materials excluding siblings would seem feasible and desirable.

The longitudinal data available at the Fels Institute for rating were observational records of the children in the natural settings of the home (in semi-annual visits), at nursery school, and at later ages in day camps and public school. One of the authors, Moss, used this rich observational material to rate 29 dimensions of behavior at four successive age periods from birth to 14 years. The age range included in each period was: birth to 3 years, 3 to 6, 6 to 10, and 10 to 14 years. One could certainly wish that the first and last of these periods had been further divided into finer age groupings. Erikson (1963), who has proposed one of the few truly developmental personality theories,* divides the age period from birth to 3 years into the three stages—"basic trust," "autonomy," and "initiative"—while he finds five more stages adequate to

---

* Erikson's theory is presented in selection 44 of this book.—
EDITOR

describe the remaining entire life span of the individual. Erikson's fourth stage, "industry vs. inferiority," coincides very nicely with Kagan and Moss's 6 to 10 year period. Of the age periods used by Kagan and Moss, the 6 to 10 year span is probably the most satisfactory.

On the other hand, giving one overall rating for years 10 to 14 for both boys and girls involves a certain discounting of the impact of puberty on behavior. There is evidence from another longitudinal investigation, the Guidance Study, that at least one of the dimensions rated by Moss, "dependence," fluctuates for girls during the age period when the largest proportion of the girls were in the pubertal cycle but does not do so during the same age span for boys (Macfarlane, Allen, and Honzik, 1954). Furthermore, it was observed that markedly dependent behavior showed a significant increase in incidence a year before menarche and declined to a much lower level at menarche. The perturbations of the dependence-independence dimension during the entire cycle of sexual maturation in girls was clear in the two independently studied groups of the Guidance Study, and it would certainly be of interest if this relationship also occurred in the Fels material.

This result is mentioned here because of its relevance to the age-period grouping and, as has been stated, the purpose of Kagan and Moss was not to portray every possible relationship but to present the continuities and discontinuities over the four specified age periods and adulthood.

One of the major strengths of this investigation is the complete independence of the adult and childhood material. Another strength lies in the fact that the senior author, Kagan, interviewed all the subjects as adults. The interviews were tape-recorded and the behavior dimensions rated by Kagan for all the subjects, and by a second psychologist for 32 subjects.

The age range of the subjects at the time of adult interview was 19 to 29 years. An effort was made to narrow this range by interviewing the older subjects first but, nevertheless, there was an age difference of approximately 10 years between the age of the oldest and youngest subject at the time of the adult interview. This means that the interviewer was a peer of the oldest subjects but would appear as a "professor" or older man to the youngest subjects. Seventy-one per cent of the women and 56 per cent of the men were married at the time of the adult interview. While this wide age-range at the time of the adult assessments is a real difficulty, it is one which could be evaluated at some later date by considering the relation of the rated dimensions to age, marital status, number of children, etc.

The actual scales used in rating behavior either during childhood or as adults are not described, but the authors report that 7-point scales were constructed and detailed behavioral referents for scale points 1, 4, and 7 provided. A word about the variables rated and their reliabilities is in order. The titles of the variables are reported but only one end of what must be a continuum is mentioned, e.g., passivity, independence. This emphasis on one end of each scale has led to some difficulties in interpretations which will be discussed later in this report. A second psychologist rated "samples of the behaviors." The reported inter-rater reliabilities are high, which is to be expected when two psychologists have access to the same narrative material in making their ratings.

In an earlier study of the constancy of personality assessments of the Oakland Growth Study sample from 14 to 33 years, Tuddenham (1959) reported inter-interviewer agreement of .61 on the average when the two interviewers differed in sex and discussed different topics. The median reliabilities reported by Kagan and Moss when the two raters were reading the same material varied from .68 for Period I (birth to 3 years) to .85 for Period IV (10 to 14 years). Kagan and Moss state that "the dissimilarity between the adolescent and adult rating situations and the low inter-rater reliabilities were two major sources of error in (Tuddenham's) study." Tuddenham perhaps erred in his emphasis on the limitations of an outstanding investigation. The expectancies of agreement should not be the same when (1) two judges rate the same material, and when (2) the ratings of two judges, or interviewers, who have each obtained different material in different contexts from the subjects, are compared. The latter condition is more akin to a validity coefficient.

Thousands of correlation coefficients were computed for the approximately 4,500 behavior ratings. These results are well organized into tables showing continuities between Periods I (birth to 3 years), II, III, and IV (10 to 14 years) and the relation of status at each of these age-periods with that at adulthood.

The number of cases for each r is not given and the effect of differences in variability on the correlations not discussed. These would seem to be sins of omission. But one superfluous result is reported and that is the relationship for the sexes combined. A good rule might be to give the findings for the sexes separately whenever the number of cases permits, only reporting results for sexes combined when the N is small or the sex differences not significant. These technical points might be thought irrelevant in a review—except that longitudinal investigations of stability and change are now coming forth with their results in increasing numbers, and comparative evaluations are going to be hard to make unless the results are fully presented, including sample size and heterogeneity.

Kagan and Moss report that the most dramatic and consistent finding in their study was that many of the behaviors exhibited by the child during Period III (6 to 10 years) and a few during Period II (3 to 6 years) were moderately good predictors of theoretically related behaviors in early adulthood. Among the adult variables which were related to analogous behaviors during the early school years were for women, "passive withdrawal from stressful situations" and "dependency on the family"; for men, "ease of anger arousal" and "sexual behavior"; and for both men and women, "involvement in intellectual mastery," "sex role identification," and "spontaneity."

Of these variables, the persistence of "spontaneity" is most impressive since it is stable and predictive for both males and females and is neither a "sex-typed" behavior nor is it an ability-related variable like achievement. Kagan and Moss consider "social interaction anxiety" to be at the opposite end of the spontaneity continuum; and they report that childhood ratings of spontaneity are predictive of spontaneity in adulthood (or "lack of adult social interaction anxiety"). They find consistency on this dimension in males from Period I (birth to 3 years) to adulthood, and in females from the 6 to 10 year period.

In at least three other longitudinal studies, investigators have reported a similar variable to be highly stable. Tuddenham (1959) reported the persistence of certain personality ratings for the young people in the Oakland Growth Study from approximately age 14 years to age 33 years, and concluded that "among the most stable variables for both sexes were several which connote spontaneity vs. inhibition." No two studies have used exactly the same variables, but in the Berkeley Growth Study a continuum which is probably highly correlated with spontaneity-inhibition is the dimension "active, extroverted vs. inactive, introverted." Bayley and Schaefer (1963) report this broad category of behavior to be the most stable and persistent of those they evaluated between birth and 18 years. In still another sample, the Berkeley Guidance Study, where the method of data collection was largely that of interviews with mothers and children over the age period 21 months to 18 years, the most consistent or stable variable of the approximately sixty considered was the dimension of "introversion vs. extroversion," and a second highly consistent dimension was "excessive reserve-spontaneity." Also in the Guidance Study sample, the most stable school behavior (according to the teachers' reports) was for boys "reserved-expressive" and for girls "somber-gay." Despite the great variation in variable description, findings of the different longitudinal studies suggest that

this dimension of outgoing responsiveness versus a retractive, inward-looking response may be one of the truly stable personality dimensions. It will be of interest to all the investigators to look more carefully at the correlates of these ratings and possible determinants of this dimension over time.

The finding of Kagan and Moss that dependent behavior in girls shows a high degree of continuity is not an isolated result. In the Guidance Study (Honzik and Macfarlane, 1964) where the ratings are based on interviews with the parents and children, girls showed a greater consistency than boys on the dependent-independent continuum during the age period 4 to 16 years. Furthermore, when as 30-year-old women they checked themselves as "dependent," there was a high probability that they had been considered dependent during the middle years of childhood, and again at 15 and 16 years. What do these facts mean? Kagan and Moss believe that "congruence with traditional standards for sex-role characteristics accounts for the differential stability of behaviors of males and females." And they elaborate that "the individual's desire to mold his overt behavior in concordance with the culture's definition of sex appropriate responses is a major determinant of the patterns of continuity and discontinuity in his development."

A major flaw in this argument with respect to dependence is that the opposite end of this continuum, non-dependence or relative independence, is also predictive for the females in the Kagan and Moss study since the correlations are based on a continuum (7-point ratings). There is a correlation of .48 between passivity during the 6 to 10 years and withdrawal behavior as an adult. This means that girls with a rating of 6 or 7 on passivity in elementary school are likely to show withdrawal behavior as adults; but it also suggests that girls with ratings of 1 or 2 (very non-passive) were *not* showing withdrawal behavior as adults. This finding suggests that behavior along this continuum becomes stabilized early. The correlations do *not* show whether or not "the individual's desire to mold his overt behavior in concordance with the culture's definition of sex appropriate responses is a major determinant of the patterns of continuity and discontinuity in his development." Only if inspection of the correlation scatters showed that there is a shift toward passivity and dependence in the females and anger arousal in males, would we be justified in concluding that the boy and girl mold their behavior in concordance with the culture's definition of sex appropriate responses.

The significant question is why are these behavioral continua maintained, and differentially so, in males and females? One possibility is that these are chance findings since they are found in one but not both sexes. However, Tuddenham (1959) found drive *aggression* to be *the* most stable of 34 variables for men, from 14 to 33 years, in the Oakland Growth Study. Dependence and passivity were not rated in the Tuddenham investigations. But the dependence-independence continuum was rated, as has been mentioned, at twelve age levels, from 4 to 16 years, in the Guidance Study and was one of the more consistent behavioral dimensions for girls but not for boys—and a high degree of consistency occurred in spite of very low correlations during the 10 to 14 year age-period when the majority of girls were pubescent.

In summary, the finding that sex appropriate or inappropriate behaviors persist was not only replicated for certain variables by Kagan and Moss, but is cross-validated in other longitudinal studies. The explanation of this sex difference is not obvious. Among the possibilities are: (1) a sex difference in variability; (2) these behavioral dimensions are constitutionally or genetically determined; (3) the environmental milieu is continuously but differentially supporting of these behavioral continua; or (4) the impact of early experiences is so overwhelming that the child's learned mode of response is maintained or continued to adulthood. The first possibility may be easily checked by looking at the variance, but the relevance of constitutional and environmental factors requires the measurement of both early response patterns and continuous measurements of the milieu.

One of the most puzzling aspects of Kagan and Moss's conclusions and interpretations is the lack of coherence between some of the findings and the theory advanced to explain their findings. They place "the construct of sex-role identification in a central position in directing the selective adoption and maintenance of several behavior domains." And yet, it seems clear that correlations showing persistence and change in behaviors are only tangentially relevant to sex-role identification. There are, of course, a number of ways of investigating the changes the boy or girl makes in his behavior to conform with traditional sex-role standards. It would not be difficult, for example, to have judges rate the characteristics of the ideal male and female and then compare the changing behaviors of the boy or girl in relation to this ideal. Kagan and Moss discuss the "hypothetical ego ideal or idealized model that embodies the essential qualities of masculinity or femininity." And they add: "Each individual has a cognitive picture of the person he would like to be and the goal states he would like to command—an idealized model of himself. . . . It would appear that the desire to be an *ideal male* or *ideal female* (italics not ours), as

defined by the individual, comprises an essential component of everyman's model. Thus the position of a response on a cognitive dimension ranging from *highly masculine* to *highly feminine* is a primary determinant of its acceptability and, therefore, of its probability of occurrence."

This discussion, with italicized emphasis, of sex-role identification as "a governor of behavior" constitutes a major segment of the summary and conclusions which suggests its importance to the authors. But the extensive data were only analyzed to show "continuities or stability of behavior" over a number of age-periods and were not considered in relation to models. Nor is there any mention of mean changes in the direction of masculine or feminine behaviors among the boys and girls. There is clearly the possibility of further analysis of the 4,500 ratings to discover the extent of, or if, indeed, "sex-role identification *is* a governor of behavior."

The authors' second conclusion is that "the early school years are a critical period" in personality development. They report that "continuity between child and adult behavior generally became manifest during the first four school years (6 to 10)." This finding is in agreement with the conclusion of Schaefer and Bayley (1963) for the Berkeley Growth Study sample, that "more enduring behavioral traits are developed during the latency period." A corollary of this finding is that prediction from the two earlier periods (birth to 6 years) is not good for a number of variables. In some instances, prediction is actually better from the 6 to 10 year period than from the 10 to 14 year period. One example is the finding that aggression-anxiety in adult males tends to be better predicted by the 6 to 10 year ratings than by the 10 to 14 year ratings. Although the sample limitations preclude a too detailed analysis of changes in the predictive power from one age-period to another, it is likely that the turbulence of adolescence may temporarily disrupt certain attitudes and personality characteristics. It is also evident that some personality constellations observed in adolescence are more highly predictive of adult personality than are the early childhood ratings. "Aggressive retaliation" in adult men is one such variable. The correlation between the adult rating of "aggressive retaliation" and "aggression to mother" during the age-period birth to 3 years is .19, but by 10 to 14 years it is .47.

One of the impressive findings of longitudinal studies is the age change in relationships, and thus in prediction. This fact also points to the impossibility of assuming that predictions made from one age-period could necessarily be made from any other age-period. It may even be found that predictions vary within the adolescent period. McKee and Turner (1961) report that "drive" ratings made in adolescence are more predictive of CPI [California Personality Inventory.—EDITOR] scales in adulthood for females than males. They suggest that the basis for this difference is the later maturing of males than females. It may well be true that for some variables 12-year ratings of girls show a similar prediction to 14-year ratings of boys. In other words, biological as well as chronological age demands consideration.

The Fels data yielded many interesting sex differences in patterns of relationships. One of the most impressive sex differences occurred in the correlates of intellectual mastery: ". . . intellectually oriented men, in contrast to the intellectual women, were less competitive, more likely to withdraw to stress." This and other results lead the authors to the conclusion that "it may be unwise to pool data for males and females without first examining the data for sex differences." One of the interesting phenomena of growth data which these authors underscore is that frequently where there are no sex differences in means and standard deviations, there may be "sex differences in patterns of intercorrelations" either at an age-period or over time. (See Schaefer and Bayley, 1963, and Honzik, 1963, for comparable findings.)

One truly exciting finding in the Fels data is what Kagan and Moss have called the "sleeper effect." The authors appear to subsume two phenomena under this heading: first, the effects on later development of specific early experiences; and second, discontinuities in personality development such that behaviors manifested in infancy or early childhood may be more predictive of comparable adult behaviors than later childhood assessments of the behavior.

An example of the first type of sleeper effect is the finding that the "maternal protection of a daughter during age 0 to 3 predicted adult withdrawal from stress ($r = .52$, $p < .01$), whereas maternal protection during ages 3 to 6 or 6 to 10 showed no relation to adult withdrawal. . . ." There is a possibility that this specific result is a chance one. However, judging by reports from other longitudinal studies, as well as the Fels investigation and the observations of perceptive persons from the beginning of time, it is more than likely that certain experiences of early childhood have far-reaching effects and that these effects may not become manifest until maturity or even later adult life. Harlow's findings for monkeys (1962)* support this hypothesis. One of the rewarding research projects of the future will be the documenting more

specifically of the origins of significant behaviors from the cumulative records of the various growth studies.

An example of the second type of sleeper effect—i.e., a period of discontinuity—is the finding that certain behaviors such as passivity and fear of bodily harm for the age-period birth to 3 years were more predictive of "love object dependency" in adult men than later assessments of these childhood variables. This predictive discontinuity has its counterpart in physical growth. During puberty, prediction of adult height is not as good as during the age-periods immediately preceding the age span when a large proportion of the youngsters are pubescent (Tuddenham, 1954). The fact of perturbations in the inter-age correlation matrices may suggest not only the periods of greater and less prediction but may also suggest the factors contributing to the continuities and discontinuities. An example of this was obtained in the Guidance Study materials, where it was noted that the age-period of lowered prediction of physical measurements in girls coincided with a period of lowered prediction in the dependence-independence continuum. This finding suggests that either the physiological changes affect the girl's behavior directly, or that the changing status of the girl approaching sexual maturity leads to a change in her dependency behavior.

In summary, there will never be a longitudinal study in which there are no methodological limitations. The investigation by Kagan and Moss has its share, some of which can still be evaluated (for example, the effect of including siblings in the correlation coefficients, and the 10-year span of the adult data). On the other hand, this developmental investigation has many strengths, including the richness of the childhood materials, high reliability of the ratings, independence of adult evaluations, and good organization of a large body of interrelationships. The results of this investigation will be discussed for a long time and compared with those of other growth studies until the ingredients of a more adequate theory of personality growth are found. Although the behaviors rated by Kagan and Moss were derived from current theory, hypotheses were not always supported and the articulation of findings and theory is not one of the strong points of this book.

The inter-age correlations show certain continuities of behavior, some of which are cross-validated in other growth studies. One such variable is "spontaneity," which is highly persistent and may be related to an introversion-extroversion dimension which Gottesman (1963) finds "most heavily influenced by genetic factors." It is clear that behaviors which are more salient in boys such

---

* For another report of Harlow's work, see selection 19 in this book.—EDITOR

as the aggression–non-aggression continuum, and those more salient in girls, such as dependency–non-dependency, are more likely to persist. This is a significant finding in our culture where sex appropriate behavior is so valued, but these results do not provide a clue as to *why* a child's status on sex relevant continua are likely to be maintained. Do these results mean that within sex constitutional factors are determining this continuity, or that sex appropriate or inappropriate behaviors are learned early?

In conclusion, a correlational analysis of consistency and change in relevant variables is an excellent first step—but it is just that. Having now found the areas and age-periods of continuity and change, the next steps will be more difficult but also more rewarding—the looking again at the individuals to see just when and under what conditions consistency and change take place. And when, with more knowledge and greater understanding, the picture becomes clearer, we may be led to more enlightened personality theory than is now available.

REFERENCES

ANDERSON, J. E. The prediction of adjustment over time. In I. Iscoe and H. Stevenson (Eds.), *Personality development in children*. Austin: Univer. Texas Press, 1960.

BAYLEY, NANCY. Consistency and variability in the growth of intelligence from birth to eighteen years. *J. genet. Psychol.,* 1949, *75,* 165–196.

BAYLEY, NANCY, & SCHAEFER, E. S. Consistency of maternal and child behavior in the Berkeley Growth Study. Symposium on personality consistency and change. *Amer. Psychologist,* 1963, *18,* No. 7.

CATTELL, R. B., BLEWETT, D. B., & BELOFF, J. R. The inheritance of personality. *Amer. J. hum. Genet.,* 1955, *7,* 122–146.

CHESS, STELLA, THOMAS, A., BIRCH, H. G., & HERTZIG, MARGARET. Implications of a longitudinal study of child development for child psychiatry. *Amer. J. Psychiat.,* 1960, *117,* 434–441.

EBERT, ELIZABETH, & SIMMONS, KATHERINE. The Brush Foundation study of child growth and development. *Soc. Res. Child Develpm. Monogr.,* 1943, *8,* No. 2.

ERIKSON, E. H. *Childhood and society.* (2nd ed.) New York: Norton, 1963.

ESCALONA, SIBYLLE, & HEIDER, GRACE M. *Prediction and outcome.* New York: Basic Books, 1959.

GEBER, MARCELLE. Longitudinal study and psychomotor development among Baganda children. In G. S. Nielsen (Ed.), *Child and education.* Copenhagen: Munksgaard, 1962.

GOTTESMAN, I. Heritability of personality: a demonstration. *Psychol. Monogr.,* 1963, *77,* No. 9 (Whole No. 572).

HARLOW, H. The heterosexual affectional system in monkeys. *Amer. Psychologist,* 1962, *17,* 1–9.

HONZIK, MARJORIE P. A sex difference in the age of onset of the parent-child resemblance in intelligence. *J. educ. Psychol.,* 1963, *54,* 231–237.

HONZIK, MARJORIE P., MACFARLANE, JEAN W., & ALLEN, LUCILE. The stability of mental test performance between two and eighteen years. *J. exp. Educ.,* 1948, *17,* 309–324.

HONZIK, MARJORIE P., & MACFARLANE, JEAN W. Prediction of specific behaviors and personality characteristics from 21 months to 30 years. (MS)

JONES, H. E., MACFARLANE, JEAN W., & EICHORN, DOROTHY H. A progress report on growth studies at the University of California. *Vita Humana,* 1960, *3,* 17–31.

MACFARLANE, JEAN W., ALLEN, LUCILE, & HONZIK, MARJORIE P. A developmental study of the behavior problems of normal children between 21 months and 14 years. *Univer. Calif. Publ. in Child Develpm.,* 1954, Vol. 2

MCKEE, J. P., & TURNER, W. S. The relation of "drive" ratings in adolescence to CPI and EPPS scores in adulthood. *Vita Humana,* 1961, *4,* 1–14.

MOORE, T., HINDLEY, C. B., & FALKNER, F. A longitudinal research in child development and some of its problems. *Brit. Med. J.,* 1954, *II,* 1132–1137.

MURPHY, LOIS B. *The widening world of childhood.* New York: Basic Books, 1962.

NEILON, PATRICIA. Shirley's babies after fifteen years: a personality study. *J. genet. Psychol.,* 1948, *73,* 175–186.

SCHAEFER, E. S., & BAYLEY, NANCY. Maternal behavior, child behavior, and their intercorrelations from infancy through adolescence. *Soc. Res. Child Develpm. Monogr.,* 1963, *28,* No. 3.

SHIRLEY, MARY M. *The first two years: a study of twenty-five babies.* Vol. 3. *Personality manifestations.* Minneapolis: Univer. Minn. Press, 1933.

SKARD, ASE. Longitudinal observations of changing family relations. In G. S. Nielsen (Ed.), *Child and education.* Copenhagen: Munksgaard, 1962.

SONTAG, L. W., BAKER, C. T., & NELSON, VIRGINIA L. Mental growth and personality development: a longitudinal study. *Soc. Res. Child Develpm. Monogr.,* 1958, *23,* No. 2.

TUDDENHAM, R. D. The constancy of personality ratings over two decades. *Genet. Psychol. Monogr.,* 1959, *60,* 3–29.

TUDDENHAM, R. D., & SNYDER, MARGARET M. Physical growth of California boys and girls from birth to 18 years. *Univer. Calif. Publ. in Child Develpm.,* 1954, Vol. 1, No. 2.

9

The Development of Social Motivation *

J. P. Scott

Inhibitory Training of Dogs: Effects of Age at Training in Basenjis and Shetland Sheepdogs †

J. P. Scott, Jane H. Shepard, and Jack Werboff

The Jackson Laboratory at Bar Harbor, Maine, has contributed much to our understanding of the interactions of genetics and experience. Two of the principal workers there were John L. Fuller (who is still at the Jackson Laboratory) and John P. Scott. The latter, represented in both parts of this dual selection, is now Regent's Professor of Psychology and director of the Center for Research on Social Behavior at Bowling Green State University in Ohio.

The first part of this selection is a portion of a longer paper that was presented at the annual invitational Symposium on Motivation held by the University of Nebraska. The second part of the selection presents portions of a specific data-based paper by Scott and two colleagues (Shepard, of the University of Georgia, and Werboff, of the University of Connecticut). These papers, together with the paper by Freedman in this section (also

done at the Jackson Laboratories), provide data both on the effects of age and on the interactions between genetics (breed of dog) and experience (types of training). If breed of dog makes such large differences in the effects of a given treatment on the dogs' behavior, is it any wonder that child psychologists cannot give a formula for how to treat children? The variations among children in certain constitutional attributes may well be analogous to breed differences in dogs, at least at the extremes of human variation.

(The Development of Social Motivation [1])

In the course of experiments on genetics and social behavior in the dog (Scott & Fuller, 1965), a colleague and I made a detailed study of the development of social behavior in these animals, beginning at birth and continuing up until one year of age. We thus had the opportunity of observing the development of all sorts of socially motivated behavior, beginning with nursing at birth and continuing with sexual and agonistic behavior at later ages. In this paper I am going to refer chiefly to one sort of social motivation that begins to appear at about three weeks of age and remains highly important throughout life. In fact, this motivation is so pervasive in the dog that it could be called a general social drive.

Besides its major importance in the life of the dog, this motivation deserves attention because it has been in the past so little studied. As I shall show, it is strongly related to a major developmental process, that of primary socialization, resulting in the formation of the first emotional attachments.

To begin with observation: a major characteristic of dogs is that they appear to dislike intensely being alone, for an animal will struggle violently to avoid solitude. Such distress can be alleviated in the ordinary pet dog by the company of familiar persons or dogs, and the accompanying motivation thus seems to rest on a relatively simple emotional base.

[1] Research described in this paper has been supported by grants from the Rockefeller Foundation, the Ford Foundation, and the National Institutes of Health (Grants M-4481 and MH-08953), and was performed at the Jackson Laboratory.

* Reprinted from J. P. Scott, "The development of social motivation," *Nebraska Symposium on Motivation*, 1967, 125–132, by permission of University of Nebraska Press. Copyright © 1967 by the University of Nebraska Press.

† J. P. Scott, Jane H. Shepard, and Jack Werboff, "Inhibitory training of dogs: effects of age at training in basenjis and Shetland sheepdogs." *The Journal of Psychology, 66*, 1967, 237–241, 248–252. Reprinted with abridgement by permission.

The physiological basis of one major system of behavior is still almost unknown, although the behavior itself is extremely common in the higher animals. Allelomimetic behavior is seen in schools of fish, flocks of birds, herds of mammals, and especially in troops of primates and groups of human beings. It is so commonly seen that it often passes unnoticed. It consists of one animal's doing what the others next to him are doing, with some degree of mutual stimulation. It frequently results in coordinated movement.

Our early experiments with this behavior involved setting up a short race course that dogs could run in approximately 10 seconds. We first worked with a miscellaneous group of dogs representing several breeds and having a varied background of experience. Each dog ran the course twice each day, once by himself and once paired with another animal, the order being reversed each day. Running time was decreased by an average of 18% in the presence of another animal. We also found that pairing a dog with an unfamiliar animal had little effect unless he was matched with a different animal each day. In this case, the average running time was increased approximately 73% (Vogel, Scott, & Marston, 1950).

While these original experiments were done under a non-competitive situation, the argument can be made that the increased motivation associated with running together was produced by the memory of former competition. Using reinforcement theory, it can be predicted than an animal which sometimes wins and sometimes loses will become strongly motivated through irregular partial reinforcement. Curt McCray and I (Scott & Mc-Cray, 1967) therefore did a carefully designed experiment involving 32 adult basenji dogs reared under comparable conditions and matched so that the pairs had no previous experience with each other and hence no memory of previous competition. In the experiment itself, one group was first run under conditions of competition and later competition was removed. In the other group the order of treatment was reversed.

The results were simple and clear-cut. A highly significant effect of running in pairs was found, but there was no difference between the competitive and the noncompetitive conditions. Dogs that lost ran equally fast whether rewarded or not. In one case, where the winner began to run slowly, the other dog always waited at the goal and allowed him to enter ahead. Competition had the effect of setting up a dominance order with respect to food but had little or no effect on motivation for running. It is therefore unlikely that the motivation produced by competition will account for allelomimetic behavior, and we can state that this behavioral system has an independent mechanism of basic motivation.

The phenomenon of enhanced performance in groups, or social facilitation, was well established in human beings in the early part of this century (Allport, 1924) and was later discovered in many animal societies (Crawford, 1939). Nice (1943), in her studies of flocking in birds, was the first to point out the relationship of social facilitation to allelomimetic behavior or, as she called it, contagious behavior.

To explain this phenomenon, we assume that the basic motivation is a tendency to do what other individuals are doing. Mutual reactions of this kind result in allelomimetic behavior and, under certain conditions, in increments of performance. The same motivation might also produce decrements in activity. While the latter has not yet been experimentally demonstrated in the lower animals, it can easily be seen in a flock of sheep lying down to rest together. . . .

THE PROCESS OF PRIMARY SOCIALIZATION

In an apparently unrelated line of work, my colleagues and I have systematically studied the development of social behavior in the dog, including all of the various behavioral systems. We first of all found that the development of the puppy falls into natural periods based on the existence of important developmental processes. There is a neonatal period of approximately two weeks, in which the major process is the establishment of neonatal nutrition, or nursing. There follows a very rapid process of transition from neonatal behavior patterns to adult behavior patterns, most of which takes place between two and three weeks of age and thus defines the transition period. Beginning at approximately three weeks of age, the process of primary socialization appears. At this point in development the puppy is readily able to form emotional attachments to other dogs, people, and inanimate objects in the environment (Scott & Fuller, 1965).

Freedman, King, and Elliot (1961) found that the peak of the process occurred at approximately six to eight weeks of age and gradually fell off thereafter, so that forming a satisfactory relationship becomes quite difficult after twelve weeks of age. The time between three and twelve weeks is therefore a critical period for the process of primary socialization.

Having established the time of this process, the next step was to discover its nature. Brodbeck (1954) had found that puppies which had been fed by mechanical means would form an attachment to human beings as readily as those which were fed by hand, and this result was later confirmed by Stanley. The process of primary socialization is therefore not dependent upon food rewards.

In 1955 Fisher devised the technique of studying this process by rearing animals in isolation except for controlled periods of social contact. None of his puppies was fed by hand. In one of his experimental groups, he punished puppies for every approach or attempt at contact, and they soon learned to stay away. However, once the punishment was discontinued, the puppies soon began making contacts with him and, if anything, showed more interest than those that had previously been uniformly rewarded. In another experimental group, the puppies were sometimes punished and sometimes rewarded for approaching. While the experiment was going on, the puppies either completely avoided the experimenter or spent much more time with him than did those puppies that were always rewarded, depending on their genetic makeup. Again, these effects disappeared after the treatment was discontinued. The process of primary socialization therefore takes place in spite of punishment and, if anything, may be facilitated by it.

Using a similar isolation technique, Fuller (1964) has shown that puppies given contact for as little as two twenty-minute periods each week during the socialization period form attachments and behave in a reasonably normal fashion. This indicates that the process of attachment can take place very rapidly. He also confirmed the critical period hypothesis by showing that isolated puppies showed no behavioral deficits if removed as early as seven weeks of age.

In still another experiment (Nunis & Trattner, 1964), my colleagues and I used the isolation technique and gave puppies two different kinds of treatment. In one group a person simply entered the large isolation box and sat with the puppy ten minutes a day when it was four to six weeks old; and in the other group, a person played actively with the puppy for a similar time. At the end of the period the puppies were given the running test. Both immediately ran to the experimenter and showed similar acquisition curves. It is evident that the process of primary socialization takes place with a person who is simply present and perceived by the puppy. As in other experiments, these puppies had not been fed by hand, and food rewards and other external stimuli appeared to be irrelevant.

Harlow and his associates have obtained similar results with rhesus monkeys. On the basis of his original experiments with artificial mothers, Harlow (1958) concluded that the acquired drive theory of primary social attachment could be discarded, and

more recent experiments (Harlow *et al.*, 1963) with infants reared by rejecting mothers indicate that in the monkey, as in the dog, the process of primary socialization goes on in spite of punishment.

The extensive literature concerned with the process of primary socialization in the social birds leads to similar conclusions. It is easy to demonstrate that a young chick or duckling can become attached to an inanimate model that never feeds it, and Hess (1964) has shown that giving an electric shock to young chicks during the critical period facilitates following rather than inhibiting it. Various experiments on the nature of models to which young chicks will become attached have shown that the models do not need to look like chickens, that they do not need to move, and finally that chicks will form attachments to a model if they merely see it at a distance (Gray, 1960). In all these experiments the process of primary socialization (or imprinting, as it is usually called in birds) goes on provided the object of attachment is present and perceived in the young animal's environment (Sluckin & Salzen, 1961). We can conclude, therefore, that the process is primarily an internal one, little affected by external stimuli and reinforcement. Again we may ask the question, What is the physiological and emotional nature of this process?

DISTRESS VOCALIZATION

Our best answer comes from a third line of experimental work. At our laboratory we had for years been conducting a series of minor experiments on a phenomenon first noticed by Emil Fredericson (1950). Beginning at about three weeks of age, a young puppy removed from its mother and littermates and placed in a strange situation begins to vocalize at a rapid rate, reaching on the average 140 vocalizations per minute in a beagle pup. The reaction is quite reliable, appearing within a minute after the puppy is moved to a strange place, and it appears the first time the puppy is exposed to the situation. At first Fredericson thought that confinement was the stimulus producing the result, but a series of later experiments showed that confinement was unimportant except that it prevented the puppy from returning to familiar places. The puppies vocalized at the same rate whether confined in large or small areas (Scott & Bronson, 1964). Isolating the puppy in a familiar area produced a relatively low rate of vocalization, which was approximately doubled by moving him into a strange place.

The essential stimuli are being removed from the proximity of familiar individuals and places. While we still have no direct evidence on the physiological nature of the emotion involved, it appears to be related to fear or loneliness. The reaction appears as soon as puppies are able to make visual discriminations, and it declines after the time of normal weaning, although there is considerable evidence that the emotion is evoked in older animals but not expressed as vocalization.

This phenomenon of emotional distress induced by putting the puppy in a strange situation suggested an experiment upon the nature of the socialization process. Our original idea was that the induction of very strong and unpleasant emotions might result in a disturbance of the process. We therefore designed an experiment in which the puppies were regularly isolated overnight from five to seven weeks of age, during the peak period of socialization, and allowed contact with human beings during three hours of each day. The primary result of the experiment was not a permanent disturbance of the relationship but rather the demonstration that the puppies under experimental conditions formed an emotional attachment to human beings more rapidly than did their littermate controls. In other words, we had speeded up the process of primary socialization, and this suggested to us that the emotion produced by isolation in a strange place is directly related to the process.

This raises the question of what happens to puppies who have never been subjected to the emotional experience of being separated from familiar individuals and surroundings and whose experience with this sort of emotion is therefore reduced rather than intensified as it was in the separation experiment described above. The first evidence along these lines came from McGill University, where twenty Scottish terriers were weaned at four weeks of age and reared in various degrees of restriction until seven to ten months old (Clarke, Heron, Fetherstonehaugh, Forgays, & Hebb, 1951; Thompson & Melzack, 1956). The idea behind the experiment was that limitation of early experience would inhibit development, and the puppies as adults showed many modifications of behavior, being more active in novel situations (Thompson & Heron, 1954a) and less competent in ability to solve a simple maze (Thompson & Heron, 1954b). They also showed unusual emotional reactions, especially in their reaction to painful stimulation. While the experiment was chiefly concerned with restriction, the result of being confined in the same cages over a period of several months was that the puppies also had no experience with moving into a strange situation until they finally emerged from the cages.

Using the same sort of technique, and confining the puppies from three to 16 weeks, Fisher (1955) showed that the development of fighting behavior could be almost completely inhibited even in the normally aggressive fox terrier breed.

Fuller and his associates (Waller & Fuller, 1961) have perfected and refined this technique, devising cages in which a single puppy can be kept and fed without contact with human hands or any visual contact outside the cage. The puppies receive all the usual physical care and grow and develop in a normal fashion. Seen through one-way vision windows, they behave perfectly normally except that there is an almost complete lack of any sort of vocalization. When first placed in the cages at three weeks, the puppies may show a small amount of distress vocalization but afterward become almost completely silent. This is, of course, what one would expect from a situation in which the puppies were always in unbroken contact with the familiar.

In contrast to their behavior in the familiar cages, the behavior of such puppies when removed at 16 weeks of age showed gross disturbances of behavior, including bizarre postures and a tendency to be unresponsive to playthings, people, and other puppies. Fuller then did a systematic series of experiments designed to elucidate the factors producing this isolation syndrome. The first assumption was that the puppies were being emotionally affected during isolation, and they were given continual treatment with tranquilizing drugs. This had no effect on the outcome.

A second hypothesis was that the puppies lacked socialization experience, and at first this hypothesis seemed to be verified. If the puppies were removed from isolation as early as seven weeks of age, or if they were given experience outside their cages in amounts as small as two 20-min. periods a week, they developed in a normal fashion. To test this further, the next experiment was to rear puppies in pairs so that they could become socialized with each other, and to provide other puppies with playthings inside their cage. Surprisingly, these puppies developed the isolation syndrome in full strength when removed from their cages.

Still another experiment was to allow the puppies visual contact with the outside world through a window. These puppies were affected, but not as severely as those reared in isolation (Fuller & Clark, 1966a, b).

We must conclude that the essential factor in preventing the development of the isolation syndrome is experience outside the cage, since the same experiences given inside produce no effect. Since the puppies behaved normally inside their cages and did not exhibit bizarre and unusual behavior until they emerged, the emergence itself must be the precipitating factor, and Fuller has had some success with alleviating the symptoms by controlling the nature of the experience upon emergence. While tranquilizing drugs had no effect if given during isolation, they markedly helped certain subjects if given just before emergence. There are also genetic differences in susceptibility to the isolation syndrome, fox terriers being more resistant than beagles.

A puppy that is isolated at a time when the distress vocalization response to a strange situation first appears and that is kept in a uniform environment thereafter has no subsequent experience with the painful emotions produced by the absence of the familiar. Furthermore, evidence from rearing litters of puppies in large fields apart from human beings indicates that there is a mounting fear of strangers beginning at about seven weeks of age. Thus we have a developmental picture of puppies beginning to react with distress to the lack of the familiar when they are about three weeks old and presumably continuing into later life. Beginning at seven weeks there develops the capacity for a stronger emotion, the fear of strangers, and this appears to be completely developed by 12 weeks. A puppy reared in normal circumstances has experience with both emotions and an opportunity to become habituated to them. A puppy reared in a completely familiar environment until 16 weeks old experiences both emotions for the first time in a massive form and apparently associates them with the whole world outside its box.

The isolation syndrome appears to be an extreme version of a milder set of symptoms, formerly seen rather commonly in dogs, the "kennel dog syndrome." For the most part this syndrome consists of unusual timidity. The dog is afraid of any strange person or strange situation. With patient care and attention the owner can eventually get such a dog to behave reasonably calmly around the house as long as everything proceeds as usual. However, if a stranger enters the home the dog may go into a fit of terror. Such dogs almost invariably have an early history of being kept for several months in the same restricted environment, usually a kennel. The situation will develop even if the dogs have the best of physical care. If prospective guide dogs are kept under kennel conditions longer than 12 weeks after birth before being taken out to be given experience in homes, an increasing proportion of them will fail when they are trained as guide dogs at one year of age (Pfaffenberger & Scott, 1959). The same result appeared in training war dogs in Russia during World War II (Krushinski, 1962). When such dogs were desperately needed, many were taken from the Pavlovian laboratories to be trained, but a large proportion of them proved to be untrainable. Breed differences were again important, German shepherd dogs being much more susceptible to the kennel dog syndrome than terrier breeds such as the Airedale.

We have begun to do experiments with certain well-known drugs, with the hope that their action might give clues to the physiological nature of the emotions involved (Scott, 1966). In moderate doses the tranquilizer chlorpromazine has the effect of slowing down the rate of vocalization, but larger doses do not produce a proportionate increase in the effect, which appears to be an indirect result of sedation rather than a direct effect of alleviating the emotion. Under this drug a puppy with his littermates will be sound asleep. Placed in a strange situation, he immediately gets on his feet and starts vocalizing, at a somewhat lower rate than usual, but without a letup. Assuming that chlorpromazine has the effect of alleviating anxiety, and defining anxiety as the emotion generated by anticipation of events in the future, we can conclude that anxiety plays little part in the emotional responses to isolation in a strange place. This suggests that this emotion is not something which is learned (although learning can obviously modify it) but rather an immediate response to the situation. . . .

Conclusion

These facts suggest that the underlying process in the phenomenon of primary socialization in the dog is a relatively simple one; namely, an unpleasant emotional state induced by unfamiliar surroundings. This emotional state is immediately relieved by a return to familiar places and contact with familiar individuals, and it would account for the rapid establishment of a social bond without external reinforcement. Internal reinforcement would, of course, take place every time separation and reunion occurred.

The nature of the behavioral relationship between a young animal and its objects of primary attachment can be modified independently by other rewards and punishments, but these do not disturb the essential nature of the process. Indeed, we have some evidence that this emotional response to isolation in a strange place completely overrides that of hunger (Scott & Bronson, 1964).

The facts further suggest that this emotional mechanism could also provide the answer to the problem of the motivational basis for allelomimetic behavior, operating in the following manner. The young puppy must very soon learn that it is unpleasant to leave a group of familiar animals and that the distressing emotion can be relieved by returning to them. In terms of reinforcement, the puppy is internally punished for leaving the group, and the operant behavior of returning to the group relieves the punishment. Avoidance of the unpleasant emotion can be maintained by doing what the other animals do and remaining with them.

Thus we have an almost absurdly simple but completely adequate explanation of the underlying motivational mechanism for allelomimetic behavior. This motivation would be strengthened by the reinforcement process over and over again in the young animal, with the result that it should be maintained strongly in adult life even if the primary emotional mechanism weakens or disappears. Actually, there is no reason to suppose that it does disappear, but rather that it is likely to be expressed in other ways than vocalization alone. The older dog in isolation may vocalize, but it is also likely to make strong efforts to escape and return to the group.

Moltz (1960) has offered an essentially similar explanation for the formation of primary social bonds (imprinting) in birds. Like young dogs, ducklings show evidence of emotional distress (called anxiety by Moltz) in unfamiliar surroundings, and this behavior is reduced or eliminated by contact with a familiar object. Familiarization takes place very rapidly in the early part of the critical period, and much less readily toward its close. The chief difference is that while Moltz postulates a single primary fear response evoked in the duckling by unfamiliar objects, two separable responses can be distinguished in the dog: a distress response to the *absence* of familiar animals and objects which declines during the latter part of the critical period, and an active avoidance response to unfamiliar animals which increases during the same period.

The motivational system postulated here not only accounts for the development and occurrence of allelomimetic behavior but also acts as a powerful and continuing source of group cohesion. Other general sorts of motivation, such as sexual behavior, also act in a positive manner to keep animals together, but not in a continuous fashion. In short, we are dealing here with a very general and pervasive kind of social motivation, one which has wide usefulness and implications.

Thus far a motivational system has been well established only in the dog. However, we have much evidence that similar phenomena exist in human beings. Allelomimetic behavior is one of the commonest kinds of human social activity, and evidence for the existence of a motivating mechanism connected with it has long been known in the phenomenon of social facilitation. Furthermore, the work of Bayley (1932) has shown that young babies, like young puppies, show distress vocalization when brought into strange surroundings. This phenomenon begins to be evident at the time when other experiments show that infants begin to be capable of visual discrimination between the strange and the familiar, roughly at about two months of age. We therefore have strong reasons

for stating the hypothesis that there exists in human beings a motivational mechanism based on an unpleasant emotion induced by the absence of the familiar. We can further state that this mechanism is strongly associated with the process of primary socialization, and that the critical period for this process extends from approximately six weeks to seven months (Scott, 1963). If these hypotheses can be confirmed, they may even be relevant to the problem of race relations, for one of the objects of integration is to cause a child to become emotionally attached to the entire human race.

What I have stated above provides a means by which much of the social behavior of dogs may be understood and controlled. In dogs there is an ever-present desire for the company of familiar places and animals, whether human or canine. A dog will work very hard and undergo much inconvenience and discomfort in order to obtain this goal, and will struggle violently if confined away from familiar places or even if isolated in a familiar one.

Not only can we use this motivation to direct a dog's behavior toward what we consider desirable ends, but also we can control its development by choosing the places and individuals to which a puppy is allowed to form primary social attachments. By social isolation we can produce a puppy who is primarily attached only to himself and his familiar nest box, and in a normally reared puppy we can determine whether his primary social relationships are developed chiefly with dogs or chiefly with people, or in a well-balanced combination between the two. A puppy removed from the litter at six to eight weeks and adopted into human society has a good start toward becoming a mentally healthy dog. (I wish that we could give an equally simple recipe for developing a mentally healthy human being.)

However, the implication here is that we can similarly control the social behavior of human beings, and particularly those infant human beings over whom we have nearly as much power as we have over the life of a family pet. What shall we do with this power?

Here I should like to interpose a word of caution. Most of us can remember having the common adolescent dream of becoming all-powerful, of being a prince in disguise who will suddenly become recognized, or of achieving magical power with which we could overcome the parents and companions who controlled us. This dream is particularly likely to occur to intellectual children, who are often isolated and disregarded by the groups in which they find themselves and who suffer from the common childhood feeling of helplessness. Most of us recover from this dream as we grow up and realize the limitations of adult power, but even a scientist may succumb to the dream of becoming a philosopher-king through his superior knowledge and start acting like one toward his children and younger associates.

The use of power to control the lives of others should always be employed with caution. The almost universal reaction of children to the exercise of power indicates that its use is almost invariably resented and resisted even when it is employed for the best possible motives. The ideal system of social control is one based on mutual understanding rather than manipulation of a herd by a superior being. Rather than seeking to control minutely the lives of children, we should attempt to get into their hands as rapidly as possible scientific information regarding behavior so that they can understand their own behavior and thus achieve self-control. The teaching of psychology is deferred until far too late in the educational process.

I have here suggested solutions to two important problems of the social behavior of the dog, that of the motivational basis of allelomimetic behavior and that of the internal nature of the process of primary socialization, and I have further suggested that both rest on the same emotional mechanism. If you examine the answer that I have given, you will see that it is not a final one. The physiological nature of the internal process has been inferred from external behavior. We still do not know where it goes on in the brain or whether visceral reactions are concerned, as they are in many other emotional reactions. Nor do we know the physical and biochemical basis of the process.

We must begin to rethink the old concept of "drive," which at the best was a collective name for unknown physiological mechanisms and was largely based on the fact that one may *feel* driven by hunger or sexual emotions. Furthermore, the motivational mechanism described here is very different from those involved in hunger and sex, from which the original drive concept was derived. The perceived reinforcements are largely internal, but the mechanism itself is under the direct control of outside circumstances. The unpleasant emotion is directly produced by the absence of familiar surroundings and individuals and is immediately relieved by returning to them. Any strengthening of this kind of motivation must be analogous to the strengthening of motivation by repeated reinforcement rather than by the accumulation of internal pressures.

A further question which this material poses is its relationship to problems of maladaptive behavior. Most of the theoretical approaches to mal-

adaptive social behavior have been based on two behavioral systems, sexual and agonistic, primarily because the behavior associated with these systems is so highly regulated and often repressed by human culture. The motivation connected with allelomimetic behavior is potentially very strong, and there are certainly situations in which individuals are placed into conflict with it by human cultural demands. Our moral codes frequently ask that we act differently from the crowd, and crowds frequently reject those who act differently from them. I would suggest that this kind of conflict can be just as severe as those resulting from the moral codes regulating sexual and agonistic behavior.

From a more practical clinical viewpoint, this raises the question of whether or not it is desirable in any form of group therapy to bring together patients with similar forms of maladaptive behavior. The theoretical effect of the group could be mutual help, but such therapy might also enhance maladaptive responses. The well-known effects of prison life upon criminal behavior may well be an example of the latter situation.

To evaluate these ideas and conclusions in the most conservative fashion, we can look at the study of the dog as at least a partial model for the study of human behavior. However different the two species are in details of development we have collected in the puppy the kind of information that needs to be gathered concerning human development and motivation. Disseminating this information has already begun to promote desirable changes in the care and training of young puppies. Similar and appropriate information needs to be collected in human beings, and we may hope that it will lead to effective and practical measures of preventive mental hygiene.

REFERENCES

ALLPORT, F. H. *Social psychology.* Boston: Houghton Mifflin, 1924.

BACON, W. E., & STANLEY, W. C. Effect of deprivation level in puppies on performance maintained by a passive person reinforcer. *J. comp. physiol. Psychol.,* 1963, *56,* 783–785.

BAYLEY, N. A study of the crying of infants during mental and physical tests. *J. genet. Psychol.,* 1932, 306–329.

BRODBECK, A. J. An exploratory study of the acquisition of dependency behavior in puppies. *Bull. Ecol. Soc. Amer.,* 1954, *35,* 73.

CANNON, W. B. *Bodily changes in pain, hunger, fear, and rage.* Boston: Branford, 1929.

CLARKE, R. S., HERON, W., FETHERSTONEHAUGH, M. L., FORGAYS, D. G., & HEBB, D. O. Individual differences in dogs: Preliminary report on the effects of early experience. *Canad. J. Psychol.*, 1951, *5*, 150–156.

CRAWFORD, M. P. The social psychology of the vertebrates. *Psychol. Bull.*, 1939, *36*, 407–466.

ELLIOT, O., & KING, J. A. Effect of early food deprivation on later consummatory behavior in puppies. *Psychol. Rep.*, 1960, *6*, 391–400.

FISHER, A. E. The effects of early differential treatment on the social and exploratory behavior of puppies. Unpublished doctoral dissertation, Pennsylvania State University, 1955.

FREDERICSON, E. Distributed vs. massed experience in a traumatic situation. *J. abnorm. soc. Psychol.*, 1950, *45*, 259–266.

FREEDMAN, D. G., KING, J. A., & ELLIOT, O. Critical period in the social development of dogs, *Science*, 1961, *133*, 1016–1017.

FULLER, J. L. Effects of experimental deprivation upon behavior in animals. *Proc. 3d World Congr. Psychiat.*, 1964, *3*, 223–227.

FULLER, J. L., & CLARK, L. D. Genetic and treatment factors modifying the post-isolation syndrome in dogs. *J. comp. physiol. Psychol.*, 1966 (a), *61*, 251–257.

FULLER, J. L., & CLARK, L. D. Effects of rearing with specific stimuli upon post-isolation behavior in dogs. *J. comp. physiol. Psychol.*, 1966 (b), *61*, 258–263.

GRAY, P. A. Evidence that retinal flicker is not a necessary condition of imprinting. *Science*, 1960, *132*, 1834–1835.

HARLOW, H. The nature of love. *Amer. Psychologist*, 1958, *13*, 673–685.

HARLOW, H. F., HARLOW, M. K., & HANSEN, E. W. The maternal affectional system of rhesus monkeys. In H. L. Rheingold (Ed.), *Maternal behavior in mammals*. New York: Wiley, 1963.

HESS, E. H. Imprinting in birds. *Science*, 1964, *146*, 1128–1139.

KRUSHINSKI, L. V. *Animal behavior; its normal and abnormal development*. New York: Consultants' Bureau, 1962.

MOLTZ, H. Imprinting: Empirical basis and theoretical significance. *Psychol. Bull.*, 1960, *57*, 291–314.

NICE, M. M. Studies in the life history of the song sparrow. *Trans. Linnaean Soc.*, 1943, *6*, 1–328.

NUNIS, T., & TRATTNER, A. Unpublished manuscript, 1964.

PFAFFENBERGER, J., & SCOTT, J. P. The relationship between delayed socialization and trainability in guide dogs. *J. genet. Psychol.*, 1959, *95*, 145–155.

SCOTT, J. P. The process of primary socialization in canine and human infants. *Monogr. Soc. Res. Child Developm.*, 1963, *28* (1), 1–47.

SCOTT, J. P. Modification of the development of social behavior. *Proc. 5th Int. Cong. Collegium Internationale Neuro-psychopharmacologicum*, 1966, in press.

SCOTT, J. P., & BRONSON, F. H. Experimental exploration of the et-epimeletic or care-soliciting behavioral system. In P. H. Leiderman & D. Shapiro (Eds.), *Psychological approaches to behavior*. Stanford: Stanford University Press, 1964.

SCOTT, J. P., & FULLER, J. L. *Genetics and the social behavior of the dog*. Chicago: University of Chicago Press, 1965.

SCOTT, J. P., & McCRAY, C. Allelomimetic behavior in dogs; negative effects of competition in social facilitation. *J. comp. physiol. Psychol.*, 1967, *63*, 316–319.

SLUCKIN, W., & SALZEN, E. A. Imprinting and perceptual learning. *Quart. J. exp. Psychol.*, 1961, *13*, 65–77.

STANLEY, W. C., & ELLIOT, O. Differential human handling as reinforcing events and as treatments influencing later social behavior in basenji puppies. *Psychol. Reports*, 1962, *10*, 775–788.

THOMPSON, W. R., & HERON, W. The effects of early restriction on activities of dogs. *J. comp. physiol. Psychol.*, 1954 (a), *47*, 77–82.

THOMPSON, W. R., & HERON, W. The effect of restricting early experience on the problem-solving capacity of dogs. *Canad. J. Psychol.*, 1954 (b), *8*, 17–31.

THOMPSON, W. R., & MELZACK, R. Early environment. *Sci. Amer.*, 1956, 38–42.

VOGEL, H. H., SCOTT, J. P., & MARSTON, M. V. Social facilitation and allelomimetic behavior in dogs. *Behaviour*, 1950, *2*, 121–143.

WALLER, M. B., & FULLER, J. L. Preliminary observations on early experience as related to social behavior. *Am. J. Ortho-psychiat.*, 1961, *31*, 254–266.

(Inhibitory Training of Dogs: Effects of Age at Training in Basenjis and Shetland Sheepdogs [1])

A. INTRODUCTION

This report is concerned with the genesis of the "kennel dog syndrome." If dogs are kept in kennels for long periods with no training other than that incidental to provision of physical care, they become virtually untrainable. If such animals are removed from the kennel at 4 months of age or later, they frequently become unsatisfactory pets, difficult to housebreak, and timid with strangers. On the other hand, if puppies are reared under laboratory-kennel conditions but are given adequate socialization experience with human handlers they are easily trainable and react normally (4).

In the course of experiments on the effects of genetic background and the development of social behavior in puppies, it was found that there might be a critical period for learning between 8 and

[1] This research was supported in part by Public Health Service Research Grant HD–01082 from the National Institute of Child Health and Human Development.

12 weeks of age. Puppies that had received preliminary training with retrieving objects at an early age performed much better at 40 weeks of age than those animals without previous training. Experiments performed at *Guide Dogs for the Blind* (where animals are given training once per week from 8 to 12 weeks and then placed in 4-H homes at 12 weeks) indicated that these animals performed well in later Guide Dog training at one year of age. If the dogs were kept in the kennels for two or more weeks beyond the normal period and given no additional training, they did not perform as well (3).

These observations have at least three possible theoretical explanations, no one of which necessarily excludes the others. The first of these explanations is that the kennel dogs are deprived of socialization experiences with human handlers during the critical period of socialization from approximately 3 to 12 weeks of age. This lack of experience would make them fearful of human handlers and would make it difficult for the dogs to develop a positive motivation for the handling reinforcement or reward associated with training. The second explanation is that these animals lack experience with anything outside of their limited kennel conditions. Fuller and Clark (1, 2) have shown that puppies, reared in tactual and visual isolation from other dogs and people from 3 weeks onward, will develop normally if removed from isolation as late as 7 weeks of age. If left in isolation as long as 16 weeks, the dogs will show grossly disturbed behavior and a lack of trainability. This "isolation syndrome" appears to be a more extreme form of the kennel dog syndrome, and may be explained on the basis of an emotional trauma when removed from the isolation cage and exposed to the outside world. This unpleasant emotional reaction may become generalized to all situations that are different from their familiar cages. A third possible explanation is that during the long period with no training and in restricted environmental conditions, the dog may develop a *negative learning set*. This negative learning set may be derived from two conditions. One is related to the dog's acquiring certain perceptual and motor patterns that are not compatible with later training, while the second condition is related to the psychological "atrophy" of certain perceptual and motor patterns that prevent the dog from acquiring information and skills. In the former case, the absence of specific training has permitted the dog to develop response patterns adaptive to its specific environment that compete with the learning of new response patterns. In the latter case, the lack of specific experiences has resulted in a deficit condition upon which it is difficult to superimpose new learning experiences.

The first two of these theories are based on the acquisition of emotional reactions, one associated with human handlers, the other with the physical environment, that interfere with the respective processes of forming emotional attachments with these two kinds of objects. The third theory is a purely cognitive one. As indicated above, these theories may represent factors with additive or interactive effects.

The present experiment is an attempt to investigate the cognitive theory of negative learning sets by controlling for the effects of environmental factors and human handling. The experiment was designed so that all animals were reared under standard laboratory kennel conditions from birth until 18 weeks of age. All training was done within the home nursery room so that physical surroundings were held constant. All puppies were given the same amount of handling and human social contact at all ages when training took place. The principal variable in the experiment was, therefore, the time of initial training, at 4 to 6, 8 to 10, and 16 to 18 weeks of age. It was expected that if an optimum period for new training exists, it should be at 8 to 10 weeks of age and that the performance of animals trained earlier and later than this time would be inferior.

In addition, the experiment provided an opportunity for measuring the retention of previous training, since all groups of animals were tested at 16 to 18 weeks of age.

The task chosen was one involving inhibitory training. Previous experiments at this laboratory (4) had largely avoided this kind of training, which is, at least hypothetically, strongly involved in the genesis of maladaptive behavior. It is, however, also a kind of training that has great importance in practical dog training, since different breeds appear to have been selected for greater and lesser capacities for inhibiting behavior. For this reason, two different breeds were selected for subjects.

B. Method

1. SUBJECTS

*S*s were purebred dogs from the colony maintained at Hamilton Station of The Jackson Laboratory. Sixteen male African basenjis from seven litters and 16 Shetland sheepdogs (nine male and seven female) from five litters were used. All pups except for four basenjis were reared with their mothers until weaned at 10 weeks of age. These four basenjis were weaned at 4 weeks of age and reared as a group because they came from litters with one or two pups. Conditions of housing, maintenance, and health care were similar to those of all dogs reared in our colony and have been previously described (4).

2. APPARATUS

The inhibitory training task required the dog to remain on a gray plywood board ($40 \times 40 \times .5$ inch) placed in the middle of the home pen. The floor of the pen surrounding the board was covered with shavings, so that the footing provided a definite cue when a pup stepped off the board. A choke collar, which was connected to a rope and pulley system, enabled E to correct the dog's responses by pulling him back onto the board from outside the pen. Because of the increased size of the dogs at 16 weeks of age, the test board was moved from the center of the pen to a wall and a heavier choke collar and pulley equipment were used. . . .

3. PROCEDURE

At 4 weeks of age, pups were assigned to each of four training groups, so that as far as possible each group represented a maximum number of litters. There were four pups in each group. The four training groups were as follows: Group I received inhibitory training at 4 to 6, 8 to 10, and 16 to 18 weeks; Group II at 4 to 6 and 16 to 18 weeks; Group III at 8 to 10 and 16 to 18 weeks; and Group IV at 16 to 18 weeks only.

Tests were conducted Monday through Friday during two successive weeks at the ages specified. Prior to the test of each day, the dogs were removed from their home pens and placed in holding cages while the apparatus was set up. For each trial, the dog was carried from the holding cage and placed on the board in its home pen. The choke collar was then attached. If the dog had moved, he was replaced at the center of the board and the collar tugged gently. E then left the pen, which started the time for the trial. If the dog placed two of his feet off the board, he was corrected by being pulled back. This started the time to criterion over again. The trial terminated when the dog either achieved the time criterion for staying on the board or received five corrections. At the termination of the trial, E carried the dog back to the holding cage, and after several minutes another dog was selected. For each trial, E recorded the number of corrections required, total time of staying on the board, and the longest single duration of staying on the board. A dog that was not being tested during a given two-week period received similar handling during each trial by E's carrying him for a similar distance down the hallway, placing him on the floor for a few seconds, picking him up, and returning him to the holding cage. The order of trials was rotated each day.

The test was designed so that a standardized regime could be followed which would still permit a good learning situation. Essentially, the puppy was required to learn a passive avoidance task reinforced by mild punishment or reward. Failure (going off the board) was punished by immediate pulling on the choke collar, and success was rewarded by immediate removal from the situation. Success on a short criterion was required before the animal could proceed to more difficult trials, and the criterion on the last trial on any day was made equal to that of the preceding successful trial, in order to ensure that the last trial of the day would ordinarily be successful. . . .

D. DISCUSSION

. . . there are major breed differences in both measures of performance. Consequently, the analysis of variance chiefly emphasizes breed differences, and any meaningful discussion of other variables in the experiment must be done by considering each breed separately.

1. OPTIMUM PERIOD FOR TRAINING

. . . the best performance in basenjis came at 8 to 10 weeks of age, as our original theory postulated, but the differences are too small to be significant with these numbers. From a statistical viewpoint, the data show only that basenjis perform equally well at the oldest two ages and more poorly at 4 to 6 weeks. In contrast, the performance of Shetland sheepdogs at the two earlier ages is approximately equal, but at the later age of testing, much superior. In the latter breed the number of corrections or punishments received by the animals is correlated inversely with their performance, the number of corrections being approximately equal at the first two ages and lower at the last. The basenjis show a corresponding picture, incurring the largest number of punishments at the earliest age and an approximately equal number at the last two ages. [Shetland sheepdogs required consistently less corrections than basenjis, and in both breeds the older the animal at the start of initial training the less corrections were required. The breed difference in the time of increasing trainability is also reflected in these data.]

In short, if there is an optimum period for initial training on this task, it is quite different in the two breeds, reaching a plateau in basenjis at 8 weeks and beyond, while performance in Shetland sheepdogs reaches a peak at 16 to 18 weeks and possibly beyond this age. None of these animals behaved like the untrainable kennel dogs, and we can conclude that the theory of negative learning sets explains only a small part, if any, of this phenomenon.

The question may be raised as to whether the improvement in Shetland sheepdogs at 16 to 18 weeks might not be the result of increasing the opportunity for performance at this age. Of the Shetland sheepdogs in Group III, none reached the criterion at 8 to 10 weeks that would have permitted extra trials at 16 to 18 weeks, whereas two of the four animals first tested at 16 to 18 weeks (Group IV) reached this criterion. The differences in performance at the two ages do not, therefore, result from the change in procedure.

2. OPTIMUM TIME FOR PREVIOUS TRAINING

Group II, first trained at 4 to 6 weeks, and Group III, first trained at 8 to 10 weeks, are the critical groups for testing this point, as both have had the same amount of experience before the final testing at 16 to 18 weeks. Shetland sheepdogs of Groups II and III are almost exactly alike. This is consistent with their original performance. In other words, there is no indication that previous training at one time or the other has any different effect in this breed. In the basenjis, Group II, which had been first trained at 4 to 6 weeks, apparently shows a better performance than the group trained at 8 to 10 weeks, but this is not significant and may be accidental. Thus there is no evidence in favor of an optimal time for previous experience.

3. AMOUNT OF PREVIOUS EXPERIENCE

As indicated above, there are no general effects of the amount of previous training. A more critical comparison is that between Group I, which has had two previous training periods, and Groups II and III, which have each had one previous period, but at the same times as Group I. In the Shetland sheepdog, Group I performed on the average better than Groups II and III, which were approximately equal. This conforms to the theory as expected, but results are not statistically significant. In basenjis, the Group I average is actually inferior to the other two, although again not statistically significant. We may conclude that while larger numbers might demonstrate that the amount of previous experience has an effect, it is certainly not a major one under these conditions.

4. BREED DIFFERENCES

Clearcut breed differences on both measures of behavior were seen and represent differences in both the timing and amount of developmental change. The two breeds show quite different developmental pictures with respect to learning this particular inhibitory task. The basenjis are poor at 4 to 6 weeks and increase their performance by 43 per cent at the later ages. The Shetland sheepdogs stay at a low level, only slightly better than basenjis, at the first two ages and then improve by 212 per cent at 16 to 18 weeks. To make a more dramatic comparison, at 16 to 18 weeks of age, 11 out of 16 Shetland sheepdogs and only two out of 15 basenjis were trained to the highest criterion of remaining on the board for a full 10 minutes. At the same age, all of the Shetland sheepdogs were trained to the maximum criterion achievable without extra trials, while only seven of the basenjis were trained to this level.

The theory of negative learning sets or carryover from training at a time when performance is poor because of immaturity is not supported by these experiments. It follows that the lack of trainability seen in the kennel dog and isolation syndromes is probably largely produced by emotional factors arising from either lack of socialization to human handlers or lack of familiarization with the physical environment in which future training takes place, or both.

These conclusions apply only to this particular task of inhibitory training. The theory of negative learning sets might still be important with other tasks, and this experiment should be followed up with one involving positive training such as that in retrieving.

The major result here is that of confirming large breed differences in reaction to inhibitory training. There are many situations in which the capacity to accept inhibitory training is very important in a dog's existence, as this may determine whether or not an animal is an acceptable pet, and certainly will determine fitness for certain kinds of complicated training, such as that involved in learning to herd sheep. Although early experience may also produce major effects on behavior, as experiments with the isolation syndrome indicate, the kinds of experiential variables used in this experiment appear to be unimportant.

The results of this experiment raise the possibility that similar genetic differences in the ability to accept inhibitory training may exist in human children. There are, of course, well-established sex differences with respect to toilet training, and similar differences may well be important at later school ages. A large part of early school and kindergarten experience is devoted to training children to sit still, and this might offer a fertile field for the study of individual genetically determined differences, both between and within the sexes. The results of this training may have considerable effect on the child's future life in school, since for a teacher the good child is the one who sits still longest.

This experiment may also have some relevance to the problem of the effects of restriction of the early environment on cognitive development in children. Our puppies were reared in what would ordinarily be considered a restricted and barren environment, but they responded to training quite effectively, with no indication that they were handicapped. The implication here is that the major effects of restriction are caused by emotional factors and that the damaging aspect of these is the result of being suddenly thrust into an unfamiliar environment.

E. SUMMARY

This experiment was designed to analyze in part the factors producing the lack of trainability associated with the "kennel dog syndrome" and, in particular, to test the hypothesis of negative learning sets acquired independently of emotional factors. Sixteen basenji and 16 Shetland sheepdog puppies were each divided into four groups given initial training on an inhibitory task beginning at three different ages: 4 to 6, 8 to 10, or 16 to 18 weeks. All animals were given equal opportunities for socialization with human handlers and training took place in the home nursery room, so that behavior would not be modified by emotional factors resulting from contact with strangers or an unfamiliar physical environment. The training regime was organized in such a way that the amounts of training were equalized but maximum opportunity for improvement was possible. The results demonstrated clearcut breed differences in responsiveness to training, and that age of training was likewise an important factor. Age at previous training and amount of previous training had no significant effects on behavior at 16 to 18 weeks, indicating that negative learning sets were not acquired either as a result of training or lack of it. Thus the kennel dog and isolation syndromes must result either from a lack of socialization or a lack of familiarization with the future environment at this critical period, or a combination of the two.

REFERENCES

1. FULLER, J. L., & CLARK, L. D. Genetic and treatment factors modifying the post-isolation syndrome in dogs. *J. Comp. & Physiol. Psychol.*, 1966, *61,* 251–257.

2. ———. Effects of rearing with specific stimuli upon post-isolation behavior in dogs. *J. Comp. & Physiol. Psychol.*, 1966, *61,* 258–263.

3. PFAFFENBURGER, C. J., & SCOTT, J. P. The relationship between delayed socialization and trainability in guide dogs. *J. Genet. Psychol.*, 1959, *95,* 145–155.

4. SCOTT, J. P., & FULLER, J. L. Genetics and the Social Behavior of the Dog. Chicago: Univ. Chicago Press, 1965.

10

Constitutional and Environmental Interactions in Rearing of Four Breeds of Dogs

D. G. FREEDMAN

If one thoroughly understood all of the data in this paper, one would have a good grasp of the interaction between heredity (breed) and experience. We are reprinting it again in our third edition because we cannot find a more cogent and succinct illustration of the points made. Freedman is now with the Committee on Human Development of the University of Chicago. His current research frequently brings biological and ethnological concepts to bear on psychological problems. He is actively pursuing research on the characteristics of newborns in many parts of the world, thus assuring greater genetic variability in the infants studied.

The initial intention of the present study was to determine the relative effects of "indulgent" and "disciplinary" modes of rearing in dogs, with particular emphasis on how each method affects the obedience of the animal at maturity. The work derived from the extensive observations of children made by D. M. Levy (1), who has shown that over-indulgent rearing may lead to psychopathy, a syndrome which involves an abnormal inability to inhibit one's impulses. The study described in this report was an attempt to deal experimentally with Levy's concept. As will be seen, the results are of interest aside from their reflection on this initial hypothesis.

Eight litters of four pups each were used. These included two litters each of Shetland sheep dogs, basenjis, wire-haired fox terriers, and beagles. Following weaning at 3 weeks of age, each litter of four was divided into two pairs equated as closely as possible on the basis of sex, weight, activity, vocalizations, maturation of eyes and ears, and reactivity to a startling stimulus. Each member of one pair was thereafter indulged, and each member of the other pair was disciplined, during two daily 15-minute periods from their third to their eighth week of age.

Indulgence consisted of encouraging a pup in any activity it initiated, such as play, aggression, and climbing on the supine handler. These pups were never punished. By contrast, the disciplined pups were at first restrained in the experimenter's lap and were later taught to sit, to stay, and to come upon command. When still older they were trained to follow on a leash. The pups were handled and tested individually by a single experimenter throughout the study. They lived in pairs in isolation boxes the remainder of the time, where members of indulged and disciplined pairs received identical treatment. The results were as follows:

At 8 weeks of age each pup was subjected to the following test: Each time a pup ate meat from a bowl placed in the center of a room, he was punished with a swat on the rump and a shout of "no!" After three minutes the experimenter left the room and, observing through a one-way glass, recorded the time that elapsed before the pup again ate. The results over 8 days of testing are summarized in Fig. 1. Basenjis tended to eat soon after the experimenter left, the method of rearing having no statistically significant effect. Shetland sheep dogs tended to refuse the food over the entire 8 days of testing. Again, the fashion of rearing had no significant effect. Beagles and wire-haired fox terriers, however, differentiated into two significantly disparate groups, depending on the condition of rearing. The Friedman non-parametric analysis of variance (2) indicates that the indulged pups took significantly longer to return to the food than did the disciplined pups ($p = 0.001$). Thus, as measured in this test, essentially the same differences in treatment had a decisive effect upon only two breeds.

Can characteristics of the breeds explain the differences in performance on this test? It was clear that, during training, beagles and wire-haired terriers were strongly oriented to the experimenter and sought contact with him continuously. Basenjis, by contrast, were interested in all phases

D. G. Freedman, "Constitutional and environmental interactions in rearing of four breeds of dogs," *Science,* 1958, *127* (3298), March 14, 585–586. Reprinted by permission.

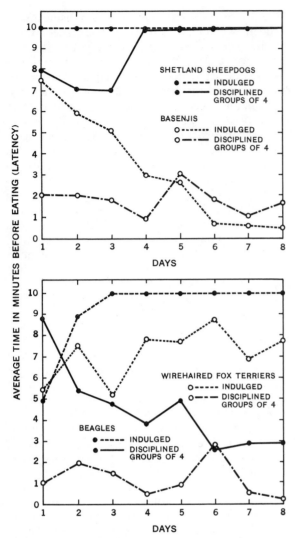

FIGURE 1. *Performance of 8-week-old puppies on the "inhibition-to-eating" test (see text for details of procedure).*

of the environment and often ignored the experimenter in favor of inanimate objects. Shetland sheep dogs showed yet another pattern; all became fearful of physical contact with the experimenter and tended to maintain distance from him. We see, then, that the two breeds that were highly attracted to the experimenter differentiated as a result of the mode of rearing, whereas the breeds that exhibited aloofness (basenjis) and excessive timidity (Shetland sheep dogs) did not. Apparently it was the strong (constitutional) attraction in interaction with indulgent treatment that enhanced the effectiveness of later punishment. It should be noted that basenjis and Shetland sheep dogs were not entirely unaffected by the differential treatment. The scores of *all* indulged animals were significantly different from those of their disciplined counterparts on five of ten tests administered. In general,

these tests indicated that the indulged pups were more active, more vocal, less timid (although more easily inhibited with punishment) than the disciplined pups.

A test of individual reactions to veterinary treatment based on vocalizations and the degree of activity during routine injections indicates that indulged pups were more vocal and active than disciplined pups in their protest ($p = 0.02$, Mann-Whitney) and that basenjis were more vocal and active than the other three breeds ($p = 0.01$, Friedman analysis of variance). It has been found at our laboratory that basenjis generally gain higher scores on this test than other breeds; hence these data suggest that similar behavior may be due in one instance to constitution (as in the basenjis) and in other instances to the conditions of rearing.

A test of the level of activity, in which the pups were observed from a hidden vantage point for 10 minutes, was administered. The testing area was 10 by 20 ft. and was demarcated into eight squares of 5 by 5 ft. each. In this setting, *disciplined* Shetland sheep dogs showed significantly less activity than any other animals ($p = 0.001$, Friedman analysis of variance). In another test the experimenter sat silently in a room for 10 minutes and recorded the amount of time the pups spent in contact with him. In this test the *indulged* Shetland sheep dogs differed significantly from all other dogs in that they rarely approached the experimenter ($p = 0.001$, Friedman analysis of variance). From these results it is clear that a specific test for a specific breed may facilitate expression of the effects of early rearing.

The conditions of rearing were continued over a second period, when the pups were 11 to 15 weeks of age, and all tests were readministered, with essentially the same results.

In the follow-up observations and tests, the indulged beagles, in contrast to all other animals, underwent dramatic changes, in time, although all animals were maintained under standard conditions. On a weekly test in which the time taken to catch each animal was recorded, these animals became exceedingly shy and wary of being caught when approached by various human beings, including the experimenter ($p = 0.05$, t test). Thus, it appears that changes in the behavior of certain animals may occur that are seemingly independent of the current environment and belatedly dependent, instead, upon the mediation of past experiences.

REFERENCES

LEVY, D. M., *Maternal Overprotection*. (Columbia Univ. Press, New York, 1943).

SIEGEL, S. *Non-parametric Statistics*. (McGraw-Hill, New York, 1956).

11

Nongenetic Transmission of Information

Victor H. Denenberg
and Kenneth M. Rosenberg

This paper supplements the previous ones because it points out that genetic factors are not the only ones that may act over more than one generation. The effects of experience are also important over more than one generation. The paper demonstrates that both a physical and a "temperamental" characteristic of rats (if one can use the word "temperament" when talking about rats) are affected by the handling experiences of their grandmothers. This finding tempts one to speculate about comparable effects in humans. Our understanding of human development is complicated by the addition of cultural effects to the apparently biological or biologically mediated effects shown in the rat. Efforts to compare different cultural groups, whose handling experiences, diet, medical status, etc. may differ markedly, become extremely complex. It is thus difficult to decide between the genetic and the experiential in assessing the causation of differences found between human cultural groups.

Dr. Denenberg is chairman of the Department of Biobehavioral Sciences at the University of Connecticut, where Dr. Rosenberg is also located. The existence of such a new department is, in itself, further demonstration of the current active concern with problems of relating biology to behavior. This is only one of several such laboratories and departments in the United States.

We have shown that one significant determinant of the rat's behaviour is the handling experience of the mother while she was an infant.[1] This experience was profound enough to modify her offspring's weaning weight and open field performance in adulthood. Thus the experience of one generation was visited on the next generation. Such a finding would appear to have broad implications for the evolution of behaviour. In this context a relevant question is: How far into the future can such effects extend? We have investigated this question by determining whether the experiences of female rats during their infancy would significantly affect the behaviour of their grandpups.

Again within an evolutionary framework, the habitat in which the animal is born and reared is known to affect profoundly his subsequent performance. We have shown that rats which are born and reared in a complex free environment between birth and weaning, or which are given free environment experience after weaning, differ along a number of behavioural dimensions from rats which are reared in standard cages during infancy and after weaning.[2–5] Thus for the laboratory rat, cages and free environments may be thought of as two different habitats. We investigated the effects of these habitats on the offspring's behaviour in this experiment.

The grandmothers' experience was as follows. At birth, litters of Purdue–Wistar rats were reduced to eight pups. Whole litters were randomly assigned to groups to be handled or not handled. Handling consisted of removing the pups from the maternity cage, leaving the mother in the cage, and placing each one into a tin can partially filled with shavings. The pups remained in the cans for 3 min and were then returned to their home cage. This procedure was followed once a day from day 1 until day 20. Non-handled controls were not disturbed between day 1 and 21, when all litters were weaned. The handled and non-handled females from these litters were the grandmothers of the animals used in this study. They were bred when

[1] Denenberg, V. H., and Whimbey, A. E., *Science 142*, 1192 (1963).

[2] Denenberg, V. H., and Morton, J. R. C., *J. Comp. Physiol. Psychol.*, 55, 242 (1962).

[3] Denenberg, V. H., and Morton, J. R. C., *Anim. Behav.*, 12, 11 (1964).

[4] Denenberg, V. H., Morton, J. R. C., and Haltmeyer, G. C., *Anim. Behav.* 12, 205 (1964).

[5] Whimbey, A. E., and Denenberg, V. H., *Multivar. Behav. Res.*, 1, 279 (1966).

Victor H. Denenberg and Kenneth M. Rosenberg, "Nongenetic transmission of information," *Nature*, 1967, *216*, 549–550. Reprinted by permission.

about 100 days old. When pregnant, the females were assigned randomly to one of two housing conditions, to be described later.

The mothers' experiences were as follows. The females were placed either into stainless steel maternity cages (15 in. × 10 in. × 7·5 in.) or into free environment boxes. These boxes were triangular compartments formed by placing a diagonal insert into a 34 in.² box. Food was scattered on the floor, water was supplied by an externally mounted bottle, and "toys" (wooden block, can, ramp. running disk) were placed into each environment. At birth, litters were cut back to eight subjects consisting of four to six females.

When weaned on day 21, the females from each litter were randomly split into two groups, one going into a stainless steel laboratory cage (11 in. × 8·25 in. × 7·5 in.), and the other into a free environment. The free environments were the same as previously described except that the diagonal partition was removed. Two or three females were placed in each laboratory cage, while ten to twelve pups shared each free environment. On day 50 the females from the free environment were placed in the same type of laboratory cages as those described above.

These females were the parents of the animals used in this study. When approximately 150 days old, one female from each litter was bred to a randomly chosen colony male. All pregnant animals were placed in stainless steel maternity cages. At birth, litters were reduced to eight pups consisting, when possible, of four males and four females. No litter contained less than four pups. The pups remained undisturbed until they were 21 days old. At this time they were placed into a 32 in.² open field consisting of sixty-four squares. An activity count was recorded each time a pup made contact with a different square. Each pup was given one 3 min test, and after this was weighed.

Table 1 presents the experimental design, the mean activity score, the mean body weight, the number of pups and the number of litters for each of the eight treatment combinations. In the statistical analysis of these data the litter was used as the unit of measurement with a sub-classification for the sex of the pup. For example, the activity scores of all males within a litter were combined and a mean was obtained; the same procedure was applied to the females. These litter sex scores were subjected to a split plot unweighted means analysis of variance.[6] All F tests were based on 1/47 degrees of freedom.

ACTIVITY

The interaction of grandmother handling × mother preweaning housing was significant at the 0·01 level (F, 7·68): descendants of non-handled grandmothers were more active than descendants of handled grandmothers if their mothers had been reared in a maternity cage between birth and weaning. Exactly the opposite pattern was obtained if their mothers had been reared in a free environment during infancy. The grandmother handling × mother postweaning housing interaction was significant (F, 5·04; $P < 0·05$): the pattern was just the opposite to that described for the previous interaction. In addition, the preweaning housing × postweaning housing interaction was significant at the 0·05 level (F, 5·77). Offspring of mothers reared in two different environments during early life (that is, cage and free environment, or free environment and cage) were more active than the offspring of mothers which had been reared only in cages or only in free environments for the first 50 days of life.

The grandmother handling × sex interaction was significant at the 0·01 level (F, 21·44). Male wean-

---

[6] Winer, B. J., *Statistical Principles in Experimental Design* (McGraw-Hill, New York, 1962).

TABLE 1
SUMMARY OF MEANS FOR ALL EXPERIMENTAL CONDITIONS

Handling experience of grandmothers of experimental subjects	Preweaning housing of mothers of experimental subjects	Postweaning housing of mothers of experimental subjects	No. of litters	No. of subjects	Open-field activity		Weaning weight (g)	
					Male	Female	Male	Female
Non-handled	Maternity cage	Laboratory cage	17	123	17·00	15·02	50·00	47·05
		Free environment	17	133	23·60	20·70	48·43	46·26
	Free environment	Laboratory cage	11	82	13·08	9·31	51·45	50·32
		Free environment	11	85	15·48	11·58	45·63	44·29
Handled	Maternity cage	Laboratory cage	12	90	11·39	18·30	49·73	48·35
		Free environment	12	86	16·32	19·17	47·07	44·76
	Free environment	Laboratory cage	11	84	25·55	24·29	44·76	42·93
		Free environment	11	86	11·35	17·46	48·76	46·91

lings were only slightly affected by the handling experience their grandmothers had received, while the females were markedly affected, with grandpups of handled females being significantly more active than grandpups of non-handled females. Finally, the preweaning housing × postweaning × sex interaction was significant at the 0·05 level (*F*, 4·55).

WEANING WEIGHT

The two main effects of grandmother handling and mother postweaning housing were both significant at the 0·05 level (*F*s of 4·55 and 5·20, respectively), while the interaction of these two factors was significant at the 0·01 level (*F*, 8·49). All three of these effects were brought about by one cell: those weanlings whose grandmothers were not handled in infancy and whose mothers were reared in laboratory cages after weaning weighed significantly more than the other three groups making up this interaction. Such groups did not differ among themselves. In addition, the grandmother handling × preweaning housing × postweaning housing interaction was significant (*F*, 18·80; *P* < 0·01), and sex was significant (*F*, 87·99; *P* < 0·01) with male weanlings weighing more than females.

These data for activity and weaning weight reveal that handling females in infancy can have an effect two generations further on; that the nature of the mother's living quarters during her early life will affect her offspring, and that these variables act in a non-additive interactive manner. The interactive nature of the variables should be emphasized: if we had merely taken the female offspring of handled and non-handled grandmothers and maintained them in standard laboratory caging conditions from birth until adulthood (first and fifth groups listed in Table 1) most of the significant findings would have disappeared. Thus the occurrence of free environment experience some time during the mother's early ontogeny was necessary for the effects of the grandmother's handling experience to express itself in the grandpups.

Others have reported findings extending into the next generation. Ginsburg and Hovda[7] reduced the incidence of death from audiogenic seizures in *dba* mice by transplanting fertilized *dba* eggs into *C57Bl* foster mothers shortly after fertilization, and Ressler[8] has shown that the strain of foster grandparent rearing young mice will influence the operant response rate of the offspring of those mice. As far as we know, the present experiment is the first documentation that the experiences which an animal has in early life will influence her unborn descendants two generations away by nongenetic mechanisms.

The nature of the mechanisms underlying these effects is not known. Both handling and free environment experience have behavioural and biological effects on the stimulated organisms.[2–5,9–12] These effects could act through changes in grandmaternal or maternal behaviour or through physiological changes which would affect the developing foetus or modify the milk supply of the grandmother or mother.

This work was supported, in part, by grants from the National Institute of Child Health and Human Development and the National Institute of Mental Health, U.S. Public Health Service.

[7] Ginsburg, B. E., and Hovda, R. B., *Anat. Rec., 99,* 621 (1947).

[8] Ressler, R. H., *J. Comp. Physiol. Psychol., 61,* 264 (1966).

[9] Denenberg, V. H., Brumaghim, J. T., Haltmeyer, G. C., and Zarrow, M. N. *Endocrinology* (in the press, 1967).

[10] Levine, S., Haltmeyer, G. C., Karas, G. G., and Denenberg, V. H., *Physiol. Behav., 2,* 55 (1967).

[11] Krech, D., Rosenzweig, M. R., and Bennett, E. J., *J. Comp. Physiol. Psychol., 53,* 509 (1960).

[12] Rosenzweig, M. R., *Amer. Psychol., 21,* 321 (1966).

12

Infantile Immunization and Adult Stature

John W. M. Whiting,
Thomas K. Landauer,
and Thomas M. Jones

This article uses data from the Berkeley and Fels studies (referred to in Honzik's paper) to examine the hypothesis that apparently stressful infant-care practices result in greater stature in adulthood. This hypothesis was generated in good part from the work of Levine and others using rats. (See the bibliography of the paper for references.) That work suggested the existence of beneficial effects (including increased size) from early physiological stress. Earlier, Whiting and his co-workers had looked at this hypothesis using cross-cultural data.

The present study provides further support for the hypothesis. In addition, it shows ways in which one can try to rule out certain explanations for the relations found, even when one cannot gain experimental control over the variables involved. An intriguing aspect of the paper is the apparent contradiction involved in finding "good" effects of

"stress." Our usual ways of thinking about stress do not encourage us to consider such possibilities. Indeed, were it not for the animal data, such a hypothesis might never have been examined.

John W. M. Whiting is professor of social anthropology at Harvard University. His work has earned him recognition as a psychologist as well as an anthropologist. Thomas Landauer is currently a research worker at the Bell Telephone Laboratories after having taught at Stanford and at Dartmouth.

There is substantial evidence that unusually stimulating events during early infancy can cause acceleration of growth in rats (see Landauer & Whiting, 1964; Levine, 1960, for reviews of this evidence). It has been postulated (Levine, 1960) that the acceleration of growth results from an alteration in endocrine balance which is brought about by the occurrence of a physiological stress reaction at an early, perhaps critical, period. Whether or not this is the proper explanation of the phenomenon, it is nevertheless empirically clear that apparently stressful experiences in early life lead to increased size at maturity in rats.

In looking for a parallel effect in humans, Landauer and Whiting (1964) studied the relation between apparently stressful infant-care practices and the adult stature of males in two independent cross-cultural samples. They found that adult males in societies in which scarification, circumcision, inoculation, or repeated molding and shaping of the limbs or cranium was practiced before the age of 2 years were a statistically significant $2\frac{1}{2}$ inches taller, on the average, than adult males in societies without such practices. The relation between infant experience and adult stature was independent of cross-cultural measures of diet, race, and several geographical factors.

There are other data which may also be interpreted as suggesting an effect of stimulation on growth in humans parallel to that observed in lower animals. Gunders (1961), in a cross-cultural study, investigated the effect on growth of separation of an infant from its mother in the first days of life, which she interprets as a stressor. She found such separation to be significantly associated with greater stature in adults. Gunders and Whiting (1964) studied the relation between hospital birth and growth. Their assumption was that hospital deliveries ordinarily involve many of the same features as do the mother-separation practices of Gunders' cross-cultural study; notably, the child

We are very grateful to Lester Sontag, director of the Fels Research Institute, and to Stanley Garn as member of the staff responsible for the materials on physical growth; to Millah Ayoub for overseeing the abstracting of materials from the Fels Institute files; to Jean Macfarlane and Marjorie Honzik of the Berkeley Guidance Study for providing us with the opportunity to use their excellent data as the basis of the study reported here; to Lincoln Moses and R. S. Srivastava for help in the statistical analyses; and to Henry Harpending who served as research assistant.

John W. M. Whiting, Thomas K. Landauer, and Thomas M. Jones, "Infantile immunization and adult stature," *Child Development,* 1968, *39,* 59–67. Reprinted by permission. © 1968 by the Society for Research in Child Development, Inc.

is removed from the warm bed of his mother and may not be fed for 24 hours or so. They studied children born in a relocation camp in Israel in which the distribution of which individuals were born in the hospital and which at home seemed to be primarily determined by how far the family's assigned tent was from the camp hospital at the time of birth. Those children born in the hospital were found to be significantly heavier at ages 3 and 4 than those born at home.

Graham et al. (Graham, 1966; Graham, Ernhart, Thurston, & Craft, 1962) found that infants who suffered anoxia at birth showed a significant faster rate of growth than a normal control group. Many of the same children were studied again at age 7. Those who had suffered perinatal anoxia were significantly ($p < .01$) taller and heavier than normals (Corah, Anthony, Painter, Stern, & Thurston, 1965). Again, it is possible to interpret anoxia at birth as a stressful stimulus which might lead to the same changes which underlie the growth-accelerating effects of early stress in animals.

While none of these data can be taken as clear evidence of a causal relation between early stress and increased growth in humans, they may all be so interpreted; and the considerable variation among them, with the exception of the commonality of their probable stressfulness to the infant, suggests that the stress-growth hypothesis is worthy of further study. In an effort in this direction, we have reanalyzed data from two longitudinal-growth studies carried out in the United States: the Fels Study (Garn, 1962; Kagan, 1964), and the Berkeley Guidance Study (Macfarlane, 1938). We have searched the medical records of the cases from these studies for the occurrence of stressful events during early life. As suggested by the results of the earlier cross-cultural work, the age of 2 years was taken as an empirical cutoff point between early and later childhood. This cutoff is used as a matter of convenience only, based on our previous results, but with the possibility held open that examination of new data will lead to its modification.

Of the various infant-care practices which were associated with increased adult stature in the cross-cultural study, in the longitudinal study samples only inoculation was found in the necessary intermediate frequency which would allow a comparison of those who had been exposed to it with those who had not been so exposed. Inoculation may be presumed to be stressful on several counts. First of all it involves a pain at the time of occurrence, but this is probably the least significant of its stressful effects. An infant who has been inoculated for smallpox ordinarily shows symptoms of distress up to 2 or 3 weeks thereafter (Spock, 1957).

In addition, recent evidence (Marshall, 1966) indicates that smallpox and other inoculations are associated with the formation of bone lines, which have often been thought to be associated with stress (Tanner, 1962, p. 130).

It is important to enter a caveat to our argument at this point. It is obvious that early inoculations in the U.S. population may be associated with many other things. Those parents who have their children inoculated early almost certainly differ in many ways from those who do not. For example there may be an association between this medical procedure and other forms of medical care. We by no means reject the possibility that the association with growth which we have observed and will report below is due to these other factors rather than to stress per se. However, we feel it is important, as a first step, to see whether inoculation, which was associated with increased stature in a cross-cultural sample of primitive societies, is similarly associated with increased stature among members of our own society. Once this empirical question has been answered, a discussion of its interpretation will become more fruitful.

While we did not present cross-cultural data separately for inoculation as compared to other forms of stress in the original report (Landauer & Whiting, 1964), a significant relation between inoculation and stature existed in those data, as indicated by the following reanalysis. There were 5 societies in the sample of 65 that were reported to systematically inoculate children before the age of 2 years. The mean stature of the adult males in these five societies was 66.8 inches as compared to 64.2 inches for the remainder of the sample, and 63.0 for those societies in which no stress before the age of 2 was reported. Each case is a society in which at least 25 individuals were measured and their heights recorded in ethnographic literature and for which detailed data on child rearing were available. The ratings on the child-care practice and stature were done by independent (blind) raters. The differences are statistically significant (for inoculated vs. not inoculated $t = 2.61$, $df = 63$, $p < .02$ two-tailed; for inoculated vs. not stressed in any way $t = 4.46$, $df = 32$, $p < .001$ two-tailed).

METHOD

MATERIALS

From the Fels study we obtained inoculation and vaccination histories, and stature measurements made at age 18 for 77 boys and 69 girls born between 1928 and 1944 in or near Yellow Springs, Ohio. From the Berkeley Guidance Study we obtained inoculation, vaccination, and summary medical histories as well as yearly stature measurements up to maturity, from 80 boys and 90 girls, all born in 1927–29 in Berkeley, California. The two samples are roughly comparable with respect to socio-economic and racial factors. However, the Fels sample contains a much larger number of children from poor and rural backgrounds, while the Berkeley sample is almost entirely urban. We also obtained adult height data, most from actual measurements, some from report, for the mothers and fathers of all children in both samples.

In an attempt to control for parental stature, and factors which might operate through association with parental stature, a statistical correction for height of mother and father was used. For these data, it was found that the sum of mother's and father's height gave the most efficient prediction of the child's terminal stature, and this sum was used as the covariate control variable in all the comparisons to be reported below. A covariance technique was used in which the height of individuals was adjusted with respect to the best fit within-group linear regression of children's stature (separately for boys and girls and for the two samples) on sum of parental heights.

For each individual in both samples, the age at which the first immunological vaccination or inoculation of any kind occurred was determined. For over half of the cases, this procedure consisted of smallpox vaccination. Following the results of the cross-cultural study, we divided the samples into those individuals who did or did not receive one or more such treatments before the age of 2 years. The number of cases was too small to make the analysis of finer age ranges possible.

RESULTS

Table 1 gives the mean 18-year statures for boys and girls in the two samples separated according to whether or not they received an immunological vaccination or inoculation before the age of 2 years. The means presented have been adjusted for heights of mothers and fathers. Separate analyses of covariance were performed for each of the four groups. The associated F ratios are given in Table 1. Only the difference for males in the Fels sample is significant by itself ($p < .04$), but the difference between the two treatment groups is in the same direction in all four groups, and the lack of significance is probably due to the rather small numbers in each. Combining the significance values for the four groups by a z transformation yields a probability of less than .02 for the full set of data. It thus appears reasonably clear that, on the average, the treated children exceeded the stature predicted from that of their parents to a greater extent than did those not treated.

INTERPRETATION

It remains to determine what interpretation may most reasonably be put on the finding that early immunization is associated with greater adult stature. One interpretation is that the relation is another instance of the growth-accelerating effect of early stress. But there are obviously other possibilities. One is that early immunization, through the protection afforded and/or through correlation with other forms of medical care, may result in less illness during the growth period and that a lack of illness contributes to adult stature. We were able to investigate the notion that illness during the growing period might be related to adult stature with the data from the Berkeley Guidance Study. Medical histories for each child were examined, abstracted, and rated by a person who did not have access to stature data for the same cases. The ratings were made in terms of the estimated number of days during which the individual had either an elevated temperature or elevated steroid hormone levels. Estimates of elevated temperature were made either from direct information given in the medical histories or from the usual course of a recorded illness, as described by standard pediatric texts. Estimates of elevated steroid levels had to be based on educated guesses, as direct evidence as to their usual course in common diseases and injuries is lacking.

Both illnesses and injuries were rated; such disparate items as severe allergic reactions, accidental ingestion of poison, rickets, infected ears, and mumps were all considered. The raters relied most heavily upon such signs as level and duration of fever, number of days of bed rest, descriptions of disability, and number of days of absence from school. When such information was only partially available, the raters relied on medical texts to determine the average course of a disease in order to make a rating. In general each illness or accident was given a rating in terms of presumed days of significantly heightened steroid levels. Each illness was given a duration rating and a severity rating. The severity ratings (1, 2, or 3) were generally "1." Ratings of "2" or "3" were reserved for definite indications of elevated steroid levels such as high fever. The total rating for each illness or accident was the product of the duration rating and the severity rating. Totals were tabulated for the years 0–2 and 2–18. A reliability coefficient of .88 was obtained between ratings on 36 separate 1-year records. While these ratings are obviously crude, they are

TABLE 1

MEAN 18-YEAR STATURE ADJUSTED FOR PARENTAL STATURE OF CHILDREN WITH AND WITHOUT EARLY IMMUNIZATION

Sample and Sex	Immunization Treatment before 24 Months	N	Adjusted (and Raw) Mean 18-Year Stature (Cm.)	F
Berkeley Guidance Study:				
Male	1 or more	38	180.31 (180.66)	1.073
	None	42	179.05 (178.74)	
Female	1 or more	48	166.61 (167.00)	2.116
	None	42	164.97 (164.52)	
Fels Growth Study:				
Male	1 or more	52	178.51 (178.73)	6.161
	None	25	175.99 (175.53)	
Female	1 or more	45	165.45 (166.35)	1.107
	None	25	164.08 (162.46)	

probably sufficient for present purposes. There was an immense range—from 31 to 195 for summary ratings for 0–18 years among children in the sample—and it is thus quite clear that large differences in the amount of illness were being reflected. Certainly if gross amount of illness has an important influence on overall growth, children with such wide differences in rated illness histories should provide some evidence thereof.

To test the relation between illness and stature, we divided the groups at the median illness rating into those with much illness in their histories and those with little illness. The mean 18-year statures, adjusted for parental height, for those with much or little illness from birth to 2 years and from 2 to 18 years are given in Tables 2 and 3. It is clear that illness, as rated, bears no appreciable relation to stature. The *F* ratios obtained from analyses of covariance for these data are all insignificant. Moreover, the average illness ratings for those with and without early immunization also do not differ appreciably (mean illness ratings were 77.4 and 78.8 for those with and without early immunization, respectively: *F* < 1.). Thus, as far as we could determine, early immunization was not associated with less illness during the growing period, and differences in illness were not associated with 18-year stature. Thus it is implausible that the observed correlation between early immunization and adult stature could have been mediated by either direct or indirect

association of early immunization with decreased morbidity.

This is not to say, of course, that better medical or other care may not still be the mediator of the immunization-growth relation observed here. It is possible that early immunization is correlated, in these samples, with more frequent correlation of serious malnutrition, with supplementary vitamin therapy, with better diets, or with any one or more of a large number of potential growth-accelerating factors. The present data, unfortunately, provide no information on such matters. The present data cannot, therefore, be used to reject these many plausible alternatives. Other evidence is needed.

DISCUSSION

This seems an appropriate place to summarize the case to date concerning the hypothesis that infantile stress leads to increased growth in humans. No single definitive test of this hypothesis has been made, nor is one likely to appear in the future, because the experimental study of the effect of early stress is not possible with human subjects as it has been with laboratory animals. To explore the hypothesis with humans it is necessary to rely on correlational data with all its well-known pitfalls. Nonetheless, confidence in the likelihood of a particular interpretation may be gradually increased by the addition of new sources of confirmatory evidence in which various alternative interpretations are successively controlled. In the original cross-cultural study, it was possible to show that the association between early stress and adult stature was independent of race, geography, and diet. It was not possible to show that the causal relation might not be in the opposite direction, that is, that tall people stressed infants, with these data, however, since parental stature could not be controlled. Nor was it possible to assess the contribution of illness during growth since such information could not be obtained. In addition, these data left open the possibility of the effect being due to other cultural variables correlated with stressful infant-care practices. Perhaps most important, the cross-cultural evidence left open the possibility of selective differential mortality resulting from early stress.

In the present study, (a) culture was held relatively constant; (b) it was possible to control for parental stature by statistical means, making the directionality of the effect, from treatment to stature rather than vice versa, more plausible; (c) the possible contribution of decreased illness could be explored; and (d) there was essentially no mortality in the sample. But it was not possible, with the present data, to control for a variety of possible third-factor effects such as diet, which *were* controlled in the cross-cultural study.

TABLE 2

ADJUSTED MEAN 18-YEAR STATURE OF BERKELEY GUIDANCE STUDY SUBJECTS IN RELATION TO ILLNESS HISTORY DURING FIRST TWO YEARS

Sex and Amount of Illness	N	Adjusted Mean (and Raw) 18-Year Stature (Cm.)	F
Male:			
High	31	180.68 (179.48)	< 1
Low	33	179.32 (180.45)	
Female:			
High	33	166.03 (165.77)	< 1
Low	37	166.78 (167.02)	

TABLE 3

ADJUSTED MEAN 18-YEAR STATURE OF BERKELEY GUIDANCE STUDY SUBJECTS IN RELATION TO ILLNESS HISTORY BETWEEN THE AGES OF 2 AND 18

Sex and Amount of Illness	N	Adjusted Mean (and Raw) 18-Year Stature (Cm.)	F
Male:			
High	30	179.58 (179.22)	< 1
Low	34	180.33 (180.65)	
Female:			
High	33	167.21 (167.10)	1.328
Low	37	165.73 (165.83)	

In the same way, the assignment of treatment to individuals was probably anything but random in the present study. But in the Gunders study of hospital births (Gunders & Whiting, 1964), the initial treatment at least approached random assignment, the proximity of parents to the camp hospital being, apparently, the chief determinant of whether infants were born in the hospital or at home. Thus, self-selection of early stress by parents who might have other features contributory to growth, such as wealth and status, were controlled in Gunders' study, but in none of the others' to date, while in her study many of the other possibilities were not controlled.

Finally, in both the Gunders hospitalization study and the present investigation of immunization, the treatment was one generally thought to be benign, and thus some question of whether its stressful aspects were the crucial ones is raised. On the other hand, this is not true of many of the treatments considered in the cross-cultural studies, nor of the birth-anoxia effect reported by Corah et al. (1965), and by Graham (1966) and Graham et al. (1962).

In summary, there now exist a number of reports of enhanced growth associated with treatment in early infancy which have been interpreted as potential stressors. While no one of the studies controls for all possible artifacts, the following possible extraneous sources of the correlation have been at least partially controlled in at least one study: diet; race; geography, including sunlight and rain; parental stature; illness and selective mortality; self-selection of treatment by parents; and direct benign effects of the treatment.

What links all of these studies and leads to comparison of their results in the first place, of course, is the interpretation that they are all instances of infantile stimulation or stress. This assumption is for the most part made on insufficient evidence, and this is probably the weakest link in the case at present. What is needed is direct evidence of a common physiological effect of such growth-enhancing infant-care practices as mother separation, hospital birth, immunization, and birth anoxia, etc., and a real understanding of how such a physiological effect, if it exists, leads to acceleration of growth.

The lack of clear understanding of the mechanism, or of definitive evidence concerning the nature and site of action of infantile experiences on growth, should not, however, obscure the existence of a very real and important relationship. It is certain that there is an association between a variety of apparently stressful infant experiences and increased growth. Elucidation of the reason for this relation cannot help but shed significant light on the processes by which differences in growth rates are determined.

REFERENCES

CORAH, N. L., ANTHONY, E. J., PAINTER, P., STERN, J. A., & THURSTON, D. Effects of perinatal anoxia after seven years. *Psychological Monographs,* 1965, *79* (Whole No. 596).

GARN, S. M. Genetics of normal human growth. In L. Gedda (Ed.), *De genetica medica.* Rome: Gregor Mendel, 1962.

GRAHAM, F. Personal communication 1966.

GRAHAM, F., ERNHART, C. B., THURSTON, D. S., & CRAFT, M. Development three years after perinatal anoxia and other potentially damaging newborn experiences. *Psychological Monographs,* 1962, *76* (Whole No. 522).

GUNDERS, S. M. The effects of periodic separation from the mother during infancy upon growth and development. Unpublished doctoral dissertation, Harvard University, 1961.

GUNDERS, S. M., & WHITING, J. W. M. The effects of periodic separation from the mother during infancy upon growth and development. Paper presented at International Congress of Anthropological and Ethnological Science, Moscow, August, 1964.

KAGAN, J. American longitudinal research on psychological development. *Child Development,* 1964, *35,* 1–32.

LANDAUER, T. K., & WHITING, J. W. M. Infantile stimulation and adult stature of human males. *American Anthropologist,* 1964, *66,* 1007–1028.

LEVINE, S. J. Stimulation in infancy. *Scientific American,* 1960, *202,* 80–86.

MACFARLANE, J. Studies in child guidance. I. Methodology of data collection and organization. *Monographs of the Society for Research in Child Development,* 1938, *3,* No. 6 (Whole No. 19).

MARSHALL, W. Personal communication. 1966.

SPOCK, B. *Baby and child care.* New York: Pocket Books, Inc., 1957.

TANNER, J. N. *Growth at adolescence.* (2d ed.) Oxford: Blackwell Scientific, 1962.

III

LEARNING AS A DETERMINANT OF BEHAVIOR

Because it is impossible to give adequate space in a book such as this to each of the schools of thought regarding the principles of learning, we have chosen one approach for major emphasis, that of reinforcement. A reinforcement theorist will seek to explain behavior by asking "What actions have been reinforced?" At times he will focus on asking "What is acting as the reinforcer for this behavior?" The latter question is particularly important when trying to eliminate undesired behaviors. At other times he will want to know what might be an effective reinforcer for the child.

We focus on reinforcement for two reasons: (1) Reinforcement theory has played a greater role than other conceptions of the learning process in stimulating and guiding research in child psychology. (2) To provide historical balance and recognize present trends in education. Since association theory with its emphasis on contiguity and practice dominated education in the past, our emphasis on reinforcement provides historical balance. Since much current work in education is strongly influenced by reinforcement, we are recognizing the present trend.

This section focuses on the role of reward and punishment in determining behavior, on the effectiveness of various types of reward, and on the continuities over time of the behaviors involved in learning. The latter is a kind of behavioral continuity that differs from the stabilities provided by biological constitution, which were examined in the previous section. Yet, it too may rest on biological substrates. The first and last selections provide broad perspectives on the topic of learning.

For surveys of various theoretical approaches to learning, the student might consult: (1) *Reward and Punishment* (Allyn and Bacon, Boston, 1965), by Frank A. Logan and Allen R. Wagner; (2) *Learning: A Survey of Psychological Interpretations* (Chandler, San Francisco, 1963), by Winfred F. Hill; and (3) *Cognitive Psychology* (Appleton-Century-Crofts, New York, 1967), by Ulric Neisser. Almost all introductory psychology texts would have one or more appropriate chapters. Chapter 11, Human Learning and Remembering, of *General Psychology* (Prentice-Hall, New Jersey, 1970), by William N. Dember and James J. Jenkins, is a recent example that has the advantage of focusing on human learning.

13

Behaviorism at Fifty

B. F. SKINNER

In this article, which appeared in Section I of the second edition of this book, Prof. B. F. Skinner looks at the role of behaviorism in our understanding of psychology, human behavior, and other sciences dealing with human behavior. Skinner, together with his students and those influenced by him indirectly, is responsible for much of the impetus to behavioral engineering taking place in classrooms, mental hospitals, homes for retarded, nursery schools, and so on. In the history of American psychology behaviorism and the psychology of learning have been closely intertwined.

Skinner is Edgar Pierce Professor of Psychology at Harvard University, where he has been since 1948. He is perhaps best known to students outside of psychology for his Walden Two, *a novel about a behaviorally engineered Utopia. His 1954 paper "The Science of Learning and the Art of Teaching" was reprinted from the Harvard Educational Review in the first edition of this book.*

We would also like to call attention to other writings of Prof. Skinner: (a) two articles in The Listener *(January 5 and January 12, 1967): "Visions of Utopia" and "Utopia through the Control of Human Behavior"; (b) his 1968 book* The Technology of Teaching *(Appleton-Century-Crofts, New York), which sums up his concerns with the educational process, including the use of teaching machines; (c)* Science and Human Behavior, *which presents his approach to learning and looks at various types of applications; and his 1971 book, "Beyond Freedom and Dignity," which is already arousing considerable controversy.*

Behaviorism, with an accent on the last syllable, is not the scientific study of behavior but a philosophy of science concerned with the subject matter and methods of psychology. If psychology is a science of mental life—of the mind, of conscious experience—then it must develop and defend a special methodology, which it has not yet done successfully. If it is, on the other hand, a science of the behavior of organisms, human or otherwise, then it is part of biology, a natural science for which tested and highly successful methods are available. The basic issue is not the nature of the stuff of which the world is made, or whether it is made of one stuff or two, but rather the dimensions of the things studied by psychology and the methods relevant to them.

Mentalistic or psychic explanations of human behavior almost certainly originated in primitive animism. When a man dreamed of being at a distant place in spite of incontrovertible evidence that he had stayed in his bed, it was easy to conclude that some part of him had actually left his body. A particularly vivid memory or a hallucination could be explained in the same way. The theory of an invisible, detachable self eventually proved useful for other purposes. It seemed to explain unexpected or abnormal episodes, even to the person behaving in an exceptional way because he was thus "possessed." It also served to explain the inexplicable. An organism as complex as man often seems to behave capriciously. It is tempting to attribute the visible behavior to another organism inside—to a little man or homunculus. The wishes of the little man become the acts of the man observed by his fellows. The inner idea is put into outer words. Inner feelings find outward expression. The explanation is satisfying, of course, only so long as the behavior of the homunculus can be neglected.

Primitive origins are not necessarily to be held against an explanatory principle, but the little man is still with us in relatively primitive form. He was

B. F. Skinner, "Behaviorism at fifty," *Science,* 1963, *140,* 3570, 951–958. Copyright 1963 by the American Association for the Advancement of Science. Reprinted with abridgement by permission. This paper . . . [was] published in *Behaviorism and Phenomenology: Contrasting Bases for Modern Psychology,* T. W. Wann, Ed., by the University of Chicago Press, 1964. It was presented at a symposium on behaviorism and phenomenology held at Rice University in March 1963. An earlier version was given as the R. M. Elliott lecture at the University of Minnesota in December 1962.

recently the hero of a television program called "Gateways to the Mind," one of a series of educational films sponsored by Bell Telephone Laboratories and written with the help of a distinguished panel of scientists. The viewer learned, from animated cartoons, that when a man's finger is pricked, electrical impulses resembling flashes of lightning run up the afferent nerves and appear on a television screen in the brain. The little man wakes up, sees the flashing screen, reaches out, and pulls a lever. More flashes of lightning go down the nerves to the muscles, which then contract, as the finger is pulled away from the threatening stimulus. The behavior of the homunculus was, of course, not explained. An explanation would presumably require another film. And it, in turn, another.

The same pattern of explanation is invoked when we are told that the behavior of a delinquent is the result of a disordered personality, or that the vagaries of a man under analysis are due to conflicts among his superego, ego, and id. Nor can we escape from primitive features by breaking the little man into pieces and dealing with his wishes, cognitions, motives, and so on, bit by bit. The objection is not that these things are mental but that they offer no real explanation and stand in the way of a more effective analysis.

It has been about 50 years since the behavioristic objection to this practice was first clearly stated, and it has been about 30 years since it has been very much discussed. A whole generation of psychologists has grown up without really coming into contact with the issue. Almost all current textbooks compromise: rather than risk a loss of adoptions, they define psychology as the science of behavior *and* mental life. Meanwhile the older view has continued to receive strong support from areas in which there has been no comparable attempt at methodological reform. During this adoptions, they define psychology as the science of behavior has emerged. Much of what it has discovered bears on the basic issue. A restatement of radical behaviorism would therefore seem to be in order.

Explaining the Mind

A rough history of the idea is not hard to trace.
. . .
The central argument [was] that behavior which seemed to be the product of mental activity could be explained in other ways. In any case, the introspectionists were prepared to challenge it. As late as 1883 Francis Galton could write (1): "Many persons, especially women and intelligent children, take pleasure in introspection, and strive their very best to explain their mental processes."

But introspection was already being taken seriously. The concept of a science of mind in which mental events obeyed mental laws had led to the development of psychophysical methods and to the accumulation of facts which seemed to bar the extension of the principle of parsimony. What might hold for animals did not hold for men, because men could *see* their mental processes.

Curiously enough, part of the answer was supplied by the psychoanalysts, who insisted that although a man might be able to see some of his mental life, he could not see all of it. The kind of thoughts Freud called unconscious took place without the knowledge of the thinker. From an association, verbal slip, or dream it could be shown that a person must have responded to a passing stimulus although he could not tell you that he had done so. More complex thought processes, including problem solving and verbal play, could also go on without the thinker's knowledge. Freud had devised, and he never abandoned faith in, one of the most elaborate mental apparatuses of all time. He nevertheless contributed to the behavioristic argument by showing that mental activity did not, at least, *require* consciousness. His proofs that thinking had occurred without introspective recognition were, indeed, clearly in the spirit of Lloyd Morgan. They were operational analyses of mental life—even though, for Freud, only the unconscious part of it. Experimental evidence pointing in the same direction soon began to accumulate.

But that was not the whole answer. What about the part of mental life which a man can see? It is a difficult question, no matter what one's point of view, partly because it raises the question of what "seeing" means and partly because the events seen are private. The fact of privacy cannot, of course, be questioned. Each person is in special contact with a small part of the universe enclosed within his own skin. To take a noncontroversial example, he is uniquely subject to certain kinds of proprioceptive and interoceptive stimulation. Though two people may in some sense be said to see the same light or hear the same sound, they cannot feel the same distension of a bile duct or the same bruised muscle. (When privacy is invaded with scientific instruments, the form of stimulation is changed; the scales read by the scientist are not the private events themselves.)

Mentalistic psychologists insist that there are other kinds of events uniquely accessible to the owner of the skin within which they occur which lack the physical dimensions of proprioceptive or interoceptive stimuli. They are as different from physical events as colors are from wavelengths of light. There are even better reasons, therefore, why two people cannot suffer each other's toothaches, recall each other's memories, or share each other's happiness. The importance assigned to this kind of world varies. For some, it is the only world there is. For others, it is the only part of the world which can be directly known. For still others, it is a special part of what can be known. In any case, the problem of how one knows about the subjective world of another must be faced. Apart from the question of what "knowing" means, the problem is one of accessibility.

PUBLIC AND PRIVATE EVENTS

One solution, often regarded as behavioristic, is to grant the distinction between public and private events and rule the latter out of scientific consideration. This is a congenial solution for those to whom scientific truth is a matter of convention or agreement among observers. It is essentially the line taken by logical positivism. . . .

. . . [It] is significant that P. W. Bridgman's physical operationism could not save him from an extreme solipsism even within physical science itself. Though he insisted that he was not a solipsist, he was never able to reconcile seemingly public physical knowledge with the private world of the scientist (2). Applied to psychological problems, operationism has been no more successful. We may recognize the restrictions imposed by the operations through which we can know of the existence of properties of subjective events, but the operations cannot be identified with the events themselves. S. S. Stevens has applied Bridgman's principle to psychology, not to decide whether subjective events exist, but to determine the extent to which we can deal with them scientifically (3).

.   .   .

If [as will be maintained below] seeing does not require the presence of things seen, we need not be concerned about certain mental processes said to be involved in the construction of such things—images, memories, and dreams, for example. We may regard a dream not as a display of things seen by the dreamer but simply as the behavior of seeing. At no time during a day-dream, for example, should we expect to find within the organism anything which corresponds to the external stimuli present when the dreamer first acquired the behavior in which he is now engaged. In simple recall we need not suppose that we wander through some storehouse of memory until we find an object which we then contemplate. Instead of assuming that we begin with a tendency to *recognize* such an object once it is found, it is simpler to assume that we begin with a tendency to *see* it. Techniques of self-management which facilitate recall—for example, the use of mnemonic devices—can be form-

ulated as ways of strengthening behavior rather than of creating objects to be seen. Freud dramatized the issue with respect to dreaming when asleep in his concept of dreamwork—an activity in which some part of the dreamer played the role of a theatrical producer while another part sat in the audience. If a dream is, indeed, something seen, then we must suppose that it is wrought as such, but if it is simply the behavior of seeing, the dreamwork may be dropped from the analysis. It took man a long time to understand that when he dreamed of a wolf, no wolf was actually there. It has taken him much longer to understand that not even a representation of a wolf is there.

Eye movements which appear to be associated with dreaming are in accord with this interpretation, since it is not likely that the dreamer is actually watching a dream on the undersides of his eyelids. When memories are aroused by electrical stimulation of the brain, as in the work of Wilder Penfield, it is also simpler to assume that it is the behavior of seeing, hearing, and so on which is aroused than that it is some copy of early environmental events which the subject then looks at or listens to. Behavior similar to the responses to the original events must be assumed in both cases—the subject sees or hears—but the reproduction of the events seen or heard is needless complication. The familiar process of response chaining is available to account for the serial character of the behavior of remembering, but the serial linkage of stored experiences (suggesting engrams in the form of sound films) demands a new mechanism.

The heart of the behavioristic position on conscious experience may be summed up in this way: seeing does not imply something seen. We acquire the behavior of seeing under stimulation from actual objects, but it may occur in the absence of these objects under the control of other variables. (So far as the world within the skin is concerned, it always occurs in the absence of such objects.) We also acquire the behavior of seeing-that-we-are-seeing when we are seeing actual objects, but it may also occur in their absence.

To question the reality or the nature of the things seen in conscious experience is not to question the value of introspective psychology or its methods. Current problems in sensation are mainly concerned with the physiological function of receptors and associated neural mechanisms. Problems in perception are, at the moment, less intimately related to specific mechanisms, but the trend appears to be in the same direction. So far as behavior is concerned, both sensation and perception may be analyzed as forms of stimulus control. The subject need not be regarded as observing or evaluating conscious experiences. Apparent anomalies of stimulus control which are now explained by appealing to a psychophysical relation or to the laws of perception may be studied in their own right. It is, after all, no real solution to attribute them to the slippage inherent in converting a physical stimulus into a subjective experience.

The experimental analysis of behavior has a little more to say on this subject. Its techniques have recently been extended to what might be called the psychophysics of lower organisms. Blough's adaption of the Békésy technique—for example, in determining the spectral sensitivity of pigeons and monkeys—yields sensory data comparable with the reports of a trained observer (4). Herrnstein and van Sommers have recently developed a procedure in which pigeons "bisect sensory intervals" (5). It is tempting to describe these procedures by saying that investigators have found ways to get nonverbal organisms to describe their sensations. The fact is that a form of stimulus control has been investigated without using a repertoire of self-observation or, rather, by constructing a special repertoire the nature and origin of which are clearly understood. Rather than describe such experiments with the terminology of introspection, we may formulate them in their proper place in an experimental analysis. The behavior of the observer in the traditional psychophysical experiment may then be reinterpreted accordingly.

MENTAL WAY STATIONS

So much for "conscious content," the classical problem in mentalistic philosophies. There are other mental states or processes to be taken into account. Moods, cognitions, and expectancies, for example, are also examined introspectively, and descriptions are used in psychological formulations. The conditions under which descriptive repertoires are set up are much less successfully controlled. Terms describing sensations and images are taught by manipulating discriminative stimuli—a relatively amenable class of variables. The remaining kinds of mental events are related to such operations as deprivation and satiation, emotional stimulation, and various schedules of reinforcement. The difficulties they present to the verbal community are suggested by the fact that there is no psychophysics of mental states of this sort. That fact has not inhibited their use in explanatory systems.

In an experimental analysis, the relation between a property of behavior and an operation performed upon the organism is studied directly. Traditional mentalistic formulations, however, emphasize certain way stations. Where an experimental analysis might examine the effect of punishment on

behavior, a mentalistic psychology will be concerned first with the effect of punishment in generating feelings of anxiety and then with the effect of anxiety on behavior. The mental state seems to bridge the gap between dependent and independent variables, and a mentalistic interpretation is particularly attractive when these are separated by long periods of time—when, for example, the punishment occurs in childhood and the effect appears in the behavior of the adult.

Mentalistic way stations are popular. In a demonstration experiment, a hungry pigeon was conditioned to turn around in a clockwise direction. A final, smoothly executed pattern of behavior was shaped by reinforcing successive approximations with food. Students who had watched the demonstration were asked to write an account of what they had seen. Their responses included the following: (i) the organism was conditioned to *expect* reinforcement for the right kind of behavior; (ii) the pigeon walked around, *hoping* that something would bring the food back again; (iii) the pigeon *observed* that a certain behavior seemed to produce a particular result; (iv) the pigeon *felt* that food would be given it because of its action; and (v) the bird came to *associate* his action with the click of the food dispenser. The observed facts could be stated, respectively, as follows: (i) the organism was reinforced *when* its behavior was of a given kind; (ii) the pigeon walked around *until* the food container again appeared; (iii) a certain behavior *produced* a particular result; (iv) food was given to the pigeon *when* it acted in a given way; and (v) the click of the food-dispenser *was temporally related* to the bird's action. These statements describe the contingencies of reinforcement. The expressions "expect," "hope," "observe," "feel," and "associate" go beyond them to identify effects on the pigeon. The effect actually observed was clear enough: the pigeon turned more skillfully and more frequently. But that was not the effect reported by the students. (If pressed, they would doubtless have said that the pigeon turned more skillfully and more frequently *because* it expected, hoped, and felt that if it did so food would appear.)

The events reported by the students were observed, if at all, in their own behavior. They were describing what *they* would have expected, felt, and hoped for under similar circumstances. But they were able to do so only because a verbal community had brought relevant terms under the control of certain stimuli, and this had been done when the community had access only to the kinds of public information available to the students in the demonstration. Whatever the students knew about themselves which permitted them to infer comparable events in the pigeon must have been learned from a verbal community which saw no more of their behavior than they had seen of the pigeon's. Private stimuli may have entered into the control of their self-descriptive repertoires, but the readiness with which they applied these repertoires to the pigeon indicates that external stimuli had remained important. The extraordinary strength of a mentalistic interpretation is really a sort of proof that, in describing a private way station, one is to a considerable extent making use of public information.

The mental way station is often accepted as a terminal datum, however. When a man must be trained to discriminate between different planes, ships, and so on, it is tempting to stop at the point at which he can be said to *identify* such objects. It is implied that if he can identify an object he can name it, label it, describe it, or act appropriately in some other way. In the training process he always behaves in one of these ways; no way station called "identification" appears in practice or need appear in theory. (Any discussion of the discriminative behavior generated by the verbal environment to permit a person to examine the content of his consciousness must be qualified accordingly.)

Cognitive theories stop at way stations where the mental action is usually somewhat more complex than identification. For example, a subject is said to *know* who and where he is, what something is, or what has happened or is going to happen, regardless of the forms of behavior through which this knowledge was set up or which may now testify to its existence. Similarly, in accounting for verbal behavior, a listener or reader is said to understand the *meaning* of a passage although the actual changes brought about by listening to or reading the passage are not specified. In the same way, schedules of reinforcement are sometimes studied simply for their effects on the *expectations* of the organism exposed to them, without discussion of the implied relation between expectation and action. Recall, inference, and reasoning may be formulated only to the point at which an experience is remembered or a conclusion is reached, behavioral manifestations being ignored. In practice the investigator always carries through to some response, if only a response of self-description.

On the other hand, mental states are often studied as causes of action. A speaker thinks of something to say before saying it, and this explains what he says, although the sources of his thoughts may not be examined. An unusual act is called "impulsive," without further inquiry into the origin of the unusual impulse. A behavioral maladjustment shows anxiety, but the source of the anxiety is neglected. One salivates upon seeing a lemon because it reminds one of a sour taste, but why it

does so is not specified. The formulation leads directly to a technology based on the manipulation of mental states. To change a man's voting behavior we change his opinions, to induce him to act we strengthen his beliefs, to make him eat we make him feel hungry, to prevent wars we reduce warlike tensions in the minds of men, to effect psychotherapy we alter troublesome mental states, and so on. In practice, all these ways of changing a man's mind reduce to manipulating his environment, verbal or otherwise.

In many cases we can reconstruct a complete causal chain by identifying the mental state which is the effect of an environmental variable with the mental state which is the cause of action. But this is not always enough. In traditional mentalistic philosophies various things happen at the way station which alter the relation between the terminal events. The effect of the psychophysical function and the laws of perception in distorting the physical stimulus before it reaches the way station has already been mentioned. Once the mental stage is reached, other effects are said to occur. Mental states alter each other. A painful memory may never affect behavior, or it may affect it an unexpected way if another mental state succeeds in repressing it. Conflicting variables may be reconciled before they have an effect on behavior if the subject engages in mental action called "making a decision." Dissonant cognitions generated by conflicting conditions of reinforcement will not be reflected in behavior if the subject can "persuade himself" that one condition was actually of a different magnitude or kind. These disturbances in simple causal linkages between environment and behavior can be formulated and studied experimentally as interactions among variables, but the possibility has not been fully exploited, and the effects still provide a formidable stronghold for mentalistic theories designed to bridge the gap between dependent and independent variables.

METHODOLOGICAL OBJECTIONS

The behavioristic argument is nevertheless still valid. We may object, first, to the predilection for unfinished causal sequences. A disturbance in behavior is not explained by relating it to felt anxiety until the anxiety has in turn been explained. An action is not explained by attributing it to expectations until the expectations have in turn been accounted for. Complete causal sequences might, of course, include references to way stations, but the fact is that the way station generally interrupts the account in one direction or the other. For example, there must be thousands of instances in the psychoanalytic literature in which a thought or memory is said to have been relegated to the unconscious because it was painful or intolerable, but the percentage of instances in which even the most casual suggestion is offered as to why it was painful or intolerable must be very small. Perhaps explanations *could* have been offered, but the practice has discouraged the completion of the causal sequence.

A second objection is that a preoccupation with mental way stations burdens a science of behavior with all the problems raised by the limitations and inaccuracies of self-descriptive repertoires. We need not take the extreme position that mediating events or any data about them obtained through introspection must be ruled out of consideration, but we should certainly welcome other ways of treating the data more satisfactorily. Independent variables change the behaving organism, often in ways which persist for many years, and such changes affect subsequent behavior. The subject may be able to describe some of these intervening states in useful ways, either before or after they have affected behavior. On the other hand, behavior may be extensively modified by variables of which, and of the effect of which, the subject is never aware. So far as we know, self-descriptive responses do not alter controlling relationships. If a severe punishment is less effective than a mild one, this is not because it cannot be "kept in mind." (Certain behaviors involved in self-management, such as reviewing a history of punishment, may alter behavior, but they do so by introducing other variables rather than by changing a given relation.)

Perhaps the most serious objection concerns the order of events. Observation of one's own behavior necessarily follows the behavior. Responses which seem to be describing intervening states alone may embrace behavioral effects. "I am hungry" may describe, in part, the strength of the speaker's on-going ingestive behavior. "I was hungrier than I thought" seems particularly to describe behavior rather than an intervening, possibly causal, state. More serious examples of a possibly mistaken order are to be found in theories of psychotherapy. Before asserting that the release of a repressed wish has a therapeutic effect on behavior, or that when one knows why he is neurotically ill he will recover, we should consider the plausible alternative that a change in behavior resulting from therapy has made it possible for the subject to recall a repressed wish or to understand his illness.

A final objection is that way stations are so often simply invented. It is too easy to say that someone does something "because he likes to do it," or that he does one thing rather than another "because he has made a choice."

The importance of behaviorism as a philosophy of science naturally declines as a scientific analysis becomes more powerful because there is then less need to use data in the form of self-description. The mentalism which survives in the fields of sensation and perception will disappear as alternative techniques prove their value in analyzing stimulus control, and similar changes may be anticipated elsewhere. Cognitive psychologists and others still try to circumvent the explicit control of variables by describing contingencies of reinforcement to their subjects in "instructions." They also try to dispense with recording behavior in a form from which probability of response can be estimated by asking their subjects to evaluate their tendencies to respond. But a person rarely responds to a description of contingencies as he would respond under direct exposure to them, nor can he accurately predict his rate of responding, particularly the course of the subtle changes in rate which are a commonplace in the experimental analysis of behavior. These attempts to short-circuit an experimental analysis can no longer be justified on grounds of expedience, and there are many reasons for abandoning them. Much remains to be done, however, before the facts to which they are currently applied can be said to be adequately understood.

BEHAVIORISM AND BIOLOGY

Elsewhere, the scientific study of man has scarcely recognized the need for reform. The biologist, for example, begins with a certain advantage in studying the behaving organism, for the structures he analyzes have an evident physical status. The nervous system is somehow earthier than the behavior for which it is largely responsible. Philosophers and psychologists alike have from time to time sought escape from mentalism in physiology. When a man sees red, he may be seeing the physiological effect of a red stimulus; when he merely imagines red, he may be seeing the same effect re-aroused. Psychophysical and perceptual distortions may be wrought by physiological processes. What a man feels as anxiety may be autonomic reactions to threatening stimuli. And so on. This may solve the minor problem of the nature of subjective experience, but it does not solve any of the methodological problems with which behaviorism is most seriously concerned. A physiological translation of mentalistic terms may reassure those who want to avoid dualism, but inadequacies in the formulation survive translation.

When writing about the behavior of organisms, biologists tend to be more mentalistic than psychologists. Adrian could not understand how a nerve impulse could cause a thought. The author of a recent article on the visual space sense in *Science* (6) asserts that "the final event in the chain from the retina to the brain is a psychic experience." Another investigator reports research on "the brain and its contained mind." Pharmacologists study the "psychotropic" drugs. Psychosomatic medicine insists on the influence of mind over matter. And psychologists join their physiological colleagues in looking for feelings, emotions, drives, and the pleasurable aspects of positive reinforcement in the brain.

The facts uncovered in such research are important, both for their own sake and for their bearing on behavior. The physiologist studies structures and processes without which behavior could not occur. He is in a position to supply a "reductionist" explanation beyond the reach of an analysis which confines itself to terminal variables. He cannot do this well, however, so long as he accepts traditional mentalistic formulations. Only an experimental analysis of behavior will define his task in optimal terms. The point is demonstrated by recent research is psychopharmacology. When the behavioral drugs first began to attract attention, they were studied with impromptu techniques based on self-observation, usually designed to quantify subjective reports. Eventually the methods of an experimental analysis proved their value in generating reproducible segments of behavior upon which the effects of drugs could be observed and in terms of which they could be effectively defined and classified. For the same reasons, brain physiology will move forward more rapidly when it recognizes that its role is to account for the mediation of behavior rather than of mind.

BEHAVIORISM IN THE SOCIAL SCIENCES

There is also still a need for behaviorism in the social sciences, where psychology has long been used for purposes of explanation. Economics has had its economic man. Political science has considered man as a political animal. Parts of anthropology and sociology have found a place for psychoanalysis. The relevance of psychology in linguistics has been debated for more than half a century. Studies of scientific method have oscillated between logical and empirical analyses. In all these fields, "psychologizing" has often had disappointing results and has frequently been rejected in favor of an extreme formalism which emphasizes objective facts. Economics confines itself to its own abundant data. Political scientists limit themselves to whatever may be studied with

a few empirical tools and techniques, and confine themselves, when they deal with theory, to formalistic analyses of political structures. A strong structuralist movement is evident in sociology. Linguistics emphasizes formal analyses of semantics and grammar.

Straight-laced commitments to pure description and formal analysis appear to leave no place for explanatory principles, and the short-coming is often blamed on the exclusion of mental activities. For example, participants at a recent symposium on "The Limits of Behavioralism in Political Science" (7) complained of a neglect of subjective experience, ideas, motives, feelings, attitudes, values, and so on. This is reminiscent of attacks on behaviorism. In any case, it shows the same misunderstanding of the scope of a behavioral analysis. In its extension to the social sciences, as in psychology proper, behaviorism means more than a commitment to objective measurement. No entity or process which has any useful explanatory force is to be rejected on the ground that it is subjective or mental. The data which have made it important must, however, be studied and formulated in effective ways. The assignment is well within the scope of an experimental analysis of behavior, which thus offers a promising alternative to a commitment to pure description on the one hand and an appeal to mentalistic theories on the other. To extend behaviorism as a philosophy of science to the study of political and economic behavior, of the behavior of people in groups, of people speaking and listening, teaching and learning—this is not "psychologizing" in the traditional sense. It is simply the application of a tested formula to important parts of the field of human behavior.

REFERENCES

1. F. GALTON, *Inquiries into Human Faculty* (London, 1883), Everyman ed., p. 60.
2. P. W. BRIDGMAN, *The Way Things Are* (Harvard Univ. Press, Cambridge, Mass., 1959).
3. S. S. STEVENS, *Am. J. Psychol. 47*, 323 (1935).
4. D. S. BLOUGH, *J. Comp. Physiol. Psychol. 49*, 425 (1956); —— and A. M. Schrier, *Science 139*, 493 (1963).
5. R. T. HERRNSTEIN and P. VAN SOMMERS, *Science 135*, 40 (1962).
6. K. N. OGLE, *ibid.*, p. 763.
7. *The Limits of Behavioralism in Political Science* (Am. Acad. Political and Social Sci., Philadelphia, 1962).

14

Effects of Adult Social Reinforcement on Child Behavior *

Florence R. Harris,
Montrose M. Wolf,
and Donald M. Baer

The Elimination of Tantrum Behavior by Extinction Procedures †

Carl D. Williams

The first paper demonstrates the principles of behavioral control through contingency management in the social setting of the nursery school. Several different behaviors are brought under control, including both desirable behaviors (which are strengthened) and undesirable ones (which are weakened). The authors of the paper, which was done at the University of Washington (Seattle) and its laboratory preschool, are Prof. Harris, director of the preschool, and Professors Baer and Wolf, now on the faculty at the University of Kansas.

The second, brief paper is an account by Carl D. Williams of the elimination of an undesirable behavior (bedtime tantrums). As in many studies of contingency of reinforcement, an individual child is the focus. Williams is a professor at the University of Miami, in Coral Gables, Florida.

(Effects of Adult Social Reinforcement on Child Behavior [1])

There is general agreement among educators that one of the primary functions of a nursery school is to foster in each child social behaviors that contribute toward more pleasant and productive living for all. However, there is no similar consensus as to precisely how this objective is to be attained. Many writers subscribe to practices based on a combination of psychoanalytic theory and client-centered therapy principles, usually referred to as a mental hygiene approach. Yet there are considerable variation and vagueness in procedures recommended, particularly those dealing with such problem behaviors as the child's hitting people, breaking valuable things, or withdrawing from both people and things. Read (1955), for example, recommends accepting the child's feelings, verbalizing them for him, and draining them off through vigorous activities. Landreth (1942) advises keeping adult contacts with the child at a minimum based on his needs, backing up verbal suggestions by an implicit assumption that the suggestion will be carried out and, when in doubt, doing nothing unless the child's physical safety is involved. In addition to some of the above precepts, Taylor (1954) counsels parents and teachers to support both desirable and undesirable behaviors and to give nonemotional punishment. According to Standing (1959), Montessori advocates that teachers pursue a process of nonintervention, following careful preparation of a specified environment aimed at "canalizing the energy" and developing "inner command." Nonintervention does not preclude the "minimum dose" of instruction and correction.

Using some combination of such guidance precepts, teachers have reported success in helping some nursery school children who showed problem behaviors; but sometimes adherence to the same teaching principles has not been helpful in modifying the behavior of concern. Indeed, it is usually not at all clear what conditions and principles may or may not have been operative. All of these precepts have in common the adult behaviors

[1] These studies were supported in part by research grants from the National Institute of Mental Health (MH–02208–07) and the University of Washington Graduate School Research Fund (11–1873). The authors are also indebted to Sidney W. Bijou for his general counsel and assistance.

† Carl D. Williams, "The elimination of tantrum behavior by extinction procedures," *Journal of Abnormal and Social Psychology,* 1959, *59,* 269. Reprinted by permission.

of approaching and attending to a child. Therefore, it seemed to the staff of the Laboratory Preschool at the University of Washington that a first step in developing possible explicit criteria for judging when and when not to attend was to study the precise effects that adult attention can have on some problem behaviors.

This paper presents an account of the procedures and results of five such studies. Two groups of normal nursery school children provided the subjects studied. One group enrolled twelve three-year-olds and the other, sixteen four-year-olds. The two teachers of the younger group and the three teachers of the older group conducted the studies as they carried out their regular teaching duties. The general methodology of these studies was developed in the course of dealing with a particularly pressing problem behavior shown by one child at the beginning of the school year. It is worth considering this case before describing the procedures which evolved from it.

The study dealt with a three-year-old girl who had regressed to an excessive amount of crawling (Harris, Johnston, Kelley, and Wolf, 1964). By "excessive" is meant that after three weeks of school she was spending most of her morning crawling or in a crouched position with her face hidden. The parents reported that for some months the behavior had been occurring whenever they took her to visit or when friends came to their home. The teachers had used the conventional techniques, as outlined above, for building the child's "security."

Observations recorded in the third week at school showed, however, that more than 80% of the child's time was spent in off-feet positions. The records also showed that the crawling behavior frequently drew the attention of teachers. On-feet behaviors, such as standing and walking, which occurred infrequently, seldom drew such notice.

A program was instituted in which the teachers no longer attended to the child whenever she was crawling or crouching, but gave her continuous warm attention as long as she was engaging in behavior in which she was standing, running, or walking. Initially the only upright behaviors that the teachers were able to attend to occurred when the child pulled herself almost to her feet in order to hang up or take down her coat from her locker, and when she pulled herself up to wash her hands in the wash basin. Within a week of the initiation of the new attention-giving procedure, the child acquired a close-to-normal pattern of on-feet behavior.

In order to see whether the change from off- to on-feet behavior was related to the differential attention given by the teachers, they reversed their procedure, making attention once again contingent only upon crawling and other off-feet behavior.

They waited for occasions of such off-feet behavior to "reinforce" with attention, while not attending to any on-feet behavior. By the second day the child had reverted to her old pattern of play and locomotion. The observational records showed the child was off her feet 80% of the class session.

To see whether on-feet behavior could be re-established, the teachers again reversed their procedure, giving attention to the child only when she was engaging in behaviors involving upright positions. On-feet behavior rose markedly during the first session. By the fourth day, the child again spent about 62% of the time on her feet.

Once the child was not spending the greater portion of her day crawling about, she quickly became a well-integrated member of the group. Evidently she already had well-developed social play skills.

As a result of this demonstration that either walking or crawling could be maintained and that the child's responses depended largely upon the teachers' attending behaviors, the teachers began a series of further experimental analyses of the relationship between teacher attention and nursery school child behavior.

PROCEDURES

A specified set of procedures common to the next studies was followed. First, a child showing problem behavior was selected and records were secured. An observer recorded all of the child's behavior, the environmental conditions under which it occurred, and its immediate consequences under conventional teacher guidance. This was done throughout the 2½-hour school session, daily, and for several days. The records gave detailed pictures of the behavior under study. In each case, it became apparent that the problem behavior almost always succeeded in attracting adult attention.

As soon as these records, technically termed "baseline" records, of the typical behavior of the child and teachers were obtained, teachers instituted a program of systematically giving differential attention to the child. When the undesired behavior occurred, they did not in any way attend to him, but remained absorbed in one of the many necessary activities of teachers with other children or with equipment. If the behavior occurred while a teacher was attending to the child, she at once turned to another child or task in a matter-of-fact and nonrejecting manner. Concurrently, teachers gave immediate attention to other behaviors of the child which were considered to be more desirable than the problem behavior. The net effect of these procedures was that the child could gain a great deal of adult attention if he refrained from engaging in "problem behavior." If under this regime of differential attention the problem behavior diminished to a stable low level at which it was no longer considered a problem, a second procedure was inaugurated to check out the functional relationship between changes in the child's behavior and the guidance procedures followed.

The second procedure was simply to reverse the first procedure. That is, when the problem behavior occurred, the teacher went immediately to the child and gave him her full, solicitous attention. If the behavior stopped, she turned to other children and tasks, remaining thus occupied until the behavior recurred. In effect, one sure way for the child to secure adult attention was to exhibit the problem behavior. This procedure was used to secure reasonably reliable information on whether the teachers' special program had indeed brought about the changes noted in the child's behavior. If adult attention was the critical factor in maintaining the behavior, the problem behavior should recur in stable form under these conditions. If it did so, this was evidence that adult attention was, technically speaking, a positive social reinforcer for the child's behavior.

The final stage of the study was, of course, to return to procedures in which attention was given at once and continuously for behaviors considered desirable. Concurrently, adult attention was again withheld or withdrawn as an immediate consequence of the problem behavior. As the problem disappeared and appropriate behaviors increased, the intense program of differential adult attention was gradually diminished until the child was receiving attention at times and in amounts normal for the teachers in the group. However, attention was given only on occasions of desirable behavior, and never (or very seldom) for the undesirable behavior.

CRYING AND WHINING

Following the above procedures, a study was conducted on a four-year-old boy who cried a great deal after mild frustrations (Hart, Allen, Buell, Harris, and Wolf, 1964). This child averaged about eight full-fledged crying episodes each school morning. The baseline observations showed that this crying behavior consistently brought attention from the teachers, in the form of going to him and showing solicitous concern. During the following days, this behavior was simply ignored. (The only exceptions to this were to have been incidents in which the child had hurt himself considerably and was judged to have genuine grounds for crying. Naturally, his hurts were to be attended to. Such incidents, however, did not occur.) Ten days of ignoring the outcries, but giving approving atten-

tion for verbal and self-help behaviors, produced a steady weakening of the crying response to a nearly zero level. In the final five days of the interval, only one crying response was recorded. The number of crying episodes on successive days is graphed in cumulative form in Fig. 1.

During the next ten days, crying was again reinforced whenever it occurred, the teachers attending to the boy on these occasions without fail. At first, it was necessary to give attention for mere grimaces that might follow a bump. The daily crying episodes quickly rose to a rate almost as high as formerly. A second ten-day period of ignoring the outcries again produced a quick weakening of the response to a near-zero level, as is apparent in the figure. Crying remained at this low level thereafter, according to the informal judgment of the teachers.

The same procedures were used in another study of "operant crying" of a four-year-old boy, with the same general results.

ISOLATE PLAY

Two studies involved children who exhibited markedly solitary play behavior. Extremely little of their morning at nursery school was spent in any interaction with other children. Instead, these children typically played alone in a quiet area of the school room or the play yard, or interacted only with the teachers. For present purposes, both of these response patterns will be called "isolate play." Sys-

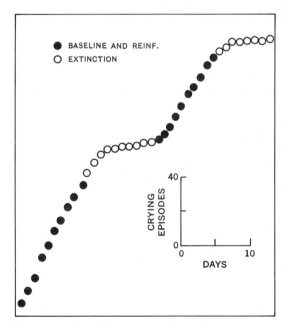

FIGURE 1. *Cumulative record of the daily number of crying episodes.*

tematic observation showed that isolate play usually attracted or maintained the attention of a teacher, whereas social play with other children did so comparatively seldom.

A plan was initiated in which the teacher was to attend regularly if the child approached other children and interacted with them. On the other hand, the teacher was not to attend to the child so long as he engaged in solitary play. To begin with, attention was given when the child merely stood nearby, watching other children; then, when he played beside another child; and finally, only when he interacted with the other child. Teachers had to take special precautions that their attending behaviors did not result in drawing the child away from children and into interaction solely with the teacher. Two techniques were found particularly effective. The teacher directed her looks and comments to the other child or children, including the subject only as a participant in the play project. For example, "That's a big building you three boys are making; Bill and Tom and Jim (subject) are all

working hard." Accessory materials were also kept at hand so that the teacher could bring a relevant item for the subject to add to the play: "Here's another plate for your tea party, Ann." In both isolate cases this new routine for giving adult attention produced the desired result: Isolate play declined markedly in strength while social play increased two- or threefold.

After about a week of the above procedure, the consequences of nonisolate and isolate play were reversed. The teachers no longer attended to the child's interactions with other children, but instead gave continuous attention to the child when he was alone. Within a week, or less, isolate play became the dominant form of activity in both cases.

The former contingencies were then reinstated: The teachers attended to social interactions by the child, and ignored isolate play as completely as they could. Again, isolate play declined sharply while social interaction increased as before. The results of one of these studies (Allen, Hart, Buell, Harris, and Wolf, 1964) are summarized in Fig. 2.

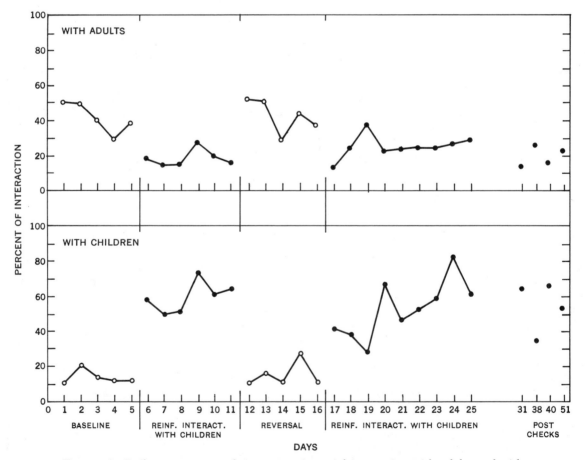

FIGURE 2. *Daily percentages of time spent in social interaction with adults and with children during approximately two hours of each morning session.*

Figure 2 shows the changes in behavior of a 4½-year-old girl under the different guidance conditions. The graph shows the percentage of play time that she spent in interaction with other children and the percentage of time spent with an adult. The remainder of her time was spent alone. It is apparent that only about 15% of this child's play time was spent in social play as long as the teachers attended primarily to her solitary play. But interacting behaviors rose to about 60% of total play time when the teachers attended only to her social play. At the same time, her interactions solely with teachers, not being reinforced, fell from their usual 40% of the child's play time to about 20%. These were considered reasonable percentages for this nursery school child. During Days 17 through 25 the schedule of adult reinforcement of social play was gradually reduced to the usual amount of attention, given at the usual irregular intervals. Nevertheless, the social behavior maintained its strength, evidently becoming largely self-maintaining.

After Day 25, the teachers took care not to attend too often to the child when she was alone, but otherwise planned no special contingencies for attending. Four checks were made at later dates to see if the pattern of social behavior persisted. It is apparent (Fig. 2, Post Checks) that the change was durable, at least until Day 51. Further checks were not possible because of the termination of the school year.

A parallel study, of a three-year-old isolate boy (Johnston, Kelley, Harris, Wolf, and Baer, unpub.) yielded similar results showing the same pattern of rapid behavioral change in response to changing contingencies for adult attention. In the case of this boy, postchecks were made on three days during the early months of school following the summer vacation period. The data showed that on those days his interaction with children averaged 55% of his play time. Apparently his social play was well established. Teachers reported that throughout the remainder of the year he continued to develop ease and skills in playing with his peers.

The immediate shifts in these children's play behavior may be partly due to the fact that they had already developed skills readily adapted to play with peers at school. Similar studies in progress are showing that, for some children, development of social play behaviors may require much longer periods of reinforcement.

EXCESSIVE PASSIVITY

A fifth case (Johnston, Kelley, Harris, and Wolf, unpub.) involved a boy noted for his thorough-going lack of any sort of vigorous play activity. The teachers reported that this child consistently stood quietly about the play yard while other children ran, rode tricycles, and climbed on special climbing frames, trees, fences, and playhouses. Teachers also reported that they frequently attempted to encourage him, through suggestions or invitations, to engage in the more vigorous forms of play available. Teachers expressed concern over his apparent lack of strength and motor skills. It was decided to select a particular form of active play to attempt to strengthen. A wooden frame with ladders and platforms, called a climbing frame, was chosen as the vehicle for establishing this activity. The teachers attended at first to the child's mere proximity to the frame. As he came closer, they progressed to attending only to his touching it, climbing up a little, and finally to extensive climbing. Technically, this was reinforcement of successive approximations to climbing behavior. Fig. 3 shows the results of nine days of this procedure, compared to a baseline of the preceding nine days. In this figure, black bars represent climbing on the climbing frame, and white bars represent climbing on any other equipment in the play yard. The height of the bars shows the percentage of the child's play time spent in such activities. It is clear that during the baseline period less than 10% of the child's time was spent in any sort of climbing activity, but that during the course of reinforcement with pleased adult attention for climbing on the frame, this behavior greatly increased, finally exceeding 50% of the child's morning. (Climbing on other objects was not scored during this period.) There then followed five days during which the teachers ignored any climbing on the frame, but attended to all other appropriate activities. The rate of climbing on the frame promptly fell virtually to zero, though the child climbed on other apparatus and was consistently given attention for this. Another five days of reinforcement of use of the climbing frame immediately restored the climbing-frame behavior to a high stable level, always in excess of 40% of the boy's play time. After this, the teachers began an intermittent program of reinforcement for climbing on any other suitable objects, as well as vigorous active play of all sorts, in an effort to generalize the increased vigorous activity. Frame-climbing weakened considerably, being largely replaced by other climbing activities, which were now scored again as data. Activities such as tricycle-riding and running were not systematically recorded due to difficulties in reliably scoring them. It is clear from the data obtained, however, that climbing activities were thoroughly generalized by this final procedure. Checks made the following school year

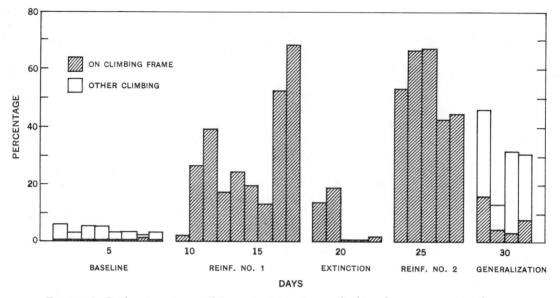

FIGURE 3. *Daily percentages of time spent in using a climbing-frame apparatus. Open bars indicate time spent in climbing on other equipment.*

in another play yard indicated that vigorous climbing had become a stable part of his behavior repertoire.

SUMMARY AND DISCUSSION

The above studies systematically examined effects of adult attention on some problem behaviors of normal preschool children. The findings in each case clearly indicated that for these children adult attention was a strong positive reinforcer. That is, the behavior which was immediately followed by a teacher's giving the child attention rose rapidly to a high rate, and the rate fell markedly when adult attention was withheld from that behavior and concurrently given to an incompatible behavior. While it seems reasonable that for most young children adult attention may be a positive reinforcer, it is also conceivable that for some children adult attention may be a negative reinforcer. That is, the rate of a behavior may decrease when it is immediately followed by the attention of an adult, and rise again as soon as the adult withdraws. Actually, for a few children observed at the preschool, it has been thought that adult attention was a negative reinforcer. This seemed to be true, for instance, in the case of the climbing-frame child. Before the study was initiated, the teachers spent several weeks attempting to make themselves positively reinforcing to the child. This they did by staying at a little distance from him and avoiding attending directly to him until he came to them for something. At first, his approaches were only for routine help, such as buttoning his coat. On each of these occa-

sions they took care to be smilingly friendly and helpful. In time, he began making approaches of other kinds, for instance, to show a toy. Finally, when a teacher approached him and commented with interest on what he was doing, he continued his play instead of stopping, hitting out, or running off. However, since his play remained lethargic and sedentary, it was decided that special measures were necessary to help him progress more rapidly. It was the use and effects of these special measures that constituted the study. Clearly, however, adult attention must be or become positively reinforcing to a child before it can be successfully used to help him achieve more desirably effective behaviors.

Studies such as those reported here seem to imply that teachers may help many children rapidly through systematic programming of their adult social reinforcements. However, further research in this area seems necessary. Some of our own studies now in progress suggest that guidance on the basis of reinforcement principles may perhaps bring rapidly into use only behaviors which are already available within the repertory of the child. If the desired behavior requires skills not yet in the child's repertory, then the process of developing those skills from such behaviors as the child has may require weeks or months. For example, a four-year-old child who could verbalize but who very rarely spoke was helped to speak freely within several days. On the other hand, a child of the same age who had never verbalized required a lengthy shaping process that involved reinforcing first any vocalization, and then gradually more appropriate sounds and combinations of sounds. The latter study was still incomplete at the close of a year of work. The time required to develop social behaviors in isolate children has likewise varied considerably, presumably for the same reasons.

Although the teachers conducted these studies in the course of carrying out their regular teaching duties, personnel in excess of the usual number were necessary. The laboratory school was staffed with one teacher to no more than six children, making it possible to assign to one teacher the role of principal "reinforcer teacher" in a study. This teacher was responsible for giving the child immediate attention whenever he behaved in specified ways. In addition, observers were hired and trained to record the behavior of each child studied. Each observer kept a record in ten-second intervals of his subject's behavior throughout each morning at school. Only with such staffing could reinforcement contingencies be precisely and consistently administered and their effects recorded.

Unless the effects are recorded, it is easy to make incorrect judgments about them. Two instances illustrate such fallibility. A boy in the laboratory preschool frequently pinched adults. Attempts by the teachers to ignore the behavior proved ineffective, since the pinches were hard enough to produce at least an involuntary startle. Teachers next decided to try to develop a substitute behavior. They selected patting as a logical substitute. Whenever the child reached toward a teacher, she attempted to forestall a pinch by saying, "Pat, Davey," sometimes adding, "Not pinch," and then strongly approving his patting, when it occurred. Patting behavior increased rapidly to a high level. The teachers agreed that they had indeed succeeded in reducing the pinching behavior through substituting patting. Then they were shown the recorded data. It showed clearly that although patting behavior was indeed high, pinching behavior continued at the previous level. Apparently, the teachers were so focused on the rise in patting behavior that, without the objective data, they would have erroneously concluded that development of a substitute behavior was in this case a successful technique. A second example illustrates a different, but equally undesirable, kind of erroneous assumption. A preschool child who had to wear glasses (Wolf, Risley, and Mees, 1964) developed a pattern of throwing them two or three times per day. Since this proved expensive, it was decided that the attendants should put him in his room for ten minutes following each glasses-throw. When the attendants were asked a few days later how the procedure was working, they said that the glasses-throwing had not diminished at all. A check of the records, however, showed that there was actually a marked decrease. The throwing dropped

to zero within five days. Presumably, the additional effort involved in carrying out the procedure had given the attendants an exaggerated impression of the rate of the behavior. Recorded data, therefore, seem essential to accurate objective assessments of what has occurred.

The findings in the studies presented here accord generally with results of laboratory research on social development reviewed in this journal by Horowitz (1963). The importance of social reinforcement was also noted by Bandura (1963) in his investigations of imitation. Gallwey (1964) has replicated the study of an isolate child discussed here, with results "clearly confirmatory of the effectiveness of the technique." Further studies in school situations that can combine the function of research with that of service seem highly desirable.

REFERENCES

ALLEN, K. EILEEN, HART, BETTY M., BUELL, JOAN S., HARRIS, FLORENCE R., & WOLF, M. M. Effects of social reinforcement on isolate behavior of a nursery school child. *Child. Develop.*, 1964, *35*, 511–518.

BANDURA, ALBERT. The role of imitation in personality development. *J. Nursery Ed.*, 1963, *18*, 207–215.

GALLWEY, MARY. Director of the Nursery School, Washington State University, Pullman, Wash., 1964. Personal communication.

HARRIS, FLORENCE R., JOHNSTON, MARGARET K., KELLEY, C. SUSAN, & WOLF, M. M. Effects of positive social reinforcement on regressed crawling of a nursery school child. *J. Ed. Psychol.*, 1964, *55*, 35–41.

HART, BETTY M., ALLEN, K. EILEEN, BUELL, JOAN S., HARRIS, FLORENCE R., & WOLF, M. M. Effects of social reinforcement on operant crying. *J. Exp. Child Psychol.* In press.

HOROWITZ, FRANCES DEGEN. Social reinforcement effects on child behavior. *J. Nursery Ed.*, 1963, *18*, 276–284.

JOHNSTON, MARGARET K., KELLEY, C. SUSAN, HARRIS, FLORENCE R., WOLF, M. M., & BAER, D. M. Effects of positive social reinforcement on isolate behavior of a nursery school child. Unpublished manuscript.

JOHNSTON, MARGARET K., KELLEY, C. SUSAN, HARRIS, FLORENCE R., & WOLF, M. M. An application of reinforcement principles to development of motor skills of a young child. Unpublished manuscript.

LANDRETH, CATHERINE. *Education of the Young Child.* New York: Wiley, 1942.

READ, KATHERINE H. *The Nursery School* (2nd ed.). Philadelphia: Saunders, 1955.

STANDING, E. M. *Maria Montessori, Her Life and Work.* Fresno: American Library Guild, 1959.

TAYLOR, KATHERINE W. *Parents Cooperative Nursery Schools.* New York: Teachers College, Columbia University, 1954.

WOLF, MONTROSE M., RISLEY, T. R., & MEES, H. L. Application of operant conditioning procedures to the behavior problems of an autistic child. *Behav. Res. Ther.*, 1964, *1*, 305–312.

(The Elimination of Tantrum Behavior by Extinction Procedures)

This paper reports the successful treatment of tyrant-like tantrum behavior in a male child by the removal of reinforcement. The subject *(S)* was approximately 21 months old. He had been seriously ill much of the first 18 months of his life. His health then improved considerably, and he gained weight and vigor.

S now demanded the special care and attention that had been given him over the many critical months. He enforced some of his wishes, especially at bedtime, by unleashing tantrum behavior to control the actions of his parents. [Readers are cautioned that some "tantrums" involve genuine loss of self-control rather than a manipulation of the parents. The causes and treatment of such tantrums differ from those of the "tyrant-like" tantrum behavior described in this article. A helpful discussion of tantrums may be found in *Emotional Problems of Living* by O. S. English and G. H. J. Pearson (New York, W. W. Norton and Co., 3rd Edition, 1963).—EDITOR]

The parents and an aunt took turns in putting him to bed both at night and for *S*'s afternoon nap. If the parent left the bedroom after putting *S* in his bed, *S* would scream and fuss until the parent returned to the room. As a result, the parent was unable to leave the bedroom until after *S* went to sleep. If the parent began to read while in the bedroom, *S* would cry until the reading material was put down. The parents felt that *S* enjoyed his control over them and that he fought off going to sleep as long as he could. In any event, a parent was spending from one-half to two hours each bedtime just waiting in the bedroom until *S* went to sleep.

Following medical reassurance regarding *S*'s physical condition, it was decided to remove the reinforcement of this tyrant-like tantrum behavior. Consistent with the learning principle that, in general, behavior that is not reinforced will be extinguished, a parent or the aunt put *S* to bed in a leisurely and relaxed fashion. After bedtime pleasantries, the parent left the bedroom and closed the door. *S* screamed and raged, but the parent did not re-enter the room. The duration of screaming and crying was obtained from the time the door was closed.

The results are shown in Fig. 1. It can be seen that *S* continued screaming for 45 min. the first time he was put to bed in the first extinction series. *S* did not cry at all the second time he was put to bed. This is perhaps attributable to his fatigue from the crying of Occasion 1. By the tenth occasion, *S* no longer whimpered, fussed, or cried when the parent left the room. Rather, he smiled as they left. The parents felt that he made happy sounds until he dropped off to sleep.

About a week later, *S* screamed and fussed after the aunt put him to bed, probably reflecting spontaneous recovery of the tantrum behavior. The aunt then reinforced the tantrum behavior by returning to *S*'s bedroom and remaining there until he went to sleep. It was then necessary to extinguish this behavior a second time.

Figure 1 shows that the second extinction curve is similar to the first. Both curves are generally similar to extinction curves obtained with subhuman subjects. The second extinction series reached zero by the ninth occasion. No further tantrums at bedtime were reported during the next two years.

It should be emphasized that the treatment in this case did not involve aversive punishment. All that was done was to remove the reinforcement. Extinction of the tyrant-like tantrum behavior then occurred.

No unfortunate side- or aftereffects of this treatment were observed. At three and three-quarters years of age, *S* appeared to be a friendly, expressive, outgoing child.

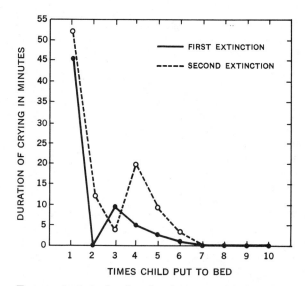

FIGURE 1. *Length of crying in two extinction series as a function of successive occasions of being put to bed.*

15

The Science of Learning and the Technology of Educational Methods

A. W. MELTON
(Abstracted by A. A. LUMSDAINE
and ROBERT GLASER)

Since Skinner's classic paper of 1954 (referred to in the introduction to Skinner's article in this section) several books concerning teaching machines have appeared. One of these is Teaching Machines and Programmed Learning: A Source Book, *edited by Arthur A. Lumsdaine and Robert Glaser. It includes an excellent appendix consisting of an annotated bibliography and abstracts of work in the field. We reprint an abstract of an article by Arthur W. Melton, professor and director of the Human Performance Center at the University of Michigan. Earlier Melton was technical director of the Air Force Personnel and Training Research Center. As these positions suggest, his horizons are not limited to laboratory studies, but reflect his contact with "real life" training situations. His article argues that those who seek to advance the science of learning and those who apply that knowledge in educational settings need each other.*

Melton asserts that "the proper question for consideration is not *whether* the science of learning and the management of learning in the classroom can be mutually supporting, but *how* this desirable—even necessary—relationship can be achieved." He states some of the assumptions and inferences underlying this assertion, some difficulties in the way of achieving a mutually supporting relationship, and some ways for overcoming these difficulties. Melton defines the field of learning in broad terms to encompass "all forms of relatively permanent modifications of behavior resulting from experience, with perhaps the exception of those modifications commonly identified as sensory adaptation and fatigue. This means that the science of learning must organize our knowledge and understanding of the acquisition of attitudes, motives, affective and emotional responses, mental sets, simple and complex discriminative acts, serial verbal and motor acts, motor and perceptual skills, meanings, concepts and abstractions, and various cognitive capabilities that go under such names as ideational problem solving, thinking, reasoning, decision-making, and even creative invention." He indicates that the relationship of education to psychology is analogous to the relation between engineering and the physical sciences or medical practice and the biological sciences. However he points out that "education is not just the straightforward application of the science of learning, any more than engineering is just a straightforward application of the physical sciences. Just as physicists discovered things that made the creation of television possible, but engineers created television, so likewise psychologists have discovered many things about the learning process, but educational technologists must design curricula and teaching machines that exploit that knowledge."

The relationship between basic research and application is a reciprocal one: "Thus, new discoveries in science make new achievements in technology feasible, and recognized sources of deficiency in technology guide the explorations of scientists." Melton discusses the recent relative isolation of educational technology and the science of learning, as evidenced in relatively low overlap in organizational membership and publication channels. He stresses the importance of what Glaser (1960a) has termed a *rapprochement* between educational psychology and the science of learning. Melton feels they have drifted apart partly as a result of "the lack of an explicit strategy for holding them together at the level of advanced training and research."

He draws a parallel between the needs for close interaction in the field of education with a similar

A. W. Melton, Some comments on "The impact of advancing technology on methods in education" by Dr. Simon Ramo, September 1959, unpublished; abstracted by A. A. Lumsdaine and Robert Glaser in their *Teaching Machines and Programmed Learning: A Source Book,* Washington: Department of Audiovisual Instruction, NEA, 1960. Reprinted by permission. The full article by A. W. Melton originally appeared in *Harvard Educational Review,* 1959, *29,* 96–106.

interaction between basic science and application which has developed in military psychology. Among the difficulties to be met, he identifies first the immaturity of the science of learning, in which "advances in empirical generalizations and in the theoretical integration of these generalizations have resulted only in *islands* of knowledge and understanding within the science of learning"; second, the inadequacy of our present taxonomy of tasks or skills; and third, confusion concerning the proper functions of applied science or technology, on the one hand, and research on the other hand. This confusion is grounded in two misconceptions—that basic and applied research are somehow antithetical (whereas actually they are complementary), and second, that the kind of learning investigated determines whether research is basic or applied (which he points out is not true).

As requirements for a profitable working relationship between the science of learning and the technology of classroom instruction, he identifies the need for a formal statement of the relationship between the two, and a concerted planning effort in which the objective is to formulate the technological and scientific problems in particular areas of education. Such planning efforts should include identification of the present "state of the art" in the management of particular types of learning, the identifying and ordering in priority of needs for improvement in such management, the identification of which aspects of problems are amenable to basic and applied research, and identification of the needs for systematic development efforts in which the available state of the art can be employed. A third major requirement is adequate facilities and subjects for research and development studies, including ready access to school populations for analytic studies. Finally, he says, "there must be a re-examination of the training of psychologists and educational psychologists with these opportunities in mind." His general conclusion is that ". . . the present low level of interest and effort in the application to the classroom of recent advances in the science of learning is a state of affairs which can be corrected. Furthermore, it seems to me that vigorous effort to apply the necessary corrective measures to both the science of learning and the technology of education is in the best interests of a healthy science of psychology and a healthy profession of education. But over-riding all these considerations is the conviction that the full realization of the human resources of this nation cannot be achieved without a science-based management of learning processes of our children. It seems to me, therefore, that we should get on with the business, so that within a few years we can know that the goals of educational psychology are at least as well supported by educators, psychologists, educational psychologists, and all of our citizens, as are the goals of military psychology."

16

Patterns of Parenthood as Theories of Learning [1]

JANE LOEVINGER

In this paper, Jane Loevinger looks at the ways in which parents implicitly follow one or another theory of learning in their child-rearing practices. The author points out the effects of the various parental theories on the actual behavior of the offspring. Loevinger, a psychologist at Washington University in St. Louis, is interested in ego development, psychometrics (or test theory), and psychoanalysis, and is the author of a test of ego development. She can be characterized as having a cognitive-developmental approach to socialization. Those concerned with ego development might want to read her paper "The Meaning and Measurement of Ego Development," in The American Psychologist *(1966, 21, 195–217).*

Gerhart Piers (in a talk which I quote from memory) has divided methods of learning into three types: learning by reinforcement, by insight, and by identification. All three types of learning unquestionably occur, and theories of learning espoused by professional psychologists must account for those facts, whatever they take as the prototype of all learning.

[1] Preparation of this note was supported by Research Grant M-1213 from the National Institute of Mental Health, Public Health Service.

Any consistent method of child-rearing contains by implication a theory of how children function, particularly how they learn. One can easily set up a correspondence between well-known patterns of parenthood and the three types of learning. Corresponding to any pattern of child-rearing there is, then, a "theory of learning," emphasizing one type of learning at the expense of others. Theories of learning held by parents are, of course, far more naive and uncomplicated than similar theories held by psychologists. To avoid confusion, the term "parental theory" may be used to distinguish the implicit learning theory.

The disciplinarian parent apparently believes that any wrong thing a child does will be continued indefinitely if the parent does not see that it is punished. While psychological research has tended to emphasize rewards as more effective than punishments as reinforcing agents, disciplinarian parents emphasize punishments as reinforcers.

Apparently insight learning is assumed to predominate by those parents, once reputed to be numerous, who believe that every demand made on a child must be rationalized and explained.

Finally, the typical permissive parent must surely believe that the socialization of his child takes place by means of the child identifying himself with the well-socialized parent.

Consider the following situation. Five-year-old Johnny is beating on his two-year-old sister Sue. Mother comes in. Let us assume that every mother will want to prevent repetition of such behavior. What will she do?

Mother One believes that if Johnny does not feel pain, he will repeat the behavior at every coincidence of impulse and opportunity. She therefore punishes him sharply, thus demonstrating her adherence to a parental reinforcement theory of learning.

Mother Two believes that Johnny can be shown how wrong his conduct is and sets about to persuade him. She believes in a parental insight theory of learning.

Mother Three believes that Johnny wants to grow up to be like his parents. If she punishes him harshly, he will learn that it is all right for the bigger one to be mean to the littler one if he or she feels like it; so his behavior is less likely to be repeated if reprimanded gently than if dealt with harshly. She believes in a parental identification theory of learning.

There is one fallacy common to all parental learning theories. Kelly (1955) points out that we are not victims of our history but only of our con-

Jane Loevinger, "Patterns of parenthood as theories of learning," *Journal of Abnormal and Social Psychology*, 1959, 59, 148–150. Reprinted by permission.

struction of that history. Kelly finds in that fact hope for the psychotherapist. But just as it gives hope for the therapist, it generates despair for the parent. A parent can decide to beat his child, but he cannot decide how the child will construe the beating. Nor, if he abstains from punishing, can he decide how the child will construe the abstention.

Rules for rearing children are beyond the scope of this note, indeed, beyond the competence of the writer. But one superordinate rule can safely be stated: Whatever the parent's theory of learning, the child will in fact be learning by an alternative method. Thus the son of Mother One is probably identifying with a punitive, disciplinarian adult; for the son of Mother Two it is being stamped in that beating on sister has no painful consequences; while the son of Mother Three has probably discerned, "Aha! I can get away with it." The explanation of why a child shifts his mode of learning to escape his parent's vigilant efforts at socialization is not difficult. He is attempting to defend the gratification of his impulses, and in this respect he is not altogether different from his parents.

The foregoing formulation helps to solve two riddles. Why is the battle between the generations fought, generation after generation, with such vigor? And why is it that experts on child-rearing are not conspicuously more successful at the art than those less expert?

The failure of expertise in child-rearing was foreshadowed in 1909 with Freud's (1925) publication of *Analysis of a Phobia in a Five-Year-Old Boy,* for little Hans was the child of two of Freud's followers. One should not make too much of the fact. He was not necessarily the most neurotic child in Vienna, merely the one that Freud had opportunity to observe and indirectly to treat. Nonetheless, the occurrence of so severe a phobia in the child was a striking omen.

Reasons have been advanced for the failure of children of experts to be vastly superior to others in their adjustment. Without disputing or discounting those reasons, one can focus on a slightly different one. The experts know what other parents did wrong, and they avoid those errors. But while they avoid the errors of parents in other houses, their children contrive to defend their instinctual gratification against the parents in their own house. In current terms, a shift in parentmanship is countered by a shift in childmanship.

The battle between the generations is commonly accounted for by the fact that parents have need to socialize their children, and the children forever battle against the socializing process. This view is the one being elaborated here. But it is not quite the whole story. A useful way to test a theory is to see what happens in the most extreme cases.

Redl and Wineman (1957) have depicted extreme cases of "children who hate." Many of the sentiments of those children, such as "Grown-ups don't want kids to have any fun," are echoed occasionally in almost all homes. But the ferocity and implacability of the war with adults is entirely disproportionate to what takes place in an ordinary household. Were their parents, then, so rigorous in their attempts at socialization? On the contrary, the parents of those children presented a picture of impulsivity no less striking than that of the children. The abuses to which the children were subjected could hardly be called punishments; they did not appear to result from any theory of how children learn but rather were crude lashing out on impulse. The picture of parent-child relations in *The Aggressive Child* is a conspicuously undesirable one, both prima facie and in terms of outcome. It serves to demonstrate that not all parents are informed by a parental theory. The battle between the generations is never more vicious than when all pretense of representing the interests of society is dropped and it becomes the parent's impulsivity versus the child's.

A general theory of the battle between generations must account for all of the cases. It must therefore read that the child's impulse gratification conflicts with the needs of society, represented by parents, to socialize him, as well as with the parent's own impulse gratification. The normal parent, to be sure, satisfies many of his desires in and through his children. But moment by moment and day by day the needs which the children gratify are not always uppermost. The presence of an infant or child in the household necessarily imposes delay or surrender on many of the parents' wishes.

The conclusions of this discussion can be stated simply, though they do not exactly simplify life. Every consistent pattern of child-rearing embodies a theory of learning, and all those parental theories are substantially wrong. However, any parental theory is better than none.

Is it possible to base one's pattern of child-rearing on a more nearly realistic theory of learning? That is an intriguing question. In view of the adaptability of the normal child in shifting his tactics to match those of his parents, such a method would require constant reconsideration and change. Yet inconsistency, so the child-rearing experts tell us, is one of the worst faces a parent can turn to his child. Possibly, however, inconsistency got its bad name not from conscientious parents trying to outwit their children but from the label being applied to such parents as Redl and Wineman have sketched.

If, as the present discussion suggests, parental

theories are more wrong than right, how does it happen that it is better to have one than not? The chief value of a parental learning theory may well be in providing a model for the child of curbing one's own impulses out of regard for the future welfare of another. The very oversimplification of parental theories may serve to make accessible to the child that his parent is acting on principle rather than on impulse. To say this is to lay emphasis on learning by identification. But probably most psychologists, whatever their professional theories, act in relation to their own children as if they expect them to learn chiefly by identification.

"All I say is by way of discourse, and nothing by way of advice. . . . I should not speak so boldly, if it were my due to be believed" (de Montaigne, 1913, p. 283).

REFERENCES

DE MONTAIGNE, M. *The essays of Michel de Montaigne.* Vol. III. C. Cotton (Trans.); W. C. Hazlitt (Ed.) London: G. Bell, 1913.

FREUD, S. Analysis of a phobia in a five-year-old boy. In *Collected papers.* Vol. III. London: Hogarth, 1925. Pp. 149–289.

KELLY, G. A. *The psychology of personal constructs.* Vol. II. *Clinical diagnosis and psychotherapy.* New York: Norton, 1955.

REDL, F., and WINEMAN, D. *The aggressive child.* Glencoe, Ill.: Free Press, 1957.

A child is an act of faith about which one grows increasingly uncertain. An adult, it might follow, is a gambler in the process of losing. Still the perpetual motion is love, and within that motion every generation has tried to save what it has already lost by teaching the losing game to its children. This state of confusion is called, by general agreement, Parenthood.

—John Ciardi

17

Interrelations and Correlates over Time in Children's Learning

HAROLD W. STEVENSON,
ANN G. FRIEDRICHS,
AND WILLIAM E. SIMPSON

*This paper is important because it makes three
departures from the usual studies of learning.
(1) It is concerned with individual differences. This
is unlike most studies, which focus on the results
of a given manipulation (e.g., type of reinforcement)
on the behavior of one or more groups, and which
do not examine the variations within the groups.
(2) It studies five different learning tasks instead
of the usual one or two. (3) It is longitudinal, relating performance on laboratory learning tasks
at one time to performance several years later.
Most studies that have been concerned with performance at different ages have looked at the
question cross-sectionally, using different children
in each of the age groups. Rarely has the same
group been studied on laboratory types of learning
tasks over a period of several years, and rarely have
the results at one period of time been related to
those at another. The data in this paper allow us to
give important new consideration to the nature or
structure of learning tasks, of learning processes,
and of their interrelations.*

*For many years, Professor Stevenson was di-
rector of the Institute of Child Development at the
University of Minnesota, where the study was done.
He is now at the University of Michigan. He is the
past president of the Society for Research in Child
Development, a national society that includes
pediatricians, nutritionists, educators, and others
concerned with research involving children. The
third author was a Post-Doctoral Fellow at Minnesota from SUNY, Oswego, N.Y., where he is an
associate professor.*

Developmental psychologists generally have
had little interest in studying the role of individual
differences in children's learning, and have concentrated their attention on the experimental analysis of independent variables. There are reasons,
however, why the investigation of individual differences also may provide important information.
Most theoretical positions have been developed
within the context of a particular type of problem,
such as paired associates, transposition, or reversal
shifts. However, theoretical mechanisms developed
to account for performance in one type of task may
have limited applicability in the discussion of other
types of tasks unless there is a reasonable degree of
consistency between Ss' performance on the
various types of tasks. Thus a better understanding
of individual differences in learning may clarify the
variables that must be included in the development
of satisfactory theories. Furthermore, investigations of interrelations among performance on
different types of learning tasks may help to explicate what we mean by the term "learning ability."
Low intercorrelations among tasks would support
the notion that learning is a composite of many
abilities, while high intercorrelations would
strengthen the conception of learning as a unitary
function. Another approach to the study of individual differences in learning is to investigate
correlates, rather than interrelations in learning.
For example, rather than compare performance on
different types of learning tasks, we may determine
the relation between learning and such factors as
intelligence. Studies of the correlates of children's
learning also may help to delineate the relation
between laboratory studies of children's learning
and everyday learning that occurs at home and

This study was supported in part by a grant (M-3519) from
the National Institute of Mental Health, United States Public
Health Service, to H. W. Stevenson, and by grants to the Center
for Research in Human Learning at the University of Minnesota
from the National Science Foundation (GS-75-541) and the
National Institute of Child Health and Human Development
(HD-01136). We are appreciative of the cooperation of the
staffs at the various schools at which the study was conducted,
and wish to thank Thomas Hertz, Terry Trowbridge, and Monica Christy, who assisted in the study. A.G.F. is now at the
University of North Carolina; W.E.S. is now at State University
of New York, College at Oswego.

school. Without information about the relation between performance in experimental tasks and in school it is impossible to determine whether laboratory research on learning is as remote from everyday life as some critics would assert.

Recently, several studies have departed from the traditional pattern described above (e.g., Cronbach & Snow 1969; Duncanson 1964; Rohwer 1970; Stake 1961). Of special interest here is the report by Stevenson, Hale, Klein, and Miller (1968), which forms the background for the present study. As part of their project, nearly 500 children in grades 3 through 7 were presented a series of nine learning and problem-solving tasks. Measures of intelligence, school achievement, and school grades were available for these Ss. Generally, the intercorrelations among tasks were of moderate strength. Correlations across the two categories of tasks were as high as those within the two categories, and the correlations between performance on the experimental tasks and measures of intelligence and long-term learning actually were higher than the intercorrelations among the tasks themselves.

The children who participated in the Stevenson et al. study resided in an area with a stable population. It seemed feasible, therefore, to extend the earlier findings by retesting a portion of these Ss. At the time the present study was undertaken, Ss who had been in the fourth grade in the original study were enrolled in the seventh grade, the highest grade for which the tasks seemed appropriate and data had been collected. By having original and retest data it was possible to compare the stability of interrelations and correlates of children's learning across a 3-year period, a type of comparison that was impossible with the cross-sectional data obtained in the original study. Since children who had not participated in the original

study also were enrolled in the seventh-grade classrooms, these "new" Ss provided a replication of the original seventh-grade sample.

It was not possible to secure enough time to permit retesting with all nine tasks. The five tasks that were selected were those that had yielded the highest correlations in the original study: paired-associate learning, discrimination learning, incidental learning, verbal memory, and anagrams.

METHOD

SUBJECTS

The Ss were 211 students, the entire enrollment in the eight classrooms of the seventh grade of a junior high school in Minneapolis, the same school attended by seventh graders in the Stevenson et al. study. Of these 211 Ss, 73 had been tested when they were enrolled in the fourth grade. This number constituted 67 percent of the original fourth-grade sample. Nearly all of the remaining 138 Ss had attended elementary schools in the same area of the city as the original Ss, but had not participated in the earlier study. Descriptive information about both groups of Ss is presented in table 1. As can be seen, the ages and IQ scores were very similar for old and new Ss.

FILMS

All tasks were presented on film and Ss responded in booklets. Complete descriptions of the procedure for each task may be found in Stevenson et al. (1968). The instructions and procedure were presented by a narrator in the films. Essentially, the tasks were as follows:

Paired associates.—Six stimulus-response pairs were used. Stimulus elements were trigrams with high association values (e.g., DAG, KOT) and response elements were common abstract words (e.g., health, joy). After the list had been presented, the first page of the response booklet appeared on the screen and the narrator gave the

TABLE 1
MEAN CA AND IQ OF Ss

Variable	Boys			Girls		
		Grade 7			Grade 7	
	Grade 4	Old Ss	New Ss	Grade 4	Old Ss	New Ss
CA (in years):						
M	9.9	12.4	12.5	9.7	12.3	12.4
SD	0.5	0.3	0.7	0.4	0.4	0.5
IQ (verbal):						
M	100.0	103.0	100.0	109.0	108.0	103.0
SD	17.4	15.7	16.5	16.2	13.1	14.5
IQ (nonverbal):						
M	106.0	111.0	109.0	119.0	115.0	112.0
SD	16.4	13.1	14.5	10.4	12.6	13.4
N (range)	34–38	33–39	61–78	33–36	30–34	43–60

instructions for responding. The projector was turned off while Ss circled the response element they thought was associated with each stimulus element. This procedure was followed for six presentations of the list, yielding a maximum score of 36 correct responses.

Discrimination learning.—The stimuli were four letterlike forms that appeared in different horizontal orders on each trial. Correct response was dictated by a cue (triangle, square, circle, diamond) that appeared above the stimulus array. On each trial S was required to look at the cue and to mark the form he thought was correct. After 8 seconds E asked the Ss to look at the screen and then pointed to the correct form. This procedure was followed for each of the 48 trials.

Incidental learning.—An 8-minute skit was filmed in sound and color. The skit took place in a living room where a man and a woman were conversing about everyday topics. A visiting woman and a delivery man appeared as part of the plot. No instructions were given before the film. Afterward, Ss were given a booklet containing 31 multiple-choice and true-false questions about incidental aspects of the content, costuming, and setting. The screen was blank while the narrator read each question.

Verbal memory.—This task was derived from the "Memory for Stories, I: The School Concert" at year X of form M of the Revised Stanford-Binet. The narrator read the instructions, indicating Ss would be asked questions about the story and then read the one-paragraph story. The standard questions contained in this subtest were printed in Ss' booklets. The maximum score was 14 points.

Anagrams.—The Ss were asked to make as many words as possible in 6 minutes from the letters contained in the word "generation." The narrator demonstrated the anagrams game with the word "federal" by constructing the words "leader," "leaf," and "deer" as examples.

PROCEDURE

The Ss were tested in their classrooms on 2 successive days. Two Es were present in each classroom. After being introduced by the teacher, one E stated that they had some films they wished to show and were interested in how individuals of Ss' ages would respond to questions asked in the films. Other than presenting this brief introduction, the Es' major function was to monitor Ss' performance and to provide clarification of individual Ss' questions. The tasks were presented in six different orders across the eight classrooms; only two of the orders were used twice.

RESULTS

AVERAGE LEVELS OF PERFORMANCE

The first question is whether performance improved over the 3-year period. The t's comparing scores obtained in grades 4 and 7 were significant (t's > 1.90, p < .05) for all but verbal memory, where performance was higher, but not significantly so, in grade 7.

A second question is whether performance was comparable for the old and new seventh graders. When t's were computed between the average levels of performance of these two groups, the only significant difference was for discrimination learning by girls ($t = 2.38$, $df = 77$, $p < .05$). It appears, therefore, that Ss gained little benefit from having performed the tasks 3 years earlier.

INTERRELATIONS AMONG TASKS

Three types of correlations were computed for the data from the "old" Ss. First, intertask correlations were computed using the data obtained at grade 4. Second, correlations were computed between performance in

TABLE 2
MEAN NUMBER OF CORRECT RESPONSES FOR EACH TASK ACCORDING TO GRADE AND SEX OF S

| | Grade 4 | | Grade 7 | | | |
| | | | Old Ss | | New Ss | |
Task	M	SD	M	SD	M	SD
			Boys			
Paired associates	20.8	8.1	29.3	8.0	28.3	8.0
Discrimination learning	30.0	10.6	38.0	8.4	37.2	9.7
Incidental learning	22.0	4.2	24.8	2.1	24.5	2.8
Verbal memory	7.0	2.8	7.8	3.3	7.7	3.0
Anagrams	14.2	5.2	16.5	7.8	15.8	7.3
			Girls			
Paired associates	23.4	8.4	31.2	5.5	28.8	6.9
Discrimination learning	31.4	11.7	39.1	7.4	34.5	9.8
Incidental learning	23.4	3.3	25.3	2.6	25.7	2.2
Verbal memory	8.1	3.0	9.1	3.3	8.4	3.4
Anagrams	17.4	6.7	20.3	6.5	21.1	8.4

grades 4 and 7. Finally, intertask correlations were computed for the data obtained at grade 7. These correlation matrices are presented in table 3.

The correlations among the tasks were higher at grade 4 than at grade 7 in seven of the 10 comparisons; thus the developmental changes in the interrelations were toward greater differentiation of learning abilities. Within-task correlations between grades 4 and 7 were significant for three of the tasks: discrimination learning, verbal memory, and anagrams. Thus seventh-grade performance could be predicted from fourth-grade performance on these tasks, but not for paired-associate or incidental learning.

The correlations between performance at grades 4 and 7 revealed several interesting effects. Of special interest is the fact that the correlations between paired-associate learning and incidental learning, verbal memory, and anagrams at grade 7 were lower than comparable correlations obtained for paired-associate learning at grade 4 and performance on the other tasks at grade 7. For example, the correlation between paired-associate learning and verbal memory at grade 7 was .29, while the correlation between paired-associate learning at grade 4 and verbal memory at grade 7 was .56; the correlation between paired-associate learning and anagrams at grade 7 was .12, while the correlation between paired-associate learning at grade 4 and anagrams at grade 7 was .41. Another way of looking at this phenomenon is to compare performance on pairs of tasks given at grades 4 and 7. For example, paired-associate learning given at grade 7

correlated .35 with verbal memory given at grade 4, while paired-associate learning given at grade 4 correlated .56 with verbal memory given at grade 7; paired-associate learning given at grade 7 correlated .04 with anagrams given at grade 4, while paired-associate learning given at grade 4 correlated at .41 with anagrams given at grade 7. In both types of comparison, therefore, the fourth-grade results for paired-associate learning have greater predictive strength than either concurrent or retrospective predictions made from the data for paired associates obtained at grade 7.

The same pattern was not found for discrimination learning. Correlations between discrimination learning and the other tasks were of the same magnitude at grade 7 as the correlations between discrimination learning given at grade 4 and the other tasks given at grade 7. Similarly, the prediction of performance was as high from grades 4 to 7 as from grades 7 to 4 when performance on discrimination learning was used as the predictive variable.

Nor was the pattern that appeared for paired-associate learning found in the correlations for incidental learning. The relations among the correlations here were similar to those obtained for discrimination learning. The most consistently high correlations with other tasks were obtained for verbal memory, whether it was given at grade 4 or 7. Anagrams given at grade 4 correlated more highly with anagrams given at grade 7 than with any of the other tasks given at grade 7, and no stronger predictions could be made from anagrams given at grade 4 than from anagrams given at grade 7.

TABLE 3
CORRELATIONS BETWEEN PERFORMANCE IN GRADES 4 AND 7

Task	1	2	3	4	5
			Grade 4		
Grade 4:					
1. Paired associates	...	.39**	.31*	.48**	.51**
2. Discrimination learning	...	...	.33**	.41**	.17
3. Incidental learning	...	...	...	.37**	.26*
4. Verbal memory	...	...	...	...	.49**
5. Anagrams	...	...	...	...	...
			Grade 7		
Grade 4:					
1. Paired associates	.19	.18	.34**	.56**	.41**
2. Discrimination learning	.35**	.39**	.09	.31*	.25
3. Incidental learning	.14	.20	.24	.42**	.23
4. Verbal memory	.35**	.29*	.40**	.46**	.45**
5. Anagrams	.04	.27*	.25	.22	.54**
			Grade 7		
Grade 7 (old Ss)					
1. Paired associates	...	.24	.21	.29*	.12
2. Discrimination learning	...	...	.04	.31*	.30*
3. Incidental learning	...	...	...	.45**	.27*
4. Verbal memory	...	...	...	...	.28*
5. Anagrams	...	...	...	...	...

* p < .05.
** p < .01.

Intercorrelations among the tasks also were computed for the new Ss in grade 7. As may be seen in tables 3 and 4, the range in values of the correlations were comparable for the new and old Ss (.11–.30 versus .04–.45).

TABLE 4
INTERRELATIONS AMONG TASKS, NEW Ss

Task	2	3	4	5
1. Paired associates	.30**	.13	.22*	.28**
2. Discrimination learning	...	.24*	.22*	.12
3. Incidental learning	...	...	.20*	.11
4. Verbal memory..................	...	...	...	.23*
5. Anagrams	...	...	...	...

* $p < .05$.
** $p < .01$.

CORRELATES OF PERFORMANCE

Intelligence. Correlations were computed between performance on the experimental tasks and IQ scores obtained from the Lorge-Thorndike test of intelligence. The correlations were computed separately for the verbal and nonverbal scores on this test; however, these two scores are highly related ($r = .73$). As can be seen in

table 5, the frequency of significant correlations was as great at grade 7 as at grade 4. There was a tendency for the correlations to be higher for the old Ss than for the new Ss in grade 7. Considering the brevity of the learning tasks and the use of group IQ scores, the correlations are substantial. There was no apparent difference in the strength of the relation between intelligence and performance on the various tasks.

Achievement scores. Scores were available at both grades 4 and 7 for the Iowa Tests of Basic Skills, a measure of long-term learning in school. Approximately three-fourths of these correlations were significant, indicating that the short-term laboratory measures of learning were related to children's learning in school. The lowest correlations were obtained for discrimination learning, and the highest for anagrams. The frequency of significant correlations was similar in grades 4 and 7, except for the correlations for the old Ss between the learning tasks and work-study skills and arithmetic. The correlations are presented in table 6.

School grades. Grades are first assigned in the Minneapolis schools in the seventh grade. Grades in four core subjects, English, social studies, science, and mathematics, were obtained for the Fall quarter of the seventh grade. These grades were correlated with per-

TABLE 5
CORRELATIONS BETWEEN PERFORMANCE ON EXPERIMENTAL TASKS AND LORGE-THORNDIKE IQ AT GRADES 4 AND 7 (OLD AND NEW Ss)

Task	IQ (Verbal)			IQ (Nonverbal)		
	Grade 4	Grade 7		Grade 4	Grade 7	
		Old Ss	New Ss		Old Ss	New Ss
1. Paired associates	.54**	.39**	.47**	.49**	.18	.56**
2. Discrimination learning	.44**	.36**	.30**	.40**	.40**	.36**
3. Incidental learning	.53**	.44**	.35**	.45**	.34**	.33**
4. Verbal memory	.68**	.56**	.36**	.51**	.49**	.22*
5. Anagrams	.57**	.62**	.45**	.58**	.69**	.37**

* $p < .05$.
** $p < .01$.

TABLE 6
CORRELATIONS BETWEEN SCORES ON IOWA TESTS OF BASIC SKILLS AND PERFORMANCE ON EXPERIMENTAL TASKS IN GRADES 4 AND 7

Task	Total Language			Total Work Study			Total Arithmetic		
	Grade 4	Grade 7		Grade 4	Grade 7		Grade 4	Grade 7	
		Old Ss	New Ss		Old Ss	New Ss		Old Ss	New Ss
1. Paired associates	.33**	.24	.42**	.40**	.23	.40**	.38**	.13	.42**
2. Discrimination learning	.15	.32**	.29*	.17	.17	.24*	.21	.23	.25*
3. Incidental learning	.32*	.31*	.35**	.32*	.24	.37**	.34*	.24	.35**
4. Verbal memory..................	.51**	.40**	.38**	.48**	.17	.28*	.50**	.42**	.20*
5. Anagrams	.54**	.58**	.53**	.55**	.30*	.52**	.55**	.63**	.52**

* $p < .05$.
** $p < .01$.

TABLE 7
CORRELATIONS OF PERFORMANCE AT GRADES 4 AND 7 WITH GRADE 7 GRADES

	Boys				Girls			
	Eng.	Soc. Stud.	Sci.	Math.	Eng.	Soc. Stud.	Sci.	Math.
Paired associates:								
Grade 4	.24	.18	.32	.51*	.31	.32	.26	.33
Grade 7	.26*	.12	.34**	.35**	.16	.24*	.35**	.29*
Discrimination learning:								
Grade 4	.25	.30	.20	.24	.20	.30	.25	.44*
Grade 7	.31**	.22	.45**	.35**	.22	.04	.24*	.27*
Incidental learning:								
Grade 4	.32	.51*	.16	.19	.55**	.56*	.50**	.53**
Grade 7	.18	.19	.29**	.26*	.39**	.26*	.13	.31**
Verbal memory:								
Grade 4	.14	.16	.38*	.31	.47**	.30	.36*	.32
Grade 7	.23*	.15	.26*	.27**	.54**	.44**	.27*	.50**
Anagrams:								
Grade 4	.32	.24	.48**	.43**	.39*	.46**	.37*	.45**
Grade 7	.52**	.22*	.43**	.42**	.53**	.43**	.32**	.42**

* $p < .05$.
** $p < .01$.

formance of all Ss on the experimental tasks in grade 7 and with that of old Ss when they were in grade 4 (see table 7). Generally, the seventh-grade correlations are lower than those obtained by Stevenson et al. (1968). There were some sex differences in the patterns of correlations. Whereas 16 of the 20 correlations between seventh-grade performance and seventh-grade grades were significant for each sex, only five of the correlations with fourth-grade performance were significant for boys, while 11 were significant for girls.

DISCUSSION

Several portions of the present results closely parallel those of Stevenson et al. (1968). The median intercorrelation among the tasks was .28 at grade 7 in the earlier study, while in the present study the median intercorrelations for old and new Ss were .27 and .22, respectively. Since the median intercorrelation among these tasks at grade 4 was .38, there is some evidence of increasing specificity in learning functions with increasing age. As in the previous study, the correlations between performance on the tasks and IQ were significant, and, as found earlier, these correlations actually were higher than the intercorrelations among the tasks themselves. For example, the median correlations found between performance on the various tasks and IQ were .44 and .36 for the old and new Ss, and .47 for the Ss in the earlier study. In spite of the fact that these correlations were significant and above the median intercorrelation among the tasks, they enable us to relate less than 25 percent of the variance in performance with variance in IQ. The

relations between performance on the experimental tasks and measures of long-term learning also were significant. The median correlations with achievement test scores were .24 and .36 for the old and new Ss in the present study, and .42 in the earlier study. The median correlations between school grades and performance on the experimental tasks were .31 for both old and new Ss, and .36 in the earlier study. In general, then, the magnitude of the correlations obtained in the two studies is quite similar.

The Ss maintained significantly stable positions within the group on discrimination learning, verbal memory, and anagrams over a 3-year period. That is, Ss who performed effectively on these tasks in the fourth grade also tended to achieve the highest scores in the seventh grade. Performance on the other two tasks, paired associates and incidental learning, did not show such stability. The failure to find significant correlations over time for paired associates was not due to unreliability of the task, since the correlations between paired associates at the fourth grade and incidental learning, verbal memory, and anagrams at the seventh grade were significant. Paradoxically, then, fourth-grade paired-associate learning predicted performance on a task like anagrams at the seventh grade better than it predicted seventh-grade paired-associate learning. A likely interpretation of this finding is that effective performance on paired-associate learning in the fourth grade involved the elaboration of the verbal materials in the production of associations and the use of other mnemonic techniques.

The *S*s who were able to do this in the fourth grade were those who were able to utilize such abilities in other verbal tasks in the seventh grade. Paired-associate learning at grade 7 may not have differentiated among the *S*s on the basis of verbal facility. The insignificant correlation between paired associates and anagrams at grade 7 would point toward this possibility.

Interestingly, incidental learning at the fourth grade was significantly correlated with seventh-grade performance on verbal memory, but was not correlated with seventh-grade incidental learning. Only on incidental learning did *S*s indicate that they remembered seeing the film before. If this were the case for most of the *S*s, what was incidental learning at grade 4 became intentional learning at grade 7. Supporting such an argument is the fact that the correlation between incidental learning and verbal memory was the highest among the tasks for the old *S*s at grade 7 and only intermediate among the correlations for the new *S*s and for *S*s at grade 4. In other words, incidental learning was related to verbal memory for all groups, but the relation was highest for *S*s who had seen the film before.

The pattern of correlations for verbal memory and discrimination learning differed from those obtained for paired associates and incidental learning. Verbal memory was a highly general function; the correlations between verbal memory at grade 4 and performance on all other tasks at grade 7 were significant, as were all of the correlations between verbal memory and the other tasks within grades 4 and 7. This high density of significant correlations was found only for verbal memory.

Because of the structure of the discrimination-learning task, a high relation between discrimination learning and the learning of paired associates would be expected. Both involved learning associations, words with nonsense syllables in the one case and abstract symbols with geometric forms in the other. Discrimination learning at grade 4 was significantly related to both paired-associate and discrimination learning at grade 7. However, paired-associate learning at grade 4 was related to neither paired-associate nor discrimination learning at grade 7. Discrimination learning was related to paired-associate learning in grade 4 but not in grade 7. Without further information, the interpretation of these relations remains unclear. Perhaps the process of paired-associate learning, at least when it involves the use of verbal materials, is changing more rapidly between grades 4 and 7 than is that of learning to discriminate among abstract symbols.

The major implications of the results of this study is that the discussion of children's learning is dependent upon an understanding of the processes underlying performance on a task, rather than upon an analysis of the structure of the task. Although this point has been made before, its importance is emphasized by the longitudinal data obtained in this study. If we consider only the structure of a task, it is impossible to predict the interrelations among tasks for either concurrent or future performance. As has been indicated, paired-associate and discrimination-learning tasks appear to have more similar structures than do paired associates and anagrams. In spite of this fact, we cannot predict later performance in discrimination learning, given information about earlier paired-associate learning. We can, however, make reliable predictions about later performance in anagrams. Without a close relation between structure and process, such as often exists in learning by adults, it becomes much more difficult to develop adequate theories of children's learning. The processes elicited by tasks with particular structures will not necessarily be comparable at one age level, nor will they be the same as those elicited by the tasks at a later age.

REFERENCES

CRONBACH, L., & SNOW, R. E. Individual differences in learning ability as a function of instructional variables. Final report, grant OEC 4–6–061269–1217, Stanford University, March 1969.

DUNCANSON, J. P. *Intelligence and the ability to learn.* Princeton, N.J.: Educational Testing Service, 1964.

ROHWER, W. Mental elaboration and proficient learning. In J. P. Hill (Ed.), *Minnesota symposia on child psychology.* Minneapolis: University of Minnesota Press, 1970.

STAKE, R. E. Learning parameters, aptitudes, and achievements. *Psychometric Monographs,* 1961, *1* (Whole No. 9).

STEVENSON, H. W.; HALE, G. A.; KLEIN, R. E.; & MILLER, L. K. Interrelations and correlates in children's learning and problem-solving. *Monographs of the Society for Research in Child Development,* 1968, *33* (7, Serial No. 123).

18

A Theoretical Framework for Personality and Social Behavior [1]

ROBERT R. SEARS

In this paper Robert Sears provides a transition between learning as a determinant of behavior and interpersonal experiences as a determinant. Indeed, Sears shows us that the two classes of determinants cannot be conceived of as separate. He focuses on the analysis of behavior in a dyadic or two-person unit. Had child and educational psychologists acted promptly on the principles Sears enunciated in this 1951 presidential address to the American Psychological Association, the fields might be further ahead in their understanding of behavior. Only recently has research design focused on two-person interaction. Bell's article in Section IV provides further discussion of this issue. Since learning in both home and school involves such dyadic relations, it is particularly discouraging to realize how long it took to effect this change in our mode of thinking and research.

Like Whiting (see Section II), Sears is a product of Yale's Institute of Human Relations during a period of active inter- and cross-disciplinary ferment. He participated in the work relating frustration to aggression that was one of the germinal products of the group at the institute. (Other products were Hull's exacting systematization of learning theory and Personality and Psychotherapy

[McGraw Hill, New York, 1950], by John Dollard [a clinical psychologist] and Neal E. Miller [an experimental psychologist]. Personality and Psychotherapy presented a simpler, more concise version of the learning theory and applied it to analysis of the therapeutic process. In short, in that period Yale influenced many behavioral scientists and spawned many of the leaders of American psychology for the next three decades.)

Sears has served as director (1942–1949) of the Iowa Child Welfare Research Station, one of the longtime active research centers. He was director of Harvard's Laboratory of Human Development (1949–1953), where he co-authored the study in the next section. Since 1953 he has been a professor at Stanford University, where he headed the Psychology Department from 1953–1962. He has now returned to the laboratory and classroom after being Dean of the School of Humanities and Science from 1962–1970.

I wish to consider some systematic aspects of personality and social psychology, and to indicate what seem to me the directions further development of these fields is likely to take. Partly these directions are dictated by more general developments in psychology and the social sciences; but partly they are matters of choice, and of estimate as to what will provide us with the most effective science of human behavior.

Perhaps the most impressive thing about both these fields is the extent to which, in recent years, they have become empirical. The opinion poll, small group observational procedures, and attitude scales have contributed notably to the precision with which the actions of groups can be measured and their future behavior predicted. Similarly, in the field of personality and motivation, such devices as the TAT, doll play, behavior unit observations, and standardized interviews have become more and more effective for providing objective and quantified statements about significant variables.

From a practical standpoint, some of these methods have been extraordinarily valuable. Market surveys, studies of morale in the military services, diagnostic analyses of disturbed children, and comparative studies of techniques of teaching have yielded findings that have much improved the quality of human output. In effect, the past decade has put in the hands of any competent technician procedures which permit the empirical discovery of facts and principles that hitherto had been the province of so-called men of wisdom. For many

---

[1] Address of the President of the American Psychological Association at Chicago, Illinois, September 3, 1951.

areas of human action, intuitively skillful lucky guessing has given way to precise and replicable investigation.

THEORY

This empirical progress has been accompanied by the construction of but a minimal amount of theory. Perhaps it could not have been otherwise. Theory does not grow in the absence of data, and until the last two decades, the data of social psychology have been meager and those of personality limited mainly to clinical observations.

Yet it is clear that further development in these fields will require an adequate theory. By a *theory* I mean a set of variables and the propositions that relate them to one another as antecedents and consequents. This involves such logical impedimenta as definitions, postulates, and theorems. And it requires the following of certain rules, such as that the definitions of variables must be mutually exclusive; that intervening variables must ultimately be reducible to operations; that the reference events specified as the consequents in theorems must be measured independently of the antecedents from which they are derived, and so on. The general procedure of theory construction is sufficiently standard that it needs no explication here.

The *findings* to be integrated are those that describe consistent relationships between behavior (or its products) and some other events. Essentially, these are the descriptive behavioral relationships that comprise the disciplines of individual and social psychology, sociology, and anthropology. Individual and group behavior are so inextricably intertwined, both as to cause and effect, that an adequate behavior theory must combine both in a single internally congruent system.

There are two main advantages of a good theory that make such a development urgent. First, it is economical in the sense that it permits many observed relationships to be subsumed under a single systematic proposition. And second, it permits the use of multiple variables and their relating principles, in combination, for the prediction of events.

These virtues have long been recognized. Several psychologists have constructed conceptual frameworks within which the facts of either social psychology or personality could be theoretically formulated. McDougall (11), Floyd Allport (1), and Kurt Lewin (10) provided them for social psychology; Freud (5), G. V. Hamilton (6), Lewin (9), Gordon Allport (2), and H. A. Murray (13) have done the same for personality. Examples of the application of theory construction to problems important in social psychology and personality are to be found in Festinger's work on communica-

tion (4), Miller's studies of displacement (12), and our own analyses of the projective process in parent-child relationships (7, 17, 18).

ACTION

Every theory must have a subject-matter. It must be a theory about something, obviously. A certain class of events must be selected for explication. These are the reference events, the consequents for which antecedents are discovered. The basic events to which behavior theory has reference are *actions*. This follows from the very nature of our interest in man. It is his behavior, the things he does, the ends he accomplishes, that concern us.

From a logical standpoint, a theory is of value to the extent that it orders a set of observations. There are many kinds of observations that can be and have been made of social and individual behavior. Some of these have involved inferred traits or needs; others have related to perceptions or to states of consciousness. By the criterion of logic, a theory that takes any of these phenomena as its basic reference events is acceptable.

But there is another criterion to be considered, the practical one. It is reasonable to ask what kind of events are important to us. On this score, action is clearly more significant than perception or traits. The clinician must make judgments about personality that will permit predictions of behavior. Will the patient attempt suicide? Will his performance at intellectual tasks continue to deteriorate? Will his level of social problem-solving improve under an anxiety-reduction therapy? Likewise, the teacher and the parent undertake methods of rearing a child with expectations that his actions will change in a particular direction. They want him to add more accurately, or paint more freely, or cry less violently when he is disappointed; even those changes commonly interpreted as perceptual, such as art or music appreciation, are evidenced in the form of choices as to where to go, what to look at, what to listen to.

The situation is even clearer with respect to social behavior. The social engineer is concerned with such questions as whether a certain parent-child relationship will establish habitually dependent behavior in the child, whether the eventual marriage of a courting couple will terminate in divorce or in the social facilitation of their mutual labors, whether citizens will buy bonds or vote for a Congressman, whether a group will be shattered or solidified by external opposition, i.e., whether there will be an increase or decrease in cooperative efforts and in-group aggression.

Aside from the fact that a behavior science, rather than a *need* or *perceptual* science, is of the greatest use to us, there is an evident practical advantage. Human beings deal with one another in terms of actions. The teacher has direct observation of the performance of her pupils. The parent or the husband or the foreman or the Congressman can have only inferential knowledge of the ideas or desires of those with whom he interacts. But he can describe the conditions that impinge on people and he can take note of the behavioral consequences. To put the argument briefly: actions are the events of most importance, and actions are most available to observation and measurement.

This is not to say that needs or motives, perceptions, traits, and other such internalized structures or processes are irrelevant. Any scientific system must contain both operational and intervening variables that are independent of the reference events forming the subject-matter of the system. But the choosing of such variables must depend on their contribution to a theory that will predict actions. There is no virtue in a descriptive statement that a person or a class of persons possesses such and such a trait or need unless that statement is part of a larger one that concludes with a specification of a kind of action to be performed. To describe a person as having *high emotionality* or *low sensitivity* or *diffuse anxiety* is systematically acceptable only if other variables are added that will, together with these internal personal properties, specify what kind of behavior can be expected from him under some specific circumstances. [See Skinner, Article 13, for further discussion of these points. —EDITOR]

DYNAMICS

By definition a theory of action is dynamic; i.e., it has to do with force or energy in motion. The term *dynamic* has been so abused by psychologists during the last half century, however, that its meaning is no longer clear. Perhaps it never was. But with successive "dynamic psychologies"—those of Freud, Morton Prince, Woodworth, Lewin, and a host of contemporary theorists—its meaning has been more obfuscated than ever. Sometimes it refers to a motivational approach, sometimes to a developmental, sometimes to an emphasis on unconscious processes. Mostly, I suspect, it merely means the theorist is revolting against what seem to him the stultifying structuralistic, unhuman inadequacies of his predecessors. It boils down to a self-attributed accolade for virtue, a promise to deal with important characteristics of real live people rather than dry and dusty processes.

This is a waste of a good word. By no means all modern psychological systems are dynamic; some are trait-based and some are need-based.

No one would deny that combinations of habit structures do exist and do provide a kind of integrated consistency in a person's behavior. Likewise, no one would attempt to order the events of human action without variables that relate to motivation, including those kinds of motivation that cannot be verbally reported by the person himself. But there is more to dynamics than motivation. There is *change*.

Changes in behavior are of two kinds. For a theory to be dynamic, both must be systematized separately but congruently. One is ongoing action, or *performance,* and the other is learning, or *acquisition.* Obviously, no predictive statement can be made about ongoing action unless certain things are known about the person's *potentialities for action.* He has certain properties that determine what kind of behavior he will produce under any given set of circumstances. His motivation is weak or strong, he is frustrated or not in various goal-directed sequences, he has expectancies of the consequences of his behavior. Unless these are known, it is impossible to have any systematization of ongoing action. And unless the *changes* in potentialities for action are systematically ordered, there is no possibility of constructing an ongoing action theory that will enable one to predict beyond the termination of any single sequence of behavior.

The combining of these two approaches to behavior has not yet been fully accomplished. The most elaborate theory of performance, or ongoing action, is that of Kurt Lewin (9), but his field theory has never been developed to care adequately for problems of personality development (learning). Similarly, the developmental theory of G. V. Hamilton (6) gave an excellent account of the acquisition of potentialities for response but did not cover so effectively the problems of ongoing action.[2]

MONADIC AND DYADIC UNITS

I have already made reference to the desirability of combining individual and social behavior into a single theoretical system. The reasons are ob-

[2] A simple behavior sequence is shown in Figure 1. The various potentialities for action are specified by S_D (motivation) and S_{cog} (cognitive structures). In large part these characteristics are a product of learning. The successful completion of a behavior sequence is a reinforcement, and this modifies the drives and habit structures of the person in certain lawful ways, these laws being part of the body of the laws of learning. In other words, there is a change in the person's potentialities for action. It is to be noted, therefore, that although Figure 1 describes a single behavior sequence, there are two ways of ordering the events that compose it. Both refer to changes, to energy in motion. To be dynamic, a theory of behavior must encompass both.

vious. In any social interaction, the interests, motives, habits or other psychological properties of the acting individuals determine to some degree the kind of interaction that will occur. The shy youngster is likely to have less stimulating learning experiences with his teacher than is a bolder one; the traveller in a foreign land who knows the language forms different kinds of friendships than the one who uses an interpreter. Conversely, the social milieu, the interpersonal relationships, within which a person acts determine his psychological properties. A man in a subordinate role cannot act as a leader; a child reared as the younger of two develops differently from one reared as the elder of two. Whether the group's behavior is dealt with as antecedent and the individual's as consequent, or vice versa, the two kinds of event are so commonly mixed in causal relationships that it is impractical to conceptualize them separately.

To wish for a combining theoretical framework is one thing, but to get it from psychologists is quite another. Sociologists have been more accustomed to think in such terms. The theoretical analyses of Cottrell (3) and of Parsons (15) have emphasized particularly the interactive processes. Among psychologists, Newcomb (14), with his exposition of role expectancy, and Festinger (4), in his studies of group cohesiveness, clearly exemplify the trend toward combination. In the main, however, in spite of their long prepossession with social influences on the individual, psychologists think monadically. That is, they choose the behavior of one person as their scientific subject matter. For them, the universe is composed of individuals. These individuals are acted upon by external events, to be sure, and in turn the external world is modified by the individuals' behaviors. But the universal laws sought by the psychologist almost always relate to a single body. They are monadic laws, and they are stated with reference to a monadic unit of behavior.

The main variables that compose such systems have been presented diagrammatically in many ways. Some are so well known as virtually to represent signatures for the theorists who devised them. There are Tolman's schematic sowbug, Hull's behavior sequence, Lewin's field structure, and Miller and Dollard's learning paradigm. These diagrams differ considerably in the kinds of variables they incorporate. Some emphasize reward and reinforcement; others do not. Some are time-oriented; others are descriptive of a nontemporal force field. All specify antecedent stimulus conditions and consequent actions, but in very different ways and with quite different systematic constructs. But there is one thing in common among them—they are all monadic.

But if personality and social behavior are to be included in a single theory, the basic monadic unit of behavior must be expandable into a dyadic one. A dyadic unit is one that describes the combined actions of two or more persons.[3] A dyadic unit is essential if there is to be any conceptualization of the *relationships* between people, as in the parent-child, teacher-pupil, husband-wife, or leader-follower instances. To have a science of interactive events, one must have variables and units of action that refer to such events. While it is possible to systematize some observations about individuals by using monadic units, the fact is that a large proportion of the properties of a person that compose his personality are originally formed in dyadic situations and are measurable only by reference to dyadic situations or symbolic representations of them. Thus, even a monadic description of a person's action, makes use of dyadic variables in the form of social stimuli.

This is exemplified in Figure 1, a diagram of a monadic behavior sequence that, as will be seen, can be expanded into a dyadic sequence. One aspect of this figure deserves comment, the *environmental event*. This concept refers to the changes produced in the environment by the instrumental activity; these are the changes necessary for the occurrence of the goal response. The teacher trying to increase participatory activity in a class of children, for example, gets her reward when the youngsters spontaneously start a team game at recess. She makes her goal response—she has achieved her aim—when the environment changes, i.e., when the children play a team game. Or a boy is seeking approbation from his father; he hits a three-bagger; his father grins with satisfaction. The grin is the boy's environmental event in his monadically conceived action sequence.

This concept achieves importance in the present context, because it is the necessary connecting link between a monadic and dyadic systematization of behavior. The framework for such a

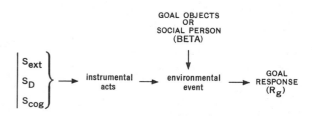

FIGURE 1. *The monadic instigation-action sequence.*

[3] Although the prefix means "two," the term is used here simply as the minimal instance of multiplicity. Similar principles would hold whether the interactors were two or more.

description is shown in Figure 2. For convenience the two persons are labelled Alpha and Beta. A dyadic situation exists whenever the actions of Beta produce the environmental events for Alpha, and vice versa. The behavior of each person is essential to the other's successful completion of his goal directed sequence of action. The drives of each are satisfied only when the motivated actions of the other are carried through to completion. The nurturant mother is satisfied by the fully-loved child's expression of satiety, and the child is satisfied by the expressions of nurturance given by his mother.

It must be made clear in this connection that environmental events are *only those changes in environment produced by the behavior of the person under consideration.* The stroke of lightning that splits a log for the tired woodcutter is not in this category, nor is the food given the newborn infant by his mother, nor the empty taxi that providentially appears when the rain is at its worst. These are certainly characteristics of the environment, manipulanda that govern in some ways the future behavior of Alpha, but they are not environmental events in the sense that the term is used here. They were not induced by any action of Alpha.

This is an important distinction. Unless the interaction of Alpha and Beta is based on something other than the fortuitously useful conjunction of their individual actions, there is no interdependence of each on the other. There is, in effect, no dyadic system, only a piling up of parallel monadic sequences.

The factor responsible for maintaining stability of the dyadic unit is exhibited in Figure 3. It is the *expectancy* of the environmental event, diagrammed in a notation similar to that used by Hull for the anticipatory goal response (8). In the present case, the anticipatory response is a fractional part of the reactions Alpha makes to those behaviors of Beta that constitute the environmental event. For example, if a child wants to be kissed good-night, his mother must lean toward him affectionately and kiss him. He, in turn,

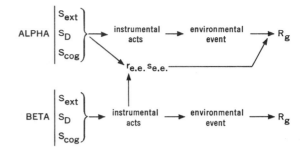

FIGURE 3. *The dyadic sequence with anticipatory responses to the environmental event.*

must slip his arms around her neck and lift his face to hers receptively. These latter movements are the ones that fractionate and become anticipatory in Alpha's behavior sequence. And as in the case of the anticipatory goal response, they elicit response-produced stimuli ($r_{ee}s_{ee}$) that become integrated into the total stimulus constellation which serves to instigate this behavior sequence on future occasions.

These anticipatory reactions to Beta's behavior are the *expectancies* that make the behavior of the two people truly interdependent. They provide the mechanism, at least within the framework of one conceptualization of the learning process, by which a dyadic behavior unit can be derived from the combining of two or more monadic units.

One can only speculate as to what variables, and what general principles, will eventually compose a dyadic behavior theory. Some of them will probably be discovered in the attempt to analyze those psychological processes that apparently result from highly particularized constellations of interpersonal relations. Identification is one such process. Reciprocal cathexis is another. A third is the process of secondary drive formation, as in the early childhood development of aggression and dependency. Other variables will likely be devised in the study of small groups. Festinger's concept of cohesiveness is a big step forward in this direction.

One way of approaching the problem would be to examine the various possibilities of reward and nonreward or punishment for Alpha and Beta. If a dyad exists on the basis of reciprocal rewards, as in the mother-child relationship, there are nevertheless possibilities of mutual interference. That is, while the dyad is held together by powerful continuing motivations and expectancies of reciprocal support, each member has the potentiality of frustrating the other. One major source of frustration is the absence of the partner, Beta, at times when Alpha needs him. Such absences would be expected to occur partly (but by no means entirely, of course) because Beta was also the

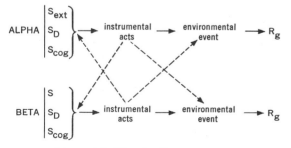

FIGURE 2. *The dyadic sequence.*

partner in dyadic relationships with other people. Now, since in young children aggression and dependency are two of the major reactions to frustration, one might reach some such hypothesis as this: that the amount of aggression and dependency that characterize a mother-child interaction will be a positive function of the number of dyadic relationships in which each is a member. Or to put it in a more testable form: everything else being held constant, a child's dependency and aggressiveness toward his mother will vary with the amount of role conflict the mother has.

Personality

In this monadic-dyadic framework, personality is a description of those properties of a person that specify his potentialities for action. Such a description must include reference to motivation, expectations, habit structure, the nature of the instigators that activate instrumental behavior, and the kinds of environmental events that such actions will produce. Furthermore, all these factors must be described in terms of the dyadic aspects of the behavior that occurs. That is, the kinds of Betas who can serve as instigators for particular responses must be specified, and the environmental events that Beta creates for Alpha must be described not only as they fit into Alpha's activity but also as they fit into the whole motivational sequence of Beta.

In behavior science, personality is sometimes treated as antecedent and sometimes as consequent. As antecedent, it is part of the total matrix that must be known in order to account for either individual or dyadic action. In recent years various approaches to personality have too much depended on assumptions of fixed traits and fixed needs. This has led to measurement procedures that do not include reference to the social stimulus conditions under which the traits or needs will be expressed. As Fillmore Sanford has said, in connection with a study of leadership, there is no trait independent of the conditions that elicit it. Leadership is a quality in a person's behavior only if there are followers who react to him as a leader. Most behavior with which the personality psychologist is concerned is either directly dyadic or is in response to symbolic representation of the dyad. Therefore, any conceptualization of the person's properties must be done with consideration of the properties of the various Betas with whom Alpha is interactive.

A simple example of the measurement problem created by these considerations arose in connection with some data on aggressive behavior collected in our laboratory (7, 17, 18). Forty preschool children were the subjects. Two main measures of aggressiveness were secured. One was overt and socially directed aggression. This measure was obtained both by teachers' rating scales and by direct observation. The other was projective or fantasy aggression displayed in doll play. By a fixed trait or need assumption, one would expect these two measures to correspond somewhat. They did—somewhat! The correlation was .13!

An analysis in terms of learning and action makes the meaning of this relationship clear. These children's mothers were interviewed concerning their methods of handling the youngsters' aggression at home. On the basis of the information it was possible to divide the children into three subgroups which had had different degrees of severity of punishment for aggression.

In Figure 4, the mother's frequency of both overt and fantasy aggression are shown for these three subgroups. It is to be noted that while the "mild" and "moderate" groups show a correspondence in amount of aggressive behavior of the two kinds, there is a radical disagreement in the "severe" punishment subgroup. These latter children, on the average, behaved rather nonaggressively in preschool, but in their doll play fantasies there was an abundance of aggression. One could ask whether these children are very aggressive or very non-aggressive. Do they have strong need for aggression or weak?

Even if these questions could be sensibly an-

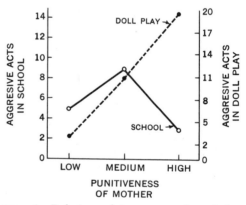

FIGURE 4. *Relation of interpersonal and fantasy aggression to maternal punitiveness. Interpersonal aggression is measured by frequency of aggressive acts occurring during four hours of observation in preschool; fantasy aggression is measured by mean frequency of aggressive acts occurring during two twenty-minute doll play sessions. Punitiveness of Mother is based on ratings of interview material concerning severity of Mother's punishment of child's aggressive acts at home. Chartered values are medians of the three groups, sizes of which are: low = 7, median = 23, high = 10.*

swered, which they cannot, the answers would be of little help in predicting the future aggressive behavior of these children. To accomplish the latter, which is our aim, there must be an analysis of the social stimulus conditions under which the future behavior is to be observed.

The minimum specification would be as to whether the behavior would be observed in a nursery school or in a permissive doll play experiment. With a conceptualization of the dyadic variables involved, however, it is possible to make a statement that goes beyond the narrow confines of these two measuring situations. In this instance, the more general statements can be made that, first, the amount of aggression will be a negative function of severity of punishment, and second, with severity of punishment held constant, the amount of aggression will vary positively with dissimilarity of the dyadic situation to the original punishment situation in the home. These are strictly monadic statements, but they assume the prior existence of dyadic experiences.

The systematization of personality development requires a different approach. When personality factors are considered as antecedents to individual or group behavior, the laws of ongoing action are involved. But when personality development is the matter for study, the laws of learning are the bases. What is needed in this case is a set of principles that will describe the way in which the child's potentialities for action—that is, his drives, habits, cognitive structures, and expectancies—are changed by the experiences he has throughout his life.

This is a difficult problem, both logically and empirically. Personality is partly the product of a life-time of dyadic action which has modified the individual's potentiality for further action. The changed potentiality is therefore partly a product of his own actions. For example, in the data concerning child aggression and severity of maternal punishment for aggression, the mother's action in punishing the child was doubtless influenced in part by the amount and kind of aggression exhibited toward her by the child. Thus, the behavior that served as an antecedent to the differential display of overt and fantasy aggression by the child was contributed to by the child himself.

Logically, and practically, a good theory requires that antecedents and consequents be entirely independent of one another. It would be most satisfactory if the child did not influence the mother's behavior, and if we could then say something about the effect of severity of punishment on later behavior. One solution to this problem appears to be a careful measurement of the child's contribution to the dyadic relationship and a partialling out of that influence in the comparison of antecedent mother behavior with consequent child behavior.

The variables that appear most promising in the study of personality development come from two main sources. One is the set of definitions and postulates that compose the laws of learning. Whether the particular formulations used by Tolman, Hull, Guthrie, or Skinner are selected seems of little importance at the moment. Those of Hull and Tolman have certain *a priori* advantages, but the main point is the use of whatever laws of learning will best serve to account for changes in potentiality for action. The theoretical formulation of the research in our own laboratory stems from Hull through Miller and Dollard.

The second source of variables lies in the conceptualization of those secondary motivational systems that arise universally as a product of the dyadic relationship between mother and child (16). These include aggression, dependency, self-reliance, responsibility, the anxieties, competition, and status-seeking as well as the various consequences of the training inherent in socialization of the primary drives of hunger, sex, fatigue, and elimination. The exact forms of behavior potentiality created in each of these motivational areas are different from child to child and culture to culture. But the biological nature of man, coupled with his universal gregariousness, gives rise to various learning experiences that every human child endures in one fashion or another.

SUMMARY

In sum, it seems to me that the most promising directions now discernible in the study of social behavior and personality require a theory that has the following properties: its basic reference events must be *actions;* it must combine congruently both *dyadic* and *monadic* events; it must account for both *ongoing action* and *learning;* it must provide a description of personality couched in terms of *potentiality for action;* and it must provide principles of personality development in terms of *changes in potentiality for action.*

REFERENCES

1. ALLPORT, F. H. *Social psychology.* Boston: Houghton Mifflin Co., 1924.

2. ALLPORT, G. W. *Personality; a psychological interpretation.* New York: Henry Holt, 1937.

3. COTTRELL, L. S. The analysis of situational fields in social psychology. *Amer. Sociol. Rev.,* 1942, 7, 370–382.

4. FESTINGER, L. Informal social communication. *In*

L. Festinger et al. *Theory and experiment in social communication.* Ann Arbor: Research Center for Group Dynamics, 1950.

5. FREUD, S. *General introduction to psychoanalysis.* New York: Boni & Liveright, 1920.

6. HAMILTON, G. V. *Objective psychopathology.* St. Louis: C. V. Mosby, 1925.

7. HOLLENBERG, E., AND SPERRY, M. Some antecedents of aggression and effects of frustration in doll play. *Personality,* 1951, *1,* 32–43.

8. HULL, C. L. Goal attraction and directing ideas conceived as habit phenomena. *Psychol. Rev.,* 1931, *38,* 487–506.

9. LEWIN, K. *A dynamic theory of personality.* New York: McGraw-Hill, 1935.

10. LEWIN, K. Constructs in psychology and psychological ecology. *Univ. Ia. Stud. Child Welf.,* 1944, *20,* 1–29.

11. McDOUGALL, W. *An introduction to social psychology.* London: Methuen, 1908.

12. MILLER, N. E. Theory and experiment relating psychoanalytic displacement to stimulus-response generalization. *J. Abn. Soc. Psychol.,* 1948, *43,* 155–178.

13. MURRAY, H. A. *Explorations in personality.* New York: Oxford Univ. Press, 1938.

14. NEWCOMB, T. M. *Social psychology.* New York: Dryden Press, 1950.

15. PARSONS, T. *The Social system.* Glencoe, Illinois: The Free Press, 1951.

16. SEARS, R. R. Personality development in contemporary culture. *Proc. Amer. Philos. Soc.,* 1948, *92,* 363–370.

17. SEARS, R. R. Relation of fantasy aggression to interpersonal aggression. *Child Develpm.,* 1950, *21,* 5–6.

18. SEARS, R. R. Effects of frustration and anxiety on fantasy aggression. *Amer. J. Orthopsychiat.,* 1951, *21,* July.

IV

INTERPERSONAL EXPERIENCES AS DETERMINANTS OF BEHAVIOR

The nature of a person's expectations of others; his ways of gaining satisfaction, of expressing his feelings, and of resolving emotional conflicts (in mature or less mature ways); the content and fervor of his ideals; and the extent of his inhibitions and guilt feelings—*all* are formed in an interpersonal context. Those who emphasize interpersonal determinants are indebted to Sigmund Freud far more than to any other theorist, a debt Bruner made clear in an opening selection of this book. Although psychoanalytic theory today represents a gradual modification and differentiation of Freud's views, his recognition of the formative impact of emotional relationships in the family stands solidly as a cornerstone of today's conceptions of personality development.

The influence of the family is not limited to the tie with father and mother. A child's gratifications and deprivations, his loves and enmities in relation to figures other than the parents may be crucial. Which relationships are important depends upon the composition of the particular family group and the roles taken by the different members. In one family, a grandmother or an uncle may be a major source of influence; in another, the relationship with brother or sister vividly colors a child's life.

As the girl or boy grows, persons outside the family are likely to be involved in an increasing proportion of the youngster's experiences. In school, the association with a teacher may become significant. A rising responsiveness of many boys and girls to children in the neighborhood rapidly eclipses their earlier orientation to the parents. (Of course, children who have older siblings may have been more oriented to them than to their parents almost from birth.) Thus, one takes into account the "peer group," which, in practice, means not only age-mates of similar status, but also children older or younger who are in a position to be of importance in a given child's day-to-day existence.

Intense and prolonged hatreds or affectional bonds formed in childhood may be forgotten in adulthood. Yet, they may still affect one's perceptions of other people, especially in circumstances that arouse inner conflict. A man who has had chronic trouble with a brother, unmitigated by sufficient happy experiences, may have difficulties in a competitive situation with a peer at work. Such difficulties may lead not only to discomfort, but also to inappropriate behavior. Several types of alternative response are possible, ranging from overt hostility to over-submissiveness. The woman whose relation with her mother was unsatisfactory may have problems in getting along with an older woman who employs her. If the picture is further complicated by unresolved difficulties the older woman had with *her* younger sister, both the supervisor and employee may behave in such distorted ways that a total impasse is reached. In such ways, the cares of childhood may live on to burden adult associations in work, marriage, and parenthood.

The first approach to gaining knowledge about interpersonal determinants of behavior was the *clinical* one of Freud and his successors. This is still the approach most used by psychiatrists and social workers, as well as by some psychologists. In this approach, hypotheses are generated from a series of cases. Such cases usually concern patients undergoing treatment for emotional tensions or for bodily disorders that represent symptoms of inner conflict. The theories and hypotheses that have grown out of such clinical studies offer a fertile field to the empirical researcher who can make the controlled investigations needed in order to test, and enrich or correct, the hard-won theoretical formulations. All articles in this section present the results of empirical, rather than clinical, research. Yet, in many instances, it was clinical work that initially gave rise to the ideas now being pursued by empirical means, which allow replication of results and are therefore more suited to verification of hypotheses. At the present stage of the scientific study of human personality and behavior, clinical studies continue to be an indispensable counterpart to the empirical ones in providing guidelines for further work.

An example of a concept now being investigated by controlled research, although it was "invented" as a result of observing patients, is "identification." The formative effects of peers, parents, and siblings are often due to the rewards and punishments they administer either knowingly *or* unwittingly (see Section III for a discussion of Learning). But it appears that principles besides those of direct learning are necessary to give adequate recognition to ways in which some human behaviors seem to be acquired. "Identification" is the term most commonly applied to a process by which behavior is influenced without punishments or rewards except those from within (including inner self-exhortation, self-criticism, and self-praise). The educational implications of identificatory learning are implicit in the following statement by Edward Joseph Shoben, Jr.:

> Psychologically, it seems sound to argue that the essential curriculum for each school child at any given time is not what is on paper in the curriculum supervisor's office. It is much more likely to be the way he perceives his teacher. The curriculum, after all, is only a statement of what the pupil is to learn. His learning proceeds through the vital and basic mediation of the teacher. What he learns, therefore, is in significant degree a function of how he reacts to and interprets the mediating adult. . . .[1]

Included in this section are papers dealing with: (1) the nature of the infant's attachment to parent and the ways in which absence of mother or father may affect offspring; (2) child-rearing practices, especially disciplinary ones; (3) the extent to which children's characteristics may cause parental behaviors rather than vice versa; (4) identification and imitation; and (5) peer influence, including the effects of siblings as a special case in connection with which the impact of birth order is also considered.

Readers who are interested in pursuing the topic of interpersonal influences from the viewpoint of psychoanalytic psychiatry and psychology will enjoy spending an evening with Dorothy W. Baruch's book *One Little Boy* (Dell Publishing Co., 1964). Another book that is very well liked by many students is *Emotional Problems of Living,* by O. S. English and G. H. J. Pearson (Third Edition, Norton, 1963). Although written dogmatically—that is, as though psychoanalytic ideas are 100 per cent right and impervious to time and further investigation— their book conveys rich insights into the inner lives of children. It also deals with the ways in which such inner lives constitute a major component in determining children's and adults' behavior.

---

[1] The Shoben paper, called "Viewpoints from related disciplines: learning theory," is from an issue of *Teachers College Record* (1959, *60*, 272–282) devoted to the topic: "What Shall the Schools Teach?" Reprinted by permission.

Those desiring more exposure to the type of data and approach used in the Sears, Maccoby, and Levin material on aggression might well enjoy reading about other areas of parental and child behavior in their book *Patterns of Child Rearing* (Row, Peterson, 1957).

19

Nature of Love—Simplified [1]

HARRY F. HARLOW
AND STEPHEN J. SUOMI

Harry Harlow has long studied ways in which the social, sexual, and parental behaviors of adult monkeys are affected by varying sorts of social contact and mothering in their early lives. Some of the more humorous papers in the psychological literature have resulted from the speeches he has given reporting his work. Everyone who has taken a recent course in Introductory Psychology is likely to recall some of this research.

Here, Harlow and Suomi describe progress in their continuing efforts to learn the exact conditions that cause attachment of the infant monkey to his mother—or mother substitute. A full understanding of those conditions will give important leads to those who study human infants. Monkeys are studied because ethical customs prevent investigators from risking emotional damage to human babies by depriving them of live mothers in order to isolate the attributes of mothers that account for their appeal to infants.

Harry F. Harlow, a past president of the Amer-

[1] This research was supported by United States Public Health Service Grants MH–11894 and FR–0167 from the National Institutes of Health to the University of Wisconsin Primate Laboratory and Regional Primate Research Center, respectively.

Requests for reprints should be sent to Harry F. Harlow, Regional Primate Research Center, University of Wisconsin, Madison, Wisconsin 53706.

Harry F. Harlow and Stephen J. Suomi, "Nature of love—simplified," *American Psychologist*, 1970, *25*, 161–168. Reprinted by permission.

ican Psychological Association, is director of the Regional Primate Research Center at the University of Wisconsin, where Stephen J. Suomi is also situated.

The cloth surrogate and its wire surrogate sibling (see Figure 1) entered into scientific history as of 1958 (Harlow, 1958). The cloth surrogate was originally designed to test the relative importance of body contact in contrast to activities associated with the breast, and the results were clear beyond all expectation. Body contact was of overpowering importance by any measure taken, even contact time, as shown in Figure 2.

However, the cloth surrogate, beyond its power to measure the relative importance of a host of variables determining infant affection for the mother, exhibited another surprising trait, one of great independent usefulness. Even though the cloth mother was inanimate, it was able to impart

FIGURE 1. *Cloth and wire surrogate mothers. (Photo by Wisconsin Primate Center and Laboratory.)*

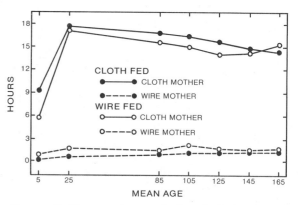

FIGURE 2. *Contact time to cloth and wire surrogate.*

to its infant such emotional security that the infant would, in the surrogate's presence, explore a strange situation and manipulate available physical objects (see Figure 3), or animate objects (see Figure 4). Manipulation of animate objects leads to play if these animate objects are age-mates, and play is the variable of primary importance in the development of normal social, sexual, and maternal functions, as described by Harlow and Harlow (1965). It is obvious that surrogate mothers, which are more docile and manipulative than real monkey mothers, have a wide range of experimental uses.

SIMPLIFIED SURROGATE

Although the original surrogates turned out to be incredibly efficient dummy mothers, they presented certain practical problems. The worst of the problems was that of cleanliness. Infant monkeys seldom soil their real mothers' bodies, though we do not know how this is achieved. However, infant monkeys soiled the bodies of the original cloth surrogates with such efficiency and enthusiasm as to present a health problem and, even worse, a financial problem resulting from laundering. Furthermore, we believed that the original cloth surrogate was too steeply angled and thereby relatively inaccessible for cuddly clinging by the neonatal monkey.

In the hope of alleviating practical problems inherent in the original cloth surrogate, we constructed a family of simplified surrogates. The simplified surrogate is mounted on a rod attached to a lead base 4 inches in diameter, angled upward at 25°, and projected through the surrogate's body for 4 inches, so that heads may be attached if desired. The body of the simplified surrogate is only

FIGURE 4. *Infant play in presence of surrogate. (Photo by Wisconsin Primate Center and Laboratory.)*

6 inches long, 2½ inches in diameter, and stands approximately 3 inches off the ground. Figure 5 shows an original cloth surrogate and simplified surrogate placed side by side.

FIGURE 3. *Infant monkey security in presence of cloth surrogate. (Photo by Wisconsin Primate Center and Laboratory.)*

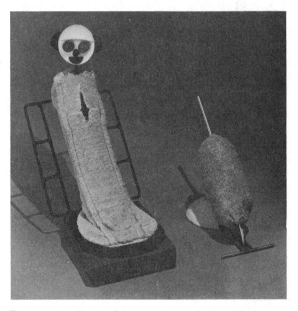

FIGURE 5. *Original surrogate and simplified surrogate. (Photo by Wisconsin Primate Center and Laboratory.)*

. . . infants readily cling to these simplified surrogates of smaller body and decreased angle of inclination. Infant monkeys do soil the simplified surrogate, but the art and act of soiling is very greatly reduced. Terry cloth slipcovers can be made easily and relatively cheaply, alleviating, if not eliminating, laundry problems. Thus, the simplified surrogate is a far more practical dummy mother than the original cloth surrogate.

SURROGATE VARIABLES

LACTATION

Although the original surrogate papers (Harlow, 1958; Harlow & Zimmermann, 1959) were written as if activities associated with the breast, particularly nursing, were of no importance, this is doubtlessly incorrect. There were no statistically significant differences in time spent by the babies on the lactating versus nonlactating cloth surrogates and on the lactating versus nonlactating wire surrogates, but the fact is that there were consistent preferences for both the cloth and the wire lactating surrogates and that these tendencies held for both the situations of time on surrogate and frequency of surrogate preference when the infant was exposed to a fear stimulus. Thus, if one can accept a statistically insignificant level of confidence, consistently obtained from four situations, one will properly conclude that nursing is a minor variable but one of more than measurable importance operating to bind the infant to the mother.

To demonstrate experimentally that activities associated with the breasts were variables of significant importance, we built two sets of differentially colored surrogates, tan and light blue; and using a 2×2 Latin square design, we arranged a situation such that the surrogate of one color lactated and the other did not. As can be seen in Figure 7, the infants showed a consistent preference for the lactating surrogate when contact comfort was held constant. The importance of the lactational variable probably decreases with time. But at least we had established the hard fact that hope springs eternal in the human breast and even longer in the breast, undressed.

FACIAL VARIABLES

In the original surrogates we created an ornamental face for the cloth surrogate and a simple dog face for the wire surrogate. I was working with few available infants and against time to prepare a presidential address for the 1958 American Psychological Association Convention. On the basis of sheer intuition, I was convinced that the ornamental cloth-surrogate face would become a stronger fear

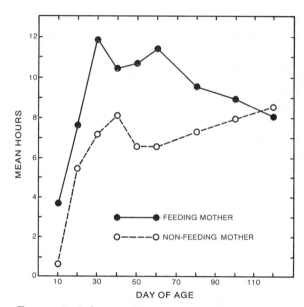

FIGURE 7. *Infant preference for lactating cloth surrogate.*

stimulus than the dog face when fear of the unfamiliar matured in the monkeys from about 70 to 110 days (Harlow & Zimmermann, 1959; Sackett, 1966). But since we wanted each surrogate to have an identifiable face and had few infants, we made no effort to balance faces by resorting to a feebleminded 2×2 Latin square design.

Subsequently, we have run two brief unpublished experiments. We tested four rhesus infants unfamiliar with surrogate faces at approximately 100 days of age and found that the ornamental face was a much stronger fear stimulus than the dog face. Clearly, the early enormous preference for the cloth surrogate over the wire surrogate was not a function of the differential faces. Later, we raised two infants on cloth and two on wire surrogates, counterbalancing the ornamental and dog faces. Here, the kind of face was a nonexistent variable. To a baby all maternal faces are beautiful. A mother's face that will stop a clock will not stop an infant.

The first surrogate mother we constructed came a little late, or phrasing it another way, her baby came a little early. Possibly her baby was illegitimate. Certainly it was her first baby. In desperation we gave the mother a face that was nothing but a round wooden ball, which displayed no trace of shame. To the baby monkey this featureless face became beautiful, and she frequently caressed it with hands and legs, beginning around 30–40 days of age. By the time the baby had reached 90 days of age we had constructed an appropriate ornamental cloth-mother face, and we proudly mounted it on the surrogate's body. The baby took one look and screamed. She fled to the back of the cage and cringed in autistic-type posturing. After some days of terror the infant solved the medusa-mother problem in a most ingenious manner. She revolved the face 180° so that she always faced a bare round ball! Furthermore, we could rotate the maternal face dozens of times and within an hour or so the infant would turn it around 180°. Within a week the baby resolved her unfaceable problem once and for all. She lifted the maternal head from the body, rolled it into the corner, and abandoned it. No one can blame the baby. She had lived with and loved a faceless mother, but she could not love a two-faced mother.

These data imply that an infant visually responds to the earliest version of mother he encounters, that the mother he grows accustomed to is the mother he relies upon. Subsequent changes, especially changes introduced after maturation of the fear response, elicit this response with no holds barred. Comparisons of effects of babysitters on human infants might be made. [Many parents have a new sitter visit the home in advance of the sitting engagement to get acquainted with the infant or young child in the reassuring presence of the mother or father. The parents thus seek to prevent a fearful response in the child at the time they leave. —EDITOR]

BODY-SURFACE VARIABLES

We have received many questions and complaints concerning the surrogate surfaces, wire and terry cloth, used in the original studies. This mountain of mail breaks down into two general categories: that wire is aversive, and that other substances would be equally effective if not better than terry cloth in eliciting a clinging response.

The answer to the first matter in question is provided by observation: Wire is not an aversive stimulus to neonatal monkeys, for they spend much time climbing on the sides of their hardware-cloth cages and exploring this substance orally and tactually. A few infants have required medical treatment from protractedly pressing their faces too hard and too long against the cage sides. Obviously, however, wire does not provide contact comfort.

In an attempt to quantify preference of various materials, an exploratory study [2] was performed in which each of four infants was presented with a choice between surrogates covered with terry cloth versus rayon, vinyl, or rough-grade sandpaper. As shown in Figure 8, the infants demonstrated a clear preference for the cloth surrogates, and no sig-

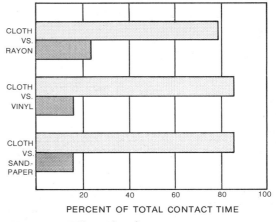

FIGURE 8. *Effect of surface on surrogate contact.*

nificant preference difference between the other body surfaces. An extension of this study is in progress in which an attempt is being made to further quantify and rank order the preference for these materials by giving infants equal exposure time to all four materials.

MOTION VARIABLES

In the original two papers, we pointed out that rocking motion, that is, proprioceptive stimulation, was a variable of more than statistical significance, particularly early in the infant's life, in binding the infant to the mother figure. We measured this by comparing the time the infants spent on two identical planes, one rocking and one stationary (see Figure 9) and two identical cloth surrogates, one rocking and one stationary (see Figure 10).

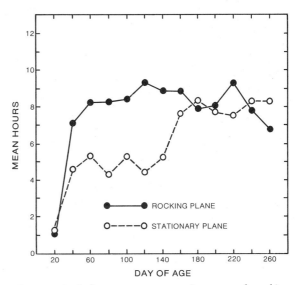

FIGURE 9. *Infant contact to stationary and rocking planes.*

---

[2] We wish to thank Carol Furchner, who conducted this experiment and the described experiment in progress.

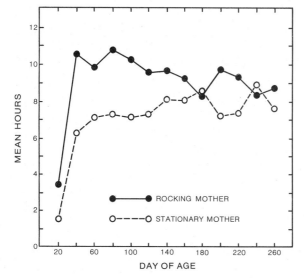

FIGURE 10. *Infant contact to stationary and rocking surrogates.*

TEMPERATURE VARIABLES

To study another variable, temperature, we created some "hot mamma" surrogates. We did this by inserting heating coils in the maternal bodies that raised the external surrogate body surface about 10° F. In one experiment, we heated the surface of a wire surrogate and let four infant macaques choose between this heated mother and a room-temperature cloth mother. The data are presented in Figure 11. The neonatal monkeys clearly preferred the former. With increasing age this difference decreased, and at approximately 15 days the preference reversed. In a second experiment, we used two differentially colored cloth surrogates and heated one and not the other. The infants preferred the hot surrogate, but frequently

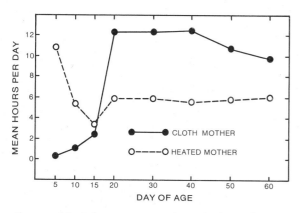

FIGURE 11. *Infant contact to heated-wire and room-temperature cloth surrogates.*

contacted the room-temperature surrogate for considerable periods of time.

More recently, a series of ingenious studies on the temperature variable has been conducted by Suomi, who created hot- and cold-running surrogates by adaptation of the simplified surrogate. These results are important not only for the information obtained concerning the temperature variable but also as an illustration of the successful experimental use of the simplified surrogate itself.

The surrogates used in these exploratory studies were modifications of the basic simplified surrogate, designed to get maximum personality out of the minimal mother. One of these surrogates was a "hot mamma," exuding warmth from a conventional heating pad wrapped around the surrogate frame and completely covered by a terry cloth sheath. The other surrogate was a cold female; beneath the terry cloth sheath was a hollow shell within which her life fluid—cold water—was continuously circulated. The two surrogates are illustrated in Figures 13 and 14, and to the untrained observer they look remarkably similar. But looks can be deceiving, especially with females, and we felt that in these similar-looking surrogates we had really simulated the two extremes of womanhood—one with a hot body and no head, and one with a cold shoulder and no heart. Actually, this is an exaggeration, for the surface temperature of the hot surrogate was only 7° F. above room temperature, while the surface temperature of the cold surrogate was only 5° F. below room temperature.

In a preliminary study, we raised one female infant from Day 15 on the warm surrogate for a period of four weeks. Like all good babies she quickly and completely became attached to her source of warmth, and during this time she exhibited not only a steadily increasing amount of surrogate contact but also began to use the surrogate as a base for exploration (see Figure 13). At the end of this four-week period, we decided that our subject had become spoiled enough and so we replaced the warm surrogate with the cold version for one week. The infant noticed the switch within two minutes, responding by huddling in a corner and vocalizing piteously. Throughout the week of bitter maternal cold, the amount of surrogate contact fell drastically; in general, the infant avoided the surrogate in her feeding, exploratory, and sleeping behaviors. Feeling somewhat guilty, we switched surrogates once more for a week and were rewarded for our efforts by an almost immediate return to previously high levels of surrogate contact. Apparently, with heart-warming heat, our infant was capable of forgiveness, even at this tender age. At this point, we switched the two surrogates daily for a total two weeks, but by this time the infant

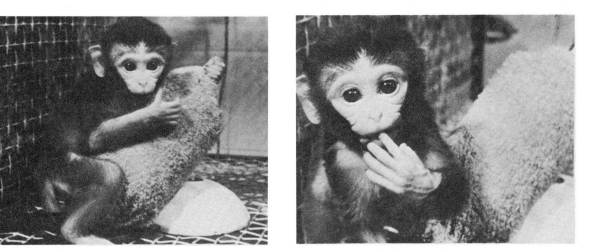

FIGURE 13. *Infant clinging to and exploring from warm simplified surrogate. (Photos by Wisconsin Primate Center and Laboratory.)*

had accepted the inherent fickle nature of her mothers. On the days that her surrogate was warm, she clung tightly to its body, but on the days when the body was cold, she generally ignored it, thus providing an excellent example of naive behaviorism.

With a second infant we maintained this procedure but switched the surrogates, so that he spent four weeks with the cold surrogate, followed by one week with the warm, an additional week with the cold, and finally a two-week period in which the surrogates were switched daily. This infant became anything but attached to the cold surrogate during the initial four-week period, spending most of his time huddling in the corner of his cage and generally avoiding the surrogate in his exploratory behavior (see Figure 14). In succeeding weeks, even with the warm surrogate, he failed to approach

FIGURE 14. *Typical infant reactions to cold simplified surrogate. (Photo by Wisconsin Primate Center and Laboratory.)*

the levels of contact exhibited by the other infant to the cold surrogate. Apparently, being raised with a cold mother had chilled him to mothers in general, even those beaming warmth and comfort.

Two months later both infants were exposed to a severe fear stimulus in the presence of a room-temperature simplified surrogate. The warm-mother infant responded to this stimulus by running to the surrogate and clinging for dear life. The cold-mother infant responded by running the other way and seeking security in a corner of the cage. We seriously doubt that this behavioral difference can be attributed to the sex difference of our subjects. Rather, this demonstration warmed our hopes and chilled our doubts that temperature may be a variable of importance. More specifically, it suggested that a simple linear model may not be adequate to describe the effects of temperature differences of surrogates on infant attachment. It is clear that warmth is a variable of major importance, particularly in the neonate, and we hazard the guess that elevated temperature is a variable of importance in the operation of all the affectional systems: maternal, mother-infant, possibly agemate, heterosexual, and even paternal.

PROSPECTIVES

Recently we have simplified the surrogate mother further for studies in which its only function is that of providing early social support and security to infants. This supersimplified surrogate is merely a board $1\frac{1}{2}$ inches in diameter and 10 inches long with a scooped-out, concave trough having a maximal depth of $\frac{3}{4}$ inch. . . . the supersimplified surrogate has an angular deviation from the base of less than 15°, though this angle can be increased by the experimenter at will. The standard cover for this supremely simple surrogate mother is a size 11, cotton athletic sock, though covers of various qualities, rayon, vinyl (which we call the "linoleum lover"), and sandpaper, have been used for experimental purposes.

> Linoleum lover, with you I am through
> The course of smooth love never runs true.

This supersimplified mother is designed to attract and elicit clinging responses from the infant during the first 15 days of the infant's life.

We have designed, but not yet tested, a swinging mother that will dangle from a frame about 2 inches off the floor and have a convex, terry cloth or cotton body surface. Observations of real macaque neonates and mothers indicate that the infant, not the mother, is the primary attachment object even when the mother locomotes, and that this swinging mother may also elicit infantile clasp and impart infant security very early in life. There is nothing original in this day and age about a swinger becoming a mother, and the only new angle, if any, is a mother becoming a swinger.

Additional findings, such as the discovery that six-month social isolates will learn to cling to a heated simplified surrogate, and that the presence of a surrogate reduces clinging among infant-infant pairs, have substantiated use of the surrogate beyond experiments for its own sake. At present, the heated simplified surrogate is being utilized as a standard apparatus in studies as varied as reaction to fear, rehabilitation of social isolates, and development of play. To date, additional research utilizing the cold version of the simplified surrogate has been far more limited, possibly because unused water faucets are harder to obtain than empty electrical outlets. But this represents a methodological, not a theoretical problem, and doubtlessly solutions will soon be forthcoming.

It is obvious that the surrogate mother at this point is not merely a historical showpiece. Unlike the proverbial old soldier, it is far from fading away. Instead, as in the past, it continues to foster not only new infants but new ideas.

REFERENCES

HARLOW, H. F. The nature of love. *American Psychologist,* 1958, *13,* 673–685.

HARLOW, H. F., & HARLOW, M. K. The affectional systems. In A. M. Schrier, H. F. Harlow, & F. Stollnitz (Eds.), *Behavior of nonhuman primates.* Vol. 2. New York: Academic Press, 1965.

HARLOW, H. F., & ZIMMERMANN, R. R. Affectional responses in the infant monkey. *Science,* 1959, *130,* 421–432.

SACKETT, G. P. Monkeys reared in visual isolation with pictures as visual input: Evidence for an innate releasing mechanism. *Science,* 1966, *154,* 1468–1472.

20

The Father in Contemporary Culture and Current Psychological Literature *

JOHN NASH

The Effect of Limited Father Absence on Cognitive Development †

F. LANDY, B. G. ROSENBERG,
AND B. SUTTON-SMITH

Having dealt with the effects of mothers or mothering, we now present an article dealing with fatherhood, a topic that psychologists have tended to neglect in the past. The topic of father-absence has become prominent in recent years because of national concern about the plight of fatherless families among the lower class, especially the black lower class, where there are high proportions of fatherless families. The assumption has often been made that boys from homes without fathers are more likely to be delinquent than those from homes where the father is present. In their review of literature on the point, Elizabeth Herzog and Cecelia Sudia found the evidence to be insufficient (Boys in Fatherless Families, Office of Child Development, Children's Bureau, U.S. Department of Health, Education, and Welfare, 1970). Nevertheless, absence of the father (or neglect by him) is likely to have deleterious effects in other ways.

The first paper of this double selection is the summary of an article reviewing our knowledge of the role of the father. The original paper has an extensive bibliography which those interested in pursuing this topic would do well to consult. The author, John Nash, is currently in the Department of Psychology at the University of Hong Kong.

The other paper deals with the effect of partial absence of fathers on the quantitative abilities of their daughters. Rosenberg is a professor of psychology at Bowling Green State University, while Landy is at Pennsylvania State University. Professor Sutton-Smith is at Teachers College, Columbia University.

(The Father in Contemporary Culture and Current Psychological Literature)

The aim of this review is to examine present day thought on the relationships between fathers and their children, and to consider the adequacy of present assumptions.

Much of the scientific literature in this field is sociological rather than psychological in content. While relatively few scientists write about the father, of those that do sociologists and anthropologists form a sizeable proportion. Much of the literature is observational rather than experimental in character and, indeed, experimental studies meeting reasonable standards of methodological sophistication, including such refinements as control groups, are scarce; but this is a difficult area in which to practice sound method. Since the primary aim of this review is to survey the field as it is, some assertions that may or may not stand up to critical examination in the future will be cited. . . .

SUMMARY

From an over-all view of the literature on fathers and their place in child-rearing, it appears that:

1. In the opinion of some sociologists, American society in particular, and probably Western industrial society in general, can be epitomized as "mother-centered" in its philosophy of child care.

2. This is in contrast to certain primitive societies with a family cooperative economy, which have typically a way of child-rearing which em-

* John Nash, "The father in contemporary culture and current psychological literature," *Child Development, 36,* 1965, 261–293. Reprinted with abridgement by permission. Copyright 1965 by The Society for Research in Child Development, Inc.

† F. Landy, B. G. Rosenberg, and B. Sutton-Smith, "The effect of limited father absence on cognitive development," *Child Development,* 1969, *40,* 941–944. Reprinted by permission. © 1969 by The Society for Research in Child Development, Inc.

phasizes father-son and mother-daughter relationships.

3. The difference can be explained by the economic history of our industrial civilization, in which the primitive family cooperative economy has been supplanted by one in which the father is usually the sole support of the family. While engaged in this economic activity, he delegates his place in child-rearing to his wife.

4. Psychologists have adopted this cultural philosophy of child care, perhaps uncritically, and many appear to have assumed that it is both the only and the most desirable pattern of child care. In consequence, the majority of psychologists have not perceived the father as important in child-rearing, and this is reflected in their writings. Some psychologists have adopted the cultural assumption so thoroughly as to ignore the father entirely or even to deny him a position of any significance.

5. This culturally determined concept of child care has further removed the father by enhancing the assumption that the rearing of children is a specifically feminine duty.

6. Clinical studies and investigations of delinquents suggest that father-child relationships, and especially those between father and son, may be of considerable etiological importance to both social and psychological abnormality.

7. Psychosexual difficulties, such as homosexuality, apparently result when a child's major identification is with the parent of the opposite sex. If this is the case, a mother-centered system is peculiarly unsuited to the needs of the boy, for while he is under cultural pressure to act as a male, he is reared predominantly by women from whom he is likely to acquire a feminine pattern.

8. Identification of child with parent is significant in sex-role and psychosexual development, and can be understood in terms of learning theory: warm, affectionate relationships and prolonged associations (in contrast to the veiled hostility of the oepidal theory) are probably among the more vital requirements to successful identifications.

9. Though as yet little understood, critical periods may be found in human development, as they almost certainly are important in the acquisition of some animal behavior.

10. There is some evidence from the few available studies of early paternal deprivation that there is a critical period during which the kind of affectional relationship with the father necessary to identification can be built up. This critical period appears to be early, and has tentatively been described as lasting from the time of weaning to entering school.

11. The role of the peer culture as a factor in sex-role development has been discussed, and its possible limitations because of its immaturity.

(The Effect of Limited Father Absence on Cognitive Development[1])

In an earlier paper the present authors contrasted the effects of father absence or presence on families of varying sibling composition (Sutton-Smith, Rosenberg, & Landy 1968). It was found that the effects of father absence varied with the size of the family and the sibling composition. While contrasts were made between the lengths of the fathers' absences and the children's ages at the time they were absent, no further examination of the character of that "absence" was presented. In the study that follows, the "absence" variable is further explored through an analysis of the effects of father shift work on children's performances. It is proposed that, when a man works on the night shift for long periods of time, his children will manifest behavioral patterns similar to those discovered in families where the father has been totally absent for a number of years, but to a lesser degree, since limited father absence is expected to have a less profound effect.

The dependent variable in this, as in the previous study, was performance on a college-entrance test, and the prediction derived from that previous study was that girls whose fathers were on shift work for long periods when the girls were between the ages of 5 and 10 years would show a depressed performance on tests of quantitative ability.

METHOD

The sample was composed of female students enrolled in a developmental psychology course who were predominantly sophomores with a median age of 19 years.

The Ss were categorized into five groups on two related dimensions of father absence: (1) the *period* in the S's life when the father worked the night shift—consecutively, no night-shift work, night shift from ages birth to 4 years, 5–9, 10 or older, and a final group whose fathers had been totally absent from the home for 10 or more years; (2) the absolute *number* of years that a father worked on the night shift—consecutively, no night-shift work, 1–5 years, 6–10 years, 11 or more years, and again a total father-absent group. It was necessary to use two different year-grouping criteria for the two absence dimensions in order to insure sufficient cell sizes. The first and last groups of each dimension were included to

[1] This study was assisted in part by grant MH 07994–05 from the National Institute of Mental Health.

provide limits within which the influence of shift work should fall. There were 20 Ss in each group. The night shift was defined as 8 consecutive hours of work with the major portion of the time falling between the hours of 8:00 P.M. and 8:00 A.M. All night-shift jobs as well as father-present jobs were of a manual nature, in an attempt to minimize socioeconomic differences between groups. Manual work was defined as factory work below the level of foreman. Forms were sent home to the father of each S to check on the accuracy of the S's report of length of absence and period of absence. The correlation coefficient between the number of years absent as reported by the subject and that reported by her father was +.98. The product-moment coefficient calculated to determine the agreement in relation to the reported period of absence was +.92.

The American College Entrance Examination (ACE) scores (Berdie, Dressel, & Kelson 1951) taken by all entering freshmen at the university were obtained from the University Counseling Center. Only the Q (quantitative) scores on the ACE were presented in the present study. For statistical purposes, all ACE scores (reported in percentiles) were converted to standard scores, and t tests were employed in the analysis. Nevertheless, median scores are also presented in the tables, as they communicate more directly than do standard scores.

RESULTS

Table 1 presents median ACE Q scores for the entire sample on the dimension of number of years of father absence. A simple analysis of variance to examine the effect of number of years of father absence (shift work) on Q scores proved to be significant ($F = 3.00$, df 4/95, $p < .05$). Multiple comparisons were undertaken employing the Newman-Keuls method (Winer 1962). The only significant difference found was between the father-present group and the total father-absent group ($p < .01$); although, directionally, scores on Q tend to decrease with the degree of father absence.

Table 2 presents median ACE Q scores for the entire sample on the dimension of age of S when father was absent. A simple analysis of variance to examine the effect of age of S when father was absent on Q scores yielded significance ($F = 3.18$, df 4/95, $p < .05$). Further analysis by Newman-Keuls revealed that, in addition to a father-present–total father-absent difference, total father-absent girls obtained significantly lower Q scores than girls whose fathers worked the night shift after they had reached the age of 10 ($p < .05$). Again, the trend for the shift-work groups indicates that the later in life father was absent on shift work, the less on Q scores.

In order to assess whether any trends were evident in the linguistic (L) portion of the ACE, a median test of the L scores was performed on the dimensions of length of father absence and period of father absence. The χ^2 values derived from both of these tests yielded probability statements in excess of .30, indicating no systematic relations between either length or period of father absence and linguistic ability.

DISCUSSION

Even though the overall F was significant for the absolute number of years of shift work, this can be accounted for almost entirely by the difference between the total father-absent group and the father-present group. The fact that the predicted depressant effect was found only in the extreme father-absent group suggests that the degree of partial father-absence becomes a relevant variable only as it approaches its upper limits.

More interesting findings emerge when Q scores are considered in terms of the *period* of father absence. The Ss whose father had worked the night shift after they had reached the age of 10 had significantly higher Q scores than the total father-absent group. This finding, coupled with the lack of difference between the total father-absent group and the 0–4 and 5–9 groups, would seem to indicate that the years from 1 to 9 compose a critical

TABLE 1
SUMMARY SCORES ON ACE FOR LENGTH OF FATHER ABSENCE

	Father Present	1–5	6–10	11+	Father Absent
ACE median scores	78.00	62.00	58.00	51.00	43.00
Z Scores	0.67	0.38	0.36	0.10	−0.12

NOTE.—$N = 20$ per category.

TABLE 2
SUMMARY SCORES ON THE ACE FOR PERIOD OF FATHER ABSENCE

	Father Present	1–4	5–9	10+	Father Absent
ACE median scores	78.00	55.00	62.00	70.00	43.00
Z Scores	0.67	0.30	0.40	0.65	−0.12

NOTE.—$N = 20$ per category.

period for the development of quantitative skills in girls, a finding also demonstrated in a previous study (Sutton-Smith et al. 1968). Thus, the important dimension to be considered in the relation of partial father absence to cognitive abilities would seem to be the period of absence.

The results of the present study show that it is feasible to treat long-term night-shift work by the father on a father-presence-absence continuum. Furthermore, as fathers who are completely absent have similar effects to fathers who are partially absent when girls are under the age of 9 years, then it is possible to define *absence* in a slightly more refined way than was previously the case. It seems now less likely that the various absence effects described in the earlier article were due to the compensatory behavior of the mother without a husband. It appears more likely that the absence effects are due simply to the decreased amount of interaction between father and child.

References

Berdie, R.; Dressel, K.; & Kelson, P. Relative validity of the *Q* and *L* scores on the ACE Psychological Examination. *Educational and Psychological Measurement,* 1951, *11,* 803–812.

Sutton-Smith, B.; Rosenberg, B. G.; & Landy, F. Father absence effects on cognitive ability in families of different sibling composition. *Child Development,* 1968, *39,* 1213–1222.

Winer, B., *Statistical principles in experimental design.* New York: McGraw-Hill, 1962.

21

Authoritarian vs. Authoritative Parental Control[1]

DIANA BAUMRIND

In this paper, Diana Baumrind of the University of California at Berkeley summarizes her work about parents' approaches to the discipline of their children. She discusses whether permissiveness is the only alternative to authoritarianism, bringing in the relevant views of such workers as Montessori, Piaget, and A. S. Neill, the author of Summerhill. *The final portions of the paper deal with the special problems of parental control of adolescents. Here she acknowledges the dilemma that confronts today's youth.*

Social protest against our political institutions, national policy, and cultural mores is so vigorous in its expression, and fundamental in its rejection of constituted authority, that it should provoke a thoughtful inquiry not only into the issues raised, but also into the conditions which legitimate authority and into those which render authority illegitimate or ineffectual.

Three years ago I wrote an article entitled *Effects of Authoritative Parental Control on Child Behavior* (2). In that article I contrasted three modes of parental control—permissive, authoritarian, and

[1] This is a revised version of a talk delivered at San Jose State College Workshop, Conflict and Adolescence, June 21, 1968, San Jose, Calif. This talk was in part supported by research grant HD0228 from the National Institute of Child Health and Development.

authoritative—in order to show that relevant arguments against the use of authoritarian parental control did not apply to authoritative parental control. I shall repeat some of those arguments because I think that they are still cogent.

However, the analysis which I made at that time is most relevant to what Dubin and Dubin (5) call the Authority Inception Period which ends at about 6 years. It deals very little with the conditions which legitimate authority in late childhood and adolescence, a matter of considerable social importance today. I will use the feminine gender to refer to the parent and the masculine gender to refer to the child.

There are a number of arguments[2] against the use of certain disciplinary techniques which are made in support of permissive childrearing which I would like to discuss briefly after defining the *permissive parent.*

As I understand the values of the permissive parent, she attempts to behave in a nonpunitive, acceptant, and affirmative manner toward the child's impulse, desires, and actions. She consults with him about policy decisions and gives explanations for family rules. She makes few demands for household responsibility and orderly behavior. She presents herself to the child as a resource for him to use as he wishes, not as an active agent responsible for shaping or altering his ongoing or future behavior. She allows the child to regulate his own activities as much as possible, avoids the exercise of control, and does not encourage him to obey externally defined standards. She attempts to use reason but not overt power to accomplish her ends.

The alternative to adult control, according to Neill, is to permit the child to be self-regulated, free of restraint, and unconcerned about expression of impulse or the effects of his carelessness.

To quote Neill:
Self-regulation means the right of a baby to live freely, without outside authority in things psychic and somatic. It means that the baby feeds when it is hungry; that it becomes clean in habits only when it wants to; that it is never stormed at nor spanked; that it is always loved and protected (14, p. 105, italics Neill's).

I believe that to impose anything by authority is wrong. The child should not do anything until he comes to the opinion—that it should be done (14, p. 114, italics Neill's).

Every child has the right to wear clothes of such a kind that it does not matter a brass farthing if they get messy or not (14, p. 115).

[2] For a more detailed treatment of the validity of such arguments, see (2).

Furniture to a child is practically nonexistent. So at Summerhill we buy old car seats and old bus seats. And in a month or two they look like wrecks. Every now and again at mealtime, some youngster waiting for his second helping will while away the time by twisting his fork almost into knots (14, p. 138).

Really, any man or woman who tries to give children freedom should be a millionaire, for it is not fair that the natural carelessness of children should always be in conflict with the economic factor (14, p. 139).

Arguments given against the use of certain disciplinary techniques:

1. It has been argued by clinically trained advocates of permissive childrearing, such as Lawrence Frank (7) or the early Spock, that *punishment has inevitable negative side effects, and is an ineffective means of controlling behavior.* However, the experimental or clinical evidence for this contention is by no means convincing. Clinical studies have tended to confuse punitive, rejecting attitudes in parents with the effects of punishment *per se* and to attribute the known negative effects of punitive and rejecting attitudes to the use of aversive stimuli, i.e., punishment, as well. Severe, unjust, and ill-timed punishment administered by an unloving parent is probably harmful as well as ineffective. However, there are some theoretical grounds to suppose that the milder forms of punishment, unlike traumatic rejection or beatings may have, like other forthright uses of power, beneficial side effects, such as the following:

a. more rapid re-establishment of affectional involvement on both sides following emotional release;
b. high resistance to similar deviation by siblings who vicariously experience punishment;
c. emulation of the aggressive parent resulting in prosocial assertive behavior;
d. lessening of guilt reactions to transgression; and
e. an increased ability of the child to endure punishment in the service of a desired end.

In addition, the proposition that punishment is an *ineffective* means of controlling human behavior may indeed be a "legend" as Solomon (20) and Walters, Parke, & Crane (21) suggest. Under conditions prevailing in the home setting, punishment may be quite effective in helping to accomplish particular objectives.

2. Another argument against the exercise of parental control is *that close supervision, high demands, and other manifestations of parental authority provoke rebelliousness* in children.

In fact, Bandura and Walters (1), Glueck and Glueck (9), and McCord, McCord, and Howard (12) found that higher demands were made by the parents of the least hostile or delinquent children. Finney (6) found that, while parental rigidity was associated with covert hostility in children, firm control was associated with conscience development.

In my own study of middle class parents of preschool children (3, 4), those parents who demanded that their children be orderly and assume household responsibilities provided more enriched and orderly surroundings, and involved themselves more conscientiously with their welfare. Perhaps that is why such demands were viewed by the child as reasonable, and did not tend to provoke rebellion.

A distinction must be made between the effects on the child of unjust, restrictive, subjective authority, when compared to rational, warm, and issue-oriented authority. There is considerable evidence that arbitrary authority but not rational authority is associated in the child with negative affect, disaffiliativeness, and rebelliousness.

3. A third argument against the imposition of authority is that *firm parental control generates passivity and dependence.* However, Hoffman's (11) results indicate that parental assertiveness, and submissiveness in the child are negatively correlated. Sears' (18) findings on early socialization and later aggression suggest that high punishment for aggression, like "reactive unqualified power assertion," does not lead to submissive behavior. My own results were that parents of the most self-reliant and approach-oriented group of children were rated highest in firm control and reactive power assertion.

4. It has been argued in support of permissive childrearing that *permissiveness frees the child from the presence and authority of the parent.* However, rather than having no effect upon him, the noninterference of an adult who is present when the child is misbehaving seems to signify approval of his behavior, not neutrality, and actually tends to increase rather than leave unaffected the incidence of that behavior. For example, Siegel and Kohn (19) demonstrated that the presence of a permissive adult increased the incidence of aggression shown by nursery school boys to somewhat younger boys. To quote Siegel and Kohn:

Two-thirds of the *S*s in the adult-present sessions were more aggressive in the second than in the first session, and all the *S*s in the adult-absent sessions were less aggressive in the second than in the first session. This finding is in confirmation of the hypothesis which was drawn from a consideration of the nature and the effects of adult permissiveness with children, and of the nature of young children's controls for aggression (19, pp. 140–141).

5. It has also been argued that *controlling parents are motivated by the Authoritarian Personal-*

ity Syndrome. Fromm used the term authoritarian personality to refer to the syndrome in which enactment of the role of inhibiting authority characterizes the individual's interpersonal relations in order to defensively protect a weak ego from any possible assault.

While parents motivated by the authoritarian personality syndrome are controlling, it does not follow that the converse is true. Some subgroups of controlling parents permit high autonomy in many areas of the child's life. Lois Hoffman et al. (10) described a subgroup of parents who were perceived by their children as both coercive and permissive of high autonomy.

I found that, whereas the parents of relatively alienated pre-school children tended to use inhibiting control, the parents of exceptionally mature children exerted even firmer control, used reason to explain their directives, and encouraged independent expression. This latter group of parents certainly did not exhibit the authoritarian personality syndrome. They were open and receptive although highly authoritative in their requirement for compliance. Thus, several investigators have identified subgroups of controlling parents who are not restrictive of children's autonomy or motivated by the authoritarian personality syndrome and have shown that children react differently to inhibiting and rational control.

It seems likely that:

Authoritarian control and permissive noncontrol may both shield the child from the opportunity to engage in vigorous interaction with people. Demands which cannot be met or no demands, suppression of conflict or sidestepping of conflict, refusal to help or too much help, unrealistically high or low standards, all may curb or understimulate the child so that he fails to achieve the knowledge and experience which could realistically reduce his dependence upon the outside world. The authoritarian and the permissive parent may both create, in different ways, a climate in which the child is not desensitized to the anxiety associated with nonconformity. Both models minimize dissent, the former by suppression and the latter by diversion or indulgence. To learn how to dissent, the child may need a strongly held position from which to diverge and then be allowed under some circumstances to pay the price for nonconformity by being punished. Spirited give and take within the home, if accompanied by respect and warmth, may teach the child how to express aggression in self-serving and prosocial causes and to accept the partially unpleasant consequences of such actions (2, p. 904).

AUTHORITARIAN VS. AUTHORITATIVE

I would like to *contrast the prototype authoritarian parent with the prototype authoritative parent*.

The *authoritarian parent* as she is generally described in the literature attempts to shape, control, and evaluate the behavior and attitudes of the child in accordance with a set standard of conduct, usually an absolute standard, theologically motivated and formulated by a higher authority. She values obedience as a virtue and favors punitive, forceful measures to curb self-will at points where the child's actions or beliefs conflict with what she thinks is right conduct. She believes in inculcating such instrumental values as respect of authority, respect for work and respect for the preservation of order and traditional structure. She does not encourage verbal give or take, believing that the child should accept her word for what is right.

The *authoritative parent* as she appears in my studies also attempts to direct the child's activities but in a rational, issue-oriented manner. She encourages verbal give and take, and shares with the child the reasoning behind her policy. She values both expressive and instrumental attributes, both autonomous self-will and disciplined conformity. Therefore, she exerts firm control at points of parent-child divergence, but does not hem the child in with restrictions. She recognizes her own special rights as an adult, but also the child's individual interests and special ways. The authoritative parent affirms the child's present qualities, but also sets standards for future conduct. She uses reason as well as power to achieve her objectives. She does not base her decisions on group consensus or the individual child's desires; but also, does not regard herself as infallible or divinely inspired.

Some quotations from Rambusch, in describing the Montessori method, illustrate the way in which authoritative control is used to resolve the antithesis between pleasure and duty, and between freedom and responsibility.

The discipline resides in three areas in a Montessori classroom: It resides in the environment itself which is controlled; in the teacher herself who is controlled and is ready to assume an authoritarian role if it is necessary; and from the very beginning it resides in the children. It is a three-way arrangement, as opposed to certain types of American education in which all of the authority is vested in the teacher, or where, in the caricature of permissive education, all of the authority is vested in the children.

When a child has finished his work he is free to put it away, he is free to initiate new work or, in certain instances, he is free to not work. But he is not free to disturb or destroy what others are doing. If the day is arranged in such a way that at a certain time the teacher must demand of the children that they arbitrarily finish what they are doing—if it is lunchtime, or recess or whatever—the child must accommodate himself to the demand of the group. It is largely a question of balance. In a Montessori class the teacher does not delude herself into believing that her manipulation of the children represents their consensus of what they would like to do. If she is manipulating them insofar as she is determining arbitrarily that this must be done at this time, she is cognizant of what she is doing, which the child may or may not be.

The importance of the responsibility in selecting matter for the child to learn is placed in the hands of those adults who are aware of what the culture will demand of the child and who are able to "program" learning in such a way that what is suitable for the child's age and stage of development is also learnable and pleasurable to him. Both Dewey and Montessori feel that interest and discipline are connected and not opposed. Dewey himself decried unrestrained freedom of action in speech, in manners, and lack of manners. He was, in fact, critical of all those progressive schools that carried the thing they call freedom nearly to the point of anarchy (17, p. 63).

The body of findings which I reviewed in the article cited, and certainly the results of my own research, support the position that authoritative control can achieve responsible conformity with group standards without loss of individual autonomy or self-assertiveness.

As Dubin and Dubin (5) point out, by the imposition of parental authority, the child in his first six years learns to express his social individuality, within the confines of what the culture will accept. He finds that there are ranges of acceptable behavior in most situations of action. By having orderly experiences with available behavioral choices, the child learns to distinguish between conforming and deviant behavior. Later when he is capable of moral judgments, he may choose to engage in deviant behavior, but he will do so prepared to endure the punishment which may follow. Hopefully he will have learned the value to him of authoritative behavior and know how to play the role behavior which is reciprocal. He will also have had his parent as a model for the role of a rational authority, a role he can himself assume at a later age.

Use of Power in Childhood and Adolescence

I believe then that the imposition of authority even against the child's will is useful to the child during the Authority Inception Period. During those early years exercise of power is a legitimate right of the parents. Indeed, power serves to legitimate authority in the mind of the child.

During childhood, power is asymmetrical in the family unit. That is, the parent's ability to exercise control over the child and to restrict his autonomy exceeds that of the child, in reciprocal interaction with his parent. The parent by virtue of her physical size, experience, and control over the sources of supply can, in most instances where there is a divergence, carry out her wishes despite the resistance of the child, and the child cannot do likewise. Parents vary of course in the extent to which they acknowledge the asymmetry of their power, or are effectively able to use power.

The major way in which parents exercise power is by manipulating the stimuli which affect the child —rewarding with positive reinforcers and punishing with aversive stimuli. The main factor which makes a parent a successful reinforcing agent or an attractive model for her child to imitate is her effective power to give the child what he needs— i.e., her control over resources which the child desires, and her willingness and ability to provide the child with these resources in such a manner and at such a time that the child will be most gratified. Both morally and practically, gratification of the child's needs is a precondition for the effective imposition of parental authority.

Piaget's analysis of the development of the idea of justice (15) suggests that the child's organization of a moral order is based upon power in the early years. In the mind of the young child, power legitimates the parent's right to exercise authority. The parent's ability to gratify the child and to withhold gratification legitimates her authority. The child has not yet reached the level of cognitive development where he can legitimate authority, or object to its imposition, on a principled basis.

The parent can accelerate the child's cognitive development both by requiring the child to accommodate at the top limit of his ability to do so, and by using reason to support her directives. Even though the specific reason may not be understood by the child, he learns that authority must ultimately be legitimated on a principled basis. By using reason, the authoritative parent teaches the child to seek the reasons behind directives and eventually to exercise his option either to conform, or to deviate and to cope with the consequences. Reason does not really legitimate authority for the young child, in the same way as power does, or in the same way as it will at adolescence.

Punishment has an informational role for the parent and the child. By setting a price on negatively sanctioned behavior, both the parent and the child can determine how important it is to the child that he perform an act which he knows will be punished at a given level of intensity. When a child repeats an act knowingly for which he has been punished moderately severely, the parent has grounds to question the legitimacy of her rejection of that act. Punishment and other manifestations of power then are an important part of the feedback which advance the parent's understanding of the child and his level of cognitive and moral development.

By early adolescence, however, power cannot

and should not be used to legitimate authority. The young person is now capable of formal operational thought. He can formulate principles of choice by which to judge his own actions and the actions of others. He has the conceptual ability to be critical even though he may lack the wisdom to moderate his criticism. He can see clearly many alternatives to parental directives; and the parent must be prepared to defend rationally, as she would to an adult, a directive with which the adolescent disagrees. Moreover, the asymmetry of power which characterizes childhood no longer exists at adolescence. The adolescent cannot be forced physically to obey over any period of time.

When a young child refuses to obey, his parent can persist until he does obey, giving him a reason based upon a principle which he may not understand, or a reason based upon the asymmetry of power, which he is sure to understand. She can say, "you must do it because I say so;" and the child will accept such a parental maneuver as legitimate even if he continues to have objections on hedonistic grounds, because he is not yet capable of principled objections.

An adolescent, on the other hand, is capable of principled objections. When an adolescent refuses to do as his parent wishes, it is more congruent with his construction of reality for the parent simply to ask him "Why not?" Through the dialogue which ensues, the parent may learn that her directive was unjust; or the adolescent may learn that his parent's directive could be legitimated. In any case, a head-on confrontation is avoided. While head-on confrontation serves to strengthen authority in the Authority Inception Period, it undermines authority during adolescence.

This does not mean that the parent relinquishes her authoritative role. It does mean that she enacts her role in a different way, one suited to the level of development of the older child. She makes limited use of power to settle parent-child divergences, and then primarily to guard her personal interests or to break a stalemate when the adolescent's objection is based, not on principle, but on pique. The adolescent can understand and be held to a contractual agreement. The adolescent, egocentric as he is, can recognize the egocentric needs of parents. More often than is admitted, a parent-child divergence involves a simple conflict of interests. The parent requires quiet and the young person wants to play loud music; if the adolescent were to come in late, his parent would lose sleep; if the working parent is to rest after dinner, the children must do the dishes. Children recognize the legitimacy of demands based on personal rights, provided that parents represent the matter as it is, and the balance of giving is well in favor of the children,

as indeed it must be if parents are to have any special rights.

The authority of the parent at adolescence stands or falls on the parent's past performance, and what she is at present, in relation to what the adolescent needs her to be. The adolescent needs a parent who has something to say that is worth listening to, and who is fully receptive to what he has to say. The adolescent needs to have someone to argue with in order to develop his own position. His parents can play this role of friendly adversary. The adolescent needs a strongly stated thesis to relate his own thinking to. A convincing antithesis requires a well-formulated thesis. The authoritative parent can state and defend her own thesis vigorously, and yet not limit the freedom of the adolescent to express and argue for his antithesis. The parent must not expect the resultant synthesis to be merely a restatement of her own thesis. By receiving the antithesis presented to her by her adolescent, the parent gains knowledge of that with which she is authorized to deal.

Receptivity does not mean listening in order to achieve conformity after talk. It does mean that an antithetical position which may threaten the stability of the system is encouraged to interact with that system. Only in that way can the system continue to perform its function. A system which cannot absorb dissent cannot survive. Revolutionary fervor is nourished by the refusal of constituted authority to receive antithesis, to be renewed by dissent. If constituted authority were as successful in absorbing dissent as Marcuse thinks it is, there would be no basis for the revolutionary fervor he advocates.

Under normal conditions, adolescents do not rebel against all authority by any means. They differentiate quite accurately between authoritarian and authoritative parental control. Pikas (16), in his survey of 656 Swedish adolescents, showed that significant differences occurred in their acceptance of parental authority, depending upon the reason for the directive. Authority which was based on rational concern for the child's welfare was accepted well by the child, while authority which was based on the adult's desire to dominate or exploit the child was rejected. The former, which he calls rational authority, is similar to "authoritative control," and the latter, which he calls inhibiting authority, is similar to "authoritarian control," as these terms are used in this discussion. Pikas' results are supported by Middleton and Snell (13) who found that parental discipline regarded by the child as either very strict or very permissive was associated with lack of closeness between parent and child and with rebellion against the parents' political viewpoints.

THE MAJOR CHALLENGE TO AUTHORITY TODAY

The major challenge to authority today is not that the young have no respect for authority, but that they have little reason to have respect for authority. Both youth and their parents are disaffected with their social institutions—with their schools, churches and their government. The mythology of affluence has been exploded. The credibility gap on issues of poverty and war has made extension of trust unfeasible, and open rebellion morally feasible. It is very difficult today for constituted authorities, even rational authorities, to have respect for themselves. Rational authorities have cause to question the legitimacy of their authority. Until relatively recently, parents could believe that by maintaining order within the family, they were upholding a higher order to which they too submitted—this higher order was defined by religious mandate, cultural tradition, or national way. Think of the basis upon which Susannah Wesley, mother of the founder of Methodism, legitimated her authority in the 18th century. These are her words:

As self-will is the root of all sin and misery, so whatever cherishes this in children insures their after-wretchedness and irreligion; whatever checks and mortifies it promotes their future happiness and piety. This is still more evident, if we further consider, that religion is nothing else than doing the will of God, and not our own: that the one grand impediment to our temporal and eternal happiness being this self-will, no indulgences of it can be trivial, no denial unprofitable. Heaven or hell depends on this alone. So that the parent who studies to subdue it in his child, works together with God in the renewing and saving a soul. The parent who indulges it does the devil's work, makes religion impracticable, salvation unattainable; and does all that in him lies to damn his child, soul and body forever (8, pp. 30–31).

Since the impediment to temporal and eternal happiness was thought to be self-will, the parent behaved in authoritarian ways because she cared for the child, not because she was weak or punitive.

While Mrs. Wesley believed that the mores of her society were divinely inspired, many parents not only know these mores are not divinely inspired, but find them in no sense inspirational. Concerning our social structure, many parents agree with their adolescents, when they in the words of Mario Savio find the operation of the machines so odious and vile as to require of them that they put their bodies on the gears and upon the wheels and upon the levers to prevent these wheels from working at all. To be more specific, these parents share the moral outrage of their adolescents at the atrocities of the Vietnam war, and the gross inequities in distribution of wealth in this country. Maintenance of structure and order is high in the hierarchy of values of authoritative parents, as we have defined these parents. What are they to do, they ask, when maintenance of structure and order conflicts with a higher value, such as killing to no just purpose. These parents feel responsible for the sins of their generation, and their faith in their own expertness is shaken. Their faith in the value of obedience, and in the possibility of constructive nonconformity is shaken. We have said that authoritative control can achieve responsible conformity with group standards without loss of individual autonomy and self-assertiveness. Conformity with group standards, if this means support of the Vietnam war, does not seem responsible to many parents today. How are they to rear their children to conform responsibly if they do not believe that it is responsible to conform? How are they to rear their children to constructively dissent if they do not believe that constructive dissent will be received by constituted authority?

In summary, I examined the criticisms directed by advocates of permissiveness against parental control and showed that to the extent that these criticisms were valid, in early childhood they were relevant to authoritarian control and not authoritative control. I contrasted the conditions and processes which legitimate authority in childhood with those which legitimate authority in adolescence. In particular, I argued that the imposition of authority by use of power is legitimate in childhood and not in adolescence, because the level of cognitive and moral development of the adolescent is such as to require that he be bound by social contract and moral principles rather than by power. Lastly, I discussed what I felt to be the fundamental challenge to authority today.

In closing, I would like to say that an increasingly larger segment of today's youth are rejecting the alternatives offered by established authority, not because they are rebellious neurotics, but because these alternatives are not morally acceptable. If their dissent is not received, and the system to which they object is not radically altered, we who are in a position of authority can expect to be confronted with what Marcuse calls the Great Refusal. We will be faced with an absolute rejection of the society and its institutions by many of our brightest and most competent youth. That absolute rejection will negate the distinction between rational and arbitrary authority, between authoritative and authoritarian adult control. If we cannot fully receive the message from the most dissenting of our youth, we may be faced with the complete withdrawal of legitimacy from rational as well as arbitrary authority by the very youth upon whom we count for cultural continuity.

REFERENCES

1. BANDURA, A., & WALTERS, R. H. *Adolescent Aggression.* New York: Ronald, 1959.
2. BAUMRIND, D. "Effects of Authoritative Parental Control on Child Behavior," *Child Development,* 1966, *37–4,* 887–907.
3. BAUMRIND, D. "Child Care Practices Anteceding Three Patterns of Preschool Behavior," *Genetic Psychology Monographs,* 1967, *75,* 43–88.
4. BAUMRIND, D., & BLACK, A. E. "Socialization Practices Associated with Dimensions of Competence in Preschool Boys and Girls," *Child Development,* 1967, *38–2,* 291–327.
5. DUBIN, E. R., & DUBIN, R. "The Authority Inception Period in Socialization," *Child Development,* 1964, *34,* 885–898.
6. FINNEY, J. C. "Some Maternal Influences on Children's Personality and Character," *Genetic Psychology Monographs,* 1961, *63,* 199–278.
7. FRANK, L. K. "Freedom for the Personality." *Psychiatry,* 140, *3,* 341–349.
8. GESELL, A. *The Guidance of Mental Growth in Infant and Child,* New York: Macmillan, 1930.
9. GLUECK, S., & GLUECK, E. *Unraveling Juvenile Delinquency.* New York: Commonwealth Fund, 1950.
10. HOFFMAN, L. ROSEN, S., & LIPPITT, R. "Parental Coerciveness, Child Autonomy, and Child's Role at School," *Sociometry,* 1960, *23,* 15–22.
11. HOFFMAN, M. L. "Power Assertion by The Parent and Its Impact on the Child," *Child Development,* 1960, *31,* 129–143.
12. McCORD, J., & HOWARD, A. "Familial Correlates of Aggression in Non-delinquent Male Children," *J. Abnorm. Soc. Psychol.,* 1961, *62,* 79–93.
13. MIDDLETON, R., & SNELL, P. "Political Expression of Adolescent Rebellion," *Amer. J. Sociol.,* 1963, *68,* 527–535.
14. NEILL, A. S. *Summerhill.* New York: Hart, 1964.
15. PIAGET, J. *The Moral Judgment of the Child.* New York: Free Press, 1965.
16. PIKAS, A. "Children's Attitudes Toward Rational Versus Inhibiting Parental Authority," *J. Abnorm. Soc. Psychol.,* 1961, *62,* 315–321.
17. RAMBUSCH, N. M. *Learning How to Learn: An American Approach to Montessori.* Baltimore: Helicon, 1962.
18. SEARS, R. R. "Relation of Early Socialization Experiences to Aggression in Middle Childhood," *J. Abnorm. Soc. Psychol.,* 1961, *63,* 466–492.
19. SIEGEL, A. E., & KOHN, L. G. "Permissiveness, Permission, and Aggression: The Effects of Adult Presence or Absence on Aggression in Children's Play," *Child Development,* 1959, *30,* 131–141.
20. SOLOMON, R. L. "Punishment," *Amer. Psychologist,* 1964, *19,* 239–253.
21. WALTERS, R. H., PARKE, R. D., & CANE, V. A. "Timing of Punishment and Observation of Consequences to Others as Determinants of Response Inhibition," *J. Exp. Child Psychol.,* 1965, *2,* 10–30.

22

Environmental Correlates of Mental Growth: Prediction from the Family Setting at 21 Months

MARJORIE P. HONZIK

Marjorie Honzik, whose writing we have sampled earlier (in Section II), is the author of this article. The data are from the major longitudinal project at Berkeley's Institute of Human Development. In this paper Dr. Honzik demonstrates associations between later IQ and the quality of relationships in the family during early childhood. Since the data show that conditions favoring the mental growth of girls are different from those benefiting boys, the findings are relevant to Section VIII (Sex as a Determinant of Behavior). It appears here that gender determines the reactions to other variables.

The search for environmental correlates of mental growth has been a long one. For many years it was thought that demographic variables—father's occupation, parents' education, social class, or other overall evaluations of family status —were environmentally relevant to the children's intelligence. These aspects of the environment certainly correlate with the child's IQ. However, the negligible relations found between the test scores of adopted children and the demographic characteristics of the adopting parents indicate that substantial correlations between parental status and child intelligence only occur when the children are related to the parents (Bishop, 1959; Burks, 1928; Leahy, 1935; Skodak & Skeels, 1949). These facts suggest that the correlations found for own children are "due primarily to the common factor of the parents' intelligence rather than to the environment acting as a causative agent" (Jones, 1954). The overall *average* effect of favorable environments is nevertheless shown by the higher average IQ of the adopted children (IQ = 106 at 13 years) than that of their true mothers (IQ = 86) who gave them up for adoption (Skodak & Skeels, 1949). The mental level is raised, but the characteristics of the environment having this effect are not known.

The concern in the present paper is in pinpointing aspects of the environment that correlate with individual differences in cognitive or mental development. The specific purpose of this report is to consider certain experiences of the child in his family during the first 2 years of life that are not highly correlated with, and therefore not likely to be directly mediated by, parental ability but *are* related to the child's intelligence and that are possibly necessary for optimal mental growth.

Suggestions as to the kinds of experiences that are relevant to accelerating and decelerating rates of mental development come from a number of sources. Ainsworth's (1962), Casler's (1961), and Yarrow's (1961) summaries of the effects of maternal deprivation suggest that the human infant who does not have adequate sensory stimulation and individualized care and affection in the first year is likely to show inadequacies in cognitive development. The significance of early affectional relations and the security-giving value of tactual comfort in relation to later adjustment and problem-solving ability is clearly shown in Harlow's experiments and observations with monkeys (1962). The beneficial effects of sensory stimulation and even stress on the development of the central nervous system, and especially of the brain, have been reported in a number of investigations of rats (Bennett, Diamond, Krech, & Rosenzweig, 1964; Levine, 1956).

This study is based on the 30-year longitudinal Guidance Study, directed by Jean W. Macfarlane and supported in part by the Ford Foundation and by U.S. Public Health Service grant MH 06238-02. A preliminary form of this paper was presented at the annual meeting of the American Psychological Association, Los Angeles, September, 1964. This paper has profited from the comments and criticisms of many colleagues. The most extensive revisions were wrought by the suggestions of Jean W. Macfarlane, M. Brewster Smith, John P. McKee, and Norman Livson.

Marjorie P. Honzik, "Environmental correlates of mental growth: prediction from the family setting at 21 months," *Child Development*, 1967, *38*, 337–364. Reprinted with abridgement by permission. © 1967 by The Society for Research in Child Development, Inc.

Studies to date are highly suggestive, but there is need for more clues as to the specific child-rearing attitudes, practices, and opportunities, and at what ages they occur, that are relevant to the development of ability. We may expect the most definitive findings from (*a*) studies of adopted children where the confounding factor of genetic parent-child similarity is controlled and (*b*) longitudinal investigations where the later effects of early experiences may be evaluated, as well as the effect of contemporaneous variables. Specific findings of the few relevant studies will be discussed after we present the results of correlating parental characteristics and family relations with the mental test scores of a group of urban children who were tested on sixteen occasions between the ages of 21 months and 30 years.

THE PRESENT STUDY

In the Guidance Study at the Institute of Human Development, the intensively studied guidance group included initially 124 children, who constituted a representative subsample of the children born in Berkeley, California, in 1928 and 1929 (Macfarlane, 1938). This group was followed from the ages of 21 months to 30 years. Sample attrition resulted largely from families moving from the area (Honzik, Macfarlane, & Allen, 1948). Fortunately, the distribution of the socioeconomic status of the subjects who continued in the study until age 30 years is similar to that of the sample first seen at 21 months. Since subjects tested at successive ages did not constitute a selected socioeconomic group, results for all children tested will be presented in the tables. Results for a core sample of subjects who remained in the study to age 18 years will be reported in Figures 5, 10, and 11.

The subjects were tested individually on the California Preschool Mental Scale at eight different ages between 21 months and 5 years, on the Revisions of the Stanford-Binet at seven different ages between 6 and 15 years, and on the Wechsler-Bellevue Intelligence Scale at 18 years (Honzik et al., 1948). The Wechsler-Bellevue Intelligence Scale block-design test was given at age 30 years.

When the children were 21 months old, the family situation was evaluated on the basis of office interviews with both parents and of home interviews and observations. Macfarlane (who conducted the office interviews) and the social workers (who visited the home) independently rated 64 specific parental characteristics and family interrelations. Macfarlane (1938) reported the agreement between her ratings and those of the psychiatric social workers. The median *r* is .56, and the average difference is .7 on a five-point rating scale. Since the raters saw the parents in quite different contexts, this degree of agreement is fairly impressive, and their averaged ratings can be expected to provide reliable assessments for consideration in relation to the children's mental test scores. The values used in the present study are weighted averages which take into account differing opportunities to observe both the family and the aspect of the family situation being rated. If one rater had a markedly better contact with a family or better opportunity to judge the situation, his or her rating was given a double weighting before the averages were computed.

This series of family variables includes characteristics and concerns of each parent, parental conflicts and agreements, and parent-child relations. The topical coverage of interviews planned by Macfarlane on which the ratings were largely based grew from the then available literature and her clinical experience with children and their parents. The inventory of items has been divided into seven categories according to content and without regard to possible relevance to the child's intelligence: Socioeconomic Conditions (4 items), Physical Status of Parents (4 items), Parental Social Adjustment (4 items), Parental Conflict (14 items), Parental Characteristics (14 items), Parental Attitudes and Concerns (13 items), and Family Affectional Relations (12 items).

Since this is an empirical survey expected to generate as well as test hypotheses, all obtained correlations between family variables and the children's test scores will be reported.

RESULTS

... If a parental characteristic or family variable is unrelated to parental education but is correlated with the child's mental test performance, we assume that this family variable is environmentally relevant to the child's mental development.... [In the original] Tables 2 through 7 give the year-by-year correlations for categories of family variables that are more highly correlated with the children's test scores.

SOCIOECONOMIC CONDITIONS

All aspects of the socioeconomic milieu are intercorrelated (Atherton, 1962) and characteristically show an increasing relation to the child's mental test performance in early childhood (Bayley, 1954; Hindley, 1961; Honzik, 1963). One aspect of socioeconomic status, *family income,* correlates with both the father's (*r* = .45, *p* < .01) and mother's (*r* = .36, *p* < .05) schooling and significantly with the daughter's test score, beginning at $3\frac{1}{2}$ years, and with the son's test score from the age of 5 years to 30 years.... This sex difference in the age of onset of a correlation between the child's test score and parental status was observed in all the above-mentioned studies and is interpreted in terms of an earlier stabilizing or maturing of the girls' abilities than the boys'. These age changes, including the sex differences, are similar for all socioeconomic variables and reflect in part, as mentioned earlier, the "shared inheritance" of parent and child, in as much as they are not obtained in studies of adopted children.

Another variable related to parental education and reflecting the socioeconomic milieu is the adequacy of the *play facilities*. The play facilities rating at 21 months is not correlated with the children's test scores until age 3 for girls and age 10 for boys (Fig. 2). The girls' scores are more highly correlated with the adequacy of play facilities than the boys'. This result is consonant with a tendency noted in a number of the correlations for aspects of the total family milieu to have greater relevance for the girls' than the boys' scores. In contrast to this sex difference is the higher correlation of the *family income* with the boys' than the girls' mental test scores at ages 18 and 30 years.

. . .

PARENTAL SOCIAL ADJUSTMENT

This category of variables yielded only two significant correlations. The fathers with *poor social adjustment* had sons with high performance IQ's on the Wechsler-Bellevue at age 18 years and above-average scores on the Wechsler-Bellevue block design at age 30 years.

. . .

PARENTAL CONFLICT

During the preschool period, lack of parental *conflict over religion* and *whether to have more children* is significantly correlated with the girls' test scores. This finding reflects a more general one that will be noted in many of the relations: a girl's mental test performance is likely to be accelerated in a milieu of parental harmony or lack of conflict. Since the girls' scores appear somewhat sensitive to parental tension, it is not surprising

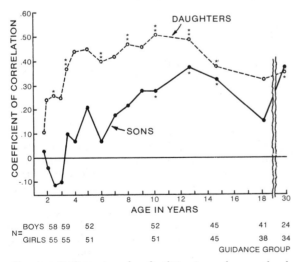

FIGURE 2. *Superior play facilities in early preschool years × child's mental test scores. *, Significant at the .05 level; **, significant at the .01 level.*

that when the tension or conflict is specifically child related, as in *discipline,* the highest correlations are obtained (see Fig. 3). The marked drop in the correlation at age 30, when only the Wechsler-Bellevue block-design test was administered, suggests that parental agreement is affecting verbal rather than performance test scores.

FIGURE 3. *Parents agree on discipline in early preschool years × child's mental test scores.*, Significant at the .05 level.*

Support for this is found in the slightly higher r with the verbal than the performance IQ on the Wechsler-Bellevue at age 18 years. The slightly negative correlations between *parental agreement* on discipline and the sons' test scores is equally impressive. Not shown in Figure 3 is the significant negative correlation ($r = -.52$, $p < .01$) between parental agreement on discipline before 2 years and the son's performance on the Wechsler-Bellevue block-design test at age 30 years. The higher correlation with the performance IQ ($r = -.28$, $p < .05$) than the verbal IQ at 18 years suggests that the 30-year correlation is not a chance one. Apparently, *parental conflict with respect to discipline* is associated with performance rather than verbal interests and skills in boys.

. . .

PARENTAL CHARACTERISTICS

None of the parental characteristics . . . is significantly related to the son's mental test scores at 21 months, but mothers who appeared *worrisome* and *tense,* somewhat *unstable,* and *highly active* and *energetic* had sons who displayed a pattern of accelerative mental growth after this age. Of these maternal variables, *worrisomeness* of the mother is correlated significantly with her education ($r = .44$, $p < .05$), but the partial r between son's test score and mother's *worrisomeness,* with mother's education held constant, is still moderate ($r_{12.5} = .30$). Mother's *energy level* is increasingly correlated with the son's and daughter's mental test scores to age 30 (Fig. 4). The fact that the course of mental growth is accelerative for young people whose mothers were, and probably continued to be, active and energetic rather than inactive and sedentary is in line with the results reported by Levine (1956) for rat pups stimulated in early infancy.

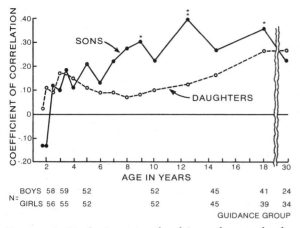

N= BOYS 58 59   52   52   45   41 24
    GIRLS 56 55 52   52   45   39 34
                                        GUIDANCE GROUP

FIGURE 4. *Mother's energy level in early preschool years × child's mental test scores. *, Significant at the .05 level; **, significant at the .01 level.*

Figure 5 gives the results for Cluster IV, which includes mother's *worrisomeness, concern about health,* and *lack of stability.*... The *r*'s are based on a core sample of children who came in for tests and interviews at least once during the following four age periods: 5–7, 8–10, 11–13, and 14–16 years. The results for this core sample are very similar to those obtained for the total group. The correlations are higher for sons than for daughters until the tenth year but are positive to year 30 for both sexes.

The apparent accelerative effect of the energetic, tense, concerned, and worrying mother is one of the clear-cut findings in this study. Mothers with these stimulating characteristics probably do more for and with their young children and may be more responsive to their children's needs and wants than are mothers who are lethargic, lack energy, and perhaps are not too concerned about their children.

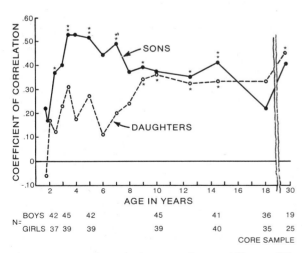

N= BOYS 42 45   42   45   41   36 19
    GIRLS 37 39 39   39   40   35 25
                                          CORE SAMPLE

FIGURE 5. *Mother worrisome and tense (Cluster IV) when child is 21 months × child's mental test scores. *, Significant at the .05 level; **, significant at the .01 level.*

Parental characteristics that are not related to the son's test scores include father's *irritability, reaction to conflict, activity* and *energy level,* and the mother's *sense of privacy.*... Parental characteristics that are unrelated to the daughter's intelligence are: father's *irritability, worrisomeness, self-confidence, stability,* and *sense of privacy* and mother's *tendency to withdraw from conflict.*...

In contrast to the positive correlations between the mother's energy level and the children's test scores (Fig. 4), the father's energy level correlated negatively with the test scores of both boys and girls.... Perhaps the more energetic father engages in more activity outside of the home and thus is not as stimulating to the children as the mother.

PARENTAL ATTITUDES AND CONCERNS

Certain family attitudes and concerns show increasing positive correlations with the children's test scores after the preschool years.... Father's *concern over health* correlates with his education ($r = .51$, $p < .01$) and with his daughter's test performance after the preschool years, but not with his son's (Fig. 6). Mother's *concern with health* is less highly correlated with her education but is significantly related to both the son's and daughter's test scores after the third year. This relation is still significant for girls at age 30 years, and almost so for boys.

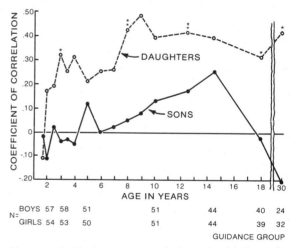

N= BOYS 57 58   51   51   44   40 24
    GIRLS 54 53 50   51   44   39 32
                                        GUIDANCE GROUP

FIGURE 6. *Father concerned about health in early preschool years × child's mental test scores. *, Significant at the .05 level; **, significant at the .01 level.*

The results shown in Figures 6 and 7 suggest that the mother's concern is relevant to the test performance of both the sons and daughters, but the father's concern has relevance only to the daughters.

Parental concern over heredity or a hereditarian point of view ... correlates with parental education and the son's and daughter's test scores. Parents given a high rating on this variable attribute much of the child's behavior to heredity. These correlations possibly reflect social-class differences in attitude in the 1930's and the additional fact that the sons and daughters of *concerned* parents tend to gain in scores.

Moss and Kagan (1958) report that "early maternal concern with achievement facilitates early intelligence test performance of boys but not girls." In the present study, *parental concern with educational achievement* is positively correlated with the test scores of both boys and girls from 3 to 30 years, but the correlations are higher with the son's than with the daughter's.... The most significant relations were obtained between the *mother's concern* and the *son's* test score. There are at least three components to this finding. When parents are *concerned,* children are likely to accelerate in test performance; and when the concern is with *achievement,* the acceleration is likely to be more marked. Additionally, the concern of the parent of the opposite sex appears somewhat more motivating than that of the parent of the same sex.

An unpredicted finding is the positive correlation between Cluster II, *parental satisfaction with father's occupation,* and the son's test performance from 5 through 18 years (Fig. 10). This relation may be a function of the son's identification with the father. An outstanding example of this effect occurred in one family where the father worked in the grandfather's business and felt caught and dominated in a situation where his abilities were not valued and only partially used. The impact of the father's dissatisfaction affected all the family. It was most pronounced in the son whose ability was above average but whose attitude became one of hopelessness. He said at 15 years, "What's the use of trying? You don't get anywhere," and he was failing in school.

Whether or not parents favored giving *sex instruction* to their sons was unrelated to their son's test performance. The daughters of parents scoring high on this variable showed accelerated patterns of test performance from 4 to 30 years, whereas the daughters of parents

who were "embarrassed by questions" or "wanted to keep the child innocent" had lower scores.

Parental *interest in the home* refers to their being pleased or dissatisfied with the housing arrangements. The father's interest in his home is positively correlated with the son's test score at 9 years. The mother's satisfaction is negatively related to the boy's test score at $3\frac{1}{2}$ years ($r = -.28$, $p < .05$) but positively related to the girl's scores at 4 and 5 years. These may be chance findings. There is no consistency or trend in the correlations.

AFFECTIONAL RELATIONS WITHIN THE FAMILY

Certain of these ratings are not only highly correlated with the children's test scores but produced some of the most clear-cut sex differences.

The son's mental test scores are negatively correlated with all aspects of *marital compatibility* (parents' sex adjustment, closeness and friendliness of the parental relationship, as well as the overall marital adjustment).... In contrast, the daughter's test scores are positively, and at certain ages significantly, related to the rating of marital adjustment.... Figure 11 presents the correlations between the *marital compatibility* cluster score and the son's and daughter's test scores for the core sample. The *friendliness of the father to the mother*...yields the largest number of significant correlations with the daughter's test scores between 21 months and 15 years. The *friendliness of mother to father* is not as highly correlated with the girl's scores at age 18 years. It appears that the father's affectional attitude toward the mother produces a family milieu conducive to the daughter's intellectual development.

A *close, friendly mother-daughter* relation correlates with the girl's test scores in the early preschool years but becomes negligible in adolescence. On the other hand, the *father-daughter* correlations are negligible early but become significant from 7 years through adolescence. The changing significance of the mother's and father's relation to the daughter is clear and is in marked contrast to the findings for the son.

Of all the family variables considered, the *closeness of the mother-son* relation is the most predictive of the boy's test performance during the age period 8 to 18 years when the r's are significant at the .01 level (cf. Fig. 12). Inasmuch as the correlation is negligible at age 30, when the Wechsler-Bellevue block design was administered..., it may be inferred that it is the verbal rather than the non-verbal test items that are contributing to the correlations between 2 and 18 years. This inference is correct. The *closeness of the mother-son* relation correlates .56 ($p < .01$) with the son's verbal IQ at 18 years but only .10 with his performance IQ. The finding that verbal competence in the male is facilitated by a close relation to the mother in the early preschool period is cross-validated in two other longitudinal investigations. Moss and Kagan (1958, p. 660) report for the Fels sample that "when a close symbiotic relationship exists between mother and son (as judged by her 'protectiveness,' 'lack of hostility,' 'preference over sibs,' and 'acceleration'), the mother's efficacy as a reinforcing agent of developmental skills is maximized."

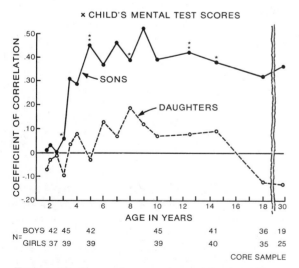

FIGURE 10. *Parental occupation satisfaction (Cluster II) when child is 21 months × child's mental test scores. *, Significant at the .05 level; **, significant at the .01 level.*

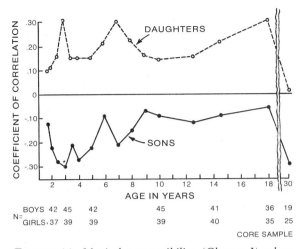

FIGURE 11. *Marital compatibility (Cluster I) when child is 21 months × child's mental test scores. *, Significant at the .05 level.*

In other words, the sons of such mothers have high IQ's at ages 3 and 6 years. Bayley and Schaefer (1964, p. 67) report for the Berkeley Growth Study sample that "mothers who evaluate their boy babies positively, behave toward them in an equalitarian way, and to some degree both grant them autonomy and express affection for them . . . have sons who tend to make below average mental scores in the first year but to make rapid gains in the next two or three years, so that by five and thereafter they are more likely to have high IQ's."

Neither of these longitudinal studies reports similar results for girls. Moss and Kagan (1958) found that "high imitative behavior of mothers" and "low maternal restrictiveness" correlate with the girl's IQ at 3 years, while Bayley and Schaefer report that "mothers who are intrusive with their girl babies" have daughters who earn low IQ's after 4 years. These results are in agreement with the Guidance Study's negligible correlations be-

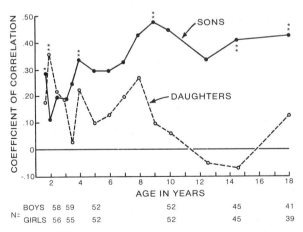

FIGURE 12. *Close bond between mother and child in early preschool years × child's mental test scores. *, Significant at the .05 level; **, significant at the .01 level.*

tween the *closeness of the mother-daughter* relation at 21 months and the daughter's mental test performance in later childhood (Fig. 12).

The finding in the Guidance Study that *marital compatibility* is positively correlated with the girl's test performance has not been reported in any other study. One explanation may be that the Guidance Study protocols include extensive interviews with the fathers. The evidence within the Guidance Study is clear. The girl whose father is concerned about her health (Fig. 6) and has a *close, friendly relationship* with the mother and with her is likely to show an above-average rate of mental development. . . . In line with Bayley and Schaefer's (1964) finding that the mother's intrusiveness is negatively related to the girl's later test scores is the finding that neither the mother's nor the father's *expressiveness of affection* is related to the girl's intelligence. Moss and Kagan (1958, p. 660) conclude "when the female child is given sufficient latitude (in terms of being non-restricted) . . . she is able to exhibit greater developmental progress as measured by the Stanford-Binet." The mental development of the girl in the current culture is accelerated when she has *compatible parents,* a father who is *friendly to the mother and daughter* but who is *not very expressive of his affection* for his daughter. . . .

DISCUSSION

We have found certain family variables assessed before the child is 2 years old to be predictive of mental growth. To the extent that these family variables are unrelated to parental ability, we may assume their influence to be environmental. The results do not clarify whether the effect of the milieu occurred before, during, or after the first 2 years. Regardless of the timing of the influence, it is clear that the family milieu as appraised before 2 years had predictive significance.

The possibility that some of the effect occurs in the first year is suggested by Yarrow's (1963) study of forty adopted infants who were tested at 6 months. Yarrow reports that the environmental variables, as evaluated during the first 6 months, that correlate with the infants' IQ's at 6 months are: *stimulus-adaptation* ($r = .85, p < .01$), *achievement stimulation* ($r = .72, p < .01$), *social stimulation* ($r = .65, p < .01$), and *affectional interchange* (including individualization, emotional involvement, acceptance) ($r = .55, p < .01$). These correlations are high and in some instances higher than any obtained in the Guidance Study, suggesting the magnitude of the impact of the contemporaneous family environment on the infant's developmental course. Yarrow's correlations may also be high because of the greater opportunity to observe maternal behavior in that study. There is essential agreement between Yarrow's findings and those of the Guidance Study. Yarrow's rating of *stimulation-adaptation* considered the extent to which materials and experiences given to the infant were adapted to his capacities. This adaptation variable appears to be related to the Guidance Study *parental concern* about physical health, heredity, etc., which shows an increasing correlation with the Guidance Study children's test scores.

A study of 118 8-year-old English children by Kent and Davis (1957) also reports that children from *unconcerned* homes have significantly lower Stanford-Binet and Wechsler Intelligence Scale for Children IQ's than children from normal homes ($p < .05$). The unconcerned parents of this English study had few ambitions for their child, were indifferent to success or failure, and gave little encouragement or guidance. The 8-year-olds in the Kent-Davis study who obtained the highest IQ's were from *demanding* homes ($p < .01$). *Demanding* parents were ambitious for their children, stimulating them and expecting them to conform to a somewhat inflexible model. These evaluations of the home were made at approximately the time the children were tested. It would be interesting to learn of the later careers of the children from demanding homes. The inflexible model might have an inhibiting effect in later childhood and adulthood.

Guidance Study results which are to some extent new and unique are the differences in the kinds of affectional relations that relate to accelerated test performance. The subtlety of the finding that the *father's friendliness,* but not *expressiveness of affection,* for the daughter is related to her intelligence is impressive. In line with this finding is the fact that if the mother-daughter relation is too *close,* the daughter's intelligence decelerates in later childhood. Additionally, we find that while the boy's mental development is unrelated to *parental compatibility,* the girl's intelligence is related not only to *parental compatibility* but also to *lack of conflict about discipline and cultural standards* and even to *parental agreement on having more children.*

Substantiation of the finding of the father's relevance to the daughter's mental growth is noted in a study by Bing (1963), who compared the child-rearing practices in families of sixty fifth-grade children divided into two groups, high and low verbal ability, as judged by the Thurstone Primary Abilities Tests. The high- and low-verbal-ability groups were "fairly well equated on 'general intelligence' as measured by total PMA scores" (Bing, 1963, p. 635). One of Bing's conclusions is so relevant to the Guidance Study results that it warrants quotation: "Many of the mothers' behavior patterns and attitudes that were investigated through the interview seemed to influence boys' cognitive development, but not girls'; on the other hand, of the very few behavior patterns pertaining to fathers

that were evaluated, two proved to be significantly associated only with girls' cognitive development. This points to the possible importance of the influence of the opposite-sex parent on the child's cognitive development. Such an influence is hard to account for in terms of our present knowledge of personality development but merits further investigation" (1963, p. 641).

In the Guidance Study results, there is a hint of the son's identification with the father. Boys show greater acceleration than girls when the *father is concerned about educational achievement* and when there is *parental satisfaction* with the *father's occupation* and the *father's income* is high. For optimal mental growth, the boy appears to need first a warm, close relation with a mother or caretaker, followed by a masculine model who not only achieves but is concerned about his son's achievement.

Bernstein (1961, p. 288) writes that "the literature of both sociology and psychology shows that sociocultural factors can depress or raise the level of educational performance." The question is "How?" There is evidence from the studies of adopted children (Bishop, 1959; Skodak & Skeels, 1949) that some of the variance in child intelligence that is correlated with social class is due in fact to hereditary factors. It is equally clear that some of the variance in intelligence is due to adverse prenatal and perinatal experiences of the underprivileged child. The neurologically intact newborn is more likely to appear in the family where pre- and paranatal care are excellent. In the present study we have explored the extent to which variance in intelligence is affected by the postnatal environment. Results from the Guidance Study and other studies suggest that the effect of the family milieu in the first 2 years of life may be substantial, since it can be demonstrated in some of its complexity even under conditions where the evaluations of the family situation were not specifically geared to investigating the effect of the family on the child's cognitive development. A distillation of the many specific correlations in the Guidance Study suggests a coherent pattern of determinants, or at least relevant family variables, that lead to acceleration or deceleration in test performance.

We do not have a conceptual model to account for all these results. A neuropsychological theory is relevant to certain of the findings (Hebb, 1949). The neurologically intact infant needs stimulation for the optimum development of his central nervous system, including the cerebral cortex. At first the need for tactual, auditory, and visual stimulation are best met in the family where the mother is responsive and actively *concerned* with the infant's welfare, even to the point of being *worrisome* and *tense* about him. We would assume here that the more responsive and more differentiated the response of the mother, the more differentiated is likely to be the baby's ability to respond. Hebb states that later learning is dependent on early learning; that is, this early learning is necessary for optimal development. Neurologists note that the earlier a deficit or injury occurs in the ontogenesis of the central nervous system, the more likely it is that development will be impaired (Yakovlev, 1959). The reverse is probably also true; the adequacy of stimulation becomes progressively less important with age. So far, the neuropsychological theory is supported, but it does not go far enough. It does not account for a series of findings that suggest that the child's personality becomes a mediating factor in his cognitive development. Affectional relations that lead to a high rate of mental growth are not explained, nor are some of the cross-sex findings or the apparent later identification of the son with his father's achievement motivation. We are in need of a more comprehensive theory that not only would account for all the results but would lead to an understanding of *what* must occur *when* for optimal cognitive development.

REFERENCES

AINSWORTH, MARY D. The effects of maternal deprivation: a review of findings and controversy in the context of research strategy. In deprivation of maternal care. A reassessment of its effects. World Health Organization, Geneva, 1962.

ATHERTON, KARYL M. A comparison of solutions obtained in factor analyses of socioeconomic variables. *Psychological Reports*, 1962, *11*, 259–273.

BAYLEY, NANCY. Some increasing parent-child similarities during the growth of children. *Journal of educational Psychology*, 1954, *45*, 1–21.

BAYLEY, NANCY, & SCHAEFER, E. S. Correlations of maternal and child behaviors with the development of mental abilities: data from the Berkeley Growth Study. *Monographs of the Society for Research in child Development*, 1964, *29*, No. 6, 1–80.

BENNETT, E. L., DIAMOND, MARIAN C., KRECH, D., & ROSENZWEIG, M. R. Chemical and anatomical plasticity of brain. *Science*, 1964, *146*, 610–619.

BERNSTEIN, B. Social class and linguistic development: a theory of social learning. In A. H. Halsey, J. Floud, and C. A. Anderson (Eds.), *Economy, education and society*. New York: Free Press, 1961.

BING, ELIZABETH. Effect of child-rearing practices on development of differential cognitive abilities. *Child Development*, 1963, *34*, 631–648.

BISHOP, LEILA. Some relationships between infants' and mothers' behavior. Unpublished doctoral dissertation, University of Chicago, 1959.

BURKS, BARBARA S. The relative influence of nature and nurture upon mental development: a comparative

study of foster parent–foster child resemblance and true parent–true child resemblance. *Yearbook of the National Society for Studies in Education*, 1928, *27*, 219–236.

CASLER, L. Maternal deprivation: a critical review of the literature. *Monographs of the Society for Research in Child Development*, 1961, *26*, No. 2, 1–64.

HARLOW, H. The development of learning in the Rhesus monkey. In W. R. Brode (Ed.), *Science in progress: twelfth series*. New Haven, Conn.: Yale University Press, 1962. Pp. 239–269.

HEBB, D. O. *Organization of behavior: a neuropsychological theory*. New York: Wiley, 1949.

HINDLEY, C. B. Social class influences on the development of ability in the first five years. In 14th International Congress of Applied Psychology, Copenhagen, 1961, *Proceedings*. Pp. 29–41.

HONZIK, MARJORIE P. Developmental studies of parent-child resemblance in intelligence. *Child Development*, 1957, *28*, 215–228.

HONZIK, MARJORIE P. A sex difference in the age of onset of the parent-child resemblance in intelligence. *Journal of educational Psychology*, 1963, *54*, 231–237.

HONZIK, MARJORIE P., MACFARLANE, JEAN W., & ALLEN, LUCILE. The stability of mental test performance between two and eighteen years. *Journal of experimental Education*, 1948, *17*, 309–324.

JONES, H. E. The environment and mental development. In L. Carmichael (Ed.), *Manual of child psychology*. New York: Wiley, 1954.

KENT, NORMA, & DAVIS, D. R. Discipline in the home and intellectual development. *British Journal of Medical Psychology*, 1957, *30*, 27–34.

LEAHY, ALICE M. Nature-nurture and intelligence. *Genetic Psychology Monographs*, 1935, *17*, 236–308.

LEVINE, S. A further study of infantile handling and adult avoidance learning. *Journal of Personality*, 1956, *25*, 70–81.

MACFARLANE, JEAN W. Studies in child guidance. I. Methodology of data collection and organization. *Monographs of the Society for Research in child Development*, 1938, *3*, No. 6, i–254.

MOSS, H. A., & KAGAN, J. Maternal influences on early IQ scores. *Psychological Reports*, 1958, *4*, 655–661.

SKODAK, MARIE, & SKEELS, H. M. A final follow-up study of one hundred adopted children. *Journal of genetic Psychology*, 1949, *75*, 85–125.

TRYON, R. C., & BAILEY, D. E. The BC TRY computer system of cluster and factor analysis. *Multivariate behavioral Research*, 1966, *1*, 95–111.

YARROW, L. Maternal deprivation: toward an empirical and conceptual re-evaluation. *Psychological Bulletin*, 1961, *58*, 459–490.

YARROW, L. Research in dimensions of early maternal care. *Merrill-Palmer Quarterly*, 1963, *9*, No. 2.

YAKOVLEV, P. I. Anatomy of the human brain and the problem of mental retardation. In P. W. Bowman & H. V. Mautner (Eds.), *Proceedings of the First International Conference on Mental Retardation*. New York: Grune & Stratton, 1959.

23

The Socialization of Aggression

Robert R. Sears,
Eleanor E. Maccoby,
and Harry Levin

This is a report on the ways in which parents deal with children's aggressiveness. It is taken from a study done at the Harvard Laboratory of Human Development when all three authors were there and Sears was the director of the Laboratory. Sears later became head of Stanford University's Psychology Department and then Dean of its School of Humanities and Science. Maccoby too is a psychology professor at Stanford. For more details of Sears's biography see Section III, No. 18. Harry Levin is chairman of the Department of Psychology at Cornell University.

The type of investigation reported here has frequently been criticized because it relies on mothers' memories and their self-reports. Such criticism is vitiated by the success of studies that have reported consistent findings about the same children in later years. Thus, the child-rearing data obtained through the mother interviews continues to have predictive value with respect to the behavior of the offspring. Confidence in the data is also bolstered by the theoretical sense the findings make. Nevertheless, retrospective reports are recognized as a fallible source of data, as Sears, Maccoby, and Levin would agree.

An even more basic question is raised by all correlational research of this type. One can never interpret the direction of cause and effect with assurance. The introduction to the next paper comments further on this topic.

Aggression, as the term is commonly used, means behavior that is intended to hurt or injure someone. Most human adults have quite a repertory of acts that fit this definition. Some of these are bold and violent, others sly and attenuated. Some are accompanied by rage or annoyance; others are done coldly and seemingly, to the perpetrator, without emotion. The complexity and subtlety of adult aggression is the end product of two or three decades of socialization by the individual's parents and peers, however, and bears little resemblance to the primitive quality of the infant's action patterns, from which it developed.

To understand the problem of aggression in child rearing, one does well to remind himself firmly that man is a mammal, and that there are certain kinds of behavior which characterize all mammals. The two that are most relevant to the problem of aggression are *fighting* and the *expression of rage*.

From the lowest quadruped to the highest biped, physical attack is used for defense. Techniques vary, depending on the sharpness of hooves, the strength of jaws, and the presence of specialized weapons like antlers. Man, being the most intelligent and inventive of all, makes use of many of the other species' techniques and adds a host of new ones that, happily, no other animal has ever dreamed of. He can bite like a dog, claw like a cat, kick like a stallion, trade insults like a howling monkey, squeeze like a gorilla; and he constructs his own clubs, blow-pipes, knives, and guns to make up for his lack of antlers and horns. The evolutionary continuity becomes crystal clear in any TV wrestling match.

In spite of this ingenuity, however, physical fighting is not the commonest form of human aggression. *Injury* is a broad term, and the socialization process develops many motives that can be thwarted. Interference with any of these motives causes pain or anguish, and if this was the intention, the interfering act was truly aggressive.

Defensive fighting is usually accompanied by expressions of rage. The older child or adult, who can report his feelings, may recognize his desire to hurt, and be very aware of his angry emotion. But this quality of aggression is attenuated, too, in the process of socialization, and there are many forms of hurt that an adult inflicts with little emotional arousal.

In a civilized society adults are rarely beaten or knifed or lashed. More often, they are hurt by attacks on their pride or status, their desire for social approval, or their feelings of affection for their families and friends. These kinds of hurt can be far more serious and more prolonged than most physical hurts. The withholding of affection by a loved spouse, for example, can have the meaning of pain that goes far beyond that from broken legs or crushed fingers. Nor do injuries that come through sheer accident, the vagaries of nature, hurt like injuries to self-esteem. Contrast them with the gratuitous insult from an admired and intimate friend, or the malicious gossip that one is "slipping" at his job, or the suggestion by a neighbor that one has been a failure in child rearing, or the rejection of a young girl seeking membership in a college sorority. And it is a strong and seasoned old man who can recall without pain his first failure as a lover—and his mistress's amusement.

Not all injuries are so great as these, of course. There are tongue-lashings that do not hurt—much—and insults that are shrugged off. There are the little obstinacies in one's friends, and the non-cooperative indifferences of one's working associates. There are the irritants of family living—a tired and sassy child, a grumpy and complaining husband, a daughter who dawdles. Since all these cause discomfort, they can be forms of aggression. Whether they are in fact, however, depends on whether the discomfort they engender was *designed* by the perpetrator to hurt someone else.

Not all acts that hurt are intended to do so. Even sophisticated and sensitive adults sometimes fail to anticipate the effects of what they do. The unanswered letter can seem a slight; the unasked question can be interpreted as indifference. With children, the problem is especially noticeable in the manipulation of physical forces. A child's innocently swinging stick only too easily turns into a painful club, the experimental bombing into a brother's broken toys.

Since these hurts are obviously unintentional, they do not qualify as *aggression* in the technical sense of the word. There are certain borderline examples, however, that are hard to be sure about. There are acts that sometimes are and sometimes are not aggressive. Most mothers consider obedience of some importance, for they use much verbal guidance in instructing and controlling their children. The children know their mothers want compliance with directions, and hence willful disobedience is widely recognized as a form of aggression. Now if a child has been told to pick up his clothes a dozen times, and if he has remembered to do this the last half-dozen times, his mother may look suspiciously at his motives if he forgets the thirteenth time. Did he just forget? Or was he angry and disobedient? People differ considerably in the degree to which they perceive an aggressive intent in the behavior of others, and what one mother calls carelessness another will call disobedience.

If we disregard borderline cases and accidents, however, there is still a great deal of human behavior that is designed to hurt. Such activity develops early in life and is a disrupting influence on family living. Later it becomes a problem for the peer group. . . .

All human societies, even all colony-living subhuman primates, have rules to limit the kinds and direction of aggression that may be expressed. The most fundamental of these is the high degree of prohibition on in-group fighting. The closer together people live, the more interdependent they are, the less they dare be aggressive toward one another. Free fighting and antagonism within the household—whether it be a nomad's hut or a suburbanite's four-bedrooms-and-two-baths—could only lead to wreckage of the family unit. Hence, all societies require that only very attenuated forms of aggression be expressed among family members, and that, within the parent-child relationship, aggression be expressed only downward. One mother described this principle with great clarity:

I. How do you handle it (if he strikes you)?
M. I don't allow it. I slap him and punish him for it, and explained that he was never to raise his hand to anyone older than himself, that he must respect older people—his mother and father especially. Never! But they do attempt it, of course; but I do think it should be checked right away.
I. How did you handle this?
M. I would just put him right in his room. Just take hold of him right at the moment and put him right in his room, and say "You mustn't do that! You never should hit your mother and father, ever; they're always right." I always make a big issue out of it.
I. That your mother and father are always right?
M. Always right; "You must never raise your hand to your mother or father."

Not all mothers felt as strongly as this one did, and different societies have different degrees of tolerance for in-family aggression, but the prohibition exists in some degree in all known societies.

Outside the family, limitations are less severe in most societies. As will be seen later, the mothers in this present study were less concerned—more permissive—about fighting between their own children and neighbor youngsters than about sibling quarreling. There were a number of instances in which mothers felt children must be encouraged to fight, to protect their own interests. Even so, there is still a good deal of necessary restriction on the more severe forms of aggression, no matter toward whom they are directed.

To insure the firm establishment of these rules, many mothers feel they must begin the control of aggression very early in the child's life. A newborn infant is not particularly dangerous, even to himself, but he represents a potential threat nevertheless. The family, indeed the whole society, has a delicate balance; the forces of aggression are being kept in check, and co-operation and love are out-weighing non-co-operation and hate. The baby is an alien who does not know all the rules. He lacks knowledge of when to hit and when not to. He has no skill at securing compliance by a *little* hurting. He cannot be counted on to channelize, to displace, or to attenuate his aggressions. He must be taught them if he is to be an acceptable member of society. . . .

PUNISHMENT AND ANXIETY

The mother's almost automatic aggressive response to her child's aggression creates a special problem in child-rearing tactics that does not seem to arise nearly so seriously in connection with other areas of child behavior. Unless a mother is busy, or annoyed to start with, dependency is likely to elicit nurturance from her, and an expression of affection will evoke its like. But aggression, being a frustration to its object, has a strong tendency to evoke counter-aggression or punishment. After all, the mother was once a child herself and learned the same ways of reacting that her child is now learning.

This built-in relationship between the aggressor and his victim has an important consequence. It means that every child grows up with the experience of being punished in some degree for his aggressive behavior. The extent and severity of such punishment differs greatly from one child to another, of course, depending on the tolerance of his parents and siblings. It is our impression, however, that the average child in our sample received more actual *punishment* (as distinguished from *non-reward*) for aggressive behavior than for any other kind of changeworthy action.

One significant effect of punishment is the production of anxiety. If the punishment is repeated many, many times through early childhood, situations that provoke aggressive feelings gradually come to arouse anxiety, too—anxiety over the danger of being punished for aggression. Eventually, the aggression itself, or the accompanying feeling of being angry, becomes sufficient to arouse anxiety. In such cases the anxiety may properly be called aggression-anxiety.

The formation of such a reaction has two kinds of consequences that are relevant to the socialization process. One is the uneasiness and discomfort that become connected with the arousal of aggressive impulses. By and large, adults in our culture do not tolerate aggression comfortably,

neither their own nor that displayed by others. It evokes too much anxiety; this may be reflected in feelings of worry, dislike, avoidance, guilt, or moral disapproval. They cannot feel fully comfortable when they are angry. They are in conflict—ambivalent—about their own impulses. The carrying through of an aggressive act is often followed not simply by the catharsis or satisfaction that one would expect from a successful action (assuming the action accomplished the intended results), but also by feelings that arise from the undercurrent anxiety. These may be shame, embarrassment, guilt, regret, self-deprecation, or even just plain fear of retaliation. A mother's uneasiness and conflict often make difficult a calm use of reason in deciding how to handle a child's aggressive actions.

A second consequence of punishment and its ensuing anxiety is the development, by the child, of techniques for avoiding punishment. The child who is consistently punished for swearing is likely to cease the practice in his parent's presence. This does not necessarily mean he will stop swearing, for punishment seems usually to have a rather localized inhibiting effect. The impulse to be aggressive is not reduced, but only the overt aggressive act that was punished. The total impulse to aggression is made stronger than ever, for the punishment is itself an additional frustration. . . .

We can turn now to the findings from our interviews. In this chapter we will describe first the ways in which the mothers handled aggression, with respect to both permissiveness and punishment. It will be seen that there was some consistency in individual mothers' attitudes, and we will indicate what some of the other personality characteristics were that were commonly associated with gentle or severe handling. Finally, we will examine the relation between these child-rearing practices and the mothers' own reports of their children's aggressiveness to discover what procedures seemed to influence such behavior. . . .

THE MOTHERS' PERMISSIVENESS
FOR AGGRESSION

In the discussion so far we have talked of aggression as a changeworthy form of behavior, particularly that directed toward the parents. This is a generalization, however, that hides a multitude of individual differences among the mothers. As might easily be predicted from what has been said of aggression-anxiety, parents differ greatly from one another in the amount of aggression they can tolerate. Some set great store by a completely non-aggressive child; others accept the inevitability of a certain amount of aggression even as late as age five; a few believe aggression is such a natural quality of early childhood behavior that they simply ignore all but the most violent episodes. . . .

In our interviews, the mothers described the ways in which children got on adult nerves, found ingenious devices for expressing annoyance or getting revenge, and in general created the social and emotional havoc that goes with anger. They also expressed their own attitudes toward their children's aggression, and gave descriptions of how this changeworthy behavior was handled. With respect to aggression of children toward their parents, the mothers were asked:

Sometimes a child will get angry at his parents and hit them and kick them or shout angry things at them. How much of this sort of thing do you think parents ought to allow in a child of (his, her) age? How do you handle it when (child's name) acts like this?

[* CASE A

M. I think he's at the age right now where you're apt to get quite a lot of it. I think as they get a little bit older, you can stop and reason with them, but right now I think that they get pretty angry at times and they do say things. And afterwards they're sorry for it, so I let him say it and it's over with, and afterwards I might say, "You weren't very nice to Mummy," and he'll generally admit it.

CASE B

I. In what ways do you get on each other's nerves?

M. I think our mutual tempers, as much as anything, as he has one, and so have I. I attempt to control it, so for instance I can understand things that he does. He gets very angry and he goes upstairs and throws things, and I can understand that perfectly. I don't know whether I was ever allowed to or whether I ever did throw things, but I wanted to, so that heaving things into the closet, I can easily understand; so that kind of thing doesn't aggravate me the way it would somebody else, and the same way with getting very angry at me. I never mind that as much, because I also get angry at him, and if I am going to, he has got to be allowed that privilege also.

CASE C

M. Well, she'll say, "I don't like you." She seldom says, "I hate you," or "I don't like you anymore," or something like that. I have let her go up to now because I feel she's just getting it out of her system. If it isn't too loud, or if she isn't too angry about it, I just let it go. If it's something that I can't turn my back on, if it's something that she's so angry about that she won't stop, then I speak to her. Otherwise she'll say, "Well, I don't like you." And I say, "Well, that's all right," or something like that. I don't pay too much attention to it because I know that she doesn't actually mean it. She means it because she isn't getting what she wants, and she doesn't mean it actually.

---

* The material in brackets, ending on page 160, is an edited version taken from Maccoby, Newcomb, and Hartley (eds.), *Readings in Social Psychology* (Holt, 1958).—EDITOR

If she kicked me or if she slapped me, I'd slap her back. I just told her that it doesn't feel good to get slapped. If she didn't want to get slapped herself, not to slap other people. The reaction would be the same in anyone that got slapped—they wouldn't like it.

CASE D

M. They never should allow him to hit them back. If he hits them, they should hit him right back. If you let him get away with it once he will always want to get away with it.

I. How do you handle it when he acts like this?

M. If he hits me I hit him back twice as hard, and if he does it again, I just get my paddle I have, and I give it to him again, and then he stops.

I. How do you handle it if he is deliberately disobedient?

M. I take off his clothes and he's in for the day and he's not to play with anything—not even his toys or anything that belongs to him—he's not to touch anything—he's to leave things alone and stay in bed.

CASE E

M. That is something I will not tolerate—my child has never done it. I mean, they have done it once in a while, both of them, but I would absolutely not tolerate it.

I. How did you teach them not to do this?

M. I don't know—I guess I just told them once, in no uncertain terms, that it was something that was never done, and I have never had any trouble with it; and if I did, I don't know just how I would cope with it, because I wouldn't stand for it.

I. How much of this sort of thing do you think a parent ought to allow?

M. I don't think they should allow it at all. I think a child should be allowed to express himself, and all that, but I don't think there is ever an exception for a child to hit his parents.

Responses of these kinds, together with much other relevant material elsewhere in the interview, enabled us to rate each mother on two dimensions: (1) her *permissiveness* for aggression, directed by the child toward herself and (2) the amount (and severity) of *punishment* she had administered to the child for such aggression. Under the heading of permissiveness we included not only the mother's stated values as to whether aggression should be allowed but also her behavior toward the child, *i.e.,* whether she actually *did* allow it or whether she always tried to take measures to prevent or stop it.

As might be expected, the two scales were correlated. That is, the mothers who were permissive about aggression, tended to use little punishment, while the nonpermissive mothers used quite a bit. But the correlation was only −.46, a low enough value to warrant considering the two dimensions separately. The two scales did not correlate more closely because there were a number of mothers who did not permit aggression from their children, but stopped it by other means than punishment.

Surprisingly, there were also a number whom we rated both quite permissive and highly punishing. In this latter group were some mothers who felt they *should* allow their children to display aggression; but they could restrain their own impulses to suppress the child's aggression only so long, and then they would blow up. When the punishment came, it was likely to be severe.

In this sample of 379 normal mothers, we found that a majority were most accurately rated at the *nonpermissive* end of our permissiveness scale. The social norm prevailing in these families was one of little tolerance about parent-directed aggression from children, although there was considerable variation in the severity with which this value was enforced.

It is of some interest to note that parents allowed somewhat more aggression from their sons than from their daughters, and that working-class parents were less permissive about aggression than parents at the middle-class level.

EFFECTS ON CHILDREN'S AGGRESSION

We turn now to a consideration of the child's aggressiveness, and will then address ourselves to the question: Does the amount of overt aggression a child displays at home have any relation to the values parents hold about aggression and the techniques they have employed in dealing with the child's aggression?]

THE SOURCES OF AGGRESSION IN THE HOME

What makes a child aggressive and quarrelsome? Among these youngsters, there were a few whose mothers could recall almost no angry behavior around home, but this was not the case for most of them. In spite of the general aura of prohibition, the majority of the youngsters had displayed many varieties and combinations of angry emotional response. Some children were more aggressive toward one parent than the other, some quarreled mainly with siblings and were pleasant toward the parents, some expressed themselves openly, and some relied chiefly on non-co-operation for their expression.

Nearly all the mothers gave fairly detailed reports of the typical forms of aggression their children displayed. It was thus possible to make a rating of *amount of aggression exhibited in the home* (excluding that toward siblings). . . .

These ratings can be compared with the mothers' reports of child-rearing practices to discover what characteristics of the latter were associated with high or low degree of reported aggression by the child.

The measures of the mothers' practices and the children's reactions were not independent. Both came from the mother herself. We cannot be certain in any particular case, therefore, that we have secured an unbiased report of the child's actual behavior. It is possible that some quality in a given mother—for instance, a sense of despair about her effectiveness as a child rearer—might lead her to give an exaggerated report about her child's aggressiveness. If we find, as we do, that mothers who felt little confidence in themselves had more (reportedly) aggressive children, we cannot tell whether this finding results from exaggerated reports by these mothers, or whether there was actually something about their behavior toward children that evoked more child aggressiveness. It would not be surprising if both were true, for the same qualities of her personality that influence her perception of the child may also induce a characteristic set of responses in him. . . .

Permissiveness and punishment. There is a constant tug of war in a child's behavior between the instigation and the inhibition of aggression. On one hand there are frustrations, threats, or other stimulating situations that tend to evoke aggressive action; on the other, there are warnings that inhibit aggression, and there are instigators to competing responses that the mother finds more desirable than aggression. One of the major research problems in the investigation of the socialization process is the discovery of just what kinds of maternal behavior fall into these classifications. What does the mother do that excites aggression in her child? What does she do that inhibits it?

The two scales of *permissiveness for aggression* and *severity of punishment for aggression* are the most obviously relevant dimensions to examine first. What should we expect of their relation to the reported amount of aggression the child shows in the home? Permissiveness, by definition, is an expression of the mother's willingness to have the child perform such acts. A simple and straightforward prediction is that children with permissive mothers will be more aggressive than children with non-permissive mothers. Similarly with punishment: if we assume that this method of discipline establishes in the child a fear of behaving aggressively then the more punitive the mother is, the more the child should avoid being aggressive. These two predictions fit together nicely. The scales for *permissiveness* and *punishment* are correlated −.46; that is, to some degree the more permissive mothers tended to be less severe in their punishment.

In point of fact, however, one of the predictions is right and the other is wrong. It is true that high *permissiveness* is associated with high aggression.

The correlation is +.23. But *punishment* works just the other way: the more severe the punishment, the more aggression the child showed. The correlation is +.16. Both these correlations are small, but they are significant, and they are artificially reduced by the negative correlation between the permissiveness and punitiveness scales. Their true importance is substantially greater, as will be seen in the next section.

We interpret these findings in this way. When a mother adopts a permissive point of view about aggression, she is saying to her child, in effect, "Go ahead and express your angry emotions; don't worry about me." She gives few signals in advance that would lead the child to fear to be aggressive. On the contrary, her attitude is one of expectancy that he *will* be, and that such behavior is acceptable. It is scarcely surprising that the child tends to fulfill her expectations. The non-permissive mother, however, does something quite different. She has an attitude that aggression is wrong, that it is not to be tolerated, and an expectancy (often very subtly expressed) that the child will not behave in such undesirable ways. When he is aggressive, she does something to try to stop it—sometimes by punishment, sometimes by other means. He, also, fulfills his mother's expectations. This dimension of permissiveness, then, is a measure of the extent to which the mother prevents or stops aggression, the non-permissive extreme being the most common.

Punishment is apparently a somewhat different matter. It is a kind of maternal behavior that occurs *after* the child's aggression has been displayed. The child has already enjoyed the satisfaction of hurting or of expressing anger—and so has had a reinforcement for aggressive action. But then he gets hurt in turn. He suffers further frustration. This should, and on the average does, incite him to more aggression. If the punishment is very severe, he may gradually learn to fear the consequences of his own actions, and the particular acts

that get most repeatedly punished may be inhibited. But the total frustration is increased, and hence the total amount of aggression displayed in the home is higher. The dimension called *severity of punishment for aggression toward parents,* then, is one measure of the amount of painful frustration that is imposed on the child without direct guidance as to what would be a more acceptable form of behavior.

It is evident from this analysis that the mothers who were most permissive but also most severely punitive would have the most aggressive children; those who were most non-permissive but least punitive would have the least aggressive ones. As may be seen in Table VII:8, this was the case for both sexes. The children of mothers in the other two groups were in between.

These findings are similar to those of an earlier study (Sears *et al.,* 1953) in one respect. In that research, 40 children were observed in nursery school. The amount of aggression they showed there was compared with their mothers' reports of the severity of punishment for aggression that they suffered at home. In that study, too, high aggression was found to be associated with severe punishment, especially in the boys. There was some indication that the most severely punished girls had become quite passive and inhibited. They displayed little activity of any kind, including aggression. When activity level was taken into consideration, they tended to be more like the boys, i.e., the more severely punished girls were *relatively* more aggressive than the less severely punished. It is interesting to note the similarity between the present findings and the earlier study, because in that research the measure of child aggression was entirely independent of the measures of child-rearing practices.

A word of caution must be said here about the interpretation of our results. We have shown that the mothers who punished their children most severely for aggression tended to report that their

TABLE VII:8

PERCENTAGE OF HIGHLY AGGRESSIVE CHILDREN IN SUBGROUPS DIVIDED ACCORDING TO WHETHER MOTHER WAS IN UPPER OR LOWER HALF OF THE DISTRIBUTION ON PERMISSIVENESS AND SEVERITY OF PUNISHMENT FOR AGGRESSION TOWARD PARENTS

	Highly Aggressive *			
	Boys		*Girls*	
Subgroup	*Per Cent*	*N* †	*Per Cent*	*N*
Low permissiveness and low punishment	3.7	27	13.3	30
Low permissiveness and high punishment	20.4	51	19.1	47
High permissiveness and low punishment	25.3	81	20.6	63
High permissiveness and high punishment	41.7	36	38.1	22

* By "highly aggressive" is meant that the child was rated by one or both raters as being in one of the two highest levels of aggression. . . .
† Number of cases.

children displayed more than the average amount of aggression toward their parents. We have implied in our discussion that the maternal behavior *caused* the child behavior. It is entirely possible, of course, that the correlation could be explained as a parental response to the child's pre-existing temperament. That is, some children may have been born with a higher level of aggressive impulses than others, and the more aggressive the child naturally was, the more his parents were forced to punish him for aggression. We have chosen to interpret the matter the other way around: that punishment by the mother bred counter-aggression in the child. Our reason is that permissiveness was also associated with aggression, and we cannot see why aggression in the child should elicit permissiveness in the mother.

Our interpretation must be tentative, however, for the other explanation of the results cannot be ruled out without further research. It is quite possible, of course, that a circular process develops: the parent's punishment makes the child aggressive, this aggression leads to further punishment, and so on. Which came first, to set the whole thing in motion, is a problem we cannot solve with our existing information. . . .

Our findings suggest that the way for parents to produce a non-aggressive child is to make abundantly clear that aggression is frowned upon, and to stop aggression when it occurs, but to avoid punishing the child for his aggression. Punishment seems to have complex effects. While undoubtedly it often stops a particular form of aggression, at least momentarily, it appears to generate more hostility in the child and lead to further aggressive outbursts at some other time or place. Furthermore, when the parents punish—particularly when they employ physical punishment—they are providing a living example of the use of aggression at the very moment they are trying to teach the child not to be aggressive. The child, who copies his parents in many ways, is likely to learn as much from this example of successful aggression on his parents' part as he is from the pain of punishment. Thus, the most peaceful home is one in which the mother believes aggression is not desirable and under no circumstances is ever to be expressed toward her, but who relies mainly on non-punitive forms of control. The homes where the children show angry, aggressive outbursts frequently are likely to be homes in which the mother has a relatively tolerant (or careless!) attitude toward such behavior, or where she administers severe punishment for it, or both.

These conclusions will certainly not astonish anyone who has worked professionally with children and their parents. Social workers, psychologists, teachers, psychiatrists, and probation officers have seen the twin effects of permissiveness and punishment many times in their own experience. What is important in the present report is the demonstration with this group of families. When one works with a few cases, particularly when most of them are quite deviant from the general population, one often has some uncertainty as to whether the relationships he sees would apply to a more normal group. Here is as normal a group of American mothers and their children as one could want for these purposes. The principles hold good.

There is another aspect to the matter worth emphasizing, however. The effects of these two aspects of control may already be known by professionals, but, even with a demonstration of this sort, they will not find ready acceptance by many others. There are two reasons.

First, *punishment is satisfying* to the parent. When a child aggresses toward his mother, he angers her, interferes with what she is doing, with her peace of mind, with her dignity and self-respect. Aggression hurts. It is meant to. And it produces in the mother the appropriate stimulation to retaliate in kind. Combined with her sense of obligation to rear her child properly, this retaliation comes out in a way she thinks of as "punishment"— that is, a form of aggression designed to have a good *training* effect on its recipient. As will be seen in a later chapter, many mothers have developed strong beliefs that punishment is a helpful method of control. (Sometimes it is, too.) These beliefs are essential to the peace of mind of such mothers. Without the conviction that "punishment is *good* for my child," these mothers would be forced to view their own behavior as retaliatory, aggressive, childish— in short, contemptible. This would not long provide a tolerable self-image. It is to be expected, then, that our demonstration of the deleterious effect of severe punishment of aggression will not be an easy finding for many people to swallow.

A second matter has to do with permissiveness. The difficulty grows out of the problem of punishment. During the last three decades there has developed, among the more literate and sensitive part of the American people, an uneasy recognition that punishment sometimes eliminates a few specific responses, but leaves a strongly hostile drive bottled up within the child. There is evidence to support this belief. With this consideration in mind, and an urgent desire to provide better mental hygiene for their children, not a few parents have developed what almost amounts to a cult of being permissive about aggression. Their aim is to avoid repression, to permit the child easier and freer expression of his impulses, and thus to prevent the development of aggression-anxiety, with its accompanying displacements, projections, and sometimes uncontrollable fantasies.

This aim is good, both for the children and the society they will compose, but whether it can be achieved by a high degree of permissiveness for expression of aggression toward the parents is a question. Does a permissive attitude, with the consequent freer expression of aggression, decrease the strength of projective fantasies? There is no indication in our own data that it does. Each of the children in the present study was tested with two 20-minute sessions of doll play. The children of the more non-permissive half of the group of mothers showed little if any more fantasy aggression under these circumstances than the children of the more permissive half. This finding is in sharp contrast to that with respect to punishment; the children of the more severely punishing mothers displayed quite significantly more fantasy aggression than the children of the less severely punishing ones (Levin and Sears, 1956). Permissiveness does not seem to decrease fantasy indications of aggressive impulses.

Permissiveness does increase the amount of aggression in the home, however, and it is worth considering what this does to the child himself. An angry child is not usually a happy child, nor is he one who receives affection and willing companionship from others. He is a source of discomfort to family and peers, and probably receives a certain amount of retaliation. He upsets his siblings, raises the level of frustration imposed on his parents, and inevitably has an increase, to some extent, of his own aggression-anxiety. There seems little advantage in all this, either to the child himself or to his parents.

These comments may seem to encourage a conclusion that parents will find it to their advantage to be somewhat non-permissive of aggression that is directed toward themselves. This can be a dangerous conclusion if the kind of permissiveness we mean is not clearly understood.

Therefore, let us be as clear as possible about the aspect of permissiveness we have in mind. A child is more likely to be non-aggressive if his parents hold the value that aggression is undesirable and should not occur. He is more likely to be non-aggressive if his parents prevent or stop the occurrence of aggressive outbursts instead of passively letting them go on, but prevent them by other means than punishment or threats of retaliation. If the parents' non-permissiveness takes the form of punishing the child (and thus leading the child to *expect* punishment) for aggressive behavior, then non-permissiveness will not have the effect of reducing the child's aggression. On the contrary, the instant that punishment enters, all the consequences of punishment that have been discussed earlier may be anticipated, including that of increasing the child's level of aggression.

One cautionary point: we are not suggesting that parents should band together in omnipotent suppression of every justifiable angry response the child makes. The right to be angry without fear or guilt is as inalienable as any other, and more important than some. But since anger interferes with constructive action in the face of many, if not most, problem situations that the child and his family face, parents are understandably anxious to keep it within reasonable bounds; and our interest has been in showing what parental actions are likely to have the desired effects and what actions are likely to have undesired side-effects.

24

A Reinterpretation of the Direction of Effects in Studies of Socialization

RICHARD Q. BELL

When research unearths associations between parental tactics of child control and children's behaviors, the usual response of psychologists has been to "explain" the children's behaviors as resulting from the parents' techniques. To what extent is it plausible to reason in reverse fashion? Could one assert that the parents' choice of one rather than another disciplinary approach is a consequence of the child's behavior rather than a cause of it? Does the severely punished child act aggressively because he has been severely punished? Or was he severely punished because of his highly aggressive behavior?

Richard Bell of the Child Research Branch, National Institute of Mental Health, takes up this question in the following paper. Readers who wish to delve further into this theme may consult the article by Lawrence V. Harper, "The Young as a Source of Stimuli Controlling Caretaker Behavior," (Developmental Psychology, 1971, 4, 73–88 or the article by Bell in the same journal (pp. 63–72), "Stimulus Control of Parent or Caretaker Behavior by Offspring."

It is not too surprising to find that most research on parent-child interaction has been directed to the question of effects of parents on children. The historian Palmer (1964) maintains that our political and social philosophy emerged in a period when there were many revolutionary or protorevolutionary movements ranging from the Carolinas to Sweden, movements directed not just against monarchical absolutism but against all constituted bodies such as parliaments, councils, assemblies, and magistracies. These institutions tended to be hereditary, either in theory or through firmly established practice. In taking a strong stand against hereditary determination of position in our society we have also stressed the malleability and susceptibility to improvement of the child. Although scientific research on parents and children is a fairly recent phenomenon, it still shows the primary influence of this broad social philosophy by emphasizing parents and educational institutions as determinants of human development.

Until recent years there have been very few findings which would indicate that this is not a fruitful approach. The prolonged helplessness of the human infant, in comparison to the early competence of some other animal infants, fits in with the picture of an organism designed to be taught and modified by the parent in the early years. It seems eminently plausible to visualize the human parent as the vehicle for the transmission of culture and the infant as simply the object of an acculturation process. The parent is the initial agent of culture, the child the object.

Because of this general view, it is often overlooked that even John Locke, to whom we are indebted for the concept of the infant as a tabula rasa, placed great emphasis in his advice to parents on early observation of congenital characteristics (Kessen, 1965, p. 67). Locke questioned the existence of innate ideas, not all innate characteristics. Currently, at least one major work on the socialization of the child has acknowledged that there are probably constitutional differences between children which affect behavior (Sears, Maccoby, & Levin, 1957, 454–455), and that the model of a unidirectional effect from parent to child is overdrawn, a fiction of convenience rather than belief (Sears et al., 1957, p. 141). The model was adopted in order to proceed with research, leaving the validity of the approach to be judged by the results.

This paper summarizes data indicating that a unidirectional approach is too imprecise and that another formulation is possible which would accommodate our social philosophy as well as new data from studies of man and other animals. Before proceeding, usage of two terms must be explained. Individual behavior sequences cannot be

Richard Q. Bell, "A reinterpretation of the direction of effects in studies of socialization," *Psychological Review, 75,* 1968, 81–95. Reprinted by permission.

referred to as exclusively genetically or experientially determined. It is possible, however, to employ experimental operations in such a way that a *difference* between two groups or between two conditions applied to the same subjects can be attributed to genetic or experiential differences. Thus the terms *genetically, congenitally,* or *experientially determined* are abstractions derived from experimental operations. For brevity, a *congenital effect* will refer to both genetic and congenital determination.

The same consideration applies to the question of whether parent and child effects can be separated. In the ordinary interaction of any parent and child we can speak only of an event sequence. However, by experimental operations we can isolate parent effects and child effects. In the remainder of this paper a child or parent effect will refer to such a derivative of an experimental operation. No implication about origin of the behavior need be drawn in this case since such studies can take as their starting point any behavior which is available at the time in the repertoire of parent or child.

We must also keep in mind that demonstration of a child effect indicates only that it plays *some* role in parent behavior. The development of the parent behavior is not explained by such a demonstration. In the same vein, Epstein (1964) has pointed out relative to studies of learning that evidence of the modifiability of a response provides no explanation of its origin.

RECENT DATA DISCORDANT WITH PARENT-EFFECT MODEL

Discordant data at the human level are still meager. This is because most research efforts have been directed to the task of testing parent effects and have not always been designed so as to permit clear interpretation of "negative" results. It will be necessary to rely upon informal observations and data generated unintentionally.

Rheingold (1966, pp. 12–13) has pointed to a compelling fact observable under ordinary circumstances in any human group containing an infant. "The amount of attention and the number of responses directed to the infant are enormous—out of all proportion to his age, size, and accomplishments." The effect of the appearance of helplessness and the powerful stimulus of distress cries were also noted. "So aversive, especially to humans, is the crying of the infant that there is almost no effort we will not expend, no device we will not employ, to change a crying baby into a smiling one —or just a quiet one."

Studies of variations in parental behavior with different children provide one other kind of data discordant with a parent-effect model. A mother of identical schizophrenic quadruplets was found to be uniformly extreme in restrictiveness with her daughters but not uniform in affection when rated against a theoretical normal group (Schaefer, 1963). Yarrow (1963, pp. 109–110) has reported that . . . [foster mothers] showed differences in behavior with infants assigned to [them] at different times. In one particularly dramatic case extreme differences in maternal care existed for two infants of the same sex and age assigned to a foster mother at the same time. Characteristics of the infants appeared to have evoked very different behavior in this foster mother and in other members of her family.

Reports of lack of uniformity of behavior of parents towards their children are not confined to intensive case studies. Stott (1941) reported a correlation of only .22 between sibling reports of a positive or negative home environment. Lasko (1954, p. 111) correlated maternal characteristics across 44 sibling pairs and found that mothers were not consistent in affection but were in restrictiveness, a finding which is in agreement with the report on the quadruplets. In a parent-effect model, it is easy to explain differences between the behavior of two parents with the same child, but awkward to accommodate a difference in the behavior of one parent toward two children. The latter difficulty is due to the fact that the parent-effect model assumes a fixed and invariantly applied repertoire. The usual method of explaining differences in behavior of a parent with different children is to postulate effects associated with ordinal position or sex of siblings. The reports on infants in foster homes could not be explained this way.

Levy (1958, p. 8) was unable to find consistency in maternal greeting behavior when the infant was brought from the nursery for a feeding, until it was noted that this behavior was a function of the state of the infant. The present author carried out separate chi-square analyses of Levy's data for each of three successive observations. There were no differences on the initial observation, but for the second and third observations it was found that infants awake or awakening were greeted, whereas those asleep were not ($p < .01$; $p < .05$, respectively). Other data in the same volume support Levy's contention that specific maternal behavior could be accounted for more by the infant's behavior than by the mother's general "maternal attitude," whether the latter was estimated from interview material or from actual observation of her behavior. Another finding with a similar implication was reported by Hillenbrand (1965). The amount the infant consumed in breastfeeding during the newborn period was highly correlated with the number of weeks the mother continued feeding at the breast, whereas the latter measure showed no correlation with personality characteristics of the mother.

One other study at the human level is best accommodated by a bidirectional model (Bell, 1964). Scores on one parent-attitude scale have been found consistently higher in mothers of children with congenital defects than in mothers of normals. Differences between groups of parents were ascribed to the effects on parents of a limitation in coping ability associated with the congenital disorder in affected children.

Research on lower animals provides stronger evidence of the stimulating and selective effect of the young. A volume edited by Rheingold (1963) covers maternal behavior from the deer mouse to the baboon and provides a number of observations on the importance of the young in shaping interactions. An example is the report of two instances in which the clinging of rhesus infants fostered with nonlactating females induced maternal responsiveness and biochemically normal lactation (pp. 268–269). In other studies offspring effects have been manipulated experimentally. Lactation in the rat has been maintained for long periods by supplying new litters of pups; number and age of pups were effective parameters (Bruce, 1961). Licking and nest-building occurred when 1-day-old pups were presented to female mice without previous [maternal] experience; short-term stimulus-specific decrements in the maternal response followed repeated presentation of 1-day-old pups, but recovery of response was shown to an older pup (Noirot, 1965). This study is the most recent in a series supporting the hypothesis that changes in the interest of the female mouse in the litter from birth to weaning depend mainly upon changes in stimuli coming from the young.

It has been shown by cross-fostering that pups from one strain of mice induced more retrieving and licking behavior than pups from another strain (Ressler, 1962). The open-field behavior of rat foster mothers has shown effects of the experience of rearing pups subjected to direct treatments such as shock (Denenberg, 1963), or indirect treatments such as subjecting their true mothers to premating and gestational stress (Joffe, 1965).

In a classic study, Beach and Jaynes (1956) manipulated appearance and behavior of offspring so as to identify specific classes of stimuli controlling parent behavior. Visual, olfactory, tactile, thermal, and movement cues from rat pups were shown to be capable of inducing maternal retrieving, being effective individually and in combination.

It is evident from the foregoing brief review that students of animal behavior have been much more aware of offspring effects on parents than investigators of human parent-child interaction; this more comprehensive view of parent-offspring interaction may be a simple consequence of availability; all phases of development are accessible to direct observation and manipulation. It is also possible that our political and social philosophy has limited scientific outlook at the human more than the animal level. The animal mother is not seen as an agent of socialization, nor her offspring as a tabula rasa.

There are many implications of this research on animal behavior. For the present purpose two are most salient. If variations in offspring behavior affect animal parents from which we expect fairly rigid patterns, even greater effects would be expected on human parental behavior, which is presumably more plastic and susceptible to all classes of influence. The other point is brought out by the variety of offspring stimulus parameters being opened up by animal studies; it should not be difficult to accept the notion of offspring effects if we consider the fact that offspring are at least sources of stimuli. Some stimulus control of human parental behavior should be expected since we take for granted the general likelihood of finding stimulus control over behavior in general.[1]

MODIFIERS OF PARENT RESPONSE

CONGENITAL DETERMINANTS

Three propositions concerning congenital determinants of later behavior will be advanced in this section. Some studies of human subjects will be cited which provide relatively clear evidence. Only reasonable inferences can be made from others. All in all, these studies suggest but by no means document the propositions which are advanced concerning child effects. The present objective is to take the first steps toward developing an alternative to existing socialization theory. A limited scheme which is merely plausible and parsimonious will serve the purpose. Provisional acceptance of this scheme will make it possible to provide concrete illustrations of how some recent findings in the research literature may be reinterpreted.

It will first be assumed that there are congenital contributors to human assertiveness, which will be taken to mean maintenance of goal-directed behavior of high magnitude in the face of barriers. Reasoning, threat of withdrawal of love, and appeals to personal and social motives can all be used

---

[1] The author is indebted to Leon J. Yarrow for suggesting this point.

to arrest ongoing child behavior in excess of parental standards, providing the child is not extreme in assertiveness. With a child who is strongly assertive a parent may more often fall back on quick tangible reinforcement or nonreinforcement. At times when the child, the parent, or both are stressed, the parent falls back further to distraction, holding, frightening verbalization, and physical punishment. The foregoing effects on parent behavior also are considered likely to issue from the behavior of hyperactive, erratic, and unpredictable children, and it is assumed that there are congenital determinants of this kind of behavior as well.

It is further assumed that a different kind of behavior is shown by parents of children congenitally low in assertiveness, activity, or sensory-motor capability. Drawing attention to stimuli, rewarding an increase in behavior, urging, prompting, and demanding are examples of parent response to these child characteristics.

It is also assumed that there are congenital contributors to differences in person orientation. Children high in person orientation attend to the behavior of their parents and reinforce social responses emanating from them. Children low in person orientation induce less nurturance from parents, and their behavior is controlled less by variations in social response of parents. They are interested in physical activity and inanimate objects. Their stimulus characteristics primarily mobilize those elements in the parent nurturance repertoires pertaining to providing and withholding physical objects and activities. Since love-oriented control techniques are less useful with these children and material reinforcers cannot always be flexibly applied, their parents more frequently show further recourse to physical punishment.

Support for a congenital contribution to assertive behavior is seen in the finding that sex differences in socialization training are pronounced in primitive cultures in which large animals are hunted (Barry, Bacon, & Child, 1957).* Furthermore, in all of the 224 primitive cultures surveyed by Murdock (1937), males were accorded roles involving fighting. Greater skeletal muscle development in males is probably an important factor, since even newborn males possess more muscle tissue, females more fat, relative to total body weight (Garn, 1958). It appears reasonable that some potential for use of muscles in physically assertive behavior can also be assumed. We would not expect the exclusive allocation of the fighting role to males if they possessed only greater skeletal muscle mass with no accompanying potential for use, or if there were equal distribution of potential between the

_____
* The article is in Section VIII of this book.—EDITOR

sexes. Males in our advanced societies do not carry spears, but it is improbable that our congenital dispositions have changed as rapidly as our cultural evolution. Even theoretical systems committed to the study of parent effects have acknowledged the probable existence of constitutional bases for sex differences in overt aggressiveness (Sears et al., 1957, p. 484).

One other line of evidence is from twin studies. Direct observation of monozygotic and dizygotic twins each month during the first year of life has shown significant heritability for an item from the Bayley Infant Behavior Profile labeled "goal directedness," which denotes absorption with a task until it is complete (Freedman, 1965). Vandenberg (1962) has pointed out that such twin contrasts in early infancy are more likely to detect genetic contributions than studies of children and adults because later social functioning shapes behavior in ways remote from the circumstances under which genetic selection took place. However, even in studies of school-age children which use the admittedly insensitive self-report questionnaires, significant heritability has been shown for groups of items interpreted as reflecting vigor (Vandenberg, 1962) and dominance (Gottesman, 1965).

Stronger evidence exists for a congenital contribution to person orientation; not only in the twin studies just cited but in several others summarized by Scarr (1965), heritability has been shown for social responsiveness or sociability, the findings cutting across age, sex, social class, and even cultural differences.

Some specific ways in which congenital factors may affect person orientation can be suggested on the basis of data from other studies. Schaffer and Emerson (1964) concluded that avoidance by some infants of being held, carried on the lap, stroked, or kissed was not accounted for by propensities of the mothers, but was due to the infant's restlessness and negative response to the restraint involved in these contacts. Infants who avoided contact showed lower intensity in later social contacts, though neither timing nor breadth of contacts was affected. There was a nonsignificant tendency for those who avoided early contacts to be males. The study is suggestive rather than conclusive because the sample of infants who avoided contacts was small.

Moss (1967) reports from day-long naturalistic observations in the home at 3 and 12 weeks that male infants were more irritable (crying, fussing), and slept less than females. This would mean that, on the average, the mother-son interaction was more one of physical caretaking, the mother being engaged in a variety of efforts to soothe males. Walters and Parke (1965) summarize evidence that the development of social response is relatively independent of the primary-drive reduction which might be expected to follow from such physical acts of caretaking. In fact, there are many reasons for expecting that greater irritability in the males would not favor development of social responses positively valued by parents (i.e., smiling, visual regard, noncrying vocalizations): *(a)* appearance of the mother at the time of crying could lead to an increase in the rate of crying, as reported for institutional infants by Etzel and Gewirtz (1967); *(b)* ministrations which follow the mother's appearance would necessarily contain some stimulation of an aversive nature, as in diaper changing or efforts to release ingested air, a point made by Rheingold (1966, p. 11); *(c)* nonaversing reinforcing elements in caretaking would be less likely to reinforce the infant's positively valued social responses since an irritable infant probably emits less of this behavior; *(d)* the mother would have less time available for purely social stimulation, and might simply wish to avoid the infant when he is quiet.

These possibilities are all consistent with Moss' (1967) finding that by the 12th week, mothers provided less stimulation of an interactional-social nature (imitation) for male than for female infants. It might also be argued that mothers imitated female infants more because of the earlier maturation of social responsiveness in females, an alternative explanation in congenital terms. Mothers could have begun differential sex-role training in social responsiveness sometime in the intervening period, but a ready explanation for initiating such training in just this period is not available. The data do not permit decisions on these different explanations, but the one selected for the present thesis seems at least as defensible as the others: Greater irritability in males led to less stimulation from mothers of the kind which should produce positively valued social responsiveness. This, in turn, may be extended developmentally using data from Bayley and Schaefer (1964, p. 44): Males were rated as less responsive to persons during 11 out of 12 developmental examinations between 10 and 36 months. Goodenough's (1957) report of sex differences in object and person orientation is typical of many other reports in the literature which indicate that males show less social orientation by the preschool period.

The research of Pasamanick, Robers, and Lilienfeld (1956) provides evidence that complications of pregnancy and delivery are associated with later behavior, and that males are more frequently affected. The foregoing studies permit an inference that there is a congenital contributor to early response to social reinforcement. If hyperactive or restless infants do not respond as well as other in-

fants to some of the early social reinforcers, it would be reasonable to expect that their later behavior would be controlled less adequately by use of love-oriented techniques which depend for their efficacy on the strength of the social bond. It could also be inferred that they would be less person-oriented, as a consequence of the less intense primary social bond.

Stechler (1964) lists a number of recent prospective studies which confirm the general validity of Pasamanick's approach, and reports his own finding that neonatal apnea was associated with low developmental quotients in the first 2 years of life. Higher irritability or crying during the newborn period and lower developmental quotients later in infancy have been reported for infants whose mothers reported fears or anxiety during pregnancy (Davids, Holden, & Gray, 1963; Ferreira, 1960; Ottinger & Simmons, 1964). We have already mentioned a study of congenital handicaps which limit sensory-motor development (Bell, 1964). Reports of congenital contributors to sensory-motor development are not limited to populations showing pathology. Kagan and Garn (1963) have reported that chest width measured from roentgenographic films of parents or their children is positively correlated with the children's perceptual-motor and language development in the preschool years.

To summarize, there is direct evidence of congenital factors contributing to two classes of child behavior which are likely to have very different effects on parents: impaired sensory-motor development, and behavior disorders involving hyperactivity. From twin studies there is evidence of a congenital contributor to person orientation and to facets of behavior which appear related to assertiveness. On the other hand, the evidence for congenital contributors to sex differences in person orientation and assertive behavior is mostly inferential. This is particularly true for assertive behavior: No relevant data on early development of sex differences could be located in the literature. In view of this, the arguments relative to assertiveness are merely advanced to indicate that congenital determination is at least reasonable. If we accept this, albeit provisionally, we can further assume that variation within the sexes on congenital grounds could also occur. Polygenetic rather than simple all-or-none determination would be favored by modern genetic theory.

DIFFERENTIATION OF PARENT RESPONSE

Parents do not have fixed techniques for socializing children. They have a repertoire of actions to accomplish each objective. Furthermore, activation of elements in the repertoire requires both cultural pressures and stimulation from the object of acculturation. Characteristics that most infants and children share, such as helplessness, evoke responses.

Another major effect of the child is shown in the parent's selective performance of elements from the caretaking repertoire. It is assumed that there are hierarchies of actions, that different children induce responses from different parts of these hierarchies. Others escalate the actions of their parents so that at one time or another, or in sequence, the entire hierarchy relevant to a certain class of child behavior may be elicited. The child in turn reinforces or fails to reinforce the parent behavior which is evoked. The repertoire changes as a function of cultural demands and also as a result of stimulation and reinforcement received from the child.

Two types of parent control repertoires must be differentiated. *Upper-limit control behavior* reduces and redirects behavior of the child which exceeds parental standards of intensity, frequency, and competence for the child's age. *Lower-limit control behavior* stimulates child behavior which is below parental standards. In other words, parent control behavior, in a sense, is homeostatic relative to child behavior. To predict interaction in particular parent-child pairs it is necessary to know the behavior characteristics of the child, the cultural demands on the parent, and the parents' own individual assimilation of these demands into a set of expectations for the child. Nonetheless, for purposes of illustration we might say that the average parent would show an increase in upper-limit control behavior in response to excessive crying in the infant, or in response to impulsive, hyperactive, or overly competent or assertive behavior in the young child. These widely different behaviors are only considered similar with respect to their effect on upper-limit control. Parental lower-limit control behavior would be stimulated by lethargy in the infant, by low activity, overly inhibited behavior, and lack of competence in the young child. Again, these are different behaviors but are assumed to be similar in effect.

It is customary to observe or rate parental behavior without reference to stimulation provided by the young. When this is done, a parent showing extreme upper-limit behavior in several areas is likely to be described as "punitive," or "restrictive," one showing extreme lower-limit behavior as "intrusive," or "demanding." Both could be considered "controlling," but according to the present conceptual scheme designed to accommodate child effects, the history of preceding interaction sequences could be quite different. The need for differentiating these two types of control

is indicated not only by the present theoretical considerations but also by the empirical findings that punitive and strict behavior is not correlated with intrusive and demanding behavior in parents of young children (Schaefer, 1959, p. 228).

REINTERPRETATION OF RECENT LITERATURE

The child-effect system of explanation which has just been developed states that parent behavior is organized hierarchically within repertoires in the areas of social response and control. Reasonable bases exist for assuming that there are congenital contributors to child behaviors which (*a*) activate these repertoires, (*b*) affect the level of response within hierarchies, and (*c*) differentially reinforce parent behavior which has been evoked.

This system will be applied next to current findings in several major areas in which parent and experiential family effects on children have been given almost exclusive consideration. The findings in most cases are from recent studies which replicate or are consistent with previous studies, or in which results are more defensible than usual because of careful attention to sampling, procedural controls, and measurement. In most cases the authors of these papers were careful not to claim that causes and effects could be clearly differentiated. The question of direction of effects may be raised nonetheless, to ascertain whether the findings are relevant to the theory which motivated the research.

Though in the discussion which follows, the evidence is organized to support the validity of a child-to-parent effect, this should not be taken to mean that an "either-or" approach to the study of parent and child effects is preferred to an interactional view. This reinterpretation is only an expedient considered necessary to direct attention to the possibility of child effects. If this possibility is admitted we can then begin the task of thinking of parent *and* child effects. The primary goal of an expanded model of the socialization process is to uncover interactions of child and parent effects as well as main effects attributable to either source.

Lefkowitz, Walder, and Eron (1963) found in 8-year-olds that peer ratings of aggression were highest and parent reports of the child's use of confession lowest where use of physical punishment was reported by the parents. Bandura and Walters (1959) reported more physical punishment used in a group of male 15- to 16-year-old repeated offenders than in nondelinquents. One theory being tested in each case was that use of punishment in the home produces frustration and conflict or affords a model of aggression which in turn produces aggressive behavior in the child.

An alternative explanation is that these children were congenitally assertive. Congenital assertiveness activated upper-limit control repertoires in parents and techniques within the repertoire were escalated toward physical punishment. Congenital hyperactivity could produce similar results.

Reviewing the area of moral development, Hoffman (1963) found consistent results in studies dealing with reaction to transgression. His interpretation was that an internalized moral orientation, indicated by confession, guilt, or reparation efforts, was fostered by an affectionate relation between the parent and child, in combination with disciplinary techniques which utilized this relation by appealing to the child's personal and social motives. One alternative explanation is that the children showing little internalization of a moral orientation were congenitally low in person orientation. Because of this their mothers were less affectionate and did not appeal to the child's personal or social values.

A study of sex-role development by Mussen and Rutherford (1963) reports findings which replicated those in a previous study. Boys 5–6 years old scoring high in masculinity on the IT test, in comparison with lows, revealed high father nurturance, punishment, and power in doll play. A high power score indicated that father figures were both highly rewarding and punishing. These findings generously supported all major contending theories: developmental identification, defensive identification, and role-theory. A congenital explanation would be that the highs were more masculine in the sense that they showed lower person orientation and higher assertiveness. The father responded with affection because the son's assertiveness and interests in physical activity and toys were sex appropriate, reinforcing his own identification vicariously through his boy. Much as he felt affectionate toward his masculine boy he found he retreated to punishment frequently because the child, being assertive and less responsive to social stimuli, could not be controlled readily by love-oriented techniques.

In the area of intelligence, Bing (1963) found that mothers of children who showed higher verbal than spatial or numerical ability had a more close and demanding relation with their children both in interviews and observation situations than did mothers of children who showed discrepant nonverbal abilities. These findings confirmed the hypothesis that discrepant verbal ability is fostered by a close relation with a demanding and somewhat intrusive mother, discrepant nonverbal abilities being enhanced by allowing the child a considerable degree of freedom. An alternative explanation would be that the high-verbal children were high in person orientation and low in assertiveness.

This is a reasonable combination of characteristics if one assumes that congenital determinants of assertiveness and person orientation are independent or at least not highly positively correlated. These children reinforced their mothers' social responses and elicited nurturant behavior. The resultant interaction intensified verbal expression because this is the primary channel of communication. The fact that these children were low in assertiveness led to lower-limit control behavior reflected in the mother's demanding and intrusive behavior.

Schaefer's (1959) summary of his own work and that of others indicates that a major portion of the variance in parent behavior can be accounted for under two dimensions described as love-hostility and autonomy-control. This is a useful finding, offering the possibility of descriptive parsimony, regardless of the question of direction of effects. However, the two-dimensional model might represent a system of effects of children on parents. The hostility extreme of the love-hostility dimension (strictness, punishment, perceiving the child as a burden) could be characterized as a parent upper-limit control pattern in response to overly assertive, unpredictable, or hyperactive behavior. The love extreme could reflect positive evaluation of children showing more modal behavior but not behavior extreme in the opposite direction.

In support of this we find in longitudinal data from the Berkeley Growth Study (Schaefer & Bayley, 1963) that calm children were evaluated positively by their mothers during the first 3 years. Children who were rapid and active were perceived as a burden during the first 15 months. The next set of measurements available for both mothers and children covered the period when the child was between 9 and 12 years. Mothers of children rated as rapid at this time were themselves rated as irritable and perceiving the child as a burden. No rating of calmness was available. A rating of the child's inactivity in this same period could not be considered a simple inverse of the activity rating made in the first 3 years, either from the standpoint of wording or correlation pattern across the sexes. If we assume that it primarily differentiated degree of inactivity running from the highly inactive to modal levels of activity, this rating becomes relevant to the autonomy versus control dimension.

The autonomy extreme of the autonomy-control dimension might reflect parents' granting autonomy to children who conform to parental expectations of capability and assertiveness. The control extreme (intrusiveness, anxiety, achievement demand, anxiety relative to the child's behavior and health) would be considered parental lower-limit control behavior in response to children low in assertiveness or sensory-motor capability. In support of this we find that mothers of male and female inactive children during the period 9–14 years were rated as intrusive and as high in achievement demand, but low in granting autonomy to the child. All relations cited from this study (Schaefer & Bayley, 1963) were consistent for both sexes and significant beyond the .05 level for combined male and female samples according to the present author's analysis of tabular material on pages 109–110 and 121–122. Data from earlier age periods could not be brought to bear on a child-effect interpretation of the autonomy-control dimension because of very differing relations between maternal and child behavior in mother-son versus mother-daughter pairs.

Social class differences in parent behavior may also be interpreted as influenced by child effects. According to Bronfenbrenner's (1958) analysis, middle-class parents show less use of physical punishment and more use of love-oriented techniques than lower-class parents. There was no clear evidence of a change in this finding in the period from 1932 to 1952, as there was for other child-rearing techniques. Complications of pregnancy and delivery are more frequent in the lower classes (Pasamanick & Knobloch, 1960), and on this basis we could expect more hyperactivity in children from lower-class samples. From the earlier discussions relative to hyperactivity we would expect to find in lower-class parents more upper-limit control behavior, of which physical punishment is a salient example, and less use of love-oriented techniques. It is clear that studies of social-class differences in the future should control for complications of pregnancy and delivery. Some class differences may be reduced in magnitude or altered qualitatively when the samples are made comparable with respect to complications of pregnancy and delivery.

Another area receiving considerable attention in the research literature is that of family structure effects such as birth order, sex of siblings, and family size and density. Data from several studies would support the assumption that differences in parent behavior with different children in the family may be primarily due to increased experience and change in availability to children as the family grows (Conners, 1963; Lasko, 1954; Waldrop & Bell, 1964). However, this does not make it possible to dismiss the possibility of child effects. Second- or later-born neonates show higher skin conductance than firstborn (Weller & Bell, 1965). There is collateral evidence that this indicates heightened arousal and greater maturity in this early period, though there is no information available on later development. Another paper summarizes data indicating that the physiology of pregnancy

and delivery is quite different for the mother with her first versus later births (Bell, 1963), raising the possibility that some differences in parent behavior with first- versus later-born children may be a response to congenital differences in the child.

A similar child effect could be operative with increases in family size and density. Since greater dependency was found in preschool children coming from large families with short intervals between siblings it was assumed that these children were simply more deprived of maternal attention (Waldrop & Bell, 1964). While this may have been true in part, further study revealed that newborns from large dense families were more lethargic (Waldrop & Bell, 1966). In this case information on later development was available and the finding was that measures of lethargy in the newborn period were correlated with later dependency. In short, there may be congenital factors operating in determining family structure effects, and credence cannot be given to an interpretation solely in terms of experiential factors until influences identifiable in pregnancy, delivery, and the newborn period are isolated.

EXAMPLES OF STUDIES DIFFICULT TO REINTERPRET

In contrast to these studies, there are others yielding data which could not be reinterpreted as a function of congenital effects contributed by the child. For example, there are studies which substitute experimenters for parents and assign children at random to experimental groups in which different "parental" treatment is administered. In one study, experimenters played the role of parents who did or did not control access to food and toy resources in familylike interactions with preschool children (Bandura, Ross, & Ross, 1963): Children imitated parents who controlled resources.* In a study of moral development, experimenters behaved with different groups of children in such a way as to create differences in the child's control over punishment and in the cognitive clarity of a task which preceded a contrived transgression (Aronfreed, 1963). Self-critical and reparative responses following transgression were maximized by prior cognitive clarity and child control. These studies used a flexible approach which can be applied to a wide variety of parent-effect parameters very rapidly. One limitation is that we do not obtain data on the cumulative effects of parents on children. The other problem is that of ownness. It is encouraging

---

* See Bandura, Ross, and Ross, "A Comparative Test of the Status Envy, Social Power, and Secondary Reinforcement Theories of Identificatory Learning," reprinted later in this section.—EDITOR

in this respect that Stevenson, Keen, and Knights (1963) in studies of social reinforcement with 4- and 5-year-olds, found effects common to fathers and male experimenters, and effects common to mothers and female experimenters. This reassures us that at least with young children it may be possible to produce results with experimenters similar to effects parents have on their own children.

One other approach involves experimental manipulation of the behavior of parents and measurement of the effects on children. This is an approach that is only slightly less flexible than the foregoing and can be carried out very rapidly. Merrill (1946) manipulated parent behavior by providing mothers in two matched groups with different feedback relative to the behavior of their children. As in the previous approach which substituted experimenters for parents, the possibility of pseudo-parent effects being produced by latent child effects is minimal where the children are assigned to experimental groups at random, or on the basis of some relevant matching variable. On the other hand, since the parent is present in the interaction, the child may respond in terms of past expectancies rather than to the manipulated behavior of the parent as such. This operates against obtaining differences in child behavior in different treatments, but where differences are obtained they can be interpreted as free of child effects.

Offspring effects can also be isolated. An example is provided in a summary of a series of studies carried out by Siegel (1963). Retardates aged 10 and 15 were classified into high- and low-verbal ability groups. Children in each group were then placed in brief interaction situations with adults who had had no previous contact with them. The adults were to assist children in learning how to assemble a puzzle. Generally, adult responses and questions with low-verbal children were more frequent but shorter and more redundant. Labeling children of similar verbal ability as high or low had no effect on the adult behavior. Support was provided for the hypothesis that linguistic level of children exerts a control over adult verbal behavior.

A second variant of the first design is suggested by the research of Yarrow (1963), already discussed, which took advantage of the assignment of young infants to foster mothers for temporary care while adoption procedures were pending. It is necessary only to measure infant characteristics prior to assignment to foster mothers and then make the assignment systematically so that each foster mother's behavior with at least two different kinds of infants could be measured.

One other approach would make it possible to obtain effects with natural parents. Clinicians frequently report that successful medication of children who are hyperactive and impulsive produces pronounced reactive changes in parent and even total family behavior. Addition of pre- and post-medication measures of parent-child and family interaction to a well-controlled study of drug effects should make it possible to evaluate this and other possible child effects.[2]

Other approaches have been mentioned in the introductory section of this paper (Bell, 1964; Levy, 1958). A detailed discussion of all possible research designs is beyond the scope of this paper, which is primarily concerned with a substantive question of how studies of socialization may be interpreted. This brief recapitulation of designs is to serve the purpose of emphasizing the fact that offspring and parent effects can be separately identified and experimentally manipulated. This will require less reliance on correlation studies of parent and child behavior upon which theories of socialization have been largely based up to the present. Even correlations obtained between parent and child behaviors from longitudinal studies offer no means of ascertaining the direction of effects, unless specially designed for the purpose. Kagan and Moss (1962) have pointed out that the problem of whether maternal hostility is a reaction to child aggression or vice versa is not solved by the demonstration of long-term relations between these maternal and child behaviors in follow-up studies.

REFERENCES

ARONFREED, J. M. The effects of experimental socialization paradigms upon two moral responses to transgression. *Journal of Abnormal and Social Psychology,* 1963, *66,* 437–448.

BANDURA, A., ROSS, D., & ROSS, S. A. A comparative test of the status envy, social power, and secondary reinforcement theories of identificatory learning. *Journal of Abnormal and Social Psychology,* 1963, *67,* 527–534.

BANDURA, A., & WALTERS, R. H. *Adolescent aggression.* New York: Ronald Press, 1959.

BARRY, H., III, BACON, M. K., & CHILD, I. L. A cross-cultural survey of some sex differences in socialization. *Journal of Abnormal and Social Psychology,* 1957, *55,* 327–332.

BAYLEY, N., & SCHAEFER, E. S. Correlations of maternal and child behaviors with the development of mental abilities: Data from the Berkeley Growth Study. *Monographs of the Society for Research in Child Development,* 1964, *29*(6, Whole No. 97).

BEACH, F. A., & JAYNES, J. Studies of maternal retrieving in rats. III. Sensory cues involved in the lactating females' response to her young. *Behaviour,* 1956, *10,* 104–125.

[2] This adaptation of drug studies was suggested by Paul H. Wender.

BELL, R. Q. Some factors to be controlled in studies of behavior of newborns. *Biologia Neonatorum*, 1963, *5*, 200–214.

BELL, R. Q. The effect on the family of a limitation in coping ability in a child: A research approach and a finding. *Merrill-Palmer Quarterly*, 1964, *10*, 129–142.

BING, E. Effect of childrearing practices on development of differential cognitive abilities. *Child Development*, 1963, *34*, 631–648.

BRONFENBRENNER, U. Socialization and social class through time and space. In E. E. Maccoby, T. M. Newcomb, & E. L. Hartley (Eds.), *Readings in social psychology*. New York: Holt, Rinehart & Winston, 1958. Pp. 400–425.

BRUCE, H. M. Observations on the suckling stimulus and lactation in the rat. *Journal of Reproduction and Fertility*, 1961, *2*, 17–34.

CONNERS, C. K. Birth order and needs for affiliation. *Journal of Personality*, 1963, *31*, 408–416.

DAVIDS, A., HOLDEN, R. H., & GRAY, G. B. Maternal anxiety during pregnancy and adequacy of mother and child adjustment eight months following childbirth. *Child Development*, 1963, *34*, 993–1002.

DENENBERG, V. H. Early experience and emotional development. *Scientific American*, 1963, *208*, 138–146.

EPSTEIN, W. Experimental investigations of the genesis of visual space perception. *Psychological Bulletin*, 1964, *61*, 115–128.

ETZEL, B., & GEWIRTZ, J. Experimental modification of caretaker-maintained high rate operant crying in a 6- and a 20-week-old infant *(Infans Tyrannotearus)*. *Journal of Experimental Child Psychology*, 1967, *5*, 303–317.

FERREIRA, A. J. The pregnant woman's emotional attitude and its reflection on the newborn. *American Journal of Orthopsychiatry*, 1960, *30*, 553–561.

FREEDMAN, D. G. Hereditary control of early social behavior. In B. M. Foss (Ed.), *Determinants of infant behaviour III*. New York: Wiley, 1965. Pp. 149–159.

GARN, S. M. Fat, body size, and growth in the newborn. *Human Biology*, 1958, *30*, 265–280.

GOODENOUGH, F. W. Interest in persons as an aspect of sex difference in early years. *Genetic Psychology Monographs*, 1957, *55*, 287–323.

GOTTESMAN, I. I. Genetic variance in adaptive personality traits. Paper presented at the 73rd annual convention of the American Psychological Association, September 1965, Chicago, Illinois.

HILLENBRAND, E. D. The relationship of psychological, medical, and feeding variables to breast feeding. Unpublished master's thesis, George Washington University, 1965.

HOFFMAN, M. L. Childrearing practices and moral development: Generalizations from empirical research. *Child Development*, 1963, *34*, 295–318.

JOFFE, J. M. Genotype and prenatal and premating stress interact to affect adult behavior in rats. *Science*, 1965, *150*, 1844–1845.

KAGAN, J., & GARN, S. M. A constitutional correlate of early intellectual functioning. *Journal of Genetic Psychology*, 1963, *102*, 83–89.

KAGAN, J., & MOSS, H. A. *Birth to maturity*. New York: Wiley, 1962.

KESSEN, W. (Ed.) *The child*. New York: Wiley, 1965.

LASKO, J. K. Parent behavior toward first and second children. *Genetic Psychology Monographs*, 1954, *49*, 97–137.

LEFKOWITZ, M. M., WALTER, L. O., & ERON, L. D. Punishment, identification and aggression. *Merrill-Palmer Quarterly*, 1963, *9*, 159–174.

LEVY, D. M. *Behavioral analysis: Analysis of clinical observations of behavior as applied to mother-newborn relationships*. New York: Thomas, 1958.

MERRILL, B. A measurement of mother-child interaction. *Journal of Abnormal and Social Psychology*, 1946, *41*, 37–49.

MOSS, H. A. Sex, age, and state as determinants of mother-infant interaction. *Merrill-Palmer Quarterly*, 1967, *13*, 19–36.

MURDOCK, G. P. Comparative data on the division of labor by sex. *Social Forces*, 1937, *15*, 551–553.

MUSSEN, P., & RUTHERFORD, E. Parent-child relations and parental personality in relation to young children's sex-role preferences. *Child Development*, 1963, *34*, 589–607.

NOIROT, E. Changes in responsiveness to young in the adult mouse. III. The effect of immediately preceding performances. *Behavior*, 1965, *24*, 318–325.

OTTINGER, D. R., & SIMMONS, J. E. Behavior of human neonates and prenatal maternal anxiety. *Psychological Reports*, 1964, *14*, 391–394.

PALMER, R. R. *The age of the democratic revolution: Vol. II. The struggle*. Princeton: Princeton University Press, 1964.

PASAMANICK, B., & KNOBLOCH, H. Brain damage and reproductive casualty. *American Journal of Orthopsychiatry*, 1960, *30*, 298–305.

PASAMANICK, B., ROBERS, M. E., & LILIENFELD, A. M. Pregnancy experience and the development of behavior disorders in children. *American Journal of Psychiatry*, 1956, *112*, 613–618.

RESSLER, R. H. Parental handling in two strains of mice reared by foster parents. *Science*, 1962, *137*, 129–130.

RHEINGOLD, H. L., (Ed.) *Maternal behavior in mammals*. New York: Wiley, 1963.

RHEINGOLD, H. L. The development of social behavior in the human infant. In H. W. Stevenson (Ed.), Concept of development: A report of a conference commemorating the fortieth anniversary of the Institute of Child Development, University of Minnesota. *Monographs of the Society for Research in Child Development*, 1966, *31*(5, Whole No. 197).

SCARR, S. The inheritance of sociability. *American Psychologist*, 1965, *20*, 524. (Abstract)

SCHAEFER, E. A circumplex model for maternal behavior. *Journal of Abnormal and Social Psychology*, 1959, *59*, 226–235.

SCHAEFER, E. Parent-child interaction patterns and parental attitudes. In D. Rosenthal (Ed.), *The Genain quadruplets*. New York: Basic Books, 1963. Pp. 398–430.

SCHAEFER, E., & BAYLEY, N. Maternal behavior, child behavior, and their intercorrelations from infancy through adolescence. *Monographs of the Society for Research in Child Development*, 1963, *28*(3, Whole No. 87).

SCHAFFER, H. R., & EMERSON, P. E. Patterns of response to physical contact in early human development. *Journal of Child Psychology and Psychiatry*, 1964, *5*, 1–13.

SEARS, R. R., MACCOBY, E. E., & LEVIN, H. *Patterns of child rearing*. Evanston, Ill.: Row, Peterson, 1957.

SIEGEL, G. M. Adult verbal behavior with retarded children labeled as "high" or "low" in verbal ability. *American Journal of Mental Deficiency*, 1963, *68*, 417–424.

STECHLER, G. A longitudinal follow-up of neonatal apnea. *Child Development*, 1964, *35*, 333–348.

STEVENSON, H. W., KEEN, R., & KNIGHTS, R. M. Parents and strangers as reinforcing agents for children's performance. *Journal of Abnormal and Social Psychology*, 1963, *67*, 183–186.

STOTT, L. H. Parent-adolescent adjustment: Its measurement and significance. *Character and Personality*, 1941, *10*, 140–150.

VANDENBERG, S. G. The hereditary abilities study: Hereditary components in a psychological test battery. *American Journal of Human Genetics*, 1962, *14*, 220–237.

WALDROP, M., & BELL, R. Q. Relation of preschool dependency behavior to family size and density. *Child Development*, 1964, *35*, 1187–1195.

WALDROP, M., & BELL, R. Q. Effects of family size and density on newborn characteristics. *American Journal of Orthopsychiatry*, 1966, *36*, 544–550.

WALTERS, R. H., & PARKE, R. D. The role of the distance receptors in the development of social responsiveness. In L. P. Lipsitt & C. C. Spiker (Eds.), *Advances in child development and behavior*. Vol. 2. New York: Academic Press, 1965. Pp. 59–96.

WELLER, G. M., & BELL, R. Q. Basal skin conductance and neonatal state. *Child Development*, 1965, *36*, 647–657.

YARROW, L. J. Research in dimensions of early maternal care. *Merrill-Palmer Quarterly*, 1963, *9*, 101–114.

Art Buchwald at Home

THE GROWN-UP PROBLEM

There has been so much discussion lately about teen-age problems that the grown-up problem is practically being ignored. And yet if you pick up a newspaper, you realize grown-ups are responsible for some of the most serious problems this country has ever faced.

For example, 60 per cent of all crime in the United States is committed by grown-ups.

The birth rate among grown-up women is four times that of teen-agers.

The divorce rate is double.

The purchasing power of grown-ups almost exceeds that of teen-agers.

Grown-ups are responsible for more daytime accidents than any other age group.

The source of these statistics is sociology Prof. Heinrich Applebaum, B.A., M.S., LL.D., Y.E.H., Y.E.H., Y.E.H., who told me in an exclusive interview that his studies showed grown-ups were drifting farther away from society all the time.

"The average grown-up," Prof. Applebaum said, "feels his children don't understand him. The more time he spends with them the less they communicate with him. So the adult feels isolated, insecure, and misunderstood. In defense he seeks out other grown-ups who feel the same way he does. Pretty soon they form gangs, go to the theater together, hold cocktail parties and dances, and before you know it you have a complete breakdown of the family."

"Why do you think grown-ups are constantly rebelling against their children, Professor?"

"I guess it's an age-old old-age problem. You have parents wanting to break away and yet not having the nerve to cut the ties completely. Grown-ups are afraid to stand up to their children, so they rebel against society instead."

"Do you think teen-agers could in some way be responsible for the behavior of their parents?"

"I definitely do," the Professor said. "Grown-ups try to emulate teen-agers. They want to do exactly what teen-agers do, which is to drink, smoke, and drive fast cars. If teen-agers didn't do these things, their parents wouldn't. For every bad adult in America, I'm sure you'll find a bad teen-ager somewhere in the background."

"Where do you think the trouble starts?"

"In the home. Teen-agers are too rough on their parents. They're always criticizing them for listening to Frank Sinatra records and reading Holiday magazine. Teen-agers don't have any patience with their mothers and fathers. They can't understand why their parents like Doris Day and Rock Hudson movies or what they see in Cary Grant. If teen-agers spent more time with grown-ups and tried to understand them, I don't think you'd have half the trouble that you have in the United States today."

"Do you mean teen-agers should spend more time at home with their parents?"

"Of course. Grown-ups need security. They want to know where their children are. They want the feeling they belong. Only teen-agers can give grown-ups this feeling."

"Professor, have you found any homes where grown-ups are leading healthy, normal, secure lives, thanks to the attention they've received from their loving teen-age children?"

"We haven't yet. But we've been looking only a year. These surveys take time."

25

Identification as a Function of the Reinforcing Quality of the Model and the Socialization Background of the Subject[1]

James C. Baxter,[2] Melvin J. Lerner, and Jerome S. Miller

The first of our selections on identification is this article by Baxter, Lerner, and Miller. Baxter is in the Department of Psychology at the University of Houston; Lerner is professor of psychology at the University of Waterloo in Ontario, Canada; and Miller is at the National Institute of Mental Health's Clinical Research Center at Lexington, Kentucky.

This article not only gives information about identification and child-rearing, but also conveys the point that various effects of upbringing may show up in adulthood only under certain (stressful) conditions. This point is an important one for developmental psychology, whether human or animal. One of the early studies to call attention to the importance of later conditions to the influence of early experiences was done by J. McV. Hunt. He showed that rats deprived of food in infancy hoarded more as adults, but only if they were stressed (suffered some food deprivation) in adult-

hood. *This idea is basic in Freudian thought and in that of Erik H. Erikson.*

Since the time of Freud's (1938) initial writing on the topic of identification, the concept has been regarded as a central variable in personality development (Bandura & Walters, 1963; Bronfenbrenner, 1960; Kagan, 1958). Two major processes of identification have been described: anaclitic identification, or the imitation of a highly valued and positively regarded model; and identification with the aggressor, or the defensive imitation of a threatening model. These two processes have been related to qualitative differences in the relationship between subject and model by a number of authors in subsequent writings (e.g., Bronfenbrenner, 1960; Carlson, 1963; Freud, 1960; Mowrer, 1950; Sanford, 1955; Sarnoff, 1962; and others). A considerable amount of research has been reported to corroborate the anaclitic process (e.g., Bandura & Huston, 1961; Helper, 1955; Mussen & Distler, 1959, 1960; Payne & Mussen, 1956; Sears, 1953; Sears, Maccoby, & Levin, 1957). The process of identification with the aggressor, on the other hand, has stimulated less research. Anecdotal accounts of the imitation of threatening models have been described (Balint, 1945; Freud, 1954), and an extensive naturalistic report of threat-based behavior in a German concentration camp has appeared (Bettelheim, 1943). Two studies have also been reported which describe stable individual differences in patterns of identification in response to threat (Carlson, 1963; Sarnoff, 1951). However, no experimental studies of the process have been reported.

Sarnoff (1951) has argued that three basic conditions are necessary for the occurrence of identification with the aggressor: an aggressor who is determined to impose his hostility upon another individual; a victim who is socially dependent upon the aggressor and who thus makes a convenient target for the aggressor's hostility; and a system of social constraints such that the victim cannot completely escape the influence of the aggressor. Anaclitic identification, on the other hand, is based on the rewarding qualities of the model, and thus would be expected to occur in a situation in which the individual is socially dependent upon a model who is supportive and nonthreatening toward him, and who makes these behaviors conditional upon the individual's behavior (Bandura & Huston, 1961).

[1] This study was supported in part by a small grant from the University of Kentucky Research Fund. The authors would like to express their appreciation to the University of Kentucky Computing Center for assisting with the data analysis. The views expressed are those of the authors and do not necessarily reflect an official position of the United States Public Health Service.

[2] At the time of this study, at the University of Kentucky.

It has been proposed that individual differences in childhood experiences affect the process of identification and influence the type of imitation shown by a person. In particular, Balint (1945) has suggested that children reared in homes in which the parents take a punitive and restrictive attitude toward pleasure-seeking activities show a decreased tolerance for frustration and anxiety. As a consequence, the children show an increased tendency to identify with available models, especially those posing a threat to their self-esteem.

Sarnoff (1951) has provided data which tend to support one aspect of Balint's position by showing that people who identify with an aggressor more strongly (e.g., anti-Semitic attitudes in Jews), do in fact ascribe more rejecting, frustrating, and hostile attitudes to their parents than do people who resist such identification. The latter report more accepting and love-oriented parental attitudes.

The present study was aimed at investigating identification in an experimental setting designed to encourage either an anaclitic (support-based) or defensive (threat-based) relationship between young adults and a model. In addition to the experimental manipulation, subjects were also differentiated for their reports of the parents' child-rearing attitudes: rejecting and hostile versus accepting and supportive. Under these conditions both anaclitic and defensive identification were expected to occur. Individual differences in degrees of identification as well as type of identification were also predicted.

METHOD

SUBJECTS

Subjects were drawn from male introductory psychology students at the University of Kentucky. All subjects were unpaid volunteers and received course credit for their participation. Only those subjects who reported having been reared in an intact parental home were eligible. Also, since other studies involving similar experimental procedures were being conducted during the same semester, only subjects who had not participated in similar studies were used. A total of 69 subjects participated, although 15 were later excluded from the sample due to failure to cooperate with the experimental instructions or failure to accept the experimental ruse (described below).[3] The remaining 54 subjects represent the final sample.

---

[3] The identification scores (described below) of all 15 subjects omitted from the sample were compared with the scores of those included in the study. In 11 out of 15 cases the scores fell within 1 standard deviation of their corresponding cell means, and in all 15 cases the scores were within 1.31 standard score units of their corresponding cell means.

APPARATUS

The room in which the experiment was conducted contained two chairs and a table, on which a microphone and one set of earphones were placed in full view. Wires from the communication equipment led to a terminal box in the wall. The earphones were connected to a tape recorder in the adjoining room. Depending on the experimental condition to which the subject had been assigned, there was also present in the room additional experimental apparatus. For one arrangement of the room, an imposing looking "shock" apparatus was placed next to the subject's chair, on an electrical apparatus rack, standing about 3 feet high. The apparatus contained a large stimulator unit with the words "shock stimulator" painted on it, a row of six patch panels above the stimulator to which a network of variously colored wires were attached, and a small unit of dials below the stimulator. Colored lights located on the stimulator and the dial unit were turned on at all times. Electrodes leading from the apparatus were resting on the table in front of the subject. Wires leading from a different outlet on the apparatus went to the adjoining room under a connecting door. A second arrangement of the room involved the chairs, table, and communication equipment, but without the shock apparatus. In this condition three rolls of quarters wrapped in standard orange-colored bank rolls with $10 and the word Quarters printed on the side in large characters were displayed on the table. One roll was "broken open," with 10 quarters piled next to the filled rolls. A pad of receipts with the words University of Kentucky printed at the top was placed next to the quarters. The third arrangement of the room included only the chairs, table, and communication equipment.

PROCEDURE

Subjects were contacted during the laboratory period of their class and asked to volunteer for an experiment in learning. When they appeared at their appointed time, they were accompanied to the experimental room by a male undergraduate experimenter. All subjects were run individually by the same experimenter, who was carefully supervised in the conduct of the study, but who was naive with respect to experimental hypotheses.

Upon entering the room, the experimenter seated the subject and told him that before beginning the main experiment he would be asked to fill out a brief questionnaire for another purpose and at the request of another experimenter. He was told that since it would take only a short time, it could be "gotten out of the way" before the main experiment. The experimenter read the instructions with the subject, answered any questions raised, and then permitted him to complete the ratings on the form while the experimenter busied himself with other papers. The questionnaire items were actually an abbreviation of the Traditional Family Ideology (TFI) Scale (Levinson & Huffman, 1955), which was obtained for the purpose of later differentiating subjects into levels of parental authoritarianism and restrictiveness toward child socialization. Fifteen items were chosen from the full scale which represented parental attitudes of authoritarian submission, conventionalism, exaggerated reliance on masculinity and femininity, moralistic rejection of impulse life, and extreme emphasis on discipline. Items were selected (or in several cases rephrased) to apply to both parents and to balance the direction of responding. A 6-point scale, ranging from very strong agreement to very strong disagreement, was provided for each item. Subjects were instructed to recall the period when they were growing up and answer the items the way they thought their parents would have responded to them.

Following completion of the TFI, the questionnaire was put aside and the subject was told that the main experiment was beginning. The experimenter read to the subject the instructions to the experiment in a standard and conversational manner. The experiment was presented as an investigation of the effectiveness of a particular method of learning an artificial language, Esperanto. He was told that he would receive a number of basic principles about the language through the earphones, and then, after he had become familiar with the principles, he would be given a list of 35 words in Esperanto one at a time and at a constant rate, to which he was to respond with the English translation.

Subjects were assigned on a random basis to one of three experimental treatments. A punishment group (run in the presence of the shock apparatus) was told that the method of learning being studied was the use of punishment as a learning technique. The subject was told that the electrodes would be attached to his left hand just before starting, and that each time he made an error in translation or failed to report the correct translation within 5 seconds, the instructor in the other room would push a button and he would receive a shock through the electrodes. He was told that the shock would be quite strong, and would probably hurt a little. He was also told that most people tend to get 15–20 shocks under these conditions, and that some get more or less, depending on how quickly they learn. Finally, he was told that he would be able to ask any questions he had later, but that there was another part to the study that he was to be told about first.

The reward group (run in the presence of the quarters and receipt pad) was given comparable instructions which stressed the expectation that the instructor in the other room would press a button after each correct translation within the time period, and the subject would be given a quarter. The experimenter demonstrated how quarters would be moved to the subject's reward pile on his side of the table, and the experimenter said that the quarters would be his winnings, and would be his to keep. The subject was also told that a receipt for his winnings would be requested, and he was led to believe that most people tend to get 15–20 quarters under these conditions, with some getting more or less, depending on how quickly they learn. The control group (run in the absence of supporting equipment) was given comparable instructions which stressed the expectation that the instructor in the other room would say "right" after each correct translation within the time period, and would say "wrong" if the translation were incorrect or too slow. Subjects were also told that most people tend to get about 15–20 correct

translations under these conditions and about the same number incorrect.

The experimental treatments, then, were designed to place the subject in a dependent relationship with the instructor in the adjoining room, who was characterized as specially trained in the material to be learned, and who was to be either punishing, rewarding, or informative while teaching the subject the language.

To measure the degree of identification present, an additional manipulation was introduced. Following the instructions concerning the task and the nature of the relationship between the subject and the instructor, the experimenter indicated that another aspect of learning was also being studied. This aspect was "what the student knows about his instructor." The subject was informed that experts think that knowing one's instructor is an important factor in learning. He was told that this was also being investigated, and that he was to overhear an interview in the adjoining room between the professor conducting the study and the subject's instructor. He was told that both the professor and the instructor knew he would be listening. He was also told that he should try to form as clear a picture of his instructor as possible while listening.

The interview was actually a 4-minute tape recording which the experimenter started in the next room by leaving the experimental room briefly, ostensibly to inform the professor and instructor that the subject was ready to begin. The content of the interview was quite general and dealt with impressions the instructor, who was identified as a graduate student, had gained of the University, Lexington, and the surrounding horse farms.

After the subject had heard the interview, he was asked to make a series of ratings about his instructor from impressions he had gained. When the ratings of the instructor were completed, the sheet was withdrawn and he was asked to rate himself on another sheet containing the same items. Finally, the self-ratings were withdrawn, and he was asked to rate the average male student at the University of Kentucky, using the same items. The ratings were made on 22 bipolar adjectival dimensions, each of which was judged on a 7-point equal-appearing interval scale. The dimensions used were obtained from Cattell's (1950) rating scale items.

Following completion of the three sets of ratings, the subject was given a booklet containing four questions about the experiment which were rated on either 31- or 36-point scales. The specific items referred to: how pleased he felt about participating in the experiment; how much he would like to be an instructor for this kind of task in a future experiment; how many correct (incorrect) responses he thought he would get in translating the words; and how valuable he felt research of this kind is. Results of the ratings on the four items proved to be unreliable, and thus were not considered further.

After the subject had completed all the ratings, he was informed that the experiment was over and he was interrogated briefly concerning his acceptance of the experimental ruse. Only those 54 subjects accepting the ruse were included in the sample. Finally, subjects were asked to avoid discussing the experiment with other students and were dismissed.

RESULTS AND DISCUSSION

Subjects were classified into six experimental groups by dividing each of the three treatment groups at the median TFI score. Six groups of nine subjects each were obtained. Comparison of TFI scores across experimental conditions was done in order to evaluate the comparability of the experimental groups with respect to the degree of authoritarianism ascribed to their parents. The three experimental groups were found to be quite comparable in levels of TFI ($Fs < 1.00$).

Product-moment correlations between the ratings of the instructor, the self, and the average male student were computed for each subject. Partial correlations between self and instructor were then obtained, with the average male student ratings controlled. In this way, characteristics attributable to male college students in general were partialed out, and a more direct measure of perceived similarity between the subject and the particular instructor was obtained. This measure was adopted as an index of identification. Transformation of these correlations to z scores was done in order to allow parametric analyses. An analysis of the variance of the transformed identification scores was then done. Table 1 summarizes these results.

It can be seen that both the experimental conditions and the individual differences in severity of childhood socialization considered separately show no reliable relation to identification scores. The interaction of the experimental conditions and levels of severity of socialization did reach significance at the .01 level, however. Mean transformed identification scores for the six groups are reported in Table 2. It can be seen from these scores that more identification occurred in high TFI subjects under the punishment condition, while the low TFI subjects tended to show more identification under both the reward and control (information) conditions. This difference in patterns of identification between TFI groups is significant at the .01 level by two-tailed t test ($t = 2.75$, $df = 48$). Individual

TABLE 2
MEAN TRANSFORMED IDENTIFICATION SCORES

Severity of socialization	Condition		
	Punishment	Reward	Control
High TFI	.89	.27	.26
Low TFI	.24	.48	.42

comparisons indicate that the differences are primarily attributable to the unusually high degree of identification shown by the high TFI subjects in the punishment condition. The high TFI punishment group differed from the other high TFI groups and from the low TFI punishment group at the .01 level, and tended to differ from the remaining low TFI groups (p's $< .10$). Considered alone, the three low TFI groups did not differ reliably between experimental conditions.

The overall pattern of results indicates rather persuasively that differences in the type of identification obtained in the present situation depend on individual differences in perceived childhood socialization experiences. Subjects who report being reared in restrictive, authoritarian homes show significantly more identification with the aggressor while subjects who report being reared in permissive, democratic homes tend to show more anaclitic identification. These results are consistent with previous data reported by Sarnoff (1951), and tend to confirm Balint's (1945) hypothesis that more severely socialized children develop tendencies to identify defensively. The absence of an overall difference in identification as a function of differences in severity of socialization alone is at variance with the second aspect of her hypothesis, however. If such differences in adjustment can be said to exist after the subjects have reached maturity, they appear to be secondary to predispositions to respond selectively to the affective quality of the situation encountered.

On the basis of the present findings a more tenable hypothesis appears to be that individuals reared in an authoritarian atmosphere, which required the development of tendencies toward defensive identification in childhood, will be more likely to identify with an aggressor as an adult. On the other hand, individuals whose patterns of identification developed in relation to supportive democratically oriented parents will be more responsive to situations which engender anaclitic identification. Such an interpretation appears to be related to differences in conformity and submission training in childhood socialization which have been emphasized in the authoritarian ideology research (Adorno, Frenkel-Brunswik, Levinson, & San-

TABLE 1
ANALYSIS OF VARIANCE OF TRANSFORMED IDENTIFICATION SCORES

Source	df	MS	F
Between cells	5		
Conditions (C)	2	.264	1.28
Socialization (S)	1	.123	<1.00
C × S	2	1.042	5.08*
Error	48	.205	
Total	53		

* $p = .01$.

ford, 1950). On the basis of their interview data, these authors have concluded that

much of the submission to parental authority in the [extremely high scoring] prejudiced subject seems to be induced by impatience on the part of the parents and by the child's fear of displeasing them [p. 385].

This threat-based training, often accomplished at the hands of extremely harsh and arbitrary parents, appears to be coextensive with the present concept of identification with the aggressor. Accordingly, the results of the high TFI groups in the present experiment are congruent with earlier clinical findings vis-à-vis the authoritarian personality.

The problem of why the conditions favoring identification were not different from the control condition in the present experiment raises an unanswered question. This result is somewhat surprising, since at least the anaclitic process of identification has been demonstrated previously by several investigators under different conditions (e.g., Bandura & Huston, 1961; Mussen & Distler, 1959, 1960). One possible explanation for the present, somewhat anomalous result appears to be that the control (information) condition was not actually as neutral as it was intended to be. That is, it may have been that the provision of information by the instructor established the anticipation of a supportive relationship. There is some evidence to support this possibility. As can be seen in Table 2, the subjects in the control condition responded quite similarly to the subjects in the reward condition. In any event, alternative control procedures appear warranted for further research using this situation.

REFERENCES

ADORNO, T. W., FRENKEL-BRUNSWIK, ELSE, LEVINSON, D. J., & SANFORD, R. N. *The authoritarian personality.* New York: Harper, 1950.

BALINT, ALICE. Identification. In S. Lorand (Ed.), *The yearbook of psychoanalysis.* Vol. 1. New York: International Univer. Press, 1945. Pp. 317–338.

BANDURA, A., & HUSTON, ALETHA C. Identification as a process of incidental learning. *Journal of Abnormal and Social Psychology,* 1961, *63,* 311–318.

BANDURA, A., & WALTERS, R. H. *Social learning and personality development.* New York: Holt, 1963.

BETTELHEIM, B. Individual and mass behavior in ex-treme situations. *Journal of Abnormal and Social Psychology,* 1943, *38,* 417–452.

BRONFENBRENNER, U. Freudian theories of identification and their derivatives. *Child Development,* 1960, *31,* 15–40.

CARLSON, R. Identification and personality structure in preadolescents. *Journal of Abnormal and Social Psychology,* 1963, *67,* 566–573.

CATTELL, R. B. *Personality: A systematic, theoretical, and factual study.* New York: McGraw-Hill, 1950.

FREUD, ANNA. *The ego and the mechanisms of defense.* (Orig. publ. 1936) London: Hogarth Press, 1954.

FREUD, S. Three contributions to the theory of sex. In A. A. Brill (Ed.), *The basic writings of Sigmund Freud.* (Orig. publ. 1905) New York: Modern Library, 1938. Pp. 553–632.

FREUD, S. *Group psychology and the analysis of the ego.* (Orig. Publ. 1921) New York: Bantam Books, 1960.

HELPER, M. M. Learning theory and the self concept. *Journal of Abnormal and Social Psychology,* 1955, *51,* 184–194.

KAGAN, J. The concept of identification. *Psychological Review,* 1958, *65,* 296–305.

LEVINSON, D. J., & HUFFMAN, PHYLLIS E. Traditional family ideology and its relation to personality. *Journal of Personality,* 1955, *23,* 251–273.

MOWRER, O. H. Identification: A link between learning theory and psychotherapy. In, *Learning theory and personality dynamics.* New York: Ronald Press, 1950. Pp. 573–616.

MUSSEN, P., & DISTLER, L. Masculinity, identification, and father-son relationships. *Journal of Abnormal and Social Psychology,* 1959, *59,* 350–356.

MUSSEN, P., & DISTLER, L. M. Child-rearing antecedents of masculine identification in kindergarten boys. *Child Development,* 1960, *31,* 89–100.

PAYNE, D. E., & MUSSEN, P. Parent-child relationships and father identification among adolescent boys. *Journal of Abnormal and Social Psychology,* 1956, *52,* 358–362.

SANFORD, R. N. The dynamics of identification. *Psychological Review,* 1955, *62,* 106–118.

SARNOFF, I. Identification with the aggressor: Some personality correlates of anti-Semitism among Jews. *Journal of Personality,* 1951, *20,* 199–218.

SARNOFF, I. *Personality dynamics and development.* New York: Wiley, 1962.

SEARS, PAULINE S. Child-rearing factors related to playing of sex-typed roles. *American Psychologist,* 1953, *8,* 431. (Abstract)

SEARS, R. R., MACCOBY, ELEANOR E., & LEVIN, H. *Patterns of child rearing.* Evanston, Ill.: Row, Peterson, 1957.

26

A Comparative Test of the Status Envy, Social Power, and Secondary Reinforcement Theories of Identificatory Learning [1]

ALBERT BANDURA, DOROTHEA ROSS,[2] AND SHEILA A. ROSS

This article is well described by its title. We might add that the test was done using three-person groups that were prototypes of those found in families. Imitation was the behavior studied. In addition to the data of the report, the student will find good brief summaries of the three theories. The senior author, Albert Bandura, is a professor of psychology at Stanford University, and one of the more prolific writers in the field of psychology.

Although it is generally assumed that social behavior is learned and modified through direct reward and punishment of instrumental responses, informal observation and laboratory study of the social learning process reveal that new responses may be rapidly acquired and existing behavioral repertoires may be considerably changed as a func-

tion of observing the behavior and attitudes exhibited by models (Bandura, 1962).

The latter type of learning is generally labeled "imitation" in behavior theory, and "identification" in most theories of personality. These concepts, however, are treated in the present paper as synonymous since both encompass the same behavioral phenomenon, i.e., the tendency for a person to match the behavior, attitudes, or emotional reactions as exhibited by actual or symbolized models. While the defining properties of identification are essentially the same in different personality theories, a host of divergent learning conditions have been proposed as the necessary antecedent variables for matching or identificatory behavior (Bronfenbrenner, 1960; Freud, 1946; Freud, 1924, 1948; Kagan, 1958; Klein, 1949; Maccoby, 1959; Mowrer, 1950; Parsons, 1955; Sears, 1957; Whiting, 1960).

In the experiment reported in this paper predictions were derived from three of the more prominent theories of learning by identification, and tested in three-person groups representing prototypes of the nuclear family. In one condition of the experiment an adult assumed the role of controller of resources and positive reinforcers. Another adult was the consumer or recipient of these resources, while the child, a participant observer in the triad, was essentially ignored. In a second treatment condition, one adult controlled the resources; the child, however, was the recipient of the positive reinforcers and the other adult was assigned a subordinate and powerless role. An adult male and female served as models in each of the triads. For half the boys and girls in each condition the male model controlled and dispensed the rewarding resources, simulating the husband dominant family; for the remaining children, the female model mediated the positive resources as in the wife dominant home. Following the experimental social interactions the two adult models exhibited divergent patterns of behavior in the presence of the child, and a measure was obtained of the degree to which the child subsequently patterned his behavior after that of the models.

According to the *status envy theory* of identification recently proposed by Whiting (1959, 1960), where a child competes unsuccessfully with an adult for affection, attention, food, and care, the child will envy the consumer adult and consequently identify with him. Whiting's theory represents an extension of the Freudian defensive identification hypothesis that identificatory be-

[1] This investigation was supported by Research Grant M-5162 from the National Institutes of Health, United States Public Health Service.

The authors are indebted to Beverly Busching, Malka Yaari, Nancy Wiggins, and John Steinbruner, who assisted in collecting the data.

[2] This research was carried out while the junior author was the recipient of an American Association of University Women International Fellowship for postdoctoral research.

Albert Bandura, Dorothea Ross, and Sheila A. Ross, "A comparative test of the status envy, social power, and secondary reinforcement theories of identificatory learning," *Journal of Abnormal and Social Psychology*, 1963, *67*, 527–534. Reprinted by permission.

havior is the outcome of rivalrous interaction between the child and the parent who occupies an envied consumer status. While Freud presents the child as in competition with the father primarily for the mother's sexual and affectional attention, Whiting regards any forms of reward, material and social, as valued resources around which rivalry may develop. The status envy theory thus predicts that the highest degree of imitation by the child will occur in the experimental condition in which the rivalrous adult consumes the resources desired by the child, with the consumer adult serving as the primary object of imitation.

In contrast to the envy theory, other writers (Maccoby, 1959; Mussen & Distler, 1959; Parsons, 1955) assume that the controller, rather than the consumer, of resources is the main source of imitative behavior. The *power theory* of social influence has received considerable attention in experimental social psychology, though not generally in the context of identification theories.

Social power is typically defined as the ability of a person to influence the behavior of others by controlling or mediating their positive and negative reinforcements. French and Raven (1959) have distinguished five types of power based on expertness, attractiveness, legitimacy, coerciveness, and rewarding power, each of which is believed to have somewhat differential effects on the social influence process. For example, the use of threat or coercion, in which the controller derives power from his ability to administer punishments, not only develops avoidance behavior toward the controller but also decreases his attractiveness and hence his effectiveness in altering the behavior of others beyond the immediate social influence setting (French, Morrison, & Levinger, 1960; Zipf, 1960). The use of reward power, in contrast, both fosters approach responses toward the power figure and increases his attractiveness or secondary reward value through the repeated association of his attributes with positive reinforcement. Attractiveness is assumed to extend the controller's power over a wide range of behavior (French & Raven, 1959).

In the present investigation power based upon the ability to dispense rewards was manipulated experimentally. In accordance with the social power theory of identification, but contrasting with the status envy hypothesis, one would predict that children will reproduce more of the behavior of the adult who controls positive reinforcers, than that of the powerless adult model, and that power inversions on the part of the male and female models will produce cross-sex imitation.

The *secondary reinforcement theory* of identification, which has been alluded to in the discussion of social power through attractiveness, has been elaborated in greatest detail by Mowrer (1950, 1958). According to this view, as a model mediates the child's biological and social rewards, the behavioral attributes of the model are paired repeatedly with positive reinforcement and thus acquire secondary reward value. On the basis of stimulus generalization, responses which match those of the model attain reinforcing value for the child in proportion to their similarity to those made by the model. Consequently, the child can administer positively conditioned reinforcers to himself simply by reproducing as closely as possible the model's positively valenced behavior. This theory predicts that the experimental condition in which the child was the recipient of positive reinforcements will yield the highest imitation scores with the model who dispensed the rewards serving as the primary source of imitative behavior.

METHOD

SUBJECTS

The subjects were 36 boys and 36 girls enrolled in the Stanford University Nursery School. They ranged in age from 33 to 65 months, although the variability was relatively small with most of the ages falling around the mean of 51 months.

An adult male and female served as models in the triads so as to reproduce possible power structures encountered in different types of family constellations. A female experimenter conducted the study for all 72 children.

DESIGN AND PROCEDURE

The subjects were assigned randomly to two experimental groups and one control group of 24 subjects each. Half the subjects in each group were males, and half were females.

High rewarding power was induced experimentally through the manipulation of material and social reinforcements, and the use of verbal structuring techniques. While accompanying the child to the experimental room, for example, the experimenter informed the child that the adult who assumed the role of controller owned the nursery school "surprise room," as well as a fabulous collection of play materials. After introducing the child to the controller, the experimenter asked whether the child may play in the surprise room. The controller explained that he was on his way to his car to fetch some of his most attractive toys, but the experimenter and the child could proceed to the room where he would join them shortly. As the controller left, the experimenter commented on how lucky they were to have access to the controller's play materials.

On the way to the experimental room they met the other adult who insisted on joining them but the experimenter informed her that she would have to obtain permission from the controller since he owned the room, and it was doubtful whether sufficient play materials were available for both the adult and the child. This brief encounter with the other adult was designed primarily to create the set that rewards were available to one person only and thereby to induce rivalrous feelings over the controller's resources.

As soon as the experimenter and the child arrived in the experimental room, they sat down at a small table and played with the few Lincoln Logs and two small cars that were provided. A short time later the other adult appeared and announced that the controller also granted her permission to play in the room.

The controller then entered carrying two large toy boxes containing a variety of highly attractive masculine and feminine toys, a colorful juice dispensing fountain, and an ample supply of cookies. As soon as the controller appeared on the scene, the experimenter departed.

For children in the Adult Consumer condition, the adult who assumed the role of consumer requested permission to play with the articles and the controller replied that, since the child appeared to be occupied at his table, the consumer was free to use the play materials. This monopolistic move by the consumer adult left the child stranded at a table with two relatively uninteresting toys.

During the 20-minute play session, the controller offered the consumer, among other things, miniature pinball machines, mechanical sparkling toys, kaleidoscopes, dolls, and actively participated with the consumer in dart games and other activities. To add to the credibility of the situation, both the controller and consumer devoted most of their attention to articles, such as the pinball machine and dart game, which could be used in adult appropriate activities. Throughout the interaction the controller was most helpful, supportive, and generous in dispensing social reinforcers in the form of praise, approval, and positive attention. The consumer, in turn, commented frequently on the controller's highly attractive resources so as to further enhance the controller's rewarding status. The consumer also verbalized considerable positive affect characteristic of a person experiencing positive reinforcements.

Approximately half way through the session, the controller remarked, "Say, you look hungry. I have just the thing for you." He then brought forth the soda fountain dispenser, poured colorful fruit juices into paper cups and served them to the consumer along with a generous supply of cookies. While the consumer was enjoying his snack, the controller turned on a "TV-radio" that played a nursery melody while a revolving dial displayed a series of storybook scenes.

Toward the end of the session, the controller informed the consumer that he will be leaving on a shopping trip to San Francisco that afternoon, and asked the consumer if there was anything special she would like him to buy for her. The consumer requested a super two-wheel bicycle, a high status object among the nursery school children. The controller promised to purchase the bicycle along with any other items the consumer might think of before the controller departed for the city.

The procedure for the Child Consumer condition was identical with that described above except the child was the recipient of the material rewards and the social reinforcement. During the session the other adult sat at the opposite end of the room engrossed in a book, and was totally ignored by the controller. In discussing the prospective San Francisco shopping trip, the controller mentioned to the child that he was planning to visit some toy stores in the city that afternoon, and asked for suggestions of attractive toys he might purchase for future play sessions with children.

For half the boys and girls in each treatment condition the male model controlled and dispensed the resources, simulating the husband dominant family; for the remaining children the female model mediated the positive resources as in the wife dominant home.

At the completion of the social interaction session the controller announced that he had a surprise game in his car that the three of them could play together. The controller then asked the other adult to fetch the experimenter to assist them with the game, and as soon as the adult departed, the controller removed the toys and assembled the imitation task apparatus.

IMITATION TASK

The imitation task was essentially the same two-choice discrimination problem utilized in an earlier experiment (Bandura & Huston, 1961), except the response repertoires exhibited by the models were considerably extended, and the procedure used in the acquisition trials was somewhat modified.

The apparatus consisted of two small boxes with hinged lids, identical in color and size. The boxes were placed on stools approximately 4 feet apart and 8 feet from the starting point. On the lid of each box was a rubber doll.

As soon as the other adult returned with the experimenter, the controller asked both the child and the experimenter to be seated in the chairs along the side of the room, and the other adult to stand at the starting point, while the controller described the game they were about to play. The controller then explained that the experimenter would hide a picture sticker in one of the two boxes and the object of the game was to guess which box contained the sticker. The adults would have the first set of turns, following which the child would play the guessing game.

The discrimination problem was employed simply as a cover task that occupied the children's attention while at the same time permitting observation of the models as they performed divergent patterns of behavior during the discrimination trials in the absence of any set to attend to or learn the responses exhibited by the models.

Before commencing the trials, the controller invited the other participants to join him in selecting a "thinking cap" from hat racks containing two identical sets of four caps, each of which had a different colored feather. The controller selected the green feathered hat, remarked, "Feather in the front" and wore the hat with the feather facing forward. The other model selected the yellow feathered hat, commented, "Feather in the back," and placed the hat on her head with the feather facing backward. The child then made his choice from the four hats in the lower rack and it was noted whether he matched the color preference, hat placement, and the verbal responses of the one or the other model.

The models then went to the starting point, the child returned to his seat, and the experimenter loaded both boxes with sticker pictures for the models' trials.

During the execution of each trial, each model exhibited a different set of relatively novel verbal and motor responses that were totally irrelevant to the discrimination problem to which the child's attention was directed. At the starting point the controller stood with his arms crossed, but at the experimenter's warning not to look, the controller placed his hands over his eyes, faced sideways, and asked, "Ready?" The other model stood with his arms on his hips, then squatted with his back turned to the boxes, and asked, "Now?"

As soon as the experimenter gave the signal for the first trial, the controller remarked, "Forward march" and began marching slowly toward the designated box repeating, "March, march, march." When he reached the box he said, "Sock him," hit the doll aggressively off the box, opened the lid and yelled, "Bingo," as he reached down for the sticker. He then remarked, "Lickit-sticket," as he pressed on the picture sticker with his thumb in the upper-right quadrant of a 24×24 inch sheet of plain white paper that hung on the wall immediately behind the boxes. The controller terminated the trial by replacing the doll facing sideways on the container with the comment, "Look in the mirror," and made a final verbal response, "There."

The other model then took her turn and performed a different set of imitative acts but equated with the controller's responses in terms of number, types of response classes represented, structural properties, and interest value. At the starting point, for example, she remarked, "Get set, go" and walked stiffly toward the boxes repeating "Left, right, left, right." When she reached the container she said, "Down and up," as she lay the doll down on the lid and opened the box. She then exclaimed, "A stickeroo," repeated, "Weto-smacko," and slapped on the sticker with the open hand in the lower-left quadrant of the sheet of paper. In terminating the trial, the model lay the doll on the lid of the container with the remark, "Lie down," and returned with her hands behind her back, and emitted the closing remark, "That's it."

The two sets of responses were counterbalanced by having the models display each pattern with half the subjects in each of the three groups.

The models performed alternately for four trials. At the conclusion of the fourth trial the controller explained that he had to check some materials in his car and while he and the other model were away the child may take his turns. Before they departed, however, the experimenter administered a picture preference test in which the models were asked to select their preferred picture from six different stickers pasted on a 5×8 inch card, after which the child was presented a similar card containing an identical set of stickers and requested to indicate his preference.

In addition to the introductory block of four trials by the models, the child's 15 total test trials were interspersed with three two-trial blocks by the models. The models were always absent from the room during the child's test series. This procedure was adopted in order to remove any imagined situational restraints against, or coercion for, the child to reproduce the models' responses. Moreover, demonstrations of delayed imitation in the absence of the model provide more decisive evidence for learning by means of imitation.

The models always selected different boxes, the right-left position varying from trial to trial in a fixed irregular order, and the controller always took the first turn. Although the models received stickers on each trial, the child was nonrewarded on one third of the trial in order to maintain his interest in the cover task.

At the beginning of each of the blocks of subjects' trials, the experimenter administered the picture preference test and the selection of stickers that matched the models' choices was recorded. In addition, on the eighth trial the models removed their hats and hung them in different locations in the room. If the child removed his hat during the session and placed it along side one or the other of the model's hats, this imitative act was also scored.

At the completion of the imitation phase of the experiment, the children were interviewed by the experimenter in order to determine whom they considered to be the controller of resources, and to assess their model preferences. The latter data were used as an index of attraction to the models. In addition, for the children in the adult consumer condition, the session was concluded by providing them the same lavish treatment accorded their adult rival.

Children in the control group had no prior social interaction with the models but participated with them in the imitative learning phase of the study. The experimenter assumed complete charge of the procedures and treated the models as though they were naive subjects. The control group was included primarily to determine the models' relative effectiveness as modeling stimuli. In addition, the models alternated between subjects in the order in which they executed the trials so as to test for the possibility of a primacy or a recency of exposure effect on imitative behavior.

IMITATION SCORES

The imitation scores were obtained by summing the frequency of occurrence of the postural, verbal, and motor responses described in the preceding section, and the hat, color, and picture preferences that matched the selections of each of the two models.

The children's performances were scored by three raters who observed the experimental sessions through a one-way mirror from an adjoining observation room. The raters were provided with a separate check list of responses exhibited by each of the two models, and the scoring procedure simply involved checking the imitative responses performed by the children on each trial. In order to provide an estimate of interscorer reliability, the performances of 30% of the children were recorded simultaneously but independently by two observers. The raters were in perfect agreement on 95% of the specific imitative responses that they scored.

RESULTS

The control group data revealed that the two models were equally effective in eliciting imitative responses, the mean values being 17.83 and 20.46 for the male and female model, respectively; nor did the children display differential imitation of same-sex ($M = 20.30$) and opposite-sex ($M = 17.92$) models. Although children in the control group tended to imitate the second model ($M = 22.21$) to a somewhat greater extent than the one who performed first ($M = 16.08$) on each trial, suggesting a recency of exposure effect, the difference was not of statistically significant magnitude ($t = 1.60$).

Table 1 presents the mean imitation scores for children in each of the two experimental triads. A $2 \times 2 \times 2 \times 2$ mixed factorial analysis of variance was computed on these data in which the four factors in the design were sex of child, sex of the model who controlled the resources, adult versus child consumer, and the controller versus the other model as the source of imitative behavior.[3] As shown in Table 2, the findings of this study clearly support the social power theory of imitation. In both experimental treatments, regardless of whether the rival adult or the children themselves were the recipients of the rewarding resources, the model who possessed rewarding power was imitated to a greater degree than was the rival or the ignored model ($F = 40.61$, $p < .001$). Nor did the condition combining resource ownership with direct reinforcement of the child yield the highest imitation of the model who controlled and dispensed the positive rewards. The latter finding is particularly surprising since an earlier experiment based on two-person groups (Bandura & Huston, 1961), demonstrated that pairing of model with positive reinforcement substantially enhanced the occurrence of imitative behavior. An examination of the remaining significant interaction effects together with the postexperimental interview data suggest a possible explanation for the discrepant results.

The differential in the controller-other model imitation was most pronounced when the male model was the con-

TABLE 1
MEAN NUMBER OF IMITATIVE RESPONSES PERFORMED BY SUBGROUPS OF CHILDREN IN THE EXPERIMENTAL TRIADS

Subjects	Objects of Imitation			
	Male	*Female*	*Female*	*Male*
	Controller	*Consumer*	*Controller*	*Consumer*
Girls	29.00	9.67	26.00	10.00
Boys	30.17	18.67	22.33	16.17
Total	29.59	14.17	24.17	13.09
	Controller	*Ignored*	*Controller*	*Ignored*
Girls	22.00	16.17	31.84	22.17
Boys	29.17	16.67	26.83	34.50
Total	25.59	16.42	29.34	28.34

[3] The assistance of Eleanor Willemsen with the statistical computations is gratefully acknowledged.

TABLE 2
SUMMARY OF THE ANALYSIS OF VARIANCE OF THE IMITATION SCORES

Source	df	MS	F
Between subjects	47	310.17	
Sex of subjects (A)	1	283.59	< 1
Sex of controller model (B)	1	128.34	< 1
Adult versus child consumer (C)	1	518.01	1.61
A × B	1	23.01	< 1
A × C	1	1.76	< 1
B × C	1	742.59	2.31
A × B × C	1	21.10	< 1
Error (b)	40	321.49	
Within subjects	48	113.24	
Controller versus other model (D)	1	2,025.84	40.61***
A × D	1	297.51	5.96*
B × D	1	237.51	4.76*
C × D	1	396.09	7.94**
A × B × D	1	256.76	5.15*
A × C × D	1	19.52	< 1
B × C × D	1	23.02	< 1
A × B × C × D	1	184.00	3.69
Error (w)	40	49.88	

* $p < .05$.
** $p < .01$.
*** $p < .001$.

troller of resources ($F = 4.76$, $p < .05$), particularly for boys. In fact, boys who were the recipients of rewarding resources mediated by the female model tended to favor the ignored male as their object of imitation. In the postexperiment interview a number of boys in this condition spontaneously expressed sympathy for the ignored male and mild criticism of the controller for not being more charitable with her bountiful resources (for example, "She doesn't share much. John played bravely even though she didn't even share. . . . She's a bit greedy.").

As a partial check on whether this factor would tend to diminish the differential imitation of the two models, six children—three boys and three girls—participated in a modified Child Consumer treatment in which, halfway through the social interaction session, the ignored adult was informed that he too may have access to the playthings. He replied that he was quite content to read his book. This modified procedure, which removed the rivalry and the exclusion of the model, yielded four times as much imitation of the controller relative to the model who was ignored by choice.

The significant triple interaction effect indicates that the differential in the controller-other model imitation was greatest when the same-sex model mediated the positive reinforcers, and this effect was more pronounced for boys than for girls.

The data presented so far demonstrate that manipulation of rewarding power had produced differential imitation of the behavior exhibited by the two models. In order to assess whether the dispensing of positive reinforcers in the prior social interaction influenced the overall level of matching responses, the imitation scores in each of the three groups were summed across models and analyzed using a Sex × Treatment design.

The mean total imitative responses for children in the Child Consumer, Adult Consumer, and the Control group were 50.21, 40.58, and 37.88, respectively. Analysis of variance of these data reveals a significant treatment effect ($F = 3.37$, $.025 < p < .05$). Further comparisons of pairs of means by the t test, show that children in the child rewarded condition displayed significantly more imitative behavior than did children both in the Adult Consumer treatment ($t = 2.19$, $p < .05$), and those in the Control group ($t = 2.48$, $p < .02$). The Adult Consumer and Control groups, however, did not differ from each other in this respect ($t = .54$).

The model preference patterns were identical for children in the two experimental conditions and consequently, the data were combined for the statistical analysis. Of the 48 children, 32 selected the model who possessed rewarding power as the more attractive, while 15 preferred the noncontrolling adult. The greater attractiveness of the rewarding model was significant beyond the .05 level ($x^2 = 5.34$). The experimental triad in which boys were the recipients of positive reinforcers while the male model was ignored, contributed the highest preference for the non-controlling adult.

In addition to the experimental groups discussed in the preceding section, data are available for 9 children in the Adult Consumer condition, and for 11 children in the Child Consumer treatment who revealed, in their post-experiment interviews, that they had actually attributed rewarding power to the ignored or the consumer adult despite the elaborate experimental manipulations designed to establish differential power status. A number of these children were firmly convinced that only a male can possess resources and, therefore, the female dispensing the rewards was only an intermediary for the male model (for example, "He's the man and it's all his because he's a daddy. Mommy never really has things belong to her. . . . He's the daddy so it's his but he shares nice with the mommy. . . . He's the man and the man always really has the money and he lets ladies play too. John's good and polite and he has very good manners.") This view of resource ownership within the family constellation was often directly reinforced by the mothers (for example, "My mommy told me and Joan that the daddy really buys all the things, but the mommy looks after things."). Children who attributed the resource ownership to the consumer or ignored female model had considerable difficulty in explaining their selection (for example, "I just knowed it does. . . . I could tell, that's how."), perhaps, because the power structure they depicted is at variance with the widely accepted cultural norm.

As shown in Table 3, models who were attributed rewarding power elicited approximately twice as many matching responses than models who were perceived by the children as possessing no control over the rewarding resources. Because of the small and unequal number of cases in each cell, these data were not evaluated statistically. The differences, however, are marked and quite

TABLE 3
IMITATION AS A FUNCTION OF ATTRIBUTED REWARDING POWER TO THE MODELS

Treatment Condition	Objects of Imitation			
	Female Controller	Male Noncontroller	Male Controller	Female Noncontroller
Adult consumer	24.0	12.3	29.8	14.6
Child consumer	18.2	6.7	35.5	16.2

in accord with those produced by the experimentally manipulated variations in power status.

DISCUSSION

To the extent that the imitative behavior elicited in the present experiment may be considered an elementary prototype of identification within a nuclear family group, the data fail to support the interpretation of identificatory learning as the outcome of a rivalrous interaction between the child and the adult who occupies an envied status in respect to the consumption of highly desired resources. Children clearly identified with the source of rewarding power rather than with the competitor for these rewards. Moreover, power inversions on the part of the male and female models produced cross-sex imitation, particularly in girls. The differential readiness of boys and girls to imitate behavior exhibited by an opposite-sex model are consistent with findings reported by Brown (1956, 1958) that boys show a decided preference for the masculine role, whereas, ambivalence and masculine role preference are widespread among girls. These findings probably reflect both the differential cultural tolerance for cross-sex behavior displayed by males and females, and the privileged status and relatively greater positive reinforcement of masculine role behavior in our society.

Failure to develop sex appropriate behavior has received considerable attention in the clinical literature and has customarily been assumed to be established and maintained by psycho-sexual threat and anxiety reducing mechanisms. Our findings strongly suggest, however, that external social learning variables, such as the distribution of rewarding power within the family constellation, may be highly influential in the formation of inverted sex role behavior.

Theories of identificatory learning have generally assumed that within the family setting the child's initial identification is confined to his mother, and that during early childhood boys must turn from the mother as the primary model to the father as the main source of imitative behavior. However, throughout the course of development children are provided with ample opportunities to observe the behavior of both parents. The results of the present experiment reveal that when children are exposed to multiple models they may select one or more of them as the primary source of behavior, but rarely reproduce all the elements of a single model's repertoire or confine their imitation to that model. Although the children adopted many of the characteristics of the model who possessed rewarding power, they also reproduced some of the elements of behavior exhibited by the model who occupied the subordinate role. Consequently, the children were not simply junior-size replicas of one or the other model; rather, they exhibited a relatively novel pattern of behavior representing an amalgam of elements from both models. Moreover, the specific admixture of behavioral elements varied from child to child. These findings provide considerable evidence for the seemingly paradoxical conclusion that imitation can in fact produce innovation of social behavior, and that within the same family even same-sex siblings may exhibit quite different response patterns, owing to their having selected for imitation different elements of their parents' response repertoires.

The association of a model with noncontingent positive reinforcement tends to increase the incidence of imitative behavior in two person groups (Bandura & Huston, 1961), whereas the addition of a same-sex third person who is denied access to desired rewards may provoke in children negative evaluations of the rewarding model and thereby decreases his potency as a modeling stimulus. These two sets of data demonstrate how learning principles based on an individual behavior model may be subject to strict limitations, since the introduction of additional social variables into the stimulus complex can produce significant changes in the functional relationships between relevant variables.

Summary

Predictions derived from 3 prominent theories of identificatory learning were tested in 3-person groups representing prototypes of the nuclear family. In 1 condition an adult assumed the role of controller of positive reinforcers. Another adult was the consumer of these resources, while the child, a participant observer in the triad, was essentially ignored. In a 2nd treatment condition, one adult controlled the rewarding resources; the child, however, was the recipient of the positive reinforcers, while the other adult was assigned a subordinate and powerless role. Following the experimental social interactions the 2 adult models exhibited divergent patterns of behavior in the presence of the child, and a measure was obtained of the degree to which the child subsequently patterned his behavior after that of the models. Children imitated primarily the model who possessed rewarding power rather than the competitor for the rewards. Moreover, power inversions on the part of the male and female models produced cross-sex imitation, particularly in girls.

References

Bandura, A. Social learning through imitation. In M. R. Jones (Ed.), *Nebraska symposium on motivation: 1962*. Lincoln: Univer. Nebraska Press, 1962.

Bandura, A., & Huston, Aletha C. Identification as a process of incidental learning. *J. abnorm. soc. Psychol.*, 1961, *63*, 311–318.

Bronfenbrenner, U. Freudian theories of identification and their derivatives. *Child Develpm.*, 1960, *31*, 15–40.

Brown, D. G. Sex-role preference in young children. *Psychol. Monogr.*, 1956, *70* (14, Whole No. 421).

Brown, D. G. Sex-role development in a changing culture. *Psychol. Bull.*, 1958, *55*, 232–242.

French, J. R. P., Jr., Morrison, H. W., & Levinger, G. Coercive power and forces affecting conformity. *J. abnorm. soc. Psychol.*, 1960, *61*, 93–101.

French, J. R. P., Jr., & Raven, B. The bases of social power. In D. Cartwright (Ed.), *Studies in social power*. Ann Arbor, Mich.: Institute for Social Research, 1959. Pp. 150–167.

Freud, Anna. *The ego and the mechanisms of defense.* New York: International Univer. Press, 1946.

Freud, S. The passing of the Oedipus-complex. In, *Collected papers*. Vol. 2. London: Hogarth Press, 1924. Pp. 269–282.

Freud, S. *Group psychology and the analysis of the ego*. London: Hogarth Press, 1948.

Kagan, J. The concept of identification. *Psychol. Rev.*, 1958, *65*, 296–305.

Klein, Melanie. *The psycho-analysis of children.* London: Hogarth Press, 1949.

Maccoby, Eleanor E. Role-taking in childhood and its consequences for social learning. *Child Develpm.*, 1959, *30*, 239–252.

Mowrer, O. H. Identification: A link between learning theory and psychotherapy. In, *Learning theory and personality dynamics*. New York: Ronald Press, 1950. Pp. 69–94.

Mowrer, O. H. Hearing and speaking: An analysis of language learning. *J. speech hear. Disord.*, 1958, *23*, 143–152.

Mussen, P., & Distler, L. Masculinity, identification, and father-son relationship. *J. abnorm. soc. Psychol.*, 1959, *59*, 350–356.

PARSONS, T. Family structure and the socialization of the child. In T. Parsons & R. F. Bales (Eds.), *Family, socialization, and interaction process*. Glencoe, Ill.: Free Press, 1955, Pp. 35–131.

SEARS, R. R. Identification as a form of behavioral development. In D. B. Harris (Ed.), *The concept of development*. Minneapolis: Univer. Minnesota Press, 1957. Pp. 149–161.

WHITING, J. W. M. Sorcery, sin, and the superego: A cross-cultural study of some mechanisms of social control. In M. R. Jones (Ed.). *Nebraska symposium on motivation: 1959*. Lincoln: Univer. Nebraska Press, 1959. Pp. 174–195.

WHITING, J. W. M. Resource mediation and learning by identification. In I. Iscoe & H. W. Stevenson (Eds.), *Personality development in children*. Austin: Univer. Texas Press, 1960, Pp. 112–126.

ZIPF, SHEILA G. Resistance and conformity under reward and punishment. *J. abnorm. soc. Psychol.*, 1960, *61*, 102–109.

27

Learning by Imitation in Kindergarten Children [1]

JUDY F. ROSENBLITH

This article on imitation is also relevant to identi-fication, which was discussed in the preceding pa-pers. The dependent variable discussed in this paper is the amount of learning of the mazes on an imitative basis. Another part of the study ex-amined the influence of the same independent vari-ables on a different kind of imitative behavior (or dependent variable), the degree to which the chil-dren chose the same color of pencil as the adult to work the mazes with. That color-matching aspect of the study was reprinted in the first edition of this book. The effects of the experimental manipula-tions on the two types of imitation are different de-spite the fact that the same Ss are engaging in both behaviors.

This study was done when the author, one of the editors of this book, was at Harvard's Laboratory of Human Development. Judy Rosenblith is pro-fessor of psychology at Wheaton College and a member of the Institute of Life Sciences at Brown University. Her research there examines the rela-tions between assessments of newborn behavior and later development.

[1] This paper is based on a dissertation submitted to Harvard University in partial fulfillment of the requirements for the Ph.D. The author would like to express gratitude to Dr. Wesley Allin-smith for his encouragement and counsel. This research was aided by a grant to the Laboratory of Human Development from the Public Health Service.

This study asks four main questions: (a) Does having a model lead to significantly greater im-provement in learning than additional experience only? (b) Is the extent of a child's learning by copy-ing an adult "leader" or model affected by the sex of that leader (considered, especially, in relation to the child's sex)? (c) Does the way in which the leader treats the child immediately before the copying session affect learning? (d) Is there an interaction between the "sex" and "treatment" variables?

The problem of imitation examined in an experi-mental framework has received its most extensive treatment in Miller and Dollard's book *Social Learning and Imitation* (4). They demonstrated that the tendency to imitate is acquired in rats and children, and that the operations of reinforcement are necessary for the establishment of imitative tendencies.

Schein (8) attempted to test the assertions of Miller and Dollard with adult *S*s. Studying the ef-fect of reward on adult imitative behavior, he found that a significant number of *S*s "learned" to imitate a model when such imitation was rewarded. He also found that the imitative response generalized to a similar but new situation. Since the absolute level of imitation was not high, Schein speculated about motives (e.g., "imitation is equivalent to cheating") which might have been operative to de-mand that his adult *S*s not imitate. Such motives all appeared less apt to be present in young chil-dren than in adults. Also, Schwartz (9) found more imitation in 9- and 10-year-olds than in 15- and 16-year-olds, suggesting that more imitation might be expected in kindergarten *S*s.

Miller and Dollard classified imitation into three categories of behavior: *same* behavior, *matched-dependent* behavior, and *copying*. They asserted that all three behaviors are learned via the princi-ples of instrumental conditioning. Learning by imi-tation is linked to their concept of copying in which one person learns to model his behavior on that of another. They further asserted that all three kinds of imitative learning respond to the same condi-tions.

In this study there was no attempt to teach the child to copy. There was reliance on the child's having learned to make imitative responses as a result of past experience in the processes of so-cialization. Generalization of this established learn-ing to imitate is what was looked for. As Miller and Dollard have said: "An analysis in terms of learn-ing principles indicated that the factor of generali-zation should play an important role in the proc-

Judy F. Rosenblith, "Learning by imitation in kindergarten children," *Child Development*, 1959, *30*, 69–80. Reprinted by per-mission of the Society for Research in Child Development.

esses determining the degree to which any leader will be reacted to as a prestigeful model" (4, p. 166). Thus, generalization to a male model from significant males in the child's life was expected, and similarly for a female model. Since the child has very little contact with the particular adults who serve as models, it was assumed that the degree to which the model is effective does stem from such generalization. Nevertheless, rewards were not excluded from the situation. The leader to be imitated or copied was not only prestigeful by virtue of age and size, but the leader's skill was emphasized by verbally rewarding his correct performance. The child was also verbally rewarded when his performance was a sufficiently close copy of the leader's (i.e., was correct).

This problem can also be examined in the theoretical framework of identification theory. Doing so poses the question of whether an adult leader of the same sex as the child might not be a more effective model for imitative behavior for 5-year-old children.

Miller and Dollard, in commenting that sex-typing may belong to a list of social conditions that may enhance or inhibit imitation or the tendency to imitate, do not tell at which age level this factor should become important. It is, however, not unreasonable to assume that at kindergarten age most children have had more reinforcement for imitating a female and hence that a female model should be more effective for both sexes. Such a view would be congruent with that expressed by Miller and Dollard or by contiguity theorists with regard to the secondary reward value which people acquire.

Most identification theories, on the other hand, would lead one to expect that a good deal of identification has taken place by the kindergarten age. Thus, one would expect that a leader of the same sex as the child should be the most effective, with considerable individual fluctuation due to differences in the stage of identification that has been reached.

Another aspect of identification theories leads to a consideration of the role of threat in the formation of identification (Freud, castration threat; Fromm, threat from authoritarian father). Mowrer (5) posits two kinds of identification. The first is developmental, it is with the mother for both sexes, threat does not play a role in it, and it is related to the learning of skills. The second kind of identification is a later form. It is with the parent of the same sex and threat may play a role. Mowrer calls this kind defensive identification, and says that it is related to character learning and is well under way by kindergarten age. In line with these considerations one might expect differences in the amount

of identification shown or generalized (hence in the effectiveness of the adult as a model for copying) according to the presence or absence of an implied threat in the adult-child relation. The contingency or uncertainty-reduction theory of effectiveness of secondary rewards would lead to the same set of expectations.

These considerations led to the following experimental manipulations: (a) the adult leader was attentive to the child for the entire period prior to the copying session for some *S*s, and (b) the adult withdrew attention from the child after half of the period and stayed withdrawn for the remainder of the period prior to the copying session for other *S*s. Such withdrawal presumably constitutes a mild threat to the child's relation to the adult.

The present study was not intended to provide an *experimentum crucis* for deciding the merits of the above theories, but only to shed light on these problems.

Procedure

The *S*s were 120 kindergarten children from two public schools in a Boston suburb composed of middle and upper-middle class residents. Each child was brought individually from the classroom to the experimental room by the *E* in order to "play a game." In this initial session the child was tested using the Porteus Maze Test (6); this test was administered with slight modifications in the instructions and procedure to make it more suitable to the age of the children.[2] The Porteus Test contains one maze for each year from 3 through 11. Two trials were allowed on each of these as in the Porteus Test. There are also mazes for 12- and 14-year-olds and adults. Porteus allows four trials for each of these mazes. In this experiment only two trials were allowed since the 5-year-old *S*s who reached the 12-year-old level or above were apt to be frustrated by four trials on such difficult mazes and want to quit the "game." The Porteus criteria for discontinuing testing were used, i.e., failure on two consecutive or on two out of three consecutive age levels.

On the basis of level of performance in this initial session children were assigned to one of four groups. Group 1 consisted of those who passed only the first two mazes, (i.e., the 3- and 4-year mazes). Group 2 consisted of those who passed a total of three or four of the mazes. Group 3 passed five mazes, and Group 4 passed six or more of the mazes. Children from each group were then assigned to each of the treatments.

One to three weeks after this initial session the

---

[2] Copies of the exact procedure may be seen in (7).

child was brought from his room by E to "have a second turn at the game." This will be referred to as the copying session. Just before arriving at the experimental room, E said to each child who was not in a control group: "You know what? I have someone else here to play the game with us." E and child then entered the room and E introduced the child to the other adult by first names. E then explained to the child that she had something to do for a while and invited the child and the other adult to go to another table in the room and play with the toys on it until E was ready to play the game.[3] The child was seated facing the table of toys and the adult at the adjacent side facing the child and/or table.

It should be noted that E essentially was treating the other adult in the same manner as the child. E did nothing to enhance the adultness or maleness (or femaleness) of the leaders except to reward their proficiency. They were not called Mr. or Mrs. and not described as fathers or mothers. However, they were adult and they were proficient at the task. During the play period the leader behaved as an adult interested in the play of the child and not as another child playing.

The experiment was first run using a male for a leader. The treatments or conditions were: (I) Male leader with a child of the same sex, leader attentive to child throughout the 10-minute period that preceded the copying session proper. (II) Male leader with a child of the same sex, leader attentive to the child for 5 minutes, then leader said: "I'm sorry, I can't play with you any more, I have to read a book." Leader then turned his chair so his back was toward the child and read a book for 5 minutes. (III) Control Ss, males, who were brought to the room by E and who immediately received two additional trials at each maze previously failed, until the criterion for discontinuing testing was reached. (IV) Male leader with a child of the opposite sex, attentive throughout (as in I). (V) Male leader with a child of the opposite sex, withdrew attention after 5 minutes (as in II). (VI) Control Ss, females, tested in the same fashion (as in III). The entire design was then repeated using a female leader.

In treatments I, II, IV, and V, at the end of the 10-minute period E said: "I'm ready to play the game now." Adult leader and child moved to the E's table. They took adjacent seats at the table on the side opposite E and facing her with the adult to the right of the child. E then said to the child: "You've played this game with me before. —— (adult) wasn't here when we played then, so how would it be if you take turns and give —— (adult) the first turn?" (We might note here that no child ever argued with the suggestion of taking turns.) The adult was then given the first maze which the child failed previously and the same instructions that the child had received. The leader did the maze correctly at a rather slow pace and with pauses at choice points accompanied by some visual search. The child watched during this period and then was given a turn at the same maze. To ensure that the child was watching the entire performance, the adult paused when he was not and only continued when the child had again turned his attention to the maze. There were two such trials on each maze failed initially (unless the child passed it correctly on the first trial, in which case there was only one), until the criterion for discontinuing testing was reached. This yields a design in which there are six treatments (including controls) and four replications (by initial level of performance). The part of the study using the male leader was started at one school and completed at the second. The repetition with the female leader was started at the second school and completed at the first.

The number of Ss decided on for each cell was based on the distribution of passes obtained by the children in the first school. Since the second school had a different distribution of passes (fewer children with a high number of passes), the number of children from groups 3 & 4 of initial performance level in each cell was decreased from 3 to 2, thus dropping the total N from an anticipated 132 to 120 (*see* Table 1).

The data to be analyzed here, in investigating the amount of learning by imitation, are the number of new mazes passed ("new passes") in the second or copying session.

RESULTS

Since the distribution of the number of new passes is not normal, and since the number of mazes passed forms only an ordinal scale, the results will be examined using nonparametric statistics.

The data in Table 2 refer to the over-all experimental design, i.e., to both the male and female leader experiments. If one applies Friedman's $\chi^2 r$ (9) to these data, one finds the p values[4] shown in Table 3. The differences found justify separate examination of pairs of treatments.

---

[3] The toys on the table were chosen for their masculine and feminine identification potential. E was actually recording the child's behavior as the child played with the toys. Ratings of these protocols for masculine and feminine identification will be examined later. The toys included shaving set and make-up kit, carpenter tools and kitchen utensils, and a family of dolls, among others.

[4] All p values reported in this paper are for a two-tailed test.

TABLE 1
EXPERIMENTAL DESIGN (NUMBER OF *S*s IN EACH CELL IS SHOWN)

Initial Performance Groups	Male *S*s			Female *S*s			
	A†(I)	*WA*†(II)	*C*†(III)	*A*(IV)	*WA*(V)	*C*(VI)	
			Male Leader*				
1	3	3	3	3	3	3	18
2	3	3	3	3	3	3	18
3	2	2	2	2	2	2	12
4	2	2	2	2	2	2	12
	10	10	10	10	10	10	60

* The entire design is repeated with a female leader.

† A stands for leader attentive throughout, WA, for withdraws attention for last half of period, and C, for controls in this and all subsequent tables.

TABLE 2
NUMBER OF NEW PASSES OBTAINED BY *S*s IN THE VARIOUS CELLS

Initial Performance Groups	Male *S*s			Female *S*s		
	A(I)	*WA*(II)	*C*(III)	*A*(IV)	*WA*(V)	*C*(VI)
			Male Leader			
1	7	6	5	5	4	2
2	9	12	8	9	6	6
3	4	6	1	4	4	2
4	6	7	1	4	5	2
Total	26	31	15	22	19	12
			Female Leader			
1	6	2	4	4	1	1
2	10	4	6	6	3	4
3	8	4	2	3	3	4
4	6	4	1	3	5	3
Total	30	14	13	16	12	12
Total	56	45	28	38	31	24

Before doing so, it is interesting to examine the data according to the sex of *S*s and of leaders. Table 3 shows the *p* values of X^2r calculated for the various combinations of sex of *S*s and of leader. Male leader and male *S*s show more influence of these manipulations.

Examination of pairs of treatments by a method described by Wilcoxon (11) shows that boys and girls who are control *S*s do not differ significantly, although there is a tendency for the control boys to improve more than the control girls. This tendency is close to the .05 level for those whose initial performance placed them in level 1. The remaining results of these comparisons are presented in Table 4. In summary it can be seen that: (a) having a model is more effective than merely having additional trials; (b) girls seem less sensitive to the experimental manipulations than are boys; (c) the female leader was less effective than the male leader; (d) attention is more effective than withdrawal of attention.

Certain qualifications of these general statements are found in the detailed results. The finding concerning the effectiveness of the male and female leaders cannot be labeled a sex difference without further replication since it is possible that individual characteristics of the leaders rather than their immediately perceptible sex characteristics were responsible. In any event, these rather major effects of sex (of both leader and child) which operate in a way that cuts across the original experimental design make the next step of analysis less apt to yield significant results.

The next step was to examine the two experiments together. Since the *S*s were not randomly assigned to treatments across both sexes of leader, some justification for combining the data is probably needed. Both leaders did have *S*s from both schools, though not equal proportions of *S*s from each. The control *S*s in both replications showed no significant difference; in fact, the rank totals are 412 for the first group and 408 for the second. It

TABLE 3

COMPARISON OF TREATMENTS EXAMINED BY THE FRIEDMAN X^2r

	p Values	
Treatments Compared	*Male Leader*	*Female Leader*
Total Table (Conditions I through VI)	.01	.09
Treatments—controls not included (Conditions I, II, IV, V)	.06	.052
Conditions involving male *S*s (Conditions I, II and III)	.04	.05
Conditions involving female *S*s (Conditions IV, V and VI)	.15	.80

TABLE 4

COMPARISONS OF PAIRS OF TREATMENTS USING THE WILCOXON RANKING METHOD

	p Values*			
	Male Leader		Female Leader	
Comparison†	*Male Ss*	*Female Ss*	*Male Ss*	*Female Ss*
A plus WA vs C	.01 (A&WA)	.01 (A&WA)	ns (A&WA)	ns (A&WA)
A vs C	.10 (A)	$.05 > p > .02$ (A)	.10 (A)	ns (A)
WA vs C	.05 (WA)	$.10 > p > .05$ (WA)	ns (WA)	ns (WA)
A vs WA	ns (WA)	ns (A)	ns (A)	ns (A)
A plus WA vs C (by initial performance groups)				
Group 1	ns (A&WA)	.05 (A&WA)	ns (C)	ns (C)
Group 2	.05 (A&WA)	ns (A&WA)	ns (C)	ns (A&WA)
Group 3 and 4	$.05 > p > .02$ (A&WA)	ns (A&WA)	.01 (A&WA)	ns (A&WA)

* Exact *p* values or *p* values larger than the .10 level are not available in the published tables. "*ns*" is used to indicate that *p* is greater than .10, i.e., is *not significant*.

† The abbreviations in the parentheses indicate which side of the comparison gave the superior performance.

thus seems reasonable to conclude that the two populations are similar enough to justify combining them for comparisons.

Analyzing the data in this way, the design yields five conditions: opposite sex attentive, opposite sex withdraws attention, same sex attentive, same sex withdraws attention, and controls. If these treatments are examined over the four replications provided by initial level groups, the X^2r is 8.85, which (with 4 *df*) has a *p* value between .06 and .07. As in the earlier analysis, the boys show a significant effect of treatments (*p* is .02) and the girls do not (*p* is .15). An extension of the Kruskal-Wallis technique[5] yields an analysis of variance the results of which are shown in Table 5.

DISCUSSION

The difference between the results for the male leader and the female leader are striking, as are the differences between the results for boys and girls. The fact that the boys tended to show more improvement than the girls may provide more ceiling

for finding differences between treatments for the boys. However, such differences between boys and girls remain puzzling since they had been equated for pretest performance. Although there was no significant difference between boys and girls as controls, the consistent superiority of all *S*s with a male leader is noted (*p* < .05 that they differ from controls by chance, but *p* < .10 that *S*s with the female leader do). Hartup (3) found that boys learned a concept formation task more quickly than girls. He speculated that the blocks involved were more salient for boys than for girls. (Note: The mazes used as a subtest on WISC correlate most highly

TABLE 5

KRUSKAL-WALLIS ANALYSIS OF VARIANCE AS EXPANDED BY HYMAN

Source of Variation	*H*	*df*	Approximate *p*
Among subcells	36.6	39	ns (.5)
Treatments	7.87	4	.10
Levels of initial performance	7.13	3	.07
Sex of *S*s	3.00	1	.09
Sex × Levels	.72	3	ns (.85)
Levels × Treatments	8.4	12	ns (.75)
Sex × Treatments	7.43	4	.11
Sex × Treatments × Levels	2.05	12	ns (.99)

[5] This extension of the Kruskal-Wallis analysis of variance was suggested to the author by Dr. R. Hyman of the Department of Social Relations at Harvard.

with block design and object assembly, about .48). Publications on the Porteus Test fail to give any information on sex differences that sheds any light on this problem.

One should also note that the level of performance on the pretest is a significant source of variation. Thus, it is wise to control for level of pretest performance in a study such as the present one. The fact that levels did not enter into any significant interaction term mitigates this conclusion. It does, however, seem (*see* Table 4) more profitable to look for certain effects of treatments at particular levels rather than in a random population or a representative one.

Now one can turn to the questions raised at the beginning of the paper.

1. Does having a model have a significant effect on the amount of improvement? The answer to this question is yes.

2. Is one sex of leader more effective in evoking learning by imitation? In particular the question raised was whether a female leader or a leader of the same sex as the child would be more effective. Actually the male leader was more effective for both sexes, though only significantly so for the girls. One possible explanation for this finding might lie in the fact that an adult male is more unusual in the school setting, hence has more reward value. Gewirtz and Baer (2), in studying the effectiveness of a social reinforcer (approval) in conjunction with social deprivation, found that the effectiveness of the isolation was qualified by an interaction which indicated that the woman was less effective relative to the man under the condition where Ss were tested immediately on removal from the play group than the condition where Ss were tested after a 20-minute period of total isolation. Our situation would seem to be closer to the former condition. Perhaps the whole school setting is one of social deprivation in respect to adult males who play a role in the life of kindergarten children. In summary, there is an effect of sex of leader, but it is not the effect anticipated from either of our theoretical approaches.

3. Does an implied threat to the relation between the child and the adult operate to enhance identification and thus enhance learning by imitation? For boys there was a tendency for those from whom the male leader withdrew attention to do better than boys with an attentive male leader; but they were better than controls at the .05 level, while the male leader attentive group were better than controls at only the .10 level. For girls, however, the effectiveness of the leader of the same sex withdrawing attention does not appear. With the female leader, as with the male, girls tend to do better when they have attention throughout.

The failure to find a relation between implied threat and better learning for girls with a female leader is particularly puzzling in view of Hartup's findings (3). In his study he found that 4-year-old girls learned a simple concept formation task twice as fast when the woman for whom they were doing it had been very nurturant for 5 minutes and then had sat "busy" at her desk for 5 minutes. This quicker learning was not shown for the 4-year-old boys in general. There are a number of differences that could account for the discrepancy: (a) He used 4- instead of 5-year-olds. (b) His task was presented by the person who withdrew instead of by a third person. (c) There were differences in the task (his Ss learned the concept that determined which of four blocks is the "right" one, ours the way to do a maze). (d) Our results also might be idiosyncratic to our female leader.[6] Hartup used two females and found no significant differences between them. (e) The nurturance which his leaders interrupted was of a more active kind (getting down on the floor and playing with the child). The possible effects of the last four differences are very difficult to speculate about. There is, however, an interesting question we might raise concerning the first point. There are reasons to expect on the basis of Freudian thinking that a girl changes her primary object from mother to father at about age 4. If that is the case, the girl may be particularly sensitive to threat from females at that age. Boys presumably do not change until resolution of the Oedipus complex, well into the fifth year on the average. In that case, 5-year-old boys might be particularly sensitive to threat from males. This interpretation would be congruent with both Hartup's and our findings. Very general support for this idea may be found by examining the data for all girls and boys in the sample who are under 5 years, 3 months, in comparison with all those who are over 5 years, 7 months. We find that the older boys improve significantly more than the younger ($p = .02$), while the older girls do not improve significantly more than the younger ($p > .10$). Unfortunately, there are too few cases to enable us to look at the operation of the attention and withdrawal of attention variables within these age subgroups.

In summary, there is equivocal evidence for threat having the effect of enhancing performance where boys with the male leader are concerned, but in no other case.

4. Is there an interaction between the sex and

---

[6] We did a spot check using another female leader for 4 children (2 boys and 2 girls, all at the same initial level of performmance). It is suggestive that there was no apparent difference between results for these 4 children and a comparable 4 from our female leader experiment.

treatment variables? Yes. This answer must be qualified by saying that we cannot be certain whether it is the sex of the leaders or other personal characteristics which account for some of the interactions. Further replications are needed to settle this issue. However, one should bear in mind that generalization from adults significant in the child's life was expected to be more important than the personal characteristics of the leaders to whom the *S*s were exposed for only a brief span of time. Also, Hartup's failure to find differences between two female adults in their effect on the children, and the lack of differences in our own small check are signs which indicate that this is a reasonable view.[7]

On the basis of the data, boys and girls both respond better to attention from the opposite sexed leader than to withdrawal. Boys, and not girls, tend to do better after withdrawal of attention from the leader of the same sex. As indicated above, the differential functioning of threat may be, in part at least, a function of the age of the *S*s. The rank orders of effectiveness of treatments for the over-all design is given in Table 6.

Summary

The effectiveness of learning by imitation was studied in a context which permitted examination of a number of variables relevant to learning and identification theories. These were: (a) the effectiveness of having a leader or model as contrasted with experience in the absence of a model; (b) the effectiveness of the sex of the leader and of the leader's sex in relation to that of the child; (c) the effectiveness of the adult leader who gives attention to the child for the entire period preceding the imitation, as contrasted with the adult who pays attention to the child for half the time and withdraws attention for the remaining half.

In general, having a model was more effective than merely having additional trials. There were important differences between the effectiveness of the male leader and the female leader. The male leader was, in general, more effective. There were also important differences between boys and girls. Boys showed more improvement. Girls seemed less sensitive to the experimental manipulations. There was a tendency for attention to be more effective than withdrawal of attention except in the case of boys with a male leader. The specific findings were examined in detail and their relation to current theories discussed. Analysis of variance on the male and female leader parts of the study combined showed effects of: (a) treatments, (b) sex of *S*s, (c) initial or pretest level of *S*s' performance on the mazes, and (d) interaction between the sex of *S*s and the treatments.

References

1. Bishop, Barbara M. Mother-child interaction and the social behavior of children. *Psychol. Monogr.*, 1951, *65*, No. 328.
2. Gewirtz, J. L., & Baer, D. M. Does brief social "deprivation" enhance the effectiveness of a social reinforcer ("approval")? *Amer. Psychol.*, 1956, *11*, 428–429.
3. Hartup, W. W. Nurturance and nurturance-withdrawal in relation to the dependency behavior of preschool children. *Child Develpm.*, 1958, *29*, 191–201.
4. Miller, N. E., & Dollard, J. *Social learning and imitation.* New Haven: Yale Univer. Press, 1941.
5. Mowrer, O. H. *Learning theory and personality dynamics.* New York: Ronald, 1950.
6. Porteus, S. D. *The Porteus Maze Test and intelligence.* Palo Alto: Pacific Books, 1950.
7. Rosenblith, Judy F. Imitation in kindergarten children. Unpublished doctoral dissertation, Radcliffe College, 1958.

---

[7] Additional evidence of this kind is provided by Bishop (1), who found that when children were brought into a play room situation with a neutral adult (female) they reacted in the same way they had earlier reacted to their mothers with respect to aggressive stimuli, cooperation, noncooperation and resistance.

Table 6
Rank Orders of Amount of Improvement

	SS-A	SS-WA	OS-A	OS-WA	C
Boys	3 (26)	1 (31)	2 (30)	5 (14)	4 (15)
Girls	3 (17)	4 (12)	1 (21)	2 (19)	5 (11)

Note.—*SS-A* stands for leader of same sex—attentive throughout;
SS-WA stands for leader of same sex—withdraws attention;
OS-A stands for leader of opposite sex—attentive throughout;
OS-WA stands for leader of opposite sex—withdraws attention;
C stands for controls, additional experience with no leader.
Figures in parentheses represent the number of new passes obtained by all subjects in that cell.

8. SCHEIN, E. H. The effect of reward on adult imitative behavior. *J. abnorm. soc. Psychol.*, 1954, *49*, 389–395.

9. SCHWARTZ, N. An experimental study of imitation. The effects of reward and age. Senior honors thesis, Radcliffe College, 1953.

10. SIEGEL, S. *Nonparametric statistics for the behavioral sciences.* New York: McGraw-Hill, 1956.

11. WILCOXON, F. Individual comparisons by ranking methods. *Biometrics Bull.*, 1945, *1*, 80–83.

28

Imitation of a Peer as a Function of Reinforcement from the Peer Group and Rewardingness of the Model

WILLARD W. HARTUP
AND BRIAN COATES

This article shows that even those nursery school children who were not accustomed to having active social interchange with the peer group are susceptible to peer influence. However, there is a difference in which peers they are affected by compared to those with more social interaction.

Willard W. Hartup is a professor at the University of Minnesota. Previously, he was associated with Iowa's Child Welfare Research Station. Brian Coates is now at the University of North Carolina at Chapel Hill.

Considerable research has been generated by the hypothesis that rewarding models are imitated to a greater extent than nonrewarding models. This hypothesis figures prominently in several general theories of identification, including the theory of anaclitic identification developed by Freud (1914), the secondary reinforcement interpretation of imitation by Mowrer (1950; 1960), and the extension

of these theories formulated by Sears (1957) and Sears, Rau, and Alpert (1965).

The formulation developed by Mowrer is particularly specific concerning the mechanisms underlying imitation. Mowrer suggested that rewards given to *S* by a model increase the secondary reinforcing value (for *S*) of behaviors manifested by the model. When *S* reproduces these behaviors, the proprioceptive feedback from the imitative acts is presumed, as a consequence of stimulus generalization, to be secondarily reinforcing. This secondary reinforcement predisposes *S* to reproduce the behavior of the model. Although Mowrer originally provided this theory as an explanation for the imitation of verbal behavior, the theory has since been extended to account for all imitative acts (Mowrer, 1960; Sears, 1957).

Both differential and experimental strategies have been used to test the prediction that rewarding models produce more imitation in children than nonrewarding models. One kind of evidence is provided by studies of the relation between parental affection and nurturance, on the one hand, and identification-related behaviors in children, on the other. Sears (1953) reported that boys with warm, affectionate fathers employed the father doll more frequently in doll play than boys of colder, less affectionate fathers. Mussen and Distler (1960) reported that fathers of highly masculine kindergarten boys were more affectionate than fathers of less masculine subjects, and, in a series of other studies by Mussen and his associates (Mussen & Distler, 1959; Mussen, 1961; Mussen & Rutherford, 1963), highly masculine boys were found to perceive their fathers as more rewarding and nurturant (as well as strong and powerful) than less masculine boys. The results of a recent study by Sears et al. (1965), however, failed to support the hypothesis that warmth and nurturance are related to identification in either girls or boys.

Experimental evidence concerning this hypothesis has been provided by Bandura and Huston (1961), who found that preschool *S*s who had received social rewards from the model during two 15-minute play periods reproduced "incidental" verbal and motor responses displayed by the model to a greater extent than *S*s experiencing nonrewarding interaction. These two groups, however, did not differ significantly in duplicating the model's choices in a discrimination task. Next, Bandura, Ross, and Ross (1963) reported that nursery school children more frequently imitated models from whom they received social and material rewards

This study was completed with the assistance of a stipend awarded to Brian Coates from grant 5–T01–MHO–6668, National Institute of Mental Health. The authors are particularly grateful to Rosalind Charlesworth for her help and to the collaborating nursery school teachers.

than models with whom they competed for such rewards. Mischel and Grusec (1966) found that the rewardingness of the model facilitated imitation, but this effect depended on the type of behavior being modeled ("aversive" or "neutral") and whether imitation was measured in terms of "rehearsal" or "transmission." More recently, Grusec (1966) reported that the model's rewardingness influenced children's imitation of self-criticism, depending on whether the model had previously used withdrawal of love, as opposed to withdrawal of material rewards.

Other evidence pertinent to the secondary reinforcement theory of imitation is provided by Rosenblith (1959), who reported that the attentiveness of the experimenter-model, as compared to attention withdrawal, enhanced imitation, but only in girls. Rosenhan and White (1967) reported no effect of the prior relation existing between *S* and model on the imitation of altruistic behavior, except that boys whose relations with the model were "negative" showed greater continuity in amount of imitation from model-present to model-absent conditions than boys whose relations with the model were positive or boys who had no prior relations with the model.

Stein and Wright (1964) reported that nurturance by an adult model affected imitation in preschool children, depending on the extent of change in the manifestation of dependency by the child during the experimental session. The *S*s who responded to withdrawal of nurturance or to isolation with *increased* dependency and *S*s who responded to continuous nurturance from *E* with *decreased* dependency imitated the model to a greater extent than *S*s whose changes in dependency were in directions opposite to those mentioned. Lastly, Kobasigawa (1965) reported that adult models who had previously dispensed social rewards and were then observed to undergo a frustration experience elicited no greater emotionality in first-grade boys than models not dispensing social reinforcement.

Many of the findings reviewed above support the secondary reinforcement theory of imitation. Simultaneously, they suggest that situational and individual differences modify the effect of reward from the model on imitation. Sex of *S*, personality characteristics, and type of response being imitated are examples of such modifiers. But what antecedents are responsible for these interaction effects? What, for example, are the antecedents of sex differences in the impact of rewarding models on imitation? Differences in the socialization history of boys and girls are probably responsible, but which?

The main purpose of this experiment was to study one likely source of variation in the effect of the model's rewardingness on imitation—*S*'s general history of reinforcement from persons resembling the model. The study was based on the hypothesis that the effects of exposure to a rewarding model, as compared to a nonrewarding model, depend on the nature of *S*'s previous experience with people who are like the model. Peers were selected as the class of models to be used. Nursery school children were believed to be appropriate *S*s because, even in nursery school groups, the range of reward frequencies exchanged among them is large.

The study was guided by the dimensional prediction stated above. Directional predictions were partially formulated prior to the experiment. For example, it was expected that rewarding peer models would produce more imitation than nonrewarding models for children with a history of frequent reinforcement from their peers. The results for children with histories of infrequent peer reinforcement were more difficult to predict because low frequencies of reinforcement from peers are often characteristic of children who are actively rejected or who are fearful in social situations. Solely on the basis of Mowrer's hypothesis, it would be expected that the rewarding-model effect would be diminished for such *S*s. To the extent that such *S*s are socially anxious, however, it is possible that nonrewarding peers may exert greater imitative influence than peers who, in the past, have been sources of reassurance and support.

The behaviors modeled in the experiment consisted of an altruistic response plus a group of verbal and motoric actions "incidental" to the altruistic act. Since the study involved peers as models and altruistic behavior as the major dependent variable, it accomplishes two secondary purposes: (*a*) it contributes to the slowly growing literature concerning the influence of peer models on the socialization of the child (e.g., Bandura & Kupers, 1964; Clark, 1965; Grosser, Polansky, & Lippitt, 1951; Hicks, 1965), and (*b*) it adds to the sparse evidence concerning imitation as a determinant of altruism (Rosenhan & White, 1967).

METHOD

Subjects

The pool from which *S*s were drawn consisted of 64 children enrolled in four groups at the Laboratory Nursery School of the University of Minnesota. This pool included all children enrolled both at the time observations were conducted in the peer group and during a later experimental period. The *S*s were 56 children from this pool. Excluded were two children who were receiving psychotherapy, two children who refused to participate, two children whose models failed to carry out the prescribed procedure, and two who were dropped to yield equal cell frequencies. These *S*s ranged in age from 3–9 through 5–4, with a mean age of 4–6.

EXPERIMENTAL DESIGN

The experimental design consisted of the following groups:

Frequent reinforcement from peers (FR):
  Rewarding peer model (RM) ($N = 12$)
  Nonrewarding peer model (NRM) ($N = 12$)
Infrequent reinforcement from peers (IR):
  Rewarding peer model (RM) ($N = 12$)
  Nonrewarding peer model (NRM) ($N = 12$)
No model (control) ($N = 8$)

ASSIGNMENT OF SUBJECTS

The initial step in the assignment of *S*s was the measurement of reinforcement frequencies occurring in the nursery school peer group. For this purpose, observations were conducted extending over a 5-week period.[1] Briefly, the observations produced 12 3-minute samples of each child's behavior, recorded in running account form by observers stationed in the nursery school. These records contained information concerning the child's activity, persons in his vicinity, and accounts of the interaction occurring between the child and other persons.

The 3-minute protocols were then rated by two judges. The records were screened for instances in which the child dispensed or received "generalized social reinforcers" (Skinner, 1953). Four types of positive social reinforcers were tabulated: *(a)* attention and approval (e.g., attending, offering praise, smiling and laughing, offering guidance or suggestions); *(b)* affection and personal acceptance (both physical and verbal); *(c)* submission (e.g., passive acceptance of another child's demands, sharing, compromise); *(d)* tokens (tangible objects).

A total of 161 protocols were rated by both raters. The ratio of agreements concerning the occurrence of social reinforcement divided by agreements plus disagreements was .77.

It was possible to compute the total number of reinforcements dispensed by each child to his peers and the number received. The latter score was assumed to be an index of the total frequency of positive reinforcement the child received from the peer group.[2] It was on the basis of these scores, which ranged from 0 to 55, that the children were divided into two groups: those above the median, for their own nursery school class, in number of

reinforcements received (frequent reinforcement group) and those below (infrequent reinforcement group). The mean number of reinforcers received from peers in the FR group was 24.9, while the mean for the IR group was 9.0.

The children in each of the two reinforcement groups were then randomly assigned to model conditions: rewarding peer model (RM) or nonrewarding peer model (NRM). The observational records for each *S* assigned to group RM were searched for the name of the like-sex peer who had given *S* the most frequent reinforcement during the observations. This peer was designated as *S*'s model. The RM *S*s had received a mean of 5.4 reinforcements from their models during the 36 minutes of observation. Next, a list was prepared for each *S* in group NRM consisting of all like-sex children in the class who had never been observed to furnish *S* with reinforcement. One child, randomly selected from this list, was designated as *S*'s model. The mean reinforcements given to the NRM *S*s by their models had, of course, been zero.

The final preliminary step consisted of establishing a testing sequence permitting all the available children to serve as *S*s. Some children participated only as *S*s; others, who were designated as models, participated first as *S*s, then were trained and served as models during subsequent sessions (not more than two for any child).

One boy and one girl from each preschool class were required to start the testing by serving as "first" models. These children were randomly selected. If this selection did not make it possible to test all of the children in that preschool class in sequence, substitute first models were picked. Those children designated as first models completed the experimental task prior to being trained as models. This group of eight children (two from each preschool class) thus comprised a no-model control group (C).

PROCEDURE

No-Model Condition

The *S* was brought to a laboratory room which contained three hats (maroon, green, and yellow) hung on pegs, three feathers (white, yellow, and orange) placed on a chair, three pencils (black, brown, and green) also hung on pegs, and a table containing a stack of dittoed mazes (simple one-turn puzzles) and three bowls. One bowl, placed in front of the child, was a receptacle for trinkets released by a dispensing device. The other bowls were placed to *S*'s left and right (counterbalanced across *S*s); one was designated as belonging to a preschool child (not known to *S*) whose picture was attached, the other was designated as *S*'s bowl. The following instructions were given:

> We have a game for you today. It is a puzzle game and these are the puzzles. (*E* displays puzzles.) The way you play this game is to draw a line from one flower to another flower, like this. (*E* demonstrates.) Now you can do some. (*S* was helped to complete two or three of the puzzles.) There is one other thing that I want to tell you about the

---

[1] A detailed description of the observational procedure can be found in Charlesworth and Hartup (1967).

[2] The extent to which the total number of positive reinforcements received serves as an index of total social interaction is not known. It was possible to compute correlations between receipt of positive and receipt of negative reinforcements for *S*s in two of the preschool groups. These correlations were .43 ($p < .10$) and .51 ($p < .05$). Incidents of nonreinforcing contacts among peers were numerous but were not tabulated.

game. Whenever you are doing a good job on the puzzle, some little cats will come out of the machine back there. They will come down this chute and fall into this bowl. Whenever some cats come down the chute I want you to put them in one of these other bowls. Either put them over here in Alec's bowl (Kathy's for female *S*s) or over here in your bowl. Alec is another boy in the nursery school. Now remember, whenever you are doing a good job on the puzzle, some little cats will come out of the machine into this bowl here and you are to put them in one of these two bowls, either in Alec's bowl or your bowl, your bowl or Alec's bowl. Do you understand? I have to do some work so I will sit in here.

Nothing further was said concerning whether *S* could keep the trinkets in his bowl at the conclusion of the session. The *E* then went into an adjoining room, left the door ajar, and seated himself out of sight. *S* was told to proceed, and after each maze was completed six trinkets were ejected through the chute. The session consisted of ten mazes, each followed by the dispensing and allocation of six trinkets. If *S* failed to pick up the trinkets, *E* urged him to do so by saying, "Put the cats in the bowls; in Alec's bowl or your bowl, your bowl or Alec's bowl."

Model Conditions

Training the model. Each child designated as a model was brought to the laboratory several days after he had participated as *S*. He was reminded of the earlier session, given an opportunity to complete two mazes, and asked to help *E* by demonstrating the game for another child from his class. The *E* stressed that it was necessary to play the game in a particular way. First, *M* was told that he should go to the hats, pick out the green one (color alternated across *S*s), attach the white feather (also alternated) to the hole in the hat, and put the hat on his head. Next, he was told to select the black pencil (color also alternated), to seat himself at the table, and begin work on the puzzles. Then *M* was instructed to pick up the six trinkets ejected after each maze, place them in a row on the table, and pick them up one at a time, placing all but the last one in Alec's (or Kathy's) bowl. The *M* was also instructed to repeat the words "One for Alec" each time a trinket was placed in "Alec's bowl." The *E* stressed that only the last trinket should be placed in *M*'s own bowl. This procedure was practiced, with *E* coaching and sometimes demonstrating, until *M* was able to perform the task with consistent accuracy. The *M* accompanied *E* to the nursery school for the purpose of inviting *S* to play the game.

Experimental session. When the children arrived in the laboratory, *E* described the game using the instructions given above. He also explained that the children would take turns and that *M* would be first. The *S* was seated so as to face *M* at a 90° angle and was told that he should try not to bother *M*. The *E* entered the adjoining room, leaving the door partly open. Then *M* was told to proceed. If *M* failed to respond or engaged in distract-

ing behavior, *E* prompted him from the other room. In no case, however, were mistakes in allocating trinkets corrected. Such mistakes were made by only two *M*s whose *S*s were subsequently excluded from the experiment.

After ten mazes, the children were told it was time for *S* to play the game. The *M* was invited to wait in the adjoining room with *E*, and the instructions were repeated briefly to *S*. When everyone had reached his appropriate spot, *S* was told to begin.

RESPONSE MEASURES

The following information was recorded by *E* (observing through a small one-way window): (*a*) whether or not *S* chose a hat, a feather, and/or a pencil and the colors of these objects; (*b*) whether or not *S* lined up the trinkets and whether the trinkets were placed in the bowls one at a time or in groups; (*c*) frequency with which *S* reproduced the verbalization of *M*; and (*d*) the particular bowl chosen for allocation of each trinket.

The response measures derived from these records included: (*a*) presence-absence of imitative hat, feather, and pencil choices; (*b*) presence-absence of "line up" behavior on each trial (ranging from 0 to 10 over entire session); (*c*) presence-absence of imitative verbalization (ranging from 0 to 6 on each trial); (*d*) number of trinkets placed in the "other's" bowl (ranging from 0 to 6 on each trial); (*e*) latency of the first nonaltruistic choice—the number of trinkets placed in "other's" bowl before placement of the first trinket in *S*'s own bowl (ranging from 0 to 7 on each trial).

RESULTS

Intercorrelations among four of the dependent measures are shown in Table 1. All of these measures represent components of the response sequence used in allocating the trinkets. The correlations, which were computed only for *S*'s who observed a model, are all significantly positive, but five are relatively small. It should be noted that the two altruism scores (frequency of "giving to other" and latency of "giving to self") are highly correlated. This relation is artifactual. Consequently, "giving to other" was used alone as the altruism index in the data analysis.

Where possible, subsequent analyses were completed with scores divided into two five-trial blocks. Inspection revealed that the treatment effects varied over time.

EFFECT OF MODEL

To assess the effects of observing a model on altruistic behavior, a one-way analysis of variance was conducted on the data for all five of the groups in the experiment. "Giving to other" scores were analyzed separately for the first and second blocks of five trials. The treatments effect was significant in all instances. For the first trial block, $F = 7.49$, $df = 4/51$, $p. < 005$; second trial block, $F = 3.39$, $df = 4/51$, $p < .02$.

Contrasts between the amount of "giving to other" in group C and in each of the model groups (*t* tests) revealed significant differences for each contrast in both trial

TABLE 1
INTERCORRELATIONS AMONG FOUR IMITATION SCORES
(*N* = 48)

Score	Giving to Other (Total)	Latency of Giving to Self (Total)	Verbali- zation (Total)	Line Up (Total)
Giving to other..	...	...	...	...
Latency of giving to self..............................	.92**	...	...	...
Verbalization..	.28*	.32*	...	...
Line up	.32*	.36*	.54**	...

* *p* < .05.
** *p* < .01.

blocks. Thus, observation of the model produced significantly more altruism than occurred when no opportunity to observe a model was provided (see Table 2).

Observing the model also affected the frequency of "incidental" behaviors. Statistical analysis was not performed, but it can be seen in Table 3 that no verbalization or "line up" behavior occurred in group C, although appreciable amounts were displayed by Ss who had observed a model.

EFFECTS OF PEER REINFORCEMENT AND REWARDINGNESS OF MODEL

The "giving to other" scores for Ss who observed models were subjected to mixed-design analysis of variance. The between-Ss factors were reinforcement from peers (FR vs. IR) and type of peer model (RM vs. NRM). The within-Ss factor consisted of trial blocks (first vs. second five trials). Mean scores for each subgroup may be seen in Table 2.

The analysis revealed a significant effect of trial blocks (*F* = 7.80, *df* = 1/44, *p* < .01), indicating that fewer altruistic responses were made during the second block of five trials than during the first. In addition, the interaction between reinforcement from peers and type of model was significant (*F* = 4.59, *df* = 1/44, *p* < .05), as was the interaction between reinforcement from peers, type of model, and trial blocks (*F* = 7.80, *df* = 1/44, *p* < .01). Further analysis revealed that the treatments effects were

TABLE 2
MEAN "GIVING TO OTHER" SCORES IN BLOCKS OF FIVE TRIALS BY REINFORCEMENT CONDITION AND TYPE OF PEER MODEL

Group	Trial Block 1	2
Frequent reinforcement:		
Rewarding model	21.00	19.25
Nonrewarding model	13.42	13.83
Infrequent reinforcement:		
Rewarding model	17.50	17.08
Nonrewarding model	22.83	18.58
No model	5.63	3.75

TABLE 3
MEAN NUMBER OF "INCIDENTAL" BEHAVIORS ACCORDING TO REINFORCEMENT CONDITION AND TYPE OF PEER MODEL

Group	Verbalization (Total)	Line-Up Responses (Total)
Frequent reinforcement:		
Rewarding model	36.83	4.50
Nonrewarding model	7.58	1.67
Infrequent reinforcement:		
Rewarding model	21.08	3.92
Nonrewarding model	18.00	3.92
No model	0.00	0.00

confined principally to the first five trials. There was a significant interaction between reinforcement from peers and type of model in the data for the first five trials (*F* = 8.44, *df* = 1/44, *p* < .01), but not for the second. During the first trials, Ss who had received frequent reinforcement from their peers imitated a rewarding peer model more frequently than a nonrewarding model (*t* = 3.17, *p* < .01). On the other hand, Ss who were observed to receive infrequent peer reinforcement imitated a nonrewarding model more frequently than a rewarding model (*t* = 2.61, *p* < .02). Additional contrasts made on the data for the first five trials revealed: (*a*) among Ss who observed a rewarding model, those with a history of frequent peer reinforcement did not differ significantly from those with a history of infrequent reinforcement (*t* = 1.41, *p* < .20); (*b*) among those who observed a nonrewarding model, Ss who had received infrequent reinforcement from the peer group imitated significantly more than those who had received frequent peer reinforcement (*t* = 4.88, *p* < .01).

Analysis of imitative verbalization scores was conducted as described for the preceding measure. None of the interactions was significant. Rather, a significant main effect of type of model was obtained (*F* = 5.39, *df* = 1/44, *p* < .02). As can be seen from Table 3, Ss who observed a rewarding model reproduced the model's verbal behaviors more frequently than Ss who observed nonrewarding models. This trend is less clear for IR Ss than for FR Ss, and the interaction between reinforcement from peers and type of model approached significance ($F = 3.53$, $df = 1/44$, $p < .10$).

"Line up" scores were collapsed over all ten trials prior to analysis because this score consisted of presence-absence on single trials. None of the main or interaction effects was significant.

The data concerning the child's behavior with the hats, feathers, and pencils were analyzed by means of χ^2. All possible contrasts between pairs of experimental groups were completed. The only significant difference to emerge from these analyses showed that FR–RM Ss reproduced the pencil choices of the model more frequently than IR–NRM Ss ($\chi^2 = 4.45$, $p < .05$).* This single finding may be attributed to chance. With respect to these particular incidental behaviors, then, the experimental conditions failed to influence differentially the child's imitative behavior.

Discussion

EFFECTS OF MODEL

Observation of altruistic models increased the frequency of altruistic behavior of the Ss, a finding which confirms the results of Rosenhan and White (1967). Since frequency of altruism was highly correlated with the latency of nonaltruistic behavior, the evidence suggests that two parameters of altruism were imitated. As pointed out earlier, however, the most conservative description of the results is in terms of one altruism index, not both.

Can it be assumed that the behavior displayed by the model was construed by S as "altruism"? It is true that S was not told explicitly that he would be able to keep the trinkets in his own bowl and that those in the other child's bowl were to be given away. Nevertheless, in postsession interviews with ten Ss, all ten thought they could keep the trinkets in their own bowl, and seven thought the trinkets in the second bowl would be given to the child whose picture was attached to the bowl. Consequently, the assumption that the experiment involved imitative effects on altruism is tenable.

Among Ss who observed a model, those showing imitative altruism tended to imitate other components of the altruistic response sequence. Most of the intercorrelations among response measures were low, however, indicating that the effects of observing a model were not highly pervasive. The experimental findings are consistent with the intercorrelations. The peer reinforcement history tended

to have significant effects on behavior which was central in the altruistic response sequence (frequency of "giving to other"). Borderline effects of peer reinforcement were found with respect to imitative verbalization, and no effects were obtained with respect to less central actions ("lining up" behavior or choices of hat, feather, and pencil). This failure of the treatment effects to generalize to all measures could simply have been a function of "response centrality." It is also possible that the treatment effects did not generalize to "lining up" scores and hat, feather, and pencil choices because these behaviors occurred much less frequently than trinket sorting or verbalization.

EFFECTS OF PEER REINFORCEMENT

The relation between rewardingness of the peer model and imitative altruism was positive when S was reinforced frequently by the peer group but negative when reinforcement was infrequent. It is known that peer reinforcement is correlated with social acceptance (e.g., Hartup, Glazer, & Charlesworth, 1967; Marshall & McCandless, 1957). Therefore, the four experimental groups were contrasted with respect to the social acceptance of the models, the acceptance of the Ss, and the friendliness existing between the models and their respective Ss. Data from a picture sociometric test were used for this purpose. First, no significant differences were found in the frequency with which the models in the four groups were chosen by their peers as "liked," as "disliked," or in total times mentioned. Similarly, the social acceptance of the Ss themselves did not differ significantly among the four groups. Finally, children in group FR–RM were significantly more friendly toward their models, as revealed by the frequency with which the model was included among S's sociometric choices, than were the children in the other three groups. However, Ss in group IR–NRM, which imitated as much as group FR–RM, were less friendly toward their models than Ss in the latter group. Thus, overall, status differences among the groups do not account for the observed differences in imitation.

It is concluded that the results support Mowrer's secondary reinforcement theory of imitation when S's history includes relatively frequent reinforcement from persons resembling the model. For infrequently reinforced Ss, the influence of model rewardingness did not diminish; rather, nonrewarding models proved to be more efficacious than rewarding ones.

One explanation for these results is based on the assumption that children who receive little reinforcement are also anxious when placed in contact with other children. For them, exposure to a non-

---

* These findings are congruent with those of Rosenblith in an aspect of the study reprinted here (Section II, article 7). In analyzing a task-irrelevant behavior (choice of color of pencil) she found that children with an attention (rewarding?) model chose the same color as the adult more than those whose adult model had withdrawn attention.—Editor

rewarding model may arouse discomfort or anxiety, adding motivation to perform the actions which the situation elicits (including, in the present instance, imitation). Exposure of such children to a rewarding model, however, could result in anxiety reduction, thereby lowering *S*'s motivation for imitative behavior.

This argument implies a dual theory of peer imitation: *(a)* when reinforcement from peers is frequent, matching the behavior of a rewarding model has greater incentive value than matching a nonrewarding model (the Mowrer hypothesis); *(b)* when peer reinforcement is not frequent, a nonrewarding model sustains or increases anxiety, whereas the presence of a rewarding model reduces such motivation for imitation. This theory is similar to the hypothesis advanced by Hill (1967) concerning the role of anxiety in task performance under social reinforcement and, in some respects, parallels the dualism in psychoanalytic theories of identification. For example, it could by hypothesized that *(a)* nurturant models are emulated (anaclitic identification) when reinforcement from persons like the model has been frequent, and *(b)* when reinforcement has been infrequent, the model who elicits anxiety (or who does not behave in such a way as to reduce it) is defensively emulated. Thus, the present speculations contain interesting implications for predicting the conditions under which anaclitic and defensive identification operate.

It is also possible to consider the present results in terms of perceived similarity. It is known that, in the peer group, the correlation between "giving reinforcement to others" and "getting reinforcement from others" is positive and high (Charlesworth & Hartup, 1967). Thus, it is possible that FR–RM *S*s perceive themselves to be similar to the model (both give as well as receive frequent reinforcements) as do IR–NRM *S*s (both receive and give few reinforcements). On the other hand, perceived similarity would not be great in the other two experimental groups, FR–NRM and IR–RM. Earlier studies have shown that if *S* perceives himself as similar to *M*, conformity is enhanced (e.g., Stotland & Patchen, 1961) as well as imitation (Maccoby, 1959; Rosekrans, 1967). The perceived similarity (or reduced dissimilarity) existing for frequently reinforced *S*s with rewarding models and for infrequently reinforced *S*s with nonrewarding models would thus account for the greater amounts of imitation shown by these two groups than by the other groups in the experiment.

The present study helps to clarify the influence of the model's rewardingness on imitation. The generality of the results needs to be assessed in further research and theoretical implications explored. It appears, however, that the child's socialization history contributes importantly to the effects on imitation of rewards from the model.

REFERENCES

BANDURA, A., & HUSTON, ALETHA C. Identification as a process of incidental learning. *Journal of abnormal and social Psychology,* 1961, *63,* 311–318.

BANDURA, A., & KUPERS, CAROL J. Transmission of patterns of self-reinforcement through modelling. *Journal of abnormal and social Psychology,* 1964, *69,* 1–9.

BANDURA, A., ROSS, DOROTHEA, & ROSS, SHEILA A. A comparative test of the status envy, social power, and secondary reinforcement theories of identificatory learning. *Journal of abnormal and social Psychology,* 1963, *67,* 527–534.

CHARLESWORTH, ROSALIND, & HARTUP, W. W. Positive social reinforcement in the nursery school peer group. *Child Development,* 1967, *38,* 993–1002.

CLARK, BARBARA S. The acquisition and extinction of peer imitation in children. *Psychonomic Science,* 1965, *2,* 147–148.

FREUD, S. On narcissism: an introduction (1914). In J. D. Sutherland (Ed.), *Collected papers of Sigmund Freud.* Vol. 4. London: Hogarth, 1957. Pp. 30–60.

GROSSER, D., POLANSKY, N., & LIPPITT, R. A laboratory study of behavioral contagion. *Human Relations,* 1951, *4,* 115–142.

GRUSEC, JOAN. Some antecedents of self-criticism. *Journal of Personality and social Psychology,* 1966, *4,* 244–253.

HARTUP, W. W., GLAZER, JANE, & CHARLESWORTH, ROSALIND. Peer reinforcement and sociometric status. *Child Development,* 1967, *38,* 1017–1024.

HICKS, D. J. Imitation and retention of film-mediated aggressive peer and adult models. *Journal of Personality and social Psychology,* 1965, *2,* 97–100.

HILL, K. T. Social reinforcement as a function of test anxiety and success-failure experiences. *Child Development,* 1967, *38,* 723–737.

KOBASIGAWA, A. Observation of failure in another person as a determinant of amplitude and speed of a simple motor response. *Journal of Personality and social Psychology,* 165, *1,* 626–631.

MACCOBY, ELEANOR E. Role-taking in childhood and its consequences for social learning. *Child Development,* 1959, *30,* 239–252.

MARSHALL, HELEN R., & McCANDLESS, B. R. A study in prediction of social behavior of preschool children. *Child Development,* 1957, *28,* 149–159.

MISCHEL, W., & GRUSEC, JOAN. Determinants of the rehearsal and transmission of neutral and aversive behaviors. *Journal of Personality and social Psychology,* 1966, *3,* 197–206.

MOWRER, O. H. Identification: a link between learning theory and psychotherapy. In *Learning theory and personality dynamics.* New York: Ronald Press, 1950. Pp. 69–94.

MOWRER, O. H. *Learning theory and the symbolic process.* New York: Wiley, 1960.

MUSSEN, P. H. Some antecedents and consequents of masculine sex-typing in adolescent boys. *Psychological Monographs,* 1961, *75* (Whole No. 506).

MUSSEN, P. H., & DISTLER, L. Masculinity, identification, and father-son relationships. *Journal of abnormal and social Psychology,* 1959, *59,* 350–356.

MUSSEN, P. H., & DISTLER, L. Child-rearing antecedents of masculine identification in kindergarten boys. *Child Development,* 1960, *31,* 89–100.

MUSSEN, P. H., & RUTHERFORD, E. Parent-child relations and parental personality in relation to young children's sex-role preferences. *Child Development,* 1963, *34,* 589–607.

ROSEKRANS, MARY A. Imitation in children as a function of perceived similarity to a social model and vicarious reinforcement. *Journal of Personality and social Psychology,* 1967, in press.

ROSENBLITH, JUDY F. Learning by imitation in kindergarten children. *Child Development,* 1959, *30,* 69–80.

ROSENHAN, D., & WHITE, G. M. Observation and rehearsal as determinants of pro-social behavior. *Journal of Personality and social Psychology,* 1967, *5,* 424–431.

SEARS, PAULINE S. Child rearing factors related to the playing of sex-typed roles. *American Psychologist,* 1953, *8,* 431. (Abstract)

SEARS, R. R. Identification as a form of behavior development. In D. B. Harris (Ed.), *The concept of development.* Minneapolis: University of Minnesota Press, 1957. Pp. 149–161.

SEARS, R. R., RAU, LUCY, & ALPERT, R. *Identification and child rearing.* Stanford, Calif.: Stanford University Press, 1965.

SKINNER, B. F. *Science and human behavior.* New York: Macmillan, 1953.

STEIN, ALETHA H., & WRIGHT, J. C. Imitation learning under conditions of nurturance and nurturance withdrawal. *Child Development,* 1964, *35,* 927–937.

STOTLAND, E., and PATCHEN, M. Identification and change in prejudice and in authoritarianism. *Journal of abnormal and social Psychology,* 1961, *62,* 254–274.

children's success at a task were deliberately altered and the resulting shifts in mother-child interaction were noted. These shifts demonstrate Bell's point that parental behavior is affected by children's characteristics, or perceived characteristics. Thus we see that Sears' argument about the importance of the dyadic relationship (Section III, article 18) has finally come to be taken seriously.

29

Differences in the Behavior of Mothers Toward First- and Later-born Children [1]

IRMA HILTON

This article takes up the topic of birth order and hence of siblings, a topic covered more fully in the companion volumes on Child Development and Educational Psychology. The effects on behavior of having brothers and sisters may be regarded as a special instance of peer influence. In addition, birth order differences may reflect differences in the ways in which the mother interacts with the child. This paper focuses on that aspect of the behavioral determinants of birth order differences. Irma Hilton shows that the mothers' behaviors with a first child tend to differ from those with a later-born child. Readers should compare these results of Hilton with those obtained on monkeys by Mitchell and Brandt (Section VIII).

As one aspect of her work, Hilton brings out a theme consonant with the position of Bell (article 24 in this section). Mothers' impressions of their

Over the past several years there has been a growing interest in birth order as a factor in determining personality characteristics. Studies with adults have suggested that first-borns can be distinguished from persons of later birth on a variety of behaviors—persuasibility, desire to affiliate, conformity (Warren, 1966). Intriguing as these findings are in and of themselves, ordinal position is not a psychologically meaningful concept. The more critical issue, therefore, is to determine if these diverse findings can be subsumed under a psychologically meaningful frame of reference—and if this frame of reference is specified, are there sufficient differences in the child training practices of parents with their firstborns and later borns to cause these different behaviors to develop.

Schachter (1959) and Sears, Maccoby, and Levin (1957) have suggested that differential dependency might be the frame of reference within which these empirically determined ordinal position differences might be integrated—firstborns are more likely to show dependency-linked behaviors. The question remains, however, whether there are sufficient behaviors peculiar to mothers with their firstborns; and if these behaviors are isolated, whether they might cause the development of greater dependency.

Previous researchers have suggested several areas of consistent variation in parental behavior towards first- and later-born children. Koch (1954) reported the parents as paying more attention to the firstborn; Rosen (1961) described the parents as talking and interacting more with the first. Stout (1960) and Lasko (1954) both reported parents to be more directive of the firstborn child. Davis (1959), McArthur (1956), Rosen (1961), Sampson (1962) and Sutton-Smith, Roberts, and Rosenberg (1964) all referred to the pressure placed on the first child to achieve and be responsible. Sears et al. (1957) noted that there seems to be an inconsistency in the training of firstborn children that does not characterize the training of later borns.

Unfortunately, however, the majority of these studies used either the retrospective reports of the

[1] This article is based upon a doctoral dissertation presented to the Department of Social Psychology of Columbia University. The study was conducted while the author held a United States Public Health Service predoctoral fellowship. The author would like to express her thanks to her chairman, Stanley Schachter; to her committee members, William J. McGuire, Richard Christie, Julian Hochberg, and William Goode; to the independent observers, Lonnie Minkoff and Susan Nachamie; to Carrie Cheek, director of the Columbia Greenhouse Nursery School, and Josephine Bliss, director of the Riverside Church Nursery School; and all the mothers and children without whom this study could not have been accomplished.

Irma Hilton, "Differences in the behavior of mothers toward first- and later-born children," *Journal of Personality and Social Psychology, 7,* 1967, 282–290.

child (usually interviewed when an adult), or the reports of parents about the manner in which they treated their children. Recent studies have shown that such data may be highly unreliable (Robbins, 1963). Accordingly, the present study was designed to observe these reported differences in an experimentally controlled interaction of mother and child. It was proposed that the inexperienced mother of the firstborn is more interfering, more inconsistent, and more extreme (either supportive or critical) in her child treatment. On theoretical grounds, greater interference (Festinger, 1954) and/or inconsistency (Martin, 1963) could stimulate the development of greater dependency.

The problem, therefore, was to get beneath the observable conclusion that certain personality traits seem to be related to ordinal position and inquire whether these birth order relationships mask some underlying psychological dynamic; that is, are they a vehicle for displaying a relationship between interference, inconsistency, extremity, and dependency?

METHOD

DESIGN AND SUBJECTS

The study involved the systematic observation of mother-child interaction in either one of two independent experimental conditions—a condition in which a child apparently failed badly at a presumed test of creativity and independent thinking (failure), and a condition in which the child apparently did very well on this test (success).

Although the major purpose of the experiment was to understand differences in mother treatment of firstborn versus later-born children, only children were included as a separate condition to illuminate the possible

child before the experimental trials. Only three mothers so contacted refused to participate.

Sixty mother-child pairs, so selected, visited the laboratory ostensibly to participate in a study of independent thinking. Half of the mothers were given to understand that their child's performance was below average (failure), and half that their child's was above average (success). The manipulations were without regard to the child's ability. In both conditions the mother observed the child for 5 minutes while he did a series of puzzles (Experimental Session 1), was given a private evaluation of his performance while the child was instructed to remain in the experimental room (Intermission 1), and was then left alone with the child for 5 minutes with instructions to do anything she felt like doing while the experimenter got some more materials (Observation 1). This sequence was repeated twice and was followed by a strong success experience for children in both conditions.

The experimental room had toys and books around and drawings on the wall. It was a large room, with two entrances, divided in half by a sliding door. The extra room was to provide a place for the experimenter to speak to the mother out of earshot of the child. The experimenter immediately explained to the child that when mother and she went to talk alone, they would be in this other room—emphasizing its proximity. While the child explored the room the mother was told that the child would do some puzzles which had been selected as representative intelligence-test items. Her function was primarily to evaluate whether the child performed in the testing situation in a way analogous to his home performance, because one of the sources of unreliability in testing was the difference between home and test performance. She was told not to interfere with or speak to the child during the 5-minute experimental sessions; but that she would have an opportunity to counsel the child during the 5-minute periods which would separate the testing sessions. The mother was then asked to make the following judgment:

How well do you expect your child to do on these puzzles?

1	2	3	4	5	6	7	8	9

Much better than most   Better than average   About average   Worse than average   Much worse than most

---

effects of a second child on the behavior of the mother and the firstborn child.

The children were approximately 4 years old; half boys, half girls—20 only children, 20 firstborns, and 20 later borns. The firstborns and later borns were from two-child families with siblings of the same sex. All were from nursery schools in the University area.

PROCEDURE

The mothers designated by the nursery school directors as having 4-year-old children with one other same-sex sibling or as having only children were contacted first by letter and then by telephone. The list designated only the age, address, and telephone number of the child so that the experimenter did not know the birth order of the

If necessary an explanation of the rating scales was given. The purpose of this initial rating was to get a base measure for the success of the manipulation as well as an index of level of aspiration or expectancy for the child.

Experimental sessions. In each of the experimental sessions the child was given a series of puzzles to do. The series of puzzles chosen was one not commercially available. The order of difficulty and the time taken to complete each puzzle was predetermined with a nursery group independent of the ones used in the sample. Each child, regardless of experimental condition, received the same initial puzzle. If the child was in the failure condition and did the puzzles easily he was given a much more difficult one to do the next time.

The experimenter used a stopwatch and allowed the child to work continuously for 5 minutes—providing new puzzles when necessary. The experimenter initiated no conversation with mother or child and answered questions as cursorily as possible; always politely reminding the mother that she was to remain inobtrusive.

Intermissions. The mother and experimenter went into the other side of the double-doored experimental room with the door ajar. The experimenter asked the mother to make some judgments about her child's performance; reiterating the problem of estimating the differences in performance between the home and school situations. The questions, presented with 9-point rating scales for answers, were: How well do you think your child is doing compared to other children who have taken this test? How well do you think your child is doing in comparison to his usual puzzle solving? How pleased or dissatisfied are you with his performance?

The function of these questions was two-fold: to provide an index of the success of the manipulation and to make the disguise of the experiment more credible to the mother.

The mother was then given either a success or failure induction. In success:

You know, _____ really did extremely well. I know it's hard for you to judge his ability relative to other children because you don't see that many others—but I can tell you that _____ did much better than most other children do. He really did extremely well. It takes the average child 7 minutes to complete as much as _____ did in five minutes.

Now I need to go upstairs for a little while to get some more materials. Will you keep him company, please, while I do?

If you'd like, you can play on the puzzles with him or do anything else you feel like doing.

In failure:

I'm afraid that _____ did rather poorly. I'm sorry to tell you this, but I guess you'd want to know, and he really was much slower than the other children. It takes the average child 4 minutes to complete this puzzle (or these two puzzles). I gave _____ 5 minutes, and he was not able to finish.

Now I need to go upstairs for a little while to get some more materials. Will you keep him company, please, while I do?

If you'd like, you can play on the puzzles with him or do anything else you feel like doing.

Observation sessions. In each of these, the experimenter left and went into the observation room with the observers for the 5-minute observation session. The experimenter maintained a running protocol while the others coded and rated. After 5 minutes the experimenter returned to the mother and child.

MEASURES

The child's dependence or independence and his mother's attitude towards him were recorded separately—with a variety of indexes available for each. Among these were coded observations, rating scales, and a checklist of overt behaviors. The observation schedules and rating scales were adapted specifically for this experiment.

OBSERVATION SCHEDULES

A category system was devised to permit scoring interaction between mother and child so that the amount and form of each subject's participation could be examined. It was hoped that these interaction data would provide information about how self-reliant children were, how autonomous the mothers permitted them to be, and what kind and amount of affect was generated in a problem-solving situation. Separate category systems were devised for the experimental observation sessions.[2]

Each experimental and observation session was coded on a separate schedule to maximize independence of judgment and to allow evaluation of change between the two periods. A unit of verbal behavior was defined as a sentence, phrase, or single word which in the observers' judgments denoted a single idea of meaning. Each discrete physical act was coded separately. If a behavior continued for more than 10 seconds it was coded again. Ten pilot sessions in which the observers' judgments were compared and discussed by the experimenter were conducted to ensure a satisfactory agreement between the two observers. The observers achieved a reliability of .92 by the start of the experimental study.

RATING SCALES

In addition to the recording and coding of specific acts, the observers made gross evaluative judgments of the mother's and child's behavior. It had been predicted that mothers of firstborns would be more inconsistent, more involved, and more extremely rated as supportive or critical. Accordingly, in each of the experimental and observation sessions the two observers judged the mothers on a 7-point scale of consistency, a 7-point scale of involvement, and a 7-point scale of support. An estimation of relaxation was included as a dimension insofar as it might modify the estimation of involvement.

With respect to the child's behavior, it had been assumed on the basis of earlier evidence that firstborn children would be more dependent and more tense (Schachter, 1959). Accordingly, the children were judged in each session as displaying dependency or tension. An estimation of the child's behavior as either cooperative or negative was included to avoid a possible confusion between negativism and independence. The observers were

---

[2] A two-page schedule of the category systems has been deposited with the American Documentation Institute. Order Document No. 9554 from ADI Auxiliary Publications Project, Photoduplication Service, Library of Congress, Washington, D.C. 20540. Remit in advance $2.50 for microfilm or $1.75 for photocopies and make checks payable to: Chief, Photoduplication Service, Library of Congress.

given explicit instruction and training in how to rate each of the seven items on the scale. The reliability and validity of the observers' judgments were assessed in 10 pilot sessions before the start of the experiment. The raters achieved a reliability of .89 before the start of the experimental trials.

OVERT BEHAVIORS

The observers recorded whether or not the child clung to the mother; whether or not the child remained at the table, drawing, when the mother and experimenter left the room to make the intersession ratings—and whether or not the child persisted in coming in after having been told to return. They also recorded who, if anyone, initiated the puzzle solving in the observation sessions.

RESULTS[3]

DEPENDENCY

Since the study was designed to examine the psychological dynamics behind affiliative-dependent behaviors linked to birth order, it was important to ascertain first that differential dependency was present.

The results indicated that firstborn and only children were significantly more dependent than later-born children.

Firstborn children were rated as significantly more dependent by the observers ($t = 5.0$, $p < .001$). They were significantly more likely to run to their mothers' side during the intermission, when the instructions had been to remain at the table, drawing, while the mother and experimenter went outside for the experimental manipulation ($\chi^2 = 4.1$, $p < .05$). They were significantly more likely to persist in this behavior when told to return ($\chi^2 = 4.1$, $p < .05$). They were significantly more likely to ask for direct help and/or reassurance ($\chi^2 = 4.6$, $p < .05$).

---

[3] Inasmuch as there were no significant differences between only children and firstborns, and only one significant difference in the behavior of mothers of only children and mothers of firstborns, these two groups were combined for the purpose of final analysis. For a more detailed breakdown, see McAlister (1965). *T* tests and interaction *t*'s were used in the instances where all or nearly all of the mothers made a response in a particular category. The χ^2 test was used in the instances where there was an irregular distribution of responses. All *t* tests are two-tailed. A Yates correction was used in all χ^2 tests where the expected frequency in a cell was less than 5. A 12-page table of frequencies of coded communication has been deposited with the American Documentation Institute. Order Document No. 9554 from ADI Auxiliary Publications Project, Photoduplication Service, Library of Congress, Washington, D.C. 20540. Remit in advance $2.50 for microfilm or $1.75 for photocopies and make checks payable to: Chief, Photoduplication Service, Library of Congress.

INTERFERENCE

The results indicated further that mothers of firstborns were seen as more involved than mothers of later borns ($t = 2.2$, $p < .05$), and were more likely to interfere with the activities of their child. Mothers of firstborns were more likely to initiate work on the puzzle, gave more task-oriented suggestions and more direct help.

Forty-nine of the children did play on the puzzles during at least one of the observation sessions. In some instances the decision to work on the puzzles was made by the mother and in some by the child. The distribution of puzzle initiations appears in Table 1. Mothers of firstborns and of only children were significantly more likely to signal the start of work on the puzzle than mothers of later borns ($\chi^2 = 7.8$, $p < .005$). The mother of the later born was more likely to wait for the child to start himself.

Further evidence of differences in the extent of interference was available from an examination of the number of task-oriented suggestions made by the mother to the child during the observation periods. Mothers of firstborns and only children gave an average of 9.1 task-oriented suggestions, mothers of later borns gave an average of 4.1. The mother of the firstborn, therefore, was not only likely to initiate and perpetuate activity—but she was also likely to continue to direct its course once begun ($t = 3.8$, $p < .001$).

Additional evidence came from an examination of the amount of direct help given by the mother to the child during the experimental period. The

TABLE 1
PUZZLE INITIATOR

	Mother	Child
Firstborns	27	7
Later borns	5	10

Note.—$\chi^2 = 7.8$, $p < .005$.

TABLE 2
SUMMARY TABLE—INTERFERENCE

Evidence	Test	Significance level
Mother gives direct help during experimental sessions (contrary to explicit instruction)	χ^2	.08
Mother initiates work on the puzzles during the observation periods	χ^2	.005
Mother gives task-oriented suggestions	t	.001
Observer ratings of involvement	t	.05

TABLE 3
MEAN NUMBER OF SUPPORTIVE AND CRITICAL STATEMENTS IN THE EXPERIMENTAL SESSIONS

TABLE 3
MEAN NUMBER OF SUPPORTIVE AND CRITICAL STATEMENTS IN THE EXPERIMENTAL SESSIONS

	Mothers of firstborns	Mothers of later borns	t
Mean no. supportive statements			
Success ($N = 30$)	3.1	1.8	.70
Failure ($N = 30$)	4.0	2.8	.85
Success and failure ($N = 60$)	7.1	4.6	1.11
Mean no. critical statements [a]			
Success ($N = 30$)	0.1	0.0	
Failure ($N = 30$)	1.0	0.4	
Success and failure ($N = 60$)	1.1	0.4	
Mean no. supportive and critical statements			
Success and failure ($N = 60$)	8.2	5.0	1.25

[a] N too small for statistical test.

mother had been told in the instructions to sit in her chair and participate as little as possible—that her role was to observe and evaluate. Eighteen of the mothers disregarded these instructions at one point or another, however, and gave direct help to their child. Of these 18, 15 were the mothers of firstborns. It appears then that even when the mothers were instructed not to participate, the mother of the firstborn was more likely to interfere with her child's activities than was the mother of a later-born child ($\chi^2 = 3.2$, $p < .08$).

IMMODERATION

It was found, furthermore, that mothers of firstborns were more extreme in their affect towards the children. The experiment was designed to elicit responses from the mother in one situation in which she would be pleased with the child's performance (success) and in another in which she would be displeased or disappointed (failure), in order to tap the extremes of her response.

The measure of the success of the manipulation to induce a perception of success or failure was the changed scale position on a 9-point scale in the mothers' answers to the questions, "How well do you expect your child to do on these puzzles?" in relation to "How well do you think your child is doing compared to other children who have taken this test?" The mothers of children in the failure condition changed their ratings to a more negative evaluation significantly more than the mothers of children in the success condition ($t = 5.3$, $p < .001$). The difference scores used were between the initial rating and the rating after Experimental Session 2.

In Table 3 the distributions of number of supportive and critical statements are presented. Although the t tests do not reach a generally accepted significance level because of the large variance for firstborns' mothers, the direction is consistent. It

is not quite accurate, however, to say simply that mothers of firstborns gave more support and criticism. The distributions are quite comparable up to the point where there are more than seven comments per mother, at which point the distribution for firstborns makes a significant climb. It would be more precise, therefore, to say that if any mother were to make an *excessive* response it would be more likely a mother with her firstborn. Of the 10 mothers who made seven or more supportive or critical comments, 9 were mothers with their firstborn children ($\chi^2 = 3.7$, $p < .06$).

A category was included for overt expressions of love and/or support (hugs, kisses, etc.) as indications of a higher level of response. Table 4 indicates even stronger differences than those found for verbal support. Mothers of firstborns were significantly more likely to make overt demonstrations of love than mothers of later borns ($t = 4.4$, $p < .001$).

INCONSISTENCY

The third area of investigation was inconsistency. How vulnerable to change was the mother's behavior when told that her child had done well or poorly? The within-trial ratings of consistency did not show any differences between the two groups, possibly because the time period was not long enough to distinguish between momentary reactions and a true

TABLE 4
MEAN NUMBER OF INSTANCES OF
DEMONSTRATIVE LOVE

Mean no. instances of demonstrative love	Mothers of firstborns	Mothers of later borns
Success	8.3	4.9
Failure	3.6	4.9
Success and failure	6.0	4.9

shift in attitude. Two other kinds of evidence were available to examine this hypothesis, however. The first was to compare differences in the level of non-verbal support; that is, to reexamine the distribution of the incidence of demonstrative love (see Table 4).

It was found that although mothers of firstborns were significantly more demonstrative than mothers of later borns, the bulk of this support came when the child was succeeding. Mothers of firstborns exhibited a higher incidence of demonstrative love when their child was doing well (success), and a significant decrement in the incidence of demonstrative love when he was failing. The later-born's mother was less extreme in her demonstrations of love, but she maintained them (interaction $t = 4.8$, $p < .001$).

The second kind of evidence was to examine the increase or decrease in amount of verbal support given by the same mother as a function of the success or failure induction. It was found than when mothers of firstborns discovered that their child was doing poorly (failure) they exhibited a significant decrement in their level of verbal support, which was not true for mothers with their later borns (see Table 5).

It seems as if the mother of the firstborn and of the only child in effect rejected her child by withdrawing love when he failed—which was made all the more potent by the extreme expectancy for demonstrations of love which she had built up when he succeeded.[4]

This same inconsistent pattern did not arise, however, in the face of a success induction. Although the differences were not significant, there

was some evidence that the mother of the later born reduced her support in the face of the child's success. This tendency may be a reflection of the lesser degree of interference by the mother with her later born. Once she was assured that the child was performing adequately, she left him alone to judge his own successes.

It did not seem surprising, however, that inconsistency appeared only when the mother of a firstborn received information that her child had done poorly. The mother of a firstborn, with less personal experience, was more susceptible to outside influence and more likely to feel that what *she* had done was wrong and had caused the child's failure. The mother of a later born, who was presumably more confident, shifted less in the induced perception of her child's failure.

SEX DIFFERENCES

Although the general trend of the ordinal position literature has indicated that firstborns are more dependent, Sampson (1965) and Singer (1964) have both suggested that the effects are not straightforward; that birth-order differences may interact with sex differences, with the firstborn boy and later-born girl the more dependent. There was no evidence in this study to support such a hypothesis. Firstborn boys and firstborn girls were consistently more dependent than later-born boys and girls.

The sex differences which did arise do not lend themselves to parsimonious explanation. There was no trend to indicate that differential dependency was more distinctly attributable to firstborns of either sex. In some areas the boys were more dependent and in others the girls were. It may be that parents tolerate dependency in boys in some areas (asking for help), but not in others (clinging). The dependency is present in both sexes, but the form in which it is manifested varies. In regard to the mothers' behavior, while there were strong con-

---

[4] Although categories had been included for criticism and overt withdrawal of love, the incidence of statements or behaviors in this area was negligible—less than 2% of total coded communication by the mother. The major means of communicating displeasure seemed to be the lessening of positive affect.

TABLE 5
SHIFT IN LEVEL OF VERBAL SUPPORT

	Firstborns		Later borns		Mean change		
	Experimental session		Experimental session		First-borns	Later borns	t
	1	2	1	2			
Mean no. supportive statements (failure condition)	3.2	0.8	1.4	1.4	−2.4	0	2.27**
Mean no. supportive statements (success condition)	1.6	1.5	1.5	0.3	−0.1	−1.2	1.40*

* $p < .15$.
** $p < .03$.

sistent distinctions in their treatment of children of differing birth orders, there were no such significant sex differences.[5]

DISCUSSION

This study experimentally confirmed the presence of differential dependency needs and suggested that firstborns are in fact interfered with more, reacted to more extremely, and treated more inconsistently. The further question is to explain how these mechanisms operate to create dependency in the child.

Initially, it is important to keep in mind in evaluating these results that this is a conception of dependence as the extent to which other people are used as sources of support and reference. It does not necessarily imply that "independence" in the sense of going out on one's own (early walking to school alone) or taking responsibility (care of younger siblings) would be a contradiction. There has been considerable mention in the literature of this independence training for firstborns (Sampson, 1965).

The distinction that must be made, however, is between psychological independence, "to thine own self be true," and the physical appearance of independence; the assumption of responsible roles. This physical demonstration of independence is frequently an internalization of the values of the adult culture—not an expression of what the child wanted to do. This point is emphasized because it is occasionally difficult to convince a parent that the firstborn child whom she has trained to go to the mailbox alone may actually be less independent than the later-born child who refuses to go.

Interference and inconsistency both undermine the child's opportunities to develop reference points for internal evaluation. Festinger (1954) has pointed out that when there are no objective or internal standards to use as reference points, one is more likely to be influenced by the attitudes of others. When the parent is inconsistent there is no stable guideline for internalizing the correct course of action. The child cannot predict outcomes on the basis of past performance, and must continue to ask for evaluation because the same behavior will elicit a varying response.

The effect of excessive interference is to create standards that the child must fulfill. He does not set his own goals, but rather achieves the ones set for him. He learns to ask for praise for his activities, and the evidence on excessive support is that *if* he achieves, he gets it. Because he does not set his own goals, he cannot determine whether they have been adequately met. His satisfactions must

come from pleasing others. There is evidence to support this interpretation in the difference between birth orders in the number of instances of praising self. The mean number per subject for firstborns was 1.32; for later borns, 2.60 ($t = 2.4$, $p < .02$). Whereas the firstborns and the only children were more likely to ask for direct help and/or reassurance, the later borns were more likely to praise themselves.

This kind of interpretation is consistent with the earlier mentioned evidence of higher and projected aspirations for the firstborn and with the evidence found by Schachter (1963) that firstborns are more likely to fulfill these goals—they are overrepresented in colleges, frequently the focus of parental planning.

It cannot be specified on the basis of this study whether there is a direct relationship between interference and dependency or inconsistency and dependency, or whether the interaction of the two creates a dependent child. It is suggested, however, that inconsistency and interference lead directly to dependency, and that extremity of reaction is the catalyst for them both. It raises the level of inconsistency and reinforces or frustrates the dependency initiated by excessive interference.

One final question for consideration is why the presence of later borns does not modify the mother's attitude toward the firstborn in the direction of making him less dependent. It had been noted earlier that although mothers' attitudes toward firstborns and only children were not significantly different, their attitudes towards first- and later-borns were. There are several possible reasons. One is that a pattern of relationships between parent and firstborn is established which becomes self-perpetuating; the parent finds himself continuing to interact more strenuously with the first. The firstborn becomes in a sense a stimulus for higher emotional arousal.

Another is that Sears et al. (1957) present evidence that the more frequently dependency responses such as clinging to the mother and resisting separation from her are punished, the greater is the strength of these dependency responses. If at some point in time the mother recognizes the greater dependency of her firstborn and tries to correct it—either because she no longer has the time to indulge these needs or because she now values independence—her rejection or punishment of these dependency responses will only increase their occurrence. There is some possibility, therefore, that the presence of the later born could make the firstborn even more dependent.

A third possibility is that the activities of the firstborn are always the new experiences for the mother—so that even in consideration of her

---

[5] For a more detailed analysis, see McAlister (1965).

greater familiarity with children, she is still a novice at each new experience with the firstborn and must try out her reactions in the new situation. By the time the later born is of similar age her attitudes towards a child in a particular situation have stabilized and she reacts more moderately and more consistently, inasmuch as she no longer feels insecure about her own competence.

This is not to say, however, that the mother is necessarily interfering, inconsistent, or intemperate with her firstborn. The variability of these responses within the framework of a significant trend emphasizes the importance of being circumspect in the interpretation. It is not one's birth order as such which predisposes one to dependency, but rather that in a particular birth order one is more likely to be exposed to the kinds of attitudes and behaviors which create dependency.

REFERENCES

DAVIS, A. American status systems and the socialization of the child. In C. Kluckhohn & H. A. Murray (Eds.), *Personality in nature, society, and culture.* New York: Knopf, 1959. Pp. 567–576.

FESTINGER, L. A theory of social comparison processes. *Human Relations,* 1954, *7,* 117–140.

KOCH, H. L. The relation of "primary mental abilities" in five- and six-year-olds to sex of child and characteristics of his sibling. *Child Development,* 1954, *25,* 209–223.

LASKO, J. K. Parent behavior toward first and second children. *Genetic Psychology Monographs,* 1954, *49,* 96–137.

MARTIN, B. Reward and punishment associated with the same goal response: A factor in the learning of motives. *Psychological Bulletin,* 1963, *60,* 441–451.

MCALISTER, I. R. Interference, immoderation, inconsistency and dependency. Unpublished doctoral dissertation, Columbia University, 1965.

MCARTHUR, C. Personalities of first and second children. *Psychiatry,* 1956, *19,* 47–54.

ROBBINS, L. C. The accuracy of parental recall of aspects of child development and of child rearing practices. *Journal of Abnormal and Social Psychology,* 1963, *66,* 261–270.

ROSEN, B. C. Family structure and achievement motivation. *American Sociological Review,* 1961, *26,* 574–585.

SAMPSON, E. E. Birth order, need achievement, and conformity. *Journal of Abnormal and Social Psychology,* 1962, *64,* 155–159.

SAMPSON, E. E. The study of ordinal position: Antecedents and outcomes. In B. Maher (Ed.), *Progress in experimental personality research.* Vol. 2. New York: Academic Press, 1965. Pp. 175–228.

SCHACHTER, S. *The psychology of affiliation.* Stanford, Calif.: Stanford University Press, 1959.

SCHACHTER, S. Birth order, eminence, and higher education. *American Sociological Review,* 1963, *28,* 757–767.

SEARS, R. R., MACCOBY, E., & LEVIN, H. *Patterns of child rearing.* Evanston, Ill.: Row, Peterson, 1957.

SINGER, J. E. The use of manipulative strategies: Machiavellianism and attractiveness. *Sociometry,* 1964, *27,* 128–150.

STOUT, A. M. Parent behavior toward children of differing ordinal position and sibling status. Unpublished doctoral dissertation, University of California, 1960.

SUTTON-SMITH, B., ROBERTS, J. M., & ROSENBERG, B. G. Sibling associations and role involvement. *Merrill-Palmer Quarterly,* 1964, *10,* 25–38.

WARREN, J. Birth order and social behavior. *Psychological Bulletin,* 1966, *65,* 38–49.

V

SETTINGS AND SPECIFIC STIMULI
AS DETERMINANTS OF BEHAVIOR

In this class of determinant we incorporate various situational influences. Immediate *instigations* such as another person's act with reference to oneself are only one part of a stimulus situation. A second aspect is the *setting:* "Where did it happen?" People act differently in differing contexts; the gymnasium evokes orders of response seldom seen in the classroom, the parlor, or the church. It is not just that basketball is played in a gym rather than a classroom, but that in the gym, additional behaviors appear; for example, boisterousness, joking, or—in some individuals—unaccustomed restraint and shyness. Such shyness might not be suspected to be part of the person's repertoire if he were seen only in other settings.

Setting is not a question solely of location; a setting can change even when the place remains the same. A classroom is not likely to remain psychologically the same environment when the teacher is out of the room for a long time. Indeed, change in the amount of structure—either in the clarity of expected behavior or in the extent of external control—often causes marked alterations in response. (For instance, some persons who are free of anxiety during the week suffer from "weekend neurosis" when deprived of the routine of their workday lives.) Research on classroom atmosphere attempts to study the effects of different emotional climates in one type of setting.

Still another influence is the impact of the various *face-to-face groups* with which an individual deals personally—his recreational cronies; his employees, employers, and competitors at work; his family at home.[1] These groups comprise a series of social systems, changes in any of which can broadly affect a person's behavior. A man's troubles in the office or a boy's anxieties in school are betrayed by actions at home. Conversely, conflict at home may damage scholastic performance. A worsening state of affairs at home may heighten the importance, to man or boy, of his boon companions outside the family. Improvements at school (for instance, a new teacher generous with praise for a girl responsive to praise) may reduce the rate of outbursts at home. It is these kinds of face-to-face relations that are dealt with in this section. The wider social systems, involving cultural and institutional memberships, are discussed under Section VI, Group Memberships.

Kurt Lewin's application of a gestalt viewpoint to understanding human social behavior stands as a landmark in the history of psychological thought. The research on group dynamics that he spawned continues to push back conceptual horizons. More recently such authors as Roger Barker and Herbert Wright have been demonstrating the alterations in behavior that accompany changes in setting. Now leading psychiatrists such as Erich Lindemann have been studying the effects of face-to-face social systems on the eruption of mental illness, especially when an "emotional hazard" such as a point of *role transition* (see introduction

---

[1] The latter was partly covered under Interpersonal Experiences in Section IV, but here we deal with the immediate relationships rather than home social learnings of the past.

to Section VII) occurs in a social system that puts undue stress on a particular individual or fails to support him in accustomed ways. Some people will show neurotic responses in any setting, but others become disturbed solely because the role relationships in which they are involved are organized in ways "unhealthful" for them. In such cases, the most appropriate treatment may be to try to change *the social system* without necessarily treating the patient directly.

Another type of stimulus that may influence behavior is the mass media. The effects of comics, movies, and TV on children have long been debated. Some psychologists, as well as laymen, assume that the depiction of violence or sex on television or in comic books will encourage children to misbehave. Others argue that experiencing a behavior such as aggression vicariously through drama may have a cathartic effect, reducing the likelihood of expression in overt behavior.

In Section V of the second edition of *The Causes of Behavior* we printed Wilbur Schramm's review of a British study on the effects of television, as well as a study by W. Paul Blakely on the effects of comic books. Both investigations failed to show the bad effects that many people had expected. Since then Bandura, his students, and others have reported an increase in subjects' aggressive behaviors after exposure to aggressive models (in person or via movie or TV). The aggressive behaviors studied have primarily been directed at inanimate objects rather than at people.

A recent study by Donald P. Hartman, "Influence of Symbolically Modeled Instrumental Aggression and Pain Cues on Aggressive Behavior" (*Journal of Personality and Social Psychology,* 1969, *11,* 280–288), contradicts the catharsis hypothesis. However, his work used delinquents as subjects. Hence, one cannot draw sound conclusions about the effects of the stimuli on normal viewers. An even more recent study on the effects of TV on aggression in the naturalistic social behavior of preschool children was reported by Aletha Huston Stein and her collaborator, Friedrich, at the 1971 meetings of the Society for Research in Child Development. They found an increase in aggressive behavior after viewing aggressive TV programs, *but* only for those Ss whose initial level of aggression was high. This study escapes one of the criticisms that can be made of much of the work on this topic, for it looked at aggressive behavior in the normal nursery school setting, not in the laboratory. The laboratory study of such behaviors always raises a question as to the extent to which the subject may perceive that he is in a respectable scientific laboratory (in the hands of powerful and wise adults) and consequently nothing really bad would be allowed to happen. Hence, any available behaviors are "safe."

Because of the disparate findings and conclusions in this field, we are not trying to cover it beyond our acknowledgment of the issues. The articles in this section, then, deal with the effects that are obtained from exposing children to particular types of influence other than those of the media. The effects of specific stimuli, settings, and face-to-face social systems are explored.

30

A Child in Distress: The Effect of Focusing Responsibility on Children on Their Attempts to Help

ERVIN STAUB

A specific stimulus in the form of verbal instruction can make a great deal of difference in the ways that subjects respond. That fact is succinctly illustrated in this brief report by Ervin Staub of the Department of Social Relations at Harvard. Staub played a recording of a child's cries of distress in order to study the conditions under which another child, in an adjoining room, will go to help when he hears the cries.

This is one of a series of studies by Staub of the pro-social behavior of helping a child in distress. The studies are trying to isolate the conditions that influence such helping responses. See, for example, "A Child in Distress: The Influence of Age and Number of Witnesses on Children's Attempts to Help" (Journal of Personality and Social Psychology, 1970, 14, 130–140) or "Helping a Person in Distress: The Influence of Implicit and Explicit 'Rules' of Conduct on Children and Adults" (same journal, 1971, 17, 137–144).

Children may learn that one should help others by adults focusing responsibility on them externally or indicating to them that they are expected to respond to another person's need. In this study the effects of indirectly focusing responsibility on children on their subsequent attempts to help another child in distress were investigated.

The subjects were 42 kindergarten and 42 first-grade boys and girls. A female experimenter asked the subject to make a drawing, but "discovered" that she had no crayon. Before she left to get crayons she went into an adjoining room ostensibly to "check on a girl who is in there." When the experimenter returned she said casually: "She's fine. I hope she doesn't climb on that chair again." This procedure aimed to communicate that there was a child alone in the adjoining room, and to suggest an explanation for the distress sounds the subject would subsequently hear. In the distress group, the experimenter then left. In the distress-responsibility group, the experimenter said: "I will leave you in charge of things, O.K.?" After the subject acknowledged this in some manner the experimenter added: "If anything happens you will take care of it." Then the experimenter left. About a minute and a half after the experimenter left the subjects heard a crash from the adjoining room, followed by sounds of distress consisting of severe crying and sobbing, which lasted 70 seconds. In a third group, the distress-help group, the procedure was the same as in the distress group, but the subjects heard sounds of distress that included calls for help. The experimenter, observing from behind a one-way mirror, recorded the subjects' behavior as active help if they went into the adjoining room or went in search of the experimenter, as volunteering information if they reported what happened on the experimenter's return to the room a minute after the distress sounds ceased, and as no help if they did neither. Scores of 3, 2, and 1 were assigned to these responses, respectively. In the case of no help, the experimenter asked questions in order to elicit a report of the distress sounds. If the subjects said in response to the most direct question that they heard nothing this was recorded as denial. All subjects were carefully debriefed.*

** Dr. Staub has provided the following description of the debriefing procedure.

"The debriefing that followed attempted to assure in two ways that the procedure would have no negative consequences for children and would leave no feelings of guilt and resentment: (a) by reassuring them that no one was suffering and that nothing was amiss and (b) by continuing the session with pleasant activities during which the experimenter behaved in a warm and nurturant manner, which was expected to further indicate to children that everything was all right and to result in an overall pleasant experience. In all cases, permission was obtained from parents for their child's participation in the experiment; neither parents nor teachers reported any adverse consequences resulting from the procedure, suggesting the success of debriefing. To minimize confusion for younger subjects, kindergarten children who did not go into the adjoining room were not told that they heard a tape recording. The experimenter told these sub-

Ervin Staub, "A child in distress: the effect of focusing responsibility on children on their attempts to help," *Developmental Psychology, 2,* 1970, 152–153. Copyright 1970 by the American Psychological Association and reprinted by permission.

An analysis of variance of helping scores showed a significant treatment effect ($F = 4.78$, $df = 1/72$, $p < .02$). The subjects in the distress-responsibility group helped significantly more than those in the distress group ($t = 3.07$, $df = 72$, $p < .01$) and marginally significantly more than those in the distress-help group ($t = 1.87$, $df = 72$, $p < .07$). The differences between groups in first grade were of the same magnitude as in the total sample, while they were insignificant in kindergarten. A number of children who did not help denied that they had heard any noise. Denial was more frequent in kindergarten than in first grade ($\chi^2 = 6.80$, $df = 1$, $p < .01$) and within kindergarten slightly greater in the distress-responsibility group than in the other two groups combined ($\chi^2 = 3.60$, $df = 1$, $p < .10$).

Thus, assignment of responsibility enhanced helping behavior, particularly in first grade. Learning to take responsibility for others' welfare may often begin through assignment of responsibility to children by socializing agents. Whiting and Whiting (1969) found that children in cultures in which mothers report that they assign important tasks to them, such as baby tending, behave more altruistically, as measured by offers of help, support, and responsible suggestions, than children in cultures in which they are assigned fewer or less responsible tasks. Denial was probably due to children's fear of disapproval for not attempting to help, which was enhanced in the group where responsibility was focused on them.

---

jects that the other child was all right now and that on her way back she saw her returning to her classroom. In addition, the experimenter went into the adjoining room and returned, saying that the room was empty now, and repeating that the other child has returned to her classroom. First graders and children who helped by going into the adjoining room were debriefed by the experimenter's telling them that they had heard a tape recording because the experimenter wanted them to draw a picture of what they thought happened when they heard the sounds. All subjects then drew a picture of either what they thought had happened, or one of their choice. Afterwards all Ss played a game, and were asked about things they liked to do, in order to end the session on a positive note."—EDITOR

REFERENCE

WHITING, J. M. W., & WHITING, B. Children in six cultures. Unpublished manuscript, Harvard University, 1969.

31

Effects of Rule Structure and Training Method on the Adoption of a Self-imposed Standard

Robert M. Liebert,
Margaret Hanratty,
and Jae H. Hill

This is one of many studies in recent years that have investigated various determinants of whether or not a child who is left to reward himself or herself for performance will adopt a stringent or lenient standard. The sort of socially acquired self-control represented by avoiding excessive self-indulgence could perhaps be considered as akin to the prosocial behaviors such as those studied by Staub (see preceding article). Verbal structuring is shown to have strong effects in appealing to S's motives or clarifying the expectations one holds for their behavior.

Though the work was done at Vanderbilt University, Robert Liebert, the senior author, is now at the State University of New York at Stony Brook.

A person's ability to impose stringent standards upon himself in the absence of external constraints is an important aspect of socially acquired self-

This study was supported, in part, by U.S. Office of Education grant OEG–2–7–070002–3005. Grateful acknowledgment is due to the administrative officials and teachers of the Nashville Metropolitan School system, without whose generous cooperation this research would not have been possible. The assistance of Donald P. Leslie, Fran Owen, and Louise M. White is also acknowledged.

control. Society continually requires its members to monitor and evaluate their own performance and set standards for the self-administration of various gratifications. Thus, a number of recent social learning studies have examined the adoption of self-reward standards by children. For example, it has been shown that important variables in influencing children's self-imposed standards include the perceived ability of the training agent (Bandura & Whalen, 1966), consistency between the agent's instructions to the subject and the behavior he subsequently models (Mischel & Liebert, 1966), the prior nurturance of the training agent and social consequences to him (Bandura, Grusec, & Menlove, 1967), and the influence of discrepancies between successively modeled standards (McMains & Liebert, 1968).

The present experiment further investigated the effectiveness of several training variables upon children's subsequent patterns of self-reward in an unmonitored situation. A recent study from our laboratory (Liebert & Allen, 1967) suggested that highly structured rules are superior to unstructured ones in transmitting high standards. Further, modeling by the training agent and direct instruction to the child were found to be equally effective. In contrast, Bee and Colle (1967) found modeling of high standards to be a wholly ineffective training procedure, a phenomenon which they tentatively attributed to the disparity between the apparent ability levels of the model and the children in their score programs. However, it may also be important to note that these investigators omitted a statement of contingency or "deservingness" from the verbal rule structure provided by their training agent. That is, instead of saying "that's a good score, that deserves a chip," the agent simply stated "that's a good score" during training. Since the direction that a child receives in a self-control often includes the verbal structuring statement made by parents or teachers, it would seem critical that the most effective type of structure be identified and the relationship of these verbalizations to method of training be determined. Thus, the present study employed three levels of rule structure: one incorporated statements of social approval and deservingness (high rule structure), the second utilized social approval only (moderate rule structure), and the third involved an explicit statement of the rule but neither of these justificatory verbalizations (low rule structure). Based on the hypothesis that these structural elements have an additive influence upon children's subsequent adherence to standards,

Robert M. Liebert, Margaret Hanratty, and Jae H. Hill, "Effects of rule structure and training method on the adoption of a self-imposed standard," *Child Development*, 1969, *40*, 93–101. Reprinted by permission. © 1969 by the Society for Research in Child Development, Inc.

it was predicted that the effectiveness of training would vary directly with the degree of rule structure involved.

As in our previous studies (Liebert & Allen, 1967; Liebert & Ora, 1968), comparison was also made between direct instruction and modeling. To the extent that one critical difference between our earlier findings and those of Bee and Colle was the latter's use of moderate rule structure, an interaction would be anticipated between rule structure and method of training. Specifically, if degree of rule structure was a critical difference between the studies, modeling and direct instruction should be equally effective under the highest and lowest levels of rule structure (see Liebert & Allen, 1967), but direct instruction should prove superior to modeling under conditions of moderate rule structure.

In life situations, training in self-control is often conducted in situations where there are no immediate temptations to deviate. Subsequently, however, children are faced with a host of circumstances in which the training agent is absent, and the contingencies are arranged so that there is considerable payoff for violating the strict standards that one has previously been taught. Consider, for example, the child who is carefully admonished by his parents not to cheat in school. Later, in actual examination situations, the parent is absent, and, at the same time, "the chips are down" with respect to the highly profitable outcome which such violations may provide. Clearly, the parental training provided must have sufficient power to transfer to this new situation. Thus, in the present study, the incentive manipulation was introduced after the training procedure. This temporal sequence, coupled with the fact that the incentive was controlled by a person other than the training agent, served the dual purpose of decreasing the similarity between training and test situations and, at the same time, increasing the parallel between the experimental sequence and its counterparts in life situations.

METHOD

SUBJECTS

The Ss were 48 children, 24 boys and 24 girls (mean $CA = 7.5$) from the second grade of a public elementary school in a lower-middle-class area of Nashville. The same adult female and adult male served, respectively, as experimenter and training agent for all Ss.

APPARATUS

The apparatus was similar to the bowling game described by Liebert and Allen (1967), with a modified display of 10 score lights arranged in the familiar wedge shape of alley bowling. The score of 5 appeared four times in the top row, the score of 10 appeared three times in the next row, 15 appeared twice in the third row, and a single 20 constituted the bottom row. In addition, a green and a red signal light indicated "start" and "game over," respectively. The apparatus contained a panel of relay switches which produced a fixed program of scores for all trials. Although the pattern of scores obtained was unchanged from the training to the testing situation, no child questioned the representation of this device as a game of skill. In previous work the bowling game has proved to be very appealing to children of this age.

Additionally a button-operated token dispenser, which delivered a stainless steel coin the size of a penny, replaced the large bowl of plastic tokens used in our earlier research.

PROCEDURE

Each S was brought separately by E from his classroom to a mobile research laboratory on the school premises. En route, E indicated that she was a representative of a toy company and that a new bowling game was being tested to see how well children liked it. Upon reaching the trailer, S was introduced to the training agent (TA), who was standing in the doorway. The TA invited S to come inside to play the game, while E excused herself. The TA briefly described the operation of the bowling game and pointed out the token dispenser, explaining to the child that he could take tokens whenever he wished. The TA then presented the relevant experimental treatment. Afterward, the TA pushed a dummy doorbell button on the pretense of calling E. An experimental confederate, who recorded S's responses and monitored the entire procedure from the trailer's observation booth, actually signaled E to return by turning on a signal light mounted on top of the trailer. When E returned, the TA excused himself. Then E reset the game and informed the subject that "this time the chips[1] would be worth valuable prizes," emphasizing that the more tokens he acquired, the better his prize would be. She then pushed back a curtain, revealing an array of attractive prizes ranging in value from $0.05 to $10.00. The S was again reminded that he could take the tokens anytime he wished. The E further instructed the child to press the doorbell button when the red light came on, indicating that the game was over. The S was also told that after he pressed the button, E would return to count his tokens and exchange them for a prize. The E then left, and the child bowled alone. The E asked whether the child enjoyed the game and counted his tokens. Each child was then given one of the less valuable displayed prizes, asked not to discuss the game with his friends, and returned to his classroom.

DIRECT INSTRUCTION VERSUS MODELING

Half of the Ss of each sex received direct instruction while the other half observed the self-reward standard

---

[1] Our experience has suggested that "chips" is a more effective term than "tokens" for young children. Thus, the former is found in all quotations of direct discourse.

exhibited by the *TA*. For all *S*s, the stringent standard for self-reward was 20, the highest obtainable score. In the direct instruction procedure, the child played and was instructed by the *TA* to take a token whenever he received a score of 20. In the modeling conditions, *S* watched the *TA* bowl and reward himself only for scores of 20. In both conditions, training consisted of 20 trials of bowling with the same fixed pattern of scores in the order 10, 5, 15, 10, 20, 5, 15, 10, 20, 5, 15, 10, 5, 20, 15, 10, 15, 5, 20, 20.

RULE STRUCTURE

One-third of the *S*s in each of the above conditions were trained under conditions of high rule structure, one-third under conditions of moderate rule structure, and one-third under low rule structure. *High rule structure* was operationalized by the *TA*'s enthusiastic utterance for each score of 20 ("20, that's a good score, that deserves a chip") and his disparaging of all lower scores (e.g., "15, that's not a very good score, that doesn't deserve a chip"). Similarly, *moderate rule structure* was communicated in the agent's approbation of 20's ("20, that's a good score—[I'll] take a chip") and parallel disapproval of lower scores (e.g., "15, that's *not* a good score—[I won't] take a chip"). Finally, for *low rule structure*, the agent merely verbalized the score obtained and the appropriate action ("20—[I'll] take a chip" or "15—[I won't] take a chip").

DEPENDENT MEASURES

The measures collected were the number of tokens which were self-administered in the presence of scores of less than 20 and scores of 20 when *S* performed alone. The latter measure was used to assess the degree to which the legitimacy of rewarding oneself for scores of 20 had been transmitted, while the former was used to assess the degree to which *S*s deviated from this stringent standard.

RESULTS

Separate three-way analyses of variance were performed on *S*s' self-administration of tokens for scores of less than 20 and for scores of 20 in the unmonitored test situation. The mean self-reward scores for all groups on both measures are presented in Table 1.

The *S*s' self-reward for scores of less than 20 revealed that the predicted effect of rule structure was obtained ($F = 4.60$, $df = 2/36$, $p < .025$). No significant influence was found for method of training ($F < 1$) or sex ($F = 2.15$, $df = 1/36$). The training × rule structure interaction, which might have identified a critical difference between our previous work and that of Bee and Colle, did not approach significance ($F = 1.72$, $df = 2/36$), nor were any of the remaining interactions significant (all F's < 1).

As anticipated, children in the 12 groups did not differ significantly in their willingless to reward themselves for scores of 20. Thus, while a tendency was found for *S*s in the modeling and direct instruction conditions to differ on this measure ($F = 3.37$, $df = 1/36$, $p < .10$),

TABLE 1
MEANS AND STANDARD DEVIATIONS OF SELF-REWARD SCORES AS A FUNCTION OF RULE STRUCTURE, TRAINING METHOD, AND SEX OF SUBJECT

A. MEAN NUMBER OF TOKENS TAKEN FOR SCORES BELOW 20

Training		Rule Structure		
		High	Moderate	Low
Modeling:				
Male	Mean =	1.50	3.00	1.75
	SD =	2.60	3.08	1.48
Female	Mean =	1.00	3.00	4.50
	SD =	1.73	3.08	4.71
Direct instruction:				
Male	Mean =	0.00	0.25	4.75
	SD =	0.00	0.42	5.07
Female	Mean =	0.50	3.75	8.00
	SD =	0.50	5.39	4.18
Overall mean		0.75	2.50	4.75

B. MEAN NUMBER OF TOKENS TAKEN FOR SCORES OF 20

Training		Rule Structure		
		High	Moderate	Low
Modeling:				
Male	Mean =	5.50	4.75	6.75
	SD =	0.86	2.95	3.03
Female	Mean =	6.25	5.00	5.25
	SD =	2.17	0.00	1.78
Direct instruction:				
Male	Mean =	4.00	2.75	5.00
	SD =	2.34	2.88	0.00
Female	Mean =	4.75	5.00	5.25
	SD =	0.83	0.00	0.86
Overall mean		5.12	4.38	5.56

neither rule structure ($F = 1.28$) nor sex ($F < 1$) differentiated among the groups. And, apart from training × sex ($F = 1.04$), the F ratios for each of the interactions was less than 1. Additionally, virtually all of the children (93.7 per cent) engaged in some self-reward for scores of 20.

Since none of the interactions for either measure approached significance, the overall outcome of the present study is best seen through an examination of mean self-reward scores for main effects. From the marginal means in Table 1 it is apparent that, with respect to violation of the standard, the predicted linear relationship between rule structure and rule adherence was obtained. Individual comparisons were performed among the three rule structure groups. These directional tests revealed that, as anticipated, high rule structure produced fewer deviations than either low or moderate rule structure ($t = 3.11$, $p < .005$; and $t = 1.75$, $p < .05$, respectively). Further, moderate rule structure tended to be superior to low rule structure ($t = 1.36$, $p < .1$).

Table 1 also reveals that, for scores of 20, the tendency toward a training effect occurred in the direction of greater self-reward by *S*s who observed the *TA* than by those who received instruction from him. Apart from the low statistical reliability of this finding, it is interesting to note that the verbalizations of the two directly instructed *S*s who did not reward themselves at all for scores of 20 (both of whom were boys) suggest they had, in fact, learned the rule. Thus, on the appearance of his first 20 when alone, one of these *S*s exclaimed, "Oh boy, I deserve a chip" (although he did not take one), and the other *S* punctuated his first two superlative scores with "20!"—his only two audible utterances in the test situation.

DISCUSSION

The results of this experiment appear to provide strong support for the hypothesis that the verbal structuring of rules can play an important role in the transmission of self-imposed standards. As predicted, children's adherence to a stringent standard for self-reward varied directly with the degree of rule structure which had been provided by a training agent. Thus, the most potent statement of the rule involved expressions of both approval and deservingness, but even an expression of approval alone tended to be superior to mere directives in influencing *S*s' subsequent self-control.

Unlike previous investigations, the present experiment provided no material incentives for the subject or the model during training. Rather, the exchange value of the token rewards was established after all tuition had been provided and immediately prior to the test situation. That subjects adhered impressively to the stringent standard (75 per cent of the children in the high structure group never engaged in self-reward for scores of less than 20) in the absence of external agents and in the face of temptations not present during training seems to provide further evidence of the power of the procedures used in inculcating the type of behavioral change frequently labeled "internalization."

Bee and Colle (1967), using verbalizations comparable to the moderate rule structure employed in the present study, found direct instruction to be superior to modeling procedures in influencing children's self-imposed standards. However, contrary to one prediction derived from their results, no evidence for the superiority of direct instruction or for a training × structure interaction appeared. Thus, at least in the absence of a sharp disparity between the apparent ability level of the child and of the training agent, modeling appears to be no less powerful than direct instruction. It would be interesting to examine systematically the influence of very capable or very high-status persons to determine whether these factors interact with the method of training which social agents provide.

Further research is underway to examine such possibilities.

Previous research has indicated that, in the absence of any training, children may be reticent to engage in any self-reward (Bee & Colle, 1967) or show no discernible patterning in their self-administered gratifications (Bee & Colle, 1967; Liebert & Ora, 1968). It is therefore important to note that virtually all subjects in the present study rewarded themselves for some or all scores of 20 when alone and that no differences among the groups appeared on this measure. Further, the relatively deviant children exposed to the lowest level of rule structure still rewarded themselves more in the presence of the five scores of 20 which they obtained than in the presence of the remaining 15 scores combined. Thus, even the weakest manipulation employed here may be sufficient to instill rudimentary self-control.

Overall, the findings of this study seem to be a consistent extension of our previous examination of the presence or absence of explanatory verbalizations (Liebert & Allen, 1967), and of studies suggesting the importance of rule structure in enhancing the effects of punishment (Walters & Cheyne, 1966) and training in self-criticism (Aronfreed, 1963; Aronfreed, Cutick, & Fagan, 1963). Taken together, these researches provide striking evidence of the importance of verbal communication for influencing children's adoption of self-imposed standards. Since the effectiveness of socialization is often measured by the liberalness of criteria which persons use in their self-regulation of rewards and punishments, identifying the antecedents of this type of socially acquired self-control seems to have particular importance.

REFERENCES

ARONFREED, J. The effects of experimental socialization paradigms upon two moral responses to transgression. *Journal of Abnormal and Social Psychology,* 1963, *66,* 437–448.

ARONFREED, J., CUTICK, R. A., & FAGAN, S. A. Cognitive structure, punishment, and nurturance in the experimental induction of self-criticism. *Child Development,* 1963, *34,* 281–294.

BANDURA, A., GRUSEC, J., & MENLOVE, F. Some social determinants of self-monitoring reinforcement systems. *Journal of Personality and Social Psychology,* 1967, *5,* 449–455.

BANDURA, A., & WHALEN, C. The influence of antecedent on reinforcement and divergent modeling cues on patterns of self-reward. *Journal of Personality and Social Psychology,* 1966, *3,* 373–382.

BEE, H. L., & COLLE, H. A. The origins of standards of excellence: modeling vs. direct reinforcement. Paper read at biennial meeting of the Society for Research in Child Development, New York, March, 1967.

LIEBERT, R. M., & ALLEN, M. K. Effects of rule structure and reward magnitude on the acquisition and adoption of self-reward criteria. *Psychological Reports,* 1967, *21,* 445–452.

LIEBERT, R. M., & ORA, J. P. Children's adoption of self-reward patterns: incentive level and method of transmission. *Child Development,* 1968, *39,* 537–544.

McMAINS, M. J., & LIEBERT, R. M. The influence of discrepancies between successively modeled self-reward criteria on the adoption of a self-imposed stand-

ard. *Journal of Personality and Social Psychology,* 1968, *8,* 166–171.

MISCHEL, W., & LIEBERT, R. M. Effects of discrepancies between observed and imposed reward criteria on their acquisition and transmission. *Journal of Personality and Social Psychology,* 1966, *3,* 45–53.

WALTERS, R. H., & CHEYNE, J. A. Some parameters influencing the effects of punishment on social behavior. Paper presented at the annual meeting of the American Psychological Association, New York, 1966.

32

Social Influence
as a Function
of Stimulus Ambiguity
at Three Age Levels [1]

KENNETH L. HOVING, NORMAN HAMM,
AND PAULA GALVIN

This study deals with a type of conformity: the responsiveness of children and adolescents to peer group standards or beliefs. We assign the article to Section V because it deals with influence of the face-to-face group of classmates, even though the classmates were not physically present when the children took their turns as research Ss.

Social influence studies on perceptual judgments have a long history in social psychology. The studies of Muzafir Sherif reported in The Psychology of Social Norms *(Harper, 1936) are cited in most introductory texts. These studies utilized a situation where the ambiguity was maximal. The amount of perceived motion of a stationary dot of light was studied in relation to the judgments of others. Perceived motion is a normally present illusion (the autokinetic effect) in the circumstances used.*

The classic study in which non-ambiguous stimuli were used was done by Solomon Asch (1952). He, Richard Crutchfield, and others have done many similar studies since then. The work reported here is a departure from most in that the degree

of ambiguity is varied, as are the ages of the subjects.

Hoving is at Kent State University in Ohio, where the study was done. Hamm is now at the University of Nebraska at Omaha.

Several recent articles have reported a nonmonotonic relationship between conformity and age. [A monotonic relation is one in which there is an increase (or decrease) in one variable for every increase in the other variable. In simple terms then, a nonmonotonic relation is one in which there is not consistency in the direction of change in the one variable as the other changes.—Editor] Costanzo and Shaw (1966) found that conformity increased from ages 7–9 to ages 11–13 and then decreased. Iscoe, Williams, and Harvey (1963) also reported increasing conformity from ages 7 through 12 in both boys and girls. Girls then decreased in conformity by age 15, but conformity in boys increased at least through age 15.

These findings are in marked contrast to those reported by Berenda (1950), who found significantly less conformity in a group of 10- to 13-year-old children than in a group of 7- to 10-year-old children. Hoving (1964) also found more conformity in second-grade (age 7) than fourth-grade (age 9) children. Hoving, Hamm, and Roehl (1967) have suggested that differences in task ambiguity may be responsible for these conflicting results. The tasks used in these studies differed in terms of the clarity with which the incorrect alternative chosen by the group differed from the objectively correct alternative. When the group's choice is clearly incorrect the subject is placed in a conflict situation in which he must either agree with the group and choose the same obviously false alternative or choose the objectively correct alternative and disagree with the group's choice. If, however, there is no objectively correct alternative and/or the subject does not perceive any difference between the group's choice and the objectively correct choice, no conflict is perceived. Thus, the subject's choice behavior should differ as a function of whether or not he perceives a conflict between objective reality and the group's choice. When conflict is perceived by the subject, it is assumed that there is an increasing tendency to choose the objectively correct alternative with increasing age. Thus, conformity should be negatively related to age on tasks that produce conflict for the subject. However, if no conflict or only minimal conflict is produced by the task (because of its high am-

[1] P. Galvin was supported under Grant NSF GY–2485 from the National Science Foundation. The authors wish to thank the administrators, teachers, and students of the Ravenna, Ohio, school system for their assistance and participation in this study.

Kenneth L. Hoving, Norman Hamm, and Paula Galvin, "Social influence as a function of stimulus ambiguity at three age levels," *Developmental Psychology*, 1969, *1*, 631–636. Reprinted by permission.

biguity), the subject may be increasingly influenced by the group's choice. Thus, conformity should be positively related to age on tasks that produce little or no conflict.

The tasks employed by Costanzo and Shaw (1966) and Iscoe et al. (1963) seem to be at least partially ambiguous and hence involved only minimal conflict for the subject. The tasks employed by Berenda (1950) and Hoving (1964) were, by contrast, clearly unambiguous and hence presented a clear-cut conflict situation to the subject. This difference in the amount of conflict produced may account for the apparent contradiction in the results of these studies.

The present study attempted to test the hypothesis that conformity behavior increases with age on tasks that produce minimal conflict, whereas conformity behavior decreases with age on tasks that produce conflict. Three levels of task ambiguity were employed at three grade levels in an attempt to evaluate this hypothesis. It was assumed that task stimuli that were maximally ambiguous would reveal the positive relationship between conformity and age, whereas the unambiguous stimuli would show the negative relationship between conformity and age.

METHOD

SUBJECTS

Subjects were 108 public school children from Grades 2, 5, and 8, equally divided as to sex and grade level. In addition, 173 subjects were used in the preexperimental procedure to empirically assess task difficulty. The subjects were drawn from a semiurban community that is largely lower middle class in terms of socioeconomic status. All of the subjects present in the classes during the period of data collecting who were at appropriate grade level for age were used.

APPARATUS

All equipment was housed in an 8×19 foot mobile trailer. A partition with a one-way mirror divided the trailer into an experimental and a control room. A modification of the Crutchfield procedure was employed. Three individual cubicles, a projection screen, and earphones were located in the experimental room. The control room contained a slide projector, electronic timers, a master control panel, and a two-way sound system and tape recorder.

Each subject's cubicle included a control box with a large green light, and a set of six small lamps arranged in three rows and two columns. A button was located beneath each column that when depressed, activated the light immediately above it and a corresponding light on the master response panel in the control room. The experimenter controlled the lights in the other two rows, although the procedure was such that the subject believed these reflected the responses of the two other subjects.

PREEXPERIMENTAL PROCEDURE

In order to objectively determine the ambiguity of a given stimulus, preexperimental sessions were conducted in classrooms located at the elementary and junior high schools from which the subjects were drawn. Preexperimental groups, of about 30 subjects each, were required to make judgments on 4 training and 44 experimental slides. Subjects were asked to determine which of two sides of a slide contained the greater number of dots. Each slide contained a varying number of white dots superimposed on a black field and was divided by a thin white line into two parts labeled Side One and Side Two. Answers were recorded on IBM answer sheets by the fifth and eighth graders; second-grade subjects circled the number of their choice on a mimeographed sheet.

Stimulus ambiguity was defined in terms of the percentage of error that the preexperimental group made when judging each of the 44 experimental slides. The unambiguous stimulus was selected on the basis of the extremely low error rate made by subjects at each grade level in the preexperimental session. More than 98% of the judgments were correct on this stimulus under noninfluence conditions. The partially ambiguous stimulus was correctly judged 80% of the time. The totally ambiguous stimulus was one in which both judgments available to the subject were equally correct, since both parts of the slide contained 15 dots. The preexperimental groups chose each side of this stimulus approximately equally in the three grade levels employed. The incorrect side contained 7 dots in the unambiguous condition and 16 in the partially ambiguous condition. One side of each slide always contained 15 dots.

PROCEDURE

In the experiment proper each of the three levels of stimulus ambiguity was presented eight times, with the side with the greater number of dots located on the right four times and on the left four times in the unambiguous and partially ambiguous series to correct for position effects. Twelve of these 24 slides, 4 at each level, were designated as test or influence slides in which the subject answered last. The subject was presented lights that indicated that the other subjects present had picked the objectively incorrect alternative on the unambiguous and partially ambiguous series and one of the equally correct alternatives on the ambiguous series. The remaining 12 slides were termed controls and were identical to the influence slides with the exception that on these trials the subject answered first. In addition, 6 slides containing other dot combinations were included. It was hoped that these slides would increase the overall credibility of the task. The slide sequence consisted of 4 training and 30 experimental slides. All subjects received the same randomly ordered sequence of slides. Each stimulus was presented for 4 seconds for each trial to reduce the subject's tendency to count the dots.

Three children of the same sex were escorted by the experimenter from their classroom to the trailer and seated in individual cubicles. A set of standardized instructions was read concurrently with the showing of four training slides. The slides were projected onto a screen located on the forward wall of the experimental room. The instructions given following the training sequence were as follows:

> On all the following pictures I want you to press the button of the side that has the most dots—button #1 if side one has the most or button #2 if side two has the most. From now on you will be able to see which choices your classmates made. If you look on your boxes, you will see three rows of lights. The bottom row belongs to each of you because it lights up when you press a button. Now let's talk for a minute about the top two rows of lights on your boxes. [The experimenter labels the top two rows with the names of the other two children present. He then explains to each subject individually that he will be able to tell how his other classmates answered by observing which light is on. The subject is then questioned with examples to determine if he understands the procedure.]

> So on all the rest of the pictures you will be able to see how the others have answered. Remember to wait for your green light before you answer. The green light tells you that it is your turn to answer. Watch the screen very carefully because you will see each picture for only a few seconds.

> Before we begin I would like you to put on the earphones that are setting in front of you. Make sure they fit comfortably. Now everyone look up at the screen.

During the experiment, a masking sound was fed through the earphones to minimize apparatus noise and subject collaboration. The experimenter manipulated the apparent choices of each peer with a master control panel; the panel also permitted the experimenter to monitor the subject's answer on each trial.

RESULTS

Two measures of social influence and an error rate measure were computed for each subject for each level of ambiguity. One measure of social influence was determined by totaling the frequency with which the subject's judgments were the same as the reference group on the influence trials. This measure of social influence is artificially inflated as it reflects errors in judgment as well as social influence. The relationship of this measure of social influence to age is graphically shown in Figure 1. The identifying numbers on the figure legends refer to the number of dots on each side of the slides used to measure social influence. The data were subjected to an analysis of variance procedure that revealed that the magnitude of social influence varied with the ambiguity of the task ($F = 235.59$, $df = 2/204$, $p < .01$), and that the magnitude of social influence at the different levels of ambiguity depended in part on the age of the subjects ($F = 11.78$, $df = 4/204$, $p < .01$). A Newman-

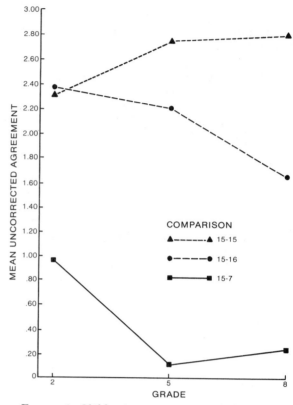

FIGURE 1. *Children's mean uncorrected agreement scores on tasks of varying ambiguity.*

Keuls test (Winer, 1962, p. 309) was computed on the differences in conformity on the ambiguous trials as a function of grade level. These tests revealed that the difference between the second and eighth grade was significant ($q = 4.81$, $r = 3/204$, $p < .01$) as was the difference between the second and fifth grade ($q = 3.63$, $r = 2/204$, $p < .05$). The difference between the fifth and eighth grade, however, was not significant.

Iscoe et al. (1963) have shown that the apparent relationship of social influence to age can be markedly distorted if error rate is not considered. Error rate was defined in the present study as the frequency with which the subject picked the side of the slide with fewer rather than more dots on the unambiguous (15–7) slide and the partially ambiguous (15–16) slide on noninfluence trials. Error rate is obviously much more difficult to define for the maximally ambiguous task (15–15). Errors were arbitrarily determined on these trials by tabulating the frequency with which the subject picked the same side under noninfluence conditions as the group chose in the influence condition. For example, on the 15–15 slide, if the group chose side one under influence conditions, an error on the slide was tabulated if the subject picked this same side when the same control 15–15 slide was shown.

Quite clearly this is a severe error measure. An analysis of variance of error rate data revealed that error rates differed as a function of ambiguity ($F = 211.59$, $df = 2/204$, $p < .01$) as well as age ($F = 5.138$, $df = 2/202$, $p < .01$). Error rate decreased with age at two levels of ambiguity as is shown in Figure 2. This figure also reveals that the greatest frequency of errors occurred on the most ambiguous slides with fewest occurring on the unambiguous slides.

A measure of social influence adjusted for error rate was also calculated. The number of errors made by each subject, calculated in the manner just described, was subtracted from his uncorrected conformity score for each level of stimulus ambiguity. This measure permits the assessment of peer influence with the differential error rate for the different difficulty levels at each age taken into account. The relationship of this measure of influence to ambiguity across age is portrayed in Figure 3. The analysis of variance of these data reveals that the magnitude of social influence differs significantly ($F = 21.9$, $df = 2/204$, $p < .01$) with the ambiguity of the task. The significant interaction of Ambiguity × Age ($F = 6.68$, $df = 4/204$, $p < .01$) indicates that children of different ages are differentially influenced by their peers depending on the ambiguity of the task.

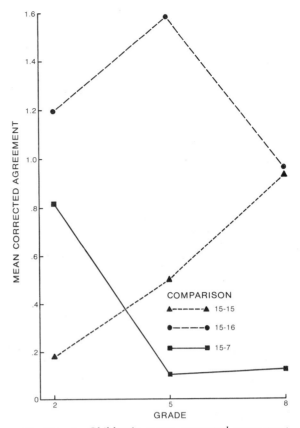

FIGURE 3. *Children's mean corrected agreement scores on tasks of varying ambiguity.*

To test the significance of the functions summarized graphically in Figure 3, a Newman-Keuls test on the corrected scores was computed. In the unambiguous condition, differences between the second and fifth grades ($q = 3.96$, $r = 3/204$, $p < .05$) and between the second and eighth grades ($q = 3.66$, $r = 2/204$, $p < .01$) were statistically significant. No difference was found between the fifth and eighth grades. In the partially ambiguous condition, only the difference between the fifth and eighth grade ($q = 3.35$, $r = 3/204$, $p < .05$) was significant. Neither the second and eighth grades nor the second and fifth grades differed significantly. In the totally ambiguous condition, the difference in conformity between the second and eighth grades was significant ($q = 4.73$, $r = 3/204$, $p < .01$), but the differences between the second and fifth and fifth and eighth grades were not significant.

DISCUSSION

The results clearly support the primary hypothesis of the present study. Conformity behavior decreases with age on tasks when the alternative chosen by the group clearly differs from the objec-

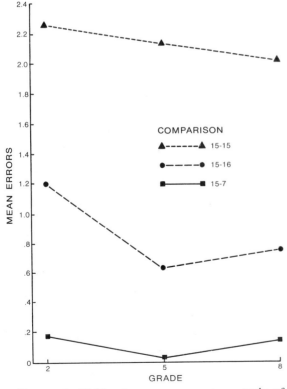

FIGURE 2. *Children's mean error rate on tasks of varying ambiguity under noninfluence conditions.*

tively correct alternative. This was shown by the line labeled 15–7 in Figures 1 and 3. Conformity behavior on tasks that are ambiguous and hence produce little, if any, conflict increases in a positive fashion with age. This was graphically demonstrated by the line labeled 15–15 in Figures 1 and 3.

These results are reflected in both the uncorrected and corrected measures of social influence. However, a comparison of Figures 1 and 3 clearly reveals the necessity of carefully specifying the criterion measures employed. In the present case, the correction for errors markedly changed the relative position of the functions describing the relationship of social influence in ambiguous tasks across age. The relationship of conformity to age on the ambiguous trials was basically the same whether a correction for errors is applied or not. This is important as the correction used for these trials is severe and in part arbitrary. The method of calculating errors for the totally ambiguous condition is one that considers a choice of the same alternative in the noninfluence condition as is chosen by the group in the influence condition as an error.

The high frequency of conformity behavior on the partially ambiguous task, Slide 15–16, may in part be explained in terms of the method used to correct for errors. Subjects at all three grade levels showed greater corrected agreement with the incorrect choice of the reference group in the partially ambiguous task than in either the totally ambiguous or unambiguous tasks. When the correction for errors is not employed, as in Figure 1, we find the level of agreement with the reference group between that found in the totally ambiguous and unambiguous situations. Quite probably, it is the elevated error rate of the totally ambiguous condition, shown in Figure 2, that accounts for the higher corrected level of agreement found in the partially ambiguous condition.

The higher corrected agreement score on the partially ambiguous condition at Grade 5 poses some difficulties since the total agreement score portrayed in Figure 1 reveals no elevation of agreement at Grade 5. However, an inspection of the error rate portrayed in Figure 2 reveals a lower error rate at this grade than at either of the other grades. This may be due to the greater difficulty of the task for subjects at Grade 2 and boredom with the task at Grade 8. In either case, when the lower error rate at Grade 5 is subtracted from the overall agreement score, we find the elevated corrected agreement score obtained at Grade 5. It is also possible that this elevation at Grade 5 may be the result of sampling error.

The motivational base responsible for conformity is commonly accepted as being at least twofold.

Deutsch and Gerard (1955), for example, have proposed a distinction between normative and informational forms of social influence. The former is thought to be controlled primarily by a need or desire for group acceptance and/or a desire to avoid disapproval, whereas informational conformity is governed by a desire for information or a desire to be correct. The operation of these motivational systems is thought to vary with the ambiguity of the task and the age of the child. The interaction of these motivational changes with task ambiguity across age may be used to tentatively account for the present results.

The need to be correct and the need for peer approval are both thought to increase in strength with age. In addition, the kinds of behavior that produce peer approval change with age. Mere agreement may be sufficient to gain peer approval only when it is compatible with the demands of objective correctness. Moreover, with age, children are increasingly able to answer questions correctly and to determine if a correct answer is possible.

These factors, in combination, may be used to at least partially account for the findings of the present study. The negative relationship between conformity and age on unambiguous tasks may be explained in the following fashion: In unambiguous tasks, the subject's need to be correct and need for peer approval are placed in direct conflict. If the subject agrees with the group to gain peer approval, he fails to satisfy his need to be correct. In the younger subjects neither need is great but apparently peer approval can be gained at this age by agreeing with the group even if the group's choice is obviously incorrect. This, when coupled with minimal opposition from the need to be correct, results in relatively large amounts of conformity at younger age levels. In older subjects we find a much stronger need to be correct coupled with the subject's presumed inability to gain peer approval for agreement when the apparent choice of the group is obviously incorrect. Hence the minimal conformity at older ages on unambiguous tasks. It is important to note that it is the decrease in the ability of older subjects to gain peer approval for agreement when the group's choice is clearly wrong, plus the increased strength of the need to be correct, that is believed to be responsible for the decrease in conformity behavior with age on unambiguous items.

The positive relationship between age and conformity on ambiguous tasks is also thought to be due to the increasing need to be correct and to gain peer approval, which occurs with age. The child's past history of reinforcement is presumed to result in his agreeing with the choices of others when in doubt as to the correct answer. Optimal satisfaction of both motivational systems occurs if the subject agrees with the choices of others in ambiguous situations. This optimizes his chances of being correct and produces maximal peer approval. As both the normative and informational motivational systems increase in strength with age, we expect and indeed do find a positive relationship between conformity and age on tasks that produce minimal or no conflict.

The frequency of agreement with the nonveridical choice of the reference group in the partially ambiguous condition is probably a function of an intermediate level of conflict produced by this task. Agreement with the group choice in the partially ambiguous condition is compatible with the subject's need for peer approval, and yet the task is sufficiently ambiguous to reduce the potential negating influence of the need to be correct. The need to be correct may motivate high levels of conformity in ambiguous situations as the subject follows the group in the hopes of being correct, whereas it motivates minimal conformity in unambiguous situations, as here the subject is motivated to choose the objectively correct alternative.

REFERENCES

BERENDA, R. W. *The influence of the group on the judgments of children.* New York: Kings Crown Press, 1950.

COSTANZO, P. R., & SHAW, M. E. Conformity as a function of age level. *Child Development,* 1966, *37,* 967–975.

DEUTSCH, M., & GERARD, H. B. A study of normative and informational social influence upon individual judgment. *Journal of Abnormal and Social Psychology,* 1955, *51,* 629–636.

HOVING, K. L. Some parameters of yielding in children. Paper presented at the meeting of the Midwestern Psychological Association, St. Louis, April 1964.

HOVING, K. L., HAMM, N. H., & ROEHL, K. Conformity in children as a function of adult vs. peer influence, hypothetical vs. real models, and degree of perceptual ambiguity. Paper presented at the meeting of the Society for Research in Child Development, New York, March 1967.

ISCOE, I., WILLIAMS, M., & HARVEY, J. Modification of children's judgments by a simulated group technique: A normative developmental study. *Child Development,* 1963, *34,* 963–978.

WINER, B. J. *Statistical principles in experimental design.* New York: McGraw-Hill, 1962.

33

Innovating Classroom Practices to Support Achievement Motivation and Ego-Development

RONALD LIPPITT,
ROBERT FOX,
AND RICHARD SCHMUCK

This paper reflects the influence of the University of Michigan's Research Center for Group Dynamics. Kurt Lewin founded the center with Ronald Lippitt and others at MIT (The Massachusetts Institute of Technology). After Lewin's death it was moved to Michigan, where Lippitt was associated with it until he and Floyd Mann founded the Center for Research on Utilization of Scientific Knowledge. Both centers are part of Michigan's huge Institute for Social Research.

Dr. Fox directs the University School in Ann Arbor. Run by the University of Michigan for local children, the school is maintained for purposes of teacher training and research. Fox's experiences at the school are doubtless reflected in the paper's sensitivity to the complex situation the educator faces when desiring to try something new.

Dr. Schmuck is at Temple University, teaching social psychology as it applies to group processes in the classroom and school.

The reader who is interested in further material about the implications of group dynamics for education will want to consult the book Learning in Social Settings, *edited by Matthew W. Miles and W. W. Charters, Jr. (Allyn and Bacon, 1970).*

Utilizing the resources of the behavioral sciences to improve classroom teaching practices is an exciting challenge. At least four types of resources are available as are a variety of ways of using them: relevant research knowledge; concepts and conceptual frameworks; diagnostic tools and methods; and scientists themselves as consultants and collaborators.

These four types of resource can be mobilized to stimulate and support an improvement process in several ways. Such patterns of improvement can be roughly classified into two types. In one the needed resources of new knowledge and practice are "imported" into the classroom and the school system from outside. In the second type of pattern the needed knowledge and resources are developed and mobilized within the classroom itself and utilized to make desired improvements. Let us look briefly at examples of these two patterns.

"IMPORTING" THE NEEDED RESOURCES

Through reading or a course or a consultant, the teacher learns about research findings and theory. In order for the materials to be useful, the teacher must perceive the information as relevant to the teaching problems with which she is coping and must be able to derive from it realistic ideas about possible action. The process of making research findings meaningful to the person who teaches has been very poorly developed in the field of education, as contrasted to such more advanced fields of research utilization as agricultural practice, medical practice, and industrial practice. In another "importing" process new educational practices developed in one setting become visible, accessible, and are adopted or adapted by another teacher. This progress requires that innovations be identified by some scanning procedure, be evaluated to eliminate those not worthy of dissemination, and then be communicated in an appropriate way which makes it possible for other teachers to understand and to adapt a new practice in their own teaching situation. One of the tragedies of American education is that so many creative teaching practice inventions consistent with the best behavioral science knowledge remain invisible and unevaluated.

INTERNAL RESOURCE DEVELOPMENT

In the second pattern of improvement the teacher is helped to collect data about her own class-

Ronald Lippitt, Robert Fox, and Richard Schmuck, "Innovating classroom practices to support achievement motivation and ego-development," in *Behavioral science frontiers in education,* ed. Eli Michael Bower and William G. Hollister. Copyright © 1967 by John Wiley & Sons, Inc. Reprinted by permission.

room situation, to interpret the findings as a diagnosis of needs and potentialities for change, and to derive designs for improvement from the diagnosis of her own classroom situation. In other words, instead of importing knowledge from outside, she is involved in creating knowledge and utilizing it for designing improvement in her practice. Typically, in this pattern, resources from outside are required to help in the process. These resources are either diagnostic tools, or a consulting scientist, or both.

The sections which follow contain the results of our experiences in using both of these patterns to help a group of elementary and secondary classroom teachers to stimulate achievement motivation and enhance the ego-development of pupils.

DIAGNOSING THE ACHIEVEMENT AND EGO-DEVELOPMENT NEEDS AND OPPORTUNITIES IN THE CLASSROOM

A pupil with high ego-strength can be characterized in two general ways. First, he has developed cognitive skills and intellectual coping mechanisms through successful classroom learning experiences. Such a pupil has mastered, without an overload of anxiety, most of the academic challenges presented to him. He is able to utilize effectively his intellectual capacities. When a child is not utilizing his academic potential in classroom performance, it is a poor situation for ego-development. In many such cases, energy is being drained off by excessive anxiety, worry, and hostile feelings, so that the pupil is not free to utilize his abilities. He is blocked or distracted or focusing on solving other types of problems.

A second characteristic of ego-strength is affective integration. Such a pupil has positive feelings about himself and others, emanating from personal feelings of strength and worthwhileness. He feels only moderate tension when relating with peers and teachers in the school setting and perceives the significant people in his life as being supportive and encouraging of his school performance and conduct.

These two aspects of ego-strength, the cognitive and the affective, are interrelated. For instance, if a pupil experiences anxiety in his relations with peers and teachers, we find that much of his attention and energy will be directed toward coping with fears and reducing tension. Such pupils often have negative feelings about themselves and perform more poorly in their school work than their intelligence levels indicate they are capable of. On the other hand, pupils who experience acceptance and support from peers and teachers often approach academic tasks with the same mobiliza-

tion of energy, effort, and expectations of adequacy and success they have experienced in these relationships. Such pupils' positive views of themselves facilitate their academic learning and the development of cognitive skills.

Considerable classroom research indicates that a pupil's interpersonal relationships condition the development of these two facets of ego-strength. Specifically, the research indicates that pupils who relate successfully to their peers and who feel relaxed and comfortable in the presence of teachers, are more likely to utilize their intellectual and emotional resources in building a strong ego. Furthermore, our research suggests that we can identify, explain, and create classroom groups with atmospheres conducive to ego-building. Teachers will be able neither to influence their pupils constructively nor to teach them academic subject matter without considering the classroom processes that offer opportunity for ego-development and enhancement. Since such problems and issues of interpersonal relations in the classroom are basic to ego-development, a teacher needs to master a style of approaching and solving these problems. One purpose of this chapter is to illustrate ways of approaching such a challenge.

First, the teacher must work toward understanding the network of interpersonal relationships in her classroom. Children attribute to each of their classmates levels of social power or ability to influence others which vary from very high to very low. Moreover, being able to do things well at school and being liked often constitute important sources of social power. Pupils assess the status of their classmates on these variables quickly at the beginning of the school year, and they maintain their judgments with relatively little variation throughout the school year.

However, even though pupils show considerable agreement when rating their peers on liking, influence, and expertness, classroom groups do differ considerably one from the other on how much consensus there is about these dimensions. In some classrooms, for instance, interpersonal acceptance and rejection are narrowly focused. Such classrooms are characterized by a large number of pupils who agree in giving high status and acceptance to only a small cluster of their classmates on a sociometric test. Along with this narrow focus on a small number of pupils, many other pupils are neglected entirely. On the other hand, some classrooms are characterized by a wide range of positive and negative choices, that is, little or no focus of interpersonal acceptance and rejection upon a few members. Such groups are distinguished by a more equal distribution of sociometric choices, by no distinct subgroups whose members receive the large proportion of preferences, and by few entirely neglected pupils.

Our research shows that classroom peer groups characterized by a wide spread of liking relations among members have positive emotional climates and that both peer group liking structure and pupil involvement in the classroom group help to fashion a pupil's perception of himself in the group. Furthermore, the research shows that this pupil evaluation of self in relation to others is associated with his attitudes toward self and school in general and that a pupil's perception of his place in the peer group, high status or low, is related also to his utilization of his ability in academic learning.

Therefore, the teacher who hopes to enhance both the cognitive skills and the affective integration of his pupils will want to learn more about the interpersonal relationships in his classroom. He will ask such questions as: Can a rejected pupil be helped to develop skills of relating to his classmates so that he will be more accepted; so that he will be listened to when he has an idea to contribute; so that he will be given support rather than negative feedback? Can the intellectual capabilities of a bright child with low social power be channeled in such a way as to be seen by his peers as resources for the group?

Besides being interested in the problems of individual pupils, the teacher who is attempting to enhance the ego-strength of his pupils looks for ways in which the general atmosphere of the classroom can become more supportive of wholesome group interaction and learning. Can pupils be taught to seek out the resources of their classmates, to be sensitive to the needs of others who may be less well-endowed than they, and to understand the effects of their own behavior on others? If the classroom atmosphere takes on some of these characteristics, it becomes a supportive setting for ego-development of all pupils.

The teacher's first step in trying to enhance pupil ego-strength through improving interpersonal relations in the classroom involves sensitivity to the dynamics of pupil behavior. The sensitive teacher learns to become objective and analytic in observing pupil behavior in the classroom and on the playground. He perceives clues of pupil aggression, underlying hostility, and negative attitudes toward academic work. He is aware of the friendship patterns in the classroom, the cliques that are influencing pupil activity, and the feelings of ostracized pupils. Perhaps he perceives that although his pupils are controlled and orderly in his presence, they are uncontrolled and disorganized in the gym and on the playground. In any case, the astute teacher is diagnostic, always attending, as best he

can, to the dynamics of pupil behavior and classroom interaction. He knows that careful observations of pupil behavior are necessary for the planning of constructive classroom change.

A teacher often finds simple diagnostic tools helpful in getting an accurate picture of a pupil's level of ego-strength, his feelings, attitudes, interpersonal relations, and academic performance. In other words, she seeks to assess the state of affairs in her classroom by having the pupils answer questions, write down their ideas, and express their feelings. Thus, she supplements the general research knowledge gathered in the study of other classrooms. Teachers have found it helpful to use such objective diagnostic inventories as, sociometric tests, attitude questionnaires, self-ratings, and achievement tests. During this diagnosis, the teacher asks: "What is it I wish to know?" Considering the answer to this question, the teacher may employ diagnostic tools similar to the following examples.

AFFECTIVE EGO-STRENGTH

Questionnaires are used often to give the teacher information concerning a pupil's emotional or affective valuations of himself. There are several types of inventories for assessing self-feelings, including the attitude survey, the sentence completion test, and the so-called "pie technique."

An example of an attitude survey item regarding personal work habits is:

How hard would you say that you are working on school work. (Circle one)
A. Very hard
B. Pretty hard
C. Not very hard
D. Not hard at all

A sentence completion item of the same general character is:

When I am doing school work, I feel _____.

Or, in measuring different aspects of feelings about self:

I like myself sometimes because _____.
When I think about other boys and girls and then think about myself, I feel _____.

The "pie technique" has been used as follows:

The plus stands for aspects about yourself that you like, the minuses for things you don't like. Place a check under the circle that stands for how you are usually.

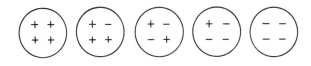

COGNITIVE EGO-STRENGTH

The teacher can assess the relationship between a child's classroom performance and his intelligence and in so doing, get one indication of his cognitive ego-strength. One procedure for doing this is as follows: the teacher first ranks all students according to their academic performance in her class. Then, she independently ranks them in order of their I.Q. score or some other measure of intelligence. The difference between positions on these rankings gives some indication of the child's utilization of intellectual potential. If a pupil ranks higher on intelligence than on achievement, he may be said to be underutilizing. If a pupil ranks higher on achievement than on intelligence, he is said to be more fully utilizing. If the class is made up of many underutilizers, the teacher should focus on improving the interpersonal atmosphere—at least as far as these underutilizers are concerned.

CLASSROOM SOCIAL RELATIONS

Sociometric questions are designed to give the teacher some indication of the social relationship among pupils in the class. He may ask pupils to select what peers they (1) like best, (2) like to work with, (3) like to play with, (4) think are smartest, (5) think like them about school, (6) like least, and so forth. In this manner, the teacher can see which pupils are friendly with one another and which are likely to make compatible work partners. In addition to getting information for grouping, she can sum and rank individual choices to find out who the peer leaders are, whether or not there are cliques, and what the general evaluation patterns are.

The major purpose of collecting such diagnostic information is to gain "leverage for thinking" creatively about the needs and potentialities of the unique teaching-learning situation of this particular classroom group.

MOVING FROM DIAGNOSIS TO ACTION

Using diagnostic information and interpretations to design a program of teaching action is a matter of disciplined professional skill. Actually the process of adopting or developing innovation in teaching practice is quite different from that in such professional fields as industry, medicine, and agriculture. A major difference is that the development or adopting of a new practice in teaching activity usually requires some re-orientation of values and attitudes as well as of behavioral skills. Such consideration of values and attitudes is not necessary in fields where the adoption of a new machine or a new fertilizer or new drug exerts no new requirements of value confrontation and skill development. Let us consider some illustrations of how a teacher can move from diagnosis to action in the classroom.

COPING WITH A COLLUSION OF IGNORANCE

A junior high teacher discovered from an analysis of his questionnaire data that the majority of the students in the classroom perceived that most of their fellow students looked down on enthusiastic participation in classroom discussion and the energetic accomplishment of homework assignments. The same questionnaire data indicated that a majority of the students would like to be more actively involved in classroom discussion and interaction with the teacher but perceived that their fellow students would be negative about this. As he reviewed these data, the teacher decided to share the information with the classroom group as a basis for discussion and mutual enlightenment as long as confidentiality was respected in the presentation of the data. He recognized, however, that there might be some embarrassment and resistance in getting into discussion. Therefore, he decided to consult with three or four of the class leaders about presenting the information and getting their collaboration in helping lead the discussion. He found them very interested in the data, ready to accept it as valid, and ready to help lead a discussion which would move the group toward a norm of enlightened participation rather than collusive withholding. With the leadership of the influential peers, the class discussion was interested, active, and enlightening. As a consequence, there were significant shifts in the pattern of group participation.

PASSIVE YOUNG LEARNERS

A second-grade teacher found that test data confirmed her observations that a significant portion of young learners who had a different racial and economic background from the majority of the class were uninterested in their work on the skills of reading. They were not openly rebellious but passive, distractable, and inattentive in the necessary drill work. The teacher and a consulting scientist discussed the data and decided that slightly older peers of the same race and background might be successful supporters and motivators of school work and might also impress upon the second graders the significance of putting energy into learning activity. With the help of the consultant, a program was designed utilizing volunteer sixth graders as teaching aides in the second grade. The sixth graders had a short seminar period each week on the techniques of being helpful. The response of the young learners was remarkable. They began to have fun working with the older peers, accepted their values about the importance of improving their achievement in reading, and began to relate more effectively to their teacher in other activities. The older peers also showed a significant upsurge in achievement motivation and in openness of collaboration with adults.

ANTI-LEARNING LEADERSHIP

From her diagnostic data collection, a fifth-grade teacher discovered that several of her high status figures in the classroom social structure were anti-schoolwork and anti-teacher in their orientation. It was clear that other members of the group were strongly influenced by this orientation. The teacher rejected several immediate derivations, such as the idea that she should try to downgrade such leadership status by direct confrontation which would have led her into a competitive struggle for leadership. After exploring a number of alternatives, she developed the plan of a classroom steering committee. She initiated the procedure by inviting four top status pupils, two of them pro-school and two anti-school, to meet with her for lunch to discuss the steering committee idea and to plan how it might work. This resulted in a classroom discussion led by the steering committee in which the question for discussion was "If a visitor came from Mars and knew nothing about classrooms and how they work, what might he see that would indicate whether we were or were not having a good day in this classroom?" Two large sheets of paper were put up in the front of the room and the steering committee recorded positive items on one and negative items on the other. Then each day one of the steering committee members served as observer and had the last few minutes of the day to state his observations on the positive and the negative list presented that day. At the end of the week, the steering committee led a discussion evaluating their week, making any revisions in the two lists, and projecting objectives for the next week. Every two weeks the steering committee rotated. Two types of things happened. Several of the negative high status figures changed their attitudes as it became clear to them what was sanctioned as desirable behavior by the classroom group. One or two of the negative high status leaders persisted in their original orientation and lost status with their peers as public group norms

emerged providing a basis for peers supporting and sanctioning each other's participation in classroom activities.

In all three of these problem-solving activities, the teacher went through several steps in the problem solving process. First of all she "brainstormed" by herself or with the help of others the possible implications of her findings and some of the alternative possibilities for action. Then there was a period of thinking out the consequences and potential "side effects" of the various courses of action. This was followed by the tentative decision to develop a particular line of action. Then she planned the line of action in detail and rehearsed her new pattern of performance. In all cases, the teacher also secured feedback from the pupils or students of response to the new classroom activity and attempted to guide and improve teaching performance in terms of an analysis of these responses.

It is time now to review some of the elements and conditions necessary for successful improvement of professional practice in the classroom. A desire to experiment is certainly important, but much creativity and enthusiasm has been lost because the professional discipline involved in the improvement of teaching practice has been ignored or neglected.

CONDITIONS FOR SUCCESSFUL CLASSROOM IMPROVEMENT ACTIONS

The creative efforts of classroom teachers to devise ways of building ego-strength in their pupils can become a major channel for improving classroom practice. However, although teachers have been exhorted to rise to their responsibilities as the key figures in effecting change in the learning environment, they are thwarted by rigid schedules, imposed curricula, lack of administrative support for changes that threaten the status quo, peer standards that discourage the seeking of advice from colleagues, lack of consultation resources, and the personal insecurity that effort to change accustomed procedures brings to the innovator. What are some of the conditions necessary to enable the teacher who has developed a plan of action such as those described in the preceding paragraphs to be successful in carrying it through the stages of initial trial, revision, further development, and evaluation? What contribution can the behavioral sciences make to the facilitation of the teacher's efforts?

Let us first look at the teacher, himself. Change in the classroom is most likely to occur if the teacher (1) is sensitive to the dynamics of the teacher-learning situation, (2) is concerned about this particular problem of building ego-strength in his pupils, (3) has some understanding of the forces which affect the development of ego-strength in children, (4) has access to resources and ideas that could be useful in bringing about change, (5) possesses the skills and tools for diagnosing the actual state of affairs within his classroom, (6) develops a strategy for altering the situation, (7) is supported by the principal and by colleagues in trying out the change plan, and (8) has professional consultation and training help available as needed, (9) has some means of evaluating the effectiveness of the change.

In exploring ways of providing for some of these conditions the University of Michigan projects have utilized a variety of techniques and procedures. For one thing, teachers have been given opportunity to experience and to examine some of the forces operating in group life and to become thoughtful about some of their own strengths and shortcomings. A technique used for this sensitivity training was the training group or "T-Group." Over a period of six weeks, within a summer workshop program, the teacher-participants came together for a series of two-hour sessions in which no agenda was provided and no leadership or rules of operation imposed. A staff member designated as "trainer" assisted the participants in focusing from time to time upon the interpersonal processes that occurred while the group engaged in interaction. It was possible to examine such aspects of group behavior as the development of group norms, friendships and influencing relationships, patterns of communication, relationships to authority and leadership, and giving and receiving feedback about the effects of our own behavior. The relevance and contribution of emotionality in group relations was also explored. These and other learnings, brought about through the opportunity to watch their own group behavior and then interpret it with the help of a skilled trainer, caused the participants to value the T-group highly among the workshop activities. They also found many occasions to explore the relevance of these new insights to pupil interaction in the classroom or to staff relationships within the school building.

Another in-service education technique was to assist teachers in learning and applying some of the concepts involving improvement of pupils' ego-strength that were described in the initial sections of this chapter.

A promising way to assist teachers in deciding upon appropriate targets for change in the classroom situation has been to help the teacher gain more information about the state of affairs in his classroom. We have seen how the teacher can learn through the use of diagnostic tools about the current peer standards toward academic work or toward the appropriateness of helping classmates.

The teacher can discover the kind of sociometric structure that exists, and can find out something of the forces from the pupil's life space or about his own self-concept. These data may give specificity to "hunches" the teacher has already had, or they may come as something of a shock. Whichever it is, the greater knowledge the teacher has about the conditions in his classroom, the better position he is in to develop an effective plan for change.

The involvement of others in the teacher's plan of action also appears to be of great significance. In some situations it was found that change efforts of teachers were best supported by teacher-administrator "change-agent" teams. In these cases, teachers who had been particularly innovative in improving their classroom practices and who were seen by other teachers as influential in the faculty power structure served with the building principal in planning ways for encouraging other teachers to consider some of the newer practices and for providing support for those who were attempting changes in their own classrooms.

Cross-building or cross-school system clinics of teachers engaged in similar types of change efforts have also proved effective. In many cases where the faculty peer standard within the school building has hampered free communication about classroom practices, teachers welcomed the opportunity to discuss plans for change and to get help on some of the obstacles faced by meeting with teachers from a distance.

Teachers have drawn upon another resource to help them bring about change—the pupils themselves. Pupil collaboration during a "try-out" phase can serve not only to build support and understanding of the change among those affected, but can also provide the teacher with useful feedback. Often the best information about the success of a plan, or about its shortcomings, can come from the pupils. Specific scales have been developed to help teachers get reaction from pupils.

It seems clear that creating the conditions for the continuous improvement of the quality of education and the development of social inventions in teaching practice is a mutual responsibility of school administrators, colleagues, the teacher herself, and also the students and their parents. The individual teacher, by herself, cannot be expected to utilize behavioral science resources creatively in an optimal way as she carries out her mission of high quality educational experience for children.

But we are very optimistic about the potentialities for the improvement of the educational experience because we have found administrators, teachers, and children usually open and eager to collaborate when they are helped to perceive new images of potentiality. Colleagues are hungry to achieve a deeper meaning from and a broader perspective on their teaching function and are ready to provide emotional support to each other. Moreover, children are ready to be invited to share in the responsibility for the adventure of learning if they are authentically and skillfully invited to do so.

The greatest stimulus to ego-development and the support of the motivation to achieve a high quality of learning activity derives from the sense of being invited into a meaningful classroom partnership. The gap between the generations must be coped with creatively in the classroom. To the degree that the adult teacher is ready to invite, listen to, and respond sensitively to the needs and influence attempts of her pupils, to that degree the child learners will be open and ready to receive and utilize the teaching efforts (that is, influence attempts) of the teacher. This respect and acceptance from the teacher is a basic ingredient of ego-development and motivation to learn. And motivating the pupils to learn is basic in the teacher's motivation to improve her teaching performance. The response of the learners is the greatest support for innovative teaching. The sharing by the teacher of power and responsibility for classroom management and learning activity is the greatest support for ego-development and motivation to learn. The growing resources of the behavioral sciences can now provide a school system, building faculty, classroom teacher, or classroom group with significant help in guiding and designing efficient group-learning experiences and effective personal growth opportunities. The challenge is to learn how to use these resources to achieve the big goal—helping children learn and grow.

REFERENCES

BARAKAT, HALIM K. *Alienation from the School System: Its Dynamics and Structure*. Ph.D. Thesis. Ann Arbor: University of Michigan, 1966.

CHESLER, MARK, RICHARD A. SCHMUCK, and RONALD O. LIPPITT. "The Principal's Role in Facilitating Innovation." *Theory into Practice, 2,* No. 5, Dec. 1963, 269–277.

CHESLER, MARK, ROBERT S. FOX, RONALD O. LIPPITT, et al. (Eds.) *The Innovation and Sharing of Teaching Practices: A Study of Professional Roles and Social Structures in Schools*. Final Report to the Office of Education, #OE 5-10-241. Ann Arbor: The Institute for Social Research (in preparation).

DENNERLL, DONALD, and MARK CHESLER. "Where Do New Teaching Practices Come From? . . . and Where Do They Go?" *Michigan Elementary Principal, 39,* No. 2, Nov.–Dec. 1964.

FOX, ROBERT S., MARGARET B. LUSZKI, and RICHARD A. SCHMUCK. *Diagnosing Classroom Learning Environments*. Chicago: Science Research Associates, Inc., 1966. (Teacher Resource Booklets on Classroom Social Relations and Learning)

FOX, ROBERT S. "In-Service Education for Innovation and Change." Paper presented to the Conference on Educational Change, Sponsored by the Illinois Demonstration Project for Gifted Youth, University of Illinois, Urbana. Feb. 28–March 2, 1966.

FOX, ROBERT S., RONALD O. LIPPITT, and RICHARD A. SCHMUCK. *Pupil-Teacher Adjustment and Mutual Adoption in Creating Classroom Learning Environments*. (mimeo)

FOX, ROBERT, RONALD O. LIPPITT, and associates, eds. *Developing Methods to Support the Creation and Spread of Innovative Teaching Practices*. Final Report to the Office of Education, #OE 4-10-197. Ann Arbor: The Institute for Social Research (in preparation).

JUNG, CHARLES, and RONALD O. LIPPITT. "The Study of Change as a Concept—in Research Utilization." *Theory into Practice, 1,* No. 1, Feb. 1966, 25–29.

LIPPITT, RONALD O. "Processes of Curriculum Change." Robert R. Leeper, ed. *Curriculum Change: Direction and Process*. Washington, D.C.: Association for Supervision and Curriculum Development, NEA, 1966, 43–59.

LIPPITT, RONALD O. "The Use of Social Research to Improve Social Practice." *American Journal of Orthopsychiatry, 35,* No. 4, July 1965.

SCHMUCK, RICHARD A., MARK CHESLER, and RONALD O. LIPPITT. *Problem Solving to Improve Classroom Learning*. Chicago: Science Research Associates, Inc., 1966. (Teacher Resource Booklets on Classroom Social Relations and Learning)

34

Psychology of Group Behavior: The Class as a Group

WILLIAM CLARK TROW,
ALVIN F. ZANDER,
WILLIAM C. MORSE,
AND DAVID H. JENKINS

In this paper the authors describe many of the classic findings of studies on human behavior in groups. They also suggest the educational applications of these findings. The first three authors (Trow, Zander, and Morse) are still at the University of Michigan. Dr. Jenkins, who died in 1968, was professor of educational psychology at Temple University.

Social psychology has been experiencing a marked development in recent years; and because of the many implications for learning situations, those tilling the educational fields should be alert to the new points of view and new findings which are emerging. This statement does not imply that individual educational psychology is to be discarded, but rather that it is now directly complemented by the basic socio-psychological concept of the group and the consideration of intra-group relationships. As long as sociologists confined their attention largely to such social groupings as crowds and mobs, criminals and delinquents, the family, and to census groups with racial and nationality characteristics, the help they could furnish to the classroom teacher was relatively slight. But with the development of field theory and the study of interaction of individuals in a face-to-face group, and more specifically with the coming of the Iowa studies of democratic, autocratic and *laissez-faire* leadership, followed by the energetic labors of those in the field of group dynamics, the picture has changed. To this has been added the later Freudian influence in the mental hygiene movement, its expansion in the area of inter-personal relationships, and the exploitation of such treatment techniques as those of group work and play therapy. We are forced to ask ourselves whether the school class is a group, and, if it is, what this should mean to educational psychologists whose task it is to introduce teachers to the principles which should aid them in developing the best possible environment for learning in their classrooms.

DEVELOPMENTAL BACKGROUND AND CONCLUSIONS FROM RESEARCH

It should be recognized at the outset that educational psychology has from the beginning devoted itself almost exclusively to modifying the responses of individuals to more or less separate stimuli. The principles of learning, derived from the performances of laboratory animals and sometimes of children, though the results were brought together statistically, have been applied to the individual learner; and his performance has been tested by presenting him with a series of tasks to perform, and measuring his success in performing them. To describe the educational psychology of the past and the present in this way is not to belittle it. Tremendous improvements have been made in instructional materials and methods as a consequence of this view. We can well feel proud of the contributions of our colleagues and wish for their continuance, for there is much more to be done. After all, individuals are individuals, and they are probably here to stay!

The single-line, teacher-pupil relationship, however, has other sources than the psychological laboratory. There seem to have been changing patterns in our educational assumptions as to the most effective and desirable learning situations for the pupil. At one time the tutorial arrangement, the scholar and the single student in a face-to-face relationship, was felt to be most nearly ideal. And it may be for certain kinds of learning. But the practical situation in our public schools has not, of course, permitted this kind of teacher-pupil ratio; so we tried to make our classes of twenty-five or more pupils into twenty-five simultaneous one-to-one relationships. At any rate we followed this pattern, in our classwork, of teacher control, assignment, and class discussion, all dependent on the

William Clark Trow, Alvin F. Zander, William C. Morse, and David H. Jenkins, "Psychology of group behavior: the class as a group," *Journal of Educational Psychology,* 1950, *41,* 322–338. Reprinted with abridgement by permission.

teacher-pupil-teacher-pupil kind of interaction. In this tradition we not only have emphasized the importance of the individual pupil and of the subject-centered curriculum, but also of individualized instruction, and the child-centered school.

This arrangement tended to be strengthened by virtue of the fact that it provided a more direct system of control. Any break in the line, with consequent spontaneous interaction among pupils, might well mean that the teacher had lost that control which he felt it necessary to maintain. If the class were allowed to become an interacting group, the behavior of the pupils would presumably not be contributing to the learning goals which the teacher had in mind. Thus, "groupiness" implied "bad discipline."

Two factors have probably contributed to the movement away from this tutorial conception of our classrooms: the increasing interest and attention being given to social learning, and the awareness that the classrooms are, potentially at least, social situations. With the acceptance of the broader social goals of learning, no longer restricted to scholarly and intellectual activities alone, dependence on the tutorial tradition began to lessen, and the potentialities of the class as a medium for instruction in social learning became clearer.

The point where modern social psychology can offer desirable additions to the individualized approach lies in a recognition of the complex nature of what has in the past been rather loosely referred to as the stimulus situation when this situation is largely made up of other persons. The exploration of this phenomenon, and of the function of perceptual and conceptual processes in relation to it, is the chief contribution of the gestalt psychologists, whose point of view the late Kurt Lewin was largely responsible for bringing over into the interaction field of social psychology. Teachers have long known that pupils responded to other stimuli than the words of wisdom emanating from behind the teacher's desk. But the teacher's task was to eliminate such distraction so far as possible. And while this is still often desirable, we are now interested in these other stimuli also, in the interactions of the pupils among themselves and with the teacher. We are asking, what are the implications of viewing the class not merely as a number of individuals in the same room, but as a group? . . .

A number of assertions from recent research in group dynamics have both theoretical and practical value for the field of educational psychology and teaching methods. This list is not exhaustive and there will be no attempt to describe the nature of the studies from which these data are derived. Many of these findings are from laboratory investi-

gations with groups, but a sufficient number of them were obtained in field-experiment settings to indicate that work of this nature can readily be done in the actual classroom setting, as well as in the laboratory. Some of these assertions are well-tested and validated. Others are less well proven. All of them have relevance and promise for educational psychology.

1. The attitudes of an individual have their anchorage in the groups to which he belongs. Present evidence makes it apparent that many attitudes can be changed more easily by making changes in certain properties of the group than by directly teaching the individuals, as individuals, even in a classroom audience situation.[9, 10]

2. The conduct and beliefs of pupils is regulated in large measure by the small groups within a classroom, such as friendship cliques, and the cohesive groups of students within a school. These groups demand conformity from their members to certain group standards, and the more cohesive the group, the greater is its power over the member.[2, 5]

3. In some instances failure to learn may be advantageously conceptualized as resistance to change, using resistance here in the same sense as the therapist uses it in his relationships with a patient.† For example, the group standards developed by persons who were learning a motor task quite similar to a previously perfected one, and who were simply told what they were to do, were entirely different from the group standards developed in a group in which the learners participated in a discussion and made group decisions about the necessity for, and the nature of, the new task to be learned. Those who participated in the discussion learned much more, more rapidly, and with much less aggression and resentment toward the persons inducing them to make this change.[2, 17]

4. When frustrations are met, highly cohesive groups maintain their effort in movement toward the group goal much more vigorously and effectively than do groups of low cohesiveness.[6]

5. Groups, especially those similar to classroom groups, can be disrupted into separate cliques; or this threat of disruption can be eliminated, by the alteration of forces which determine the attractiveness of the group for the members. (For example, helping them to become aware of the strength of attraction they have for each other, or the degree to which membership in the group provides a way to achieve things they value highly.) This condition can be brought about most easily when the

---

† It should be noted, however, that failure to change may not be due to such "resistance." There may be an inadequate set, unsatisfactory motivation, inability to comply with the demands of the goal or a rational nonacceptance of a new position.

members become aware of the forces influencing them, but it can also be effected by an outsider, such as a teacher, who adroitly helps the group to change the impact and strength of these forces surrounding and within their group.[16]

6. The training of persons for effective social action such as performance in school or civic service, can lead to greater effectiveness of effort by the trainees if they are members of a group which is being trained to work as a group, than will result if they are merely individuals in an audience situation.[11]

7. The amount of interaction among students in a class is determined in part by group factors. For example, in highly cohesive groups arriving at a decision that has general approval, the person whose viewpoint is too different from that of the rest will be rejected—that is, ignored. In a less well knit group, in which the discussion is not directed to a group decision, the deviate member is likely to get more comments directed to him than the person whose ideas are quite similar to those of the rest of the group.[15]

8. When the members see themselves competing for their own individual goals which make coöperative effort impossible, there is disruption of the ready communication of ideas, the coordination of efforts and the friendliness and pride in one's group which are basic to class harmony and effectiveness. The competitive grading system commonly used today is an illustration in that it creates mutually exclusive goals among the members of a class group.[3, 4]

9. The group climate or style of group life can have an important influence on the members' personalities. One such style of group life can develop hostile, obedient, uncreative "goldbrickers"; another can produce confused, purposeless, competitive drifters; and still another can mould coöperative, flexible, purposeful, turn-taking, we-spirited persons. The group climate that produces such effects is created by the resultant of a number of group properties which can be combined in various ways, among which are the leadership style of the teacher or that of those who function most as group leaders, the degree of cohesiveness, which has already been mentioned, the group-member skills, the suitability of the group process for the task in hand, the techniques employed by the teacher to satisfy his ego and other needs, and the tension-release patterns used by the group.[12, 18]

10. The reasons for the occasional failure of project methods, and other teaching procedures which depend upon effectively functioning groups often lie in the ineffective use of group problem-solving methods, or in the unskillful handling of group procedures. Groups can help themselves to mature and improve their ability as a learning or producing team by diagnosing their own failures and planning ways of repairing their own deficiencies. Students of group development have devoted much attention to methods of group diagnosis, ways of presenting the findings to a group, and methods for alleviating a group's procedural difficulties.

11. Certain forms of classroom behavior may be recognized as mechanisms developed for relieving tensions somewhat similar to those employed by an individual in relieving his tensions. For example, they employ patterns of group behavior which help avoid difficult tasks or unpleasant situations. These mechanisms are often difficult to identify since they may either be wrongly perceived by the teacher as signs that the group is keeping busy, or they may be accepted as the usual troubles one gets into by the use of committee methods.[13]

12. Difficulties in the transfer of verbal learning to social behavior can often be overcome by the use of that form of role-playing referred to as reality practice, in which the participants try-out the behavior they are expected to use in a situation from which all threat has been removed. Inhibition blindnesses, or fears of "learning" certain content, or behaving in unaccustomed ways can be removed by the use of a "cultural-island," a situation where new group standards are generated while away from the source of the inhibitions. This procedure is effectively used in excursions, conferences, summer camps, and other group activities in which the person is under the pressure of group standards that are different from those at home, and so he dares to adopt forms of behavior which might be quite desirable for him, but which he might hesitate to try out in his accustomed environment for fear of adverse criticism.[7]

Thus we can safely accept the view that group phenomena definitely affect the progress of learning, as well as the kind of learning that takes place. The educational significance of this view derives from the fact that the pupil's attitudes as well as his behavior patterns are modifiable. Increased motivation in participating in the classroom activities, and consequently in learning, derives from several different potential sources in a group atmosphere where good mental hygiene prevails.

Three such potential sources of increased motivation will be considered. The first of these sources lies in the method of *goal determination*—the extent to which the goals of the class are determined by the entire group including both pupils and teachers, in a truly co-participant sense. When this procedure is followed, the child will feel that he has some control over his own destiny and, therefore, is able to accept the group goals which he helped select as being his own personal goals. They are things which he himself wants to do and, therefore, he is more likely to follow through on them. The absence of such codetermined objectives does not mean the absence of group standards, but some of these standards are not likely to be the ones which the teacher would choose, or the ones which best promote learning. Such group standards as the "gentlemen's mark" of C, and the group rejection of the student who is too "eager," are familiar to all. Thus group standards in a classroom may inhibit good learning as well as accelerate it.

The second source of increased motivation lies in the extent to which the teachers and the pupils build a *supportive atmosphere* in the classroom, one which helps each child to realize that he is an accepted group member. When this condition maintains, each child has his own "area of freedom," within which he is free to make his own decisions. This area can often be much wider than is ordinarily supposed by teachers who are constantly making pupils' decisions for them. Although the group may not approve of everything a pupil does, it still accepts him as a person. In this kind of an atmosphere the child is able to develop a greater feeling of security with his fellows. In addition—and this is the important contribution to learning—he is likely to feel freed from personal threat and criticism and, therefore, more willing to go ahead and try new things without fear, realizing that if he fails he will not be rejected either by the class or by the teacher. Thus failure can be a very positive learning experience because, once the emotional threat is removed, the child can look at his abilities and limitations far more objectively and with greater awareness of what next steps are required for his learning. It would seem that little learning can occur if the child is denied positive opportunities to make errors.

A third potential source of increased motivation lies in the extent to which the various members of the class are accepted as *participating members*. When they are so accepted, each can benefit from the knowledge, skills, and abilities of all the other members. They are no longer dependent primarily or solely on the teacher for all information and guidance. Besides offering the possibility of the development of broader understandings, this gives to each pupil the opportunity to be a contributor to the group, and the classroom becomes, then, a situation for mutual exchange, for mutual sharing. Research is beginning to show the increased productivity of groups which have this coöperative pattern of relationship.[3] Goal determination by the group, a supportive atmosphere, and a participating membership, then, constitute three conditions of group organization of great effectiveness in developing motivation which contribute to the promotion of effective learning.

THE ROLES OF A TEACHER

What can the teacher do to develop and maintain these conditions conducive to learning? There are three fundamental roles which cover the things a teacher does. Actually these are not discrete parts of the teacher's job, but they do carry quite different implications. The roles that will be discussed are the following: (1) the instructional role, (2) the role of the democratic strategist, and (3) the role of the therapist. Following this, we will ask how the teacher selects the proper role, and how the actual operation of this role can be evaluated.

First, the *instruction role*. It is obvious that the concept of what a teacher should do has changed over the years. To the Hoosier schoolmaster the matter was quite simple. He was the drill sergeant. The cadence of recitation was akin to the sound of marching feet. As master of the drill, he called the steps. This teacher also held the role of academic authority; not only did he choose the school experiences, but he was also revered for his great storehouse of information. His very person was the embodiment of learning, and he was categorically right. This fundamental instructional role has mellowed with the years. Now the teacher does not always have to know. He operates as an adult with superior learning to be sure, but serves more as a resource person explaining, telling, and demonstrating. His drillmaster's uniform has been exchanged for the Socratic garb, for his instruction is more concerned with fostering the students' power to think and reason. This major "informational role" of the teacher is often discussed and is perhaps quite well understood. But it should be clear that this role itself is not exclusively the property of the teacher. At times, especially as the content of the course falls within the experience of the students, the class members share or take over the instructional role. As we come to understand more about the dynamics of the classroom, we realize that the way in which this role is handled by the teacher has important effects on the total learning situation.

A second major role which the teacher must play is that of *democratic strategist*. This has been discussed by other writers under the heading of "group formation." With the goal of pupil participation the teacher must provide the occasion for the introduction of processes to facilitate teacher-pupil planning. To play this role successfully two things are required: a high regard for democratic values, and their implications, and a high level of psychological insight into group factors and individual personality. In the role of a democratic strategist, the teacher helps the group utilize various methods of progress evaluation, and the information about their progress which they secure. He further helps them see and clarify their accomplishments, blocks, and failures, as well as the values in democratic group action. Thus, the task is more than that of being merely an exponent of democratic education. This role becomes one of activating democratic processes by helping the class to experience democratic goals and relationships in the design of their everyday classroom experiences.

Understanding the dynamic forces which are affecting the class as a group and those which the techniques bring into play makes possible a contribution to democratic learning because our democratic ethics have established the educational goals and values. Techniques are selected in terms of their potentiality for contributing to the democratic goals of the group at the particular time. It should be pointed out that on the basis of a different set of ethics for the same condition in a group, different techniques would be selected in order to achieve the goals determined by these differing ethics. However, since it is a contribution toward democratic learning that is desired, it is essential that teachers become as skilled as possible in understanding and working with their classroom groups. For a lack of such skill is likely to result in conditions which are quite the opposite of democratic, even though democratic techniques were supposedly being used. Democratic techniques do not exist *per se;* a technique is democratic only to the extent that it serves as a means to help the group achieve its democratic goals at a particular time. For example, the democratic technique of voting has been used as a very effective method of imposing some small minority opinion on the group.

A third important role of the teacher can be subsumed under the title of *therapist*—a combination of clinician and group worker. Lest someone remonstrate at this obligation, let him be reminded that, willingly or not, every teacher plays this role. Sometimes it is somewhat separate from other functions, but more often it is embedded in the classroom life while other functions predominate. No teacher avoids being a group worker, although some are more successful than others and some do crude jobs to be sure. The role of therapist implies group management to the end of helping all of the children toward individual and social adjustment. This means a degree of permissiveness, the establishment of rapport with each child, and the conduct of the work without the teacher's ego becoming involved. Such masterful, objective, "impersonal" human relationships are hard to come by. No one

person is able to meet the differential needs of thirty-five or more children and serve as a cushion to soften the blows of harsh reality dealt out by the child's peer culture. But one tries. To do this the teacher must so act as to be the implicit embodiment of an acceptable code of behavior. Time and time again the mores of mental hygiene are illustrated as the teacher relates to the children, to their feelings and to their problems.

It is through the supportive atmosphere previously discussed that the teachers' therapeutic work is carried on. In a conflict situation pupils may come to the teacher as a judge or decision maker. The case need not be handled arbitrarily, but it must be handled. Teachers can never be neutrals but are continually interpreting "the law" as it applies in individual cases. In the therapist role, the teacher shares insights concerning human behavior, helps to get at causes of conflict and to find methods of resolving it. Sometimes the teacher serves this end by just being a friend, or he may provide, or himself be, an example with whom the child can identify in the Freudian sense. At any rate, the teacher must be an expert in human relations, understanding both the group and the individual.

In general teachers play this role least adequately of all. They tend toward being moralists, policemen, or punitive agents expecting good character to be developed by decree. While we have much to learn in applying the therapist role to the teacher, we already understand enough to know that such a playing of the role spells failure. The reason for such failure may often be that the teacher, having personal needs, tends to exploit the situation to satisfy these needs. We have in mind the need to be loved, the desire to avoid conflict, or pressures from latent hostility as examples. A very common attitude is the desire for dependency, where the teacher is happy if the students remain attached and dependent. Redl [14] has written a very interesting paper approaching this from a slightly different angle in which he shows how teachers tend to orient the whole atmosphere so that it plays into a masochistic or sadistic syndrome, to take only two examples. This is a complicated study in depth psychology, fraught with controversy. But it is not without point to us.

SITUATION AND CHOICE OF ROLE

From the point of view we have been discussing, it will be seen that there is no single complex of roles a teacher plays. The different legitimate objectives of a classroom demand different emphases. Certainly groups of children differ in their leadership qualities, and other individual and group factors need to be studied and understood. The question the teacher would then ask is: "What technique will contribute most effectively, in terms of the dynamics of my class at this time, to the goals and values which are held by the class (or myself, depending on who determines the goals)?" Two things are needed in selecting the techniques: (1) a knowledge of the dynamics of the technique itself, and (2) a knowledge of the goals and values of the group.

Knowledge about groups will help materially in gaining an understanding of the dynamics of a particular technique, and of the kinds of forces in the group which it brings into play in a positive (or negative) manner under specified conditions. To know these dynamics is important. Otherwise the teacher may fall into the trap of thinking that certain techniques are "good" *per se,* forgetting that a technique will contribute to the group only as it is able to draw on the positive forces present in the group at the time. If the condition of the group is different at a particular time, the "good" technique may bring out all that is "bad" in the group, causing him to wonder why it didn't work, or to blame the group for "not cooperating."

SOME TYPICAL CUES FOR ROLE CHANGES

How is it possible to determine which role to play at a particular time? What are the characteristics of a group which will serve as cues for shifting roles? One such cue is group "apathy." If the group is lethargic and passive, one must start searching for reasons. Is it the course content? The teaching methods? A general atmosphere of repression? Children who do not become boisterous at times are living under the control of teachers who are misers of freedom.

Another cue is to be found in the rapidity of "spread of disorder." In a group with adequate morale and goal involvement, disturbances do not spread easily. If one child upsets the room, individual work with that child is, of course, indicated. But more important is the signal it gives about the group condition. If a "bad actor" is a source of rapid contagion, the bond of common purpose must be weak indeed. This condition may be caused by such a simple thing as the need for a change of activity due to a requirement for over-long attention to a specific task. It may be a tension for muscle discharge, or it may go far beyond this to a fundamental dissatisfaction with the teacher behavior.

Other cues for further diagnosis and role modification include the presence of isolates, cliques, scapegoating, exclusiveness, extreme competitiveness, and the like. How much do teachers know about diagnosing these things? Indeed, how much help can educational psychologists give? Once the

teacher really understands the situation and appreciates its deeper aspects, the role complex to meet the situation can usually be found. The task of the educational psychologist is to see that teachers are so trained that they will understand the dynamics of that situation.

Understanding more about the dynamics of groups helps the teacher in a variety of ways toward increasing his effectiveness in the roles that are appropriate in different situations. As more is learned about the theory and research on groups, new ways of thinking about the classroom situation will at first be gained, ways which may have been overlooked before. The importance of effective communication will come to be recognized in giving instructions and in expressing ideas. The relationships between the various pupils in the class will be studied, how they feel about each other, and the leader-group relationships, and gradually the teacher will become aware of his own behavior in the class and the kinds of effect it has on the pupils.

Of course, it is not easy to take one's knowledge into the classroom and become immediately aware of these complex interrelationships. Often it takes considerable training in observation and experience to be able to see, especially at the time it is happening, what is occurring in the group and what its casual relationships and potential effects are. The transition from "book learning" to "observation skill" is a difficult one to make, but it must be made if knowledge about groups is to contribute to teaching effectiveness. . . .

REFERENCES

1. WILLIAM C. BAGLEY. *School Discipline.* New York: Macmillan. 1917.
2. LESTER COCH and JOHN R. P. FRENCH, JR. "Overcoming Resistance to Change." *J. Human Relations,* Vol. I, *4,* 1948.
3. MORTON DEUTSCH. "An Experimental Study of the Effects of Cooperation and Competition upon Group Process." *J. Human Relations,* Vol. II, *3,* 1949.
4. ———. "A Theory of Cooperation and Competition." *J. Human Relations,* Vol. II, *2,* 1949.
5. LEON FESTINGER, KURT BACK, and STANLEY SCHACHTER. *Social Influence* (pre-publication book manuscript, mimeographed). Chapter VI, "The Operation of Group Standards" and Chapter X, "A Theory of Group Structure and Group Standards."
6. JOHN R. P. FRENCH, JR. "Organized and Unorganized Groups under Fear and Frustration." *Iowa Studies in Child Welfare, Studies in Vector and Topological Psychology,* Vol. XX, 1944.

7. CHARLES E. HENDRY, RONALD LIPPITT, and ALVIN ZANDER. *Reality Practice as Educational Method.* Psychodrama Monographs, No. 9, 1944, p. 36. *Sociometry,* May 1944.

8. DAVID JENKINS. "Feedback and Group Self-evaluation." *J. Social Issues,* Vol. IV, 2, 1948.

9. KURT LEWIN. "Group Decision and Social Change." In Newcomb and Hartley, *Readings in Social Psychology.* New York: Henry Holt, 1947, pp. 330–344.

10. _____. *Resolving Social Conflicts.* New York: Harper Bros., 1948. Chapter IV.

11. RONALD LIPPITT. *Training in Community Relations.* New York: Harper Bros., 1949, p. 286.

12. RONALD LIPPITT and R. K. WHITE. "An Experimental Study of Leadership and Group Life." In Newcomb and Hartley, *Readings in Social Psychology.* New York: Henry Holt, 1947, pp. 315–329.

13. T. MAIN and M. NYSWANDER. *Some Observations on the Third National Training Laboratory in Group Development.* (mimeographed)

14. FRITZ REDL. "Group Emotion and Leadership." *Psychiatry.* Vol. V, 4, 1942, pp. 573–596.

15. STANLEY SCHACHTER. *Deviation, Rejection, and Communications.* Doctoral dissertation, University of Michigan, 1950.

16. JOHN THIBAUT. *The Relationship of Group Cohesiveness to Inter-Group Status Differences.* Doctoral Dissertation, Massachusetts Institute of Technology, 1949.

17. ALVIN ZANDER. "Resistance to Change—Its Analysis and Prevention," *Advanced Management,* Vol. XV, 1, Jan. 1950, pp. 9–12.

18. _____. "Within the Bonds of Freedom." *Childhood Education,* Vol. XXIV, 1, Sept. 1947.

35

Introduction to "An Application of Psychoanalysis to Education"

LAWRENCE S. KUBIE

This is a brief passage by Lawrence Kubie, a prominent psychiatrist and psychoanalyst. In it he expresses his faith that a new kind of classroom climate can reduce neurotic interference with the learning process. (See Kubie's widely read book The Neurotic Distortion of the Creative Process *[New York: Farrar, Straus and Giroux, 1970].) A related paper that might have been placed in this section is that by Terry Borton included in Section XII.*

Throughout our educational system a realization is growing that both intellectual development and creativity will continue to be seriously hampered unless we find out how to make emotional maturation a part of education. Consequently educators are preoccupied increasingly with the difficult problems attendant on the attempt to introduce self-knowledge-in-depth into the main stream of formal education. They recognize that if this is to be done at all, it must start in the kindergarten and continue throughout the elementary grades, grammar school, high school, college and graduate years.

"Progressive education" was one of the early efforts in this direction. Originally, however, this involved a misapplication to education processes of techniques which are sometimes essential in formal psychotherapy. The predictable failures of these well-meant but inept efforts caused the climate of education to swing back temporarily to an opposite extreme, i.e., back to the old-fashioned techniques of drill and grill, and more drill and more grill.

A newer realization of the full complexity of these problems is now developing, i.e., that there is an incessant interaction between universal but subtly masked neurotic mechanisms and the educational process, and that as a result of this interplay education is blocked and distorted. The relationship between the two is evidently so close, that both must be solved if either is to be solved.

This does not, however, force us to the impossible conclusion that every teacher must be an analytically trained psychotherapist or that every school child must be psychoanalyzed. It brings us rather to conclude that all education should be conducted in an atmosphere in which the universal and recurrent emotional disturbances and repressive tendencies of childhood can be resolved as soon as they arise, and before they become chronic. The child's fifth freedom is the right to know what he feels; but this does not carry with it any right to act out his feelings blindly. This will require a new mores for our schools, one which will enable young people from early years to understand and feel and put into words all the hidden things which go on inside of them, thus ending the conspiracy of silence with which the development of the child is now distorted both at home and at school. If the conspiracy of silence is to be replaced by the fifth freedom, children must be encouraged and helped to attend to their forbidden thoughts, and to put them into words, i.e., to talk out loud about love and hate and jealousy and fear, about curiosity over the body, its products and its apertures; about what goes in and what comes out; about what happens inside and what happens outside; about their dim and confused feelings about sex itself; about the strained and stressful relationships within families, which are transplanted into schools. All of these are things about which school must help children to become articulate in the schoolroom.

Once any child becomes free in this sense then his great preconscious creative capacity will be freed from the retarding weight of pedestrian, literal, conscious processes, and at the same time from the distortions which arise out of neurotogenic and psychotogenic unconscious processes.

Lawrence S. Kubie, Introduction to Richard M. Jones, *An Application of Psychoanalysis to Education*, 1960, pp. vii–viii. Reprinted by permission of the authors and the publisher, Charles C. Thomas.

VI

GROUP MEMBERSHIPS
AS DETERMINANTS OF BEHAVIOR

The groups and institutions or organizations to which an individual belongs or with which he identifies himself are another important determinant of behavior. Face-to-face groups such as the family, whose impact is largely a matter of interpersonal influence (see Section IV), are not included here, nor do we refer to the classroom or playground groups, which were covered under settings and specific stimuli in Section V. Rather, we deal with (1) the society or culture in which a man is reared; (2) his connections with various organizations and societal institutions; (3) his economic and other role relations with his fellow men; and (4) the "reference groups" to which he belongs or with which he is identified (his membership in a caste, a social class, an ethnic or national group; political leanings; religious affiliation; and residence in a rural or urban area, etc.). Because sociology, social or cultural anthropology, and social psychology are in large part represented by this topic, the selections included here are merely illustrative of some realms of possible inquiry.[1] Such growing sub-disciplines as educational sociology and educational anthropology will increasingly demand study in their own right. In fact, W. W. Charters and N. L. Gage have produced a book entitled *Readings in the Social Psychology of Education* (Boston: Allyn and Bacon, 1963). The student especially interested in this area will find other useful papers in that collection.

Although some of the articles reprinted here and in other sections of the book do deal with socio-economic variables, it is hardly possible to give as much attention to *poverty* as a culture or subculture as a lot of contemporary writing does. Hence, we would like to direct your attention to several sources in this specific area. The poverty literature is important in relation to the extensive social action that is current or contemplated. Much of the social action to date has suffered from inadequate understanding of the psychological characteristics of persons toward whom the programs were directed. In the opinion of some, the fact that programs are directed toward a given group *by others* is one of the things that may be wrong. Vernon L. Allen has edited a book entitled *Psychological Factors in Poverty* (Markham Publishing Co., 1970). The papers in it represent a number of viewpoints. A very different attitude toward poverty can be found in the book *Blaming the Victim,* by William Ryan (Pantheon, 1971). That book attacks the often cherished idea, expressed sometimes subtly and sometimes not, that poor people are responsible for their own misfortune.

---

[1] It may be helpful to give a rough idea of the differing preoccupations of the principal disciplines mentioned. By and large, anthropologists are concerned with differences between societies, sociologists study differences between groups in the same society, and psychologists are interested in differences among individuals in the same group. Although there is increasing overlap of interests among all three fields, there are characteristic distinctions in viewpoint. The fact that most adult Americans use alarm clocks might be called to our attention by an anthropologist because of variations among peoples or cultures in technological development or in attitudes toward time and toward work. He might contrast behaviors of Americans with those of Italians or of Zulus. A sociologist might investigate attitudes toward time and work among religious or economic groups within a culture, comparing the groups to discover differences and seek explanations of them. Either psychologists or sociologists might investigate changes in such attitudes between the ages of 14 and 24 or differences between sorority members and non-members in their views and habits. Only psychologists would seek meaning in the fact that Suzie Snoozy neglects to set her alarm clock at night.

36

The Effect of Psychological Environment on Childbirth: Combined Cross-Cultural and Experimental Approach [1]

NILES NEWTON [2]

This imaginative paper looks at the impact of group membership on the birth process. Cultural attitudes toward the process of birth, and more broadly toward sex, appear to influence the speed and ease of labor. Hypotheses derived from this anthropological perspective were tested using laboratory mice. Despite what we assume to be the uncomplicated psyches of mice, we find analogous and even more dramatic effects of disturbances on the delivery of mice pups. This is not the first time that laboratory animals have been used to test the effects of "psychological" variables. The effects of stress (or "anxiety") during pregnancy on the later behavior of offspring were investigated earlier by Thompson. The fact that a number of workers failed to replicate Thompson's results led to the discovery that the effects found depended on the particular strain of rats used. There was an interaction between environmentally produced "anxiety" and the biological or genetic characteristics of the organisms being studied.

[1] Adapted from a paper presented at the XIX International Congress of Psychology in London, July 31, 1969, entitled "Impact of Collaborating with Margaret Mead." This work was supported in part by the John R. and Doris J. Haire Foundation.

[2] The author gratefully acknowledges the insights, guidance and training given her by Margaret Mead, Ph.D., in the use and interpretation of intercultural materials pertaining to childbearing in the course of their collaboration in writing a review of the cross-cultural literature in this area (Mead and Newton, 1967).

One might argue that the manipulations involved in influencing the birth process of the mice hardly makes them members of a "group," unless it is of the defined experimental group. However, because the hypotheses are derived from consideration of group differences, the study is included in this section. One should note that such hypotheses based on group differences always direct our attention away from the fact that there are individual differences within the groups.

*The author, Niles Newton, is at the Northwestern University Medical School. She is author of a number of monographs and chapters in books, and has written a book for parents (*Family Book of Child Care, Harper & Row, 1957*). She also teaches a course on the psychology of childbearing and reproduction.*

The patterning of birth varies tremendously from culture to culture. This is particularly notable in studying data from contrasting preliterate cultures. Take, for instance, the example of the Cuna Indians of Central America (DeSmidt, 1948; Marshall, 1950; Stout, 1947) and the Siriono Indians of Bolivia, South America (Holmberg, 1950), groups that differ dramatically in their handling of birth.

Ideally, the Cuna girls did not learn of the existence of either coitus or childbirth until the final stages of the marriage ceremony. Pregnancy was seen by the Cuna as a time of anxiety and rising fear of childbirth. Each day the pregnant woman went to the house of the medicine man, who specialized in prenatal care and childbirth, for a cup of freshly brewed medicine tea. Labor, however, was too "hidden" for the medicine man to attend. Children and men, even husbands and medicine men, were excluded from the labor area. The midwives kept the medicine man informed of the progress of the labor. He chanted and supplied medications in response to the labor progress reports. Labor under these circumstances was frequently prolonged and so extreme that unconsciousness of the laboring woman occurred at times.

In contrast to this, the Siriono patterned birth as an easy, open process, in keeping with their relaxed sexual attitudes. Birth took place in a communal hut and was a public event freely witnessed by men as well as women. The mother labored in a hammock while groups of women gathered, gossiping about their own labors and wondering whether the coming baby would be a boy or a girl. No help, however, was given to the mother during the usual normal labor. She herself tied the child-

Niles Newton, "The effect of psychological environment on childbirth: Combined cross-cultural and experimental approach," *Journal of Cross-Cultural Psychology, 1,* 1970, 85–90. Reprinted by permission.

birth rope over her hammock to pull during contractions. She dug the earth under the hammock to cushion the baby's fall. The grunts and groans of labor did not appear to bother others within earshot. When the baby was born it slid over the edge of the hammock, dropping a few inches to the ground. This casual treatment of labor had an interesting accompaniment—extremely short labor durations. Seven of the eight labors observed by the recording anthropologist lasted only one to three hours. The eighth one, which took longer, resulted in the birth of twins.

From the psycho-physiological point of view[3] there is a marked difference—the Cuna girl in a culture which handled labor with frightening ritual tended to have an extreme experience in labor with unconsciousness and prolonged labor occurring at times. In contrast to this, the relaxed, casual Siriono had startlingly quick labors, far quicker not only than the Cuna appear to have had, but also far quicker than the labors of a typical woman in Western industrial cultures.

The rarity with which birth occurs at inconvenient times and places also becomes notable as one goes through anthropological accounts of birth in various cultures from many parts of the world (Mead & Newton, 1967). Of course, birth in a taxi-cab in the United States or by the roadside among agricultural and migrant people receive consideration and attention—perhaps only because they are actually so rare. The typical pattern of birth is that it usually takes place in an environment in which the mother feels safe, suggesting psychological as well as physiological triggering mechanisms.

If labor is really so markedly affected by environmental and cultural variations, this is indeed a fact of significance. It has important implications for the psychological management of women in labor—a problem met every day all over the world.

EXPERIMENTAL CONFIRMATION

Unfortunately, the nature of most anthropological material is such that it can suggest but not prove a point. Associative relationships cannot demonstrate cause and effect even when sufficient data are available to obtain significantly low probabilities. Experimental psychology can, however, take up insights gleaned from anthropological data and

put them to controlled test. After developing hypotheses about birth based on the study of cross-cultural materials with Margaret Mead, they were tested experimentally in a series of experiments with mice.

The first experiment took up the problem of labor speed (Newton, Foshee, & Newton, 1966a). Since anthropological accounts seem to indicate that the swiftness of labor varies markedly from one society to another, mice were systematically disturbed (and presumably frightened) by subjecting them to complete olfactory, kinesthetic and visual change for one minute after the birth of their second pup. A laboratory assistant gently picked up the mouse and placed it in cupped hands, completely enclosing it for one minute. The control group was not disturbed. Two types of subjects were used: in Experiment A all the mice used had experienced only routine handling. Experiment B was identical to Experiment A except that all mice in both control and disturbed groups had been previously subjected to 15 periods of systematic human handling which included hand-cupping.

The undisturbed mice delivered their next pups in about 12 to 13 minutes (see Table 1). The disturbed mice were markedly slower in delivering the next pup. Labor after disturbance was significantly slower ($p < .05$) in both Experiment A and Experiment B. In each experiment the disturbed mice took over eight minutes longer than the controls to produce the next pup, a slowing of labor by about 65% to 72%.

The next anthropologically-based theory tested experimentally was that birth tends to be confined to more convenient or safe places, suggesting environmental as well as biochemical control of the labor mechanism (Newton, Foshee, & Newton, 1966b). Two environments for delivery were used. One was a glass fish bowl with a little bedding from cat cages to give it a strange odor; the other was a familiar cage complete with nesting box. Each expectant mouse at term was moved between these two environments at regular intervals.

During each time period the same number of

---

[3] Under some circumstances culturally determined variations in body mechanics during labor may influence its course. The experimental and cross-cultural data on this point have recently been extensively reviewed (Mead and Newton, 1967, 205–215). However, since both the Cuna and the Siriono deliver in hammocks it is unlikely that the differences in the difficulty of their labors can be chiefly attributable to variations in body position during delivery.

TABLE 1
EFFECTS OF DISTURBANCE ON LABOR SPEED

Groups	Minutes between birth of second and third pup (Means)	Parturient mice involved (N)
Experiment A:		
Controls	13.2	16
Disturbed	21.8	12
Experiment B:		
Controls	12.0	11
Disturbed	20.7	15

TABLE 2
RELATION OF ENVIRONMENT TO NUMBER OF PUPS DELIVERED

Groups	Number of pups born in familiar cage with shelter	Number of pups born in glass bowls with cat odor
First born pups of parturient females moved:		
Hourly	9	4
Every two hours	10	2
Total pups born to parturient females moved:		
Hourly	66	45
Every two hours	72	42

mice were in each type of cage. However, equal numbers of births did not occur in the two contrasting environments (see Table 2). Significantly more first born pups ($p < .01$) and total number of pups ($p < .05$) were born in familiar cages with nesting boxes than in the fish bowls. Only six first births took place in the glass fish bowl with cat odor as compared with 19 in the other cages. The mice under experimental conditions seemed to act like the women of many different cultural groups insofar as they appeared to avoid giving birth in a strange, open environment.

The third experiment (Newton, Peeler, & Newton, 1968) involved continuous disturbances during labor—a technique applied to laboring women in some societies. Mice were disturbed continuously by being moved every two hours from one glass bowl to another. The control group was alternated every two hours between one cage with shelter to a similar one (see Table 3). The mean elapsed time before the birth of the first pup was significantly longer for the continuously disturbed than for the control group mice ($p < .05$). The median delay in the appearance of the first pup was almost nine hours longer for the continuously disturbed group than for the controls, which is a considerable amount of time in view of the fact that the average mouse gestation in the strain used lasts only about 19 days.

Even more important, however, was what happened to offspring mortality rates (see Table 3). Significantly ($p = .036$) more dead pups were born to mice continuously disturbed than to the control group. The adverse psychological environment during parturition appears to have raised the mortality rate about 54%.

If *Homo sapiens* are as sensitive as mice to psychological environment during parturition, it is possible that preliterate cultures using patterned disturbance in labor actually have developed an indirect method of population control. In our so-

TABLE 3
EFFECT OF CONTINUOUS DISTURBANCE ON TIME OF
FIRST DELIVERY AND PUP MORTALITY

Group	Hours to first delivery		Total pups found	
	Mean	Median	Dead	Alive
Control	12.77	10.00	28	321
Experimental	17.10	18.50	43	306

ciety the effect of taking a poverty mother in labor away from her familiar environment and placing her in a hospital environment, which may be extremely strange to her, may be one factor contributing to the higher infant mortality rates of this group.

CONCLUSIONS

A series of psychological experiments were based on hypotheses suggested by anthropological data. Both cross-cultural and experimental data on mice suggest that equanimity may be conducive to more effective labors.

The gap between anthropological insight and experimental psychology is not too great to be bridged. Indeed, experimental psychologists can learn much from the breadth and variety of material available from anthropological sources.

REFERENCES

DeSMIDT, L. S. *Among the San Blas Indians of Panama.* New York, the author, 1948.

HOLMBERG, A. R. *Nomads of the Long Bow: The Siriono of Eastern Bolivia.* Washington: Smithsonian Institution, Institute of Social Anthropology, Publication 10, 1950.

MARSHALL, D. S. *Cuna folk: conceptual scheme involving dynamic factors of culture, as applied to the Cuna*

Indians of Danien. Unpublished manuscript, Department of Anthropology, Harvard University, 1950.

MEAD, M., & NEWTON, N. Cultural patterning of perinatal behavior. *Childbearing: Its Social and Psychological Aspects.* Richardson, S. A., & Guttmacher, A. F. (Eds.), Baltimore: Williams & Wilkins, 1967.

NEWTON, N., FOSHEE, D., & NEWTON, M. Experimental inhibition of labor through environmental disturbance. *Obstetrics and Gynecology,* 1966a, *27,* 371–377.

NEWTON, N., FOSHEE, D., & NEWTON, M. Parturient mice: effects of environment on labor. *Science,* 1966b, *151,* 1560–1561.

NEWTON, N., PEELER, D., & NEWTON, M. Effect of disturbance on labor: an experiment using 100 mice with dated pregnancies. *American Journal of Obstetrics and Gynecology,* 1968, *101,* 1096–1102.

STOUT, D. B. *San Blas Cuna Acculturation: Introduction.* New York: Viking Fund Publications in Anthropology, No. 9, 1947.

37

Perceptual Articulation
and Task Effectiveness
in Several Israel Subcultures

Ilana Preale, Yehuda Amir,
and Shlomo Sharan (Singer)

This selection looks at the effects of ethnic and class or caste memberships in a culture that differs from our own in a variety of ways. Though the ethnic groups are different from those of interest in our own society, the problems are not very different. Perhaps the greater distance from us of the cultures described will help us gain more perspective on similar group differences in our own culture.

In addition to looking at the different ethnic subcultures, the study compares children raised on a kibbutz (or communal settlement) with those raised in the usual family settings. The behaviors that are examined, performance on perceptual tasks, also have a considerable history of study, both in our own culture and cross-culturally. The authors of the study are Israeli and are located in Israel. Preale and Amir are at Bar-Ilan University. Sharan is at Tel-Aviv University.

Evidence from various sectors of Israel society points to the presence of distinct differences in levels of achievement typical of the country's major cultural subgroups, namely Jews of Western ethnic origin and Middle-Eastern ethnic origin (i.e., individuals from countries whose dominant culture is Moslem). Children of Middle-Eastern background evidence lower levels of academic achievement and

are less represented in institutions of higher learning than their peers from Western ethnic backgrounds (Ortar, 1967; Smilansky & Yam, 1969; Statistical Abstract of Israel, 1969). Middle-Eastern Jews are less represented in executive managerial positions in Israel and occupy lower positions in the civil service than do individuals of Western ethnic backgrounds (Civil Service Commission, 1968; Statistical Abstract of Israel, 1969).

Another major subculture in Israel is the kibbutz movement, comprised of approximately 240 voluntary collectives based on a socialist ideology of the economic and social equality of its members. Data from achievement ratings in the Israel Defense Forces indicate that kibbutz-born soldiers are generally more effective than comparable groups not born and raised in a kibbutz (Amir, 1969). Also during the first 2 years of life kibbutz children achieved higher scores on several measures of motor and intellectual development than their urban peers (Cohen-Raz, 1968). The task for research is to illuminate the social-psychological variables which can aid in explaining these intergroup differences.

Witkin's (Witkin, Dyk, Faterson, Goodenough, & Karp, 1962) notion of styles of perceptual articulation has proved to be of considerable heuristic value for the investigation of interethnic differences. A well-articulated or field-independent perceptual style, in contrast to a more global, field-dependent style according to the Witkin group, is characterized by the individual's tendency to perceive figures as clearly distinguished from their backgrounds and an ability to actively impose structure on relatively unstructured perceptual fields. Differentiated or articulated perception also encompasses the individual's experience of himself as possessing an identity distinctly independent of his social environment. Studies of interethnic differences in perceptual articulation (Berry, 1966; Dawson, 1967; Witkin, 1967) have reported that members of cultural or ethnic groups which foster individual autonomy evidenced more articulated perceptual functioning than did individuals from societies stressing conformity and dependence on authority, such as may be found in tradition-oriented groups.

This approach appears particularly applicable to the investigation of psychosocial intergroup differences in Israel for two reasons: (a) There is some evidence that these subgroups in Israel, that is, those of Middle-Eastern and of Western origin and those raised in or outside of the kibbutz, place differential emphasis on subordination to authority and on the acquisition of individual autonomy. The Middle-Eastern family, in contrast with the family of Western origin, is more tradition oriented with an authoritarian, patriarchal structure which tends to foster subordination to authority and restriction of emotional autonomy (Feitelson, 1954; Kohls, 1956; Smilansky, 1968; Weintraub, 1962). Investigators of kibbutz education and socialization processes agree that the kibbutz strives to cultivate emotional autonomy and self-reliance while shunning those forms of punishment, for example, which foster conformity to and dependence upon authority figures (Bar-Yosef, 1959; Faigin, 1958; Rabin, 1965; Spiro, 1965; Talmon, 1965); (b) the ability to analyze and organize the perceptual field appears to be essential to the successful execution of complex social tasks such as positions of leadership in military settings. An officer is required to make decisions based on a careful analysis of the perceptual field; to differentiate various aspects of the total situation in terms of their mutual relationship; and to demonstrate considerable independence in acting on the inferences he draws from this analysis. These functions appear to be related to Witkin's notion of the field-dependence-independence variable. Thus, perceptual articulation may account, in part at least, for the intersubgroups' differences in social task achievement such as those cited above.

Emphasis on autonomy in the child-rearing process was found by Witkin to correlate significantly with a well-articulated, field-independent mode of perceptual functioning. From the evidence reviewed earlier, therefore, one would anticipate a positive relationship between measures of perceptual articulation and achievement on complex social tasks. Furthermore, it seems reasonable to anticipate that members of social subgroups tending to foster emotional autonomy would evidence an articulated, field-independent style of perception more than would members of those groups which emphasize conformity and dependence on authority.

METHOD

SUBJECTS AND PROCEDURE

The present study consisted of two major intergroup comparisons as follows: (a) 88 males of Middle-Eastern ethnic background ages 19 and 20 years contrasted with 112 of their peers of Western origin all of whom fell within the Stanine 6 range of intelligence (104–110 IQ); (b) 145 males born and raised in a kibbutz contrasted with 145 of their peers of Western origin born and raised in Israel from a nonkibbutz setting. These men constituted a random sample of subjects representing their respective subcultures selected from a population of officer candidates in the Israel Defense Forces. The latter group

of kibbutz and nonkibbutz Western males was comprised of two subgroups: Group 1 consisted of 60 kibbutz members and a control group of 60 nonkibbutz individuals. The IQ range of this group was restricted to the Stanine 6 level. Group 2 was comprised of kibbutz ($n = 85$) and nonkibbutz ($n = 85$) individuals who were matched on the basis of mean group IQ score (Mean IQ = 114). Individual IQ scores of these subjects were scattered over the entire range of IQ scores ordinarily found among the candidates for officer training.

Witkin et al. (1962) reported a significant relationship between level of perceptual articulation and measures of general intelligence, so that it was considered advisable to control for IQ level in the present study. In both intergroup comparisons, level of intelligence was controlled on the basis of two tests currently employed by the Israel army, namely a modification of Raven's Progressive Matrices and an Otis-type examination. Results from each test were transformed into standard scores and subsequently combined giving equal weight to each test. This combined score was again standardized and divided into stanines. The average reliability coefficient of the combined score, as routinely employed in the Israel Army, is .95.

As indicated, in two out of the three intergroup comparisons in this study, subjects were restricted to the Stanine 6 IQ range. Subjects in these two groups were preselected in order to insure that the mean standard scores for all groups would be the same. This was done for each IQ measure individually as well as for their combined score.

Some comments are relevant here regarding procedures for the selection of officer training candidates in the Israel army. Acceptance to officer training school depends upon successful completion of a battery of tests designed to assess the candidates' suitability for officer rank. Included in the battery were a variety of situational tests to evaluate the candidates' capacity for leadership in the field, for decision making under stress, and for advance planning and judgement under varying environmental conditions. The tests for perceptual articulation are not routinely included in the personnel selection battery but were appendaged to the battery for purposes of this research project only. In order to avoid possible contamination between perceptual articulation scores and the score on the officer's selection examination, no information was given to the examiners regarding results on the former tests.

TABLE 1

PEARSON *r* CORRELATIONS BETWEEN FOUR MEASURES OF PERCEPTUAL ARTICULATION

Test	Embedded Figures	Block Design	Picture Completion	Figure Drawing
Embedded Figures	—	.34	.33	.22
Block Design		—	.35	.19
Picture Completion			—	.16
Figure Drawing				—

Note.—$N = 200$.

MEASURES

The four tests employed in this study are described by Witkin as evaluating "analytic field approach." Three of the tests were found to load heavily on the same factor, while the fourth, the human figure drawing test, was also found to be related to analytical field approach (Witkin et al., 1962, p. 129). Two of the tests, Block Design (BD) and Picture Completion (PC), were taken from Wechsler's well-known intelligence scale and require no further description. The Embedded Figures Test (EFT) employed in this study was a version proposed by Witkin and modified by Jackson (1964). It consists of 16 geometrical designs embedded in a larger, complex figure. The subject must locate the embedded figure within a specified time limit and give a response scored either right or wrong, so that the possible range of scores is 0–16. In addition to these three tests, each subject was requested to draw two human figures (HFD), first a male and afterwards a female figure. This test assessed the relative degree of sophistication with which the individual perceives the human body. Marlen's scoring method (cited by Witkin et al., 1962, pp. 118–129) was used to evaluate the drawings, and scores ranged from 1, reflecting the highest level of articulation of the body percept, to 5, reflecting markedly primitive figures. In order to check the Hebrew version of the instructions and interrater reliability for evaluating the figure drawings, a pretest was conducted with 24 subjects. Interrater reliability for three judges ranged from .85 to .94.

All individuals participating in the Middle-Eastern–Western group comparison were administered all four of the perceptual articulation tests, namely: EFT, BD, PC, and HFD. Participants in the kibbutz-nonkibbutz Group 1 were assessed with three tests of perceptual articulation: EFT, BD, and HFD. In Group 2, due to limitations of time and circumstances, it was possible to employ only the EFT. The sample of kibbutz subjects examined in this study constituted the total population of kibbutz candidates available for testing for an entire year.

PREDICTIONS

The predictions were as follows:
1. Subjects of Middle-Eastern ethnic origin would achieve lower scores on each of the four tests assessing perceptual articulation than would subjects of Western ethnic origin.
2. Kibbutz subjects would achieve higher scores on tests of perceptual articulation than would nonkibbutz subjects.
3. There would be a significantly positive correlation between measures of perceptual articulation and ratings on the final examination for officer selection.

RESULTS

Before presenting the results, it is of interest to note the intercorrelations of the four measures of perceptual articulation reported in Table 1. These intercorrelations are markedly lower than those reported by Witkin et al. (1962) for the same tests. All intercorrelations are nevertheless significant.

Data relevant to Prediction 1 regarding interethnic differences in perceptual articulation are presented in Table 2. Interethnic differences were significant on all four tests to the effect that subjects of Middle-Eastern origin achieved lower levels of perceptual articulation than did their Western peers.

It may be noted that the criterion for including individuals in their respective ethnic groups was their birthplace or that of their father. Thus, the criterion encompassed individuals born abroad as well as those born in Israel. An analysis of variance revealed no significant differences in measures of perceptual articulation between native and foreign-born Israelis within each ethnic group.

Table 3 summarizes findings relevant to Prediction 2 regarding the comparison of kibbutz with nonkibbutz Western groups. The data support the prediction to the effect that the kibbutz males achieved higher levels of perceptual articulation than did those not born and raised in a kibbutz. All findings are significant except for results on the BD test, for which the results were not statistically significant.

A Pearson's *r* correlation was used to test Prediction 3 to the effect that there will be a positive relationship between level of achievement on tests for officer selection and level of perceptual articulation. The findings are summarized in Table 4. All correlations between the two variables were found to be statistically significant.

The findings of this study are consistent with the evidence cited earlier to the effect that members of Western ethnic origin achieve higher levels of

TABLE 2
LEVEL OF PERCEPTUAL ARTICULATION IN WESTERN AND MIDDLE-EASTERN ETHNIC GROUPS

Test	Western	Middle-Eastern	t
Embedded Figures [a]			
M	8.21	6.59	2.55**
SD	4.56	4.37	
Block Design [a]			
M	33.14	30.07	3.01***
SD	7.53	6.75	
Picture Completion [a]			
M	14.73	13.55	2.78***
SD	3.04	2.89	
Figure Drawing [b]			
M	2.64	2.99	2.23*
SD	1.17	.99	

[a] Larger means indicate higher level of articulation.
[b] Smaller means indicate higher level of articulation.
* $p = .05$.
** $p = .02$.
*** $p = .01$.

TABLE 3
LEVEL OF PERCEPTUAL ARTICULATION IN KIBBUTZ AND NONKIBBUTZ SUBJECTS

Test	Kibbutz	Nonkibbutz	t
Embedded Figures [a]			
Group 1			
M	9.98	7.88	2.36*
SD	4.55	4.87	
Group 2			
M	12.06	10.60	2.36*
SD	3.79	4.18	
Block Design [a]			
M	31.41	32.49	ns
SD	8.68	7.22	
Figure Drawing [b]			
M	2.47	3.05	2.51*
SD	1.32	1.07	

[a] Larger means indicate higher level of articulation.
[b] Smaller means indicate higher level of articulation.
* $p = .02$.

performance on complex tasks than do individuals of Middle-Eastern background. It might be argued, therefore, that the correlation reported in Table 4 between level of perceptual articulation and level of task achievement on the officer selection tests stems from the fact that one ethnic group is consistently low and the other group consistently high on both variables, while within each ethnic group itself the correlation between task achievement and perceptual articulation might not obtain. Separate correlations were therefore calculated for Middle-Eastern and Western groups individually, and no significant differences were found between the correlations of each group. This finding indicates that the relationship between the two variables, that is, task achievement and perceptual articulation, obtains independently in each ethnic subgroup.

DISCUSSION

The results obtained in this study support the hypotheses to the effect that (a) subjects of Western ethnic origin achieved a higher level on four measures of perceptual articulation than did subjects of Middle-Eastern ethnic origin (Table 2);

TABLE 4
CORRELATIONS BETWEEN MEASURES OF PERCEPTUAL ARTICULATION AND SCORES ON OFFICER SELECTION EXAMINATIONS

Test	r	p
Embedded Figures	.33	.01
Block Design	.23	.01
Picture Completion	.34	.01
Figure Drawing	.17	.05

(b) subjects raised in a kibbutz setting achieved higher scores on two out of three measures of perceptual articulation than did subjects of Western background not raised in a kibbutz (Table 3); (c) there was a positive correlation between measures of perceptual articulation and level of achievement on a series of psychological and situational tests designed to evaluate candidates for officer training in the Israel Defense Forces (Table 4).

Before proceeding to the implications of these findings, some comments may be made on the low intercorrelations found here between the various measures of perceptual articulation (Table 1) in contrast to the relatively higher intercorrelations reported by Witkin et al. (1962). It is likely that the highly restricted range of IQ scores of the present population is the major factor which contributed to these low correlations. Witkin's work revealed a relationship between perceptual articulation and intelligence, so that relatively low-order correlations should be anticipated in a group preselected on the basis of similar IQ.

The present study sought to limit the possible effects of the interrelation between general intelligence and perceptual articulation by controlling for general intelligence. Despite this attempt, however, it is possible that the measures employed here did not succeed fully in achieving this goal in respect to the Middle-Eastern–Western group comparison. As indicated above, there is evidence that in the total population, the Middle-Eastern and Western groups differ in level of general intelligence. One might argue, therefore, that due to the "regression to the mean" effect stemming from the lack of reliability in the initial assessment of general intelligence, the tests of perceptual articulation were merely repeated measures of the same general functions of intelligence. It must be noted, however, that this argument does not obtain in respect to the kibbutz-nonkibbutz comparison. Additional analysis of data gathered in another study (Amir, 1969) indicates that there is no difference in level of general intelligence between these two Western groups (i.e., kibbutz- and nonkibbutz-reared males) in the total population. Therefore, there is a firm basis to conclude that general intelligence between kibbutz and nonkibbutz groups of Western origin was adequately controlled in the present study. Hence, the finding that measures of perceptual articulation discriminated between the two latter groups when general intelligence was restricted to a narrow range indicates that tests of perceptual articulation cannot be construed as repeated measures of general intelligence.

Findings obtained in this study testify to the relationship between membership in several Israel subcultures and level of perceptual articulation. No direct information was obtained in this study regarding possible psychosocial factors within each subculture which would shed light on the sources of these intergroup differences. Sociological studies suggest a possible connection between child-rearing practices typical of the various subgroups studied here and cognitive outcomes such as perceptual articulation. Kibbutz children are raised by several socializing agents whose roles and relationship to the child are highly differentiated. On the other hand, the child-rearing functions of socializing agents in the family of Middle-Eastern origin are more stereotyped and less differentiated than in the urban family of Western ethnic background. One might conjecture that these socialization variables exert considerable influence on the development of the intergroup difference found here. However, one may certainly invoke other factors as potential sources of these differences, such as social class and its associated variables, or even the relative emphasis which parents in the various subcultures place upon perceptual differentiation in the behavior of their children. Clear-cut conclusions about these issues must await results obtained from further research. However, the relationship found here (Table 4) between level of perceptual articulation and task achievement on the one hand, and between perceptual articulation and group membership on the other hand, points to perceptual articulation as a possible intervening variable which could contribute to the relationship between group membership and level of task performance.

References

AMIR, Y. The effectiveness of the kibbutz born soldiers in the Israel Defence Forces. *Human Relations,* 1969, *22,* 333–344.

BAR-YOSEF, R. The patterns of early socialization in the collective settlements in Israel. *Human Relations,* 1959, *12,* 345–360.

BERRY, J. W. Temne and Eskimo perceptual skills. *International Journal of Psychology,* 1966, *1,* 207–229.

CIVIL SERVICE COMMISSION. *Comparative study of the composition of the civil service* [Hebrew]. Jerusalem: Ministry of the Treasury, 1968.

COHEN-RAZ, R. Mental and motor development of kibbutz, private-home and institutionalized infants [Hebrew]. *Megamot: Behavioral Sciences Quarterly,* 1968, *15,* 366–387.

DAWSON, J. Z. M. Cultural and physiological influences upon spatial perceptual processes in West Africa. *International Journal of Psychology,* 1967, *2,* 115–128; 171–185.

FAIGIN, H. Social behavior of young children in the kibbutz. *Journal of Abnormal and Social Psychology,* 1958, *56,* 117–129.

FEITELSON, D. Some changes in the educational patterns of the Kurdish community in Israel [Hebrew]. *Megamot—Child Welfare Research Quarterly,* 1954, *6,* 275–297.

JACKSON, D. N., MESSICK, K. S., & MAYERS, C. T. Evaluation of group and individual forms of embedded figures measures of field independence. *Educational and Psychological Measurement,* 1964, *24,* 177–192.

KOHLS, M. Culture patterns and adjustment processes of Moroccan immigrants from rural areas [Hebrew]. *Megamot—Child Welfare Research Quarterly,* 1956, *7,* 345–376.

ORTAR, C. Educational achievements as related to socio-cultural background of primary school graduates in Israel [Hebrew]. *Megamot: Behavioral Sciences Quarterly,* 1967, *15,* 220–230.

RABIN, A. I. *Growing up in the kibbutz.* New York: Springer, 1965.

SMILANSKY, S. *The effects of sociodramatic play on disadvantaged pre-school children.* New York: Wiley, 1968.

SMILANSKY, M., & YAM, Y. The relationship between family size, ethnic origin, father's education and students' achievement [Hebrew]. *Megamot: Behavioral Sciences Quarterly,* 1969, *16,* 248–273.

SPIRO, M. E. *Children of the kibbutz.* New York: Schocken Books, 1965.

Statistical abstract of Israel. Jerusalem: Central Bureau of Statistics, 1969, 20.

TALMON, Y. The family in a revolutionary movement—the case of the kibbutz in Israel. In M. F. Nimkoff (Ed.), *Comparative family systems.* Boston: Houghton Mifflin, 1965.

WEINTRAUB, D. Patterns of social change of ethnic groups in immigrant settlements [Hebrew]. Unpublished doctoral dissertation, Hebrew University, Jerusalem, 1962.

WITKIN, H. A., DYK, R. B., FATERSON, H. F., GOODENOUGH, D. R., & KARP, S. A. *Psychological differentiation.* New York: Wiley, 1962.

WITKIN, H. A. A cognitive-style approach to cross-cultural research. *International Journal of Psychology,* 1967, *2,* 233–250.

38

A Comparative Analysis of Fantasy Need Achievement among High and Low Achieving Male Hawaiian-Americans [1]

BARBARA B. SLOGGETT,
RONALD GALLIMORE,
AND EDWARD S. KUBANY

This study too is interested in the effects of a given culture. Sloggett, Gallimore, and Kubany focus on the ways in which culture may modify the relations between a variable such as need achievement and actual achievement. Although it can be considered a cross-cultural study, the cultures are found in the state of Hawaii. The authors are all affiliated with the University of Hawaii, where Gallimore has been involved in studies of indigenous Hawaiians and (to a lesser extent) other ethnic groups.

The degree to which need achievement as measured by fantasy productions can be studied in the same ways in different cultural groups is an interesting question in itself. The paper by Kubany, Gallimore and Buell in the same issue of the new publication Journal of Cross-Cultural Psychology sheds further light on this question. We cannot reprint it in its entirety, but quote its concluding discussion as a good background for the paper by Sloggett et al.

It is evident from the data that contemporaneous social factors may influence the manifestation of achievement-oriented activity, at least among Filipinos. Subjects in the public condition, under the surveillance of the experimenter, selected a moderate risk on 75 out of 100 trials (chance equals 33/100), significantly more than subjects in the relatively anonymous, private condition. These results are consistent with the notion that Filipinos are highly concerned with social cues as guidelines for behavior. The glaring avoidance of easy risks by subjects in the public condition provides some further support for this conclusion. That is, in the face of public evaluation, acceptance of a moderate or difficult challenge might be construed as more socially desirable than taking the "easy" way out. Among Filipinos, striving for a "sense of accomplishment" may be considerably less important than the social consequences of such striving. The most obvious implication is that analysis of specific forms of achievement-oriented behavior among Filipinos should take into account the context in which such behavior does or does not occur; i.e., whether achievement-oriented behavior is considered as "competitive," "showing off," "expected," or "for the good name of the family."

Our principal intent was not to demonstrate the sensitivity of Filipinos to situational cues; that aspect is incidental. Rather, we have sought to illustrate in an isolated instance the danger of exporting American psychological methodologies and conceptions to non-Western groups. While the study was concerned with the behavior of a specific group, the findings reflect on some broader theoretical issues. Previous studies of achievement-oriented behavior have typically ignored the possible effects of extrinsic motives such as the desire for acceptance or social approval. Investigators have usually assumed that a subject may be concerned with cooperating with the experimenter's demands to perform a task, but that this concern does not systematically affect the degree of achievement-oriented behavior. However, the present findings and other recent experimental evidence (Atkinson & O'Connor, 1966; Gallimore, 1969; Klinger, 1967) suggest that under certain circumstances extrinsic factors may operate to enhance preference for moderately difficult tasks; for example, Gallimore (1969) reported that fantasy n Affiliation scores, but not resultant achievement motivation scores (TAT n Ach minus test anxiety scores), predicted intermediate risk taking among indigenous Hawaiians. Underscoring the potential effects of situational cues, Klinger (1967) recently found that subjects exposed to achievement-oriented models produced more fantasy achievement than subjects exposed to affiliative or neutral models. These findings raise doubts about the cross-cultural generality of the theory of achievement motivation (Atkinson & Feather, 1966) and draw attention to the potential importance of situational and social factors which have been neglected in most previous research on achievement motivation.[1]

[1] The research was supported by an NIMH research grant to the Bernice Pauahi Bishop Museum, Honolulu, and by the Social Science Research Institute, University of Hawaii. Alan Howard, Roland Tharp, and Anthony Marsella are due our appreciation for many contributions to this work.

[1] Kubany, Gallimore, and Buell, "The Effects of Extrinsic Factors on Achievement-Oriented Behavior: A Non-Western Case." Used by permission.

Barbara B. Sloggett, Ronald Gallimore, and Edward S. Kubany, "A comparative analysis of fantasy need achievement among high and low achieving male Hawaiian-Americans," Journal of Cross-Cultural Psychology, 1, 1970, 53–61. Reprinted by permission.

Investigating psychological motivation among ethnic minorities whose social problems are a matter of national concern is an endeavor of considerable importance. Most studies of *n* Ach (Barberio, 1967; McClelland, 1961; Mingione, 1965; Nuttall, 1964; Veroff, Atkinson, Feld, & Gurin, 1960) data have been collected in a fashion which has permitted only between group comparisons. Missing, in most cases, is analysis of within ethnic group relationships between *n* Ach and relevant indices, except for the abundant studies of Americans of Caucasian descent (Atkinson & Feather, 1966). For example, there are almost no studies comparing psychological motivation between academically successful and academically unsuccessful Afro-Americans. Nevertheless it has been generally assumed that the relationship between *n* Ach and achievement holds for ethnic groups of non-Western origins. Other writers, for example DeVos (1968), have seriously questioned this view, suggesting that *n* Ach, either theoretically or empirically need not be expected to relate to achievement within all cultural groups. The present study examined this question by comparing high and low achieving (HA and LA) indigenous Hawaiians on a fantasy measure of *n* Ach. The indigenous Hawaiians were drawn from two disparate populations. A low achieving (LA) Hawaiian group consisted of individuals living in a suburb of Honolulu which had been the focus of a year of participant observation and ethnographic analysis completed prior to the study reported here (Gallimore & Howard, 1968). The particular community and the majority of Hawaiians are plagued by educational problems confronting other impoverished American ethnic minorities. More particularly, the levels of educational achievement in this Hawaiian community were among the lowest in the entire State. The high achieving (HA) Hawaiian group was selected from a private school established in the last century specifically for Hawaiian children and which currently accepts, on a state-wide basis, only academically talented and accomplished Hawaiian youngsters. This group, in contrast to the LA group, was almost entirely from middle-class families with fathers in skilled or white-collar jobs; thus, for a variety of reasons, the LA Hawaiians should write fewer *n* Ach stories.

For purposes of contrast, small samples of Filipinos and Japanese were obtained.

METHOD

SUBJECTS

The *S*s, all males, included 31 LA Hawaiians—10th, 11th, and 12th graders from a high school in a low-income area. From the same school, 13 Japanese and 15 Filipinos from similar grades were also selected. The LA Hawaiians were living on lands leased by the Department of Hawaiian Homelands to individuals of at least 50 percent Hawaiian ancestry. The HA Hawaiian *S*s were 48 students attending a private school established for children of Hawaiian ancestry. Entrance to this school is based on academic ability and achievement, with the student population being selected on a state-wide basis. Average Hawaiian ancestry (self-report) was 49.50 and 43.45 percent for the LA and HA groups respectively.

English is spoken by almost all residents of Hawaii although, for some, particularly Hawaiians and Filipinos, a dialect of English, known as "pidgin," is the primary language.

MATERIALS

Merbaum (1961),[2] following an exacting psychometric procedure, developed a set of 12 TAT-like pictures in which racial cues were made deliberately ambiguous. That is, *S*s of any race or ethnic group could interpret the drawings as portraying people of any race they chose. The stimuli were line drawings representing school, work, or neutral scenes, such as a boy in a school hall, a boy standing on a street corner, etc. Of the original 12 pictures used by Merbaum (1961), six were eliminated from the Hawaii study because of the presence of cues not common to the Islands; e.g., a man on a farm tractor.

PROCEDURE

The picture stimuli were administered in a group setting at the respective schools; the instructions were identical to those employed by Merbaum (1961). Each of the pictures for which stories were to be written was reproduced on a separate page and accompanied by the four questions ordinarily used by *n* Ach researchers, including Merbaum (1961). Scoring followed the usual procedure; reliability of scoring was assessed by comparison of scores assigned by an experienced graduate student to stories scored by expert scorers as reported in Atkinson (1959). The degree of reliability was highly satisfactory, ranging from .80 to .94. The scorer had no knowledge of the samples or the purposes of the study.

Intelligence and achievement test scores were obtained from school records. The intelligence measure available was the total test score on the California Test of Mental Maturity (CTMM) and the achievement tests were the Scholastic Test of Educational Progress (STEP) in reading and math. Unfortunately, test data were not available for all *S*s.

RESULTS

Because of the multiplicity of possible comparisons and for simplicity of presentation, all statistical levels reported are two-tailed though some directional hypotheses were clearly suggested; e.g., Japanese were expected to have higher *n* Ach scores than the LA Hawaiians. For

---

[2] Merbaum's doctoral dissertation was published under her married name of Mingione (1965).

the same reasons, conservative *post hoc* comparisons of *n* Ach levels (Hays, 1963) were performed.

Table 1 presents the intelligence test scores for the four groups of boys. An analysis of variance yields a highly significant F of 17.07 (p < .01, *df* = 3/74). By *post hoc* analysis, the HA Hawaiians had significantly higher intelligence test scores than both the Filipinos and LA Hawaiians, who had the lowest scores, and were nonsignificantly higher than the Japanese. The Japanese also had significantly higher intelligence test scores than the LA Hawaiians.

Table 1 also presents the means and standard deviations among the groups in reading and math achievement. The overall analyses of variance for reading and math achievement were both highly significant. For reading achievement, F = 38.48 (p < .01, *df* = 3/78) and for math achievement, F = 23.91 (p < .01, *df* = 3/77). Consistent with the intelligence test scores, the data indicated that the HA Hawaiians had the highest achievement scores, both in math and reading. In math achievement, the HA Hawaiians scored significantly higher than both the Filipinos and LA Hawaiians and nonsignificantly higher than the Japanese, who also scored significantly higher than the Filipinos and LA

Hawaiians. The same relationships hold for reading achievement, with the single exception that the HA Hawaiians also had significantly higher reading achievement scores than the Japanese.

The classification of the two Hawaiian groups as LA and HA respectively was confirmed by the data, albeit on less than the entire *n* Ach sample. On each of the three measures, the HA Hawaiians were higher than the low achievers. The Japanese and Filipino boys, from groups less noted for academic problems, were generally intermediate to the two Hawaiian groups.

Table 2 presents the *n* Ach means and standard deviations for each of the four groups. Comparing the *n* Ach means for each of the four male groups, an overall analysis of variance was significant beyond the .01 level (F = 4.38, *df* = 3/103). All possible paired comparisons were made using the *post hoc* technique suggested by Hays (1963). Table 2 shows there was no significant difference in *n* Ach between the HA and LA Hawaiian groups. The one significant difference was between the Japanese and LA Hawaiians (p < .05) with the Japanese-HA Hawaiian difference marginally significant (p < .10). The Filipinos scored nonsignificantly intermediate to the Japanese and Hawaiian groups.

TABLE 1

MEANS, STANDARD DEVIATIONS, AND SIGNIFICANCE LEVELS FOR MALES IN ALL GROUPS ON ACHIEVEMENT AND INTELLIGENCE TESTS *

	California Test of Mental Maturity (CTMM)			
	HA Hawaiian	LA Hawaiian	Japanese	Filipino
N	39	19	8	12
$\bar{X}$	113.87	90.58	105.13	100.00
SD	10.29	12.52	15.59	10.62
High Achieving Hawaiian	—		NS	.01
Low Achieving Hawaiian	.01	—	.01	NS
Japanese			—	
Filipino			NS	—
	STEP–Reading			
N	44	13	12	13
$\bar{X}$	69.55	13.92	50.67	20.08
SD	19.73	11.42	28.17	17.49
High Achieving Hawaiian	—		.05	.01
Low Achieving Hawaiian	.01	—	.01	NS
Japanese			—	
Filipino			.05	—
	STEP–Math			
N	43	13	12	13
$\bar{X}$	68.67	18.31	47.83	18.31
SD	24.83	17.25	32.45	16.06
High Achieving Hawaiian	—		NS	.01
Low Achieving Hawaiian	.01	—	.05	NS
Japanese			—	
Filipino			.05	—

* The variability in Ns reflects incomplete school records of some of the boys in the samples.

TABLE 2
MEANS, STANDARD DEVIATIONS, AND SIGNIFICANCE LEVELS FOR BOYS IN ALL GROUPS ON *n* ACHIEVEMENT

	HA Hawaiian	LA Hawaiian	Japanese	Filipino
N	48	31	13	15
$\overline{X}$	2.27	1.77	4.77	4.13
SD	2.86	2.23	3.92	4.12
High Achieving Hawaiian	—		.10	NS
Low Achieving Hawaiian	NS	—	.05	NS
Japanese			—	
Filipino			NS	—

The marked differences in variability reflected by the standard deviations shown in Table 2 prompted an additional form of analysis in terms of the percentage of subjects within each ethnic group who wrote at least one *n* Ach theme. The percentages of boys within each group who wrote from zero to three stories with an *n* Ach theme are presented in Table 3. The rank order of the various groups of boys in Table 3 is identical to the rank order shown in Table 2. It appears that the differences in Table 2 are not simply an artifact of the extreme variability reflected by the standard deviations. The *n* Ach differences among the Japanese and Hawaiian groups become more striking when viewed in this manner; it is evident that the Hawaiians produced an extremely small absolute amount of *n* Ach imagery. While 54 percent of the Japanese boys wrote *n* Ach themes in response to at least two cards, only 15 percent of the HA Hawaiians and only 3 percent of the LA Hawaiians wrote *n* Ach themes in response to more than one of the six pictures. For comparative purposes, it might be noted that 58 percent of the rural Caucasian males in Merbaum's (1961) study wrote *n* Ach themes in response to more than one of the same six pictures; thus, the Merbaum pictures had a stimulus value for the Japanese approximately equal to that observed for the rural Caucasians. Similarly, 24 percent of the Afro-Americans in Merbaum's study wrote *n* Ach themes to two or more pictures, compared to 33 percent of the Filipinos in the present study.

The Japanese wrote more *n* Ach themes than the LA Hawaiians and, as might be expected, also had higher intelligence and achievement test scores than the LA Hawaiians. However, the relationships between the HA Hawaiians and the other groups are not nearly so clear. For example, in spite of the fact that the HA Hawaiians had lower *n* Ach scores than the Japanese, they had nonsignificantly higher intelligence and math achievement test scores and significantly higher reading

TABLE 3
PERCENTAGE OF BOYS WRITING VARIOUS NUMBERS
OF *n* ACHIEVEMENT THEMES

	0	1	2	3	4	5	6
High Achieving Hawaiians	54%	31	13	2			
Low Achieving Hawaiians	56	41	3				
Japanese	31	15	54				
Filipinos	33	33	20	13			

achievement scores than the Japanese. Further, while the HA Hawaiians had substantially higher intelligence and achievement scores than the LA Hawaiians, there was no significant difference in *n* Ach between the HA and LA group. There was no *n* Ach difference in spite of the fact that the HA Hawaiian boys wrote longer stories ($\overline{X}$ number of words = 410, SD = 121), though not significantly longer, than the LA Hawaiians ($\overline{X}$ = 372, SD = 107).

To analyze the within ethnic group relationships between *n* Ach and actual accomplishment, Pearson product-moment correlations were computed between *n* Ach, intelligence, reading achievement and math achievement for each of the groups separately, and for all groups combined. These correlations are reported in Table 4. Among the Japanese, *n* Ach correlated significantly with intelligence and reading achievement and nonsignificantly with math achievement scores. However, among the Filipinos and both of the Hawaiian groups, there were no significant correlations between *n* Ach and intelligence nor between *n* Ach and achievement test scores. For all groups combined, however, *n* Ach correlated significantly with both reading and math achievement and intelligence; however, the magnitude of these correlations is small, ranging from .15 to .26. Of course, the attenuated distribution of *n* Ach scores, particularly in the LA Hawaiian group, substantially reduced the possibility of a significant correlation between *n* Ach and the achievement and intelligence tests.

DISCUSSION

In terms of experience, ability, achievement, and social status, there was every reason to believe that the HA Hawaiian boys ought to have written more *n* Ach themes than their LA counterparts. But they did not. In view of the performance of the Japanese and Filipinos, there appears to be no reason to attribute their performance to a lack of "pull" of the picture stimuli. These findings challenge the usefulness of the notion that Hawaiian boys do poorly in school because they lack *n* Ach.[3] As

---

[3] Comparable data for females yielded no differences in *n* Ach among Hawaiians, Japanese, and Filipinos; thus, the Discussion applies only to males. The female data were not reported, since there is a general lack of agreement about relationship of *n* Ach to female personality.

TABLE 4
WITHIN ETHNIC GROUP CORRELATION OF *n* ACHIEVEMENT WITH ACHIEVEMENT AND INTELLIGENCE TEST SCORES

| *n Ach* | Hawaiians | | | | | | | | | |
| | High Achieving | | Low Achieving | | Japanese | | Filipino | | All Groups | |
	N	r	N	r	N	r	N	r	N	r
CTMM	79	.14	40	.19	21	.46**	18	.25	288	.15**
STEP–Reading	86	.05	30	−.14	27	.37*	21	−.02	309	.26***
STEP–Math	86	.08	30	−.07	27	.26	21	.35	309	.24

* $p < .10$
** $p < .05$
*** $p < .01$

previously indicated, the HA Hawaiian boys were students enrolled in a private school which selects pupils on the basis of ability and achievement. The LA Hawaiian sample, on the other hand, was drawn from a public high school and, as a group, was characterized by low levels of academic success, high truancy, dropout or push-out rates and other school behavior problems associated with impoverished areas.

The conclusion that Hawaiian males are poor scholars because they lack *n* Ach is a "deficiency" explanation (Gallimore, 1969); at best, it explains why Hawaiian children do not behave as middle-class Caucasian children do, but it does not explain what motivates those among the Hawaiian children who do achieve. Thus the issue becomes what motive, if not *n* Ach, is associated with achievement for Hawaiian males. One preliminary study (Gallimore, 1969) indicates that, for Hawaiian high school boys, fantasy *n* Affiliation and not *n* Ach, is correlated with achievement-oriented behavior in a risk taking task. This finding is consistent with the ethnographic data (Gallimore & Howard, 1968) which clearly reflected the importance attached by Hawaiians to affiliative rewards; thus, it is possible that among Hawaiians, both HA and LA, those individuals whose preferences for affiliative reinforcement are particularly strong may be motivated to work especially hard at achievement tasks in order to gain the approval of others. Consistent with this notion is the finding by Sloggett (1969) that affiliative reinforcers were more effective than individual rewards in a program designed to foster academic improvement among a group of male Hawaiian high school dropouts.

In general, the data suggest that attempts to explain the problems of American ethnic minorities in terms of psychological motives must first assess what is valued by the members of the respective groups. If there are variations across ethnic groups in the motivational antecedents of achievement, then attempts to foster higher achievement—for example, among Afro-American youngsters in ghetto schools—may fail if it is

assumed that *n* Ach is or can be a primary motive. It is likely that greater success could be achieved if the schools were organized to take advantage of the motives operative within particular ethnic groups.

REFERENCES

ATKINSON, J. W. (Ed.) *Motives in fantasy, action, and society.* Princeton: Van Nostrand, 1959.

ATKINSON, J. W., & FEATHER, N. T. *A theory of achievement motivation.* New York: Wiley, 1966.

BARBERIO, R. The relationship between achievement motivation and ethnicity in Anglo-American and Mexican-American junior high school students. *Psychological Record,* 1967, *17*(2), 263–266.

DEVOS, G. A. Achievement and innovation in culture and personality. In E. Norbeck, D. Price-Williams, & W. M. McCord (Eds.). *The study of personality: an interdisciplinary approach.* New York: Holt, Rinehart, & Winston, 1968.

GALLIMORE, R. Variations in the motivational antecedents of achievement among Hawaii's ethnic groups. Paper read at East-West Conference on Culture and Mental Health, Social Science Research Institute, Honolulu, Hawaii, 1969. (Proceedings in press.)

GALLIMORE, R., & HOWARD, A. (Eds.) *Studies in a Hawaiian Community: Na Makamaka O Nanakuli.* Pacific Anthropological Records No. 1. Honolulu: Department of Anthropology, B. P. Bishop Museum, 1968.

HAYS, W. L. *Statistics for psychologists.* New York: Holt, Rinehart, & Winston, 1963.

MCCLELLAND, D. C. *The achieving society.* Princeton: Van Nostrand, 1961.

MERBAUM, A. D. *Need for achievement in Negro and white children.* (Doctoral dissertation, University of North Carolina) Ann Arbor, Michigan: University Microfilms, 1961. No. 62-3140.

MINGIONE, A. D. Need for achievement in Negro and white children. *Journal of Consulting Psychology,* 1965, *29*(2), 108–111.

NUTTALL, R. L. Some correlates of high need for achievement among urban northern Negroes. *Journal of Abnormal and Social Psychology,* 1964, *68,* 593–608.

SLOGGETT, B. B. *Behavior modification of the underachieving rural Hawaiian: An experimental classroom.* Pacific Anthropological Records No. 5. Honolulu: Department of Anthropology, B. P. Bishop Museum, 1969.

VEROFF, J., ATKINSON, J. W., FELD, S. C., & GURIN, G. The use of thematic apperception to assess motivation in a nationwide interview study. *Psychological Monographs,* 1960, *74*(12), 32 pp.

39

Interpersonal Spacing in Natural Settings *

James C. Baxter

The first few selections in this section dealt with the effects of culture, or membership in a particular culture, on behavior. This article is concerned with behaviors that appear to be primarily influenced by ethnic origin. The study was done in a state that has a variety of minority groups (i.e., groups of ethnic origin other than northern or central European). While the article's title may suggest that it should be in Section V (Settings), ethnic origin proves to be the more important "cause of behavior." The study could also have been put in Sections VII (Age) or VIII (Sex), since those variables were also investigated.

Interpersonal spacing is currently a topic of considerable amounts of research, as well as being of intrinsic interest. Another reason for including this study is to point out the possibility of doing research in real life (not just in laboratory settings) and without disturbing the research subjects.

The author of the paper is in the Psychology Department of the University of Houston, where he has also worked in the Counseling Service.

* This investigation was supported in part by National Institute of Dental Research Grant, DE 138-05, awarded to Richard I. Evans. Appreciation is expressed to Douglas Jackson for serving as the primary rater throughout the study and to Susan J. Fiester and Steven D. Kantor for serving as reliability raters.

A principle which has gained recognition in recent years is that people from different cultural backgrounds learn to define and utilize geographic space in different ways. Thus, culturally differentiated groups tend to prefer different spatial arrangements of participants involved in social interactions, and usually prefer to interact with each other at different interpersonal distances—some tightly clustered, others more widely spaced (Little, 1968). While the quality and type of interaction involved affects the spacing adopted (Hall, 1966; Little et al., 1968), a given type of interaction also tends to be conducted at different distances in different cultures. An acceptable distance for a personal conversation between adult males of equivalent status under given conditions in an Arab culture, for example, may be quite unacceptable or even anxiety arousing in a Northern European culture (Hall, 1966).

A number of investigations from a variety of research traditions have tended to confirm these general observations (Patterson, 1968; Sommer, 1966). Groups which have received most attention have been East European, Arabic, and Mediterranean cultures. E. T. Hall (1966) has argued that, in general, these groups tend to interact under much more proximal conditions and frequently can be seen touching each other during encounters. A substantial amount of anecdotal data has supported this contention. Systematic data from Watson and Graves (1966) have demonstrated such differences between Arabs and Americans under standardized real life conditions, and Little (1968) has supported the finding with a variety of cultural groups using symbolic tasks.

The extension of work of this sort would appear to be necessary and quite useful. A number of promising implications from such data can be identified in areas such as interpersonal and social processes and in environmental design. For example, it could be argued that people interacting more proximally expose themselves to a much different "view" of each other, and therefore utilize different cues in the interaction process (Frede et al., 1968). From a design standpoint, considerably different spatial requirements are imposed by people preferring interpersonal closeness and contact (Alexander, 1967).

While the dominant cultural heritage in the United States has been Northern European, significant minorities from other backgrounds exist. To the extent that such subcultures show corresponding or similar differences in space usage, they may prefer different interaction conditions and, therefore, may require certain design alterations

James C. Baxter, "Interpersonal spacing in natural settings," *Sociometry*, 1970, *33*, 444–456. Reprinted by permission.

for optimal interpersonal function (Carr, 1967). Very little information is available to date regarding preferred interaction distances of subcultural groups in this country. A study by Willis (1966) is an exception, and provides a beginning point for investigation. He used either black or white experimenters of both sexes as observers of the social greeting distances of either black or white subjects in several types of natural settings. While his results were complex, one finding relevant to the present investigation was that black subjects generally tended to greet others (especially other blacks) at greater distances. He also found that greeting distances involving one or more women were shorter. That is, they apparently delayed greetings and social interaction until the interpersonal distance was much smaller. While not specifically focusing on these issues, an early study by Efron (1941) also reported differences in body contact and spacing patterns. He studied East European Jewish and Southern Italian subcultures as they conversed on New York City streets. In general, he found greater closeness and more physical contact among his Jewish subjects. However, these observations were quite secondary to other emphases of the investigation. They also provide no information on spacing patterns of other subgroupings such as age and sex combinations.

The present investigation was designed to examine the distances at which people interacted with each other in several natural settings. Three subcultural groupings, along with three sex combinations and three age levels were studied in two types of settings. The general location chosen for the observations was the Houston zoo. This setting was selected because it is an attractive location, consistently drawing large numbers of people to fixed observation points. Further, representatives of all the major ethnic and social groupings of the city can be found in large numbers, and they typically are seen interacting spontaneously under pleasant circumstances in natural groupings. The groupings are very often family units, but also reflect social and some fraternal groupings.

Two person groups of Anglo-, Black-, or Mexican-American ethnic composition were divided into three sex combinations: two males, two females, or one male and one female; and into three age levels: adults, adolescents, and children. Finally, observations were made in both indoor and outdoor settings.

While the purpose of the investigation was primarily exploratory, several expectations were formulated on the basis of previous work. In general, the Mexican groups were expected to interact most proximally (Hall, 1966), while the Negro groups were expected to interact at greatest

distances (Willis, 1966). Groups composed of one or two females were expected to interact most closely (Sommer, 1962; Willis, 1966), although the absence of sex differences in some previous research (Baxter and Phelps, 1970; Little et al., 1968) made this expectation quite reserved. Differences in spacing in different settings were also expected. In general, subject groups were expected to interact more proximally in indoor settings (Baxter and Phelps, 1970; Little, 1965). Finally, while little research has focused specifically on the issue, observers often agree that young children interact with each other and with adults under more proximal conditions (cf. Argyle and Dean, 1965), especially when excited or threatened. Thus, the children were expected to interact more proximally under present conditions.

METHOD

After some pilot observations of interaction patterns and traffic flow in the zoo, four locations were chosen for the observations. These locations were two indoor settings: the Toucan bird exhibit in the aviary and the baby gorilla exhibit in the children's zoo; and two outdoor settings: the Diana monkey cage in the primate area and the Kodiak bear enclosure in the heavy mammal area. These locations were selected because the traffic flow was moderately heavy, people usually tended to pause briefly and interact with each other while observing the animals, and each setting had a bench opposite it, on which an observer could position himself. These benches were approximately 10 feet from the observation area in each case and were generally out of view of people passing by.

As people passed each of the settings they were classified for ethnic, sex, and age grouping, and distance ratings were made and inconspicuously recorded on a tabulation sheet. The following procedure was used in classifying subjects and making ratings. Two person groups were identified in terms of how they approached an observation setting from previous exhibits. If they came to the setting in a two person grouping, they were considered for classification. Other types of groupings were ignored. Further, ethnic classification was made on the basis of external appearance and language. Black subjects were identified on the basis of skin color and physiognomic features, while Mexican subjects were identified on the basis of appearance and language, if possible. Most remaining subjects, with the exception of obvious orientals, were classified as Anglo. Any cues available were taken into consideration, and doubtful subjects were ignored. Three sex groupings were identified: male-male, male-female, and female-female combinations. The final classification was made on the basis of age. When both members of the pair were 20 years of age or above, they were classified as adult; when both were between 10 and 20, they were classified as adolescent; and when both were between five and 10, they were classified as children. Pairs which crossed age or ethnic groups were ignored.

Thus, several criteria determined whether subjects were included in the present sample. They had to approach an observation area in a pair grouping, and they could not be carrying children or large parcels nor be pushing strollers. Moreover, they had to be classifiable into one of the ethnic and age groupings. Any pairs meeting these conditions were rated, regardless of how they arranged themselves upon stopping at the exhibit. While it cannot be estimated with certainty, perhaps one-tenth to one-fifth of the people passing the settings were classifiable, and therefore became subjects. In all, 859 subject pairs were included in the present observations.

Interpersonal distance judgments were made by one rater as he observed a pair approach an observation setting and stop to look at the exhibit. When the pair passed a previously designated point on their way to the setting, the observer began a fixed timing interval. After 10 seconds had elapsed, he judged the distance between the pair to the nearest one-quarter foot from nose to nose. Typically, this caught subjects standing side-by-side looking at the animal. Of course, the judgment was made at that time, no matter what the actions or positions of the pair were. The 10 second interval was introduced for two reasons. It took the decision of when to judge the interpersonal distance out of the rater's hands. It also allowed the subjects enough time to "settle" into an observation position, but not so long an interval that many potential subjects had passed out of the observation area before it had elapsed.[1]

The observations were made at varying time periods during the months of June and July, 1969. Primary emphasis was placed on weekends, although weekdays were also used. On each observation day, observations were made at all settings.

One adult male judge who was unacquainted with the specific expectations of the investigation served as the rater throughout the period of the study. A considerable amount of discussion with and training of the rater preceded the point at which he began making ratings, and periodic visits and observations by the author throughout the course of the observations helped maintain his concern with accuracy. Two additional raters, one man and one woman, were trained as alternate raters about half-way through the observation period. Their ratings were intended to provide an overall estimate of the primary rater's reliability. The alternate raters judged distances with the primary rater at varying times during the middle period of observation. In all cases, agreement of the judgments regarding the ethnic group, age level, and sex combination of subjects to be rated was quite high. Distance measurements were recorded separately by the two raters. The delay interval was timed by the primary rater in all cases. The timing of each rating was signaled to the comparison rater by the pri-

mary rater; although no other communication occurred between raters during rating sessions. Comparisons of rating patterns were not made until the completion of all ratings to be made by each comparison rater. The ratings of the primary judge correlated .94 with his female comparison rater for 38 subject pairs and .88 with his male comparison rater for 68 subject pairs. The means of the raters' judgments were within .55 feet of each other using the female comparison and .11 feet using the male comparison. In general, the level of classification and rating agreement was quite high and appeared to be adequate for present purposes.

RESULTS

The interpersonal distance ratings of the primary rater were entered into a four-way analysis of variance design and analyzed according to an unweighted means solution. Main factors of the design were defined by: the ethnic group of the subject pair (Anglo-, Black-, or Mexican-American), the age level category of the subjects (adult, adolescent, or child), the sex combination of the subjects (male-male, male-female, or female-female), and the location of the observations (indoor or outdoor). Results of this overall analysis are summarized in Table 1. The means of the 54 cells of the design are also presented for examination in Table 2.

Seven of the 15 comparisons attained significance at conventional levels of confidence, and an eighth comparison approached significance ($p < .10$). The most impressive result of the analysis is the difference in spacing attributable to ethnic groupings ($F = 126.57$; $df = 2/805$; $p < .001$). This effect is quite sizable, and accounts for approximately 32 percent of the total variability of the sample (Vaughan and Corbollis, 1969). Evaluation of the individual means involved indicates

TABLE 1
SUMMARY OF THE ANALYSIS OF THE VARIANCE
OF INTERPERSONAL DISTANCE RATINGS

Source	d.f.	M.S.	F
Ethnic Group (E)	2	34.53	126.57****
Age (A)	2	10.24	37.53****
Sex (S)	2	3.48	12.77****
Location (L)	1	0.33	1.20
E × A	4	0.53	1.96*
E × S	4	2.08	7.64****
E × L	2	1.54	5.65***
A × S	4	0.77	2.82**
A × L	2	0.04	< 1.00
S × L	2	0.39	1.45
E × A × S	8	0.78	2.87***
E × A × L	4	0.12	< 1.00
E × S × L	4	0.14	< 1.00
A × S × L	4	0.27	1.01
E × A × S × L	8	0.16	< 1.00
Error	805	0.27	...

**** $p < .001$.
*** $p < .005$.
** $p < .025$.
* $p < .10$.

---

[1] During the pilot investigation period, observations were made on 120 subject pairs for purposes of refining procedures. A 15 second interval was used during this period. However, it proved to be too long, since a high percentage of the adult Negro males were found to have moved beyond the observation area within this time. The shorter interval corrected this problem in most cases.

TABLE 2
MEAN INTERPERSONAL DISTANCE RATINGS FOR EACH COMBINATION OF ETHNIC, AGE, SEX, AND LOCATION CONDITIONS

Ethnic Group	Sex Combination	Indoor			Outdoor		
		Adult	Adolesc.	Child.	Adult	Adolesc.	Child.
Anglo	M–M	2.72	2.71	2.07	2.72	2.47	2.05
	M–F	2.33	2.04	1.89	2.59	2.22	1.92
	F–F	2.45	2.03	1.94	2.46	2.41	2.21
Black	M–M	3.15	2.67	1.81	3.16	2.84	2.20
	M–F	2.77	2.01	2.14	2.99	2.63	2.26
	F–F	2.89	2.89	2.64	2.83	2.96	2.99
Mexican	M–M	2.14	2.34	2.09	1.97	2.11	1.75
	M–F	1.65	1.94	1.57	1.83	1.65	1.50
	F–F	2.00	1.56	1.39	1.67	1.54	1.30

that the Mexican groups stood closest ($\overline{X} = 1.78$; N = 160), Anglos were intermediate ($\overline{X} = 2.29$; N = 427), and Blacks stood most distant ($\overline{X} = 2.66$; N = 272). Analysis of the differences between means by *t*-tests indicates that each ethnic group differs from the other significantly (*t*'s > 7.40; *p*'s < .001).[2] It is also of interest to note that the order of the ethnic group means was maintained in each of the three first-order interactions where ethnic groupings were distinguished for age and sex classifications and for observation setting. Thus, the expectation of differential spacing of the three ethnic groups was clearly supported.

The age groupings also differed significantly in the interpersonal distances adopted (F = 37.53; df = 2/805; *p* < .001). This effect is moderately large, and accounts for approximately 10 percent of the total variance of the sample. Individual means revealed that the children interacted most proximally ($\overline{X} = 1.99$; N = 257), adolescents were intermediate ($\overline{X} = 2.28$; N = 212), and adults interacted at greatest distances ($\overline{X} = 2.46$; N = 390). All three individual comparisons were significant (*t*'s > 3.60; *p*'s < .001), and the order of the age groups remained consistent when the groups were distinguished for ethnic and sex classifications and for location of observation. Again, results were consistent with expectations guiding the study.

A final main effect which attained significance is attributable to the sex groupings of the subjects (F = 12.77; df = 2/805; *p* < .001). However, while the effect is reliable, only about three percent of the total variability of the sample is controlled by the sex groupings of the subjects. Individual comparisons revealed that the male-female groups interacted most proximally ($\overline{X} = 2.11$; N = 386), the female-female groups were intermediate ($\overline{X} = 2.23$; N = 238), and the male-male groups were most distant ($\overline{X} = 2.39$; N = 235). Again, all three groupings differed significantly from each other (*t*'s > 2.40; *p*'s < .02). In contrast to the other main effects, however, the order of the sex groupings did not remain constant within the ethnic and age combinations and across observation settings. In any case, the result is in

general agreement with prior expectations. The modest level of the effect and its inconsistency across groups is interesting, since previous work has been inconsistent in reporting sex differences in spacing.

Four interactions reached conventional levels of significance. Of these, the ethnic group by sex group comparison (E × S) and the ethnic group by sex group by age group comparison (E × S × A) appear most meaningful. These interactions account for approximately eight and nine percent of the total sample variance, respectively. Examination of the patterns of means involved indicates that the Anglos and Blacks showed sex group differences such that the male-female groups stood closest and the male-male groups stood most distant in relation to each other. The Mexicans showed a different pattern, however. For them, the female-female group interacted most proximally, while the male-male group was most distant. Examination of the second-order interaction of these factors with age (i.e., E × S × A) revealed that the ethnic differences in which of the sex groupings interacted most proximally was clearest for adolescents and adults, but was absent among the children. The Anglo children essentially failed to show sex group effects, while both the Mexican and Black children showed strong, albeit different patterns. The female-female group interacted most proximally within the Mexican groups and at the greatest distance within the Black groups.

Two additional interactions attained significance, each of which accounted for approximately two percent of the total sample variability. The age by sex group comparison (A × S) revealed that the sex combination differences were most pronounced within the adolescent groups, and were minimal within children's groups. However, the most interesting effect is attributable to the ethnic group by location of observation comparison (E × L). Evaluation of group means reveals that while the Anglos interacted at approximately the same distances both in the indoor locations and in the outdoor settings, this is not true of the Blacks and Mexicans. Indeed, their patterns of interaction are reversed (*t* = 3.36; df = 4.28; *p* < .001), with the Mexicans interacting more closely in outdoor settings and the Blacks interacting more closely in indoor settings. Thus, the general expectation that subjects would cluster more tightly in indoor

---

[2] The pooled error term derived from the analysis of variance table was used for the comparison of all simple effects.

settings was not supported. This pattern only occurred in the Black groups.

The final comparison, the ethnic group by age group interaction ($E \times A$), attained significance at a marginal level of confidence and actually accounts for only one percent of the total variance. The means contained in this comparison reveal that the ethnic group differences are most pronounced among adults, and tend to be less noticeable among adolescents and children.

DISCUSSION

The pattern of results reveals striking ethnic, age, and sex group effects in interpersonal spacing. In fact, approximately 67 percent of the total variability of the sample was controlled by these effects and their combinations. The most impressive single finding, however, is attributable to the ethnic group membership of the subject pairs. The tendency for Mexican subjects of all ages and sex groupings to interact most proximally is consistent with Hall's (1966) and Little's (1968) reports that Mediterranean cultures, and presumably American subcultures of this origin, interact at closer distances. Indeed, they not only stood closer together, but informal observation also suggested that they very frequently touched each other and often held each other by the hand or arm or one member stood with his arm around the waist of the other. This was rarely observed in the Anglo and Black groups. The tendency for Blacks to stand at greater distances is consistent with Willis' (1966) findings concerning greeting distances. Thus, the present results reveal rather small but exceedingly consistent subcultural differences between subjects interacting in natural settings in pre-established groupings.

The age group differences also achieved significance and were associated with a meaningful proportion of the total variability. Perhaps most interesting, however, is the fact that the ethnic group differences in spacing were present even in the youngest subject groups. While the size of these differences increased with age, their presence in the children's groups suggests that schemata of appropriate spatial arrangements are learned early in the childhood period and persist into adulthood. These data, while interesting also tend to add support to other studies (cf. Baxter and Phelps, 1970; Fisher, 1967; Weinstein, 1967) of the importance of spatial schemata in young children. The present data corroborate this generalization using unobtrusive ratings of children in natural interaction.

Sex group differences were extremely reliable, although quite minor in the present data. While significant differences were found, they generally controlled rather small proportions of the variance, and were inconsistently maintained across age and ethnic groupings. While it is correct to conclude that groupings with one or two female members interacted more proximally under most conditions, the differences were generally slight. Perhaps a variety of factors contributed to the weak and inconsistent effects. One factor may have been the variability in role relationships among the participants. It may be, for example, that more family units including spouses, siblings, etc., were observed in some ethnic groupings as compared with others, where more nonfamilial groupings may have occurred. It seems reasonable to expect that if greater control could be exerted over the role relationships of subjects observed, more dependable sex differences would emerge.

An especially interesting, although somewhat minor effect, can be seen in the ethnic group by location of observation result. The Anglo groups tended to interact consistently in both interior and exterior settings. However, the Mexican groups clustered more closely when interacting outdoors, while the Black groups clustered more when indoors. The basis for this contrast is entirely unclear. If it can be assumed, however, that clustering is increased with external threat (Feshbach and Feshbach, 1963; Latané, 1969; Schachter, 1959) it may be possible that the groups tend to feel more exposed or threatened in different types of physical settings. Of course, physical factors such as the differing levels of background noise, heat, ambient light, etc. could also influence the differential spacing patterns. Interesting implications for setting design intended for use by different subcultural groups are evident, however. If this result can be shown to be dependable and subject to replication, it would seem reasonable to think in terms of designing fewer open, exposed spaces in areas intended primarily for Mexican-American use. Perhaps the prevalence of wall enclosed spaces in Spanish architecture is a guide to the validity of such an implication.

The present ethnic group by location of observation differences also tend to cast some light on inconsistencies in previous data. Little (1965) expected to find differences in doll placement distances when indoor vs. outdoor settings were involved. He reasoned that tighter clustering would occur in indoor settings since, in general, the degree of interpersonal intimacy expected in indoor locations was greater. His overall results were inconsistent. In some comparisons, he found closer placements in outdoor settings, in others he found a tendency for tighter clustering in indoor settings. Since Little used white adults as subjects, the present Anglo adult groups would seem most comparable. For these groups, the present results are entirely consistent with Little's data. Essentially, they failed to respond differently to different locations. On the other hand, a study by Baxter and Phelps (1970) also sought indoor vs. outdoor differences in spacing. The reasoning involved was the same as that developed by Little. In that study, the result emerged as expected. That is, closer doll placements occurred in indoor settings as contrasted with outdoor locations. The Baxter-Phelps study used Negro preschool children as subjects. Thus, the present data indicating that Black-American subjects show the expected effect of clustering more tightly together when indoors is also consistent with the earlier Baxter-Phelps data. The overall result, then, clearly indicates that differences in interpersonal clustering in indoor vs. outdoor settings depends on the subcultural membership of the subjects. This area would appear to warrant further investigation aimed at determining the basis for the differences.

E. T. Hall (1966) has observed that interacting with people at different distances has the effect of exposing one to differing types and intensities of sensory data. For example, very close contact allows tactile, olfactory and thermal information essentially unavailable to subjects interacting under more distant conditions. The quality and intensity of visual and auditory information can be said to vary similarly. Thus, groups interacting under differing spacing conditions may be relying to varying degrees on different channels of information and may be employing different communication mechanisms. The present data suggest that such differences may be present among ethnic, age, and sex groupings when they interact under spontaneous conditions.

Some final implications of the present results seem worthy of note. Since the various subject groupings tend to adopt consistent, albeit slight, differences in spacing, it would seem reasonable to assume that both participants in the interactions may be contributing to establishing and maintaining their desired spatial arrangement. Indeed, observing the subjects as they interact in these settings leads one very quickly to the impression that the spacing process is an intricate one which is contributed to by both parties. As soon as one member leans too close, the other smoothly compensates. When one member moves too far away, the other quickly closes the gap. Further, it would appear that the process proceeds outside awareness, for the most part, and is usually very smooth and rapid in its operation.

Given the substantial ethnic group and age differences in spacing, it would follow that cross-group interactions would be interesting to examine. That is, given that an adult Mexican male and an adult Black male interacted under specified conditions, it would follow that they would both tend to "work" toward inconsistent spacing arrangements. Since inappropriately close spacing has been shown to be anxiety arousing (Baxter and Deanovich, 1970; Felipe and Sommer, 1966), one of the participants would be expected to be uncomfortable in the situation. Assuming that inappropriately distant spacing may be seen as rejecting or inappropriately formal, the other participant may be expected to view the encounter as equally unsatisfying. No direct data are available on the matter at present. However, the present study suggests that investigations along these lines would prove especially significant in terms of delineating subtle determinants of social encounter processes and their outcomes.

REFERENCES

ALEXANDER, CHRISTOPHER, 1967, "The city as a mechanism for sustaining human contact." Pp. 60–102 in W. R. Ewald (ed.), *Environment for Man.* Bloomington: Indiana University Press.

ARGYLE, MICHAEL AND JANET DEAN, 1965, "Eye contact, distance and affiliation." *Sociometry 28* (July): 289–304.

BAXTER, JAMES C. AND BETTYE F. DEANOVICH, 1970, "Anxiety arousing effects of inappropriate crowding." *Journal of Consulting and Clinical Psychology,* in press.

BAXTER, JAMES C. AND ANN T. PHELPS, 1970, "Space utilization in pre-school children." Unpublished manuscript.

CARR, STEPHEN, 1967, "The city of the mind." Pp. 197–226 in W. R. Ewald (ed.), *Environment for Man.* Bloomington: Indiana University Press.

EFRON, DAVID, 1941, *Gesture and Environment.* New York: King's Crown Press.

FELIPE, NANCY AND ROBERT SOMMER, 1966, "Invasions of personal space." *Social Problems 14* (April): 206–214.

FESHBACH, SEYMOUR AND NORMA FESHBACH, 1963, "Influence of the stimulus object upon the complementary and supplementary projection of fear." *Journal of Abnormal and Social Psychology 66* (May):498–502.

FISHER, RHODA L., 1967, "Social schema of normal and disturbed school children." *Journal of Educational Psychology 58* (April):88–92.

FREDE, MARTHA C., DONALD B. GAUTNEY AND JAMES C. BAXTER, 1968, "Relationships between body image boundary and interaction patterns on the MAPS test." *Journal of Consulting and Clinical Psychology 32* (October):575–578.

HALL, EDWARD T., 1966, *The Hidden Dimension.* Garden City: Doubleday.

LATANÉ, BIBB, 1969, "Gregariousness and fear in laboratory rats." *Journal of Experimental Social Psychology 5* (January):61–69.

LITTLE, KENNETH B., 1965, "Personal space." *Journal of Experimental Social Psychology 1* (August):237–247.

———, 1968, "Cultural variations in social schemata." *Journal of Personality and Social Psychology 10* (September):1–7.

LITTLE, KENNETH B., Z. JOSEPH ULEHLA AND CHARLOTTE HENDERSON, 1968, "Value congruence and interpersonal distance." *Journal of Social Psychology 75* (August):249–253.

PATTERSON, MILES, 1968, "Spatial factors in social interactions." *Human Relations 21* (November):351–361.

SCHACHTER, STANLEY, 1959, *The Psychology of Affiliation.* Stanford: Stanford University Press.

SOMMER, ROBERT, 1962, "The distance for comfortable conversation: A further study." *Sociometry 25* (March):111–116.

———, 1966, "Man's proximate environment." *Journal of Social Issues 22* (October):59–70.

VAUGHAN, GRAHAM M. AND MICHAEL C. CORBOLLIS, 1969, "Beyond tests of significance: Estimating strength of effects in selected ANOVA designs." *Psychological Bulletin 73* (September):204–213.

WATSON, O. MICHAEL AND THEODORE D. GRAVES, 1966, "Quantitative research in proxemic behavior." *American Anthropologist 68* (August):971–985.

WEINSTEIN, LAURA, 1967, "Social experience and social schemata." *Journal of Personality and Social Psychology 6* (August):429–434.

WILLIS, FRANK N., JR., 1966, "Initial speaking distance as a function of the speakers' relationship." *Psychonomic Science 5* (June):221–222.

Social Class Differences in Some Aspects of the Nonverbal Communication between Mother and Preschool Child [1]

TERRY HORE

The question of language development in different race and/or class groups will be dealt with in Section IX of this book. This paper, addressed to nonverbal aspects of communication, is placed here because social class is the crucial variable in the study. Nonverbal communication is getting increased attention currently in a variety of contexts, ranging from mother-infant interactions to encounter groups.

The following study was done in Canada, but its author, Dr. Terry Hore, is now at Monash University in Victoria, Australia.

Until recently, the study of communication has been regarded as synonymous with the study of language. Mead (1964) traced the roots of European and American linguistic research methodologies, and found that, whereas the meticulous analysis of written texts originates from Europe, the American tradition has developed from the observation of the language of non-literate peoples. This observation of people in the act of speaking has emphasized not only what people say, but also how they say it.

There is little doubt of the existence and im-

portance of the nonverbal aspects of the communication system in the life of the preverbal child; the child devises ways of telling what he wants. Church (1966a) has called this method "concrete enactment," and described a situation where a child who wants to be lifted up will hold out his arms. Neither can it be denied that these nonverbal methods of communicating are present when adults interact, for examples of such message transmission are seen frequently: the smile, the nod, the glance. But apart from observations of children's behaviour which have described nonverbal language incidentally (Church, 1966b), this method of communication has received little attention from child development researchers. Since 1925 there has been marked growth in interest in the linguistic aspect of communication, and developmental stages have been set for such variables as length of sentence, vocabulary and complex sentence types. Throughout these studies it has been a common finding that there is a marked positive relationship between socio-economic status (SES) of the family and the linguistic development of the child. The studies of Davis (1937) and McCarthy (1930) showed that middle class as opposed to working class children use more mature sentence forms and longer sentences at an earlier age. Deutsch (1963) showed that the differences which were present at Grade 1 were greater at Grade 5; an occurrence which Deutsch called the "cumulative deficit phenomenon." In addressing themselves to the question of why such SES differences exist researchers have become interested in the language environment, and the interaction of mothers with their pre-school child. The work of Hess & Shipman (1965, 1966) is an example of the latter. On the basis of the research cited previously, it can be assumed that there are differences in language "maturity" between mother-child samples taken from different SES levels. However, no experimental evidence was found to show differentiation in nonverbal language use by people from different SES groups. Robson (1967), for example, commenting on the role of eye-to-eye contact in maternal-infant attachment, suggested that early contingency experience may also determine the extent to which older children and adults rely upon and utilize nonverbal forms of communication. The majority of information on nonverbal behaviour has come from the study of adults in psychotherapy. Patients have unconsciously communicated information by bodily posture (Scheflen, 1964), physical contact (Spradlin, Rosenberg & Sanford, 1961) or glancing behaviour (Robson, 1967; Ruesch,

[1] This paper is based upon work carried out at the Department of Educational Psychology, University of Alberta, Canada.

1955). However, to this point, it is not known what relationship nonverbal language has to SES or what relationship it has to verbal communication.

There are some hints in the literature which may lead to the formulation of a tentative relationship from which testable hypotheses can be derived. For example, Ruesch (1955) saw the development of language as a transition from the nonverbal to the verbal. Szasz (1961) said something similar: "Since the use of iconic (body) signs is the simplest communicational device known to man, communication of this type varies inversely with knowledge and learning ... conversations in this protolanguage can occur only if the participants in the communication process do not readily speak a higher level of language (p. 121)." Within different SES groups Degerando (in Chamberlain, 1900) stated that rich children understood more words and less actions whereas poor children understood less words and more actions. More recently, Bernstein (1960) commented on the need for the "restricted code" user to employ nonverbal channels for the transmission of personal intent because he does not have the verbal facility enjoyed by the user of [an] "elaborated code." The foregoing comments seem to suggest that the relationships of nonverbal to verbal communication and of nonverbal communication to SES are both negative, that is, the more verbal facility one has, the less reliant one will be on the employment of the nonverbal channel.

Commencing from the assumption that the higher SES groups have greater verbal facility than a corresponding lower SES group, the general hypothesis was deduced that higher SES groups use nonverbal communication less than lower SES groups. More specifically, it was hypothesized that when mothers and children interact, high SES pairs show less (a) physical contact; (b) physical closeness; (c) mutual glances.

THE STUDY

SAMPLE

The total group of non-working mothers with 5-year-old children was drawn from the census records of two areas of the City of Edmonton, Canada, which were representative of high and low income families.[2] The final sample of 15 high and 15 low income subjects was randomly drawn from the larger purposive sample. The children were matched for age and intelligence, as measured by the Peabody

Picture Vocabulary Test (PPVT). Apart from having no employment outside the home, the mothers were not matched. As expected, the high SES mothers used more complex[3] language than the low SES mothers (Practical Task, $t(28) = 2 \cdot 75$, $p < \cdot 05$, one-tailed test; Verbal Task, $t(28) = 3 \cdot 10$, $p < \cdot 05$, one-tailed test). There was no difference between the children of the two groups in the complexity of the language used during either task. The high SES group contained 7 boys and 8 girls, and there were 8 boys and 7 girls in the low SES group.

PROCEDURE

Recently, evidence has been accumulating regarding the significance of eye-to-eye contact or "glancing" behaviour in maternal-infant attachment (Robson, 1967). This behaviour is so fleeting that it requires recording equipment capable of freezing the action as well as providing for innumerable play-backs. Previous techniques to measure these variables have varied from an interval notation system (Merrill, 1946) to an elaborate shorthand (Birdwhistell, 1952), to the use of tape recordings (Hess & Shipman, 1965) and filmed sequences (Katz, 1964). The investigation described here made extensive use of videotaped recordings, to instruct the subjects and to record the interaction of the mother and child. An Interaction Timer was constructed to count and time the occurrence of each event, i.e., glance. The two other nonverbal variables measured were physical contact, and physical closeness without contact. Physical contact did not occur during the verbal task in any of the pilot studies and for this reason the discussion of this variable is restricted to its occurrence within the practical task only. In order to quantify physical closeness without contact, a grid was constructed to fit over the television monitor which divided the screen vertically into three parts. A tally was made each time the heads of mother and child appeared in the central portion simultaneously. Except for physical contact, measures were taken under two different task situations.

One task was largely manipulative and required the mother and child to work together with a toy,[4]

---

[2] The fathers of the high SES families earned over $10,000 (Canadian) per year. The fathers of the low SES families were manual workers earning less than $5,000 (Canadian) per year.

[3] Language complexity was operationally defined as "average number of words per communication unit." Loban (1963) outlined the division of spoken language called a communication unit, which approximates the more complex analysis of syntax; it requires a phonological division of the subjects' speech, without encompassing meaning, and a further subdivision into groups of words which cannot be divided further without the loss of essential meaning. These final groups of words are communication units.

[4] "Etch-a-sketch" No. 505, Peter Austin Mfg. Co. Ltd., Toronto, Canada.

the second task was mainly verbal, requiring the
mother and child to tell each other stories based
upon four cards from the supplement to the Children's Apperception Test. Since pilot studies had
indicated that the presence of the investigator
disturbed the mother-child interaction, this interaction was observed on a television monitor outside the testing area. The pilot studies had also
enabled the investigator to construct the testing
area in such a way as to obtain full profile shots of
mother and child simultaneously from a concealed
unattended camera. The mothers had been told
that a recording would be made but the children
were not aware that their reactions would be recorded.

Comparisons were made between the two SES
groups by individual *t* tests on each pair of means
for each nonverbal measure. (Parallel nonparametric tests, Welch's *t* prime for unequal variances
and the Mann-Whitney *U* test, were carried out.
The results were compatible with those from the
parametric analyses.) A significance level of ·05
was adopted.

On completion of the home visits where the intelligence test was given and rapport established
with mother and child, each mother brought her
child to the television studio at the University of
Alberta, where she was instructed, *via* two videotaped films, how to lead her child through the two
tasks. The order of presentation of the tasks to the
child was alternated for each half of each SES
group, and each task was only presented when the
child and mother had successfully completed an
orientation task designed to overcome any uneasiness in the experimental situation.

RESULTS

The high and low SES groups did not differ on the
cumulative time taken to complete either of the
two tasks, so that the data which follow were based
upon the total time spent working on each task.

Hypothesis (a). This hypothesis was supported
by the data (see Table 1); the low SES mother-child
pairs showed a greater amount of physical contact
during the practical task than the high SES pairs.

Hypothesis (b). Table 2 summarizes the data
which showed that there was no difference between
the high and low SES groups, in terms of physical
closeness, on the practical or the verbal task.

Hypothesis (c). The data presented in Table 3
did not support this hypothesis, in fact the direction
was the reverse of the expectation. That is, the high
SES pairs engaged in more, not less, mutual glances

TABLE 1
PHYSICAL CONTACT

Measure	Practical task	
	Low SES	High SES
Means	6·40	1·87
Standard deviations	9·27	2·50
No. of subjects	15	15
t (28)	1.76*	

* *p* < .05, one-tailed test.

than the low SES pairs. The implications of this
result are discussed in the next section.

DISCUSSION

The groups did not differ in the amount of physical
closeness in either task. This may have resulted
from the crudeness of the measuring device which
was not sensitive to small movements. Physical
contact was found to discriminate between the
groups: this contact was usually initiated by the
mother and was seen as an indication of the tendency of the low SES mother to steer her child
physically rather than verbally. The occurrence of
this contact generally followed two or three verbal
directives which were ignored, whereupon obedience was manually effected.

During the verbal task, visual interaction was
more frequent in favour of the high SES pairs. On
the practical task there was no difference between
the SES groups when "mutual" glances were tallied
and timed; it appeared that the task-oriented behaviour required by this task itself prevented this
form of interaction from occurring.

Subsequent investigations of "unreciprocated"
glancing behaviour during the verbal task revealed
that the high SES mother spent more time looking
at her child than the low SES mother. This had two
results, first, the high SES child had fewer of his
glances unreciprocated, hence the result of more
"mutual" glances being recorded by this group;
secondly, the low SES child who looked at his
mother more often than the high SES child failed
to receive the direct visual attention of his mother.
Jensen (1967) considered that gesture and facial
expression were parts of the differential reinforcement behaviour which he believed was more persistently carried out in the middle class homes (high
SES in this study). It is suggested that "glancing"
behaviour is part of this reinforcement behaviour
and was differentially employed by the SES groups
described here. Brown & Bellugi (1964) commented
that the middle class child learns by feedback from
his parents, who reduce or expand the child's expression to incorporate the correct grammatical

TABLE 2
PHYSICAL CLOSENESS

Measure	Practical task		Verbal task	
	Low SES	High SES	Low SES	High SES
Means	2·67	5·60	1·13	0·20
Standard deviations	4·45	8·12	2·73	0·75
No. of pairs	15	15	15	15
t (28)	1·19		1·23	

TABLE 3
MUTUAL GLANCES

Measure	Practical task		Verbal task	
	Low SES	High SES	Low SES	High SES
Means	0·20	0·67	6·87	16·00
Standard deviations	0·40	1·07	4·94	11·27
No. of pairs	15	15	15	15
t (28)	−1·522[a]		−2·778[ab]	

[a] Result was in reverse direction to expectation.
[b] For a two-tailed test, this result would have been significant, $p < .01$.

elements. The present study suggested that this feedback may not be singularly verbal, but may include concomitant nonverbal components, i.e., glances.

The results warn future investigators against treating nonverbal variables as homogeneous in their effect on the interaction process. It may be speculated that there is a continuum in nonverbal communication, parallel to the verbal, from less to more complex or mature. The results suggested that glancing behaviour is more "complex" than physical contact. In turn this could mean that culturally handicapped children are more than verbally handicapped by their environment; they may also be deficient in the nonverbal aspects of their exchanges with adults. Teachers should be alerted to the power of the nonverbal channels of communication as a means of influencing behaviour. Commenting on the effects of teacher expectations on teacher behaviour and pupil performance, Rosenthal & Jacobson (1968) suggested that teachers look more frequently at those children from whom they expected better performance. This is similar to the events recorded in this investigation, for at six years of age the children did not differ significantly in the number of times they looked at their mothers. What did differ was the number of times their mothers looked at them.

The study raises interesting questions for further research. Will it be possible to describe the nonverbal aspects of communication in such a way as to place them along a continuum? Such a description would facilitate research into the total communication process. Why did the high SES mothers look at their children more than the low SES mothers? Exline & Winters (1965) have demonstrated that there is a greater affective involvement, and willingness to relate to another, between individuals who participate in mutual glances; it may be important therefore to examine the affective components of the mothers' personality structure. The frequency with which a mother looks at her child may be one of the unconscious ways she "encourages excellence" (McClelland, 1961) but this awaits further investigation.

Although it has been a common finding that social class differences exist in the use of language, it is not known whether nonverbal communication is also used differentially by different SES groups. Videotaped recordings were made of the interactions between 2 divergent SES groups of 15 mothers and their preschool children in 2 situations. Data were analyzed with respect to three nonverbal variables. It was found that low SES mothers used more physical contact during a practical task; no difference existed between the SES groups on physical closeness during the tasks; the high SES mother-child pairs exchanged more mutual glances. The implications of these results for teachers are discussed.

REFERENCES

BERNSTEIN, B. Language and social class. *British Journal of Sociology*, 1960, *11*, 271–276.

BIRDWHISTELL, R. L. *Introduction to kinesics.* Louisville: University of Louisville Press, 1952.

BROWN, R. & BELLUGI, U. Three processes in the child's acquisition of syntax. *Harvard Educational Review,* 1964, *34,* 133–151.

CHAMBERLAIN, A. F. *The child: A study in the evolution of man.* London: Walter Scott, 1900.

CHURCH, J. *Language and the discovery of reality.* New York: Vintage, 1966. (a)

CHURCH, J. (Ed.) *Three babies: Biographies of cognitive development.* New York: Random House, 1966. (b)

DAVIS, E. A. The development of linguistic skill in twins, singletons with siblings and only children from age 5 to 10 years. *Institute of Child Welfare Monograph,* 1937, No. 14.

DEUTSCH, M. The disadvantaged child and the learning process. In A. H. Passow (Ed.), *Education in depressed areas.* New York: Teachers College, 1963. Pp. 163–180.

EXLINE, R. V. & WINTERS, L. C. Affective relations and mutual glances in dyads. In S. S. Tomkins & C. E. Izard (Eds.), *Affect, cognition and personality.* New York: Springer, 1965. Pp. 319–350.

HESS, R. D. & SHIPMAN, V. Early blocks to children's learning. *Children,* 1965, *12,* 189–194.

HESS, R. D. & SHIPMAN, V. Cognitive elements in maternal behaviour. Paper presented at the 1st Annual Minnesota Symposium on Child Psychology, May, 1966.

JENSEN, A. R. Social class and verbal learning. In J. P. de Cecco (Ed.), *The psychology of language, thought and instruction.* New York: Holt, Rinehart and Winston, 1967. Pp. 103–117.

KATZ, R. L. Body language: A study in unintentional communication. Unpublished doctoral dissertation, Harvard University, 1964.

LOBAN, W. D. *The language of elementary school children.* Champaign, Illinois: National Council of Teachers in English, 1963.

McCARTHY, D. M. Language development of the preschool child. *Institute of Child Welfare Monograph,* 1930, No. 4.

McCLELLAND, D. C. Encouraging excellence. *Daedalus,* 1961, *90,* 711–724.

MEAD, M. Vicissitudes of the study of the total communication process. In Sebeok, T. A., Hayes, A. S. and Bateson, M. C. *Approaches to semiotics.* The Hague: Mouton, 1964. Pp. 277–287.

MERRILL, B. A measurement of mother-child interaction. *Journal of Abnormal and Social Psychology,* 1946, *41,* 37–49.

ROBSON, K. S. The role of eye-to-eye contact in maternal-infant attachment. *Journal of Child Psychology and Psychiatry and Allied Disciplines,* 1967, *8,* 13–27.

ROSENTHAL, R. & JACOBSON, L. *Pygmalion in the classroom.* New York: Holt, Rinehart & Winston, 1968.

RUESCH, J. Nonverbal language and therapy. *Psychiatry,* 1955, *19,* 323–330.

SCHEFLEN, A. E. The significance of posture in communication systems. *Psychiatry,* 1964, *27,* 316–331.

SPRADLIN, J. E., ROSENBERG, S. & SANFORD, M. Interaction among retarded children as a function of their relative language skill. *American Psychologist,* 1961, *16,* 396. (Abstract).

SZASZ, T. S. *The myth of mental illness.* New York: Hoeber-Harper, 1961.

41

Race, Class, Family, and School Achievement[1]

STEVEN R. TULKIN

Steven Tulkin also looks at SES as an independent variable together with race and family. The dependent variable is school achievement. This study was published prior to the Jensen report referred to in the introduction to Section II on biological bases of behavior. It exemplifies a typical approach, but it is methodologically superior to many other studies because of the controls it was able to establish. The number of subjects used was also greater than in many other studies. Tulkin is in the department of psychology at State University of New York at Buffalo.

[1] This report summarizes and expands certain aspects of an investigation conducted while the author was at the Department of Psychology, University of Maryland. Marvin G. Cline was very helpful in both planning the investigation and interpreting the results. The research was carried out as part of the Reading Ability and Outcome Study of the Mental Health Study Center (National Institute of Mental Health). J. R. Newbrough and Dee Norman Lloyd were especially helpful throughout the investigation. Grateful appreciation is also extended to Victor Rice, supervisor of testing and research of the Prince George's County (Maryland) Board of Education; Leo Walder, University of Maryland, and John Muller, Harvard University, for their help in obtaining and analyzing the present data; and to Thomas F. Pettigrew, J. R. Newbrough, and Jerome Kagan for their thoughtful comments on the present paper. Computer analyses were supported by the Computer Science Center of the University of Maryland and by a Field Foundation Grant to the Laboratory of Social Relations of Harvard University.

The debate surrounding heredity versus environmental influences on the development of intelligence is one of the oldest in the social sciences. The effects of characteristics such as social class have been acknowledged since Binet's work with intelligence testing (Binet & Simon, 1916). Although many social scientists interpret racial differences in tested intelligence and school achievement as resulting from social class differences, so-called "caste" differences, and various other environmental influences (Pettigrew, 1964, pp. 132–135), the advocates of the heredity view can still be heard (Burt, 1958; McGurk, 1959; Shuey, 1958, 1966). Still others have argued that the question has not been answered and insist that genetic differences be further investigated rather than assumed not to exist (Ingle, 1964).

The problem is a complex one, involving the interaction of race (caste), social class, family environments, and sex differences, as well as methodological questions such as random sampling and use of "culturally biased" tests. All of these problems must be considered when attempting to examine this complex question.

There have been many hypotheses about how these various factors influence intelligence. Some have related differential environmental experiences of Negroes and whites to differential academic performance. Deutsch (1960), for example, related racial differences on intelligence and achievement tests to the fact that the Negro student, not being a part of the majority culture, finds that identification with a set of majority culture symbols is not personally relevant. This "racial" difference is seen as existing all along the social class continuum, and, in fact, Deutsch and Brown (1964) reported that racial differences are greatest in the upper socioeconomic status (SES) groups. Similarly, Roen (1960) hypothesized that the psychological experiences of socioeconomic exclusion and generally more erratic family ties negatively influence the emerging personalities or self-perceptions of Negroes, especially as these relate to their intellectual potentials.

These authors, then, have suggested that Negro students—because of special environmental experiences associated with being Negro Americans—tend to be alienated from the majority culture, to have family backgrounds which are less conducive to the development of intellectual skills, and to have personality traits which themselves limit intellectual performance.

In contrast to the view that racial differences are found in each social class, Bloom, Whiteman, and

Deutsch (1963) found that the relationships between social class and various family and environmental conditions are very similar in white and Negro samples. In fact, they reported that the association of environmental conditions with social class tends to be stronger than with race, and they tentatively concluded that "social class may be a more potent variable than race in predicting to environmental and attitudinal factors [p. 10]" which have been shown to be related to test scores on intelligence and achievement tests.

Sex has also been found to relate to measures of intelligence and school achievement. Kennedy Vande, and White (1963), for example, reported that although in the first grade there are no differences in the achievement scores of 1,800 Negro students, with each higher grade sex differences become greater. By Grade 6, achievement scores of the females are more than three-fourths of a grade level higher than the scores of the males. This is consistent with a report by Mingione (1965) that among Negroes the girls have a greater need for achievement than the boys, as would be expected, according to Veroff, Atkinson, Feld, and Gurin (1960), as a natural result of matriarchal Negro families.

This brief review serves to illustrate the complex interactions of race, social class, and sex, all of which may influence scores on tests of intelligence and school achievement. The majority of studies which have attempted to control these three factors have still found significant differences between racial groups, as is reported in both of Shuey's (1958, 1966) reviews of the literature. However, rather than conclude, as Shuey did, that the differences are caused by a genetic factor, one must ask whether, in fact, the groups studied were really equated. It has been shown that the more closely white and Negro groups are equated, the smaller are the differences that are found. McCord and Demerath (1958), for example, controlled for social class, father's occupation, nationality, generation of entry into America, and the "personality and emotional climate of the home." They found no significant differences among racial groups. However, in addition to the fact that this study has been criticized for its methodology (Shuey, 1966), the data were mostly on lower-middle- and lower-class subjects. The relationships among these factors in the middle and upper classes remain unstudied.

The present research is a study of a group of upper and lower SES Negroes and whites in which differences on intelligence and achievement tests are examined from the points of view of race, social class, family environments, and sex. Of particular interest is the extent to which environmental variables relate to differences between Negroes and whites on measures of intelligence and school achievement, and whether test-score differences are reduced as more of these environmental factors are controlled.

METHOD

The subjects were 389 fifth- and sixth-grade students from a suburban Maryland school system. They were divided into two SES groups (upper and lower), two racial groups (Negro and white), and two sexes, yielding eight groups (see Table 1). Background information was obtained from the students' permanent record cards. SES was determined by a modification of the Hollingshead (1957) Two-Factor Index of Social Position (occupation and education), with Levels 1 and 2 being used as upper SES and Level 5 as lower SES. Students from SES Levels 3 and 4 were not included in the sample. The Lorge-Thorndike Intelligence Test (Level Three) and the Iowa Tests of Basic Skills were administered by the local school system as a part of its regular testing program, and scores were obtained from the records.

A specially developed questionnaire consisting of items related to cultural participation, family participation, and family structure was also administered. The Cultural Participation Scale consists of four 1-point items (visit library, visit museum, attend concert, and read newspaper) and five items on which 1 point was given for each time an activity was performed (books read in previous 2 months, culturally related trips, etc.). The Family Participation Scale has two parts: time spent with parents (I), and verbal interaction between children and parents (II). In Section I, 1 point is given for each activity of the child in which one or both parents participate (Sunday activities, trips, visits to museums, libraries, etc.). In Section II, the student uses a scale from 0 to 3 to indicate how often he talks with parents about homework, personal problems, what to do on a rainy day, what he reads in the newspapers, and what is going on in school. These scores are summed and added to the total from Section I. Family-structure items include a crowdedness ratio (number of people living in the house divided by the number of rooms), data on maternal employment, marital status of parents, and number of siblings.

The questionnaire was developed in three stages: (*a*) testing of construct validity, (*b*) pretesting the instructions and vocabulary to improve clarity, and (*c*) obtaining sample distributions from pretest subjects on the Cultural Participation Scale, the Family Participation Scale, and the family-structure indexes.

TABLE 1

RACE, CLASS, AND SEX DISTRIBUTION OF SAMPLE POPULATION

SES	White		Negro		Total
	Male	*Female*	*Male*	*Female*	
Upper	70	67	29	23	189
Lower	48	37	57	58	200
Total	118	104	86	81	389

Construct validity is based on a set of judgments by 10 members of the professional staff of the Mental Health Study Center (National Institute of Mental Health). Each of the judges rated all questions on the amount of relationship to the desired construct. Following this, the questionnaire was pretested with students from one white and one Negro classroom and administered by individual interview to two students representing each of the eight cells shown in Table 1. Questions which were ambiguous to the subjects or were not discriminating in the same direction as the total scale were modified or eliminated.

Analysis of the data consisted of two major phases. First, the data were analyzed on the basis of race and class only. Significance tests were computed on all variables, and an attempt was made to control further for environmental differences by use of a multivariate analysis of variance in which the environmental differences were statistically controlled through the use of covariate adjustors.[2] Correlations were also examined within each race-class group. In Phase 2, the data were examined to determine the importance of sex differences.

RESULTS

Table 2 presents race within class comparisons of the means, standard deviations, and significance levels of the test scores and home and family scales. Three-fourths of the tests yield significant differences in the upper SES group, while half of the differences are significant in the lower SES group. In the upper SES group, there are differences on both verbal and nonverbal tests, while differences in

[2] The program used was the Multivariate Analysis of Variance, General Linear Hypothesis Model, Biometric Laboratory, George Washington University.

the lower SES group are found only on nonverbal measures. On the family variables, there are racial differences on the crowdedness ratio in both SES groups, a difference in the number of siblings, and a difference on the Family Participation Scale in the lower SES group only.[3] (Univariate analyses of variance were done on each test separately and yielded identical significance levels.)

SES group differences were also tested within each race (upper white versus lower white and upper Negro versus lower Negro). On *every measure* presented in Table 2, social class differences are significant beyond the .001 level of confidence. Thus the breakdown into SES groups yields a greater number and larger differences than does the breakdown into racial groups.

In order to determine if other home and family differences existed among racial groups of similar SES background, comparisons were made on two other variables, broken homes and maternal employment. Tables 3 and 4 present these data. Again it appears that controlling for SES does not equate white and Negro samples. Broken homes are more common, proportionately, in the upper SES Negro group than in the upper SES white group. In fact, there is no significant difference between upper and lower SES Negro groups. Similarly, maternal employment seems to vary more along racial than SES lines.

[3] Since large racial differences were also found on "social desirability" questions that were asked in the questionnaire, and since "faking" was much easier on the Family Participation Scale, this latter difference may be largely attributable to social desirability.

TABLE 2
MEANS, STANDARD DEVIATIONS, AND SIGNIFICANCE LEVELS FOR STANDARD TESTS AND FAMILY SCALES

	Upper SES white		Upper SES Negro		Lower SES white		Lower SES Negro	
	M	SD	M	SD	M	SD	M	SD
Verbal IQ	114.48	14.56	109.15**	12.88	92.67	12.84	90.04	12.08
Nonverbal IQ	112.10	12.20	107.81*	11.79	95.41	13.57	91.01**	12.38
Vocabulary achievement[a]	6.22	1.38	5.88	1.18	4.40	.78	4.51	.65
Reading achievement	5.92	1.50	5.44*	1.38	4.12	.88	4.11	.92
Language achievement	6.42	1.44	6.16	1.38	4.48	.98	4.44	1.04
Work study achievement	5.80	1.00	5.42***	.74	4.48	.64	4.26*	.66
Arithmetic achievement	5.75	.83	5.33***	.76	4.74	.68	4.36****	.67
Total achievement	6.06	1.13	5.64***	.93	4.48	.72	4.36	.84
Crowdedness	.72	.25	.92***	.43	1.28	.54	1.73****	1.12
Cultural participation scale	13.89	3.98	13.60	3.83	7.82	3.79	8.44	4.27
Family participation scale	15.58	4.54	16.87	4.48	11.27	4.48	13.24***	5.46
No. siblings	2.47	1.60	2.08	1.36	3.34	2.00	4.97***	2.56

Note.—Significance levels represent difference between white and Negro means within each SES group.
[a] Achievement test scores are reported as "grade equivalents."
* $p = .05$.
** $p = .02$.
*** $p = .01$.
**** $p = .001$.

TABLE 3
INTACT AND BROKEN HOMES BY RACE AND CLASS

SES	White		Negro	
	Intact	*Broken*	*Intact*	*Broken*
Upper	126	11	42	10
Lower	66	19	91	24

Note.—Difference between upper and lower SES groups is significant for the white sample by chi-square analysis at $p < .01$. Difference between white and Negro upper SES groups is significant by chi-square analysis at $p < .05$.

In an attempt to further equate the groups in light of the environmental differences reported above, a multivariate analysis of variance was performed in which the environmental measures were used as covariate controls.[4] Table 5 presents this analysis both with and without the covariate controls. It can be seen that while the covariate controls reduce the size of the F for race in the upper SES group, they do not change the race effect in the lower SES group. Univariate analyses of variance on the individual tests also showed that individual F ratios in the upper SES group were all reduced by the introduction of the covariates, while none of the ratios were reduced in the lower SES group. The present measures, then, were unable to account for the test-score differences between the racial groups at the lower SES level.

More information about the above relationships can be seen in the correlations between total achievement and the other variables in each race-class group (Table 6). Two important relationships are evident. Significant SES differences are seen within each racial group in the correlations of verbal intelligence to total achievement. Verbal intelligence accounts for a much larger portion of the variance of total achievement in the upper SES groups. Since racial differences on these correlations are minimal, it appears that the extent to which a student achieves at a level which is correlated with his verbal intelligence tends to be more

---

[4] Since there are no reliable racial differences on the Cultural Participation Scale or the Family Participation Scale, these scales are not used as covariate controls.

TABLE 5
MULTIVARIATE ANALYSIS OF VARIANCE ON INTELLIGENCE AND ACHIEVEMENT TESTS WITH AND WITHOUT COVARIATE CONTROLS [a]

Effect	F			
	Upper SES		Lower SES	
	Without	*With*	*Without*	*With*
Race	2.34*	1.52	5.55**	5.57**
Sex	3.91**	3.55**	7.05**	7.88**
Race × Sex	0.86	0.98	1.12	1.12

[a] Covariate controls are intact home, maternal employment, and crowdedness ratio.
* $p = .05$.
** $p = .01$.

strongly related to SES than to race. Second, Table 6 shows that none of the home and family scales are significantly correlated with total achievement in the lower SES Negro group. This corroborates the previous assertion that factors other than those controlled in the present study are affecting the scores of the lower SES Negroes.

Since Table 5 has shown that the sex effect is highly significant in both SES groups, the data were also examined to determine if the racial differences discussed above are found in both males and females. Reanalysis of the racial differences controlling for sex showed that in the upper SES group all of the significant differences were attributable to racial differences between the male groups, while none of the differences between the female groups reached an acceptable level of significance. At the lower SES level, for the most part, the pattern was reversed, and differences were more often significant in the female group. Some sex differences in correlations were also obtained when the data presented in Table 6 were analyzed separately by sex groups.[5]

DISCUSSION

Shuey (1966) contended that racial differences in tested intelligence cannot be explained on the

---

[5] A more detailed presentation of the data on sex differences is available from the author.

TABLE 4
MATERNAL EMPLOYMENT BY RACE AND CLASS

SES	White			Negro		
	Employed full time	*Employed part time*	*Not employed*	*Employed full time*	*Employed part time*	*Not employed*
Upper	33	17	87	31	8	12
Lower	32	4	49	59	27	29

Note.—Difference between upper and lower SES groups is significant for the white sample by chi-square analysis at $p < .05$. Differences between white and Negro upper and lower SES groups are both significant by chi-square analysis at $p < .001$.

TABLE 6

CORRELATIONS BETWEEN TOTAL ACHIEVEMENT AND
OTHER MAJOR VARIABLES

Variable	Upper SES white	Lower SES white	Upper SES Negro	Lower SES Negro
Verbal IQ	.81**	.64**	.81**	.62**
Nonverbal IQ	.63**	.54**	.57**	.43**
Cultural Participation Scale	.36**	.34**	.40**	.12
Family Participation Scale	.00	.26*	.21	−.01
Crowdedness	−.11	−.08	−.31*	−.10

Note.—For Verbal IQ, correlations in upper SES groups are significantly higher than correlations in lower SES groups.

* $p = .05$.
** $p = .01$.

basis of environmental differences, and that research evidence points to the presence of some "native differences" in intelligence between white and Negro samples. One cannot deny that most studies previously reported have found racial differences, regardless of the controls that have been employed. It is possible from the present findings, however, to question whether all of these previous studies have adequately equated the racial groups. Equating experimental groups is difficult even when one draws samples from a relatively homogeneous population. Attempting to equate the environments and psychological experiences of individuals from different racial groups is a considerably more complex problem. It would seem that Shuey's argument is based largely on the weight of poorly controlled research. The present study demonstrates that controlling for SES (social class) alone does not equate white and Negro students on their home environments. When these family influences are controlled, the racial groups are certainly more similar, although still not "equated." Differences between these groups in the present study are minimal. No differences are found, in fact, between upper SES whites and Negroes when broken homes, maternal employment, and crowdedness of the home are controlled, and no differences are found between upper SES white and Negro females—even without the additional covariate controls. These results are contrary to the previous finding that racial differences are more pronounced in upper SES groups (Deutsch & Brown, 1964), although quite possibly this difference could be accounted for by the different measures of social class employed by the two investigations, or other uncontrolled characteristics of the populations studied.

The fact that the present analysis failed to eliminate racial differences among the lower SES students merits further discussion. First, it should

be pointed out that at the time of the study over 90% of the Negro students in the present sample attended all-Negro schools. Research has shown that this factor by itself is significant as a determinant of the level of school performance (United States Commission on Civil Rights, 1967). In addition, the present correlational analysis (Table 6) has shown that in the lower SES Negro group (compared with the lower SES whites), a larger amount of the variance of total achievement is not accounted for either by intelligence or by the home and family variables that were employed in the present investigation. This is perhaps where the "caste" analogy (Dreger & Miller, 1960) is most useful. Many lower SES Negroes seem to be at a distinct social class level, and, therefore, equating lower class groups appears to be particularly difficult, at least with the type of procedures used in the present study. Even on so-called "culture-fair" tests, significant differences are found. With the present subjects, for example, Tulkin and Newbrough (1968) found no significant differences on Raven's Progressive Matrices between upper SES groups, but did find a significant difference between the lower SES groups.

How can one explain a racial difference that is found among lower SES students and not among upper SES students? Pettigrew (1964) noted that the economic floor for lower class Negroes is "distinctively below" the floor of the whites. A recent review of economic trends among Negroes in the United States based on the 1960 census (Brimmer, 1966) supports this argument and further demonstrates that economic differences between the races are greatest at the lower income level. Furthermore, the difference between whites and nonwhites with incomes in the upper fifth group decreased since 1947, while the gap between white and nonwhite incomes in the bottom fifth group actually increased during that 13-year period. Brimmer (1966) concluded that within the Negro community "the middle and upper income groups are getting richer, while the lowest income group is getting poorer [p. 267]." The psychological feelings of hopelessness and helplessness resulting from this economic situation would be quite difficult to control statistically.

Another variable not usually considered when studying racial differences in academic performance is prematurity. Prematurity is related to intelligence (Kagan & Henker, 1966) and is more frequent in Negroes than in whites (Abramowicz & Kass, 1966). Here also, however, differences are greatest at the lower SES levels. Block, Lippsett, Redner, and Hirschl (1952), for example, found that the racial difference in the prematurity rates for the lower SES group is more than $2\frac{1}{2}$ times larger than the difference in the upper SES group.

These findings point to the need for multidisciplinary studies to determine how the environment influences intellectual growth and behavior in general, and to determine the extent to which these environmental influences interact with "genetic predispositions." Poorly controlled research only adds confusion to the attempt to define the relationships between environmental backgrounds of students and their performance on tests of intelligence and achievement. Specifically, controls for race, class, sex, and home and family variables—including income—are prerequisites for meaningful results. The present study suggests that with adequate control measures it is possible to demonstrate that racial groups are not significantly different on measures of intelligence and school achievement. Although results are still inconclusive concerning the measures necessary to equate racial groups at the lower social class level, they do suggest that intellectual differences are not to be found between different racial groups with similar social class status and experiences.

Intelligence and achievement test scores and home and family information were collected from 389 5th- and 6th-grade students. Controlling for social class, racial differences were found on both test scores and family measures. When family differences were also statistically controlled, there were no significant racial differences on test scores in the upper socioeconomic group, although differences remained significant in the lower socioeconomic group. It was suggested that economic differences between the racial groups might be related to the present findings, and further research was suggested on environmental factors which could account for the racial difference among the lower socioeconomic groups.

REFERENCES

ABRAMOWICZ, M., & KASS, E. H. Pathogenesis and prognosis of prematurity. *New England Journal of Medicine,* 1966, *275,* 878.

BINET, A., & SIMON, T. *The development of intelligence in children.* (Trans. by E. S. Kite) Baltimore: Williams & Wilkins, 1916.

BLOCK, H., LIPPSETT, H., REDNER, B., & HIRSCHL, D. Reduction of mortality in the premature nursery: II. Incidence and causes of prematurity: Ethnic, socioeconomic and obstetric factors. *Journal of Pediatrics,* 1952, *41,* 300–304.

BLOOM, R., WHITEMAN, M., & DEUTSCH, M. Race and social class as separate factors related to social environment. Paper presented at the meeting of the American Psychological Association, Philadelphia, September, 1963.

BRIMMER, A. F. The Negro in the national economy. In J. P. Davis (Ed.), *The American Negro reference book.* Englewood Cliffs, N.J.: Prentice-Hall, 1966.

BURT, C. The inheritance of mental ability. *American Psychologist,* 1958, *13,* 1–15.

DEUTSCH, M. Minority group and class status as related to social and personality factors in scholastic achievement. *Monographs of the Society for Applied Anthropology,* 1960, No. 2.

DEUTSCH, M., & BROWN, B. Some data on social influences in Negro-white intelligence differences. *Journal of Social Issues,* 1964, *20,* 24–35.

DREGER, R. M., & MILLER, K. S. Comparative studies of Negroes and whites in the United States. *Psychological Bulletin,* 1960, *57,* 361–402.

HOLLINGSHEAD, A. *The Two-Factor Index of Social Position.* New Haven, Conn.: Author, 1957.

INGLE, D. J. Racial differences and the future. *Science,* 1964, *146,* 375–379.

KAGAN, J., & HENKER, B. A. Developmental psychology. *Annual Review of Psychology,* 1966, *17,* 1–50.

KENNEDY, W. A., VANDE, R. V., & WHITE, J. C. Normative sample of intelligence and achievement of Negro elementary school children in the southeastern United States. *Monographs of the Society for Research in Child Development,* 1963, *28*(6).

McCORD, W. M., & DEMERATH, N. J., III. Negro versus white intelligence: A continuing controversy. *Harvard Educational Review,* 1958, *28,* 120–135.

McGURK, F. Negro versus white intelligence: An answer. *Harvard Educational Review,* 1959, *29,* 54–62.

MINGIONE, A. D. Need for achievement in Negro and white children. *Journal of Consulting Psychology,* 1965, *29,* 108–111.

PETTIGREW, T. F. *A profile of the Negro American.* Princeton, N.J.: Van Nostrand, 1964.

ROEN, S. R. Personality and Negro-white intelligence. *Journal of Abnormal and Social Psychology,* 1960, *61,* 148–150.

SHUEY, A. M. *The testing of Negro intelligence.* Lynchburg, Va.: Randolph-Macon Women's College, 1958.

SHUEY, A. M. *The testing of Negro intelligence.* (2nd ed.) New York: Social Science Press, 1966.

TULKIN, S. R., & NEWBROUGH, J. R. Social class, race, and sex differences on the Raven (1956) Standard Progressive Matrices. *Journal of Consulting and Clinical Psychology,* 1968, *32,* in press.

UNITED STATES COMMISSION ON CIVIL RIGHTS. *Racial isolation in the public schools.* Washington, D.C.: United States Government Printing Office, 1967.

VEROFF, J., ATKINSON, J. W., FELD, S., & GURIN, G. The use of thematic apperception to assess motivation in a nationwide interview study. *Psychological Monographs,* 1960, *74*(12, Whole Number 499).

42

Chaotic Reinforcement:
A Socioeconomic Leveler[1]

JEAN L. BRESNAHAN
AND WILLIAM L. BLUM

This brief article examines the effects of reinforcement history (as provided in the laboratory) on the efficiency of learning. These variables might make it appear that the study should have been placed in Section III (Learning). However, the variables and their interrelations are examined within groups that differ in social class. The difference between the social classes in the effects of the experimental manipulation is of primary interest. Hence, the paper is included under Group Memberships.

The study was done at Emory University, where Jean Bresnahan, the senior author, received her Ph.D. and is now on the faculty.

Previous work (Bresnahan, 1966; Bresnahan, Ivey, & Shapiro, 1969) showed that low-socioeconomic-level children do not adopt a win-stay lose-shift strategy in a concept-acquisition task. It was hypothesized from these data that low-socioeconomic-level children perform less successfully on concept-attainment problems because of their inconsistent reinforcement histories. A study was planned, therefore, to investigate whether the in-troduction of chaotic reinforcement into the histories of high-socioeconomic-level children would lead to a comparable decrement in their performance.

Other researchers have taken another approach to this problem. They have used successive training procedures under which the performance of low-socioeconomic-level children improves. Since Harlow's (1949) paper on learning to learn, experimenters have hypothesized that with appropriate experience, the difference in the asymptotic behavior of originally discrepant groups can be attenuated or reduced to zero (e.g., Scholnick & Osler, 1969). However, learning not to learn is also a phenomenon which provides direct information regarding the establishment, if not the remediation, of low-socioeconomic-level performance.

The following experiment was designed to examine the effects of random (chaotic) reinforcement in a subsequent concept-acquisition task. Levine (1962) had demonstrated that the performance of college students on a concept-acquisition task was significantly lowered after random reinforcement. The effect was pronounced for even as few as four random reinforcement trials. In the usual concept-acquisition experiment, different values of the relevant stimulus dimension are consistently reinforced, for example, triangle is always correct and circle is always wrong. In the present design, the first n trials were randomly reinforced, that is, triangle was correct on one-half of the trials and circle was correct on one-half of the trials; after the n random trials, with no clues given to the subject, the actual concept-acquisition trials began and consistent reinforcement continued thereafter.

METHOD

SUBJECTS

The subjects were 60 first graders, with a mean age of 7.0 years, enrolled in the Cobb County, Georgia, school system. One-half of the subjects were from a high socioeconomic level and one-half from a low socioeconomic level; in each socioeconomic-level group one-half were boys and one-half girls. Considering socioeconomic level, sex, and experimental conditions, there were 12 independent groups of 5 subjects each.

Three indexes were used to determine socioeconomic level: residence, occupation of parents, and education of parents. All subjects were at the extreme ends of the Warner-Meeker-Eells scale (Warner, Meeker, & Eells, 1949); the high group corresponded to Categories 1 and 2, and the low group corresponded to Categories 6 and 7 on the scale. In the former group the parents were professionals, semiprofessionals, and proprietors of large

[1] This research was supported in part by Contract No. 6–062707–2127 from the Office of Education. The authors express their appreciation to the administrators and teachers of Cobb County, Georgia.

businesses; in the latter group the parents were crafts-men, semiskilled workers, and unskilled workers. In the high-socioeconomic-level group, most fathers were college graduates; in the low-socioeconomic-level group, most parents had a seventh- to tenth-grade education. The schools from which the subjects were chosen were either predominantly high or low in socioeconomic level, and the subjects were selected only if their socioeconomic level corresponded to the predominant socioeconomic level of the school.

APPARATUS

The apparatus used was a Lehigh Valley Electronics Company Human Intelligence Panel. Mounted on the panel were a dual multistimulus response key apparatus and a 1¢ reinforcement delivery system. The experimental procedure was controlled by automated electronic equipment and all responses and stimuli were recorded on a six-channel event recorder.

PROCEDURE

Each subject was individually seated in front of the Lehigh Valley console on which two different figures on two different colored backgrounds were presented on each trial. The subject's task was to choose between the two stimuli. A finger press against a stimulus activated a microswitch.

Each correct response was rewarded with a penny. The use of a correction procedure required the subject to press the correct key if his initial response did not result in a reward. No penny was given for a response correction.

The following instructions were given to each subject by the experimenter.

> We're going to play a little game. There will be lights in these two openings like this [the experimenter pointed to each one]. Do you see them? If you press the correct one both lights will go out, and a penny will drop here [the experimenter pointed to dispenser]. If you press the wrong one, then go ahead and press the correct one so you'll get another turn. Here's the way it works [the experimenter pressed the correct one]. See, that one was correct so both the lights went out and a penny dropped down here. [The experimenter then pressed the wrong one.] See, that one was wrong so I'll go ahead and press the correct one in order to get another turn. Do you understand how to play? Try to get as many correct as you can. Leave the pennies in here [the experimenter pointed to the dispenser] and after we're finished you can take them all home.

The subject was then told to wait for the lights to change before beginning to play the game. The subject was allowed to use only one hand and was corrected if he failed to do so. For the instructions, the subject was presented with stimuli different from those used for the test trials; in the left opening was a plus sign on a yellow background and in the right opening an X on a blue background. The test stimuli consisted of a triangle and a circle, one on a red background and the other on a green background. The four permutations of form and color, GT–RC, RC–GT, GC–RT, RT–GC, appeared with equal frequency in an unsystematic order.

The 30 subjects in each socioeconomic-level group were divided into three subgroups of 10 subjects each. One-third of the subjects began immediately on the concept-acquisition task in which the triangle was always reinforced. One-third of the subjects had 6 trials on which the triangle and circle were randomly reinforced prior to the beginning of concept formation. One-third of the subjects had 12 trials on which triangle and circle were randomly reinforced prior to the beginning of concept formation. The red or green color and the positions of the circle and the triangle were never relevant stimuli. All subjects were run at least 42 trials. If a criterion of 12 correct responses in succession was not reached within the first 42 trials, the run was continued until the criterion was reached, up to a maximum of 120 trials.

RESULTS

Previous work with the same population (Bresnahan, 1966) had shown a significant difference between the IQs of the two socioeconomic-level groups, but no significant correlation between IQ and performance on the concept-acquisition task. Given the random distribution of IQs throughout the three experimental groups of each socioeconomic level, it is clear that even a true overall correlation between IQ and performance could not survive the significant experimental interaction to be reported in the following paragraphs.

The number of errors in the first 42 trials, divided into seven blocks of 6 trials each, can be seen in Table 1. An analysis of variance [was] calculated from these data . . . [is shown in Table 2.] Three main effects were significant: socioeconomic level, number of random reinforcements, and trials. The high-socioeconomic-level children made fewer errors than the low-socioeconomic-level children on all tasks combined, $F = 5.429$, $df = 1/48$, $p < .05$. Errors increased with an increase in the number of random reinforcements, $F = 9.065$, $df = 2/48$, $p < .001$. Errors decreased over the seven blocks of trials, $F = 6.300$, $df = 6/288$, $p < .001$. When the interaction of Socioeconomic Level × Number of Random Reinforcements was partitioned into two orthogonal comparisons, 12 and 6 versus 0, and 12 versus 6, only the former was significant, $F = 5.362$, $df = 1/48$, $p < .01$. This significant result can be explained by the fact that with 6 or 12 random reinforcements the high-socioeconomic-level subjects became progressively more similar to the low-socioeconomic-level subjects in performance (Figure 1). There were almost identical results from the high- and low-socioeconomic-level subjects run under 12 prior random reinforcements. The significant Socioeconomic Level × Trials interaction, $F = 2.867$, $df = 6/288$, $p < .05$, resulted from the fact that the high-socioeconomic-

TABLE 1
NUMBER OF ERRORS IN FIRST 42 TRIALS OF CONSISTENT REINFORCEMENT

No. of random reinforcements	Blocks of six trials							
	1	*2*	*3*	*4*	*5*	*6*	*7*	*Total*
High SEL								
12	33	31	20	19	24	24	28	179
6	29	26	26	18	17	23	12	151
0	18	13	13	6	2	3	1	56
Total	80	70	59	43	43	50	41	386
Low SEL								
12	31	27	24	30	22	24	22	180
6	25	28	25	25	25	16	25	172
0	24	16	25	22	22	16	20	145
Total	80	71	77	77	69	56	67	497
Grand total	160	141	136	120	112	106	108	883

level children improved more than the low-socio-economic-level children over trials (Table 1).

Nonparametric statistical tests computed on the data for number of trials to criterion in 120 trials yielded the same general results. Tests for independent samples (Wilcoxon, 1947) were used to compare the high-socioeconomic-level scores with the low-socioeconomic-level scores. After either 12 or 6 random reinforcements there was no significant difference between the two socioeconomic-level groups. After 0 random reinforcements, the number of trials to criterion was significantly different ($T = 76.5$, $p < .05$); the overall result combining the three Ts also yielded a significant difference between the high- and low-socioeconomic-level groups ($T = 255$, $p < .01$).

The number of errors for each of the six groups shown in Figure 1 was significantly superior to the chance level of 21 errors per subject; the smallest z value so obtained was 2.928.

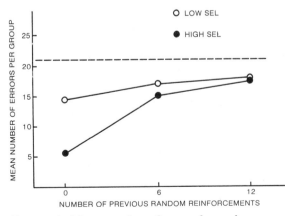

FIGURE 1. *Mean number of errors for each group of 10 subjects for 42 trials. (The broken line denotes chance level of performance; SEL = socioeconomic level.)*

DISCUSSION

This experiment demonstrated that the introduction of random reinforcement produces typically low-socioeconomic-level behavior in high-socioeconomic-level subjects. It was shown that this result was not a simple consequence of all concept acquisition degenerating to a chance level. Both number of errors and trials to criterion revealed that the high-socioeconomic-level performance progressively approached and ultimately equaled the ineffectual low-socioeconomic-level performance. The data add credibility to the hypothesis that the inferior performance of low-socioeconomic-level children is a function of their chaotic or inconsistent reinforcement histories.

REFERENCES

BRESNAHAN, J. L. The effect of task and incentive on concept acquisition with children from two socioeconomic levels. Unpublished doctoral dissertation, Emory University, 1966.

BRESNAHAN, J. L., IVEY, S. L., & SHAPIRO, M. M. Developmentally defined obviousness in concept formation tasks. *Developmental Psychology*, 1969, *1*, 383–388.

HARLOW, H. F. The formation of learning sets. *Psychological Review*, 1949, *56*, 51–65.

LEVINE, M. Cue neutralization: The effects of random reinforcements upon discrimination learning. *Journal of Experimental Psychology*, 1962, *63*, 438–443.

SCHOLNICK, E. K., & OSLER, S. F. Effect of pretest experiences on concept attainment in lower- and middle-class children. *Developmental Psychology*, 1969, *1*, 440–443.

WARNER, W. L., MEEKER, M., & EELLS, K. *Social class in America.* Chicago: Science Research Associates, 1949.

WILCOXON, F. Probability tables for individual comparisons by ranking methods. *Biometrics*, 1947, *3*, 119–122.

43

A Note on the Relation
of Reading Failure
to Peer-Group Status
in Urban Ghettos

WILLIAM LABOV AND CLARENCE ROBINS

This paper examines the relation of an out-of-school variable to an aspect of school performance. It is important to note, when we talk about the relation between the two variables, that we cannot talk about the direction of causation. That is, of course, true of all correlational studies. It is likely that the relations between the variables are complexly circular. This point does not in any way vitiate the suggestions the authors make for unusual use of para-professional helpers.

Implicitly, at least, the authors interpret their findings in terms of the school's failure to reach those students who have strong ties to the peer culture. Recently, there have been a number of charges made that the schools do not just passively fail to educate many of the students, but that they actively operate to prevent their education. For one example of such an approach, see "Student Social Class and Teacher Expectations: The Self-fulfilling Prophesy in Ghetto Education," by Ray C. Rist (Harvard Educational Review, 1970, 40, 411–451). Rist's longitudinal, observational study of children from kindergarten entry through second grade examines the relations between the "caste" systems of the classroom and of the society. Another, and much more direct, indictment of the schools for seeking failure (even if unconsciously) is provided by Annie Stein, who has spent 35 years as a research analyst and has long been concerned with racial imbalance in various school systems.

Her article "Strategies of Failure" appeared in the May 1971 issue of the Harvard Educational Review.

The authors of the article reprinted here are William Labov and Clarence Robins. Professor Labov, the senior author, is professor of psychology at the University of Pennsylvania. Robins is a graduate student in sociology at Adelphi University.

For the past several years, we have been studying certain conflicts between the vernacular of the urban ghettos and schoolroom English, especially in relation to reading failure.[1] We work primarily with peer-groups of Negro boys within the culture of the street, since we believe that the major controls upon language are exerted by these groups rather than the school or the home. Our research has recently revealed a sharp and striking relationship between participation in this street culture and reading failure. The pattern is so clear and plainly so important in understanding the educational problems of ghetto areas, that we are sending this brief note to all those who have shown interest in our progress reports.

THE POPULATIONS CONCERNED

In the summer of 1965, we interviewed a sample of 75 Negro boys, age 10 to 12 years, in a geographically random sample of "Vacation Day Camps" in Harlem. Boys had to be enrolled by their parents in these recreational programs, held in schoolyards and playgrounds, so that there was a bias of selection for children from intact families with support for educational goals. Nevertheless, we found that the majority of these 10–12-year-olds had serious difficulty in reading aloud such second- and third-grade sentences as

Now I read and write better than Alfred does.
When I passed by, I read the sign.

---

[1] Data in this research note is the product of Cooperative Research Project 3288, "A Study of the Non-standard English of Negro and Puerto Rican Speakers in New York City," under OE-6-10-059. Preliminary linguistic findings of this research are published in "Some Sources of Reading Problems of Negro Speakers of Non-Standard English," in A. Frazier (Ed.), *New Directions in Elementary English* (Champaign, Ill.: N.C.T.E., 1967), pp. 140–167, and available in "Some Suggestions for Teaching Standard English to Speakers of Non-Standard Urban Dialects," submitted to the Bureau of Curriculum Research of the Board of Education of the City of New York.

William Labov and Clarence Robins, "A note on the relation of reading failure to peer-group status in urban ghettos," *The Record—Teachers College*, 1969, *70*, 395–405. Reprinted by permission.

In August of 1965, we turned to the study of groups of boys in their natural associations on the streets of South Central Harlem. Our normal method of work was to interview a few individuals, locate their peer group and become acquainted with it; we then studied the language of the peer group in spontaneous interaction, and recorded the remaining individuals in face-to-face interviews. We used this approach first in studying two pre-adolescent groups in a low-income project, the "Thunderbirds" and the "Aces," against the general population of the project. We then began the study of the major adolescent groups that dominated the tenement areas from 110th Street to 118th Street between Sixth and Eighth Avenues. One of our staff members, Mr. John Lewis, acted as a participant-observer in the area. With his help, we followed two major adolescent groups, each composed of many subgroups, for two years. These groups were known as the "Cobras" and the "Jets." [2]

Our knowledge of the social structure, history, activities, and value systems of these groups is an essential aspect of the finding to be presented in this note. We traced the history of group relations and explored the value systems through individual face-to-face interviews, meetings with small groups of two or three close friends, and group sessions with six to twelve boys. In all these sessions, involving the most excited physical and verbal interaction, each person's statements and ideas were recorded on a separate track from a microphone several inches away from his mouth. We also studied group behavior in various field trips with the boys, and recorded their interaction en route. Most importantly, our participant-observer saw the boys every day on the streets, and met with them in their hang-outs and our "club-house." He was present at several moments of crisis when fighting was about to break out between the two major groups.

We also interviewed a number of isolated individuals in the same tenement areas, who were definitely not members of these groups, but who often knew about them. We are able then to assert that we reached all the major "named" groups in the area, although we did not have a representative sample of all adolescent boys. In the same areas we completed a stratified random sample of 100 adults, but only in the low-income projects did we

relate our groups quantitatively to the total population. [3]

THE STREET GROUPS

The larger associations which bear the names "Jets" or "Cobras" are known to the boys as "clubs." They are not to be confused with the groups which are organized within recreation centers by adults, which are also called "clubs" and sometimes overlap in membership. The groups we studied are initiated by the boys themselves, and are disapproved of by the adults in the neighborhood. [4]

The structure and value systems of these groups are partly inherited from the period of gang violence of the 1940's and 1950's. The frequency of group fighting, however, is comparatively low. These are not "gangs" in the sense of groups which frequently fight as a unit. Nevertheless, a major source of prestige for the leaders is skill in fighting, and individual fights are very common. The inter-group conflicts which do occur are the most important sources of group cohesion; they become a fixed part of the mythology and ideology of the group, and the obligation to support one's fellow members in a group fight is strongly felt by many members.

The general value systems of these groups conform to the lower class value pattern which has been described by Walter B. Miller. [5] The focal concerns of the groups are *toughness, smartness, trouble, excitement, autonomy,* and *fate.* Intelligence or smartness is used and valued as a means of manipulating others, rather than a means of obtaining information or solving abstract problems. The specific values of the Negro nationalist movement are reflected in some groups more than others. The members of the "Cobras," within the period that we worked with them, moved from a moderately nationalist position to deep involvement with the militant Muslim religion and its complex ideology. [6] This ideology involved the members in a strong interest in learning and abstract knowledge;

---

[2] The names "Cobras" and "Jets" are here used as cover symbols for a complex of formal groups which changes over time. The "Cobras," in particular, was originally a group formed by mergers of several groups which in turn underwent mergers with other groups under successive changes in nationalist orientation.

[3] See below for relative sizes of street groups and isolated population in one project.

[4] The "Thunderbirds" are a partial exception here, since the club was formed in a recreation center (and was successively re-formed with different names); however, the identity of the group was not confined to the center, and it contained members who had been banned from the center.

[5] "Lower Class Culture as a Generating Milieu of Juvenile Delinquency," *Journal of Social Issues, 14,* 1958, pp. 5–19.

[6] As noted above, the "Cobras" underwent a number of organizational transformations, with new officers, and merged with other groups as nationalist orientation increased.

but the general value systems of all the groups were such that school learning was seen as hostile, distant, and essentially irrelevant.

The groups have a formal structure which may include four officers: president, vice-president, prime minister and war-lord. Junior organizations are often formed by the appointment of a younger brother of an officer to a leading position among the 10-to-13-year-olds. However, this formal structure can be misleading. The day-to-day activities of the boys [7] are in smaller, informal hang-out groups, determined by geography and age; an individual's association with the larger group is often a matter of formal definition of his identity more than anything else.[8] Yet the ultimate sanction of the larger group and its fighting role is often referred to.

Sources of prestige within the group are physical size, toughness, courage and skill in fighting; skill with language in ritual insults, verbal routines with girls, singing, jokes and story-telling; knowledge of nationalist lore; skill and boldness in stealing; experience in reform schools; and connections with family members or others which provide reputation, money, hang-outs, marijuana, or other material goods. Success in school is irrelevant to prestige within the group, and reading is rarely if ever used outside of school.[9]

GROUP MEMBERSHIP

Full participation in the group consists of *endorsement* of this set of values, and *acceptance* of a set of personal obligations to others within the same environment and value system. The criterion of formal membership ("you are a Jet" or "you are not a Jet") is often disputed. A few individuals want to be members and are rejected; others could easily be members but do not care to. Full membership, as we define it, means that the individual is thoroughly involved with the values and activities of the group, and is defined as a member both by himself and by others. If some but not all of these criteria are fulfilled, we term the individual a "marginal member." The clearest evidence for full membership as against marginal status is provided by the symmetrical and asymmetrical relations in a socio-metric diagram.[10] If an individual on the outskirts of the group wants to be a member, yet is prevented by the influence of other environments (family, school) and other value systems, he is classed with other non-members. In each area there are "social groups" which are strongly influenced by adult organizations: we do not include membership in such groups in the category of membership which we are studying.

It has been shown in many similar situations that group membership is a function of age.[11] Boys 8-to-9 years old are definitely outsiders for the groups we are studying, and they have only a vague knowledge of group activities. Membership is strongest in the 13-to-15-year-old range, and falls off rapidly in the later teens. A few 18-or-19-year-old boys act as seniors, especially if younger brothers are serving as officers, but as a rule older boys drift off into different activities.

It is difficult to estimate the percentage of boys who are full participants in the street culture. However, in the one 13-story low income project which we studied intensively,[12] there were 22 boys 10-to-12 years old. Their relationships to the major peer group, the "Thunderbirds," were as follows:

members	marginal members	non-members
12	3	7

Our general experience would indicate that 50 to 60 per cent of the boys in the age range 10-to-16 are full participants in the street culture we are studying here.

READING RECORDS

In all of our individual interviews, we used a number of special reading tests developed to yield specific information on the vernacular phonology and grammar.[13] However, the most direct evidence for reading performance in schools is obtained from the Metropolitan Achievement Test given every year in the New York City schools. With the help of the New York City Board of Education, we were able to study recently the academic records of 75 pre-adolescent and adolescent boys with whom we

---

[7] Major activities are flying pigeons, playing basketball, playing cards, petty theft, playing pool, smoking marijuana, hanging out . . . although not all members participate in all of these activities. The groups as formal wholes have relatively few activities.

[8] The problem of group identity, and the obligations which accompany membership, is not fully solved.

[9] As one indication of the importance of reading in the group, we may consider one pair of boys who were best friends and saw each other every day. One read extremely well, the other not at all: the other's performance was a total surprise to each.

[10] The most important data is derived from the question, "Who are the guys [cats] you hang out with?", supplemented with other questions on group leaders, best friends, and all other mentions of individuals in relevant roles.

[11] Cf. Peter Wilmott, *Adolescent Boys in East London*. London: 1966, p. 35. In answer to a question on main companions in spare time, 57 per cent of those 14–15 years old indicated a group of other males; 44 per cent of those 16–18 years old; and only 32 per cent of those 19–20 years old.

[12] The building studied here is 1390 Fifth Avenue.

[13] Gray's Oral Reading Test was also given to a section of the population for further calibration on school approaches to reading.

had worked in the years 1965 to 1967. The substance of this report is the correlation between the Metropolitan Achievement Reading Test and group membership.

Figure 1 shows the correlation between grade level and reading achievement for 32 boys we interviewed in the 110th-120th Street area who are not members of the street culture, or whose group status is unknown (from the Vacation Day Camp series). The horizontal axis is grade level at the time of the test; the vertical axis the Metropolitan Achievement Test score. Each individual's score and grade are indicated by the location of an *x*. The diagonal lines group together those who are reading on grade level [0], one to three years above grade level [+3 − +1], or one to six years behind grade level [−1 − −6]. As one would expect, there are a good many boys who are two years behind grade, which is average in New York City, but there are also quite a few on grade and some ahead of grade level. Eleven of the 32 boys are on grade or above. The general direction of the pattern is upward, indicating that learning is taking place.

Figure 2 shows the same relationships for 43 boys who are members or marginal members of street groups in South Central Harlem. Each indi-

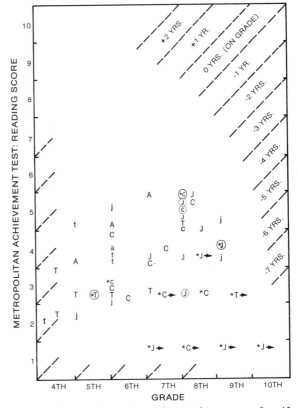

FIGURE 2. *Grade and reading achievement for 43 members of street groups in South Central Harlem, T,t = "Thunderbirds," A,a = "Aces," C,c = "Cobras," J,j = "Jets," other symbols: see text*

vidual is represented by a letter symbolizing the group of which he is a member or to which he is most closely related. Upper case letters are full members, and lower case marginal members. The over-all pattern is entirely different from Figure 1: no one is reading above grade, only one boy reading on grade, and the great majority are three or more years behind. Moreover, there are *no* boys who are reading above the fifth grade level, no matter what grade they are in. At each grade, the reading achievement for these boys forms a lower, more compact group than for the same grade in Figure 1. The close concentration of boys in the eighth grade below the fifth grade level shows a limitation on achievement which is quite striking. On the whole, Figure 2 shows very little learning as compared to Figure 1.[14]

The lower achievement of group members does not indicate over-all deficiency in verbal skills. Many of these boys are proficient at a wide range of

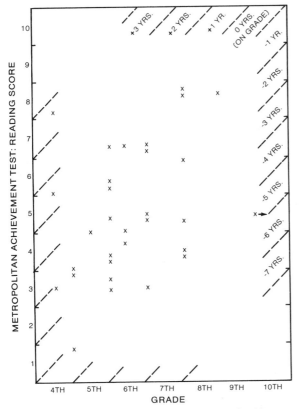

FIGURE 1. *Grade and reading achievement for 32 non-members of street groups in South Central Harlem*

[14] There is a close correlation between reading achievement and the Pintner-Cunningham IQ test (given in the early grades in New York City in former years) in Figure 1, and less markedly in Figure 2.

verbal skills appropriate for group activity: the verbal leaders are indicated by circles in Figure 2. While several are clustered near the highest point of achievement, there are other verbal leaders near the bottom of the diagram.

These findings are merely preliminary to our main body of correlations; we will shortly be able to provide more detailed data on a larger sample. There are a total of 170 boys whose reading abilities and language scores have been studied, and we will be able to correlate reading skill with many other factors besides membership in the street culture. However, the patterns revealed by Figures 1 and 2 are so striking that we thought all those interested in the problem should be aware of them as soon as possible.

WHAT IS TO BE DONE?

The over-all view given by Figure 2 strongly reinforces our view that the major problem responsible for reading failure is a cultural conflict. The school environment and school values are plainly not influencing the boys firmly grounded in street culture. The group which does show learning contains a large percentage of boys who do not fit in with street culture—who reject it or are rejected by it. For the majority, Figure 2 confirms indirect evidence that teachers in the city schools have little ability to reward or punish members of the street culture, or to motivate learning by any means.

The usual statistics on reading achievement in urban ghettos are alarming, but they do not reveal the full extent of reading failure. Research inside the schools cannot discriminate membership in the street culture from non-membership, and educators are therefore not aware of the full extent of the cultural barrier between them and their students.

It should be understood that the educational goals of the adult Negro community are the same as that of our society as a whole. Our subjective evaluation tests, for example, show that adults in Harlem are almost unanimous in their norms of correct speech and the goals for language teaching in school. Many of the members of the street culture gradually break away and acquire these adult norms in their twenties. However, these norms are of little value for those who do not have the skills to put them into effect.

The reading failure that we have documented here is typical of other performance on the academic records. The pattern of failure is so widespread, in many urban areas, that one cannot hold responsible any one system, school or teacher. The majority of these boys have not learned to read well enough to use reading as a tool for further learning. For many of them, there is no realistic possibility of graduating from high school and acquiring the skills needed for the job market. In this particular note we are dealing only with the formal aspect of educational failure. In later publications, we will attempt to document the pessimism and despair with which these adolescents view their immediate future.

The absolute ceiling of Figure 2 is of course an artifact of the limited sample. We know from our own tests that there are group members who read very well, whose school records are not presently available. But even these rare individuals view the educational system with a profound cynicism. The majority of those who learn from the system are located in Figure 1.

We do not believe that the present college-educated teaching staff, Negro or white, has the specific knowledge of the street culture to solve this problem alone. Negro teachers raised in ghetto areas are not members of the *current* street culture. With a few rare exceptions, we find that success in

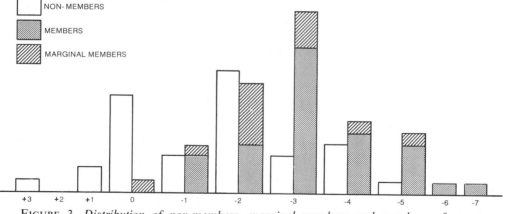

FIGURE 3. *Distribution of non-members, marginal members and members of street culture by years behind grade*

education removes the individual from his culture so effectively that his knowledge of it becomes quite marginal. The specific knowledge of the street culture which is needed is only available to those who are in constant interaction with the peer groups on the streets. Part of the reason is that the value system, though quite general, is intensely *local* in focus. The factors that control language behavior are often local and immediate: what happened last year, last month, or yesterday to that particular sub-group is the best stimulus for evoking spontaneous speech. And the general configurations of the culture change rapidly even though the value system remains intact: a teacher raised in Harlem in the 1950's, returning to the streets today, would find it difficult to understand how and why gang fighting is no longer in style.

We hope to elaborate on these problems of communication in later publications. Here we would like to indicate briefly the form of one proposal we believe will be effective in solving the problem of Figure 2.

We propose that a cultural intermediary be introduced into the classroom in the person of a young Negro man,[15] 16 to 25 years old, with high school

level reading skills, but not a college graduate. We propose the creation of a special license to allow this young man to carry out the following functions:

1. to acquaint the teacher with the specific interests of members of the class and help design reading materials centering on these interests.
2. to provide effective rewards and punishments that will motivate members of street culture for whom normal school sanctions are irrelevant.
3. to lead group discussion on topics of immediate concern to members of the class.
4. to lead boys in sports and other recreational activities in school time.
5. to maintain contact with boys outside of school, on the streets, and help organize extra-curricular activities.

We are well aware of the difficulties that any school system will have in absorbing such outside elements. The situation in most ghetto schools is plainly desperate enough so that many educators will be willing to endorse a proposal that may create such difficulties. We suggest that summer training schools be held for such special license teachers, in which regular teachers will participate, to develop jointly techniques for cross-cultural cooperation. At such training schools, it will also be possible to provide regular teachers and special license teachers with specific linguistic data of the type generated by our principal direction of research.

---

[15] We specifically designate a male for this role, in contrast to a number of proposals for "para-professionals" in the schools which utilize women from the community or from college training courses. We cannot elaborate on the importance of sex differentiation here, except to indicate that we believe it is a matter of prime importance.

VII

AGE OR DEVELOPMENTAL STAGE AS A DETERMINANT OF BEHAVIOR

It is very likely that, when pressed, no theorist would maintain that chronological age per se is an important determinant of behavior. We can characterize as "maturationists" a number of authors who believe both that many psychological characteristics appear in a predictable sequence and that the absolute age for reaching a given stage of development varies among individuals. Despite their explicit statements on the importance of such individual variations in the age at which a stage is reached, some "authorities" have written in such a fashion that their readers have focused on absolute ages. The author may describe the "typical" behaviors for given ages (e.g., Gesell), or he may give age labels to the stages he discovers (e.g., Piaget). A more reasonable reading of these authors' materials would be to accept the ages stated as mere approximations while recognizing the assumption of such workers that the developmental stage reached is a crucial determinant of behavior.

Some of the most important workers whose thinking is (or was) dominated by a belief in the sequential orderliness of development are Jean Piaget[1] and the late Arnold Gesell, both mentioned above, and Myrtle McGraw and the late Heinz Werner. They have all tended to assume that the contrasts they find between younger and older human beings are found in the development of all individuals. Because Gesell believed that the attributes he saw as unfolding sequentially were biologically determined, we have also commented on his work in Section II (Biological Bases for Behavior).

Psychoanalytic theory has a developmental aspect in its concept of psychosexual stages.[2] Although the stages themselves are considered to be biologically determined, life experiences are considered important in creating the behaviors held characteristic of each developmental stage. Inherited capacities appearing in accordance with chronological maturation interact with interpersonal influences to produce behavior. Consequently, a change in either the inherited capacities or the interpersonal experiences can alter the outcome of the interaction. Thus, individual differences, which have been of little interest to Piaget and Gesell, are accounted for in psychoanalytic theory by variations not only in hereditary tendencies, but also in emotional histories.

Some theorists stress the idea that certain ages or periods may be "critical." A period may be critical in two senses: (1) if certain experiences or learnings do not take place at that time, development cannot proceed properly; or (2) if certain experiences occur at that time, they may have more serious negative consequences than if they occurred either earlier or later. For example, it has been speculated that if the opportunity for language learning or for the development of social contacts and affectional bonds is not present at the proper time, later the

---

[1] For a detailed view of Piaget's contributions, see the book by John H. Flavell, *The Developmental Psychology of Jean Piaget,* D. Van Nostrand Co., Inc., Princeton, N.J., 1963.

[2] The term "psychosexual stages" refers to stages in the socialization of pleasure needs, and is not limited to "sexual" in the American use of the term.

child will not be able to speak properly or to form close attachments with others. Much of the germane work to date, however, has been based on rather loose analogies to ethological and embryological findings. The reader is referred to Bettye Caldwell's article "The Usefulness of the Critical Period Hypothesis in the Study of Filiative Behavior," which appeared in the *Merrill-Palmer Quarterly* (1962, *8*, 229–242) and was reprinted in the second edition of *The Causes of Behavior*.

We have not attempted to organize the selections in this section on exactly the lines dictated by these theoretical concerns. Instead, the section commences with two general papers that span a range of stages of development. Both of these owe much of their intellectual heritage to the psychoanalytic approach. Following these is a discussion of the rather astonishingly extensive capacities of the human infant to receive sensory stimulation and to learn. Then come two articles that focus on the period of adolescence. Completing this section is an article that describes the developmental theory of one of the most important psychologists of today, Jean Piaget.

The reader who is not acquainted with the writings of anthropologists on the topic of normality of adolescent difficulties may wish to refer to Margaret Mead's paper "Adolescence in Primitive and Modern Society," in Maccoby, Newcomb, Hartley (Eds.), *Readings in Social Psychology* (Henry Holt & Co., Inc., 1958). She reports the discovery of human societies in which adolescence is a period without turmoil and tension. A classic paper in a similar vein is Ruth Benedict's "Continuities and Discontinuities in Cultural Conditioning." It has been reprinted in at least two collections of readings (Martin and Stendler, *Readings in Child Development* [Harcourt, Brace & Co., 1954], pp. 142–148) and should be readily available to readers. A recent book by Daniel Offer, *The Psychological World of the Teen-ager* (Basic Books, Inc., 1969), presents a point of view contrary to the tenor of some of the articles presented in this section, that adolescence even in American society is by no means a time of surliness and rebellion, but rather is often a smooth and comfortable period.

Additional articles that relate to phases of development appear elsewhere in this book, for example, the Scott papers in Section II.

44

A Healthy Personality for Every Child

"A Healthy Personality for Every Child," adapted from the writings of Erik H. Erikson, was prepared for a White House conference. Erikson is a psychoanalyst noted for his clinical studies of children and for his theoretical work greatly enlarging upon and enriching Freudian developmental concepts. His book Childhood and Society *(New York: W. W. Norton & Co., Inc., 1950, rev. 1963) is a classic. Recently, Erikson has written noted books about Martin Luther* (Young Man Luther) *and Mahatma Gandhi* (Gandhi's Truth). *Erikson has been professor of human development at Harvard University since 1960. For many years before that he was at University of California in Berkeley.*

Many attempts have been made to describe the attributes of healthy personality. They have been put succinctly as the ability to love and the ability to work. A recent review of the literature suggests that the individual with a healthy personality is one who actively masters his environment, shows a unity of personality, and is able to perceive the world and himself correctly. Clearly, none of these criteria applies to a child. It seemed to us best, then, to present for the Conference's consideration an outline that has the merit of indicating at one and the same time the main course of personality development and the attributes of a healthy personality.

This developmental outline was worked out by Erik H. Erikson, a psychologist and practicing psychoanalyst who has made anthropological field studies and has had much experience with children. It is an analysis that derives from psychological theory, to which is added knowledge from the fields of child development and cultural anthropology. The whole is infused with the author's insight and personal philosophy.

In each stage of child development, the author says, there is a central problem that has to be solved, temporarily at least, if the child is to proceed with vigor and confidence to the next stage. These problems, these conflicts of feeling and desire, are never solved in entirety. Each shift in experience and environment presents them in a new form. It is held, however, that each type of conflict appears in its purest, most unequivocal form at a particular stage of child development, and that if the problem is well solved at that time the basis for progress to the next stage is well laid.

In a sense personality development follows biological principles. Biologists have found that everything that grows has a groundplan that is laid out at its start. Out of this groundplan the parts arise, each part having its time of special ascendancy. Together these parts form a functioning whole. If a part does not arise at its appointed time, it will never be able to form fully, since the moment for the rapid outgrowth of some other part will have arrived. Moreover, a part that misses its time of ascendancy or is severely damaged during its formative period is apt to doom, in turn, the whole hierarchy of organs. Proper rate and normal sequence is necessary if functional harmony is to be secured

Personality represents the most complicated functioning of the human organism and does not consist of parts in the organic sense. Instead of the development of organs, there is the development of locomotor, sensory, and social capacities and the development of individual modes of dealing with experience. Nevertheless, proper rate and proper sequence are as important here as in physical growth, and functional harmony is achieved only if development proceeds according to the groundplan.

In all this it is encouraging for parents and others who have children in charge to realize that in the sequence of his most personal experiences, just as in the sequence of organ formation, the child can be trusted to follow inner laws of development, and needs from adults chiefly love, encouragement, and guidance.

A Healthy Personality for Every Child: A digest of the Fact Finding Report to the Midcentury White House Conference on Children and Youth, 1951, 6–25.

The operation of biological laws is seen, also, in the fact that there is constant interplay between organism and environment and that problems of personality functioning are never solved once and for all. Each of the components of the healthy personality to be described below is present in some form from the beginning, and the struggle to maintain it continues throughout life.

For example, a baby may show something like "autonomy" or a will of his own in the way he angrily tries to free his head when he is tightly held. Nevertheless, it is not until the second year of life that he begins to experience the whole conflict between being an autonomous creature and a dependent one. It is not until then that he is ready for a decisive encounter with the people around him, and it is not until then that they feel called upon to train him or otherwise curb his free-questing spirit. The struggle goes on for months and finally, under favorable circumstances, some compromise between dependence and independence is reached that gives the child a sense of well-being.

The sense of autonomy thus achieved is not a permanent possession, however. There will be other challenges to that sense and other solutions more in keeping with later stages of development. Nevertheless, once established at two or three years of age, this early sense of autonomy will be a bulwark against later frustrations and will permit the emergence of the next developmental problem at a time that is most favorable for its solution.

So it is with all the personality components to be described. They appear in miniature early in life. The struggle to secure them against tendencies to act otherwise comes to a climax at a time determined by emergence of the necessary physical and mental abilities. There are, throughout life, other challenges and other responses but they are seldom so serious and seldom so decisive as those of the critical years.

In all this, it must be noted in addition, there is not the strict dichotomy that the analysis given below suggests. With each of the personality components to be described, it is not all or nothing: trust *or* mistrust, autonomy *or* doubt, and so on. Instead, each individual has some of each. His health of personality is determined by the preponderance of the favorable over the unfavorable, as well as by what manner of compensations he develops to cope with his disabilities.

THE SENSE OF TRUST

The component of the healthy personality that is the first to develop is the sense of trust. The crucial time for [its] emergence is the first year of life. As with the other personality components to be described, the sense of trust is not something that develops independent of other manifestations of growth. It is not that the infant learns how to use his body for purposeful movement, learns to recognize people and objects around him, and also develops a sense of trust. Rather, the concept "sense of trust" is a short-cut expression intended to convey the characteristic flavor of all the child's satisfying experiences at this early age. Or, to say it another way, this psychological formulation serves to condense, summarize, and synthesize the most important underlying changes that give meaning to the infant's concrete and diversified experience.

Trust can exist only in relation to something. Consequently a sense of trust cannot develop until the infant is old enough to be aware of objects and persons and to have some feeling that he is a separate individual. At about three months of age a baby is likely to smile if somebody comes close and talks to him. This shows that he is aware of the approach of the other person, that pleasurable sensations are aroused. If, however, the person moves too quickly or speaks too sharply the baby may look apprehensive or cry. He will not "trust" the unusual situation but will have a feeling of uneasiness, of mistrust, instead.

Experiences connected with feeding are a prime source for the development of trust. At around four months of age a hungry baby will grow quiet and show signs of pleasure at the sound of an approaching footstep, anticipating (trusting) that he will be held and fed. This repeated experience of being hungry, seeing food, receiving food, and feeling relieved and comforted assures the baby that the world is a dependable place.

Later experiences, starting at around five months of age, add another dimension to the sense of trust. Through endless repetitions of attempts to grasp for and hold objects, the baby is finally successful in controlling and adapting his movements in such a way as to reach his goal. Through these and other feats of muscular coordination the baby is gradually able to trust his own body to do his bidding.

The baby's trust-mistrust problem is symbolized in the game of peek-a-boo. In this game, which babies begin to like at about four months of age, an object disappears and then reappears. There is a slightly tense expression on the baby's face when the object goes away; its reappearance is greeted by wriggles and smiles. Only gradually does a baby learn that things continue to exist even though he does not see them, that there is order and stability in his universe. Peek-a-boo proves the point by playful repetition.

Studies of mentally ill individuals and observations of infants who have been grossly deprived of affection suggest that trust is an early-formed and important element in the healthy personality. Psychiatrists find again and again that the most serious illnesses occur in patients who have been sorely neglected or abused or otherwise deprived of love in infancy. Similarly, it is a common finding of psychological and social investigators that individuals diagnosed as a "psychopathic personality" were so unloved in infancy that they have no reason to trust the human race and, therefore, no sense of responsibility toward their fellow men.

Observations of infants brought up in emotionally unfavorable institutions or removed to hospitals with inadequate facilities for psychological care support these findings. A recent report says: "Infants under six months of age who have been in an institution for some time present a well-defined picture. The outstanding features are listlessness, emaciation and pallor, relative immobility, quietness, unresponsiveness to stimuli like a smile or a coo, indifferent appetite, failure to gain weight properly despite ingestion of diets which are entirely adequate, frequent stools, poor sleep, an appearance of unhappiness, proneness to febrile episodes, absence of sucking habits."[1]

Another investigation of children separated from their mothers at six to twelve months and not provided with an adequate substitute comes to much the same conclusion: "The emotional tone is one of apprehension and sadness, there is withdrawal from the environment amounting to rejection of it, there is no attempt to contact a stranger and no brightening if a stranger contacts him. Activities are retarded and the child often sits or lies inert in a dazed stupor. Insomnia is common and lack of appetite universal. Weight is lost, and the child becomes prone to current infections."[2]

Most significant for our present point, these reactions are most likely to occur in children who up to the time of separation at six to nine months of age had a happy relation with their mothers, while those whose relations were unhappy are relatively unaffected. It is at about this age that the struggle between trusting and mistrusting the world comes to a climax, for it is then that the child first perceives clearly that he and his environment are things apart. That at this time formerly happy infants should react so badly to separation suggests, indeed, that they had a faith which now was shattered. Happily, there is usually spectacular

change for the better when the maternal presence and love are restored.

It is probably unnecessary to describe the numerous ways in which stimuli from without and from within may cause an infant distress. Birth is believed by some experts to be a painful experience for the baby. Until fairly recently doctors were likely to advise that babies be fed on schedule and that little attention be paid to their cries of hunger at other times. Many infants spent many of the waking hours of the first four months doubled up with colic. All of them had to be bathed and dressed at stated times, whether they liked it or not. Add to these usual discomforts the fact that some infants are handled rather roughly by their parents, that others hear angry words and loud voices, and that a few are really mistreated, and it will not be difficult to understand why some infants may feel the world is a place that cannot be trusted.

In most primitive societies and in some sections of our own society the attention accorded infants is more in line with natural processes. In such societies separation from the mother is less abrupt, in that for some time after birth the baby is kept close to the warmth and comfort of its mother's body and at its least cry the breast is produced. Throughout infancy the baby is surrounded by people who are ready to feed it, fondle it, otherwise comfort it at a moment's notice. Moreover, these ministrations are given spontaneously, wholeheartedly, and without that element of nervous concern that may characterize the efforts of young mothers made self-conscious and insecure by our scientific age.

We must not exaggerate, however. Most infants in our society, too, find smiles and the comfort of mother's soft, warm body accompanying their intake of food, whether from breast or bottle. Coldness, wetness, pain, and boredom—for each misfortune there is prompt and comforting relief. As their own bodies come to be more dependable, there is added to the pleasures of increasing sensory response and motor control the pleasure of the mother's encouragement.

Moreover, babies are rather hardy creatures and are not to be discouraged by inexperienced mothers' mistakes. Even a mother cat has to learn, and the kittens endure gracefully her first clumsy efforts to carry them away from danger. Then, too, psychologists tell us that mothers create a sense of trust in their children not by the particular techniques they employ but by the sensitiveness with which they respond to the children's needs and by their over-all attitude.

For most infants, then, a sense of trust is not difficult to come by. It is the most important element in the personality. It emerges at the most

[1] Harry Bakwin, "Emotional Deprivation in Infants," *Journal of Pediatrics,* October, 1949, *35*, 512–529.

[2] John Bowlby, M.D., Summary of Dr. René Spitz's observations, unpublished manuscript.

vulnerable period of a child's life. Yet it is the least likely to suffer harm, perhaps because both nature and culture work toward making mothers most maternal at that time.

THE SENSE OF AUTONOMY

The sense of trust once firmly established, the struggle for the next component of the healthy personality begins. The child is now twelve to fifteen months old. Much of his energy for the next two years will center around asserting that he is a human being with a mind and will of his own. A list of some of the items discussed by Spock under the heading, "The One Year Old," will serve to remind us of the characteristics of that age and the problems they create for parents. "Feeling his oats." "The passion to explore." "He gets more dependent and more independent at the same time." "Arranging the house for the wandering baby." "Avoiding accidents." "How do you make him leave certain things alone?" "Droppings and throwing things." "Biting humans." "The small child who won't stay in bed at night."

What is at stake throughout the struggle of these years is the child's sense of autonomy, the sense that he is an independent human being and yet one who is able to use the help and guidance of others in important matters. This stage of development becomes decisive for the ratio between love and hate, between cooperation and wilfulness, for freedom of self-expression and its renunciation in the make-up of the individual. The favorable outcome is self-control without loss of self-esteem. The unfavorable outcome is doubt and shame.

Before the sense of autonomy can develop, the sense of trust must be reasonably well-established and must continue to pervade the child's feeling about himself and his world. Only so dare he respond with confidence to his new-felt desire to assert himself boldly, to appropriate demandingly, and to hurl away without let or hindrance.

As with the previous stage, there is a physiological basis for this characteristic behavior. This is the period of muscle-system maturation and the consequent ability (and doubly felt inability) to coordinate a number of highly conflicting action patterns, such as those of holding on and letting go, walking, talking, and manipulating objects in ever more complicated ways. With these abilities come pressing needs to use them: to handle, to explore, to seize and to drop, to withhold and to expel. And, with all, there is the dominant will, the insistent "Me do" that defies help and yet is so easily frustrated by the inabilities of the hands and feet.

For a child to develop this sense of self-reliance and adequacy that Erikson calls autonomy, it is necessary that he experience over and over again that he is a person who is permitted to make choices. He has to have the right to choose, for example, whether to sit or whether to stand, whether to approach a visitor or to lean against his mother's knee, whether to accept offered food or whether to reject it, whether to use the toilet or to wet his pants. At the same time he must learn some of the boundaries of self-determination. He inevitably finds that there are walls he cannot climb, that there are objects out of reach, that, above all, there are innumerable commands enforced by powerful adults. His experience is much too small to enable him to know what he can and cannot do with respect to the physical environment, and it will take him years to discover the boundaries that mark off what is approved, what is tolerated, and what is forbidden by his elders whom he finds so hard to understand.

As problems of this period, some psychologists have concentrated particularly on bladder and bowel control. Emphasis is put upon the need for care in both timing and mode of training children in the performance of these functions. If parental control is too rigid or if training is started too early, the child is robbed of his opportunity to develop, by his own free choice, gradual control of the contradictory impulses of retention and elimination.

To others who study child development, this matter of toilet training is but a prototype of all the problems of this age-range. The sphincters are only part of the whole muscle system, with its general ambiguity of rigidity and relaxation, of flexion and extension. To hold and to relinquish refer to much more than the bowels. As the child acquires the ability to stand on his two feet and move around, he delineates his world as me and you. He can be astonishingly pliable once he has decided that he wants to do what he is supposed to do, but there is no reliable formula for assuring that he will relinquish when he wants to hold on.

The matter of mutual regulation between parent and child (for fathers have now entered the picture to an extent that was rare in the earlier stage) now faces its severest task. The task is indeed one to challenge the most resourceful and the most calm adult. Firmness is necessary, for the child must be protected against the potential anarchy of his as yet untrained sense of discrimination. Yet the adult must back him up in his wish to "stand on his own feet," lest he be overcome by shame that he has exposed himself foolishly and by doubt in his self-worth. Perhaps the most constructive rule a parent can follow is to forbid only what "really matters" and, in such forbidding, to be clear and consistent.

Shame and doubt are emotions that many primitive peoples and some of the less sophisticated individuals in our own society utilize in training children. Shaming exploits the child's sense of being small. Used to excess it misses its objective and may result in open shamelessness, or, at least, in the child's secret determination to do as he pleases when not observed. Such defiance is a normal, even healthy response to demands that a child consider himself, his body, his needs, or his wishes evil and dirty and that he regard those who pass judgment as infallible. Young delinquents may be produced by this means, and others who are oblivious to the opinion of society.

Those who would guide the growing child wisely, then, will avoid shaming him and avoid causing him to doubt that he is a person of worth. They will be firm and tolerant with him so that he can rejoice in being a person of independence and can grant independence to others. As to detailed procedures, it is impossible to prescribe, not only because we do not know and because every situation is different but also because the kind and degree of autonomy that parents are able to grant their small children depends on feelings about themselves that they derive from society. Just as the child's sense of trust is a reflection of the mother's sturdy and realistic faith, so the child's sense of autonomy is a reflection of the parents' personal dignity. Such appears to be the teaching of the comparative study of cultures.

Personal autonomy, independence of the individual, is an especially outstanding feature of the American way of life. American parents, accordingly, are in a particularly favorable position to transmit the sense of autonomy to their children. They themselves resent being bossed, being pushed around; they maintain that everybody has the right to express his opinion and to be in control of his affairs. More easily than people who live according to an authoritarian pattern, they can appreciate a little child's vigorous desire to assert his independence and they can give him the leeway he needs in order to grow up into the upstanding, look-you-in-the-eye kind of individual that Americans admire.

It is not only in early childhood, however, that this attitude toward growing children must be maintained. As was said at the outset, these components of the healthy personality cannot be established once and for all. The period of life in which they first come into being is the most crucial, it is true. But threats to their maintenance occur throughout life. Not only parents, then, but everybody who has significant contact with children and young people must respect their desire for self-assertion, help them hold it within bounds, and avoid treating them in ways that arouse shame or doubt.

This attitude toward children, toward all people, must be maintained in institutional arrangements as well. Great differences in educational and economic opportunity and in access to the law, discrimination of all kinds are threats to this ingredient of mental health. So, too, may be the over-mechanization of our society, the depersonalization of human relations that is likely to accompany large-scale endeavor of all kinds.

Parents, as well as children, are affected by these matters. In fact, parents' ability to grant children the kind of autonomy Americans think desirable depends in part on the way they are treated as employees and citizens. Throughout, the relation must be such as affirms personal dignity. Much of the shame and doubt aroused in children result from the indignity and uncertainty that are an expression of parents' frustrations in love and work. Special attention must be paid to all these matters, then, if we are to avoid destroying the autonomy that Americans have always set store by.

THE SENSE OF INITIATIVE

Having become sure, for the time being, that he is a person in his own right and having enjoyed that feeling for a year or so, the child of four or five wants to find out what kind of person he can be. To be any particular kind of person, he sees clearly, involves being able to do particular kinds of things. So he observes with keen attention what all manner of interesting adults do (his parents, the milkman, the truck driver, and so on), tries to imitate their behavior, and yearns for a share in their activities.

This is the period of enterprise and imagination, an ebullient, creative period when phantasy substitutes for literal execution of desires and the meagerest equipment provides material for high imaginings. It is a period of intrusive, vigorous learning, learning that leads away from the child's own limitations into future possibilities. There is intrusion into other people's bodies by physical attack, into other people's ears and minds by loud and aggressive talking. There is intrusion into space by vigorous locomotion and intrusion into the unknown by consuming curiosity.

By this age, too, conscience has developed. The child is no longer guided only by outsiders; there is installed within him a voice that comments on his deeds, and warns and threatens. Close attention to the remarks of any child of this age will confirm this statement. Less obvious, however, are experts' observations that children now begin to feel guilty for mere thoughts, for deeds that have been imagined but never executed. This, they say, is the explanation for the characteristic nightmares of this age period and for the over-reaction to slight punishment.

The problem to be worked out in this stage of

development, accordingly, is how to will without too great a sense of guilt. The fortunate outcome of the struggle is a sense of initiative. Failure to win through to that outcome leaves the personality overburdened, and possibly over-restricted by guilt.

It is easy to see how the child's developing sense of initiative may be discouraged. So many of the projects dreamed up at this age are of a kind which cannot be permitted that the child may come to feel he is faced by a universal "No." In addition he finds that many of the projects are impossible of execution and others, even if not forbidden, fail to win the approval of the adults whom he has come to love. Moreover, since he does not always distinguish clearly between actuality and phantasy, his over-zealous conscience may disapprove of even imaginary deeds.

It is very important, therefore, for healthy personality development that much leeway and encouragement be given to the child's show of enterprise and imagination and that punishment be kept at a minimum. Boys and girls at this stage are extraordinarily appreciative of any convincing promise that someday they will be able to do things as well, or maybe better, than father and mother. They enjoy competition (especially if they can win) and insistence on goal; they get great pleasure from conquest. They need numerous examples of the kinds of roles adults assume, and they need a chance to try them out in play.

The ability that is in the making is that of selecting social goals and persevering in the attempt to reach them.

If enterprise and imagination are too greatly curbed, if severe rebukes accompany the frequently necessary denial of permission to carry out desires, a personality may result that is over-constricted. Such a personality cannot live up to its inner capacities for imagination, feeling, or performance, though it may over-compensate by immense activity and find relaxation impossible.

Constriction of personality is a self-imposed constriction, an act of the child's over-zealous conscience. "If I may not do this, I will not even think it," says conscience, "for even thinking it is dangerous." Resentment and bitterness and a vindictive attitude toward the world that forces the restriction may accompany this decision, however, and become unconscious but functioning parts of the personality. Such, at least, is the warning of psychiatrists who have learned to know the inmost feelings of emotionally handicapped children and adults.

This developmental stage has great assets as well as great dangers. At no time in life is the individual more ready to learn avidly and quickly, to become big in the sense of sharing obligation and performance. If during this preschool period the child can get some sense of the various roles and functions that he can perform as an adult, he will be ready to progress joyfully to the next stage, in which he will find pleasurable accomplishment in activities less fraught with phantasy and fear.

There is a lesson in this for later periods of personality development as well. As has been said before, these conflicts that come to a head at particular periods of a child's life are not settled once and for all. The sense of initiative, then, is one that must be continually fostered, and great care must be taken that youngsters and young people do not have to feel guilty for having dared to dream.

Just as we Americans prize autonomy, so too do we prize initiative; in fact, we regard it as the cornerstone of our economic system. There is much in the present industrial and political mode of life that may discourage initiative, that may make a young person think he had best pull in his horns. What these tendencies are and what they may do to youngsters and to their parents, who too must feel free if they are to cultivate the sense of initiative in their children, is a subject that warrants much serious discussion.

THE SENSE OF ACCOMPLISHMENT

The three stages so far described probably are the most important for personality development. With a sense of trust, a sense of autonomy, and a sense of initiative achieved, progress through the later stages is pretty well assured. Whether this is because children who have a good environment in their early years are likely to continue to be so favored, or whether it is because they have attained such strength of personality that they can successfully handle later difficulties, research has not yet made clear. We do know that nearly all children who get a good start continue to develop very well, and we know that some of those who start off poorly continue to be handicapped. Observations of this sort seem to support psychological theory in the conclusion that personality is pretty well set by about six years of age. Since, however, some children develop into psychologically healthy adults in spite of a bad start, and since some who start well run into difficulties later, it is clear that much research is needed before this conclusion can be accepted as wholly correct.

To return to the developmental analysis, the fourth stage, which begins somewhere around six years of age and extends over five or six years, has as its achievement what Erikson calls the sense of industry. Perhaps "sense of accomplishment" would make the meaning clearer. At any rate, this is the period in which preoccupation with phantasy subsides, and the child wants to be engaged in real tasks that he can carry through to completion. As with the other developmental stages, there are foreshadowings of this kind of interest long before six years of age. Moreover, in some societies and in some parts of our own society children are trained very early to perform socially useful tasks. The exact age is not the point at issue. What is to be pointed out is that children, after a period characterized by exuberant imagination, want to settle down to learning exactly how to do things and how to do them well.

In contrast to the preceding stages and to the succeeding ones, this stage does not consist of a swing from a violent inner upheaval to a new mastery. Under reasonably favorable circumstances this is a period of calm, steady growth, especially if the problems of the previous stages have been well worked through. Despite its unspectacular character, this is a very important period, for in it is laid a firm basis for responsible citizenship. It is during this period that children acquire not only knowledge and skills that make for good workmanship but also the ability to co-operate and play fair and otherwise follow the rules of the larger social game.

The chief danger of this period is the presence of conditions that may lead to the development of a sense of inadequacy and inferiority. This may be the outcome if the child has not yet achieved a sense of initiative, or if his experiences at home have not prepared him for entering school happily, or if he finds school a place where his previous accomplishments are disregarded or his latent abilities are not challenged. Even with a good start the child may later lapse into discouragement and lack of interest if at home or school his individual needs are overlooked—if too much is expected of him, or if he is made to feel that achievement is beyond his ability.

It is most important for health of personality, therefore, that schools be conducted well, that methods and courses of instruction be such as will give every child the feeling of successful accomplishment. Autobiographies of juvenile delinquents show time and again a boy who hated school—hated the fact that he was marked out as stupid or awkward, as one who was not as good as the rest. Some such boys find in jobs the sense of accomplishment they miss at school and consequently give up their delinquent ways. Others, however, are handicapped in job finding and keeping by the very fact that in school they did not develop the sense of industry; hence they have work failure added to their other insecurities. Nor is delinquency the only or the most likely outcome of lack of success in school. Many children respond in a quieter way, by passive acceptance of their inferiority. Psychologically they are perhaps even more harmed.

Our Puritan tradition maintains that children will not work except under the spur of competition, so we tend to fear the suggestion that all should succeed. To help children develop a sense of accomplishment does not mean, however, merely giving all of them good marks and passing them on to the next grade. Children need and want real achievement. How to help them secure it, despite differences in native capacity and differences in emotional development, is one of the school's most serious challenges.

School, of course, is not the only place in which children at this stage of development can secure the sense of industry. In work at home there are many opportunities for a child to get a feeling of mastery and worthwhile endeavor. Rural youth groups and their urban counterparts cater to this need, and many recreation programs put as much emphasis on work as on play. School, however, is the legally constituted arrangement for giving instruction to the young, so it is upon teachers that the professional responsibility for helping all children achieve a sense of industry and accomplishment rests.

In addition to aiding personality development in this way, teachers have many opportunities for reconfirming their pupils' sense of trust, autonomy, and initiative or for encouraging its growth in children who have been somewhat hampered by previous life experiences. Teachers cannot work alone, of course, either in aiding a child in the development of new capacities or in strengthening old ones. Jointly with parents and others they can do much, not only for children of already healthy personality but also for many whose development has been handicapped.

THE SENSE OF IDENTITY

With the onset of adolescence another period of personality development begins. As is well known, adolescence is a period of storm and stress for many young people, a period in which previous certainties are questioned and previous continuities no longer relied upon. Physiological changes and rapid physical growth provide the somatic base for the turmoil and indecision. It may be that cultural factors also play a part, for it has been observed that adolescence is less upsetting in some societies than in others.

The central problem of the period is the establishment of a sense of identity. The identity the adolescent seeks to clarify is who he is, what his role in society is to be. Is he a child or is he an adult? Does he have it in him to be someday a husband and father? What is he to be as a worker and an earner of money? Can he feel self-confident in spite of the fact that his race or religion or national background makes him a person some people look down upon? Over all, will he be a success or a failure? By reason of these questions adolescents are sometimes morbidly preoccupied with how they appear in the eyes of others as compared with their own conception of themselves, and with how they can make the roles and skills learned earlier jibe with what is currently in style.

In primitive societies adolescents are perhaps spared these doubts and indecisions. Through initiation rites, often seemingly cruel in character, young people are tested out (and test themselves out) and are then welcomed into a socially recognized age category in which rights and duties and mode of living are clearly defined. In our society there are few rituals or ceremonies that mark the change in status from childhood to youth. For those who have religious affiliations, confirmation, joining the church, may serve this purpose in part, since the young people are thereby admitted, in this one segment of their lives at least, to the company of adults. Such ceremonies serve, in addition, to reaffirm to youth that the universe is trustworthy and stable and that a way of life is clearly laid out.

Graduation ceremonies might play a part in marking a new status were it not that, in present-day America, status is so ill defined. What rules of law and custom exist are too diverse to be of much help. For example, legal regulations governing age of "consent," age at which marriage is permitted, age for leaving school, for driving a car, for joining (or being required to join) the Army or Navy mark no logical progressions in rights and duties. As to custom, there is so much variation in what even families who live next door to each other expect or permit that adolescents, eager to be on their way, are practically forced into standardizing themselves in their search for status. In this they are ably abetted by advertisers and entertainers who seek their patronage, as well as by well-meaning magazine writers who describe in great detail the means by which uniformity can be achieved.

In this urge to find comfort through similarity, adolescents are likely to become stereotyped in behavior and ideals. They tend to form cliques for self-protection and fasten on petty similarities of dress and gesture to assure themselves that they are really somebody. In these cliques they may be intolerant and even cruel toward those they label as different. Unfortunate as such behavior is and not to be condoned, intolerance serves the important purpose of giving the group members at least the negative assurance that there is something they are not.

The danger of this developmental period is self-diffusion. As Biff puts it in *The Death of a Salesman,* "I just can't take hold, Mom. I can't take hold of some kind of a life." A boy or girl can scarcely help feeling somewhat diffuse when the body changes in size and shape so rapidly, when genital maturity floods body and imagination with forbidden desires, when adult life lies ahead with such a diversity of conflicting possibilities and choices.

Whether this feeling of self-diffusion is fairly easily mastered or whether, in extreme, it leads to delinquency, neurosis or outright psychosis, depends to a considerable extent on what has gone before. If the course of personality development has been a healthy one, a feeling of self-esteem has accrued from the numerous experiences of succeeding in a task and sensing its cultural meaning. Along with this, the child has come to the conviction that he is moving toward an understandable future in which he will have a definite role to play. Adolescence may upset this assurance for a time or to a degree but fairly soon a new integration is achieved, and the boy or girl sees again (and with clearer vision) that he belongs and that he is on his way.

The course is not so easy for adolescents who have not had so fortunate a past or for those whose earlier security is broken by a sudden awareness that as members of minority groups their way of life sets them apart. The former, already unsure of themselves, find their earlier doubt and mistrust reactivated by the physiological and social changes that adolescence brings. The latter, once secure, may feel that they must disavow their past and try to develop an "American" personality.

Much has been learned and written about the adolescent problems of the boys and girls whose early personality development has been impaired. How they can be helped, if their disorders are not too severe, is also fairly well known. The full implications of these findings for parents, teachers, and others who would guide youth are still to be worked out but, even so, there is considerable information.

Less well understood are the difficulties and the ways of helping adolescents who grew up in cultures that are not of the usual run. These boys and girls may have been privileged in having had a childhood in which there was little inhibition of sensual pleasures, and in which development proceeded by easy, unself-conscious stages. For them, difficulties arise if their parents lose trust in themselves or if their teachers apply sudden correctives, or if they themselves reject their past and try to act like the others. The new role of middle-class adolescent if often too hard to play. Delinquency or bizarre behavior marks the failure.

How to reach these boys and girls, how to help

them attain their desire, is a matter not well understood. It is clear, however, that they should not be typed by pat diagnoses and social judgments, for they are ever ready to become the "bums" that they are called. Those who would guide them must understand both the psychology of adolescence and the cultural realities of the day. There is trust to be restored and doubt and guilt and feelings of inferiority to be overcome. The science of how to do this is still pretty much lacking, though here and there teachers, clergymen, probation officers and the like are highly successful in the task.

Hard though it be to achieve, the sense of identity is the individual's only safeguard against the lawlessness of his biological drives and the authority of an over-weening conscience. Loss of identity, loss of the sense that there is some continuity, sameness, and meaning to life, exposes the individual to his childhood conflicts and leads to emotional upsets. This outcome was observed time and again among men hard pressed by the dangers of war. It is clear, then, that if health of personality is to be preserved much attention must be given to assuring that America makes good on its promises to youth.

THE SENSE OF INTIMACY

After the sense of identity, to a greater or less extent, is achieved it becomes possible for the next component of the healthy personality to develop. This is the sense of intimacy, intimacy with persons of the same sex or of the opposite sex or with one's self. The youth who is not fairly sure of his identity shies away from interpersonal relations and is afraid of close communion with himself. The surer he becomes of himself, the more he seeks intimacy, in the form of friendship, love and inspiration.

In view of the early age at which boy and girl attachments are encouraged today, it may seem strange to put the critical period for the development of the sense of intimacy late in adolescence. The explanation is that, on the one hand, sexual intimacy is only one part of what is involved, and, on the other, boy-girl attachments of earlier age periods are likely to be of a somewhat different order. Regarding the latter point, it has been observed by those who know young people well that high-school age boys and girls often use each other's company for an endless verbal examination of what the other thinks, feels, and wants to do. In other words, these attachments are one means of defining one's identity.

In contrast to this use of friendship and companionship, boys and girls late in adolescence usually have need for a kind of fusion with the essence of other people and for a communion with their own inner resources. If, by reason of inadequacies in previous personality development, this sense of intimacy cannot be achieved, the youth may retire into psychological isolation and keep his relations with people on a formal, stereotyped level that is lacking in spontaneity and warmth or he may keep trying again and again to get close to others, only to meet with repeated failure. Under this compulsion he may even marry, but the role of mate is one he can rarely sustain, for the condition of true two-ness is that each individual must first become himself.

In this area of personality development as in the others, cultural factors play a part in sustaining or in discouraging the individual in his development. American culture is unusually successful in encouraging the development of the feelings of independence, initiative, industry, and identity. It is somewhat less successful in the area of intimacy, for the culture's ideal is the subordination of sexuality and sensuality to a life of work, duty, and worship.

Consequently, American adolescents are likely to be unsupported by their parents and to find little confirmation in story or song for their desire to sense intimately the full flavor of the personality of others. In many of them, then, the sense of intimacy does not develop highly and they have difficulty in finding in close personal relations the outlet for tension that they need.

There is some evidence that a change in conventions and customs in this respect is in the making, however. Too abrupt change in any such cultural matter is not to be urged, but it is to be hoped that gradual, frank discussion can bring about gradual alteration in attitude and overcome the dangers inherent in the traditional rigidity.

THE PARENTAL SENSE

"Parental sense" designates somewhat the same capacity as that implied in the words, creativity or productivity. The individual has normally come to adulthood before this sense can develop fully.

The parental sense is indicated most clearly by interest in producing and caring for children of one's own. It may also be exhibited in relation to other people's children or by a parental kind of responsibility toward the products of creative activity of other sorts. The mere desire for or possession of children does not indicate that this component of the healthy personality has developed. In fact, many parents who bring their children to child guidance clinics are found not to have reached this stage of personality development.

The essential element is the desire to nourish and nurture what has been produced. It is the ability to regard one's children as a trust of the community, rather than as extensions of one's own personality or merely as beings that one happens to live with.

Failure to develop this component of the healthy personality often results in a condition which has not been adequately categorized clinically. Although a true sense of intimacy has not developed, the individual may obsessively seek companionship. There is something of egotism in this as in his other activities, a kind of self-absorption. The individual is inclined to treat himself as a child and to be rivalrous with his children, if he has any. He indulges himself, expects to be indulged, and in general behaves in an infantile or immature manner.

There are both individual and social explanations of the failure to develop an adequate parental sense. Individually, the explanation may be found in the inadequate development of the personality components previously described. In some people this failure goes far back. Because of unfortunate experiences in childhood they did not arrive at a firm sense of trust, autonomy, and the rest. In others it is only inadequacies in later stages, especially in the development of the sense of intimacy, that are at fault.

Socially, as has been suggested throughout this analysis, healthy personality development depends upon the culture's ideals and upon the economic arrangements of the society. In order that most people may develop fully the sense of being a parent, the role of parent, both mother and father, must be a respected one in the society. Giving must rank higher than getting, and loving than being loved. The economy must be such that the future can be depended upon and each person can feel assured that he has a meaningful and respected part to play. Only so can most individuals afford to renounce selfish aims and derive much of their satisfaction from rearing children.

The Sense of Integrity

The final component of the healthy personality is the sense of integrity. In every culture the dominant ideals, honor, courage, faith, purity, grace, fairness, self-discipline, become at this stage the core of the healthy personality's integration. The individual, in Erikson's words, "becomes able to accept his individual life cycle and the people who have become significant to it as meaningful within the segment of history in which he lives."

To continue Erikson's description, "Integrity thus means a new and different love of one's parents, free of the wish that they should have been different, and an acceptance of the fact that one's life is one's own responsibility. It is a sense of comradeship with men and women of distant times and of different pursuits, who have created orders and objects and sayings conveying human dignity and love. Although aware of the relativity of all the various life styles that have given meaning to human striving, the possessor of integrity is ready to defend the dignity of his own life style against all physical and economic threats. For he knows that, for him, all human dignity stands or falls with the one style of integrity of which he partakes."

The adult who lacks integrity in this sense may wish that he could live life again. He feels that if at one time he had made a different decision he could have been a different person and his ventures would have been successful. He fears death and cannot accept his one and only life cycle as the ultimate of life. In the extreme, he experiences disgust and despair. Despair expresses the feeling that time is too short to try out new roads to integrity. Disgust is a means of hiding the despair, a chronic, contemptuous displeasure with the way life is run. As with the dangers and the solutions of previous periods, doubt and despair are not difficulties that are overcome once and for all, nor is integrity so achieved. Most people fluctuate between the two extremes. Most, also, at no point, either attain to the heights of unalloyed integrity or fall to the depths of complete disgust and despair.

Even in adulthood a reasonably healthy personality is sometimes secured in spite of previous misfortunes in the developmental sequence. New sources of trust may be found. Fortunate events and circumstances may aid the individual in his struggle to feel autonomous. Imagination and initiative may be spurred by new responsibilities, and feelings of inferiority be overcome by successful achievement. Even late in life an individual may arrive at a true sense of who he is and what he has to do and may be able to win through to a feeling of intimacy with others and to joy in producing and giving.

Evidence of such changes is found in the case records of psychiatrists and social workers. Common sense observation attests that similar changes in health of personality are sometimes accomplished without benefit of any form of psychotherapy. Much remains to be learned about this, however, especially about how life itself may serve as therapeusis.

For the healthy personality development of children and youth it is necessary that a large proportion of adults attain a sense of integrity to a considerable degree. Not only parents but all who deal with children have need of this quality if they are to help children maintain the feeling that the universe is dependable and trustworthy. Integrity is relatively easily attained and sustained when the culture itself gives support, when a meaning to life is clearly spelled out in tradition and ceremony, and roles are clearly defined. Our culture, with its rapidly changing technology and its diversity of value standards, leaves much for the individual to work out for himself. In the American dream, however, and the Judaeo-Christian tradition on which it is based there are values and ideals aplenty. In the interest of the welfare of children and youth, in order that a generation of happy individuals and responsible citizens be reared, it is highly important that these values and ideals be brought into prominence and that the promise of American life be kept.

45

Competence and the Psychosexual Stages of Development

ROBERT W. WHITE

Robert W. White, Professor Emeritus at Harvard University, is the author of the widely used text The Abnormal Personality *(Ronald, 3rd ed., 1964). In the following classic article he comments on Erikson's elaboration of Freud's developmental stages. He suggests a new motivational dimension —competence—that he would add to the body of theory about ego psychology. Many lines of evidence have been brought to bear in support of this concept.*

The purpose of this paper is to reconsider a part of psychoanalytic theory, the part that deals with stages of emotional development. It will be necessary first, however, to show why I think it important to look again at a theory that has survived nearly half a century of critical onslaught and that enjoys enduring high esteem among clinicians. This will require a short exposition of the concept of competence and of certain related concepts which I have discussed at length elsewhere (1959). As you will see, my use of these concepts puts me at variance with theories that make drive the necessary condition for activity and learning; at variance, therefore, with Freud's theory of instincts. The concept of competence, moreover, leads to an idea of the ego that is different from the one we usually

find in discussions of psychosexual stages. Freud's theory of these stages undoubtedly occupies a secure historical position. It will stand in the history of thought as an astonishing first approximation to a theory of growth in its dynamic aspects. Nevertheless, I believe that the time has come when its continued use will only block further insights. The theory that illuminated us all as a first approximation may only hinder us in reaching those closer approximations that always mark the forward steps in a scientific pilgrimage.

In broadest outline, Freud's theory is that the most important features of childhood development, the ones that are fateful for emotional well-being and for the shape of personality, have their motive power in sexual energy or libido. Conceiving sexuality broadly to include the obtaining of pleasure from various zones of the body, he postulated a maturational sequence whereby first the mouth, then the anal zone, finally the genitals become the dominant source of libidinal gratification. Aggressive impulses, fused with libidinal ones, enter importantly during the anal stage and from then on, but the movement from one stage to another is determined biologically by the sequence of libidinal changes. The latency period * and the final genital stage likewise come into existence through developments strictly in the sphere of sexual energy. Thus it is possible to speak of psychosexual stages, and Freud intended the double adjective to be taken quite literally. It is libido, he said, that makes demands upon the mind, that calls forth psychic activity, that constitutes the motivating force behind the development of the mental apparatus (Freud, 1905, 1908, 1913, 1923).

The great virtue of this theory lies, of course, in its gathering and ordering of the confusingly diverse facts of development. For the first three and the last stages it provides us with a model or prototype of behavior: the infant at the breast, the child on the toilet, the phallic child concerned about genital impulses toward family members, the physically mature adult in the heterosexual relation. It tells us, moreover, that these prototypes are truly basic, that events in these situations are really the

---

* *Latency period*—The period of life corresponding roughly to the kindergarten and elementary school years when, in the psychoanalytic conception, children have gained control of— or are less preoccupied than formerly with—their body-pleasure needs and primitive impulsiveness. Oral, anal, and sexual interests are said to be less evident or more disguised, i.e., to be relatively "latent," remaining so until the resurgence of sexuality in adolescence.—EDITOR

Robert W. White, "Competence and the psychosexual stages of development," reprinted from *Nebraska Symposium on Motivation, 1960*, 97–104, 106–108, 133–138, by permission of the author and the University of Nebraska Press. Copyright © 1960 by the University of Nebraska Press.

most important things that happen, so that if we know just these aspects of a person's history we know all that counts. Each prototype involves not only libidinal and aggressive energies but also frustrations, anxieties, defenses, ego developments, and relations with other people. But all these other things are brought to pass by the instincts, and we are thus permitted to place them in a subordinate relation to the central libidinal events. The theory thus achieves a heroic simplification. Right or wrong, it rescued us historically from a tangled mass of facts and made it possible for the first time to think coherently about emotional development.

Freud's ideas on this subject were completed nearly forty years ago. His ideas concerning the libido itself, a highly mobile and general source of energy, look anything but plausible in the light of recent research on motivation. Many psychoanalysts, however, retain the libido model as a working tool, finding that it greatly helps them to understand their patients' problems. Other workers have proposed more or less extensive revisions in the theory of development. In the writings of Horney (1939), Thompson (1950), and Fromm (1947), for instance, emphasis is shifted sharply from instinctual roots to human relations, especially those between child and parents. These neo-Freudians treat motivation in an offhand, pluralistic way, with perhaps special accent on security and anxiety. Development really turns, they believe, on a series of crises in parent-child relations, crises which arise because the parents, acting both for themselves and for the culture, make successive demands upon the infant that put the relation under strain. The libido model is thus displaced in favor of an interpersonal model.

One might suppose that this change of model would sweep away the prototypes provided by psychosexual theory. But the fact is that only Sullivan (1953) has seriously attempted to revise the scheme of crises in strictly interpersonal terms. With most of the revisionists the oral, anal, phallic, and genital prototypes live on, either quite literally or in such guises as "neurotic trends" and "character orientations." The familiar stages, no longer libidinal, are still considered to be crucial. This situation is most clearly recognized by Silverberg (1952), who translates Freud's stages into *"areas of experience . . .* presented to the children of western civilization by parents performing the task of acculturating their offspring." Each area has its typical problem: deprivation in the oral area; obedience, conformity, and rebelliousness in the anal; rivalry and genitality in the phallic area. It is thus contended that the prototypes originally provided by libido theory are adequate models for the crucial events in the child's interpersonal develop-ment. Feeding, toilet training, and the Oedipal triangle are still the fateful battlefields of growth.

The thesis of this paper can be set forth at this point in the form of two propositions. I shall contend, first, that *the child's emotional development cannot be adequately conceptualized by an exclusive libido model,* no matter how liberally we interpret this concept. Second, I shall try to show that *when the prototypes derived from libido theory are translated into interpersonal terms they still do not constitute adequate models for development.* The best of these prototypes is undoubtedly the feeding child of the oral stage, who cuts a prominent figure even in Sullivan's revision, but from then on the models simply miss part of the significant problems of growth. In particular they fail to embody the development of competence, and they tend to direct attention away from certain crises in the growth of the child's sense of competence. This weakness is attested most eloquently by the lack of a clear-cut model for the latency period, when competence is a central theme. What is needed, I shall argue, is a clearly conceived *competence model* that can be used throughout the stages. Sexual and interpersonal models will be needed too, but we can never do justice to emotional development until we work up a competence model to put beside them.

COMPETENCE AND SENSE OF COMPETENCE

By presenting my theme in this way I have placed a great burden on the word "competence," and I must now give this concept a fuller introduction. Let me say at the outset that it is not something I have invented. It has been distilled from the writings of a great many workers in animal psychology, child development, research on personality, and psychopathology—workers whose only common quality is a certain disenchantment with prevailing concepts of drive. It is a way of saying what I believe many voices have been saying, especially during the last twenty years. Among those who have moved in this direction, it seems to me, are Erikson, Hartmann, and other workers who are trying to carry psychoanalytic ego psychology forward from the point at which Freud left it. I am therefore not trying to promote a novel idea, but rather to find suitable expression for a concept which, suppressed for a time by the immensely popular drive theories, has lately begun to throw out restless derivatives in every direction.

Competence means fitness or ability. The competence of an organism means its fitness or ability to carry on those transactions with the environment which result in its maintaining itself, growing, and flourishing. Some parts of the environment must if possible be fought off, but other parts can safely be enjoyed, and still others can be ingested and transformed into materials for self-maintenance and growth. Some organisms are born more or less fully equipped with patterns of behavior that produce effective interactions with favorable surroundings. This is not the case with the higher animals, least of all with man, who has to learn almost everything that is useful in dealing with his world, yet who immeasurably surpasses all other living creatures in his ultimate ability to subdue and transform the environment to his own use. Man's prowess as a learner has long been an object of wonder. How does he do it, and when does he get it all done?

Theories in which drive is the central motivational concept deal quite simply with this problem. Drives arise from lacks and deficits. They are powerful and persistent internal stimuli which arouse the organism from homeostatic bliss and promote activities that ultimately eliminate the deficit, thus reducing the drive. Reduction of drive supplies the selective principle whereby patterns of behavior are retained or discarded. Our knowledge of the world and our competence in dealing with it are thus acquired in the course of satisfying our constantly recurring needs. We learn what helps us to reduce drives.

There have recently been some startling departures from this orthodoxy—not, as one might suppose, among soft-headed students of personality, but in the very heartland of hardheadedness, the animal laboratory. In a series of experiments Sheffield and others (1950, 1951, 1954) have shown that instrumental learning can take place without drive reduction, indeed under circumstances where one can suppose only that drive level is being increased. Olds and Milner (1954) have found a connection between reinforcement and the electrical stimulation of certain areas of the brain. A whole series of workers, including Harlow (1953), Butler (1958), Montgomery (1954), Berlyne (1950), and Myers and Miller (1954), have pointed out that animals show persistent tendencies toward activity, exploration, and manipulation even when all known primary drives have been satiated. Clearly the original drive model, based on hunger and other internal deficits, stands in need of extensive revision.

One way of accomplishing this revision is to postulate new drives not hitherto included in the list. In addition to hunger, sex, and the avoidance of pain we must attribute an exploratory drive and perhaps an activity drive to the higher animals, even a manipulative drive to those forms that have free use of the forelimbs. These new drives are like the older ones, it is argued, in that they provoke activity and lead to the reinforcement of instrumental learning. I find myself unable to climb aboard this drive bandwagon because I am so impressed by the differences between the old and new drives. Exploration and manipulation have nothing to do with deficits, they appear to arise in the nervous system without visceral stimulation, and they produce instrumental learning without any sign of consummatory response or drive reduction. Call them drives if you are fixated on that term, but remember that in doing so you have destroyed the original conception of drive, including Freud's conception of the instincts. Remember that you are separating drives from visceral deficits and somatic cravings, so that hunger and sex must be treated as special cases rather than as prototypes for the whole idea. But if you do remember these things, what good are you getting out of the concept of drive? I prefer to leave the word in its excellent original meaning so that we can look with a fresh eye at the adaptive significance of activity, manipulation, and exploration.

The theory that we learn what helps us to reduce our viscerogenic drives will not stand up if we stop to consider the whole range of what a child must learn in order to deal effectively with his surroundings. He has much to learn about visual forms, about grasping and letting go, about the coordination of hand and eye. He must work out the difficult problem of the constancy of objects. He must put together an increasingly varied repertory of skilled acts such as locomotion and the use of words. He must learn many facts about his world, building up a cognitive map that will afford guidance and structure for his behavior. It is not hard to see the biological advantage of an arrangement whereby these many learnings can get under way before they are needed as instruments for drive reduction or for safety. An animal that has thoroughly explored its environment stands a better chance of escaping from a sudden enemy or satisfying a gnawing hunger than one that merely dozes in the sun when its homeostatic crises are past. Seen in this light, the many hours that infants and children spend in play are by no means wasted or merely recuperative in nature. Play may be fun, but it is also a serious business in childhood. During these hours the child steadily builds up his competence in dealing with the environment.

Careful study of exploratory play, even in the first year of life, shows it to have the characteristics of directedness, selectivity, and persistence. Piaget's observations (1952) make it plain that the child seeks opportunities to investigate his surroundings and will go to no little trouble to find them. My proposal is that activity, manipulation, and exploration, which are all pretty much of a piece in the infant, be considered together as aspects of competence, and that for the present we assume that one general motivational principle lies behind them. The word I have suggested for this motive is *effectance* because its most characteristic feature is seen in the production of effects upon the environment. At first these effects may consist of any changes in sensory input that follow upon activity or exertion, but before long the child becomes able to intend particular changes and to be content only with these. The experience that goes with producing such changes I have designated as the *feeling of efficacy*. Effectance is to be conceived as a neurogenic motive, in contrast to a viscerogenic one. It can be informally described as what the sensori-neuromuscular system wants to do when it is not occupied with homeostatic business. Its adaptive significance lies in its promotion of spare-time behavior that leads to an extensive growth of competence, well beyond what could be learned in connection with drive reduction.

This, then, is the new motivational base from which I want to reconsider the stages of psychosexual development. But I must make it clear that my procedure will not consist merely of introducing a neglected motive and fighting for its recognition against the claims of sexuality and aggression. If the problem could be so easily solved, it would have been solved long ago. The difficulty is that effectance does not pursue a separate life. It does not typically come into sharp, decisive conflict with drives. It can be mobilized alone, as in the child's play or in the adult's fascination with puzzles, but it is often mobilized in close connection with other needs. The feeling of efficacy can be experienced alone, but it is often merged with other satisfactions, as when, for example, a campus Don Juan reduces his sexual drive while also congratulating himself on the success of his technique of seduction. Because of this high tendency toward fusion it is not profitable to carry on the analysis of later development in terms of effectance and feelings of efficacy. Competence is built up out of all kinds of interactions with the environment, including those due to effectance alone and those due to much more complex patterns of motives. Our interest from here on will be in *competence* and its very important subjective aspect, which I am calling *sense of competence*. And we shall not find it profitable to look for the sense of competence as if it were a separate thing in personality; rather, we must become aware of the *aspect of competence in a wide variety of actions and experiences.*

Sense of competence can be seen as the cumulative product of one's history of efficacies and inefficacies. It comes to operate in new behavior as a kind of set: we judge whether or not we can jump over a brook or carry out a proposed task. It also comes to be much cherished, so that we feel truly elated at new proofs of our ability and deeply humiliated when we cannot do something we supposed was within our power. The sense of competence thus has strong motivational backing, doubtless from a variety of sources. Its importance in personality will be more readily apparent if we bear in mind that it applies to interactions with people as well as to dealings with the inanimate environment. Just as the child explores his physical surroundings, finding out what he can do with objects and what they will do to him, so he investigates his human environment, learning what he can make people do and what he can expect of them. Sense of social competence may well be the more important of the two, though I think we should beware of the current fashion of discussing personality as if it grew in a physical vacuum where tumbles and bumps, victories of locomotion, and struggles with refractory objects are held to exist only insofar as they elicit social responses. We do not live exclusively in a social environment, but we live there importantly, and it is often harder to develop a stable sense of one's social competence than to know what one can accomplish with material objects.

COMPETENCE AND EGO PSYCHOLOGY

I should like now to indicate the relation between these ideas and some of the recent advances in psychoanalytic ego psychology. As you will see, there is a great deal of similarity when we talk on the level of general concepts. There are also many common implications for the psychosexual stages, though only Erikson has tried to reconsider these stages in a systematic way. . . .

[We omit here some material about writers other than Erikson.]

It is in the work of Erikson (1950, 1959) that one finds the most far-reaching attempt to extend the range of ego psychology. Erikson's eight stages in the development of the ego constitute, it seems to me, a major advance in psychoanalytic theory. For the first time the latency period is given a significance of its own. Likewise for the first time the problems of growth are seen as continuing beyond young adulthood when haply the goal of genital primacy has been achieved. But the most important step is the systematic relating of the child's unfolding capacities to his encounters with the social environment. Erikson sees early development as a process of mutual regulation between child and parents. The child's changing capacities and the parents' changing demands lead to a series of decisive encounters, the outcomes of which are fateful for future growth. Later on, these encounters involve the social environment more broadly conceived; in this way, Erikson achieves the social relatedness that is the virtue of neo-Freudian theories without falling into their vice of losing touch with the biological roots of behavior.

Erikson's description of development is remarkably inclusive. In his concept of zones he retains the essence of libido theory, though with a somewhat altered meaning. With the concept of mutual regulation he draws in the best features of the interpersonal model. With his idea of modes he introduces competence, describing at each stage the motor and cognitive capacities that determine the character of the crisis. Erikson's account therefore seems to have everything the heart could desire. But it has one thing I wish it did not have, namely, an implied close connection between zones and modes which I think can lead only to confusion.

In recasting libido theory Erikson undertakes to avoid the scientific crudeness of Freud's formulation by a generous broadening of the biological base. Zonal sensitivities are but part of the picture; the progression from oral to anal to phallic stages is determined by a general ripening of sensory-motor capacity as a whole. The concept of mode captures these broader possibilities. Thus the oral stage, called "oral-sensory," is dominated by the incorporative mode, which means that everything the infant does, even his visual and tactile exploration, has the character of a taking in of experience. The anal stage, renamed "muscular-anal," represents more advanced prowess in motor and manipulative control. It is dominated by the retentive and eliminative modes, which show themselves alike in bowel functions and in the familiar manipulative sequence characterized by grasping and a little later by letting go and throwing away. Likewise the "locomotor-genital" stage brings to full flower the intrusive mode, which includes "the intrusion into other bodies by physical attack; the intrusion into other people's ears and minds by aggressive talking; the intrusion into space by vigorous locomotion; the intrusion into the unknown by consuming curiosity" (Erikson, 1950, p. 83). Erogenous zones and neuromuscular competence are thus seen as strictly isomorphic, set in the same patterns of interaction with the environment.

My discontent with this idea comes from my belief that in trying to put the stages of development on a broader base Erikson has not sufficiently disengaged himself from the old libidinal prototypes. He wants to assign significance to the growth of competence, but he describes this growth in generalizations carried over directly from the original theory. Incorporation, retention, elimination, and intrusion precisely describe the zonal impulses demanded by straight libido theory. Erikson then asks us to believe that these modes successively characterize virtually all the important things a young child does in the course of growth. This seems to me rather dubious, and I prefer a different strategy for finding out about it. It seems to me safer to treat visual exploration, manipulation, locomotion, and the many other aspects of competence as functions developing in their own right, more or less autonomously, without any presumed relation to zonal pleasures or presumed similarity to zonal impulses. By using the competence model in this way we can protect ourselves from unwarranted generalizations while yet leaving the facts free to tumble back into the old psychosexual stages if that is how they really look.

Let us proceed to re-examine the stages in the light of what I have said about effectance, feeling of efficacy, competence, and sense of competence, and let us see what happens. . . .

THE FINAL GENITAL STAGE

We come now to the last stage in psychosexual development, the stage at which newly strengthened sexual impulses bring about the possibility of genital primacy. In view of the great length of this paper you will be happy to hear that I shall have few words to say about the final stage. The plot is already clear. A prolonged fifth act would add little to whatever impact it may already have made. Obviously I would have words of praise for the more orthodox description of adolescence as given, for instance, by Anna Freud (1937, 1958), Bernfeld (1938), and Helene Deutsch (1944). Obviously there is great illumination in the treatment of this period as a time of increased instinctual drive and threat to established patterns of ego control. Certainly it is fruitful to look upon some aspects of adolescent behavior as a struggle to maintain and expand one's defenses. You would expect me also to mention some merit in the interpersonal model as developed, for instance, by Sullivan (1953), who described the task of late adolescence as that of establishing "a fully human or mature repertory of interpersonal relations." But then you would predict complaints on my part about the neglect of competence and the failure of the two models to capture whole ranges of behavior that are essential for full understanding. To spell out what you can so easily anticipate would be a bad anticlimax to anything as dramatic as adolescence and genital primacy.

Perhaps the one thing I should do is to indicate the kinds of behavior in adolescence that I consider important, well handled by a competence model, and neglected by libido and interpersonal models. Since the adolescent is reaching adult size, strength, and mental development, the behavior in question lies in the realm of serious accomplishment—serious in the terms either of the youth culture or of adult society. I am referring to the adolescent equivalent of what Erikson calls a *sense of industry* in the latency period, and I see this problem as continuing rather more strongly after puberty than seems to be implied in Erikson's account. No doubt I bring to this judgment an occupational bias different from that of a therapist. My professional life is spent among late adolescents whose sexual problems and social relations have for the most part not overwhelmed them. We talk together about their plans for study, their abilities and limitations, their struggles with materials to be learned and skills to be attained, their occupational leanings, career plans, and concerns about modern society as the scene of their future endeavors. We talk, in other words, mostly about their competence, and I do not believe that understanding is fostered by interpreting these concerns too much as displacements of instinctual drives, defense mechanisms, or interpersonal relations. They are real.

Adolescents today learn how to drive cars. Some of them learn to compete against adult records in sports, occasionally breaking them. Some of them become part of the football, band, and cheerleader complex that plays such an important part in community entertainment. Some of them try their hands at building workable radio sets, at scientific exploration, at editing newspapers, at writing stories and verse, at musical and dramatic performances, at political activity. Some of them with fewer opportunities or talents put their maturing bodies to heavy work or their maturing minds to white-collar office jobs. All this belongs in the sphere of work, and work, as Schilder (1942) so cogently argued, is importantly a phenomenon of competence. These happenings create many crises, many defeats, many victories for the sense of competence. Once again there are large spheres in which the adolescent can be suffering losses or making gains in ego strength. In theorizing about the subject we must not foreclose the possibility that these developments significantly affect what happens in the erotic and interpersonal realms.

I shall say no more about this stage of development except to launch my last complaint against the models bequeathed us by psychosexual theory. The model proffered by libido theory is that of heterosexual relations, and their ideal form is embodied in the concept of genital primacy. It is not argued, of course, that we all successfully become genital primates, but the ideal type serves to indicate the problems of the period. The sexual act itself plays a prominent part in genital primacy, reminding us that Freud's oft-mentioned broadened conception of sex sometimes touched base again in what no one has ever denied to be sexual. In libidinal terms, the regular discharge of genital tensions serves also to drain some of the energy from pregenital tensions, thus making the control and sublimation of the latter an easy problem for the ego. Erikson (1950) prefers "to put it more situationally: the total fact of finding, via the climactic turmoil of the orgasm, a supreme experience of the mutual regulation of two beings in some way breaks the point off the hostilities and potential rages caused by the oppositeness of male and female, of fact and fancy, of love and hate. Satisfactory sex relations thus make sex less obsessive, overcompensation less necessary, sadistic controls superfluous." Erikson's further account of what "the utopia of genitality" should include—mutual trust and a willingness to share lives in the interest of securing a happy development for the children—is something I commend to you all as an uncommonly beautiful statement of what we should aspire to in family life. It is an interpersonal statement as well as a libidinal one. I like it so well that I am sorry to point out that it has only the slightest relation to competence and to that other sphere of human concern—work.

Unfortunately the climactic turmoil of the orgasm is completely the wrong model for work. This is not to say that good sexual relations may not sometimes free a person from gnawing hates and doubts that have interfered with his capacity to work. But the emphasis of the idea of orgastic potency and mutuality is on an essential loss of ego, a drowning of all other considerations in the immense involuntary experience of the sexual relation. He who takes the ego to bed with him will never get a gold star for genital primacy. The orgastic model has virtue for certain human activities requiring a temporary submergence of self, such as inspiration, creative imagination, and thoroughly relaxed play. But it will never do for the serious, stable, lasting concerns of human life, the realm that I am trying to designate as work. This is the sphere in which the ego must always keep a firm hand on the helm.

Work requires a certain constancy of effort. There must be sustained endeavor with control of wayward impulses that distract from the requirements of external reality and social roles. There must be a capacity for persistent return to tasks, sometimes dull in themselves, that form part of the job requirement or that belong in a long-range plan to achieve remote goals. There must be a quality of reliability, so that one keeps promises and lives up to the obligations one has assumed. Even the fashion for being spontaneous and natural, even the bright vision of self-fulfilling work in Fromm's (1955) sane society, even Marcuse's (1955) fantasy of a nonrepressive civilization in which all work becomes libidinal pleasure cannot exorcize the true and somewhat stern nature of reality. And even Ernst Kris (1952), no enemy of psychoanalytic theory, reminded us that artistic creation required, in addition to a phase of inspiration, a second phase characterized by "the experience of purposeful organization and the intent to solve a problem." When we call an artist "merely competent" it is a weak form of praise, but if he were "merely inspired," without a certain rather high minimum of competency, we would never even see or hear his products.

I should like to close with a short coda on the words "merely competent." I particularly do not want to be misunderstood concerning the part to be assigned to competence and the sense of competence in human development. As a simple and sovereign concept it will never do. A person developed wholly along lines of competence, with no dimensions of passion, love, or friendliness, would never qualify for maturity. Competence is not intended to describe such experiences as enjoying food, immersing oneself in a sexual relation, loving children, cherishing friends, being moved by natural beauty or great works of art; nor is it designed to swallow up the problems created by aggression and anxiety. This is what I meant by saying that the competence model must always be used in conjunction with other models that do full justice to such things as hunger, sexuality, and aggression. It may hurt one's desire for logical simplicity to suppose that several models are needed to understand a problem. Yet I think no one can claim a probability that human nature was designed in the interests of logic.

It is my conviction, in short, that Freud's discoveries were of epoch-making importance, that psychoanalytic ego psychology has taken effective steps to fill out some of the undeveloped parts of Freud's theories, and that Erikson in particular has accomplished a synthesis that promises good things for future understanding of the growth of personality. But I also believe that our understanding cannot be rounded out by stretching Freud's concepts in a vain attempt to cover everything, or by calling everything interpersonal as if body and material world did not exist. We should add to the picture a meticulous consideration, at every level, of the growth of the child's capacity both for action and for understanding. We should try to be as shrewd in detecting the vicissitudes of the sense of competence as Freud was with sexuality, ag-

gression, and defense. It is to encourage such a development that I have had so much to say about the concept of competence.

Summary

Even an idea as monumental as Freud's theory of the psychosexual stages of development can come to have an adverse effect upon scientific progress if it is believed too literally too long. Libido theory provided a series of models for critical phases in emotional growth: feeding, toilet training, the Oedipus situation, latency, and the adult heterosexual relation. These models are largely preserved in revisions of Freud, though changed to interpersonal terms, and they continue to dominate the thinking of workers in psychoanalytic ego psychology. In this paper it is maintained that the models are in certain respects inadequate and misleading. In particular, they encourage us to neglect a range of facts which is ordered here under the concept of competence. If these facts are slighted, it is held, there can be little hope of further progress in psychoanalytic ego psychology or in closing the gap between this and other theories of development.

The concept of competence subsumes the whole realm of learned behavior whereby the child comes to deal effectively with his environment. It includes manipulation, locomotion, language, the building of cognitive maps and skilled actions, and the growth of effective behavior in relation to other people. These acquisitions are made by young animals and children partly through exploratory and manipulative play when drives such as hunger and sex are in abeyance. The directed persistence of such behavior warrants the assumption of a motivation independent of drives, here called effectance motivation, which has its immediate satisfaction in a feeling of efficacy and its adaptive significance in the growth of competence. Effectance motivation can be likened to independent ego energies in the psychoanalytic scheme. The child's actual competence and his sense of competence are built up from his history of efficacies and inefficacies, and sense of competence is held to be a crucial element in any psychology of the ego.

It is proposed that libidinal and interpersonal models for critical points in development be supplemented by a competence model. For the oral stage this means taking serious account of the growth of manipulative prowess and experimentation as seen both in the child's many hours of play and in his zeal for self-help in feeding. For the anal stage it means attributing importance to negativism in the sphere of giving and receiving commands, an early crisis in social competence, and to the enormous growth of motility with its constant influence upon self-esteem. Neither development is adequately implied in the anal-erotic model. For the phallic stage it means detecting the consequences of growth in locomotion, linguistic understanding, and imagination; it also means noticing the child's waxing ability to comprehend and try out various social roles, in many of which he receives encouragement. The Oedipus model, with its foreordained inexplicable defeat, cannot be considered typical for the period. During latency the chief developments are in the sphere of competence; this is clear in Erikson's account of the sense of industry and Sullivan's of competition and compromise. For the final genital stage the competence model invites us to take seriously the adolescent's continuing concern with sense of industry and with social competence, problems that confront him with new crises in their own right. The heterosexual relation does not provide an adequate model for all the serious concerns of this stage of life, nor can they be fully conceptualized in terms of instinctual drive and defense.

In short, the competence model is held to supplement in significant ways the models of development derived from psychoanalysis. By directing attention to action and its consequences and to the vicissitudes of the sense of competence, it should help to speed the construction of an adequate ego psychology.

REFERENCES *

BERLYNE, D. E. Novelty and curiosity as determinants of exploratory behavior. *Brit. J. Psychol.,* 1950, *41,* 68–80.

BERNFELD, S. Types of adolescence. *Psychoanal. Quart.,* 1938, *7,* 243–253.

BUTLER, R. A. Exploratory and related behavior: A new trend in animal research. *J. indiv. Psychol.,* 1958, *14,* 111–120.

DEUTSCH, HELENE. *The psychology of women,* Vol. I. New York: Grune & Stratton, 1944.

ERIKSON, E. H. *Childhood and society.* New York: Norton, 1950.

ERIKSON, E. H. Identity and the life cycle: selected papers. *Psychol. Issues,* 1959, Monograph 1.

FREUD, ANNA. *The ego and the mechanisms of defence.* (Trans. by C. Baines.) London: Hogarth, 1937.

FREUD, ANNA. Adolescence. *Psychoanal. Stud. Child,* 1958, *13,* 255–278.

FREUD, S. *Three contributions to the theory of sex.*

(1905). (Trans. by A. A. Brill.) New York and Washington: Nerv. and Ment. Dis. Pub. Co., 1930.

FREUD, S. Character and anal erotism (1908). *Collected papers.* (Trans. under supervision of J. Riviere.) New York: Basic Books, 1959. Vol. II, 45–50.

FREUD, S. The predisposition to obsessional neurosis (1913). *Collected papers.* (Trans. under supervision of J. Riviere.) New York: Basic Books, 1959. Vol. II, 122–131.

FREUD, S. The infantile genital organization of the libido (1923). *Collected papers.* (Trans. under supervision of J. Riviere.) New York: Basic Books, 1959. Vol. II, 244–249.

FROMM, E. *Man for himself.* New York: Rinehart, 1947.

FROMM, E. *The sane society.* New York: Rinehart, 1955.

HARLOW, H. F. Mice, monkeys, men, and motives. *Psychol. Rev.,* 1953, *60,* 23–32.

HORNEY, KAREN. *New ways in psychoanalysis.* New York: Norton, 1939.

KRIS, E. *Psychoanalytic explorations in art.* New York: International Univer. Press, 1952.

MARCUSE, H. *Eros and civilization.* Boston: Beacon Press, 1955.

MONTGOMERY, K. C. The role of the exploratory drive in learning. *J. comp. physiol. Psychol.,* 1954, *47,* 60–64.

MYERS, A. K., AND MILLER, N. E. Failure to find a learned drive based on hunger; evidence for learning motivated by "exploration." *J. comp. physiol. Psychol.,* 1954, *47,* 428–436.

OLDS, J., AND MILNER, P. Positive reinforcement produced by electrical stimulation of septal area and other regions of rat brain. *J. comp. physiol. Psychol.,* 1954, *47,* 419–427.

PIAGET, J. *The origins of intelligence in children.* (Trans. by M. Cook.) New York: International Univer. Press, 1952.

SCHILDER, P. *Goals and desires of men.* New York: Columbia Univer. Press, 1942.

SHEFFIELD, F. D., AND ROBY, T. B. Reward value of a non-nutritive sweet taste. *J. comp. physiol. Psychol.,* 1950, *43,* 471–481.

SHEFFIELD, F. D., ROBY, T. B., AND CAMPBELL, B. A. Drive reduction vs. consummatory behavior as determinants of reinforcement. *J. comp. physiol. Psychol.,* 1954, *47,* 349–354.

SHEFFIELD, F. D., WULFF, J. J., AND BACKER, R. Reward value of copulation without sex drive reduction. *J. comp. physiol. Psychol.,* 1951, *44,* 3–8.

SILVERBERG, W. V. *Childhood experience and personal destiny.* New York: Springer, 1952.

SULLIVAN, H. S. *The interpersonal theory of psychiatry.* New York: Norton, 1953.

THOMPSON, C. *Psychoanalysis: evolution and development.* New York: Hermitage, 1950.

WHITE, R. W. Motivation reconsidered: The concept of competence. *Psychol. Rev.,* 1959, *66,* 297–333.

---

* For a more extensive list of references, see original paper. —EDITOR

46

Learning Capacities
of the Human Infant [1]

Lewis P. Lipsitt [2]

This article describes a program of research in infant behavior. Infancy, an age period that received very little attention for many years, is now a topic of great interest and concern. Lewis Lipsitt, professor of psychology at Brown University, has an extensive laboratory in a large maternity hospital in Providence, Rhode Island. The recent advances in technology have been fully utilized to insure the reliability of his experimental methods.

INTRODUCTION

HISTORICAL ORIENTATION

The field of child development has traditionally relied on psychometric or "maturity-measuring" techniques. Though these are founded on the use of morphological models borrowed from structural biology (Gesell, 1954; Harris, 1957), they have been used even for assessing the behavioural properties of the young organism and for seeking principles explaining the origins of later behaviour in the history of the organism (Lipsitt, 1963). It has been implicitly assumed that intellectual endowment is genetically determined and essentially constant; proper attention has not been paid to the behavioural consequences of experiential precursors. These attitudes and assumptions have almost pre-empted the search for, and discovery of, the special capacities of infants to receive sensory stimulation in all modalities and to learn. The studies of Pratt (1954), Irwin (1943), and Marquis (1931, 1941) were notable exceptions.

No thoughtful observer or researcher of infant behaviour would deny the obvious fact that some behavioural differences are related to age. Nevertheless the human newborn can no longer be regarded as a spinal creature who can have no capacity for learning or cognitive activity because of absence or reduction of myelination or cerebral convolutions (Elkonin, 1957).

The normal human infant shows an exceptional talent for differential responding, conditioning, and discrimination learning. These are often achieved in a matter of minutes, particularly when the responses are relevant to the maintenance of life, or to evolutionary selection, or when they provide opportunity to explore the environment. I hold no brief for any particular mode of learning or for any special theoretical model for the understanding of specific learning effects that may be induced in the immature organism. A constricted view of the possible mechanisms whereby experimental circumstances may work their wonders would limit the accumulation of knowledge in this area, as did the premature conclusion that the structural properties of the immature organism could not possibly permit learning to occur. It would be equally senseless to allow a monolithic learning-theory orientation to shut off possible lines of inquiry as it was to permit the tyranny of an exclusive developmental-structural dogma. Indeed, it may well be that we are only beginning to understand some of the very special learning skills of the young human (Hinde, 1966).

It should no longer surprise us that organisms do not inevitably get better and better at whatever they do with increasing age. Of course there has always been acceptance of a statute of limitations for the aged in this connection; but apologists have generally considered the frailties of age to be the result of a superimposition of disease and deformity rather than a "true" developmental effect. The effectiveness of some types of stimulation, and the organism's capacity for response, become dimin-

[1] The research reported here and the writing of the present paper were supported largely by a grant to the author from the U.S. Public Health Service, National Institutes of Health (Grant No. HD 03911).

[2] The author expresses his gratitude to the staff of Providence Lying-In Hospital, where so much of the newborn research reported here has been carried out.

Lewis P. Lipsitt, "Learning capacities of the human infant," in *Brain and Early Behavior: Development in the Fetus and Infant*, R. J. Robinson, ed. New York: Academic Press, 1969, 227–249. Reprinted with abridgement by permission.

ished in many different ways with increasing age; with respect to some human attributes the developmental decline or social destruction of a response may begin at birth. The human newborn is as good at the palmar grasp, at the Babkin response, at rooting, and even at sucking soon after birth as he will ever be again. [The Babkin response is an inborn rooting reflex in which the mouth opens in response to pressure on the palm.—EDITOR] Some of the body's glands decrease proportionately in size from birth on, while others increase and then decrease in both size and function. So, too, may certain behavioural capacities of the "growing" organism either "atrophy" or wax then wane with increasing age. It is perhaps time for someone to present the thesis that the newborn human creature is about as competent a learning organism as he can become.

RESEARCH PROGRAMME

For the past decade, I have been fortunate to have a laboratory for sensory assessment and conditioning in one of the larger U.S. maternity hospitals. Many of the infants first studied during the newborn period, along with small populations of infants from private paediatric practices, have been available subsequently for behaviour studies at various intervals throughout the first year. The eventual aim of this research programme is to document longitudinal changes (or constancies) in the learning and sensory properties of the child at least through the first year of life. The success of such studies depends heavily upon the prior development of appropriately reliable experimental stimulation techniques and upon the initial documentation of behaviour-phenomena worth pursuing across an extensive age-span. For these reasons, and because longitudinal data-cells require more time to fill, the results available thus far are concerned predominantly with the behaviours that occur at specific young ages and with the stimulating conditions necessary to elicit them. Although our concern is with processes or changes in behaviour occurring over periods of time or with repetitive stimulation, the time courses to which I shall refer here will, with two exceptions, be of relatively short duration.

. . .

BRIEF REVIEW OF PREVIOUS FINDINGS

As a background for the present paper, some of the previous studies carried out in these laboratories and reported in detail elsewhere will first be reviewed. Several studies (Lipsitt, 1967; Engen and Lipsitt, 1965; Engen, Lipsitt, and Kaye, 1963)

have clearly demonstrated that habituation occurs in the human newborn; repetitive presentation of stimulation of moderate intensity, in this case odorants, produces response decrement over successive trials, and subsequent recovery of response whether to totally new odorants or to olfactory stimuli which were components of previously habituated compounds. Such behaviour suggests that the human newborn processes information in a rather sophisticated way, suppressing response to non-threatening stimulus signals but alerting once again if a novel stimulus, even in the same sensory modality, should be introduced suddenly. Moreover, the phenomenon of response recovery to components of previously habituated compounds indicates that some central nervous system mechanism is probably involved in the discrimination, since peripheral factors and fatigue are ruled out by the technique.

With respect to sucking behaviour, it has been established that the human newborn is keenly sensitive to momentary differences in intraoral stimulation and that reinforcing circumstances associated with the sucking act may increase (or diminish) sucking-response frequency. In a study (Lipsitt and Kaye, 1965) which compared the sucking behaviour of infants who were administered either nipple, tube, or nipple-tube-alternation sequences of trials, it was shown that the sucking rate is greater with an ordinary nipple than with a less flexible and less rounded tube, that nipple-sucking is adversely affected by the previous administration of the tube, and that tube-sucking is made easier by previous nipple-sucking. The evidence of these lasting effects of previous experience brings us closer to an understanding of the role of prior experience in the determination of infants' behaviour.

. . .

The work of our laboratory has recently been increasingly concerned with the exploration of conditioning techniques using responses of the infant that may be presumed to have functional significance for the survival of the organism and for the maximization of exploratory arousal. The human infant seems capable of making many responses which have the consequence of increasing stimulus input. The assimilation of such stimulus input often results in arousing still further "searching" activity. When this relationship between the organism and the environment has progressed to a maximum (to be determined for each subject, for each type of stimulus, and for various reinforcing conditions) the stimulation loop is often "turned off" by the subject who now manifests satiation, fatigue, or habituation. This cycle of events can perhaps be best understood in operant behavioural terms, but it must be acknowledged, if not insisted, that respondent behaviour has an important role in the cycle.

RECENT STUDIES

THE NEWBORN INFANT

Conditioned head-turning. Elaborating upon techniques earlier reported by Papoušek (1959, 1960, 1961), Siqueland and Lipsitt (1966) used both tactile stimulation and nutritive reinforcement to condition head-turning in neonates. The general procedure requires tactile stimulation of the infant at the corner of the mouth, a procedure that characteristically elicits ipsilateral head-turning in 25–35 per cent of the trials prior to conditioning. Such "rooting" is usually considered to be respondent behaviour, since it requires a specific eliciting stimulus. The procedure used in these studies involved the systematic reinforcement of the respondent as if it were an operant or instrumental behaviour. Thus, on conditioning trials in which the infant turned his head appropriately in response to the tactile stimulus, a nipple was quickly placed in the baby's mouth, allowing it to suck and to be nutritively reinforced. In all these studies, auditory stimuli preceded and occurred simultaneously with the tactile stimulus, in order (1) to determine whether classically-conditioned anticipatory head-turning might increase in frequency over conditioning trials, and (2) to afford an opportunity to study discriminative behaviour as well as non-differential conditioning behaviour.

In our first study the procedure was to sound a buzzer for 5 seconds, during the latter half of which the left cheek of the subject was stroked. If the infant responded ipsilaterally, dextrose was administered for 2 seconds. Eighteen subjects in the second and third days of life received thirty trials of conditioning, with 30-second inter-trial intervals, while another 18 matched control subjects received the same programme of stimulation, subject for subject, but were given the dextrose, on appropriate trials, 8–10 seconds after termination of the tactile stimulus. Response to the tactile stimulus increased strikingly in the experimental group— from approximately 30 per cent to 80 per cent— while the matched control group merely declined in the frequency of ipsilateral head-turning.

In an elaboration of the technique, two groups of infants 2–4 days old were studied to see whether differential reinforcement for two responses, left versus right head-turning, would lead to discriminative responding. Now two auditory stimuli were used, a tone and the buzzer, and trials were alternated between the left and the right cheeks, the

buzzer being associated with touch to one side and tone with touch to the other. The tone and buzzer were each the positive stimulus for a random half of the subjects, and a basal assessment period enabled application of the positive stimulus to the less favoured head-turning side. For the 20 experimental subjects, reinforcement was presented after ipsilateral turns to the positive stimulus (R^{S+}), but not after turns to the negative stimulus (R^{S-}). Twenty control subjects received the same total number of reinforcements, subject for subject, but dextrose reinforcement was presented 8–10 seconds after tactile stimulation and was not contingent upon head-turning. Learning was reflected in relative shifts in percentages of R^{S+} and R^{S-} over trials. The shift occurred in the experimental group, which rose in R^{S+} responding from approximately 20 per cent to 75 per cent, while the control group declined from 20 per cent. Learned differentiation of head-turning behaviour in the newborn was thus substantiated.

Next, in an attempt to induce a still more difficult differentiation, the two auditory stimuli served as positive and negative cues for reinforcement at one side only. Sixteen infants, aged 48 to 116 hours, were divided into two groups: for one the tone was positive and the buzzer negative, while for the other the designations were reversed. Turns to right-sided stimulation in the presence of one auditory stimulus were reinforced, while right turns in the presence of the other auditory stimulus were not. After original training $S+$ became $S-$, and $S-$ became $S+$ in each group. As previously, stimulus presentations occurred on a 30-second inter-trial interval basis, and tactile stimulation overlapped the last half of the tone or buzzer. Under such conditions, responding to the positive stimulus increased sharply, from approximately 25 per cent to 70 per cent, while response to the negative stimulus changed negligibly. Upon reversal of the stimulating conditions, the expected shift in behaviour was such that the previously negative and now positive stimulus eventually generated reliably more ipsilateral responses than the previously positive and now negative stimulus.

In none of these three studies did conditioned subjects demonstrate a reliable increase in classical anticipatory responding during the sound-stimulus presentations, but it is apparent from the differential behaviour established in the third study that the auditory stimuli had discriminative signal functions.

Free-operant head-turning. In a further study of reinforcement patterns and extinction in human newborns Siqueland (1968) demonstrated large differences in free-operant head-turning behaviour, during extinction, as a function of differences in reinforcement schedules during acquisition. An apparatus for the continuous polygraphic monitoring of head-turning activity was used, and a 10° head-turn arc in either direction was adopted as the required operant. Three groups of eight newborns each in the third and fourth days of life were given 5-second presentations of a non-nutritive nipple as reinforcement. Conditioning procedures involved a 3-minute baseline period, 25 reinforcements, a 5-minute extinction period, 15 additional reinforcements, and a second extinction period of 3 minutes. Training in one group was on a continuous (100 per cent) schedule, and a Ratio group received one reinforcement for every two responses early in learning and one for every three responses later. A third group received reinforcement for each 20-second period in which a head movement was *not* made (that is, a 10° movement delayed reinforcement for 20 seconds). The groups were thus equated on total number of reinforcements, prior to each extinction period, while their patterns of reinforcement varied.

The analysis of data was concerned with extinction behaviour. It is very clear that the three groups varied greatly in frequency of head-turns during both of the extinction conditions. The Ratio group gave reliably more responses than the Continuous Reinforcement group, and the third group produced the fewest responses. In fact, reliable increases in responding over the course of extinction were evidenced by the third group, as would be expected by the fact that for this group conditioning involved the suppression of head-turns.

While the Siqueland-Lipsitt studies demonstrated strong learning effects in a situation involving nutritive reinforcement, the Siqueland study shows very clearly that opportunity to suck non-nutritively may also serve as a powerful reinforcing event. This study is also the first clear demonstration of free operant conditioning in a situation that does not rely on eliciting stimulation as in the Papoušek and the Siqueland-Lipsitt studies.

Temporal conditioning. Marquis (1941) has shown that human infants within the first 10 days of life are capable of adjusting their activity patterns and sleep-waking cycles (Irwin, 1930) to temporally controlled feeding schedules. To explore the capacity of the neonate for short-term temporal conditioning Ambrose and Lipsitt (unpublished) studied temporal responsivity under three different modes of stimulation: auditory, vestibular, and olfactory. Two methods were used to assess whether temporal conditioning occurred: (1) presentation of mock or test trials after a series of stimulations to determine whether responses would occur at the accustomed time of stimulus presentation, and (2) examination of increased responding, over training trials, to determine whether there is an increased tendency for anticipatory responses to be made in the interval immediately preceding the customary stimulus presentation time. To provide vestibular stimulation Ambrose designed a motor-driven baby rocker which automatically moves the baby up and down through an excursion of 3 inches at controlled rates of speed. Besides the vestibular stimulation of rocking, the infants in the present study received olfactory stimulation from anise oil on a cotton-swab, and sound stimulation produced by dropping a pegged wooden ball through a constant distance to a wooden surface. The auditory stimulus was an 87-dB clack of noise, of essentially momentary duration, while the odorant presentation and rocking stimulation lasted 5 seconds on each trial. Three groups, each of five infants, received the stimulus types in different orders: (1) sound, odorant, rocking, (2) odorant, sound, rocking, and (3) rocking, sound, odorant. Each of the three stimuli was presented to each infant on eight successive occasions, then was followed by three "mock" trials during which the polygraph record was marked at the regular 30-second interval (the interval between all stimulations). No stimulation whatever was administered on mock trials.

The analysis of responding was concerned with respiration, heart rate, and motility, the latter represented in either the electromyographic or stabilimetric records (these being almost perfectly correlated). The response of greatest concern was that occurring during the nine mock trials. The period for response-assessment was a 5-second unit of time. The first such period began 30 seconds after the previous stimulus presentation and the subsequent ones were at 30-second intervals. A response was defined simply as any change in pattern form or frequency relative to a baseline period. Baseline was the 5-second interval immediately preceding this time unit, unless an anticipatory response occurred, in which case the 5-second unit immediately preceding that interval was used. When two judges were unable to make identical judgements concerning the occurrence of response on mock trials, the trial was scored "uncertain." In the case of heart-rate change a stringent criterion was adopted: a change of two beats or more per 5-second interval (24 beats per minute) was required. Responding during the mock trials was compared with control intervals which were of comparable duration but which followed each mock trial by 15 seconds. Each subject then had nine opportunities to respond during mock trials and nine opportunities during control intervals. The mean number of responses made during mock trials was 4·53, as compared with mean control-interval responding of 2·46, a difference resulting in a t of 4·55, significant at the ·01 level (df = 14).

Although the magnitude of the temporal-conditioning effect as found here is not great, further corroboration of infant capacity for such learning has been found by Fitzgerald and associates (1967) for pupillary responding (although not for eyelid blinking), and further study of such phenomena seems warranted.

The "Bronshtein effect."   Ever since the reports of Bronshtein and his colleagues (1958) American researchers in neonatal behaviour have been fascinated by the possibility of suppressing ongoing behaviour by external stimulation. The phenomenon is now commonly referred to as the Bronshtein effect; for example, if an infant has a nipple in his mouth and is sucking ordinarily (that is, is engaging in sucking behaviour dictated by his idiosyncratic congenital patterns under no special conditions of external stimulation), the sudden introduction of an extraneous stimulus such as a sound, visual stimulus, or odour will tend to disrupt the sucking pattern. The phenomenon has been interpreted as one of external inhibition or the arousal of orienting behaviour which competes with other ongoing behaviour (Sokolov, 1963; Lynn, 1966).

In connection with the disruption of ongoing behaviour through the introduction of external competing stimulation, Bronshtein reported that habituation of such disruption occurs over successive stimulus presentations. Thus although the introduction of a tone at first had a marked effect upon the sucking pattern this effect diminished progressively with increasing experience. In our laboratory two studies have failed to replicate the Bronshtein suppression effect (Kaye and Levin, 1963), but other investigators (Keen, 1965; Haith, 1966) have been able to document it clearly.

Semb and Lipsitt (1968) completed an investigation in which the Bronshtein suppression effect without habituation has been clearly demonstrated in newborns. The study was designed to provide optimal conditions for its occurrence in that the tonal stimulation was introduced on specific occasions when the child was sucking, not on a random-presentation or a temporally locked basis. At the same time, and in the same subjects, the obverse response to that of sucking-suppression was studied. On occasions when the infant was not sucking, the same tone was systematically introduced. Under these conditions activation of sucking is readily induced; in fact activation of sucking in the presence of a non-sucking state of the infant

occurs about twice as frequently as the sucking-suppression phenomenon.

. . .

OLDER INFANTS IN THE FIRST YEAR

Conjugate reinforcement.   At this point I should like to leave consideration of the newborn to discuss recent advances in techniques for studying behaviour in the older infant. It is our eventual aim to have techniques for longitudinal study of learning proficiency and for the study of specific stimulating circumstances and their short-term effects on behaviour. In studies of learning in infants, various environmental events must be sought which promote and sustain some measured behaviour. Although it is apparent to most investigators of child behaviour that infants and children engage in much behaviour that seems "self-reinforcing" only recently have there been systematic attempts to incorporate such behaviour into basic psychological theory or to study its origins parametrically. White (1959) introduced the term "competency striving," Butler (1953) the term "curiosity motivation," and Harlow, Harlow and Meyer (1950) spoke of the "manipulation drive" to refer to behaviour occurring in the absence of apparent or traditional primary drives. Hunt (1965) has spoken of infants as having a need for sensory input and opportunity to experience "recognitive familiarity," and in a physiological context Pfaffmann (1960) spoke of "the pleasures of sensation." However, in studies involving sensory input as reinforcement rather than more vital consequences of response, reinforcers often lose their effectiveness, due to adaptation or boredom, before the associative process has been demonstrated or explored extensively (Lipsitt, 1963). Recently Lindsley and co-workers (1961) and Lindsley (1962, 1963) implemented and investigated a type of reinforcement that shows promise in infant conditioning.

Conjugate reinforcement involves the presentation of a continuously available event contingent upon response, such that the event's intensity varies directly and immediately with response strength (for example, rate or intensity). The prototype is the hand-generator flashlight in which illumination intensity is controlled directly by the response rate and pressure on a trigger or dynamometer handle. Compared with episodic schedules in which reinforcement is provided either by delivery of pellets or candies, or by punitive circumstances with discrete onsets and offsets, the conjugate type of response-consequent permits (1) closer analysis of periodic changes in the value of reinforcing stimuli, and (2) maintenance of the subject in the observation situation for fairly long periods of time.

In our first use of the conjugate reinforcement technique (Lipsitt *et al.*, 1966) 12-month-old subjects were seated in an infant chair attached to a box containing a manipulandum, a clear plastic panel. Response to the manipulandum activated a power supply which was designed to vary the light intensity inside the box according to changes in the response rate. Opportunity to see inside the box, which was otherwise dark, was proportionate to the response rate, and transition from low to high brightness and *vice versa* was gradual rather than sudden. In the box a colourful clown picture was rotated continuously. An electrical counter enabled cumulative recording of response every 15 seconds. The procedure involved the use of a basal period of no reinforcement for responding, followed by a conditioning session in which visual reinforcement was available, followed by extinction, then reconditioning, then re-extinction. The behaviour of infants in this situation even for as short a period as 15 minutes supported the efficacy of conjugate reinforcement in the study of infant learning; response rates increased from basal levels through conditioning and decreased when reinforcement was withheld.

Mobiles for conjugate reinforcement. Recently a former student of our laboratory conducted a study using her own 2-month-old infant and five other children of the same age. Following suggestions of Uzgiris and Hunt (1965), Rovee and Rovee (1969) hung a mobile over the infants' cribs. The infants were familiarized with the mobile for several weeks before the experimental procedure began. For four of the infants, the experimental session lasted 27 minutes, and for two others the session lasted 46 minutes. For the experimental session, the infants were loosely clothed with legs exposed and feet bare. Observations were made from the foot of the crib, with the observer out of view of the child. The 27-minute procedure involved a 3-minute baseline period during which the operant level of right-foot kicks was established, a 15-minute acquisition period involving conjugate reinforcement wherein the mobile was linked to the child's leg via a light string, and a 5-minute extinction period in which the string connecting the child's limb with the mobile was detached. The two subjects serving in the 46-minute session received a 10-minute re-acquisition period followed by 5 minutes of re-extinction. The operant response conditioned was that of leg flexions, and the reinforcement was that of visual feedback from the moving mobile. It should be emphasized that the mobile always remained in position during the basal and extinction phases, but limb movements during these phases were not instrumental in activating movement of the object.

Reliability tests indicated that limb movement increased, relative to the basal level, when the mobile could be moved by the leg and that detachment of the string connection resulted in diminution of leg activity.

The Rovees observed that the behaviour of the infants changed qualitatively as well as quantitatively over the course of the sessions. Gross, diffuse body activity occurred early in the sessions, but after experience in operating the mobile the infant used smooth direct thrusts of the limb to which the cord was attached. During the reinforcement phases intense kicking was often followed by rather long pauses, during which the infant remained still but kept his gaze fixed on the swaying figures.

Following the Rovees' work, another study was conducted by Leslie Smith on her own child between the ages of 2 and 5 months. She tested the infant with a multitude of mobile objects varying in colour and form; some were offered with associated sound stimulation. In this study, movements were registered by an automatic counter. As in Rovee's study, it was shown that a 2-month-old infant quickly learns to move his limb appropriately to activate the visual reinforcer, and that limb movement increases during reinforcement periods and diminishes during extinction periods. Interesting findings from this pilot investigation include the strong suggestion that with increased experience in the situation the infant begins to "test" the effect of the response, so that after some training the infant comes to recognize quickly when his responses are effective and when not and adjusts his behaviour accordingly and rapidly. The mobile-reinforcement situation provides a potentially sensitive procedure by which to assess infants' preferences for various types of stimulation. For example, when the child in the Smith study was presented with a red mobile its response rate was consistently higher than when it was presented with an otherwise identical but white mobile.

The Smith data show clearly that infants will behave in a mobile-movement situation for very long periods of time without apparent fatigue or satiation except as indicated by occasional pauses. To be sure, the technique is hampered by the occasional occurrence of fussy or crying behaviour—such activity increases limb-movement responses considerably—and for purposes of assessing cognitive processes it would appear that the procedure ought to be "shut off" during fussy periods of this sort. On the other hand these studies suggest that crying itself might become an important subject for study. It seems that crying occurs rather frequently some minutes after the onset of an extinction condition, as if the crying may be generated by the frustration of expectation. It was noted that the crying could sometimes be abated by re-institution of a conditioning period.

Sucking and visual stimulation. Over the past 2 years Siqueland has developed a line of research in which infants as young as 3 months of age can control the visual input which they receive by sucking on an automatic nipple linked to a slide projector. The presentation of visual stimuli or the experimental withdrawal of these stimuli is contingent upon the infants' making high-amplitude sucking responses. When high-amplitude sucking is required to activate the projector light, infants rapidly adjust the intensity of sucks to produce higher illumination, much as previously described in the conjugate reinforcement situation.

In one experiment Siqueland sought to determine whether non-nutritive sucking could be studied in 4-month-old children by the use of visual reinforcers. Subjects were 30 infants assigned to one of three groups: *Gp C* (control baseline), *Gp R* (reinforcement group), and *Gp W* (stimulus withdrawal group). The first group provided a baseline reference for 10 minutes of non-reinforced sucking, and the other groups received a 13-minute session consisting of conditioning, extinction, reconditioning, and re-extinction. For *Gp R* reinforcement was contingent on sucking during the conditioning periods, and for *Gp W* sucking resulted in withdrawal of the visual stimulus, each criterion suck resulting in a 5-seconds delayed onset of the visual stimulus. For both groups, eight chromatic 35 mm slides showing geometric forms, cartoon figures, and human faces were presented for 30 seconds each in 4-minute conditioning blocks.

The reinforcement group showed rapid acquisition of criterion sucks, while the baseline group showed negligible change in such behaviour. *Gp W* showed a slight decrease in the ratio of high-amplitude sucking. The evidence clearly shows that heterogeneous visual stimulation may function in a reinforcing capacity to maintain sucking behaviour in infants of 4 months.

Another of Siqueland's studies compared the sucking behaviour of three age groups (4-, 8- and 12-months) in the visual reinforcement situation again using the sucking response as the operant. Highly reliable differences in sucking rates were obtained among the three age groups during a baseline-assessment session lasting 5 minutes.

Siqueland next attempted re-establishment of sucking behaviour in 12-month-old infants when such behaviour is operative in enhancing visual stimulation. Two groups of ten infants received different sets of visual stimuli. One group was shown four coloured slides four times each over two 4-minute sessions, and the other group was shown a set of eight slides twice each. The results showed dramatic increases in sucking rate for both groups as compared with baseline controls of the same age. Reliable response decrements were also obtained after reinforcement ended. Moreover, although predicted differences between the two groups were not obtained during initial conditioning and extinction phases, apparent stimulus familiarization (satiation) effects were reflected in a decreasing response rate for the 4-stimulus group during reconditioning as compared with high stable rates for the 8-stimulus group. Siqueland's work continues to explore which stimulus parameters, including comparisons across modalities, are influential in controlling an infant's sucking behaviour. The apparent ease with which infants learn to control their visual environment by appropriate sucking behaviour is interesting because many observers of infants have noted that visual exploratory behaviour is often most intense in a child that is engaged in sucking. Many a mother has reported that she can most easily attract the child's gaze to hers when the infant is feeding. In the earliest days of life, sucking and visual exploratory behaviour seem to have an intimate relationship.

PROSPECTS FOR THE FUTURE

It only remains to be said that as we progress in our studies of human behaviour in the first year of life some of the seeming complexities become better understood through experimental analyses and careful measurement of the relationships between the response and the environmental feedback. Experimental techniques based on some traditional notions about the reinforcing functions of environmental stimulation have been immensely useful in leading to knowledge about the control of behaviour by stimuli. However, it must also be admitted that experimentalists must pay more attention to the ordinary non-laboratory circumstances under which the human organism generally lives and to which he seems, all things considered, remarkably well adapted. The ecologists in America (for example, Wright, 1960; Barker, 1951) and the ethologists in Europe (for example, Hinde, 1966; Eibl-Eibesfeldt, 1967) have done the field of experimental child psychology a great service in calling for increased attention to the naturalistic habitat and the built-in response repertoire of the human child. A healthy consequence is that conjugate reinforcement phenomena, for instance, are now being seriously explored by child experimentalists.

It does appear at present that modifications and embellishments of traditional classical and operant conditioning techniques seem quite in order for the further advance of understanding of infant learning behaviour. The enormous amount of effective learning which takes place during the first year of life in infants reared "naturally" is seldom accomplished under conditions exactly like those used in the laboratory to study basic acquisition and extinction processes. In real life learning trials are almost never deliberately spaced, the stimulating conditions are seldom well-controlled, and much of the infant's learning gives the appearance of occurring fortuitously.

The proper scientific study of a natural phenomenon is not usually the exploration of the fortuitous. Nevertheless it is quite possible that by taking advantage of the changing state of the baby from moment to moment, including the momentary changes in its condition of curiosity, and by using variant rather than constant stimulation conditions experimenters might understand better some of the learning processes that have often proved refractory in the well-controlled laboratory situation. It is apparent to me, for instance, that most early learning is neither of a purely classical conditioning nor of a purely operant variety, but is some sort of amalgamation of these. The Siqueland-Lipsitt finding with respect to conditioned head-turning is a case in point, inasmuch as the procedure fulfilled both respondent and operant requirements, providing both eliciting and emitting stimulus conditions. It is sometimes necessary or desirable to use an eliciting stimulus to potentiate a response which can then be reinforced operantly, thus increasing the probability of the occurrence of that response in the absence of the eliciting stimulation on future occasions. For example, the process of conditioning the sucking behaviour of a newborn with an initially low-probability level of sucking might be facilitated by pressing the infant's palms when the nipple is in the mouth, thus eliciting a higher sucking rate. This higher sucking rate may then be reinforced through feeding, eventually allowing the eliciting stimulation of the palm-press to be faded out. In a sense, we might most readily engender learned behaviour in the immature organism by violating the basic requirements of the classical and operant conditioning paradigms. The head-retraction response in the presence of a smothering stimulus may well be of this type, whereby it first occurs as an elicited or respondent behaviour but becomes a learned operant in the course of development; thus the older child positions his head so as to preclude smothering even before an actual threat of respiratory occlusion occurs. Similarly, it is not unlikely that smiling behaviour in children first occurs primarily as respondent behaviour which is supplanted or overshadowed later in ontogeny by a predominantly operant mode of occurrence (Bijou and Baer, 1965).

REFERENCES

BARKER, R. G. 1951. *One boy's day.* Harper, New York.

BIJOU, S. W. and BAER, D. M. 1965. *Child development II: Universal stage of infancy.* Appleton-Century-Crofts, New York. Pp. 3–7.

BRONSHTEIN, A. I., ANTONOVA, T. G., KAMENSTKAYA, A. G., LUPPOVA, N. N. and SYTOVA, V. A. 1958. On the development of the functions of analysers in infants and some animals at the early stage of ontogenesis. In *Problemy evolyutaii fisiolgicheskikh funkisii.* Akademiya Nauk, Moscow and Leningrad. Transl. (Off. of Tech. Servs. Report No. 60–61066, 1960. Pp. 106–116) obtainable from U.S. Dept. of Commerce, Office of Technical Services, Washington, D.C.

BUTLER, R. A. 1953. Discrimination learning by rhesus monkeys to visual exploration motivation. *J. comp. physiol. Psychol. 46,* 95–98.

EIBL-EIBESFELDT, I. 1967. Concepts of ethology and their significance in the study of human behaviour. In H. W. Stevenson, E. Hess, and H. L. Rheingold (Eds.), *Early behavior: comparative and developmental approaches.* Wiley, New York. Pp. 127–146.

ELKONIN, D. B. 1957. The physiology of higher nervous activity and child psychology. In B. Simon (Ed.), *Psychology in the Soviet Union.* Routledge & Kegan Paul, London. Pp. 47–68.

ENGEN, T. and LIPSITT, L. P. 1965. Decrement and recovery of responses to olfactory stimuli in the human neonate. *J. comp. physiol. Psychol. 59,* 312–316.

ENGEN, T., LIPSITT, L. P. and KAYE, H. 1963. Olfactory responses and adaptation in the human neonate. *J. comp. physiol. Psychol. 56,* 73–77.

FITZGERALD, H. E., LINTZ, L. M., BRACKBILL, Y. and ADAMS, G. 1967. Time perception and conditioning of an autonomic response in human infants. *Percept. Mot. Skills. 24,* 479–486.

GESELL, A. 1954. The ontogenesis of infant behavior. In L. Carmichael (Ed.), *Manual of child psychology.* Wiley, New York. Pp. 335–373.

HARLOW, H. F., HARLOW, M. K. and MEYER, D. R. 1950. Learning motivated by a manipulation drive. *J. exp. Psychol. 40,* 228–234.

HARRIS, D. B. 1957. (Ed.), *The concept of development.* Univ. of Minnesota Press, Minneapolis.

HINDE, R. A. 1966. *Animal behaviour: a synthesis of ethology and comparative psychology.* McGraw-Hill, New York.

HUNT, J. McV. 1965. Traditional personality theory in the light of recent evidence. *Am. Scient. 53,* 80–96.

IRWIN, O. C. 1930. Amount and nature of activities of

newborn infants under constant external stimulating conditions during the first ten days of life. *Genet. Psychol. Monogr. 8,* 1–92.

IRWIN, O. C. 1943. The activities of newborn infants. In R. G. Barker, J. S. Kounin, and H. F. Wright (Eds.), *Child behavior and development.* McGraw-Hill, New York. Pp. 29–47.

KAYE, H. and LEVIN, G. R. 1963. Two attempts to demonstrate tonal suppression of non-nutritive sucking in neonates. *Percept. Mot. Skills. 17,* 521–522.

KEEN, R. 1965. Effects of auditory stimuli on sucking behavior in the human neonate, *J. exp. child Psychol. 1,* 348–354.

LINDSLEY, O. R. 1962. A behavioral measure of television viewing. *J. advert. Res. 2,* 2–12.

LINDSLEY, O. R. 1963. Experimental analysis of social reinforcement: terms and methods. *Am. J. Orthopsychiat. 33,* 624–633.

LINDSLEY, O. R., HOBIKA, J. H. and ETSTEN, B. E. 1961. Operant behavior during anesthesia recovery: a continuous and objective method. *Anesthesiology. 22,* 937–946.

LIPSITT, L. P. 1963. Learning in the first year of life. In L. P. Lipsitt and C. C. Spiker (Eds.), *Advances in child development and behavior.* Vol. 1. Academic Press, New York. Pp. 147–195.

LIPSITT, L. P. 1967. Learning in the human infant. In H. W. Stevenson, E. H. Hess, and H. L. Rheingold (Eds.), *Early behavior: comparative and developmental approaches.* Wiley, New York. Pp. 225–247.

LIPSITT, L. P. and KAYE, H. 1965. Changes in neonatal response to optimizing and non-optimizing sucking stimulation. *Psychon. Sci. 2,* 221–222.

LIPSITT, L. P., PEDERSON, L. J. and DeLUCIA, C. A. 1966. Conjugate reinforcement of operant responding in infants. *Psychon. Sci. 4,* 67–68.

LYNN, R. 1966. *Attention, arousal and the orienting reaction.* Pergamon, Oxford.

MARQUIS, D. P. 1931. Can conditioned responses be established in the newborn infant? *J. genet. Psychol. 39,* 479–492.

MARQUIS, D. P. 1941. Learning in the neonate: the modification of behavior under three feeding schedules, *J. exp. Psychol. 29,* 263–282.

PAPOUŠEK, H. 1959. A method of studying conditioned food reflexes in young children up to the age of six months. *Pavlov J. Higher Nerv. Activ. 9,* 136–140.

PAPOUŠEK, H. 1960. Conditioned motor alimentary reflexes in infants. *Cesk. Pediat. 15,* 861–872, 981–988.

PAPOUŠEK, H. 1961. Conditioned head rotation reflexes in the first months of life. *Acta paediat., Stockh. 50,* 565–576.

PFAFFMANN, C. 1960. The pleasures of sensation. *Psychol. Rev. 67,* 253–268.

PRATT, K. C. 1954. The neonate. In L. Carmichael (Ed.), *Manual of child psychology.* Wiley, New York. Pp. 215–291.

ROVEE, C. K. and ROVEE, D. 1969. Conjugate reinforcement of infant exploratory behaviour. *J. exp. Child Psychol. 8,* 33–39.

SEMB, G. and LIPSITT, L. P. 1968. The effects of acoustic stimulation on cessation and initiation of non-nutritive sucking in neonates. *J. exp. Child Psychol. 6,* 585–597.

SIQUELAND, E. R. 1968. Reinforcement patterns and extinction in human newborns. *J. exp. Child Psychol. 6,* 431–442.

SIQUELAND, E. R. and LIPSITT, L. P. 1966. Conditioned head-turning in human newborns. *J. exp. Child Psychol. 3,* 356–376.

SOKOLOV, E. N. 1963. Higher nervous functions: the orienting reflex. *A. Rev. Physiol.* 545–580.

UZGIRIS, I. and HUNT, J. McV. 1965. A longitudinal study of recognition learning. Paper read at the biennial meeting of the Society for Research in Child Development, Minneapolis, Minnesota.

WHITE, R. W. 1959. Motivation reconsidered: the concept of competence. *Psychol. Rev. 66,* 297–333.

WRIGHT, H. F. 1960. Observational Child Study. In P. H. Mussen (Ed.), *Handbook of research methods in child development.* Wiley, New York. Pp. 71–139.

47

Adolescence [1]

ANNA FREUD

An article by Anna Freud of London, England, follows. Her contributions to psychoanalytic theory are probably exceeded only by those of her father, Sigmund Freud. In her discussion of the problems of the adolescent, she emphasizes personality differences among adolescents in coping with the stresses of their age period. Among her books are The Ego and the Mechanisms of Defense *(1948, rev. 1966) and* Normality and Pathology in Childhood: Assessments of Development *(1965), both published by the International Universities Press, New York City.*

This paper is a provocative version of her long-famed descriptions of adolescent defenses against anxiety and guilt. Freud closes her article with an important discussion of the normality of adolescent difficulties.

I. ADOLESCENCE IN THE PSYCHOANALYTIC THEORY

INTRODUCTION

I return to the subject of adolescence after an interval of twenty years. During this time much has

[1] The content of this paper is based on material collected in the Hampstead Child-Therapy Clinic with the aid of grants by The Field Foundation, Inc., New York, The Foundations' Fund for Research in Psychiatry, New Haven, Connecticut, The Ford Foundation, New York, The Psychoanalytic Foundation, Inc., and The Grant Foundation, Inc., New York.

happened in analytic work to throw added light on the problems concerned and to influence the conditions of life for young people, whether normal or abnormal. Nevertheless, in spite of partial advances, the position with regard to the analytic study of adolescence is not a happy one, and especially unsatisfactory when compared with that of early childhood. With the latter period, we feel sure of our ground, and in possession of a wealth of material and information which enables us to assume authority and apply analytic findings to the practical problems of upbringing. When it comes to adolescence, we feel hesitant and, accordingly, cannot satisfy the parents or educational workers who apply for help to us and to our knowledge. One can hear it said frequently that adolescence is a neglected period, a stepchild where analytic thinking is concerned.

These complaints, which come from two sides, from the parents as well as from the analytic workers themselves, seem to me to warrant closer study and investigation than they have received so far. . . .

II. CLINICAL APPLICATIONS

What follows is an attempt to apply at least some of our hard-won insights to three of the most pressing problems concerning adolescence.

IS THE ADOLESCENT UPSET INEVITABLE?

There is, first, the ever recurrent question whether the adolescent upheaval is welcome and beneficial as such, whether it is necessary and, more than that, inevitable. On this point, psychoanalytic opinion is decisive and unanimous. The people in the child's family and school, who assess his state on the basis of behavior, may deplore the adolescent upset which, to them, spells the loss of valuable qualities, of character stability, and of social adaptation. As analysts, who assess personalities from the structural point of view, we think otherwise. We know that the character structure of a child at the end of the latency period represents the outcome of long drawn-out conflicts between id and ego forces. The inner balance achieved, although characteristic for each individual and precious to him, is preliminary only and precarious. It does not allow for the quantitative increase in drive activity, nor for the changes of drive quality which are both inseparable from puberty. Consequently, it has to be abandoned to allow adult sexuality to be integrated into the individual's per-

Anna Freud, Adolescence, *Psychoanalytic Study of the Child,* 1958. Reprinted by permission of International Universities Press and the author.

sonality. The so-called adolescent upheavals are no more than the external indications that such internal adjustments are in progress.

On the other hand, we all know individual children who as late as the ages of fourteen, fifteen or sixteen show no such outer evidence of inner unrest. They remain, as they have been during the latency period, "good" children, wrapped up in their family relationships, considerate sons of their mothers, submissive to their fathers, in accord with the atmosphere, ideas and ideals of their childhood background. Convenient as this may be, it signifies a delay of normal development and is, as such, a sign to be taken seriously. The first impression conveyed by these cases may be that of a quantitative deficiency of drive endowment, a suspicion which will usually prove unfounded. Analytic exploration reveals that this reluctance to "grow up" is derived not from the id but from the ego and superego aspects of the personality. These are children who have built up excessive defenses against their drive activities and are now crippled by the results, which act as barriers against the normal maturational processes of phase development. They are, perhaps more than any others, in need of therapeutic help to remove the inner restrictions and clear the path for normal development, however "upsetting" the latter may prove to be.

IS THE ADOLESCENT UPSET PREDICTABLE?

A second question which we are asked to answer frequently concerns the problem whether the manner in which a given child will react in adolescence can be predicted from the characteristics of his early infantile or latency behavior. Apart from the more general affirmative answer given by Ernest Jones (1922), only one among the authors named above has made clear and positive assertions in this respect. Siegfried Bernfeld (1923), when discussing his protracted type of male adolescence and its characteristics, established the links between this form of puberty and a specific type of infantile development based on the following three conditions: (a) that the frustration of infantile sex wishes has been shattering for the child's narcissism; (b) that the incestuous fixations to the parents have been of exceptional strength and have been maintained throughout the latency period; (c) that the superego has been established early, has been delineated sharply from the ego, and that the ideals contained in it are invested with narcissistic as well as with object libido.

Other and less precise answers to the same question are scattered through the literature. We find the opinion that, in the majority of cases, the mani-

festations of the adolescent process are not predictable since they depend almost wholly on quantitative relations, i.e., on the strength and suddenness of drive increase, the corresponding increase in anxiety causing all the rest of the upheaval.

I suggested in another place (1936) that adolescence brings about occasionally something in the nature of a spontaneous cure. This happens in children whose pregenital activities and characteristics remained dominant throughout latency until the increase in genital libido produces a welcome decrease in pregenitality. This latter occurrence, on the other hand, can be matched by a corresponding one which produces the opposite effect: where phallic characteristics have remained dominant during latency, the increase in genital libido produces the effect of an exaggerated and threatening aggressive masculinity.

It seems to be generally accepted that a strong fixation to the mother, dating not only from the oedipal but from the preoedipal attachment to her, renders adolescence especially difficult. This latter assertion, on the other hand, has to be correlated with two recent findings of a different nature which we owe to work done in our Hampstead Child-Therapy Clinic. One of these findings is derived from the study of orphaned children who were deprived of the relationship to a stable mother figure in their first years. This lack of a mother fixation, far from making adolescence easier, constitutes a real danger to the whole inner coherence of the personality during that period. In these cases adolescence is preceded frequently by a frantic search for a mother image; the internal possession and cathexis of such an image seems to be essential for the ensuing normal process of detaching libido from it for transfer to new objects, i.e., to sexual partners.

The second finding mentioned above is derived from the analyses of adolescent twins, in one case children whose twin relationship in infancy had been observed and recorded in minute detail (Burlingham, 1952). In their treatments it transpired that the "adolescent revolt" against the love objects of infancy demands the breaking of the tie to the twin in no lesser degree than the breaking of the tie to the mother. Since this libidinal (narcissistic as well as object-directed) cathexis of the twin is rooted in the same deep layer of the personality as the early attachment to the mother, its withdrawal is accompanied by an equal amount of structural upheaval, emotional upset, and resulting symptom formation. Where, on the other hand, the twin relationship survives the adolescent phase, we may expect to see a delay in the onset of maturity or a restrictive hardening of the character of the latency period similar to the instances mentioned above in which the childhood love for the parents withstands the onslaught of the adolescent phase.

To return to the initial question: it seems that we are able to foretell the adolescent reactions in certain specific and typical constellations but certainly not for all the individual variations of infantile personality structure. Our insight into typical developments will increase with the number of adolescents who undergo analysis.

PATHOLOGY IN ADOLESCENCE

This leaves us with a third problem which, to my mind, outweighs the preceding ones so far as clinical and theoretical significance are concerned. I refer to the difficulty in adolescent cases to draw the line between normality and pathology. As described above, adolescence constitutes by definition an interruption of peaceful growth which resembles in appearance a variety of other emotional upsets and structural upheavals.[3] The adolescent manifestations come close to symptom formation of the neurotic, psychotic or dissocial order and merge almost imperceptibly into borderline states, initial, frustrated or fully fledged forms of almost all the mental illnesses. Consequently, the differential diagnosis between the adolescent upsets and true pathology becomes a difficult task.

For the discussion of this diagnostic problem I leave most other authors in the field to speak for themselves and summarize my own impressions based on past and present clinical experience.

In 1936, when I approached the same subject from the aspect of the defenses, I was concerned with the similarity between the adolescent and other emotional disturbances rather than with the differences between them. I described that adolescent upsets take on the appearance of a neurosis if the initial, pathogenic danger situation is located in the superego with the resulting anxiety being felt as guilt; that they resemble psychotic disturbances if the danger lies in the increased power of the id itself, which threatens the ego in its existence or integrity. Whether such an adolescent individual impresses us, then, as obsessional, phobic, hysterical, ascetic, schizoid, paranoid, suicidal, etc., will depend on the one hand on the quality and quantity of the id contents which beset the ego, on the other hand on the selection of defense mechanisms which the latter employs. Since, in adolescence, impulses from all pregenital phases rise to the surface and

defense mechanisms from all levels of crudity or complexity come into use, the pathological results —although identical in structure—are more varied and less stabilized than at other times of life.

Today it seems to me that this structural description needs to be amplified, not in the direction of the similarity of the adolescent to other disorders but in that of their specific nature. There is in their etiology at least one additional element which may be regarded as exclusive to this period and characteristic for it: namely that the danger is felt to be located not only in the id impulses and fantasies but in the very existence of the love objects of the individual's oedipal and preoedipal past. The libidinal cathexis to them has been carried forward from the infantile phases, merely toned down or inhibited in aim during latency. Therefore the reawakened pregenital urges, or— worse still—the newly acquired genital ones, are in danger of making contact with them, lending a new and threatening reality to fantasies which had seemed extinct but are, in fact, merely under repression.[4] The anxieties which arise on these grounds are directed toward eliminating the infantile objects, i.e., toward breaking the tie with them. Anny Katan (1937) has discussed this type of defense, which aims above all at changing the persons and the scene of conflict, under the term of "removal." Such an attempt may succeed or fail, partially or totally. In any case, I agree with Anny Katan that its outcome will be decisive for the success or failure of the other, more familiar line of defensive measures which are directed against the impulses themselves.

A number of illustrations will serve to clarify the meaning of this assumption.

(I) Defense Against the Infantile Object Ties. Defense by Displacement of Libido. There are many adolescents who deal with the anxiety aroused by the attachment to their infantile objects by the simple means of flight. Instead of permitting a process of gradual detachment from the parents to take place, they withdraw their libido from them suddenly and altogether. This leaves them with a passionate longing for partnership which they succeed in transferring to the environment outside the family. Here they adopt varying solutions. Libido may be transferred, more or less unchanged in

---

[3] Adolescence, of course, is not the only time in life when alterations of a physiological nature cause disturbances of mental equilibrium. The same happens in later years in the climacterium; and recently, Grete L. Bibring has given a convincing description of similar damage to the equilibrium of mental forces during pregnancy.

[4] An important clinical instance of this can be found in adolescent girls with anorexia nervosa. Here the infantile fantasies of oral impregnation receive added impetus from the new real possibilities of motherhood opened up by genital development. Consequently, the phobic measures adopted against the intake of food on the one hand and identification with the mother on the other hand are overemphasized to a degree which may lead to starvation.

form, to parent substitutes, provided that these new figures are diametrically opposed in every aspect (personal, social, cultural) to the original ones. Or the attachment may be made to so-called "leaders," usually persons in age between the adolescent's and the parents' generation, who represent ideals. Equally frequent are the passionate new ties to contemporaries, either of the same or of the opposite sex (i.e., homosexual friendships) and the attachments to adolescent groups (or "gangs"). Whichever of these typical solutions is chosen, the result makes the adolescent feel "free," and revel in a new precious sense of independence from the parents who are treated, then, with indifference bordering on callousness.

Although the direction taken by the libido in these instances is, in itself, on lines of normality, the suddenness of the change, the carefully observed contrast in object selection, and the overemphasis on the new allegiances mark it as defensive. It represents an all too hasty anticipation of normal growth rather than a normal developmental process.

It makes little further difference to the emotional situation whether the libidinal flight is followed by actual flight, i.e., whether the adolescent also "removes" himself bodily from his family. If not, he remains in the home in the attitude of a boarder, usually a very inconsiderate one so far as the older and younger family members are concerned.

On the other hand, the withdrawal of cathexis from the parents has most decisive consequences for the rest of the defensive processes. Once the infantile objects are stripped of their importance, the pregenital and genital impulses cease to be threatening to the same degree. Consequently, guilt and anxiety decrease and the ego becomes more tolerant. Formerly repressed sexual and aggressive wishes rise to the surface and are acted on, the actions being taken outside the family in the wider environment. Whether this acting out will be on harmless, or idealistic, or dissocial, or even criminal lines will depend essentially on the new objects to which the adolescent has attached himself. Usually the ideals of the leader, of the adolescent group, or of the gang, are taken over wholeheartedly and without criticism.

Adolescents of this type may be sent for treatment after their actions have brought them into conflict with their schools, their employers, or the law. As far as psychoanalytic therapy is concerned, they seem to offer little chance for the therapeutic alliance between analyst and patient without which the analytic technique cannot proceed. Any relationship to the analyst and, above all, the transference to him would revive the infantile attachments

which have been discarded; therefore the adolescent remains unresponsive. Also, the escape from these attachments has suspended the feeling of internal conflict, at least temporarily; consequently, the adolescent does not feel in need of psychological help. A. Aichhorn had these points in mind when he maintained that adolescents of the dissocial and criminal type needed a long period of preparation and inner rearrangement before they could become amenable to analytic treatment. He maintained that the latter would be successful only if, during this preparation in a residential setting, the adolescent made a new transference of object love, reawakened his infantile attachments, internalized his conflicts once more, in short, became neurotic.

To try and analyze an adolescent in his phase of successful detachment from the past seems to be a venture doomed to failure.

Defense by Reversal of Affect. A second typical reaction to the same danger situation, is, although less conspicuous outwardly, more ominous in nature inwardly.

Instead of displacing libido from the parents—or, more likely, after failing to do so—the adolescent ego may defend itself by turning the emotions felt toward them into their opposites. This changes love into hate, dependence into revolt, respect and admiration into contempt and derision. On the basis of such reversal of affect the adolescent imagines himself to be "free" but, unluckily for his peace of mind and sense of conflict, this conviction does not reach further than the conscious surface layer of his mind. For all deeper intents and purposes he remains as securely tied to the parental figures as he has been before; acting out remains within the family; and any alterations achieved by the defense turn out to his disadvantage. There are no positive pleasures to be derived from the reversed relationships, only suffering, felt as well as inflicted. There is no room for independence of action, or of growth; compulsive opposition to the parents proves as crippling in this respect as compulsive obedience to them can prove to be.[5] Since anxiety and guilt remain undiminished, constant reinforcement of defense is necessary. This is provided in the first place by two methods: denial (of positive feeling) and reaction formations (churlish, unsympathetic, contemptuous attitudes). The behavioral picture that emerges at this stage is that of an uncooperative and hostile adolescent.

Further pathological developments of this state of affairs are worth watching. The hostility and

[5] S. Ferenczi has pointed to this effect of "compulsive disobedience" many years ago.

aggressiveness, which serve as a defense against object love in the beginning, soon become intolerable to the ego, are felt as threats, and are warded off in their own right. This may happen by means of projection; in that case the aggression is ascribed to the parents who, consequently, become the adolescent's main oppressors and persecutors. In the clinical picture this appears first as the adolescent's suspiciousness and, when the projections increase, as paranoid behavior.

Conversely, the full hostility and aggression may be turned away from the objects and employed inwardly against the self. In these cases, the adolescents display intense depression, tendencies of self-abasement and self-injury, and develop, or even carry out, suicidal wishes.

During all stages of this process, personal suffering is great and the desire to be helped intense. This, in itself, is no guarantee that the adolescent in question will submit to analytic therapy. He will certainly not do so if treatment is urged and initiated by the parents. Whenever this happens, he will consider analysis as their tool, extend his hostility or his suspicions to include the person of the analyst, and refuse cooperation. The chances are better if the adolescent himself decides to seek help and turns to analysis, as it were, in opposition to the parents' wishes. Even so, the alliance with the analyst may not be of long duration. As soon as a true transference develops and the positive infantile fantasies come into consciousness, the same reversal of affect tends to be repeated in the analytic setting. Rather than relive the whole turmoil of feelings with the analyst, many adolescent patients run away. They escape from their positive feelings, although it appears to the analyst that they break off treatment in an overwhelmingly strong negative transference.

Defense by Withdrawal of Libido to the Self. To proceed in the direction of increasing pathology:

Withdrawal of libido from the parents, as it has been described above, does not, in itself, decide about its further use, or fate. If anxieties and inhibitions block the way toward new objects outside the family, the libido remains within the self. There, it may be employed to cathect the ego and superego, thereby inflating them. Clinically this means that ideas of grandeur will appear, fantasies of unlimited power over other human beings, or of major achievement and championship in one or more fields. Or, the suffering and persecuted ego of the adolescent may assume Christ-like proportions with corresponding fantasies of saving the world.

On the other hand, the cathexis may become attached to the adolescent's body only and give rise there to the hypochondriacal sensations and feelings of body changes that are well known clinically from initial stages of psychotic illness.

In either case analytic therapy is indicated as well as urgent. Treatment will dispel the appearance of severe abnormality if it reopens a path for the libido, either to flow backwards and recathect the original infantile objects, or to flow forward, in the direction described above, to cathect less frightening substitutes in the environment.

What taxes the analyst's technical skill in these cases is the withdrawn state of the patient, i.e., the problem of establishing an initial relationship and transference. Once this is accomplished, the return from narcissistic withdrawal to object cathexis will relieve the patient, at least temporarily.

I believe there are many cases where the analyst would be wise to be content with this partial success without urging further treatment. A further, and deeper, involvement in the transference may well arouse all the anxieties described above and, again, lead to abrupt termination of the analysis due to the adolescent's flight reaction.

Defense by Regression. The greater the anxiety aroused by the object ties, the more elementary and primitive is the defense activity employed by the adolescent ego to escape them. Thus, at the extreme height of anxiety, the relations with the object world may be reduced to the emotional state known as "primary identification" with the objects. This solution with which we are familiar from psychotic illnesses implies regressive changes in all parts of the personality, i.e., in the ego organization as well as in the libido. The ego boundaries [6] are widened to embrace parts of the object together with the self. This creates in the adolescent surprising changes of qualities, attitudes and even outward appearance. His allegiance to persons outside himself betrays itself in these alterations of his own personality (i.e., his identifications) rather than in an outflow of libido. Projections, together with these identifications, dominate the scene and create a give-and-take between the self and object which has repercussions on important ego functions. For example, the distinction between the external and internal world (i.e., reality testing) becomes temporarily negligible, a lapse in ego functioning which manifests itself in the clinical picture as a state of confusion.

Regression of this kind may bring transitory relief to the ego by emptying the oedipal (and many of the preoedipal) fantasies of their libidinal cathexis.[7] But this lessening anxiety will not be long-

---

[6] See P. Federn (1952) and, following him, T. Freeman et al. (1958).

[7] See in this connection M. Katan (1950).

lived. Another and deeper anxiety will soon take its place which I have characterized on a former occasion (1951) as the fear of emotional surrender, with the accompanying fear of loss of identity.

(II) Defense Against Impulses.   Where the defenses against the oedipal and preoedipal object ties fail to achieve their aim, clinical pictures emerge which come nearest to the borderline toward psychotic illness.

The "Ascetic" Adolescent. One of these, the "ascetic" adolescent, I have described before as fighting all his impulses, preoedipal and oedipal, sexual and aggressive, extending the defense even to the fulfillment of the physiological needs for food, sleep, and body comfort. This, to me, seems the characteristic reaction of an ego, driven by the blind fear of overwhelming id quantities, an anxiety which leaves no room for the finer distinctions between vital or merely pleasant satisfactions, the healthy or the morbid, the morally permitted or forbidden pleasures. Total war is waged against the pursuit of pleasure as such. Accordingly, most of the normal processes of instinct and need satisfaction are interfered with and become paralyzed. According to clinical observation, adolescent asceticism is, with luck, a transitory phenomenon. For the analytic observer it provides precious proof of the power of defense, i.e., of the extent to which the normal, healthy drive derivatives are open to crippling interference by the ego.

On the whole, analytic treatment of the ascetic type does not present as many technical difficulties as one would expect. Perhaps, in these individuals, defense against the impulses is so massive, that they can permit themselves some object relationship to the analyst and, thus, enter into transference.

The "Uncompromising" Adolescent. Another, equally abnormal adolescent, is described best as the "uncompromising" type. The term, in this instance, does refer to more than the well-known conscious, unrelenting position adopted by many young people who stand up for their ideas, refuse to make concessions to the more practical and reality-adapted attitudes of their elders, and take pride in their moral or aesthetic principles. "Compromise," with these adolescents, includes processes which are as essential for life as, for example, the cooperation between impulses, the blending of opposite strivings, the mitigation of id strivings by interference from the side of the ego. One adolescent whom I observed in analysis did his utmost, in pursuit of this impossible aim, to prevent any interference of his mind with his body, of his activity with his passivity, his loves with his hates, his realities with his fantasies, the external de-

mands with his internal ones, in short, of his ego with his id.

In treatment this defense was represented as a strong resistance against any "cure," the idea of which he despised in spite of intense suffering. He understood correctly that mental health is based in the last resort on harmony, i.e., on the very compromise formations which he was trying to avoid.

III. THE CONCEPT OF NORMALITY IN ADOLESCENCE

Where adolescence is concerned, it seems easier to describe its pathological manifestations than the normal processes. Nevertheless, there are in the above exposition at least two pronouncements which may prove useful for the concept: (1) that adolescence is by its nature an interruption of peaceful growth, and (2) that the upholding of a steady equilibrium during the adolescent process is in itself abnormal. Once we accept for adolescence disharmony within the psychic structure as our basic fact, understanding becomes easier. We begin to see the upsetting battles which are raging between id and ego as beneficent attempts to restore peace and harmony. The defensive methods which are employed either against the impulses, or against the object cathexis, begin to appear legitimate and normal. If they produce pathological results, this happens not because of any malignancy in their nature, but because they are overused, overstressed, or used in isolation. Actually, each of the abnormal types of adolescent development, as it is described above, represents also a potentially useful way of regaining mental stability, normal if combined with other defenses, and if used in moderation.

To explain this last statement in greater detail: I take it that it is normal for an adolescent to behave for a considerable length of time in an inconsistent and unpredictable manner; to fight his impulses and to accept them; to ward them off successfully and to be overrun by them; to love his parents and to hate them; to revolt against them and to be dependent on them; to be deeply ashamed to acknowledge his mother before others and, unexpectedly, to desire heart-to-heart talks with her; to thrive on imitation of and identification with others while searching unceasingly for his own identity; to be more idealistic, artistic, generous, and unselfish than he will ever be again, but also the opposite: self-centered, egoistic, calculating. Such fluctuations between extreme opposites would be deemed highly abnormal at any other time of life. At this time they may signify no more than that an adult structure of personality takes a long time to emerge, that the ego of the individual in question does not cease to experiment and is in no hurry to close down on possibilities. If the temporary solutions seem abnormal to the onlooker, they are less so, nevertheless, than the hasty decisions made in other cases for one-sided suppression, or revolt, or flight, or withdrawal, or regression, or asceticism, which are responsible for the truly pathological developments described above.

While an adolescent remains inconsistent and unpredictable in his behavior, he may suffer, but he does not seem to me to be in need of treatment. I think that he should be given time and scope to work out his own solution. Rather, it may be his parents who need help and guidance so as to be able to bear with him. There are few situations in life which are more difficult to cope with than an adolescent son or daughter during the attempt to liberate themselves.

IV. SUMMARY

In the foregoing papers the author has reviewed and summarized some of the basic literature on adolescence, as well as her own views on the subject. Her former description of the defensive processes in adolescence has been amplified to include specific defense activities directed against the oedipal and preoedipal object ties.

BIBLIOGRAPHY

AICHHORN, A. (1925), *Wayward Youth*. New York: Viking Press, 1948.

BERNFELD, S. (1923), Uber eine typische Form der männlichen Pubertät. *Imago*, IX.

BURLINGHAM, D. (1952), *Twins*. New York: International Universities Press.

FEDERN, P. (1952), *Ego Psychology and the Psychoses*. New York: Basic Books.

FREEMAN, T., CAMERON, L. J. and McGHIE, A. (1958), *Chronic Schizophrenia*. New York: International Universities Press.

FREUD, A. (1936), *The Ego and the Mechanisms of Defense*. New York: International Universities Press, 1946. See Chapters X and XI.

FREUD, A. (1951), A Connection between the States of Negativism and of Emotional Surrender (Horigkeit). Paper read at the International Psycho-Analytical Congress, Amsterdam, August 1951. Summary in *Int. J. Psa.*, XXXIII, 1952, p. 265.

JONES, E. (1922), Some Problems of Adolescence. *Papers on Psycho-Analysis*. London: Bailliere, Tindall & Cox, fifth edition, 1948.

KATAN-ANGEL, A. (1937), The Role of Displacement in Agoraphobia. *Int. J. Psa.*, XXXII, 1951.

KATAN, M. (1950), Structural Aspects of a Case of Schizophrenia. *This Annual*, V.

48

Crises in Normal Personality Development

GORDON W. ALLPORT

This article, by the late Gordon W. Allport, deals with crises in the personality development of "normal" college students. Allport deals with his topic in relation to autobiographical materials supplied by his students. His discussion is not from a Freudian point of view. Vicissitudes of adjustment to college, motherhood, etc., have a lesson for preventive work in mental health. A study of the transition points in life may permit forecasting (or at least early recognition of) periods of emotional difficulty, which then may be palliated, often in fairly simple ways. Examples of such role changes are getting a new brother or sister, entering school, developing sexually in early adolescence, leaving home in late adolescence, and experiencing major changes in adulthood (entering military service, marrying, being pregnant, giving birth, moving, changing jobs, and being bereaved). Indeed, the relatively fixed age, within our society, of some of these role changes may contribute to the apparent relation of developmental periods to chronological age.

There is one trick every teacher knows: When trapped in a state of ignorance throw the question back to the class. Without suspecting the teacher's predicament, bright students will often rescue him.

This is the strategy I employed to learn something about crises in normal personality development. I passed along the assignment to my class of 100 captive undergraduates, and they obligingly provided me, through their own autobiographical writing, with the insights that I articulate now. Parenthetically, let me say that in my opinion no teacher or counselor has the right to require intimate autobiographical documents from students. Yet when given a completely free choice, the large majority will choose to write in the autobiographical vein. For the few who would find the experience too threatening, it should not be prescribed.

. . .

It is in middle and late adolescence, . . . according to Erikson (3), that the identity crisis is in the ascendance.* The young person seems to be moving from past childhood into present adulthood in a jerky manner. Development is not continuous like a hill; rather, it is episodic like a flight of stairs. It is this episodic or crisis character of development that brings both challenge and opportunity to the guidance officer.

NATURE OF CRISIS

What precisely is a "crisis"? It is a situation of emotional and mental stress requiring significant alterations of outlook within a short period of time. These alterations of outlook frequently involve changes in the structure of personality. The resulting changes may be progressive in the life or they may be regressive. By definition, a person in crisis cannot stand still; that is to say, he cannot redact his present traumatic experience into familiar and routine categories or employ simple habitual modes of adjustment. He must either separate himself further from childhood and move toward adulthood, or else move backward to earlier levels of adjustment which may mean becoming disorganized, dropping out of school, escaping from the field, developing hostilities and defenses, and in general becoming a thorn in the flesh of the teacher, the parent, the counselor, the dean, and occasionally of the police. Sometimes, following a crisis, the adolescent will become stabilized anew after four or five weeks of severe disorganization; but in many cases the trauma retards development for a year or more, and may even leave a life-long scar.

_____

* Erikson's views are stated at the beginning of this section in "A Healthy Personality for Every Child."—EDITOR

Gordon W. Allport, "Crises in normal personality development," *Teachers College Record*, 1964, *66* (3), 235–241. Reprinted, with slight abridgement, by permission.

Turning now to my data, drawn from college undergraduates, we ask first about the phenomenology of crisis. What does it "feel" like to the student? Common is a sense of numbness and apathy. Upon entering college, the youth finds fewer strict role-prescriptions than at home. He is no longer tied to his domestic filial role, to the highly structured routine of high school, to his siblings, to his church connections, to his teen-age sub-cultures. He has left his possessions behind—his stamp collection, his television, his girl friends, his boy friends. All his familiar roles are in suspension. As one students writes,

> The complete freedom of college is itself a crisis. For the first time I live in close contact with people who are not members of my family. They don't even resemble people I have known before. They have different opinions, different origins, and different emotions. I feel numbed by it all.

Interestingly enough, this sense of hollowness does not necessarily have its maximum effect during the freshman year. The excitement of new scenes and especially frequent correspondence with and visits back to the home town keep the silver cord intact. The student feels that he should prove to his parents, teachers, friends, that he can master the college environment and thus please them and win their approval as he has done in the past. The impending crisis has not yet overwhelmed him (or her—for what I am saying is as true for college girls as for boys).

It is the sophomore year that seems (from my data) to be the year of crisis *par excellence*. Suddenly it becomes no longer tolerable to live one's life for the edification of people "back home." The time has come for the child of the past to be separated once and for all from the adult of the present. Here are typical phenomenological statements of this stage of the crisis:

> I feel I have been dragged into something against my will.
>
> I feel like a rat in a maze.
>
> I want to be a law unto myself, but cannot.
>
> It seems suddenly that the decisions I make must be valid for the rest of my life.
>
> To shake off parental norms and values seems to me the most important thing I must do.

The life of the past and the life of the future seem suddenly to be at cross purposes. There is often an intolerable feeling of suspended animation. Recrystallization is not yet possible. The youth is waiting still to make a choice of careers, a suitable marriage, and to find an integrative philosophy of life which his diverse college courses are too discordant to supply.

APATHY AND ANXIETY

It is small wonder that apathy and a paralysis of will often occur. But apathy is only a mask for anxiety. The whole framework of life is disturbed. Whereas the majority of students contrive gradually to build a new framework in spite of, or perhaps because of, the goads of anxiety, yet a large minority cannot cope with the situation unaided.

From my data, I would estimate that three-quarters are able to take the progressive road in creating their new frame of existence. About one-quarter cannot immediately do so. Proof of this point is that the dropout rate during undergraduate years is surprisingly high—over 20 per cent at Harvard, about three-quarters of the cases representing voluntary withdrawals (2). The dropouts present a special problem of guidance. Blaine and McArthur (2) write,

> The drop-outs as a group ultimately do quite well if properly handled. We attempt to establish a relationship, however brief or tenuous, with these students, not so much to prevent their leaving school, but rather in the hope of giving them some insight into the determinants of their difficulties so that their dropping out can be ultimately converted into a meaningful constructive experience instead of mere failure.

After a year or two of constructive work elsewhere, the majority of voluntary dropouts return to college and graduate. But they could not have met their crisis by remaining in the environment that was the context of their conflict.

The regressive road is surprisingly common. Among eventual dropouts, but also among other students, we find such self-destroying behavior as quitting classes, a compulsion to do trivial things, playing bridge until four A.M., drinking bouts, feelings of unreality, fugues, and general debauchery. The candid documents received startle me a bit by the extent of plain juvenile delinquency among my innocent-appearing students:

> One student finding himself unable to handle his conflicts over choice of career and over friction with his roommate, indulged in plagiarism on a term paper in such a way that he would be caught and forcibly separated from college. In this case a wise instructor, catching him in the transgression, turned the occasion into constructive counseling, forgave the deed, and put the lad onto the progressive rather than regressive road.

Here I venture a theoretical digression. The problem, as I see it, is one of interiorizing motivation. To put it in a student's words: "I am fed up with having everybody else cheer me on. I want to work to please myself rather than others, but I don't know how to do it." This plaintive statement points to a serious dilemma in our educational process. In school, the child is rewarded and punished by good grades and bad grades. Even in college, As and Bs are pats on the back, Ds and Fs are punishment. To gain love, the student must read books and toe the academic line. Finally, he obtains his degree (which is a symbol of academic love) and is freed from this external form of motivation. What then happens?

We know that a shockingly high percentage of college graduates rarely or never read another book after receiving their bachelor's degree. Why should they? Their love now comes from their employer, their wife, their children, not from the approval of parents and teachers. For them, intellectual curiosity never became a motive in its own right. External rewards are appropriate props in early childhood. But we educators, being limited by current inadequate theories of learning, do not know how to help the student free himself from the props of reward and develop a functionally autonomous zeal for learning. With our slavish dependence on reinforcement theory, I think it surprising that we arouse as much internal motivation as we do. In any event, we cannot be proud of the many educational cripples who after graduation, lacking the routine incentive of college, sink into intellectual apathy.

CRISIS AREAS

The counselor or teacher, of course, cannot wait for better theories of learning. He is confronted here and now with crises in the concrete. Four areas of conflict, judging from my data, are especially common.

INTELLECTUAL CRISES

First, there are students whose problem is one of intellectual malplacement. Among my cases, a large number report that in primary and secondary school they were too bright for their class. The penalty is one of boredom lasting down into college work, which they still do not find challenging enough for their abilities. At the same time, double promotions in elementary and high school are not a solution. To be placed with older children often creates social difficulties far more serious than boredom. In fact, the evil consequences reported from double promotion are so numerous that we should challenge this particular solution of the bright child's dilemma.

The opposite type of intellectual crisis is also common. It is the deep disturbance that often results in college from intensified competition. It is statistically impossible for most students to maintain the same relative superiority in college that they enjoyed in high school. While this fact does not trouble the majority, it is a critical experience for those who depend on scholarship aid or who frame their self-image almost entirely in terms of scholarly preeminence. They are suffering a severe narcissistic wound.

SPECIFIC INFERIORITIES

A second area of crisis is the old, familiar "inferiority complex." Besides the sense of intellectual inferiority just described, we encounter deep disturbance due to physical handicaps or to plain physical appearance, with resulting shyness, loneliness, and misery. To be poor at athletics creates a crisis for males, probably more acute in high school than in college. To be a member of a minority group likewise creates an inevitable crisis somewhere along the line. Here again I suspect the major adjustments and defenses are prepared before the college age. Occasionally, the inferiority concerns guilt due to moral lapses. One student is still haunted by her dishonesty which enabled her to pass a certain course three years ago. She has felt miserable ever since about this critical experience and badly needs a means of expiation.

In this connection we may speak of religious crises. While they are uncommon in my sample, Havens (5) estimates that at any given time 12 per cent of college students have a critical concern, and sometimes acute crises, due to their religious conflicts. I suspect the concern is even more widespread, but since it pertains to one's whole ground of being, it is seldom configured as a specific crisis at a given moment of time.

Another area, seldom mentioned but surely important, is the ideological crisis of modern society as a whole. Youth is inevitably worried, as are adults, by our uncertain future. Elsewhere I have discussed the withdrawal of American youth from their social and political context (4). Both the earlier and present data show an almost exclusive concern among American youth with their own lives. Compared with autobiographies of youth in other cultures, the American documents are far more self-centered, more privatistic. They are too baffled to articulate their distress, and so take refuge in their private concerns.

SEX AND FAMILY *

SEX CONFLICTS

Needless to say, our candid discussions of crises frequently, in fact usually, report acute sex conflicts. Extremely common are breakups in boy-girl relationships which are usually taken as a disaster only slightly less fatal than the end of the world. Such breakups are so recently experienced that college students do not realize that they will, in spite of their present feelings, eventually make a good recovery.

We should face the fact that at least in the early years of college life crises in the sexual sphere are for the most part frankly genital in their reference. The biological drive is so powerful that the youth is concerned with it almost by itself. Its integration into mature love, into marriage, into career plans, into an embracing philosophy of life, exceeds his present capacity. He is likely to think that genitality by itself is maturity. Sexual gratification is frankly the aim, often with devastating consequences. At this stage of development, the students have much to say about sex and little to say about mature love.

FAMILY CONFLICTS

I have left until last the most pervasive area of conflict and crisis. I am referring, of course, to the situation that exists between every adolescent and his parents. It is not enough to say that adolescent rebellion against the parents is the rule. Of course it is; but my documents show that the whole history of the relationships from the time of earliest memories is important. Almost any irregularity in normal family life is felt bitterly and may trouble a student even into adulthood. A mother who is neglectful or self-centered, or perhaps overpossessive and neurotic, leaves traumatic traces in the child's life. A father who is ineffectual and weak, or cruel, or absent (if only for wartime service) leaves the child with a lasting feeling of protest.

One document of unusual maturity notes that many college students seem to need their parents as scapegoats. They find it comfortable to blame parents for their own shortcomings. Perceiving that their parents are not all-powerful, all-wise, and all-perfect, they can say, "Well, no wonder I am having a hard time growing up; they didn't raise me right." Thus, an adolescent, having no genuine ground for complaint, may yet soak himself in self-pity, not being mature enough to relate his re-

---

* In order to interpet the material which follows, the reader should know that the majority of students in this study were males.—EDITOR

stricted image of his parents to the totality of human nature—not yet ready to appreciate the fact that his parents, considering human limitations, may have done a good job. Even if the job was not especially good, the adolescent seems not yet able to appreciate his parents' good intentions as an important value in their own right. From talking with many parents, I hazard the hypothesis that normally it is not until the age of 23 that a child encounters his parents on a mature, adult-to-adult basis.

This brief account of crises emanating from the parent-child relationship leads me to a final point. My students were required to discuss their crises from the point of view of personality theory. They were free to employ any of the theories they were studying in my course. Most of them took Freud. (I may add that the reason was not because Freud was their instructor's favorite author.)

THE CONDITIONS OF THEORY

Now my observation is this: Their Freudian interpretations seemed to fit well if and when the family situation in early life was disturbed. When the father was absent or ineffectual, when the mother was notably aggressive, when there was deliberate sex stimulation within the family—in such cases, it seems that the Oedipal formula provides a good fit, together with all its theoretical accoutrements of identification, superego conflict, defense mechanisms, castration threats, and all the rest.

When, on the other hand, the family life is reasonably normal and secure, a Freudian conceptualization seems forced and artificial. If we say, by way of rough estimate, that 60 per cent of the students try a Freudian conceptualization of their own cases, about 10 per cent turn out to be wholly convincing and theoretically appropriate. The remaining 50 per cent appear to be somehow contrived and badly strained.

I am wondering whether the same ratio might be applicable to cases that come to counselors. If a counselor or a therapist approaches every client or patient with the preconceived belief that his life must fit a Freudian frame of conceptualization, he may win in a minority of the cases, but lose in the majority.

Even where a Freudian approach is clearly justified, exclusive adherence to it may distract the counselor from many significant developments within the life—for example, from the present functional significance of religious and aesthetic values, from the competence and interests that extend beyond the neurotic core, from the client's conscious plans for the future, and from his "will to meaning" and existential concern with life as a whole.

Every person concerned with guidance, or for that matter with teaching, needs as background some general theory of the nature of human personality (1).* Our tendency, I fear, is to draw our theories from the realm of illness and deviance. It is somehow tempting to apply psychiatric rubrics to all personalities, for psychiatric rubrics are vivid, incisive, dramatic, and easy. Our conceptual banners bear such sloganized concepts as Oedipal complex, character disorder, identity diffusion, schizoid, acting out, and maybe an array of dimensions drawn from the Minnesota Multiphasic Personality Inventory. All such concepts, of course, have their proper place. But personality theory for guidance and teaching needs also to be woven of less lurid fabrics.

Youth, whatever neurotic threads may lie in his nature, is busy with his realistic perceptions, with his gradual learning and quiet coping, with the slow extension of selfhood, with noncritical failures and

successes, with developing a generic conscience and a personal style of life. Even in the throes of crisis, he seeks in undramatic ways to consolidate his gains and continue on the path of becoming. A theory of personality adequate to undergird the art of guidance will keep such nondramatic facts in mind. Crises in normal personality development are important, but so too is the slow growth of each youth's unique style of life.

REFERENCES

1. ALLPORT, G. W. Psychological models for guidance. *Harvard educ. Rev.,* 1962, *32,* 373–381.
2. BLAINE, G. B., & McARTHUR, C. C. *Emotional problems of the student.* New York: Appleton-Century-Crofts, 1961.
3. ERIKSON, E. *Childhood and society.* New York: Norton, 1950.
4. GILLESPIE, J. M., & ALLPORT, G. W. *Youth's outlook on the future.* New York: Doubleday, 1955.
5. HAVENS, J. A study of religious conflict in college students. *J. sci. Stud. Relig.,* 1963, *3,* 52–69.

* The article cited here is to be found in Section I of *The Causes of Behavior: Readings in Child Development and Educational Psychology.*—EDITOR

49

Jean Piaget
and the World of the Child[1]

Read D. Tuddenham[2]

Read Tuddenham, professor of psychology at the University of California, Berkeley, has written the following appreciation of Jean Piaget, one of the world's foremost psychologists. It is difficult to realize that Piaget, whose influence is immense today, was neglected for many years. This neglect was for several reasons, among them the fact that no translations of his current work were available. Today, huge numbers of research studies are inspired by Piaget's theory.

Piaget's conceptions are cognitive, and this article might have been placed in Section IX. It appears in this section because of his emphasis on stages of development. The interested reader should examine Tuddenham's list of references, which includes a few of Piaget's basic books. One of Piaget's latest books is Science of Education and the Psychology of the Child *(New York: Grossman, 1970).*

[1] Public lecture given at Berkeley on May 23, 1964, as a part of the University of California fete celebrating the four hundredth anniversary of the founding of the University of Geneva.

[2] The author wishes to acknowledge his indebtedness to earlier writers on Piaget, not all of whom could be mentioned in the lecture. However, special acknowledgment is owing to Flavell (1962) in connection with the biographical account, and to Wolff (1960) for portions of the summary of theory.

. . .

It is difficult to characterize Piaget's work, for it is both deep and broad in scope. He has been in turn a biologist, psychologist, philosopher, and logician, and in all four fields he has made major contributions. He is currently Professor of Psychology at the University of Geneva and at the Sorbonne.

. . .

Since his book, the *Language and Thought of the Child,* appeared in 1923, Piaget and his collaborators have published more than 20 full-length books and largely filled 30 bulky annual volumes of the *Archives de Psychologie;* in all, over 180 major studies covering thousands of pages, of which the barest fraction has been translated into English.

. . .

For those who did not attend [Piaget's lecture at Berkeley in March (1964)], a word of description may not be amiss.

Imagine a man approaching 70, a man of average build, of clear and ruddy complexion, and with snow-white hair worn long over his collar. He moves deliberately, but his blue eyes sparkle with youth, good humor, and zest. Benevolent enough, but not heavy enough, to look like Santa Claus, he reminds one faintly of the pictures of Franz Liszt that have come down to us. A man of great vigor, he still bicycles the several miles from his home to his office in the Palais Wilson and back again each day; and despite a man-killing schedule of conferences and meetings here in Berkeley, he wore out relays of us who tried to entertain him, and had energy left to spare for private hikes in Strawberry Canyon.

. . .

Born in Neuchâtel in 1896, he published his first paper when he was 10 years old on an albino sparrow he found hopping in the public garden. His interest soon turned to molluscs. Before he was 21, he had published 20 papers on molluscs and related topics, and had been offered sight unseen the curatorship of molluscs at Geneva while still in secondary school. He took his baccalaureate at Neuchâtel in 1915 followed by his doctorate in 1918.

Throughout these early years he read widely in other fields—religion, philosophy, and psychology. He came thus to the view that biology should contribute to the solution of classical problems in epistemology, but realized that something was needed to bridge the two. In later years, his developmental psychology came to provide the link, culminating in his three-volume work of 1950 on

Read D. Tuddenham, "Jean Piaget and the world of the child," *American Psychologist, 21,* 1966, 207–217. Copyright 1966 by the American Psychological Association, and reproduced with abridgement by permission.

genetic epistemology, unfortunately still untranslated.

After receiving his doctorate, his interests shifted more explicitly to psychology, and he left Neuchâtel to visit and study at various other centers, including Bleuler's psychiatric clinic and the Sorbonne. Binet had died in 1911, but in Paris, Piaget was given the opportunity by Simon, Binet's collaborator in the Simon-Binet tests, to work in Binet's old laboratory at a Paris grade school. The problem suggested was a standardization of Burt's reasoning tests on Paris school children. Although Piaget was not much interested in the psychometric aspects of the problem, he found himself fascinated by the processes whereby the child achieved his answers—and wrong answers were often more enlightening than right ones.

The psychiatric examining procedures learned at Bleuler's clinic were pressed into service to elucidate the child's reasoning, and came ultimately to constitute the *méthode clinique* by which much of Piaget's data have been collected. This method of intensive interrogation is common enough among psychiatrists, but it is likely to scandalize the American psychologist trained in the canons of objectivity and standardization of procedure, because it risks leading the child and putting words in his mouth. Yet in skillful hands, it yields subtle insights which our "measurement" approach precludes.

. . .

In all the vast corpus of Piaget's work are there unifying trends or concerns which can serve to orient us in this brief survey? Apart from his zoological studies and a few mathematical papers on logic as such, the central preoccupation has been with epistemology—the fundamental problem of how we come to know our world. But this problem is approached, not via traditional philosophical speculation, but rather via scientific observation and experimentation, although sometimes of an unconventional kind. The subjects are infants, children, and adolescents, and the emphasis is always developmental.

Some of this work is on perception, and is concerned with discovering the laws of perceptual development and the differences between perceptual and cognitive functions. To this end, the Geneva workers have shown a persistent interest in optical illusions. For example, they have systematically altered various aspects of the stimulus configuration and measured the magnitude and direction of the observer's errors as a function of his age. These perception studies, over 40 in number, are more rigorous and quantitative than the studies on cognitive development, and substitute for the *méthode clinique* the traditional experimental approach.

In summary, Piaget finds a general tendency, though by no means a linear one, nor one found in all instances, whereby perceptual judgments grow more accurate with age. However, he regards perceptual development as essentially continuous, and he does not consider that the developmental stages, which are so important in his cognitive theory, exist in the perceptual domain. Indeed, he has repeatedly contrasted the perceptual versus the conceptual or inferential process even in the young child, and emphasized that the two functions follow very different paths in development. Wohlwill (1962) has suggested that Piaget's denial of stages in perception while affirming them for cognition stems not from the finding that ontogenetic change in perception is necessarily more gradual, but rather because the differences between successive perceptual achievements are only quantitative, whereas one can find structural criteria—that is to say the presence or absence of particular logical operations—to differentiate the stages of conceptual development.

Time precludes further discussion of the Geneva work on perception, though it constitutes a large and important body of data and interpretation for the perception psychologist. Let us turn instead to the more familiar studies concerned with reasoning and inference.

To throw Piaget's contributions into sharper focus, let us digress briefly to consider the epistemological problem, one of the great imponderables which have engaged man's attention at least since the golden age of Greek philosophy. Now philosophers often ask questions in ways which admit of no final answer. They thus get a great deal of mileage out of them, and the same controversies keep recurring, century after century.

. . .

Obviously such questions as, "Is there an external reality?" or even merely, "What is knowledge?" can lead only to speculative controversy. If the epistemological problem is formulated in more restricted terms of *how* is knowledge acquired, rather than *what* is knowledge, it may become susceptible of scientific experimental attack.

Returning to Piaget, it is clear that his genius has lain in his resourcefulness in investigating the more manageable question, "How does knowledge develop and change?" As you can see, Piaget's epistemology is at once empirical—even experimental—and developmental in orientation. Leaving aside the question of whether the world is real, he has observed and recorded the activities of the child from earliest infancy to adolescence in acquiring the strategies for coping with it.

. . .

Let us turn first to Piaget's theory of cognitive development. Here a confusing situation arises for the English-speaking student. Piaget's [four] important books of the early 1920s were translated fairly promptly into English in the first flurry of interest in his work. These volumes—*Language and Thought of the Child, Judgment and Reasoning in the Child, The Child's Conception of Physical Causality,* and *The Moral Judgment of the Child*—are widely available. It is their contents—the famous inquiries about what makes clouds move, the origins of dreams, the basis of rules for games, and a host of other such topics—which come to mind for many people when Piaget is mentioned.

Now these works were gradually superseded in Piaget's theoretical formulations, but the point has not been sufficiently appreciated. In this country, there was a decline of interest in Piaget during what Koch (1959) has called the "Age of Theory" in American psychology—roughly from the early '30s to the end of the war—a tough-minded period dominated by the rules of "hypothetico-deduction" and "operational definition" and animated by belief in the imminence of a precisely quantitative behavior theory. Piaget's work was not easily reconciled with the fashions of the period, and little was translated. Now the tide has turned, and at least a portion of Piaget's recent work is available in English, not to mention several excellent "explanations" of him by Wolff (1960), Wohlwill (1960), Hunt (1961), and especially Flavell's comprehensive volume of 1963. However, the essential continuity of development of Piaget's ideas is obscured by the discontinuity of translation. So different are the recent works from the old ones, that to read them one must master a new vocabulary and a new theoretical formulation, and this time the task is made more difficult by the heavy emphasis upon propositions of symbolic logic to explicate the developmental stages of reasoning.

To the early Piaget belonged the painstaking compilation of the forms of verbal expression according to age level from 3 years to 10 years: the demonstration that children's "explanations" of phenomena pass through *stages,* from early animistic, through magical and artificialist forms, to rational thought, and that at each level, the child constructs a systematic "cosmology" according to the modes of reasoning available to him at that stage. The empirical bases for these findings were the children's verbalizations as elicited by the *méthode clinique,* with its inherent risks of misinterpretation of what the child is trying to express. Piaget was severely and perhaps unjustly criticized on this account, for he was sharply aware of the problem. As he put it (1929),

It is so hard not to talk too much when questioning a child, especially for a pedagogue! It is so hard not to suggest! And above all, it is so hard to find the middle course between systematization due to preconceived ideas, and incoherence due to the absence of any directing hypothesis! . . . In short, it is no simple task, and the material it yields needs to be subjected to the strictest criticism [p. 8].

In retrospect, Piaget (1952a) recognizes that his method in those years was much too exclusively verbal.

I well knew that thought proceeds from action, but believed then that language directly reflects the act, and that to understand the logic of the child one has to look for it in the domain of verbal interactions. It was only by studying the patterns of intelligent behavior of *the first two years* that I learned that for a complete understanding of the genesis of intellectual operations, manipulation and experience with objects had first to be considered [p. 247].

As Piaget notes, the shift from reliance on verbalization to observation and experiment is most important for genetic epistemology because it permits one to study infants as well as the later stages of growth, and by more or less comparable methods.

The cognitive theory starts from the central postulate that motor action is the source from which mental operations emerge. The *action* of the organism is central to the acquisitions of the operations (i.e., ideas, or strategies), which we acquire for coping with the world. In the Hegelian dialectical form which his lectures often assume, Piaget contrasts his emphasis upon the active interplay of organism and environment, both with the environmentalist view in which experience or conditioning is impressed upon a passive organism, and with the nativist view that intellectual capabilities exist preformed and merely unfold in the course of development.

Motor action is *adaptive,* and so are the cognitive activities which more and more replace overt motor behavior. Piaget's biological orientation is seen in his assertion that intelligence is an adaptation, and only one aspect of biological adaptation. Intelligence is an organizing activity which extends the biological organization. With respect to intelligence, a subject to which Piaget has given much attention, it should be noted that his interest is in the typical, not in the range of variation. For him, the word "intelligence" lacks the mental-testing connotations with which it is usually invested in English, and corresponds rather to "intellect" or to intellectual activity or adaptation.

Life is a continuous creation of increasingly complex forms, and a progressive balancing of these forms with the environment [Piaget, 1952b, p. 3].

Intellectual adaptation is the progressive differentiation and integration of inborn reflex mechanisms under the impact of experience. The differentiation of inborn reflex structures and their functions give rise to the mental operations by which man conceives of objects, space, time, and causality, and of the logical relationships which constitute the basis of scientific thought [Wolff, 1960, p. 9].

Another central postulate is that intellectual operations acquired by interaction between organism and environment are acquired in a *lawful sequence*. It should be emphasized again that Piaget's concern is with elucidating the sequence, *not* with establishing exact age norms for its stages. It should also be noted that Piaget has set out to write the ontogenetic history of cognition—*not* a complete account of personality development. What lies outside the cognitive domain is rigorously excluded.

The innate equipment consists of reflexes present at birth. A few reflexes, e.g., yawning or sneezing, are relatively fixed and unmodifiable by experience, though some, like the Babinski, change with maturation. The majority of reflexes, for example, grasping, *require* stimulation for their stabilization, are modified as a result of experience, and constitute the basic behavioral units from which more complex forms of behavior emerge. Most important, the feedback from the activation of a reflex alters all subsequent performance of that reflex. Thus, behavior is simultaneously determined by: first, the inborn structure; second, past activations, i.e., experience; and third, the particular present situation.

Now corresponding to each innate reflex there is assumed to exist in the mind a reflex *schema,* which will not become a stable structure unless repeatedly activated by external stimulation. The concept of schema is difficult. It is described as a flexible mental structure, the primary unit of mental organization. It is too invested with motor connotations to translate as "idea"; and being initially innate, it can hardly be a memory trace. Yet it covers both. . . .

When a reflex responds to a suitable external stimulus, the total sensory perception *and* motor activity are incorporated into the schema of that reflex, and change it; so that when the reflex is again stimulated, the schema has been modified. The stimulus is never again experienced in quite the same way, nor is the response quite the same. Thus the schema is invoked to account for the modification of response, *and* for the alteration of perception in the course of learning. In other words, the organism experiences and reacts to the environment always in terms of an existing organization. All experiences of a particular kind are molded into the already present schema, and in turn alter it according to the reality conditions. Hence, experiences are not recorded as isolated stimulus-response connections, or engrams impressed on a passive brain field, but are integrated into a constantly changing structure.

For the dual aspects of learning, Piaget has used the terms *assimilation* and *accommodation*. He points out first that there exists a fundamental coordination or tuning of the organism to its environment. We have eyes and skin receptors preadapted for the photic and thermal radiation found on earth, ears for sensing rapid waves of pressure in earth's atmosphere, and so forth. There exists, moreover, a fundamental tendency of organisms to take in substances and stimulations for which there already exist the appropriate internal structures and organization. This taking in is called *assimilation.* At a biological level, it refers to the physical incorporation of suitable nutrients into organic structure. At a primitive psychological level, it refers to the incorporation of the sensory and motor components of a behavioral act into the reflex schema they have activated. At more complex levels, assimilation refers to the tendency of the mental apparatus to incorporate ideas into a complex system of thought schemata.

Parallel to assimilation is the function of *accommodation,* i.e., the process by which a schema *changes* so as to adapt better to the assimilated reality. At the biological level, accommodation refers to modification of the organism in response to stimulation, e.g., skin tanning in response to sunlight, or muscle growth in response to exercise. At the lowest psychological level, it refers to the gradual adaptation of the reflexes to new stimulus conditions—what others have called conditioning or stimulus generalization. At higher levels it refers to the coordination of thought patterns to one another and to external reality.

While assimilation and accommodation seem not too far from conventional learning theory, the concept of *aliment* is more unfamiliar. Whatever can be assimilated to a schema is aliment for that schema. Now the aliment is not the *object* which seems from the point of view of the observer to activate behavior, but rather those properties of the object which are assimilated and accommodated to. For example, a nursing bottle filled with milk may be organic aliment for the metabolism, sucking aliment for the reflex sucking schema, and visual aliment for the visual schema. And if the idea strikes you as bizarre that a reflex requires to be fed, as it were, by appropriate stimulation, consider Riesen's (1947) report on the degeneration of the visual apparatus in chimpanzees reared in the dark—or the more familiar degeneration of unstimulated muscles when polio destroys the motor pathways.

Why the careful distinction between an object and its properties? Because for the infant the object does not exist! The idea of an object grows gradually out of the coordination of several schemata—that which is perceived by several sensorial avenues *becomes* the object. At first, the infant has not even awareness of the boundaries of his own body. Objects in the perceptual field—including his own hands and feet—are responded to according to the infant's limited reflexive repertoire. He sucks in response to oral stimulation, grasps in response to palmar stimulation, but makes no attempt to grasp the nursing bottle which he competently sucks, or to follow visually the bottle he can clutch if placed in his hand. Only gradually, by a process called generalizing assimilation, do stimuli which were initially specific aliment for one schema become aliment for other schemata. In parallel accommodation, a schema becomes attuned to more complex inputs, and tends to become coordinated with other schemata which are simultaneously activated. When this happens, things previously known tactilely by being grasped can be recognized by sight alone. Similarly, grasping attempts of increasing accuracy can be directed toward sources of visual stimulation. In such a fashion does the baby come to populate the world with objects, one of which is his own body, which supplies him at once with visual, tactile and kinesthetic stimuli—and when he cries, with auditory ones.

However, the infant still does not attach the concept of permanence to objects. "Out of sight" is quite literally "out of mind." One of Piaget's most interesting experiments—and one which can be repeated by any parent of an infant—concerns the growth of the idea of permanent objects. If you catch a young baby's attention with a small toy, and then hide it, he will make little response. When somewhat older, he will show diffuse motor behavior. If now he once happens to touch it, he will gradually learn to search more efficiently where the object is hidden. However, if the object is hidden in a different place, in full sight of the baby, he will search not where he saw it hidden, but where previously he had touched it. It is an intellectual achievement of some magnitude when the very young child learns to coordinate the space of things seen with the space of things touched, and seeks to touch an object where hitherto he has only seen it.

We can conclude our rapid survey of Piaget's basic concepts with a brief reference to *equilibrium*. Bruner (1959), otherwise most sympathetic, regards the notion of equilibrium as excess baggage, contributing to Piaget a comforting sense of continuity with biology, but offering little else. Perhaps the idea of disequilibrium is more easily described. A schema is in disequilibrium if adaptation (i.e., assimilation and accommodation) to the stimulus is incomplete.

It seems to me that the ideas of equilibrium and disequilibrium constitute most of Piaget's theory of motivation, which is a rather underelaborated part of his psychological system. The organism has a basic need to continue contact with an object as long as adaptation to it is incomplete—or, as Piaget would say, as long as the corresponding schema is in disequilibrium. The need for commerce with an object persists until the child's behavior has been wholly adapted to whatever novelty it presents, that is to say, it persists until the child has acquired mastery. Once accommodation is complete and assimilation is total, the schema is said to be "in equilibrium," and there is no further adaptation. There is, in short, no learning without a problem.

Further, two *schemata* are in disequilibrium until they have mutually accommodated and assimilated, and thereby been integrated into a new superordinate mental structure. This tendency to integrate schemata into more and more complex wholes is assumed by Piaget to be a native propensity of the mind, and as fundamental as the tendency toward equilibrium in physical systems. To put the matter in less cosmic terms, the person strives continually for more and more comprehensive mastery of his world. At each *stage,* however, he is concerned with those things which lie just beyond his intellectual grasp—far enough away to present a novelty to be assimilated, but not so far but what accommodation is possible. Phenomena too simple—i.e., already in equilibrium—and phenomena too complex for present adaptation are ignored in favor of those in the critical range. Anyone who has ever watched the persistence, and resistance to satiation, of a baby intent on mastering a developmental task—for example, learning to walk—will agree with Piaget as to the strength of the motivation, whether or not he accepts Piaget's thermodynamic metaphor.

What then are the general *stages* of intellectual development, and how may they be characterized? Piaget's stages are one of the best known aspects of his work, but he has not been altogether consistent either in the number of them or in the names assigned. Moreover, the stages are linked to particular chronological ages only rather loosely, and

Piaget has himself offered data to show that the age at which a particular stage is reached differs for different content domains. For example, conservation (i.e., invariance under transformation) of a plastic object, such as a lump of clay, is acquired first with respect to mass, a year or so later with respect to weight, and a couple of years after that with respect to volume. Moreover, the Geneva group are concerned to demonstrate the invariance of the *sequence* of stages, not the age at which a given stage is achieved. In Martinique the children are 4 years retarded compared to those in Montreal (Laurendeau & Pinard, 1963), and certain Brazilian Indians appear never to achieve the last stage—but the sequence is everywhere the same.

When Piaget visited Berkeley, he deplored the preoccupation of American psychologists with accelerating a child's progress through the successive stages, and commented on recent work of Gruber, who found that kittens achieve awareness of the permanence of objects in 3 months, the human baby only in 9 months; but the important fact is that the cat never acquires the power to think in terms of formal logic, and the human being may!

The more recent books from Geneva usually divide development into four stages: the sensorimotor, from birth to 2 or 3 years; the preoperational stage, from around 2 to around 7 years; the stage of concrete operations, from roughly 7 years to 11 or 12; and finally the stage of formal operations. Each stage in turn has substages—no less than six for the sensorimotor period alone—which we shall not have time to describe today.

The sensorimotor period as a whole (i.e., from birth up to age 2) carries the child from inborn reflexes to acquired behavior patterns. It leads the child from a body-centered (i.e., self-centered) world to an object-centered one. During this period the various sensory spaces, of vision, touch, and the rest, are coordinated into a single space and objects evolve from their separate sensory properties into *things* with multiple properties, permanence, and spatial relationships to other objects. Altogether this stage comprises a most important set of intellectual achievements.

The preoperational stage (2 years to around 7 years) covers the important period when language is acquired. This permits the child to deal symbolically with the world instead of directly through motor activity, though his problem solving tends to be "action ridden." The child is himself still the focus of his own world, and space and time are centered on him. Time is only "before now," "now," and "not yet"; and space moves as the child moves. When he is taken for an evening walk, the moon follows *him*. Traces of this attitude

are present even in adults, who often locate places and things in terms of distance and direction from themselves, rather than in terms of objective spatial relationships. By a process of "decentering," the child during this stage learns gradually to conceive of a time scale and of a spatial world which exist independent of himself. In dealing with physical objects and quantities, the child pays attention to one aspect to the neglect of other aspects. He concludes, for example, that there is more water in a glass graduate than in a beaker—though he has just seen it poured from the one vessel into the other—because in the graduate the column of water is taller, and the child neglects the reduction in diameter.

The stage of concrete operations has its beginnings as early as age 6 or 7. Now the child grows less dependent upon his own perceptions and motor actions and shows a capacity for reasoning, though still at a very concrete level. Among his "logical" acquisitions are classifying, ordering in series, and numbering. Asked to put a handful of sticks in order by length, he need no longer make all the pair comparisons but can pick out the longest, then the longest one left, and so forth, until the series is complete. When shown that Stick A is longer than Stick B, and Stick B is longer than Stick C, he can infer without actual demonstration that A is longer than C.

Here at Berkeley, my students and I have been developing test materials based on Piaget experiments, and intended to measure the abilities of children in the primary grades, i.e., at the transition point from the perceptual attitude of the preoperational stage to the reasoning attitude of the stage of concrete operations. Thus far, fifteen tests have been developed and administered to more than 300 school children. Although we abandoned the *méthode clinique* for a strictly standardized psychometric approach, we have observed precisely the same types of behavior which Piaget had previously reported.

The last of Piaget's major stages of intellectual development begins usually somewhere around 11 or 12 years and matures a couple of years later. He calls it the stage of formal operations. Now the child can deal with abstract relationships instead of with things, with the form of an argument while ignoring its content. For the first time he can intellectually manipulate the merely hypothetical, and systematically evaluate a lengthy set of alternatives. He learns to handle the logical relationships of Identity (I), Negation (N), Reciprocity (R), and Correlation (C), which permit him to deal with problems of proportionality, probability, permutations, and combinations.

I have just referred to the INRC logical group whose acquisition marks the last stage of intellectual growth. In Piaget's writings over the years, the characteristics of each stage and the differences between them have increasingly been formulated in the notation of symbolic logic—a circumstance which does not increase the comprehensibility of his latest books for nonmathematicians.

Nevertheless, this transition to the language of formal logic is of profound importance for Piaget's theory because it provides a set of explicit, mathematical models for cognitive structure, and serves as a vehicle to describe in a unified way the findings of experiments very different in content. The unity and economy of the logical theory as contrasted with his earlier multiplicity of explanatory terms—egocentrism, syncretism, animism, realism, etc.—is obvious. However, Piaget's critics have sometimes found the mathematical formulation strained, and have accused Piaget of distorting intellectual development to force it into the categories of formal logic.

Piaget's point of view may have been misunderstood. As he phrases it (1957),

The aim is . . . to study the application of logical techniques to the psychological facts themselves. . . . The question whether the structures and operations of logic correspond to anything in our actual thought, and whether the latter conforms to logical laws, is still an open one. . . . On the other hand, the algebra of logic can help us to specify psychological structures, and put into calculus form those operations and structures central to our thought processes. . . . The psychologist welcomes the qualitative character of logic since it facilitates the analyses of the actual structures underlying intellectual operations, as contrasted with the quantitative treatment of their behavioral outcome. Most "tests" of intelligence measure the latter, but our real problem is to discover the actual operational mechanisms which govern such behavior, and not simply to measure it [pp. xvii–xviii].

Many psychologists who acknowledge the brilliant originality of many of Piaget's experiments, and the enormous importance of his empirical contribution taken as a whole, continue nevertheless to reject the formal, mathematical theory which lies closest to Piaget's heart. Yet one of the most impressive parts of Piaget's discussions here in Berkeley concerned the isomorphism between his stages and the most basic structure of mathematics itself.

Piaget points out that if one considers not the content, but the architecture, as it were, of the various branches of mathematics, one discovers first a level where the prototype structure is the group and the type of reversibility is inversion or negation. Next comes a level where structures of order, such as the lattice, are typical, and reversibility is not inversion but reciprocity. Last comes the level of topology with key concepts of neighborhood, boundary, etc. Now the first of these three levels is the oldest, one part of it, Euclidean geometry, going back to the Greeks. The second level, typified by projective geometry, dates from the late seventeenth century; and the last, or topological, level is a product only of the nineteenth century. Taken in sequence, each level is more general, i.e., involves *fewer* axioms than the preceding, and the entire sequence might theoretically be expected to have developed in the opposite order. Now the curious part, is that the sequence of acquisition of mental operations by children follows not the historical sequence, but the theoretical sequence. Small children of 3 years of age, who for example are quite unable even to copy a simple geometrical figure such as a square, have no difficulty differentiating between a closed figure like a circle and an open one like a cross, and they can easily follow instructions in putting a second circle, however imperfectly drawn, inside, or outside, or even half in and half out of the experimenter's circle. Further evidence of young children's grasp of topological principles is seen in their sure knowledge of the forms into which a sphere, such as a balloon, can be deformed—i.e., sausagelike, flat sided, or dimpled figures, etc.— and those forms such as the torus or doughnut, which cannot be obtained by deformation of a sphere. Later, with the shift from the preoperational stage to the stage of concrete operations at age 6 or 7, the child learns to handle relations of order— seriation, transitivity, reciprocal relationships, and the rest to which I have already referred. Only with the approach of adolescence does he spontaneously utilize the propositional algebraic structures which are the oldest development in the history of mathematics.

What finally are the implications of Piaget's work for fields other than psychology and mathematics? Certainly they have a major bearing upon education.

If Piaget is correct—and much work now substantiates his empirical findings at least in broad outline—methods of education will be most effective when they are attuned to the patterns of thought which are natural to a child of the age concerned. It may not be true that you can teach a child *anything* if your approach is correct, but it does look as if you can teach him a great deal more than anyone might have guessed. Of course, teachers long before Piaget recognized intuitively that a child learned better when problems were approached at a concrete rather than at an abstract level. But there is more to it than that. Bruner, at Harvard, and others in this country are attempting to find ways to introduce children to some of the abstract ideas of mathematics—for example, the algebraic concept of squaring a number—by concrete, geometric models. They hope thus possibly to accelerate a child's progress—a goal which Piaget has his reservations about. Perhaps the most dramatic evidence of a revolution which owes a great deal of its impetus to Piaget is the new elementary school mathematics, in which children even in the lower grades are being taught, and learning, and actually enjoying learning basic arithmetical and geometrical ideas introduced via set theory, which most of their parents have never heard of.

I could not better conclude this appreciation of Piaget than by quoting from William James (1890) who wrote 75 years ago in his famous *Principles of Psychology* as follows: "To the infant, sounds, sights, touches and pains form probably one unanalyzed bloom of confusion [p. 496]." We can now go beyond the philosopher's speculations and describe in some detail how the unanalyzed "bloom of confusion" of the infant becomes the world of the child—in which not only objects, but time, space, causality and the rest acquire a coherent organization. And we owe this achievement in large measure to the analyses of Jean Piaget.

REFERENCES

BRUNER, J. S. Inhelder and Piaget's *The growth of logical thinking*. I. A psychologist's viewpoint. *British Journal of Psychology*, 1959, *50*, 363–370.

FLAVELL, J. H. Historical and bibliographic note. In W. Kessen & Clementina Kuhlman (Eds.), Thought in the young child. *Monographs of the Society for Research in Child Development*, 1962, *27*(2, Whole No. 83).

FLAVELL, J. H. *The developmental psychology of Jean Piaget*. Princeton, N.J.: Van Nostrand, 1963.

HUNT, J. McV. *Intelligence and experience*. New York: Ronald Press, 1961.

JAMES, W. *The principles of psychology*. New York: Holt, 1890.

KOCH, S. (Ed.) *Psychology: A study of a science*. Vol. 3. *Formulations of the person and the social context*. New York: McGraw-Hill, 1959.

LAURENDEAU, MONIQUE, & PINARD, A. *Causal thinking in the child, a genetic and experimental approach*. New York: International Universities Press, 1963.

PIAGET, J. *The child's conception of the world*. New York: Harcourt, Brace, 1929.

PIAGET, J. Autobiography. In E. G. Boring (Ed.), *A history of psychology in autobiography*. Vol. 4. Worcester, Mass.: Clark Univer. Press, 1952. (a)

PIAGET, J. *The origins of intelligence in children*. (2nd ed.) New York: International Universities Press, 1952. (b)

PIAGET, J. *Logic and psychology*. New York: Basic Books, 1957.

RIESEN, A. H. The development of visual perception in man and chimpanzee. *Science*, 1947, *106*, 107–108.

WOHLWILL, J. F. Developmental studies of perception. *Psychological Bulletin*, 1960, *57*, 249–288.

WOHLWILL, J. F. From perception to inference: A dimension of cognitive development. In W. Kessen and Clementina Kuhlman (Eds.), Thought in the young child. *Monographs of the Society for Research in Child Development*, 1962, *27*(2, Whole No. 83).

WOLFF, P. H. The developmental psychologies of Jean Piaget and psychoanalysis. *Psychological Issues*, 1960, *2*(1, Whole No. 5).

VIII

SEX AS A DETERMINANT OF BEHAVIOR

Under many conditions, knowing a person's gender is important if one wishes to predict how he or she will behave. As an explanatory concept, sex or gender is (and has been) the center of considerable controversy. Are behavioral sex differences rooted in the contrasting biological make-up of males and females? Are they determined by differences in the ways boys and girls are taught to act in conformity with the role ascribed to each sex, as culturally prescribed or as viewed by the particular parents?

Anthropologists have contributed some answers. The contrasts between males and females observed in certain societies are different from the contrasts in others. By providing us with knowledge of the range of behaviors adopted by each of the sexes in various cultures, anthropologists have shown us that certain behaviors are clearly not determined by biological sex. The work of Margaret Mead on this topic is particularly well known (e.g. *Male and Female,* Morrow, 1949).

The differences between the sexes are not to be found solely in the biological aspects of anatomy and reproductive functions. M. F. Ashley Montagu has said that "females are more durable and males more unendurable." The female appears to be biologically sounder than the male at every stage, and can expect to outlive the male. Although more males are conceived than females, more males are lost in spontaneous abortion or miscarriage, and in neonatal and infant deaths. In the living of life, males appear to have more problems. Reading disabilities are more frequent among males, as are at least certain types of emotional disturbances (according to some data in our society). The second part of Montagu's statement refers to the fact that differences in activity level and metabolic rates may contribute to making the male more assertive, more difficult to live with—more "unendurable."

Once we leave the area of biological viability, all differences in behavior between the sexes are due to the action of experience on the genetic substrate. One should note that even genetically there are not just two separate populations (male and female) in the world. The genetic anomalies of the sex chromosomes provide numerous combinations, or "sexes."[1] However, the behavioral effects of the genetic anomalies are poorly understood, though behavioral gender roles seem to be determined primarily by child rearing.

The anthropological evidence that many or perhaps most sex differences other than anatomical are learned has led some psychologists to act as though sex differences did not really exist—that is, as if they were not "real," *only* learned. Researchers even formed their samples by including males and females together as though sex would not affect the results. At present, interest in sex differences has come in for a revival. One reason for this is the fact that research data analyzed separately for the two sexes have frequently revealed that girls and boys responded to the experimental conditions disparately or even in opposite directions.

At the 1961 meeting of the American Psychological Association, Dorothy

---

[1] See Section II, Article 7, for further discussion relevant to this topic.

Eichorn, on the basis of some of her work, commented: "If you want to predict the behavior of a male, you must know the male. If you want to predict the behavior of a female, you must know the situation." This statement implies not only that there are differences between males and females, but that male behavior and female behavior must be explained or predicted by different theories. Such a statement does not prejudge whether the differences exist because of biology or because of the interaction of our culture with biological factors. Indeed, any time we use classifications such as sex and race, which appear to be biologically based, or such as "first-born," which appears to reflect experiential differences, we lose a great deal of information that might help us understand or predict behavior. We would always improve our prediction if we knew an individual's personal characteristics, not just which group he belonged to. However, when we have access to no other information, knowledge of membership in such groups may be helpful in predicting behavior.

One must carefully distinguish between using classifications like race, sex, or birth order as an aid in scientific understanding and using them to assign individuals to one treatment or another. This is especially true when the treatment affects opportunities for schooling or jobs. The values of democracy call for equal opportunity for each sex. Even if it should turn out that one kind of educational milieu would be better, on the average, for males and another for females, children should be assigned to educational programs on the basis of their individual characteristics, not just because they happen to be members of a particular biological or social group. This point is not only relevant for sex or race, which are biologically defined groups, but for groups defined by age, birth position in the family, or social class. Age is an imperfect way of defining readiness for school (or readiness for retirement). While position in the family, or birth order, is not an important basis for discrimination in the United States today, some Western cultural groups of the past have accorded great favoritism (in terms of education and inheritance) to the first-born son, regardless of his individual merits or characteristics. Such practices still exist in some parts of the world and to some degree in Western cultures.

Sex differences, conceived of as a product of both biological attributes and learning, may be created or molded in a variety of ways:

1. Certain behaviors are often reinforced more in one sex than in the other.
2. Interpersonal experiences are frequently different according to one's sex.
3. Individuals may belong to groups that have members of only one sex and that mold their behavior accordingly.

To recapitulate, *sex* as an explanatory concept can be *biological* (Section II), or it can be an intermediate variable in such explanatory systems as those stressing *learning* (Section III), *interpersonal experiences* (Section IV), *settings and instigations* (Section V), or *group memberships* (Section VI). From whichever of these standpoints one conceives of sex as a variable in determining behavior, it may also play a role in relation to the other determinants considered in this book (e.g., cognitive and motivational). In most sections, some papers have analyzed or discussed their research data in terms of each sex separately. Some have limited their studies to subjects of only one sex. Such a decision may have been dictated by theoretical or practical concerns. Some theoretical issues are best investigated in one sex only. Discrepant findings for the two sexes may be difficult to deal with in theoretical terms, or the money may be lacking to permit study of a sample large enough to be analyzed for each sex separately.

For those students interested in pursuing this topic in greater depth, we recommend the following sources (listed alphabetically):

1. Daniel G. Brown, "Sex Role Development in a Changing Culture," *Psychological Bulletin,* 1958, *55,* 232–242 (or in either previous edition of this book).
2. Josef E. Garai and Amram Scheinfeld, "Sex Differences in Mental and Behavioral Traits," *Genetic Psychology Monographs,* 1968, *77,* 169–299.
3. David B. Lynn, *Parental and Sex Role Identification* (McCutcheon, 1969). This small book incorporates materials from a number of his articles.
4. John Money, "Developmental Differentiation of Femininity and Masculinity Compared," in *Potential of Women,* edited by S. M. Farber and R. H. L. Wilson (McGraw-Hill, 1963).
5. Paul Mussen and Eldred Rutherford, "Parent-Child Relations and Parental Personality in Relation to Young Children's Sex Role Preferences," *Child Development,* 1963, *34,* 589–607 (and in the second edition of *The Causes of Behavior,* 1966).
6. Robert R. Sears, "Development of Gender Role" in *Sex and Behavior,* edited by Frank A. Beach (Wiley, 1965).

In addition, numerous references will be found in the bibliographies of the various articles in this section.

50

A Cross-cultural Survey
of Some Sex Differences
in Socialization [1]

HERBERT BARRY III,
MARGARET K. BACON,
AND IRVIN L. CHILD

This article gives some cross-cultural perspective on the socialization practices for the two sexes. It thus exemplifies the type of anthropological contribution referred to in the introduction to this section. The paper is based on materials from the Human Relations Area Files developed at Yale University, where the authors were located. The files, copies of which now exist at various universities, contain information about the living practices of human beings in societies around the globe. They are an important source of data for testing hypotheses in psychology and child development, as well as in anthropology.

The survey shows that there are common elements across societies in how the sexes are differentiated. These findings could be used to bolster the idea that biology dictates the communalities. However, the data also show that there are exceptions, thus highlighting the role of cultural determinism. The authors' analysis indicates that the needs of a society or culture influence the variations. This is congruent with the relatively small sex differentiation in our own society. The fact that the differentiation made between maleness and femaleness is less in the United States (and in modern or technological cultures generally) than in many other cultures does not mean that there is an absence in the U.S. of discrimination based on sex.

Barry, a psychologist interested in psychopharmacology as well as cross-cultural research, has a research appointment in the School of Pharmacy at the University of Pittsburgh. Bacon is in the Department of Anthropology at Livingston College of Rutgers University. Child is professor of psychology at Yale University.

In our society, certain differences may be observed between the typical personality characteristics of the two sexes. These sex differences in personality are generally believed to result in part from differences in the way boys and girls are reared. To the extent that personality differences between the sexes are thus of cultural rather than biological origin, they seem potentially susceptible to change. But how readily susceptible to change? In the differential rearing of the sexes does our society make an arbitrary imposition on an infinitely plastic biological base, or is this cultural imposition found uniformly in all societies as an adjustment to the real biological differences between the sexes? This paper reports one attempt to deal with this problem.

DATA AND PROCEDURES

The data used were ethnographic reports, available in the anthropological literature, about socialization practices of various cultures. One hundred and ten cultures, mostly nonliterate, were studied.[2] They were selected primarily in terms of the existence of adequate ethnographic reports of socialization practices and secondarily so as to obtain a wide and reasonably balanced geographical distribution. Various aspects of socialization of infants and children were rated on a 7-point scale by two judges (Mrs. Bacon and Mr. Barry). Where the ethnographic reports permitted, separate ratings were made for the socialization of boys and girls. Each rating was indicated as either confident or doubtful; with still greater uncertainty, or with

[1] This research is part of a project for which financial support was provided by the Social Science Research Council and the Ford Foundation. We are greatly indebted to G. P. Murdock for supplying us with certain data, as indicated below, and to him and Thomas W. Maretzki for suggestions that have been used in this paper.

[2] Most of the societies we used are listed by name in H. Barry III, I. L. Child, and M. K. Bacon, Relation of child training to subsistence economy, *American Anthropologist*, 1959, *61*, 51–63.

Herbert Barry III, Margaret K. Bacon, and Irvin L. Child, "A cross-cultural survey of some sex differences in socialization," *Journal of Abnormal and Social Psychology*, 1957, 55, 327–332. Reprinted by permission.

complete lack of evidence, the particular rating was of course not made at all. We shall restrict the report of sex difference ratings to cases in which both judges made a confident rating. Also omitted is the one instance where the two judges reported a sex difference in opposite directions, as it demonstrates only unreliability of judgment. The number of cultures that meet these criteria is much smaller than the total of 110; for the several variables to be considered, the number varies from 31 to 84.

The aspects of socialization on which ratings were made included:

1. Several criteria of attention and indulgence toward infants.
2. Strength of socialization from age 4 to 5 years until shortly before puberty, with respect to five systems of behavior; strength of socialization was defined as the combination of positive pressure (rewards for the behavior) plus negative pressure (punishments for lack of the behavior). The variables were:

    (a) Responsibility or dutifulness training. (The data were such that training in the performance of chores in the productive or domestic economy was necessarily the principal source of information here; however, training in the performance of other duties was also taken into account when information was available.)
    (b) Nurturance training, i.e., training the child to be nurturant or helpful toward younger siblings and other dependent people.
    (c) Obedience training.
    (d) Self-reliance training.
    (e) Achievement training, i.e., training the child to orient his behavior toward standards of excellence in performance, and to seek to achieve as excellent a performance as possible.

Where the term "no sex difference" is used here, it may mean any of three things: (a) the judge found separate evidence about the training of boys and girls on this particular variable, and judged it to be identical; (b) the judge found a difference between the training of boys and girls, but not great enough for the sexes to be rated a whole point apart on a 7-point scale; (c) the judge found evidence only about the training of "children" on this variable, the ethnographer not reporting separately about boys and girls.

SEX DIFFERENCES IN SOCIALIZATION

On the various aspects of attention and indulgence toward infants, the judges almost always agreed in finding no sex difference. Out of 96 cultures for which the ratings included the infancy period, 88 (92%) were rated with no sex difference by either judge for any of those variables. This result is consistent with the point sometimes made by anthropologists that "baby" generally is a single status undifferentiated by sex, even though "boy" and "girl" are distinct statuses.

On the variables of childhood socialization, on the other hand, a rating of no sex difference by both judges was much less common. This finding of no sex difference varied in frequency from 10% of the cultures for the achievement variable up to 62% of the cultures for the obedience variable, as shown in the last column of Table 1. Where a sex difference is reported, by either one or both judges, the difference tends strongly to be in a particular direction, as shown in the earlier columns of the same table. Pressure toward nurturance, obedience, and responsibility is most often stronger for girls, whereas pressure toward achievement and self-reliance is most often stronger for boys.

For nurturance and for self-reliance, all the sex differences are in the same direction. For achievement there is only one exception to the usual direction of difference, and for obedience only two; but for responsibility there are nine. What do these exceptions mean? We have reexamined all these cases. In most of them, only one judge had rated the sexes as differently treated (sometimes one judge, sometimes the other), and in the majority of these cases both judges were now inclined to agree that there was no convincing evidence of a real difference. There were exceptions, however, especially in cases where a more formal or systematic training of boys seemed to imply greater pressure

TABLE 1
RATINGS OF CULTURES FOR SEX DIFFERENCES OF FIVE VARIABLES OF CHILDHOOD SOCIALIZATION PRESSURE

Variable	Number of Cultures	Both Judges Agree in Rating the Variable Higher in		One Judge Rates No Difference, One Rates the Variable Higher in		Percentage of Cultures with Evidence of Sex Difference in Direction of		
		Girls	Boys	Girls	Boys	Girls	Boys	Neither
Nurturance	33	17	0	10	0	82%	0%	18%
Obedience	69	6	0	18	2	35%	3%	62%
Responsibility	84	25	2	26	7	61%	11%	28%
Achievement	31	0	17	1	10	3%	87%	10%
Self-reliance	82	0	64	0	6	0%	85%	15%

on them toward responsibility. The most convincing cases were the Masai and Swazi, where both judges had originally agreed in rating responsibility pressures greater in boys than in girls. In comparing the five aspects of socialization we may conclude that responsibility shows by far the strongest evidence of real variation in the direction of sex difference, and obedience much the most frequently shows evidence of no sex difference at all.

In subsequent discussion we shall be assuming that the obtained sex differences in the socialization ratings reflect true sex differences in the cultural practices. We should consider here two other possible sources of these rated differences.

1. The ethnographers could have been biased in favor of seeing the same pattern of sex differences as in our culture. However, most anthropologists readily perceive and eagerly report novel and startling cultural features, so we may expect them to have reported unusual sex differences where they existed. The distinction between matrilineal and patrilineal, and between matrilocal and patrilocal cultures, given prominence in many ethnographic reports, shows an awareness of possible variations in the significance of sex differences from culture to culture.

2. The two judges could have expected to find in other cultures the sex roles which are familiar in our culture and inferred them from the material on the cultures. However, we have reported only confident ratings, and such a bias seems less likely here than for doubtful ratings. It might be argued, moreover, that bias has more opportunity in the case ambiguous enough so that only one judge reported a sex difference, and less opportunity in the cases where the evidence is so clear that both judges agree. Yet in general, as may be seen in Table 1, the deviant cases are somewhat more frequent among the cultures where only one judge reported a sex difference.

The observed differences in the socialization of boys and girls are consistent with certain universal tendencies in the differentiation of adult sex role. In the economic sphere, men are more frequently allotted tasks that involve leaving home and engaging in activities where a high level of skill yields important returns; hunting is a prime example. Emphasis on training in self-reliance and achievement for boys would function as preparation for such an economic role. Women, on the other hand, are more frequently allotted tasks at or near home that minister most immediately to the needs of others (such as cooking and water carrying); these activities have a nurturant character, and in their pursuit a responsible carrying out of established routines is likely to be more important than the development of an especially high order of skill.

Thus training in nurturance, responsibility, and, less clearly, obedience, may contribute to preparation for this economic role. These consistencies with adult role go beyond the economic sphere, of course. Participation in warfare, as a male prerogative, calls for self-reliance and a high order of skill where survival or death is the immediate issue. The childbearing which is biologically assigned to women, and the child care which is socially assigned primarily to them, lead to nurturant behavior and often call for a more continuous responsibility than do the tasks carried out by men. Most of these distinctions in adult role are not inevitable, but the biological differences between the sexes strongly predispose the distinction of role, if made, to be in a uniform direction.[3]

The relevant biological sex differences are conspicuous in adulthood but generally not in childhood. If each generation were left entirely to its own devices, therefore, without even an older generation to copy, sex differences in role would presumably be almost absent in childhood and would have to be developed after puberty at the expense of considerable relearning on the part of one or both sexes. Hence, a pattern of child training which foreshadows adult differences can serve the useful function of minimizing what Benedict termed "discontinuities in cultural conditioning" (1).

The differences in socialization between the sexes in our society, then, are no arbitrary custom of our society, but a very widespread adaptation of culture to the biological substratum of human life.

VARIATIONS IN DEGREE OF SEX DIFFERENTIATION

While demonstrating near-universal tendencies in direction of difference between the socialization of boys and girls, our data do not show perfect uniformity. A study of the variations in our data may allow us to see some of the conditions which are associated with, and perhaps give rise to, a greater or smaller degree of this difference. For this purpose, we classified cultures as having relatively large or small sex difference by two different methods, one more inclusive and the other more selective. In both methods the ratings were at first considered separately for each of the five variables. A sex difference rating was made only if both judges made a rating on this variable and at least one judge's rating was confident.

In the more inclusive method the ratings were

---

[3] For data and interpretations supporting various arguments of this paragraph, see Mead (2), Murdock (3), and Scheinfeld (6).

dichotomized, separately for each variable, as close as possible to the median into those showing a large and those showing a small sex difference. Thus, for each society a large or a small sex difference was recorded for each of the five variables on which a sex difference rating was available. A society was given an over-all classification of large or small sex difference if it had a sex difference rating on at least three variables and if a majority of these ratings agreed in being large, or agreed in being small. This method permitted classification of a large number of cultures, but the grounds for classification were capricious in many cases, as a difference of only one point in the rating of a single variable might change the over-all classification of sex difference for a culture from large to small.

In the more selective method, we again began by dichotomizing each variable as close as possible to the median; but a society was now classified as having a large or small sex difference on the variable only if it was at least one step away from the scores immediately adjacent to the median. Thus only the more decisive ratings of sex difference were used. A culture was classified as having an over-all large or small sex difference only if it was given a sex difference rating which met this criterion on at least two variables, and only if all such ratings agreed in being large, or agreed in being small.

We then tested the relation of each of these dichotomies to 24 aspects of culture on which Murdock has categorized the customs of most of these societies [4] and which seemed of possible significance for sex differentiation. The aspects of culture covered include type of economy, residence pattern, marriage and incest rules, political integration, and social organization. For each aspect of culture, we grouped Murdock's categories to make a dichotomous contrast (sometimes omitting certain categories as irrelevant to the contrast). In the case of some aspects of culture, two or more separate contrasts were made (e.g., under form of marriage we contrasted monogamy with polygyny, and also contrasted sororal with nonsororal polygyny). For each of 40 comparisons thus formed, we prepared a 2×2 frequency table to determine relation to each of our sex-difference dichotomies. A significant relation was found for six of these 40 aspects of culture with the more selective dichotomization of overall sex difference. In four of these comparisons, the relation to the more inclusive dichotomization was also significant. These relationships are all given in Table 2, in the form of phi

[4] These data were supplied to us directly by Professor Murdock.

TABLE 2
CULTURE VARIABLES CORRELATED WITH LARGE SEX DIFFERENCES IN SOCIALIZATION, SEPARATELY FOR TWO TYPES OF SAMPLE

Variable	More Selective Sample		More Inclusive Sample	
	ϕ	N	ϕ	N
Large animals are hunted	.48*	(34)	.28*	(72)
Grain rather than root crops are grown	.82**	(20)	.62*	(43)
Large or milking animals rather than small animals are kept	.65*	(19)	.43*	(35)
Fishing unimportant or absent	.42*	(31)	.19	(69)
Nomadic rather than sedentary residence	.61**	(34)	.15	(71)
Polygyny rather than monogamy	.51*	(28)	.38**	(64)

* $p < .05$.
** $p < .01$.
Note.—The variables have been so phrased that all correlations are positive. The phi coefficient is shown, and in parentheses, the number of cases on which the comparison was based. Significance level was determined by x^2, or Fisher's exact test where applicable, using in all cases a two-tailed test.

coefficients, along with the outcome of testing significance by the use of x^2 or Fisher's exact test. In trying to interpret these findings, we have also considered the nonsignificant correlations with other variables, looking for consistency and inconsistency with the general implications of the significant findings. We have arrived at the following formulation of results:

1. Large sex difference in socialization is associated with an economy that places a high premium on the superior strength, and superior development of motor skills requiring strength, which characterize the male. Four of the correlations reported in Table 2 clearly point to this generalization: the correlations of large sex difference with the hunting of large animals, with grain rather than root crops, with the keeping of large rather than small domestic animals, and with nomadic rather than sedentary residence. The correlation with the unimportance of fishing may also be consistent with this generalization, but the argument is not clear.[5] Other cor-

[5] Looking (with the more inclusive sample) into the possibility that this correlation might result from the correlation between fishing and sedentary residence, a complicated interaction between these variables was found. The correlation of sex differentiation with absence of fishing is found only in nomadic societies, where fishing is likely to involve cooperative activity of the two sexes, and its absence is likely to mean dependence upon the male for large game hunting or herding large animals (whereas in sedentary societies the alternatives to fishing do not so uniformly require special emphasis on male strength). The correlation of sex differentiation with nomadism is found only in nonfishing societies; here nomadism is likely to imply large game hunting or herding large animals, whereas in fishing

relations consistent with the generalization, though not statistically significant, are with large game hunting rather than gathering, with the hunting of large game rather than small game, and with the general importance of all hunting and gathering.

2. Large sex difference in socialization appears to be correlated with customs that make for a large family group with high cooperative interaction. The only statistically significant correlation relevant here is that with polygyny rather than monogamy. This generalization is, however, supported by several substantial correlations that fall only a little short of being statistically significant. One of these is a correlation with sororal rather than nonsororal polygyny; Murdock and Whiting (4) have presented indirect evidence that co-wives generally show smoother cooperative interaction if they are sisters. Correlations are also found with the presence of either an extended or a polygynous family rather than the nuclear family only; with the presence of an extended family; and with the extreme contrast between maximal extension and no extension of the family. The generalization is also to some extent supported by small correlations with wide extension of incest taboos, if we may presume that an incest taboo makes for effective unthreatening cooperation within the extended family. The only possible exception to this generalization, among substantial correlations, is a near-significant correlation with an extended or polygynous family's occupying a cluster of dwellings rather than a single dwelling.[6]

In seeking to understand this second generalization, we feel that the degree of social isolation of the nuclear family may perhaps be the crucial underlying variable. To the extent that the nuclear family must stand alone, the man must be prepared to take the woman's role when she is absent or incapaci-

tated, and vice versa. Thus the sex differentiation cannot afford to be too great. But to the extent that the nuclear family is steadily interdependent with other nuclear families, the female role in the household economy can be temporarily taken over by another woman, or the male role by another man, so that sharp differentiation of sex role is no handicap.

The first generalization, which concerns the economy, cannot be viewed as dealing with material completely independent of the ratings of socialization. The training of children in their economic role was often an important part of the data used in rating socialization variables, and would naturally vary according to the general economy of the society. We would stress, however, that we were by no means using the identical data on the two sides of our comparison; we were on the one hand judging data on the socialization of children and on the other hand using Murdock's judgments on the economy of the adult culture. In the case of the second generalization, it seems to us that there was little opportunity for information on family and social structure to have influenced the judges in making the socialization ratings.

Both of these generalizations contribute to understanding the social background of the relatively small difference in socialization of boys and girls which we believe characterizes our society at the present time. Our mechanized economy is perhaps less dependent than any previous economy upon the superior average strength of the male. The nuclear family in our society is often so isolated that husband and wife must each be prepared at times to take over or help in the household tasks normally assigned to the other. It is also significant that the conditions favoring low sex differentiation appear to be more characteristic of the upper segments of our society, in socioeconomic and educational status, than of lower segments. This observation may be relevant to the tendency toward smaller sex differences in personality in higher status groups (cf. Terman and Miles, 8).

The increase in our society of conditions favoring small sex difference has led some people to advocate a virtual elimination of sex differences in socialization. This course seems likely to be dysfunctional even in our society. Parsons, Bales, *et al.* (5) argue that a differentiation of role similar to the universal pattern of sex difference is an important and perhaps inevitable development in any social group, such as the nuclear family. If we add to their argument the point that biological differences between the sexes make most appropriate the usual division of those roles between the sexes, we have compelling reasons to expect that the decrease in differentiation of adult sex role will not

societies nomadism evidently implies no such special dependence upon male strength. Maximum sex differentiation is found in nomadic nonfishing societies (15 with large difference and only 2 with small) and minimum sex differentiation in nomadic fishing societies (2 with large difference and 7 with small difference). These findings further strengthen the argument for a conspicuous influence of the economy upon sex differentiation.

[6] We think the reverse of this correlation would be more consistent with our generalization here. But perhaps it may reasonably be argued that the various nuclear families composing an extended or polygynous family are less likely to develop antagonisms which hinder cooperation if they are able to maintain some physical separation. On the other hand, this variable may be more relevant to the first generalization than to the second. Occupation of a cluster of dwellings is highly correlated with presence of herding and with herding of large rather than small animals, and these economic variables in turn are correlated with large sex difference in socialization. Occupation of a cluster of dwellings is also correlated with polygyny rather than monogamy and shows no correlation with sororal vs. nonsororal polygyny.

continue to the vanishing point. In our training of children, there may now be less differentiation in sex role than characterizes adult life—so little, indeed, as to provide inadequate preparation for adulthood. This state of affairs is likely to be especially true of formal education, which is more subject to conscious influence by an ideology than is informal socialization at home. With child training being more oriented toward the male than the female role in adulthood, many of the adjustment problems of women in our society today may be partly traced to conflicts growing out of inadequate childhood preparation for their adult role. This argument is nicely supported in extreme form by Spiro's analysis of sex roles in an Israeli kibbutz (7). The ideology of the founders of the kibbutz included the objective of greatly reducing differences in sex role. But the economy of the kibbutz is a largely nonmechanized one in which the superior average strength of men is badly needed in many jobs. The result is that, despite the ideology and many attempts to implement it, women continue to be assigned primarily to traditional "women's work," and the incompatibility between upbringing or ideology and adult role is an important source of conflict for women.

NOTE ON REGIONAL DISTRIBUTION

There is marked variation among regions of the world in typical size of sex difference in socialization. In our sample, societies in North America and Africa tend to have large sex difference and societies in Oceania to have small sex difference. Less confidently, because of the smaller number of cases, we can report a tendency toward small sex differences in Asia and South America as well. Since most of the variables with which we find the sex difference to be significantly correlated have a similar regional distribution, the question arises whether the correlations might better be ascribed to some quite different source having to do with large regional similarities, rather than to the functional dependence we have suggested. As a partial check, we have tried to determine whether the correlations we report in Table 2 tend also to be found strictly within regions. For each of the three regions for which we have sizable samples (North America, Africa, and Oceania) we have separately plotted 2 x 2 tables corresponding to each of the 6 relationships reported in Table 2. (We did this only for the more inclusive sample, since for the more selective sample the number of cases within a region would have been extremely

small.) Out of the 18 correlations thus determined, 11 are positive and only 3 are negative (the other 4 being exactly zero). This result clearly suggests a general tendency for these correlations to hold true within regions as well as between regions, and may lend further support to our functional interpretation.

SUMMARY

A survey of certain aspects of socialization in 110 cultures shows that differentiation of the sexes is unimportant in infancy, but that in childhood there is, as in our society, a widespread pattern of greater pressure toward nurturance, obedience, and responsibility in girls, and toward self-reliance and achievement striving in boys. There are a few reversals of sex difference, and many instances of no detectable sex difference; these facts tend to confirm the cultural rather than directly biological nature of the differences. Cultures vary in the degree to which these differentiations are made; correlational analysis suggests some of the social conditions influencing these variations, and helps in understanding why our society has relatively small sex differentiation.

REFERENCES

1. BENEDICT, RUTH. Continuities and discontinuities in cultural conditioning. *Psychiatry,* 1938, *1,* 161–167.

2. MEAD, MARGARET. *Male and female.* New York: Morrow, 1949.

3. MURDOCK, G. P. Comparative data on the division of labor by sex. *Social Forces,* 1937, *15,* 551–553.

4. MURDOCK G. P., and WHITING, J. W. M. Cultural determination of parental attitudes. The relationship between the social structure, particular family structure and parental behavior. In M. J. E. Senn (Ed.), *Problems of infancy and childhood: Transactions of the Fourth Conference,* March 6–7, 1950. New York: Josiah Macy, Jr. Foundation, 1951. Pp. 13–34.

5. PARSONS, T., BALES, R. F., *et al. Family, socialization and interaction process.* Glencoe, Ill.: Free Press, 1955.

6. SCHEINFELD, A. *Women and men.* New York: Harcourt, Brace, 1944.

7. SPIRO, M. E. *Kibbutz: Venture in Utopia.* Cambridge: Harvard Univer. Press, 1956.

8. TERMAN, L. M., and MILES, CATHERINE C. *Sex and personality.* New York: McGraw-Hill, 1936.

51

On the Meaning of Behavior:
Illustrations
from the Infant

Jerome Kagan

This paper raises methodological, or even philosophical, issues that are crucial to an understanding of most of the articles in this book.

One often forgets that a given behavior may have many different meanings. The author deals with this and other important general points in the context of specific data. He considers changes in the meaning of certain behaviors (visual fixation and vocalization) that depend on the age or sex of the infant. We have chosen to put the paper in this section rather than in Section VII because we feel that the points raised apply to sex as a determinant of behavior more than to age. Meanings of behaviors are also considered in relation to the social class of the infants, so that a portion of the paper is relevant to Section VI.

Professor Kagan is a leading figure in child psychology. He has been at Harvard University since 1964, after some years at the Fels Research Institute.

Psychology's assigned responsibility in the scientific academy is to understand the relations among events, behaviors, and internal psychological structures. The laws that link psychological structures to stimulus events, on the one hand, and to behaviors, on the other, seem to be of preferential importance, and modern biology may provide useful analogies as we search for the form of these laws. Specifically, the problems inherent in the relation of genetic structure to manifest characteristics (the genotype-phenotype relation) are remarkably similar to the problems inherent in the relation between psychological structures and overt behaviors. Consider two central principles from modern genetics as illustrations.

The first principle states that phenotypes resist change and remain constant despite changes in genotype (Mayr 1966). The experimental proof of this principle is contained in the observation that the distribution of phenotypes for a particular trait in the F_1 generation does not always reveal the true genetic structure of each offspring. Analogously, the pattern of overt responses remains similar despite changes in internal structure. A newly acquired idea does not typically change the overt action of the individual, and powerful probes are required to reveal the presence of new acquisitions.

A second genetic principle states that there is a greater potential for variability in the genotype than in the phenotype (Mayr 1966). There are, for example, a limited number of visible hues that a given flower can exhibit, but a much larger number of different biochemical structures, each of which results in the same hue. It is estimated that man's approximately 150,000 genes permit a potential variety of 6.4×10^{13} different genotypes but actually produce a far smaller number of phenotypically different individuals. Analogously, it is proposed that there is far less potential variety in the classes of overt responses a human being can display than there is in the combinations of psychological structures that can mediate responses. That is, there are more constraints on variety in behavior than there are on variety in psychological structures. Anatomical as well as social constraints (which take the form of rules) limit seriously the total variety of responses an organism can issue. There are a limited number of ways one can press a bar, sip martinis, or cry. But each of these delineated responses can serve many different combinations of motives, expectancies, standards, and beliefs. This image of a relatively limited set of behaviors to be mapped on a larger set of internal psychological structures provides the central theme of this paper.

Presidential address to Division 7 of the American Psychological Association, San Francisco, California, September 2, 1968. Preparation of this manuscript was facilitated by research grant MH 08792 from the National Institute of Mental Health and a grant from the Carnegie Corporation of New York.

Jerome Kagan, "On the meaning of behavior: illustrations from the infant," *Child Development, 40,* 1969, 1121–1134. Reprinted by permission. © 1969 by The Society for Research in Child Development, Inc.

One of psychology's problems is to discern the meaning of its behavioral phenotypes, which is a way of saying that it must find the psychological structures each response class serves. Since responses do not exist independent of organisms and situations, it is necessary, at a minimum, to acknowledge the species, age, and sex of the organism and the stimulus context in which he is behaving. We should not inquire about the cause of smiling, but must constrain the question by denoting, at a minimum, the age, sex, and context in which the behavior occurred. Consider some popular dependent variables in contemporary psychology: anxiety, rapid eye movements, ease of conditioning, EEG desynchronization, achievement themes, risk taking, or affiliative behavior. These are vital and extensively researched phenomena, but the flavor of the work occasionally implies that a particular score or magnitude on one of these variables has a univocal meaning, regardless of the age or sex of the organism or the context in which he is behaving.

This general issue could be discussed in relation to many different response dimensions. This paper shall consider the issue with relation to two easily quantified responses displayed by the infant: duration of orientation toward a visual stimulus (typically called fixation time) and nonmorphemic vocalization. The intention is to persuade the reader that the meaning of these responses is a serious function of the age and sex of the agent making the response, in children under 2 years of age. Investigation of fixation time has the longer history; Fantz (1961) chose this variable in his pioneering studies of perceptual dynamics in the young infant. Nonmorphemic vocalization, oddly enough, has not been popular with investigators. Less than 1 percent of studies of infants during the last 50 years chose nonmorphemic vocalization in the first year as a dependent variable worthy of quantification. Investigation of reflexes, sitting, crawling, creeping, and morphemic speech have been, by contrast, extremely popular. It is possible that the pragmatic and evaluative biases of these early investigators led to this selectivity. One can see positive progression or growth in motor skill and vocabulary, whereas babbling of infants appears to idle. Let us turn now to the differential meaning of fixation time as a function of age.

AGE AND FIXATION TIME

Duration of fixation of a visual stimulus seems to change its primary loyalty at least three times during the first 3 years of life. During the first 6–8 weeks the infant has an unlearned disposition to fixate events that have a high rate of change in their physical parameters. Movement and contour contrast possess high rates of change, and newborns are dramatically more attentive to moving lights than to static ones, to stimuli with a high degree of black-white contour than to stimuli with minimal contour contrast (Haith 1966; Salapatek & Kessen 1966). But this apparently unlearned disposition eventually competes with an acquired determinant by the time the infant is 12 weeks old.

The degree of discrepancy between the stimulus and an acquired schema becomes an important determinant of fixation time at this age. A schema is an internal representation of a stimulus, where the term *representation* refers to a particular arrangement of the distinctive elements of the stimulus. The principles by which elements acquire distinctiveness are not known, and this is one of psychology's most challenging problems. However, the hypothesis states that once a schema has been formed, events that are discrepant from that schema—alterations in the arrangement or form of the distinctive elements of the schema—will elicit longer fixations from the infant than events perfectly representative of the schema or events having no relation to schema. That is, there is a curvilinear relation between fixation time and degree of discrepancy between schema and external event. Support for this hypothesis is found in the pattern of fixation times of 4-month-old infants to schematic representations of human faces and meaningless designs. Achromatic illustrations of male faces elicit fixation times twice as long as those elicited by random shapes of varying number of turns which are extremely novel and contain greater contour contrast than the faces (McCall & Kagan 1967a). Moreover, the 4-month-old studies a regular schematic face longer than one which has the same facial components disarranged (Haaf & Bell 1967). Final support for the discrepancy hypothesis comes from a study in which 3-month-old infants were exposed to a novel three-dimensional stimulus at home for 1 month and then shown that stimulus and three transformations of the standard at 4 months of age. Control children viewed all four stimuli for the first time at 4 months. The experimental infants who viewed the standard at home showed shorter fixation times to all four stimuli than the controls. The discrepancy effect emerged for girls who showed longer fixation times to the transformations than to the standard they viewed at home (McCall & Kagan 1967b).

Although the definitive study is yet to be performed, there is tentative support for the notion that very familiar and very novel stimuli elicit shorter fixation times than events that are only moderately discrepant from established schema. But this generalization is probably not true until the infant is at least 3–4 months old and has had time to establish some schema. [The advanced psychology student may want to compare with Helson's concept of adaptation level.—EDITOR]

A third determinant of fixation time—in addition to high rate of change and discrepancy—first appears during the last third of the first year and becomes prominent by 2 years. It concerns the meaningfulness of the event and is defined by the density of hypotheses associated with a class of events. With age, a child acquires both a more articulated schema for a particular class of events, as well as a set of associations and hypotheses which he activates when he is exposed to an event that is discrepant from his schema. The activation of these hypotheses leads to prolonged fixations. The child's attention is maintained because he is trying to construct the familiar from the discrepant; he is actively trying out cognitive hypotheses that will permit him to assimilate the event. The more knowledge he has about a class of stimuli, the longer he can work at this construction. The child's attention remains riveted on the stimulus in approximate proportion to the density of these hypotheses.

In sum, three factors appear to control duration of fixation in the infant: high rate of change in the physical parameters of the stimulus operating during the opening weeks of life, to which is added moderate discrepancy at about 3 months and activation of hypotheses at 9–10 months. It is suggested that these factors supplement each other; an event that has contrast, is discrepant, and engages meaningful hypotheses should elicit longer fixations from an 18-month-old than a stimulus with only one or two of these characteristics.

Data on age changes in fixation time to representations of human faces provide a test of the usefulness of these assumptions. A set of four different three-dimensional representations of a male face was presented to the same sample of 150 children at 4, 8, 13, and 27 months of age. All infants were Caucasian and first born. Figure 1 illustrates the four faces.

Fixation times were highest at 4 months, lowest at 8–13 months, and intermediate at 27 months. The long fixations at 4 months reflect the fact that the stimuli were discrepant from the infant's acquired schema for his parent's face. Fixation times dropped at 8–13 months because the faces were much less discrepant but did not elicit any hypotheses. The fixation times began to rise between 13 and 27 months as a consequent of the meaningfulness vector. The largest increase in fixation time between 13 and 27 months occurred for the face that had eyes, nose, and mouth rearranged (scrambled face), suggesting the comple-

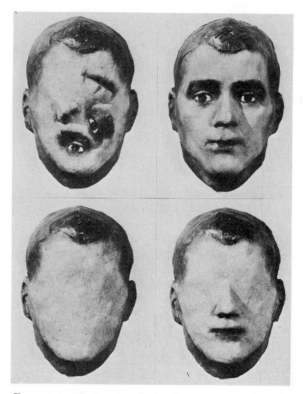

FIGURE 1. *Flesh-colored clay faces presented to the infants.*

mentary action of discrepancy and meaningfulness.

Independent data gathered by Finley (1967) corroborate these ideas and extend the age function to 3 years of age. Finley saw three cross-sectional samples of 1-, 2-, and 3-year-old children. One group was composed of peasant Mayan Indians living on the Yucatan peninsula; the second was a middle-class group from Cambridge. The Indian children saw the faces of a Mayan male; the Cambridge children saw a Caucasian male face. The fixation times increased linearly with age and also showed a stimulus by age interaction, with the rearranged face showing the largest increase in fixation time between 2 and 3 years of age. Figure 2 combines the longitudinal data with those gathered by Finley for the regular, rearranged, and blank faces—three faces that were used in both investigations. There was an almost perfect U-shaped function relating fixation time and age; and the greatest increase in fixation time from 1 to 3 years occurred for the rearranged, or scrambled, face. This stimulus by age interaction reflects the joint action of discrepancy and density of hypotheses. The scrambled face was more difficult to assimilate than the other two and elicited a richer set of hypotheses in the service of this assimilation. Some of the children's spontaneous comments are consonant with this suggestion. One 2-year-old

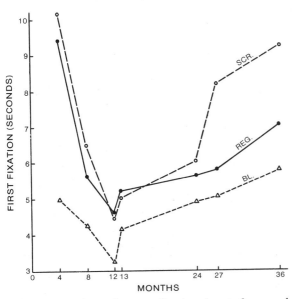

FIGURE 2. *Relation between fixation time to faces and age (several samples combined).*

child said, "What happened to his nose, who hit him in the nose?" Another said, "Who that, mommy? A monster, that a monster, mommy?"

SOCIAL CLASS AND FIXATION TIME

Additional support for the assumption that meaningfulness begins to control fixation time toward the end of the first year is found in the degree of covariation between educational level of the child's family and fixation time from 4 through 27 months. There was no relation between educational level of the infant's family and duration of fixation at 4 months for either sex. At 13 and 27 months, however, there were significant positive correlations—in the high 30s—between these variables, although slightly higher for girls than for boys. Since upper-middle-class children are likely to be taught a richer set of symbolic structures surrounding faces than lower-middle-class infants, the former should possess richer nests of hypotheses to the faces and display longer fixations. The increasing correlation between educational level of the parents and fixation time as the child grows is congruent with the presumed role of meaningfulness on fixation time.

STABILITY OF FIXATION TIME

The data on intraindividual stability of fixation time support the assumptions regarding the changing determinants of this response. If fixation time at 4 months is primarily controlled by degree of discrepancy, whereas at 8 and 13 months it begins

to be controlled by activation of hypotheses, there should be minimal continuity for fixation time from 4 to 8 or from 4 to 13 months. But if a child's rate of acquisition of hypotheses to the faces remains relatively constant, there might be moderate stability from 8 to 13 months. These expectations were generally confirmed. There was minimal intraindividual stability of fixation time from 4 to 8 or from 4 to 13 months for this group of 150 infants. However, there was moderate stability of fixation time to the faces from 8 to 13 months for girls ($r = 0.51$, $p < .01$). The correlation for boys was lower and nonsignificant. The sex difference in degree of continuity of fixation time to the faces is concordant with the sex differences in magnitude of association between educational level of the family and fixation time at 1 year. Rate of acquisition of hypotheses to the faces seems to be more constant and more closely tied to the educational level of the family among girls than boys.

The entire corpus of data is, at the least, congruent with the proposition that duration of fixation of a visual event comes under the influence of different processes during the opening 3 years. The meaning of a 10-second fixation time to a face depends on the age of the child, which is shorthand for implying a particular stage of cognitive development.

SEX AND VOCALIZATION

The vocalization data illustrate the importance of the child's sex in understanding the meaning of a response. Students of comparative psychology often find sexual dimorphisms in behavior (i.e., a given situation leads to different responses in the two sexes; see Hamburg & Lunde 1966). For example, a fear-inducing stimulus more often leads to motor freezing in the female monkey than in the male but leads to motor excitability in the male. The babbling of the young infant may display a sexual dimorphism. Nonfretful, nonmorphemic vocalization to auditory and visual stimulation during the first half year seems to be more clearly in the service of an excitability that accompanies information processing in girls than in boys. The boys' vocalizations seem to reflect an excitability that more often accompanies boredom or motor restlessness than the processing of information. Before considering evidence for this suggestion, it should be noted that the average vocalization time during a 30-second stimulus presentation averaged only 2 seconds at 4, 8, and 13 months. Vocalization, like fixation time, was longer at 4 months than at 8 or 13 months. With only one major exception, vocalization time was independent of fixation time, cardiac deceleration, or frequency of smiling during the first year. Moreover, there were no sex differences in mean vocalization time or variability at any age. Boys and girls vocalized equally often, but the pattern of correlates of this response was unequivocally different for the two sexes. [Remember Eichorn's point (see Intro., Sec. 8)—ED.]

THE LINK TO ATTENTIVENESS

Vocalization was more closely associated with independent indexes of active information processing among girls than boys. For example, among girls, duration of vocalization to representations of faces at 4 months predicted duration of orientation, at 8 months of age, to a speaker baffle which was the source of human speech. At 8 months, each child listened to a set of four taped stimuli, read by a male voice, in which meaning and inflection were varied. There were four sets of sentences, each lasting 20 seconds. The four stimuli were (1) high meaning read with high inflection, (2) high meaning read with low inflection, (3) low meaning (nonsense) read with high inflection, and finally (4) low meaning read with low inflection. The girls who vocalized to a photograph of a male face at 4 months looked longer at the speaker baffle than the girls who did not vocalize ($r = 0.35$, $p < .01$). No such relation emerged for boys ($r = -0.01$). This relation was even more dramatic when general attentiveness at 4 months was controlled. All infants who showed short fixation times to the faces at 4 months (based on a median split) were eliminated from the analysis. The group of highly attentive 4-month infants was then divided into those who vocalized versus those who did not vocalize at 4 months. The vocalizing girls looked significantly longer at the speaker than the nonvocalizing girls; the relation for boys was in the reverse direction.

A second instance of covariation between vocalization and an index of attentiveness involved a contemporaneous relation between vocalization and magnitude of cardiac deceleration to the presentation of the male voice at 8 months. Investigation of cardiac deceleration has a short history, partly for technical reasons concerning amplifiers, but partly because of the theoretical prejudices spawned by arousal theory. The Laceys (Lacey 1959; Lacey, Kagan, Lacey, & Moss 1963) demonstrated that cardiac deceleration, not acceleration, was a common reaction when an adult was attending to an auditory or visual event. Subsequent work verified this phenomenon in infants and indicated its usefulness in studies of attention distribution in preverbal children (Lewis, Kagan, Campbell, & Kalafat 1966). A working hypothesis is that, other things being equal, an obvious deceleration is most likely to occur in an infant when

the stimulus is a moderate discrepancy from an existing schema, that is, when the event surprises the infant. A long fixation is least likely to be accompanied by a cardiac deceleration when the event is very novel or too familiar. The phrase "double take" is an apt description of the infant's appearance when he shows a deceleration to a visual or auditory stimulus. This look of surprise is typically accompanied by a sudden quieting and a large cardiac deceleration. It is assumed that the infants who showed large decelerations to the auditory sentences at 8 months were more attentive than those who did not decelerate. Many infants showed large cardiac decelerations to the sentences at 8 months, but there were no sex differences in average deceleration. Similarly, many infants vocalized after the auditory stimulus terminated, during the 10-second interstimulus period when the room was silent. Again, there were no sex differences in average vocalization during this quiet period. But if vocalization is an index of excitability occasioned by information processing, then the girls who were most attentive to the sentences as they were being presented—as indexed by cardiac deceleration—should have vocalized the most when the voice terminated. This relation held for girls but not for boys. There was a significant positive association between magnitude of deceleration during the stimulus and vocalization following its termination for the girls ($r = 0.3$, $p < .01$) but not for the boys ($r = 0.1$, $p =$ N.S.).

A third instance of covariation between attentiveness and vocalization among girls is seen in the degree of correlation between fixation time and vocalization time to the regular face at 4 months. There was a significant positive association between looking and babbling for the girls, but none for the boys.

A fourth instance of a preferential link between early babbling and later attentiveness in girls was contained in the significant correlation between vocalization to the faces at 8 months and the tendency to engage in long periods of uninterrupted play with toys when these children were 27 months old. Once again, this relation was absent for the boys.

Finally, vocalization among the girls differentiated among stimuli that elicited equal fixation times, while vocalization among the boys failed to differentiate among these stimuli. The 4-month-old girls vocalized significantly more to the regular face than to the scrambled clay face on the first presentation of these two stimuli. The boys showed equivalent vocalization to these two faces.

Independent data gathered by Michael Lewis and the author on 6-month-old infants seen at the Fels Institute also revealed differentiated use of vocalization by girls, but not by boys. The infants were shown a series of faces and geometric forms in random order. Girls vocalized significantly more to the faces than to the forms; the boys showed equivalent vocalization to both classes of stimuli. An auditory episode that followed the visual series contained a strange male voice and a strange female voice reading prose. Girls vocalized more to the female than to the male voice; the boys babbled equally to both voices.

In addition to the preferential association between vocalization and varied indexes of information processing, vocalization was also more stable across ages for girls than for boys. Vocalization to all four clay faces at 4 or 8 months predicted vocalization to these faces at 13 months ($r = 0.34$, $p < .05$; $r = 0.47$, $p < .01$ for girls); there was no stability for the boys ($r = 0.00$; $r = -.14$).

The sex differences in stability of vocalization and degree of association with indexes of attentiveness imply that nonmorphemic babbling reflects the excitement generated by information processing more faithfully in girls than in boys. This speculation is supported by the work of others. Cameron, Livson, and Bayley (1967) have reported that high scores on a vocalization factor derived from the Bayley Intelligence Scale during the second half of the first year predicted Stanford-Binet IQ scores during childhood and adulthood for girls (r ranged from 0.4 to 0.6), but not for boys. Moore's (1967) longitudinal study of middle- and working-class London infants also provides relevant evidence. At 6 and 18 months of age, each of 41 boys and 35 girls was assigned a speech quotient from the Griffith's Infant Scale. High scores index frequency and variety of babbling to people's voices and music. The speech quotient was more stable for girls than for boys across the period 6–18 months ($r = 0.52$ for girls but only -0.01 for boys).

There are two complementary interpretations of this sexual dimorphism for infant babbling. One explanation assumes, first, that samples of Cambridge, Berkeley, or London mothers differ in their tendency to accelerate the cognitive development of their infants. Second, the disposition to accelerate the infant leads mothers to initiate different actions with daughters than with sons. It is suggested that an accelerating mother is more likely to engage in frequent, reciprocal vocalization with her daughter than with her son. As a result, the infant girl establishes a strong disposition to babble when excited by interesting events. In essence, it is suggested that there is greater variability among mothers of daughters than among mothers of sons in practices that involve reciprocal vocalization and stimulation of vocalization when the child is

processing information. There is some support for this point of view.

Part of our longitudinal sample was observed in the home when the infants were 4 months old. As reported elsewhere, well-educated mothers of daughters were more likely than poorly educated ones to engage in distinct face-to-face vocalization with their daughters and to respond to the girls' babbling within 10 seconds of its occurrence. Among boys, there was no relation between the mother's education and the occurrence of these practices (Kagan 1968). Additional support for this argument comes from a study in which mothers were interviewed during their pregnancy and rated on a variable called "quality and affective excitability of mother's speech." When the infants of these mothers were 3 months old, the mother-child interaction was observed in the home. The personality dimension rated during pregnancy covaried with auditory and visual stimulation of daughters (but not sons), and with physical affection toward sons (but not daughters). These data support the idea that a particular type of mother may display different patterns of handling toward sons and daughters as early as 12 weeks of age (Moss and Robson 1968).

A second interpretation, not exclusive of the first, argues for a basic sex difference in organization of the central nervous system. It is possible that vocalization is a more prepotent reaction for girls than boys when the infant is in the state of arousal created by processing information. This suggestion gains credence from comparative studies showing dramatic sex differences within primate strains in typical reactions to arousal states (Hamburg & Lunde 1966; Harlow 1965), and from observations of primates in natural contexts, suggesting that specific vocal sounds (such as squeals) are more often noted in females than males (Jay 1965). This explanation assumes that the sexes differ in their preferred reaction to that state designated as "stimulus excitement." The infant girl is likely to vocalize; the infant boy is more likely to react with motor quieting or skeletal motor discharge. If this is true, then babbling in the 4–8-month-old infant will be a more faithful index of attentional dynamics for girls than for boys.

SUMMARY

In general, there was minimal intraindividual continuity for the fixation and vocalization variables from 4 to 8 months, but moderate, and in some cases surprisingly good, continuity from 8 to 13 months, especially for girls. The emergence of this stability during the latter half of the first year is concordant with anthropometric data suggesting that stable physical growth dimensions begin to emerge about 6 months of age (Acheson 1966).

The more impressive stability of fixation and vocalization time for girls over boys matches the human biological data. Acheson (1966) has written that it is difficult to find a physiological or physical growth dimension that is not more stable for girls than for boys, and we are tempted to call upon biological factors as agents lobbying for continuity of these psychological dimensions in the girl. The stronger correlation for girls between social class and fixation time at 13 months has an interesting analogue in the fact that similar results emerge for older children. For example, grades in school, IQ scores, and decision times each show greater covariation with social class among girls than among boys. This pattern is not restricted to white populations; the correlation between maternal and child IQ at 4 years is markedly higher for girls ($r = 0.39$, $p < .001$) than for boys ($r = 0.15$) from black, urban families (Hess, Shipman, Brophy, & Bear 1968). It is suggested that this phenomenon is due to the fact that mothers of different social classes in the United States differ more dramatically in their acceleratory practices toward their daughters than toward their sons.

Finally, these data are relevant to the problem of mapping behavior on psychological structure. The U-shaped function relating age and fixation time to faces over the period 4–36 months is persuasive of the need to invent different determinants for fixation time. The importance of sex is a bit more controversial. It is not common for a psychologist to give the same task to subjects varying widely in age and assume that the behavior of all the age cadres derives from the same structures. However, there are many psychologists who deny the relevance of sex differences. They either pool sexes regularly or fail to specify whether the subjects were boys or girls. Most of the responses psychologists quantify are not sexually dimorphic. But some are, and since we do not know which ones, it seems appropriate to examine all corpuses of data for such differences before accepting the null hypothesis. This examination means not only checking means and variances but also looking at patterns of relations among variables.

A specific magnitude for a specific response often serves many different forces. The mapping of these magnitudes on the set of varied determinants will require rigorous theory and a keen sensitivity to nature's subtle messages. Von Békésy (1964, p. 728) gave a hint about the source of his own inductive creations when he noted that he chose da Vinci as his model because "da Vinci did not try to outdo nature with his fantasy, but, quite the opposite, he tried to learn from nature. It was this simple finding that gave me, in my student years, the hope that perhaps I would be able to produce something of enduring interest."

REFERENCES

ACHESON, R. M. Maturation of the skeleton. In F. Falkner (Ed.), *Human development*. Philadelphia: Saunders, 1966. Pp. 465–502.

CAMERON, J.; LIVSON, N.; & BAYLEY, N. Infant vocalizations and their relationship to mature intelligence. *Science*, 1967, *157*, 331–333.

FANTZ, R. L. The origin of form perception. *Scientific American*, 1961, *204*, 66–72.

FINLEY, G. E. Visual attention, play and satiation in young children: a cross-cultural study. Unpublished doctoral dissertation, Harvard University, 1967.

HAAF, R. A., & BELL, R. Q. The facial dimension in visual discrimination by human infants. *Child Development*, 1967, *38*, 893–899.

HAITH, M. M. The response of the human newborn to visual movement. *Journal of Experimental Child Psychology*, 1966, *3*, 235–243.

HAMBURG, D. A., & LUNDE, D. T. Sex hormones in the development of sex differences in human behavior. In E. E. Maccoby (Ed.), *The development of sex differences*. Stanford, Calif.: Stanford University Press, 1966. Pp. 1–24.

HARLOW, H. F. Sexual behavior in the rhesus monkey. In F. A. Beach (Ed.), *Sex and behavior*. New York: Wiley, 1965. Pp. 234–265.

HESS, R. D.; SHIPMAN, V. C.; BROPHY, J. E.; & BEAR, R. M. The cognitive environments of urban preschool children. Project report, Graduate School of Education, University of Chicago, November 1968.

JAY, P. The common langur of North India. In I. DeVore (Ed.), *Primate behavior*. New York: Holt, Rinehart & Winston, 1965. Pp. 197–249.

KAGAN, J. On cultural deprivation. In D. C. Glass (Ed.), *Biology and behavior: environmental influences*. New York: Rockefeller University Press, 1968. Pp. 211–250.

LACEY, J. I. Psychophysiological approaches to the evaluation of psychotherapeutic process and outcome. In E. A. Rubenstein & M. B. Parloff (Eds.), *Research in psychotherapy*. Washington, D.C.: National Publishing Co., 1959. Pp. 160–208.

LACEY, J. I.; KAGAN, J.; LACEY, B.; & MOSS, H. A. The visceral level: situational determinants and behavioral correlates of autonomic response patterns. In P. H. Knapp (Ed.), *Expressions of the emotions in man*. New York: International Universities Press, 1963. Pp. 161–196.

LEWIS, M.; KAGAN, J.; CAMPBELL, H.; & KALAFAT, J. The cardiac response as a correlate of attention in infants. *Child Development*, 1966, *37*, 63–72.

McCALL, R. B., & KAGAN, J. Attention in the infant: effects of complexity, contour, perimeter, and familiarity. *Child Development*, 1967, *38*, 939–952. (a)

McCall, R. B., & Kagan, J. Stimulus-schema discrepancy and attention in the infant. *Journal of Experimental Child Psychology*, 1967, *5*, 381–390. (b)

Mayr, E. *Animal species and evolution.* Cambridge, Mass.: Belknap Press, 1966.

Moore, T. Language and intelligence: a longitudinal study of the first eight years. *Human Development*, 1967, *10*, 88–106.

Moss, H. A., & Robson, K. The role of protest behavior in the development of the mother-infant attachment. Paper presented at the meeting of the American Psychological Association, San Francisco, 1968.

Salapatek, P., & Kessen, W. Visual scanning of triangles by the human newborn. *Journal of Experimental Child Psychology,* 1966, *3*, 113–122.

Von Békésy, G. Concerning the pleasure of observing and the mechanics of the inner ear. Nobel Lecture in Physiology or Medicine for 1961. In *Nobel lectures in physiology or medicine.* Vol. 3. *1942–1962.* Amsterdam: Elsevier, 1964. Pp. 722–746.

52

Behavioral Differences Related to Experience of Mother and Sex of Infant in the Rhesus Monkey[1]

G. MITCHELL AND E. M. BRANDT

This brief note by Mitchell and Brandt shows differences in the ways monkey mothers treat their offspring according to the sex of the baby. While the sexes receive different treatment, the data suggest that individual differences in offspring (as well as in mothers) may play a considerable role in child rearing among the Rhesus. Differences in the behavior of male and female infant monkeys are also shown. On the one hand, the findings of these differences in the rhesus (a species less influenced than humans are by culture) could be taken to underline the importance of biological factors. On the other hand, the mother's experience as a mother has the most influence on her behavior in the first three months of her infant's life, even though the sex of the infant becomes more impor-

tant after three months. These facts complicate the interpretation.

Dr. Mitchell and Dr. Brandt are both at the National Center for Primate Biology of the University of California at Davis.

The Mitchell and Stevens (1968) *Macaca mulatta* mothers and infants, studied from 1 to 3 months, were used in the present study. The effects of maternal experience and the sex of the infant on maternal and infant behavior were evaluated again in the second 3 months.

Eight multiparous monkey mothers were matched with eight primiparous mothers for date of delivery and sex of infant. An observation cage was divided into two $3 \times 3 \times 3$ foot cubicles by a $3/8$-inch sheet of transparent Acrylite. In six of twelve 16-minute sessions for any given matched pair, each mother-infant pair was observed in one side of the cage with a neutral mother-infant stimulus pair in the other side. A different stimulus pair was used for the next six sessions. Frequencies and durations were recorded on a clock counter device. All reported results are significant beyond the .05 level.

Primiparous mothers stroked their own infants and, particularly mothers of females, threatened the stimulus infants more often than multiparous mothers (stroke, $\bar{X} = 20$ versus 5 times; threat, $\bar{X} = 19$ versus 5 times); multiparous mothers bit their own infants (particularly male infants) while the primiparous did not ($\bar{X} = 2$ versus 0 times).

While mothers of females, particularly multiparous, looked at the environment longer than mothers of males ($\bar{X} = 17$ versus 14 minutes), mothers of males, particularly primiparous, looked at and lipsmacked at the stimulus infant longer than mothers of females (look, $\bar{X} = 5$ versus 3 minutes; lipsmack, $\bar{X} = .5$ versus .2 minute). Mothers of males threatened and (especially the multiparous mothers) bit their own infants more often than mothers of females (threat, $\bar{X} = 3$ versus 0 times; bite, $\bar{X} = 2$ versus 0 times), but they also submitted passively to their infants more often ($\bar{X} = 14$ versus 4 times). Mothers of females, more often than mothers of males, restrained ($\bar{X} = 2$ versus 0 times) and retrieved their infants ($\bar{X} = 5$ versus 1 time) and threatened the stimulus mothers ($\bar{X} = 5$ versus 1 time).

Male infants looked at their mothers' bodies longer than female infants ($\bar{X} = 1.4$ versus .7 minutes), who looked at their mothers' faces more often ($\bar{X} = 29$ versus 18 times). Female infants (particu-

[1] This research was supported by National Institutes of Health Grant FR–00169 to the National Center for Primate Biology, and Grants MH 17425–01 to the first author and HD 04335–01 to the second author.

An extended report of this study may be obtained without charge from G. Mitchell, National Center for Primate Biology, University of California, Davis, California 95616, or for a fee from the National Auxiliary Publications Service. Order Document No. 00956 from National Auxiliary Publications Service of the American Society for Information Science, c/o CCM Information Sciences, Inc., 909 Third Avenue, New York, New York 10022. Remit in advance $2.00 for microfiche or $5.00 for photocopies and make checks payable to: Research and Microfilm Publications, Inc.

larly of multiparous mothers) looked at the observers and at the stimulus mothers more often than male infants (looked at observer, $\bar{X} = 24$ versus 13 times; looked at stimulus mother, $\bar{X} = 106$ versus 71 times); while male infants, as compared to female infants, play-imitated with the stimulus infants longer ($\bar{X} = 1$ versus 0 minute), oral-explored the environment more often (especially primiparous infants) ($\bar{X} = 37$ versus 15 times), climbed longer ($\bar{X} = 4$ versus 2 minutes), ran-jumped more often ($\bar{X} = 56$ versus 12 times), and threatened the stimulus infant longer ($\bar{X} = .1$ versus .0 minute).

The factors of maternal experience and sex of infant do affect the behaviors of mother and infant rhesus monkeys. In the second 3 months, maternal experience wanes in importance as a factor influencing maternal or infant behavior, as the sex of the infant becomes the more important factor. One can best characterize mothers of males as "punishers," mothers of females as "protectors," male infants as "doers," and female infants as "watchers." The mother plays a role in prompting the greater independence and activity that is typical of males.

[Primiparous mothers are those with first offspring. Multiparous mothers have had previous offspring.—EDITOR]

REFERENCE

MITCHELL, G., & STEVENS, C. W. Primiparous and multiparous monkey mothers in a mildly stressful social situation: First three months. *Development Psychobiology*, 1968, *1*, 280–286.

53

It Score Variations by Instructional Style

NORMAN L. THOMPSON, JR.,
AND BOYD R. MCCANDLESS

Because the It score is frequently used to assess the degree of sex-role stereotyping in children's choices or preferences, the methodological problems concerning this scale are important as well as instructive with respect to matters of research method. In this study, Thompson and McCandless used both black and white lower class Ss. Since all Ss were lower class, generalization of the findings is limited. But Ss were of two races, so the attendant cultural variation gives the findings greater scope. In particular, it enables us to see that biological sex interacts with the socially mediated factors that are linked to race to produce effects of the differing instructions. The level of sex-role stereotyping is also affected by race in interaction with sex.

Norman L. Thompson, Jr. is on the education faculty at the University of Pennsylvania. Boyd R. McCandless spent a number of years at the Iowa Child Welfare Research Station and was its director from 1951 to 1960. Since 1966 he has been professor of psychology and education at Emory

This research was supported in part by a U.S. Office of Education Small Grant to the Emory Division of Educational Studies, and by the Atlanta Education Improvement Program, Ford Foundation. Miss Elizabeth Perry of the Atlanta Education Improvement Program assisted centrally in data collection. This paper was presented March 1, 1969, at the meeting of the Southeastern Psychological Association, New Orleans.

University. He is also the editor of Developmental Psychology, *published by the American Psychological Association.*

The concept of sex-role identification occupies an important position in the attempt to understand personality development. A major research problem in the area concerns measurement. Thus, the authors of the present study have focused on Brown's (1956) It Scale for Children (ITSC), a widely used instrument for assessing sex-role development in children. This technique purports to measure sex-role preference, defined by Brown (1956) as "behavior associated with one sex or the other that the individual would like to adopt, or that he perceives as the preferred or more desirable behavior" (p. 3).

In the standard procedure, the child is presented with a modified stick figure, "It," which is assumed to be sexless. The task for the child is to choose what "It" likes in a series of pictures of various sex-typed items. The assumption behind the test is that the child considers himself as "It" and that the activities he chooses for "It" are actually those he would choose for himself (McCandless 1967).

The major criticism leveled against the instrument is that "It" actually looks like a boy, rather than a neuter figure. Therefore, many children make choices for a boy figure rather than projecting their own choices onto "It" (Brown 1962). There is considerable evidence to support such a criticism. Sher and Lansky (1968) found that girls as well as boys tended to see "It" as a male when asked the sex of the figure. They also found that boys tended to say "boy" and girls tended to say "girl" when asked the sex of the "It" figure while it was concealed in an envelope. When these children were then shown "It," more girls changed their attributions to "boy" than boys changed their attributions to "girl." Additional support for the hypothesis that "It" possesses masculine cues comes from the results of a study by Hartup and Zook (1960).

Lansky and McKay (1963) eliminated the possible masculine stimulus effect of "It" by testing kindergarten children with the figure concealed in an envelope. They found that boys were more variable than girls in this situation. Endsley (1967) obtained different results in a study in which he tested half the 3- to 5-year-old children with the standard instructions and half with "It" concealed in an envelope. He found that boys were less variable than girls under both conditions. There were no differ-

Norman L. Thompson and Boyd R. McCandless, "It score variations by instructional style," *Child Development, 41,* 1970, 425–436. Reprinted by permission. © 1970 by The Society for Research in Child Development, Inc.

ences in the mean scores between the two conditions for the boys or girls. He thus found no support for the contention that "It" possesses a masculine bias.

Sher and Lansky (1968) tested kindergarten children randomly assigned to one of three different sequences. The first sequence began with the standard instructions. The second sequence began with "It" concealed in an envelope. In the third sequence, the children were first asked to attribute a sex to the picture of "It." The task for these latter children was to respond to the choices for an "It" of the sex they attributed to the figure. The results indicated that there were no differences among the three conditions for boys. However, the girls were more feminine on the concealed condition than on the other two conditions. As girls and boys also tended to see "It" as a boy when asked the figure's sex, Sher and Lansky concluded that it is likely the "It" figure contains predominantly masculine cues. ITSC scores may reflect the child's attempt to match a sex-typed figure with its appropriate objects. Thus it appears the test may measure sex-role knowledge rather than sex-role preferences.

The present study was designed to explore further the effects of the instructions used with the ITSC. Three different sets of instructions were employed in the study. These instructions were designed to produce variations in the test situation ranging from projective to semiprojective to objective.

A second purpose was to explore the effects of the examiner's sex on the children's performance. It is possible that the examiner's sex has a systematic effect on the children's performance. However, this had not been previously tested.

The third purpose of this study was to add normative data for the ITSC for lower-class Negro and white children. Hartup and Zook (1960) found no social class differences among their preschool-aged Ss. In a study of older children, Hall and Keith (1964) found socioeconomic class differences, largely among the boys. Thomas (1966) tested deprived and nondeprived Negro and nondeprived white children. The results indicated that sex-role preferences mature more slowly among deprived Negro children than among nondeprived Negro and white youngsters. The feminine role had greater prestige among the deprived Negroes, while the masculine role had greater prestige among the nondeprived whites. The relative prestige of the two roles among the nondeprived Negroes was in transition but closer to that found among the whites. The present study is an extension of such work.

The final purpose was to explore the relationship between sex-role preference as measured by the

ITSC and sex-role adoption as measured by teacher ratings.

Six hypotheses can be formally tested in connection with the four main objectives of the study:

1. When boys are compared with girls in ITSC (*a*) the boys' mean scores for all three instructions will be significantly higher (more masculine) than the girls'; (*b*) the boys' variances for the three instructions will be significantly smaller than the girls', except for condition *C*. This double hypothesis comes directly from Brown's results (1956, 1957).

2. Data do not permit a directional hypothesis about the effect of the sex of the examiner on Ss' performance. However, information is needed.

3. This set of hypotheses concerns the performance of the girls on the ITSC. (*a*) There will be a significant difference between the mean scores of instructions *A* (standard instructions) and *B* ("It" is concealed). The *A* score will be higher (more masculine). (*b*) There will be a significant difference between the mean scores of instructions *A* and *C* ("It-is-you"). The *A* score will be higher. (*c*) There will be a significant difference between the mean scores of instructions *B* and *C*. The *B* mean score will be higher.

Hypothesis 3*b* is based on Hartup and Zook's (1960) results; hypotheses 3*a* and 3*c*, on those of Sher and Lansky (1968).

4. The fourth set of hypotheses relates to the performance of the boys on the ITSC. (*a*) There will be no significant difference between the mean scores of instructions *A* (standard) and *B* (concealed). (*b*) There will be no significant difference between the mean scores of instructions *A* and *C* ("It-is-you"). (*c*) There will be no significant difference between the mean scores of instructions *B* and *C*.

Hypothesis 4*b* comes from Hartup and Zook (1960), while hypotheses 4*a* and 4*c* are based on Sher and Lansky's (1968) findings.

5. This set of hypotheses pertains to racial differences in performance on the ITSC. (*a*) Negro boys will score significantly more feminine than white boys on instructions *A* and *B*. (*b*) Negro girls will score significantly more feminine than white girls on instructions *A* and *B*. (*c*) Negro boys will be significantly more variable than white boys.

This set of hypotheses is based on Thomas's (1966) results.

6. There will not be a significant relation between sex-role preference as measured by the ITSC and sex-role adoption as measured by teacher ratings. This hypothesis is based on Ward's (1969) results. He found that sex-role preference develops before the age of five, while sex-role adoption comes later.

METHOD

SUBJECTS

The *S*s were 72 prekindergarten children, 36 boys and 36 girls, ranging from 51 to 66 months with a mean age of 57.50 months. The mean ages in months and standard deviations, respectively, for the four racial and sex groups were as follows: Negro boys, 55.94 and 2.68; Negro girls, 56.56 and 3.75; white boys, 58.33 and 3.61; and white girls, 59.17 and 3.09. Although the children were born at approximately the same time, the testing schedule necessitated testing each school at different times during the late winter and spring of the year. Fifty-eight of the *S*s were enrolled in a special prekindergarten program for deprived children in three schools of the Atlanta, Georgia, public school system. Two of the schools were entirely Negro, while the third was predominantly white. The remaining 14 *S*s were enrolled in Project Head Start classes in the same neighborhoods as the *S*s in the special prekindergarten program. These classes were racially mixed. All *S*s were deprived, lower-class children (McCandless 1968).

Subjects from each school were assigned to each of the treatment groups. Assignment was random except that the groups were matched for race and sex. Only one *S* refused to be tested, and she was replaced by a class-mate. Two *S*s refused to be tested by a male examiner and were consequently tested by a female examiner.

PROCEDURE

The ITSC was administered individually in private rooms of the schools. Half of the *S*s were tested by a male examiner and half by a female examiner. Each *S* was given the ITSC three times in one day according to his assigned sequence. Due to the sporadic attendance of many of the *S*s, it was not feasible to lengthen the time between testings. One-third of the *S*s were randomly assigned to the *ABC* sequence, one-third to the *BCA* sequence, and one-third to the *CAB* sequence. The instructions were:

A (standard instructions).—These instructions were the same as Brown's (1956). The figure was called "It" and was visible to the child throughout this portion of the test.

B (concealed instructions).—This technique was developed by Lansky and McKay (1963). The figure remained in the envelope, and the child was told, "There is a child named 'It' in the envelope."

C ("It-is-you" instructions).—These instructions were developed by Hartup and Zook (1960). The figure was identified as the same sex as the child throughout this portion of the test.

The sections of the ITSC were administered according to Brown's manual (1956). However, the 16 pictured toys were presented in two groups of eight rather than one group of 16 pictures. Each group contained four boys' toys and four girls' toys arranged in the numbered order of the cards. Each *S* was instructed to choose four from each of the two groups.

The weighted scoring method developed by Brown (1956) was employed. Each masculine choice receives a positive score, and a feminine choice receives a 0. The possible scores range from 0 (most feminine) to 84 (most masculine).

TEACHER RATINGS

Sex-role adoption was measured by ratings of the *S*s' behavior by the head and assistant teachers. The ratings were based on the teachers' observations of the *S*s' behavior throughout the school year, or the entire summer Head Start program. The masculine rating scale was developed by Biller (1969). The feminine scale was constructed by McCandless and Thompson for this study and was based on Biller's masculine scale.

Each scale contains 16 items describing various behaviors. The masculine scale has nine items characteristic of masculine behavior in young children and seven items characteristic of feminine behavior. The feminine scale contains 10 items characteristic of feminine behavior in young children and six items characteristic of masculine behavior. The teacher is asked to rate the child on a scale ranging from *very frequently* to *never* for each item of behavior. The masculine scale is scored so that a high score indicates masculine behavior and a low score indicates nonmasculine behavior. The feminine scale is scored in such a manner that a low score indicates feminine and a high score indicates nonfeminine behavior. This scoring procedure was employed so that the scoring direction on these scales corresponded to the scoring direction of the ITSC.

The percentages of agreement between the two teachers was computed by comparing the teachers' responses on each item. A disagreement of one step gave a score of 75 percent agreement on that item, a disagreement of two steps gave a score of 50 percent agreement, etc. The overall percentages of agreement between the pairs of teachers ranged from 72.5 to 89.3 for the masculine scale and from 76.6 to 86.7 for the feminine scale.

RESULTS

The age differences among the various racial and sex groups were examined. The difference between boys and girls for both Negro and white was not significant (black, $t = .554$, $df = 34$; white, $t = .730$, $df = 34$). The difference between Negro and white girls was significant at the .05 level of confidence ($t = 2.212$, $df = 34$). The difference between Negro and white boys was also significant at the .05 level of confidence ($t = 2.176$, $df = 34$). Although these mean differences are significant, the differences of 2.66 months between the two groups of girls and 2.39 months between the boys are small for the overall age of the children. Correlations between age and the various instructions of the ITSC are given in table 1. The only significant correlations work *against* the hypothesis regarding racial differences between boys, and *for* the hypothesis concerning girls.

An analysis of variance was performed on the order effect of the various instructional conditions for boys and girls. A nonsignificant *F* of .580 ($df = 2$) was obtained among the orders for boys, and a nonsignificant *F* of .348 ($df = 2$) was obtained for the girls. The order in which the children received the ITSC does not affect the scores significantly.

TABLE 1
CORRELATIONS BETWEEN AGE AND INSTRUCTIONAL CONDITIONS OF THE ITSC

Group	A (Standard)	B (Concealed)	C ("It-Is-You")
Negro boys	−.68**	.32	−.13
White boys	.16	.13	.13
Negro girls	−.51*	.16	.09
White girls	.06	.00	.07

* $p < .05$.
** $p < .01$.

TABLE 2
MEANS AND STANDARD DEVIATIONS OF SUBJECTS ON THE ITSC

Group	A		B		C	
	Mean	SD	Mean	SD	Mean	SD
Males	54.22	17.60	56.67	16.13	61.50	15.28
Negro	46.78	14.73	53.33	13.03	56.56	14.76
White	61.67	17.08	60.00	18.12	66.44	14.15
Females	40.58	18.19	36.11	13.25	27.81	15.98
Negro	35.56	14.84	37.61	13.08	26.72	14.46
White	45.61	19.76	34.61	13.25	28.89	17.30

A separate analysis of variance that involved four factors—sex of child, sex of examiner, race, and instructions—revealed that the effects of the child's sex were significant (F for 1 $df = 70.85$). This result, bearing on the validity of the ITSC, supports hypothesis 1a: Boys will score higher than girls. As shown in table 2, the boys' mean scores were consistently higher than the girls' for all instructional conditions. The various combinations of variances were examined by F tests for each subgroup. Hypothesis 1b (boys less variable than girls) was not supported, nor were there between-race differences in variance.

No hypothesis was made concerning the effect of the examiner's sex on the performance of the Ss. The results of the analysis of variance indicate that it produced no effect ($F = 0.188$).

The sex of child by instruction interaction was significant at less than the .01 level (F was 9.891 for 2 df). The effects of instructions were examined by means of t tests for correlated means. The results of these tests for boys and girls, separated by race, are shown in table 3. Hypothesis 3a, which states that the girls' mean scores under A (standard instructions) will be higher (more masculine) than those under B (concealed instructions) is not supported for the total group. Hypothesis 3b, that the girls will score higher on A than on C ("It-is-you"), was supported for the total group and for white girls. Hypothesis 3c, which states that the girls will score higher on B than C, was supported for the total group and for black girls. The hypothesis was not supported for white girls. The hypothesis about effects of instructions on boys' performance, 4a ($A = B$), 4b ($A = C$), and 4c ($B = C$), were all supported for the total group and for the white boys. However, the Negro boys were more masculine on both B and C than on A.

The analysis of variance indicated that race is a significant factor in ITSC scores. The data, which are summarized in table 4, show that the Negro boys were more feminine than white boys on the three instructional conditions combined.[1] On the individual instructions the Negro boys were significantly more feminine than white boys on A, with condition C ("It-is-you") reaching borderline significance. It is doubtful that the age difference between Negro and white boys produced these results. There were no significant correlations for boys between age and ITSC score except −.68 on A for the

TABLE 3
TESTS BETWEEN THE INSTRUCTIONAL CONDITIONS FOR NEGRO AND WHITE SUBJECTS

Group	A–B	A–C	B–C
Males	0.935	0.826	1.404
Negro	2.408*	2.843*	0.944
White	0.390	1.000	1.322
Females	1.149	3.803***	2.726*
Negro	0.522	1.898	2.201
White	2.080	3.611**	1.677

* $p < .05$.
** $p < .01$.
*** $p < .002$.

[1] This difference cannot be accounted for by different father-absent ratios for the ethnic groups. For Negro boys, 14 fathers were living at home and four were absent, while the white boys had 12 present and six absent. The Negro girls had 10 fathers present with eight absent, and the white girls had 14 present with four absent. In addition, one father-absent Negro girl had a grandfather living at home. An analysis was done to see if there were any differences in ITSC performances between father-absent and father-present children. Due to the small N's for children separated by sex and race, the data were collapsed over race. There were no significant differences between father-absent and father-present children for any instructional condition. The full data may be obtained from the authors.

TABLE 4
t TESTS BETWEEN NEGRO AND WHITE SUBJECTS

Group	A	B	C	Total
Males...............	2.722**	1.233	1.992*	2.673**
Females...........	1.678*	.664	.397	.858

* *p* < .10.
** *p* < .02.

Negro boys (see table 1). This indicates that the older the Negro boy, the more feminine he is likely to score under the standard instructions. If there had been no age difference between the two groups of boys, the difference on *A* might have been larger. There was no difference between the Negro and white girls on the combined instructional conditions. On the individual instructions, only *A* (standard) approaches significance. The differences on *B* and *C* are not significant. Therefore, hypothesis 5*a* was partially supported, while 5*b* was not supported. Nor was hypothesis 5*c* supported; it states that the Negro boys will be significantly more variable than white boys.

Hypothesis 6 states that there will be no significant relationship between sex-role preference as measured by the ITSC and sex-role adoption as measured by the teacher ratings. The results (table 5) support the hypothesis, except for the white boys. It may be that sex-role preference and sex-role adoption are coming into congruence by the approximate age of 5 years for lower-class white boys but not for the other groups.

The correlations among the treatments are reported in table 6. These indicate that the Negro boys were consistent across instructions, with the correlation between *B* and *C* reaching borderline significance (*p* < .10). The white boys were only consistent between conditions *A* and *B*. There was no consistency among the Negro girls across instructions; the white girls were consistent between *B* and *C*, with the correlation between *A* and *C* reaching borderline significance (*p* < .10).

DISCUSSION

The data from this study clearly suggest that race is an important variable in the responding to the ITSC. The type of instructions used did not affect the performance of the white boys, but the Negro boys were significantly more feminine on the standard instructions than on the concealed or "It-is-you" conditions. It is possible that the white boys' attitudes concerning their own sex role have de-

TABLE 5
CORRELATION FOR TEACHERS' RATINGS WITH ITSC

Group	A	B	C
Males			
Negro	−.029	−.216	.004
White....................	.512*	.301	.479*
Females			
Negro	.134	−.489*	.355
White....................	−.017	.247	.001

* *p* < .05.

TABLE 6
CORRELATIONS AMONG TREATMENTS

	A–B	A–C	B–C
Negro boys	.662***	.510*	.458
White boys	.475*	.170	−.198
Negro girls	.286	.093	−.163
White girls	.121	.440	.576**

* *p* < .05.
** *p* < .02.
*** *p* < .01.

veloped consistently with their knowledge of the masculine sex role. The Negro boys made more feminine choices when the "It" figure was shown but not identified as being one sex or the other. Perhaps they see "It" as feminine. Such a conclusion is reasonable if, as has been suggested, the feminine role is preferred in lower-class black culture (Rainwater 1966).

There is some support for the hypothesis that white girls respond to masculine cues in the "It" figure when, as in standard instructions, the figure is not identified by sex. This was not true for Negro girls. This difference could be due to the relative prestige of the sex roles in the two subcultures. For lower-class white girls, a neutral figure may be seen as masculine because the masculine role is more favored. Lower-class Negro girls may be similar to white boys, in that their sex-role attitudes have developed consistently with their knowledge of cultural advantage for their sex. However, the patterning of the Negro girls' scores suggests an additional possibility. The mothers of these girls may be more assertive and engage in more "masculine" activities than mothers in many other groups in the United States. These daughters are probably reinforced for imitating these activities. Although on the one hand the Negro girls may be learning what is typically the feminine role in our society, on the other they are learning the attitudes associated with the assertive role lower-class black women are forced to play.

The evidence from this study, in conjunction with previous studies (Hartup & Zook 1960; Lansky & McKay 1963; Sher & Lansky 1968), supports the conclusion that standard "It" instructions measure variables in addition to sex-role preference, at least for white girls and Negro boys. Use of these instructions to measure which sex role a child prefers may thus be suspect.

The Negro boys in this study scored more feminine than white boys on the ITSC, while the Negro girls were more feminine than white girls only under standard instructions. Only the Negro boys and white girls were consistent across instructions. (The only exception to this was the correlation between standard and concealed instructions for the white girls.)

These results fall into a reasonable pattern if we look at the possible meaning of each instructional condition. The standard instructions are semiprojective in the sense that they reflect an interaction between the "projective" or "true" self and social expectations. These expectations vary according to whether the child sees "It" as a boy or girl. "It" under concealed instructions is most likely a projective test. The "It-is-you" instructions induce clear social expectations which are overridden only for high-autonomy children with inappropriate sex preference.

Regardless of the stimulus conditions, the Negro boys in the sample did not vary their response pattern. This may be because they have few adequate male models in their coculture. This, plus possible reinforcement for feminine "good behavior" activities, may account for their rather feminine scores. The white girls may be exposed to similar social dynamics. They live in a coculture which provides unattractive feminine models, and where males are clearly dominant and more highly valued. The nonsignificant *AB* correlation for these girls may be due to the small *N* and random variation; it may be due to mixed perceptions of "It" by the *S*s, some seeing "It" as male and responding according to social expectations, while others respond projectively.

The relationship between ITSC performance and teachers' ratings of behavior supports hypotheses about the deleterious effects of a predominantly feminine-dominated subculture on the Negro boys and a masculine-dominated subculture on the white girls. For neither group is there a translation into behavior, as seen by teachers, of either their "true" preference or their social expectations. It is possible that they do not perceive the social expectations, or that they perceive these expectations but do not have adequate models. In contrast, it appears that white boys perceive appropriate sex-role behavior and exhibit it.

The Negro girls seem to see that femininity for "true" selves (as measured by the projective condition) calls for a strong male social posture. This fits with the model of a matriarchal society in which a true woman has to be strong. There is no relationship between the behavior of these girls and the standard instructions, since the scores represent an interaction between responses shaped projectively, by expectations, or both. The correlation obtained between behavior and condition *C* (knowledge of social expectations) suggests that they may perceive the social expectations of the general society and translate them into action that is perceived as appropriately feminine by the teachers.

This study indicates the importance of racial socially mediated factors in the development of sex-role attitudes and behaviors in lower class children. Gewirtz and Stingle (1968) believe that their generalized imitation paradigm can account for the attitudes and behaviors that are usually subsumed under identification. This suggests that research is needed in the lower-class Negro and white communities to determine the types of models available to the children, and especially the types of behaviors reinforced by adults in these groups.

REFERENCES

Biller, H. B. Father dominance and sex-role development in kindergarten age boys. *Developmental Psychology,* 1969, *1,* 87–94.

Brown, D. G. Sex-role preference in young children. *Psychological Monographs,* 1956, *70* (14, Whole No. 421).

Brown, D. G. Masculinity-femininity development in children. *Journal of Consulting Psychology,* 1957, *21,* 197–202.

Brown, D. G. Sex-role preference in children: methodological problems. *Psychological Reports,* 1962, *11,* 477–478.

Endsley, R. C. Effects of concealing "It" on sex-role preferences of preschool children. *Perceptual and Motor Skills,* 1967, *24,* 998.

Gewirtz, J. J., & Stingle, K. G. Learning of generalized imitations as the basis for identification. *Psychological Review,* 1968, *75,* 374–397.

Hall, M., & Keith, R. A. Sex-role preference among children of upper and lower social class. *Journal of Social Psychology,* 1964, *62,* 101–110.

Hartup, W. W., & Zook, E. A. Sex-role preferences in three- and four-year-old children. *Journal of Consulting Psychology,* 1960, *24,* 420–426.

Lansky, L. M., & McKay, G. Sex-role preferences of kindergarten boys and girls: some contradictory results. *Psychological Reports,* 1963, *13,* 415–421.

McCandless, B. R. Children: behavior and development. (2d ed.) New York: Holt, Rinehart & Winston, 1967.

McCandless, B. R. Predictor variable of school success of slum children. Paper presented at the meeting of the American Psychological Association, San Francisco, August 1968.

Rainwater, L. Crucible of identity: the Negro lower class family. *Daedalus,* 1966, *95,* 172–217. (Republished in T. Parsons and K. B. Clark (Eds.), *The Negro American.* Boston: Beacon, 1967. Pp. 166–204.)

Sher, M. A., & Lansky, L. M. The It scale for children: effects of variations in the sex-specificity of the It figure. *Merrill-Palmer Quarterly,* 1968, *14,* 323–330.

Thomas, P. J. Sub-cultural differences in sex-role preference patterns. *Dissertation Abstracts,* 1966, *26,* 6894–6895.

Ward, W. D. The process of sex-role development. *Developmental Psychology,* 1969, *1,* 163–168.

54

Stimulus Preference and Discrimination Learning [1]

Lenore A. DeLucia

This study helps us answer the question, "Does a child begin school with a set of attitudes and preferences that affect his responsiveness to instruction?" The study uses one of psychology's classical techniques—psychophysics—to examine kindergartners' preferences for various toys. (Psychophysical methods, which demand many judgments, have been relatively little used with children since early in the century.) Toys previously scaled by adults for their sex-appropriateness were the stimuli for the children. Thus, it is possible to see the degree to which children's preferences parallel adult judgment of sex-appropriateness. Using a simple discrimination as to which of two toys is "correct" (arbitrarily set), the study goes on to see whether the learning of children is affected by their degree of preference for the stimuli used in the learning task. From the results we see that in our culture, at least, the child takes to school many "built-in" preferences that may influence his (her) learning there.

Dr. Lenore DeLucia is a professor of psychology at Rhode Island College. She prepared this paper especially for this volume.

Abstract

These studies were undertaken to ascertain whether kindergarten children would have stable and similar preference values for toys and whether these preference values would affect discrimination learning. Preference values were determined by the method of paired comparisons and compared with adult judgments of the sex appropriateness of the same toys. Two-choice discrimination problems were devised with the more preferred stimulus being correct for some Ss and the less preferred for others. Ss did have consistent preferences (both within S stability and consistency between Ss). Discrimination was markedly affected by the preferences. Ss learned significantly faster if the more preferred of the two stimuli was the correct one.

The present experiments were designed to clarify the role that stimulus preference plays in children's discrimination learning. Does a child's preference for one or the other of the stimuli in a discrimination problem influence his learning about those stimuli? First, the preference values of several stimuli were determined for a group of kindergarten children. Then the effect on learning of manipulating the pairs of stimuli according to these preference values was determined.

THE FIRST STUDY: PSYCHOLOGICAL SCALING

This study was designed to answer the following questions.

1. What are the preference values of the stimuli judged?
2. Would given Ss be consistent in their preference judgments?
3. Would there be agreement among children on their preferences for the various stimuli?
4. Does agreement among Ss (if found) show an ordering of the preferences according to some criterion?

The stimuli used were toys and the criterion investigated was sex-appropriateness.

The psychological scaling technique that appeared best suited for use with young children was the method of paired comparisons. This method was used successfully by Witryol and Fisher (1960) with preschool children to determine the incentive values of various objects.

In order to make use of the results of scaling to manipulate the stimuli on a group basis in the second study, it was necessary to demonstrate agreement among Ss on their order of preference among the stimuli, for if individual Ss turned out to show internally consistent preferences which were idiosyncratic (not consistent with those of

[1] This paper is based upon a dissertation submitted to Brown University in partial fulfillment of the requirements for the Ph.D. The author is especially indebted to Dr. Gerald R. Levin and Dr. Judy F. Rosenblith.

other *S*s) one could make statements only about the individual's preferences and would be limited from making generalizations about the preference order for a group.

PROCEDURE

*S*s were 12 boys and 12 girls from the kindergarten of the Broad Street School in Providence, Rhode Island.[2] Their mean age was 5 years, 10 months. The apparatus was a device for presenting two pictures and obtaining an objective discrete response measure (choice). (See Fig. 1.) The apparatus consisted of a wooden panel topped by two large rings. The rings were placed so that *E* could flip a picture from her side to the *S*s' side. Directly below both stimulus locations on the *S*s' side of the apparatus was a shelf on which two response bars were mounted. When a bar was depressed it actuated a microswitch which turned on one of two lights on *E*'s side of the panel thus informing *E* as to which bar had been depressed. The stimuli used were 24 black and white photographs of children's toys. The toys are listed in Table 1 together with their scale values to be explained later.

In a complete paired comparison matrix for 24 stimuli there are 276 pairs to be judged. Since this number of comparisons exceeds what one can expect from 5- and 6-year-olds in a single session, the matrix was split into four stimulus series with 69 comparisons in each. Every comparison was randomly assigned to one of the four series. Each stimulus was presented an equal number of times on the right and left side of the apparatus. The stimulus series were presented in different orders to different *S*s. The four sessions were administered over a period of from 6 to 16 days. Each session took approximately 15 minutes.

An *S* was brought to the experimental room by the *E* and seated in front of the apparatus. *E* asked the child to pretend that he (she) was in a toy store and could have one of the two toys pictured. The child was to tell *E* which toy he (she) would rather have by pressing the bar under the toy he (she) chose.

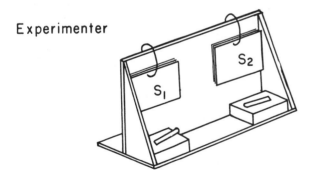

Experimenter

S_2

S_1

Subject

FIGURE 1. *Schematic drawing of the apparatus.*

[2] The author expresses her appreciation to the Providence School Department and principals and teachers of the Broad Street School, the Mary E. Fogarty School and the Sackett Street School for their help in the collection of the data.

TABLE 1
SCALE VALUES OF TOYS

	Boys	Girls
convertible	.00	.73
dump truck	.03	.34
* tool set	.05	.10
airplane	.06	.22
racing car	.12	.16
erector set	.19	.35
football	.25	.00
wheelbarrow	.33	.20
banjo	.35	1.33
* tractor	.40	.40
wading pool	.51	.83
alphabet ball	.62	.79
blackboard	.72	.56
roller skates	.74	.73
* rocking horse	.76	.96
teddy bear	.84	.53
* telephone	1.11	1.22
jump rope	1.16	.92
dish cabinet	1.20	1.29
sewing machine	1.23	.87
* broom set	1.46	1.38
doll-wardrobe	1.61	1.41
doll buggy	1.67	1.43
* cosmetics	1.69	1.86

* Stimuli used in the Second Study. Their selection is discussed in detail later in this paper.

RESULTS

Scale values were obtained for each stimulus using Thurstone's (1927) Case V model. The scale was constructed to order the toys from most to least preferred for boys and from least to most preferred for girls. This makes it easy to compare scale values on a given stimulus for boys and girls. For boys, then, the higher the scale value, the less the toy is preferred; but for girls, the higher the scale value, the *more* the toy is preferred. These scale values are shown in Table 1. The difference between the scale values for any two stimuli reflects the difference in the proportion of *S*s who prefer one to the other. If two stimuli are equally preferred, 50% of *S*s prefer one and 50% the other.[3]

Consistency was examined for each *S*. If *S* is consistent, it means that if he prefers A to B and also prefers B to C, then he must prefer A to C. If *S* judges C as preferred to A, the three comparative judgments are said to form a circular triad. The most powerful test for the consistency of an *S* takes into account the number of

[3] Statistical determination of scale values proceeds by transforming the proportion data to Z scores or deviation scores. The Z score is one estimate of the distance between stimulus A and stimulus B. It is obtained from the proportion of *S*s who preferred stimulus A to stimulus B. Since each of these stimuli was compared with every other stimulus we have a number of estimates of the relative distance between stimulus A and B in relation to all other stimuli judged. An average of all these estimates provides the scale value for that stimulus.

circular triads *S* makes. The fewer circular triads, the more consistent the judgments. This is tested by Kendall's (1948) coefficient of consistency. The probability value associated with this coefficient reflects the likelihood of making the observed number of circular triads by chance. In a 24 by 24 matrix such as this there are over 10,000 possible circular triads. The number actually observed for *S*s in this study ranged from 36 to 504. Chance could account for 36 triads 99 times out of 100 and even for 504 triads 60 times in 100. Thus no *S* showed any statistically significant inconsistencies.[4]

Consistency among *S*s was examined next. Kendall's (1948) coefficient of agreement measures the extent of agreement among *S*s.[4] Perfect agreement would yield a *u* of 1.00. The obtained *u*'s (.24 for boys, .23 for girls) reflect agreement among *S*s' judgments that is significant at the .001 level. The relation between the consistency of an individual's preference choices and his agreement with the group was also checked by comparing consistency coefficients and agreement coefficients. *S*s who showed greater consistency in their individual preferences also showed higher agreement with the group (rho = .71 for boys and .54 for girls).

The agreement between the scale values determined for each stimulus by boys and by girls was tested. There was a high negative correlation (*r* = −.83), i.e., stimuli most preferred by girls tended to be least preferred by boys.

Next the relation between the preference scale values for the children and the sex-appropriateness of the toys was examined. In a previous study (DeLucia, 1963) these same toys had been rated by a group of college students. They had been instructed to assign each toy a rating based on how appropriate it was for one sex or the other. These ratings yielded scale values of the sex-appropriateness of the toys. These adult sex-appropriateness values are highly related to the preference scale values of the children. The rank order correlations between the two are .92 for boys and .87 for girls.

The Second Study: Discrimination Learning

The problem of stimulus preference in discrimination learning received little attention in early studies. More recently, however, it has been studied indirectly by inferring stimulus preferences from the response patterns during the learning process (Behar, 1961; Harlow, 1950; Levine, 1959; and Moon and Harlow, 1955). It has also been studied by assuming that the first response made during discrimination learning reflects a preference for that stimulus (Harlow and Hicks, 1957). Stimulus preference is one of several error factors which Harlow (1950), Levine (1959) and Behar (1961) have been able to isolate in discrimination learning by means of the learning set experiments. Harlow and Hicks (1957) found that monkeys learned dis-

crimination problems faster when the preferred stimulus was correct than when it was incorrect. They also showed that the effect of stimulus preference was strongest early in learning and decreased with increasing numbers of trials. In a study of oddity learning (Moon and Harlow, 1955) stimulus preference accounted for a significant number of errors during the first block of problems, but such errors became infrequent during later blocks of problems.

The tendency to form preferences and respond on the basis of those preferences appears to be a response set which is built into organisms at a relatively early age. Levine's (1959) developmental data on monkeys showed that stimulus preference responses accounted for a significant number of errors during discrimination learning by 60-day-old *S*s. Data on the development of stimulus preference are also available from a few child studies. Spears (1966) demonstrated consistent stimulus preferences in 4-month-old human infants. He found that these infants were not only consistent in their own preferences, but that there was also close agreement among *S*s. Simmons (1964) used an operant discrimination task with one-year-old infants. During a sixty-second baseline period the infants were shown red and blue lights which were subsequently to be used in discrimination learning. The number of responses made to each stimulus during this period was her measure of preference. She found that more of her *S*s had high response rates to red than to blue, hence suggested that most infants prefer red. The preferences of somewhat older children were studied by Stewart (1958). Using both nursery school children and fourth graders, she found that the older children exhibited more consistent preferences, but that both age groups were significantly consistent in their preferences.

The present experiment requires *S* to respond to one stimulus (and not the other) when one stimulus is more preferred (or sex-appropriate) than the other. It asks the following sets of questions:

1. Is learning to respond to the "correct" (arbitrarily designated) stimulus any easier or faster when it is also the more preferred (or sex-appropriate)? If preference affects the learning, is the effect more pronounced early in learning?

2. What effect on learning does the position on the preference scale of the two stimuli have? If both stimuli are highly preferred, does learning occur at a different rate than if both stimuli are low in preference value? What is the effect of having both stimuli of medium preference value?

3. Are there sex differences in any of these results? Do boys and girls learn equally well when the problems involve sex-typed materials?

---

[4] This is based on Kendall's test of significance for *u*, a test which is based on the X^2 distribution.

PROCEDURE

Stimuli were chosen for the discrimination learning problems using the preference scaling data in such a way as to fulfill the following requirements. There were to be three pairs of stimulus objects, each to be used in a different discrimination problem. One problem was to have stimulus objects both of which were high on the preference scale, though one higher than the other (referred to subsequently as the HP problem, meaning high preference); another problem was to have stimuli which were both low in preference value, though one lower than the other (LP or low preference problem); the third problem was to have stimuli from the center portion of the preference scale, but with one stimulus more preferred than the other (MP or medium preference problem). In terms of the sex-appropriateness of the stimuli, one pair would contain two masculine toys, one two feminine toys, and the third would have one masculine and one feminine toy. For boys, then, the two masculine toys would be the HP problem and for girls they would be the LP problem. In addition, the magnitude of the difference in preference scale values for a pair of toys was to be about the same for boys as for girls. And the magnitude of the difference in preference scale values for the two objects in a pair was to be about the same for all three pairs.

These considerations led to choosing the tool set and tractor as one pair, the broom set and cosmetics kit as the second, and the rocking horse and telephone as the third. Table 2 shows the design of the experiment. For half of the groups, the more preferred of the two stimuli was correct and for the others the more preferred was incorrect. In other words, some children received reinforcement for responding to their preferred stimulus object and others were incorrect when they did so. For girls the more preferred members of the pairs are the cosmetics, telephone and tractor. It is the reverse for the boys.

All combinations of the three variables, correctness of preferred stimulus, preference locus of the stimulus pair (HP, MP or LP), and sex of *S* were studied. Within each sex, *S*s were randomly assigned to one of the six groups.

*S*s were 193 children from the kindergartens of three Providence public schools. Their ages ranged from 5 years, 3 months to 6 years, 7 months, and the mean was 6 years, 0 months. Their mean I.Q. was 95 on the Lorge-Thorndike Intelligence Test, Form A.

The apparatus was basically the same as that in Fig. 1. The modifications were the addition of : (1) a large red jewel light to the top center portion, and (2) two swinging doors in front of the stimulus area so that stimuli could be put in place without *S* seeing them until E opened the swinging doors (simultaneously).

The discrimination problem was introduced to each *S* as a game. The object was to press the bar under the stimulus which *S* thought would turn on the light. *S*s were instructed that if they turned on the light a sufficient number of times they would receive a prize. The prizes were small plastic charms of animals, musical instruments, or toys.

*S*s were allowed 48 trials of discrimination learning. Trials were discontinued prior to this if the criterion of learning (six consecutive correct responses) was reached. All correct responses were followed by a two-to-three-second presentation of the red light.

It should be noted that three statistical analyses were performed. In all cases Lindquist Type III analyses of variance were used. Two analyses (one for boys and one for girls) involved the variables of (1) preferred stimulus correct or incorrect, (2) locus on the preference dimension, and (3) trials. In the third analysis sex differences were analyzed by collapsing trials and using trials-to-criterion data instead of the number of correct responses per block of trials.

TABLE 2
STIMULI AND GROUPS IN DISCRIMINATION LEARNING

Group	N	Designated as correct	(Scale value)	Designated as incorrect	(Scale value)	Experimental manipulation
BOYS						
High Preference Toys	15	tool set	(.05)	tractor	(.40)	Preferred stimulus correct
High Preference Toys	15	tractor	(.40)	tool set	(.05)	Preferred stimulus incorrect
Medium Preference Toys	15	rocking horse	(.76)	telephone	(1.11)	Preferred stimulus correct
Medium Preference Toys	15	telephone	(1.11)	rocking horse	(.76)	Preferred stimulus incorrect
Low Preference Toys	15	broom set	(1.46)	cosmetics	(1.69)	Preferred stimulus correct
Low Preference Toys	15	cosmetics	(1.69)	broom set	(1.46)	Preferred stimulus incorrect
GIRLS						
Low Preference Toys	15	tractor	(.40)	tool set	(.10)	Preferred stimulus correct
Low Preference Toys	15	tool set	(.10)	tractor	(.40)	Preferred stimulus incorrect
Medium Preference Toys	15	telephone	(1.22)	rocking horse	(.96)	Preferred stimulus correct
Medium Preference Toys	15	rocking horse	(.96)	telephone	(1.22)	Preferred stimulus incorrect
High Preference Toys	15	cosmetics	(1.86)	broom set	(1.38)	Preferred stimulus correct
High Preference Toys	15	broom set	(1.38)	cosmetics	(1.86)	Preferred stimulus incorrect

*S*s were included in the data analysis only if they had preferences for the toys consistent with those of the *S*s on whom the preference values had been established. If *S*s had preferences greatly different from those used for scaling, there would be no basis for generalizing the preference values of the original sample to the present sample. To check on this a three-item paired comparison test was devised. The pairs were chosen such that the *S*s in the scaling study who were internally consistent in their 276 judgments agreed among themselves on their responses to these three pairs. The pairs used were racing car with doll buggy, blackboard with doll buggy, and racing car with blackboard. The first member of each pair is the more preferred for boys and the second for girls. With position of each member randomized, the pairs were presented in random order at the conclusion of the discrimination learning. This timing was used to avoid calling attention to the preference characteristics or sex-appropriateness of the stimulus objects used in the learning phase. Any *S* who made more than one inconsistent choice was eliminated from the main sample and another tested until there were 15 in each of the final groups. If a girl, for instance, preferred both the racing car and the blackboard to the doll buggy, she was considered inconsistent with others of her sex and eliminated. Thirteen *S*s did not pass this consistency test. Data analyses are based on the remaining 180 *S*s.

RESULTS

Preferred stimulus correct or incorrect:

The main question of this part of the study concerned the effect on learning of *S*s' having the preferred stimulus as correct or incorrect in a discrimination problem. Figure 2 shows that in 5 out of 6 cases, groups that had their preferred stimulus as correct learned more efficiently than the comparable group that had the preferred stimulus as incorrect. The only reversal was for the boys in the MP group and differences were small. Figure 3 shows the results of pooling the data so that all *S*s with the preferred stimulus correct can be compared with all *S*s having it incorrect.

Analysis of the trials-to-criterion measure showed that preferred stimulus correct groups required fewer trials than did the preferred stimulus incorrect group ($F = 10.45$, $df = 1,168$, $p = .001$).

The related question asked whether the effects of stimulus preference would be stronger early in learning than later as Harlow and Hicks (1957) had found for monkeys. As can be seen in Figure 2, five of the six group comparisons show only minor differences between preferred-correct and preferred-incorrect curves early in learning (on the early blocks of trials) with some tendency to an increased difference over trials. The interaction between trials and the stimulus value (correct or incorrect) was statistically significant for girls ($p = .05$). It did not reach the usual significance levels for boys ($p = .25$). For girls, at least, it can be said that learning occurred at a significantly faster rate when the preferred stimulus was correct.

The response of *S*s on trial one, the only trial not influenced by any reinforcement, can also be analyzed to determine the early effects of stimulus preference value.

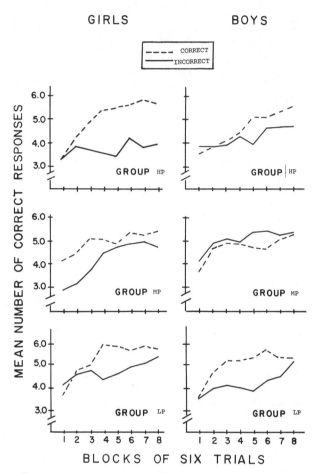

FIGURE 2. *Mean number of correct responses during the discrimination learning of HP, MP, and LP problem with the preferred stimulus correct or incorrect.*

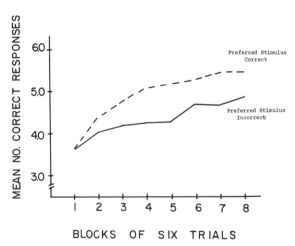

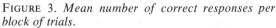

FIGURE 3. *Mean number of correct responses per block of trials.*

*S*s' choices on trial one do not show marked bias toward one or the other of the stimuli.

Location on the preference scale:

Question 2 asked whether the rate of learning would be different if both stimulus objects were highly preferred (HP) or nonpreferred (LP), or were from the central portion of the scale though with one on the preferred side (MP). Analysis of variance showed this variable to be unimportant ($p = .25$ for both sexes).

Sex differences:

Separate analyses of the data for boys and girls showed an interaction of stimulus preference and trials, significant only for girls. Girls who had the preferred stimulus as correct in the discrimination problem learned more rapidly than those who had it as incorrect. There was a non-significant trend in this direction for boys.

The correctness of the preferred stimulus was consistent in its effectiveness despite the fact that the actual objects differed for boys and girls. Because the stimuli were sex-typed, the preferred toy for a boy was a nonpreferred toy for a girl. Had a group of boys and girls been given the same problem, i.e., the same two stimuli to discriminate using the same toy as correct for both, one sex would have had its preferred stimulus correct and the other would have had it as incorrect. On the basis of the effects of correctness-incorrectness found here, one could predict which sex would make more correct responses. To give a concrete example, using cosmetics as correct when paired with the broom set, cosmetics is the more preferred stimulus for girls, but for boys the broom set is the more preferred, so their preferred stimulus is incorrect. Thus one would expect that even though the problem may appear to be the same for boys and girls it is not, and girls would make more correct responses because the correct stimulus is their preferred toy. This is indeed the result that was obtained, for those two groups of *S*s. Two other groups of *S*s had the same problem, but with the broom set as the correct stimulus. Thus boys would be expected to make more correct responses on this problem. This was the case. In five of the six group comparisons shown in Figure 4 the children for whom the correct choice was the preferred stimulus performed better in learning the problem than those for whom it was nonpreferred. Five out of six comparisons in the expected direction is possible fewer than 11 times in 100 by chance.

DISCUSSION

What kinds of behaviors or processes might serve to explain the results? Zeigler and Wyckoff (1961) suggest that the preference characteristics of stimulus objects affect the number of observing responses made to those objects. It may be that the preferred stimulus acts as its own reinforcer for the observing response. Wyckoff's (1952) data indicate that if one of the two stimuli in a discrimination problem is preferred, a high level of observing responses will be maintained. This is true regardless of whether the preferred stimulus is the correct or incorrect one in the discrimination problem.

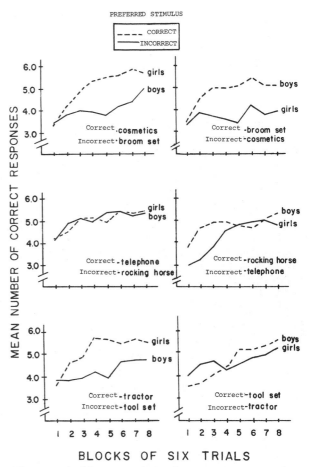

FIGURE 4. *Mean number of correct responses in each block of six trials. Shown are the comparisons in which both boys and girls had the same problem but for one sex the preferred stimulus was correct and for the other sex the preferred stimulus was incorrect.*

In order to account for the present results in Wyckoff's terms, an additional problem must be considered. Any explanation for the different speeds of learning and level of learning attained by the preferred-correct and preferred-incorrect groups must account for the fact that both groups had the exact same stimuli in their problems. A complete explanation cannot be based only on the notion that a discrimination problem including a preferred stimulus increases *S*s' observing response. According to Wyckoff it would do so regardless of the correctness or incorrectness of the preferred stimulus. However, in this study the groups do not show equal amounts of learning. The consistently better learning of the preferred-correct groups cannot be attributed to the preference characteristics of the two stimuli alone. The reinforcement value of the preferred stimulus must, in some part, be responsible for the differential learning of the two groups.

Another model of discrimination learning has been proposed by Zeaman and House (1961). The response set in their theory is termed "attention." They have found that one stimulus dimension which exerts considerable control in gaining the S's attention is stimulus novelty. They consider novelty a "preferred aspect" of a stimulus situation, and have demonstrated that the introduction of a novel stimulus has led to the learning of discrimination problems which were judged too difficult for the Ss. What if this "preferred aspect" were measured in a way other than novelty? Why not measure the stimulus preference itself? Is it possible that the preferred stimulus "exercises strong control over attention"? Can it be that reinforcement of the preferred stimulus object increases that stimulus's attention value more than reinforcement of the nonpreferred stimulus increases the attention value of the nonpreferred stimulus object?

Another possible explanation for the effect of stimulus preference on discrimination learning comes from another study by Zeaman and House (1962) in which they studied the relative speed in learning of approach and avoidance tendencies in discrimination learning problems by retardates. They found that approach tendencies developed more rapidly than avoidance tendencies early in discrimination learning. In the present study, one could hypothesize that children in the preferred stimulus-correct groups viewed the problem as one of approaching the preferred stimulus, whereas those in the incorrect groups had to learn to avoid the preferred stimulus. In such a case the superiority of the preferred-correct groups might be explained in terms of their learning an approach tendency, Zeaman and House having found approach to be learned more quickly than avoidance.

The present study demonstrated the superior learning of the preferred-correct groups. However, early in learning there were no differences between the groups. There was an increasing difference in speed of learning as trials progressed. An attention theory might suggest that Ss were responding on the basis of some other response set which was more potent early in learning. Were the Ss initially inattentive to the relevant dimension in this experiment? One can check to see whether Ss were responding to position. The right hand stimulus was chosen by 61% of the girls and 69% of the boys on the first trial. While position clearly does not account for all errors, it does appear that right position responses were more prominent than stimulus preference responses on trial one.

In this experiment, the two items in a pair of stimuli in each learning problem were not very different from one another in stimulus preference value. Both stimuli of a pair were distinctly preferred or dis-

tinctly nonpreferred for two problems, and both were medium in preferredness for one problem. Such an arrangement may limit the amount of stimulus preference demonstrated early in learning. It is possible that if the difference in preference value between the two stimuli in a problem were increased, the effects of preference would be more powerful early in learning.

While other experiments which vary parameters such as that above will make possible fuller comprehension of the phenomena observed in this study, the present results make it imperative to give consideration to stimulus preference in discrimination learning studies. It is also clear that the data of such studies should be analyzed separately for the two sexes where both are used as Ss. In addition to these obvious extrapolations from this work, we call attention to the fact that such results have implications for school learning situations as well. Much of school learning is in the form of discrimination learning. Learning the difference between the words "dad" and "bad" requires the discrimination of the letters "d" and "b"; learning that a gold star is more valuable than a red star requires another form of discrimination. Teachers have often been cautioned to arrange discrimination learning situations in such a way that children have a high likelihood of making the correct response. The implications of this study are that the best arrangement of a discrimination learning situation is one in which one takes advantage of the child's built-in preferences for one or the other of the stimulus objects and designates the preferred stimulus as correct, or where that is impossible, alters the original preference before presenting the discrimination problem.

REFERENCES

1. BEHAR, I. Analysis of object-alternation learning in rhesus monkeys. *J. comp. physiol. Psychol.*, 1961, *54*, 539–542.
2. DeLUCIA, LENORE A. The toy preference test: a measure of sex-role identification. *Child Develpm.*, 1963, *34*, 107–117.
3. HARLOW, H. F. Analysis of discrimination learning by monkeys. *J. exp. Psychol.*, 1950, *40*, 26–39.
4. HARLOW, H. F. and HICKS, L. H. Discrimination learning theory: uniprocess vs. duoprocess. *Psychol. Rev.*, 1957, *64*, 104–109.
5. KENDALL, J. G. *Rank correlation method.* Charles Griffin, London: 1948.
6. LEVINE, J. A model of hypothesis behavior in discrimination learning set. *Psychol. Rev.*, 1959, *66*, 353–366.
7. MOON, L. E. and HARLOW, H. F. Analysis of oddity learning by rhesus monkeys. *J. comp. physiol. Psychol.*, 1955, *48*, 188–194.

8. SIMMONS, MAE WILLIAMSON. Operant discrimination in human infants. *Child Develpm.*, 1964, *35*, 737–748.

9. SPEARS, W. C. Visual preferences in the four-month-old infant. *Psychonomic Science*, 1966, *4*, 237–238.

10. STEWART, B. R. Developmental differences in the stability of object preferences and conflict behavior. *Child Develpm.*, 1958, *29*, 9–18.

11. THURSTONE, L. L. A law of comparative judgment. *Psychol. Rev.*, 1927, *34*, 273–286.

12. WITRYOL, S. L. and FISCHER, W. F. Scaling children's incentives by the method of paired comparisons. *Psychol. Rep.*, 1960, *7*, 471–474.

13. WYCKOFF, L. B. JR. The role of observing responses in discrimination learning, Part I. *Psychol. Rev.*, 1952, *59*, 431–442.

14. ZEAMAN, D. and HOUSE, B. J. *Role of attention in retardate discrimination learning*. University of Connecticut and Psychological Laboratories of the Mansfield State Training School. Progress Report No. 3, Nov. 1961.

15. ZEAMAN, D. and HOUSE, B. J. Approach and avoidance in the discrimination learning of retardates. *Child Develpm.*, 1962, *33*, 355–372.

16. ZEIGLER, H. P. and WYCKOFF, L. B. JR. Observing responses and discrimination learning. *Quart. J. exp. Psychol.*, 1961, *13*, 129–140.

55

Children's Textbooks
and Personality Development:
An Exploration
in the Social Psychology
of Education

IRVIN L. CHILD, ELMER H. POTTER,
AND ESTELLE M. LEVINE

*In this paper, the authors point out some of the
incidental "teaching" that takes place in our
schools. Specifically, they show us what the textbooks teach with respect to the definition of sex
roles. Although the study is relatively old, it is
doubtful that the intervening years have brought
much real change in the ways in which girls are
portrayed in our textbooks. In addition, the methodology used in this study is still highly adaptable
to all kinds of projects that readers of this book
might want to undertake.*

*We would like to call attention to a related prob-
lem of current concern—our school texts fail to
portray racial and other minorities. Thus, they
handicap the learning of children who cannot find
appropriate identification figures in their school
"readers." This is one aspect of the problem of
"relevance" in school materials.*

*Irvin L. Child is a professor in Yale's Depart-
ment of Psychology. Elmer H. Potter (now Ethe-
lyn H. Klatskin) is in the Department of Pediatrics
at Yale University Medical School. Mrs. Estelle
Levine, an undergraduate student at the time of
the study, is no longer in the field of psychology.*

INTRODUCTION

In the application of psychology to the study of
formal education in our society, attention has been
directed primarily at intellectual aspects of education. A few notable studies, such as those by the
Character Education Inquiry (1) and by Jones (2),
have been concerned with the development of
ideals and morals in the school situation. But for
the most part, psychologists have directed their
attention to the study of intellectual aptitudes and
achievements—their measurement, the factors
influencing them, and their predictive value.

Yet intellectual achievements and aptitudes are
only one aspect of the child's behavior that schools
are capable of influencing. Also of tremendous importance is another aspect: the motives that children develop, the ways they learn to satisfy their
motives, the expectations they acquire about the
consequences of trying to satisfy their motives in
various ways. It is around this motivational aspect
of the educational process that this study is centered.

The motivational influences of education are
significant both in themselves and in relation to
intellectual development. They are important in
themselves because education should be directed
at training children to become well-adjusted and
responsible adults as well as adults equipped with
intellectual skills. But a person's very acquisition
of information and understanding, and most of all
the use he will make of it, depends upon motivational aspects of his personality. Hence the attainment of the intellectual aims of education is itself
dependent upon the motives developed in children.
This study represents, then, one of several beginnings that have been and are being made in the social psychology of education in our society—the
study of the role of the educational system in shaping not merely the intellect but the general personality of the child.

The specific objective of this study is the analysis of certain content of the world of ideas which
confronts children in the process of education,
from the point of view of the probable effect of that
content on the motivation of their behavior. Just
what that means will be made clear through the
discussion, in the rest of this chapter, of the way
the content was analyzed.

SELECTION OF MATERIAL

THE BOOKS CHOSEN

The material chosen for analysis consisted of certain portions of the content of general readers intended for use in the third grade. Printed material
was selected, rather than the content of what was

Irvin L. Child, Elmer H. Potter, and Estelle M. Levine, "Children's textbooks and personality development: An exploration in
the social psychology of education," *Psychological Monographs, 60,* No. 3, 1946, 1–7, 43–53. Copyright 1946 by the American
Psychological Association, and reproduced by permission.

said by teachers in classrooms, because of the accessibility of printed material, and because a manageable sample of it must of necessity reflect accurately certain educational practices in the country at large. The choice of the third-grade level was made on the grounds of convenience for the purpose of this study: textbooks for the first and second grades have such very simple content that few passages are susceptible of the kind of analysis that we have undertaken, while readers from the fourth grade up, on the other hand, begin to have such complex material that the analysis would be more laborious and less reliable.

We chose for our purpose all of the general third-grade readers we were able to find which had been published since 1930. (Excluded were third-grade readers intended primarily to teach special topics such as science, social studies, or arithmetic, and one reader which deviated greatly from all the others in containing considerable material on religion.) In all, 30 books were included in the analysis.

SELECTION OF CONTENT FROM THE BOOKS

. . . The general criterion for selection was that the story contain characters in action, since the child's behavior would be affected only by his generalizing from that of individuals in the stories to his own behavior. This resulted in the exclusion of [some] types of material . . . but the material analyzed included well over three quarters of the content of the books. Altogether, 914 stories were analyzed.

A story is often, however, a cumbersome and complex unit for analysis and comparison. . . . The unit for analysis, therefore, was not the story but the *thema.* A thema is a sequence of psychological events consisting of (1) a situation or circumstances confronting a person, (2) the behavior (internal and external) with which the person responds, (3) the consequences of the behavior as felt by the person himself (3). In the 914 stories used, 3409 thema were found and analyzed, an average of almost 4 thema per story. In the presentation of quantitative data in the rest of this monograph, the number of thema is always the basic quantity dealt with.

METHOD OF ANALYSIS

. . . SUMMARY OF PROCEDURE

The outline of the analysis given above will now be briefly summarized, together with some indication of the actual technique used in recording the data.

The first step was to read each story in a given book and determine whether it was suitable for the purposes of the analysis. If it was suitable, the sec-

TABLE 1

CATEGORIES OF BEHAVIOR EMPLOYED IN ANALYZING THE CONTENT OF THIRD-GRADE READERS, WITH THE NUMBER OF THEMA IN WHICH EACH CATEGORY WAS FOUND

Category *	*Number of Thema in Which It Appears*
Objectless behavior	
Activity	264
Passivity	89
Sentience	82
Elation	55
Behavior primarily in relation to things and events	
Cognizance	351
Achievement	221
Construction	75
Imaginality	31
Acquisition	177
Retention	33
Order	43
Altruistic social behavior (generally leading to simultaneous gratification of other person's needs)	
Affiliation	364
Nurturance	266
Succorance	176
Deference	184
Egoistic social behavior (generally competing with other person's needs)	
Aggression	206
Dominance	152
Recognition	175
Autonomy	122
Rejection	21
Avoidance behavior	
Harmavoidance	212
Blamavoidance	72
Infavoidance	38

* For definition of terms, see Glossary at end of article.—EDITOR

ond step was to identify all the separate thema in the story that fitted the pattern of analysis. When these thema were identified, a file card was prepared for each one. It was labeled appropriately to identify the story and the book and then the following information was entered on it:

1. The type of story
2. Whether the character was central or antisocial
3. The classification of the character according to age, sex, humanity, etc.
4. The behavior displayed, classified according to Murray's system of needs (3)
5. Notes on the circumstances surrounding the behavior
6. The classification of the consequences of the behavior.

OVERALL FINDINGS AND DISCUSSION

CULTURAL FORCES INFLUENCING PERSONALITY

The observations that have been reviewed on the treatment of various categories of behavior in children's readers can leave no doubt that this treatment is such as to encourage the development of certain motives and to discourage others. A tabulation of the percentage of reward, punishment, and no consequence for the various categories of behavior, presented in Table 2, brings out this general point quite clearly. The categories are arranged here in order of relative frequency of reward, and this order may be taken as one indication of the degree of encouragement or discouragement of the development of each one. In considerable part, of course, this order reflects general cultural norms—for example, in the high value placed on affiliation, nurturance and cognizance, and in the frequent punishment of aggression, retention and rejection. To this extent the analysis of the contents of the readers does not stand alone but is useful as symptomatic of probable characteristics of other kinds of content of the world of ideas that reach children—what teachers say to them in classes, morals that their parents point up to them, the content of stories they read elsewhere.

But the entire impact of cultural forces on personality manifested in these readers is not shown in a simple listing of the treatment of the several categories separately. There are also certain generalities which can be found running through the whole series of categories, generalities about particular ways of achieving ends which are most likely to lead to success or to failure.

Perhaps the most striking case of this sort is the repeated reward of effort or work as a way of reaching goals. In the discussion of acquisition, it was shown that effortful ways of acquiring things are the most frequently rewarded; similar observations were made in connection with achievement and construction. Even in the case of the relatively objectless need for activity, the more purposeful instances of activity which require more work are more frequently rewarded. Here certainly are some of the forces leading to the development of a motive to work or put forth effort. This motive is sometimes very important in adults or older children, and may activate them for a long time, even when the effort leads to no external reward. It needs explanation, because of marked contrast with the general tendency for human beings and other organisms to avoid work or effort when it is not necessary. The motive is doubtless developed in large part through social learning, and we have in this reading matter an example of the kinds of social influences that lead to its development.

TABLE 2

PERCENTAGE OF REWARD, PUNISHMENT, AND NO CONSEQUENCE FOR EACH CATEGORY OF BEHAVIOR (IN ALL OF THE 3409 THEMA WHICH WERE ANALYZED)

Category of Behavior	Percent of Thema in Which the Behavior Is Rewarded	Percent of Thema in Which the Behavior Is Punished	Percent of Thema in Which Behavior Results in No Consequence (i.e., neither Rewarded nor Punished)
Construction	96	1	3
Sentience	96	4	0
Elation	95	4	1
Cognizance	86	9	5
Succorance	84	10	6
Affiliation	82	8	9
Nurturance	82	5	12
Achievement	80	10	9
Recognition	79	13	8
Activity	74	9	16
Dominance	74	16	8
Blamavoidance	71	15	14
Imaginality	71	6	23
Order	70	2	28
Acquisition	64	31	3
Passivity	54	26	20
Deference	52	10	38
Harmavoidance	49	39	12
Autonomy	48	40	12
Retention	42	48	10
Aggression	35	52	11
Rejection	14	62	24
Infavoidance	8	74	18
All categories	71	17	12

Another special emphasis is on the acquisition of skills, on learning. This is, of course, evident in the first place from the high frequency of cognizant behavior and its high proportion of reward. It also appears in the treatment of achievement; there it was observed that the most frequently rewarded mode of achievement was by the acquisition of new skills, even more frequently rewarded than achievement through the display of skills formerly acquired.

Despite the emphasis on learning, there is in these third-grade readers little encouragement of intellectual activity as such. The cognizance is usually directed at simple isolated information rather than a quest for understanding. Sentience, as it appears in the readers, is only rarely concerned with esthetic appreciation which goes beyond the admiration of simple manmade objects or of nature. Activity is ordinarily physical, and in only one case intellectual in nature. The achievements, even those involving the acquisition of a skill, can in most cases hardly be spoken of as intellectual. Similarly in constructive behavior: only one story about construction concerns a non-material product, a poem.

It should be noted, moreover, that the acquisition of skills or knowledge which is rewarded is generally that which is dependent upon persons in a superior position—for example the gaining of knowledge by children through questioning parents or teachers. In this sense, too, there is less emphasis on intellectual activity than might appear, since there is relatively little encouragement of original thinking on the part of the central character.

A distinction is also made between satisfying needs in socially approved ways, which tends to be rewarded, and satisfying them in disapproved ways, which tends to be punished. For example, in the case of retention, retention which is defined as socially or individually useful and permissible, such as saving money, is rewarded; on the other hand, retention which is defined as selfish is punished. Similarly for recognition: there is heavy reward for exhibiting one's capacities so long as social rules are followed; but when rules are broken, as by exhibiting oneself at the wrong time or making claims about one's powers that are not justified, then the behavior is punished. Dominance and aggression provide examples of other modes of behavior where social rules set down certain conditions as making the behavior permissible and certain other conditions as not. In these cases the conditions have to do with what other needs, if any, are served at the same time; if dominance or aggression does not serve some other approved purpose, or if it serves other disapproved purposes such as selfish acquisition or retention, it is punished.

PROBLEMS OF ADJUSTMENT

In the ways that have just been indicated, material such as that in the readers provides lessons to children, encouraging or discouraging the development of motives in a way that on the whole is likely to lead to more satisfactory adjustment in our society. But at the same time there are certain respects in which this material is failing to contribute to good adjustment.

A major defect of the readers from this point of view is what might be called their unrealistic optimism. Behavior directed at affiliation and nurturance, for example, is almost always rewarded in the readers. There are very few cases of failure.

It is impossible to compare the proportion of success here with that obtaining in children's everyday life. Yet from the point of view of contributing to the solution of problems of everyday life, failures ought to receive a larger proportion of attention, for it is they that pose problems.

It may indeed be true that the encouragement of affiliative and nurturant needs in this reading is of little consequence, because the much stronger pressures from the real environment are already working in that same direction, and the contribution from here can be little more. But there is a very great opportunity for reading matter, such as in these textbooks, to point up possible solutions for frustrations often encountered by the child in seeking for gratification of these needs. In that case, such reading matter should include a larger number of accounts of how children get around obstacles in their attempts to satisfy affiliative and nurturant needs—stories in which expression of these needs first meets with punishment or rebuff and only attains success when some new method of approach more suited to the environment is hit upon.

For children who have encountered failure in their everyday life, the easy attainment of goals such as nurturance and affiliation in the readers may be so unrealistic as to have little effect in strengthening their desire for such goals. Suggestions as to how these needs may be satisfied despite serious difficulties might, on the other hand, through their realism to such children, contribute to strengthening the needs.

A similar sort of unrealism was commented on in the discussion of infavoidance. While the content of these readers might do a great deal towards strengthening a desire for achievement in competitive success, there is very little about those children—perhaps the majority—who frequently experience failure in competition, and few suggestions about how such children can find some satisfactory way of adjusting to their failure. Such material might be more beneficial than what is actually found in contributing to the better adjustment of those children whose present adjustment is unsatisfactory.

A similar failure to make positive suggestions is found in the treatment of aggression and acquisition. Here are two needs, certainly universally present in children, which lead to serious problems of adjustment because of their frequent interference with desires of other and more powerful persons.

Children's reading matter might be quite useful in furthering satisfactory adjustment if it were able to pose models for the child of ways to satisfy these needs when they are prevented from the most direct and immediately satisfactory expression. While there are certainly some incidents which might be useful in this way, the general tendency in the readers is, instead, for these needs simply to be overlooked in the child characters. It is as though the writers were inclined to solve problems of aggression and acquisition in children by trying to convince children that they do not have these needs, that they are experienced only by adults, animals and supernatural creatures. To a certain extent the child's real social environment may be cooperating with the readers in this direction, through a tradition that children do not hate or covet and are basically nice unless they are led to be otherwise. But the fact probably is that every child does hate and does covet, and that in his efforts to do so he is being repeatedly rebuffed by the more powerful persons in his environment. Those persons are apt often not to have the psychological insight necessary for redirecting these interests of the child into channels where they can have more success. Here then is a valuable potential role of children's reading matter.

Another possible inadequacy of the reading matter, one much more difficult to judge, is concerned with maturity. It is notable in the content of these readers that independent action initiated by child characters, and indeed by anyone, is more likely to be punished than similar behavior which is performed under the direction of a superior. Cognizance, for example, is rather frequently punished when it is undertaken on the child's own initiative and leads to pursuit of knowledge directly by the child's own exploratory behavior, whereas it is almost always rewarded if knowledge is gained through dependence upon authority. Autonomous behavior, too, is generally punished except in the case where the kind of autonomy is that desired by the child's elders. (There is an exception to this in the case of nurturance, which is more often rewarded when it is spontaneously initiated by the character himself.)

There can be no doubt that if children continue to be trained in this way as they grow older, the effect on their potentialities as adults will be a bad one. It may indeed be that a considerable proportion of adult maladjustment in marriage and occupational life is due to the discouragement of autonomy and independence by the educational system up to the point where an adolescent or young adult leaves it. On the other hand, it may of course be argued that the amount of independence encouraged by the content of these readers is quite appropriate for the particular age level at which the readers are directed. Certainly the development towards autonomy must be a gradual process and a considerable amount of dependence on superiors

is necessary, not only at this age but on into adult life. For this reason it is impossible to make a conclusive judgment about the wisdom of this aspect of the content of the readers.

DIFFERENTIAL TREATMENT OF THE SEXES

Perhaps the most striking single finding of this study is the extent to which a differentiation is made between the roles of male and female in the content of these readers. To the extent that boys identify with male characters, and girls with female characters, this difference both in itself and as a reflection of facts that hold true of many other sources of influence on children, must have a profound significance on the differential development of personality in the two sexes.

Some of the differentiation can be seen in the mere frequency with which the two sexes appear among the characters displaying the various categories of behavior. Female characters, for example, are relatively more frequent among those displaying affiliation, nurturance, and harmavoidance. On the other hand, females are less frequent, relatively, among characters displaying activity, aggression, achievement, construction, and recognition. Girls and women are thus being shown as sociable, kind and timid, but inactive, unambitious and uncreative.

This picture is further added to by considering the relative proportion of male and female characters among the subsidiary characters who are objects related to the satisfaction of the needs of the central characters. The most important findings here refer to nurturance and cognizance. The persons nurtured by a central character are in the majority female, suggesting that females are in a relatively helpless position. The persons who supply information to central characters who are seeking for knowledge are, in contrast, predominantly male. It will be recalled that even among unrelated adults who supply knowledge to children, the majority are male despite the obvious fact that the most important such persons of the real environment are the child's teachers, who are mostly women. Males, in short, are being portrayed as the bearers of knowledge and wisdom, and as the persons through whom knowledge can come to the child.

In all these respects, a distinction in role is being made between the sexes which may indeed have a certain validity as of our society of the present time, but which seems much more a survival of former practices. The many schoolgirls who will at some future time have to make their own living are failing, if they identify with female characters, to receive the same training in the development of motives for work and achievement that boys are receiving. To the extent that this distinction is characteristic of many other aspects of the training the child receives from his environment, it should cause little wonder that women are sometimes less fitted for creative work and achievement than men of similar aptitude, for there is certainly much difference in the motivational training they receive for it. It has been a common assumption that the education of the two sexes is virtually the same in American public schools, except for differences in vocational training. Here is clear evidence that the education is not the same, even at early levels of grammar school and even when the boys and girls are mixed together, as they usually are, in the same classroom. Not only does the informal training of boys and girls at home and in the community differ, but even the formal education they are receiving in the classroom differs.

It has been shown in several instances that the differential treatment of the sexes goes further than mere correspondence with this stereotype of different categories of behavior as being more conspicuous in a particular sex. There are several striking instances where females are shown as being definitely inferior from a moral point of view. In the discussion of passivity it was shown that female characters are portrayed as lazy twice as often, relatively, as male characters. In the discussion of acquisition it was seen that female characters are shown as acquiring in socially disapproved ways much more often, relatively, than males, and much less frequently by the most approved routes of work and effort.

In view of the social values of our society, it can also be said that the facts already cited above are relevant here. Insofar as female characters are shown as not often achieving, constructing, obtaining recognition or engaging in activity, they are being shown in an unfavorable light by the general standards of our society. But on the other hand, in that female characters are being shown as more frequently affiliative, nurturant, or unaggressive, they may perhaps be said to be receiving the more favorable treatment. While it is not true, then, that female characters are uniformly shown in a more unfavorable light, the balance is certainly in that direction.

The most striking single fact of all, however, about the difference between the sexes is that female characters do simply tend to be neglected. Of all the central characters in all these thema (excluding central characters who consist of a group of mixed sex), 73% are male and only 27% are female. Male characters are thus over two and a half times as frequent as female ones. The same tendency is found, though not so strikingly, in the characters who are objects of, or cooperators in, the satisfaction of the needs of the central characters; here the proportion of males is 63% and of females 37%.

There can be no excuse for this greater attention to males in the claim that males have achieved more in society and hence that there is more to write about them. These stories are, with few exceptions, not about individuals of outstanding achievement but simply about the life of everyday people. The implication of this difference for a girl is that being female is a pretty bad thing, that the only people even in everyday life who are worth writing about or reading about are boys and men. If the content of these readers is typical of other social influences, small wonder that girls might develop for this reason alone an inferiority complex about their sex.

DIFFERENTIAL TREATMENT OF ADULTS AND CHILDREN

The human characters in the stories were readily divisible into two groups according to age—adults and children. The treatment of these two groups differed markedly, and in ways that raise interesting problems about the effect of these stories on the children who read them.

There are, first of all, great differences in the relative frequency of the various categories of behavior. Children are much lower than adults in the incidence of aggression and acquisition. In adults, aggression and acquisition are the most frequently appearing categories of behavior, whereas in children these two are of very low incidence. . . .

That children are shown as more socialized is demonstrated also by the relative frequency of different kinds of rewards. It was noted in connection with several categories of behavior, especially affiliation and nurturance, that children are shown as more frequently receiving only internal rewards. This generalization holds true for all of the behavior in the readers taken as a whole. A summary of the percent of each type of reward in all four types of character is presented in Table 3. . . . Now internal rewards are dependent upon socialization, for they are rewards that a person administers to himself

TABLE 3
KINDS OF REWARDS FOR ALL CATEGORIES OF BEHAVIOR:
PERCENTAGE DISTRIBUTION IN EACH CHARACTER TYPE

| Character Type | *Percentage Distribution of Kinds of Reward in Each Character Type* | | | |
	Internal	Social	Material	Automatic
Children	34	23	36	6
Adults	16	26	53	4
Animals	24	18	50	8
Fairies	16	34	43	8

because he is well socialized, because he is able to feel good or virtuous at having done the right thing, even if no reward is offered by an external agency.

That children are shown as more socialized than adults, perhaps points up more clearly than anything else the role that the content of these readers must be more or less consciously intended to play in the moral education of children. If the readers are intended for inculcating proper behavior in children, then it must seem only natural at first glance that it is the child characters who especially should be shown as displaying the desired forms of behavior. But a serious question may be raised as to whether the readers are likely to accomplish the purpose in this way. A more sophisticated consideration of the probable effect of the content of these readers would suggest that there is considerable probability that children pattern their behavior more after that of the adult characters than after that of the child characters. There is ample reason to suppose that children imitate adults, especially their parents, much more than they do their age-mates, and particularly with reference to deep-seated motivational tendencies. If this be true, then for purposes of the moral education of the children who read these stories, the adult characters should be shown as at least as well socialized as the child characters.

Whether this criticism is justified does, of course, depend upon factual determination of whether children are more likely to be influenced by the behavior portrayed in adult characters than in child characters. But on general psychological grounds, this does seem so likely as to give the criticism considerable weight. . . .

TREATMENT OF ANIMALS AND FAIRIES

Animals are the central characters in 17% of the thema, ranking second to child characters in frequency. Their behavior can be expected to influence the children reading about them not only because of the frequency of their occurrence, but also because most of them are shown as young animals who appear in a parent-child relationship. They are usually portrayed as anthropomorphic characters endowed with speech, and their relationship to the physical and social environment closely approximates the subordinate position in which children also find themselves.

The pattern of their behavior is in most instances similar to that of children: they, like the child characters, are shown as rewarded for dependent, socially conforming behavior. There are a few striking exceptions to this parallelism, however. The major differences in child and animal behavior are in the more frequent occurrence of aggression among animals (where it ranks second in frequency), and also of autonomy. . . . Their aggression is also usually of the more undesirable form, unprovoked aggression, while their instances of autonomy are most frequently instances of disobedience to authority. These, as has been pointed out, are the most frequently punished forms of aggression and autonomy.

To a certain extent, then, animal characters seem to furnish an outlet for the expression in child-like characters of aggressive and rebellious tendencies. Since these needs are predominantly punished, the animal characters

serve the function of teaching the lesson that whenever asocial tendencies are expressed, they are punished. Thus they have a double purpose: they remove the necessity of showing child characters as exhibiting undesirable behavior, while at the same time yielding an object lesson as to the results of such behavior should it be manifested. It is as though the writers felt that, to a child reading animal stories, the behavior is detached enough from the child so that he would not copy it, and yet plausible enough for him to accept the moral that aggressive and autonomous asocial behavior leads to certain punishment. . . .

Indirectly, then, the readers do admit the existence of aggression in young persons (i.e., young animals or young fairies). Yet here, too, there is little constructive suggestion as to how to handle such tendencies. When characters are shown as aggressive, punishment follows, without an indication of suitable substitute outlets.

SIGNIFICANCE OF VARIOUS STORY TYPES

. . . It is apparent [however] that the various types of stories do serve a function, and that this is related to the types of characters appearing in them. For the stories represent various degrees of realism in portraying behavior, from the prosaic everyday story, through the idealized hero and the humanized animal story, to the frankly unrealistic fairy story. It is significant, therefore, that most of the behavior of the children is portrayed against a realistic, everyday background. For if the children are able to differentiate between the real and the unreal, they will tend to be more influenced by behavior which is possible for them. And even where they do not make this distinction, the very fact that such behavior more closely resembles theirs is likely to make for greater generalization to their own behavior. It is important to note, therefore, that the pattern of behavior for children in the readers, which was summarized earlier in this chapter, is the one pattern of behavior for any character type that is most consistently presented realistically. It is reinforced and emphasized by the medium of its presentation—the everyday story. . . .

Fairy stories . . . [permit] the expression of antisocial egoistic behavior in an unreal situation where the reader will be less likely to copy it. It is probably also true, however, that presentation of such behavior in very unrealistic circumstances fails to contribute to a child's learning ways for handling the similar anti-social tendencies he must cope with in everyday life. In this respect, it is consistent with the whole treatment of children's behavior in the readers that these categories of behavior which are handled unrealistically within themselves, are further treated so by having them displayed primarily in an unrealistic situation.

The total picture of adult behavior is also somewhat clarified by noting how very often it is placed in the unrealistic setting of the fairy story. It will be remembered that adults are frequently shown as conforming less often to socially approved behavior than are children. The interpretation of this pattern is less ambiguous when it is noted that it frequently occurs in the fairy story. In fact, the relative frequency of the various categories of behavior in the fairy story corresponds quite closely to their relative frequency in the adult characters. Again the fairy stories are apparently serving as an outlet for the expression of anti-social needs, in situations where children will be less likely to generalize from the behavior. . . .

Since animal stories are composed almost exclusively of animal characters, the interpretation of them is similar to that for the characters: they permit the expression of rebellious and asocial tendencies in a situation where the child will not be very likely to copy such undesirable behavior. . . .

BIBLIOGRAPHY

1. HARTSHORNE, H. and MAY, M. A. *Studies in deceit.* New York: Macmillan, 1928.
2. JONES, V. *Character and citizenship training in the public schools.* Chicago: Univ. of Chicago Press, 1936.
3. MURRAY, H. A., *et al. Explorations in personality.* New York: Oxford Univ. Press, 1938.

[See original for more extensive bibliography, including the books analyzed.—EDITOR]

GLOSSARY

COGNIZANCE. Refers to behavior that evinces an "inquiring attitude . . . To explore (moving and touching). To ask questions. To satisfy curiosity. To look, listen, inspect. To read and seek knowledge." One of the needs listed by Murray.*

CONSTRUCTION. Refers to behaviors of organizing and building. One of the needs listed by Murray.*

DEFERENCE. "To admire and willingly follow a superior . . . To co-operate with a leader. To serve gladly." One of the needs listed by Murray.*

INFAVOIDANCE. "To avoid failure, shame, humiliation, ridicule. To refrain from attempting to do something that is beyond one's powers. To conceal a disfigurement." One of the needs listed by Murray.*

NURTURANCE. "To nourish, aid or protect a helpless [person]. To express sympathy. To 'mother' a child." One of the needs listed by Murray.*

SENTIENCE. ". . . refers to the inclination for sensuous gratification, particularly from objects in contact with the body: taste sensations and tactile sensations." One of the needs listed by Murray.*

SUCCORANCE. "To seek aid, protection, or sympathy. To cry for help. To plead for mercy. To adhere to an affectionate, nurturant parent. To be dependent." One of the needs listed by Murray.*

---

* Henry A. Murray *et al., Explorations in Personality* (New York: Oxford University Press, 1938), pp. 77–83.

56

Race, Social Class, and the Motive to Avoid Success in Women[1]

PETER J. WESTON[2]
AND MARTHA SHUCH MEDNICK

The final article in this section presents a study of college women and deals with a kind of variable that is of particular concern to the women's liberation movement. The motive to avoid success has often been alleged to be one of the chief handicaps to woman's achievement in our society. Here we have an empirical study of the problem in the context of both race and class differences. It could thus have been put in Section VI.

Such a motive, which seems in the majority culture in the United States to be more characteristic of women than men, is greatly influenced by experiential factors. This, at least, is the implication of the differences found between races. Because the samples do not permit all of the possible race and class comparisons, one is glad to see that the authors anticipate further work in this area. Indeed some of that work is alluded to in the additional results that Dr. Mednick has provided for us. Dr. Martha Shuch Mednick is on the faculty of Howard University.

Horner (1968) successfully reconciled some of the confusion in research on achievement motiva-

tion in women by postulating and demonstrating an avoidance motive called the motive to avoid success (M-s).[3] This psychological barrier to intellectual achievement is defined as "the expectancy or anticipation of negative consequences as a result of success in competitive achievement situations." In the case of women, the specific negative consequences may be social rejection by men, loss of affection, friendship or one's datable or marriageable quality (Horner, 1968, p. 22). According to Horner, when a girl achieves intellectually, she anticipates that she will be regarded as unfeminine. Horner's data support the existence of such a motive in fantasy productions; she also successfully predicted women's problem solving behavior in intellectually competitive situations by using M-s scores. Tangri (1969) also demonstrated that senior level college women express M-s with greater frequency than do junior level girls.

It has been observed by a number of investigators that the motivations and aspirations expressed by black women follow a pattern different from those expressed by white women (Moynihan, 1965; Frazier, 1939, 1962; Pettigrew, 1965). Forces inherent in the social system have had a deleterious effect on black family life as evidenced, for example, by the high percentage of black families headed by women (Clark, 1965; U.S. Department of Labor, 1965). It is commonly asserted that this has resulted in a sex-role identity pattern in which women are more dominant and aggressive and permitted, and indeed, encouraged to be aspiring and intellectually striving. This overt image is partially confirmed by studies of aspirations of black high school students in which girls express higher aspirations than boys (Thompson, 1965); black parents' aspirations for their daughters are higher than for their sons. This finding was not obtained by Gurin and Katz (1966) in their massive study of motivation and level of aspiration in students in Southern black colleges in which college women expressed lower aspirations than the men, seemingly following the pattern of the larger society. The aspirations of these women seemed to be a reflection of the women's realistic perceptions of the opportunities available to them. We maintain, however, that while a girl may lower and be realistic about her aspirations, she may nevertheless maintain fantasies of success and achievement and not avoid dominance and aggressive intellectual

[1] Based on a thesis by the senior author submitted to Howard University in partial fulfillment of the requirements for the M.A. in Psychology.

[2] Now at the University of Michigan.

[3] This study addresses itself to a comparison of women from several cultural subgroups within the American (U.S.) society. Cross-society or national comparisons are projected for future research by the second author.

Peter J. Weston and Martha T. Mednick, "Race, social class, and the motive to avoid success in women," *Journal of Cross-Cultural Psychology, 1,* 1970, 284–291. Reprinted by permission.

mastery. Furthermore, the dynamics involved in her achievement orientation may still be quite different from those of the white women. With this in mind, a series of studies have been undertaken with the goal of exploring the personality and motivational dynamics influencing expressed aspirations and actual career planning in black college women.

A few words must be added about the variable of social class. The possibility of social class differences among black women must be anticipated. The black middle class has been described as "out-middle classing" white middle class in terms of their values. Furthermore, since middle class life is generally more male dominated and family life more stable (Frazier, 1962), it is reasonable to expect that the black middle class college woman will be less dominant and striving than her lower class counterpart.

The present study simply sought to compare black women with white women, not on aspirations, but in fantasy productions to a situation with an intrinsic theme of intellectual competition.

The following hypotheses were tested:

1. Black college women will exhibit fewer M-s responses than white college women.
2. Lower class black women will have fewer M-s responses than middle class black women.

METHOD

SUBJECTS

The *S*s were 63 undergraduate women enrolled at Bluefield State College and 22 enrolled at American University.[4] The breakdown of these *S*s by race and social class is given in Table 1. Social class was determined by occupation and educational level of the parents.

TABLE 1

NUMBER OF SUBJECTS FROM EACH SCHOOL BY RACE AND SOCIAL CLASS

	American University		*Bluefield State*	
Race	*Middle class*	*Lower class*	*Middle class*	*Lower class*
Black	10	1	22	28
White	11	0	13	0

[4] Bluefield State is a four year liberal arts college in West Virginia whose undergraduate population is approximately 50.8% black. (U.S. Department of Health, Education and Welfare, 1967; Bluefield Registrar's Office, 1969). The undergraduate population of American University (Washington, D.C.) is 4–4.8% black (Statistical Office, American University, 1969).

MATERIALS

Verbal TAT cues[5] such as those used by Horner and a brief questionnaire requesting socio-economic information were administered to each subject. The four cues in order of presentation were as follows:

1. After first term finals, Anne finds herself at the top of her medical school class.
2. A young woman is talking about something important with an older person.
3. Jennifer has just been informed that her three-act play will be produced in New York this coming season.
4. Susan is sitting in a chair with a smile on her face.

Cues 1 and 3 were designed to elicit success imagery while cues 2 and 4 were non-arousal or neutral cues and, as such, were not scored for M-s but served as buffers in the experimental situation.

PROCEDURE

The *S*s were seated in a classroom and given a questionnaire containing the four verbal cues. The cues were presented in the order stated above. All *S*s received the following instructions:

> You are going to see a series of verbal leads or cues and I would like you to tell a story that is suggested to you by each one. Try to imagine what is going on in each. Then tell what the situation is, what led up to the situation, what the people are thinking and feeling and what they will do. In other words, write as complete a story as you can, a story with plot and characters. You will have twenty seconds to look at each verbal cue and then five minutes to write your story about it. Write your first impressions and work rapidly. I will keep time and tell you when it is time to finish your story and to get ready for the next cue. Remember there are no right or wrong answers or kinds of stories, so please feel free to write whatever story is suggested to you when you look at a cue. Spelling, punctuation, and grammar are not important. What is important is to write out as fully and as quickly as possible the story that comes into your mind as you imagine what is going on in each cue.

Thus, the *S*s were required to write brief five-minute stories in response to each of the four cues which were observed for twenty seconds. The stories were written around the following four questions spaced on an answer sheet:

[5] The use of verbal cues appear as effective in eliciting imagery as the TAT pictures and have been used by numerous investigators (Atkinson, Horner, Tangri, McClelland, 1959; Bachman et al., 1967). Of course, these are ideally suited to studies in which race comparisons are to be made, since the problem of changing the pictures of identity figures does not arise.

1. What is happening? Who are the persons?
2. What has led up to this situation? What has happened in the past?
3. What is being thought? What is wanted? By whom?
4. What will happen? What will be done?

The instructions given are standard for the TAT; their general tone is to urge the Ss to produce stories and not to think in terms of right or wrong answers.

The M-s scores were obtained from a content analysis of the fantasies. The first and third cues were scored for M-s independently by two trained raters using the coding directions described by Horner (1968). A general decision was made concerning the presence or absence of M-s imagery and only results agreed upon by both raters were considered.[6] Any imagery (i.e., statement in the story) which suggested or anticipated negative consequences as a result of success was considered fear of success imagery. More specifically, this meant that someone in the story was being placed in an undesirable or negative situation (e.g., losing the friendship of close associates, being socially rejected especially by men, feeling guilt, despair, or doubting one's normality or femininity) because of success in an intellectually competitive situation.

Thus, in scoring the stories for M-s when there was negative imagery reflecting concern about the success, the following criteria were used:

a. negative consequences because of the success
b. anticipation of negative consequences because of the success
c. negative affect because of the success
d. instrumental activity away from present or future success
e. any direct expression of conflict about success.

Also scored was any evidence of:

f. denial of the situation described by the cue
g. bizarre, inappropriate, unrealistic or non-adaptive responses to the situation described by the cue.

No score was given when the stories contained no indication of negative consequences, negative affect

or concern about negative consequences of success. This comprised the "low M-s" category in analysis. A score of 1 indicated that the S's responses reflected mild concern about possible negative consequences of success while a score of 2 was given when there was mention of severe negative consequences of success.[7] Scores of 1 and 2 comprised the "high M-s" category. A score of 3 was assigned to those stories of a bizarre, inappropriate or unrealistic nature. These stories were not used in the analysis of M-s.

After writing the stories, each S was asked to answer the questionnaire described above. The designation of social class level was determined on the basis of the answers to those questions.

RESULTS

The M-s data were evaluated separately for each success cue and for the two schools. These means and standard deviations are presented in Table 2.

The significance level of all group differences was evaluated by means of the Fisher Exact Probability Test (1956). Table 3 shows the findings from the Bluefield and American University samples.

The hypothesis with regard to race differences was supported for both cues and at both schools. Class differences within the Black group were not significant, in contradiction to our second hypothesis. This, of course, was only observed at Bluefield State, but was consistent for both cues.

[The absence of a social class difference has since been confirmed in additional samples, according to Dr. Mednick. In a Master's Thesis by Bright conducted at Howard University in 1970, 28% of 125 women tested (all Black) manifested M-s on the "Anne" cue. Other studies at Black schools in the Southeast by Puryear (M.S. Thesis, 1971) found a similar rate (N = 165). In all samples, incidence of M-s and social class level were unrelated. The stability of this finding is suggested further by the fact that sex of experimenter does not affect the results: in all these additional samples the experimenter was a woman, in contrast with the first,

[6] For the sample of 85 Ss the raters agreed upon 91.8% of the responses to cue 1; there was 81.2% agreement on responses to cue 3.

[7] There were seven such stories in the Bluefield sample: five were in response to cue 1 and two to cue 3. No such stories appeared in the American University sample.

TABLE 2
M-s MEANS AND STANDARD DEVIATIONS FOR THE TWO SCHOOLS AND THE TWO CUES

| | Bluefield State | | | | | | American University | | | | | |
| | Cue 1 | | | Cue 3 | | | Cue 1 | | | Cue 3 | | |
Race and class	N	M	SD	N	M	SD	N	M	SD	N	M	SD
White Middle	13	1.25	.59	13	.73	.75	11	1.13	.73	11	.44	.50
Black Middle	22	.16	.49	22	.11	.31	10	.30	.64	10	0	0
Black Lower	28	.24	.42	28	0	0	1	0	0	1	0	0

TABLE 3
MOTIVE TO AVOID SUCCESS AS RELATED TO RACE AND SOCIAL CLASS

	Bluefield State sample				American University sample			
	Cue 1		Cue 3		Cue 1		Cue 3	
Race and class	High M-s	Low M-s	High M-s	Low M-s	High M-s	Low M-s	High M-s	Low M-s
White Middle	11	1	6	5	6	2	4	5
Black Middle	2	17	2	16	2	8	0	9
	$p = .00001$		$p = .018$		$p = .28$		$p = .041$ $(\alpha = .05)$[1]	
Black Lower	6	19	0	19	NR[2]	NR	NR	NR
Black Middle	2	17	2	16	NR	NR	NR	NR
	$p = .170$		$p = .23$					

Note—Fisher probability test used for all analyses.
[1] $\alpha = .05$ for all tests
[2] NR—no respondents

wherein the instruments were administered by a man.—EDITOR]

DISCUSSION

The race difference hypothesis was supported; social class, on the other hand, does not seem to affect M-s imagery.

The stories of black Ss displayed very little M-s. The following are examples of stories written by these Ss. A response to cue 1:

Anne is very pleased because upon completion of finals, she finds herself at the top of her medical school class. Anne has studied diligently for long and hard hours. She has always wanted to be a part of the medical profession. Although she studied constantly, she never dreamed of being number one in her class. She wants to pursue a medical career and she is convinced that she can master the work. Her parents and boyfriend will be proud of her. She will continue in medical school graduate and go on to become a leader in her profession.

An example of a response to cue 3:

Jennifer has majored in drama school. Although she is only a junior, she has been writing little three-act plays, one of which has brought her much success. She is, of course, delighted because she never anticipated that any of her work would ever be produced. Jennifer had fancied herself more as an actress than a playwright. She will continue to write more plays. Eventually, Jennifer will write and star in her own productions, moving on to Hollywood, making motion pictures and receiving an Oscar.

In contrast, the display of fear of success imagery is quite clear in the stories of white Ss. Examples

of such stories are the following: Typical responses to cue 1:

Anne and her fellow classmates are sitting around 'shooting the bull.' Final exams, naturally, is the topic of discussion. Two or three people seem to dominate the conversation, and Anne is sitting quietly off to one side, her facial expression is one of mixed emotions. Anne has always been a good student and medicine is her 'thing.' She has worked many long and hard hours to achieve the goal she has reached, with very little time for fun. Anne wonders whether it is really worth it, as she seems to be left out of the 'fun crowd' and ignored by the guys because she is a 'brain.' The only time she is noticed is when someone needs help with homework. Anne will let her studies go and become a party girl.

and

Anne is in George Washington Medical School. The persons involved are the ten girls and fifty guys in Anne's first year in medical class. Anne graduated at the top of her class at Jackson College for Women. She was an anthropology major. Anne's friends and parents are proud. Some of the guys in her class are jealous and there's some tension in the class. Anne will marry Jack, a second year medical student and she won't finish medical school.

A response to cue 3:

Jennifer has worked very hard to achieve this success despite lack of encouragement from Bill, her boyfriend. Bill feels that success will change her. She will go to New York and her play will be a flop. She will come back to Bill. However, Bill is engaged. Jennifer realizes her mistake and lost dream and becomes a nun.

Horner (1968) has suggested that the high M-s found in white Ss is probably due to the aggressive overtones of intellectual competition needed for success in these areas, since aggression has been socially linked to a lack of femininity and its display is seen as leading to negative consequences (i.e., social rejection). The present findings suggest that success in intellectually competitive situations does not elicit similar fear in the black college woman. This may be related to the different sex role patterns since, as noted above, the nature of American society has placed black women in more dominant roles than those assumed by black men or by white women. Accordingly, intellectual mastery is not threatening and professional achievement may in fact not lead to rejection by the male. A successful woman is an economic asset and attractive rather than threatening to a black man. Hence, success as here projected is not to be feared. It may also be argued that the aspirations depicted in these situations are so unrealistic for any black person that the girls do not actually project themselves into their stories, do not identify with the characters and therefore have nothing to fear. For the present this must stand as an alternative explanation though there is some evidence that this is not the case. It would be difficult to argue that the American University sample sees such career goals as completely unattainable. While the Bluefield women may view themselves, as well as their potential husbands, as being unlikely to achieve high status professional careers, the girls attending a white urban university may have realistic aspirations of this sort. It is interesting to note here that in a study of black upper-middle class sorority women attending the University of Michigan, M-s scores matched those of white women on that campus, indicating that at some point up the social-educational status ladder fears of such success may appear.[8] We are now proceeding with several studies designed to illuminate the dynamics of M-s in these women as well as their actual career aspirations and the degree of their commitment to these aspirations. Problem solving performance of high and low M-s scorers in competition with men will be examined. Of course, if low M-s is simply a result of the unreality of the goals implied in the cue, and fear of being intellectually dominant over men does exist, this should be demonstrated in a face to face competitive task.

A final comment about the absence of social class differences needs to be made. It has been suggested (Horner, personal communication) that a black woman needs to be of upper-middle or upper class status before a fear of success is generated. The Michigan findings tend to support this notion but we could not examine this in our data. Social class differences will be examined in more detail in data about to be collected at Howard University.

REFERENCES

CLARK, KENNETH B. *Dark ghetto*. New York: Harper and Row, 1965.

DAVIS, A., & HAVIGHURST, R. J. Social class and color differences in child-rearing. In C. Kluckhohn, H. A. Murray, & D. M. Schneider. (Eds.), *Personality in nature, society and culture*. (third ed.) New York: Alfred A. Knopf, 1959, chap. 18.

FRAZIER, E. F. *Black bourgeoisie*. New York: Collier Books, 1962.

GURIN, P., & KATZ, D. *Motivation and aspiration in the Negro college*. Final report, U.S. Department of Health, Education and Welfare, 1966.

HORNER, M. S. Sex differences in achievement motivation and performance in competitive and non-competitive situations. Unpublished doctoral dissertation, University of Michigan, 1968.

MOYNIHAN, D. P. *The Negro family*. Washington, D.C.: Office of Policy Planning and Research, United States Department of Labor, 1965.

PETTIGREW, L. *A profile of the Negro American*. Princeton: D. Van Nostrand Company, 1964.

SIEGEL, S. *Non-parametric statistics for the behavioral sciences*. New York: McGraw-Hill, 1956.

TANGRI, SANDRA S. Role-innovation in occupational choice among college women. Unpublished doctoral dissertation, University of Michigan, 1969.

THOMPSON, D. In Moynihan, D. (Ed.). *The Negro family*. U.S. Department of Labor, 1965.

UNITED STATES DEPARTMENT OF LABOR. *The Negroes in the United States: their economic and social situations*. Bulletin No. 1511, U.S. Department of Labor, 1965.

UNITED STATES DEPARTMENT OF LABOR. *Extent of unemployment among non-white men, 1955–63*. Bureau of Labor Statistics, 1965.

WESTON, P. J. *Race, social class and the motive to avoid success in women*. Unpublished Master's Thesis, Howard University, 1969.

---

[8] Personal communications from Matina S. Horner and Sandra G. Tangri.

IX

COGNITIVE DETERMINANTS
AND RESULTS

Among American psychologists, a fundamental challenge to the tradition of behaviorism has emerged within the last few years—cognitive psychology. Behaviorists, especially learning theorists of the S–R (stimulus–response) reinforcement persuasion featured in Section III, focus on overt acts. In order to learn how behavior is determined, they study the ways responses can be changed by environmental events (stimuli) under the control of the experimenter. Cognitive theorists, on the other hand, emphasize the *knowledge* that an individual has, how he organizes his world, and how he integrates new information with that which he already possesses. The impetus giving rise to the cognitive point of view arose from the enormous difficulty—some say impossibility—of dealing with complex human behavior in S–R terms. The complexity of language, especially, argues for this approach. Man is qualitatively different from lower animals in terms of his symbolic capacities—his ability to use language. The production of novel utterances is a creative accomplishment that cannot be accounted for in simple S–R terms.[1] Noam Chomsky's major contributions to linguistic theory (transformational-generative grammar) have done much to further the acceptance of the cognitive point of view. Both Bruner and Ausubel (see Section XI) are representatives of a cognitive orientation, an attitude that is rapidly becoming the theoretical preference of many workers in child development and educational psychology.

Jean Piaget has probably been the single most important influence on today's conceptions of cognitive development. According to Piaget, the child passes through a series of stages, the order of which is invariant; that is, the same for all children. Tuddenham's discussion of Piagetian theory was placed in Section VII because of Piaget's strong emphasis on the correlation of age with developmental stages. In this section there are two additional articles about Piagetian notions.

The measurement of intelligence has been a primary concern of many psychologists, especially those in the field of education. Intelligence is one of the key variables in influencing the outcome of education and in determining the nature of the training that should be given. The problems of intelligence and its measurement are related to biological issues. Biological bases for intelligent behavior are discussed by Scott in Section II. Indeed, historically the question of hereditary *vs.* experiential determinants has dominated discussions of intelligence. Not content to think of intelligence as merely that which is measured by intelligence tests, many psychologists (as well as lay people) have tended to reify intelligence and then to engage in lengthy discussions about the degree to which "it" is innately or biologically determined. Recently, psychologists have found it more fruitful to think in terms of *intelligent behaviors* rather than "intelligence" and to turn attention to the interactions of heredity and environment in determining intelligent behaviors. The introduction to Section II and Tulkin's article in Section VI deal with the influence of race and social class on intelligence.

---

[1] The behaviorists, of course, argue that this phenomenon can indeed be accounted for in S–R terms. See B. F. Skinner's *Verbal Behavior*. (New York: Appleton-Century-Crofts, 1957.)

57

Cognitive Capacity
and Cognitive Competence [1]

MORTON BORTNER
AND HERBERT G. BIRCH

One of the central theses of the cognitivist's position is that actual performance is quite different from underlying capacity (often called "competence"). While in the behaviorist tradition performance is usually accepted as a fairly good indicator of "what has been learned" (even though the theoretical distinction between learning and performance is often acknowledged), the cognitive viewpoint emphasizes that one must know a considerable amount about the particular concepts, abilities, and strategies of the subject, as well as the particular conditions of training and task demand, in order to determine the degree to which performance accurately reflects capacity. Morton Bortner is professor and Kennedy Foundation Scholar at Yeshiva University. Herbert Birch, who holds both the Ph.D. and the M.D. degree, is professor of pediatrics at the Albert Einstein College of Medicine.

[1] This is a revision of a paper read at the annual conference of the American Association on Mental Deficiency, San Francisco, May 12–17, 1969. The report is based on projects supported, in part, by the Joseph P. Kennedy, Jr., Foundation, the U.S. Office of Education Grant OEG–0–8–071272–3317 (032), the National Institute of Child Health and Human Development Grant HD 00719, the Association for the Aid of Crippled Children, and the National Association for Retarded Children.

In this paper we wish to argue that it is essential to make a distinction between cognitive capacity and cognitive performance if we are to be most effective in developing approaches to the habilitation and education of mentally subnormal children. Such a distinction, though rarely stated explicitly, is not new and has its roots in the very first efforts directed at developing special training procedures for the improvement of function in the mentally subnormal. It was a distinction which underlay Itard's disagreement with Pinel as to the worthwhileness of trying to teach Victor, the "wild boy" of Aveyron (Itard, 1801). Pinel was dominated by the 18th Century attitude which tended to view mental subnormality as a unitary phenomenon in which cognitive functions were fixed, and to lump mentally defective children into a homogeneous mass with individuals differing from one another primarily in the severity of their deficits and in the nature of associated physical and behavioral signs.

Itard, stimulated by the French revolution and its doctrine of the improvability of man, argued that Victor's defects derived at least as much from his faulty opportunities for development as from his biologic limitations. In Itard's view, Victor's behavior did not reflect his capacity but only his currently available competence. Itard saw his task as that of raising performance to the limits imposed by capacity. The difference between Itard and Pinel was therefore not merely a disagreement between persons, but between epochs. When Itard decided to work with Victor, it was therefore in courageous opposition to established opinion expressed by Pinel that the child was "an incurable idiot, inferior to domestic animals" (Kanner, 1964). Itard's experience over a 5-year period—though depressing for him since Victor failed to reach a normal level of intellectual and social functioning—constituted one of the most successful failures in the history of special education. It demonstrated that even a severely mentally subnormal child could learn, and produced a variety of training strategies, methods, and approaches through which such improvement could be effected. Itard's work made it clear that Victor's performance did not necessarily reflect his capacity directly, and that special methods were essential in dealing with handicapped children if competence were to approach the limits of capacity.

Despite Itard's demonstration that mentally subnormal children could improve in their adjustment to their environment, Seguin had to transcend authoritative gloom and doom, as exemplified by

Morton Bortner and Herbert G. Birch, "Cognitive capacity and cognitive competence," *American Journal of Mental Deficiency, 74,* 1970, 735–744. Reprinted by permission.

Esquirol's opinion that educational efforts were useless and that "no means are known by which a larger amount of reason or intelligence can be bestowed upon the unhappy idiot, even for the briefest period" (Kanner, 1964). Seguin's insistence that something could be done to bridge the gap between capacity and performance, however, foreshadowed the common assumption underlying the work of such modern researchers as Luria, Tizard, Lewis, House and Zeaman, O'Connor and Hermelin, Zigler, and the Clarkes. All these workers view cognitive performance as not necessarily providing an accurate reflection of cognitive capacity. They have been able to demonstrate that changes in training procedures, task organization, social circumstances, and motivation, as well as characteristics of the examiner, all significantly influence the level of performance.

The scope of the present paper did not permit us to review in detail the history of attitudes toward capacity and performance. Rather, it was our feeling that studies relevant to the question have been so scattered that at no point have they been sufficiently integrated and related to general principles of psychological development. We have attempted, therefore, to relate them to work in the general psychology of development in the hope that a more fully expressed conceptualization of the distinction between cognitive capacity and cognitive performance would be helpful in the guidance and development of practices for the care and habilitation of mentally subnormal children.

We began this effort by considering some of the studies from our own laboratories. In these studies, we raised the question of the degree to which children possessed concepts which were not available for use when they performed under ordinary free-field conditions (Birch & Bortner, 1966). It was found that when young children were presented with a model object and asked to select from among three alternatives that object which "belonged" with the model, the children matched on the basis of stimulus properties. Thus, if the model object were a red button, and the alternatives for matching were a red lipstick case, a blue poker chip, and a spool of thread, the young children selected either the lipstick case, which agreed with the model in color, or the poker chip, which had the same shape. Older children, in contrast, ignored the stimulus properties and selected the thread, which had a functional relation to the button, as the object which "belonged" with it. Did the younger children fail to select the thread because they did not understand its functional relationship to the button, or did they possess the concept but not have it available for use? This question could be examined by testing the hypothesis that

the younger children did indeed possess the concept, i.e., had it as one of their capacities but did not utilize it under conditions in which their behavior could be guided by information at a sensory level. If this hypothesis were true, it would be expected that a comparable group of young children, confronted with the task under conditions in which competition from sensory properties was reduced, would manifest their possessed functional concept in performance. We presented this and other problems under conditions in which the alternative choices contained no striking sensory attributes which matched the model. Behavior was not dominated by sensory properties under these altered conditions, and almost all of the young children made functional selections. Many of them, when requested to rationalize their choice of thread to go with a red button, stated, "You sew a button with it."

Clearly, these normal young children possessed functional concepts, but they were not available for use when the task was presented in such a way as to place their hierarchically organized and age-specific determining tendencies in competition with their much weaker tendency to be responsive to functional attributes. Such a tendency is not restricted to children and is, in a more general sense, a feature of human problem solving (Birch & Rabinowitz, 1951; Duncker, 1945; Maier, 1930; Woodworth & Sells, 1935).

When this technique for differentiating between capacity and competence was applied to brain-damaged children, essentially the same findings obtained (Birch & Bortner, 1967). The tendency to use such abstractions as class membership and functional characteristics as bases for matching was facilitated in brain-damaged children when the competition of immediately present stimulus properties was systematically reduced. Moreover, the brain-damaged children were able to match in terms of function as frequently and correctly under conditions where the competition between conceptual category or function and stimulus properties was reduced as did normal children who had to choose in the context of stimulus competition. These results demonstrated that brain-damaged children did in fact possess, and under certain conditions could use, higher-order abstractions. However, their expression of such abstract capacity was inhibited in the presence of stimulus competition and only became evident when such competition was reduced.

The findings in these studies suggested the possibility that changes in problem solving and cognitive style as a function of age are based upon alterations in hierarchical selection set rather than simply on the acquisition of new concepts or new capacities. This suggestion received support in the study by Mehler and Bever (1967) in which conservation of number was studied in very young children. In general, Piaget's approach was utilized. Clay pellets were arranged in two rows, with the shorter row containing the larger number of pellets. When the children were asked to point to the row with "more," Piaget's reported finding of nonconservation was confirmed, with the children choosing the longer row (the one containing fewer pellets). However, when M & M candies were substituted for the pellets and the response called for was nonverbal, i.e., when the children were permitted to take and eat the row of their choice, the children more frequently took the shorter row with more candies—apparently demonstrating conservation in action. Some children responded incorrectly in their verbal judgments of which clay row had "more" whereas in the M & M row they chose the correct row to eat. Apparently, in one case (clay pellets) "more" meant visual extent, whereas in the other (M & M candies) it meant "more" things to eat. Hence, the particular task set appeared to have influenced both the children's definitions of "more" and their performance. The content of the task apparently defined a set which drew selectively upon the children's possessed capacities—leading to selections based on visual-perceptual responses to extent in one instance and on responses linked to an amount concept in the other.

Dryman, Birch, and Korn (1970) found a similar dissociation between capacity and performance in the problem solving of older children. In their study, 6-year-old children were presented with a task in which a floating bead had to be extracted from a test tube that was one-third full of water. The children were asked how they would get the bead out. First responses were manipulative. Approximately a third of the children offered or verbalized a float-up solution. They were then confronted with the tube and bead on a table with tweezers and other tools as well as two bottles of water. Not one of the children who had verbalized the correct solution poured water into the tube as his *first* response. All the children tended to be dominated by the manipulative opportunities present despite the fact that the tweezers and other objects were not effective tools. After failing with these objects, some of the children used the water, but half of the children who had verbalized a float-up solution *never* used this strategy in their efforts. Instead, they perseveratively and repetitively were dominated by their manipulative sets.

Thus, there are age-specific sets, motive-specific sets (M & M), and task-specific sets, all of which define different fragments of capacity which are expressed in performance. The gap is broader or narrower in accordance with the goodness of fit between the structure of the task demand and the nature of the relation between the subject's motivation and his capacities.

These studies supported the assumption that a meaningful distinction could be made between capacity (representing the potential of the individual) and performance (representing the level at which the individual responds). Moreover, the performance of the individual did not appear directly to reflect his capacity, but rather seemed to represent that fragment of his capacities which was in accord with the particular conditions of demand. This general proposition has led workers in Britain, Russia, and America to be concerned with delineating the appropriate conditions for making demands which, in turn, would lead to performance that more truly reflected the capacities of the subnormal individual than he ordinarily exhibited.

These different workers have had different emphases. The British group emphasized work habilitation and the productivity of subjects, with special concern for the development of training methods that would permit the individual to engage in productive work through an appropriate tapping of potentials that are dormant under most task conditions. The American work, which has overlapped somewhat with this view, has had a primarily motivational emphasis, and has, in general, shown how level of performance varies both qualitatively and quantitatively as a result of the selective manipulation of conditions of demand and of reward. The Russian emphasis has been on the "second signal system" (language) and ways in which deficiencies in this area could be overcome with appropriate training, resulting in a fuller expression of capability. All three groups have been concerned with the gap between capacity and performance in the cognitive functioning of subnormal children.

Lewis (1960) summarized the British approach to the distinction between capacity and performance by pointing to such studies as those of O'Connor and Tizard (1956), who demonstrated that acquisition of a skill improved strikingly for retarded individuals when social conditions in the workshop were manipulated. The focus of British concern was on work habilitation, productivity, defining of work conditions and motives, and the development of training methods. Manipulation of work (learning) conditions (Clarke, 1957; Tizard & Loos, 1954) resulted in the employment of retarded patients who for years had been viewed as unemployable.

Another approach to the problem of the influence of motivational factors on cognitive functioning has been pursued by the Clarkes, who have advanced the notion that the complexity of the task may be a factor in the transfer of learning and that this can be used to advantage by the retarded child. They have reported that transfer is facilitated when practice in categorizing is offered to the subject, and when superordinate categories are formed. Manipulation of conditions is thus possible which then enhances and improves cognitive performance (Clarke & Cookson, 1962; Clarke & Cooper, 1964; Clarke, Cooper, & Clarke, 1967; Clarke & Clarke, 1967; Clarke & Cooper, 1967; Clarke, Clarke, & Cooper, in press; Clarke, 1968).

More generally, Tizard and Grad (1961) found considerable differences in the abilities of retarded individuals which could not be attributed to differences in level of intelligence, i.e., defects of temperament were among the noncognitive handicaps exhibited by these individuals. Such a view has much in common with the American tendency to shift the emphasis from intelligence alone to other features of personality. The work of Thomas, Chess, Birch, Hertzig, and Korn (1963), with normal children, has constituted one such search for those relatively stable noncognitive characteristics which are identifiable from early infancy and which help to define the child's later functioning.

Another search for the motivational or noncognitive components of learning is illustrated in the work of Zigler and his associates. In response to suggestions by Lewin (1936) and Kounin (1941) that retarded children are more cognitively rigid (e.g., more perseverative) than normal children, and thus less capable in satiation, motoric, and concept-switching tasks, Zigler and others have proposed a motivational hypothesis. They suggested that the observed differences on these tasks were related to the child's responsiveness to verbal support, approval, and in general, social reinforcement (Shallenberger & Zigler, 1961; Zigler, 1966; Zigler & Butterfield, 1966). The effectiveness of such reinforcement was seen as interacting with a number of factors in the child's personal and social context, including anxiety level of the subject (Walters & Ray, 1960), sex of the examiner in relation to sex of the subject (Gewirtz & Baer, 1958; Stevenson, 1961), chronological age or mental age of subject (Stevenson, 1961), social class of the subject (Douvan, 1956; Zigler, 1962; Zigler & DeLabry, 1962) relationship of the examiner to the subject (McCoy & Zigler, 1965), imitativeness of the subject (Turnure & Zigler, 1964) and nature of the incentive (Cantor & Hottell, 1955; Ellis, 1962; Gordon, O'Connor & Tizard, 1955; Heber, 1959; Wolfensberger, 1960; Zigler & Unell, 1962). Most importantly, social reinforcement was thought to be related to the nature and extent of the social deprivation in the child's background (Butterfield

& Zigler, 1965; Clarke & Clarke, 1959; Clarke, Clarke & Reiman, 1958; Green & Zigler, 1962; Shepps & Zigler, 1962; Zigler, 1961, 1962; Zigler, Hodgden & Stevenson, 1958), with greater deprivation leading to greater responsiveness to social reinforcement.

House and Zeaman have sought to define those conditions of a noncognitive nature which lead to improved cognitive performance, and have identified such contributing factors as novelty (Zeaman, House & Orlando, 1958), sequence of easy to hard (House & Zeaman, 1960), and various conditions of reward (House, Orlando & Zeaman, 1957; House & Zeaman, 1958a, 1958b; Zeaman & House, 1962).

Luria and his colleagues have emphasized the significance of language development for the more general process of mental development (Liublinskaya, 1957; Luria, 1961; Luria & Vinogradova, 1959). Luria also stressed the interaction of the child and the teacher (offering verbal help) as an educational event wherein "what the child can do today with the help of the teacher he will be able to do by himself tomorrow." This rise in performance level, then, was related to what Vygotsky had called the "zone of potential development"—an apparent reference to capacity. Luria appeared to be concerned with the distinction between capacity and performance, in his implicit focus upon the fact that the child was capable of doing more, and with the consequent need to bridge this gap through verbal help from the teacher.

Luria suggested that there are two signal systems, one governing motor behavior and the other verbal behavior. In the normal child, the second system (language) guides and regulates action, and this regulation forms the basis for voluntary behavior. In the severely subnormal child, language does not develop sufficiently to assume this orienting function, and the result is a loose connection between verbal and motor behavior. This theory has led a number of investigators to study language functions in subnormal children in order to explore the conditions which facilitate learning of words (Hermelin & O'Connor, 1964; O'Connor & Hermelin, 1963), learning sets (O'Connor & Hermelin, 1959a) and the relation of words to sensory-motor behavior (O'Connor & Hermelin, 1959b).

In comparative psychology, too, the problem of possession and availability was exemplified in the work of Lashley and Yerkes. They sought to determine whether or not rats were capable of distinguishing geometric forms one from another. Yerkes and Watson's (1911) work with the discrimination box had clearly indicated that, under the conditions of performance defined by the use of the box at that time, rats were totally incapable of making form discriminations but, instead, made discriminations based merely upon relative brightness. Lashley, on the basis of his naturalistic observations of rats, believed that this was an underestimation of the rat's capacity and repeated Yerkes' experiments. However, after thousands of trials of experience, the performance of the rats in Lashley's experiments was no better than was the case with completely naive rats. It was not until 19 years later (Lashley, 1930) that he conceptualized the problem in a new way. He argued that the rat was an organism that was primarily responsive to the kinesthetic, tactile, and olfactory aspects of a situation, and that when the conditions of a task were ones in which these nonvisual cues dominated the animal's responsiveness, the response made to a visual stimulus would be at a level considerably below his capacity. Thus, it could be argued that the rat possessed the ability to discriminate forms but did not exhibit this capacity under the particular conditions of testing. With the goal of reducing nonvisual stimuli and of focusing "attention" on the visual task, Lashley developed the jumping apparatus in which the movements of the animal were restricted by placing him upon a small platform. Under these conditions, the animal's attention was more readily directed to, and forced to focus upon, the properties of the visual stimuli. Once this technique was introduced, Lashley was able to demonstrate that those rats which previously could not make form discriminations in thousands of trials were now able to exhibit this capacity in 20 to 30 trials. An organism, therefore, which for years had been declared as lacking in the capacity to develop form discriminations now evidenced such a capacity.

An analogous controversy existed in physiological psychology between Malmo and Jacobsen with respect to the functions of the frontal lobes. Jacobsen (1934) found that monkeys which had their frontal lobes removed bilaterally lost their ability to engage in a delayed response. Malmo and Kleinsasser (1942) questioned whether the animals really had lost this ability, and suggested the alternative view that bilateral frontal lobe extirpation led to increased vulnerability to retroactive inhibition. Such inhibition, they asserted, interfered with the learning upon which the delayed response was based. If this were true, then the performance of the animals was not truly reflecting their capacity with respect to either single-trial learning or the ability to engage in delay. They changed the nature of the delay period from one in which the lights were on (giving the animals the opportunity to respond to other visual stimuli and so, retroactively, to inhibit the initial visual learn-

ing) to a delay period sustained in total darkness. When this was done, delayed response was exhibited by animals with bilateral frontal lobectomy. These results, again, indicated that a distinction had to be made between an animal's capacity to engage in a given level of behavior and its manifestation of this capacity in performance.

Related findings are those of Geschwind, who described a patient with neurological impairment who could not name colors but who could nevertheless recognize their correct names when this information was presented in either oral or written form (Geschwind & Fusillo, 1966). Another patient (Geschwind & Kaplan, 1962), even while giving an incorrect verbal description of an object, effectively demonstrated the correct use of the object. In both of these cases, the performance of the patients did not reflect their understanding until the task requirements were adapted from ones requiring a verbal response to ones requiring some other kind of response.

Similar concerns have been expressed by Pribram and others in their judgments of the consequences of brain extirpations on behavior. They have argued that deterioration in performance need not always be interpreted as a loss of the capacity to perform, that the primary mechanism that has been interfered with in many instances is the motivation of the animal to perform, and that if this motivation is restored, performance will again reflect intact capacity (Pribram, 1966; West, 1960).

Additional conclusions deriving from experimental and comparative psychology dealing with the difference between capacity and performance can be found in the studies of Tryon (1940) on the genetics of intelligence in rats. Tryon selectively bred a group of rats which performed well and a group which performed poorly on an enclosed alley maze. By breeding bright with bright and dull with dull animals, he raised two colonies of rats which were consistent in their maze brightness and maze dullness. Tryon's data were interpreted as demonstrating that intelligence was heritable, and that breeding bright with bright and dull with dull resulted in increased differentiation between the two groups of rats with respect to general intellectual capacity. Overlooked in Tryon's discussion was the possibility that the specific learning task he was using was one that was dependent rather explicitly upon information deriving from nonvisual cues. Therefore, what Tryon might have been breeding for was not intelligence in general but, rather, responsiveness to certain features of environmental information in one of his groups of rats, as contrasted with responsiveness to alternative features of environmental information in his other rats. The failure to consider this problem became apparent when one of Tryon's students, Searle, repeated the experiment with these strains.

Searle (1949) found that, on elevated mazes which permitted greater opportunities for visual cues to operate, Tryon's dull rats performed as well as the so-called bright rats. Moreover, he noted that temperamental differences of a complex nature existed between the two strains and concluded:

[When] all types of apparatus situations are considered there is no evidence that Dulls are generally inferior ... [and] differences in the maze learning ability represent differences in patterns of behavior traits rather than in *degrees* of any single psychological capacity [pp. 319–320].

This suggested that what had been bred for was not a difference in general intellectual capacity but, rather, differences in sensory sensitivity and temperamental stability.

The latter conclusion was supported more recently by the findings of Fuller and Thompson (1960) in the area of behavior genetics. They compared five dog breeds on seven behavioral measures. Although there were differences among the breeds, different breeds appeared to be superior learners on different types of learning tasks. On tasks eliciting motivational and emotional responses, even greater differences were found among breeds. These findings led Birch (1968) to conclude that:

learning ability is by no means a unitary trait, and that in different organisms different patterns of responsiveness, of motivation, of emotionality, and of antecedent history contribute substantially to determining which sub-grouping will learn most effectively under conditions of different instruction and task demand ... [and] that differences in learning achievement whether measured by intelligence tests or by school achievement in human beings, represent the products of different degrees of goodness of fit between the learner, the task, and, in particular, the instructional mode [p. 56].

All of the findings discussed thus far involve the following concepts. The first is the concept that stimuli in the environment compete to dominate the behavior of the individual. The second is the concept that preponderant set or directional style in individuals determines (either on an habitual basis, or on the basis of prior focused training, or on the basis of intrinsic physiologic differences) those aspects of environmental stimulation to which the individual will respond. The third concept involves the motivation of the organism and

the degree to which this motivation acts both to elevate level of activity and to make explicit the direction of activity. (In this sense, one differentiates between drive, which represents an elevation of action level, and motive, which is a directed and selective organization of such increased energetics toward defined goals and specified features of the environment.) The fourth point is the problem of interference with competences, as illustrated by the Malmo–Jacobsen controversy. The fifth point embraces the totality of ideas considered above and involves the idea that differences in learning achievement represent products of different degrees of goodness of fit between the organism and the environment. Certain kinds of fit between organism and environment result in directionalities of behavior and in the successful expression of selected features of the individual's capacities, whereas environmental modifications may encourage other types of performance which reflect quite different capacities.

The concept of the hierarchical organization of response systems is relevant here. This general concept was recently advanced by Birch (1962) and suggests that one of the ways in which organisms differ from one another is in the hierarchical organization of their sense systems. In the development of the normal individual, the telereceptor system gradually comes to dominate over visceral and proximal reception. Complex patterning of behavior, e.g., reading readiness, comes to be organized around the dominant use of auditory and visual information. Thus, certain kinds of reading disability may stem from the inadequate development of an appropriate hierarchical organization of sensory systems, and thus may be the result of the failure of visual system dominance.

Little empirical work is available in this area. Bakker (1966, 1967) has been doing systematic studies within the context of this hypothesis on individuals with reading disabilities, and has demonstrated certain differences in the hierarchy of visual and kinesthetic responsiveness of normal and backward readers. Using a psychophysical method to determine differences in responsiveness to visual and kinesthetic stimuli, and using a difference-threshold procedure, he reported that visual and kinesthetic discrimination capacities were more similar in backward readers than in normal readers in whom visual discrimination was far superior to kinesthetic discrimination. He inferred that there was less dominance of the visual over the kinesthetic system in backward readers.

Clearly, the point of view being developed is related to the issue of behavioral individuality. We have been focusing upon those features of cognitive individuality which may contribute to the gap between capacity and performance. The areas of social psychology and personality development yield related findings. For example, examiner effects on intelligence test scores represent manifestations of the ways in which incorrect estimates of capacity may be obtained on the basis of differences in attitude or in style of approach of the examiner to the child. Thus, the studies of Haggard (1954) and of Anastasi and DeJesus (1953) on social background, atmosphere, and examiner effects indicate that the ethnicity of the examiner, the style with which the examiner approaches the child, and the degree to which the child is familiar with the test circumstances and test atmosphere all contribute to both the level of performance itself and the degree to which the child's performance is a more or less accurate reflection of his capacity.

Our consideration of the relation between cognitive capacity and cognitive performance in mentally subnormal children, as well as in normal children and experimental animals, permits a general conclusion. It is clear from all these data that performance levels under particular conditions are but fragmentary indicators of capacity. Possessed concepts and skills, and particular conceptual abilities, as well as levels of learning when manifested in performance, all reflect the interaction between possessed potentialities and the particular conditions of training and task demand. Glaring differences occur in the estimates of potential when meaningful alterations are made in the conditions for performance. It is clear that we have but begun to explore the universe of conditions for learning and performance which will facilitate most effectively the expression of the potentialities for adaptation which exist in mentally subnormal children. Clearly, the most effective facilitation of development will be dependent on the ingenuity with which such conditions are elaborated. It is to be hoped that placing this question in the broader context of psychology will contribute to the invention of more effective strategies for training and for the maximation of competence.

REFERENCES

ANASTASI, A., & DeJESUS, C. Language development and non-verbal IQ of Puerto Rican preschool children in New York City. *Journal of Abnormal and Social Psychology,* 1953, *48,* 357–366.

BAKKER, D. Sensory dominance in normal and backward readers. *Perceptual and Motor Skills,* 1966, *23,* 1055–1058.

BAKKER, D. Sensory dominance and reading ability. *Journal of Communication Disorders,* 1967, *1,* 316–318.

BIRCH, H. G. Dyslexia and the maturation of visual function. In J. Money (Ed.), *Reading disability: Progress and research needs in dyslexia.* Baltimore: Johns Hopkins Press, 1962. Pp. 161–169.

BIRCH, H. G. Boldness and judgment in behavior genetics. In M. Mead, T. Dobzhansky, E. Tobach, & R. Light (Eds.), *Science and the concept of race.* New York: Columbia University Press, 1968. Pp. 49–58.

BIRCH, H. G., & BORTNER, M. Stimulus competition and category usage in normal children. *Journal of Genetic Psychology,* 1966, *109,* 195–204.

BIRCH, H. G., & BORTNER, M. Stimulus competition and category utilization in brain damaged children. *Developmental Medicine and Child Neurology,* 1967, *9,* 402–410. (Also in S. Chess & A. Thomas, (Eds.), *Annual progress in child psychiatry and child development.* New York: Bruner/Mazel, 1968.)

BIRCH, H. G., & RABINOWITZ, H. S. The negative effect of previous experience on productive thinking. *Journal of Experimental Psychology,* 1951, *41,* 121–125.

BUTTERFIELD, E. C., & ZIGLER, E. The influence of differing institutional social climates on the effectiveness of social reinforcement in the mentally retarded. *American Journal of Mental Deficiency,* 1965, *70,* 48–56.

CANTOR, G. N., & HOTTELL, J. V. Discrimination learning in mental defectives as a function of magnitude of food reward and intelligence level. *American Journal of Mental Deficiency,* 1955, *60,* 380–384.

CLARKE, A. D. B. A symposium: The social adjustment of the mentally deficient: I. Recent English research. *American Journal of Mental Deficiency,* 1957, *62,* 295–299.

CLARKE, A. D. B. The need of the mentally retarded for complex learning experiences. Paper read at Symposium on Education of the Moderately and Severely Retarded, Ostend, Belgium, April 1968.

CLARKE, A. D. B., CLARKE, A. M., & REIMAN, S. Cognitive and social changes in the feebleminded: Three further studies. *British Journal of Psychology,* 1958, *49,* 144–157.

CLARKE, A. D. B., & CLARKE, A. M. Recovery from the effects of deprivation. *Acta Psychologica, Amsterdam,* 1959, *16,* 137–144.

CLARKE, A. M., & CLARKE, A. D. B. Learning transfer and cognitive development. In G. Jervis, & J. Zubin (Eds.), *Psychopathology of mental development.* New York: Grune & Stratton, 1967.

CLARKE, A. M., CLARKE, A. D. B., & COOPER, G. M. The development of a set to perceive categorical relations. In H. C. Haywood (Ed.), *Social-Cultural Aspects of Mental Retardation.* New York: Appleton-Century-Crofts, 1970, in press.

CLARKE, A. D. B., & COOKSON, M. Perceptual-motor transfer in imbeciles: A second series of experiments. *British Journal of Psychology,* 1962, *53,* 321–330.

CLARKE, A. D. B., & COOPER, G. M. Age and perceptual-motor transfer of training. *Perceptual and Motor Skills,* 1964, *19,* 849–850.

CLARKE, A. M., & COOPER, G. M. Conceptual transfer in preschool children as a function of prior training. *Psychonomic Science*, 1967, *9*, 307–308.

CLARKE, A. M., COOPER, G. M., & CLARKE, A. D. B. Task complexity and transfer in the development of cognitive structures. *Journal of Experimental Child Psychology*, 1967, *5*, 562–576.

DOUVAN, E. Social status and success striving. *Journal of Abnormal and Social Psychology*, 1956, *52*, 219–223.

DRYMAN, I., BIRCH, H. G., & KORN, S. J. Verbalization and action in the problem-solving of six-year-old children. Unpublished manuscript, Yeshiva University, 1970.

DUNCKER, K. On problem-solving. *Psychological Monographs*, 1945, *58*, (5, Whole No. 270). (Translated by L. S. Lees.)

ELLIS, N. R. Amount of reward and operant behavior in mental defectives. *American Journal of Mental Deficiency*, 1962, *66*, 613–617.

FULLER, J. L., & THOMPSON, W. R. *Behavior genetics*. New York: Wiley, 1960.

GESCHWIND, N., & FUSILLO, M. Color naming defects in association with alexia. *Archives of Neurology*, 1966, *15*, 137–146.

GESCHWIND, N., & KAPLAN, E. A human cerebral deconnection syndrome. *Neurology*, 1962, *12*, 675–685.

GEWIRTZ, J., & BAER, D. The effect of brief social deprivation on behaviors for a social reinforcer. *Journal of Abnormal and Social Psychology*, 1958, *56*, 49–56.

GORDON, S., O'CONNOR, N., & TIZARD, J. Some effects of incentives on the performance of imbeciles on a repetitive task. *American Journal of Mental Deficiency*, 1955, *60*, 371–377.

GREEN, C., & ZIGLER, E. Social deprivation and the performance of retarded and normal children on a satiation type task. *Child Development*, 1962, *33*, 499–508.

HAGGARD, E. A. Social status and intelligence: An experimental study of certain cultural determinants of measured intelligence. *Genetic Psychology Monographs*, 1954, *49*, 141–186.

HEBER, R. Motor task performance of high grade mentally retarded males as a function of the magnitude of incentive. *American Journal of Mental Deficiency*, 1959, *63*, 667–671.

HERMELIN, B., & O'CONNOR, N. Short term memory in normal and subnormal children. *American Journal of Mental Deficiency*, 1964, *69*, 121–125.

HOUSE, B. J., ORLANDO, R., & ZEAMAN, D. Role of positive and negative cues in the discrimination learning of mental defectives. *Perceptual and Motor Skills*, 1957, *7*, 73–79.

HOUSE, B. J., & ZEAMAN, D. Visual discrimination learning in imbeciles. *American Journal of Mental Deficiency*, 1958, *63*, 447–452. (a)

HOUSE, B. J., & ZEAMAN, D. Reward and non-reward in the discrimination learning of imbeciles. *Journal of Comparative and Physiological Psychology*, 1958, *51*, 614–618. (b)

HOUSE, B. J., & ZEAMAN, D. Transfer of a discrimination from objects to patterns. *Journal of Experimental Psychology*, 1960, *59*, 298–302.

ITARD, J. M. G. *De l'éducation d'un homme sauvage*. Paris: Goujon, 1801.

JACOBSEN, C. F. The effects of extirpation of the frontal association in monkeys upon complex adaptive behavior. *Psychological Bulletin*, 1934, *31*, 636–637.

KANNER, L. *A history of the care and study of the mentally retarded*. Springfield, Ill.: Charles C Thomas, 1964.

KOUNIN, J. Experimental studies of rigidity: I. The measurement of rigidity in normal and feebleminded persons. *Character and Personality*, 1941, *9*, 251–273.

LASHLEY, K. The mechanism of vision: I. A method for rapid analysis of pattern vision in the rat. *Journal of Genetic Psychology*, 1930, *37*, 353–460.

LEWIN, K. *A dynamic theory of personality*. New York: McGraw-Hill, 1936.

LEWIS, A. The study of defect. *American Journal of Psychiatry*, 1960, *117*, 289–305.

LIUBLINSKAYA, A. A. The development of children's speech and thought. In B. Simon (Ed.), *Psychology in the Soviet Union*. Translated by J. Ellis, M. Ellis, and others. Stanford, Calif.: Stanford University Press, 1957.

LURIA, A. R. An objective approach to the study of the abnormal child. *American Journal of Orthopsychiatry*, 1961, *31*, 1–16.

LURIA, A. R., & VINOGRADOVA, O. S. An objective investigation of the dynamics of semantic systems. *British Journal of Psychology*, 1959, *50*, 89–105.

MAIER, N. R. F. Reasoning in humans: I. On directions. *Journal of Comparative Psychology*, 1930, *10*, 115–143.

MALMO, R. B., & KLEINSASSER, A. J. Interference factors in delayed response in monkeys after removal of the frontal lobes. *Psychological Bulletin*, 1942, *39*, 492–493.

McCOY, N., & ZIGLER, E. Social reinforcer effectiveness as a function of the relationship between child and adult. *Journal of Personality and Social Psychology*, 1965, *1*, 604–612.

MEHLER, J., & BEVER, T. G. Cognitive capacity of very young children. *Science*, 1967, *158*, 141–142.

O'CONNOR, N., & HERMELIN, B. Some effects of word learning in imbeciles. *Language and Speech*, 1959, *2*, 63–71. (a)

O'CONNOR, N., & HERMELIN, B. Discrimination and reversal learning in imbeciles. *Journal of Abnormal and Social Psychology*, 1959, *59*, 409–413. (b)

O'CONNOR, N., & HERMELIN, B. Recall in normals and subnormals of like mental age. *Journal of Abnormal and Social Psychology*, 1963, *66*, 81–84.

O'CONNOR, N., & TIZARD, J. *The social problem of mental deficiency*. London: Pergamon Press, 1956.

PRIBRAM, K. H. (ED.), *Brain and behavior*. Baltimore: Penguin, 1966. 2 vols.

SEARLE, L. V. The organization of hereditary maze-brightness and maze-dullness. *Genetic Psychology Monographs*, 1949, *39*, 279–325.

SHALLENBERGER, P., & ZIGLER, E. Rigidity, negative reaction tendencies, and cosatiation effects in normal and feebleminded children. *Journal of Abnormal and Social Psychology*, 1961, *63*, 20–26.

SHEPPS, R., & ZIGLER, E. Social deprivation and rigidity in the performance of organic and familial retardates. *American Journal of Mental Deficiency*, 1962, *67*, 262–268.

STEVENSON, H. Social reinforcement with children as a function of CA, sex of E and sex of S. *Journal of Abnormal and Social Psychology*, 1961, *63*, 147–154.

THOMAS, A., CHESS, S., BIRCH, H. G., HERTZIG, M., & KORN, S. *Behavioral individuality in early childhood*. New York: New York University Press, 1963.

TIZARD, J., & GRAD, J. C. *The mentally handicapped and their families; a social survey*. London: Oxford University Press, 1961.

TIZARD, J., & LOOS, F. The learning of a spatial relations test by adult imbeciles. *American Journal of Mental Deficiency*, 1954, *59*, 85–90.

TRYON, R. C. Genetic differences in maze learning ability in rats. *Yearbook of the National Society for the Study of Education*, 1940, *39*(1), 111–119.

TURNURE, J., & ZIGLER, E. Outer-directedness in the problem solving of normal and retarded children. *Journal of Abnormal and Social Psychology*, 1964, *69*, 427–436.

WALTERS, R., & RAY, E. Anxiety, isolation and reinforcer effectiveness. *Journal of Personality*, 1960, *28*, 358–367.

WEST, R. W. *Childhood aphasia: Proceedings of Institute on Childhood Aphasia. Stanford University School of Medicine*. Chicago: National Society for Crippled Children and Adults, 1960.

WOLFENSBERGER, W. Differential reward as motivating factors in mental deficiency research. *American Journal of Mental Deficiency*, 1960, *64*, 902–906.

WOODWORTH, R. S., & SELLS, S. B. An atmospheric effect in formal syllogistic reasoning. *Journal of Experimental Psychology*, 1935, *18*, 451–460.

YERKES, R. B., & WATSON, J. B. Methods of studying vision in animals. *Behavior Monographs*, 1911, *1*, 1–90.

ZEAMAN, D., & HOUSE, B. J. Approach and avoidance in the discrimination learning of retardates. *Child Development*, 1962, *33*, 355–372.

ZEAMAN, D., HOUSE, B. J., & ORLANDO, R. Use of special training conditions in visual discrimination learning with imbeciles. *American Journal of Mental Deficiency*, 1958, *63*, 453–459.

ZIGLER, E. Social deprivation and rigidity in the performance of feebleminded children. *Journal of Abnormal and Social Psychology*, 1961, *62*, 413–421.

ZIGLER, E. Social deprivation in familial and organic retardates. *Psychological Reports*, 1962, *10*, 370.

ZIGLER, E. Motivational determinants in the performance of retarded children. *American Journal of Orthopsychiatry*, 1966, *36*, 848–856.

ZIGLER, E., & BUTTERFIELD, E. C. Rigidity in the retarded: A further test of the Lewin-Kounin formulation. *Journal of Abnormal Psychology*, 1966, *71*(3), 224–231.

ZIGLER, E., & DeLABRY, J. Concept switching in middle class, lower class and retarded children. *Journal of Abnormal and Social Psychology*, 1962, *65*, 267–273.

ZIGLER, E., HODGDEN, L., & STEVENSON, H. W. The effect of support and nonsupport on the performance of normal and feebleminded children. *Journal of Personality*, 1958, *26*, 106–122.

ZIGLER, E., & UNELL, E. Concept-switching in normal and feebleminded children as a function of reinforcement. *American Journal of Mental Deficiency*, 1962, *66*, 651–657.

58

The Effect of Task Complexity on Reflection-Impulsivity [1]

REGINA M. YANDO
AND JEROME KAGAN

Children differ substantially in the way in which they approach problem-solving and other cognitive tasks, and they manifest their own particular style in many different circumstances. Jerome Kagan, professor of developmental psychology at Harvard, has done extensive investigation of one such cognitive style, the tendency of a child to be reflective or impulsive. Regina Yando is a member of the Research Department of the Fernald School, Waltham, Massachusetts.

Though substantial progress has been made in recent years in studying and modelling human problem solving, relatively little account has been taken of the effects of individual differences upon the problem-solving process. This paper describes research investigating the effects of one such individual difference variable. The disposition to evaluate one's cognitive product is likely to be an important determinant of the quality of the final solution, especially in problem situations where multiple solution hypotheses are available. Decision time is often a good index of the degree to which a problem solver pauses to evaluate his answer.

Classical studies of the decision time variable (e.g., Morin & Forrin, 1963; Hyman, 1953) have largely been concerned with establishing the relation between decision time and the amount of information (either stimulus or response) available to the subject. Other investigations (Kagan, 1966b), however, have studied decision time in problem situations that hold the amount of information constant. These studies have revealed that some individuals consistently display fast or slow decision times when faced with problems containing a fixed number of alternative responses. This individual difference variable has been described as the reflection-impulsivity dimension.

Previous investigations of reflection-impulsivity have demonstrated its long-term stability, generality across varied task situations, and predictive validity to a variety of problem-solving situations (Kagan, 1965a,b). However, the stability of this disposition across problems with varying numbers of alternative responses has not been investigated. Specifically, this study asks whether children previously classified as reflective or impulsive retain their preferred style of response under conditions which vary the number of alternative responses.

METHOD

SUBJECTS

The *S*s were second-grade children from four public elementary schools in Fargo, North Dakota. The schools were chosen from a total of 13 elementary schools as being most representative of the general socioeconomic level of this city of 50,000 people. The parents of all second-grade children in the four selected schools were sent a letter requesting permission to test their children. An affirmative reply was received from approximately 200 of the 360 families, and 60 boys and 60 girls were randomly selected from the 200 for the initial phase of testing.

The age range was 6–11 to 8–6, and the IQ range (Kuhlmann-Anderson) was 91 to 135 (mean of 106 for boys, 109 for girls). These scores were obtained at the beginning of the school year; the technical manual for the seventh edition of the Kuhlmann-Anderson reports for grade 2 a test-retest reliability of .85 and an odd-even score reliability of .95. The correlation of the Kuhlmann with the Stanford-Binet (forms L and L–M) is reported to be .65 for grades 2 and 3. No child had been retained in any grade, and no gross physical anomalies (specifically visual) were detected in any of the children.

[1] Supported by NSF University Grant GU–1877 (North Dakota State University) and MH–8792 from NIMH. The assistance of the North Dakota State University psychology students, particularly Sheila Emblin, is gratefully acknowledged. The cooperation of the administrative officials, principals, and teachers of the Fargo City school system made this study possible.

Regina M. Yando and Jerome Kagan, "The effect of task complexity on reflection-impulsivity," *Cognitive Psychology, I,* 1970, 192–200. Reprinted with abridgement by permission.

TEST MATERIALS

Performance on the Matching Familiar Figures (MFF) Test has been regarded as the primary index of the reflection-impulsivity dimension. In the standard form of this task, the child is presented a picture of a familiar object (standard) and six similar variants, only one of which is identical to the standard. The test consists of two initial practice items and 10 test items, each comprised of a standard and six variants. The standard appears alone on the top page of a book and the variants on the bottom page. The instructions request the child to find the picture on the bottom page that is exactly like the picture on the top page. If the child makes the correct response, he is praised; if incorrect, he is told that his response is not correct, and he is asked to try again until he finds the correct variant. The two major variables scored are: (a) response time to the child's first solution hypothesis and (b) total number of errors on each test item. The child's final scores are the mean response time to the first solution hypothesis across all 10 test items and the total number of errors. Figure 1 shows a typical test item.

In order to test the stability of a child's preferred style of response in problems having varying numbers of alternative responses, 10 different forms of the MFF were constructed. Like the original MFF, the new forms consisted of 10 items (standard and variants), each item on a given form having the same number of variants. Where the original MFF had six variants per item, however, the 10 new forms had 2, 3, 4, 5, 7, 8, 9, 10, 11, and 12 variants per item. Each item was entirely different from any other item appearing on any of the forms. The same directions and the same two practice items (containing six variants) were used with each of the 10 new forms.

PROCEDURE

Ten trained male and female advanced psychology students were randomly assigned to test individually 8 to

9 Ss each week. Es tested a different group of children each week and were never aware of the previous test results on the children. Neither the examiners nor the children were aware of the purpose of the study.

Initially, each child was administered the original six variant MFF as a classification test. On the basis of his performance on this test, a child was classified as reflective (response time above the median, error score below the median), impulsive (response time below the median, error score above the median), or nonextreme (all children not identified as reflective or impulsive). Median splits were performed within each sex separately. Random selection from this remaining group narrowed the sample to 14 boys and 14 girls in each of the three classifications (84 children total).

Following the initial classification, each of the 84 Ss was seen weekly on the same day for 10 consecutive weeks. A different form of the MFF was administered to each S each week in order of increasing difficulty (i.e., during the first week, all Ss were administered the 2 variant form; during the second week, the 3 variant form, etc.).

RESULTS

RESPONSE TIME

Mean response times across the 10 weeks are presented in Fig. 2. Response time data were subjected to a $3 \times 2 \times 10$ (Classification Tempo × Sex × Number of Alternatives) repeated measures analysis of variance. The between aspects of the analysis revealed significant main effects for Classification Tempo [$F(2/78) = 21.11$, $p < .001$] and Sex [$F(1/78) = 5.63$, $p < .05$]. The Classification Tempo × Sex interaction was not significant. Newman-Keuls (Winer, 1962) analysis of the nature of the tempo effect revealed that reflective children obtained significantly higher response times than both nonextreme ($p < .01$) and impulsive children ($p < .01$). The difference between the nonextreme and impulsive children was also significant at the .05 level. The sex differ-

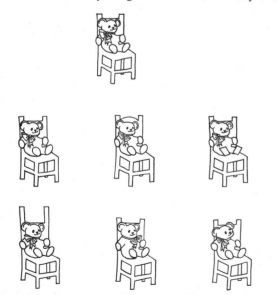

FIGURE 1. *Sample item from Matching Familiar Figures Test.*

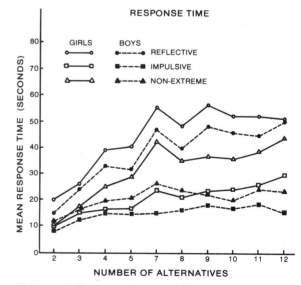

FIGURE 2. *Response time as a function of number of alternatives for the initial classification group.*

ence was produced by the nonextreme girls who showed significantly longer response times than nonextreme boys ($p < .05$). The within portion of the analysis revealed a significant main effect for Number of Alternatives [$F(9/702) = 42.81$, $p < .001$] and significant interactions between Sex × Number of Alternatives [$F(9/702) = 2.71$, $p < .001$] and Classification Tempo × Number of Alternatives [$F(2/702) = 4.11$, $p < .001$]. The triple interaction was not significant. The nature of these effects can be clearly seen in Fig. 2. Although all groups showed a gradual increase in time as the number of alternatives increased, this effect was more dramatic for reflective children and nonextreme girls than for impulsive children and nonextreme boys.

ERROR SCORES

Mean total error scores across the 10 weeks are presented in Fig. 3. Error data were subjected to a 3 × 2 × 10 (Classification Tempo × Sex × Number of Alternatives) repeated measures analysis of variance. The between aspects of the analysis revealed significant main effects for Classification Tempo [$F(2/78) = 17.93$, p $< .001$] and Sex [$F(1/78) = 8.54$, $p < .01$], but the interaction was not significant. Newman-Keuls analysis revealed all tempo groups (reflective $\overline{X} = 3.10$, nonextreme $\overline{X} = 6.84$, impulsive $\overline{X} = 11.64$) to be significantly different from each other at the .01 level. Moreover, the girls in each classification group made significantly fewer errors than the boys in the corresponding group. The within portion of the analysis revealed a significant main effect for Number of Alternatives [$F(9/702) = 38.67$, $p < .001$] and significant interactions between Sex × Number of Alternatives [$F(1/702) = 5.03$, $p < .001$] and Classification Tempo × Number of Alternatives [$F(2/702) = 6.09$, $p < .001$]. The triple interaction was not significant. The nature of these effects can be clearly seen in Fig. 3.

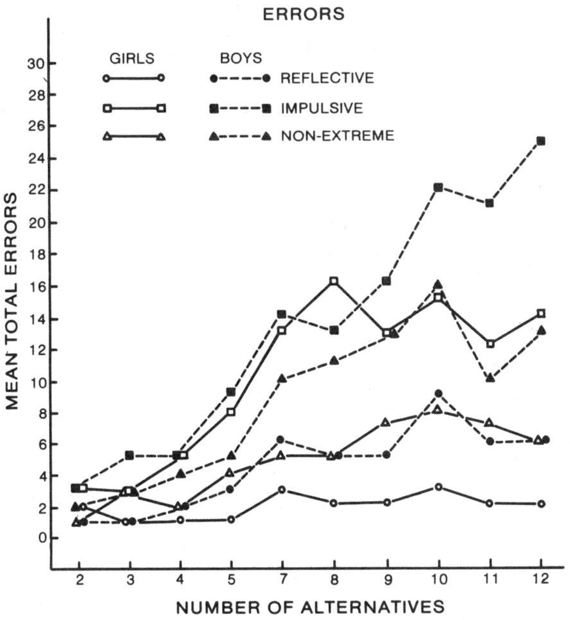

FIGURE 3. *Errors as a function of the number of alternatives for the initial classification group.*

Impulsive children and boys in general showed the most significant increase in errors as the number of alternatives on each task increased. However, task complexity had little, if any, effect on reflective girls.

STABILITY

The children tended to retain their rank order for response time and errors, for the interweek Pearson Product Moment correlations were high. The median correlation was .73 ($p < .01$) for response time and .68 ($p < .01$) for errors. The range was .46 to .92 ($p < .01$) for response time and .22 to .87 ($p < .01$) for errors. The relation between errors and response time was in accord with earlier findings; there was a negative relation between errors and response time for each of the 10 tests (median $r = -.57$).

CLASSIFICATION

Although the data reveal that as a group children maintained their respective classifications over time and across problems with varying alternative responses, it is of interest to inspect the individual cases within each classification. In order to do this, each child was reclassified (reflective, impulsive, or nonextreme) on the basis of the median response time and error scores obtained for each of the 10 sets of data; thus yielding 10 classifications for each child. This analysis revealed that 7 boys and 9 girls of the 28 children initially classified as impulsive retained an impulsive classification for *each* of the 10 forms of the MFF; of the 28 initially classified as reflective, 7 boys and 8 girls retained a reflective classification; and 10 boys and 8 girls retained a nonextreme classification.

The trends evidenced for the total group (Figs. 2 and 3) were more dramatic for this select sample. The consistently reflective *S*s showed no increase in errors despite increasing task difficulty across the 10 weeks. Impulsive *S*s, on the other hand, showed no increase in response time over the 10 weeks despite increasing task difficulty. The mean response time for impulsive *S*s for the 12 variant test was about 12 sec, only slightly larger than the mean response time of 9 sec for the 2 variant test. These values are to be contrasted with mean response times for the reflective *S*s; 58 sec for the 12 variant test and 17 sec for the easy 2 variant test.

RELATION TO IQ

Among boys, the group administered IQ score was independent of response time (range: $r = .06$ to .22, none significant) and errors (range: $r = .00$ to $-.36$, with only one coefficient significant at the .05 level). Among girls, however, there was a weak positive relation between IQ and response time (5 of 11 coefficients significant at the .05 level; range: $r = .14$ to .36), and a consistent negative relation between IQ and errors (8 of 11 coefficients significant at the .05 level; range: $r = -.26$ to $-.40$).

DISCUSSION

The reflection-impulsivity dimension was remarkably stable across problems with differing numbers of alternative responses. The child's preferred approach to the task was a better predictor of both errors (for reflective children) and response time (for impulsive children) than task difficulty. That is, regardless of task difficulty, reflective children committed few errors; impulsive children responded quickly and committed many errors. These findings, together with the apparent stability of this dimension over a 10-week period, support the notion that reflection-impulsivity is an important characteristic of the child's psychological organization. It should be noted, however, that since the number of alternatives increased linearly each week there is a confounding of difficulty with previous experience with the task.

The reflective children are actively considering alternative hypotheses during their longer decision times, for earlier work has demonstrated that they make many more visual scans of the standard and variants than the impulsives (Kagan, Pearson, & Welch, 1966a). Moreover, the reflective children tend to examine all the variants before offering a solution; the impulsives often respond after examining only a few (Vurpillot, 1968; Nelson, 1968; Sigelman, 1966).

The tendency to be reflective or impulsive is likely to have multiple determinants. Our preferred interpretation is that reflective children experience greater anxiety over error than impulsives. Reflectives seem to be overly concerned with making a mistake and thus subject their answers to scrutiny. A recent experimental study indicated that response times increase following a failure experience designed to arouse anxiety over error (Messer, 1968). Moreover, 11-year-old boys who display symptoms associated with low anxiety (aggression, cheating) were more impulsive than boys of the same social class who displayed symptoms associated with high anxiety (fears, obsessions, nightmares).[2] Although anxiety over error is admittedly only one potential determinant of reflection-impulsivity, we view it as the most salient.

Lower class and "culturally deprived" children tend to be impulsive (Kagan, 1966a). The inferior intellectual performance displayed by these children may be due, in part, to an impulsive attitude, in addition to deficits in cognitive resources. Although impulsivity is not the sole cause of error, a child who consistently attacks a problem with this preferred strategy may experience repeated failure.

Agents of educational change have typically con-

centrated upon curriculum and the incentive value of classroom materials and paid less attention to individual differences in children of similar competence. The concern has been with *what* rather than *how* the child is to be taught. Previous data (Yando & Kagan, 1968; Kagan, Pearson, & Welch, 1966b) suggest that modification of the decision strategy of the children may have subsequent effects on his problem-solving ability. It is urged that research in instructional and testing procedures acknowledge the significance of the preferred strategy of the learner.

REFERENCES

HYMAN, R. Stimulus information as a determinant of reaction time. *Journal of Experimental Psychology*, 1953, *45*, 188–196.

KAGAN, J. Individual differences in the resolution of response uncertainty. *Journal of Personality and Social Psychology*, 1965, *2*, 154–160. (a)

KAGAN, J. Reflection-impulsivity and reading ability in primary grade children. *Child Development*, 1965, *36*, 609–628. (b)

KAGAN, J. Reflection-impulsivity: the generality and dynamics of conceptual tempo. *Journal of Abnormal Psychology*, 1966, *71*, 17–24. (a)

KAGAN, J. Developmental studies in reflection and analysis. In A. H. Kidd & J. L. Rivoire (Eds.), *Perceptual development in children*. New York: International Press, 1966. Pp. 497–522. (b)

KAGAN, J., PEARSON, L., & WELCH, L. Conceptual impulsivity and inductive reasoning. *Child Development*, 1966, *37*, 583–594. (a)

KAGAN, J., PEARSON, L., & WELCH, L. The modifiability of an impulsive tempo. *Journal of Educational Psychology*, 1966, *57*, 359–365. (b)

MORIN, R. E., & FORRIN, B. Response equivocation and reaction time. *Journal of Experimental Psychology*, 1963, *66*, 30–36.

NELSON, T. F. The effects of training in attention deployment on observing behavior in reflective and impulsive children. Unpublished doctoral dissertation, University of Minnesota, 1968.

SIGELMAN, E. Y. Observing behavior in impulsive and reflective children. Unpublished doctoral dissertation, University of Minnesota, 1966.

VURPILLOT, E. The development of scanning strategies and their relation to visual discrimination. *Journal of Experimental Child Psychology*, 1968, *6*, 637–650.

WINER, B. J. *Statistical principles in experimental design*. New York: McGraw-Hill, 1962.

YANDO, R., & KAGAN, J. The effect of teacher tempo on the child. *Child Development*, 1968, *39*, 27–34.

---

[2] S. Weintraub, personal communication.

59

Children's Conceptions of Psychological Causality

MARTIN WHITEMAN

This article is another example of the extensive literature that has been based on the seminal works of Jean Piaget. In this article, Martin Whiteman, a member of the faculty of the Columbia University School of Social Work, looks at the development of children's notions about psychological causality. The article is also valuable for its discussion of how the interview technique was used with young children.

Piaget's pioneering explorations have brought forth a number of investigations of the child's conception of physical causality. However, there has been relatively little investigation of the child's conceptions of psychological causality. It would seem as appropriate to ask a child, "What makes people angry?" as it is to ask him "What makes clouds move?" Yet, systematic explorations of the child's developing awareness of the causes of another person's behavior are lacking. This lack is particularly poignant since, as adults, we are continually making inferences about the causes of other people's behavior. An important problem, then, is how and when such causal inferences are learned.

A major set of concepts used by people in explaining behavior comprises the so-called mechanisms of adjustment. People, in their everyday behavior, do seem to use as explanatory devices those behaviors that psychologists have conceptualized as rationalizations or displacements or projections, for example, rationalization ("He's using that as an excuse"), displacement ("He's just taking out all his troubles on me"), projection ("Well, that's the way he is himself and he thinks everybody is that way"). From a theoretical point of view, it is important to understand how and when such explanatory ideas become part of the conceptual repertoire of the child. Psychologists of such widely differing theoretical persuasion as Anna Freud (1946) and Hilgard (1949) have pointed to the importance of such mechanisms for maintenance of self-esteem. However, there has been no attempt to study directly the cognitive development of such notions, which are as important in their own right as the development by the child of conceptions of space, time, and physical causality.

Piaget has drawn a basic distinction between the preoperational intuitive stage (around 4–7 years) and the concrete operational stage (around 7–11 years). According to Piaget (1950) and Flavell (1963), there is a major revision in the child's thought at around 7 years, enabling him to conceptualize certain types of relations and classes. A major achievement of the operational child is his ability to decenter from a focus on the perceptually dominant to an emphasis on the more invariant but less salient properties of stimulus displays, as illustrated by the operational child's ability to conserve conceptually an object's substance or length despite changes in the object's appearance or location. Similarly, one would expect that the operational as compared to the younger preoperational child should have greater ease in decentering from the more obvious overt behaviors to the less obvious underlying motivations as described by the adjustment mechanisms. Furthermore, Laurendeau and Pinard (1962), replicating early Piaget investigations (1929; 1930),

This research was supported by a grant from the National Institute of Mental Health (No. MH–10578–01). A preliminary report was made at the 1965 meeting of the Eastern Psychological Association at Atlantic City. Grateful acknowledgment is made to Anita G. Bardin, Judith F. Levine, Sherrie F. Miller, and Judith L. Ryan for their contribution to the interviewing and to the coding of the data gathered in phase 2. Dr. Lassar K. Gotkin of the Institute for Developmental Studies, Department of Psychiatry, New York Medical College, was most helpful in securing the cooperation of the teachers and of the administration of the public schools in which the work was done. Miss Jean Lloyd and Mrs. Goldie Haile, kindergarten teachers, are thanked for their cooperation in expediting the interviewing of the children.

Martin Whiteman, "Children's conceptions of psychological causality," *Child Development, 38,* 1967, 143–155. Reprinted with abridgement by permission. Copyright 1967 by The Society for Research in Child Development, Inc.

have shown striking differences between these two age levels in their ability to apprehend physical causality. It becomes pertinent, therefore, to explore the differences between such contrasting age groups in their explanations of psychological causality as well as to relate such differences to conceptions of physical causality.

The general aim of this study is to explore the feasibility of using interviews with children at two age levels, the 5–6-year range and the 8–9-year-old span, in order to study developing conceptions of psychological causality.

The study comprised two separate phases. The specific aims of phase 1 were to *(a)* devise usable categorizations and scoring systems for the assessment of psychological causality, *(b)* study the homogeneity among items in order to determine whether reliable and meaningful indexes might be formed, and *(c)* study developmental and intellectual differences with respect to such indexes of psychological causality. The second phase had as its purposes: *(a)* the objectification and standardization of the interviewing procedure devised in phase 1, *(b)* the replication of phase 1 with comparable but somewhat larger samples to assess the reliability of phase 1 findings with respect to developmental and intellectual differences in the understanding of psychological causality, and *(c)* the extension of phase 1 results through the study of the relation between grasp of psychological causality and understanding of physical causality.

PHASE 1

METHOD

Subjects. The subjects comprised 42 children. The 21 younger children comprised an experimental kindergarten class in Harlem, New York City. Stanford-Binet IQ's were available for these children. For each kindergarten child, a separate roster of third-grade children from the same school was prepared. The third graders on each roster had been matched with the kindergarten child with respect to sex and IQ as assessed by group test. For each kindergarten child, a third grader was then selected from the appropriate roster by random sampling. For each grade, the average IQ was 101 with a standard deviation of 10. All children were Negro or Puerto Rican. The kindergarten children were in the 5–6-year range, while the third graders fell in the 8–9-year span.

The interview. The interviews were conducted by the writer and dealt with the child's tape-recorded responses to questions about each of seven stories. Each story read to the child exemplified

in rudimentary form a different mechanism of adjustment, that is, displacement, wishful dreaming, projection, regression, repression, rationalization, and denial. The instructions to the child and the stories themselves were as follows:

"I'm going to tell you some stories about a little girl called Jane. In each of these stories Jane does something different from what she usually does. I want you to tell me why she did it. Here's the first story." (For boys, "Johnnie" was substituted for "Jane" in all the stories, and "toy soldiers" for "dolls" in the first story.)

1. Displacement: "There was once a little girl named Jane. One day her mother promised that Jane's favorite dessert, ice cream, would be served at supper. But Jane's mother forgot to buy the ice cream, and so there wasn't any ice cream for dessert. Jane didn't say anything to her mother about the ice cream. After supper Jane went to play with her dolls and did something she never did before. She spanked her dolls. Why did she spank her dolls?"

2. Wishful dreaming: "One day Jane looked at T.V. and saw a girl who had a wonderful bicycle. Jane herself didn't have a bicycle and couldn't even ride one. That night Jane dreamed that her father bought her a bicycle and that she was riding all over the block on it. How come she had such a dream?"

3. Projection: "Jane was a good girl, but there was one thing she never liked to do. She didn't like to share her toys with the other kids. She always wanted to keep her toys to herself and not let the other kids use them. One day Jane's mother told her that they were going to visit another family where there was another little girl who was Jane's age. Jane and this other little girl could play together. But Jane looked unhappy and said, 'I bet she won't want to share any of her games and toys.' Why did Jane say this when she didn't even know the other little girl?"

4. Regression: "One day Jane didn't feel well. She had a headache and didn't want to eat. She began to act just like her baby brother. She talked baby talk; she wanted to suck her baby brother's milk bottle; and she even wanted to be held in her mother's arms just like a baby. Why did she act this way?"

5. Repression: "One day Jane's mother bought her a new pair of gloves. She warned Jane not to lose the gloves, because Jane had lost the last pair. One afternoon Jane lost her gloves coming back from school. She knew she had to tell her mother. But when she got home, she forgot to tell her. When Jane went out to play in the afternoon, she told her friends about the lost gloves. But that night she forgot to tell her mother. The next morning at breakfast Jane again forgot to tell her mother. Why did she keep forgetting to tell her mother about the lost gloves?"

6. Rationalization: "One day Jane's mother gave her a big bowl of spinach. Jane said, 'I'm not going to eat the spinach because it makes you very fat!' Why did Jane say that about the spinach when she liked to eat fattening things like ice cream and candy?"

7. Denial: "Jane wanted very much to go to her friend's birthday party. On the day of the party she fell

sick and couldn't go. But Jane said, 'I didn't want to go to that party anyway!' Why did Jane say that?"

There was an attempt in each story to focus questions or probes on certain key elements, for example, whether the child grasped the role of the ice cream disappointment in arousing anger in the displacement story, or whether the child saw Jane as really wanting to go to the party in the denial story.

In order to gain some control on memory and language differences, an attempt was made to pose alternatives, to recapitulate part of the stories in the questions, and in some cases to suggest causal possibilities as a kind of testing-of-the-limits procedure.

Each story was coded according to the degree in which the motivation of the child in the story situation was grasped. Thus, in the displacement story, the highest score was given to the children who attributed the spanking of the doll to the ice cream deprivation, who spontaneously or in response to probes cited an appropriate emotional reaction to the ice cream deprivation, that is, being mad or sad, and had some psychological explanation for spanking the doll rather than the mother. A lower score was assigned to sequences which related the ice cream deprivation to the spanking, but offered no psychological reason for spanking the doll rather than the mother. At a lower level, the spanking was conceived as the doll's fault, with no apprehension of the possible causal role of the ice cream incident. Thus, the doll was conceived as bad or dirty or ugly or jumping too much.

Statistical treatment. The feasibility of combining the responses to the various stories into an index was explored. A Motivation Index was constructed by cumulating weights for each of the seven stories. For the entire group, this total index score was then correlated with each of the subscores derived from particular stories.

RESULTS

The individual stories. Table 1 indicates that the stories proved difficult even for the older children. The percentage of older children showing the highest level of understanding (level 4 in Table 1) ranges from 5 per cent for the rationalization story to 38 per cent for the displacement story, with a median of 19 per cent. The repression and displacement stories proved the easiest for the older children, while the rationalization and regression stories proved the most difficult. For the younger children, the highest level could be reached only in the case of the repression story, and this with only one child. With more lenient criteria (success

TABLE 1

DISTRIBUTION OF 21 YOUNGER CHILDREN (AGES 5 AND 6) AND MATCHED OLDER CHILDREN (AGES 8 AND 9) IN RESPONSE CATEGORIES OF PHASE 1 STORIES

Story and Age Group	Level of Understanding					x^{2a}
	0	1	2	3	4	
Displacement:						
Younger	...	3	15	3	0	
Older	...	0	5	8	8	11.08***
Wishful dreaming:						
Younger	3	10	3	5	0	
Older	0	4	5	8	4	2.77
Projection:						
Younger	4	4	12	1	0	
Older	0	0	9	9	3	9.09**
Regression:						
Younger	6	6	4	5	0	
Older	0	5	12	2	2	4.08*
Repression:						
Younger	...	...	10	10	1	
Older	...	...	6	8	7	.75
Rationalization:						
Younger	2	18	1	0	0	
Older	0	11	8	1	1	4.90*
Denial:						
Younger	...	14	3	4	0	
Older	...	8	3	6	4	2.08

a Corrected for discontinuity. Adjacent scoring categories for each story combined to form median dichotomies for the x^2 analysis.
* Significant at .05 level.
** Significant at .01 level.
*** Significant at .001 level.

at levels 3 or 4), the percentage of success for the younger children ranged from 48 per cent in the case of the repression story to 0 per cent for the rationalization story, with a median of 10 per cent. Rationalization and projection were the most difficult stories for the younger children while repression, regression, and wishful dreaming proved relatively easier. Most of the older children (71 per cent as compared to 10 per cent of the younger children) were able to show comprehension of Jane's underlying motivation in at least three stories (using the more lenient level 3 or 4 criterion). The application of more rigorous criteria for comprehension, with greater concentration on the spontaneous answers of the child (level 4), disclosed that 76 per cent of the older children were able to reach the highest level on at least one story as compared to 5 per cent of the younger group.

Table 1 also indicates that, when the scores for each story were dichotomized at the median, significant age differences appeared in the case of the displacement, projection, regression, and rationalization stories.

With respect to the displacement story, the older children tended to attribute the spanking to the ice cream deprivation. The younger children tended to attribute the spanking to the intrinsic naughtiness of the doll. In the projection story, some of the older children tended to attribute Jane's statement about the other girl's not sharing to Jane's own behavior. Thus, Jane's remark is seen as a projection of her own disinclination to share. As one child put it: "Just because she don't share her things, she might believe that girl would be as evil as she." More usually, however, Jane's remark was seen as occasioned by the other girl's reaction to Jane's own habit of not sharing. The younger children had difficulty seeing Jane's own nonsharing as the direct or indirect cause of her thinking the other child would not share. The younger children tended to refer more to the other girl as directly causing Jane's remark, for example: "Jane says the other girl won't share because the girl was strange." In the regression story, the older children more readily perceived the advantages of acting like a baby. The younger children may have mentioned the illness as cause, but had difficulty in seeing the child wanting to be treated as a baby when ill. Finally, in the rationalization story, the younger child was more prone to believe that Jane said she would not eat the spinach because it makes you very fat because Jane actually thought that the spinach made you very fat, that she did not just say it but really believed it. The older child tended to attribute Jane's saying that spinach makes you very fat because she didn't want to eat it.

. . .

The Motivation Index. The analysis of variance of the Motivation Index revealed the expected and highly significant age differences. Ninety per cent of the younger children scored below the median score of the older children. The more intelligent children tended to score significantly higher when the dichotomies of those above 100 IQ and those at 100 or below were used. Rhos of .40 and .15 between IQ and Motivation Index were found for the older and younger children, respectively. Neither of these coefficients is significant. However, the analysis of variance revealed a significant interaction between grade and IQ. Thus, IQ differences on the Motivation Index were stronger among the older children than among the younger children. Sex differences on the Motivation Index were not significant, but there was a significant interaction between sex and intelligence. Differences between intelligence levels were more clearly related to the Motivation Index in the case of the boys, with the less intelligent boys scoring lower. However, among the girls, the difference between intelligence levels on the Motivation Index was minimal and in a reversed direction, with the less

intelligent girls scoring slightly but not significantly higher.

PHASE 2

METHOD

Subjects. The phase 2 subjects comprised seventy children—36 kindergarten children and 34 third graders. As in phase 1, the younger children were in the 5–6-year range, the older in the 8–9-year span, and all children were Negro or Puerto Rican. Two kindergarten classes were used, both taught by the same teacher. Of the 47 kindergarten children interviewed, the records of 11 children were not used either because of difficulty in comprehending their answers or, more frequently, because they simply replied "don't know" to most of the questions on the psychological causality interview. The 34 third-grade children were randomly selected from the entire third-grade roster of this particular school. The IQ data based on group tests were available for 27 of the 34 third graders. The mean IQ was 97, with a range from 75 to 133. For the kindergarten group, Stanford-Binet IQ data were available, but only for 24 out of the 36 children. However, these IQ's were based on a random sample of children from the two kindergarten classes. For the kindergarten group, the mean IQ was 94, with a range from 71 to 116. Forty-two per cent and 53 per cent of the kindergarten and third graders, respectively, were male. In order to replicate an analysis performed on 21 matched pairs in phase 1, twenty pairs of kindergarten and third-grade children matched in IQ were selected. The mean IQ of the twenty phase 2 kindergarteners and twenty matched third graders was 93.

Procedure. Six of the seven stories used in phase 1 were administered to the two groups. The repression story was omitted in order to shorten the administration time. In addition, the projection story was revised so as to impress upon the respondent that Jane did not know the other child. However, the paramount change in phase 2 was the use of a standardized interview with standardized probes and a standard sequence of probes. The standardized probes were explicit wordings of questions to be asked the child. The sequence of such probes was also specified for the interviewers. Directions were given to the interviewers about when to probe for a new element of the concept in question and when to stay with the same point, altering the question in order to see whether the child could succeed with more information. The stories were administered in a randomized order.

In contrast to phase 1, the interviews were not conducted by the writer but by four graduate students of the Columbia University School of Social Work. A number of sessions were devoted to a discussion of the specific rationales of the study, of underlying theoretical issues, and of methodological problems in interviewing young children. Pilot interviewing was conducted by three of the students at a neighboring day-care center, after which further discussion was held regarding ambiguities or difficulties arising in the interviewing situation.

Scoring categories were devised, both for the initial responses to the story and the responses to questions by the interviewer. As in phase 1, there was an attempt to arrange the categories in each story hierarchically, with the higher-numbered categories including more of the elements of the concept studied. The scoring system involved categorizing the children for each story at three levels. Level 3 was assigned to children whose responses at any point in the interview included all of the elements of the concept for any particular story, whether or not the grasp of the concept was maintained or lost following further questioning. Level 2 included children whose responses at any point showed comprehension of some but not all elements of the concept, while level 1 was assigned to children whose responses at no point showed an understanding of any of the key elements of the explanatory concept.

In addition to the questionnaire on psychological causality, a series of questions dealing with physical causality was also posed. These questions dealt with the attribution of life to various objects and were designed to reveal animistic tendencies in the child. The questionnaire was originally constructed by Laurendeau and Pinard (1962) in their replication of Piaget's work on physical causality. The child was asked whether each of 21 objects was alive. In the present study, the score of this Animism Scale was the number of correct responses given by child. The reliability of this measure for the combined group was .84, as assessed by the Kuder-Richardson Formula 20 (Gulliksen, 1950, pp. 220–227).

RESULTS AND DISCUSSION

The individual stories. The stories were scored independently by two sets of raters. For the coding of the elements of each story based on the initial response of 36 children, the percentage of agreement was 96 per cent. The percentage of agreement ranged from 89 per cent for the Denial story to 100 per cent for the dream wishing story. For the coding of the elements of each story based on both initial and probed-for responses of 28 children, the overall percentage of agreement was 85 per cent, with a range from 75 per cent for rationalization to 93 per cent for the wishful dreaming story. Table 2 reveals that the older children consistently scored higher than the younger group, with five of the six items significant at least on the .01 level. The failure of the rationalization story to yield significant differences between the two graders may be due to the relatively low interrater reliability of coding for this item. From the point of view of age differentiation, the new interview procedure seems at least as effective as the one reported on in phase 1. However, the increment in significant age differentiation on the part of the stories may be at least partly due to the increased sample size in phase 2. The displacement, projection, and regression stories which were significant differentiators between age levels in phase 1 also show significant differentiation in phase 2. Additionally, the denial and wishful dreaming stories which did not yield significant differences in phase 1 do so in phase 2.

. . .

Motivation Index 2. [The analysis of variance] reveals that the age differences on Motivation In-

TABLE 2

PERCENTAGES OF 36 YOUNGER CHILDREN (AGES 5 AND 6) AND 34 OLDER CHILDREN (AGES 8 AND 9) IN RESPONSE CATEGORIES OF PHASE 2 STORIES

Story and Age Group	Level of Understanding [a]			x^2
	1	2	3	
Displacement:				
Younger	31	69	0	7.52*
Older	3	79	18	$df = 1$
Wishful dreaming:				
Younger	30	61	9	17.83**
Older	3	50	47	$df = 2$
Projection:				
Younger	78	8	14	25.41**
Older	15	15	70	$df = 1$
Regression:				
Younger	25	67	8	10.59*
Older	12	47	41	$df = 2$
Rationalization:				
Younger	36	64	0	.75
Older	26	65	9	$df = 1$
Denial:				
Younger	50	42	8	13.70**
Older	24	29	47	$df = 2$

[a] For displacement, projection, and rationalization, scoring categories 2 and 3 were combined in the x^2 analysis, with correction for discontinuity.

* Significant at .01 level.

** Significant at .001 level.

dex 2 were highly significant. As anticipated, the older children scored considerably higher than the younger. Ninety-four per cent of the kindergarten group fell below the median score of the third graders, which parallels the comparable figure of 90 per cent found with Motivation Index 1. However, this and a separate analysis of variance (not shown) failed to reveal significant IQ differences, nor IQ interactions with age and sex—contrary to the results of phase 1. The younger children were significantly more animistic than the older ones. Twice as many kindergarten children as third graders fell into a high animism group ($P <$ .01). The above analyses suggest that conceptions of psychological causality (as assessed by Motivation Index 2) and of physical causality (as assessed by the Animism Scale) both develop with age. However, the limited relation between the two measures points to the independence in the rate and timing of their respective development within the individual child.

The relation between age and conceptions of psychological causality appears stronger than the relation between age and conceptions of physical causality (see Table 3). Thus when one selects children who are relatively homogeneous with respect to the Motivation Index, the relation between age and the Animism Scale is not statistically significant. However, when the selection is of children who are relatively homogeneous on animism score, the relation between age and Motivation Index is still highly significant. Similarly, a comparison of the five kindergarten children and eight third graders with comparable MA's (about 7 years)

revealed that the younger children averaged about four points *below* the older on the Motivation Index but about four points *above* the older on the Animism Scale. This suggests the importance of chronological rather than mental age in the development of conceptions of psychological causality.

SOME CONCLUDING POINTS

The relative difficulty of the younger child in *(a)* differentiating between observed locus of effect and inferred locus of cause and *(b)* decentering from a focus on overt behavior to a more covert intent would not be inconsistent with Piaget's distinction between the "intuitive" child (ages 4–7) and the "concrete operational" child (ages 7–11). It would, therefore, be worthwhile to explore the Motivation Index scores of children who have and have not attained conservation of substance, for example, since the latter is a criterion for the concrete operation stage. However, the operation of more specific experiential factors is suggested by the differential ease of the items within age groups, the lack of strong or consistent correlations of the Motivation Indexes with IQ, the importance of chronological age over and above mental age differences, the relative independence of the Motivation Indexes from the Animism Scale, and the sex differences on Motivation Index 1. It is also possible that age differences in psychological causality may take a different form within groups of higher socioeconomic standing where the child's linguistic experiences and explanatory encounters with adults are differently patterned.

Behavioral correlates need exploration. Certain patternings of responses to the stories may be related to particular behavioral patterns. Thus, ease in grasping projection stories, where blame is externalized, may be related to acting-out behavior. The Motivation Index might be correlated with measures of ability to shift role, to understand the other's viewpoint, and with avoidance of what Piaget (1932) has conceptualized as objective morality. One would expect the growth of understanding of psychological causality to parallel the growth of moral judgments based on the other's underlying intentions, rather than on his overt behaviors.

TABLE 3

RELATIONS BETWEEN AGE AND (*a*) ANIMISM SCALE, WITH MOTIVATION INDEX 2 CONTROLLED; (*b*) MOTIVATION INDEX 2, WITH ANIMISM SCALE CONTROLLED

| | Age Group | | | | | |
| | 5 and 6 years | | 8 and 9 years | | | |
	N	%	N	%	x^2	P
Animism Scale[a]:						
Higher	9	64	8	35		
					1.98	> .05
Lower...............	5	36	15	65		
Motivation Index 2[b]:						
Higher	0	0	14	82		
					14.97	< .001
Lower...............	11	100	3	18		

[a] Higher and lower levels defined by score ranges on the Animism Scale of 5–12, and 13–21, respectively. The 37 subjects are all within the 11–14 range on the Motivation Index 2.

[b] Higher and lower levels defined by score ranges on the Motivation Index of 13–16 and 7–12, respectively. The 28 subjects are all within the 16–19 range on the Animism Scale.

REFERENCES

FLAVELL, J. *The developmental psychology of Jean Piaget.* Princeton, N.J.: Van Nostrand, 1963.

FREUD, ANNA. *The ego and the mechanisms of defence.* New York: International Universities Press, 1946.

GULLIKSEN, N. *Theory of mental tests.* New York: Wiley, 1950.

HILGARD, E. Human motives and the concept of the self, *American Psychologist,* 1949, *4,* 374–382.

LAURENDEAU, MONIQUE, & PINARD, A. *Causal thinking in the child.* New York: International Universities Press, 1962.

PIAGET, J. *The child's conception of the world.* New York: Harcourt, Brace, 1929.

PIAGET, J. *The child's conception of physical causality.* London: Kegan Paul, 1930.

PIAGET, J. *The moral judgment of the child.* London: Kegan Paul, 1932.

PIAGET, J. *The psychology of intelligence.* New York: Harcourt, Brace, 1950.

60

Egocentrism in Adolescence

DAVID ELKIND

David Elkind, professor of psychology at the University of Rochester, is one of the leading interpreters of Piaget in the United States. One of his latest books is Children and Adolescents: Interpretive Essays on Jean Piaget *(New York: Oxford University Press, 1970). In this article, Elkind describes the forms in which egocentrism appears at each stage of cognitive development, up to adolescence.*

Within the Piagetian theory of intellectual growth, the concept of egocentrism generally refers to a lack of differentiation in some area of subject-object interaction (Piaget, 1962). At each stage of mental development, this lack of differentiation takes a unique form and is manifested in a unique set of behaviors. The transition from one form of egocentrism to another takes place in a dialectic fashion such that the mental structures which free the child from a lower form of egocentrism are the same structures which ensnare him in a higher form of egocentrism. From the developmental point of view, therefore, egocentrism can be regarded as a negative by-product of any emergent mental system in the sense that it corresponds to the fresh cognitive problems engendered by that system.

Preparation of this paper was supported in part by grant No. 6881 from the Office of Education.

Although in recent years Piaget has focused his attention more on the positive than on the negative products of mental structures, egocentrism continues to be of interest because of its relation to the affective aspects of child thought and behavior. Indeed, it is possible that the study of egocentrism may provide a bridge between the study of cognitive structure, on the one hand, and the exploration of personality dynamics, on the other (Cowan, 1966; Gourevitch & Feffer, 1962). The purpose of the present paper is to describe, in greater detail than Inhelder and Piaget (1958), what seems to me to be the nature of egocentrism in adolescence and some of its behavioral and experiential correlates. Before doing that, however, it might be well to set the stage for the discussion with a brief review of the forms of egocentrism which precede this mode of thought in adolescence.

FORMS OF EGOCENTRISM IN INFANCY AND CHILDHOOD

In presenting the childhood forms of egocentrism, it is useful to treat each of Piaget's major stages as if it were primarily concerned with resolving one major cognitive task. The egocentrism of a particular stage can then be described with reference to this special problem of cognition. It must be stressed, however, that while the cognitive task characteristic of a particular stage seems to attract the major share of the child's mental energies, it is not the only cognitive problem with which the child is attempting to cope. In mental development there are major battles and minor skirmishes, and if I here ignore the lesser engagements it is for purposes of economy of presentation rather than because I assume that such engagements are insignificant.

SENSORI-MOTOR EGOCENTRISM (0–2 YEARS)

The major cognitive task of infancy might be regarded as *the conquest of the object.* In the early months of life, the infant deals with objects as if their existence were dependent upon their being present in immediate perception (Charlesworth, 1966; Piaget, 1954). The egocentrism of this stage corresponds, therefore, to a lack of differentiation between the object and the sense impressions occasioned by it. Toward the end of the first year, however, the infant begins to seek the object even when it is hidden, and thus shows that he can now differentiate between the object and the "experience of the object." This breakdown of egocentrism

David Elkind, "Egocentrism in adolescence," *Child Development, 38,* 1967, 1025–1034. Reprinted by permission. Copyright 1967 by The Society for Research in Child Development, Inc.

with respect to objects is brought about by mental representation of the absent object.[1] An internal representation of the absent object is the earliest manifestation of the symbolic function which develops gradually during the second year of life and whose activities dominate the next stage of mental growth.

PRE-OPERATIONAL EGOCENTRISM (2–6 YEARS)

During the preschool period, the child's major cognitive task can be regarded as *the conquest of the symbol*. It is during the preschool period that the symbolic function becomes fully active, as evidenced by the rapid growth in the acquisition and utilization of language, by the appearance of symbolic play, and by the first reports of dreams. Yet this new capacity for representation, which loosed the infant from his egocentrism with respect to objects, now ensnares the preschool children in a new egocentrism with regard to symbols. At the beginning of this period, the child fails to differentiate between words and their referents (Piaget, 1952b) and between his self-created play and dream symbols and reality (Kohlberg, 1966; Piaget, 1951). Children at this stage believe that the name inheres in the thing and that an object cannot have more than one name (Elkind, 1961a, 1962, 1963).

The egocentrism of this period is particularly evident in children's linguistic behavior. When explaining a piece of apparatus to another child, for example, the youngster at this stage uses many indefinite terms and leaves out important information (Piaget, 1952b). Although this observation is sometimes explained by saying that the child fails to take the other person's point of view, it can also be explained by saying that the child assumes words carry much more information than they actually do. This results from his belief that even the indefinite "thing" somehow conveys the properties of the object which it is used to represent. In short, the egocentrism of this period consists in a lack of clear differentiation between symbols and their referents.

Toward the end of the pre-operational period, the differentiation between symbols and their referents is gradually brought about by the emergence of concrete operations (internalized actions which are roughly comparable in their activity to the elementary operations of arithmetic). One consequence of concrete operational thought is that it enables the child to deal with two elements, properties, or relations at the same time. A child with concrete operations can, for example, take account of both the height and width of a glass of colored liquid and recognize that, when the liquid is poured into a differently shaped container, the changes in height and width of the liquid compensate one another so that the total quantity of liquid is conserved (Elkind, 1961b; Piaget, 1952a). This ability, to hold two dimensions in mind at the same time, also enables the child to hold both symbol and referent in mind simultaneously, and thus distinguish between them. Concrete operations are, therefore, instrumental in overcoming the egocentrism of the preoperational stage.

CONCRETE OPERATIONAL EGOCENTRISM (7–11 YEARS)

With the emergence of concrete operations, the major cognitive task of the school-age child becomes that of *mastering classes, relations, and quantities*. While the preschool child forms global notions of classes, relations, and quantities, such notions are imprecise and cannot be combined one with the other. The child with concrete operations, on the other hand, can nest classes, seriate relations, and conserve quantities. In addition, concrete operations enable the school-age child to perform elementary syllogistic reasoning and to formulate hypotheses and explanations about concrete matters. This system of concrete operations, however, which lifts the school-age child to new heights of thought, nonetheless lowers him to new depths of egocentrism.

Operations are essentially mental tools whose products, series, class hierarchies, conservations, etc., are not directly derived from experience. At this stage, however, the child nonetheless regards these mental products as being on a par with perceptual phenomena. It is the inability to differentiate clearly between mental constructions and perceptual givens which constitutes the egocentrism of the school-age child. An example may help to clarify the form which egocentrism takes during the concrete operational stage.

In a study reported by Peel (1960), children and adolescents were read a passage about Stonehenge and then asked questions about it. One of the questions had to do with whether Stonehenge was a place for religious worship or a fort. The children (ages 7–10) answered the question with flat statements, as if they were stating a fact. When they were given evidence that contradicted their statements, they rationalized the evidence to make it conform with their initial position. Adolescents, on the other hand, phrased their replies in proba-

---

[1] It is characteristic of the dialectic of mental growth that the capacity to represent internally the absent object also enables the infant to cognize the object as externally existent.

bilistic terms and supported their judgments with material gleaned from the passage. Similar differences between children and adolescents have been found by Elkind (1966) and Weir (1964).

What these studies show is that, when a child constructs a hypothesis or formulates a strategy, he assumes that this product is imposed by the data rather than derived from his own mental activity. When his position is challenged, he does not change his stance but, on the contrary, reinterprets the data to fit with his assumption. This observation, however, raises a puzzling question. Why, if the child regards both his thought products and the givens of perception as coming from the environment, does he nonetheless give preference to his own mental constructions? The answer probably lies in the fact that the child's mental constructions are the product of reasoning, and hence are experienced as imbued with a (logical) necessity. This "felt" necessity is absent when the child experiences the products of perception. It is not surprising, then, that the child should give priority to what seems permanent and necessary in perception (the products of his own thought, such as conservation) rather than to what seems transitory and arbitrary in perception (products of environmental stimulation). Only in adolescence do young people differentiate between their own mental constructions and the givens of perception. For the child, there are no problems of epistemology.

Toward the end of childhood, the emergence of formal operational thought (which is analogous to propositional logic) gradually frees the child from his egocentrism with respect to his own mental constructions. As Inhelder and Piaget (1958) have shown, formal operational thought enables the young person to deal with all of the possible combinations and permutations of elements within a given set. Provided with four differently colored pieces of plastic, for example, the adolescent can work out all the possible combinations of colors by taking the pieces one, two, three and four, and none, at a time. Children, on the other hand, cannot formulate these combinations in any systematic way. The ability to conceptualize all of the possible combinations in a system allows the adolescent to construct contrary-to-fact hypotheses and to reason about such propositions "as if" they were true. The adolescent, for example, can accept the statement, "Let's suppose coal is white," whereas the child would reply, "But coal is black," This ability to formulate contrary-to-fact hypotheses is crucial to the overcoming of the egocentrism of the concrete operational period. Through the formulation of such contrary-to-fact hypotheses, the young person discovers the arbitrariness of his own

mental constructions and learns to differentiate them from perceptual reality.

ADOLESCENT EGOCENTRISM

From the strictly cognitive point of view (as opposed to the psychoanalytic point of view as represented by Blos [1962] and A. Freud [1946] or the ego psychological point of view as represented by Erikson [1959]), the major task of early adolescence can be regarded as having to do with *the conquest of thought*. Formal operations not only permit the young person to construct all the possibilities in a system and construct contrary-to-fact propositions (Inhelder & Piaget, 1958); they also enable him to conceptualize his own thought, to take his mental constructions as objects and reason about them. Only at about the ages of 11–12, for example, do children spontaneously introduce concepts of belief, intelligence, and faith into their definitions of their religious denomination (Elkind, 1961a; 1962; 1963). Once more, however, this new mental system which frees the young person from the egocentrism of childhood entangles him in a new form of egocentrism characteristic of adolescence.

Formal operational thought not only enables the adolescent to conceptualize his thought, it also permits him to conceptualize the thought of other people. It is this capacity to take account of other people's thought, however, which is the crux of adolescent egocentrism. This egocentrism emerges because, while the adolescent can now cognize the thoughts of others, he fails to differentiate between the objects toward which the thoughts of others are directed and those which are the focus of his own concern. Now, it is well known that the young adolescent, because of the physiological metamorphosis he is undergoing, is primarily concerned with himself. Accordingly, since he fails to differentiate between what others are thinking about and his own mental preoccupations, he assumes that other people are as obsessed with his behavior and appearance as he is himself. *It is this belief that others are preoccupied with his appearance and behavior that constitutes the egocentrism of the adolescent.*

One consequence of adolescent egocentrism is that, in actual or impending social situations, the young person anticipates the reactions of other people to himself. These anticipations, however, are based on the premise that others are as admiring or as critical of him as he is of himself. In a sense, then, the adolescent is continually constructing, or reacting to, *an imaginary audience*. It is an audience because the adolescent believes that he will be the focus of attention; and it is imaginary because, in actual social situations, this is not usually the case (unless he contrives to make it so). The construction of imaginary audiences would seem to account, in part at least, for a wide variety of typical adolescent behaviors and experiences.

The imaginary audience, for example, probably plays a role in the self-consciousness which is so characteristic of early adolescence. When the young person is feeling critical of himself, he anticipates that the audience—of which he is necessarily a part—will be critical too. And, since the audience is his own construction and privy to his own knowledge of himself, it knows just what to look for in the way of cosmetic and behavioral sensitivities. The adolescent's wish for privacy and his reluctance to reveal himself may, to some extent, be a reaction to the feeling of being under the constant critical scrutiny of other people. The notion of an imaginary audience also helps to explain the observation that the affect which most concerns adolescents is not guilt but, rather, shame, that is, the reaction to an audience (Lynd, 1961).

While the adolescent is often self-critical, he is frequently self-admiring too. At such times, the audience takes on the same affective coloration. A good deal of adolescent boorishness, loudness, and faddish dress is probably provoked, partially in any case, by a failure to differentiate between what the young person believes to be attractive and what others admire. It is for this reason that the young person frequently fails to understand why adults disapprove of the way he dresses and behaves. The same sort of egocentrism is often seen in behavior directed toward the opposite sex. The boy who stands in front of the mirror for 2 hours combing his hair is probably imagining the swooning reactions he will produce in the girls. Likewise, the girl applying her makeup is more likely than not imagining the admiring glances that will come her way. When these young people actually meet, each is more concerned with being the observed than with being the observer. Gatherings of young adolescents are unique in the sense that each young person is simultaneously an actor to himself and an audience to others.

One of the most common admiring audience constructions, in the adolescent, is the anticipation of how others will react to his own demise. A certain bittersweet pleasure is derived from anticipating the belated recognition by others of his positive qualities. As often happens with such universal fantasies, the imaginary anticipation of one's own demise has been realized in fiction. Below, for example, is the passage in *Tom Sawyer* where Tom sneaks back to his home, after having run away with Joe and Huck, to discover that he and his friends are thought to have been drowned:

> But this memory was too much for the old lady, and she broke entirely down. Tom was snuffling, now, himself—and more in pity of himself than anybody else. He could hear Mary crying and putting in a kindly word for him from time to time. He began to have a nobler opinion of himself than ever before. Still, he was sufficiently touched by his aunt's grief to long to rush out from under the bed and overwhelm her with joy—and the theatrical gorgeousness of the thing appealed strongly to his nature too—but he resisted and lay still.

Corresponding to the imaginary audience is another mental construction which is its complement. While the adolescent fails to differentiate the concerns of his own thought from those of others, he at the same time over-differentiates his feelings. Perhaps because he believes he is of importance to so many people, the imaginary audience, he comes to regard himself, and particularly his feelings, as something special and unique. Only he can suffer with such agonized intensity, or experience such exquisite rapture. How many parents have been confronted with the typically adolescent phrase, "But you don't know how it feels...." The emotional torments undergone by Goethe's young Werther and by Salinger's Holden Caulfield exemplify the adolescent's belief in the uniqueness of his own emotional experience. At a somewhat different level, this belief in personal uniqueness becomes a conviction that he will not die, that death will happen to others but not to him. This complex of beliefs in the uniqueness of his feelings and of his immortality might be called *a personal fable*, a story which he tells himself and which is not true.

Evidences of the personal fable are particularly prominent in adolescent diaries. Such diaries are often written for posterity in the conviction that the young person's experiences, crushes, and frustrations are of universal significance and importance. Another kind of evidence for the personal fable during this period is the tendency to confide in a personal God. The search for privacy and the belief in personal uniqueness leads to the establishment of an I-Thou relationship with God as a personal confidant to whom one no longer looks for gifts but rather for guidance and support (Long, Elkind, & Spilka, 1967).

The concepts of an imaginary audience and a personal fable have proved useful, at least to the writer, in the understanding and treatment of troubled adolescents. The imaginary audience, for example, seems often to play a role in middle-class delinquency (Elkind, 1967). As a case in point, one young man took $1,000 from a golf tournament purse, hid the money, and then promptly revealed himself. It turned out that much of the motivation for this act was derived from the anticipated response of "the audience" to the guttiness of his action. In a similar vein, many young girls become pregnant because, in part at least, their personal fable convinces them that pregnancy will happen to others but never to them and so they need not take precautions. Such examples could be multiplied but will perhaps suffice to illustrate how adolescent egocentrism, as manifested in the imaginary audience and in the personal fable, can help provide a rationale for some adolescent behavior. These concepts can, moreover, be utilized in the treatment of adolescent offenders. It is often helpful to these young people if they can learn to differentiate between the real and the imaginary audience, which often boils down to a discrimination between the real and the imaginary parents.

The Passing of Adolescent Egocentrism

After the appearance of formal operational thought, no new mental systems develop and the mental structures of adolescence must serve for the rest of the life span. The egocentrism of early adolescence nonetheless tends to diminish by the age of 15 or 16, the age at which formal operations become firmly established. What appears to happen is that the imaginary audience, which is primarily an anticipatory audience, is progressively modified in the direction of the reactions of the real audience. In a way, the imaginary audience can be regarded as hypothesis—or better, as a series of hypotheses—which the young person tests against reality. As a consequence of this testing, he gradually comes to recognize the difference between his own preoccupations and the interests and concerns of others.

The personal fable, on the other hand, is probably overcome (although probably never in its entirety) by the gradual establishment of what Erikson (1959) has called "intimacy." Once the young person sees himself in a more realistic light as a function of having adjusted his imaginary audience to the real one, he can establish true rather than self-interested interpersonal relations. Once relations of mutuality are established and confidences are shared, the young person discovers that others have feelings similar to his own and have suffered and been enraptured in the same way.

Adolescent egocentrism is thus overcome by a twofold transformation. On the cognitive plane, it is overcome by the gradual differentiation between his own preoccupations and the thoughts of others; while on the plane of affectivity, it is overcome by a gradual integration of the feelings of others with his own emotions.

Summary and Conclusions

In this paper I have tried to describe the forms which egocentrism takes and the mechanisms by which it is overcome, in the course of mental development. In infancy, egocentrism corresponds to the impression that objects are identical with the perception of them, and this form of egocentrism is overcome with the appearance of representation. During the preschool period, egocentrism appears in the guise of a belief that symbols contain the same information as is provided by the objects which they represent. With the emergence of concrete operations, the child is able to discriminate between symbol and referent, and so overcome this type of egocentrism. The egocentrism of the school-age period can be characterized as the belief that one's own mental constructions correspond to a superior form of perceptual reality. With the advent of formal operations and the ability to construct contrary-to-fact hypotheses, this kind of egocentrism is dissolved because the young person can now recognize the arbitrariness of his own mental constructions. Finally, during early adolescence, egocentrism appears as the belief that the thoughts of others are directed toward the self. This variety of egocentrism is overcome as a consequence of the conflict between the reactions which the young person anticipates and those which actually occur.

Although egocentrism corresponds to a negative product of mental growth, its usefulness would seem to lie in the light which it throws upon the affective reactions characteristic of any particular stage of mental development. In this paper I have dealt primarily with the affective reactions associated with the egocentrism of adolescence. Much of the material, particularly the discussion of the *imaginary audience* and the *personal fable* is speculative in the sense that it is based as much upon my clinical experience with young people as it is upon research data. These constructs are offered, not as the final word on adolescent egocentrism, but rather to illustrate how the cognitive structures peculiar to a particular level of development can be related to the affective experience and behavior characteristic of that stage. Although I have here only considered the correspondence between mental structure and affect in adolescence, it is possible that similar correspondences can be found at the earlier levels of development as well. A consideration of egocentrism, then, would seem to be a useful starting point for any attempt to reconcile cognitive structure and the dynamics of personality.

REFERENCES

BLOS, P. *On adolescence.* New York: Free Press, 1962.

CHARLESWORTH, W. R. Development of the object concept in infancy: methodological study. *American Psychologist,* 1966, *21*, 623. (Abstract)

COWAN, P. A. Cognitive egocentrism and social interaction in children. *American Psychologist,* 1966, *21*, 623. (Abstract)

ELKIND, D. The child's conception of his religious denomination, I: The Jewish child. *Journal of genetic Psychology,* 1961, *99*, 209–225. (a)

ELKIND, D. The development of quantitative thinking. *Journal of genetic Psychology,* 1961, *98*, 37–46. (b)

ELKIND, D. The child's conception of his religious denomination, II: The Catholic child. *Journal of genetic Psychology,* 1962, *101*, 185–193.

ELKIND, D. The child's conception of his religious denomination, III: The Protestant child. *Journal of genetic Psychology,* 1963, *103*, 291–304.

ELKIND, D. Conceptual orientation shifts in children and adolescents. *Child Development,* 1966, *37*, 493–498.

ELKIND, D. Middle-class delinquency. *Mental Hygiene,* 1967, *51*, 80–84.

ERIKSON, E. H. Identity and the life cycle. *Psychological issues.* Vol. 1, No. 1, New York: International Universities Press, 1959.

FREUD, ANNA. *The ego and the mechanisms of defense.* New York International Universities Press, 1946.

GOUREVITCH, VIVIAN, & FEFFER, M. H. A study of motivational development. *Journal of genetic Psychology,* 1962, *100*, 361–375.

INHELDER, BÄRBEL, & PIAGET, J. *The growth of logical thinking from childhood to adolescence.* New York: Basic Books, 1958.

KOHLBERG, L. Cognitive stages and preschool education. *Human Development,* 1966, *9*, 5–17.

LONG, DIANE, ELKIND, D., & SPILKA, B. The child's conception of prayer. *Journal for the scientific Study of Religion,* 1967, *6*, 101–109.

LYND, HELEN M. *On shame and the search for identity.* New York: Science Editions, 1961.

PEEL, E. A. *The pupil's thinking.* London: Oldhourne, 1960.

PIAGET, J. *The child's conception of the world.* London: Routledge & Kegan Paul, 1951.

PIAGET, J. *The child's conception of number.* New York: Humanities Press, 1952. (a)

PIAGET, J. *The language and thought of the child.* London: Routledge & Kegan Paul, 1952. (b)

PIAGET, J. *The construction of reality in the child.* New York: Basic Books, 1954.

PIAGET, J. *Comments on Vygotsky's critical remarks concerning "The language and thought of the child" and "Judgment and reasoning in the child."* Cambridge, Mass.: M.I.T. Press, 1962.

WEIR, M. W. Development changes in problem solving strategies. *Psychological Review,* 1964, *71*, 473–490.

61

How Shall the Disadvantaged Child Be Taught?

Marion Blank and Frances Solomon

Consideration of the problems of disadvantaged children has led to the development of "intervention" programs, which seek to provide a stimulating environment for the child, different from what he finds at home. The great emphasis placed on preschool programs today reflects convictions about the crucial importance of the early years for later development. Few quarrel with the goal of intervention, but the way in which an intervention program should be shaped is the subject of much debate. Professor Marion Blank, a member of the faculty of the Albert Einstein College of Medicine, has developed a language-based program that offers individualized instruction. In this article, co-authored by Frances Solomon, also at Albert Einstein College of Medicine, the program is illustrated in a series of dialogues between a teacher and a four-year-old child, and then the teaching is analyzed. (See also Miriam Goldberg's paper in Section XII.)

An eclectic approach to the teaching of language is usual in most preschool programs for disadvan-

This research was supported by U.S. Public Health Service grant K3-MH-10, 749. The authors wish to thank Miss E. Johnson and the staff of the Bronx River Day Care Center for their cooperation and participation in this research.

taged children. Since their language deficiencies are extensive, it is hoped that the presentation of a massive array of possibly fruitful techniques is bound to lead to learning. In contrast, the present authors (Blank, 1968; Blank & Solomon, 1968) have presented the hypothesis that the deprived child's verbal weakness is so overwhelming that it blinds one to his more subtle but basic deficiency. This deficiency is the lack of a symbolic system for thinking. In order to develop this system, language is essential—but not all language is equally useful. In particular, we outlined a series of techniques in which the child was taught to use language so as to organize thoughts, to reflect upon situations, to comprehend the meaning of events, and to choose among alternatives. For example, one technique required the child to develop simple cause-and-effect models; for example, if the room is too bright when he comes in, he might be asked, "How can we make it darker in here?" These techniques are in direct contrast to methods focused mainly on enlarging vocabulary for description and communication.

We further postulated that this type of teaching could not be done in the group situation. In observing children, even in small group settings, we have found that they often "tune out" when the teacher attempts to structure a lesson. Once that occurs, almost infinite teaching skill is required to re-engage the child's attention without losing the interest of the rest of the group. Therefore it was decided to conduct the teaching on the basis of short (15-minute), one-to-one sessions between the teacher and the child.

An exploratory program using these techniques was conducted with a group of 22 disadvantaged children ranging in age from 3 years 3 months to 4 years 7 months (Blank & Solomon, 1968). The children were divided into four groups, two tutored and two untutored, matched as closely as possible for age, sex, and Stanford-Binet IQ scores. In one tutored group, each of six children received individual teaching five times per week; in the second tutored group, six children received the same teaching three times per week. The tutoring involved taking the child for this short period from his classroom to a familiar room in the school. One untutored group of three children had daily individual sessions, but no attempt was made to tutor them. These children were exposed to the identical materials and were permitted to engage in any activity of their choice. This group was included to control for the possible role of individual attention alone in facilitating intellectual performance.

Marion Blank and Frances Solomon, "How shall the disadvantaged child be taught?" *Child Development, 40,* 1969, 47–61. Reprinted by permission. Copyright 1969 by The Society for Research in Child Development, Inc.

Another untutored group of seven children remained in the regular nursery school program with no additional attention. After 3 months (approximately 12 and 7 hours of tutoring for the tutored groups, respectively) the mean IQ increases in groups tutored five and three times per week were 14.5 and 7.0 points, respectively; in the untutored groups the changes were 2.0 and 1.3 points.

In order to demonstrate these techniques in actual use, this paper presents two sessions with one of the 4-year-old children from the study. The sessions cover a 3-month period so as to illustrate the growth in her capacity to handle and structure cognitive material. A third session between this child and a nursery school teacher not trained in these techniques is also included here. We recorded a number of such sessions with teachers from established nursery schools. This was done to investigate the possibility that teachers might spontaneously adopt this approach to abstract thinking if permitted the opportunity of working on a one-to-one basis.

The commentary accompanying the dialogue is directed toward diagnosing both the deficiencies of the child's thinking and the success of the teacher's methods in overcoming these deficiencies. "Success," of course, is evaluated according to the rationale of our philosophy of teaching abstract thinking.

Session 1

Julie was a highly impulsive, voluble 4-year-old of Puerto Rican background. She was charming, but a will-o'-the-wisp. Many deficiencies obscured her latent brightness; chief among them was an attention span even shorter than that of her peers.

A teacher trained in the principles of the program is seen here conducting one of the first sessions with Julie. The dialogue reads slowly, but actually covered only 5 minutes of a 15-minute session.

After the child had been in the room for several minutes, the teacher introduced some drawing materials:

Dialogue	*Interpretation*
TEACHER: I'm going to draw a picture, and then you're going to make one just like it. I'll give you a paper. What color crayon would you like to use?	Teacher's statements are designed to: (1) Tune child in to intended activity; (2) Have her make a specific verbal choice which will determine her next action.
JULIE: Yellow. [Child chooses correctly, immediately starts drawing in usually impulsive manner.]	Had child's choice not been consistent with verbalization, teacher would have initiated interchange to correct child.
TEACHER: *Wait.* Don't draw anything yet.	Teacher attempts to delay impulsivity.
JULIE: [Halts and focuses.]	
TEACHER: [Draws a circle.] What did I draw?	Teacher was not concerned with label per se, but rather, with posing a question so as to keep the child's attention.
JULIE: A ball.	
TEACHER: Could you make that ball? Make one just like mine.	Using child's word, teacher utilizes imitation as a means of getting child to complete a simple task.
JULIE: [Succeeds.]	
TEACHER: Good, now, I'm going to make a line *across* the ball. Can you do that? [Teacher draws a line across the circle.]	Teacher is trying to integrate another concept into the work. Almost any elementary but relevant concept which would have increased the complexity of the situation would have been suitable (e.g., drawing another figure inside the circle).
JULIE: [Draws an incorrect line from top to bottom of a circle.]	Child has merely responded to the word "line." She has not heeded the total direction.
TEACHER: No, you drew it from the top to the bottom. We want it to go across [Teacher indicates desired direction.]	
JULIE: [Draws line independently and correctly.] Now I went across.	Child's appropriate verbalization indicates understanding.
TEACHER: Very good. You know, we can also call a ball a circle. Do you know what I'm going to do with this circle? I'm going to get a green crayon and I'm going to fill in the *bottom half* of my circle. Would you like to get a green crayon and do the same thing? Fill it in so it looks like mine.	Since understanding is apparent, teacher introduces (1) the consensually validated label of circle, (2) again increases complexity by the dual idea of *bottom* and *color*. To help child handle this increase in complexity, teacher perseveres with imitation ("do the same thing"). It would have been better here had the teacher not used the phrase "would you like . . ." since it lends itself to the child's using an automatic response of "no." Since choice was not at issue, a specific demand such as "please get" could have been put forth.

JULIE: I like this color. I like all colors. I like flowers, too. I got that kind of crayon. I like brown—it's dark. We could play in the dark and we be scared.

TEACHER: But we're working with the green.

This talk typifies the random associations of young children's thinking. Judgment is required to differentiate this from a creative use of spontaneous language.

Teacher evaluates child's monologue as rambling and refuses to be led by it. She attempts to refocus child so that the child can experience the opportunity of completing an assignment.

JULIE: [Continues drawing but keeps up rambling conversation.] I got my new clothes. I gotta lot of new clothes in my house.

TEACHER: Would you work a little faster on this bottom one?

Since rapid tempo for this child is pleasurable, teacher introduces it to aid the child in completing her work.

JULIE: [Completes task.]

TEACHER: Very good. Now, look what I'm going to do. I'm going to get a purple crayon. I'm going to make the top of my circle purple. Look how fast I do it. Can you do yours like this?

Tempo retained as a means of handling child's short attention span.

JULIE: Fast—right? [Completes task.]

Child responds well to incorporating tempo into task.

TEACHER: Show me the top of the circle.

Teacher maintains concept of directionality.

JULIE: [Accomplishes task.]

TEACHER: Show me the bottom of your circle.

Normally, opposites are not taught together. If child did not know "top," teacher would not go on to "bottom." Since the child knew, the teacher could attempt to introduce the opposite concept.

JULIE: [Does as she is asked.]

TEACHER: Very good, Julie. Turn your paper upside down. Now show me which is the top.

This action is designed as a first step in enabling the child to see that top is a relative concept.

JULIE: [Points to bottom.]

This response shows that the child's concept of top is tied to the specific place designated originally. This error is typical in the development of a concept from the specific to the general.

TEACHER: No, this is the top now. [Points to area.] The top is always the highest place. Everything has a top. When you turned your paper upside down, this became the top. Show me the top of your head.

Direct answers are usually avoided since the aim of the teaching is self-discovery. However, most factual information cannot be arrived at independently; therefore, the teacher gives this information. Teacher now begins to offer many examples of the concept.

JULIE: [Gestures correctly.]

TEACHER: Show me the top of the chair.

JULIE: [Satisfies this demand.]

Child is responding appropriately to concept posed by teacher. Thus, even though her response is nonverbal, it reflects thinking.

TEACHER: Show me the top of my boots.

Teacher specifically uses a low object to demonstrate that objects close to ground also have a "top."

JULIE: [Points correctly.]

TEACHER: Now, show me the top of the paper.

JULIE: [Points correctly.]

TEACHER: Show me the top of your drawing.

JULIE: [Gestures correctly.] The top is up here.

Child's correct response does not mean that she has a secure grasp of the concept, but she is developing a glimmering of the idea.

The teacher then reviewed the activities up to this point by having the child describe what they had done in that session (e.g., drawing, circle, across, top, bottom, same, color, etc.). Aid was given to help the child recall any significant omissions, and *she was made to ascertain whether her answers were correct*. If, for instance, she said she had used the color red, she was asked to find the drawing and determine if red was, in fact, the color used. If the child was unable to answer a question, the teacher might offer alternatives such as, "Did we draw a circle or a box?" Thus, assistance was given when needed, but the direct answer was rarely given. A basic precept of this study is that a self-discovered answer is most effective for the development of thinking.

This simple review of recent activities is a memory-strengthening task which is not to be confused with the aimless reporting elicted by questions such as, "What did you do yesterday?" Any answers given by the child to a question like the latter cannot be verified by the teacher. As a result, she has no means of demonstrating to the child whether his verbalizations correspond to reality. Therefore, all questions requiring memory in our program were restricted to verifiable events. These principles were continued throughout the teaching and are evident in the session that follows.

SESSION 2

The following dialogue with Julie is from a session held 3 months later. After entering the room, the teacher says:

TEACHER: Do you remember what we did when you were here yesterday?

JULIE: Yes.

TEACHER: What did we do?

JULIE: I don't know.

TEACHER: Let's see if I can help you. Is there anything on this table that we worked with the last time? [A limited variety of materials is present.]

JULIE: [Points to blackboard.]

TEACHER: That's just pointing. Tell me what we did.

JULIE: We did—we did a square.

TEACHER: Right. What did we do with the square?

JULIE: [Hesitates.]

TEACHER: Think about it for a minute.

JULIE: We took it off. [Child refers to erasing.]

TEACHER: Good. Now, what did we use to take it off?

JULIE: I don't know.

TEACHER: [Brings blackboard forward.] All right—what would you do if you had a square on here and you wanted to get rid of it? How could you get it off?

JULIE: Maybe we could use paper.

TEACHER: Why could we use paper? What would it do?

JULIE: It could take it off. It could rub it off.

TEACHER: Fine. Now, remember what we did? We didn't use paper to take off the square. Do you remember what it was we *did* use?

JULIE: A sponge.

TEACHER: Very good. Would you get the sponge for me and wet it? Get a paper towel and wet that too. Wet them both.

JULIE: [Goes to sink in room and reaches, not for the requested items, but for the soap.]

TEACHER: [Follows child over to sink.] Do we need the soap?

JULIE: No. [Takes sponge and piece of paper toweling and starts to return to seat.]

The type of recall expected by now from child extends over greater time spans but is still verifiable. By contrast, in the early session, recall was restricted to tasks in the immediate session.

Despite her affirmative answer to the previous question, the automatic negative response follows.

Teacher presents visual aid to prod memory.

Child's gesture is correct.

Although a gesture would have been acceptable in an earlier session, teacher now demands a description, since child is capable of responding in language.

Without being given any hints, the child correctly describes the object she drew.

The teacher is making the child recount the next step in the past sequence.

Teacher makes a judgment that child can answer and delays offering help.

The pause has offered the child a chance to reflect. Her impulsive first answer has been replaced by accurate memory.

Teacher is continuing to focus on interrelated sequence of past events.

Since child is encountering difficulty, teacher chooses a slightly easier level by offering a question which has several alternative answers (e.g., "What could you use to get it off?"). The child is thereby no longer limited to the past, where only one answer (the thing that actually happened) is correct.

Child is more successful with this relaxation in demand.

Teacher's question is to make child aware of the relationship between the object and the action for which it can be used.

Child grasps this connection and expresses herself in clear language.

Child's answer is correct. The reduced complexity helped her recall the past sequence.

This chain of commands is to help the child practice retaining several elements at one time.

This behavior illustrates the easy distractibility of a young child.

Teacher attempts to give aid by focusing on problem at hand.

Child has executed one segment of complex command in selecting the correct objects.

TEACHER: Do you remember what I asked you to do with the paper and sponge?

Teacher is offering assistance to help child remember last part of command. This emphasis on memory is intentional, since once a child has a grasp of how to relate past to present events, he has made a major gain in thinking.

JULIE: Uh huh. Wet them.

TEACHER: Fine. Then, do that.

JULIE: [Wets toweling and sponge.] They are full of water.

Spontaneously verbalizes observation.

TEACHER: Do you need all that water?

JULIE: [Shakes head to indicate "no."]

Offers question to help child arrive at simple cause-and-effect relation.

TEACHER: What could you do to get rid of the water that you don't need?

Child's response is correct on action level.

JULIE: [Squeezes water from both sponge and paper.]

TEACHER: What did you do?

Even when child acts appropriately, he may not understand the rationale for the action. Teacher's question was designed to elicit this awareness.

JULIE: The water comes out.

TEACHER: That's fine Julie. You really didn't need all that water. [They return to the table.] Now, I'd like you to draw something for me on the blackboard.

JULIE: What color?

TEACHER: What color would you like to use?

The specific color is not integral to completing the task. Therefore, here and whenever possible, teacher gives child the opportunity to exercise choice.

JULIE: Green [and selects green crayon].

As opposed to random grabbing, this action follows a specific direction.

TEACHER: Green is fine. Draw some green lines for me.

JULIE: I'll make some big ones.

TEACHER: Okay. We can work with big ones. Oh! Those are very big lines. What will happen if you wipe the sponge on those lines?

Since child's wish is not in conflict with the goal of the lesson, the teacher incorporates it into the lesson. The question is designed to help the child predict future events.

JULIE: I don't know.

TEACHER: Think about it, Julie. If you put this sponge over your lines and wipe them, what will happen?

Even though teacher thought child could not predict the outcome, she posed this question to help child recognize that a significant event is about to occur.

JULIE: [Moves sponge over drawing.]

TEACHER: What's happening to the lines, Julie?

JULIE: [With surprise.] They're not there anymore!

By having been focused, child gets a flash of insight that an interesting process is occurring. By contrast, when given no direction, children frequently just accept common phenomena without understanding. For example, if teacher had merely said "erase it," child would have done so without any recognition of the processes involved.

TEACHER: [Holds sponge down to prevent child from lifting it.] If I lift up the sponge, what color is going to be on the sponge?

Another question to help child predict future events.

JULIE: White.

Child automatically responds to word "color" by naming any color.

TEACHER: Why white?

Regardless of whether child's answer is correct or incorrect, teacher makes child justify response.

JULIE: Green.

TEACHER: Tell me why you said green? Why do you think it will be green?

This question is asked so that child begins to recognize that prediction is based on observation and must be justified.

JULIE: 'Cause I wipe it off.

The action she describes is one aspect of the cause-and-effect idea that teacher is trying to develop.

TEACHER: What did you wipe off?

This question is to bring in other aspects necessary for the completion of the cause-and-effect idea.

JULIE: The green color.

TEACHER: Let's see if you're right. [Lifts sponge.] Green! You're right. Very good.

Achieves correct answer.

Shows child that prediction was correct.

The discussion went on to consider issues such as the effects on the sponge of erasing different colors, what happens to the chalk after it is erased, how to get chalk out of a sponge, comparison of sponge and paper toweling as erasers, and so forth.

This lesson, which lasted 20 minutes, was conducted with interest and enthusiasm on the part of the child who 3 months before could not maintain a set for more than a few minutes.

The lesson that follows was given in the same week as Session 2. It was taught by one of the nursery school teachers who had been invited to visit the program. The teacher was told to teach a cognitively oriented lesson that she deemed appropriate for this age child.

SESSION 3

On this particular day, there were boxes of small plants in the room which the children were to plant outside. As she entered, Julie immediately looked at these flowers. The teacher noticed this and said:

TEACHER: Have you seen the flowers?

JULIE: I saw a beautiful flower outside.

Because the specific referent was not designated (i.e., the flowers in the room), child reacted only to the word "flower."

TEACHER: A beautiful flower? What color was it?

Teacher is led away from her initial referent and poses an unverifiable question.

JULIE: I don't know. It's a beautiful flower.

It is not possible to ascertain whether child's response is a superficial verbalization or an accurate description.

TEACHER: Did you put it in the ground?

Teacher appears to assume that child's comments reflect true interest. Thus, rather than initiating productive dialogue, teacher has limited herself to a very confined area.

JULIE: I picked it up.

TEACHER: You picked it up? What kind was it?

JULIE: I don't know.

TEACHER: Was it little and yellow? Maybe it was a dandelion? Did you plant the flower? Was it a seed and now it's a flower?

This response is likely to be a simple rote association.

Teacher here poses another unverifiable question.

Teacher's questions involve multiple concepts, including an understanding of plant metamorphosis. This example illustrates the paradox of many pre-school language programs, in which it is common to ask extremely complex questions couched in deceptively simple terms. Because of the apparent simplicity, it is often not deemed necessary to give the aids necessary for grasping what are, in fact, complex ideas.

JULIE: [Nods.]

TEACHER: Why don't you draw a picture of the flower and then we can see what color it is.

Teacher assumes that child's poverty of language prohibits explanation and that if the verbal requirements are replaced through drawing, child's knowledge will be revealed. This may, in fact, be true. However, since child's drawing is not verifiable, teacher cannot determine its accuracy. Thus, dialogue with seeming conceptual content can often be aimless.

JULIE: I'd like to do any color flower.

TEACHER: I'd love to have a drawing of it.

In keeping with her permissive orientation, teacher drops her original request and follows child's superficial comment. If child were moving toward a productive idea of her own, this permissive acceptance would prove valuable.

JULIE: I'm gonna make a beautiful flower.

TEACHER: Good.

JULIE: What's this? [The child is referring to the design from the table which comes through on her drawing.]

TEACHER: That's the table cloth coming up; the pattern.

Child is beginning to observe and question her surroundings.

Teacher answers directly. The information requested by child is not simply factual but could be deduced by child herself through proper questioning.

An interchange about flowers then continued on the assumption that the child, in fact, had something definite she wanted to draw. The teacher did attempt to stimulate the child's recall of the specific flower but for this purpose again used unverifiable questions. After the child had drawn several flowers, the teacher said:

TEACHER: Do you know how many flowers you have there now?

JULIE: Three. I'm 5 years old.

Teacher here is attempting to lead child away from narrowness of flowers per se and integrate it with another concept, that is, number.

Child's association of one number with another has an understandable basis. However, her spontaneous use of the same words for a variety of phenomena (age, objects, etc.) suggests that she does not have a clear understanding of the concept of number. Although one would not expect greater understanding in a young child, one must be aware that confusion exists.

TEACHER: You're 5 years old? Maybe you could make flowers for how old you are. Do you know how many more you would need?

JULIE: Five.

Teacher assumes that child can make an equation between numbers in terms of years and numbers of objects.

Child does not answer question but, rather, repeats her response to earlier question.

TEACHER: Five *altogether*. And how many do you have here?

Teacher makes attempt to dissect the problem for simplification. However, the complexity involved requires an almost endless dissection, for example, "Five equals the number of years you are; each flower represents one year; the flowers do not equal the desired number of years; additional flowers must be drawn; you need to consider the number of flowers you have drawn relative to the desired number five, etc." This fantastic complexity is far beyond child's ability to comprehend, but is in effect what has been asked of her.

JULIE: I'll make one more. What kind of brown is this? It's a tree.

Child shows a primitive understanding that *more* is needed, but not specifically how much or why. Her leading back to color may be a combination of avoiding a difficult issue or another intrusion of an impulsive idea.

TEACHER: Oh, that's pretty, Julie. That's very, very, nice.

Topic of numbers has been discarded without any advance in child's knowledge.

JULIE: I bet it's time to wake up now.

Child is referring to the nap time of the rest of the nursery group.

TEACHER: What time do you get up?

Teacher has misinterpreted child's referent to mean the time she wakes up at home. This confusion is reasonable, and where teaching time is unlimited, it is of no special significance. In a language program with a highly restricted time element, however, it hampers the few opportunities available to teach a child how to interpret correctly other people's frames of reference.

JULIE: I get up five o'clock.
TEACHER: In the morning? [Incredulously.] Do you really wake up at five o'clock in the morning?
JULIE: I do.

It is likely that child is perseverating the "five" from the earlier discussion.

TEACHER: And what time do you come to school?
JULIE: I don't know what time—nighttime?
TEACHER: No.
JULIE: I think so; I got a clock. I'm tired.

This dialogue again illustrates the type of communication between a child and teacher which is often mistaken for a conceptual discussion (i.e., time, hours, daytime, nighttime, etc.). Child's lack of awareness of the absurdity of being in nursery school at night indicates that she is in a discussion beyond her depth. In her effort to respond, child is led to rely on prattle alone.

DISCUSSION

We believe that the first two dialogues illustrate the marked changes that occurred in this child after only 6 hours of tutoring. These 15-minute sessions took place three times a week over a 3-month period. Nine hours would have been the optimum during this time span, but absences reduced the total possible time allocated.

The changes in the behavior were corroborated

by a rise of 12 points from 86 to 98 on the Stanford-Binet Intelligence Test. Similar changes which were statistically significant occurred for the total group of 12 children tutored as Julie had been. Although Julie's rise was only 12 points, one child's IQ rose 28 points. These changes occurred across a wide behavioral range including control of impulsivity, increase of attention span, and greater enjoyment in learning.

Verbal skills alone were not an indication of Julie's growth (and may well not be a good indicator for other children). For example, as her hyperactive state became more controlled, her initial *rate* of verbalization declined. In place of her scattered language outpouring, she began to harness the language skills she possessed and use them in a relevant and directed manner. No measures exist for discerning this growth in quality versus quantity of verbalization in the young child, although such measures are sorely needed.

It may be argued that any one-to-one situation may bring about this type of change. However, when the same nursery school teacher met with a control group of three children on an individual but nonteaching basis, there was no significant change. A relationship with an involved and warm adult has often been suggested as the missing link to learning. We submit that such a relationship is fruitless from a cognitive view, unless the time is structured and directed toward a language for cognition.

The session with the visiting teacher was included to offer clues as to why the one-to-one situation fails to develop thinking skills. We recognize that the dialogue is shown to a disadvantage in that the teacher was new to the situation and not well known to the child. However, it is representative of the type of session we recorded by a number of cooperating nursery school teachers. In addition, we feel that this sequence epitomizes the traditionally child-centered and permissive Gestalt of nursery school philosophy (see review by Weikart, 1967). In this type of program, which is designed to meet the needs of the middle-class child, language and intellectual development are placed *last* in a list of desired attributes to be developed. Even when cognitive skills are taught, the philosophy of "what does the child *want* to do" is the pervasive element.

This philosophy was clearly illustrated in the visiting lesson where the teacher severely limited the scope of the material by continuing to focus on casual comments of the child. Regardless of whether she mistook these remarks for real interest or whether she was guided by a consideration for a child's words, the teacher missed the opportunity to lead Julie toward developing the higher level concepts of which she was capable.

On the other hand, when the teacher did initiate material, she posed seemingly simple questions which, in reality, were of enormous complexity. Since the teacher did not have the techniques for analyzing where the child's difficulty lay, she assumed that the concepts involved were well beyond the child. The failure to recognize the complexity of her questions reinforces the philosophy that thinking cannot be accelerated but must merely wait until the child is "ready." The teacher thus abdicates her leadership in favor of the ephemeral concept of "readiness." Consequently, she sees her role as merely structuring the surroundings so as to set the stage for the spontaneous emergence of reasoning.

If this is the viewpoint of many nursery schools attended by middle-class children, the question arises as to how these children develop cognitive skills without special tutoring. It is generally assumed that they absorb them at home. However, if the middle-class teacher *avoids* fostering these skills, might not the middle-class parent similarly avoid this type of dialogue? Evidence indicates that, compared to the lower class, there is a much greater richness of verbal interchange between parent and child in the middle-class home (Freeburg & Payne, 1967). Thus, language is pervasive in these homes, and the child is exposed "naturally" to language skills throughout the day. The middle-class person is not accustomed to being limited to a special time (i.e., 15-minute periods) focused upon these skills, nor to the necessity for having such focusing. When a relevant situation arises, the middle-class parent will encourage discussion with his children. Such situations arise "normally" during the course of the day and are therefore taken for granted. However, such times rarely emerge during the course of the day of the lower-class child. These opportunities must be created for him. Consequently, the teaching situation may appear artificial and constricted, since the 15-minute period must be utilized with a maximum of efficiency in order to grasp every possible opportunity for cognitive growth.

REFERENCES

BLANK, M. A methodology for fostering abstract thinking in deprived children. Paper presented at Ontario Institute for Studies in Education conference on "Problems in the Teaching of Young Children," Toronto, March, 1968.

BLANK, M., & SOLOMON, F. A tutorial language program to develop abstract thinking in socially disadvantaged preschool children. *Child Development*, 1968, *39*, 379–390.

FREEBURG, N. E., & PAYNE, D. T. Parental influence on cognitive development in early childhood: a review. *Child Development*, 1967, *38*, 65–87.

WEIKART, D. P. Preschool programs: preliminary findings. *Journal of Special Education*, 1967, *1*, 163–181.

62

Language and Cognition: Current Perspectives from Linguistics and Psychology

JOHN B. CARROLL

The view that non-standard dialects in general, and lower-class black English in particular, are not adequate for the development of organized, higher-order thought has been widespread. The counter-view is maintained with at least equal fervor. John B. Carroll, as chairman of the Linguistic Society of America's Committee on Language and Cognitive Development, presents very cogently the alternative point of view. It becomes apparent quickly that the controversy is far from being solely a theoretical one; it has important educational, social, and political implications. The reader will want to review the previous article by Blank and Solomon in light of Carroll's paper. Also, see the paper by Labov and Robins in Section VI.

Dr. Carroll, a leading educational psychologist, psychometrician, and psycholinguist, was formerly at Harvard University and is now Senior Research Psychologist at Educational Testing Service, Princeton, New Jersey.

In a series of papers published in the late 1950's and early 1960's, the British sociologist Basil Bernstein (3, 4) proposed a distinction between two forms of language that has caught the attention of educators and educational psychologists on both sides of the Atlantic. One form is what he called "public" language, the other is what he called "formal" language. Later, he renamed these forms as the "restricted code" and the "elaborated code," respectively. It was not Bernstein's drawing of the distinction between these two forms of language that was of particular moment; it was what Bernstein said about them, namely that the "public" or "restricted" code tended to be limited to short, highly stereotyped utterances whose symbolism is descriptive and concrete, whereas the "formal" or "elaborated" language is rich in qualification and complexity. The implication was that the user of the "restricted" code is unable to convey any careful, logical analysis of a situation, or even to conceive of a situation in any analytic terms, whereas the user of the "formal" or "elaborated" code was not so handicapped. In a number of empirical studies, Bernstein claimed to have been able to demonstrate the existence of these two types of language and to show their correlation with social-class differentiation.

Actually, Bernstein's views on the difference between these two codes and the effect of the difference on thinking have never been entirely clear, and as has been pointed out by Lawton (7), these views have undergone certain changes in emphasis over the course of the years. Lawton believes that Bernstein did not really mean to say that the linguistic code actually influences the form of thought; rather he argued that thought, and the kind of language used to express that thought, is a function of the social situation and the individual's perception of his role in society. Lawton also points out that the alleged correlation between language code and social class is not as great as some of those who quote Bernstein might have us think: on occasion, lower-class persons can use the "elaborated" code, and even in Bernstein's early presentations of his theory, it was emphasized that middle-class persons use *both* the restricted code and the elaborated code, depending upon the social situation.

Be that as it may, Bernstein's ideas have been much discussed. As frequently happens when new ideas are discussed by people who hear about them only second-hand, Bernstein's ideas have been watered down, modified, and oversimplified. It has been assumed that Bernstein's "restricted code" is one in which it is impossible to formulate thought of any high degree of logical complexity, and it has also been assumed that lower-class persons, being limited to the use of a "restricted" code, are unable to formulate logical thought. Bernstein did not make any such simplistic claims. I refer you to Lawton's analysis of Bernstein's writings for a more accurate statement of what Bernstein actually said.

John B. Carroll, "Language and cognition: Current perspectives from linguistics and psychology." Presented April 19, 1971, at the IRA Pre-Convention Institute on Reading, Language and Non-Standard Dialects. Reprinted by permission.

In their book *Teaching Disadvantaged Children in the Pre-School*, the educational psychologists Bereiter and Engelmann (*1*) cited Bernstein's theories as claiming that "the speech of lower-class people follows a linguistic code . . . that is inadequate for expressing personal or original opinions, for analysis and careful reasoning, for dealing with anything hypothetical or beyond the present, and for explaining anything very complex." According to these writers, Bernstein "sees the [lower-class] child . . . as being trapped by the restrictions of [his] linguistic code and unable to operate at the high conceptual and logical level that is required in formal education." They go on to describe the "language problems of culturally deprived children" (i.e., lower-class black children), making such points as these:

1. "The speech of the severely deprived children seems to consist not of distinct words, but rather of whole phrases or sentences that function like giant words. . . . These 'giant word' units cannot be taken apart by the child and recombined. . . . Instead of saying 'He's a big dog,' the deprived child says 'He bih daw.' Instead of saying 'I ain't got no juice,' he says 'Uai-ga-na-ju'" (p. 34).

2. It is not merely a problem of "faulty pronunciation," but of an "inability to deal with sentences *as sequences of meaningful parts*" (italics in the original). The lower-class black child cannot repeat sentences with any degree of complexity; he tends to "give merely an approximate rendition of the over-all sound profile of the sentence" (p. 35).

3. The "culturally deprived" child cannot distinguish sentences that differ with respect to structure words or inflections (p. 35).

4. "Many disadvantaged children of preschool age come very close to the total lack of ability to use language as a device for acquiring and processing information" (p. 39).

It is true that Bereiter and Engelmann acknowledge that "studies by Loban and others have been cited as evidence that culturally deprived children do possess all the necessary elements of English grammar and syntax, even though they make scanty use of some of them." But, they continue, "what is crucial . . . is not the extent to which their language is technically capable of conveying thoughts and information but the extent to which the children themselves are able to use language in this way" (p. 39).

It is worthy of note that Bereiter and Engelmann apply Bernstein's notion of a "restricted code" to the language of lower-class black children, who speak a form of English that is a distinct, non-standard dialect. While there are dialect differences in England between middle-class and lower-class speech, Bernstein was thinking not so much of dialect differences as of differences in speech styles and modes of formulating thought. Thus, it is easy to gain the false impression, from Bereiter and Engelmann's statements, that lower-class black English *is* what Bernstein would call a restricted code, whereas standard English is an "elaborated code." The fact of the matter is that if there is any validity in Bernstein's distinction between "restricted" and "elaborated" codes, it could operate just as well in standard English as in some nonstandard form of English such as what is loosely called "lower-class black English." We all use a "restricted" code when we are in casual social situations in which there is quick interchange of simple information, feelings, and opinions that we do not have to formulate carefully.

I have quoted extensively from Bereiter and Engelmann only because they give the most explicit statement available of a view that seems to be widespread: that lower-class black English is "a basically nonlogical mode of expressive behavior which lacks the formal properties necessary for the organization of thought" (*2*, pp. 112–113). It may be that Bereiter and Engelmann no longer hold to this view, but the impression that it has made is sufficiently common among educators that it deserves comment and rebuttal. Also, this view reflects social attitudes toward nonstandard languages that linguists feel are misguided and wrong. There are, in fact, many myths about language that are commonly believed and repeated: that simple folk have exceedingly small vocabularies, that the languages of "primitive" tribes are extremely simple and incapable of expressing thought, and that when a person does not speak "grammatically," he is not thinking correctly. The widespread acceptance of such ideas is alarming to linguists, not only because they are scientifically untenable, but also because they reflect social attitudes that are rightly to be regarded as snobbish, undemocratic, and antithetical to social progress.

It was for this reason that the Linguistic Society of America last year appointed a Committee on Language and Cognitive Development, of which I am chairman, to prepare materials that would seek to inform educators and the public at large concerning linguists' knowledge about the nature of language, the adequacy of different languages or forms of language for formulating thought, and the nature of language development in the individual. The present address is a brief summary of some of the facts, principles, and views that linguists hope to have made more widely known. These include not only things that linguists as linguists know, but also some facts and conclusions that have been reached in the psychology of language.

Let me lay down some general principles that

will guide our later consideration of the particular problems of nonstandard dialects:

1. Language is a complex human phenomenon that takes the same general form wherever it is found. It permits the expression of a certain very wide range of information, experiences, feelings, and thoughts, and it does so in somewhat the same way regardless of the particular form of the language or the culture of the user, as long as the language is a so-called "natural language" that is used from childhood on as a native language by its users. This is true whether the language is one such as English, Russian, Chinese, or Indonesian used by a highly developed culture, or one such as Bantu, Navaho, or Fijian, used by a less technically advanced culture. (There are, of course, certain modes of expression, such as music or higher mathematics, that are outside the province of language, but they are equally excluded from all natural languages.)

2. In saying that all languages have the same general form, we mean that all languages possess units for expressing particular concepts and rules whereby utterances are constructed to indicate the social purpose of the utterance and the particular relationships among concepts that are to be communicated. Languages do, of course, differ somewhat in the concepts they select for use in expression, and they vary widely in the particular rules they employ for constructing utterances. Nevertheless, all languages have ways of referring to all the kinds of beings, objects, substances, events, and relationships encountered in common human experience. They all have ways of communicating ideas of space, time, number, negation, condition, opposition, specificity, class membership, quality, and the like, many of these ideas being of a highly abstract nature. In general, it is true that anything that can be said in one language can be said in any other language, if one ignores the special cultural connotations and conceptual references that may attach to the utterances of a given language, and if one excludes the problem of translating advanced technical ideas from one language to another.

3. Language systems are neutral with respect to truth or logic; a language system does not force its speakers to make true or logical statements as opposed to untrue or illogical statements.

4. Except for languages with very small numbers of speakers living in close association, it is common to find minor or even major variations in the pronunciation, vocabulary, or grammar of a language across the various groups using it. Different forms of a language are technically known as *dialects*, and to say that a person speaks a dialect has no derogatory or pejorative force. (I am speaking a particular dialect of English right now!) Dialect variation occurs both in the languages of advanced civilization (witness all the dialects of English) and in those of aboriginal groups. It is often the case, too, that one or more dialects of a language acquire higher status than others; high-status dialects are generally called standard dialects, while dialects of lesser status are often regarded as "nonstandard." This is not at all because a high-status form of a language is necessarily any better equipped to communicate ideas or formulate thought, but simply because the speakers of that dialect have attained generally higher social status and power (and often, more education) than the speakers of other dialects, through the operation of political, economic, and other social forces. The phenomenon of "standard" vs. "nonstandard" dialects is found throughout the world, even in the case of aboriginal languages like Bantu or Fijian, and speakers of nonstandard dialects are generally well aware of the low status accorded their dialects, regardless of their actual social status.

5. Speakers of any language, or any dialect, use that language in many different styles, depending upon the particular social situation in which they find themselves on a given occasion. These styles or registers vary in many ways, generally along a dimension of formality vs. informality. For example, Martin Joos in his essay *The Five Clocks* (5) distinguishes five styles that speakers and writers of standard English may affect: frozen, formal, consultative, casual, and intimate. But he also notes that styles vary in the dimensions of age, "breadth," and "responsibility" (with some overtones of relations with the "standard-nonstandard" dimension mentioned above). Speakers of nonstandard dialects are capable of similar variation in styles of speech.

6. It is usually the case that the various dialects of a language, whether standard or nonstandard, are mutually intelligible at least to some extent. The more similar the dialects are in their pronunciation, vocabulary, and grammar, the more they are mutually intelligible. Depending upon the amount of exposure to them, and other factors, speakers can learn to understand a number of different dialects better than would otherwise be normal for them. Some speakers can speak and be understood in two or more dialects, often in different levels or registers of these dialects.

7. Within the speakers of a given dialect, there will be certain variations in *competence*, that is, knowledge of the system of the language and the rules by which the system is put together, so to speak. In the main, this variation occurs in the individual's knowledge of vocabulary. That is, some speakers know more words, and more about the different uses of words, than others. There may

be some variation also in competence with respect to grammatical rules, and even some variation with respect to basic pronunciation rules. These variations in competence depend to an unknown extent on differences in basic mental capacities, in amount of education, or in amount of exposure to other speakers of the language. Through appropriate education or training, individuals can be helped to reach higher levels of competence, but we do not necessarily know what the best training methods are to achieve this goal, nor do we know how to predict the maximum level of competence that an individual can achieve after such training.

8. In addition, even among speakers who have the same degree of "competence" (technically defined as above), there will be variation in what we may call *performance characteristics*, that is, in verbal fluency and creativeness, in reasoning power, in social perception, and other individual traits that affect the individual's use of language, whether in speaking, understanding, reading, or writing. Of course, the more the individual knows about the language, the more likely it is that he will be able to use it fluently, creatively, and intelligently, but it remains true that skill in language use is not only a matter of language competence but of many other factors in the individual's make-up.

9. The course of a child's acquisition of his native language, whatever that language may be, is normally regular and predictable. While there are individual differences in rate of development that may be associated with some combination of hereditary and environmental factors, every child passes through certain distinct stages of development in his learning of the phonological, lexical, and grammatical characteristics of his language. Furthermore, he learns whatever language or variety of language he is exposed to. (Sometimes he learns several languages, or varieties of language, at the same time.) By the time he is about five, the normal child has learned *most* of the characteristics of his language that enable him to use it in ordinary communication with peers and with adults, although he will learn much more about his language as he grows older and is exposed to more advanced uses of it.

10. The developmental stages through which a child passes in learning his language are quite possibly correlated with the child's mental development. Frankly, we do not know much, as yet, about this correlation or how it operates. There are those who believe that language development leads and guides mental development, and there are those who believe that, on the contrary, mental development leads language development. There is no *a priori* way of resolving this question, and it is difficult even to interpret the few empirical

studies that bear on it. On the basis of several lines of reasoning and the available evidence, I incline to the belief that mental development tends to lead and proceed in advance of language development— that a given stage of language development cannot be attained until the appropriate mental capacity for that development has matured. I believe also that the adequate development of mental maturity is only a *necessary* condition, not a sufficient condition, for language development. Obviously, the child must be exposed to language in situations that are meaningful to him before he can learn it. If this view is correct, the absence of a given phase of language development cannot be taken necessarily as evidence for a deficit in mental maturity; it could equally well be evidence for a deficiency in the environmental conditions in which the child is placed.

Armed with these general propositions and principles, we may now re-examine some of the views that have been put forth by such writers as Bernstein, Bereiter and Engelmann, and others.

To say that there exists a "restricted code" in no sense implies that the basic form of a speaker's language is incapable of allowing him to formulate thought of any degree of logical complexity. If one takes the total range of linguistic devices available to the speaker of any natural language, and in fact usually within the competence of that speaker, one finds that these devices would permit the expression of any thought or relationship that one might desire to express (except, of course, for highly technical discourse for which vocabulary might be lacking). Neither British lower-class English, nor lower-class black English is incapable of expressing complex thought. The linguist William Labov (6) has given a number of examples of lower-class black English in which quite complex thoughts are expressed, for example, one in which a youngster tells a slightly older black interviewer that there can't be a heaven because it could only have been made by a God, but since nobody really knows what God is like, he doesn't exist and therefore couldn't have made a heaven.

Note, however, that this youngster was speaking in a social situation in which he felt perfectly free to talk. If Bereiter's slum children appeared to speak in "grunts" or "giant words," it may have been because they found themselves in a situation which inhibited their speech in certain ways.

Bernstein's "restricted code" is properly to be interpreted as a style or mode of speaking in which the speaker finds no need to formulate thoughts carefully and with adequate qualification. It has little or nothing to do with the basic language system in which the speech is couched, and it is merely an accident if the particular speech patterns used under such conditions appear to be less complex on the average.

Bereiter and Engelmann's notion that their slum children speak in "giant words" and are unable to perceive speech as a sequence of meaningful sounds is patently wrong, as it violates the second proposition I have enunciated above, that all languages have a certain form, with rules for constructing utterances out of basic elements. No language has any provision for constructing "giant words" that are unanalyzable in terms of simpler elements and that would convey what might otherwise be conveyed by a sentence. Neither the famous compound words of German nor the polysynthetic words of a language like Eskimo can be conceived of as "giant words" constructed out of whole cloth, independent of other elements in the language. Bereiter and Engelmann's very examples belie their allegations: The child who said "Uai-ga-na-ju" (for "I ain't got no juice") *constructed* his utterance from basic elements according to a fairly complex set of rules; he could have said "I ain't got no milk" or "I got some juice" or "If you don't give me no juice, I ain't got none" or literally hundreds of other utterances on this general pattern.

Since all languages are neutral with respect to truth or logic, it cannot be the case that nonstandard forms of English are illogical. Under certain conditions, black English omits the copula *to be*, as in the utterance "He sick," a fact from which it is sometimes concluded that black English is "illogical." As it happens, standard Russian also omits the copula in sentences of this type, but I hope nobody would argue that Russian is "illogical." The same goes for the argument that languages that use the double negative are illogical. Black English is similar to French, Spanish, and Old English in using the double negative.

Lower-class black English is admittedly a nonstandard dialect of English but I believe the status in which it is regarded, like the status of many other nonstandard dialects, would be improved if the public realizes that it is just as highly structured and just as capable of communicating thought as a standard dialect. Even if Bernstein's distinction between "restricted" and "elaborated" codes is accepted, there can be both "restricted" and "elaborated" codes, or modes of speaking, in nonstandard dialects as well as in standard ones.

Also, just as standard dialects can be used in various styles, so also can nonstandard dialects be used in various styles. It is possible to reinterpret Bereiter and Engelmann's reports of the speech of their slum children by saying that these children were speaking in a special style—a style adopted whenever the children found themselves in a minority position.

Children speaking a nonstandard dialect cannot be expected necessarily to comprehend standard English, although the evidence says that they understand standard English better than speakers of standard English understand *their* dialect. This fact is not adequately taken into account in a variety of psychological tests. For example, children who speak nonstandard dialects get unfairly low scores on certain subtests of the widely-used Illinois Test of Psycholinguistic Abilities (*8*) that require the child to follow the grammatical distinctions observed by standard English. It is a grave mistake, often made, to interpret these low scores as indicating a retarded state of language development or, worse still, a retarded state of mental development. The Manual of the ITPA fails to recognize this problem or to warn against such misinterpretations. A fairer test would be one that is designed in terms of the nonstandard dialect in question.

There may be some justice in the claims of Bereiter and Engelmann, and others who have prepared programs of language improvement for speakers of nonstandard English, that some of these children have not learned the words for certain concepts, even in their own dialects, because one can expect differences in the extent to which children have learned such words. The mistake that is often made, however, is to assume that the nonstandard dialect in question lacks these words or has no way of expressing these concepts. Programs of language "improvement," i.e., programs in which children are taught the standard dialect, should be based on careful analyses of what stock of words and concepts is possessed by the nonstandard dialect. It will frequently turn out that a child who seems not to possess a particular feature of a standard dialect already knows a corresponding feature in his nonstandard dialect.

From the proposition that language acquisition is a natural and regular course of development we can draw the inference that the child who learns a nonstandard dialect learns it in much the same way as do children who acquire standard dialects. If the child's acquisition of a nonstandard dialect is viewed in its own terms rather than in terms of the extent to which he acquires the standard dialect, it will not appear as distorted and unusual as it is often thought to be.

To sum up the argument of this paper, I would emphasize the incorrectness and fallaciousness of the apparently widespread belief that speaking a nonstandard dialect is somehow a sign of a deficiency in thought or of mental development.

There may be some connection between language and thought, but it is not exhibited in nonstandard speech. Our children who are speakers of nonstandard dialects—whether they be blacks, Puerto Ricans, or Chicanos, are not the victims of undeveloped language codes. Their languages have principles and rules similar to those that govern any language.

REFERENCES

1. BEREITER, CARL, and SIEGFRIED ENGELMANN. *Teaching Disadvantaged Children in the Pre-School.* Englewood Cliffs, N.J.: Prentice-Hall, 1966.

2. BEREITER, CARL; S. ENGELMANN; JEAN OSBORN; and P. A. REIDFORD. "An Academically Oriented Pre-School." In Fred M. Hechinger (Ed.), *Pre-School Education Today.* New York: Doubleday, 1966. Pp. 105–135.

3. BERNSTEIN, BASIL. "Some Sociological Determinants of Perception: An Inquiry into Sub-Cultural Differences." *British Journal of Sociology, 9* (June, 1958), 159–174.

4. BERNSTEIN, BASIL. "Linguistic Codes, Hesitation Phenomena, and Intelligence." *Language and Speech, 5* (January, 1962), 31–46.

5. JOOS, MARTIN. *The Five Clocks.* New York: Harcourt Brace Jovanovich, 1967.

6. LABOV, WILLIAM. "The Logic of Non-Standard English." In Frederick Williams (Ed.), *Language and Poverty: Perspectives on a Theme.* Chicago: Markham Publishing Co., 1970. Pp. 153–189.

7. LAWTON, DENIS. *Social Class, Language, and Education.* New York: Schocken Books, 1968.

8. PARASKEVOPOULOS, JOHN N., and SAMUEL A. KIRK. *The Development and Psychometric Characteristics of the Revised Illinois Test of Psycholinguistic Abilities.* Urbana: University of Illinois Press, 1969.

63

Personality and IQ Change[1]

Jerome Kagan, Lester W. Sontag,
Charles T. Baker,
and Virginia L. Nelson

*This article addresses itself to the interactions be-
tween personality and intelligence in terms of IQ
change. The paper is from The Fels Research
Institute for the Study of Human Development, the
locus of one of the earliest-begun and broadest
longitudinal studies. (Honzik's article in Section II
is another example of the longitudinal approach.)
The techniques used by Kagan et al. to assess
personality are two well-known projective techniques—the Rorschach Ink Blots and the TAT or
Thematic Apperception Test. As mentioned earlier,
Professor Kagan is now at Harvard University.
Lester W. Sontag is Director Emeritus of Fels
Research Institute, Antioch College; Charles T.
Baker is assistant resident psychiatrist at Van-
couver General Hospital, University of British
Columbia, Canada; and Virginia L. Nelson was
formerly a research assistant at the Fels Research
Institute.*

Research on mental development during the last
twenty years has indicated that a child's IQ score
does not necessarily remain constant with age

[1] This investigation was supported in part by a research grant
(PHS M 1260) from the National Institute of Mental Health
of the National Institutes of Health, United States Public
Health Service. The writers wish to thank Dr. Seymour B.
Sarason for his critical reading of the manuscript.

(2, 3, 4, 10). Several reports (9, 10, 12) suggest
that changes in environmental conditions can depress or raise IQ level and it is sometimes implied
that these changes may be explained by recourse
to personality variables. The purpose of this paper
is to demonstrate that changes in IQ during childhood are correlated with certain personality predispositions as inferred from projective test data.
The personality variables under study include
(a) need for achievement, (b) competitive strivings,
(c) curiosity about nature, and (d) passivity.

Performance on an IQ test is assumed to be a
function of at least two major variables: the variety
of skills and abilities the person brings to the test
situation and his motivation to perform well on the
test (2, 6). Since the IQ scores of some children
change markedly during the school years, it seems
plausible to assume that those children who show
marked increases in IQ have a very strong motivation to acquire or develop the various intellectual
skills tapped by an IQ test and to perform well in
a testing situation. It is suggested that need for
achievement, competitive strivings, and curiosity
about nature motivate the acquisition and improvement of cognitive abilities and by so doing facilitate increases in tested IQ.

The social environment often awards praise
and recognition for intellectual accomplishment,
and school age children with a high need for
achievement might seek to gratify this need through
intellectual activity. Thus it was predicted that
children showing marked increases in IQ would
produce more achievement imagery on the TAT
than those with minimal gains in IQ.

Secondly, the school environment emphasizes
competitive intellectual activity, and children with
strong competitive needs would be highly motivated to acquire the intellectual skills which result
in successful competition with one's classmates.
Thus it was predicted that children showing IQ
gains would show more competitive strivings than
children displaying minimal gains in IQ. In choosing an index of competitive strivings, besides the
related measure of TAT achievement fantasy, it
was decided to use aggressive content on the
Rorschach. The bases for this choice rested on the
assumptions that (a) incidence of aggressive
imagery reflected degree of aggressive motivation
and (b) competition was a socially accepted form of
aggressive behavior. For in competition, as in
aggression, the child desires to defeat another
individual and assert his superiority over him. The
population of children in this study is predominantly
middle class and apt to place strong inhibitions on

Jerome Kagan, Lester W. Sontag, Charles T. Baker, and Virginia L. Nelson, "Personality and IQ change," *Journal of Abnormal
and Social Psychology*, 1958, *56*, 261–266. Reprinted by permission.

direct overt expression of aggression. Therefore, there would be a tendency for the individual with high aggressive motivation to seek socially accepted channels for aggressive expression such as competitive activity with peers. Thus it was predicted that children showing IQ gain would report more Rorschach aggressive content than those with minimal gain because of their greater competitive predisposition.

A third motive that might facilitate a child's acquisition of knowledge and skills in dealing with the environment could be curiosity about nature. Interest in birth, death, sexual anatomy, and other processes of nature is a frequent phenomenon in young children. It is suggested that the more intense this curiosity the greater the motivation to acquire the habits which would gratify this motive. Since reading, questioning, and manipulating the environment are effective behavioral methods of gratifying one's curiosity, it might be expected that the highly curious child would be more likely to develop these skills and therefore apt to gain in IQ score. The TAT measure used to evaluate curiosity was presence of themes of interest in nature and its phenomena. For the Rorschach, it was hypothesized that concern with the body might reflect, in part, heightened interest in natural processes, and it was suggested that anatomy content might be more frequent for children who showed marked IQ gains than for those with minimal increases in IQ. It is recognized that many clinical psychologists regard anatomy content in adults as indicative of psychopathology. This study is concerned with the correlates of IQ gain rather than psychopathology, and it is not implied that children who show increases in IQ are completely free of conflict. Secondly, it was felt that the determinants of anatomy content for children might be different from those which produce this content in adults.

A final prediction dealt with the predisposition to behavioral passivity. The children who show IQ gains have been characterized as having high need achievement, competitive strivings, and curiosity about the environment. This constellation of motives implies that when these children are confronted with a problem, they would have a tendency to attack and attempt to solve the problem rather than withdraw from the situation or seek help. On this basis, it was predicted that children who showed IQ gains would be less likely than those with minimal IQ increases to characterize their TAT heroes as passive in attitude or behavior.

The Fels Research Institute is uniquely equipped to test these ideas about IQ change since it has continuous longitudinal information on the development of a sample of normal children. These data include intelligence and projective tests, observations of the children, and reports on the parent-child interaction. In a recent study, Sontag, Baker, and Nelson (11) related personality information on a sample of children with changes in IQ and found that those children who showed marked increases in IQ were rated as more competitive, more likely to display self-initiated behavior and less passive than those who showed decreases in IQ. The TAT and Rorschach protocols were not utilized in making these personality ratings, and the results from this study served as a major stimulus for the present investigation.

METHOD

A sample of 140 Fels subjects (*S*s), 70 of each sex, were chosen for study because a fairly complete record of test information was available on them. From ages 2½ to 6, the Stanford-Binet intelligence test (1916 or 1937 revision) was administered to most *S*s twice yearly, on their birthdays and six months after their birthdays. From ages 6 to 12, most *S*s received alternately Form L or Form M of the 1937 revision annually on or near each *S*'s birthday. All of the tests were administered by one of the authors (VLN). The mean IQ of the Fels population is near 120, with standard deviation varying from 14 to 20 IQ points.

In order to obtain groups of *S*s who showed the most change in IQ score from ages 6 to 10, a smoothed longitudinal plot of each *S*'s IQ was prepared by averaging the mean of three consecutive test scores around each age. This procedure is explained in detail in other reports (1, 10, 11). This technique tends to eliminate erratic variations in IQ and hopefully furnishes a more valid measure of IQ changes. Then each *S*'s smoothed IQ at age 6 was subtracted from his smoothed IQ at age 10, and this distribution of differences, positive if *S* gained in IQ and negative if *S* lost in IQ, was divided into quartiles. This report deals with the projective test information on those *S*'s in the two extreme groups: those who increased and those who decreased the most in IQ score. These will be called Group A, the IQ ascenders, and Group D, the IQ descenders, respectively. There was no significant difference between the mean IQ of the two extreme quartiles at age six, the means being 119 and 116 for Groups A and D respectively. The average amount of increase in IQ for Group A was larger (plus 17 points) than the corresponding decrease for the members of Group D (minus 5 points) and while 46 per cent of Group D lost five or more points, every child in Group A gained 10 or more points during the years 6 through 10. The mean IQ of the entire sample of 140 tends to increase slightly from ages 6 to 10, probably as a result of practice effects with the same test. Since every *S* in Group D showed a decrease in IQ, it might be inferred that the members of Group D did not benefit from practice and familiarity with the test, and it is probably more accurate to view Group D *S*s in this light rather than as *S*s who showed marked decreases in IQ score.

The projective tests used in the analysis were the Rorschach and selected TAT pictures. Two factors governed the choice of the TAT cards which were analyzed. Because the protocols were gathered over a period of years, there was not complete comparability for all Ss for the number of cards administered. Secondly, the specific hypotheses of the study dictated the cards chosen for analysis and Cards 1, 3 BM, 3 GF, 5, 6 BM, 12 F, 14, and 17 BM were selected for analysis. The age at which the TAT protocols were administered ranged from 8-9 to 14-6 with median at 11-6 and 80 per cent of the protocols obtained between the ages of 11 and 12. The age at which the Rorschachs were administered ranged from 6-5 to 13-6 with median at 10-5 and 63 per cent of the sample having had the test between ages 10 and 11. Since the Rorschach and TAT were administered by different examiners there was no comparability with respect to inquiry or probing. Thus, the analysis of both the Rorschach and TAT were restricted to the S's spontaneous verbalization to the stimulus before any questions or inquiry were conducted by the examiner. The protocols were scored for the following fantasy categories.

1. *Need achievement on the TAT.* Achievement imagery on the TAT was scored according to the definition of McClelland et al. (8); and themes involving a reference to competition with a standard of excellence were scored achievement imagery.

2. *Rorschach aggression.* The definition of aggressive content on the Rorschach included (*a*) people, animals, or creatures engaged in physical or verbal aggression, e.g., fighting or quarreling, (*b*) explosive objects or explosions, e.g., volcanoes, bombs exploding, fireworks, and (*c*) objects or animal parts normally regarded as instruments of aggression, e.g., spears, rifles, clubs, guns, knives, horns, and claws.

3. *Intellectual curiosity about nature.* For the TAT, curiosity was defined in terms of themes in which someone is interested in the processes or phenomena of nature. Curiosity on the Rorschach was restricted to anatomy or X-ray responses of internal organs or boney parts, e.g., stomach, backbone, ribs.

4. *Passivity.* Because of the limited amount of thematic material in the spontaneous performance, themes of passivity were limited to stories in which the central figure was described as sleepy, tired, or resting.

The fantasy categories were independently scored by the senior author and an assistant without knowledge of the S's IQ scores.[2] Reliability was very high because of the limited amount of content scored for each response and the objectivity of the definitions. Percentage of agreement for the three TAT categories was 95 per cent and for the two Rorschach categories 99 per cent.

RESULTS

Although there was a total of 70 Ss in the two extreme quartiles, not all of the Ss had Rorschach or TAT data for the age range under study. Table 1 shows the distri-

[2] The writers wish to thank Mary Schnurer for her assistance in assessing the reliability of the scoring.

TABLE 1

DISTRIBUTION OF Ss BY SEX AND DIRECTION OF IQ CHANGE USED IN THE ANALYSIS OF THE TAT AND RORSCHACH

Group	TAT		Rorschach	
	Boys	Girls	Boys	Girls
Group A	22	11	22	10
Group D	10	20	9	18
Both groups	32	31	31	28

bution of Ss, by sex and direction of IQ change, for the TAT and Rorschach analyses. Because there are approximately twice as many boys as there are girls in Group A, all comparisons were first made separately by sex and results were only combined if the direction of the result for both boys and girls in the same IQ group was in the predicted direction.

1. *Need Achievement.* All achievement themes, save one, occurred to Cards 1 and 17 BM. The typical achievement story to Card 1 concerned a boy who wanted to master the violin and/or become a famous violinist, while the typical achievement theme to 17 BM involved competitive activity with regard to rope climbing. Table 2 shows the percentage of Ss in each group reporting achievement imagery plots to Cards 1, 17 BM, and to both pictures.

For both Cards 1 and 17 BM, more male and female Ss in Group A report achievement imagery than the boys or girls of Group D. For Card 1, the difference between Group A and Group D girls is reliable at the .03 level; the difference for boys is in the predicted direction but not significant. For Card 17 BM, the difference between Group A and Group D boys is significant ($P = .03$) and in the predicted direction for girls. All P values are for one tail and were evaluated using the exact method suggested by Fisher (5). When the sexes were pooled, comparisons between Groups A and D were significant not only for Cards 1 and 17 BM separately but also for the number of Ss telling achievement imagery to both Cards 1 and 17 BM ($P < .10$, .03, and .01 respectively). Thus, the Ss who showed increases in IQ were more prone to structure Cards 1 and 17 BM in terms of achievement oriented behavior than the Ss in Group D.

2. *Aggressive Content on Rorschach.* There was no significant difference between Groups A and D or be-

TABLE 2

PERCENTAGE OF Ss REPORTING ACHIEVEMENT IMAGERY TO CARDS 1 AND 17 BM

TAT Card	Group A			Group D		
	Boys	Girls	Boys and Girls	Boys	Girls	Boys and Girls
Card 1	36.4	50.0	40.6	27.3	15.0	19.4
Card 17 BM	36.4	30.0	34.4	0.0	15.0	9.7
Cards 1 and 17 BM	22.7	10.0	18.8	0.0	0.0	0.0

tween boys and girls with respect to the mean number of responses per protocol, and the mean for the entire sample was 27 responses. There was no difference between Group A and Group D girls with respect to percentage of each group reporting one or more aggressive responses per protocol (30.0 per cent for Group A versus 33.0 per cent for Group D). However, the difference between Group A and D boys approached significance with 59.1 per cent of the former and 22.2 per cent of the latter reporting one or more aggressive images ($P = .07$). Thus, the prediction of a correlation between IQ increase and aggressive imagery held only for the boys. Because of the tentativeness of this result and the more speculative nature of the hypothesis relating competitive striving and aggressive content, an attempt was made to validate this finding by analyzing a later Rorschach protocol for the boys in Groups A and D. Not all of the boys had Rorschachs administered to them at a later age, and only 15 Ss in Group A and five in Group D were available for analysis. The median ages at the time of administration were 13-8 and 15-0 for Groups A and D respectively, and there was no significant difference in the lengths of the protocols of the two groups. The results were in the same direction for 86.7 per cent of Group A, and 20.0 per cent of Group D reported one or more aggressive images, and this difference is highly significant ($P = .01$).

3. *Intellectual Curiosity.* The only TAT card eliciting curiosity plots was Card 14, and the typical theme described a person gazing at or interested in the stars or the heavens. Table 3 shows the percentage of each group telling such themes to Card 14.

Both the boys and girls in Group A told more themes of interest in the stars or heavens than the males and females in Group D ($P = .14$, $P = .10$, respectively) and combining of the sexes yielded a highly significant difference between Groups A and D ($P < .01$).

4. *Anatomy and X-Ray Responses on the Rorschach.* There was no difference between Group A and Group D girls reporting one or more anatomy responses (30.0 per cent versus 38.9 per cent for Groups A and D respectively). For the boys, 31.8 per cent of Group A and 0.0 per cent of Group D reported anatomy or X-ray imagery, a difference that approached significance ($P = .06$). This finding was also validated on the same sample of 20 boys that was used to check the differences in aggressive content. The results were in the same direction with 60.0 per cent of Group A and 20.0 per cent of Group D reporting anatomy content ($P = .15$).

5. *Passivity.* Card 3 BM accounted for most of the passivity themes and the groups were compared with respect to the incidence of stories to Card 3 BM in which the central figure was sleepy, tired, or resting. Table 4

TABLE 3
PERCENTAGE OF Ss REPORTING THEMES OF
CURIOSITY TO CARD 14

Sex	Group A	Group D
Boys	40.9	18.2
Girls	30.0	5.0
Boys and girls	37.5	9.7

TABLE 4
PERCENTAGE OF Ss REPORTING THEMES OF
PASSIVITY TO CARD 3 BM

Sex	Group A	Group D
Boys	9.1	27.3
Girls	10.0	45.0
Boys and girls	9.4	38.7

shows the percentage of each group telling such themes. Both the boys and girls in Group D showed more passivity themes than the boys and girls in Group A. Although only the difference for the girls was significant ($P = .06$), when the sexes were pooled the difference was highly reliable ($P < .03$).

Cards 3 GF, 5, 6 BM, and 12 F did not furnish data relevant to the hypotheses under test and these results are not summarized.

DISCUSSION

In the main, the hypotheses about the differences between Groups A and D have been verified. Boy and girl ascenders produced more TAT achievement imagery and curiosity about nature than Group D children and male ascenders displayed more aggressive content on the Rorschach than the boys in Group D. The higher incidence of aggressive imagery for the boys who gained in IQ was interpreted as reflecting stronger competitive motivation. Finally, the Ss in Group D were presumed to have a more passive orientation since they were more likely to perceive the ambiguous figure on Card 3 BM as sleeping or tired. The relation between Rorschach anatomy content and IQ gain was the most tentative finding.

The results are interpreted as indicating that high motivation to achieve, competitive strivings, and curiosity about nature may motivate the acquisition of intellectual skills and knowledge which, in turn, facilitates increases in tested IQ. If one accepts the generally assumed notion that boys are more competitive and achievement oriented than girls, the fact that there were twice as many boys in Group A as there were girls supports the present interpretation. A recent study using the Edwards Personal Preference Schedule found that high school boys obtained higher need achievement scores than high school girls (7).

These results are not interpreted as indicating that strong achievement, competitive, and curiosity motives are the only variables involved in producing gains in IQ. The Ss in this study are all average or above in IQ and there is not adequate sampling of children with lower IQ levels. One would not expect Ss with low IQs or language handicaps to suddenly show an interest in reading despite achievement needs or intellectual curiosity.

The child who spends increased time reading because of a heightened interest in natural processes must have already learned the basic reading skills so that his behavior is not a difficult or unlikely choice for him.

Similarly, needs for achievement and successful competition should only motivate attempts at improvement of intellectual abilities in a social milieu where praise, recognition, and superior status are awarded for such accomplishment. That is, achievement-oriented children from homes in which intellectual activity was praised would probably be more likely to master intellectual skills than achievement-oriented children from homes in which such accomplishment was not rewarded. In a cultural environment where athletic ability, fighting prowess, or success with the opposite sex was highly valued, one might expect the child to choose these behavioral channels to gratify his achievement and competitive needs. The parents in the Fels population are predominantly middle class and tend to place importance on intellectual accomplishment. A large majority of the parents have attended college, and since enrollment in the Fels program is voluntary it might be inferred that only parents who valued knowledge and scientific pursuits would be predisposed to become part of the research population. Thus, the children under study tend to come from homes which value intellectual ability.

Study of the educational attainment of the parents of the *S*s in Groups A and D revealed no significant difference between the groups with respect to the percentage of families in which both parents attended college (57.1 per cent for Group A versus 42.9 per cent for Group D; $P > .30$). Although there is a slight difference favoring the educational level of Group A families, the difference was not dramatic. There may be important differences between Groups A and D with respect to the differential encouragement of intellectual achievement, but measurement of these differences would probably require variables more refined than educational level of the parents. However, even though parental emphasis on intellectual activity may increase the child's desire to improve his cognitive skills, the child's predisposition to adopt or rebel against parental values should selectively influence his motivation to strive for intellectual accomplishment. Thus, the type of relation between parent and child may be an important factor in this process.

Finally, there is the possibility that genetic and/or constitutional variables may play a role in facilitating marked IQ changes. There is considerable data indicating that genetic factors influence IQ level but less evidence relevant to the role of these variables in producing childhood increases in IQ score. For most of the children in our population, IQs tend to level off during the ages 6–10 and most of the marked changes in level occur during the preschool years. However, the exact relationship between genetic variables and IQ change has yet to be determined. The phenomenon of IQ increase during the school years is admittedly complex and it is not implied that the child's motives are the major factor. However, it is suggested that personality needs may influence this process. Perhaps the most accurate generalization is that for middle-class children with average or above IQ levels, strong achievement, competitive, and curiosity needs may facilitate IQ gains by motivating the child to master intellectual skills.

A final implication of these findings is that they add indirect evidence for the usefulness of the Rorschach and TAT as research instruments. Validation of a predicted relationship between TAT achievement imagery and IQ gain increases one's confidence in the hypothesis that TAT plots can serve as an index of achievement-oriented tendencies. The results of the Rorschach analysis suggest that aggressive content may be an index of an individual's aggressive predispositions but not necessarily a measure of his tendency to express direct, physical aggression. Although Sontag, Baker, and Nelson (11), using behavioral observations, rated the boys in Group A as more competitive than those in Group D, there was no difference between these groups with respect to intensity or incidence of direct verbal or physical aggression or destruction of property. We have assumed that competition is a socially approved form of aggressive behavior and the higher incidence of aggressive content for Group A boys was presumed to be a result of their more intense competitive strivings. Some clinicians who use projective tests are too prone to focus on predictive statements about direct, physical aggression when confronted with a protocol containing aggressive content. One is apt to overlook the fact that the individual may have alternative behavioral channels for expression of aggressive motives.

Summary

For a group of 140 boys and girls in the Fels Research population on whom continuous Binet IQ data were available, a distribution of IQ change was obtained by subtracting each *S*'s smoothed IQ at age 6 from his smoothed IQ at age 10. This distribution of differences was divided into quartiles, and the Rorschach and TAT protocols of the upper (maximum increase in IQ) and lower (maximum decrease in IQ) quartiles were analyzed and compared. The results showed that in comparing the *S*s who showed IQ increases with those showing IQ decreases, the former had, on the TAT, significantly more (*a*) achievement imagery on Cards 1 and 17 BM and (*b*) themes of curiosity about nature on Card 14, and significantly fewer themes of passivity on Card 3 BM. For the boys only, more of the *S*s who increased in IQ had anatomy responses and aggressive imagery on the Rorschach. The results were interpreted as indicating that high need achievement, competitive striving, and curiosity about nature are correlated with gains in IQ score because they may facilitate the acquisition of skills that are measured by the intelligence test.

REFERENCES

1. BAKER, C. T., SONTAG, L. W., and NELSON, VIRGINIA L. Specific ability in IQ change. *J. consult, Psychol.,* 1955, *19,* 307–310.
2. BAYLEY, NANCY. Mental growth in young children. *Yearb. Nat. Soc. Stud. Educ.,* 1940, *39,* (II), 11–47.
3. BAYLEY, NANCY. Consistency and variability in the growth in IQ from birth to eighteen years. *J. genet. Psychol.,* 1949, *75,* 165–196.
4. BRADWAY, KATHERINE. IQ constancy on the Revised Stanford-Binet from the preschool to the junior high school level. *J. genet. Psychol.,* 1944, *65,* 197–217.
5. FISHER, R. A. *Statistical methods for research workers.* (5th ed.) Edinburgh: Oliver & Boyd, 1934.
6. HAGGARD, E. A., DAVIS, A., and HAVIGHURST, R. J. Some factors which influence performance of children on intelligence tests. *Amer. Psychol.,* 1948, *3,* 265–266.
7. KLETT, C. J. Performance of high school students on the Edwards Personal Preference Schedule. *J. consult. Psychol.,* 1957, *21,* 68–72.
8. MCCLELLAND, D. C., ATKINSON, J. W., CLARK, R. A., and LOWELL, E. L. *The achievement motive.* New York: Appleton-Century-Crofts, 1953.
9. RICHARDS, T. W. Mental test performance as a reflection of the child's current life situation: A methodological study. *Child Develpm.,* 1951, *22,* 221–233.
10. SONTAG, L. W., BAKER, C. T., and NELSON, VIRGINIA L. Personality as a determinant of performance. *Amer. J. Orthopsychiat.,* 1955, *25,* 555–562.
11. SONTAG, L. W., BAKER, C. T., and NELSON, VIRGINIA L. Mental growth and personality development. *Monogr. Soc. Res. Child Develpm.,* in press.
12. WELLMANN, BETH L., and MCCANDLESS, B. R. Factors associated with Binet IQ changes of preschool children. *Psychol. Monogr.,* 1946, *60,* No. 2 (Whole No. 278).

64

The Discovery
and Encouragement
of Exceptional Talent

LEWIS M. TERMAN

The following paper by Lewis M. Terman, a former president of the American Psychological Association, gives a further view of testing in this country. The general framework stresses the importance of discovering and making use of talent— a concern that received a great deal of emphasis in the years immediately following Sputnik. Terman himself devoted most of his life (he died in 1956) to the longitudinal study of the gifted, developing many kinds of tests in the process. The Stanford-Binet Test, the most widely used American form of the Binet-Simon Test, derives its name from the fact that Terman and his colleagues developed it at Stanford University. Together with the two Wechsler Tests (WISC and WAIS), the Stanford-Binet is a mainstay of individual testing of intelligence in the United States.

One of the issues raised by Terman concerns "readiness." Gesell, Piaget, McGraw, and other "maturationists" have all influenced educational thinking about the problem of "readiness" to learn. We would like to stress further an incidental point made by Terman, that it is important not to make the child wait until long after he is ready. Although not explicitly addressed to the topic, the paper by Terman helps to point out the inadequacy of chronological age as a basis for deciding readiness for education.

The following remarks were made by Professor E. C. Tolman, introducing Professor Terman in the first Walter Van Dyke Bingham lecture at the University of California at Berkeley, March 25, 1954:

Tonight we honor, and give thanks to, the memory of Walter Van Dyke Bingham. As Chairman of this country's first Department of Applied Psychology at the Carnegie Institute of Technology; as one of the two succeeding small groups of expert psychologists who developed the intelligence and classification tests used in the two World Wars; and as one who, in many prominent and key positions both in government and in industry, devoted almost his entire professional activity to the problems of the selection, management, and encouragement of personnel, Walter Bingham nonetheless remained profoundly disturbed at our prodigious waste of talent—at our society's failure to discover and encourage potential leaders.

And so at his death he left a memorandum desiring that money from his estate be used to support a series of annual lectures on "The Discovery and Development of Exceptional Abilities and Capacities." These lectures, for which we are grateful, are Walter Bingham's continuing contribution toward a better, a more free, and a more happy society.

The lectures are to be given at different universities and by those individuals who have made significant contributions to the problem of discovering and fostering high ability. This is the first lecture. And it is more than right that Professor Lewis M. Terman should have been chosen as the first lecturer. For Lewis Terman, in his development of the Stanford-Binet test and in his study of the gifted children, has made this country's outstanding research contribution to the problem of the discovery and understanding of intelligence.

At the close of the lecture, Mrs. Bingham, whom we have the honor of having with us tonight, will present two illuminated scrolls, one to the University of California, selected by a committee of the American Psychological Association as the locale for the first lecture (this scroll will be received by Dean Alva R. Davis in the name of the University); and one to Professor Terman, selected by the same committee as the first lecturer.

I take great professional and personal pleasure in introducing Lewis M. Terman, Professor Emeritus of Psychology, Stanford University, who will speak on "The Discovery and Encouragement of Exceptional Talent."

I am deeply sensible of the honor of being invited by the American Psychological Association, through its special committee, to give the initial lecture in the Walter V. Bingham Lectureship series.

I am especially happy that Chancellor Kerr and the psychology department of the University of

Lewis M. Terman, "The discovery and encouragement of exceptional talent," *American Psychologist*, 1954, 9, 221–230. Reprinted by permission.

California graciously acceded to my request that the address be given here, where I have many friends and where so much notable research has been done on the mental, physical, and personality development of children; where such famous experiments have been made on the purposive behavior of rats, both gifted and dull; where authoritarian minds have been so exhaustively probed; and where the recently established Institute of Personality Assessment is engaged in such promising investigations.

Before beginning my lecture I should like to pay tribute to the life work of the late Walter Van Dyke Bingham, at whose request this lectureship was established by Mrs. Bingham. Born in Iowa in 1880, young Walter early demonstrated his exceptional gifts by skipping both the third and fourth grades and by graduating from high school at the age of 16. As a freshman in college he was the youngest in his class and the only one to make a straight A record. After graduating from Beloit College he taught in high schools for four years, then entered the graduate school of the University of Chicago and in 1908 won his doctorate in psychology with honors. From 1908 to 1910 he was instructor at Teachers College and assistant to Edward L. Thorndike. In 1910 he was appointed assistant professor at Dartmouth to teach all their classes in psychology, but when he left there five years later the staff included an instructor and two full professors, all selected by Dr. Bingham. His rare ability to recognize exceptional talent is indicated by the fact that both of these professors became college presidents.

From 1915 to 1924 Dr. Bingham was professor of psychology and head of the division of applied psychology at the Carnegie Institute of Technology, and it was here that he found the opportunity he had long wanted to promote large-scale investigations in applied psychology. The faculty he assembled for that purpose was one of the most distinguished ever brought together anywhere in this country. Among them were J. B. Miner, L. L. Thurstone, Walter Dill Scott, Kate Gordon, and E. K. Strong. Three others appointed as consultants were F. L. Wells, G. M. Whipple, and Raymond Dodge. It was this faculty that, under the wise leadership of Dr. Bingham, laid the solid foundation for vocational and industrial psychology in America.

When our country entered the war in 1917, nearly all of the Carnegie group were soon engaged in psychological work either for the Surgeon General or for the War Department or for both. Dr. Bingham was a member of Yerkes' committee of seven that devised the army mental tests, in 1917–18 was a member of the Committee on Classification of Personnel (the committee charged with devising and administering vocational tests in all the army camps), and in 1918–19 was Lt. Colonel in the Personnel Branch of the Army General Staff.

During World War II even greater service was rendered by Dr. Bingham as chief psychologist for the Office of Adjutant General from 1940 to 1946. In this capacity he and his committee were responsible not only for the Army General Classification Test that was administered to the many millions of inductees, but also for advising on the entire program of psychological services in the armed forces. In this capacity too he was in position to influence the selection of men best qualified to head the various branches of military psychology. I have no doubt that the extraordinary success of the work accomplished by psychologists during the war was largely due to his leadership and to his judgment of men.

If time permitted, I should like to tell you about his more than 200 publications, about the great variety of problems they dealt with, and the contributions they made in several fields of psychology, but I am sure that if Dr. Bingham were here he would want me to get on with our scheduled program.

I have often been asked how I happened to become interested in mental tests and gifted children. My first introduction to the scientific problems posed by intellectual differences occurred well over a half-century ago when I was a senior in psychology at Indiana University and was asked to prepare two reports for a seminar, one on mental deficiency and one on genius. Up to that time, despite the fact that I had graduated from a normal college as a Bachelor of Pedagogy and had taught school for five years, I had never so much as heard of a mental test. The reading for those two reports opened up a new world to me, the world of Galton, Binet, and their contemporaries. The following year my MA thesis on leadership among children (10) was based in part on tests used by Binet in his studies of suggestibility.

Then I entered Clark University, where I spent considerable time during the first year in reading on mental tests and precocious children. Child prodigies, I soon learned, were at that time in bad repute because of the prevailing belief that they were usually psychotic or otherwise abnormal and almost sure to burn themselves out quickly or to develop postadolescent stupidity. "Early ripe, early rot" was a slogan frequently encountered. By the time I reached my last graduate year, I decided to find out for myself how precocious children differ from the mentally backward, and accordingly chose as my doctoral dissertation an experimental study of the intellectual processes of fourteen boys, seven of them picked as the brightest and seven as the dullest in a large city school (11). These subjects I put through a great variety of intelligence tests, some of them borrowed from Binet and others, many of them new. The tests were given individually and required a total of 40 or 50 hours for each subject. The experiment contributed little or nothing to science, but it contributed a lot to my future thinking. Besides "selling" me completely on the value of mental tests as a research method, it offered an ideal escape from the kinds of laboratory work which I disliked and in which I was more than ordinarily inept. (Edward Thorndike confessed to me once that *his* lack of mechanical skill was partly responsible for turning *him* to mental tests and to the kinds of experiments on learning that required no apparatus.)

However, it was not until I got to Stanford in 1910 that I was able to pick up with mental tests where I had left off at Clark University. By that time Binet's 1905 and 1908 scales had been published, and the first thing I undertook at Stanford was a tentative revision of his 1908 scale. This, after further revisions, was published in 1916. The standardization of the scale was based on tests of a thousand children whose IQ's ranged from 60 to 145. The contrast in intellectual performance between the dullest and the brightest of a given age so intensified my earlier interest in the gifted that I decided to launch an ambitious study of such children at the earliest opportunity.

My dream was realized in the spring of 1921 when I obtained a generous grant from the Commonwealth Fund of New York City for the purpose of locating a thousand subjects of IQ 140 or higher. More than that number were selected by Stanford-Binet tests from the kindergarten through the eighth grade, and a group mental test given in 95 high schools provided nearly 400 additional subjects. The latter, plus those I had located before 1921, brought the number close to 1,500. The average IQ was approximately 150, and 80 were 170 or higher (13).

The twofold purpose of the project was, first of all, to find what traits characterize children of high IQ, and secondly, to follow them for as many years as possible to see what kind of adults they might become. This meant that it was necessary to select a group representative of high-testing children in general. With the help of four field assistants, we canvassed a school population of nearly a quarter-million in the urban and semiurban areas of California. Two careful checks on the methods used showed that not more than 10 or 12 per cent of the children who could have qualified for the group in the schools canvassed were missed. A sample of

close to 90 per cent insured that whatever traits were typical of these children would be typical of high-testing children in any comparable school population.

Time does not permit me to describe the physical measurements, medical examinations, achievement tests, character and interest tests, or the trait ratings and other supplementary information obtained from parents and teachers. Nor can I here describe the comparative data we obtained for control groups of unselected children. The more important results, however, can be stated briefly: children of IQ 140 or higher are, in general, appreciably superior to unselected children in physique, health, and social adjustment; markedly superior in moral attitudes as measured either by character tests or by trait ratings; and vastly superior in their mastery of school subjects as shown by a three-hour battery of achievement tests. In fact, the typical child of the group had mastered the school subjects to a point about two grades beyond the one in which he was enrolled, some of them three or four grades beyond. Moreover, his ability as evidenced by achievement in the different school subjects is so general as to refute completely the traditional belief that gifted children are usually one-sided. I take some pride in the fact that not one of the major conclusions we drew in the early 1920's regarding the traits that are typical of gifted children has been overthrown in the three decades since then.

Results of thirty years' follow-up of these subjects by field studies in 1927–28, 1939–40, and 1951–52, and by mail follow-up at other dates, show that incidence of mortality, ill health, insanity, and alcoholism is in each case below that for the generality of corresponding age, that the great majority are still well adjusted socially, and that the delinquency rate is but a fraction of what it is in the general population. Two forms of our difficult Concept Mastery Test, devised especially to reach into the stratosphere of adult intelligence, have been administered to all members of the group who could be visited by the field assistants, including some 950 tested in 1939–40 and more than 1,000 in 1951–52. On both tests they scored on the average about as far above the generality of adults as they had scored above the generality of children when we selected them. Moreover, as Dr. Bayley and Mrs. Oden have shown, in the twelve-year interval between the two tests, 90 per cent increased their intellectual stature as measured by this test. "Early ripe, early rot" simply does not hold for these subjects. So far, no one has developed postadolescent stupidity!

As for schooling, close to 90 per cent entered college and 70 per cent graduated. Of those graduating, 30 per cent were awarded honors and about two-thirds remained for graduate work. The educational record would have been still better but for the fact that a majority reached college age during the great depression. In their undergraduate years 40 per cent of the men and 20 per cent of the women earned half or more of their college expenses, and the total of undergraduate and graduate expenses earned amounted to $670,000, not counting stipends from scholarships and fellowships, which amounted to $350,000.

The cooperation of the subjects is indicated by the fact that we have been able to keep track of more than 98 per cent of the original group, thanks to the rapport fostered by the incomparable field and office assistants I have had from the beginning of the study to the present. I dislike to think how differently things could have gone with helpers even a little less competent.

The achievement of the group to midlife is best illustrated by the case histories of the 800 men, since only a minority of the women have gone out for professional careers (15). By 1950, when the men had an average age of 40 years, they had published 67 books (including 46 in the fields of science, arts, and the humanities, and 21 books of fiction). They had published more than 1,400 scientific, technical, and professional articles; over 200 short stories, novelettes, and plays; and 236 miscellaneous articles on a great variety of subjects. They had also authored more than 150 patents. The figures on publications do not include the hundreds of publications by journalists that classify as news stories, editorials, or newspaper columns; nor do they include the hundreds if not thousands of radio and TV scripts.

The 800 men include 78 who have taken PhD degree or its equivalent, 48 with a medical degree, 85 with a law degree, 74 who are teaching or have taught in a four-year college or university, 51 who have done basic research in the physical sciences or engineering, and 104 who are engineers but have done only applied research or none. Of the scientists, 47 are listed in the 1949 edition of *American Men of Science*. Nearly all of these numbers are from 10 to 20 or 30 times as large as would be found for 800 men of corresponding age picked at random in the general population, and are sufficient answer to those who belittle the significance of IQ differences.

The follow-up of these gifted subjects has proved beyond question that tests of "general intelligence," given as early as six, eight, or ten years, tell a great deal about the ability to achieve either presently or 30 years hence. Such tests do not, however, enable us to predict what direction the achievement will take, and least of all do they tell us what personality

factors or what accidents of fortune will affect the fruition of exceptional ability. Granting that both interest patterns and special aptitudes play important roles in the making of a gifted scientist, mathematician, mechanic, artist, poet, or musical composer, I am convinced that to achieve greatly in almost any field, the special talents have to be backed up by a lot of Spearman's g, by which is meant the kind of general intelligence that requires ability to form many sharply defined concepts, to manipulate them, and to perceive subtle relationships between them; in other words, the ability to engage in abstract thinking.

The study by Catharine Cox of the childhood traits of historical geniuses gives additional evidence regarding the role of general intelligence in exceptional achievement. That study was part of our original plan to investigate superior ability by two methods of approach: (*a*) by identifying and following living gifted subjects from childhood onward; and (*b*) by proceeding in the opposite direction and tracing the mature genius back to his childhood promise. With a second grant from the Commonwealth Fund, the latter approach got under way only a year later than the former and resulted in the magnum opus by Cox entitled *The Early Mental Traits of Three Hundred Geniuses* (1). Her subjects represented an unbiased selection from the top 510 in Cattell's objectively compiled list of the 1,000 most eminent men of history. Cox and two able assistants then scanned some 3,000 biographies in search of information that would throw light on the early mental development of these subjects. The information thus obtained filled more than 6,000 typed pages. Next, three psychologists familiar with mental age norms read the documentary evidence on all the subjects and estimated for each the IQ that presumably would be necessary to account for the intellectual behavior recorded for given chronological ages. Average of the three IQ estimates was used as the index of intelligence. In fact two IQ's were estimated for each subject, one based on the evidence to age 17, and the other on evidence to the mid-twenties. The recorded evidence on development to age 17 varied from very little to an amount that yielded about as valid an IQ as a good intelligence test would give. Examples of the latter are Goethe, John Stuart Mill, and Francis Galton. It was the documentary information on Galton, which I summarized and published in 1917 (12), that decided me to prepare plans for the kind of study that was carried out by Cox. The average of estimated IQ's for her 300 geniuses was 155, with many going as high as 175 and several as high as 200. Estimates below 120 occurred only when there was little biographical evidence about the early years.

It is easy to scoff at these post-morten IQ's, but as one of the three psychologists who examined the evidence and made the IQ ratings, I think the author's main conclusion is fully warranted; namely, that "the genius who achieves highest eminence is one whom intelligence tests would have identified as gifted in childhood."

Special attention was given the geniuses who had sometime or other been labeled as backward in childhood, and in every one of these cases the facts clearly contradicted the legend. One of them was Oliver Goldsmith, of whom his childhood teacher is said to have said "Never was so dull a boy." The fact is that little Oliver was writing clever verse at 7 years and at 8 was reading Ovid and Horace. Another was Sir Walter Scott, who at 7 not only read widely in poetry but was using correctly in his written prose such words as "melancholy" and "exotic." Other alleged childhood dullards included a number who disliked the usual diet of Latin and Greek but had a natural talent for science. Among these were the celebrated German chemist Justus von Liebig, the great English anatomist John Hunter, and the naturalist Alexander von Humboldt, whose name is scattered so widely over the maps of the world.

In the cases just cited one notes a tendency for the direction of later achievement to be foreshadowed by the interests and preoccupations of childhood. I have tried to determine how frequently this was true of the 100 subjects in Cox's group whose childhood was best documented. Very marked foreshadowing was noted in the case of more than half of the group, none at all in less than a fourth. Macaulay, for example, began his career as historian at the age of 6 with what he called a "Compendium of Universal History," filling a quire of paper before he lost interest in the project. Ben Franklin before the age of 17 had displayed nearly all the traits that characterized him in middle life: scientific curiosity, religious heterodoxy, wit and buffoonery, political and business shrewdness, and ability to write. At 11 Pascal was so interested in mathematics that his father thought it best to deprive him of books on this subject until he had first mastered Latin and Greek. Pascal secretly proceeded to construct a geometry of his own and covered the ground as far as the 32nd proposition of Euclid. His father then relented. At 14 Leibnitz was writing on logic and philosophy and composing what he called "An Alphabet of Human Thought." He relates that at this age he took a walk one afternoon to consider whether he should accept the "doctrine of substantial forms."

Similar foreshadowing is disclosed by the case histories of my gifted subjects. A recent study of the scientists and nonscientists among our 800 gifted men (15) showed many highly significant differences between the early interests and social attitudes of those who became physical scientists and those who majored in the social sciences, law, or the humanities. Those in medical or biological sciences usually rated on such variables somewhere between the physical scientists and the nonscientists.

What I especially want to emphasize, however, is that both the evidence on early mental development of historical geniuses and that obtained by follow-up of gifted subjects selected in childhood by mental tests point to the conclusion that capacity to achieve far beyond the average can be detected early in life by a well-constructed ability test that is heavily weighted with the g factor. It remains to be seen how much the prediction of future achievement can be made more specific as to field by getting, in addition, measures of ability factors that are largely independent of g. It would seem that a 20-year follow-up of the thousands of school children who have been given Thurstone's test of seven "primary mental abilities" would help to provide the answer. At present the factor analysts don't agree on how many "primary" mental abilities there are, nor exactly on what they are. The experts in this field are divided into two schools. The British school, represented by Thomson, Vernon, and Burt, usually stop with the identification of at most three or four group factors in addition to g, while some representing the American school feed the scores of 40 or 50 kinds of tests into a hopper and manage to extract from them what they believe to be a dozen or fifteen separate factors. Members of the British school are as a rule very skeptical about the realities underlying the minor group factors. There are also American psychologists, highly skilled in psychometrics, who share this skepticism. It is to be hoped that further research will give us more information than we now have about the predictive value of the group factors. Until such information is available, the scores on group factors can contribute little to vocational guidance beyond what a good test of general intelligence will provide.

I have always stressed the importance of *early* discovery of exceptional abilities. Its importance is now highlighted by the facts Harvey Lehman has disclosed in his monumental studies of the relation between age and creative achievement (8). The striking thing about his age curves is how early in life the period of maximum creativity is reached. In nearly all fields of science, the best work is done between ages 25 and 35, and rarely later than 40. The peak productivity for works of lesser merit is usually reached 5 to 10 years later; this is true in some twenty fields of science, in philosophy, in most kinds of musical composition, in art, and in literature of many varieties. The lesson for us from Lehman's statistics is that the youth of high achievement potential should be well trained for his life work before too many of his most creative years have been passed.

This raises the issue of educational acceleration for the gifted. It seems that the schools are more opposed to acceleration now than they were thirty years ago. The lockstep seems to have become more and more the fashion, notwithstanding the fact that practically everyone who has investigated the subject is against it. Of my gifted group, 29 per cent managed to graduate from high school before the age of $16\frac{1}{2}$ years (62 of these before $15\frac{1}{2}$), but I doubt if so many would be allowed to do so now. The other 71 per cent graduated between $16\frac{1}{2}$ and $18\frac{1}{2}$. We have compared the accelerated with the nonaccelerated on numerous case-history variables. The two groups differed very little in childhood IQ, their health records are equally good, and as adults they are equally well adjusted socially. More of the accelerates graduated from college, and on the average nearly a year and a half earlier than the nonaccelerates; they averaged higher in college grades and more often remained for graduate work. Moreover, the accelerates on the average married .7 of a year earlier, have a trifle lower divorce rate, and score just a little higher on a test of marital happiness (14). So far as college records of accelerates and nonaccelerates are concerned, our data closely parallel those obtained by the late Noel Keys (3) at the University of California and those by Pressey (9) and his associates at Ohio State University.

The Ford Fund for the Advancement of Education has awarded annually since 1951 some 400 college scholarships to gifted students who are not over $16\frac{1}{2}$ years old, are a year or even two years short of high school graduation, but show good evidence of ability to do college work. Three quarters of them are between $15\frac{1}{2}$ and $16\frac{1}{2}$ at the time of college entrance. A dozen colleges and universities accept these students and are keeping close track of their success. A summary of their records for the first year shows that they not only get higher grades than their classmates, who average about two years older, but that they are also equally well adjusted socially and participate in as many extracurricular activities (17). The main problem the boys have is in finding girls to date who are not too old for them! Some of them have started a campaign to remedy the situation by urging that more of these scholarships be awarded to girls.

The facts I have given do not mean that all gifted children should be rushed through school just as rapidly as possible. If that were done, a majority with IQ of 140 could graduate from high school before the age of 15. I do believe, however, that such children should be promoted rapidly enough to permit college entrance by the age of 17 at latest, and that a majority would be better off to enter at 16. The exceptionally bright student who is kept with his age group finds little to challenge his intelligence and all too often develops habits of laziness that later wreck his college career. I could give you some choice examples of this in my gifted group. In the case of a college student who is preparing for a profession in science, medicine, law, or any field of advanced scholarship, graduation at 20 instead of the usual 22 means two years added to his professional career; or the two years saved could be used for additional training beyond the doctorate, if that were deemed preferable.

Learned and Wood (7) have shown by objective achievement tests in some 40 Pennsylvania colleges how little correlation there is between the student's knowledge and the number of months or years of his college attendance. They found some beginning sophomores who had acquired more knowledge than some seniors near their graduation. They found similarly low correlations between the number of course units a student had in a given field and the amount he knew in that field. Some with only one year of Latin had learned more than others with three years. And, believe it or not, they even found boys just graduating from high school who had more knowledge of science than some college seniors who had majored in science and were about to begin teaching science in high schools! The sensible thing to do, it seems, would be to quit crediting the individual high school or the individual college and begin crediting the individual student. That, essentially, is what the Ford Fund scholarships are intended to encourage.

Instruments that permit the identification of gifted subjects are available in great variety and at nearly all levels from the primary grades to the graduate schools in universities. My rough guess is that at the present time tests of achievement in the school subjects are being given in this country to children below high school at a rate of perhaps ten or twelve million a year, and to high school students another million or two. In addition, perhaps two million tests of intelligence are given annually in the elementary and high schools. The testing of college students began in a small way only 30 years ago; now almost every college in the country requires applicants for admission to take some kind of aptitude test. This is usually a test of general aptitude, but subject-matter tests and tests of special aptitudes are sometimes given to supplement the tests of general aptitude.

The testing movement has also spread rapidly

in other countries, especially in Britain and the Commonwealth countries. Godfrey Thomson devised what is now called the Moray House test of intelligence in 1921 to aid in selecting the more gifted 11-year-olds in the primary schools for the privilege of free secondary education. This test has been revised and is given annually to about a half million scholarship candidates. The Moray House tests now include tests of English, arithmetic, and history. In 1932 the Scottish Council for Research in Education (18) arranged to give the Moray House test of intelligence (a group test) to all the 90,000 children in Scotland who were born in 1921, and actually tested some 87,000 of them. The Stanford-Binet tests have been translated and adapted for use in nearly all the countries of Europe and in several countries of Asia and Latin America. Behind the Iron Curtain, however, mental tests are now banned.

I have discussed only tests of intelligence and of school achievement. There is time to mention only a few of the many kinds of personality tests that have been developed during the last thirty-five years: personality inventories, projective techniques by the dozen, attitude scales by the hundred, interest tests, tests of psychotic and predelinquent tendencies, tests of leadership, marital aptitude, masculinity-femininity, et cetera. The current output of research on personality tests probably equals or exceeds that on intelligence and achievement tests, and is even more exciting.

Along with the increasing use of tests, and perhaps largely as a result of it, there is a growing interest, both here and abroad, in improving educational methods for the gifted. Acceleration of a year or two or three, however desirable, is but a fraction of what is needed to keep the gifted child or youth working at his intellectual best. The method most often advocated is curriculum enrichment for the gifted without segregating them from the ordinary class. Under ideal conditions enrichment can accomplish much, but in these days of crowded schools, when so many teachers are overworked, underpaid, and inadequately trained, curriculum enrichment for a few gifted in a large mixed class cannot begin to solve the problem. The best survey of thought and action in this field of education is the book entitled *The Gifted Child,* written by many authors and published in 1951 (16). In planning for and sponsoring this book, The American Association for Gifted Children has rendered a great service to education.

But however efficient our tests may be in discovering exceptional talents, and whatever the schools may do to foster those discovered, it is the prevailing *Zeitgeist* that will decide, by the rewards it gives or withholds, what talents will come to flower. In Western Europe of the Middle Ages, the favored talents were those that served the Church by providing its priests, the architects of its cathedrals, and the painters of religious themes. A few centuries later the same countries had a renaissance that included science and literature as well as the arts. Although presumably there are as many potential composers of great music as there ever were, and as many potentially great artists as in the days of Leonardo da Vinci and Michelangelo, I am reliably informed that in this country today it is almost impossible for a composer of *serious* music to earn his living except by teaching, and that the situation is much the same, though somewhat less critical, with respect to artists.

The talents most favored by the current *Zeitgeist* are those that can contribute to science and technology. If intelligence and achievement tests don't discover the potential scientist, there is a good chance that the annual Science Talent Search will, though not until the high school years. Since Westinghouse inaugurated in 1942 this annual search for the high school seniors most likely to become creative scientists, nearly 4,000 boys and girls have been picked for honors by Science Service out of the many thousands who have competed. As a result, "Science Clubs of America" now number 15,000 with a third of a million members—a twenty-fold increase in a dozen years (2). As our need for more and better scientists is real and urgent, one can rejoice at what the talent search and the science clubs are accomplishing. One may regret, however, that the spirit of the times is not equally favorable to the discovery and encouragement of potential poets, prose writers, artists, statesmen, and social leaders.

But in addition to the over-all climates that reflect the *Zeitgeist,* there are localized climates that favor or hinder the encouragement of given talents in particular colleges and universities. I have in mind especially two recent investigations of the differences among colleges in the later achievement of their graduates. One by Knapp and Goodrich (4) dealt with the undergraduate origin of 18,000 scientists who got the bachelor's degree between 1924 and 1934 and were listed in the 1944 edition of *American Men of Science.* The list of 18,000 was composed chiefly of men who had taken a PhD degree, but included a few without a PhD who were starred scientists. The IBM cards for these men were then sorted according to the college from which they obtained the bachelor's degree, and an index of productivity was computed for each college in terms of the proportion of its male graduates who were in the list of 18,000. Some of the results were surprising, not to say sensational. The institutions that were most productive of future scientists between 1924 and 1934 were not the great universities, but the small liberal arts colleges. Reed College topped the list with an index of 132 per thousand male graduates. The California Institute of Technology was second with an index of 70. Kalamazoo College was third with 66, Earlham fourth with 57, and Oberlin fifth with 56. Only a half-dozen of the great universities were in the top fifty with a productivity index of 25 or more.

The second study referred to was by Knapp and Greenbaum (5), who rated educational institutions according to the proportion of their graduate level in the six-year period from 1946 to 1951. Three kinds of awards were considered: a PhD degree, a graduate scholarship or fellowship paying at least $400 a year, or a prize at the graduate level won in open competition. The roster of awardees they compiled included 7,000 students who had graduated from 377 colleges and universities. This study differs from the former in three respects: (a) it deals with recent graduates, who had not had time to become distinguished but who could be regarded as good bets for the future; (b) these good bets were classified according to whether the major field was science, social science, or the humanities; and (c) data were obtained for both sexes, though what I shall report here relates only to men. In this study the great universities make a better showing than in the other, but still only a dozen of them are in the top fifty institutions in the production of men who are good bets. In the top ten, the University of Chicago is third, Princeton is eighth, and Harvard is tenth; the other seven in order of rank are Swarthmore 1, Reed 2, Oberlin 4, Haverford 5, California Institute of Technology 6, Carleton 7, and Antioch 9. When the schools were listed separately for production of men who were good bets in science, social science, and the humanities, there were eight that rated in the top twenty on all three lists. These were Swarthmore, Reed, Chicago, Harvard, Oberlin, Antioch, Carleton, and Princeton.

The causes of these differences are not entirely clear. Scores on aptitude tests show that the intelligence of students in a given institution is by no means the sole factor, though it is an important one. Other important factors are the quality of the school's intellectual climate, the proportion of able and inspiring teachers on its faculty, and the amount of conscious effort that is made not only to discover but also to motivate the most highly gifted. The influence of motivation can hardly be exaggerated.

In this address I have twice alluded to the fact that achievement in school is influenced by many things other than the sum total of intellectual abilities. The same is true of success in life. In closing I will tell you briefly about an attempt we made a dozen years ago to identify some of the nonintellectual factors that have influenced life success among the men in my gifted group. Three judges, working independently, examined the records (to 1940) of the 730 men who were then 25 years old or older, and rated each on life success. The criterion of "success" was the extent to which a subject had made use of his superior intellectual ability, little weight being given to earned income. The 150 men rated highest for success and the 150 rated lowest were then compared on some 200 items of information obtained from childhood onward (14). How did the two groups differ?

During the elementary school years, the A's and C's (as we call them) were almost equally successful. The average grades were about the same, and average scores on achievement tests were only a trifle higher for the A's. Early in high school the groups began to draw apart in scholarship, and by the end of high school the slump of the C's was quite marked. The slump could not be blamed on extracurricular activities, for these were almost twice as common among the A's. Nor was much of it due to difference in intelligence. Although the A's tested on the average a little higher than the C's both in 1922 and 1940, the average score made by the C's in 1940 was high enough to permit brilliant college work, in fact was equaled by only 15 per cent of our highly selected Stanford students. Of the A's, 97 per cent entered college and 90 per cent graduated; of the C's, 68 per cent entered but only 37 per cent graduated. Of those who graduated, 52 per cent of the A's but only 14 per cent of the C's graduated with honors. The A's were also more accelerated in school; on the average they were six months younger on completing the eighth grade, 10 months younger at high school graduation, and 15 months younger at graduation from college.

The differences between the educational histories of the A's and C's reflect to some degree the differences in their family backgrounds. Half of the A fathers but only 15 per cent of the C fathers were college graduates, and twice as many of A siblings as of C siblings graduated. The estimated number of books in the A homes was nearly 50 per cent greater than in the C homes. As of 1928, when the average age of the subjects was about 16 years, more than twice as many of the C parents as of A parents had been divorced.

Interesting differences between the groups were found in the childhood data on emotional stability, social adjustments, and various traits of personality. Of the 25 traits on which each child was rated by parent and teacher in 1922 (18 years before the

A and C groups were made up), the only trait on which the C's averaged as high as the A's was general health. The superiority of the A's was especially marked in four volitional traits: prudence, self-confidence, perseverance, and desire to excel. The A's also rated significantly higher in 1922 on leadership, popularity, and sensitiveness to approval or disapproval. By 1940 the difference between the groups in social adjustment and all-round mental stability had greatly increased and showed itself in many ways. By that time four-fifths of the A's had married, but only two-thirds of the C's, and the divorce rate for those who had married was twice as high for the C's as for the A's. Moreover, the A's made better marriages; their wives on the average came from better homes, were better educated, and scored higher on intelligence tests.

But the most spectacular differences between the two groups came from the three sets of ratings, made in 1940, on a dozen personality traits. Each man rated himself on all the traits, was rated on them by his wife if he had a wife, and by a parent if a parent was still living. Although the three sets of ratings were made independently, they agreed unanimously on the four traits in which the A and C groups differed most widely. These were "persistence in the accomplishment of ends," "integration toward goals, as contrasted with drifting," "self-confidence," and "freedom from inferiority feelings." For each trait three critical ratios were computed showing, respectively, the reliability of the A–C differences in average of self-ratings, rating by wives, and ratings by parents. The average of the three critical ratios was 5.5 for perseverance, 5.6 for integration toward goals, 3.7 for self-confidence, and 3.1 for freedom from inferiority feelings. These closely parallel the traits that Cox found to be especially characteristic of the 100 leading geniuses in her group whom she rated on many aspects of personality; their three outstanding traits she defined as "persistence of motive and effort," "confidence in their abilities," and "strength or force of character."

There was one trait on which only the parents of our A and C men were asked to rate them; that trait was designated "common sense." As judged by parents, the A's are again reliably superior, the A–C difference in average rating having a critical ratio of 3.9. We are still wondering what self-ratings by the subjects and ratings of them by their wives on common sense would have shown if we had been impudent enough to ask for them!

Everything considered, there is nothing in which our A and C groups present a greater contrast than in drive to achieve and in all-round mental and social adjustment. Our data do not support the theory of Lange-Eichbaum (6) that great achievement usually stems from emotional tensions that border on the abnormal. In our gifted group, success is associated with stability rather than instability, with absence rather than with presence of disturbing conflicts—in short with well-balanced temperament and with freedom from excessive frustrations. The Lange-Eichbaum theory may explain a Hitler, but hardly a Churchill; the junior senator from Wisconsin, possibly, but not a Jefferson or a Washington.

At any rate, we have seen that intellect and achievement are far from perfectly correlated. To identify the internal and external factors that help or hinder the fruition of exceptional talent, and to measure the extent of their influences, are surely among the major problems of our time. These problems are not new; their existence has been recognized by countless men from Plato to Francis Galton. What is new is the general awareness of them caused by the manpower shortage of scientists, engineers, moral leaders, statesmen, scholars, and teachers that the country must have if it is to survive in a threatened world. These problems are now being investigated on a scale never before approached, and by a new generation of workers in several related fields. Within a couple of decades vastly more should be known than we know today about our resources of potential genius, the environmental circumstances that favor its expression, the emotional compulsions that give it dynamic quality, and the personality distortions that can make it dangerous.

REFERENCES

1. COX, CATHARINE C. *The early mental traits of three hundred geniuses.* Vol. II of *Genetic studies of genius*, Terman, L. M. (Ed.). Stanford: Stanford Univer. Press, 1926.

2. DAVIS, W. Communicating science. *J. atomic Scientists*, 1953, 337–340.

3. KEYS, N. The underage student in high school and college. *Univer. Calif. Publ. Educ.*, 1938, *7*, 145–272.

4. KNAPP, R. H., and GOODRICH, H. B. *Origins of American scientists.* Chicago: Univer. of Chicago Press, 1952.

5. KNAPP, R. H., and GREENBAUM, J. J. *The younger American scholar: his collegiate origins.* Chicago: Univer. of Chicago Press, 1953.

6. LANGE-EICHBAUM, W. *The problem of genius.* New York: Macmillan, 1932.

7. LEARNED, W. S., and WOOD, B. D. The student and his knowledge. *Carnegie Found. Adv. Teaching Bull.*, 1938, No. 29.

8. LEHMAN, H. C. *Age and achievement.* Princeton: Princeton Univer. Press, 1953.

9. PRESSEY, S. L. *Educational acceleration: appraisals and basic problems.* Columbus: Ohio State Univer. Press, 1949.

10. TERMAN, L. M. A preliminary study in the psychology and pedagogy of leadership. *Pedag. Sem.,* 1904, *11,* 413–451.

11. TERMAN, L. M. Genius and stupidity: a study of some of the intellectual processes of seven "bright" and seven "dull" boys. *Pedag. Sem.,* 1906, *13,* 307–373.

12. TERMAN, L. M. The intelligence quotient of Francis Galton in childhood. *Amer. J. Psychol.,* 1917, *28,* 209–215.

13. TERMAN, L. M. (Ed.), *et al. Mental and physical traits of a thousand gifted children.* Vol. I of *Genetic studies of genius,* Terman, L. M. (Ed.). Stanford: Stanford Univ. Press, 1925.

14. TERMAN, L. M., and ODEN, M. H. *The gifted child grows up.* Vol. IV of *Genetic studies of genius,* Terman, L. M. (Ed.). Stanford: Stanford Univ. Press, 1947.

15. TERMAN, L. M. Scientists and nonscientists in a group of 800 gifted men. *Psychol. Monogr.,* 1954, *68,* in press.

16. WITTY, P. (Ed.) *The gifted child.* Boston: Heath, 1951.

17. *Bridging the gap between school and college.* New York: The Fund for the Advancement of Education, 1953.

18. *The intelligence of Scottish children.* Scottish Council for Research in Education. London: Univer. of London Press, 1933.

"I think that children are more intelligent and less experienced than most parents realize. I have tried to treat my son as if he were a beloved companion with whom I was traveling in a country where I had been before and he had not."

Frederick Lewis Allen
(quoted in *Reader's Digest,*
February 1959, page 28)

65

Mental Tests and the Creation of Opportunity

Lee J. Cronbach

Lee J. Cronbach, Vida Jacks Professor of Education at Stanford University, is a noted authority on educational and psychological measurement. He has written widely on this topic (e.g., with Goldine C. Gleser, Psychological Tests and Personnel Decisions, *second edition, Urbana: University of Illinois Press, 1969) and in the area of educational psychology in general. He and Patrick Suppes co-edited* Research for Tomorrow's Schools: Disciplined Inquiry for Education *(New York: Macmillan, 1969).*

In this article, Cronbach reviews the history of the testing movement and some of the recent efforts in the field. The use of standardized tests, especially those that assess intelligence or scholastic aptitude, has been criticized recently on many grounds. This issue is taken up in Section II's introduction, and in Wayne Holtzman's article in Section XI.

Modern mental testing has a hundred-year history. Francis Galton's *Hereditary Genius,* published in 1869,[1] was the first thrust of the testing movement. Fascinated by the variety of human differences, Galton opened a laboratory in London where he tested all comers for keenness of hearing, strength of squeeze, reaction time, and the sensory

discriminations which he hypothesized to be the roots of intellect. While his studies and those of many later investigators were purely scientific, the investigations were inspired by a social philosophy and gave rise to a chain of social policies.

Galton, like Jefferson, and like Mill and other nineteenth-century reformers, believed in a natural aristocracy of intellect. It was only rational to bring the best talents into the most responsible positions. An aristocracy had to be supplanted by an elite selected on the basis of individual merit, to "defeat"—in Jefferson's words—"the competition of wealth and birth."[2] An open system of *laissez faire* competition could in theory bring to the top the individuals fittest to survive. Educational and vocational opportunity would not be open, however, if judgments of merit were impressionistic, and colored by awareness of the young person's family connections. The objective mental test, the Civil Service examination, and other formal tests came into use as liberal devices, intended to break down the barriers of caste and class so as to bring every talent to fruition.

The high-water mark of the testing movement in the United States and Great Britain came in the period from 1945 to 1960. This was the period when the "11-plus" examination opened or closed the door to the British grammar school, the university, and the professional career. This was the period when American desires to develop scientific "manpower" led to an enormous expansion of testing and guidance, under the National Defense Education Act. Some remarks by George Stoddard reflect clearly the then prevailing view of the social value of testing. The remarks take on added significance from the fact that Stoddard was a liberal, had vehemently attacked the hereditarian view of intelligence, and had been critical of many testing techniques. Nonetheless, challenged to describe any outstanding social contribution that social science had made, Stoddard's first thought was to cite the fruits of testing. "We know [now]," said Stoddard,

that if we conduct a search for the kind of scientific and humane scholarly ability which we seek in high-school and college students, for example, we discover that Jefferson's ideal is sound—we will find such ability in every level of population, and one cannot tell, either, simply by looking at the parents or the success of the parents. . . . I do not see how we could have found good

---

[1] Francis Galton, *Hereditary Genius* (London, 1869).

[2] Thomas Jefferson, in letter to John Adams, October 28, 1813. Lester J. Cappon (ed.), *Adams-Jefferson Letters* (Chapel Hill, N. C., 1959) 2: pp. 387–392.

Lee J. Cronbach, "Mental tests and the creation of opportunity," *Proceedings of the American Philosophical Society, 114,* 1970, 480–487. Reprinted by permission.

airplane pilots without our new and practical knowledge of vocational testing. I do not see how we can carry on good business and industrial enterprises from this time forward without using in guidance and counseling our testing knowledge. . . . [We know from recent large-scale testing that] we probably could have twice as many men and women in college without diluting the mental ability at all. They just are not there now, not because of mental deficiency, but probably because of economic stringency.[3]

Yet it is just because of the thrust toward expanded educational opportunities that Stoddard's enthusiasm, and indeed the optimism of my own title, appear a bit out of tune with the present. Since about 1965, those most vocally concerned with equalizing opportunity have been united in their opposition to tests, and to intelligence tests in particular. In 1969, for example, a motion was put before the College Entrance Examination Board, and seriously debated, whose effect would have been to stop the use of the Scholastic Aptitude Test (SAT) for admission of minority and low-income students. The motion finally passed was milder, but within even this most orthodox body the suspicion of tests was evident. In Japan, the opposition of New Left students has blocked the introduction of tests of the SAT type, thus ironically keeping in force the advantage a youngster wins by going to the prestige schools in earlier years. In England, the Labour Party and its sociologist advisers are intent on bringing educational differentiation to an end. In the last decade or so the elite grammar schools have been open to poor students selected strictly on the basis of tested merit, who then received government tuition grants. The aim was to remove the economic barrier to the best education. In 1970, however, the Labour government was in its last weeks insisting that the tuition grants go to students selected at random from the community, without regard to ability. To generalize: in the countries where testing has been most trusted, it is now much distrusted. In many developing countries, however, in these same recent years, policy makers have turned to testing programs as their one best hope of locating talented persons and distributing limited educational resources fairly.

It is not my intention here to debate specific policy proposals, or even to examine criticisms of common testing practices. The practices and proposals rest on scientific understandings, or misunderstandings. In the past fifteen years the scientific aspects of mental ability have been con-

sidered afresh, and a substantial degree of consensus reached. Sometimes the consensus is a return to principles enunciated by Spearman and Binet at the turn of the century, principles that were lost to view in subsequent practice. Sometimes the consensus is only an agreement that research has been concentrating on the wrong questions, and that major advances in mental testing must wait upon extensive empirical inquiry of a radically new type. This paper attempts to set forth that consensus.

What Mental Tests Measure

The layman is often confused by the connotations of the word "intelligence," thinking that the tests claim to measure some capacity or potential distinct from performance. But the psychologist knows that he is observing and evaluating the person's behavior as he is confronted with certain tasks, at a certain point in his life. The test examines presently developed abilities. Task performance expresses not intellect alone, but the person's whole life-style as it has been shaped by his culture. Anxiety in the presence of an adult examiner of a different social class, readiness to persist in troublesome tasks, willingness to dig systematically into a problem—such aspects of personality are as much a factor in test performance as are strictly intellectual skills. Intellect cannot be tested apart from personality, or from the subject's social response to the examiner; this insight is an old one, present even in the pioneer writings of Alfred Binet.

The insight was lost as testers moved away from Binet's clinical view toward an emphasis on the statistical and objective aspects of tests. Tests are standardized only with respect to what the examiner does. How the subject reacts is not capable of being standardized. He may rise to the challenge with enthusiasm, he may accept it resignedly, or he may escape unwelcome pressure by making minimal, passive, discouraged responses. If the child does not rise to the test in the spirit in which it is given, his score will be depressed. This is likely with the child whose home has not created pride in achievement, and also with the older person who has had trouble in meeting past demands of teachers.

Even with the best of effort, a person with poor schooling will do badly on a test that stresses school material. Originally the testers set out to identify individuals who were more capable in reasoning and judgment than their past school records showed. But over a period of time the tests drifted in their content.

Figure 1 suggests a simple way of looking at mental tests. At one extreme are tasks that call

---
[3] George D. Stoddard, in James B. Conant and others, "Prospects for the Scientific Study of Human Relations," *University of Chicago Round Table*, 1947, No. 510.

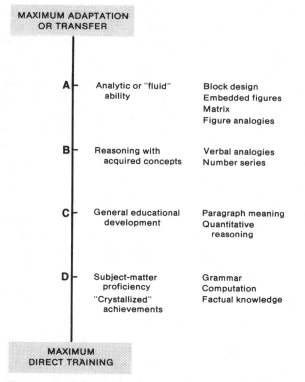

FIGURE 1. *Scheme for distinguishing among ability tests. From L. J. Cronbach,* Essentials of Psychological Testing *(ed. 3, New York, 1970), p. 282. Reproduced by permission of Harper and Row.*

upon "crystallized" abilities—to use the psychologist's current jargon. These tasks demand recall of what one has been taught, or demonstration of a well-rehearsed skill. Although there is a certain tendency for the crystallized abilities to go together, they are not much unified—save as the person with more or better schooling tends to pick up more of them. One can have a fine science vocabulary and a scanty one in the arts; within science, one may know more words from genetics and fewer from astronomy. So tests at the crystallized end of the scale tend to be dragnets, that seine in and weigh up a sample of the person's past learning. Tests at level *D*, and the slightly less routine performances at level *C*, are good predictors of success in school and college and often are good predictors of success in occupational training. Since selectors have been looking for tests that predict, the tests in practical use have been increasingly measures of crystallized, education-loaded performances.

Fluid ability, at the upper end of the scale, is relatively neglected, even though the tasks that measure it are clearly intellectual, and require analysis, judgment, and self-discipline. Let us look at two of the tasks. Figure 2 displays the Embedded Figures task in one of its many versions. The person is directed to locate and mark the

simple figure where it appears somewhere in the complex drawing at the right.

The task is introduced with a few simple examples such as, for example, locating a triangle where it appears in the letter A. Then the subject is asked to solve increasingly difficult problems. In figure 2, each simple figure at the left can be located in the figure to its right. The person must analyze carefully, ignoring the confusion caused by the irrelevant lines of the complex figure, and carefully verifying his proposed answer. The problem at the top is fairly simple, since there is only one reasonable place to look for the solution. (Rotation of the simple figure is not allowed.) The second problem has two acceptable solutions, in which the "box" fits into either the upper or lower three-fifths of the complex rectangular pattern. The third problem requires even more careful discrimination, since simple perception cannot identify the correct combination of lines in the right-hand figure.

For many years this task was thought of as rather specialized, and separate from general intelligence, but there is now a great deal of evidence that people who do well on this do well on other fluid reasoning tasks. Embedded Figures of course has almost nothing to do with school learning, through it does call for a diligence that the culture

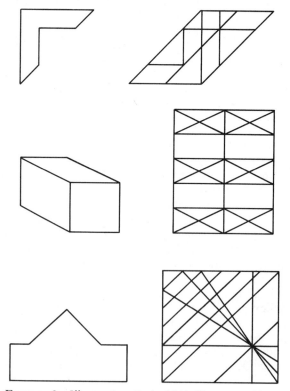

FIGURE 2. *Illustrative Embedded Figure problems From Cronbach, 1970: p. 241. Reproduced by permission of Harper and Row.*

may or may not have instilled. There is also a cultural component in the use of straight lines. In a culture where villages have wandering paths instead of straight streets, and where straight lines are used in art and architecture, the necessary figural perception will not be developed.

There are many measures of fluid ability, all of which pick out much the same persons as high scorers. I shall give only one further example, the matrix (fig. 3).

To select the one of the six choices that completes the pattern within the rectangle is a suitable problem for the six-year-old. The second problem is typical of the usual matrix test; in each rectangle, there is one rule for changing the figures as one moves from left to right, and another rule for change as one moves downward. Applying both rules in conjunction gives choice 2 as the right answer. In the third problem, which is designed to challenge even college graduates, the person must construct the answer instead of selecting among six choices. The solution is identical to the figure in the upper right-hand cell, since the circle in the third column must be of the largest size and the vertical line must be in the lowest possible position. This solution also satisfies the "third row" rule, as the circle touches the upper edge.

Fluid and crystallized tests tend to agree in their assessments, at least of persons from the same culture and educational level. But the agreement is modest. Among the 15 persons out of 100 who score lowest in crystallized ability, only about five will also be in the bottom 15 on fluid ability, and at

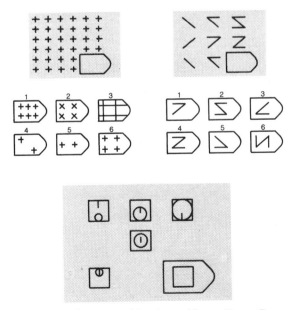

FIGURE 3. *Illustrative Matrix problems. From Cronbach, 1970: p. 270. Reproduced by permission of Harper and Row.*

least five will be at or above average in fluid ability. Of those in the average range on crystallized ability, a healthy number will score very high—or very low—on fluid, analytic ability.

Tasks at level *A* of the scale are unquestionably susceptible to training. Effective strategies for attacking any one of the tasks can be identified and directly taught. Marcia Linn,[4] in a recent study at Stanford, trained fourth-graders to do matrix problems. Just 65 minutes of training raised scores dramatically. The training evidently did not produce a general increase in fluid ability, as the trained children did not, on the average, show improvement on tests other than the matrix. A close look at the data suggests that the training produced changes in style of problem solving that raised the mental-test scores of some children and lowered the scores of others.

A chief question in the study was whether the children who ranked high in matrix performance before training would also rank high after training. It has been suggested by the Russian psychologist Vygotsky[5] that many bright but unsophisticated children will rank considerably higher after they have had a chance to become familiar with the kind of problem the test presents, and that the score after training is a more valid indication of educability. In the Linn study there were considerably larger changes in rank than would be expected from error of measurement alone, though there was still a correlation between pre-test and post-test scores.

Different children learned different things from the training. On the pre-test, as is expected from other research on fluid ability, the various items ranked children in about the same way. After training the items fell into two distinct groups, and many students scored high on just one of the two groups. Thus what was originally a single ranking on mental ability became a double ranking. How the trained children rank depends on the kind of problem presented and the kind of attack to which those particular problems yield. We are not able to evaluate the predictive significance of the post-test scores.

This brings us to the matter of ability to learn. A combination of flimsy data and flimsier methodology led many psychologists, in the years following 1940, to argue that mental tests do not measure ability to learn. The proper conclusion is highly complex, and I shall have to confine myself to the sketchiest of statements. It is true that learning of

[4] Marcia C. Linn, *Effects of a Training Procedure on Matrix Performance and on Transfer Tasks* (Stanford University, 1970).

[5] Lev Semeon Vygotsky, *Thought and Language* (New York, 1962).

discriminations or word strings—straightforward memory tasks—has little relation to tested mental ability.

When there is meaningful material to learn, however, success does usually relate to mental-test scores.[6] If the test includes a measure of vocabulary, and the learning requires study of a text that contains uncommon words, there is a direct tie to account for the relationship. But there is now increasing evidence that the analytic powers measured by tests at levels *A* and *B* of figure 1 (the more fluid tests) do relate to success in learning connected or conceptual materials.[7] The findings are mysteriously inconsistent; if a study employs, say, six learning tasks, the tests are likely to predict success on only four of them. It is clearly unsound to postulate a single "ability to learn." How well a person will learn depends, apparently, on characteristics of the task and on the instructional procedure. There is also a substantial chance element in success on any one of the isolated learning tasks the psychologist usually sets for his subject, which keeps relations weak.

THE QUEST FOR INTERACTIONS

There was an odd shift in thinking about individual differences in the years after *The Origin of Species* was published. In Darwin's view, natural selection operates to favor whatever species or subspecies has characteristics suited to a particular set of conditions. Change the environment, and a different kind of organism is favored. But Spencer spoke of "survival of the fittest," and even Darwin was seduced by the phrase, never noting its non-Darwinian implication that some organisms are fitter than others for *every* environment. The notion of a general adaptive ability or a general in-

telligence, which marked the first century of the testing movement, ignores the fundamental principle that it is the interaction between the traits of the organism and the demands of the environment that makes for survival or elimination.

The intent to identify superior individuals led psychologists to a standard methodology for choosing tests. If a test is to select students, for example, a group of applicants is tested, all of them are admitted, and in due time success is measured, perhaps by a grade-point average. Then a plot relating the scores on the aptitude test to the outcome is made, such as we see in figure 4. In a random sample of applicants, the average achievement would be at the level of the dot in the center of the figure. But when the low scorers are eliminated, the average outcome goes up, as indicated by the arrow. The more severely the applicant group is cut back, the higher the average outcome. Evidence like this is traditionally the basis for concluding that the test is validly selecting a relatively fit group.

This kind of predictive power is relevant when educational places are few and one must be selective. It is irrelevant when one is interested in universal education. The British, with their 11-plus examination, were trying to decide which children should go to grammar school and which to secondary modern. A general ability test ought to predict success in school, but if it predicts equally well in both schools, it is worthless for decision making. Figure 5 shows hypothetical results that might be found under alternative educational treatments. Think of treatment *A* as the grammar school.

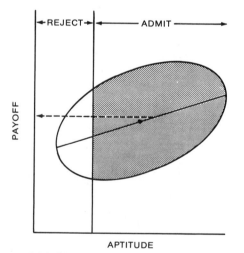

FIGURE 4. *Achievement expected when selection is based on a valid predictor. From Cronbach, "The Two Disciplines of Scientific Psychology,"* Amer. Psychologist *12 (1957): p. 680. Copyright 1967 by the American Psychological Association and reproduced by permission.*

---

[6] The conclusions given here are drawn from a critical summary of research on learning and aptitude-treatment interactions. See Lee J. Cronbach and Richard E. Snow, *Individual Differences in Response to Instruction* (Stanford University, 1969). Obtainable from the ERIC system of the United States Office of Education, under the number ED–029001.

[7] Perhaps the strongest single finding is a correlation of 0.73 between Stanford-Binet scores and the progress made by kindergarten children when instructed in a variety of school tasks (printing one's name, constructing a mosaic of blocks, etc.). Reported by J. A. R. Wilson and Mildred C. Robeck, "A Comparison of the Kindergarten Evaluation of Learning Potential (KELP), Readiness, Mental Maturity, Achievement, and Ratings of First-Grade Teachers," *Educ. Psychol. Measurement* 24 (1964): pp. 409–414. Substantial correlations with learning of military skills such as map reading were found by Taylor and Fox. J. E. Taylor and W. L. Fox, *Differential Approaches to Training* (Alexandria, Virginia, 1967). One of the better studies of laboratory learning is H. W. Stevenson and R. D. Odom, "Interrelationships in Children's Learning," *Child Development* 36 (1965): pp. 7–19.

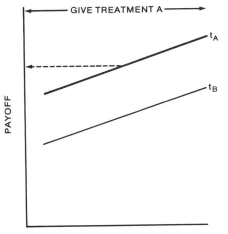

FIGURE 5. *Outcomes when students are assigned to alternative kinds of instruction. Cronbach, 1957: p. 680. Copyright 1957 by the American Psychological Association and reproduced by permission.*

According to the upper line, high scorers on the test do better in that school. The lower line shows a similar relation in the secondary modern school; but it implies that the grammar school accomplishes more than the secondary modern, on the average, for pupils at every ability level. If that is the case, every pupil should be sent to the grammar school. If there are not enough grammar-school places for everyone, the test cannot tell us which pupils will find the grammar school especially advantageous.

One ought to pick out the pupils peculiarly suited to the grammar school, and the ones peculiarly ready to take advantage of the secondary modern program. A test for this purpose would have to have relations like those (again hypothetical) displayed in figure 6. The two prediction functions cross. There is an interaction, in the formal sense of that statistical term. High scorers profit most from one treatment, low scorers from the other. The pupil's success depends on the environment to which he is sent.

We should be seeking out the kind of test that predicts well for one kind of instruction, and that for another kind of instruction predicts badly or gives reverse predictions (i.e., where "low" scores on the test forecast good response to that instruction). Such a concept presses us to invent mutually compatible educational procedures and tests. Research on interaction is a new style in psychology. It integrates the traditional experimental comparison of treatments with the statistical method of checking up on predictions.[8]

Ideally this paper would be climaxed with a

solid demonstration that new tests, linked to correspondingly diverse educational procedures, enhance the proportion of learners who do well in school. The search for interactions is much too new, however, to provide solid results. Nearly ten years elapsed between the first emphasis on interactions in the middle 1950's and the launching of an appreciable number of studies. There were a number of false starts, and most of the hypotheses that seemed promising at the outset were knocked down by the evidence. Where an investigator did succeed in detecting a certain interaction, other investigators generally were unable to substantiate the conclusion. An important reason for such inconsistencies, presumably, was unintentional changes in the instructional procedures from one study to another.

I shall describe just one illustrative study that is representative of the best current efforts. Teacher training at Stanford makes much use of "microteaching," a laboratory arrangement in which the trainee presents a ten-minute lesson to a few pupils. After viewing a videotape of his work, possibly alongside a critic teacher, the trainee then teaches the lesson to another group of pupils. The trainee is encouraged to use certain techniques. In the experiment before us he was taught to pose analytic questions to his class rather than questions whose answers could simply be recalled.[9] This technique

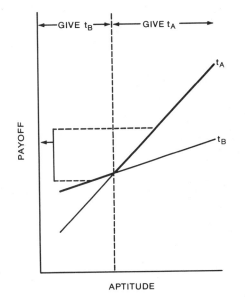

FIGURE 6. *Outcomes when students are assigned to alternative kinds of instruction, interaction present. Cronbach, 1957: p. 680. Copyright 1957 by the American Psychological Association and reproduced by permission.*

---

[8] Lee J. Cronbach, "The Two Disciplines of Scientific Psychology," *Amer. Psychologist* 12 (1957): pp. 671–684.

[9] Mary Lou Koran, *The Effects of Individual Differences on Observational Learning in the Acquisition of a Teaching Skill*

was demonstrated on videotape by a master teacher. It was thought that some trainees would learn well from the video demonstration and that others would do better if given only the typescript of the sound track. Two kinds of test showed up as relevant aptitudes (fig. 7).

One was an Embedded Figures measure of fluid ability. The second was a test in which the subject sees a silent film of a person in action and later answers questions about what he has seen. The effect of training was judged by the extent to which the trainee did ask analytic questions during his third microlesson. The trend of results with the videotape is shown by the plane seen edge-on. This treatment worked well for those with good Film Memory scores. Embedded Figures had little to do with success. The procedure that relied on the typescript was, on the average, less effective than the video treatment. But, on the average,

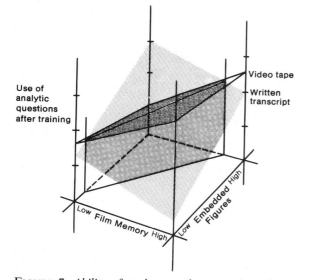

FIGURE 7. *Ability of student teachers to ask analytic questions as a function of aptitude and kind of training. Based on data of Koran, Snow, and McDonald (see footnote 9). This figure from Cronbach, 1970: p. 449. Reproduced by permission of Harper and Row.*

(Stanford University, 1969). See also Mary Lou Koran, Richard E. Snow, and Frederick J. McDonald, "Teacher Aptitude and Observational Learning of a Teaching Skill" (in preparation).

The statistical analysis used in these reports leads perhaps to an incorrect emphasis on the unique predictive power of Embedded Figures. Many intellectual tasks at levels *A, B,* and *C* of figure 1, including the Verbal score of the Graduate Record Examination, had relations similar to that for Embedded Figures, though a bit weaker. The best conclusion is probably that mental abilities such as are usually tested forecast success in learning from the transcript, rather than that Embedded Figures is uniquely relevant. Film Memory, however, does perform uniquely, here and in an earlier study. Richard E. Snow, Joseph Tiffin, and Warren F. Seibert, "Individual Differences and Instructional Film Effects," *Jour. Educ. Psychol. 56* (1965): pp. 315–326.

the transcript was likely to be the better way of teaching for the trainee with high fluid ability. Good film memory was, if anything, slightly disadvantageous. If this interaction is confirmed in further studies, one would recommend using videotape with one kind of student and printed material with students having a different ability pattern. It is not, however, a simple matter of assigning all cases in the rear corner of the aptitude diagram to printed instruction, and all cases forward of the interaction line to learn from videotape. Using videotapes is more expensive, and there is an intermediate region where its small superiority does not offset its greater cost.

This and other findings suggest that students have different ways of reacting to instruction. The typescript requires active imagination and interpretation on the part of the student, and it is not surprising that students with high fluid ability can manage that best. One suspects that the video presentation overloads the mentally active student, giving him too much information to process, and that its pacing interferes with his active efforts. The student who learns well from films may be inclined to soak up impressions passively; whatever the explanation, his superiority on the film test carries over to superior learning from a videotaped model.

The thrust of this kind of research is to explain mental ability as a set of skills in analyzing situations. One kind of response is effective in coping with one kind of instruction; with another kind of instruction, another set of responses works best. If this thinking is ultimately supported by substantial bodies of evidence, we will have confirmed that there are many kinds of ability to learn and will have made strides toward sorting them out.

The fact that the test of fluid ability forecasts success in only some kind of learning then appears as a virtue rather than as a shortcoming. The students high in fluid ability can be taught by a method that calls on that aptitude; very likely, it will be a method that resembles commonplace school procedures. The students low in fluid ability can reach the same level of attainment through some other instructional method. Thus equality of opportunity will mean something other than identity of opportunity.

It is not new to suggest that different students should be taught by different methods. What is new is to offer the possibility of systematic research that will, in time, define clearly identifiable types of students and distinctive educational environments suited to each type. When the school can offer alternative ways to learn, and the tester can route the student into the classroom where he will succeed, testing can properly be credited with the creation of opportunity.

66

Stimulation, Enjoyment, and Originality in Dyadic Creativity

E. PAUL TORRANCE

The final paper in this section is addressed to a topic that has aroused great interest in recent years—creativity. Many tests of creativity have been devised; typically, such tests require that a student (1) produce answers instead of choosing from among a set of suggested answers, and (2) give multiple answers, not just one. For example, a student is asked to list all the ways he can think of to use a brick; this type of item comes from one of the most widely used tests, developed by J. P. Guilford (see his "Three Faces of Intellect," American Psychologist, 14, 469–479). Unfortunately, the correlation among the several tests of creativity is not very high, so that the identification of "creative" children depends strongly on which test you use!

One of the psychologists whose names are most associated with the investigation of creativity is E. Paul Torrance of the University of Georgia, the author of this article.

The history of creative achievement as it has been written is largely the story of individual creativity. There have been of course the rare but well-known instances of dyadic creativity such as that of Wilbur and Orville Wright, Marie and Pierre Curie, Charles and William Mayo, William and Karl Menninger, and Frederick Banting and Charles Best. Less well known was Alexander Graham Bell's Thomas A. Watson; Robert H. Goddard's wife, Esther; Thomas Edison's John Krueski and other collaborators. In behavioral science there have been the well-known husband and wife teams such as Sheldon and Eleanor Glueck, and Lois and Gardner Murphy, Thelma and Edward L. Thurstone, Margaret and Harry Harlow, Anne Roe and George Gaylord Simpson, and others. Also familiar is the expression, "Behind every great man is a great woman." Perhaps the underlying dynamic of this truth springs from the dyadic creativity of the husband-wife interaction. Thus, dyadic creativity may be more common and more important than is apparent from the history of creative achievement.

Neither the literature of social psychology and group dynamics nor creativity has anything specific to say about dyadic creativity. One of the few psychologists who have attempted to describe the nature of dyadic creativity is Henry A. Murray (1964). He conceptualizes dyadic creativity as dealing with two interdependent regions of imagination operating as a single system. In the dyadic interaction, both members of the dyad try to translate their imaginations into actual, overt reciprocations and collaborations. Murray (1964) uses the analogy of "two people singing a duet and making up the music as they go along [p. 639]." He attempts to formulate the concept of dyadic creativity in terms of different kinds of zestful and capable transmissions resulting in appreciative receptions. In this formulation, the member of the dyad who acts as the transmittor in one instance may function as the receptor in another.

The present investigation arose from the author's research in the broader area of group dynamics and creative functioning and his interest in classroom procedures that facilitate creative functioning. In a study with 5-year-old children he (Torrance, 1969) had found a greater willingness to undertake difficult tasks in dyads than in individual and large group conditions. In a pilot study with both 5-year-old children and college students he (Torrance, 1970) had found that a higher level of originality is attained on creative thinking tests by both members of a dyad than by individuals working alone. The investigation reported herein represents an attempt to explore further the dynamics of dyadic creativity with particular emphasis on the feelings of members of dyads about their own stimulation, enjoyment, and originality. It was hypothesized that individuals taking a test of creative thinking in dyads would attain a higher level of creativity and experience stronger feelings of stimulation, enjoyment, and originality of expression than individuals working alone under standard conditions.

METHOD

SUBJECTS

The subjects were 100 juniors and seniors enrolled in three classes of introductory educational psychology at the University of Georgia. They were about equally divided between majors in elementary education and secondary education; 74 were female and 26 were male. The subjects were assigned randomly to the experimental and control conditions.

MEASURES

The Ask-and-Guess Test of the Torrance Tests of Creative Thinking, Form A (Torrance, 1966) was used as the warm-up task and the Product Improvement Test of this same battery was used as the test task. This task calls for the subject to produce ideas for improving a stuffed toy elephant so that it will be more fun for children to play with and requires 10 minutes. Responses are scored according to a standardized scoring guide for fluency, flexibility, and originality. Extensive reliability and validity data are reported in the norms-technical manual.

A set of 10-point rating scales was used in obtaining self-ratings of feelings of stimulation, enjoyment, and originality of expression. To permit chi-square analyses the 10-point scales for stimulation and enjoyment were collapsed to 3-point scales (High, points 1 and 2; Moderate, 3 and 4; Low, 5 and above). The 10-point scale for self-ratings of originality was collapsed to a 4-point scale (Highly Original, points 1 and 2; Fairly Original, points 3 and 4; Not Very Original, points 5 and 6; Unoriginal and Commonplace, 7 and above).

EXPERIMENTAL TREATMENT

The subjects within each of the three classes were assigned to dyads and to standard, individual, or control conditions. The test booklets had been marked in advance to designate specific dyads and were shuffled thoroughly before being drawn by subjects. Members of dyads were instructed to sit side by side and to call out their responses to one another as they wrote them. They were encouraged to hitchhike on one another's responses and permit themselves to be sparked by one another. They were forbidden, however, to copy or repeat one another's responses.

To provide warm-up and practice in working in dyads, the Ask-and-Guess Test was administered. This test consists of three 5-minute tasks: asking questions about a picture, making guesses about the causes of the action depicted in the picture, and making guesses about the consequences of the action depicted. Instructions for the test task were as follows:

> In the middle of this page is a sketch of a stuffed toy elephant of the kind you can buy in most dime stores for about one to two dollars. It is about six inches tall and weighs about a half pound. In the spaces on this page and the next one, list the cleverest, most interesting and unusual ways you can think of for changing this toy elephant so that children will have more fun playing with it. Do not worry about how much the change would cost. Think only about what would make it more fun to play with as a toy.

The rating scales were administered immediately after the subjects completed the test task.

Data were obtained for 100 subjects on the test task but the rating scales of two of the experimental and two of the control subjects could not be used.

RESULTS

The means, standard deviations, and F ratios for the scores on fluency, flexibility, and originality on the Product Improvement Test under dyadic and standard, individual, or control conditions are reported in Table 1. These data indicate that the experimental treatment had a very strong effect on the creative functioning of the subjects in this study as measured by the fluency, flexibility, and originality scores of the Product Improvement Test. The results for flexibility and originality are especially strong.

Table 2 presents the data to permit a comparison of the self-ratings of the experimental and control subjects on feelings of stimulation and enjoyment

TABLE 1

MEANS, STANDARD DEVIATIONS, AND F RATIOS FOR SCORES OF FLUENCY, FLEXIBILITY, AND ORIGINALITY ON PRODUCT IMPROVEMENT TEST UNDER DYADIC AND INDIVIDUAL CONDITIONS

| Measure | Dyads | | Individual | | |
	M	SD	M	SD	F
Fluency	23.7	8.75	19.0	6.32	9.38*
Flexibility	10.0	2.63	7.6	2.35	22.27*
Originality	27.1	13.86	18.2	9.13	14.36*

Note.—$n = 50$ for each condition.
* $p < .01$.

TABLE 2

SELF-RATINGS OF FEELINGS OF STIMULATION AND ENJOYMENT ON CREATIVITY TEST TASK IN DYADS AND INDIVIDUAL CONDITION

| Variable | Dyads | | | Individual | | | |
	High	Moderate	Low	High	Moderate	Low	x^2
Stimulation	34	12	2	25	17	6	4.20*
Enjoyment	39	7	2	27	13	8	7.56*

Note.—$n = 50$ for each condition.
* $p < .05$.

on the test task. It will be noted from these data that the subjects in the experimental or dyadic condition expressed greater feelings of stimulation and enjoyment than the subjects in the control or standard administration of the test.

The data on the self-ratings of originality on the test task are reported in Table 3 for the experimental and control subjects. From these data, it is clear that the subjects in dyads sensed in their performance on the test task a stronger feeling of having produced highly original responses than did subjects working alone as under standard testing conditions.

DISCUSSION

The data yielded by the experiment described herein give strong support to the author's hypothesis that individuals taking a test of creative thinking in dyads would attain a higher level of functioning and experience stronger feelings of stimulation, enjoyment, and originality of expression than individuals working alone under standard test conditions. It should be recognized that these results were obtained from college students who have reasonably good skills in communicating with one another. If similar results could be obtained from disadvantaged children and young people and potential school dropouts, the implications for compensatory education for these groups would be quite promising. It is known from a variety of studies that students in these groups are deficient in verbal skills and perform rather poorly on verbal tests of the kind used in this study. Many observers (Riessman, 1962; Taba & Elkins, 1966), however, have noted that disadvantaged children and youth are quite articulate in their peer groups.

TABLE 3

SELF-RATINGS OF ORIGINALITY ON CREATIVITY TEST TASK IN DYADS AND INDIVIDUAL CONDITION

Rating	Dyads	Individual
Highly original	17	3
Fairly original	18	20
Not very original	10	15
Unoriginal, commonplace	3	10

Note.—$n = 50$ for each condition. $x^2 = 14.64$, $p < .001$.

The rationale supported by the findings of this study offers promise as a guide in devising classroom procedures to facilitate a higher level of creative functioning in the classroom. The production of original responses places the thinker in a minority of one and being a minority of one makes a person uncomfortable psychologically and requires courage and considerable ego strength. This makes children and young people in formal classroom situations reluctant to express their original ideas even on paper. Since disadvantaged children and youth, potential school dropouts, and the like are especially lacking in self-esteem and weak in ego strength, they are especially vulnerable to classroom pressures against originality of expression. If dyadic interaction can provide the support and stimulation necessary to reduce the pressures against originality of expression, the use of dyadic arrangements in classrooms might possibly result in a higher level of mental functioning among students, especially among disadvantaged children and young people, potential school dropouts, and others who require such psychological support and stimulation. The data also suggest that greater attention might profitably be given the entire problem of dyadic creativity.

REFERENCES

MURRAY, H. A. Dyadic creations. In W. G. Bennis, E. E. Schein, D. E. Berlew, & F. I. Steele (Eds.) *Interpersonal dynamics.* Homewood, Ill.: Dorsey Press, 1964.

RIESSMAN, F. *The culturally deprived child.* New York: Harper & Row, 1962.

TABA, H., & ELKINS, D. *Teaching strategies for the culturally disadvantaged.* Chicago: Rand McNally, 1966.

TORRANCE, E. P. *Torrance Tests of Creative Thinking: Norms-technical manual.* Princeton, N.J.: Personnel Press, 1966.

TORRANCE, E. P. Peer influences on preschool children's willingness to try difficult tasks. *Journal of Psychology,* 1969, *72,* 189–194.

TORRANCE, E. P. Influence of dyadic interaction on creative functioning. *Psychological Reports,* 1970, *26,* 391–394.

X

MOTIVATIONAL DETERMINANTS AND RESULTANTS

Here we deal with psychological conditions, states, or processes that influence human behavior. In the main, these affect a person's use of his abilities more than the existence of the abilities, a topic that was covered in Section IX; hence, our somewhat oversimplified use of the term "motivational." Examples of the kinds of inner disposition with which the present section deals are need for achievement and level of aspiration.

Another example is intellectual efficiency. Under certain circumstances, functioning is spurred by anxiety and sharpened by perfectionism or conscientiousness, as Grimes and Allinsmith show in their paper. Under other circumstances, however, anxiety proves disorganizing. In the first article in this section, Weisskopf discusses personality tendencies that adversely affect mental performance.

Other personality characteristics discussed in Section X include the positive traits of frustration tolerance (delay of gratification) and generosity. Although the attributes presented in this section are themselves determinants of behavior, they are also the resultants of other determinants—those described in the foregoing parts of this book.

67

Intellectual Malfunctioning and Personality

Edith A. Weisskopf

Here Edith Weisskopf (now Weisskopf-Joelson) describes many ways in which intellectual functioning may be adversely affected by personality factors. The personality factors, in turn, may stem from a variety of determinants. Dr. Weisskopf-Joelson is a professor of psychology at the University of Georgia, after many years at Purdue.

It is one of the traditional tasks of the psychologist to evaluate the intellectual potentialities of individuals. The traditional tool for such evaluation is the intelligence test. At the same time, experience with the use of intelligence tests has shown that this instrument has serious limitations. If, for instance, of two individuals with the same IQ, one behaves considerably more "intelligently" outside the test situation than the other one, it becomes evident that intelligent behavior is affected by factors which may not be measured by traditional intelligence tests.[1] More specifically, these factors are thought to be personality traits, such as persistence, emotional stability, curiosity, etc. However, it would be erroneous to say that these

personality factors affect the degree to which an individual behaves intelligently outside the test situation without ever influencing the scores on intelligence tests. That psychometric performance also may be influenced by personality factors is a tacit assumption made by clinical psychologists (62) and corroborated by various studies which submit the components of intelligence to factorial analysis (3, 9, 61).

Thus, a child with a comparatively high IQ, who functions on a low academic level, may be handicapped by personality factors unfavorable for high academic achievement. In this case, these unfavorable personality factors depress the individual's academic achievement more than they depress his psychometric performance. Stoddard (58) indicates that the nature of the psychometric situation prevents certain personality factors from having an effect on test scores, while the same factors may be of potent influence on intellectual achievement outside the test situation. The ability to concentrate one's effort and interest over a long period of time on a problem, for example, is a factor which may have little effect on psychometric performances, since each problem in such performances requires only a very short amount of time. On the other hand, the ability to make a persistent effort may be an important factor affecting intellectual achievement outside the test situation. In other cases, nonintellective factors may depress test scores as much as they depress performance outside the test situation. For example, this is the case with certain individuals who are described as being pseudofeebleminded. The test scores of such individuals fall within the feebleminded range. Their behavior outside the test situation is in agreement with the test scores, i.e., on a defective level. Yet, there may be indicators in these individuals' performance on tests and projective techniques as well as in their present and past behavior outside test situations which make the clinician suspect that nonintellective personality factors rather than low intellectual ability are responsible for the defective behavior. Such suspicion is, of course, of great practical importance to the clinician, since unfavorable personality traits may yield to therapeutic effort. Thus, in studying nonintellective factors inhibiting intellectual functioning, the psychologist should not limit himself to cases where he finds a discrepancy between psychometric score and performance outside the test situation.

It will be noted that no attempt has been made, thus far, to draw, by definition, a line of demarcation between intellective and nonintellective fac-

---

[1] The statement that the term "intelligence" as used in the field of intelligence testing has a different meaning from the same term as used in everyday language expresses the same idea in different words.

Edith A. Weisskopf, "Intellectual malfunctioning and personality," *Journal of Abnormal and Social Psychology,* 1951, *46,* 410–423. Reprinted by permission.

tors. Wechsler says "personality traits *enter into* the effectiveness of intelligent behavior and, hence, into any global concept of intelligence itself" (62, p. 82). If this is the case, the question may arise how these personality traits can be distinguished from "intellective" factors. Probably the only way to distinguish the two kinds of factors is by enumeration, not by definition. We speak traditionally of the ability to do arithmetical computation or to grasp spatial relationships as intellective factors, while we do not include curiosity under the same heading. The recognition that intelligent behavior is influenced by every aspect of the personality may induce the psychologist to do away completely with any line of demarcation between intellective and nonintellective factors.

Part of the psychological literature on nonintellective factors affecting intelligence deals with the correlation of personality traits as measured by personality tests with intelligence as measured by intelligence tests (43). This is a perfectly legitimate and fruitful approach. But this approach should not exclude another type of approach, in which the problem of total personality and intelligence is not seen as a correlational investigation between isolated traits but as a causal investigation of the effect of various aspects of the case history of individuals on their intellectual functioning. The intelligence of individuals is studied as affected by parent-child relationship, and by the complicated dynamic interaction of impulses and defense mechanisms, by the vicissitudes of psychosexual development, and the like. It is highly important that we psychologists, the traditional evaluators of intelligence, should give this dynamic approach to the study of intelligence the emphasis it deserves.

It is the purpose of this article to survey some of the dynamic personality factors as this is a survey of case studies of individuals rather than large-scale statistical investigations. The individuals studied are handicapped in intellectual functioning by emotional factors. In some cases psychotherapy has greatly increased their intellectual efficiency. Here, as in so many instances, the study of abnormal personalities serves as a magnifying glass to help us take notice of factors which are present to a lesser degree in the normal personality. The same emotional factors which cause pathological intellectual blocking in some individuals may, by being present in different degrees, become responsible for quantitative and qualitative differences in intelligence within the normal range.

Another fruitful and "magnifying" source for getting acquainted with the influence of personality factors on intelligence are case studies of geniuses, i.e., of individuals with whom such factors play a strongly enhancing rather than a blocking role.

However, such studies are not included in the present paper.

This article is a discussion of some emotional factors which have been identified in the course of intensive study of individuals as possible blocks for the unhampered functioning of cognition. In most cases a combination of these etiological factors, rather than one single factor, is responsible for intellectual blocking.

ETIOLOGICAL FACTORS [2]

LACK OF PARENTAL REWARD

It is well known that the emotional relationship of parents with their children may influence the children's intellectual efficiency. Thus, parental rejection may be a factor which blocks the child in the progress of his intellectual development. There are various possible connections between parental rejection and learning disabilities. The author has pointed out one connection in a previous treatment (63), the main points of which are as follows:

Learning processes of any kind and at any age are connected with frustration of more or less serious degree. The child feels frustrated when he has to learn to drink from a cup instead of a nipple. It is frustrating, too, for him to adjust the functioning of his bowels to the demands and taboos of the society in which he lives. Also, the acquisition of knowledge and skills at school is frustrating to a certain degree. What is it, then, that makes children put up with all the thwarting "do's and dont's" which are impressed on them? It is obvious that children could never be induced to put on the tight corset of cultural demands unless they are given some reward which makes it worth while for them. Maybe the most powerful reward is love and approval, especially when given by the parents or parent substitutes. Thus, if the child develops intellectually, if he learns to master the three R's and to acquire the skill which enables him to perform the little tricks required by psychometric scales, he does it partly in exchange for approval, love, and security.[3] If he does not get this reward because he has no parents or parent substitutes, or because the responsible adults fail to give love and security, he may fail to learn what is expected from him by society and to develop intellectually in the desired direction. This is usually an unconscious

---

[2] The sections in the following discussion are somewhat overlapping.

[3] This statement does not negate heredity as a factor in the determination of intellectual differences. However, this article is concerned with the effect of environmental rather than hereditary factors.

psychological mechanism rather than conscious malingering. Such a child appears dull to the superficial observer. However, he may actually be like a good businessman, who does not deliver the merchandise unless the price has been paid; sometimes it is smart to be dull.

Thus, if we encounter parents who seem to reject their children because they are dull and do not get along at school, we find frequently that the cart has been put before the horse. The children may be rejected because they are dull, but they may be dull because they are rejected.

DESIRE TO PUNISH THE PARENT

In our culture the most potent satisfiers of children's needs, namely the parents, are, at the same time, the most potent frustrators. Such a culture can be expected to create a frequent desire in children to punish their parents. This desire may be present even though the relationship between the parents and children is a "normal" one. It may become strongly enhanced by such maladaptive factors as domination, neglect, etc. Because of societal taboos and the child's dependence on his seemingly powerful, omnipotent parents, the hostile impulses of children against their parents remain frequently unconscious. For the same reason, punishing actions against the parents have often to be undertaken in an indirect, camouflaged manner whereby the connection between the action and its punishing significance may remain entirely unconscious. The refusal to eat, or to defecate regularly, is often an unconscious way of punishing parents, characteristic for the preschool child, but often carried on far beyond the first years of life, and even into adulthood. The refusal to develop intellectually—for example, to progress at school—may have the same unconscious significance (4, 5, 6, 52). The following example illustrates the above.

Shirley, an 18-year-old girl, was referred to the author for psychotherapy because of her inability to meet the academic requirements of a junior college. Her Wechsler-Bellevue IQ was 120. She showed considerable blocking in her social relationships. She was overcome with feelings of despair and anxiety whenever she was in social contact with contemporaries, but she felt perfectly at ease with her parents and their friends. Her academic difficulties at school, however, were probably not a mere outcome of her inability to associate with people of her own age, since she exhibited the same blocking towards academic achievement when taking individual instructions from a tutor. Shirley's mother underwent psychotherapy simultaneously with Shirley. She was a woman who had great difficulties in accepting a feminine role. Her marriage and pregnancy forced her to give up her aim of getting graduate academic training and becoming a lawyer. She unconsciously resented Shirley

for this reason. When Shirley reached school age and proved to have good intellectual endowment, her mother transferred her professional ambitions from herself to her daughter, hoping that Shirley would get a higher education and reach the goal which she herself had to give up. Shirley's father was a pediatrician and very fond of children. He wanted to have another child, a desire which met with strong resistance on the part of the mother. Shirley remained the only child. The father's arguments in favor of having a second child centered especially around the idea that Shirley's development might suffer by her being the only child. The mother tried to pacify her feelings of guilt about the matter by making herself believe that Shirley would associate with many other children and never be lonely on account of her onliness. Thus, the mother had two main ambitions for her daughter. She wanted her to get a higher education, and she wanted her to be a sociable person who is surrounded by and enjoys the company of a large number of contemporaries.

It is remarkable that Shirley blocked in exactly the activities which were most important to her mother, namely, in her association with contemporaries and in her intellectual growth. In the course of Shirley's therapy it became apparent that behind a façade of extreme submission she harboured a tremendous amount of resentment against her mother. The material brought out in the course of her treatment suggested that the two main symptoms of her neurosis were partially determined by her unconscious desire to hit her mother's two most sensitive spots.

Edith Buxbaum (12) cites another case where learning difficulties appear to be a device to punish the parents.

A girl with academic difficulties was constantly admonished by her mother to study. The girl stated that her mother thought she was unable to do her school work without constant nagging. In the course of treatment the therapist advised the mother to stop any kind of interference with the girl's learning process. The mother followed this advice and stopped nagging, whereupon the girl remarked that she would now show her mother how wrong she was to think that her daughter would only progress in school under constant nagging. From then on the girl made good progress. The author comments that the girl was apparently able to make progress, or not to make progress, in order to spite her mother.

DESIRE FOR SELF-PUNISHMENT

Like many other neurotic symptoms, intellectual blocking may be brought about by an unconscious desire for self-punishment and, thus, for atonement of guilt feelings (5). These guilt feelings may stem from some of the sources discussed in this paper, or from other sources. The fact that a very high prestige premium is put on intellectual achievement in certain strata of society facilitates the use of learning disabilities as a self-punishing device.

Individuals whose intellect serves in the function of self-punishment frequently torture themselves through many other devices besides failure; for example, by compulsive pedantry in their intellectual work, through exaggeratedly long studying hours, etc. (7, 34, 38).

DESIRE FOR MASOCHISTIC GRATIFICATION

Intellectual blocking may be unconsciously enjoyed as a masochistic pleasure by the afflicted individual. The desire to obtain such masochistic gratification may be among the etiological factors of pseudostupidity (30, 32, 39). As is well known, this desire may be a factor in the etiology of many other psychological disorders.

DESIRE TO MAINTAIN AN INFANTILE LEVEL OF GRATIFICATION

Intellectual malfunctioning may be a manifestation of a conscious resistance against growing up. Every step which the child undertakes in his development toward maturity brings about the necessity to forego more infantile gratifications. Thus, developmental progress is often accompanied by considerable nostalgia. Growing up means losing the privilege of entertaining sweet, dependent, protected relationships which are based on self-centered receiving rather than on a give-and-take basis. For example, the satisfaction of passive, irresponsible sucking at the mother's breast has to be given up, first for the sake of more active, less convenient cup-and-spoon feeding, which lacks the intimate physical contact with the mother and burdens the child with heavy responsibility, and much later for the strenuous and inconvenient activity of making a living. Intellectual growth, too, means renouncement of the satisfaction of dependent needs. Learning to read may mean to a child not being read to (32); learning to think may mean not being thought for; learning to orient himself in his environment may mean not being guided and protected. The child who is excessively afraid of losing infantile gratifications may block in his intellectual development (39, 44, 51).

Mahler-Schoenberger (44) reports on an 18-year-old boy suffering from pseudoimbecility. His behavior was seriously retarded. He walked with a shuffling gait like an automaton and sat with his arms listlessly hanging at his side. His mother and his siblings felt toward him as towards a small child and treated him accordingly. They exchanged kisses and caresses with him, a form of behavior in which they could not have indulged if the patient were a normal 18-year-old boy. Mahler-Schoen-

berger considers the desire of obtaining such infantile gratification one of the etiological factors of the boy's neurosis.

In this connection it may be interesting to note that clinical workers are frequently concerned as to whether the mentally retarded child will encounter rejection by his parents and whether the parents will show favoritism towards the normal siblings. The opposite danger is discussed less frequently, namely, that the parents, especially the mother, may develop an unduly strong attachment toward the defective child, so that the normal sibling may be at a disadvantage. In many ways mentally retarded children may offer certain libidinal satisfactions to parents which the normal child cannot supply, namely, complete, helpless dependence without the threat of a second childbirth, i.e., of a painful separation from the child at the time of adolescence. Such helplessness may satisfy the parents' need to protect, or to dominate. In a more indirect manner it may also satisfy the parents' dependency needs, since it offers them the possibility of identifying with a completely dependent individual. The parents may, thus, enjoy the care of a feebleminded child directly and vicariously. In this manner, *true* mental retardation may offer certain libidinal satisfactions to the child and to his parents. *Pseudo*retardation, on the other hand, may be caused by the unconscious desire of the child to gain such satisfaction, and unconsciously encouraged through the same desire in the parents.

A graduate student of the author who worked in an institution for the feebleminded remarked jokingly that if he would ever adopt a child, it would have to be a Mongolian imbecile. The remark was, of course, not serious, but humorous in a grim way. However, a genuine emotion may have given rise to his statement, namely, the sweet feeling of attachment which many adults experience towards creatures who are and will forever remain helpless. It is known that Mongolians with their characteristic clinging behavior often become the favorites of institutional staff members.

The previous discussion also throws some light on the problems of children who show intellectual regression, such as deterioration of speech, reading, or other mental skills, at the time of the birth of a younger sibling. At that time the advantages of the infant's way of life and the futility of trying to capture the parents' attention by "academic sophistication" seem especially apparent to the older child. If the child could express his feelings, he would say something like, "Why did I have to go through all the troubles of growing up, when this helpless and stupid baby receives so much affection?"

In this connection it may be enlightening to compare the attitude of adults toward children of very superior intelligence and toward less intelligent children. We often find that superior children are to a lesser degree recipients of adults' protective warmth. Many adults are inclined to handle superior children with objective detachment. Thus, the unconscious desire to avoid such curtailment in warmth and affection may result in intellectual blocking with children of superior ability. Gumpert (27) says about the American woman that "she would rather be loved than respected" (p. 163). The same may be true for some children of superior intellect.

DISPLACEMENT OF ATTITUDES TOWARD ORAL AND ANAL IMPULSES UPON INTELLECTUAL PROCESSES

The well-adjusted infant gets great satisfaction from the intake of food. The mouth seems to be the most important organ of his body. He may develop a variety of attitudes toward oral gratification, depending on the person who feeds him and the manner in which he is fed and weaned. His oral development may proceed unhampered or be subject to various disturbances. For example, he may fail to experience the normal satisfaction of feeding due to the absence of a secure emotional relationship with the mother or due to various other factors. In this case he may refuse the normal amount of food intake. In many instances, drinking and eating may become a tool by the help of which the child rewards or punishes his mother, or food intake may turn into an antidote against anxiety and insecurity. In the latter case the child may eat an excessive amount of food.

Similarly, defecation is an important source of pleasure for the child. During an early period in his life he likes to smell, touch, and smear his bowel movements. He may be as proud of his feces as an adult individual is proud of personal achievement. His mother usually indicates to him that it is a prerequisite for friendly acceptance in the family and society to acquire a somewhat negative attitude toward anal activities and anal products. She also trains him to limit his defecation to specific times and conditions. The well-adjusted child is able to give up his anal freedom without too much frustration in order to please his mother. However, the anal development can also undergo various disturbances. This may occur if the relationship between mother and child is an unfavorable one, so that the child is unable to give up anal pleasures for her sake. If, for example, she tries to enforce toilet training in a hostile, rigid, and nonsympathetic manner, the normal development may be seriously endangered. The child may become overcompliant or rebellious. In the former case he may adjust as far as overt behavior is concerned, but "boil inside" about the environment's impingement upon "his private life." In the latter case he may refuse to conform to anal etiquette and annoy his mother by developing training difficulties. Constipation, for example, is at times a form of protest which enjoys great popularity among toddlers. No wonder, since it fulfills so many purposes at the same time. It is a symbolic expression of the child's unwillingness to give, a method of punishing the mother, a way of getting attention and feelings of power, and a secret device to increase anal stimulation.

Needless to say, the attitudes toward orality and anality which are acquired during early childhood may persist into adulthood (1, 2, 21). The gourmet, the drunkard, the worrier about digestion, the ulcer patient, the chronically constipated individual are examples of continuations of oral or anal conflicts. However, attitudes toward oral or anal matters can also be displaced upon certain other fields. Experience has taught us that displacement is often facilitated by similarity between the person, object, or situation *from* which displacement takes place, and the person, object, or situation *upon* which the individual displaces (49). For example, attitudes toward parents are more often displaced upon older persons in an authoritarian position than upon younger subordinates. Thus, attitudes towards orality and anality are most likely displaced upon activities which possess certain similarities with drinking, eating, and defecating. Intellectual activities show such similarities. Learning is similar to drinking and eating inasmuch as it is an intake and assimilation process. In reading and in listening to lectures, knowledge is taken in and assimilated. Intellectual activity is also a giving-out process, and as such it resembles defecation. Writing, answering the teachers' questions, etc., are examples of this aspect of intellectual work. According to psychoanalytic theory, various disturbances of oral and anal development may thus be displaced upon intellectual activities, and such displacement may result in intellectual disturbances (1, 2, 4, 25, 32, 36, 37, 55, 56, 59). In this manner, the refusal to take food may be transformed into the inability to grasp and assimilate subject matter. Likewise, the tendency to be constipated, when displaced upon intellectual functions, may result in unwillingness or inability to express ideas, for example, to answer questions, to recite in class, etc.[4]

---

[4] According to the psychoanalytic school, speech disturbances may be caused by oral as well as anal displacement. Speaking is performed with the mouth and, thus, invites oral

Moreover, the similarity of intellectual activities to pregenital (oral and anal) sexual activities may make the individual feel guilty about intellectual work, and such guilt may block mental development.[5]

One of Bornstein's (7, p. 393), intellectually blocked patients made the following statement: "I lack milk for my brain, for my thinking" (translated by the present author). The remark may indicate a possible connection between orality and mental retardation in this case.

Chidester and Menninger (15) report on a boy, Henry, who received psychoanalytic treatment at the Southard School from the age of 12 to the age of 15 years. When treatment was begun, his IQ on the 1916 Binet was 65. In the course of therapy the IQ rose to 90. Oral and anal displacement was, according to the author's interpretation, one of the emotional factors responsible for his intellectual malfunctioning. He was especially weak in arithmetic and writing. He would irritate his teachers by his extreme slowness in giving answers. Before he underwent treatment he spoke so slowly that it sometimes took him 15 minutes to complete a sentence. However, he was a good and eager reader. His intellectual pattern was one of taking in without giving out. The same pattern could be observed also in nonacademic situations. His relationship to other children was one of taking without giving. He requested gifts from them, took their possessions, asked questions, but never volunteered any information. He had the habit of collecting old cans and other odd objects, which he never used. Instead, he liked to hoard them in his room and was deeply upset if anybody tried to remove them.

That Henry displaced oral attitudes upon the reading process was suggested by various indications. He was, for example, occasionally punished by being prevented from reading the newspaper. He stated that he then felt "as mad as a hungry bear" (p. 621). At such occasions he would look for discarded food in garbage cans. The interpretation that Henry's resistance against speaking or writing is connected with anal retention gains probability from the fact that he exhibited so many adjustment patterns characteristic of the anal retention phase, such as hoarding. Similarly, he expressed his resistance against his analysis in a passively stubborn, rather than in an actively aggressive, manner. During periods of resistance he refused to groom himself. He also became constipated frequently and remained in the bathroom for hours even though there was a line of children waiting

outside. All these are characteristically anal forms of behavior. One day he made an interesting statement with the purpose of explaining his reluctance to communicate with other people in and outside the school situation. He said he was hesitant to express ideas since that meant giving them away; the more you said, the less you retained for yourself. In his magical thinking he seemed to equate the expression of ideas with the expulsion of matter.

DISPLACEMENT[6] OF INHIBITIONS FROM SPECIFIC, THREATENING ASPECTS OF COGNITION TO INTELLECTUAL ACTIVITY IN GENERAL

Inhibitions caused by guilt feelings. (a) Sexual curiosity. In certain strata of society the attitude of adults towards children's sexual knowledge is, in many ways, diametrically the opposite of their attitude toward other kinds of knowledge. This rather obvious fact becomes especially apparent if we examine the literature on sex education written for parents and teachers of young children. Many authors, for example, make statements to this effect:

A frank way of discussing the facts of life will, they say, stop the child's curiosity and interest in these matters and will put an end to his preoccupation and his questions. Now let us compare this alleged aim of sex education with the aim of any other branch of education. Is there any other field in which the teacher aims at squelching the children's intellectual thirst, at suffocating interest and curiosity, and at stopping further questions? On the contrary, educators measure the success of their teaching not so much according to the amount of knowledge or information they transmit, but according to the interest they create. Questions, stimulated curiosity, attempts to make further investigations are considered criteria of success in teaching. Thus, the aims of sex education appear to be the exact opposite of the aims of education in any other field (26).

It is no wonder that many children develop guilt feelings about their knowledge and curiosity concerning sexual matters. According to psychoanalytic theory, such guilt feelings do not always remain limited to knowledge about sex. Again, displacement upon similar stimuli may take place, i.e., the guilt feelings may spread to intellectual activity in general. Since the guilt is irrational, it usually remains unconscious, but may result in serious blocking of intellectual functioning (6, 52).

---

displacement. On the other hand, it is an expulsion process and, therefore, lends itself to anal displacement.

If the displaced oral and anal disturbances have originated as a response to lack of emotional reward, as protest against growing up, or as a device to punish the parents, then we find an overlapping between the first, second, and fifth sections above and the present section of this paper. However, learning difficulties can arise as an effect of the previously discussed factors without the detour of oral and anal displacement.

[5] For such cases, the present section of this paper overlaps with the section immediately below.

---

[6] In many instances where the term "displacement" is used in this paper, it would be more correct to use the term "displacement or stimulus generalization" since the exact nature of the mechanism cannot be determined. (See Miller [49] regarding the distinction between the two mechanisms.)

The author treated an 11-year-old boy who was making poor progress at school. His school achievement improved considerably after treatment for several months. The main topic of conversation during the counseling sessions was "the facts of life." The boy had very drastic misconceptions about reproduction. His foster parents had never given him any sex information. He had acquired most of his knowledge from an older boy, whom he met secretly, against the wish of his foster parents. He considered the conversations about sex which he carried on with this boy as "bad." The treatment sessions taught him that it was not necessarily bad to talk, to know, or to be curious about sex. This relief of his guilt feelings about a specific type of knowledge may be one of the factors which decreased his blocking against school work.

Sylvester and Kunst (60) report about an interesting fantasy of a boy with a reading disability.

He daydreamed that his father had invented a big machine and had cautioned the boy to stay away from it. It was a dangerous machine which made terrific noises. However, the boy disregarded his father's warning and looked at the machine. As an effect of this disobedience, he was forced to run with closed eyes for many years so that the machine could not catch him. He then pretended in his daydream the *he* was the inventor of the machine, and that he was not permitted to make any further inventions. The fantasy suggests that the boy feels guilty about curiosity, knowledge, and intellectual creativity, and that he believes it is safest to "keep his eyes closed." Since the boy is suffering from a reading disability, guilt may be one of the etiological factors of his difficulty.

Thus, the conventional parental reasoning—that if curiosity about sexual matters is suppressed, children will turn their thinking "to more wholesome and constructive matters"—may be a fallacy. In many cases the results may be the opposite from what the parents expect (see 56).

(*b*) *Aggression and sadism.* The above discussion indicates that intellectual blocking may result from guilt feelings about a specific *kind* of knowledge and subsequent displacement upon intellectual work in general. Similarly, guilt feelings about a specific *aspect* of knowledge may develop and be displaced upon intellectual functioning in general. For example, the aggressive and sadistic aspect of thinking may, thus, become an instigator of learning difficulties (5, 6, 8, 22, 32, 33, 37, 38, 39, 40, 41, 54).

There are various connections between the acquisition of knowledge, and aggression and sadism. One possible connection becomes apparent during preschool age, when the toddler tears apart toys, such as dolls, or living creatures, such as beetles, in order to investigate what is inside. Also the desire to know what is inside the human body

may become associated with the aggressive desire to tear apart and to destroy.

Sylvester and Kunst (60) report about an eight-year-old boy who was placed in a subnormal room at school even though he was of superior intelligence. His behavior during play therapy suggested strong aggression against the mother. He stated that the mother doll did not want to carry her baby since the baby might kick her. Finally the boy tied the baby doll to the mother doll's arm in order to prevent him from kicking. It also became apparent that the boy was filled with strong curiosity as to what was in his mother's body. During his play with dolls, he expressed the desire to tear the mother doll apart in order to see what was inside. Thus, intellectual curiosity and aggression were closely associated in the boy's personality structure. Furthermore, the situation was aggravated by the fact that the mother was seriously sick. The boy's magical thinking made his own aggressive desires responsible for her disease. In this manner, his guilt feelings were greatly increased. Finally, displacement of guilt from the aggressive aspect of "wanting to know" to intellectual functioning in general took place, and the boy developed a serious learning disability.

Aggression and intellectuality may become associated in various other ways. Intellective learning, for example, has a strong competitive aspect in certain strata of society. With some individuals competition may become the main motive for learning. Competition, however, implies aggression. Again, guilt feelings about competitive aggression may be displaced upon learning in general. Guilt feelings about competition are especially likely to arise in a culture where cooperative and competitive ideals are taught simultaneously. While tribes such as the Mundugumor stress competition and tribes such as the Arapesh preach mainly cooperative ideals (48), Western civilization finds itself in between the two contradictory ideals of competition and cooperation. Both attitudes are taught simultaneously. Thus, Western man is quasi forced to go out in the rain without getting wet. Indoctrinated with the ideal of competition, he finds it difficult to cooperate, and his training in cooperation makes him feel guilty about competitive activities.

In addition, some of the words used synonymously with "intelligent" and "stupid" suggest an association between intelligence and aggression in people's thinking, for example, the terms "sharp" and "dull." Similarly, Landauer (35) points out that the German word "albern," meaning stupid, is derived from the obsolete word "alvari," meaning good or friendly.

Since intellectual work is related to a higher degree to the masculine role in our culture than to feminine activity, women often use their intellect as a device to compete aggressively with men. If such competition becomes the major motivating factor of intellectual endeavor, the ensuing guilt may become a serious block to progress.

Especially strong guilt feelings about competitive aggression are likely to arise in the Oedipus situation and in sibling rivalry, since the victims of aggression in these situations are people who should be loved, and not hated, according to the mores of our society. Thus, it is not surprising that the etiology of pseudostupidity is often connected with Oedipal hatred (4, 7) and aggressive competition against siblings (37, 40, 41).

Bornstein (7) reports a case of a $12\frac{1}{2}$-year-old girl with whom Oedipal competition resulted in guilt and intellectual retardation. Learning, for this girl, was partially motivated by the desire to gain the affection of her father and of men in general. She was convinced that her mother and teacher were afraid of her competition for the attention of men and, therefore, did not want her to progress intellectually. The girl interpreted any encouragement she received from her mother or teacher as an insincere, strategic device designed to give her a false belief of achievement in order to prevent her from further striving.

Thus, it seems that intellectual endeavor may become associated with, and work in the service of, various impulses. The fate of intellectuality will then depend upon the fate of these impulses. If the intellect functions "in the service" of aggression, and if the individual feels guilty about aggression and tends to repress it, the servant intellect may share the fate of his master—and intellectual blocking may result.

Inhibitions caused by failure. Serious failure in specific intellectual endeavors may result in inhibition of intellectual functioning in general (32).

A child may be unsuccessful in his first attempts to master academic subject matter, not due to lack of intellectual endowment, but due to more extraneous factors such as a bad teacher, or a visual or auditory defect. The discouraging experience may condition the child in such a manner that he remains intellectually blocked even after all obstacles have been removed, e.g., after he has been placed with a better teacher or after his physical defects have been corrected.

According to psychoanalytic theory, such blocking is especially frequently instigated by children's failures in their investigations about sexual matters. These investigations are especially liable to meet with failure, since most adults tend to increase the obstacles of such endeavors or, at least, not to offer much constructive help. Moreover, his own psychosexual immaturity often prevents the young thinker from finding the truth. Instead, he may lose himself in a maze of contradictory hunches and fantastic sexual theories (8, 18, 23). Such "first failure" may have "a crippling effect forever after" (23, p. 68).

Inhibitions caused by miscellaneous other threats. Guilt about knowing and the threat of failure are not the only factors which can cause negative attitudes toward specific types of cognition. Knowledge may become threatening in many other ways. In such cases also, the individual may avoid a specific piece of knowledge, and the avoidance response may become displaced upon other or all intellective activity.

A ten-year-old boy was referred for psychiatric treatment because of various neurotic disturbances. When his mother was pregnant with his sister, he had denied to himself the coming of the child, even though informational and observational clues should have led him to the correct conclusion. He patterned his behavior to the slogan, "What I don't know doesn't hurt me." Displacement of this response was a partial cause of his reading disability, according to the author's interpretation (60).

Also, Freud's little Hans may have become a victim of "protective stupidity" when he said about his baby sister that "her widdler [penis] is still quite small" (24, p. 155), since the knowledge that girls do not possess penises may be of considerable threat to boys (see 51). In a sarcastic footnote to little Hans's remark, Freud draws a parallel between Hans's error and an erroneous statement made by philosophers:

We can go a step further in vindicating little Hans's honour. As a matter of fact, he behaved no worse than a philosopher of the school of Wundt. In the view of that school, consciousness is the invariable characteristic of what is mental, just as in the view of little Hans a widdler is the indispensable criterion of what is animate. If now the philosopher comes across mental processes, the existence of which has to be inferred, but about which there is not a trace of consciousness to be detected— for the subject, in fact, knows nothing of them, although it is impossible to avoid inferring their existence—then, instead of saying that they are unconscious mental processes, he calls them *semi*-conscious. The widdler is still very small (24, p. 155)!

Just as in Hans's case, the difficulty of the philosopher to accept fully the concept of the unconscious may be a defense against threatening insight. Hermann (28) illustrates a similar kind of blocking, using Semmelweis' great discovery of the causes of childbed fever as an example. Semmelweis was bewildered by his observation that many more women died in a maternity ward attended by physicians than in a ward attended by midwives. Finally he found the explanation: the physicians examined their patients after they had conducted autopsies and, thus, killed them by infecting them. This understanding led to the introduction of prophylactic measures against childbed fever. Semmelweis' colleagues showed considerable resistance against the new discovery. Semmelweis was ignored, ridiculed, and even fired from his position (16). Such resistance may be partly due to the fact that the knowledge of having killed some of their patients, even though inadvertently, was highly threatening to many gynecologists. One of Semmelweis' young collaborators was especially strongly affected by this threat. He had treated a cousin of his some time before the discovery was made. The woman had died from childbed fever. Semmelweis' discovery made it clear to the young doctor that he had killed his own cousin. He committed suicide. One could speculate that the young doctor, even though he was aware of all the necessary premises, could hardly have discovered the cause of childbed fever himself, since the threat of the discovery would have resulted in blocking.

The statement that a stimulus might remain unrecognized because it is threatening may seem a paradox, since it is hard to conceive how an individual could respond to a characteristic of a stimulus, namely its threatening nature, without previous recognition of the stimulus. However, clinical observation of this phenomenon is in agreement with various experimental findings. Postman, Bruner, and McGinnies (53), for example, found that subjects recognize tachistoscopically exposed stimulus words less quickly when these words are connected with areas on which the subject puts little value than when they are connected with highly valued areas. Thus, a scientist may recognize words such as "logical" more quickly than words such as "wealthy." The question arises how this scientist would "know" that the exposed word belonged to an area of low value, and therefore build up defenses against the word before he was able to read it. A similar riddle arises in McGinnies' study (47), where it was found that subjects show significantly stronger GSR's during the *pre*-recognition phase of emotion-evoking words such as "whore" as compared to neutral words such as "apple" (see 11, 46). The protective stupidity of individuals who don't become aware of threatening material, as well as the paradoxical results of these experimental investigations, are covered by Bruner and Postman's statement that "the threshold for affective avoidance response is frequently lower than the threshold for veridical report" (10, p. 27). In other words, subjects respond to "emotional tones" of stimuli before they recognize other characteristics of the stimulus situation.

It is tempting to speculate on the implications of

"protective stupidity" for clinical research. Some clinicians are especially attracted by research topics which are closely connected with their own unresolved personal problems. Thus, stuttering clinicians may become interested in speech defects, etc. Such personal involvement in the area of one's research may become a serious block. As is well known, insight into the etiological factors of his own neurotic disturbances may be threatening to the individual. Therefore, any material contributing to such insight may be repressed. The removal of such repression usually encounters considerable resistance and often requires deep-reaching and time-consuming psychotherapeutic procedures. Consequently, if a scientist engages in research to discover psychological phenomena in other individuals which are closely related to his own repressions, he may encounter considerable difficulties. Like the previously discussed clinical cases, he may become a victim of protective blocking. Much of the pseudo-efficiency and pseudo-exactness of psychological research may be an expression of the unconscious desire to avoid discovery rather than to achieve it, i.e., to seek security in a blind alley and, at the same time, "cheat the ego" into mistaking the blind alley for a road leading to the goal. Some investigations of this kind remind one of the following cartoon:[7] An elderly woman is seen copying a painting in an art gallery. The huge picture shows a nude and luscious nymph courted by a faun; an incidental little bird is seen in the corner of the painting. The copyist, disregarding the essence of the original, copies the bird only, with perfect technique, in an exacting and painstaking manner.

On the other hand, personal involvement in the area of one's research may be a strong incentive and have a constructive effect on the progress of research. This is especially the case when the type of repression discussed in the previous paragraphs is absent or incomplete.

Personal involvement may affect the psychotherapist in a similar manner as the research worker. When a patient discusses conflictive topics which correspond to repressed problem areas in the therapist's personality, the therapist may unconsciously block the patient's progress, e.g., by diverting him to less threatening topics (42).

DESIRE TO POSSESS "A MAGIC CAP OF INVISIBILITY" (44)

When analyzing the previously mentioned 18-year-old pseudoimbecile (44), Mahler-Schoenberger

---

[7] The source of this cartoon could not be identified.

calls the boy's intellectual retardation "a magic cap of invisibility." Thereby she postulates a possible etiological factor of his disturbance. The term "magic cap of invisibility" refers to the "tarnkappe" in the Niebelungen Saga, which made Siegfried invisible and enabled him, thus, to engage in various kinds of socially unacceptable behavior without being discovered. By the help of his cap of invisibility he could witness situations from which he would otherwise be barred, remaining unnoticed by others. Similarly, Mahler-Schoenberger's patient is made "invisible" by his pseudo-imbecility, i.e., invisible as an adult male with normal impulses. This invisibility makes it possible for him to obtain surreptitious gratifications from which normal adults are usually excluded. For example, he is able to satisfy his curiosity about his brothers' sexual life. One brother and his sweetheart, a married woman, engage in heavy necking in the presence of the patient, who is considered too dull to understand. For the same reason, the patient is permitted to enter the bedroom where another brother and his bride are in bed with each other. According to Mahler-Schoenberger, this gain obtained from the retardation is one of the etiological factors responsible for the boy's pseudofeeblemindedness.

More generally speaking, children may gain various satisfactions of their curiosity by wearing the "magic cap of stupidity." They may attempt purposely to appear naive in order to encourage adults in carrying on conversations about tabooed knowledge in their presence. If, instead of conscious suppression of the behavioral manifestations of understanding, repression of actual understanding takes place, "the magic-cap mechanism" becomes an etiological factor of intellectual blocking.

Jones gives a vivid description of children's attempt to appear stupid in order to gain forbidden information:

"When a mother chats with her intimate friend over various private topics, frequently the child will resort to the strangest devices in order to stay in the room and listen to the conversation. Then when someone remarks him, and by her looks insinuates a doubt as to the propriety of conversing in his presence, he will interrupt his innocent crooning over his toys and indulge in exaggeratedly foolish antics, to disarm as it were, the suspicions of the company—by convincing them of his thorough simplemindedness and innocence" (31, p. 484).

By using "the magic-cap mechanism" of pseudo-stupidity, the individual can get away with the expression of other unacceptable impulses besides sexual curiosity, e.g., with the expression of aggression (20, 31, 32, 35). Landauer (35) reports

about two children who showed much interest in the fact that a woman living on the floor above them was expecting a baby. On the day the woman gave birth to the baby, the children broke a window in their own apartment. The mother asked who had done it. She received the reply that the window had been broken by the stork, who had mistakenly tried to enter through the window of their apartment instead of flying into the apartment upstairs. At this reply the mother broke out in laughter. The children were not punished for the breakage.

DESIRE TO AVOID SELF-EVALUATION

Some individuals fail intellectually because they do not make any effort to succeed. Such "lazy" individuals are often extremely ambitious. Their ambition may be so strong that they could not bear to become aware of their limitations. Since they do not make any effort to succeed, they can avoid getting a realistic and possibly disappointing conception of their capacity. Thus their laziness enables them to excuse their failure and to cling to the magical belief that they would be champions if they would care to participate in the contest (6, 17).

DESIRE TO BE THE RECIPIENT OF LOVE RATHER THAN OF ENVY AND AGGRESSION[8]

The desire to succeed and the desire to be liked by one's fellow men are frequently incompatible. Success in climbing the ladder of achievement is often accompanied by loss of love. The successful individual may endanger himself by becoming the target of envy and aggression. Such envy and aggression against a successful person may be attitudes which are actually existing, or they may be projections on the part of the successful individual. In other cases actually existing aggression may be exaggerated in the recipient's perception through the mechanism of projection. Three kinds of projection, as described by Cattell (14), may be at work to produce such distortion. One is projection in the psychoanalytic sense, a mechanism by which individuals attempt to remain unaware of their own ego-alien impulses by ascribing them to the outside world. Thus, especially people who themselves have strongly competitive, aggressive attitudes which they cannot accept, may perceive their fellow men as more aggressive than they actually are. Another type of projection is called by Cattell,

---

[8] This section is, in many ways, closely related to the section, "Desire to Maintain an Infantile Level of Gratification." However, it is believed that the emphasis under these two headings is sufficiently different to justify separate discussion.

"Projection of Press Required by Emotional State" (PRES projection). When this mechanism is at work, the individual may be fully aware of his own attitudes. However, he distorts his perception of the outside world in a way which helps him to justify his own feelings. Thus, Murray (50) found that girls whose anxiety had been aroused experimentally, perceived photographs of faces as being more hostile than they had perceived them before the arousal of anxiety. Similarly, the hostile competitor may justify his uncooperative attitude toward his fellow men by perceiving them as more hostile than they actually are. Or he may expect hostility as a retaliation for his own feelings and, thus, perceive expected rather than actual hostility. Finally, Cattell distinguishes a further type of projection, "Naive Inference from Personal Experience" (NIPE projection). People with limited knowledge about their fellow men may naively assume that all individuals have attitudes similar to their own. This type of projection may also be applicable to the hostile competitor's view of the world around him. He may naively shape his perception of other individuals according to his own image.

Thus, the successful competitor may experience discomfort due to perceived hostility, regardless of whether his perception is realistic or distorted. He may attempt to avoid discomfort by avoiding achievement (29, 54).

A very bright student of the author excelled in class by her stimulating contributions to the discussion, and by the quality of her written work. However, after a few weeks of class work her contributions dropped noticeably in quality and quantity. In conversation with the author she stated that several remarks made by her colleagues were reported to her, indicating that her intellectual superiority made her unpopular with her classmates. Thus, she decided to control her behavior at school in such a way that she would appear less outstanding. We would hesitate to designate this girl as a case of intellectual blocking, because her plan not to excel was conscious, intentional, and reversible through deliberate decision. However, the study of individuals' attitudes toward success in intellectual activities or in any other field indicates that the tendency to "hold back" in order to avoid hostility can lie anywhere on a continuum from complete conscious intention to entirely unconscious blocking. For example, "holding back" may start as a consciously planned maneuver and later develop into an automatic, uncontrollable habit.

Brilliant, well-educated, and sophisticated young women occasionally engage in diplomatic malingerings when associating with men in social situations such as dates. They try to hide their knowledge and sophistication in order not to be threatening to their companion and, thus, to enjoy the pleasures of unambivalent male affection rather than to be frustrated by the ambivalent emotional relationship of competitors and the pseudo-triumph of Pyrrhic victory (32). In other cases, the expectation of loss of gratification may automatically inhibit their intellectual development, without conscious planning or even against conscious planning. Every step which a man undertakes toward vocational success makes him more desirable as a love object, but every step undertaken by a woman in the same direction may make her less desirable as a partner for love and marriage. The conflict between two goals may become an etiological factor for the automatic inhibition of activity directed toward either goal.

The role played by the innocent, unsophisticated fool in myth, fairy tale, and fiction may serve as an illustration of the statement that intellectual blocking may be caused by fear of hostility. The fool in folk literature and other fiction is often an appealing figure, loved by everybody, envied by nobody (35). Since he is at the bottom of the ladder already, nobody can push him down.

Conclusion

The above is a discussion of some connecting bonds between intelligence and total personality. The discussion claims neither completeness nor originality. The emotional factors affecting thought processes covered in this paper have been described by others. However, the treatment of these topics is scattered through the psychiatric and psychological literature and interwoven with various other material. The author considered it a worth-while undertaking to extract pertinent material from various sources in order to present a more systematic discussion of intellect and total personality. Moreover, much of the subject matter surveyed in this paper is, in its original source, expressed in the often highly esoteric language of psychoanalysis, and interwoven with other psychoanalytic material which may be less acceptable to psychologically trained clinicians. In the author's opinion the above presentation discusses important aspects of intelligence, with emphasis on dynamic connections rather than quantitative comparisons. This approach has been relatively neglected by psychological investigators. Yet the objective research training of the academic psychologist is badly needed for the study of these aspects. Most emotional factors affecting intelligence have been ascertained "intuitively" rather than by objective methods. It will require all the ingenuity of psychologists to plan research designs which corroborate or disprove some of the "hunches" discussed in this paper.

REFERENCES

1. ABRAHAM, K. Contributions to the theory of the anal character. In *Selected papers*. London: Hogarth, 1927.

2. ABRAHAM, K. The influence of oral erotism on character formation. In *Selected papers*. London: Hogarth, 1927.

3. ALEXANDER, W. P. Intelligence, concrete and abstract. *Brit. J. Psychol. Monogr. Suppl.*, 1935, *6*, No. 19.

4. BERGLER, E. Zur Problematik der Pseudodebilität. *Int. Z. Psychoanal.*, 1932, *18*, 528–538.

5. BLANCHARD, PHYLLIS. Reading disabilities in relation to difficulties of personality and emotional development. *Ment. Hyg., N. Y.*, 1936, *20*, 384–413.

6. BLANCHARD, PHYLLIS. Psychoanalytic contribution to the problem of reading disabilities. *Psychoanal. Stud. Child.*, 1946, *2*, 163–187.

7. BORNSTEIN, BERTA. Zur. Psychogenese der Pseudodebilität. *Int. Z. Psychoanal.*, 1930, *16*, 378–399.

8. BORNSTEIN, BERTA. Beziehungen zwischen Sexual- und Intellektentwicklung. *Z. psychoanal. Pädag.*, 1930, *4*, 446–454.

9. BROWN, W. M. Character traits as factors in intelligence test performance. *Arch. Psychol., N. Y.*, 1923, *10*, No. 65.

10. BRUNER, J. S., and POSTMAN, L. Perception, cognition, and behavior. *J. Personality*, 1949, *18*, 14–31.

11. BRUNER, J. S., and POSTMAN, L. On the perception of incongruity: A paradigm. *J. Personality*, 1949, *18*, 206–223.

12. BUXBAUM, EDITH. Uber schwierige, insbesondere faule Schuler. *Z. psychoanal. Pädag.*, 1930, *4*, 461–466.

13. CATTELL, R. B. Temperament tests. I. Temperament. *Brit. J. Psychol.*, 1933, *23*, 308–329.

14. CATTELL, R. B. Projection and the design of projective tests of personality. *Character & Pers.*, 1944, *12*, 177–194.

15. CHIDESTER, LEONA, and MENNINGER, K. A. The application of psychoanalytic methods to the study of mental retardation. *Amer. J. Orthopsychiat.*, 1936, *6*, 616–625.

16. DE KRUIF, P. *Men against death*. New York: Harcourt, Brace, 1932.

17. FREUD, ANNA. *The ego and the mechanisms of defence*. London: Hogarth, 1937.

18. FREUD, S. Three contributions to the theory of sex. In *The basic writings of Sigmund Freud*. New York: Modern Library, 1938.

19. FREUD, S. *A general introduction to psychoanalysis*. Garden City, N. Y.: Garden City Pub. Co., 1938.

20. FREUD, S. On the psychopathology of everyday life. In *The basic writings of Sigmund Freud*. New York: Modern Library, 1938.

21. FREUD, S. Character and anal eroticism. In *Collected papers, Vol. II*. London: Hogarth, 1949.

22. FREUD, S. The predisposition to obsessional neurosis. In *Collected papers, Vol. II*. London: Hogarth, 1949.

23. FREUD, S. On the sexual theories of children. In *Collected papers, Vol. II*. London: Hogarth, 1949.

24. FREUD, S. Analysis of a phobia in a five-year-old boy. In *Collected papers, Vol. III*. London: Hogarth, 1949.

25. GLOVER, E. Notes on oral character formation. *Int. J. Psycho-Anal.*, 1925, *6*, 131–154.

26. GRUENBERG, SIDONIE M. *We, the parents*. New York: Harper, 1939.

27. GUMPERT, M. *First papers*. New York: Duell, Sloan and Pearce, 1941.

28. HERMANN, I. Begabtheit und Unbegabtheit. *Z. psychoanal. Pädag.*, 1930, *4*, 408–416.

29. HORNEY, KAREN. *The neurotic personality of our time*. New York: Norton, 1937.

30. JACOBSOHN, EDITH. Lernstörungen beim Schulkind durch masochistische Mechanismen. *Int. Z. Psychoanal.*, 1932, *18*, 242–251.

31. JONES, E. Simulated foolishness in hysteria. *Papers on Psychoanal.* London: Wood, 1913.

32. KLEIN, E. Psychoanalytic aspect of school problems. *Psychoanal. Stud. Child.*, 1949, *4*, 369–390.

33. KLEIN, MELANIE. A contribution to the theory of intellectual inhibition. *Int. J. Psycho-Anal.*, 1931, *12*, 206–218.

34. LAFORGUE, R. Die Mechanismen der Selbstbestrafung und ihr Einfluss auf den Character des Kindes. *Z. psychoanal. Pädag.*, 1930, *4*, 104–114.

35. LANDAUER, K. Zur psychosexuellen Genese der Dummheit. *Z. Sexual Wissenschaft und Sexualpolitik*, 1929, *16*, 12–22.

36. LISS, E. Libidinal fixations as pedagogic determinants. *Amer. J. Orthopsychiat.*, 1935, *5*, 126–131.

37. LISS, E. Emotional and biological factors involved in learning processes. *Amer. J. Orthopsychiat.*, 1937, *7*, 483–488.

38. LISS, E. Learning: Its sadistic and masochistic manifestations. *Amer. J. Orthopsychiat.*, 1940, *10*, 123–128.

39. LISS, E. Learning difficulties. *Amer. J. Orthopsychiat.*, 1941, *11*, 520–523.

40. LISS, E. The failing student. *Amer. J. Orthopsychiat.*, 1941, *11*, 712–717.

41. LISS, E. Examination anxiety. *Amer. J. Orthopsychiat.*, 1944, *14*, 345–348.

42. LORAND, S. *Technique of psychoanalytic therapy.* New York: Int. Univ. Press, 1946.

43. LORGE, I. Intelligence and personality as revealed in questionnaires and inventories. *Yearb. nat. Soc. Stud. Educ.,* 1940, *39,* Pt. I, 275–281.

44. MAHLER-SCHOENBERGER, MARGARET. Pseudoimbecility: A magic cap of invisibility. *Psychoanal. Quart.,* 1942, *11,* 149–164.

45. MCCARTHY, DOROTHEA. Personality and learning. *Amer. Coun. Educ. Stud.,* 1948, Ser. I, No. 35.

46. MCCLEARY, J., and LAZARUS, R. Autonomic discrimination without awareness. An interim report. *J. Personality,* 1949, *18,* 171–179.

47. MCGINNIES, E. Emotionality and perceptual defense. *Psychol. Rev.,* 1949, *56,* 244–251.

48. MEAD, MARGARET (ed.). *Cooperation and competition among primitive peoples.* New York: McGraw-Hill, 1937.

49. MILLER, N. E. Theory and experiment relating psychoanalytic displacement to stimulus response generalization. *J. abnorm. soc. Psychol.,* 1948, *43,* 155–178.

50. MURRAY, H. A. The effect of fear upon estimates of the maliciousness of other personalities. *J. soc. Psychol.,* 1933, *4,* 310–329.

51. OLDEN, CHRISTINE. Headline intelligence. *Psychoanal. Stud. Child.,* 1946, *2,* 263–269.

52. PEARSON, G. H. J., and ENGLISH, O. S. *Common neuroses of children and adults.* New York: Norton, 1937.

53. POSTMAN, L., BRUNER, J. S., and MCGINNIES, E. Personal values as selective factors in perception. *J. abnorm. soc. Psychol.,* 1948, *43,* 148–153.

54. SCHMIDEBERG, MELITTA. Intellektuelle Hemmungen und Aggression. *Z. psychoanal. Pädag.,* 1930, *4,* 467–477.

55. SCHMIDEBERG, MELITTA. Intellectual inhibition and disturbances in eating. *Int. J. Psycho-Anal.,* 1938, *19,* 17–22.

56. SCHMIDT, VERA. Die Entwicklung des Wisstriebes bei einem Kinde. *Imago. Lpz.,* 1930, *16,* 246–289.

57. SPEARMAN, C. *The abilities of man.* New York: Macmillan, 1927.

58. STODDARD, G. D. *The meaning of intelligence.* New York: Macmillan, 1947.

59. STRACHEY, J. Some unconscious factors in reading. *Int. J. Psycho-Anal.,* 1930, *11,* 322–331.

60. SYLVESTER, EMMY, and KUNST, MAY S. Psychodynamic aspects of the reading problem. *Amer. J. Orthopsychiat.,* 1943, *13,* 69–76.

61. WEBB, E. Character and intelligence. *Brit. J. Psychol. Monogr. Suppl.,* 1915, *1,* No. 3.

62. WECHSLER, D. Cognitive, conative, and non-intellective intelligence. *Amer. Psychologist,* 1950, *5,* 78–83.

63. WEISSKOPF, EDITH A. The influence of mental hygiene on intellectual development. *Publ. Welf. Ind.,* 1945, *55,* 8, 19–20.

68

Daydreams and Children's Favorite Books *

LILI E. PELLER

Stages in the Development of the Sense of Reality †

SANDOR FERENCZI

At times, motives that might disrupt concentration find expression in behaviors that are harmless and sometimes even beneficial. In the first paper of this double selection, Lili Peller conveys the idea that enjoyment of literature, one of the more graceful self-indulgences available to man or woman, stems in large part from the need to deal with inner conflicts that are not fully resolved—even in adults. She describes the latent meanings she discerns in the plots of children's books—meanings that account for the satisfaction readers gain from specific types of literature. Prior to her death, Peller was a lay analyst in New York and a member of the faculty of the Philadelphia Association for Psychoanalysis.

Adding a footnote to the discussion of the meanings of children's literature, we quote the conclusion of a classic paper written by one of the pioneers of psychoanalytic theory, the late Sandor Ferenczi.

. . . In recent decades the esteem for writers of children's books has greatly risen, in line with the general tendency to relish a much wider range of productions in all fields of art (for instance, primitive, exotic, psychotic, and frankly amateurish art). In keeping with this trend, a publisher sometimes even brings out a story written and illustrated by a child. Such a book may be very appealing because its author is so genuine, so earnest, so involved in his own writing—but as a story it usually falls flat.

But a child can spin a daydream with such emotional intensity that he will remember it in later years; indeed, he may live his life under its spell. This is especially true when at a time of inner turmoil, he encounters his own, his private daydream woven into a story. Sometimes we discover only in analysis the strong grip that an early story has had on a person's life. Usually it is one scene of the story or one story character which is vested with emotional significance.

"The poet arouses in us emotions of which we hardly believed ourselves capable" (Freud, 1908). If the adult reader cherishes this ability of the poet, the child with his unlimited eagerness to savor life is wide open to the magic of the storyteller.

A fear or anxiety which remains covered up in everyday life may become broadly visible through the child's reaction to a story. But while a tale may frighten a child, it may give relief too. He discovers that he is not the only one in the world who harbors fears or hatred or spite, emotions that are socially unacceptable. Thus the recent well-meant endeavors to purge stories of all cruelties, of all mean feelings and of vengeance may actually increase a child's guilt feelings and the burden he carries unaided. . . .

I am going to discuss a number of typical childhood fantasies and some of the stories built on them. [Not all the story types discussed in the original are included in these excerpts.—EDITOR] Let us start with a plot intended for the very young.

THE FANTASY OF LOSS AND RETURN

A child loses his mother and, after dangerous adventures, is reunited with her. Any number of

[1] Paper presented at the Annual Meeting of the American Psychoanalytic Association in Chicago, May, 1957. A first version had been presented at the Hampstead Child Therapy Clinic, London, 1956.

* Lili Peller, "Daydreams and children's favorite books," *The Psychoanalytic Study of the Child*, 1959, *14*, taken from 414–433. Reprinted by permission of the International Universities Press, Inc., New York

† Excerpt from "Stages in the development of the sense of reality," in Sandor Ferenczi, *Sex in Psychoanalysis* (New York: Basic Books, Inc., 1950), pp. 238–239. Reprinted by permission.

stories use this plot. Because it appeals to the youngest listener, the child in the story is often an animal child. This has the advantage that more gruesome adventures can be included. With an animal as the central figure, the storyteller can introduce the cannibalistic fears and fantasies of young children and thus increase the drama (see, e.g., *The Story about Ping, the Duckling; Peter Rabbit; Curious George, the Monkey*). It is the child who acts out, who runs away, but his leaving is often preceded by some fault or negligence of his mother (or protector) mentioned very casually, and hardly noticed by the reader—the story really gains momentum with the child's escapade.

Let us look at the best known story for very young children, *The Tale of Peter Rabbit*. His mother warns him not to go *near* Mr. McGregor's garden. She has hardly left on her shopping trip when Peter runs right into that forbidden territory. He finds it absolutely full of delicacies, young radishes and tender salad leaves, but Peter's happiness in stuffing himself is very short-lived. He is chased and almost caught and killed. Is it all Peter's fault? It looks this way, yet it never would have happened if his mother had not considered a shopping trip more important than looking after her children.

And so it goes also in the other stories. Curious George would not have ended up in jail had his protector not left him alone on their very first day in the big city where George was surrounded by gadgets tempting him to manipulate them. It is the mother who, by turning her attention temporarily to other matters, loosens the bond between herself and the child (A. Freud, 1953). Even in this simplest type of story there is a conscious plot and another one which reaches consciousness for a brief moment, then sinks back to the preconscious or unconscious. Yet this part contributes to the story's emotional appeal as well as to the motivation and the plausibility of the story hero's conduct. In all art, essential parts remain on the unconscious or preconscious level, and the nursery tale is no exception.

In these stories for very young readers, animals feel, behave, and talk like human beings. But these fantastic elements are not essential; the very same daydream may also be expressed in a cogently realistic story; see e.g., *Oley, the Sea Monster*. Oley is a baby seal that gets picked up and carried away by a sailor while his mother dives for some food. An exciting adventure story follows, with funny and deeply moving events—but nothing that could not have happened in reality. The book even carries a map showing the route through the Great Lakes, the St. Lawrence and around Nova Scotia by which Oley swam back to his mother.

Tales of *fantasy* and realistic "true" stories are considered to be basically different, yet we find that every childhood fantasy can become the backbone for either type of story.

The Fantasy of the Reversal of Roles

The young son (the small one, the simpleton), the shy one who always is left out of things, proves to be stronger than all his older brothers when a great danger arises. Thus he not only slays the dragon and wins the princess, he also rescues his friends or his father's kingdom—in short, he becomes the beloved and admired benefactor. This is the core of many fairy tales, in which it is often the third, the youngest son whom nobody has taken seriously, and who wins after his older brothers have failed.[3] This is the plot of *Hop o' My Thumb*, of John Ruskin's famous *The King of the Golden River*, and also of the Biblical legend of Joseph and his brothers. The contrast of who seems to be strong and powerful and who is small and helpless, and the sudden unexpected reversal of roles provide the spice of these stories. Again there are completely realistic stories with the same plot, for instance the French story *Moustachio*. Moustachio is the smallest dog in his village, indeed, ridiculously small. Yet on the day of the great hunt, he is the one who finds and holds the vicious wild boar at bay until his master comes and fires the deadly shot. The storyteller's skill, his use of relevant details, makes the improbable victory plausible. . . .

Heroic Tale—Oedipal-Level Stories

In these tales the hero obtains the goals of oedipal wishes in a form which is acceptable to the ego of the latency child. What we know of other latency fantasies also applies here: their ingredients are akin to those which in stories, dramas, operas, and ballads appeal to an adult audience. The essentials of these fantasies have been presented by Freud (1908, 1909b), and its juvenile version was studied

---

[3] Why is it usually the *third* son who wins? We may think of the symbolic significance of the number three (Abraham, 1923). However, reasons of plot construction offer another explanation. Were the story to speak of one older and one younger brother, the contest between them would resemble too closely the father-son contest, and thus conjure up the oedipal struggle; on the other hand, the account of deeds of a larger number of brothers might be too lengthy, too repetitious—three is the smallest crowd. Finally, the story of the youngest son who succeeds where his older brothers lost out may be a faint memory of archaic conditions where elder sons were murdered or exiled while the youngest, born when the father's strength was declining, stood a better chance of becoming his heir.

by Friedlaender (1942), whose work remains to be of basic importance.

The hero or the heroine lives with one parent or some relatives. Thus at the outset of the story the parents, or at least the parent of the same sex, have been eliminated without the hero's guilt. The grownups in the story accept the child hero as one of them, not as a child. The story depicts the hero's struggle against adverse circumstances and against the villain or villains. But being fearless, resourceful, and a paradigm of many virtues, his eventual triumph is assured.

Friedlaender mentions the following favorite books which use this fantasy: *David Copperfield, Jane Eyre, Treasure Island, Emil and the Detectives;* Anna Freud (1936) has already pointed to *Little Lord Fauntleroy,* and to various fairy tales. Friedlaender attributes the overwhelming popularity of *Jane Eyre* to the fact that in this story the oedipal wish attains a "relatively undisguised" fulfillment. Here I do not follow her. It is the very art of storytelling that the fulfillment of the primal wish is achieved and at the same time skillfully veiled. Occasionally, it even remains barred from consciousness. There is only one other alternative left to the artist: a hero (or heroine) who attains undisguised gratification goes to his own destruction—like Oedipus. But Jane, after long and tragic trials and tribulations, eventually marries her man, and they live fairly happily ever after. Throughout the story, Jane is a very proper girl. I do not agree that in her story the oedipal fantasies "break through in almost bare-faced fashion." Yet Friedlaender is right in one point: the gratification in *Jane Eyre* seems more direct than, for instance, in *Treasure Island* or *David Copperfield.*

A remark of Freud helps us to understand Jane Eyre's seemingly more overt wish fulfillment. In his story the poet may incorporate the boy's version of the oedipal wish—centering on gratification of aggression and ambition—or the poet may build the story on the feminine counterpart and focus on direct libidinal gratification: a prince charming who leads the heroine home. But it is a difference of focus only—both versions contain or allude to both gratifications, the erotic and the ambitious one....

THE STORIES FOR "HAVE NOTS"

This group may not seem to be a counterpart to the others mentioned so far, but rather a catch-all term for a number of types, namely, for all stories which owe their special appeal less to the tale they spin or to the story characters they bring to life than to the *milieu* they describe. This discrepancy disappears when we extend the meaning of the term "daydream" to indicate not only a narrative, a sequence of events, but also a static *tableau,* the vision of a blissful scene, which includes the daydreamer in his enjoyment of a coveted environment. The readers of these tales are recruited from the ranks of those who pine for an ambient not attainable to them in reality. Here we think of the story describing ways and joys of *teenagers* for those who are still too timid or too young for them; there are the stories of *school life,* i.e., life in a British public school for those who are too young, or, more often, who do not quite belong to the socioeconomic strata who can afford such a school (Orwell, 1939). There are *nature, mystery, adventure, big game* and *Wildwest* stories for those who are barred from these experiences in reality. One generation ago, youthful readers loved historical novels which took them into a romanticized past. Today, stories of space travel have partly replaced them.

Of course, all these stories have also a hero; he has satellites and adversaries; there is a plot, and the story may represent hack-writing or may be well done—in either event a great deal of the attraction is due to the coveted milieu into which the readers are transposed. This is their bait; and this formula is by no means restricted to juveniles but accounts for the popularity of many books, movies, and plays for all ages.

Books may give pleasure through more than one fantasy. Biographies enable the reader to identify with a father image. You have to be famous to rate a biography, and achieving fame can be translated into psychoanalytic concepts as achieving a flamboyant oedipal victory. But a well-written biography does more than this: by reporting personal anecdotes, by letting the reader in on trivial day-by-day incidents, it fosters in him the illusion of hobnobbing with the great and the mighty. This is our reason for mentioning biographies here among the "Have Not" stories. (Receiving factual information may of course be also highly pleasurable, but is outside our topic.)

I suspect that the countless "How-To-Do-It" books, pamphlets and magazines describing hobbies and skills of amateurs are cherished not only by the "doers," to whom they deliver technical information, but also (or mainly?) by the "idlers," for whom they substitute for the doing. Not only an imaginative tale, also a sober step-by-step account can incite and feed daydreams.

I have presented typical daydreams paraphrasing the important emotional constellations of childhood. There is the relationship of the little child to the protective and despotic preoedipal mother. The young child cannot fight her, nor oppose her— the drama is restricted to the possibility of escape and return or rescue. The Loss-and-Return fantasy is really an elaboration of the infant's earliest play activity, the peek-a-boo game. There the plot also consists of separation and reunion.

Several types of daydream mirror the oedipal tension. The Reversal-of-Roles fantasy deals with the relationship to older siblings and to the early father, experienced as fearfully big and strong. The Hero and Heroine fantasies refer more directly to the oedipal constellation. The Bad-Boy stories glorify open defiance of all father images. Actually both the Hero and the Bad-Boy stories tell of oedipal victory, but the bad boy's triumph is quickly attained and short-lived, while the hero attains his goal the slow and arduous way. There are the fantasies of having a twin, an alter ego, or a most faithful companion; and finally the last-mentioned omnibus group which "sells" admission to the coveted but unattainable milieu. Thus daydreams born and fomented by all basic childhood constellations seem covered—but the best group of stories for the young child is still to be discussed.

THE EARLY TALE

I am speaking of such universal favorites as the *Christopher Robin* stories, *The Story of Dr. Dolittle,* the *Mary Poppins* books, and Grahame's *The Wind in the Willows.* In some respect, the books of *Babar, the Elephant* also belong here.

In all groups discussed so far we find books which are little masterpieces and others where the writer has learned the formula and uses it glibly. But in this last group I know of no such hackwriting. These are tales which cannot easily be imitated. If not handled by a literary master, the plot would fall apart, and there would not be left a story worth the telling.

In *Winnie-the-Pooh,* for instance, there is a group of toy animals who for all intents and purposes are alive, although they are at the same time plain stuffed animals. Each one lives in his own house—but all are within easy walking distance from each other. They share adventures and expeditions and all kinds of pleasures and hardships. Winnie-the-Pooh is not their leader, but ranks first in seniority, he is *primus inter pares.* And he is a conceited, greedy, but lovable toy bear. The real leader, the figure who turns up in emergencies, is Christopher Robin, the five-year-old to whom they all belong. Only a few lines of each chapter deal with C.R. in person, but when he is badly needed he is right at hand. The personality of each toy animal emerges clearly and so do the positive, the likeable as well as the weaker qualities of its character.

Now let us take a quick glance at *Dr. Dolittle.* He is an elderly, smallish, shy doctor. The drawings show him pot-bellied, bald, a rather ridiculous figure. His outstanding qualities are his simplicity and kindness. No part of the globe is too distant to travel to when he learns about sick animals in need of his magical cure. His home is in the English country side; originally his sister kept house for him, but she became disgusted and left when the doctor refused to give up the crocodile who ate up the linoleum. As the tale begins, the good doctor lives all alone with his faithful animals, a parrot, a dog, a baby pig, an owl, a duck, and a monkey. These, his household companions, are introduced by name and drawn as individual characters. Besides them are nameless throngs of animals who move in and out of the story.

The central figure of another classic series is *Mary Poppins,* the governess whom the eastwind blows into the home of four children at number Seventeen Cherry Tree Lane. The pictures show her rather unkindly as an old-fashioned, bony spinster with quite shabby yet frilly clothing and accessories. She is at times harsh, moody, often snappy in her commands and answers—but she works magic and enjoys a terrific reputation with various mysterious personages. Her children have wonderful adventures and thus are willing to put up with her occasional bad days.

And, finally, *The Wind in the Willows (The Wind in the Reeds,* as it was originally called) tells the story of four devoted friends, Toad, Rat, Mole and Badger. Each one has his own house and each house is quite different from the others. Rat lives at the bank of the busy river. Toad is rich and keeps residence in a splendid mansion, Badger's ancient and many-chambered home is in the Wild Woods, and Mole has very modest ("compact," his friends call it) quarters underground. Among the friends there is continuous visiting, passing by and dropping in, and staying for hours and days and sumptuous meals. These casual visits alternate with adventures undertaken jointly by two or three of them. The Almighty Protector of this chummy group appears only once. He is the Piper-at-the-Gates-of-Dawn, whose presence is felt long before he is seen, whose sweet chant is heard before he appears as a faun-shaped figure. Yet his animals know that in distress he will be at their side.

The togetherness of these friends, their deep loyalty, fills the books and shows in their cozy visits as well as in their wild and glorious adventures. Their enemies are nameless and faceless flocks of animals. A few incidentally introduced humans stay at the fringe of the narrative and their feelings remain hazy and are not really woven into the story. They appear and disappear as their function in the story requires not growing into story characters.

Here are four obviously very diverse tales. They differ not only in plot, in characters, in style, they also appeal to different age groups and are far apart in their literary levels. What, then, do they have in common? In each story we find a Group of loyal friends and we find a Protector who can work magic (at least in the eyes of his entourage; whatever five-year-old Christopher plans or figures out appears as magic to his toy animals). Every member of this group has unique gifts and skills and foibles. In the animal stories there is usually one of a kind, one of a species, and animals who in reality could never live together, like a badger and a toad, or a pig and a parrot, are intimates. No member of the circle is defined as either young or old, as male or female.[5] The magician-protector's sex is given, but he (or she) is of an age or appearance where genital maleness or femaleness is of little consequence. . . .

The magician-protector stays offstage or near the wings and the friends' actions and their feelings really carry the story. The character of each one of them is etched distinctly, although age and sex are left vague. In these tales *the two great dichotomies, male-female, old-young,* which pervade and shape our life and bring so much pressure upon the ego of the young child, are mostly nonexistent. These stories seem to say: "See what good times and how much adventure you can have if you just forget and ignore those things."

The friends in these stories are devoted to one another, yet their love is conflict-free. There is no jealousy. Let us see what else is absent. Family relations of all kinds are nonexistent or they are at the very fringe of the story, and the feelings of these incidental relatives for one another are lukewarm in comparison with the ardent loyalty and the intimacy welding the friends together. The exception here is a parent's love for its small, helpless baby. Kanga loves Roo, Otter loves Little Portly.

In all the chapters of contented home life or risky adventures nothing happens that would suggest a comparison between what Tom does and what Dick does, or between their appearance. And perhaps as a further assurance against the pressure of comparison, of jealousy and competition, most of them belong to different species. Who will compare a monkey with an owl or a mole with a toad? The members of the closely knit circle are not measured against one another. And more than this: their earlier self is not compared with their later self. They are the same people at the end of the story as they were when we first met them. This, too, is in sharp contrast to the hero of the oedipal tale, who at the close of the story is not only in different circumstances, but is changed, an "improved" person. The good and the sly and bad people he met, the events he went through, joy and sorrow, love and loneliness—have molded him. The endearing characters of Lofting's, of Milne's and of Grahame's tales remain throughout the story

what they were at the very beginning. Each one is as boastful or greedy, or as kind or gullible as we found him when he first entered. This is not because these stories, by and large, appeal to younger children who are but little aware of the passage of time. After all, heroes intended for a very young age group (e.g., Pinocchio or Bambi) grow up and change, and this recasting of their inner self becomes an essential part of the story. But the heroes of the Early Tale are static characters.[6]

The reader of the oedipal story identifies with the hero and with his success, and by doing so he vicariously shares the hero's pressures, The charm of the Early Tale may be due to their complete absence.

Frequently the characters of these stories wear animal masks.[7] These are the masks of animals rather than real animals. Not only do they talk and wear clothes, but besides giving them a few convincing and specific animal features, there is no attempt to present a biologically correct picture of their animal life. Why, then, are these animal masks employed by the writer? A human character who in a story is not defined according to his approximate age remains so vague, so insipid, that he does not win our interest, and a human being whose sex remains undefined arouses anxiety. In the Early Tale the animals are depicted with just enough authentic detail to screen the absence of those features which are usually indispensable for creating a plausible character, i.e., the missing age and sex. *The animal mask supports the mechanism of denial.* The paucity of concrete features gives them a heraldic quality.

In the preoedipal phase the child is almost unaware that there are men and women. The difference he perceives is between him and the adults, the persons who can fulfill his wishes or deny them all. The world is divided into children and grown-ups. In the oedipal phase he is aware of sexual differences but likely to forget that other division which formerly loomed so large, he is cocky enough to consider himself the equal of his parents. I know that I am over-simplifying—yet basically this is correct: from being innocent of one of the great dichotomies (male-female) the child turns to ignore the other one (child-adult). Time and again, however, this dichotomy is sharply brought to his attention. He is only a child and thus can neither

---

[5] Exception: the children in the *Mary Poppins* stories. And the general principle may as well be stated here: I am presenting a story structure which exists in the abstract, yet is violated in one or the other point in each story. In relation to the perfect fantasy each story is like a web torn in a different spot in every instance and thus the pattern, i.e., the basic daydream, can be reconstructed by bringing them side by side and comparing them.

[6] In the discussion in London, 1956, Dr. B. Lantos pointed to their similarity with the inhabitants of the Garden Eden whose serene life flowed along without strife, murder, or sexuality.

[7] The Pogo characters of Walt Kelly, which use the childish form of the comic strip to amuse adults and to bootleg some biting social and political criticism, also are animal masks, also one of a kind and nondescript in their sex and age.

be his mother's partner nor his father's successful competitor. In his happy moments he succeeds in denying that he is small and unequipped for being a lover, but painful experiences bring him brusquely back to reality. That a child envies the grownups has always been known, but Freud pointed to the direct and gross male (or female) aspirations which go with the wish to be big. These fantastic aspirations make the child's happy illusions and his downfalls so intense and potentially traumatic.

At this point I thought I had discovered a new way of looking at the oedipal constellation. But then I happened to scan the last pages of Little Hans's case history and came across the daydreams he produced at the end of his analysis (Freud, 1909b). Hans has two "happiness fantasies" (*"Glücksfantasien"*), which testify to his newly-won ability to cope with the pressures in his life. The plumber comes in one fantasy to screw off his buttocks and his penis and to give him larger ones instead; in the other, Hans has many children and takes them to the toilet, wipes their behind, their "podl," in short, does everything a mother does with her little children.

With these fantasies Hans has regained his former cheerfulness. They provide the gratifications from which reality excludes him because he is only a little boy. With the first fantasy he denies the gulf separating the boy from the grown man, while the second cancels the difference between male and female. The Early Tale employs the opposite technique: the confining and often painful dichotomies are blissfully absent or irrelevant for the story characters.

The Early Tale builds on the defense mechanisms of denial. A quick glance at another story character may clarify what is being done here. *Peter Pan* is a little boy who refuses to grow up—that is, he is well aware of the difference between old and young, but says NO to something he does not like, he *negates* the need to grow up. The Early Tale goes one step further: there nobody heard of such a thing as growing up. The animal friends are a delightful mixture of childishness and grownupness.[8]

At the core of every successful story there is a universal daydream. The tale begins, the curtain rises, the reader identifies with the hero, and enjoys experiences inaccessible to him in reality. The intensity and the grip of emotions he finds in the story would at times be painful in real life.

The pleasure yielded by a daydream is intense, yet definitely restricted. The storyteller makes the daydream articulate, hence communicable, and he

makes it ego-syntonic, thereby changing and multiplying the enjoyment. The hack-writer takes the daydream and uses it pretty much "as is." The poet paraphrases and veils it, and he even destroys some of its easy and glib gratification.

Earlier studies had assumed that the story in which we meet our own daydream makes it fully conscious by lending words to it. I believe that essential parts of a story, of its plot, of the story characters' motivations and conflicts remain unconscious or preconscious and *for this very reason* arouse our emotions, our sympathy most effectully. Here a good children's story shares the dynamics of all art.

Many nursery tales employ magical features, i.e., denial in fantasy. Miracles happen with complete ease and make the story possible. The well-known traditional fairy tales are very old and come to us from a time when adults, too, believed in magic. In a preliterate world the laws of reality have less validity, they are less stringent for the reasoning of anyone, child or adult.

The storyteller, like the poet, must believe in the tale he spins. If he makes a conscious effort to write "for little children," his story is likely to sound concocted or it becomes pedantic. This may explain why the majority of fairy tales written today are so trite and syrupy. But recent decades have given us one type of story where fantastic happenings are closely interwoven with highly realistic and prosaic details which in a way deny the first denial. The reader is shuttled between the two, and this double denial may account for the story's ability to hold his interest.

The sincere modern fairy tale is at home in both the world of magic and denial in fantasy *and* in the well-observed world of sober, everyday reality.

We have discussed daydreams, paraphrasing important human relationships and aspirations, and we also took a close look at one type of contemporary fairy tales. Because these stories usually appeal to young children and because they remind us of a simple, carefree age, we called them "Early Tales." In these stories, problems of genital sexuality and the slow encroachments of death are eliminated. Yet thanks to the poet's art, the sutures where these powerful realities were cut out from the fabric of human life are invisible.

---

[8] Suppression is the conscious attempt to forget something, while repression refers to the unconscious mechanism. I am using negation and denial in a parallel fashion.

BIBLIOGRAPHY

JUVENILES AND NOVELS

BARRIE, J. M. (1906), *Peter Pan.*
BRONTË, C. (1847), *Jane Eyre.*
BURNETT, F. H. (1886), *Little Lord Fauntleroy.*
COLLODI, C. (1880), *The Adventures of Pinocchio.*

De Brunhoff, J. (1933), *Babar, the Elephant.**

Dickens, C. (1850), *David Copperfield.*

Ets, M. (1947), *Oley, the Sea Monster.*

Flack, M. (1933), *The Story about Ping.*

Grahame, K. (1908), *The Wind in the Willows.*

Kästner, E. (1929), *Emil and the Detectives.*

Lofting, H. (1920), *The Story of Dr. Dolittle.**

Milne, A. A. (1926), *Winnie-the-Pooh.**

Potter, B. (1902), *The Tale of Peter Rabbit.**

Rey, A. H. (1941), *Curious George.**

Rigby, D. (1947), *Moustachio.*

Ruskin, J. (1851), *The King of the Golden River.*

Salten, F. (1926), *Bambi.*

Stevenson, R. L. (1883), *Treasure Island.*

Travers, P. (1934), *Mary Poppins.**

PSYCHOANALYTIC AND GENERAL

Abraham, K. (1923), Two Contributions to the Study of Symbols. *Clinical Papers and Essays on Psychoanalysis.* New York: Basic Books, 1955.

Buxbaum, E. (1941), The Role of Detective Stories in a Child's Analysis, *Psa. Quart.,* X.

Fraiberg, S. (1954), Tales of the Discovery of the Secret Treasure. *This Annual,* IX.

Freud, A. (1936), Chapter VI: Denial in Phantasy. *The Ego and the Mechanisms of Defense.* New York: International Universities Press, 1946.

Freud, A. (1953), On Losing and Getting Lost. Presented at the International Psychoanalytical Congress, London.

Freud, S. (1906), The Relation of the Poet to Day-Dreaming. *Collected Papers,* IV. London: Hogarth Press, 1925.

Freud, S. (1909b), Family Romances. *Collected Papers,* V. London: Hogarth Press, 1950.

Friedlaender, K. (1942), Children's Books and Their Function in Latency and Prepuberty. *Am. Imago,* III.

Orwell, G. (1939), Boys' Weeklies. In *A Collection of Essays by George Orwell.* New York: Doubleday, 1954.

* First volume of a series.—Editor

(Stages in the Development of the Sense of Reality)

In fairy-tales ... phantasies of omnipotence are and remain the dominating ones. Just where we have most humbly to bow before the forces of Nature, the fairy-tale comes to our aid with its typical motives. In reality we are weak, hence the heroes of fairy-tales are strong and unconquerable; in our activities and our knowledge we are cramped and hindered by time and space, hence in fairy-tales one is immortal, is in a hundred places at the same time, sees into the future and knows the past. The ponderousness, the solidity, and the impenetrability of matter obstruct our way every moment: in the fairy-tale, however, man has wings, his eyes pierce the walls, his magic wand opens all doors. Reality is a hard fight for existence; in the fairy-tale the words "little table, be spread" are sufficient. A man may live in perpetual fear of attacks from dangerous beasts and fierce foes; in the fairy-tale a magic cap enables every transformation and makes us inaccessible. How hard it is in reality to attain love that can fulfill all our wishes! In the fairy-tale the hero is irresistible, or he bewitches with a magic gesture.

Thus the fairy-tale, through which grown-ups are so fond of relating to their children their own unfulfilled and repressed wishes, really brings the forfeited situation of omnipotence to a last, artistic presentation.

69

Compulsivity, Anxiety, and School Achievement [1]

JESSE W. GRIMES
AND WESLEY ALLINSMITH

Grimes and Allinsmith assert that someday class-room placement of students of all ages may take personality as well as ability into account. Instructional techniques may also be gauged to personality. Data show that scholastic achievement can be far more dependent on the interaction between the teaching method and the motivational and personality attributes of the child than upon either class of variable taken alone.

Jesse Grimes is now associated with the Reading Laboratory of the Newton, Massachusetts, schools. Wesley Allinsmith, one of the editors of this book, is a professor of psychology at the University of Cincinnati.

The problem of the child in the task of learning to read is of serious concern to psychologists, as well as to educators, parents, and children themselves. Among the many possible causes of reading retardation, some, such as physical handicaps or low intelligence, are obvious. Others are more subtle. Recent psychological research suggests that certain motivational and perceptual characteristics of children may interact with common techniques used in the teaching of reading. Individual differences in such factors as selective perception or emotional needs may dispose pupils to find that one or another method of teaching makes learning easier, more palatable, or more satisfying. The classroom procedure that is effective for some children may prove to be deleterious to the performance or development of others. If a clear-cut association can be shown between school achievement and an interaction of pupil personality and teaching method, the implications will be far-reaching for the psychology of learning and instruction as well as for teaching the specific skill of reading.

Each person restructures any stimulus into a unique pattern that fits his own expectations, conceptions, values, taboos, and wishes. Learning becomes a function of what the individual does to the material as well as of the actual content of the material. Studies of perceptual defense (Spence, 1957; Lowenfeld, 1956) and clinical observations of children with learning difficulties (Weisskopf, 1951) have given evidence of perceptual distortions that protect the individual from conscious recognition of unwanted or feared stimuli. Bruner (1951) emphasizes the factor of expectation, interpreting his research as evidence that the individual perceives by using a set of cues which he has learned from his particular experiences to associate with certain situations.

A child's personal reconstruction of stimuli in perception may be vastly different from reality as a consequence of his unique needs, anxieties, or ambitions. For instance, when a teacher kindly remarks, "I know you will do well," some children may perceive severe threat, perhaps unconsciously generalizing from earlier traumatic experiences when an authority figure demanded performance beyond their capacities. When a teacher attempts to be democratic and permissive, some other children's conflicts over making decisions in the absence of direction may cause them to perceive only disorganization, danger, and confusion. If the teacher as well as the child is unaware that what is seen or heard is not being interpreted realistically, it is impossible for the teacher to help the pupil perceive correctly.

It seems probable that one cannot teach a single lesson in a particular manner with any assurance that *all* children will have perceived the content as intended or will attend to it as hoped, free of

[1] This investigation was part of a program of studies conducted at the Harvard Laboratory for Research in Instruction under the direction of Dr. John B. Carroll, who gave much help during the collection and analysis of data. We are grateful also to Celeste T. Forbes and to Dr. Beverly Allinsmith, Dr. Leonard M. Lansky, and Dr. Judy F. Rosenblith for their deft criticisms of the manuscript.

Jesse W. Grimes and Wesley Allinsmith, "Compulsivity, anxiety, and school achievement," *Merrill-Palmer Quarterly*, 1961, *7*, 247–271. Reprinted by permission.

crippling anxiety or other preoccupation. If almost all children are to be reached and some degree of unity established in the perception of a given fact or generalization, a differentiation of teaching methods may be required. Interest in these problems led to an investigation of ways in which reading is currently taught.

METHODS OF INSTRUCTION IN READING

There are two major schools of thought about the teaching of reading, and each group leans upon psychological principles to support the method advocated. Much controversy between the groups has been publicized in recent years, particularly as an aftermath of Flesch's *Why Johnny Can't Read* (1955) which provoked a rebuttal by Carroll (1956). A summary of the two systems is presented below.

One group would initiate reading instruction through systematic presentation of sounds and their letter symbols, and teaching for competence in the skill of "sounding out" the words encountered in reading. This "phonics" method is basically a system of rules; the child learns that the word symbols have been built from the letter elements in an orderly manner.

Most such systems begin with a limited number of letters. The children are drilled in the sound-letter associations. Syllables and words are built by the child through the use of known word elements, with new letters and letter combinations presented systematically, followed by drill, and then by usage in word attack. The phonics approach is usually followed by an emphasis upon thought-getting when the child actually begins to read, with whole words becoming automatically recognized *after* the child establishes the skill of word analysis. Proponents of the system argue that since the child has already acquired much of the spoken language, his greatest need in learning to read is to achieve mastery of the translation of the alphabetical symbols.

In contrast to the method in which phonics is emphasized from the outset, the "whole-word" or "look-and-say" approach to initial reading instruction has been advocated by many educators in recent decades and is in wide use throughout the United States. Instruction begins with narrative reading material. The child is taught to recognize whole word configurations in association, with meaning, thus developing a "sight vocabulary" through repetitive exposure to a limited but gradually expanding number of words.

The original "sight vocabulary" of 50 to 200 words is learned through memorization of total word forms with little or no attention to the alphabetical details of word construction. The words that are taught are chosen for their concept and interest value rather than in accordance with any designed plan for systematizing word recognition. The whole-word approach is *followed* by instruction in a variety of word attack skills including phonics, but the latter is taught incidentally, i.e., when the teacher perceives the need during the on-going process of reading for meaning. In the procedure, generalizations are made, and used later in attempts at word analysis, but there is seldom a systematic follow-through with isolated drills to establish the learning of one generalization at a time in an ordered fashion. Other word attack techniques accompanying the sight method encourage the child to make "trial responses" on unfamiliar words, i.e., to make intelligent guesses, on the basis of clues gained from pictures, text, or configuration.

Proponents of the whole-word method argue that since the only real objective of reading is to derive meaning from the printed words, skill in achieving this objective can best be attained through successful and rewarding experience in actual reading. They argue further that an early emphasis upon phonic analysis impedes the child in the process of thought-getting, and that the irregularities in spelling render this approach confusing. In contrast, advocates of phonics allege that many children taught with a sight emphasis cannot analyze new words effectively and do poorly in composition because they fail to differentiate nuances of spelling.

Of course individual teachers can be found who use a combination of techniques from both systems. Nevertheless, one emphasis has tended to exclude the other in many educational settings. The major differences between the two systems are found in (a) the timing of the introduction of phonics instruction; (b) the degree of systemization of phonics instruction; (c) the emphasis upon phonics as a basic tool in word attack; and (d) the encouragement of trial responses on the basis of clues other than letter-sound associations.

Many researchers have investigated the differential effectiveness of the two methods. The results are inconclusive and contradictory, often showing no significant differences in reading skill between groups taught one way and those taught another, but usually finding a substantial and about equal number of children in *both* systems who do not achieve satisfactorily in reading and whose underachievement or relatively poor performance is not explained by the usual "causes" of school failure, such as low intelligence or clear-cut emotional problems. After reviewing the literature, Witty and Sizemore (1955) concluded that while differences in method of reading instruction may produce different qualities of reading skill, they are inconsequential when overall skill is judged. Others have voiced opinions that many children learn to read more successfully through the whole-word approach, but that certain children seem to make better progress through a systematic study of phonics.

INTERACTION OF PERSONALITY AND METHODS

This latter observation suggests that there may be an interaction between children's personality characteristics and methods of teaching. Until recently there has been almost no attempt through research to discover whether one teaching method may have been more effective than another for certain students because of the students' individual characteristics.

The few relevant studies, all within the past decade, have in every case dealt with college students. Wispe (1953), Smith, *et al.* (1956), and McKeachie (1958) have reported experiments which suggest that teaching methods interact with student personality characteristics. In all these experiments some students were placed in recitation or lecture sections where expectations were clearly defined, while other students were placed in seminar-like sections where they were free to establish objectives and course procedures. In one instance, Smith, *et al.,* the more highly structured sections were taught in a cold, impersonal, even punitive manner, while the unstructured sections were conducted in a warm, supportive, and permissive atmosphere. In all three instances, a type of student was identified who appeared to demand a high degree of structuring in the learning situation in order to make optimum progress. Wispe describes such students as personally insecure and dependent:

In the first place, this insecurity demands an abnormal amount of structuring of the situation, so that tensions arising out of the fear of doing the wrong thing can be reduced. . . . When this kind of student, who is disposed toward a highly dependent type of educational system, with desires for direction that cannot be met by any "normal" amount of instructor-structuring of the situation, is placed in a permissive section, the real conflict comes to the fore. Being intensely frustrated, and lacking the personal security to make the best of a bad situation this student becomes rigid, intropunitive, and vindictive in his evaluation of sections and instructors. To this student the permissive section meetings are "absolutely worthless," a place where intellectual confusion is heaped upon personal anxiety. (pp. 176–177)

Such reports suggest a promising method of attack on the problem at hand. The two methods of teaching reading described may be viewed as providing contrasting amounts of structure imposed in the definition of the task. From the above reports, two different pupil personality tendencies

appear relevant: anxiety and compulsivity, tendencies for which there is much descriptive evidence in the literature. If an interaction does exist between teaching methods and these two personality types, we should find that highly anxious or highly compulsive children will perform successfully when exposed to one method of instruction while similar children will do less well or even fail when taught by the other method. Before making a prediction, we need to look at (a) structure in teaching, (b) the nature of anxiety and compulsivity.

STRUCTURE AS A DIMENSION IN THE TEACHING OF READING

Structure in teaching involves the availability of cues within the whole that give certainty of meaning, definiteness of form, or clearly understood expectations. Usually this means that material is presented sequentially in such a way that when new stimuli are introduced, the learner is able to recognize familiar elements and attack each problem on the basis of prior learning of fundamental skills, facts, or principles. In structured teaching, the child is made aware of all expectations through carefully defined rules; when new situations are presented, the child is prepared to act with certainty on the basis of previously taught information.[2]

We believe that the two methods of teaching reading provide different amounts of structure. The phonics method, because of its reliance upon rules, systematic arrangement, and provision for certainty in problem-solving, appears to represent a high degree of structuring. The whole-word method, particularly in its earlier stages, can be judged as relatively unstructured because of its lack of discipline in word attack, and its encouragement of "intelligent guessing" on the basis of loosely defined clues.

PERSONALITY TENDENCIES

Anxiety and compulsivity, the two personality characteristics chosen for the investigation of a possible interaction with methods, are discussed below to determine what evidence exists that would enable us to predict the direction of interaction.

---

[2] "Structure," as a term long applied to educational practices, has recently taken on a special color as a result of Bruner's (1960) writings. He uses the term with a meaning which differs somewhat from ours. To him, structure is an attribute of the curriculum concerned with the sequence of the *conceptual principles* taught and their application to the mastery of later material. (We are using "structure" in a more traditional sense as referring to the clarity of procedure to be followed in a given task and the explicitness of the connections between one task and the next. This usage does not exclude Bruner's theme.)

Compulsivity. Fenichel (1945) describes the need for being systematic and for clinging to known routine and clear guide-rules as it occurs in the obsessive-compulsive, as well as the tendency of such persons to classify ideas rigidly in logical categories and to think in black and white terms. Meticulous preoccupation with small, insignificant details and with the letter of the law are noted in many cases with a frequent inability to see the forest for the trees.

Murphy (1947) offers a functional description of the compulsive personality: "Everything that is free, uncontrolled, spontaneous is dangerous. Papa will spank. Play safe; put the books back in the right place; rule the note-paper neatly; pay your bills on the first of the month; be good." (p. 748)

Frenkel-Brunswik (1952) pursued the task of demonstrating the inhibitory and paralyzing effects of harsh discipline upon the initiative and imagination of children. In homes with a rigid orientation she found that discipline was often based upon an expectation of the quick learning of external, superficial rules. Her description of the behavior of children from such homes is typical of the syndrome of compulsivity:

In order to reduce conflict and anxiety and to maintain stereotyped patterns, certain aspects of experience have to be kept out of awareness. . . . The clinging to the familiar and precise detail can go hand in hand with the ignoring of most of the remaining aspects of the stimulus configuration, resulting in an altogether haphazard approach to reality. (pp. 487–489)

Children of this type exhibited an extreme intolerance of ambiguity. Ambiguity seems to be perceived as a warning of the uncertainty of continued well being and tends to evoke fear or anxiety. It is as though the individual would prefer to see anything "certain" rather than remain in a state of flux, often accepting superficial clarity at a cost of maladaptive behavior.

In summary, the compulsive person appears to have exaggerated conceptions about exactness and order, and is oriented motivationally and perceptually by these concerns. Compulsives are described as relatively rigid, preoccupied with small details, inhibited in spontaneity, conforming, perfectionistic, seeking certainty, and intolerant of the ambiguous or incongruous situation. Of course these adjectives apply in marked degree only to disordered personalities (or to some fairly well-adjusted people in periods of stress). But obsessive-compulsive *tendencies* can be observed in so many children who are clinically within the normal range that we found it possible to categorize our sample of "normal" public school pupils as

relatively "high," "medium," or "low" in compulsivity. It seems logical to predict that the structured phonics program would facilitate school progress for children who show evidence of "high" compulsivity compared with similar children exposed to an unstructured whole-word reading program. The latter approach would probably be perceived by such children as disorganized and unsystematic, and they could be expected to have difficulty in complying with the requirement to guess in ambiguous situations.

Anxiety. Anxiety as a universal experience of human beings and as a factor in neurosis has long been recognized as a key psychological phenomenon, but only recently has there been a concentrated attack upon it as a personality variable in normal subjects. People measured as highly anxious have been shown to perceive more intense threat in a greater variety of circumstances (Heath, 1956). It appears that anxiety is a response to stress or to the perception of threat. When experienced at an optimum level for the subject, such anxiety *facilitates* problem-solving behavior (Sarason, 1957) but at an intense level it exerts a disorganizing effect (Castaneda, 1956), diminishing the powers of discrimination and thinking.

Korchin and Levine (1957) analyzed types of errors and rate of learning verbal material and found that the more anxious subjects differed little from non-anxious in the amount learned when dealing with simple and logically associated material, but that the differences were significant when difficult or unfamiliar material was presented, particularly if it was contradictory to previous knowledge. Their interpretation was, "In the situation in which the subject has to make a novel adjustment and cannot utilize existing behavior patterns, the possibility of failure and the consequent loss of self-esteem can further release anxiety and further reduce the subject's ability to develop appropriate behavior." (pp. 234–240) A similar point is made by Ausubel, *et al.* (1953).

Noll (1955) investigated the relation of anxiety to the learning and retention of verbal material. He found that the more difficult the task, the more difficult it was for highly anxious subjects to habituate to the learning situation, but that they were able to do so when required to master a series of tasks that aided in the structuring of the succeeding tasks. When task difficulty was thus structured, the anxious subjects performed as well as or better than the other group.

These findings seem directly applicable to the problem of this study, and justify forecasting the direction of an interaction between anxiety and methods of teaching beginning reading. We predicted that if learning experiences are highly structured as in the phonics method of teaching reading, the child with high anxiety will make greater progress in school than similar children in the unstructured setting.

Thus the structured phonics approach should allow anxious children as well as compulsive children to do better than they would have with the unstructured, whole-word method.

Research Procedure

Selection of Schools Representing Methods of Reading Instruction

Two city school systems were chosen to be representative of the methods of instruction required for this study. Trained independent observers surveyed the methods of teaching primary reading throughout the two communities, using objective checklists. Classroom observations and studies of curricula were made in the first three grades, obtaining evidence of actual practices. In one system, all schools initiated reading through teaching the alphabet, using a systematic phonics program with phonics drill held separately from reading practice, and through an emphasis upon "sounding out" as the major word-attack tool. In the other school system all primary grade teachers were using the whole-word approach as the initial instructional technique followed by incidental phonics begun late in the first grade and continued throughout the primary grades. Objective categorizing of the data confirmed the classification of each school as structured or unstructured according to the dimension of structure discussed earlier in this paper.

Further differences were noted in the general conditions in the classrooms in the two school systems. In the structured schools, the classroom atmosphere was found to be more authoritarian and cold, the curriculum more traditional. In the unstructured schools, child expression and meaningful experience were emphasized throughout the curriculum, and the teachers were more democratic and permissive.

Control of Socio-Economic Status

It would have been desirable for the two communities to have differed only in respect to the variable being investigated: the degree of structure in teaching method. The structured schools were in an industrial city, with three-family tenement houses typical of the residential areas, but with one rather sizeable section of middle-class homes. The unstructured schools were in a large suburban community, predominantly middle- to upper-middle class, but fringed by an industrial area. In order to equate the samples on socio-economic status, we chose schools in both cities on the basis of socio-economic status of the neighborhoods. School principals and guidance workers made ratings of the various neighborhoods and the research team made independent observations of houses and dwelling areas. An objective scale was developed for rating school neighborhoods from these data. Equal proportions of children in each

city were drawn from upper-lower and lower-middle class neighborhoods.

Subjects

Individual differences in maturation and the development of readiness for learning to read indicate that not until the third grade have most children had ample opportunity to demonstrate their capacity for school achievement. Therefore, third grade children were chosen as subjects for this study.

For purposes of sample selection only (individual tests were given later) we obtained group test scores of reading achievement and intelligence from school records of the entire third grade population in each school system.[3] The subjects for this study were randomly selected from stratified areas of the distribution, one third as under-achievers, one third medium, and one third over-achievers. Children whose reading scores were at least one standard deviation below the regression line of each total third grade school population were considered under-achievers for the purposes of sample selection. Over-achievers were at least one standard deviation above the regression line in their school system. The final sample was not significantly different from a normal distribution in regard to reading achievement or intelligence test scores. Twenty-four classrooms in twelve unstructured schools furnished 156 cases, 87 boys and 69 girls. Eight classrooms in three structured schools furnished 72 cases, 36 boys and 36 girls. Administrative restrictions necessitated the smaller sample size in the structured schools.

It was assumed that the sampling procedure was purely random with respect to the personality variables under investigation.

Rating Scale of Compulsivity

An interview schedule of open-ended questions and a multiple choice questionnaire[4] were prepared, and one parent of each of the sample children was seen in the home. The parent was asked to describe the child's typical behavior in certain standard situations in which there was an opportunity to observe tendencies toward perfectionism in demands upon self and others, irrational conformity to rules, orderliness, punctuality, and need for certainty. The interviewers were instructed not to suggest answers and, as much as possible, to record the parents' actual words as they described the child's behavior in home situations.

The rating scale of compulsivity was constructed by first perusing the interview records, categorizing all evidence related to compulsivity, then arranging a distribution on such information apart from the case

---

[3] In structured schools, the California Test of Mental Maturity was used as a measure of intelligence; in unstructured schools, the Kuhlmann-Anderson Intelligence Test. Reading achievement was recorded from scores on the Paragraph Meaning Subtest of Stanford Achievement Test, Form J, in both school systems.

[4] These and other instruments used in the study are given in the report of Grimes (1958) on which this article is partly based.

records. Final ratings were made on the basis of a point system which was developed after studying the distributions of actual behaviors recorded and assigning weight values to each type of behavior that was deviant from the discovered norms. Children scoring high in compulsivity were those who gave evidence of tension or emotionality in situations where there was lack of organization or conformity to standards and expectations, or who made exaggerated efforts to achieve these goals.[5] The low compulsive child was one who appeared relatively unconcerned about such matters. For instance, the following statement was rated low in compulsivity, "She's naturally quite neat about things, but it doesn't bother her at all if her room gets messy. But she cleans it up very well when I remind her."

MEASUREMENT OF ANXIETY

Castaneda, *et al.* (1956) revised the Taylor Anxiety Scale for use with children. The Taylor Scale was adapted from the Minnesota Multiphasic Personality Inventory, with item selection based upon clinical definitions of anxiety. There is much research evidence (Taylor, 1956) to validate the use of the instrument in differentiating individuals who are likely to manifest anxiety in varying degrees. Reliability and validation work with the Children's Anxiety Scale by Castaneda, *et al.* demonstrated results closely similar to the findings with the adult scale. Although the Taylor Scale was designed as a group testing device, in this study it was individually administered by psychologically trained workers who established rapport and assisted the children in reading the items.[6]

RELATIONSHIP OF ANXIETY TO COMPULSIVITY

The question may be raised whether or not we are dealing with a common factor, in anxiety and compulsivity. The two ratings yield a correlation of +.04, which is not significantly different from zero; therefore, we have measured two different characteristics. In theory, compulsive behavior is a way of diminishing anxiety, and one

---

[5] In order to fit the theoretically-defined compulsive character we scored deviant behavior in either direction as compulsive: those whose need for orderliness was exaggerated, those who were rebelliously disorderly, and those who inconsistently oscillated between the extremes.

[6] The work of Alpert and Haber (1960) raises the question whether a test of situational anxiety specific to schooling, e.g., one of test anxiety, might have been more appropriate and revealing than the Taylor Children's Scale of general anxiety used in the present study. Such an instrument was not available at the time these data were collected. Since that time the Sarason (1960) scale of test anxiety for children has been developed. It is interesting to note that even though Alpert and Haber found no correlation between the Taylor Scale and academic achievement with college students, Castaneda found significant negative correlations between the Taylor Children's Scale and achievement scores, foreshadowing one aspect of the results reported below. Perhaps the contradiction arises from an absence, among those gaining entrance to college, of students whose general anxiety inhibits rather than facilitates school performance.

might expect a negative association except for the possibility that for many children the obsessive-compulsive defenses are not sufficient to quell the amount of anxiety they suffer. The issue of interaction between anxiety and compulsivity will be taken up later.

CRITERION MEASUREMENT

In the primary grades, reading permeates almost every aspect of school progress, and the children's early experiences of success or failure in learning to read often set a pattern of total achievement that is relatively enduring throughout the following years. In establishing criterion measurements, it was therefore thought best to broaden the scope beyond the reading act itself. The predicted interaction effect should, if potent, extend its influence over all academic achievement.

The Stanford Achievement Test, Form J, was administered by classroom teachers, consisting of a battery of six sub-tests: Paragraph Meaning, Word Meaning, Spelling, Language, Arithmetic Computation, and Arithmetic Reasoning. All of these subtests involve reading except Arithmetic Computation. Scores are stated in grade-equivalents on a national norm. The battery median grade-equivalent was used in data analysis in this study.

The Wechsler Intelligence Scale for Children was administered to each sample third grade child by a clinical worker. The relationship of intelligence test scores to school achievement is a well-established fact (in this case, $r = .506$ $p < .001$); therefore, in the investigation of the present hypothesis, it was necessary to control this factor.

The criterion score used in the statistical analysis is an index of over- or under-achievement. It is the discrepancy between the actual attained achievement test score and the score that would be predicted by the I.Q. For example, on the basis of the regression equation, a child with an I.Q. of 120 in this sample would be expected to earn an achievement test score of 4.8 (grade equivalent). If a child with an I.Q. of 120 scored 5.5 in achievement, his discrepancy score would be +.7, representing .7 of one year of over-achievement. A child with an I.Q. of 98 would be expected to earn an achievement test score of 3.5. If such a child scored 3.0, his discrepancy score would be −.5, representing .5 of one year of under-achievement. In this manner, the factors measured by the intelligence test were controlled, allowing discovered differences in achievement to be interpreted as resulting from other variables.

RESULTS

TEST OF INTERACTION OF COMPULSIVITY AND TEACHING METHODS

Tables 1 and 2 present the results of the statistical analysis of the data when compulsivity is used as the descriptive variable. Figure 1 portrays the mean achievement scores of each sub-group graphically. First of all, as we had surmised, the highly compul-

TABLE 1

THE EFFECT OF TEACHING METHOD ON SCHOOL ACHIEVEMENT OF CHILDREN RATED LOW, MEDIUM,
OR HIGH IN COMPULSIVITY

| | Mean Years of Over- or Under-Achievement | | | | | | |
| | Low Compulsivity | | Medium Compulsivity | | High Compulsivity | | |
Teaching Method	Years	N	Years	N	Years	N	t Ratio Hi vs. Low
Structured	+.05	17	+.45	36	+.82	19	2.89[a]
Unstructured	−.28	42	−.36	57	−.12	56	.99
t-ratio	1.65[a]				4.15[b]		

[a] $p < .01$ (2 tail)
[b] $p < .001$ (1 tail)

TABLE 2

ANALYSIS OF VARIANCE[c] OF HI VS. LOW COMPULSIVITY

Source of Variance	s.s.	d.f.	Mean Sq.	F
Between method groups	40.73	1	40.73	17.12[a]
Between trait groups	21.51	1	21.51	9.04[a]
Interaction	9.26	1	9.26	3.89[b]
Error		131	2.38	

[a] $p < .01$ (2 tail)
[b] $p < .05$ (1 tail)
[c] Corrected for unequal frequencies.

sive children in the structured setting score significantly better ($p < .001$) on achievement than do similar children in the unstructured schools. It can be seen too that when we contrast levels of compulsivity within the structured schools, the high compulsive children do better ($p < .01$). No signifi-

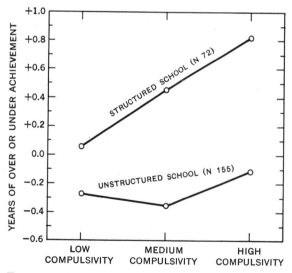

FIGURE 1. *Graph of test results showing mean school achievement of children categorized as to compulsivity.*

cant difference was found in achievement between high and low compulsive children within the unstructured school. The hypothesis of there being an interaction between compulsivity and teaching method was supported, in this case, at the .05 level.

While we had expected that compulsive children in the unstructured school setting would have difficulty when compared to those in the structured, we were surprised to find that the achievement of the high compulsives within the schools where the whole-word method is used in beginning reading compares favorably with that of the low compulsives.[7] Indeed their achievement scores were somewhat better on an absolute basis although the difference was not significant. We speculate that compulsives in the unstructured schools are under greater strain because of the lack of systemization in their school setting, but that their need to organize (for comfort) is so intense that they struggle to induce the phonic rules and achieve in spite of the lack of direction from the environment.[8]

It is interesting to note that medium compulsives in the unstructured schools made the lowest achievement scores (though not significantly

---

[7] This could have been foretold from a careful reading of Frenkel-Brunswik (1952) or from listening to our colleague Dr. Leonard M. Lansky who anticipated that the compulsive person is one who is inclined to make blind stabs at any possible solution. One might then speculate that difficulty in guessing under lack of structure would occur only in the case of those compulsive children who were also highly anxious. The achievement of such children who are anxious is compared below with those compulsive children low in anxiety. The trend is in line with the expectation although it is not significant with the small number of cases.

[8] If this is true, we would expect that high compulsives in the unstructured schools would develop skill in phonics to a greater extent than the low compulsive children. Scores were available on a test of phonics skill, and again intelligence was controlled. Analysis revealed that high compulsives in unstructured schools learned phonics significantly ($p < .01$) more successfully than low compulsives.

TABLE 3
THE EFFECT OF TEACHING METHOD ON SCHOOL ACHIEVEMENT OF CHILDREN RATED LOW, MEDIUM, OR HIGH IN ANXIETY

	Mean Years of Over- or Under-Achievement						
	Low Anxiety		*Medium Anxiety*		*High Anxiety*		*t Ratio Hi vs. Low*
Teaching Method	*Years*	*N*	*Years*	*N*	*Years*	*N*	
Structured	+.39	27	+.43	27	+.60	18	.80
Unstructured	+.002	51	−.24	46	−.49	59	3.34[b]
t-ratio	2.07[a]				4.88[c]		

[a] $p < .05$ (2 tail)
[b] $p < .01$ (2 tail)
[c] $p < .001$ (1 tail)

lower). Possibly their compulsivity was not strong enough to cause them to build their own structure.

Our conjecture is, then, that regardless of the manner in which school lessons are taught, the compulsive child accentuates those elements of each lesson that aid him in systematizing his work. When helped by a high degree of structure in lesson presentation, then and only then does such a child attain unusual success.

TEST OF INTERACTION OF ANXIETY AND TEACHING METHODS

The statistical analyses of achievement in relation to anxiety and teaching methods and the interactions of the two are presented in Tables 3 and 4. Figure 2 is a graph of the mean achievement scores of each group. As predicted, the highly anxious children in the unstructured schools score more poorly ($p < .001$) than those in the structured schools. The interaction effect, which is significant at the .01 level, can be seen best in the contrast of mean scores. While high anxiety children achieve significantly less well ($p < .01$) in the unstructured school than do low anxiety children, they appear to do at least as well as the average in the structured classroom.

The most striking aspect of the interaction demonstrated is the marked decrement in performance suffered by the highly anxious children in unstructured schools. According to the theory proposed, this is a consequence of the severe condition of perceived threat that persists unabated for the anxious child in an ambiguous sort of school environment. The fact that such threat is potent in the beginning reading lessons is thought to be a vital factor in the continued pattern of failure or under-achievement these children exhibit. The child with high anxiety may first direct his anxiety-released energy toward achievement, but because his distress severely reduces the abilities of dis-

TABLE 4
ANALYSIS OF VARIANCE[c] OF HI VS. LOW ANXIETY

Source of Variance	*s.s.*	*d.f.*	*Mean Sq.*	*F*
Between method groups	54.27	1	54.27	26.22[a]
Between trait groups	1.87	1	1.87	.90
Interaction	12.09	1	12.09	5.83[b]
Error		151	2.07	

[a] $p < .01$ (2 tail)
[b] $p < .01$ (1 tail)
[c] Corrected for unequal frequencies.

crimination and memorization of complex symbols, the child may fail in his initial attempts to master the problem. Failure confirms the threat, and the intensity of anxiety is increased as the required learning becomes more difficult, so that by the time the child reaches the third grade the decrement in performance is pronounced.

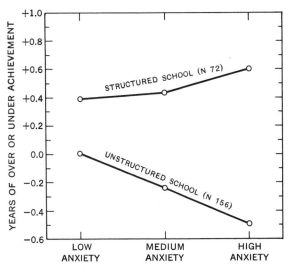

FIGURE 2. *Graph of test results showing mean school achievement of children categorized as to anxiety.*

The individual with high anxiety in the structured classroom may approach the learning task with the same increased energy and lowered powers of discrimination. But the symbols he is asked to learn are simple. As shown earlier, the highly anxious individual may be superior in his memorizing of simple elements. Success reduces the prospect of threat and his powers of discrimination are improved. By the time the child first attacks the actual problem of reading, he is completely familiar and at ease with all of the elements of words. Apparently academic challenge in the structured setting creates an optimum of stress so that the child with high anxiety is able to achieve because he is aroused to an energetic state without becoming confused or panicked.

Sarason, *et al.* (1960), present evidence that the anxious child will suffer in the test-like situation, and that his performance will be impaired unless he receives supporting and accepting treatment from the teacher. Although the present study was not a direct replication of their investigations, the results do not confirm their conclusion. Observers, in the two school systems studied here, judged the teachers in the structured schools to be more impersonal and demanding, while the atmosphere in the unstructured schools was judged to be more supporting and accepting. Yet the highly anxious child suffered a tremendous disadvantage only in the unstructured school, and performed as well or better than average in the structured setting. Our results lead us to guess that the study by Sarason, *et al.,* was done entirely in "modern," unstructured schools. It seems probable to us that the child who perceives danger in the test-like situation associates that danger not only with the authoritative parent-like status of the teacher, but also with the degree of his own adequacy for mastering the situation. It is apparent that warm, understanding treatment alone does not mitigate that threat, and indeed, may accentuate it in a classroom situation which shifts from accustomed warm support to more authoritative discipline on the day of achievement testing.

Shands (1954) mentioned two factors that may be effective in relieving anxiety: (a) the availability of a pattern of behavior (the present authors assumed that a structured program should excel in offering a guide to behavior) and (b) the availability of a pattern of relationship, i.e., dependence upon some other person. Sarason, *et al.,* have concentrated on personal relationships and support as a means of allaying anxiety and presumably making it possible for the child to achieve. The present study shows that even in the absence of such support, the condition of structure is so potent that it will have

a significant beneficial effect upon the achievement of the anxious child. But with support available and structure missing, the anxious child risks failure. The feeling the teacher imparts to such a child is evidently not so influential as the extent to which the teacher lets the child know exactly what is expected, and structures the learning in simple, logically-ordered steps. Of course teachers should not exacerbate children's anxiety, but it may be that they should be less concerned with allaying anxiety on the assumption that in doing so they are providing a sufficient condition for learning, and more concerned with teaching in a manner that allows the child to make optimum "use" of his existing anxieties.

Sarason, *et al.,* argue well that the influence of the teacher goes well beyond what is measured in an achievement test, and that the supportive and benign attitudes and behavior they recommend would have far-reaching effects in improving mental health. This is probably true as far as it goes, but the positive value of academic success cannot be discounted, nor can the seriously disruptive effects of school failure or underachievement. We then have to raise the question: Is there any reason why teachers cannot provide both conditions prescribed by Shands? Many complex interacting factors are at work in any classroom. While the results of a number of studies have indicated the rewarding advantages of warmth and friendliness on the part of the teacher, e.g., Withall's (1951) investigations have demonstrated that a greater degree of general progress can be expected in a warm, assuring climate, yet in the present study we find that such emotional support is of little avail in the absence of structure. This discovery enables us to postulate that if the highly anxious children in the structured schools had experienced a greater degree of warmth and security in interpersonal relationships, they might have made even greater gains as Sarason, *et al.,* would expect.

The implications of these findings may reach further. Interpretations of both psychoanalytic and non-directive concepts have led many workers in the fields of counseling and ecucational therapy as well as remedial reading to spend months—or even years!—in establishing a "proper" relationship, with no sense of urgency about actual instruction. Meantime the children continue to fail in school and their anxiety mounts. It is entirely possible too that when actual tutoring itself is conducted in an unstructured, non-directive way, it cannot meet certain needs of children whose symptoms include anxiety and loss of self-esteem through continued school failure. If ways can be found to accelerate educational progress through more directive and structured teaching without hampering the work of the psychotherapist, the time and professional investment often taken to treat learning difficulties might be reduced.

DIFFERENCES IN THE TOTAL SAMPLES

A highly significant difference was found between the two towns in the means of achievement criterion scores ($p < .001$), indicating that the structured school system was more successful in bringing about a generally higher level of student achievement. The magnitude of the difference in terms of grade equivalents as depicted in Figures 1 and 2 might at first seem spectacular, and an answer to the nation's prayer for guidance in furthering early school performance, but the differences call for qualification. We raise a question first about the causation of the differences, and then state our uncertainty whether such achievement is the most important goal for education at this level.

A possible factor other than teaching method in accounting for the differences may be cultural variations between the two communities. The attempt to equate socio-economic status may not have been sufficient, based as it was on house and dwelling area. Data established that incomes were lower in the structured school community, and interviewers gained the impression that a larger proportion of income was used there to keep up residence appearances, while certain cultural values seemed less highly prized than in the other community. It is possible that school achievement in primary grades, particularly skill development, is stressed to a greater extent in the homes of the structured school community. At the same time, the conditions ordinarily expected to motivate reading growth were found to be more prevalent in the homes of the unstructured school community: these homes contain more books, the parents read more to their pre-school children, they provide more tutoring, and have higher expectations for future academic and vocational attainments for their children. It appears that there may be two different types of achievement motivation in the two communities, and future research should control this factor.

If the achievement differences between systems are due to the differences in schooling methods, several questions may be asked regarding the desirability of such achievement, and whether or not it is attained at too great a cost. It is probable that more of the total school time in the structured schools was devoted to practice of skills, thereby producing students able to read, spell, and work arithmetic problems, but for all we know, less

advanced in other areas of development. The general scholastic superiority in the structured schools of this study may possibly be attributed to this factor of extra practice.

The achievement test used in this study essentially measures skill in fundamental tool subjects, and does not measure the breadth of the child's understanding and behavior in other respects. For instance, we have no evidence about the creativity of one set of children or the other. We do, however, have scores on the California Test of Personality. Children in the unstructured schools scored higher ($p < .001$) than in the structured schools. This fact may indicate a greater degree of social adjustment.

It may be, too, that the attainment of skill proficiency is the only rewarding element in the school environment in these particular structured schools, i.e., perhaps the children find that they must achieve in the limited sphere of the three R's to gain any approbation.

Anderson, *et al.* (1956) found that systematic instruction resulted in faster initial progress in skill development but that after a few years, children taught by a technique emphasizing child expression and meaningfulness of each task caught up or surpassed those who continued in the systematized learning situation. Our results, then, do not necessarily point to a clear superiority of one method over another as a recommended approach for teaching *all* children. Our goal is to call attention to the possible need for creating methods of instruction attuned to the type of pupil, or for seeking a single method that does not handicap any pupils. Indications are that many primary grade children might be helped by a more formal structure in their earlier school learnings.

TEST OF INTERACTION OF ANXIETY AND COMPULSIVITY

The results of the study open up several new questions, at least one of which can be investigated through further analysis of these data. When ratings in one personality factor are held constant, will the other factor exert a significant influence, or are the discovered differences a result of an interaction of anxiety and compulsivity such that neither has an effect without the other?

In this analysis, each school system, the structured and unstructured, is considered separately. Within each system four groups of children are studied: HiComp-HiAnx, HiComp-LoAnx, LoComp-HiAnx, LoComp-LoAnx. In order to obtain larger frequencies in each category, the cutting point for each extreme group was moved closer to the median score on compulsivity and anxiety than in the previous three-way categorization. The resulting smaller medium groups were removed from consideration. This recategorization was done without reference to achievement scores, and the cutting points then set so that one third of the cases would fall in the excluded median group. The mean achievement score of each new group and the frequencies above and below the local medians are presented in Table 5. Results of

non-parametric tests of significance of differences between groups are shown in Tables 6 and 7. Since the overall differences between groups in each school are significant as shown in Table 6, we may interpret each specific difference in terms of the personality categorization.

At once apparent is the successful academic performance of the HiComp-HiAnx children in the structured schools. As a group they are more than a year advanced in achievement! Apparently,

TABLE 5
MEAN ACHIEVEMENT AND FREQUENCIES ABOVE AND BELOW LOCAL MEDIANS OF CHILDREN CATEGORIZED ACCORDING TO COMBINATIONS OF HIGH AND LOW ANXIETY AND COMPULSIVITY

| | Structured Schools | | | |
	HiComp-HiAnx	HiComp-LoAnx	LoComp-HiAnx	LoComp-LoAnx
Above local median	8	7	3	4
Below local median	0	7	8	9
Mean achievement criterion scores	+1.24	+.42	+.08	+.08

| | Unstructured Schools | | | |
	HiComp-HiAnx	HiComp-LoAnx	LoComp-HiAnx	LoComp-LoAnx
Above local median	11	22	5	10
Below local median	11	11	16	11
Mean achievement criterion scores	−.22	+.16	−.68	−.14

TABLE 6
NON-PARAMETRIC SIGNIFICANCE TESTS OF THE FREQUENCIES IN TABLE 5 (MOOD'S LIKELIHOOD RATIO TEST)

School System	Groups Compared	d.f.	χ^2
Structured	HiComp-HiAnx X HiComp-LoAnx X LoComp-HiAnx X LoComp-LoAnx	3	15.336[b]
Unstructured	HiComp-HiAnx X HiComp-LoAnx X LoComp-HiAnx X LoComp-LoAnx	3	9.834[a]

[a] $p < .03$ (2 tail)
[b] $p < .01$ (2 tail)

TABLE 7
SIGNIFICANCE OF DIFFERENCES BETWEEN PERSONALITY CATEGORIES WITHIN EACH SCHOOL SYSTEM, TESTED BY CHI SQUARE CORRECTED FOR CONTINUITY. PROBABILITIES ARE TWO-TAILED

| | Structured Schools | | Unstructured Schools | |
	d.f.	χ^2	d.f.	χ^2
HiComp-HiAnx X HiComp-LoAnx	1	5.867[b]	1	1.528
LoComp-HiAnx X LoComp-LoAnx	1	.035	1	2.593
HiComp-HiAnx X LoComp-HiAnx	1	10.455[d]	1	3.154[a]
HiComp-LoAnx X LoComp-LoAnx	1	1.033	1	1.929
HiComp-LoAnx X LoComp-HiAnx	1	1.325	1	9.429[c]
HiComp-HiAnx X LoComp-LoAnx	1	9.692[d]	1	.024

[a] $p < .10$ [c] $p < .01$
[b] $p < .02$ [d] $p < .005$

when the school systematizes the learning experiences for such children in accordance with their need for orderliness, their anxiety is facilitating rather than disorganizing.[9]

This interpretation is supported by the comparable data of the other groups, each of which is significantly different from the HiComp-HiAnx. The HiComp-LoAnx children are evidently benefited by lesson structure in satisfying their need for organization but apparently lack some of the drive of the HiComp-HiAnx group.

In the unstructured school, the data again indicate an interaction of the two personality variables. The HiComp-LoAnx group makes the best record while the LoComp-HiAnx group does poorly, and the difference is significant at the .01 level. The child with low anxiety is evidently not threatened by the lack of structure, and if he has the organizational power to systematize his own learning tasks, he is able to master the achievement problem reasonably well. However, when little structure is provided in the school experiences, children with high anxiety and no personal drive to systematize for themselves are in serious trouble. The anxiety serves to disrupt problem-solving ability to a striking degree.

The same analyses were repeated but with sex held constant, and the results are closely similar to those shown above. We still find for both sexes the poor performance of LoComp-HiAnx in the unstructured school, and in the case of girls (there was a dearth of boys in the comparison) the marked high performance of HiComp-HiAnx in the structured school.

ALTERNATE INTERPRETATIONS OF STRUCTURE

What we have really shown definitely, of course, is merely that there are interactions among compulsivity, anxiety, and school system attended. The question is, what causes these findings. Although we have chosen the matter of structure in methods of teaching reading to account for the variations, there may, in fact, be at least three meanings. a) The influence of teaching method may reflect *not* the structure of phonics but a generally-structured manner of teaching and classroom management if such existed in one school system more than another. Clarity of directions, explicitness about the applications of principles taught, and precise knowledge on the part of the child as to what is expected of him are characteristics of a structured manner of teaching. b) The

findings of interaction between pupil personality and teaching method may be due to the structure provided in phonics, along with whatever structure through sequencing and rule-teaching may have existed in other subject-matter areas. c) Pupil personality may have been interacting with one or more attributes of teaching method other than the provision of structure.

We have no evidence that interpretation (c) is incorrect, but the concordance with personality theory of the interactions that we discovered leads us to reject it as an explanation of our findings. Our skepticism of interpretation (a) is less easy to defend: we made no measurements of structure in teaching manner. Yet it seems to us that structure of this type might be provided equally well by a teacher in either system.[10] During their three years in school, our 156 whole-word-taught children had been taught by 87 different teachers, and our 72 phonics-taught children had experienced 31 different teachers. Individual differences among teachers must have been great in both school systems. We have considerable confidence that if structure in teaching manner had been constantly greater in one system than in the other, this fact would not have gone undetected by our team of observers.

The methods of teaching reading were accurately determined, and the structure of the phonics program was the only clear-cut difference that was found to be constant across school systems. Therefore, we feel justified in accepting interpretation (b) as an explanation of the interactions of personality tendencies with teaching methods. This does not rule out the possibility that if degree of structure in teaching manner were experimentally varied it would produce similar results. It seems probable that structure provided by phonics[11] in conjunction with that in the whole classroom experience would produce even more striking benefits for highly anxious or highly compulsive children.

---

[9] Their "overachievement" may of course mask serious neurotic problems by causing them to be regarded as model children.

[10] Earlier in this paper, it was mentioned that the team of observers had noted a more authoritarian and cold atmosphere in the structured schools. We do not consider this to be evidence of general structure in teaching manner. The more traditional curriculum that was also noted may or may not indicate a greater degree of structure in the organization of subject-matter.

[11] Should further investigations show interpretation (b) to be valid, the needed structure might be provided by means other than the alphabetic or phonics approach. Brown (1958) describes a method in which the rules of pronunciation and spelling are defined to children early in their study of reading, but word recognition is used from the start for necessary words like "and" and "the," without which meaningful material cannot be read. Also, Richards and Gibson (1957) have prepared materials using a structured whole-word program, teaching the child in his first lessons to discriminate letter, sound, and meaning within closely similar sentences.

We must acknowledge an important caution about the provision of structure in teaching. The continuance of structuring too far in later schooling may perpetuate dependence upon those in authority positions. Because of this danger McKeachie (1951) wrote of structured techniques, "... we still may not grant that it is the most desirable method to be used in our educational system which has as its aim preparation for life in a democracy." We suggest that if particular children's desperate need for structure in certain types of learning can be satisfied during the early school years with failure prevented and their literacy assured, ways to reduce the need for continuance of such structure may be gradually introduced later.

ALTERNATE INTERPRETATIONS OF PERSONALITY CHARACTERISTICS

We have implied a causal relationship—that because of existing tendencies toward compulsivity or anxiety, a child may need structure in teaching. The reverse might be argued, that failure or success in learning to read contributed to or actually caused the personality characteristics that we observed. Since we have no personality measures of the children before they entered first grade, we cannot deny this possibility, but our examination of the results leads us to discount it as an explanation of the findings.

The reverse argument gains plausibility from the common observations that children who are retarded in reading often are emotionally maladjusted and that with wise remedial instruction and consequent success in learning to read, the signs of maladjustment may disappear. This is doubtless often true, but the argument is weakened if those signs are not the same as the ones measured by our instruments. And indeed, the behaviors exhibited by pupils and recognized by teachers as maladjustment are not those revealed by our tests of compulsivity and anxiety. Each of our sample children was placed on a five-point scale of emotional adjustment by the first, second, and third grade teachers who had taught them. The scaled continuum ran from (1) well adjusted and secure, to (5) poorly adjusted, insecure, apprehensive. Teacher ratings were then compared with our measures of compulsivity and anxiety, and also with school achievement. Non-parametric analysis showed that teacher ratings of maladjustment were negatively related ($p < .05$) to school achievement, but not related to anxiety or compulsivity. Thus children's emotional reactions in the classroom are not indicative of the more subtle personality characteristics measured in our instruments, and the data do not confirm the supposition that the degree of school success actually causes the personality tendencies that we measured.

School failure will probably cause certain manifestations of emotional behavior in most children, but if we are reasoning soundly, it can hardly account for the interactions that we found. While low achievement in the unstructured school may heighten tension, it does not seem reasonable that high achievement would cause a *high* rating on the same test of anxiety for some children in the *structured* school! Also it is not reasonable that compulsivity, as measured by emotionality in certain home-like situations, would be changed substantially by variations of methods of teaching at school. Therefore, we feel justified in interpreting our data to mean that the differential in teaching methods (that we see in the structure provided in systematic phonics) interacts with personality characteristics such that highly anxious and/or highly compulsive children are helped in school achievement by the introduction of structure in teaching.

POSSIBLE APPLICATIONS

Do we seriously envisage the differentiation of teaching methods according to pupils' personality tendencies? Upon first hearing this suggestion, educators may throw up their hands in horror! But homogeneous grouping done by means of achievement or intelligence test scores is, after all, common practice. Already the skilled teacher tries as best he can to individuate instruction for certain pupils within his classroom based upon his intuitive judgments of personal needs. When the results of studies like ours have hardened in the kiln of replication, they may foretell the wide use of personality tests to distinguish those children who will particularly benefit by increased structure (or other techniques) in their school experiences.

A final implication concerns those doing counseling or educational therapy with children afflicted by learning difficulties. In some cases where emphasis has been placed upon allaying anxiety, it may prove effective to provide concomitantly a high degree of structure in the remedial teaching.

SUMMARY

In this study we tested the hypothesis that there is an interaction between teaching method and pupils' personality characteristics in determining school achievement. We anticipated that highly anxious or highly compulsive children who are taught reading initially by "structured" methods stressing phonics will show more achievement by the third grade than similar children taught in other schools where the "unstructured" word recognition approach to beginning reading is used. Our expectation is supported by the findings.

We also examined the effects of personality variables with teaching method held constant. Under structured teaching, compulsive children do substantially better than less compulsive children, but compulsivity makes no difference in the unstructured settings. Anxiety, in contrast, makes no difference under structured conditions; it is in the unstructured settings that high anxiety impedes scholastic performance.

Anxiety and compulsivity, which are not correlated in our sample, interact with one another as well as with teaching method. Children who are both highly anxious *and* highly compulsive overachieve strikingly in the structured environment, and those who are highly anxious but *low* in compulsivity underachieve in the unstructured schools.

Thus choice of instructional methods makes a big difference for certain kinds of pupil, and a search for the "best" way to teach can succeed only when the learner's personality is taken into account.

REFERENCES

ALPERT, R., AND HABER, R. N. Anxiety in academic achievement situations. *J. abnorm. soc. Psychol.,* 1960, *61,* 207–215.

ANDERSON, I. H., HUGHES, B. O., AND DIXON, W. R. Relationships between reading achievement and method of teaching. *Univer. Michigan, sch. of educ. bull.,* 1956, *7,* 104–108.

AUSUBEL, D. P., SCHIFF, H. M., AND GOLDMAN, M. Qualitative characteristics in the learning process associated with anxiety. *J. abnorm. soc. Psychol.,* 1953, *48,* 537–547.

BROWN, R. *Words and things.* Glencoe, Ill.: Free Press, 1958, 78–79.

BRUNER, J. S. Personality dynamics and the process of perceiving. In R. Blake and G. Ramsey (Eds.), *Perception: An approach to personality.* New York: Ronald, 1951.

BRUNER, J. S. *The process of education.* Cambridge, Mass.: Harvard Univer. Press, 1960.

CARROLL, J. B. The case of Dr. Flesch. *Amer. Psychologist,* 1956, *11,* 158–163.

CASTANEDA, A. Reaction time and response amplitude as a function of anxiety and stimulus intensity. *J. abnorm. soc. Psychol.,* 1956, *53,* 225–228.

CASTANEDA, A., McCANDLESS, B. R., AND PALERMO, D. S. The children's form of the manifest anxiety scale. *Child develpm.,* 1956, *27,* 317–326.

FENICHEL, O. *The psychoanalytic theory of neurosis.* New York: Norton, 1945.

FLESCH, R. *Why Johnny can't read.* New York: Harper, 1955.

FRENKEL-BRUNSWIK, ELSE. The inhibitory effects of an authoritarian home regime on the emotional and cognitive patterns of children. In J. Frosh (Ed.), *Annual survey of psychoanalysis* (Vol. 3). New York: Internat. Univer. Press, 1952.

GRIMES, J. W. The interaction of pupil personality with methods of teaching reading in determining primary grade achievement. Unpublished doctoral dissertation, Harvard Univer., 1958.

HEATH, D. H. Individual anxiety thresholds and their effect on intellectual performance. *J. abnorm. soc. Psychol.,* 1956, *52,* 403–408.

KORCHIN, S. J., AND LEVINE, S. Anxiety and verbal learning. *J. abnorm. soc. Psychol.,* 1957, *54,* 234–240.

LOWENFELD, J., RUBENFELD, S., AND GUTHRIE, G. M. Verbal inhibition in subception. *J. gen. Psychol.,* 1956, *54,* 171–176.

McKEACHIE, W. J. Anxiety in the college classroom. *J. educ. Res.,* 1951, *55,* 153–160.

McKEACHIE, W. J. Students, groups, and teaching methods. *Amer. Psychologist,* 1958, *13,* 580–584.

MURPHY, G. Personality. New York: Harper, 1947.

NOLL, J. O. An investigation of the relation of anxiety to learning and retention. *Dissert. Abstr.,* 1955, *15.*

RICHARDS, I. A., AND GIBSON, CHRISTINE M. *First steps in reading English.* New York: Washington Square Press, 1957.

SARASON, I. G. Effect of anxiety and two kinds of motivating instructions on verbal learning. *J. abnorm. soc. Psychol.,* 1957, *54,* 166–171.

SARASON, S. B., DAVIDSON, K. S., LIGHTHALL, F. F., WAITE, R. R., AND RUEBUSH, B. K. *Anxiety in elementary school children.* New York: Wiley, 1960.

SHANDS, H. C. Anxiety, anaclitic object, and the sign function: Comments on early developments in the use of symbols. *Amer. J. Orthopsychiat.,* 1954, *23,* 84–97.

SMITH, D. E. P., WOOD, R. L., DOWNER, J. W., AND RAYGOR, A. L. Reading improvement as a function of student personality and teaching method. *J. of educ. Psychol.,* 1956, *47,* 47–59.

SPENCE, D. P. A new look at vigilance and defense. *J. abnorm. soc. Psychol.,* 1957, *54,* 103–108.

TAYLOR, JANET A. Drive theory and manifest anxiety. *Psychol. Bull.,* 1956, *53,* 303–320.

WEISSKOPF, EDITH A. Intellectual malfunctioning and personality. *J. abnorm. soc. Psychol.,* 1951, *46,* 410–423.

WISPE, LAUREN G. Evaluating section teaching methods in the introductory course. *J. educ. Res.,* 1951, *45,* 162.

WITHALL, J. The development of the climate index. *J. educ. Res.,* 1951, *45,* 93–100.

WITTY, P., AND SIZEMORE, R. A. Phonics in the reading program: A review and an evaluation. *Elem. English,* 1955, *32,* 355–371.

70

The Teacher's Role in the Motivation of the Learner

PAULINE S. SEARS
AND ERNEST R. HILGARD

The book from which this selection was taken (see credit line below) is a valuable source for those concerned with research in the field of education. In it, Pauline S. Sears and Ernest R. Hilgard review the literature on a vast topic. Dr. Sears, like her husband Robert and her co-author Hilgard, is a product of graduate training at Yale University. She has long been active in research in child psychology. At Stanford University she has concentrated more and more on research with educational implications. Ernest Hilgard, also a professor at Stanford, is a former president of the American Psychological Association.

The significance of motivation for learning is usually assumed without question. On the one hand, the promise of reward or the threat of punishment provides means by which the teacher can keep the pupil at work; on the other hand, interest, curiosity, and self-selected goals keep the learner at work without pressure from the teacher. The teacher has a choice between using specific goads or enlisting self-activating motives, or perhaps employing some combination of these. The considerations that bear on what can or should be done are the present concern.

MOTIVATION IN LEARNING THEORY

The straightforward relationship between motivation and learning is not supported by experimental studies of learning as these are carried out and described by psychologists. One obstacle to experimentation is the uncertain distinction between learning and performance as they relate to motivation: It may be that learning (habit formation) arises through simple contiguous association, independent of motivation, while motivation affects the utilization of habit, that is, performance. For purposes, such as those of instruction, the distinction between learning and performance becomes somewhat less important, since what keeps the pupil performing is also likely to keep him learning. Still, if the distinction is important in theory it may also have some importance in practice. For example, some relatively low-pressure learning, such as browsing in a library, may be quite important, even though it goes on at a low level of motivation. When motivation is aroused, the results of this browsing may be capitalized on, thus providing an illustration in practice of the distinction that the experimentalists make in theory.

There is considerable turmoil within learning theory at the present time, as other chapters of the 1964 yearbook indicate. The once dominant need-drive-incentive theory, interpreting reinforcement as drive-reduction, has been undergoing searching re-examination. The drives usually studied (hunger, thirst, pain) were always treated as aversive drives, from which relief was sought; now the "neglected drives" of curiosity, manipulation, activity, and achievement, which emphasize the positive side of something sought rather than the negative of something to be escaped, have come to the fore.[1]

Secondary reinforcements, that is reinforcing situations supposed to have been derived from primary ones based on primitive drives, turn out not always to be secondary at all, and their properties are quite complex. Lawrence and Festinger[2] have shown in a series of provocative experiments that small or intermittent rewards, if they are sufficient to keep an organism at the task, tend to

[1] Ernest R. Hilgard, "Motivation in Learning Theory," in *Psychology: A Study of a Science,* Vol. V. Edited by S. Koch. New York: McGraw-Hill Book Co., 1963.

[2] Douglas H. Lawrence and Leon Festinger, *Deterrents and Reinforcement: The Psychology of Insufficient Reward.* Stanford, California: Stanford University Press, 1962.

Pauline S. Sears and Ernest R. Hilgard, "The teacher's role in the motivation of the learner," *Theories of Learning and Instruction,* Sixty-third Yearbook of the National Society for the Study of Education, Part I, 1964, 182–209. Reprinted by permission.

yield responses more resistant to extinction than large and regular rewards; they attribute this to the "extra attractions" that have to be adduced to justify the amount of work expended for the slight reward obtained.

The drive theory itself has been subjected to criticism by those who see learning becoming attached to cue-stimuli, whether these cues are internal or external.[3] Thus we do not need a "doorbell-answering-drive" to make us respond to a ringing doorbell: the ringing bell is both cue and drive.

The literature on motivation has been summarized in a large number of recent books, many of which have little to say about human motivation. One of the broader studies is that of Rethlingshafer,[4] which includes animal studies but is more particularly concerned with human motives.

Despite the uncertainty about the precise relationship between motivation and learning, the general importance of motivation in relation to the learner's absorption in his task, his resistance to distraction, his favorable attitudes toward school, can scarcely be denied. Thus, some problems of detail (e.g., that excessive motivation may in some cases hinder learning) need not confuse us or prevent our paying confident attention to motivation as important in classroom learning.

MOTIVES WHICH TEACHERS CAN UTILIZE OR AROUSE

A distinction has to be made between a motivational disposition and an aroused motive. A motivational disposition is a relatively enduring tendency to be prone to certain forms of motivational arousal, although at any one time that motive may be dormant. Thus, a person might be characterized as having a voracious appetite, which means that he is easily aroused by food; yet at any one time he may be satiated. Hunger is an aroused motive; the enduring characteristic of having a good appetite is a motivational disposition. In the same way some children are easily aroused to aggression, easily become dependent, or anxious. When so characterized, their motivational dispositions are being described.

SOCIAL MOTIVES: WARMTH AND NURTURANCE

Social motives have to do with one's relationships to other people. The desire to affiliate with others is one class of dependable human motivational dispositions found in parent-child relations, friendships, and as an important aspect of sex and marriage. Because the teacher is an adult, the affiliative motive often takes the form of dependency, that is, the child is the welcome recipient of the warmth and nurturance of the adult. There is evidence that such warmth and nurturance clearly relate to performances by young children on concept formation, memory, and maze performance, and affect the imitation of irrelevant behavior performed by adults. A nurturant adult, who then withdraws that nurturance, leads the child to make great efforts to restore the warm interaction. Most of the experimental evidence comes from tests made over short periods of time, and it would be valuable to know how these relationships endure through time. These conclusions are supported by the studies of Hartup,[5] Rosenblith,[6] Bandura and Huston,[7] Gewirtz,[8] and Gewirtz and Baer.[9]

The investigations just mentioned are chiefly laboratory-type studies designed to examine the effect of manipulation of nurturant variables upon child behavior. That their conclusions have implications for the classroom can be documented by studies of teacher warmth and pupil behavior. For example, Cogan[10] found that warm and considerate teachers got an unusual amount of original poetry and art from their high-school students.

[3] For example, see William K. Estes, "Stimulus Response Theory of Drive," in *Nebraska Symposium on Motivation,* pp. 114–68 (Edited by Marshall R. Jones. Lincoln, Nebraska: University of Nebraska Press, 1958); and Evan R. Keislar, "A Descriptive Approach to Classroom Motivation," *Journal of Teacher Education,* XI (June, 1960), 310–15.

[4] Dorothy Rethlingshafer, *Motivation as Related to Personality.* New York: McGraw-Hill Book Co., 1963.

[5] Willard W. Hartup, "Nurturance and Nurturance-Withdrawal in Relation to the Dependency Behavior of Preschool Children," *Child Development,* XXIX (June, 1958), 191–203.

[6] Judy F. Rosenblith, "Learning by Imitation in Kindergarten Children," *Child Development,* XXX (1959), 69–80. [See Section IV, no. 27 in this book.—EDITOR]

[7] Albert Bandura and Aletha C. Huston, "Identification as a Process of Incidental Learning," *Journal of Abnormal and Social Psychology,* LXIII (1961), 311–18.

[8] Jacob L. Gewirtz, "A Program of Research on the Dimensions and Antecedents of Emotional Dependence," *Child Development,* XXVII (1956), 206–21.

[9] Jacob L. Gewirtz and Donald M. Baer, "The Effect of Brief Social Deprivation on Behaviors for a Social Reinforcer," *Journal of Abnormal and Social Psychology,* LVI (1958), 49–56; Jacob L. Gewirtz and Donald M. Baer, "Deprivation and Satiation of Social Reinforcers as Drive Conditions," *Journal of Abnormal and Social Psychology,* LVII (1958), 166–72; Jacob L. Gewirtz, Donald M. Baer, and Chaya H. Roth, "A Note on the Similar Effects of Low Social Deprivation on Young Children's Behavior," *Child Development,* XXIX (1958), 149–52.

[10] Morris L. Cogan, "The Behavior of Teachers and the Productive Behavior of Their Pupils," *Journal of Experimental Education,* XXVII (December, 1958), 89–124.

Reed[11] found that teachers higher in warmth favorably affected pupils' interest in science. He found that the utilization of intrinsic interest by the teacher and the teacher's personal warmth were highly correlated; this would seem to justify some emphasis upon warmth of personality in the selection of teachers who are to be trained to make use of pupils' intrinsic motivation.

EGO-INTEGRATIVE MOTIVES: THE ACHIEVEMENT MOTIVE

A group of motives that serve to maintain self-confidence and self-esteem have sometimes been referred to as ego-integrative motives. These have been variously characterized as motives of self-actualization[12] or of competence.[13] The achievement motive may be taken as a convenient representative of this group of motives, for it has been the subject of numerous investigations.

Our society is achievement-oriented, and it is not surprising that the desire to meet standards of excellence motivates some students. Any such motivational disposition is, however, quite complex, and without some clarification we confuse motives of social competition (the desire for prestige or power) with those of meeting standards of excellence in a skill or in scientific or artistic production. The earlier studies on level of aspiration, concerned more with aroused motives, have been supplemented by studies of persistent achievement motives, initiated by McClelland and his associates,[14] and since carried on by many others.[15]

Because the achievement motive is so obviously related to classroom behavior, we shall return to it in other contexts.

CURIOSITY AND OTHER COGNITIVE MOTIVES

Among the "neglected drives" that have more lately come to prominence we may recognize a group that can be called cognitive because they are concerned with "knowing" the environment or the relationships among things and ideas. Pavlov long ago recognized what he called a "What-is-it reflex," by which he referred to curiosity in animals. The exploratory motives have been reintroduced by Harlow;[16] Berlyne[17] has brought out his own work and that of others in book form. This group of motives also includes manipulative motives[18] and activity motives.[19] These are related to what in the past have been called *intrinsic* motives, that is, motives that reside in the task itself rather than external to it (i.e., *extrinsic* motives, such as rewards or prizes).

These motives, too, are so important in school learning that further attention will be paid to them. All of these motives—social, ego-integrative, and cognitive—are open to manipulation in one way or another by the teacher. We turn now to how this may be done and what consequences can be expected.

THE SCHOOL ENVIRONMENT AND INSTRUCTIONAL PROCEDURES AS THEY BEAR UPON MOTIVATION

The general atmosphere of the school may determine which motives are aroused and, hence, which children will profit most from the school. This follows if some children respond more to one kind of motivation than to another; if all are to be served, some flexibility is essential. Within the general atmosphere the particular instructional methods and emphases also affect the utilization of motivational potential for learning. . . .

THE SCHOOL ENVIRONMENT AND ATMOSPHERE

It is well known that the socioeconomic backgrounds of the pupils affect their school motivation, particularly achievement motivation. This is well attested in numerous studies of subcultures

[11] Horace B. Reed, "Implications for Science Education of a Teacher Competence Research," *Science Education,* XLVI (December, 1962), 473–86.

[12] A. H. Maslow, *Motivation and Personality.* New York: Harper & Bros., 1954.

[13] R. W. White, "Motivation Reconsidered: The Concept of Competence," *Psychological Review,* LXVI (1959), 297–333.

[14] David C. McClelland, John W. Atkinson, Russell A. Clark, and Edgar L. Lowell, *The Achievement Motive.* New York: Appleton-Century-Crofts, 1953.

[15] For example, *Motives in Fantasy, Action, and Society* (Edited by John W. Atkinson. Princeton, New Jersey: Van Nostrand Co., 1958); and V. J. Crandall, "Achievement," in *Child Psychology,* pp. 416–59 (Sixty-second Yearbook of the National Society for the Study of Education, Part I. Edited by Harold W. Stevenson. Chicago: Distributed by University of Chicago Press, 1963).

[16] H. F. Harlow, "Learning and Satiation of Response in Intrinsically Motivated Complex Puzzle Performance by Monkeys," *Journal of Comparative and Physiological Psychology,* XLIII (1950), 289–94.

[17] D. E. Berlyne, *Conflict, Arousal, and Curiosity.* New York: McGraw-Hill Book Co., 1960.

[18] H. F. Harlow and G. E. McClearn, "Object Discrimination Learned by Monkeys on the Basis of Manipulation Motives," *Journal of Comparative and Physiological Psychology,* XLVII (1954), 73–76.

[19] W. F. Hill, "Activity as an Autonomous Drive," *Journal of Comparative and Physiological Psychology,* XLIX (1956), 15–19.

within America, such as those of Rosen[20] and Strodtbeck.[21] To the extent that school success (and continuing in school) is associated with higher occupational level, vocational aspiration can often be taken as a measure of achievement motivation. While the father's occupation has little relation to school success in the early grades, by the time the pupil reaches junior high school, his achievement is likely to be more related to his father's occupation than to his intelligence level.[22] These facts need to be recognized by the teacher; the inevitability of poor motivation on the part of those from lower occupational groups need not be accepted, but the need for special motivational efforts is obvious.

Let us suppose that a school wishes to stress problem-solving and creativity, in line with the current emphasis upon cognitive motives. How, then, can an atmosphere be created in which such motives will be aroused? The question has been studied by Shaftel, Crabtree, and Rushworth,[23] who point out that the teacher in dealing with the young child must do the following things: (*a*) make sure that the emotional climate of the classroom is suitable for the development of a healthy self-concept, (*b*) evoke problems when they are not immediately apparent to the children, (*c*) stimulate a problem-solving climate, which involves the process of search, rather than focusing on one right answer, and (*d*) plan a curriculum which stimulates problem-solving, by the use of experience units, construction activities, science experiments, group work, dramatic play, and role-playing.

A book by Taba[24] goes into specifics on the development of curricula and teaching methods which will release cognition and serve to satisfy cognitive needs. She makes use of some of the reflections about intelligence and experience recounted by Hunt,[25] and some of the observations of Piaget.[26] (The new interest in Piaget is evidenced in many places; a very able summary of his work has appeared.[27])

The old concept of ability grouping, as simplifying the task of the teacher, has been examined in a new light by Thelen.[28] He proposes that some teachers find given students, selected on the basis of the teacher's purposes, more "teachable" than others. When pupils are grouped in accordance with this criterion, the teacher tends to be more satisfied with his class, to like the pupils better, and to give them higher grades. The pupils, in turn, tend to be more orderly and more manageable, more cooperative, and more satisfied with the activities. They like each other better, and the class appears to be more cohesive than classes not selected on this basis. The achievement gains in these classes depended on the purposes of the teacher. When achievement was central among the teacher's purposes, these teachable groups did better. For some teachers achievement was not a central goal; their students did not do as well by achievement criteria.

ACTIVITIES CAPITALIZING ON COGNITIVE MOTIVATION

It is difficult to unravel those aspects of instruction that should be called motivational from those that are merely successful for whatever reason. It can be assumed that a kind of program that leads to spontaneous effort, to absorption in learning, and to results that yield the self-esteem that comes from reaching goals that are self-set by the learner must be well-grounded in appropriate motivation. In part, these results come about without direct concern for motivation through a kind of contagion of interest when problems are well set up, so that search leads to creative answers. Much of modern curriculum-planning concerns itself with the structure of knowledge and with the kind of thinking that is divergent rather than convergent; when conditions are appropriate, motivation appears to take care of itself.

Thus, major curricular studies in specific fields, such as the Biological Sciences Study Group[29]

[20] Bernard C. Rosen, "Race, Ethnicity, and the Achievement Syndrome," *American Sociological Review*, XXIV (1959), 47–60.

[21] Fred L. Strodtbeck, "Family Interaction, Values, and Achievement," in *Talent and Society: New Perspectives in the Identification of Talent*. Edited by David C. McClelland *et al*. Princeton, New Jersey: D. Van Nostrand Co., 1958.

[22] Joseph A. Kahl, *The American Class Structure*. New York: Rinehart & Co., 1957.

[23] Fannie R. Shaftel, Charlotte Crabtree, and Vivian Rushworth, "Problem-solving in the Elementary School," in *Problems-approach in the Social Studies*, pp. 25–47. Edited by Richard E. Gross. Washington: National Education Assn., 1960.

[24] Hilda Taba, *Curriculum Development: Theory and Practice*. New York: Harcourt, Brace & World, 1962.

[25] J. McV. Hunt, *Intelligence and Experience*. New York: Ronald Press, 1961.

[26] Jean Piaget, *The Psychology of Intelligence* (London: Routledge & Kegan Paul, 1950); Jean Piaget, *The Origins of Intelligence in Children* (Translated by Margaret Cook. New York: International Universities Press, 1952).

[27] John H. Flavell, *The Developmental Psychology of Jean Piaget*. Princeton, New Jersey: D. Van Nostrand Co., 1963.

[28] Herbert A. Thelen, "Development of Educational Methods for Different Types of Students." Chicago: Department of Education, University of Chicago, 1960 (duplicated).

[29] Bentley Glass, "Renascent Biology: A Report on the AIBS Biological Curriculum Study," *School Review*, LXX (Spring, 1962), 16–43.

and the Physical Sciences Study Group,[30] try to get the student to learn not only content but also the strategy and approaches of the scientist. In so doing, it is anticipated that as a by-product the student will wish to adopt a pattern of behavior conducive to productive thinking.

Suchman[31] has developed a program for training in inquiry skills with reference to science instruction. He conceives that some dissonance is necessary for development of such skills: a puzzling problem, a lack of structure. However, induction of relational constructs or discovery depends on existing conceptual systems in the child. Hunt[32] has suggested that controlling intrinsic motivation is a matter of providing an organism with circumstances that provide a proper level of incongruity with the residues of previous encounters with such circumstances that the organism has stored in his memory—the "problem of the match" between incoming information and that already stored.

Some experiments have been directed specifically to the problem of the conditions under which new ideas are freely developed. Torrance[33] divided all pupils in a university experimental school from the first to the sixth grade into four experimental groups at each grade level. Four conditions were created by two conditions of training and two sets of verbal instructions regarding output. The training conditions consisted in teaching two groups the principles for developing new ideas as suggested by Osborn,[34] while the other two groups, not taught any principles, were told that they would receive prizes for the best performance. The two sets of verbal instructions, combined with the two training conditions, were, first, a motivation to produce as many ideas as possible; second, a motivation to produce clever, original, and unusual ideas. In general, the results were in the expected direction: the special training in principles produced desired results beyond those produced by the promise of prizes, and the specific instructions to produce clever and unusual responses yielded more of them than the request for mere quantity of ideas. However, this was a short-range experiment and leaves unanswered the question: Would a series or pattern of exercises or training produce a permanent change in thinking abilities or cognitive style of a student?

How a teacher can produce divergent rather than convergent thinking is well illustrated by some studies by Gallagher.[35] There appears to be a correspondence between the sorts of statements the teacher makes and those the students make, as these are studied at the junior high school level. Thus, the profile of divergent ideas produced by the students corresponds rather closely to the pattern set by the teacher. In those sessions during which the teacher asks for more divergent production, the percentages of student responses in this direction are correspondingly high. Only a slight increase in the teacher's percentage of divergent questions brings forth a large increase in divergent production by the student. A single question, such as "What would have happened were the United States colonized from the west coast to the east instead of vice versa?" can bring forth as many as 15 or 20 responses, each related to a divergent idea. This illustration points again to the close relationship between content and motivation: The motivation here is to keep curiosity alive, and the only motivational device needed is to ask the right questions, and not to stifle curiosity by sticking too closely to facts that are to be memorized.

The introduction of mechanical aids to instruction, such as audio-visual aids and teaching machines, raises interesting motivational questions. Part of the appeal of the teaching machine is to the manipulative motives, and at the least an active process is substituted for a passive one. Smedslund[36] analyzes the orienting response, the overt response, and the reinforcement, and decides that the teaching machine relies entirely on extrinsic motivation. His analysis is, however, incomplete, for the program of a teaching machine need by no means be cut-and-dried, and sustained only by the reward of "right." A well-designed teaching program brings out cognitive motivation, and provides the intrinsic satisfactions that come with competence. At least the learner knows that he is learning, a result, alas, that is often not yielded for some pupils in the same classrooms. The chief criticism of too general reliance on teaching machines is that the learning process is essentially sedentary and isolated, even though the learner is active in finding his way through the program. Much of creative search involves moving about and active interchange with others.

[30] Gilbert C. Finlay, "The Physical Science Study Committee," *School Review*, LXX (Spring, 1962), 63–81.

[31] J. Richard Suchman, "Inquiry Training: Building Skills for Autonomous Discovery," *Merrill Palmer Quarterly*, VII (1961), 147–69.

[32] Hunt, *op. cit.*

[33] *Guiding Creative Talent*. Edited by Paul Torrance. Englewood Cliffs, New Jersey: Prentice-Hall, Inc., 1962.

[34] Alex F. Osborn, *Applied Imagination: Principles and Procedures of Creative Thinking*. New York: Charles Scribner's Sons, 1957.

[35] *A Report on a Conference of Research on Gifted Children*. Edited by James J. Gallagher. Washington: U.S. Department of Health, Education, and Welfare, U.S. Office of Education, Cooperative Research Branch, 1963.

[36] J. Smedslund, personal communication, 1961.

OBSERVED TEACHER INTERACTION
WITH CHILDREN

Teacher behavior has such a strong effect upon pupil motivation that it is worthwhile to review some of the observational studies that show how this comes about. For purposes of this review, these interactions will be grouped under three topics: (*a*) *affective* interaction, in which emotional-attitudinal variables, those most often considered in connection with positive mental health, will be in the foreground; (*b*) *evaluative* interaction, in which the teacher judges and criticizes, rewards and punishes; and (*c*) *cognitive* interaction, in which emphasis is essentially nonaffective and non-evaluative of achievement but encourages problem-solving, intellectual ferment, originality, and creativity.

Affective interaction between teacher and pupils. The teacher's responsibility for maintaining discipline in the classroom brings to the fore the affective consequences of various rewarding and punishing techniques, though these are by no means the only sources of affective influence of teachers upon students. Other aspects include the general warmth of the atmosphere that is created, the tolerance of some release of feeling on the part of the child, the protection of the individual egos, the satisfaction of individual needs. The techniques of control are, however, readily open to observation, and a number of studies have been directed toward them.

In an experiment in regular classrooms with eighth- and ninth-grade children, Kounin, Gump, and Ryan[37] studied the effects of three "desist techniques." Under one condition the teacher was punitive and intense. When a pretrained male student got up while slides were being shown and sharpened his pencil the teacher stalked toward him saying, "Hey you, who do you think you are?" in a firm, irritated voice; put her arm on his shoulders in a gesture of pushing him into his seat and said, "Now sit down! If you ever do that again, I'll really make trouble for you."[38] A second condition involved a matter-of-fact reprimand—i.e., "Don't do that again. Please sit down in your seat now." Under the third condition the teacher indicated her awareness of the behavior but did nothing about it. When the effects on the audience children were compared under the three conditions, the punitive technique was found to result in "the subjects' rating the *deviancy* as 'most serious,' the

degree of *interference* with attention to the task as 'greatest,' the *teacher* as 'making too much of an issue' over the event, the experience 'most discomforting,' and the *teacher* 'best able to maintain order in a class of tough kids.'"[39] The simple reprimand resulted in the students reporting the highest ratings for teacher fairness and paying more attention to the lesson after witnessing the event. Under the "ignoring" condition, pupils rated the teacher highest in her liking for children but thought the misbehavior most likely to recur.

In another study,[40] three pairs of punitive versus nonpunitive first-grade teachers were selected from three elementary schools. The 174 children in these teachers' classrooms were individually interviewed about what they thought was "the worst thing to do in school" and were asked for their explanations of why these misconducts were bad. Regarding their responses as expressions of their preoccupations, it was concluded that children who have punitive teachers, as compared with children who have nonpunitive teachers, manifest more aggression in their misconducts; are more unsettled and conflicted about misconduct in school; are less concerned with learning and school-unique values; and show some, but not consistent, indication of a reduction in rationality pertaining to school misconduct. A theory that children with punitive teachers develop less trust of school than do children with nonpunitive teachers was also presented to explain some of the findings.

Some hypotheses concerning the types of social power that are exercised in classrooms were tested in a correlational study by Rosenfeld and Zander.[41] Among other findings were the following:

1. Two forms of coercion by teachers are discriminated by students: disapproval of inadequate performance, and disapproval when the performance is as good as the student feels he can do. The first type has little effect on future aspiration or performance, while the second has a deleterious effect on both aspiration and future performance.

2. Two forms of reward are also discriminated by students. When rewards are showered indiscriminately, tendencies to accept the teacher's influence are lowered; when rewards are limited to adequate performances, the teacher's influence is increased.

---

[37] Jacob S. Kounin, Paul V. Gump, and James J. Ryan, "Explorations in Classroom Management," *Journal of Teacher Education*, XII (June, 1961), 235–46.

[38] *Ibid.*, p. 237.

[39] *Ibid.*

[40] Jacob S. Kounin and Paul V. Gump, "The Comparative Influence of Punitive and Nonpunitive Teachers upon Children's Concepts of School Misconduct," *Journal of Educational Psychology*, LII (February, 1961), 44–49.

[41] Howard Rosenfeld and Alvin Zander, "The Influence of Teachers on Aspirations of Students," *Journal of Educational Psychology*, LII (February, 1961), 1–11.

The ways in which teachers exercise power, as indicated by these types of reward and punishment, have additional consequences in affecting the favorableness or negativeness of student attitudes toward the teacher and toward course content.

While rewarding and punishing behavior affect teacher influence, there are many other affective interactions between teachers and pupils. Della Piana and Gage [42] found, for example, that some pupils are more concerned about feelings and personal relationships, while others are mainly achievement-oriented. Classes made up predominantly of pupils of the first type tend to accept the teacher whom they like, and to reject the teacher whom they dislike, on personal grounds; classes composed of pupils of the second type pay less attention to teacher warmth in estimating their acceptance or rejection of particular teachers. It often turns out that what is important for one pupil is not important for another; this is one reason why cookbook formulas for good teaching are of so little use and why teaching is inevitably something of an art.

Another subtle influence of affective responsiveness of teachers has to do with creativity. A rather plausible principle from psychoanalysis is that creativity involves some freedom in the use of unconscious or preconscious processes. These processes tend to be less critical and more impulsive than the more rational and analytical processes, and hence are likely to call for some tolerance on the teacher's part. The process of partial or limited regression has been called "regression in the service of the ego" by Kris; [43] the importance of something similar has been stressed by Kubie, [44] who believes that too much emphasis upon convergent thinking in the early years leads to a neurotic distortion of the creative process. That is, the child becomes frightened or anxious over that part of the normal play of his own fantasy life which does not follow the "rules" of evidence and logic.

Thus Spaulding [45] found strong negative relations between the expression of creativity in elementary-aged children and teacher behavior characterized as formal group instruction, using shame as a punishment technique. Sears [46] has shown that there are positive correlations between creativity and teachers' rewarding by personal interest in the child's ideas, accompanied by a high frequency of listening to the child. Such teaching techniques probably provide an atmosphere in which the child can permit himself more leeway in expression of unconventional ideas without threat of devastating criticism. Torrance [47] has emphasized the pressures toward conformity, away from creativity, exerted by the peer group of classmates. Competition may increase such pressures. Teachers may be able to provide an atmosphere which reduces these pressures somewhat. It is interesting that, in the aforementioned Sears study, much the same teacher behavior which tended to be related to creativity in the children was also positively related to the degree in which children in the classroom liked one another. A peer group in which there are good feelings between the children probably is more tolerant of nonconformist behavior than one in which the children like each other less.

The competitive situation of the classroom is almost inevitably anxiety-provoking for some children, and the handling of this anxiety in one form or another becomes an important task for the teacher. There is a large literature on this topic, concerned both with anxiety in general and with the special anxieties arising in the test situation so often confronted in school. [48] The results are complex and, in some cases, contradictory. The subtlety of the relationships involved is well illustrated by a study by Sarason, Mandler, and Craighill [49] in which it was found that (*a*) low-anxious college students did better, in general, on a laboratory task than high-anxious subjects, and (*b*) pressure to complete the task improved the performance for low-anxious subjects, but did not do so for high-anxious ones. It appears that anxiety is interfering enough, without adding new components to it through pressure; low-anxious subjects, working without interference, can accept the exhortation to do better.

[42] G. M. Della Piana and N. L. Gage, "Pupils' Values and the Validity of the Minnesota Teacher Attitude Inventory," *Journal of Educational Psychology*. XLVI (March, 1955), 167–78.

[43] Ernest Kris, *Psychoanalytic Explorations in Art*. New York: International Universities Press, 1952.

[44] L. S. Kubie, *Neurotic Distortions of the Creative Process*. New York: Noonday Press, 1952.

[45] R. Spaulding, "Achievement, Creativity, and Self-concept Correlates of Teacher-Pupil Transactions in Elementary Schools." Urbana, Illinois: University of Illinois (U.S. Office of Education Cooperative Research Project No. 1352), 1963 (mimeographed).

[46] Pauline S. Sears, "The Effect of Classroom Conditions on Strength of Achievement Motive and Work Output of Elementary-School Children." In press, 1963.

[47] Torrance, *op. cit.*

[48] Seymour B. Sarason *et al., Anxiety in Elementary-School Children* (New York: John Wiley & Sons, 1960); Britton K. Ruebush, "Anxiety," in *Child Psychology*, pp. 460–516 (Sixty-second Yearbook of the National Society for the Study of Education, Part I. Edited by Harold W. Stevenson. Chicago: Distributed by the University of Chicago Press, 1963).

[49] Seymour B. Sarason, George Mandler, and Peyton G. Craighill, "The Effect of Differential Instructions on Anxiety and Learning," *Journal of Abnormal and Social Psychology*, XLVII (April, 1952), 561–65.

The interplay between anxiety and achievement has been studied by Flanders[50] in experimentally produced climates, characterized on the one hand as "learner-centered" and on the other as "teacher-centered." In the learner-centered climate the teacher was acceptant and supportive of the student and problem-centered in approach; in the teacher-centered climate the teacher was directive and demanding, often deprecating, in his behavior toward the individual. Anxiety was estimated from physiological measures (pulse rate, galvanic skin responses) and by the direction and intensity of movements of a lever operated by the students to indicate positive and negative feelings. The major conclusions were:

1. When a conflict arises, student behavior oriented to the handling of interpersonal anxiety takes precedence over behavior oriented toward achievement.
2. The "teacher-centered" behavior of directing, demanding, and using private criteria in deprecating a student leads to hostility to the self or the teacher, aggressiveness, or occasionally withdrawal, apathy, and even emotional disintegration.
3. The "learner-centered" behavior of accepting the student, being evaluative or critical only by public criteria, and being usually supportive, elicited problem orientation, decreased interpersonal anxiety, and led to emotionally readjusting and integrative behavior.

In these days of emphasis upon cognitive processes, it is quite possible for the pendulum to swing too far, and hence to defeat the attainment of the very cognitive goals that are being sought. If cognition is made synonymous with achievement and competition for excellence, the concomitantly aroused anxiety may defeat the development of the very creativity and problem-solving orientation that is being sought. Hence the teacher's awareness of the affective interaction with pupils is as important in a curriculum directed toward cognition as one with other goals, such as those of social competence or personal adjustment. Much of the abstract discussion of educational goals overlooks the essential interrelatedness of low anxiety and high performance, and the need for teacher warmth if the climate to create is to be provided.

Evaluative interaction between teacher and pupils. As indicated in the foregoing section, teacher evaluation can be by private criteria or by public criteria; in the one case the evaluation is likely to be punitive and to arouse hostility; in the other case it is likely to be informative and hence lead to better learning.

A very interesting experiment was done by Page[51] with high school and junior high school students and a large number of teachers. The teachers graded objective tests of their students and then randomly assigned each paper to one of three groups. The group-one pupil was given back his paper with no comment except the mark. Each group-two pupil was given a stereotyped comment from excellent if his score was high to "let's raise this grade." Every C student, for example, received his mark with the notation, "perhaps try to do still better?" For group three, the teacher wrote a personal comment on every paper, saying whatever she felt would encourage that particular pupil. On the next objective test, groups two and three outperformed group one. The personalized comments seemed to have a greater effect than the standardized comments, but even a very short standard comment written on the paper produced measurable improvement. The greatest improvement was found in the failing students in group three, who received an encouraging personal note.

This study points up the motivational significance of evaluative practices that go beyond the indication of right or wrong answers. Personal interest of the teacher in the student's progress is shown to be effective.

. . .

Without reviewing further studies at this point, it is perhaps sufficient to point out that a teacher's evaluative activities go far beyond marking papers; they include attention to many experiences of success and failure, of expanded or restricted autonomy, of immediate and long-term goal-setting, of recognition of individual progress, and of attitudinal response to divergent behavior. These evaluative behaviors have the characteristics of positive and negative reinforcers, and, as such, are motivationally relevant to learning.

Cognitive interaction between teacher and pupils. To the extent that the teacher imparts skill and knowledge and teaches the approaches to solving problems and creating products that are both novel and valuable, he is having a cognitive interaction with pupils. This is the most readily understood purpose of teaching, but it is by no means easy to categorize the processes that are involved. They include methods, such as lecture, discussion, individual projects; they include content-related matters, such as structuring the problem and developing content-relevant understandings. Attempts at categorizing, such as those of Medley and

---

[50] Ned A. Flanders, "Personal-Social Anxiety as a Factor in Experimental Learning Situations," *Journal of Educational Research,* XLV (October, 1951), 100–110.

[51] E. B. Page, "Teacher Comments and Student Performance," *Journal of Educational Psychology,* XLIX (1958), 173–81.

Mitzel,[54] Smith,[55] and Wright and Proctor [56] are none too satisfactory, being either very general or at such a commonsense level as to have no element of newness in them. Thus, Wright and Proctor [57] classify the content of what teachers of mathematics say to their pupils as promoting (*a*) ability to think, (*b*) appreciation of mathematics, and (*c*) curiosity and initiative. The effort to devise such categories has value, however, in that it calls attention to the fact that what the teacher says to the pupil goes beyond the exposition of subject matter.[58]

Spaulding,[59] using tape recordings from 21 elementary teachers, identified empirically components of teacher behavior similar to the more global behavior syndromes discussed by Anderson,[60] Withall,[61] and Lewin, Lippitt, and White.[62] Support was given to the prediction that self-concepts of children would be higher in classrooms in which the teacher was "socially integrative" and "learner supportive." Spaulding's description of the behavior found to be positively related to self-concept was as follows: "calm, acceptant transactions in general with private, individualized instruction and a concern for divergency, attention to task, and the use of task-appropriate procedures and resources."

However, a test of the predictions involving "democratic" teacher behavior [63] failed to gain support. Neither pupil self-concepts, achievement, nor creativity was found to be related to this pattern of behavior.

All of these pupil outcomes were positively correlated to a modest degree with the component described as follows: "business-like lecture method with insistence upon attention to task and conformity to rules of procedure." [64] In the case of scores on reading achievement, this correlation was strongly significant. Ryans [65] also found business-like methods and warmth related to students' behavior. For elementary-school classes, high positive relationships were noted between observers' assessments of "productive pupil behavior" (e.g., assessments presumed to reflect pupil alertness, participation, confidence, responsibility and self-control, initiating behavior, and so on) and observers' assessments of previously identified patterns of teacher behavior which seemed to refer to understanding, friendly classroom behavior; organized, businesslike classroom behavior; and stimulating, original classroom behavior.

For secondary-school classes, low positive relationships appeared to obtain between productive pupil behavior and the above-named categories of teacher behavior, with a tendency for the stimulating, original teacher classroom-behavior pattern to show a slightly higher correlation with pupil behavior than the understanding, friendly or the organized, businesslike teacher behavior patterns.

A narrower definition of pupil task-oriented behavior was used by Sears.[66] Time samples of the percentage of time elementary-school children were attentive to the assigned task were found strongly related to teacher behavior. If children work steadily during a large proportion of class time, their teachers tend to give rewards in evaluative terms, to the group rather than to the individual, without show of interest in individual personalities. They tend to teach by statement and by giving of information. Thus the teacher behavior related to task-oriented work is very different from that associated with children's production of creative responses. It was also found that high frequencies of task-oriented behavior, as defined here, did not relate to achievement as reflected in test scores. The quiet, apparently industrious groups did not achieve more.

The teaching methods just described could be characterized as directive on the part of the teacher.

[54] Donald M. Medley and Harold E. Mitzel, "Measuring Classroom Behavior by Systematic Observation," in *Handbook of Research on Teaching*, pp. 247–328. Edited by N. L. Gage. Chicago: Rand McNally & Co., 1963.

[55] B. Othanel Smith, "A Study of the Logic of Teaching: A Report on the First Phase of a Five-Year Research Project." Washington: U.S. Office of Education, 1959 (duplicated).

[56] E. Muriel J. Wright and Virginia H. Proctor, *Systematic Observations of Verbal Interaction as a Method of Comparing Mathematics Lessons*. St. Louis, Missouri: Washington University (U.S. Office of Education Cooperative Research Project No. 816), 1961.

[57] *Ibid.*

[58] For problems of cognitive interactions as related to particular subject matters, see the chapters in the 1964 yearbook by Bruner on mathematics and by Carroll on reading. *The Handbook of Research on Teaching (op. cit.)* contains excellent comprehensive reviews of significant studies.

[59] Spaulding, *op. cit.*

[60] Harold H. Anderson, "Domination and Socially Integrative Behavior," in *Child Behavior and Development*, pp. 459–84. Edited by Roger G. Barker, Jacob S. Kounin, and Herbert F. Wright. New York: McGraw-Hill Book Co., 1943.

[61] John Withall, "Development of a Technique for the Measurement of Socioemotional Climate in Classrooms," *Journal of Experimental Education*, XVII (March, 1949), 347–61.

[62] Kurt Lewin, Ronald Lippitt, and R. K. White, "Patterns of Aggressive Behavior in Experimentally Created 'Social Climates,'" *Journal of Social Psychology*, X (1939), 271–99.

[63] *Ibid.*

[64] *Ibid.*, p. 119.

[65] David G. Ryans, "Some Relationships between Pupil Behavior and Certain Teacher Characteristics," *Journal of Educational Psychology*, LII (April, 1961), 82–90.

[66] Sears, *op. cit.*

Stern[67] has reviewed 34 studies (largely of college classes) comparing nondirective with directive instruction in influencing two types of learning outcome: (*a*) gain in achievement of cognitive knowledge and understanding, and (*b*) attitude change toward self or others. The following quotation summarizes the findings:

In general, it would appear that amount of cognitive gain is largely unaffected by the autocratic or democratic tendencies of the instructor. The majority of investigators who have attempted to measure differences in achievement report no particular advantage for either approach. . . . Regardless of whether the investigator was concerned with attitudes toward the cultural outgroup, toward other participants in the class, or toward the self, the results generally have indicated that non-directive instruction facilitates a shift in a more favorable, acceptant direction.[68]

However, in connection with student reactions to nondirective instruction, "at least as many students feel dissatisfied, frustrated, or anxious in a nondirective classroom as consider it valuable." Nondirective instruction, as practiced by some instructors, may be more laissez faire than learner-centered, and may arouse latent anxieties in students with precarious ego-strength. The next section considers the interaction of student predisposition and teaching method.

CHILD PERSONALITY, TEACHER PERSONALITY, AND THEIR CONSEQUENCES FOR THE MOTIVATION OF THE LEARNER

It has not been possible, in attempting to indicate some of the influences of teachers upon pupils, to avoid occasional mention of differences in pupils (and teachers) that affect the results, not entirely related to the specific classroom behavior of the teacher or specific instructional techniques. In this section we shall call attention more specifically to some of the personality factors that influence the acceptability of different methods of teaching.

PUPIL PERSONALITY AND THE CONDITIONS FAVORING ACHIEVEMENT

As one illustration, consider the differences between the independent, autonomous student and the one who is dependent-prone, that is, is likely to turn for support to adult authority. These relationships among students of eighth-grade geometry have been studied by Amidon and Flanders.[69]

The primary purpose of this study was to determine the effects of direct versus indirect teacher behavior and of clear versus unclear student perception of the learning goal on the achievement of eighth-grade geometry students. A specially trained teacher role-played both a very direct and a very indirect teacher in a laboratory situation involving 140 eighth-grade pupils, chosen from a larger population on the basis of high scores on a test of dependency proneness. All students were randomly assigned to one of the following four experimental treatments: direct teacher influence with clear goals, direct teacher influence with unclear goals, indirect teacher influence with clear goals, and indirect teacher influence with unclear goals.

Students in the various classifications were then compared on the basis of pre- and post-achievement tests in geometry. No differences were found between the clear-goal and unclear-goal treatments, indicating that in this study, at least, achievement of dependent-prone students was not affected by perception of the learning goal. An analysis of the direct and indirect treatments indicated that the children taught by the indirect teacher learned more than did the children taught by the direct teacher.

The results of this study take on additional meaning when compared with the results of Flanders[70] using the same experimental design. Flanders found no differences (among the four experimental conditions) in the total group of 560 students who ranged from very high to very low on the dependence scale. Apparently, dependent-prone students are more sensitive to types of teacher influence than are independent-prone students as measured by scores on the test for dependence proneness.

Whether or not a particular type of student can learn when he is exposed to a particular style of teaching has interested a number of researchers. Smith[71] and Wispe[72] have both shown that when

[67] George G. Stern, "Measuring Non-cognitive Variables in Research on Teaching," in *Handbook of Research on Teaching, op. cit.*, p. 427.

[68] *Ibid.*, p. 428.

[69] Edmund Amidon and Ned A. Flanders, "The Effects of Direct and Indirect Teacher Influence on Dependent-prone Students Learning Geometry," *Journal of Educational Psychology*, LII (December, 1961), 286–91.

[70] Ned A. Flanders, "Teacher Influence, Pupil Attitudes, and Achievement." Minneapolis: University of Minnesota (U.S. Office of Education Cooperative Research Project no. 397), 1960 (mimeographed).

[71] Donald E. P. Smith, "Fit Teaching Methods to Personality Structure," *High School Journal*, XXXIX (December, 1955), 167–71.

[72] Lauren G. Wispe, "Evaluating Section Teaching Methods in the Introductory Course," *Journal of Educational Research*, XLV (November, 1951), 161–86.

students are classified by the use of personality test data, they respond differently to highly organized (versus loosely organized) classroom activities in a college remedial reading course [73] and to college lecturing (versus group discussion) techniques [74] in Freshman sociology.

Asch,[75] Kagen and Mussen,[76] and Livson and Mussen [77] have studied the reactions of dependent-prone persons in various kinds of experimental situations. They concluded that dependent-prone individuals are more likely to comply with authority figures and conform to group pressures than the less dependent-prone. Their results suggest that a dependent-prone student might become overly concerned with following the suggestions and directions of a teacher and more dependent on support and encouragement.

Kagan, Sontag, Baker, and Nelson,[78] working from the Fels Institute longitudinal data, studied the 35 subjects who had gained the most on I.Q. retest, and the 35 who had lost the most. The ascending I.Q. group was characterized by independence, mastery, high need achievement, and curiosity. The descending I.Q. group showed dependence and an attitude that competition was not emotionally comforting. Thus, there seems to be a relation between motivational dispositions and the production represented by scores on an intelligence test. The more active and achievement-motivated subjects the data suggest, interact more effectively with their environment in ways which provide for increase in I.Q. Much of the teacher's interaction with pupils must be directed toward arousal of such motivation.

Gains in achievement for children of superior mental ability were found related, in Sears' study,[79] to various teacher behaviors which may provide such arousal. These included the frequency with which the teacher emphasizes the expanding and amplifying of ideas, giving of alternatives and possibilities rather than of straight statements of facts,

and also the amount of listening to the child done by the teacher. These methods essentially stimulate but do not direct, and for bright children they seem to be effective in connection with achievement.

Another illustration of pupil personality as affecting responsiveness to teaching is that of Grimes and Allinsmith concerned with compulsivity and anxiety. . . . [A summary of the Grimes and Allinsmith material is here omitted because the original article is reprinted in this book (X, 69).—EDITOR]

It appears that instructional methods make a difference for certain kinds of pupils, and a search for the preferred method of teaching can succeed only when consideration is given to the personality of the learner. On the other hand, many of the relationships cited are of only moderate size and based on selected samples of teachers. Definitive answers to questions of results of different instructional techniques await replication of new samples.

TEACHING PERSONALITY AND TEACHING EFFECTIVENESS

Heil, Powell, and Feifer [81] have related pupil achievement to interaction between teacher and pupil personalities. Three teacher and four pupil personality types were identified. The various teacher-pupil combinations were compared in terms of measures of pupil achievement, teacher knowledge, and classroom ratings. The well-integrated (self-controlling) teachers were the most effective with all types of students, whereas the weakly integrated (fearful) teachers were ineffective with everyone except the children identified as "strivers." The third type of teacher (turbulent) identified by these investigators is similar to a defensively intellectual person in using intellectualization as a mechanism of defense. The turbulent teachers were found to be effective with children who had been categorized as "conformers" or "strivers," particularly in mathematics and science achievement. They were ineffective with "opposers" and "waverers," two classroom-problem types requiring interpersonal skills to which these teachers were totally indifferent. The behavior of the "self-controlled teacher" suggests the importance of consistency, structure, routine activities, and orderliness—especially for "opposing" or "wavering" (anxious) children. The criterion measure in this study was simply scores on achievement tests.

[73] Donald E. P. Smith, *op. cit.*

[74] Wispe, *op. cit.*

[75] Solomon E. Asch, "Effects of Group Pressure upon the Modification and Distortion of Judgments," in *Groups, Leadership, and Men.* Edited by H. Guetzkow. Pittsburgh: Carnegie Press, 1951.

[76] Jerome Kagan and Paul H. Mussen, "Dependency Themes on the TAT and Group Conformity," *Journal of Consulting Psychology,* XX (1956), 19–27.

[77] Norman Livson and Paul H. Mussen, "The Relation of Control to Overt Aggression and Dependency," *Journal of Abnormal and Social Psychology,* LV (1957), 66–71.

[78] Jerome Kagan, Lester W. Sontag, Charles T. Baker, and Virginia L. Nelson, "Personality and I.Q. Change," *Journal of Abnormal and Social Psychology,* LVI (1958), 261–66. [See Section IX, no. 64 in this book.]

[79] Sears, *op. cit.*

[81] L. M. Heil, Marion Powell, and I. Feifer, *Characteristics of Teacher Behavior Related to the Achievement of Children in Several Elementary Grades.* Washington: U.S. Department of Health, Education, and Welfare, Office of Education, Co-operative Research Branch, 1960.

It was earlier pointed out that teacher warmth tends to be associated with the encouragement of creativity. Sears[82] found that teachers who like pupils tend to have pupils who like each other. Other aspects of teacher behavior related to the pupils' liking of each other include the manner in which such teachers use rewards and punishments. Rewards tend to be individualized, directed to the person, rather than to the group; punishments, however, are more often group-directed, hence reducing the sting of individual criticism. Children perhaps show liking for each other under these circumstances because the teaching techniques allow for social interchange without tension engendered by personal evaluation.

Thus, the teacher as a motivating agent operates in two interrelated ways. First, teacher personality and behavior act through a kind of contagion, in which the teacher becomes a model for appropriate behavior. The principles at work here are those of imitation and identification. Second, the teacher, as an administrator of rewards and punishments, wields power and creates a structure in which learning occurs. Here the principles are the more usual ones of positive and negative reinforcement. In addition, and in subtle ways, the child becomes an independent seeker and learner, satisfying his curiosity in his own ways and at his own pace.

The consequence of displaying interest in the individual child and his ideas, of acting in a warmly encouraging manner rather than in a critically evaluative one, is to produce a creative child, with a liking for the other children. The consequence of "efficient" teaching, in which the quiet industrious classroom is the goal, comes about through group methods and frequent evaluation, with a product neither high in conventional subject-matter achievement nor characterized particularly by new ideas or child-to-child affiliation. However, businesslike, well-organized teaching together with individualized attention to the student is associated with favorable learning outcomes, and structure appears to be favorable, at least on a short-term basis, for more anxious or dependent students. There are suggestions, however, that dependent students tend to become more dependent on authority figures with directive teaching, and that their achievement may be better in certain situations with less directive teaching.

SUMMARY AND CONCLUSIONS

The turmoil in learning theory at the present time is reflected also in the uncertainty about the relationship between motivation and learning. Some extreme positions assert that motivation affects only performance, not learning; another viewpoint is that motivation is an irrelevant category, and that all learning is eventually under the control of the stimulus. These uncertainties within the more abstract discussions of learning theory need not detract from the practical importance of motivation in applied settings, where the distinction between learning and performance becomes less important, and where motivational dispositions are as relevant as motivational arousal.

The kinds of motives that the teacher can utilize and arouse are not the ones most often studied in the animal laboratory (hunger, thirst, and pain), but have more to do with personal and social motives that characterize children growing up in a particular culture. Even in the laboratory there is a turn away from deprived states to positive motives, such as activity, curiosity, and manipulation, to "hope" rather than "fear" as fundamental. Among the motives that the teacher necessarily uses in one way or another are the social (illustrated by warmth and nurturance), the ego-integrative (illustrated by the achievement motive), and the cognitive (illustrated by curiosity).

The school environment and atmosphere contribute to the arousal and support of particular motives. Various socioeconomic backgrounds bring children to school with different expectations of achievement. The ways in which pupils are grouped may affect their teachableness by given teachers. The ways in which the school is set up will determine whether or not creativity will be encouraged.

The current interest in making schools more intellectually exciting can be described as an effort to enhance and capitalize upon cognitive motivation. Most of the new curricula more or less take for granted that if students are free to work out their own solutions to problems, if they have an opportunity for divergent rather than merely convergent thinking, intrinsic motivation appears to be readily aroused.

Efforts to see how, in fact, teachers affect students have led to extensive observations of teacher behavior, to attempts to relate this behavior to certain consequences in the behavior, attitudes, and achievements of pupils. These interactions are conveniently classified as affective, evaluative, and cognitive. Affective consequences arise through teacher efforts to maintain control by way of reward and punishment; many other affective consequences are related to the anxieties created by the competitive situation in classrooms. Evaluation can be done individually in such a manner as to threaten self-esteem, or it can be done according to group standards and thus be less threatening.

---

[82] Sears, *op. cit.*

The nonacademic behavior of students is of course evaluated, particularly in the effort to maintain discipline; the judgment of severity of pupil problems tends today to conform more nearly to that of clinicians than formerly. Cognitive interaction of teachers and pupils lies at the heart of instruction. Some plausible conjectures about autocratic and democratic atmospheres do not appear to be supported by some recent studies; businesslike and matter-of-fact approaches tend to yield achievement as well as creativity. At the same time, support is given to nondirective approaches, apparently because they keep alive the searching behavior important to divergent thinking. Teachers who are insistent on quiet, orderly behavior, who teach by informative statements, produce task-oriented behavior favorable to convergent thinking; teachers who show personal interest and who avoid critical individual evaluation tend to favor the more creative products of divergent thinking.

Child personality affects the ability to profit from particular kinds of teaching. Compulsive and anxious children respond differently from those less compulsive and less anxious; for example, those high in these characteristics do very well ("overachieve") in structured situations; those who are highly anxious, but low in compulsivity, do poorly ("underachieve") in an unstructured setting. Dependency tendencies also affect the profit from particular kinds of teaching. Hence, teachers must know their pupils and must be flexible in their approaches if they are to have the most favorable results.

Teacher personality also has an influence on teaching effectiveness. This is to be expected because of the importance of the teacher as a "model" for pupil behavior. In some comparisons of self-controlling, fearful, and turbulent teachers, best results, by achievement measures, were obtained by the self-controlled teachers. Another dimension—that of warmth—appears to affect creativity, the warmer teachers encouraging divergent behavior. While perhaps there is little the teacher can do about his own personality, some self-awareness is no doubt helpful in avoiding extremes of unfavorable influence. Those responsible for teacher selection may be helped to make wiser choices when the results of some of these studies become better established.

The problems of motivation are so intertwined with problems of personality that an adequate account of motivation in relation to learning cannot rest solely on the findings of the learning laboratory. A classroom is a social situation, with a power structure, including peer relationships, and adult-child relationships; hence the most favorable motivational conditions need to take all of these factors into account, recognizing that the teacher is both model and reinforcer and, in ways not fully understood, a releaser of intrinsic motives.

71

Attention in Delay of Gratification [1]

WALTER MISCHEL
AND EBBE B. EBBESEN

In recent years, Walter Mischel has directed our attention to the conditions that affect a child's willingness to delay gratification (get a larger reward later instead of a smaller one immediately). The present study expands the earlier work by examining how the visual presence or absence of either of the rewards affects the child's willingness to wait. You may find yourselves surprised by the ability of very young children to wait a long time. The findings have strong implications with respect to the validity of the saying "out of sight, out of mind."

Mischel is a professor of psychology at Stanford University, where he and his collaborator, Ebbe Ebbesen, conducted this investigation.

The concept of voluntary postponement of immediate gratification for the sake of more distant long-term gains has a central place in conceptualizations of the development of complex human behavior. Formulations stressing the role of voluntary delay of reward range from the possible origins of "psychopathy" and antisocial be-

havior (e.g., Mowrer & Ullmann, 1945) to characterizations of societal and cultural adaptation patterns in terms of the renunciation of immediate gratifications in favor of disciplined seeking of more substantial future gains. At the empirical level, extensive experimental work has been done on delay of reward in animals (e.g., Renner, 1967). Surprisingly, although voluntary delay behavior has been assumed to be a critical component of such concepts as "ego strength," "impulse control," and "internalization," relatively little attention has been devoted to it in empirical work on human social behavior.

One line of research has tried to apply psychoanalytic concepts concerning ego functions to motoric inhibition and impulse control (e.g., Singer, 1955). Most of the resulting empirical work has relied on highly indirect measures of delayed gratification and ego control, mainly inferred from human movement responses on the Rorschach (e.g., Spivack, Levine, & Sprigle, 1959).

In contrast, the present research is part of a larger project to investigate delay of reward with more direct behavioral measures. For example, subjects were required to choose among actual alternatives that varied in delay time and value (e.g., immediate smaller versus delayed but larger rewards) in realistic situations (e.g., Mischel, 1966). Past research in this vein has investigated the organization of self-control by exploring the relationship between various preference patterns for immediate smaller rewards or delayed larger rewards and other theoretically relevant aspects of personality functioning. The network of associations found here so far indicates, for example, significant relations between preference for delayed rewards and indexes of achievement orientation, social responsibility, age, sociocultural and rearing conditions, and intelligence (e.g., Klineberg, 1968; Mischel, 1961a, 1961b, 1961c; Mischel & Metzner, 1962). Relations have also been found with resistance to temptation (Mischel & Gilligan, 1964) and with severity of psychological disturbances (Shybut, 1968). Correlational studies were supplemented in recent years by experiments to investigate more precisely the determinants of voluntary delay of reward and similar forms of self-control in laboratory situations (e.g., Mischel & Staub, 1965; Mischel, Grusec, & Masters, 1969). As a result of both correlational and experimental studies, some of the determinants of choice preferences for delayed rewards are becoming clearer (Mischel, 1966, 1968).

Although choice preferences for immediate or

[1] This study was supported by Research Grant M6830 from the National Institutes of Health, United States Public Health Service. Grateful acknowledgment is due to Jerry Zadny for serving as an experimenter.

Walter Mischel and Ebbe B. Ebbesen, "Attention in delay of gratification," *Journal of Personality and Social Psychology*, 1970, *16*, 329–337. Reprinted by permission.

delayed rewards are beginning to be understood, the psychological mechanisms through which persons manage to bridge the temporal delay of reward required for attainment of deferred gratification remain remarkably unstudied. In spite of its seemingly evident importance, little is known about the self-regulatory mechanisms during the actual delay period when the individual must engage in the waiting dictated by his choice of delayed, larger gratification. Past research has studied verbal choice preferences between rewards varying in value and in the delay time required to attain them, but just how subjects are able to wait during the temporal delay remains unknown. Given that one has chosen to wait for a larger deferred gratification, how can the delay period be managed? The mechanisms that maintain goal-directed delay seem especially important, considering the fact that the ability to sustain self-imposed delay for the sake of larger but delayed consequences appears to be a chief component of most complex higher order human behavior. A main purpose of the present research, therefore, was to investigate the psychological processes that mediate sustained waiting behavior for delayed gratification.

Freud's (1959) classic discussion of the transition from primary to secondary process is one of the few theoretical treatments of how delay of gratification may be bridged. According to the psychoanalytic formulation, ideation arises initially when there is a block or delay in the process of direct gratification discharge (Rapaport, 1967, p. 315). During such externally imposed delay, according to Freud, the child constructs a "hallucinatory image" of the physically absent need-satisfying object. Gradually, as a result of repeated association of tension reduction with goal objects, and the development of greater ego organization, the imposed delay of satisfying objects results in the substitution of hallucinatory satisfactions and other thought processes that convert "free cathexes" into "bound cathexes" (e.g., Freud, 1959; Singer, 1955). In spite of much psychoanalytic theorizing and speculation about the role of the mental representation of blocked gratifications in the development of delaying capacity, the process remains far from clear.

In their theoretical discussion of impulse control, Jones and Gerard (1967) reasoned that "time-binding," or the capacity to bridge delay of gratification, probably hinges on self-instructional processes through which the individual increases the salience of the delayed consequences or outcomes of his action. In their view, any factors (situational or within the individual) that make delayed consequences more salient should enhance impulse control and voluntary delay. Their position, while

emphasizing the self-instructional aspects of attention to deferred outcomes, also implies covert self-reinforcement processes through which the subject may reinforce his own waiting behavior by vividly anticipating some of the positive consequences to which it will lead. Finally, a cognitive-developmental view might lead one to expect that young children may readily forget the delayed outcomes for which they are waiting, and hence cease to wait unless they are reminded of the relevant contingencies and rewards involved in the delay-of-gratification paradigm.

In line with all the foregoing arguments, it seems most plausible that conditions that help the individual to attend mentally to the delayed reward for which he is waiting should help him to sustain the delay. Operationally, these speculations would suggest that any cues that make the delayed gratification more salient—that help the person to make deferred consequences more psychologically vivid or immediate (e.g., by letting him look at them, by visualizing them in imagination, or by reminding him of the object for which he is waiting)—should facilitate waiting behavior. Such expectations also seem congruent with the results of earlier work on choice of immediate but smaller versus delayed but larger rewards (Mahrer, 1956; Mischel, 1966; Mischel & Metzner, 1962; Mischel & Staub, 1965). These earlier studies showed that an important determinant of choice preference for delayed rewards is the individual's expectation or "trust" that he will really get the delayed (but more valuable) outcome. Consequently, conditions that increase the salience or visibility of the delayed gratification may enhance the subject's willingness to wait by increasing his subjective probability that the delayed outcome will really materialize and be available after the waiting time ends.

In light of the foregoing considerations, one might expect that voluntary delay behavior is facilitated when the subject converts, as it were, the deferred or delayed object into more tangible form by making it psychologically more immediate, as by providing himself with representations or physical cues about it. The most direct way to increase the salience of the deferred outcomes and to focus attention on them would be to have them physically present and facing the subject, so that he can attend to them readily and vividly. To investigate how attention to delayed and immediate outcomes influences waiting behavior for them, a first step would be to manipulate the availability of those outcomes for attention during the delay time.

Previous research on preference for delayed rewards has been conducted mainly with subjects at least 6 years of age or older. Preliminary observations of the actual waiting behavior of nursery school children suggested, however, that the capacity to wait for long-term goals and to inhibit both immediate gratification and motoric activity seems to develop markedly at about ages 3–4. It was hoped, therefore, that research with subjects in this young age range should be especially informative in revealing some of the processes that underlie the genesis of goal-directed waiting.

A first requirement was a paradigm in which such very young children would be willing to remain in an experimental room, waiting entirely alone for at least a short time without becoming upset and debilitatingly anxious. As an initial step (after the usual play periods for rapport building) each child was taught a game in which he could immediately summon the experimenter by a simple signal. This step was practiced repeatedly until the child clearly understood that he could immediately terminate his waiting period in the room simply by signaling for the experimenter, who regularly returned from outside as soon as the child signaled. After this critical procedure had been clearly established, the child was introduced to the relevant contingency. He was shown two objects (e.g., snack-food treats), one of which he clearly preferred (as determined by pretesting); to attain the preferred object he had to wait for it until the experimenter returned "by himself." The child was, however, entirely free throughout this waiting period to signal at any time for the experimenter to return; if he signaled, he could have the less preferred object at once, but would forego the more desirable one later.

To manipulate the extent to which children could attend to the reward objects while they were waiting, the rewards were removed from the experimental room in all combinations, creating four conditions with respect to the objects available for attention. In one condition, the children waited with both the immediate (less preferred) and the delayed (more preferred) reward facing them in the experimental room, so that they could attend to both outcomes. In another group neither reward was available for the subject's attention, both rewards having been removed from his sight. In the remaining two groups either the delayed reward only or the immediate reward only was left facing the child and available for attention while he waited. The dependent measure was the length of time before each child voluntarily terminated the waiting period.

In accord with the previously discussed theoretical ideas, it was predicted that conditions in which the delayed reward was present and visually available would enhance attention to it and hence increase voluntary delay time for it. It was anticipated that the condition in which the child was left

without either reward would make it most difficult to bridge the delay time and therefore lead to the shortest waiting. In addition it was expected, although less confidently, that the condition in which both the delayed and immediate reward were available for attention would best facilitate waiting time. This condition might permit the subject to compare and contrast the two outcomes, possibly providing himself with persuasive arguments and self-instructions to help him delay long enough to achieve his preferred gratification. On the other hand, one might also plausibly expect maximum delay when the child could focus his attention on the delayed reward without being tempted by the immediate gratification—that is, the condition in which the delayed reward was present for attention but the immediate one was not.

METHOD

SUBJECTS AND EXPERIMENTERS

The subjects were 16 boys and 16 girls attending the Bing Nursery School of Stanford University. Three other subjects were run but eliminated because of their failure to comprehend the instructions as described later. The children ranged in age from 3 years, 6 months, to 5 years, 8 months (with a median age of 4 years, 6 months). The procedures were conducted by two male experimenters. Eight subjects (4 males and 4 females) were assigned randomly to each of the four experimental conditions. In each condition each experimenter ran 2 males and 2 females in order to avoid systematic biasing effects from sex or experimenters.

PROCEDURE

The procedures were designed to develop a new method for studying delay behavior experimentally with young subjects. The development of this method was one of the chief goals of the project, and the procedures therefore are described in considerable detail.

In the week prior to the start of the experiment, the two male experimenters spent a few days playing with as many children in the nursery school as they could. These nurturant sessions were designed so that the children would more readily agree to accompany the experimenters to the "surprise room" and, once there, would be at ease. After obtaining the child's consent to go to the surprise room, the experimenter escorted the child to the experimental room.

The experimental room was a small private chamber containing a table, on which lay five ½-inch-long pieces of pretzel and an opaque cake tin. A chair was in front of the table, and on a second chair there was an empty cardboard box. Under the cake tin on the table were five 2-inch-long pretzels and two animal cookies. On the floor near the chair with the cardboard box were four battery-operated toys. On one wall, at right angles with the table, was a one-way mirror. Apart from these objects, the room was empty. The experimenter pointed out the four toys, and before the child could begin to play with the toys, asked the child to sit in the chair which was in front of the table. He then demonstrated each toy briefly in a friendly manner, saying with enthusiasm after each demonstration that they would play with the toys later on, placing each toy in the cardboard box out of sight of the child. These references to the toys were designed to help relax the children and also to set up an expectancy that both the child and experimenter would play with the toys sometime later on in the session (thus, terminating the delay period would not mean having to terminate play in the surprise room).

The next phase required teaching the child the technique for terminating the waiting period and summoning the experimenter at will. For this purpose the experimenter said:

> Sometimes I have to go out of the room and when I do, you can bring me back. Do you see these tiny pretzels? [The experimenter pointed to the five $\frac{1}{8}$-inch pieces of pretzel that would serve as signals.] Well, if I go out of the room and you eat one of these pretzels you can make me come back into the room. You can make me come back! Let's try it. I'll go out of the room now and shut the door. As soon as I do, you eat one of the pretzels and make me come back.

The instructions were repeated, if necessary, until the child seemed to understand them completely.

The experimenter then left the room and shut the door, observing through a small viewing hole in the door when the child ate the pretzel. As soon as the child put the pretzel in his mouth, the experimenter returned, laughing playfully and exclaiming how well the child brought him back into the room. To insure that the child learned reliably how to bring the experimenter back, this sequence was repeated four times with four of the five small pieces of pretzel, still leaving the last small piece lying next to the as yet unopened cake tin.

Next the experimenter lifted the cake tin, revealing the two sets of reward objects lying there (two cookies and five 2-inch pretzels). The experimenter asked the child which of the two rewards he liked better, and after the child chose, said:

> Oh well, you know what? In order for you to eat those _____ [naming the preferred reward] you will have to wait here in your chair and sit very still. I have to go out of the room for a while and when I come back you can eat those _____ [preferred reward] all up. You can take them off the table and eat them right up. But, you know, sometimes, I'm gone a long time and if you want to bring me back you can. Do you know how to bring me back? [All children did know how.] That's right. You eat that little piece [pointing to signal] and I have to come back. But I have to tell you something else. If you eat that and make me come back you can't have_____ [preferred reward]. You can't have them. But you can have all the _____ [naming less preferred reward]! If you sit very still in your chair

until I come back *by myself,* then you can eat the _____ [preferred reward]! But if you want to make me come back all you have to do is eat that [pointing to signal] and I'll come back; but then you can't have the _____ [preferred reward]; but you can have all the _____ [less preferred].

Thus the instructions faced the child with a choice: he could either continue waiting for the more preferred reward until the experimenter returned, or he could stop waiting by bringing the experimenter back. If he stopped waiting, then he would receive the less favored (but more immediately available) reward and forego the more preferred one. The waiting contingencies were repeated once more, and then, to assess if the subject understood them, the experimenter asked three questions: "Can you tell me how to bring me back"? "What happens if you eat the pretzel"? "But what happens if you sit very still in your chair and wait for me to come back by myself?" Three children were unable to answer these questions correctly and were therefore excluded from the data a priori.

At this point the experimenter was informed of the condition in which the subject was to be placed by consulting a slip of paper concealed in the room. This method assured that the experimenter remained unaware of the subject's experimental condition until the last possible moment in the procedure. Depending on the condition and the child's choice of preferred reward, the experimenter picked up the cake tin and along with it either nothing, one of the rewards (the more preferred reward or the less preferred reward), or both. The physical arrangement was such that the rewards, if left, were directly in front of the child at about shoulder level. In all conditions the signal for summoning the experimenter was left on the table in front of the child. Thus, depending upon the condition to which the child had been assigned, he was left waiting either with both the delayed and immediate rewards, with either the delayed but more preferred or the immediate but less preferred reward, or with neither reward available for attention. Finally, in all conditions the experimenter excused himself to leave, and as he was leaving, resummarized the waiting instructions and reminded the child that "no matter what you do, whether you sit and wait for me to come back by myself or whether you bring me back.... No matter what you do, we're going to play with my toys when I get back," This instruction was included to stress that the child's waiting behavior would not affect his later play period in the surprise room.

Waiting time was scored from the moment the experimenter shut the door. The experimenter returned either as soon as the child signaled or after 15 minutes—the criterion time—if the child did not signal. To determine whether or not the child remembered the waiting contingencies, when the experimenter finally returned he asked the child, "What happens now?" All children answered this question correctly. Subjects were also asked why they had or had not waited. Children who waited to criterion were allowed to eat the chosen, more preferred reward. Those who did not wait to criterion were allowed to eat the unchosen reward. Thereafter each child played with the toys for a while and then was escorted back to his nursery school playroom.

RESULTS

In accord with the previously discussed theorizing, it was expected that as the degree of attention paid to the delayed rewards increased, the length of time which the children waited would increase. To determine whether or not this prediction was fulfilled, the mean length of time waited (in minutes) was computed for each of the four attention conditions and is depicted in Table 1. Inspection of these results revealed that unexpectedly, the children waited longest when the rewards were entirely absent—that is, in the condition in which neither the delayed nor the immediate reward was available for attention during the waiting period. Furthermore, the children waited the shortest length of time when both the delayed and the immediate rewards were facing them during the waiting session. These results were exactly opposite to the predictions.

An analysis of variance of the mean delay times (Table 2) demonstrated that the overall effect of attentional conditions was significant ($F = 4.42$, $df = 3/28$, $p < .025$). To determine the relative contribution of the conditions to the overall effect, orthogonal contrasts were computed (Winer, 1962). The first orthogonal contrast (C_1 in Table 2) compared the effect of having any reward present for attention with having no reward present during the delay period. This comparison yielded an F of 9.52 ($p < .005$, $df = 1/28$). Thus, children waited much longer for rewards when the rewards were absent than when any rewards were left available for attention. The second orthogonal contrast (C_2) compared mean delay times when both rewards were present with mean delay times when either the delayed or the immediate reward was available for attention. The results of this contrast suggested a slight trend toward shorter delay when both rewards were present for attention, rather than when only one reward was present ($F = 3.45$, $df = 1/28$, $p < .1$). The final contrast (C_3), comparing

attention to the delayed reward with attention to the immediate reward, was not statistically significant ($F < 1$).

The absolute mean waiting times were probably depressed by the low maximum waiting period used, that is, 15 minutes. Ten subjects out of the total 32 in the study waited the maximum time. Table 3 shows the number of subjects in each condition who waited the full 15 minutes. An overall frequency analysis yielded a significant chi-square ($\chi^2 = 11.07$, $p < .025$, $df = 3$). Note that not a single child waited the maximum time in the condition in which both rewards were available, whereas 6 out of 8 children waited the maximum time when neither reward was present. These results further support the findings of the parametric analysis, showing greatest delay of gratification when the reward objects were not available for attention. In summary, children who were given the opportunity to attend to any of the rewards while they were waiting delayed less long than children who could not attend to any rewards while waiting.

FOLLOW-UP DATA

To test the stability of these findings, a partial replication was conducted in later follow-up work. In this replication, the method was altered in one major way. It was recognized that interpretation of the reported results might be somewhat hampered by the fact that the signal for terminating the delay

TABLE 2
ANALYSIS OF VARIANCE FOR MEAN WAITING
TIMES (IN MINUTES) IN EACH
ATTENTION CONDITION

Source	df	MS	F
Between	3	144.2	4.42**
C_1	1	310.5	9.52***
C_2	1	112.4	3.45*
C_3	1	9.8	< 1
Error	28	32.63	

* $p < .10$.
** $p < .025$.
*** $p < .005$.

TABLE 1
MEAN MINUTES AND STANDARD DEVIATIONS OF
WAITING TIME FOR A DELAYED REWARD
AS A FUNCTION OF ATTENTION

Statistic	Available for attention			
	No rewards	Both rewards	Delayed reward	Immediate reward
M	11.29	1.03	4.87	5.72
SD	6.84	2.39	6.57	6.43

TABLE 3
NUMBER OF CHILDREN WAITING THE MAXIMUM
TIME (15 MINUTES) IN EACH
ATTENTION CONDITION

Situation	Rewards available for attention			
	None	Both	Delayed	Immediate
Not waiting	2	8	6	6
Waiting	6	0	2	2

involved eating a tiny pretzel, and that pretzels also were the rewards. Therefore, instead of the tiny pretzel, a desk bell was used as the signal to terminate the delay period in the follow-up.

Subjects of comparable age from the same nursery school were run in the two conditions that had yielded the main effects. Namely, 12 children were left waiting with neither the delayed nor immediate rewards present and 12 with both rewards present.

The findings clearly supported the previous results. The mean waiting time for the condition in which neither reward was present for attention was 8.9 minutes ($SD = 5.26$), while the mean waiting time when both rewards were visible was only 3.09 minutes ($SD = 5.59$). These means were significantly different in the same direction found previously ($t = 2.61$, $df = 22$, $p < .025$). We therefore may conclude that this attentional condition produced reliable differences in the length of time that children delayed gratification (regardless of the signal used to terminate the delay period).

DISCUSSION

Throughout this study unexpected results emerged. A first surprise was the long duration of the waiting periods that many of these young children were able to maintain under some conditions. In pilot work, for example, some of the preschool youngsters waited for the preferred reward quietly by themselves, seated alone in a chair for periods sometimes exceeding 1 hour—an observation that is surprising, considering the widespread belief that young children are incapable of sustained delay of gratification. Moreover, throughout the entire study not a single child violated the stated contingency rule by consuming the preferred but delayed reward before the experimenter's return.

The experimental conditions exerted potent effects on the children's delay behavior, as seen in the finding that six out of eight children waited the maximum 15-minute time when they could attend to neither the immediate nor the delayed rewards, whereas the mean waiting time was about 1 minute when they could attend to both rewards. These differences between conditions suggest that it is inappropriate to conceptualize delay of gratification as if it hinged on an all-or-none "ability." Instead, most of the subjects in the present study, in spite of their young age, seemed capable of delay of gratification; the extent to which they did delay depended critically on the specific conditions of the delay period.

The initial theorizing about delay behavior led to predictions of results which were the direct opposite of the obtained findings. It was predicted that

attention to the outcomes available in the choice situation while waiting would enhance delay behavior; instead it sharply reduced delay of gratification. Extensive observations of the children's behavior during the delay period provided some clues for a better understanding of the mechanisms through which they mediated their own goal-directed waiting.

One of the most striking delay strategies used by some subjects was exceedingly simple and effective. These children seemed to facilitate their waiting by converting the aversive waiting situation into a more pleasant non-waiting one. They devised elaborate self-distraction techniques through which they spent their time psychologically doing something (almost anything) other than waiting. Instead of focusing prolonged attention on the objects for which they were waiting, they avoided looking at them. Some children covered their eyes with their hands, rested their heads on their arms, and found other similar techniques for averting their eyes from the reward objects. Many seemed to try to reduce the frustration of delay of reward by generating their own diversions: they talked to themselves, sang, invented games with their hands and feet, and even tried to fall asleep while waiting—as one child successfully did. These elaborate self-distractions occurred mainly in the rewards-absent condition and almost never in the both-rewards-present condition, since in the latter group the children quickly terminated the delay period.

These observations, while obviously inconclusive, suggest that diverting one's attention away from the delayed reward (while maintaining behavior directed toward its ultimate attainment) may be a key step in bridging temporal delay of reward. That is, learning *not* to think about what one is awaiting may enhance delay of gratification, much more than does ideating about the outcomes.

These observations also seem consistent with theoretical considerations which (post hoc) could correctly predict the obtained results. Namely, from the perspective of "frustrative nonreward" theory (e.g., Amsel, 1958, 1962; Wagner, 1966), the occurrence of non-reward when reward is expected elicits a primary frustration reaction. Congruent with this formulation, when the anticipation of reward is increased, the aversive frustration effect also should be greater. Hence one might predict that cues that enhance the salience of anticipated but still unavailable (delayed) rewards should increase the aversiveness of the delay period. Presumably the greater and more vivid the anticipation of reward, the greater the frustration generated by its delay. This line of reasoning would suggest that conditions that decrease the subjects' attention to the blocked reward—and that distract him by internal or overt activity from the frustrative delay of reward—would make it less aversive for him to continue his goal-directed waiting and hence permit him to wait longer for delayed gratifications. These theoretical expectations seem closely congruent both with the obtained findings and with the more informal observations of the children's delay behavior.

The present terminology focuses on the frustrative aspects of not being able to immediately obtain the preferred reward in the delay-of-gratification paradigm. The same theoretical considerations, however, apply to the aversiveness of the waiting period and of the continuous decisional conflict (between terminating versus waiting longer). In part, attending to the rewards in the waiting paradigm may be aversive, because it increases the frustration of anticipating the attainment of a blocked reward; in part it may be frustrative, because it enhances the aversiveness of the waiting situation and accentuates the ongoing decisional conflict. All of these sources of frustration seem an integral part of the delay-of-gratification situation, and attention to them makes effective delay behavior more difficult.

It is of considerable interest that delay behavior was about the same, regardless of whether the reward in front of the child was the immediately available one or the delayed, more preferred outcome. This finding seems most clearly to contradict any Freudian theoretical expectations that a mental focus on the delayed outcome (rather than the immediate gratification) serves to bridge temporal delay of gratification by providing an internal or "hallucinatory" representation of the desired but deferred or blocked outcome.

It might also be thought that the children's waiting behavior in the present situation depends on implicit "experimenter demands." Such speculations would predict that the presence of the delayed reward should serve as a cue to the subject that waiting for the delayed outcome is expected by the experimenter. Similarly the condition in which only the immediate reward is present should cue less lengthy waiting and enhance willingness to terminate the delay and settle for the immediate outcome. These interpretations are untenable, however, because waiting times were similar in the condition in which only the delayed reward was present and the condition in which only the immediate reward was present.

One further alternative interpretation that may be suggested is that attention to the rewards simply decreases their subjective value through some sort of habituation process, and therefore subjects wait less long. In that case one would expect the attention to the delayed reward to result in its subjective devaluation and hence predict shorter waiting when the delayed reward is present, as indeed occurred. The same reasoning, however, also would predict that the presence of the immediate reward should lead to its devaluation and hence generate longer waiting times for the more preferred and absent delayed outcome. The finding that the presence of only the immediate reward in fact led to less delay argues against such a habituation or value-reduction interpretation of the role of attention in delay behavior.

Throughout the present study it has been assumed that the content of subjects' ideation while waiting would be correlated with the attentional conditions to which they were assigned. Thus it was assumed that making reward(s) available for attention by facing the subject with them would increase the likelihood that he would actually attend to them during the delay period. While this assumption seems straightforward and parsimonious, it might conceivably be argued that subjects would actually attend mentally more to the reward objects when the rewards were not physically present than when they were facing them. In that unlikely event, however, one would again have to predict a difference in waiting time between the immediate reward only and delayed reward only conditions. Presumably subjects would then be fantasizing and thinking more about the absent outcome, which should lead to different waiting times in the immediate reward and delayed reward only attention conditions.

The lack of significant difference in waiting time when the subjects faced the immediate reward or the delayed one does seem understandable from the perspective of frustrative nonreward theory. When the subject attends to the immediate reward and is tempted to take it, he is frustrated by recalling the contingency that attainment of it now prevents his getting the preferred reward later. When the subject attends to the delayed reward, he is frustrated by the fact that he wants it now but cannot have it yet. When he attends to both objects, both of the above aversive frustrations occur, and hence delay tends to be most difficult—as was the case. In contrast, when the rewards are not visually present for attention, and therefore not made mentally salient, the subject can more easily avoid the frustration of blocked reward by engaging in various distraction maneuvers both overtly and in his thought processes.

Thus perhaps the most compelling interpretation of the findings may be in terms of the frustrativeness of delay of reward: the presence of the rewards serves to increase the magnitude of the frustration effect and hence decreases delay of gratification by making the waiting period more difficult. The overall findings tentatively suggest that learning to inhibit frustrative ideation, and to divert attention away from temptations by focusing, externally and internally, on competing and less frustrating stimuli, may be essential steps for mastery of delay of gratification. If that is true, then the attentional and cognitive processes through which people manage to transform aversive and frustrative conditions into bearable ones by generating their own frustration-reducing distractions become intriguing questions for future research on self-control. Such research should help us to understand more definitively the mechanisms underlying the present findings.

REFERENCES

AMSEL, A. The role of frustrative nonreward in non-continuous reward situations. *Psychological Bulletin,* 1958, *55,* 102–119.

AMSEL, A. Frustrative nonreward in partial reinforcement and discrimination learning. *Psychological Review,* 1962, *69,* 306–328.

FREUD, S. (1911) Formulations regarding the two principles in mental functioning. In *Collected papers.* Vol. 4. New York: Basic Books, 1959.

JONES, E., & GERARD, H. B. *Foundations of social psychology.* New York: Wiley, 1967.

KLINEBERG, S. L. Future time perspective and the preference for delayed reward. *Journal of Personality and Social Psychology,* 1968, *8,* 253–257.

MAHRER, A. R. The role of expectancy in delayed reinforcement. *Journal of Experimental Psychology,* 1956, *52,* 101–105.

MISCHEL, W. Delay of gratification, need for achievement, and acquiescence in another culture. *Journal of Abnormal and Social Psychology,* 1961, *62,* 543–552. (a)

MISCHEL, W. Father-absence and delay of gratification: Cross-cultural comparisons. *Journal of Abnormal and Social Psychology,* 1961, *62,* 116–124. (b)

MISCHEL, W. Preference for delayed reinforcement and social responsibility. *Journal of Abnormal and Social Psychology,* 1961, *62,* 1–7. (c)

MISCHEL, W. Theory and research on the antecedents of self-imposed delay of reward. In B. A. Maher (Ed.), *Progress in experimental personality research.* Vol. 3. New York: Academic Press, 1966.

MISCHEL, W. *Personality and assessment.* New York: Wiley, 1968.

MISCHEL, W., & GILLIGAN, C. F. Delay of gratification, motivation for the prohibited gratification, and responses to temptation. *Journal of Abnormal and Social Psychology,* 1964, *69,* 411–417.

MISCHEL, W., GRUSEC, J., & MASTERS, J. C. Effects of expected delay time on the subjective value of rewards and punishments. *Journal of Personality and Social Psychology,* 1969.

MISCHEL, W., & METZNER, R. Preference for delayed reward as a function of age, intelligence, and length of delay interval. *Journal of Abnormal and Social Psychology,* 1962, *64,* 425–431.

MISCHEL, W., & STAUB, E. Effects of expectancy on waiting and working for larger rewards. *Journal of Personality and Social Psychology,* 1965, *2,* 625–633.

MOWRER, O. H., & ULLMAN, A. D. Time as a determinant in integrative learning. *Psychological Review,* 1945, *52,* 61–90.

RAPAPORT, D. On the psychoanalytic theory of thinking. In M. M. Gill (Ed.), *The collected papers of David Rapaport.* New York: Basic Books, 1967.

RENNER, K. E. Temporal integration: An incentive approach to conflict resolution. In B. A. Maher (Ed.), *Progress in experimental personality research.* Vol. 4. New York: Academic Press, 1967.

SHYBUT, J. Delay of gratification and severity of psychological disturbance among hospitalized psychiatric patients. *Journal of Consulting and Clinical Psychology,* 1968, *32,* 462–468.

SINGER, J. L. Delayed gratification and ego development: Implications for clinical and experimental research. *Journal of Consulting Psychology,* 1955, *19,* 259–266.

SPIVACK, G., LEVINE, M., & SPRIGLE, H. Intelligence test performance and the delay function of the ego. *Journal of Consulting Psychology,* 1959, *23,* 428–431.

WAGNER, A. R. Frustration and punishment. In R. N. Haber (Ed.), *Research on motivation.* New York: Holt, Rinehart & Winston, 1966.

72

Generosity in Nursery School Boys

ELDRED RUTHERFORD
AND PAUL MUSSEN

*Psychologists have focused a great deal of their
energy and attention on the study of human difficulties—on the troubled or the anti-social and
troublesome. Since the classic study by Lois Bar-
clay Murphy* (Social Behavior and Child Personality: An Exploratory Study of Some Roots of
Sympathy *[Columbia University Press, 1937]),
relatively little research has been done on prosocial behaviors. Recently, there has been a cheer-
ing trend toward more work on desirable attributes.
One instance is the work of Staub (see Section V).
This study of generosity by Paul Mussen and Eldred Rutherford is another instance of such investigations.*

*Mussen and Rutherford have long collaborated,
as evidenced by selections authored by them in
previous editions of this book. Mussen is professor of psychology at the University of California
at Berkeley. In 1970 he edited a new edition of the
famous* Carmichael's Manual of Child Psychology
*(Wiley). Rutherford has taught psychology for
some years at California's San Jose State College.*

This study was supported by the National Institute of Child
Health and Human Development, U.S. Public Health Service,
under research grant HD 01650. The authors wish to express
their appreciation to Mrs. Natasha Wist, of San Jose State
College, for her invaluable assistance in collecting and analyzing
the data for this study.

The now classic studies of Hartshorne and May
(1928–1930) started a long series of investigations
of children's conscience, strength of character,
moral characteristics, and judgments. While there
are some exceptions (Grinder, 1962; Sears, Maccoby, & Levin, 1957; Sears, Rau, & Alpert, 1965),
these have generally been less concerned with the
personality correlates and familial antecedents of
moral behavior and standards than with establishing patterns of behavior reflecting underlying moral
dispositions or traits (e.g., Aronfreed, 1961; Burton, 1963; Johnson, 1962; Kohlberg, 1963). This
is somewhat surprising in view of the fact that
parental teaching, guidance, and treatment have
ordinarily been considered crucial for the acquisition of high standards of moral behavior.

Students of socialization view the development
of superego or conscience, like sex typing, as a
major product of the child's identification with his
parents. There is evidence that the acquisition of
sex-appropriate patterns of interests and activities
(sex typing) is a consequence of what Mowrer has
termed "developmental identification" (Mowrer,
1952)—identification motivated by warmth and
affection toward the model, in this case, the like-
sexed parent.

But the relation between moral behavior and developmental identification, if it exists, has yet to be
established empirically. Data from several investigations indicate that high levels of conscience
development are associated with positive, affectionate attachment to nurturant parents, but the correlations are small and the evidence does not seem
compelling. For example, Sears et al. (1957)
showed that a child's tendency toward confessing
transgression, as reported by the mother, was related to parental warmth, as rated by an interviewer. Resistance to temptation has also been
found to be related to some criteria of dependency
(and, presumably, parental nurturance) among
nursery school children (Sears et al., 1965).

Most research on moral development, like that
mentioned above, has been focused on prohibitions,
the proscriptive "thou shalt not" aspects of morality, such as resistance to temptation, cheating, and
stealing. Although Hoffman (1963) dealt with
"consideration for others" as a dependent variable,
relatively little research attention has been given
to other behaviors that reflect more altruistic, inter-
personally oriented kinds of morality—compassion,
generosity, cooperation, sympathy. Operational
definitions of high conscience typically involve
either compliance with rules about prohibited behavior or guilt about transgressions. Perhaps this

Eldred Rutherford and Paul Mussen, "Generosity in nursery school boys," *Child Development*, 1968, *39*, 755–765. Reprinted
by permission. © 1968 by the Society for Research in Child Development, Inc.

research emphasis on prohibitions is due to the fact that, in the moral training of young children in our culture, proscriptive rules are more readily conveyed and more strongly emphasized than more positive, altruistic values. Certainly parents and other agents of socialization have many opportunities to "teach" children those proscriptive rules by rewarding approved responses and by punishing behaviors that violate such rules. Direct tuition may be the primary source of the child's acquisition of these proscriptions; parental identification—modeling one's behavior after the parents'—may play a comparatively minor role here.

Moreover, the products of identification are presumably *patterns* of behavior rather than isolated, restricted, discrete responses. If the tendency to resist temptation is a result of the process of identification, this characteristic would be positively related to other moral behaviors. But Hartshorne and May (1928–1930) found only low, though positive, correlations among various types of moral behavior. Children were not highly consistent in their behavior. For example, cheating in one situation was not generally predictive of cheating in another situation. This suggests that acquiring proscriptive rules of morality depends upon specific learning experiences rather than on identification with parents.

It is, of course, possible that proscriptive rules of behavior are "taught" by means of reward and punishment, while more positive—perhaps more complex—characteristics are acquired by means of developmental identification with a model. If this is true, the development of such characteristics as altruism, cooperation, generosity, and sympathy would be associated with warm, nurturant parent-child relationships.

This is in fact the first hypothesis of the present study, which is focused on one aspect of moral behavior—generosity. More specifically, this hypothesis states that high levels of generosity in young children will be related to perceptions of their like-sexed parent (the primary identificand) as warm, affectionate, and nurturant.

In addition, if a high level of generosity is a consequence of the identification process, it should be one aspect of a *pattern* of moral behaviors correlated with other positive characteristics. The second major hypothesis of the study, therefore, is that generosity is positively related to such characteristics as cooperation, altruism, sympathy, and kindness.

METHODS

The subjects of the study were middle-class Caucasian boys between the ages of 4-6 and 4-11, en-

rolled in nursery schools in a large California city. This age group was considered most appropriate to test the hypothesis about the relation between parent-child interactions and the acquisition of moral behavior, since it may be assumed that during these years parental and familial influences predominate over the kinds of peer influences that may be prepotent later on.

THE ASSESSMENT OF GENEROSITY

The initial sample consisted of 63 boys in seven nursery school classes who were observed individually in a structured situation designed to assess level of generosity. Subjects considered high and low in generosity on the basis of their performance in this situation were selected for further study.

Each subject was taken to a small room by a "teacher" (investigator's assistant). The teacher presented him with 18 identical pieces of candy, all of them of a kind he had previously chosen from a wide assortment as the most desirable. He was also given three plastic bags and was told that one was for him and the other two were for "the two children in the nursery school you like best." He was then asked to divide the candies into the three bags, putting as many as he wanted in his own bag, which he could take home with him at the end of the day. Pretesting of this technique indicated that children of this age readily understood the instructions and knew that keeping more candies for themselves meant that there would be fewer candies for their two friends. The *generosity score* was simply the number of candies the subject gave away.

The range of possible scores was, of course, 0–18. The mean for all 63 boys tested initially was 10.7. Fourteen of the 63 subjects, the nongenerous group, got scores of zero, that is, they kept all 18 candies. The generous (high) group, 17 boys, donated 15 or more candies to their friends. These two groups of boys were selected for further study.

Ratings of generosity by the boys' teachers were used to assess the validity of this situational measure of generosity. These teachers were asked to sort name cards, each giving the name of a boy in her class, into five piles, pile one for those "who are among the most generous, least selfish nursery school boys I have ever known" and pile five for those "who are among the most selfish, least generous nursery school boys I have known." Pile three contained the names of boys "who seem about average in generosity, neither highly generous nor highly selfish in their behavior." Ratings of 1–5 were assigned to the boys on the basis of this sort. The mean ratings for the groups of boys who scored generous and nongenerous in their disposition of the candy were 2.12 and 3.36, respectively

($t = 3.13$, $p < .01$, $df = 20$). It may be assumed that teachers' ratings were based on extensive observations of their pupils' behavior. The generosity measure used in this study therefore appears to be generally valid, that is, scores in the structured situational test reflect generalized tendencies to behave generously.

DOLL PLAY

The hypotheses were tested by relating generosity scores to data derived from children's responses in doll play, a situational test of competitiveness, and a series of 21 teachers' ratings (the Fels scales [Baldwin, 1948]).

Twenty-two of the subjects (12 generous and 10 nongenerous boys) responded to a projective, semi-structured doll-play situation, administered by *E*, using a standardized set of instructions. The boys' responses were used in testing both major hypotheses of the study. Using a simple set of family dolls (mother, father, and child), each subject played out, and thus completed, seven incomplete stories. These were specifically designed to elicit the child's attitudes toward his parents and his perceptions of them, as well as some self-concepts —particularly those aspects related to feelings of generosity, hostility, and sympathy. The following two stories are illustrative:

PARENT-CHILD RELATIONS STORY

SCENE.—In the house, parent dolls are in their bed, and the child doll is in his.
INSTRUCTIONS.—"It's late at night. Everyone is asleep. Suddenly the boy has a bad dream and wakes up very frightened. What do you think he will do? Show me."

SELF-CONCEPT STORY

SCENE.—Mother in kitchen by window looking into yard, child doll and two other children are in yard.
INSTRUCTIONS.—"Mother calls to her son to come in and get cookies. The boy brings the last three cookies in the house—there are no more—for him and friends. But just then, another friend comes to play. Now there are four children and only three cookies. What will the boy do? Show me."

The assumption underlying the interpretation and scoring of these stories is that the child's descriptions of the hero reflect his self-concepts, and what he says about the parent dolls reveals his attitudes toward his own parents. Thus it is assumed that the child who portrays the child hero as behaving generously sees himself as a generous person and the one who describes the doll father as nurturant considers his own father to be nurturant.

Each story was recorded verbatim and scored for presence or absence of the following variables: (*a*) Father Nurturance or Mother Nurturance (FN or MN) (the hero or other children receive help, attention, or reassurance from the father or mother); (*b*) Father Sympathy or Mother Sympathy (FS or MS) (the father or the mother comforts a child in distress); (*c*) Child Dependency (CD) (a child seeks help from another person—usually a parent or parents); (*d*) Child Sympathy (CS) (the hero attends to another child's distress); (*e*) Child Generosity (CG) (the hero shares a limited supply of valuable goods, e.g., toys, cookies, with other children); and (*f*) Interpersonal Hostility (IH) (verbal or physical expression of aggression between participants in the story).

In order to eliminate bias, all scoring was done "blind," that is, the scorer had no knowledge of the subject's generosity status. The reliability of the scoring system was checked by having two psychologists score the stories independently. The two scorers agreed perfectly in 91 per cent of the scores of the 22 protocols (154 stories).

The subject's score for each doll-play variable was the total number of stories in which it appeared.

COMPETITION GAME

After the doll-play stories had been completed, each subject participated with the investigator in a "racing game," which was based on one of Murphy's situational tests (Murphy, 1956). In nine races, the child raced a doll against the investigator's doll along the length of a yardstick on the floor. The investigator moved his doll at a constant, moderately slow speed, and the child could win or lose the race with a large or small margin of victory. In no instance did the subject permit the investigator to win. The competitiveness score was the subject's average margin of victory for all nine races.

TEACHER'S RATINGS

Nursery teachers rated each of the 31 generous and nongenerous subjects they knew on 21 nine-point rating scales, the Fels scales (Baldwin, 1948). These scales describe a number of characteristics directly relevant to a test of the second major hypothesis of the study. These were: affectionateness, aggressiveness, competitiveness, conscience, friendliness, gregariousness, kindness, leadership, obedience, patience, quarrelsomeness, sensitiveness, shyness, suggestibility, tenacity.

Unfortunately, it was impossible to evaluate the interrater reliability of these ratings because no child was rated by more than one teacher.

RESULTS AND DISCUSSION

The first hypothesis of the study maintains that the acquisition of moral behavior is a product of developmental identification. If this hypothesis is valid, high levels of generosity in young boys, an index of moral development, should be related to perceptions of their fathers as warm, nurturant, and affectionate. The boy's relation with his father was assumed to be most crucial, since that parent is ordinarily the boy's principal identificand.

The hypothesis was tested by comparing the doll-play FN scores of the generous and nongenerous groups. The results of this comparison are presented in Table 1, which gives the mean scores of the two groups in FN and MN and in the child variables assessed by means of the doll-play techniques.

The data clearly support the first hypothesis: the mean FN score of the highly generous boys was significantly higher than that of the boys low in generosity. Generosity in young boys is in fact related to variables underlying developmental identification, specifically to their perceptions of their fathers as warm and nurturant. These data may therefore be interpreted as being entirely consistent with, and thus supportive of, the developmental identification hypothesis which holds that a child's identification with a parent is motivated by his feelings of warmth and affection for that parent.

Since the child's perceptions of his parents were assessed on the basis of his verbalized responses in a doll-play situation, it might be argued that the child's generosity is an antecedent rather than a consequent of his perceptions of his father. The child's descriptions of the doll-play figures may be projections of his own generous characteristics. If this were the case, these findings would have no bearing on the problem of the relation between strength of identification and the acquisition of behaviors related to superego development.

While there are no data in this study that permit direct refutation of this argument, there are a number of reasons for believing that it is not valid. For one thing, while the generous and nongenerous boys differed significantly in FN scores, the two groups did not differ significantly in MN scores, in the degree to which they attributed nurturant, affectionate characteristics to the mother in their stories. If characteristics attributed to doll-play figures were simply projections of the subjects' feelings about themselves, the generous boys would portray *both* parents as highly nurturant and giving. The fact that generous boys view the father as more nurturant does not seem consistent with the argument that descriptions of him are projections of the child's self-concepts. The finding is more consistent with the developmental identification hypothesis.

Furthermore, although there were no direct assessments of parent-child relationships in the present study, the findings of other investigations indicate that the child's perceptions of parental warmth and nurturance are highly correlated with actual parental behavior, at least as the latter is evaluated in parental interviews (Mussen & Distler, 1960; Mussen & Rutherford, 1963). For these reasons, it seems most plausible to regard these positive, nurturant perceptions of the fathers as determinants, rather than consequents, of the child's level of generosity. This is of course what would be predicted on the basis of the developmental identification hypothesis.

Another finding from the doll-play data seems particularly pertinent to the first hypothesis. This involves parental sympathy, a characteristic that was seldom depicted in these subjects' stories. In fact, only six subjects told stories in which the father comforted a child in distress (e.g., holding a hurt child; telling a child "don't worry, you'll feel all right in a minute"; taking a child into the house "for a cookie so he will feel better"). All six of

TABLE 1

MEAN SCORES OF BOYS HIGH AND LOW IN GENEROSITY ON PARENTAL AND SELF-PERCEPTION (DOLL PLAY) VARIABLES

Variable	*High* (N = 12)	*Low* (N = 10)	*d*	*t*	*p* [a]
Parental:					
Mother Nurturance (MN)	2.25	1.90	0.35	0.83	N.S.
Father Nurturance (FN)	1.40	0.17	1.23	2.24	< .05
Child:					
Generosity	2.00	1.10	0.90	2.65	< .02
Sympathy	1.08	1.10	0.02	0.06	N.S.
Hostility	0.42	1.20	0.78	2.17	< .05
Dependency	1.67	3.70	2.03	3.43	< .01

[a] *p* is for two-tail tests (*df* = 20).

these boys were in the highly generous group; none of the boys in the nongenerous groups told a story involving parental sympathy. Application of a χ^2 test to the data, with Yates's correction, yielded a a value of 4.59 ($p < .05$).

This finding, although based on only relatively few subjects, suggests that fathers of generous boys, in addition to being warm and nurturant in their relationships with their sons, are more likely to respond to a child's distress with sympathy and attempts to comfort him. If, as we assumed, the child's descriptions of the fathers in his stories accurately reflect his perceptions of his own father's behavior, the fathers of generous boys are apparently more likely than the others to provide models of sympathy, generosity, altruism, and compassion. It may be suggested that paternal nurturance serves a double function: it motivates the child to emulate the father's behavior and, at the same time, it provides a model of behavior that is essentially kind and considerate. The father's sympathy and compassion may be conceptualized by the child as generosity. In identifying with the father, he incorporates this characteristic and behaves in generous ways.

The second general hypothesis of the study holds that, if a high level of generosity is a consequent of identification with the parents, it should be part of a *pattern* of moral behaviors, not a discrete, isolated characteristic. If this hypothesis is valid, level of generosity would be positively correlated to such characteristics as cooperation, altruism, lack of interpersonal aggression, and sympathy.

Several of the techniques used in the study provided data for testing this hypothesis. Certain aspects of the child's self-concept—some of them related to morality—were assessed by means of doll play. Comparisons of the means of the generous and nongenerous groups on the relevant doll-play child scores are summarized in Table 1. These data provide some general support for the hypothesis that moral characteristics are positively intercorrelated. On the basis of the characteristics attributed to the children in their doll-play stories, it may be inferred that highly generous boys, in contrast to those low in generosity, are motivated to behave generously and have less feeling of hostility and aggression toward others.

As Table 1 indicates, generous boys show significantly less dependency in their stories than the nongenerous group. While dependency (or its reverse, independence) is not generally considered a moral quality, this finding seems highly consistent with the second hypothesis. Being generous to others undoubtedly requires some impulse control, some capacity for suppressing desires for immediate gratification (such as taking all the available

candy). The development of such capacity—and the maturity it implies—would certainly seem to depend upon identification with an adult model. This would be particularly true of boys identifying with their fathers because independent behavior, in our culture, is commonly regarded as a masculine sex-typed characteristic. The relation between high levels of generosity and a strong sense of independence may therefore be interpreted as indicating that generosity is part of a pattern of characteristics acquired through identification with the father.

Children who manifest high levels of generosity would be expected to be less fiercely competitive than those who are not generous. The subjects' reactions in the structured competitive situation (racing) in which they all participated indicated that this is true. The average lead of the nongenerous boys over the investigator-competitor, based on nine races, was 3.69 inches, while the corresponding margin for boys who were highly generous was only 2.65 inches ($t = 2.13$, $p < .05$). Behaviorally, then, high generosity seems to be part of a pattern which involves less intense interpersonal competition, less need to win out over a competitor by a great margin.

Each subject was rated by his teacher on 21 characteristics (the Fels scales), and these ratings were also used to test the second hypothesis. Table 2 summarizes the data for the two groups.

The groups differed significantly, or nearly significantly, in 5 of the 21 rated characteristics. Four of the five differences were in directions consistent with findings from doll play or the competition situation and were supportive of the second hypothesis. Thus, in comparison with boys low in generosity, those who were highly generous were rated as more kindly, less competitive (or more cooperative)—consistent with the behavioral measure—less aggressive and less quarrelsome—consistent with less interpersonal hostility in doll play.

In addition, the generous boys were regarded by their nursery school teachers as less gregarious than their nongenerous peers. Apparently their activities are less directed toward others and toward the group. They appear to be more independent and self-sufficient. This is very likely another reflection of their relatively low dependency needs, already noted in their doll-play stories. From this point of view, relatively low ratings in gregariousness may be regarded as an indication of a sense of independence that is a product of identification with the father.

In sum, the relevant data from the doll-play techniques, from a behavioral test of competitiveness, and from teachers' ratings (which are pre-

TABLE 2
PERSONAL CHARACTERISTICS OF BOYS HIGH AND LOW IN GENEROSITY

Rating Variable	High ($N = 17$)	Low ($N = 14$)	d	t	p [a]
Gregariousness	3.00	5.23	2.23	2.75	< .02
Competitiveness	3.18	5.07	1.89	2.44	.02
Quarrelsomeness	3.53	4.78	1.25	1.91	< .10
Kindness	3.35	2.28	1.07	1.92	< .10
Aggressiveness	3.12	4.50	1.38	1.66	.10
Patience	4.65	3.64	1.01	1.20	N.S.
Tenacity	3.88	3.31	0.57	0.79	N.S.
Affectionateness	3.53	4.54	1.01	1.19	N.S.
Leadership	3.29	4.64	1.35	1.48	N.S.
Masculinity	2.53	3.15	0.62	0.95	N.S.
Obedience	3.65	2.78	0.87	1.21	N.S.
Apprehensiveness	3.76	4.57	0.81	1.02	N.S.
Sensitiveness	3.29	3.50	0.21	0.26	N.S.
Shyness	4.88	4.21	0.67	0.74	N.S.
Suggestibleness	3.18	3.77	0.59	0.84	N.S.
Cheerfulness	2.53	2.36	0.17	0.24	N.S.
Conscience	4.38	4.57	0.19	0.24	N.S.
Curiosity	2.53	3.56	1.03	1.47	N.S.
Emotional control	3.71	3.77	0.06	0.07	N.S.
Gross activity	2.53	3.26	1.09	1.57	N.S.
Friendliness	2.59	2.00	0.59	1.07	N.S.

[a] p is for two-tail tests ($df = 20$).

sumably based on extensive sampling of the overt behavior of the children) are highly supportive of the second hypothesis. Generosity as tested in the situational tests used in this study does appear, as the second hypothesis predicts, to be part of a pattern of interrelated, altruistic characteristics. Apparently, then, generosity is not an isolated, discrete bit of moral behavior that develops independently of other types of behavior that are manifestations of high moral standards governing interpersonal relations. This is precisely what one would expect if this characteristic were a result of an identification process in which the identificand is actually a model of behavior indicative of generosity, rather than the outcome of specific experiences involving positive and negative reinforcements for generous and nongenerous behavior.

REFERENCES

ARONFREED, J. The nature, variety, and social patterning of moral responses to transgression. *Journal of Abnormal and Social Psychology*, 1961, *63*, 223–241.

BALDWIN, A. Socialization and the parent-child relationship. *Child Development*, 1948, *19*, 127–136.

BURTON, R. V. The generality of honesty reconsidered. *Psychological Review*, 1963, *70*, 481–500.

GRINDER, R. Parental child-rearing practices, conscience, and resistance to temptation of sixth grade children. *Child Development*, 1962, *33*, 802–820.

HARTSHORNE, H., & MAY, M. A. *Studies in the nature of character*, Vol. 1: *Studies in deceit;* Vol. 2, *Studies in self-control;* Vol. 3, *Studies in the organization of character.* New York: Macmillan, 1928–1930.

HOFFMAN, M. L. Parent discipline and the child's consideration for others. *Child Development*, 1963, *34*, 573–588.

JOHNSON, R. A study of children's moral judgments. *Child Development*, 1962, *33*, 327–354.

KOHLBERG, L. The development of children's orientations toward a moral order, I: Sequence in the development of moral thought. *Vita Humana*, 1963, *6*, 11–33.

MOWRER, O. H. Identification: a link between learning theory and psychotherapy. In *Learning theory and personality dynamics*. New York: Ronald, 1952. Pp. 573–616.

MURPHY, L. B. *Personality in young children*. New York: Basic Books, 1956.

MUSSEN, P., & DISTLER, L. Child-rearing antecedents of masculine identification in kindergarten boys. *Child Development*, 1960, *31*, 89–100.

MUSSEN, P., & RUTHERFORD, E. Parent-child relations and parental personality in relation to young children's sex-role preferences. *Child Development*, 1963, *34*, 589–607.

SEARS, R. R., MACCOBY, E. E., & LEVIN, H. *Patterns of child-rearing*. Evanston, Ill.: Row, Peterson, 1957.

SEARS, R. R., RAU, L., & ALPERT, R. *Identification and child-rearing*. Stanford, Calif.: Stanford University Press, 1965.

XI

SPECIFIC EDUCATIONAL IMPLICATIONS

The papers in this section focus on instructional issues. To varying degrees all of the determinants of behavior discussed in previous parts of the book affect the behaviors subsumed under the label "educational implications." It will be obvious to the reader that many of the articles in other sections might well have been placed here. We have chosen to place those items elsewhere, instead of concentrating them all in this section, to underscore the fundamental continuity of the fields of child development and educational psychology.

The important distinction to be made is not between child development and educational psychology, but, rather, between (1) both of these topics, as aspects of the science of psychology, and (2) educational practice. The aim of psychology is to develop systematic knowledge about behavior, to seek answers to questions that might be highly abstract; the goal of education is to determine policy, to design and implement educational programs. The psychologist's role, in the search for knowledge, allows him the luxury of waiting until all the data are in—until he is satisfied with his answer to a question. The educator, on the other hand, must make decisions: he must select and train teachers, and adopt a curriculum for the year. The classroom teacher must make myriad decisions every day— there is often no opportunity to test out alternative strategies. When faced by a first-grader who has a temper tantrum during the arithmetic lesson, the teacher *must* adopt a course of action.

How can the practitioner use the general knowledge that is offered by the psychologist? He must take from the research and theory whatever he can use to make informed decisions and to make his actions as effective as possible. It is hoped that he will look closely at what he has done, in order to evaluate his decisions. One can indeed conceptualize the role of the teacher as one of "hypothesis-making" and "hypothesis-testing." That is done by Frederick J. Mc-Donald in his book *Educational Psychology*, second edition (Belmont, California: Wadsworth Publishing Co., 1965).

Is the task fundamentally one of applying findings from basic research? N. L. Gage, professor of educational psychology at Stanford University and editor of the extremely useful *Handbook of Research on Teaching* (Chicago: Rand McNally and Co., 1963), says:

> What *must* [the teacher] do, if his behavior is to have the desired effect on the comprehension of his youngsters? How can the behavior of one person, a teacher, have an effect on another person's comprehension of a concept or principle? . . .
>
> My answer, in very general terms, is that the teacher will manipulate the learner's environment, in accordance with the laws of logic and cognition, in the same way that he can influence another person's perceptions by manipulating the environment in accordance with the laws of perception. . . .
>
> The teacher, by the same token, can compel us to comprehend concepts and principles, depending on whether the stimuli or ideas themselves exist in certain patterns, whether they have certain relationships to one another,

and, of course, on whether the pupil has certain cognitive capacities, sets, and the like.[1]

Compare this with Bruner's statement:

> ... Part of the failure of educational psychology was its failure to grasp the full scope of its mission. It has too readily assumed that its central task was the application of learning theory to education—or, in turn, the application of personality or of group dynamics or whatnot. In fact, none of these efforts produced a major contribution to educational practice largely because the task was not really one of application in any obvious sense, but of formulation. Learning theory, for example, is distilled from descriptions of behavior in situations where the environment has been arranged either for the convenience of observing learning behavior or out of a theoretical interest in some special aspect of learning—reinforcement, cue distinctiveness, or whatnot. But a theory of instruction, which must be at the heart of educational psychology, is principally concerned with *how* to arrange environments to *optimize* learning according to various criteria—e.g., to optimize transfer or retrievability of information or whatnot.[2]

When you have finished your reading (and the course) you may lean toward one or the other of these views. And if you get practical experience, you may modify these views over time.

Recent work on the psychology of reading provides a good example of a "new style" in educational research. The plethora of studies of educational methods, comparing their effectiveness in typical classrooms, has, unfortunately, produced very little useful information. This has resulted in more stress on basic research. At first, much of the basic research focused on a rather narrow definition of "reading," that is, the ability to "decode" from an unfamiliar orthographic code to the already-mastered speech code. Most recently, other aspects of reading—especially comprehension—have attracted attention, reflecting the strong influence of cognitive psychology. The articles on reading in this section will show the student how a curriculum area is attacked. The reader is also urged to examine other articles which involve reading, including those by Labov and Robins in Section VI and Grimes and Allinsmith in Section X.

In today's rapidly changing world, the promise of technology is great. Programmed instruction is now coming of age in the form of computer-assisted instruction. Teaching machines have provoked both a great deal of work and a good deal of debate. The current models (both theoretical and actual) are based on the earlier work of B. F. Skinner. Sidney L. Pressey, long at Ohio State University and now at the University of Arizona, is generally credited with being the first to devise a "teaching machine." As is frequently the case, the climate was not favorable at the time, and not much development occurred. (This is in marked contrast to what happened to Skinner's invention of a teaching machine.) Pressey has written an article critical of the ways the new devices are being used.[3]

Educational technology provides one way to cope with an important reality, the enormous amount of individual variation among students. There has been a long history of research on individual differences—witness the development

---

[1] From N. L. Gage, Toward a cognitive theory of teaching, *Teachers College Record*, 1964, *65*, 408–412 (p. 410).

[2] From J. S. Bruner, Education as social invention, *The Journal of Social Issues*, 1964, *20*, 21–33 (p. 32).

[3] "A puncture of the huge 'programming' boom?" *Teachers College Record*, 1964, *65*, 413–418.

and importance of testing. However, as Gerald S. Lesser, professor of developmental psychology at Harvard University, points out, knowledge of individual differences is not enough. We must add to that knowledge a "... range of instructional alternatives to fit particular children. We must discover how to adjust and adapt our instructional strategies—the choice of curriculum, its content, level, sequence, pace, and style of presentation—to the differences we have identified among students. Given an enlarged understanding of individual differences, it becomes obvious that, instead of seeking a single 'best' instructional arrangement, the teacher's task is that of building options in the instructional arrangements needed to fit particular learners." These words are taken from Professor Lesser's new book *Psychology and Educational Practice* (Glenview, Ill.: Scott, Foresman and Co., 1971). The student may wish to look at that book after reading the relevant articles in this volume, such as the one by Yando and Kagan in Section IX, and Grimes and Allinsmith's in Section X.

73

The Growth of Mind[1]

JEROME S. BRUNER

This selection, by Jerome S. Bruner, professor of psychology and director of the Center for Cognitive Studies at Harvard University, was Bruner's presidential address to the American Psychological Association. In the paper he probes the relation between cognitive development and pedagogy.

These past several years, I have had the painful pleasure—and it has been both—of exploring two aspects of the cognitive processes that were new to me. One was cognitive development, the other pedagogy. I knew, as we all know, that the two were closely related, and it was my naive hope that, betimes, the relation would come clear to me. Indeed, 2 years ago when I first knew that in early September 1965 I would be standing here, delivering this lecture, I said to myself that I would use the occasion to set forth to my colleagues what I had been able to find out about this vexed subject, the relation of pedagogy and development. It seemed obvious then that in 2 years one could get to the heart of the matter.

The 2 years have gone by. I have had the privilege of addressing this distinguished audience

[1] Address of the President to the Seventy-third Annual Convention of the American Psychological Association, Chicago, September 4, 1965.

(Bruner, 1964) on some of our findings concerning the development of cognitive processes in children, and I have similarly set forth what I hope are not entirely unreasonable ideas about pedagogy (Bruner, in press). I am still in a very deep quandary concerning the relation of these two enterprises. The heart of the matter still eludes me, but I shall stand by my resolve. I begin on this autobiographical note so that you may know in advance why this evening is more an exercise in conjecture than a cataloguing of solid conclusions.

What is most unique about man is that his growth as an individual depends upon the history of his species—not upon a history reflected in genes and chromosomes but, rather, reflected in a culture external to man's tissue and wider in scope than is embodied in any one man's competency. Perforce, then, the growth of mind is always growth assisted from the outside. And since a culture, particularly an advanced one, transcends the bounds of individual competence, the limits for individual growth are by definition greater than what any single person has previously attained. For the limits of growth depend on how a culture assists the individual to use such intellectual potential as he may possess. It seems highly unlikely—either empirically or canonically—that we have any realistic sense of the furthest reach of such assistance to growth.

The evidence today is that the full evolution of intelligence came as a result of bipedalism and tool using. The large human brain gradually evolved as a sequel to the first use of pebble tools by early near-man. To condense the story, a near-man, or hominid, with a slightly superior brain, using a pebble tool, could make out better in the niche provided by nature than a near-man who depended not on tools but on sheer strength and formidable jaws. Natural selection favored the primitive tool user. In time, thanks to his better chance of surviving and breeding, he became more so: The ones who survived had larger brains, smaller jaws, less ferocious teeth. In place of belligerent anatomy, they developed tools and a brain that made it possible to use them. Human evolution thereafter became less a matter of having appropriate fangs or claws and more one of using and later fashioning tools to express the powers of the larger brain that was also emerging. Without tools the brain was of little use, no matter how many hundred cubic centimeters of it there might be. Let it also be said that without the original programmatic capacity for fitting tools into a sequence of acts, early hominids would never have started the epigenetic progress that brought them to their present state. And as human groups stabilized tools became more complex and "shaped to pattern," so that it was no longer a matter of reinventing tools in order to survive, but rather of mastering the skills necessary for using them. In short, after a certain point in human evolution, the only means whereby man could fill his evolutionary niche was through the cultural transmission of the skills necessary for the use of priorly invented techniques, implements, and devices.

Two crucial parallel developments seem also to have occurred. As hominids became increasingly bipedal, with the freed hands necessary for using spontaneous pebble tools, selection also favored those with a heavier pelvic bony structure that could sustain the impacting strain of bipedal locomotion. The added strength came, of course, from a gradual closing down of the birth canal. There is an obstetrical paradox here: a creature with an increasingly larger brain but with a smaller and smaller birth canal to get through. The resolution seems to have been achieved through the immaturity of the human neonate, particularly cerebral immaturity that assures not only a smaller head, but also a longer period of transmitting the necessary skills required by human culture. During this same period, human language must have emerged, giving man not only a new and powerful way of representing reality but also increasing his power to assist the mental growth of the young to a degree beyond anything before seen in nature.

It is impossible, of course, to reconstruct the evolution in techniques of instruction in the shadow zone between hominids and man. I have tried to compensate by observing contemporary analogues of earlier forms, knowing full well that the pursuit of analogy can be dangerously misleading. I have spent many hours observing uncut films of the behavior of free-ranging baboons, films shot in East Africa by my colleague Irven DeVore with a very generous footage devoted to infants and juveniles. I have also had access to the unedited film archives of a hunting-gathering people living under roughly analogous ecological conditions, the !Kung Bushmen of the Kalahari, recorded by Laurance and Lorna Marshall, brilliantly aided by their son John and daughter Elizabeth.[2] I have also worked directly but informally with the Wolof of Senegal, observing children in the bush and in French-style schools. Even more valuable than my own in-

formal observations in Senegal were the systematic experiments carried out later by my colleague, Patricia Marks Greenfield (in press).

Let me describe very briefly some salient differences in the free learning patterns of immature baboons and among !Kung children. Baboons have a highly developed social life in their troops, with well-organized and stable dominance patterns. They live within a territory, protecting themselves from predators by joint action of the strongly built, adult males. It is striking that the behavior of baboon juveniles is shaped principally by play with their peer group, play that provides opportunity for the spontaneous expression and practice of the component acts that, in maturity, will be orchestrated into either the behavior of the dominant male or of the infant-protective female. All this seems to be accomplished with little participation by any mature animals in the play of the juveniles. We know from the important experiments of Harlow and his colleagues (Harlow & Harlow, 1962) how devastating a disruption in development can be produced in subhuman primates by interfering with their opportunity for peer-group play and social interaction,

Among hunting-gathering humans, on the other hand, there is *constant* interaction between adult and child, or adult and adolescent, or adolescent and child. !Kung adults and children play and dance together, sit together, participate in minor hunting together, join in song and story telling together. At very frequent intervals, moreover, children are party to rituals presided over by adults—minor, as in the first haircutting, or major, as when a boy kills his first Kudu buck and goes through the proud but painful process of scarification. Children, besides, are constantly playing imitatively with the rituals, implements, tools, and weapons of the adult world. Young juvenile baboons, on the other hand, virtually never play with things or imitate directly large and significant sequences of adult behavior.

Note, though, that in tens of thousands of feet of !Kung film, one virtually never sees an instance of "teaching" taking place outside the situation where the behavior to be learned is relevant. Nobody "teaches" in our prepared sense of the word. There is nothing like school, nothing like lessons. Indeed, among the !Kung children there is very little "telling." Most of what we would call instruction is through showing. And there is no "practice" or "drill" as such save in the form of play modeled directly on adult models—play hunting, play bossing, play exchanging, play baby tending, play house making. In the end, every man in the culture knows nearly all there is to know about how to get on with life as a man, and every woman as a woman—

[2] I am greatly indebted to Irven DeVore and Educational Services Incorporated for the opportunity to view his films of free-ranging baboons, and to Laurance and Lorna Marshall for the opportunity to examine their incomparable archives. DeVore and the Marshalls have been generous in their counsel as well.

the skills, the rituals and myths, the obligations and rights.

The change in the instruction of children in more complex societies is twofold. First of all, there is knowledge and skill in the culture far in excess of what any one individual knows. And so, increasingly, there develops an economical technique of instructing the young based heavily on *telling* out of context rather than *showing* in context. In literate societies, the practice becomes institutionalized in the school or the "teacher." Both promote this necessarily abstract way of instructing the young. The result of "teaching the culture" can, at its worst, lead to the ritual, rote nonsense that has led a generation of critics from Max Wertheimer (1945) to Mary Alice White (undated) of Teachers' College to despair. For in the detached school, what is imparted often has little to do with life as lived in the society except insofar as the demands of school are of a kind that reflect *indirectly* the demands of life in a technical society. But these indirectly imposed demands may be the most important feature of the detached school. For school is a sharp departure from indigenous practice. It takes learning, as we have noted, out of the context of immediate action just by dint of putting it into a school. This very extirpation makes learning become an act in itself, freed from the immediate ends of action, preparing the learner for the chain of reckoning remote from payoff that is needed for the formulation of complex ideas. At the same time, the school (if successful) frees the child from the pace setting of the round of daily activity. If the school succeeds in avoiding a pace-setting round of its own, it may be one of the great agents for promoting reflectiveness. Moreover, in school, one must "follow the lesson" which means one must learn to follow either the abstraction of written speech—abstract in the sense that it is divorced from the concrete situation to which the speech might originally have been related—or the abstraction of language delivered orally but out of the context of an ongoing action. Both of these are highly abstract uses of language.

It is no wonder, then, that many recent studies report large differences between "primitive" children who are in schools and their brothers who are not: differences in perception, abstraction, time perspective, and so on. I need only cite the work of Biesheuvel (1949) in South Africa, Gay and Cole (undated) in Liberia, Greenfield (in press) in Senegal, Maccoby and Modiano (in press) in rural Mexico, Reich (in press) among Alaskan Eskimos.

What a culture does to assist the development of the powers of mind of its members is, in effect, to provide amplification systems to which human beings, equipped with appropriate skills, can link themselves. There are, first, the amplifiers of action —hammers, levers, digging sticks, wheels—but more important, the programs of action into which such implements can be substituted. Second, there are amplifiers of the senses, ways of looking and noticing that can take advantage of devices ranging from smoke signals and hailers to diagrams and pictures that stop the action or microscopes that enlarge it. Finally and most powerfully, there are amplifiers of the thought processes, ways of thinking that employ language and formation of explanation, and later use such languages as mathematics and logic and even find automatic servants to crank out the consequences. A culture is, then, a deviser, a repository, and a transmitter of amplification systems and of the devices that fit into such systems. We know very little in a deep sense about the transmission function, how people are trained to get the most from their potential by use of a culture's resources.

But it is reasonably clear that there is a major difference between the mode of transmission in a technical society, with its schools, and an indigenous one, where cultural transmission is in the context of action. It is not just that an indigenous society, when its action pattern becomes disrupted falls apart—at a most terrifying rate—as in uncontrolled urbanization in some parts of Africa. Rather, it is that the institution of a school serves to convert knowledge and skill into more symbolical, more abstract, more verbal form. It is this process of transmission—admittedly very new in human history—that is so poorly understood and to which, finally, we shall return.

There are certain obvious specifications that can be stated about how a society must proceed in order to equip its young. It must convert what is to be known—whether a skill or a belief system or a connected body of knowledge—into a form capable of being mastered by a beginner. The more we know of the process of growth, the better we shall be at such conversion. The failure of modern man to understand mathematics and science may be less a matter of stunted abilities than our failure to understand how to teach such subjects. Second, given the limited amount of time available for learning, there must be a due regard for saving the learner from needless learning. There must be some emphasis placed on economy and transfer and the learning of general rules. All societies must (and virtually all do) distinguish those who are clever from those who are stupid—though few of them generalize this trait across all activities. Cleverness in a particular activity almost universally connotes strategy, economy, heuristics, highly generalized skills. A society must also place emphasis upon how one derives a course of action from what one has learned. Indeed, in an indigenous society, it is almost impossible to separate what one does from what one knows. More advanced societies often have not found a way of dealing with the separation of knowledge and action—probably a result of the emphasis they place upon "telling" in their instruction. All societies must maintain interest among the young in the learning process, a minor problem when learning is in the context of life and action, but harder when it becomes more abstracted. And finally, and perhaps most obviously, a society must assure that its necessary skills and procedures remain intact from one generation to the next—which does not always happen, as witnessed by Easter Islanders, Incas, Aztecs, and Mayas.[3]

Unfortunately, psychology has not concerned itself much with any of these five requisites of cultural transmission—or at least not much with four of them. We have too easily assumed that learning is learning is learning—that the early version of what was taught did not matter much, one thing being much like another and reducible to a pattern of association, to stimulus-response connections, or to our favorite molecular componentry. We denied there was a problem of development beyond the quantitative one of providing more experience, and with the denial, closed our eyes to the pedagogical problem of how to represent knowledge, how to sequence it, how to embody it in a form appropriate to young learners. We expended more passion on the part-whole controversy than on what whole or what part of it was to be presented first. I should except Piaget (1954), Kohler (1940), and Vygotsky (1962) from these complaints—all until recently unheeded voices.

Our neglect of the economy of learning stems, ironically, from the heritage of Ebbinghaus (1913), who was vastly interested in savings. Our nonsense syllables, our random mazes failed to take into account how we reduce complexity and strangeness to simplicity and the familiar, how we convert what we have learned into rules and procedures, how, to use Bartlett's (1932) term of over 30 years ago, we turn around on our own schemata to reorganize

what we have mastered into more manageable form.

Nor have we taken naturally to the issue of knowledge and action. Its apparent mentalism has repelled us. Tolman (1951), who bravely made the distinction, was accused of leaving his organisms wrapt in thought. But he recognized the problem and if he insisted on the idea that knowledge might be organized in cognitive maps, it was in recognition (as a great functionalist) that organisms go somewhere on the basis of what they have learned. I believe we are getting closer to the problem of how knowledge affects action and vice versa, and offer in testimony of my conviction the provocative book by Miller, Galanter, and Pribram (1960), *Plans and the Structure of Behavior*.

Where the maintenance of the learner's interest is concerned, I remind you of what my colleague Gordon Allport (1946) has long warned. We have been so concerned with the model of driven behavior, with drive reduction and the *vis a tergo* that, again, until recently, we have tended to overlook the question of what keeps learners interested in the activity of learning, in the achievement of competence beyond bare necessity and first payoff. The work of R. W. White (1959) on effectance motivation, of Harlow and his colleagues (Butler, 1954; Harlow, 1953) on curiosity, and of Heider (1958) and Festinger (1962) on consistency begins to redress the balance. But it is only a beginning.

The invention of antigradation devices, guarantors that skill and knowledge will be maintained intact, is an exception to our oversight. We psychologists have been up to our ears in it. Our special contribution is the achievement test. But the achievement test has, in the main, reflected the timidity of the educational enterprise as a whole. I believe we know how to determine, though we have not yet devised tests to determine, how pupils use what they learn to think with later in life—for there is the real issue.

I have tried to examine briefly what a culture must do in passing on its amplifying skills and knowledge to a new generation and, even more briefly, how we as psychologists have dealt or failed to deal with the problems. I think the situation is fast changing—with a sharp increase in interest in the conversion problem, the problems of economy of learning, the nature of interest, the relation of knowledge and action. We are, I believe, at a major turning point where psychology will once again concern itself with the design of methods of assisting cognitive growth, be it through the invention of a rational technology of toys, of ways of enriching the environment of the crib and nursery, of organizing the activity of a school, or of devising a curriculum whereby we transmit an

---

[3] I have purposely left out of the discussion the problems of impulse regulation and socialization of motives, topics that have received extended treatment in the voluminous literature on culture and personality. The omission is dictated by emphasis rather than evaluation. Obviously, the shaping of character by culture is of great importance for an understanding of our topic as it bears, for example, upon culture-instilled attitudes toward the uses of mind. Since our emphasis is upon human potential and its amplification by culturally patterned instrumental skills, we mention the problem of character formation in passing and in recognition of its importance in a complete treatment of the issues under discussion.

organized body of knowledge and skill to a new generation to amplify their powers of mind.

I commented earlier that there was strikingly little knowledge available about the "third way" of training the skills of the young: the first being the play practice of component skills in prehuman primates, the second the teaching-in-context of indigenous societies, and the third being the abstracted, detached method of the school.

Let me now become highly specific. Let me consider a particular course of study, one given in a school, one we are ourselves constructing, trying out, and in a highly qualitative way, evaluating. It is for schools of the kind that exist in Western culture. The experience we have had with this effort, now in its third year, may serve to highlight the kinds of problems and conjectures one encounters in studying how to assist the growth of intellect in this "third way."

There is a dilemma in describing a course of study. One begins by setting forth the intellectual substance of what is to be taught. Yet if such a recounting tempts one to "get across" the subject, the ingredient of pedagogy is in jeopardy. For only in a trivial sense is a course designed to "get something across," merely to impart information. There are better means to that end than teaching. Unless the learner develops his skills, disciplines his taste, deepens his view of the world, the "something" that is got across is hardly worth the effort of transmission.

The more "elementary" a course and the younger its students, the more serious must be its pedagogical aim of forming the intellectual powers of those whom it serves. It is as important to justify a good mathematics course by the intellectual discipline it provides or the honesty it promotes as by the mathematics it transmits. Indeed, neither can be accomplished without the other. The content of this particular course is man: his nature as a species, the forces that shaped and continue to shape his humanity. Three questions recur throughout:

> What is human about human beings?
> How did they get that way?
> How can they be made more so?

In pursuit of our questions we explore five matters, each closely associated with the evolution of man as a species, each defining at once the distinctiveness of man and his potentiality for further evolution. The five great humanizing forces are, of course, tool making, language, social organization, the management of man's prolonged childhood, and man's urge to explain. It has been

our first lesson in teaching that no pupil, however eager, can appreciate the relevance of, say, tool making or language in human evolution without first grasping the fundamental concept of a tool or what a language is. These are not self-evident matters, even to the expert. So we are involved in teaching not only the role of tools or language in the emergence of man, but, as a necessary precondition for doing so, setting forth the fundamentals of linguistics or the theory of tools. And it is as often the case as not that (as in the case of the "theory of tools") we must solve a formidable intellectual problem ourselves in order to be able to help our pupils do the same. I should have said at the outset that the "we" I employ in this context is no editorial fiction, but rather a group of anthropologists, zoologists, linguists, theoretical engineers, artists, designers, camera crews, teachers, children, and psychologists. The project is being carried out under my direction at Educational Services Incorporated, with grants from the National Science Foundation and the Ford Foundation.

While one readily singles out five sources of man's humanization, under no circumstances can they be put into airtight compartments. Human kinship is distinctively different from primate mating patterns precisely because it is classificatory and rests on man's ability to use language. Or, if you will, tool use enhances the division of labor in a society which in turn affects kinship. So while each domain can be treated as a separate set of ideas, their teaching must make it possible for the children to have a sense of their interaction. We have leaned heavily on the use of contrast, highly controlled contrast, to help children achieve detachment from the all too familiar matrix of social life: the contrasts of man versus higher primates, man versus prehistoric man, contemporary technological man versus "primitive" man, and man versus child. The primates are principally baboons, the prehistoric materials mostly from the Olduvai Gorge and Les Eyzies, the "primitive" peoples mostly the Netsilik Eskimos of Pelly Bay and the !Kung Bushmen. The materials, collected for our purposes, are on film, in story, in ethnography, in pictures and drawings, and principally in ideas embodied in exercises.

We have high aspirations. We hope to achieve five goals:

1. To give our pupils respect for and confidence in the powers of their own minds
2. To give them respect, moreover, for the powers of thought concerning the human condition, man's plight, and his social life
3. To provide them with a set of workable models that make it simpler to analyze the nature of the social

world in which they live and the condition in which man finds himself

4. To impart a sense of respect for the capacities and plight of man as a species, for his origins, for his potential, for his humanity

5. To leave the student with a sense of the unfinished business of man's evolution

One last word about the course of study that has to do with the quality of the ideas, materials, and artistry—a matter that is at once technological and intellectual. We have felt that the making of such a curriculum deserved the best talent and technique available in the world. Whether artist, ethnographer, film maker, poet, teacher—nobody we have asked has refused us. We are obviously going to suffer in testing a Hawthorne effect* of some magnitude. But then, perhaps it is as well to live in a permanent state of revolution.

Let me now try to describe some of the major problems one encounters in trying to construct a course of study. I shall not try to translate the problems into refined theoretical form, for they do not as yet merit such translation. They are more difficulties than problems. I choose them, because they are vividly typical of what one encounters in such enterprises. The course is designed for 10-year-olds in the fifth grade of elementary school, but we have been trying it out as well on the fourth and sixth grades better to bracket our difficulties.

One special point about these difficulties. They are born of trying to achieve an objective and are as much policy bound as theory bound. It is like the difference between building an economic theory about monopolistic practices and constructing policies for controlling monopoly. Let me remind you that modern economic theory has been reformulated, refined, and revived by having a season in policy. I am convinced that the psychology of assisted growth, i.e., pedagogy, will have to be forged in the policy crucible of curriculum making before it can reach its full descriptive power as theory. Economics was first through the cycle from theory to policy to theory to policy; it is happening now to psychology, anthropology, and sociology.

---

* A Hawthorne effect is an effect often observed when new procedures are introduced. It consists of an increase in productivity, irrespective of changing conditions of work, because of improvement in mental attitude of the workers as a result of their being subjects in an experiment. For example, not only may production increase if lighting conditions are bettered, it may also increase if they are worsened. Because of discovery of this effect, we know that heightened performances of workers or students who are participants in a new plan or program may not be indicative of the long-term value of the innovation but may, in some cases, be solely the consequence of raised morale.—EDITOR

Now on to the difficulties. The first is what might be called *the psychology of a subject matter*. A learned discipline can be conceived as a way of thinking about certain phenomena. Mathematics is one way of thinking about order without reference to what is being ordered. The behavioral sciences provide one or perhaps several ways of thinking about man and his society—about regularities, origins, causes, effects. They are probably special (and suspect) because they permit man to look at himself from a perspective that is outside his own skin and beyond his own preferences—at least for awhile.

Underlying a discipline's "way of thought," there is a set of connected, varyingly implicit, generative propositions. In physics and mathematics, most of the underlying generative propositions like the conservation theorems, or the axioms of geometry, or the associative, distributive, and commutative rules of analysis are by now very explicit indeed. In the behavioral sciences we must be content with more implicitness. We traffic in inductive propositions: e.g., the different activities of a society are interconnected such that if you know something about the technological response of a society to an environment, you will be able to make some shrewd guesses about its myths or about the things it values, etc. We use the device of a significant contrast as in linguistics as when we describe the territoriality of a baboon troop in order to help us recognize the system of reciprocal exchange of a human group, the former somehow provoking awareness of the latter.

There is nothing more central to a discipline than its way of thinking. There is nothing more important in its teaching than to provide the child the earliest opportunity to learn that way of thinking—the forms of connection, the attitudes, hopes, jokes, and frustrations that go with it. In a word, the best introduction to a subject is the subject itself. At the very first breath, the young learner should, we think, be given the chance to solve problems, to conjecture, to quarrel as these are done at the heart of the discipline. But, you will ask, how can this be arranged?

Here again the problem of conversion. There exist ways of thinking characteristic of different stages of development. We are acquainted with Inhelder and Piaget's (1958) account of the transition from preoperational, through concrete operational, to propositional thought in the years from preschool through, say, high school. If you have an eventual pedagogical objective in mind, you can translate the way of thought of a discipline into its Piagetian (or other) equivalent appropriate to a given level of development and take the child onward from there. The Cambridge Mathematics

Project of Educational Services, Incorporated, argues that if the child is to master the calculus early in his high school years, he should start work early with the idea of limits, the earliest work being manipulative, later going on to images and diagrams, and finally moving on to the more abstract notation needed for delineating the more precise idea of limits.

In "Man: A Course of Study," (Bruner, 1965) there are also versions of the subject appropriate to a particular age that can at a later age be given a more powerful rendering. We have tried to choose topics with this in mind: The analysis of kinship that begins with children using sticks and blocks and colors and whatnot to represent their own families, goes on to the conventional kinship diagrams by a meandering but, as you can imagine, interesting path, and then can move on to more formal and powerful componential analysis. So, too, with myth. We begin with the excitement of a powerful myth (like the Netsilik Nuliajik myth), then have the children construct some myths of their own, then examine what a set of Netsilik myths have in common, which takes us finally to Lévi-Strauss's (1963) analysis of contrastive features in myth construction. A variorum text of a myth or corpus of myths put together by sixth graders can be quite an extraordinary document.

This approach to the psychology of a learned discipline turns out to illuminate another problem raised earlier: the maintenance of interest. There is, in this approach, a reward in understanding that grows from the subject matter itself. It is easier to engineer this satisfaction in mathematics, for understanding is so utter in a formal discipline—a balance beam balances or it does not: therefore there is an equality or there is not. In the behavioral sciences the payoff in understanding cannot be so obviously and startlingly self-revealing. Yet, one can design exercises in the understanding of man, too—as when children figure out the ways in which, given limits of ecology, skills, and materials, Bushmen hunt different animals, and then compare their predictions with the real thing on film.

Consider now a second problem: *how to stimulate thought in the setting of a school.* We know from experimental studies like those of Bloom and Broder (1950), and of Goodnow and Pettigrew (1955), that there is a striking difference in the acts of a person who thinks that the task before him represents a problem to be solved rather than being controlled by random forces. School is a particular subculture where these matters are concerned. By school age, children have come to expect quite arbitrary and, from their point of view, meaningless demands to be made upon them by adults—the result, most likely, of the fact that adults often fail to recognize the task of conversion necessary to make their questions have some intrinsic significance for the child. Children, of course, will try to solve problems if they recognize them as such. But they are not often either predisposed to or skillful in problem finding, in recognizing the hidden conjectural feature in tasks set them. But we know now that children in school can quite quickly be led to such problem finding by encouragement and instruction.

The need for this instruction and encouragement and its relatively swift success relates, I suspect, to what psychoanalysts refer to as the guilt-ridden oversuppression of primary process and its public replacement by secondary process. Children, like adults, need reassurance that it is all right to entertain and express highly subjective ideas, to treat a task as a problem where you *invent* an answer rather than *finding* one out there in the book or on the blackboard. With children in elementary school, there is often a need to devise emotionally vivid special games, story-making episodes, or construction projects to reestablish in the child's mind his right not only to have his own private ideas but to express them in the public setting of a classroom.

But there is another, perhaps more serious difficulty: the interference of intrinsic problem solving by extrinsic. Young children in school expend extraordinary time and effort figuring out what it is that the teacher wants—and usually coming to the conclusion that she or he wants tidiness or remembering or to do things at a certain time in a certain way. This I refer to as extrinsic problem solving. There is a great deal of it in school.

There are several quite straightforward ways of stimulating problem solving. One is to train teachers to want it and that will come in time. But teachers can be encouraged to like it, interestingly enough, by providing them and their children with materials and lessons that *permit* legitimate problem solving and permit the teacher to recognize it. For exercises with such materials create an atmosphere by treating things as instances of what *might* have occurred rather than simply as what did occur. Let me illustrate by a concrete instance. A fifth-grade class was working on the organization of a baboon troop—on this particular day, specifically on how they might protect against predators. They saw a brief sequence of film in which six or seven adult males go forward to intimidate and hold off three cheetahs. The teacher asked what the baboons had done to keep the cheetahs off, and there ensued a lively discussion of how the dominant adult males, by showing their formidable mouthful of teeth and making threatening gestures had turned the trick.

A boy raised a tentative hand and asked whether cheetahs always attacked together. Yes, though a single cheetah sometimes followed behind a moving troop and picked off an older, weakened straggler or an unwary, straying juvenile. "Well, what if there were four cheetahs and two of them attacked from behind and two from in front. What would the baboons do then?" The question could have been answered empirically—and the inquiry ended. Cheetahs *do not* attack that way, and so we do not know what baboons *might* do. Fortunately, it was not. For the question opens up the deep issues of what might be and why it is not. Is there a necessary relation between predators and prey that share a common ecological niche? Must their encounters have a "sporting chance" outcome? It is such conjecture, in this case quite unanswerable, that produces rational, self-consciously problem-finding behavior so crucial to the growth of intellectual power. Given the materials, given some background and encouragement, teachers like it as much as the students.

I should like to turn now to the *personalization of knowledge.* A generation ago, the progressive movement urged that knowledge be related to the child's own experience and brought out of the realm of empty abstractions. A good idea was translated into banalities about the home, then the friendly postman and trashman, then the community, and so on. It is a poor way to compete with the child's own dramas and mysteries. A decade ago, my colleague Clyde Kluckhohn (1949) wrote a prize-winning popular book on anthropology with the entrancing title *Mirror for Man.* In some deep way, there is extraordinary power in "that mirror which other civilizations still hold up to us to recognize and study . . . [the] image of ourselves [Lévi-Strauss, 1965]." The psychological bases of the power are not obvious. Is it as in discrimination learning, where increasing the degree of contrast helps in the learning of a discrimination, or as in studies of concept attainment where a negative instance demonstrably defines the domain of a conceptual rule? Or is it some primitive identification? All these miss one thing that seems to come up frequently in our interviews with the children. It is the experience of discovering kinship and likeness in what at first seemed bizarre, exotic, and even a little repellant.

Consider two examples, both involving film of the Netsilik. In the films, a single nuclear family, Zachary, Marta, and their 4-year-old Alexi, is followed through the year—spring sealing, summer fishing at the stone weir, fall caribou hunting, early winter fishing through the ice, winter at the big ceremonial igloo. Children report that at first the three members of the family look weird and un-

couth. In time, they look normal, and eventually, as when Marta finds sticks around which to wrap her braids, the girls speak of how pretty she is. That much is superficial—or so it seems. But consider a second episode.

It has to do with Alexi who, with his father's help, devises a snare and catches a gull. There is a scene in which he stones the gull to death. Our children watched, horror struck. One girl, Kathy, blurted out, "He's not even human, doing that to the seagull." The class was silent. Then another girl, Jennine, said quietly: "He's got to grow up to be a hunter. His mother was smiling when he was doing that." And then an extended discussion about how people have to do things to learn and even do things to learn how to feel appropriately. "What would you do if you had to live there? Would you be as smart about getting along as they are with what they've got?" said one boy, going back to the accusation that Alexi was inhuman to stone the bird.

I am sorry it is so difficult to say it clearly. What I am trying to say is that to personalize knowledge one does not simply link it to the familiar. Rather one makes the familiar an instance of a more general case and thereby produces awareness of it. What the children were learning about was not seagulls and Eskimos, but about their own feelings and preconceptions that, up to then, were too implicit to be recognizable to them.

Consider finally the problem of *self-conscious reflectiveness.* It is an epistemological mystery why traditional education has so often emphasized extensiveness and coverage over intensiveness and depth. We have already commented on the fact that memorizing was usually perceived by children as one of the high-priority tasks but rarely did children sense an emphasis upon ratiocination with a view toward redefining what had been encountered, reshaping it, reordering it. The cultivation of reflectiveness, or whatever you choose to call it, is one of the great problems one faces in devising curriculum. How lead children to discover the powers and pleasures that await the exercise of retrospection?

Let me suggest one answer that has grown from what we have done. It is the use of the "organizing conjecture." We have used three such conjectures —what is human about human beings, how they got that way, how they could become more so. They serve two functions, one of them the very obvious though important one of putting perspective back into the particulars. The second is less obvious and considerably more surprising. The questions often seemed to serve as criteria for determining where they were getting, how well they were understanding, whether anything new was emerging. Recall Kathy's cry: "He's not human doing that to the seagull." She was hard at work in her rage on the conjecture what makes human beings human.

There, in brief, are four problems that provide some sense of what a psychologist encounters when he takes a hand in assisting the growth of mind in children in the special setting of a school. The problems look quite different from those we encounter in formulating classical developmental theory with the aid of typical laboratory research. They also look very different from those that one would find in an indigenous society, describing how children picked up skills and knowledge and values in the context of action and daily life. We clearly do not have a theory of the school that is sufficient to the task of running schools—just as we have no adequate theory of toys or of readiness building or whatever the jargon is for preparing children to do a better job the next round. It only obscures the issue to urge that some day our classical theories of learning will fill the gap. They show no sign of doing so.

I hope that we shall not allow ourselves to be embarrassed by our present ignorance. It has been a long time since we have looked at what is involved in imparting knowledge through the vehicle of the school—if ever we did look at it squarely. I urge that we delay no longer.

But I am deeply convinced that the psychologist cannot alone construct a theory of how to assist cognitive development and cannot alone learn how to enrich and amplify the powers of a growing human mind. The task belongs to the whole intellectual community: the behavioral scientists and the artists, scientists, and scholars who are the custodians of skill, taste, and knowledge in our culture. Our special task as psychologists is to convert skills and knowledge to forms and exercises that fit growing minds—and it is a task ranging from how to keep children free from anxiety to how to translate physics for the very young child into a set of playground maneuvers that, later, the child can turn around upon and convert into a sense of inertial regularities.

And this in turn leads me to a final conjecture, one that has to do with the organization of our profession, a matter that has concerned me greatly during this past year during which I have had the privilege of serving as your President. Psychology is peculiarly prey to parochialism. Left to our own devices, we tend to construct models of a man who is neither a victim of history, a target of economic forces, or even a working member of a society. I am still struck by Roger Barker's (1963) ironic truism that the best way to predict the behavior of a human being is to know where he is: In a post office he behaves post office, at church he behaves church.

Psychology, and you will forgive me if the image seems a trifle frivolous, thrives on polygamy with her neighbors. Our marriage with the biological sciences has produced a cumulation of ever more powerful knowledge. So, too, our joint undertakings with anthropology and sociology. Joined together with a variety of disciplines, we have made lasting contributions now that the emphasis is shifting to the problems of alleviating stress and arranging for a community's mental health. What I find lacking is an alignment that might properly be called the growth sciences. The field of pedagogy is one participant in the growth sciences. Any field of inquiry devoted to assisting the growth of effective human beings, fully empowered with zest, with skill, with knowledge, with taste is surely a candidate for this sodality. My friend Philip Morrison once suggested to his colleagues at Cornell that his department of physics grant a doctorate not only for work in theoretical, experimental, or applied physics, but also for work in pedagogical physics. The limits of the growth sciences remain to be drawn. They surely transcend the behavioral sciences cum pediatrics. It is plain that, if we are to achieve the effectiveness of which we as human beings are capable, there will one day have to be such a field. I hope that we psychologists can earn our way as charter members.

REFERENCES

ALLPORT, G. Effect: A secondary principle of learning. *Psychological Review*, 1946, *53*, 335–347.

BARKER, R. On the nature of the environment. *Journal of Social Issues*, 1963, *19*, 17–38.

BARTLETT, F. *Remembering*. Cambridge, England: Cambridge Univer. Press, 1932.

BIESHEUVEL, S. Psychological tests and their application to non-European peoples. *Yearbook of Education.* London: Evans, 1949. Pp. 87–126.

BLOOM, B., & BRODER, L. Problem solving processes of college students. *Supplementary Educational Monograph, No. 73.* Chicago: Univer. Chicago Press, 1950.

BRUNER, J. The course of cognitive growth. *American Psychologist*, 1964, *19*, 1–15.

BRUNER, J. Man: A course of study. *Educational Services Inc. Quarterly Report*, 1965, Spring-Summer, 3–13.

BRUNER, J. *Toward a theory of instruction*. Cambridge: Harvard Univer. Press, in press.

BUTLER, R. A. Incentive conditions which influence visual exploration. *Journal of Experimental Psychology*, 1954, *48*, 19–23.

EBBINGHAUS, H. *Memory: A contribution to experimental psychology.* New York: Teachers College, Columbia University, 1913.

FESTINGER, L. *A theory of cognitive dissonance.* Stanford: Stanford Univer. Press, 1962.

GAY, J., & COLE, M. Outline of general report on Kpelle mathematics project. Stanford: Stanford University, Institute for Mathematical Social Studies, undated. (Mimeo)

GOODNOW, JACQUELINE, & PETTIGREW, T. Effect of prior patterns of experience on strategies and learning sets. *Journal of Experimental Psychology,* 1955, *49,* 381–389.

GREENFIELD, PATRICIA M. Culture and conservation. In J. Bruner, Rose Olver, & Patricia M. Greenfield (Eds.), *Studies in cognitive growth.* New York: Wiley, in press. Ch. 10.

HARLOW, H., & HARLOW, MARGARET. Social deprivation in monkeys. *Scientific American,* 1962, November.

HARLOW, H. F. Mice, monkeys, men, and motives. *Psychological Review,* 1953, *60,* 23–32.

HEIDER, F. *The psychology of interpersonal relations.* New York: Wiley, 1958.

INHELDER, BARBEL, & PIAGET, J. *The growth of logical thinking.* New York: Basic Books, 1958.

KLUCKHOHN, C. *Mirror for man.* New York: Whittlesey House, 1949.

KOHLER, W. *Dynamics in psychology.* New York: Liveright, 1940.

LÉVI-STRAUSS, C. The structural study of myth. *Structural anthropology.* (Trans. by Claire Jacobson &

B. Grundfest Scharpf) New York: Basic Books, 1963. Pp. 206–231.

LÉVI-STRAUSS, C. Anthropology: Its achievements and future. Lecture presented at Bicentennial Celebration, Smithsonian Institution, Washington, D. C., September 1965.

MACCOBY, M., & MODIANO, NANCY. On culture and equivalence. In J. Bruner, Rose Olver, & Patricia M. Greenfield (Eds.), *Studies in cognitive growth.* New York: Wiley, in press. Ch. 12.

MILLER, G., GALANTER, E., & PRIBRAM, K. *Plans and the structure of behavior.* New York: Holt, 1960.

PIAGET, J. *The construction of reality in the child.* New York: Basic Books, 1954.

REICH, LEE. On culture and grouping. In J. Bruner, Rose Olver, & Patricia M. Greenfield (Eds.), *Studies in cognitive growth.* New York: Wiley, in press. Ch. 13.

TOLMAN, E. Cognitive maps in rats and men. *Collected papers in psychology.* Berkeley & Los Angeles: Univer. California Press, 1951. Pp. 241–264.

VYGOTSKY, L. *Thought and language.* (Ed. & trans. by Eugenia Hanfmann & Gertrude Vakar) New York: Wiley, 1962.

WERTHEIMER, M. *Productive thinking.* New York & London: Harper, 1945.

WHITE, MARY A. The child's world of learning. Teachers College, Columbia University, undated. (Mimeo)

WHITE, R. W. Motivation reconsidered: The concept of competence. *Psychological Review,* 1959, *66,* 297–333.

74

The Use of Advance Organizers in the Learning and Retention of Meaningful Verbal Material

David P. Ausubel

This article poses issues with respect to the organizational framework a person has on which he can "hang" new information. These issues are very important in terms of curriculum design, for the structure of the subject matter must be understood thoroughly in order to develop effective instruction. The selection is by David P. Ausubel, professor of educational psychology at the City University of New York.

The purpose of this study is to test the hypothesis that the learning and retention of unfamiliar but meaningful verbal material can be facilitated by the advance introduction of relevant subsuming concepts (organizers). . . . It is reasonable to suppose (Ausubel, Robbins, & Blake, 1957) that new meaningful material becomes incorporated into cognitive structure in so far as it is subsumable under relevant existing concepts. . . .

In the present study, appropriate and relevant subsuming concepts (organizers) are deliberately introduced prior to the learning of unfamiliar academic material, in order to ascertain whether learning and retention are enhanced thereby in accordance with . . . theoretical premises. . . .

David P. Ausubel, "The use of advance organizers in the learning and retention of meaningful verbal material," *Journal of Educational Psychology,* 1960, *51,* 267–272. Reprinted by permission.

METHOD

SUBJECTS

The experimental population consisted of 120 senior undergraduate students (78 women and 32 men) in four sections of an educational psychology course at the University of Illinois. All Ss were enrolled in one of eight teacher education curricula at the secondary school level. Students specializing in industrial education and in vocational agriculture were excluded from the study since they had received specific instruction in the topic covered by the learning passage. The experiment was conducted separately in each section as a required laboratory exercise and was performed during regularly scheduled class hours. In order to maximize ego-involvement, Ss were informed that after the data were processed their individual scores, as well as the class results, would be reported to them.

LEARNING PASSAGE AND TEST OF RETENTION

The learning material used in this study was a specially prepared 2,500-word passage[1] dealing with the metallurgical properties of plain carbon steel. Emphasis was placed on such basic principles as the relationship between metallic grain structure, on the one hand, and temperature, carbon content, and rate of cooling, on the other. Important factual information (e.g., critical temperatures), however, was also included, and basic principles were also applied to such technological processes as heat treatment and tempering.

The metallurgical topic was chosen on the basis of being generally unfamiliar to undergraduates in liberal arts and sciences (i.e., not ordinarily included in chemistry courses), but still sufficiently elementary to be both comprehensible and interesting to novices with no prior background in the field. The criterion of unfamiliarity was especially crucial because the purpose of the study was to ascertain whether advance organizers could facilitate retention in areas of knowledge *new* to learners. By using unfamiliar material it was also possible to ensure that all Ss started from approximately the same baseline in learning the material. Empirical proof of unfamiliarity was sought, therefore, by administering the retention test on the steel passage to a comparable group of naive Ss who had *not* studied the material; but although this latter group of Ss made scores which, on the average, were only slightly and not significantly better than chance, it was evident from later analysis of the experimental data that scores earned by Ss who *had* studied the passage were related to both sex and field of specialization. Male students and majors in science and art were better able to learn and retain the steel material than were female students and majors in English, foreign languages, music, and the social sciences. Hence, the criterion of unfamiliarity was not completely satisfied, in

[1] Appreciation is expressed to Robert M. Tomlinson for assistance in the preparation of the learning passage.

as much as these differences undoubtedly reflected, in part, variability in relevant incidental experience influencing the learnability of the material.

Knowledge of the steel passage was tested by a 36-item multiple-choice examination with a corrected split-half reliability of .79. Test questions covered principles, facts, and applications, and were selected by an item analysis procedure from a larger population of items. Scores on the test showed a satisfactory range of variability and were distributed normally. Since it was intended as a power test, no time limit was imposed.

PROCEDURE

It was first necessary to equate experimental and control groups on the basis of ability to learn an unfamiliar scientific passage of comparable difficulty. The passage used for this purpose was concerned with the endocrinology of human pubescence and was approximately 1,800 words long. *Ss* were given 20 minutes to read and study this material, and were tested immediately thereafter by a 26-item multiple-choice test with a corrected split-half reliability of .78. (The unfamiliarity of the material had been previously ascertained by administering the test to a comparable group of naive *Ss* who had not studied the passage, and obtaining a mean score only slightly and not significantly greater than chance.) Test scores on the pubescence passage were normally distributed and correlated .64 on a product-moment basis with test scores on the steel passage. *F* tests were performed on the variance ratios of the pubescence material test scores for all possible combinations of the four sections, and none approached significance at the .05 level of confidence. It was considered justifiable, therefore, to treat the retention scores of experimental and control groups on the steel passage as if derived, respectively, from one large class rather than from four separate sections.

Ss in each of the four sections were matched on the basis of test scores on the pubescence material and assigned to experimental and control groups. Experimental and control treatments were then administered simultaneously to experimental and control *Ss*, respectively, within each section. This procedure was possible because the two treatments consisted of studying identical appearing introductory passages differing only in content. The use of this procedure also provided the important methodological advantage of holding instructor, class, and situational variables constant for both groups. Each introductory passage of approximately 500 words was studied twice, 5 minutes each time, by the appropriate group of *Ss*. The two occasions were 48 hours and immediately before exposure to the main learning passage.

The experimental introductory passage contained background material for the learning passage which was presented at a much higher level of abstraction, generality, and inclusiveness than the latter-passage itself. It was designed to serve as an organizing or anchoring focus for the steel material and to relate it to existing cognitive structure. Principal emphasis was placed, therefore, on the major similarities and differences between metals and alloys, their respective advantages and limi-

tations, and the reasons for making and using alloys. Although this passage provided *Ss* in the experimental group with relevant background concepts of a general nature, it was carefully designed not to contain specific information that would confer a direct advantage in answering any of the questions on the steel test. This latter criterion was tested empirically and shown to be warranted when a comparable group of *Ss* made only a slightly better than chance mean score on the steel test after studying the introductory passage alone.

The control introductory passage, on the other hand, consisted of such historically relevant background material as the historical evolution of the methods used in processing iron and steel. This type of introductory material is traditionally included in most textbooks on metallugry and is presumably intended to enhance student interest. In contrast to the introductory passage given to the experimental group, it contained no conceptual material that could serve as an ideational framework for organizing the particular substantive body of more detailed ideas, facts, and relationships in the learning passage.

It was methodologically necessary to provide this control treatment in order that any obtained difference between experimental and control groups could be attributed to the particular nature of the experimental introductory passage (i.e., to its organizing properties) rather than to its presence per se.

Both groups studied the steel passage for 35 minutes and took the multiple-choice steel test 3 days later. Since it was evident from a comparison of test scores on the steel and pubescence passages that scores on the steel test were related to *Ss*' sex and major field, it was necessary to hold these latter factors (as well as pubescence test scores) constant. Hence, it was no longer possible to use the originally matched pairs of *Ss* within each section. Sufficient *Ss* were also not available to rematch individual pairs of *Ss* on all three variables. By matching experimental and control *Ss* across sections, however, it was possible to equate two groups of 40 *Ss* each for sex, pubescence scores, and field of specialization. The crossing of sectional lines in this rematching procedure was justifiable in view of the intersectional homogeneity of variance.

RESULTS AND DISCUSSION

The mean steel test score of the experimental group was 16.7, as compared to 14.1 for the control group and a mean chance score of 7.2 (one-fifth of 36).[2] The standard deviations of the two groups were 5.8 and 5.4, respectively. The difference between the means[3] of the experimental and control groups

---

[2] The distribution of steel test scores for both experimental and control groups did not deviate significantly from the norm. Appreciation is expressed to Pearl Ausubel for assistance in the processing of the data.

[3] The standard error of the difference for equated groups was calculated according to a method described by Edwards (1954, pp. 282–288).

TABLE 1
RETENTION TEST SCORES OF EXPERIMENTAL AND
CONTROL GROUPS ON LEARNING PASSAGE

Group	Type of Introduction	Mean	SD
Experimental	Substantive	16.7	5.8
Control	Historical	14.1	5.4

Note.—Chance Score on the multiple-choice test of 36 items is 7.2. The difference between the means in this table is reliable at between the .05 and .01 level of confidence.

was significant at the .05 level and nearly at the .01 level for a one-tailed test.

The obtained difference in retention between experimental and control groups, although statistically significant, would undoubtedly have been even greater if the learning passage used for matching purposes had been in the same subject matter field as the steel material (i.e., if the relationship between the two sets of scores were higher than that indicated by the correlation of .64 between the steel and pubescence scores.) Another experimental condition probably detracting from the difference between the two groups was the fact that the steel material was not completely unfamiliar to many Ss. Because of some prior general familiarity with the contents of the steel passage, many Ss already possessed relevant and stable subsuming concepts. These obviously rendered less significant the potential learning advantages conferable by advance organizers.

It could be argued, of course, that exposure to the experimental introduction constituted in effect a partial substantive equivalent of an additional learning trial. Actually, however, any substantive repetition was at most very indirect, since the introductory passage consisted of much more inclusive and general background material than was contained in the learning task itself, and also provided no direct advantage in answering the test items. Furthermore, according to behavioristic (interference) theory, prior exposure to similar but not identical learning material induces proactive inhibition rather than facilitation.

Advance organizers probably facilitate the incorporability and longevity of meaningful verbal material in two different ways. First, they explicitly draw upon and mobilize whatever relevant subsuming concepts are already established in the learner's cognitive structure and make them part of the subsuming entity. Thus, not only is the new material rendered more familiar and meaningful, but the most relevant ideational antecedents are also selected and utilized in integrated fashion. Second, advance organizers at an appropriate level of inclusiveness provide optimal anchorage. This promotes both initial incorporation and later resistance to obliterative subsumption.

The appropriate level of inclusiveness may be defined as that level which is as proximate as possible to the degree of conceptualization of the learning task—relative, of course, to the existing degree of differentiation of the subject as a whole in the learner's cognitive background. Thus, the more unfamiliar the learning material (i.e., the more undifferentiated the learner's background of relevant concepts), the more inclusive or highly generalized the subsumers must be in order to be proximate. If appropriately relevant and proximate subsuming concepts are not available, the learner tends to use the most proximate and relevant ones that are. But since it is highly improbable, however, that we can count on the spontaneous availability of the most relevant and proximate subsuming concepts, the most dependable way of facilitating retention is to introduce the appropriate subsumers and make them part of cognitive structure prior to the actual presentation of the learning task. The introduced subsumers thus become advance organizers or anchoring foci for the reception of new material.

Even though this principle seems rather self-evident it is rarely followed in actual teaching procedures or in the organization of most textbooks. The more typical practice is to segregate topically homogeneous materials into separate chapters, and to present them throughout at a uniform level of conceptualization in accordance with a logical outline of subject matter organization. This practice, of course, although logically sound is psychologically incongruous with the postulated process whereby meaningful learning occurs, i.e., with the hierarchical organization of cognitive structure in terms of progressive gradations of inclusiveness, and with the mechanism of accretion through a process of progressive differentiation of an undifferentiated field. Thus, in most instances, students are required to learn the details of new and unfamiliar disciplines before they have acquired an adequate body of relevant subsumers at an appropriate level of inclusiveness.

As a result, both students and teachers are often coerced into treating meaningful materials as if they were rote in character, and students consequently experience unnecessary difficulty and reduced success in both learning and retention. The teaching of mathematics and science, for example, still relies heavily on rote learning of formulas and procedural steps, on recognition of stereotyped "type problems," and on mechanical manipulation of symbols. In the absence of clear and stable concepts which can serve as anchoring points and organizing foci for the incorporation of new meaningful material, students are trapped in a morass of confusion and have little choice but to rotely memorize learning tasks for examination purposes. The traditional historical introduction to new and primarily nonhistorical subject matter concepts possibly enhances student interest, but lacks the necessary substantive content to serve this organizing function (see examples under *Procedure* section above).

The pedagogic value of advance organizers obviously depends in part upon how well organized the learning material itself is. If it contains built-in organizers and proceeds from regions of lesser to greater differentiation (higher to lower inclusiveness), rather than in the manner of the typical textbook or lecture presentation, much of the potential benefit derivable from advance organizers will not be actualized. Regardless of how well-organized learning material is, however, it is hypothesized that learning and retention can still be facilitated by the use of advance organizers at an appropriate level of inclusiveness. Such organizers are available from the very beginning of the learning task, and their integrative properties are also much more salient than when introduced concurrently with the learning material.

SUMMARY AND CONCLUSIONS

An empirical test was made of the hypothesis that the learning and retention of unfamiliar but meaningful verbal material could be facilitated by the advance introduction of relevant subsuming concepts (organizers). Experimental and control groups of 40 undergraduate *S*s each were equated on the basis of sex, field of specialization, and ability to learn unfamiliar scientific material. The learning task consisted of a 2,500-word passage of empirically demonstrated unfamiliarity, dealing with the metallurgical properties of steel. On two separate occasions, 48 hours and immediately prior to contact with the learning task, experimental *S*s studied a 500-word introductory passage containing substantive background material of a conceptual nature presented at a much higher level of generality, abstraction, and inclusiveness than the steel material itself. This passage was empirically shown to contain no information that could be directly helpful in answering the test itsms on the steel passage. Control *S*s similarly studied a traditional type of historical introduction of identical length. Retention of the learning material was tested 3 days later by means of a multiple-choice test. Comparison of the mean retention scores of the experimental and control groups unequivocally supported the hypothesis.

The facilitating influence of advance organizers on the incorporability and longevity of meaningful learning material was attributed to two factors: (*a*) the selective mobilization of the most relevant existing concepts in the learner's cognitive structure for integrative use as part of the subsuming focus for the new learning task, thereby increasing the task's familiarity and meaningfulness; and (*b*) the provision of optimal anchorage for the learning material in the form of relevant and appropriate subsuming concepts at a proximate level of inclusiveness.

The suggestion was offered that the greater use of appropriate (substantive rather than historical) advance organizers in the teaching of meaningful verbal material could lead to more effective retention. This procedure would also render unnecessary much of the rote memorization to which students resort because they are required to learn the details of a discipline before having available a sufficient number of key subsuming concepts.

REFERENCES

AUSUBEL, D. B., ROBBINS, LILLIAN C., and BLAKE, E., JR. Retroactive inhibition and facilitation in the learning of school materials. *J. Educ. Psychol.,* 1957, *48,* 334–343.

EDWARDS, A. L. *Statistical methods for the behavioral sciences.* New York: Rinehart, 1954.

75

Training Kindergarten Children to Discriminate Letter-Like Forms [1]

JOANNA P. WILLIAMS

Letter recognition is one of the first tasks that a beginning reader faces, and it often proves a difficult one. How should we best structure our teaching of this skill? At what age is such training undertaken most effectively? The author of this article, Joanna P. Williams, is associate professor of education at the University of Pennsylvania and is an editor of this volume.

To learn to differentiate and recognize letters is one of the primary steps in learning to read, and this task is often a major source of difficulty in reading instruction (Vernon, 1957). Not only are certain letters of the alphabet quite similar in form to others, but in some cases they are merely rotations and reversals of others, e.g., *b*, *d*, and *q*, *p*. These letters, in fact, produce the most confusion and difficulty (Smith, 1928; Gibson et al., 1962; Popp, 1964).

Many practice materials have been designed to handle this problem. Some stress discrimination training (matching-to-sample and sorting pictures, symbols, or actual letters), whereas others empha-

size reproduction training of some type (tracing or copying). Reading methods themselves vary as to the emphasis placed on instruction in writing. While some methods stress it (Fernald, 1943; Spalding and Spalding, 1957), typically instruction in writing is not emphasized today. In fact, at least one recently developed method (Moore, 1963) puts off writing until later stages of training.

There is little empirical evidence as to the relative effectiveness of discrimination training and reproduction training, and it is difficult to make predictions from theory. It is generally held that one should train directly the behavior which is to be tested. According to this principle, training in discrimination should be given if the criterion is some type of recognition skill. On the other hand, it can be argued that increasing the degree of active participation, by requiring the subject to reproduce the material in some manner, might lead to superior performance even on a recognition task.

Gibson (1962) has hypothesized that improvement of visual discrimination depends on learning the distinctive features of the forms to be discriminated, that is, those dimensions of difference that distinguish the stimuli. Precise specification of the critical features of letters of the alphabet, of course, will be a difficult task (Gibson, 1966).

The present experiment is concerned not with the nature of the critical features themselves, but rather with the effectiveness of different training methods in ensuring that attention is focused on the critical features, whatever they may be. Maccoby and Bee (1965) have suggested that a subject must take account of more attributes of a form in order to reproduce it than to discriminate it from other forms. For example, children who can reproduce certain distinctive features of a form may fail to draw them in proper relation to each other, although they can recognize the form in an array perfectly. The authors propose that the lag in development between discrimination and reproduction may be accounted for by a difference in the number of attributes of the model necessary for the two tasks.

Maccoby and Bee presented no data directly relevant to the question of training, but it seems likely that reproduction training could produce better recognition of forms than discrimination training because it would force the subject to attend to more criterial attributes. That is, if the subject must abstract more distinctive features in reproduction training in order to solve the training task, he then will have available more cues for the new discriminations presented in testing.

Furthermore, whether or not reproduction training forces closer attention to the stimuli is likely to

[1] This research was supported in part by the Cooperative Research Program, U.S. Office of Education, and in part by the William T. Carter Foundation, University of Pennsylvania. The author is indebted to JoAnne Koltnow for her assistance in the collection and analysis of the data.

Joanna P. Williams, "Training kindergarten children to discriminate letter-like forms," *American Educational Research Journal*, 6, 1969, 501–514. Reprinted with abridgement by permission.

depend on the similarity of the standard and the other stimuli from which it must be distinguished. For example, there are few critical features that differentiate between two very similar stimuli. During training, while the subject is attempting to hit upon a feature that *is* a distinctive one, he will focus on many features, and will be more likely to abstract features that are critical for differentiation of the standard in a different test situation.

This experiment compares three conditions: (1) discrimination training where the comparison stimuli are quite different from the standard; (2) discrimination training where the comparison stimuli are transformations (rotations and reversals) of the standards; and (3) reproduction training. It is predicted that (2) will be more effective than (1), because (2) forces attention during training to more of the critical features of the forms. If reproduction training does in fact produce discrimination of more attributes than discrimination training, then (3) will be most effective. If not, then reproduction training will be less effective than (2) and perhaps even than (1).

The experiment had an additional purpose. Gibson et al. (1962) suggested that transformation types are more important as "predictors of identifiability" than are the characteristics of the standards themselves. That is, when used as comparison stimuli in a discrimination task, certain transformations (notably the right-left reversal) are more confusing than others, no matter what the nature of original stimulus.

Actually, two separate experiments are reported here. In the first, children who had just begun kindergarten were run. The second experiment, similar to the first but using subjects who had more school experience, was done in order to assess the effectiveness of the training conditions at a more advanced level.

METHOD

Subjects: Subjects were kindergarten pupils enrolled in a Philadelphia elementary school. Experiment 1, which involved 32 of these children, was conducted during the first month of the kindergarten year. Another 32 Ss participated (Experiment 2) after they had completed $3/4$ of their first school year. All Ss were between the ages of four and one-half and five and one-half years old at the time of testing. An additional 11 children were dropped from the sample because they were uncooperative ($N = 2$) or because they were absent on the second day of testing. Within each experiment, Ss were assigned randomly to one of the four training conditions, with the restriction that the sexes be represented equally in each group.

Materials: The stimuli consisted of six non-symmetrical letter-like forms, modified from those designed by Gibson et al. (1962) to follow the constraints of printed upper case capitals. Four transformations of these standard stimuli were also used: right-left reversal, up-down reversal (mirror image), 180° rotation, and 90° rotation. The standards and their transformations are shown in Figure 1. Twelve additional stimuli were also used, different from the six standards but constructed according to the same set of rules. These forms (individually and in combination) were printed in red on white 5″ × 8″ cards.

Training: The basic training conditions were (1) Discrimination, and (2) Reproduction training.

1. DISCRIMINATION TRAINING

The training task consisted of delayed matching-to-sample task, in which S was asked to identify the standard after it was removed from view. This visual memory task was used because it approximates the perceptual learning tasks involved in actual reading more closely than does simple discrimination training (Wohlwill and Wiener, 1964).

Three of the six standards described above were placed in an array in front of S. (Half the Ss were shown three of the standards, chosen randomly from the six, and the other Ss were shown the other three.) Twelve cards, on each of which were two forms (one of the standards and another form), were presented in sequence, and S's task was to choose the form on each card which was exactly the same as one of the three standards. When S made a correct choice, E praised him and gave him a small gummed star. (These stars were traded at the end of training for a larger sticker.) When S's response was incorrect, E pointed to the correct stimulus and said, "No, this is the one just like the one above." The presentation of all twelve cards constituted one training trial. There were five trials,

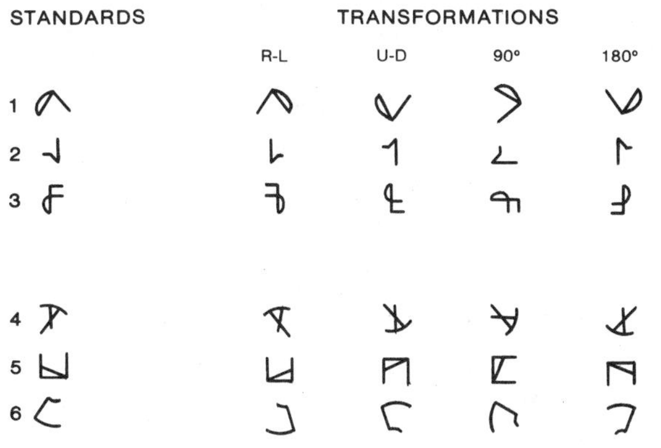

FIGURE 1. *The standards and their transformations.*

with the cards presented in a different random order on each trial. The standards remained exposed during the first two trials, after which they were removed. The time taken in training depended on the *S*'s own response rate. The total time taken for the five trials was recorded for each *S*.

There were three discrimination training groups ($n = 8$ in each group). In all cases, each of the three standards was represented on four of the twelve cards. The comparison stimuli varied among the groups.

(a) *Difficult (D-1):* The comparison stimuli were right-left reversal and 180° rotation transformations. There were two of each for each standard, and they were balanced as to whether they were placed to the right or the left of the standard on the card.

(b) *Difficult (D-2):* The comparison stimuli were up-down reversal and 90° rotation transformations, arranged as above.

(c) *Simple (S):* The comparison stimuli were four forms other than those used as the standards. Half the *S*s in this group were shown one set of forms, and for the other half, a completely different set of comparison stimuli was used.

2. REPRODUCTION TRAINING (R)

As in each of the discrimination groups, there were eight *S*s in this group. The three standards were presented in an array as in discrimination training. However, no other forms were presented. *S* was asked to trace (twice) and copy (three or four times) each standard. The order in which the three standards were presented for reproduction was balanced over *S*s. The training time for each individual *S* in this condition was matched with the time taken by an *S* in one of the discrimination training groups being represented equally. Approximately the same number of stars was given as in the other groups.

The order in which the three standards were placed in front of *S* at the beginning of training was balanced within and across groups. Half the *S*s were given one set of three standards, and the other half were given the other three standards.

Experiment 2: The design of this experiment was similar to that described above, except that three, and not five, training trials were given. On the first trial, the standards were exposed, and on the other two they were hidden. This was the only modification in the design.

Testing: A series of three tests was administered immediately upon the completion of training, and the same series of tests was repeated 24 hours afterwards.

Test 1 (& Retest 1) consisted of a series of 24 cards (5″ × 8″) on each of which was drawn two forms, one standard and one other. Each of the three standards was presented four times with dissimilar forms (those used in *S* training) and once each with the four transformations. The cards were divided into two sets of twelve; and half the *S*s received one set first and the other *S*s, the other set first. The cards within each set were presented in a different random order to each *S*. *S* was required to point to the standard on each card. No feedback was given on this or any of the tests.

Test 2 (& Retest 2) consisted of a series of 15 cards. On each card (8½″ × 11″) were printed two sets of three forms each. One set contained one of the three standards. The other set contained a transformation of that standard. The other four forms, two in each set, had not previously been seen by the *S*. Each standard was presented five times, once paired with each of the four transformations and once paired with one of the other forms used in Group *S* training. The standard and its comparison stimulus were always placed in the middle of their respective sets. The cards were presented in a different random order for each *S*. *S* was required to point to the set which contained the standard.

Test 3 (& Retest 3) consisted of twelve cards (8½″ × 11″). On each card were placed two pairs of forms. One pair consisted of two of the three standards; the other pair consisted of one standard and a transformation of one of the other two standards. The cards were presented in a different random order for each *S*. *S* was required to point to the pair which contained the two standards.

RESULTS

· · ·

The relative difficulty of the three tests was assessed by comparing the proportion of errors made on each of the three tests and their retests. The proportion of errors increased as a function of how much the test differed from the training task ($F = 6.07$, $df = 2/380$; $p < .01$). The performance in the second experiment was significantly superior to that in the first ($F = 144.13$, $df = 1/190$, $p < .01$), even though these subjects had received fewer training trials. There was no interaction between the two variables.

Performance on each of the three tests was analyzed as a function of the training conditions, the particular set of three standard stimuli to be discriminated, and the time of testing. *Experiment 1:* On all three tests, differences among training methods were significant (*Test 1:*

F = 4.27, p < .05; Test 2: F = 9.57, p < .01; Test 3: F = 3.27, p < .05; all df = 3/24). The two sets of standards did not differ *(the respective Fs were 2.88, 2.11, and <1, df = 1/24).* On Test 1, there were fewer errors on the retest than on the original test *(F = 5.17, df = 1/24, p < .05),* and there was a tendency for the retest to show fewer errors on the other two tests, although those differences did not reach significance. None of the interactions reached significance.

Experiment 2: There were no differences among training methods *(Test 1: F < 1; Test 2: F = 1.53; Test 3: F = 1.54; df = 3/24),* nor were there differences in the standards used *(the Fs were 4.19, 3.29, and <1, df = 1/24).* As in the first experiment, there were fewer errors on the retest than on the original test in Test 1 *(F = 5.07, df = 1/24, p < .05),* and on the other two sets, the retest performance remained superior, though not significantly so *(F = 1.81 and <1, df = 1/24).* There were no significant interactions.

The next analysis concerned differences among training methods as a function of the type of transformation with which the standard was compared. Each of the three test and retest combinations was analyzed separately. Because of the significant differences between the two experiments, they were subjected to separate analyses. There were practically no errors on those comparison stimuli which were totally dissimilar from the standards and not simply transformations of them. Because these errors were so negligible, those items were excluded from the analyses.

Experiment 1: Type of training was a significant variable, of course. Specific comparisons on Test 1 indicated that the two difficult training procedures were not different *(F < 1; df = 1/28),* but were significantly superior *(i.e., showed fewer errors)* to the simple discrimination and the reproduction training *(F = 12.90, df = 1/28, p < .01).* The simple discrimination training and the reproduction training did not differ *(F = 1.23, df = 1/28).* Exactly the same pattern was seen on the other tests....

On all three tests there was a tendency for Group S to show more errors in training than Group R, but this trend never reached significance. The other main effect, type of transformation, also reached significance on Test 1 and Test 3, although not on Test 2. (An analysis of the specific differences among the transformations is presented below.) There was no interaction between type of training and type of transformation.

Experiment 2: Type of transformation was a significant variable. However, type of training did not reach conventional levels of significance. There were no interactions.

Further analysis was done in order to assess the differences among the various transformations. The proportion of errors made on each of the four transformations was computed for each of the six standards individually. While the order of the difficulty on the transformations depended on the particular stimulus, there was indeed a reliable difference among the transformation types *(F = 5.09, df = 3/20, p < .01).* Specific comparisons showed that the right-left reversal *(R-L)* was more difficult than the up-down reversal *(U-D),* the 90° rotation and the 180° rotation *(F = 14.18; df = 1/20; p < .01).* These other transformations did not differ among themselves.

DISCUSSION

In Experiment *1,* as predicted, discrimination training in which the comparison stimuli were transformations was superior to discrimination training where the comparison stimuli were totally different forms. This suggests that the comparisons involving minimally different stimuli did force the subject to attend to and abstract more attributes of the standard, which were then available for new test comparisons. Reproduction training was not as effective as discrimination-with-transformations, but was as effective as the simple discrimination training. These results suggest that in reproduction training the subject was focusing on the standards to the same extent at least as in simple discrimination training, though less than in the discrimination-with-transformation training. Thus, in terms of the Gibson hypothesis, it is suggested that the number of attributes that will be abstracted by reproduction training as compared to discrimination training does indeed depend on the similarity of the forms used in the discrimination training.

The fact that the right-left reversal was more difficult than the other transformations corroborates the findings of Wohlwill and Wiener (1964), Huttenlocher (1967), and, to some extent, Gibson et al. (1962). However, the difficulty of specific transformations did vary as a function of the particular stimulus: transformations other than the right-left reversal were distinctly more difficult for two of the six standards. The Gibson et al. (1962) conclusion that the transformation types are more important as "predictors of identifiability" than are the characteristics of the standard itself does not seem warranted on the basis of the present study. It might prove instructive to analyze a set of stimuli in order to specify the variables that determine the order of difficulty of the transformations.

Although the number of training trials had been decreased in Experiment 2 in order to approximate the degree of training achieved in Experiment *1,* overall performance in Experiment 2 was significantly superior. The important comparison, that of the three types of training, showed no significant differences in Experiment 2, suggesting that the question of whether reproduction training or discrimination training is more effective does indeed depend on the level of the subject. The factor or factors responsible for this difference as a function of level cannot, of course, be determined by the present data.

The crucial point is that even after a rather small amount of training at an appropriate level (i.e., at the beginning of the kindergarten year), there were significant differences among the training groups. These data indicate clearly that the effectiveness of readiness training does indeed depend on the particular technique used, and that there would be wide variation in the effectiveness of typically-used readiness materials. While special attention is often given to practice on rotations and reversals, usually too much time is devoted to copying and tracing or to discrimination exercises that—according to these data—are relatively ineffective. Moreover, such systematic training is sometimes given only in remedial work, that is, after a child has already developed some difficulty. The present experiment suggests (1) that more time be devoted to discrimination training that involves comparison of letters with their transformations, and (2) that this type of training be given early. It is quite effective at the very start of kindergarten, and obviously, if the occurrence of certain relatively common perceptual confusions could be minimized by appropriate training techniques introduced in the begin-

ning stages of instruction, there should be less necessity later for remedial techniques.

REFERENCES

FERNALD, G. M. *Remedial Techniques in Basic School Subjects*. New York: McGraw-Hill Book Co., Inc., 1943. 349 pp.

GIBSON, E. J. "Experimental Psychology of Learning to Read." *The Disabled Reader*. (Edited by J. Money), Baltimore: Johns Hopkins Press, 1966. 421 pp.

GIBSON, E. J., GIBSON, J. J., PICK, A. D., and OSSER, H. "A Developmental Study of the Discrimination of Letter-Like Forms." *Journal of Comparative and Physiological Psychology* 55: 897–906; No. 6, 1962.

HUTTENLOCHER, J. "Children's Ability to Order and Orient Objects." *Child Development* 38: 1169–1176; December 1967.

MACCOBY, E. E., and BEE, H. L. "Some Speculations Concerning the Lag Between Perceiving and Performing." *Child Development* 36: 367–377; June 1965.

MOORE, O. K. *Autotelic Responsive Environments and Exceptional Children*. Hamden, Conn.: Responsive Environments Foundation, 1963.

POPP, H. M. "Visual Discrimination of Alphabet Letters." *Reading Teacher* 17: 221–226; January 1964.

SMITH, N. B. "Matching Ability as a Factor in First Grade Reading." *Journal of Educational Research* 19: 560–571; November 1928.

VERNON, M. D. *Backwardness in Reading*. Cambridge, England: Cambridge University Press, 1958. 227 pp.

WOHLWILL, J. F., and WIENER, M. "Discrimination of Form Orientation in Young Children." *Child Development* 35: 1113–1125; December 1964.

76

Attentional Process in Reading: The Effect of Pictures on the Acquisition of Reading Responses

S. JAY SAMUELS[1]

The use of pictures in beginning reading texts has usually been encouraged. The pictures are considered to be an effective way of attracting the child's attention to the reading task. But is this assumption really valid? S. Jay Samuels, associate professor of educational psychology at the University of Minnesota, presents evidence that pictures may in fact be detrimental.

Psychologists have long been aware of the central role of attentional processes in learning. Pavlov and his associates found that in order to classically condition animals, distracting stimuli which competed for the animal's attention had to be eliminated. To accomplish this, they worked in a specially constructed soundproofed building with partitions separating experimenter and animal. The mere presence of the experimenter or the sound of footsteps in the experimental situation seriously prolonged the conditioning procedure (Osgood, p. 311, 1953). Distracting background stimuli not only interfere with the learning of animals but with the learning of humans as well. The ability of the

[1] The author would like to express his appreciation to Joseph Jenkins for his help in data collection and data analysis for Experiment I, and to Edwin Myers for his help in data collection and data analysis in Experiment II.

individual to withhold attention selectively from irrelevant and distracting background stimulation seems to be implicated in reading disability, according to Santostefano, Rutledge, and Randall (1965). It appears that when distracting stimuli are present the performance of the underachiever undergoes greater disruption than does the performance of the more capable student (Baker & Madell, 1965; Silverman, Davids, & Andrews, 1963).

The purpose of the present study was to test the hypothesis that when pictures and words are presented together, the pictures would function as distracting stimuli and interfere with the acquisition of reading responses. Pictures may be used as prompts when the reader cannot read a word in the text, but pictures may miscue and divert attention from the critical task of attending to the printed words. In order to test this hypothesis two experiments were conducted. Experiment I was designed as a laboratory study to test the effect of pictures on naïve subjects (Ss) under conditions unlike those found in classrooms. Since findings derived from laboratory settings are often subject to the criticism that they could not be replicated in less artificial situations, Experiment II was designed to test the effect of pictures on less naïve Ss using a procedure which was similar to that used in actual classrooms.

EXPERIMENT I

METHOD

Subjects. Thirty children who had kindergarten experience and who were enrolled in a prefirst grade summer program were randomly assigned to one of three experimental treatments. The Ss were pretested to assure that no one was able to read the words used in the experiment.

Design. A simple, randomized design was used. Ten Ss were randomly assigned to the no-picture, 10 to the simple-picture, and 10 to the complex-picture condition.

Materials. The pretest materials consisted of four 5 × 8 inch index cards with either "boy," "bed," "man," or "car," typed on them. There was one word typed on each card.

For the warm-up trials, four novel, nonsense figures that had been created for a study on reading were used (Jeffrey & Samuels, in press). The figures were highly discriminable from each other and sufficiently dissimilar from letters in the Roman alphabet to make generalization from the other unlikely. The figures were placed on

5 × 8 inch index cards, one to a card. The *S*s had to learn to associate a number with each figure. The numbers were 1, 2, 3, and 4.

For the experiment proper, a primary typewriter was used to type the words, boy, bed, man, and car, at the bottom of 5 × 8 inch index cards, one word to a card. The same words were presented in the no-picture, simple-picture, and complex-picture conditions.

For learning trials in the no-picture condition, there was a word at the bottom of each card but no picture was present.

For learning trials in the simple-picture condition, the words were typed at the bottom of each card as in the no-picture condition. Above each word was a simple black and white drawing portraying the object that the word symbolized. Previous work with the pictures indicated they could reliably elicit the same verbal response as was typed at the bottom of the card.

For learning trials in the complex-picture condition, the words were typed at the bottom as in the no-picture condition. Above each word was a colorful picture which had been cut out of a reading primer. The pictures were complex in that they pictorially represented more than the word which was at the bottom of the card. For example, the picture attached to the card with the word "boy" at the bottom showed a boy holding his dog. The boy was pointing to a horse in the background.

The cards used for the test trials were the same for all conditions. At the bottom of the test cards the four words, boy, bed, man, and car, were typed in lower case with the primary typewriter, one word to a card. There were no pictures on any of the test cards.

PROCEDURE

The experimenter worked individually with the *S*s during all phases of the procedure. A pretest was given to each *S*. The *S* was told, "Today, we are going to play a game. In this game we are going to learn some words. First, let us see if you already know what the names of the words are." The four words were shown to the *S*. If he was able to read any of the words, he was eliminated.

Following the pretest a warm-up was given to each *S* to acquaint him with the nature of the learning task. The *S* was told, "Before we learn the new words, let us practice on some numbers. I will show you a card with a funny-looking number on it and I want you to tell me what the number is. If you don't know the number's name I will tell you what it is. You should try to tell me what the number is before I tell you. Do you understand what we are to do? All right? Then, what do you do when I show you a card with a number on it?" Each card was shown to *S* for an approximate 4-second interval. At the end of the anticipation interval *S* was told the number. The cards were presented in three random orders. Each *S* was given six warm-up trials.

When the warm-up was over, *S* was given the first learning trial. He was told, "All right, now let us see how we can learn the new words. I will show you a card with a word on it and I want you to tell me what the word's name is. If you don't know the word's name I will tell you. You should try to tell me the name before I tell you.

Do you understand?" Each card was shown to the *S* for 4 seconds. Then he was told the name. The *S* was scored for a correct response if he said the appropriate word before feedback was given.

Following the first acquisition trial, the first test trial was given. The test card was presented for 4 seconds and *S* had to give the correct response during this interval. No feedback was given during test trials. Acquisition trials and test trials were alternated. Each *S* received 10 learning trials and 10 test trials. The stimuli for all phases of the procedure were presented in three random orders.

RESULTS

Separate analyses were computed for responses during acquisition trials and for responses during test trials. During acquisition trials pictures were present as incidental cues for the picture conditions. During test trials pictures were not present.

On the acquisition trials, as seen in Table 1, the mean number of correct responses given for the no-picture condition was 25.30; for the complex picture condition it was 36.90; and for the simple-picture condition it was 39.40. Comparing the simple-picture to the no-picture condition during acquisition, *S*s in the simple-picture condition gave significantly more correct responses ($t = 9.02$, $df = 18$, $p < .01$). Comparing the complex-picture to the no-picture condition, *S*s in the complex-picture condition gave significantly more correct responses ($t = 7.42$, $df = 18$, $p < .01$).

On the test trials, where incidental cues were absent for all conditions, the no-picture group excelled. As seen in Table 2, the mean number of correct responses given on the tests by *S*s in the no-picture condition was 19.20; for *S*s in the simple-picture condition it was 11.30; and for *S*s in the complex-picture condition it was 11.60.

TABLE 1

MEANS AND STANDARD DEVIATIONS FOR
TREATMENTS ON ACQUISITION TRIALS

Treatment	M	SD
No-picture	25.30	7.23
Simple-picture	39.40	1.26
Complex-picture	36.90	6.34

TABLE 2

MEANS AND STANDARD DEVIATIONS FOR
TREATMENTS ON TEST TRIALS

Treatment	M	SD
No-picture	19.20	7.93
Simple-picture	11.30	5.79
Complex-picture	11.60	4.93

Comparing the simple-picture to the no-picture condition on the test trials, Ss in the no-picture condition recognized significantly more words ($t = 4.02$, $df = 18$, $p < .01$). Comparing the complex-picture to the no-picture condition, Ss in the no-picture condition recognized significantly more words ($t = 3.87$, $df = 18$, $p < .01$).

DISCUSSION

The purpose of Experiment I was to test the hypothesis that when related pictures and words are presented together, the presence of pictures would retard the acquisition of reading responses. This experiment used naïve Ss under conditions unlike those found in classrooms. The results disclosed that during the 10 acquisition trials, when pictures were available as incidental cues for appropriate verbal responses for Ss in the picture conditions, Ss in these conditions gave significantly more correct responses than did Ss in the no-picture condition. On the 10 critical test trials, when pictures were not available as incidental cues, Ss in the no-picture condition gave significantly more correct responses. Acquisition and test trials were purposely alternated so that Ss in the picture conditions would be aware that the printed words were important stimuli. Despite the alternation of acquisition and test trials, Ss in the picture conditions tended to use pictures rather than words as cues. It would appear that pictures functioned as distracting stimuli in that they drew attention away from the printed words. A similar finding has been reported by Underwood (1963) and Samuels and Jeffrey (1966). They report that in paired-associate learning, under certain conditions, an S may extract from the stimulus complex an incidental cue to which the response gets attached. When the stimulus complex is presented, the S may give the correct response, but for the wrong reasons. For example, when presented h-o-r-s-e, the child says "horse." He may have attached the response to the letter "h," however. When the stimulus h-o-u-s-e is presented, he says "horse" since he attends only to the one letter.

Subsequent to the completion of Experiment I, two doctoral dissertations were conducted which tested the effect of pictures on reading acquisition. Despite methodological differences, these studies lend additional support to the finding that the presence of pictures retards reading acquisition. Using kindergarteners, Braun (1967) found significant differences in reading acquisition favoring the no-picture group on seven of eight comparisons. Harris (1967), who used kindergarteners from a low socioeconomic background, found significant differences in acquisition on four of eight comparisons, favoring

the no-picture group. Harris attributed his failure to find significance on more comparisons to the generally low level of learning for all his Ss regardless of experimental condition. In both studies, all comparisons which did not reach significance were in the predicted direction.

EXPERIMENT II

METHOD

Subjects. Fifty-two students from a Minneapolis public school with 7 months first-grade experience were used as Ss.

Design. A treatment by levels design was used. The Ss were divided into two matched groups. There were 26 Ss in the picture and 26 Ss in the no-picture condition. Half the Ss in each condition were designated as above and the other half as below the median based on pretest scores. The same test was used as pretest and posttest for all Ss, regardless of condition.

Materials. A pretest and posttest were used in this study. Both tests were exactly the same. The test was constructed by typing in large type each of the 50 different words used in the story "Fun at Blue Lake" on 3×5 inch index cards, one word to a card.

The reading material for the no-picture and picture condition was the same. A story called "Fun at Blue Lake" was written. It was 106 words long and contained 50 different words. The words were typed in large type and the story was mimeographed. A book was made for each S. The story, "Fun at Blue Lake," was pasted on the right face of the book for both conditions. The Ss in the picture condition had a picture from a reading primer pasted on the left face of the book. The picture showed a cabin in the woods with a lake in the foreground. At the lakeshore was a family and their dog. In the no-picture condition the left face of the book was blank. When the books were opened Ss in the picture condition saw the text on the right and a picture on the left. The Ss in the no-picture condition saw a blank page on the left and the text on the right.

PROCEDURE

Several days before the experiment proper was run, Ss were pretested on the 50 words used in the story. The pretest consisted of showing each of the 50 words used in the story to S. The words were exposed one at a time to S, allowing 10 seconds for a response. The Ss were then matched on pretest scores and randomly assigned to either the picture or no-picture condition.

Reading instruction was given to both conditions simultaneously. The groups were separated in the room so that Ss in the no-picture condition were unable to see the pictures of the Ss in the picture condition. Reading instruction was given to small groups. At no time were there more than eight Ss in the room. The instructional procedure paralleled that used in typical classrooms. Instruction consisted of motivating and building background for the story, reading for a purpose, silent reading, and then oral reading. The Ss were instructed to raise their hands during silent reading if they were unable to read any word. The experimenter went about whispering the words to the children who requested help. The experimenter was careful to give help to students in both groups and both groups were given opportunities to read aloud.

Immediately following reading instruction, the *S*s were given the posttest. They were tested by four assistants on the 50 words used in the story in a similar manner to that which was used in the pretest.

RESULTS

Two comparisons were made to test differences in word recognition on the posttest. In the first comparison, as seen in Table 3, above-median *S*s in the picture condition recognized a mean of 43.15 words while above-median *S*s in the no-picture condition recognized a mean of 42.08 words. This difference was not significant. In the second comparison, below-median *S*s in the picture condition recognized a mean of 23.69 words, while below-median *S*s in the no-picture condition recognized a mean of 26.23 words. This difference was significant ($t = 2.73$, $df = 12$, $p < .01$, one-tailed test).

DISCUSSION

Experiment II was designed to test the effect of pictures on reading acquisition using a procedure which was similar to that used in classrooms. The *S*s in this experiment had 7 months of formal reading instruction. No significant difference was found in reading acquisition between the picture and no-picture condition among the better readers. Among the poorer readers, *S*s in the no-picture condition learned to read significantly more words than did *S*s in the picture condition. The results of Experiment II support the findings of Silverman, Davids, and Andrews (1963) and Baker and Madell (1965) in that performance of the less capable student was affected more by distracting stimuli than was the performance of the more capable student.

Several questions are raised by the two experiments. Considering the effect which pictures had on reading acquisition of naïve and less capable students, one may wonder if it is good practice to put pictures in reading primers. Another question left unanswered is how the more capable student uses pictures when they are available. It would seem advisable to continue the investigation of the role of pictures in readers in terms of motivation, student attitude towards reading, and attentional processes.

REFERENCES

BAKER, R. W., & MADELL, T. O. A continued investigation of susceptibility to distraction in academically underachieving and achieving male college students. *Journal of Educational Psychology*, 1965, *56*, 254–258.

BRAUN, C. The efficacy of selected stimulus modalities in acquisition and retention of sex-typed textual responses of kindergarten children. Unpublished doctoral dissertation, University of Minnesota, 1967.

HARRIS, L. A. A study of the rate of acquisition and retention of interest-loaded words by low socio-economic kindergarten children. Unpublished doctoral dissertation, University of Minnesota, 1967.

JEFFREY, W. E., & SAMUELS, S. J. The effect of method of reading training on initial learning and transfer. *Journal of Verbal Learning and Verbal Behavior*, 1967, *6*, 354–358.

OSGOOD, C. E. *Method and theory in experimental psychology*. New York: Oxford University Press, 1953.

SAMUELS, S. J., & JEFFREY, W. E. Discriminability of words and letter cues used in learning to read. *Journal of Educational Psychology*, 1966, *57*, 337–340.

SANTOSTEFANO, S., RUTLEDGE, L., & RANDALL, D. Cognitive styles and reading disability. *Psychology in the Schools*, 1965, *2*, 57–62.

SILVERMAN, M., DAVIDS, A., & ANDREWS, J. M. Powers of attention and academic achievement. *Perceptual and Motor Skills*, 1963, *17*, 243–249.

UNDERWOOD, B. J. Stimulus selection in verbal learning. In C. N. Cofer & B. S. Musgrave (Eds.), *Verbal behavior and learning, problems and processes*. New York: McGraw-Hill, 1963. Pp. 33–48.

TABLE 3

WORD RECOGNITION SCORES ON POSTTEST FOR ABOVE AND BELOW MEDIAN SUBJECTS FOR TREATMENTS

Reading ability	M	SD
Below median		
No-picture treatment	26.23	8.48
Picture treatment	23.69	7.69
Above median		
No-picture treatment	42.08	4.57
Picture treatment	43.15	6.05

77

Fear Arousal, Persuasion, and Actual Versus Implied Behavioral Change: New Perspective Utilizing a Real-Life Dental Hygiene Program [1]

RICHARD I. EVANS, RICHARD M. ROZELLE,
THOMAS M. LASATER,
THEODORE M. DEMBROSKI,
AND BEM P. ALLEN

Ever since World War II, when researchers contributed a great deal of knowledge about how to help soldiers to keep up their morale, how to get housewives to cook the cuts of meat not normally used, etc., there has been a substantial amount of work on persuasive communication. This article evaluates the effectiveness of fear-arousal as a persuasive technique. It has obvious relevance to strategies used in anti-smoking and cancer detection campaigns, and it also has relevance to the classroom. The senior author, Richard I. Evans, is professor of psychology at the University of Houston, where Rozelle is associate professor of psychology. Lasater is assistant professor of dentistry and psychology at the University of Alabama in Birmingham; Dembroski is assistant professor of psychology at Florida Presbyterian College; and Allen is assistant professor at Western Illinois University.

The present report presents the results of an investigation designed to explore the differential impact of various patterns of appeals on retention, intention to behave, reported behavior, and, most significantly, on actual behavior. The focus on the effects of persuasive communications on actual behavior and the utilization of an innovative behavioral measure (Evans, Rozelle, Lasater, Dembroski, & Allen, 1968) in the present study is responsive in general to the growing need for research in social psychology which examined the effects of persuasion on actual behavior, as well as on attitudes, beliefs, and intended or reported behavior. More specifically, it attempts to utilize as a criterion a specific behavioral measure to further explore the effect of fear arousal in persuasion communications.

In his review of research in the fear arousal area during the past 15 years, Higbee (1969) pointed to inconsistencies in the findings. In spite of such contradictions in the literature, the present authors agree with Higbee and suggest further that there exists at least some evidence for the following generalizations: (*a*) Generally, high fear is more effective than low fear, or there is no difference between the two in changing intentions to behave, self-report of behavior, or actual behavior. (*b*) The effect is usually greatest immediately following the communication and dissipates with time. (*c*) The effects of fear-arousing communications are more clearly demonstrated through changes in reported intentions to behave, attitudes toward the topic of the appeal, or for self-reports of behavior than for changes in actual behavior. (*d*) At least some minimum level of affect arousal coupled with instructions appears to be involved in most of the fear-arousal studies. (*e*) There have been few if any comparisons made between effectiveness of negative (fear) appeals and positive (optimistic) appeals. (*f*) There is a need in fear-arousal studies

[1] This research was supported in the context of Psychology Research Training Grant 5 TI DE 138 from the National Institute of Dental Research under the direction of the first author. Thanks are expressed for the fine cooperation of the Aldine Independent School District, Houston, Texas, and in particular, Superintendent W. W. Thorne and Nurse Barbara Wallace. Special thanks are expressed to Dean Sumter S. Arnim of the University of Texas Graduate School of Biomedical Sciences for his advice from a dental perspective in the adapting of the disclosing tablet (which he developed clinically) to the special requirements of our investigation and contributing the supply of dental kits used in the study through his affiliation with the Procter and Gamble Company. Thanks are expressed to psychology graduate student and NIDR trainee William Forbes for his able assistance in some additional statistical calculations and preparation of tables and to Miriam Thompson for her fine job in the preparation of the manuscript.

This paper was presented at the meeting of the American Psychological Association, Miami Beach, Florida, September 1970, during the special Cattell Research Awards Session as the third recipient of the 1970 awards.

to not only examine the immediate effects of the communication, but to examine the relative long-term effects as well. (*g*) There may be an over-riding need that aside from affect arousal, the instructions in such studies should be quite specific. (*h*) Learning and retention as well as anxiety may be crucial considerations in studies in the effectiveness of communications.

The Present Study

The present study was designed both to further clarify issues suggested in the above eight generalizations and to consider some yet unexplored considerations in the area of affect-arousing communications. It utilizes the pretest-treatment-posttest design found in virtually all the affect-arousing communication studies reported in the literature.

An innovative aspect of the present study is the inclusion of a novel behavioral measure of toothbrushing behavior, which was developed to fill the need for more adequate criteria of behavior in such studies.

Another aspect of the present study rarely found in previous studies is the utilization of three post-treatment periods: immediately following the presentation of the message, 5 days after the presentation, and 6 weeks after the presentation.

Still another aspect of the present study not often found in previous ones is the inclusion of a positive (optimistic) affect appeal. It is possible that fear-arousal appeals may not have the persuasive effectiveness of an appeal emphasizing positive consequences. Because positive consequences are often not visible, examining the effects of positive appeals are difficult in some health communications. However, because of its nature, the dental hygiene situation permits the inclusion of positive affect appeals.

Given a certain amount of motivation, subjects need also to know when and where to behave and have access to the necessary equipment needed to behave if persuasion is to be effective in line with the findings of Leventhal, Singer, and Jones (1965). It was in response to this consideration that the procedure was included of giving each subject a dental care kit, as well as the detailed recommendations for its use. In fact, one plausible explanation for the relative ineffectiveness of high fear as a persuasive condition found in the Janis and Feshbach (1953) study is the possibility that inadequate recommendations were provided with the high-fear message. For example, Janis and Feshbach (1953) reported the following quotes from subjects in the high-fear condition: "Leave out the slides that show the rottiness of the teeth and have more in about how to brush your teeth; I don't think you should have shown so many gory pictures without showing more to prevent it [p. 83]."

So the present investigation is an extension of the basic approach utilized in the earlier study (Evans et al., 1968), more systematically reexamining and extending several facets of the problem of fear-arousal persuasive communications, the background of which were reviewed by Janis (1967) and Higbee (1969). To more completely measure our knowledge of the impact of persuasive communications, measures of information retained and anxiety were also included.

On the basis of the rationale thus presented and generalizations in terms indigenous to the interaction of the independent and dependent variables in the present investigation, the following hypotheses were formulated: (*a*) The high-fear appeal generates a higher degree of anxiety than a low-fear appeal; the least amount of anxiety is generated by the positive appeal. (*b*) No significant differences are obtained in information retention among any of the conditions. (*c*) The high-fear, low-fear, and positive appeals generate a significantly greater intention to behave, in accordance with the recommendations, than the recommendations only and the elaborated recommendations. (*d*) The high-fear, low-fear, and positive appeals generate a significantly greater report of behavior in accordance with the recommendations than the recommendations only and the elaborated recommendations. (*e*) The high-fear, low-fear, and positive appeals generate a significantly greater behavior change in accordance with the recommendations than the recommendations only and the elaborated recommendations.

The present investigation thus explores the relative impact on the anxiety level, information retained, and on intended, reported, and actual toothbrushing behavior (as measured by the "disclosing wafer" technique) of persuasive communications involving high fear arousal, low fear arousal, a positive affect message, elaborated dental hygiene instructions presented without affect, and simple dental hygiene instructions presented without affect.

Method

The present investigation was conducted in the context of an ostensible program of dental hygiene training. The programs were part of the physical education curricula of the junior high schools in an independent school district near Houston, Texas, thus insuring a natural setting for the study.

Subjects

Students from the independent school district constituted the population from which the present sample was drawn. Subjects were 394 junior high school children from the population. The administration of a questionnaire which yielded demographic data covering the subject population at the various schools indicated that the subjects ranged from 12 to 15 years of age and that all subjects were homogeneous with respect to socioeconomic level, roughly lower middle-class. It was necessary to gain permission from subjects' parents for their participation. Therefore, only subjects who returned a permission slip that indicated parental acceptance were included in the sample. There appeared to be an approximate 70% return rate. However, upon further investigation, it was discovered that some of the teachers had misplaced return slips, so this 70% may be a substantial underestimate of the actual return rate.

One junior high school was randomly selected for the presentation of two fear communications. Another was randomly selected for the presentation of the positive communication and the elaborated recommendations communication. A third was randomly selected for presentation of the recommendations only and to provide a control group which received no communications. However, the group intended as a control was not considered in the analysis of the results because the class had been dismissed to attend a track meet on the occasion of the fourth subject contact. Classes selected for the various messages were counterbalanced with respect to time of day (morning versus afternoon).

PERSUASIVE APPEALS (INDEPENDENT VARIABLES)

Five varieties of persuasive appeals were used in all. Three of the persuasive appeals, high fear, low fear, and positive, were each followed by an identical set of specific recommendations. A fourth communication consisted only of a set of these specific recommendations. A fifth communication condition consisted of an elaboration of the specific recommendations utilized in the other four appeals.

The positive communication began with a non-specific reference to the good health and popularity obtainable by those who take proper care of their teeth. This section was followed by the chronicle of a boy and his sister. Events in the lives of these two persons were integrated with their dental history, and several slides of these persons were shown. It was emphasized that both had always taken proper care of their teeth and that both had always been popular and otherwise socially successful. A cause and effect relationship between proper dental care and popularity was thus suggested. The communication ended with the suggestion that anyone can be healthy and popular if he takes proper care of his teeth.

The specific recommendations which were included in all communication conditions (see the discussion of Leventhal & Singer, 1965) began with a suggestion that procedures for the proper care of the teeth do exist and can, in fact, be stated. This suggestion was followed by the presentation of a step-by-step procedure concerning how to care for the teeth. This consisted of four specific recommended steps:

1. Brush your teeth with toothpaste in your usual way, but as thoroughly as you can and remember to brush the back of your teeth. Try to brush all of your teeth and be sure to clean in between your teeth. After brushing them as clean as you can, rinse your mouth thoroughly with water.
2. Clean more thoroughly in between the teeth. The dental floss is used to help clean the places a toothbrush misses. This is easy to do. Cut off a piece of dental floss about a foot or so long. Wrap the floss around your index finger and grab the loose end with your other hand, so about an inch of floss is left between your hands. Slip the floss between each pair of teeth by moving it gently back and forth. Then scrape the floss against both sides of the teeth until you feel they are clean.
3. Chew the disclosing wafer and swish it around your teeth to see if you have missed any places.
4. Spot brush the few remaining places away and remember these places you've missed the next time you're brushing your teeth.

The "dental care kit" (produced by Procter and Gamble) was given to all subjects at the conclusion of each message. The kit contained some disclosing wafers, a toothbrush, some toothpaste, and a cylinder of dental floss. Each kit contained a precise set of printed instructions which consisted of a restatement of the step-by-step recommendations presented in the communications presented orally.

The remaining communication condition was included in the light of results reported by Leventhal et al. (1965) which suggest the importance of elaborating instructions. These elaborated recommendations were combined with the set of recommendations which were included in all other communications, but were more detailed in describing proper dental hygiene practices.

An actor was hired and trained to present the various communications. This individual was chosen because he looked mature and had the appearance of a professional person. The actor, although identified as only a member of the research team, was told to speak with authority and confidence.

DEPENDENT VARIABLES

The behavioral measure. Arnim (1963) developed a "disclosing wafer" which, when chewed, stains the plaque on the teeth red and thereby reveals the amount of this plaque. According to Arnim, this has proven to be a reliable indicator of dental hygiene behavior involving toothbrushing and use of dental floss. Using the disclosing wafer and a technique for photographing the teeth and gums, Evans et al. (1968) standardized a 5-point scale for rating plaque concentration which reflects such dental hygiene behavior. This scale was utilized to measure dental hygiene behavior in the present investigation. The ratings ranged from 1 (very clean) to 5 (very dirty).

Reported behavior. Reported behavior was measured by subjects' responses to a question eliciting information concerning the relative frequency of toothbrushing be-

542	XI—Specific Educational Implications

havior. The alternatives were scored from 1 (never) to 5 (two times a day).

Anxiety. A gross measure of anxiety was used to determine the degree to which affect was aroused by the communications. Using four questions which requested subjects to report their own anxiety level, scores of 4 (high anxiety) to 20 (no anxiety) were recorded.

Intention to behave. Intention to behave was determined from subjects' responses to two questions eliciting estimates of intended frequency of engaging in dental hygiene behavior. Scores ranged from 2 (lowest intention to behave) to 10 (greatest intention to behave).

Information retained. The measure of information retained by the subject was composed of five multiple-choice questions covering only the content of the specific recommendations which were present in all communication conditions. Scores ranged from 4 (lowest retention) to 16 (highest retention).

Also administered in the present investigation were various attitudinal and personality measures including the Locus of Control scale (Rotter, 1966), Dogmatism scale (Rokeach, 1960), the Social Approval Scale (Crowne & Marlowe, 1964), and a measure of attitudes indirectly related to the dependent variables. Results of this aspect of the study and related theoretical and methodological considerations involving instruments with the exception of the Social Approval Scale have been reported elsewhere (Allen, 1969; Dembroski, 1969; Lasater, 1969). Complete results of the findings concerning the Social Approval Scale will be reported elsewhere.

PROCEDURE

The experimental portion of the present investigation consisted of five subject contacts. Each subject contact involved a visit by three experimenters and their assistants to three junior high schools.

First subject contact. The first subject contact took place 6 weeks after the permission slips were distributed to potential subjects to avoid the possibility of subject reactivity to the permission slips.

The experimenters introduced themselves and their assistants. One of the experimenters told the subjects that they were to take part in a dental health program as part of their physical education class requirements. Following this brief introduction, the subjects were told how to complete the questionnaire booklets. Assurances of anonymity were given to the subjects.

After the questionnaire booklets had been administered, the procedure for utilizing the dental wafer and photographing subjects' gums and teeth was implemented.

Second subject contact. The second subject contact took place 1 week after the first and involved the administration of the personality and attitudinal measures.

Third subject contact. The third subject contact occurred 1 week after the second, and the persuasive com-

munications were presented. The anxiety, intention to behave, reported behavior, and retention measures were administered. Since only three schools were made available for the present investigation and five experimental groups were to be formed, a system for combining conditions within schools was developed.

Fourth subject contact. The fourth subject contact occurred 5 days after the third. The procedures were repeated involving the behavior measure and measures of reported behavior, intention to behave, anxiety, and retention were once again administered.

Fifth subject contact. The fifth subject contact occurred approximately 6 weeks after the presentation of the communications (third subject contact). The same measures which were obtained during the fourth subject contact were again administered.

RESULTS

While all conditions were homogeneous with reference to socioeconomic level, an erratic pattern of differences was obtained among conditions for the preexposure measures of reported behavior and actual behavior. As a result, difference scores[6] were used in the analysis of these measures for the purpose of assessing relative change among treatment conditions. Since there were no precommunication measures obtained for anxiety, retention of information, and intention to behave, means for each of these were obtained on each of the three postcommunication measurement occasions and used for the analyses of these measures. The data were analyzed by means of analysis of variance using the unweighted means formula for unequal ns with repeated measures given by Winer (1962, pp. 374–378). The n for each analysis was the number of subjects measured on all pretest and posttest occasions. Differences between the various treatment conditions were assessed by t tests.

---

[6] In developing an analysis for the present investigation, the writers were immediately confronted with the often-discussed problem of developing a plausible rationale for the use of difference scores when there are initial differences between the comparison conditions. It would seem that the decision whether or not to use difference scores is in the final analysis rather an an arbitrary one. In this instance in a complex field setting where it was virtually impossible to insure preexperimental equivalence, the investigators concluded that since the effects of the independent variables were ultimately in terms of merely grossly effecting existing health habits, this use of change scores was at least reasonably justified. An alternative approach, the after-only design, of course, would have automatically assumed preexperimental equivalence, which is not by definition taken for granted in the analysis utilizing change scores. In summary, because of the intrinsic nature of quasi-experimental studies such as this, it would appear to justify the use of pre-post test difference scores as at least one plausible solution to this difficult problem.

Reported anxiety. A main effect was observed for reported anxiety ($F = 14.3$, $df = 4/364$, $p < .001$). In support of the first hypothesis, subjects in the high-fear condition displayed the greatest amount of anxiety immediately following the communication and were significantly higher in anxiety than the low-fear-appeal condition ($t = 2.22$, $p < .05$) and the positive-appeal condition ($t = 6.40$, $p < .001$). In further support of the first hypothesis, the low-fear-appeal condition was higher in anxiety than the positive-appeal condition ($t = 4.4$, $p < .001$). A significant main effect was obtained for time ($F = 6.5$, $df = 2/728$, $p < .001$). The magnitude of the differences between conditions decreased over time, and, although the rank order of the conditions was somewhat altered on the 5-day and 6-week postcommunication measure, no significant reversals for relative amount of anxiety were obtained. Also found was a significant interaction between time and condition ($F = 5.3$, $df = 8/728$, $p < .01$).

Information retained. Contrary to the second hypothesis, a significant main effect was observed for information retention ($F = 4.25$, $df = 4/364$, $p < .005$). The positive-appeal-condition groups retained significantly more information than all the other condition groups (high fear, $t = 4.1$, $p < .001$; low fear, $t = 2.6$, $p < .01$; recommendations only, $t = 2.4$, $p < .05$; elaborated recommendations, $t = 2.2$, $p < .05$). The elaborated-recommendation groups in comparison with the other groups retained the second greatest amount of information. They retained significantly more information than the high-fear-condition group ($t = 2.3$, $p < .05$). A significant difference was also obtained between the amount of retention in the recommendations-only-condition groups and the high-fear groups ($t = 2.4$, $p < .05$), with the recommendations-only-condition group retaining the greater amount of information. A main effect was observed for time ($F = 47.0$, $df = 2/728$, $p < .001$). The magnitude of the differences between the information-retention means generally decreased over time with no significant reversals in rank order among the conditions occurring. The differences attenuated to such an extent that there were no significant differences between any of the conditions on the 6-week posttest measure. Also obtained was a significant interaction between time and initial level of cleanliness ($F = 2.5$, $df = 8/728$, $p < .05$).

Intention to behave. A significant main effect was obtained for intention to behave ($F = 4.37$, $df = 4/364$, $p < .005$). Partial support of the hypotheses was obtained as the high- and low-fear conditions reported mutually equal and stronger intentions to behave than were expressed in the

positive and elaborated recommendation groups (high fear versus positive, $t = 2.4$, $p < .05$; high fear versus elaborated recommendations, $t = 2.5$, $p < .05$; low fear versus positive, $t = 2.9$, $p < .01$; low fear versus elaborated recommendations, $t = 3.1$, $p < .01$). A significant main effect was obtained for time ($F = 46.5$, $df = 2/728$, $p < .001$). For every condition the intention to behave decreased over time. On the 6-week postcommunication measure, the only significant differences were between the high-fear condition and both the positive ($t = 2.7$, $p < .01$) and the recommendations-only conditions ($t = 2.1$, $p < .05$). Thus, the high-fear appeal seemed to have the greatest effect in sustaining an intention to behave in accordance with the message. Parenthetically, no significant interaction effect was obtained between time and condition.

Reported behavior change. A significant main effect was obtained for reported behavior change ($F = 2.7$, $df = 4/364$, $p < .05$). Figure 1 presents the mean reported behavior change scores for the five conditions of the experiment (the change scores consist of the difference between the score for the measurement occasion indicated and that of the precommunication measure). The mean reported behavior score taken immediately after the subject had been exposed to the communication was more similar to the precommunication score than that of the 5-day postcommunication score, because it referred to toothbrushing practices prior to exposure to the communication. There were no significant differences among the change scores taken on the immediate postcommunication measure. As Figure 1 shows, there was considerable improvement for reported toothbrushing practices within

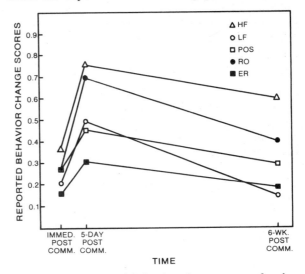

FIGURE 1. *Reported behavior change scores for the treatment groups.*

all five conditions 5 days after exposure to the communications. The group hearing the high-fear appeal showed the greatest amount of reported behavior change, followed by the recommendations-only group, low-fear, positive-, with the elaborated-recommendations appeal group reporting the least change. In general, the data fail to support the fourth hypothesis. But the change for the high-fear and recommendations-only groups was significantly greater than for the elaborated-recommendations group (high fear versus elaborated recommendations, $t = 3.1$, $p < .01$; recommendations only versus elaborated recommendation, $t = 2.6$, $p < .01$). None of the other t values were significant, however. As Figure 1 shows, there was a marked reduction in reported behavior change between the 5-day and the 6-week postcommunication measure. A significant effect was obtained for time ($F = 21.68$, $df = 2/728$, $p < .001$). All of the appeal groups showed a regression to precommunication reported behavior levels. Six weeks after exposure to the communication the high-fear group again displayed the greatest reported change, and again was followed by the recommendations-only group. Also obtained was a significant interaction effect between time and initial level of cleanliness ($F = 3.5$, $df = 4/728$, $p < .01$).

Behavior change.   A significant main effect was obtained for behavior change (tooth cleanliness ratings—$F = 4.92$, $df = 4/364$, $p < .01$). The mean behavior change scores for the five treatment conditions are presented in Figure 2. Change scores involved only two postcommunication measures, since, unlike that for reported behavior change, the disclosing tablet was not used immediately after exposure to the message. Although all of the groups showed increased tooth cleanliness, the group

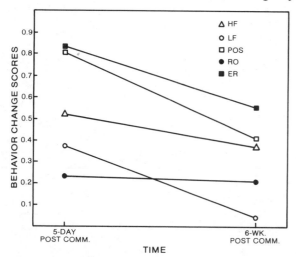

FIGURE 2. *Behavior change scores for the treatment groups.*

showing the greatest change from precommunication to 5-day postcommunication was the elaborated-recommendations condition. The positive appeal was second in magnitude of behavior change, followed by the high-fear, low-fear, and recommendations-only conditions, respectively. In partial support of the fifth hypothesis, the positive and high-fear conditions yielded significantly greater change than did the recommendations-only condition (positive versus recommendations only, $t = 3.6$, $p < .001$; high fear versus recommendations only, $t = 2.0$, $p < .05$). Contrary to the fifth hypothesis, the elaborated recommendations condition yielded significantly greater behavior change than did the high-fear, low-fear, and recommendations-only conditions (high fear versus elaborated recommendations, $t = 2.1$, $p < .05$; low fear versus elaborated recommendations, $t = 3.2$, $p < .01$; recommendations only versus elaborated recommendations, $t = 4.2$, $p < .001$). A significant main effect was also obtained for time ($F = 21.01$, $df = 1/364$, $p < .001$). Figure 2 shows that 6 weeks after exposure to the communication, all of the treatment groups showed a regression to their precommunication cleanliness levels.

Actual behavior versus reported behavior change. It is important to note that although significant effects of appeals were obtained for both reported behavior and the measure of actual behavior, evidence of their differences as criterion measures is supported by examining Figures 1 and 2. The conditions which yielded significant changes in report of behavior were high fear and recommendations only. On the other hand, the conditions which yielded significant changes in the measure of actual behavior were elaborated recommendations and the positive-appeal condition, with the high-fear condition proving to be only moderately effective.

In addition, as would be logically expected, the main effect of the initial level of tooth cleanliness was very large for the reported behavior and actual behavior measures ($F = 13.98$, $df = 2/364$, $p < .01$ and $F = 40.18$, $df = 2/364$, $p < .01$, respectively). This simply indicates that those subjects having cleaner teeth before the experiment both reported and exhibited less change after exposure to the communications than those having dirtier teeth.

DISCUSSION

It appears that in the present investigation as a whole, some very provocative results from the tests of the various hypotheses were obtained which bear on various issues presented by Higbee (1969) concerning the overall problems involved in fear-arousal communication investigations over the past several years.

1. Once again, serious doubt has been cast concerning the generality of any principle which suggests that high fear arousal is or is not as effective as other appeals. In fact, the findings in the present study, which show the surprising effectiveness of a positive motivating appeal, as well as the effectiveness of the elaborated recommendations, raise questions concerning the necessity of using fear arousal at all in order to effect behaviors such as the one sought in the present study. The results involving elaborated recommendations would agree essentially with the observations incorporated in the reports of Leventhal and his coinvestigators.

2. The fact that this investigation was implemented within a natural setting utilizing a unique measure of behavior change provides additional evidence concerning the general theoretical notion that attitude or reported behavior and actual behavior do not necessarily correspond. However, it should be stressed that the measure of reported behavior unfortunately may not be recording the same type of activity as the measure of actual behavior (reported frequency of brushing teeth versus a direct indicator of the cleanliness of teeth). Additionally, it should be pointed out that the recommendations never referred to the frequency of brushing teeth as a desirable response. However, Pearson product-moment correlations between information retention and both reported and actual behavior failed to reach significance within *any* of the appeal groups. Thus, it is difficult to determine whether or not the actual behavior measure recorded a response that resulted from an information input that differed from the reported behavior measure.

3. The finding of a 6-week postcommunication regression through the utilization of a time-series dimension underlines the limitations of investigations involving only immediate postcommunication measures of the effects of persuasive appeals. It also suggests strongly that such research designs would be enhanced by schedules of repeated presentations or other reinforcers of messages.

The first and second authors of the present report are now completing an investigation which attempts to deal with these variables in another school setting. This investigation also is attempting to validate more precisely the measure of actual behavior and uses a more parallel measure of reported behavior. Responding to the need for evaluating the effects of repeated reinforcement of the message, a technique of interschool competition has been introduced.

REFERENCES

ALLEN, B. P. The relationships among the effects of persuasive appeals, toothbrushing behavior, attitude toward dental hygiene, intention to behave, and reported behavior. Unpublished doctoral dissertation, University of Houston, 1969.

ARNIM, S. S. The use of disclosing agents for measuring tooth cleanliness. *Journal of Periodontology,* 1963, *34,* 227–245.

CROWNE, D. P., & MARLOWE, D. *The approval motive.* New York: Wiley, 1964.

DEMBROSKI, T. M. Locus of control and the effectiveness of persuasive communications: Changing dental health practices as measured by a chemical agent. Unpublished doctoral dissertation, University of Houston, 1969.

EVANS, R. I., ROZELLE, R. M., LASATER, T. M., DEMBROSKI, T. M., & ALLEN, B. P. New measure of effects of persuasive communications: A chemical indicator of toothbrushing behavior. *Psychological Reports,* 1968, *23,* 731–736.

HIGBEE, K. L. Fifteen years of fear arousal: Research on threat appeals: 1953–1968. *Psychological Bulletin,* 1969, *72,* 426–444.

JANIS, I. L. Effects of fear arousal on attitude: Recent developments in theory and experimental research. *Advances in Experimental Social Psychology,* 1967, *4,* 166–224.

JANIS, I. L., & FESHBACH, S. Effects of fear-arousing communications. *Journal of Abnormal and Social Psychology,* 1953, *48,* 78–92.

LASATER, T. M. An examination of the relationships among dogmatism, cognitive and behavioral changes, and persuasive communications within the context of a dental health program. Unpublished doctoral dissertation, University of Houston, 1969.

LEVENTHAL, H., & SINGER, R. P. Order of affect arousal and recommendations as determinants of attitude change. New Haven, Conn.: Author, 1965. (Mimeo)

LEVENTHAL, H., SINGER, R. P., & JONES, S. Effects of fear and specificity of recommendation upon attitudes and behavior. *Journal of Personality and Social Psychology,* 1965, *2,* 20–29.

ROKEACH, M. *The open and closed mind.* New York: Basic Books, 1960.

ROTTER, J. B. Generalized expectancies for internal vs. external control of reinforcement. *Psychological Monographs,* 1966, *80*(No. 1, Whole No. 699).

WINER, B. J. *Statistical principles in experimental design.* New York: McGraw-Hill, 1962.

78

The Metropolitan Educational Park

THOMAS F. PETTIGREW

In his provocative book Toward a Theory of Instruction *(Harvard University Press, 1966), Bruner
says that "... each generation must define afresh
the nature, direction, and aims of education to
assure such freedom and rationality as can be
attained for a future generation. For there are
changes both in circumstances and in knowledge
that impose constraints on and give opportunities
to the teacher in each succeeding generation. It is
in this sense that education is in constant process
of invention. . . ."*

*The demands of our society for innovation in
education become stronger all the time. In this
article, Thomas Pettigrew, professor of social
psychology at Harvard University, considers new
ways to structure the schools, suggesting the metropolitan educational park as a possibility.*

The need for radically new designs for American
public education was never more immediate and
obvious. For a variety of reasons, only a few of
which are racial in character, the present structure
of our schools is inadequate to meet the heavy demands placed upon them by our society. But as a
social psychologist who specializes in race relations, I shall dwell principally on racial reasons for
why I strongly support one possible new structural
design for public education.

My reasoning begins with the following facts
from relevant social science research:

1. Interracial schools featuring cross-racial acceptance
   have significant benefits, especially in the early grades,
   for both white and black children.
2. Schools with significant numbers of middle-class children have significant benefits for less-advantaged
   children regardless of race.
3. Public schools in the United States are rapidly becoming *less,* not more, heterogeneous both in terms
   of race and social class.
4. In small cities and towns, the remedies for this growing separation are well known—district-wide redraw-
   ing of school lines within a district, the pairing of
   schools, careful placement of new schools, alteration
   of feeder systems, and conversion of more schools
   into district-wide specialized institutions.
5. The problem is most intense in the large central city,
   brought about basically by: (a) the anti-metropolitan
   manner in which our school districts are drawn and
   operated; (b) the growing racial and class ecological
   divisions between central cities and their suburbs;
   (c) the depletion of the central city's pool of middle-
   class white children by large parochial and private
   school systems; and, finally, (d) the cynical and willful
   planning by major school systems to achieve maximum racial and class segregation. Here the techniques
   for heterogeneous schools in smaller localities are
   mere palliatives at best and counter-productive at
   worst.

Armed with these data-supported observations,
one is soon led to consider new ways to structure
our public schools in metropolitan areas which are
not based on anti-metropolitan, "neighborhood
school" assumptions. Actually, the four basic
reasons just cited for the growing intensity of big
city race and class segregation of schools provide
the form and direction for future efforts. Thus, large
educational complexes drawing from wide attendance areas will be essential. These attendance
areas will generally have to include both central
city and suburban territory in order to ensure the
optimal stable racial mix. The sites for these facilities must not only be convenient to the mass
transit network but must also be on racially "neutral turf." Such locations would avoid immediate
public labeling of the school as "white" or "Negro."

Racial specifications are by no means the only
criteria for future remedies. Public schools in our
largest cities have lost their former pre-eminence
as the innovative educational leaders. Berkeley,
California, Newton and Brookline, Massachusetts,
and a host of other smaller communities are now the
pace-setters. Thus, the plans for the future should
accent and facilitate innovation. Indeed, future

Thomas F. Pettigrew, "The metropolitan educational park," *The Science Teacher, 36,* 1969, 23–26. Reprinted by permission.

public schools should possess facilities which could rarely be duplicated by expensive private schools if they are to compete effectively for the children of advantaged parents. Such arrangements, of course, will cost considerable money; thus, a final criterion must be significant federal support of capital costs.

Several designs would meet these criteria; but let's consider one design as illustrative. Ringing our major cities with educational parks, each of which serves both inner city and suburban students, offers one basic plan—*the metropolitan park plan.* Each park would be located on "neutral turf" in an inner-ring suburb or just inside the central city boundary; and it would be so placed that the same spoke of the mass transit system could bring both outer-ring suburban children into the park and inner-city children out to it. The attendance area of each park would ideally cut out a metropolitan pie-slice containing a minimum of 12,000 to 15,000 public school students, with the thin end of the slice in the more dense central city and the thick end in the more sparse suburbs.

But what incentive could generate the metropolitan cooperation necessary for such a plan? A number of systems have considered educational parks, but they usually find the capital costs prohibitive. Moreover, many systems are currently hard-pressed for expansion funds—especially as referenda for school construction bonds continue to be defeated throughout the nation. Federal funding, then, on a massive scale will obviously be needed, though it must be dispersed in a far more careful and strategic manner than the everybody-gets-his-cut, "river and harbors bill" principle of the 1965 Elementary and Secondary Education Act. As long as alternate federal funding for capital costs is available, many school systems—particularly those in bad faith—will not choose to join a metropolitan park plan. Therefore, future federal construction grants must: involve more than one urban district and the consortium must always include the central city (note that any one park would not require the entire metropolitan area to join the proposal—though some coordination would be necessary, perhaps through review by each area's metropolitan planning commission); require racial and social desegregation—and, hopefully, integration—in every school involved (metropolitan involvement makes this requirement feasible); and exclude alternate routes for federal building funds (though if the first two criteria are met, the proposal need not adopt the metropolitan park plan as the model).

A 15,000 student, forty-to-fifty-million dollar park, 90 percent of it paid by the federal government, would be a powerful inducement. But is such

federal funding possible in the near future? The answer, as with many other domestic questions, rests with the termination of the Vietnam war. Nothing like the Vietnam war costs, of course, would become available for the domestic scene. Yet, at such a time, a two-billion-dollars-a-year school construction program—enough for building roughly forty parks annually—is not unlikely. Here lies both a greater opportunity and an equally great danger. If the money is distributed in the easy fashion of the 1965 Education Act to individual school districts, the anti-metropolitan effects could be disastrous for both race relations and public education. Federal building money spent in such a manner would further insulate aloof suburbia and institutionalize *de facto* school segregation in the inner city for at least another half-century. School construction money is likely to be made available by the federal government after Vietnam. The vital question is: What will be its form and effects?

The educational park idea is not a panacea; there can be elegantly effective and incredibly ineffective parks. Yet ample federal funding combined with the nation's planning and architectural genius should be able to set a new standard and direction for public schools. This combination has successfully been applied to public facilities ranging from interstate highways to magnificent airports. Now the combination should be applied to the benefit of children.

From high-rise structures to multiple-unit campuses, educational parks themselves can be planned in a variety of ways. The most widely discussed design would involve a reasonably large tract of land (80 to 100 acres as a minimum) and no fewer than 14 or 15 schools serving grades from kindergarten through high school. One educator has visualized a campus design for 18,000 students consisting of two senior high, four junior high, and eight elementary schools. If the park were to serve an especially densely populated section, it would be best if it did not include the entire grade spectrum so that it could still cover a reasonably expansive and heterogeneous attendance area. In general, however, an educational park resembles a public university. Both include a variety of educational programs for a large group of students of varying abilities. And like public universities in our major cities, some parks could consist of high-rise structures and some could develop a more spacious campus atmosphere with numerous buildings. Hopefully, the metropolitan park could usually follow the campus model since sufficient space would generally be obtainable at suburban-ring locations.

Apart from offering racial remedies, the metropolitan park concept has a number of distinct advantages. First, there are considerable savings that accrue from consolidation; centralized facilities, such as a single kitchen, need not be duplicated in each of the park's units. Savings on capital costs, too, would accrue from simultaneous building of many units at one location. These savings, however, do not necessarily mean that the total construction and operating costs would be less than those for the same student capacity spread out in traditional units. The advantage is that for essentially the same cost, metropolitan parks could boast significantly better facilities than traditional schools. Consequently, each child would be receiving far more per educational dollar in the metropolitan park.

The improved centralized facilities of the park should maximize innovations and individualized instruction. It is difficult to institute new approaches to learning in old settings. A prime finding of social change research is that new norms are easier to introduce in new institutions. The metropolitan park offers a fresh and exciting setting that should encourage new educational techniques and attract the more innovative members of the teaching profession. In addition, the park presents a rare design opportunity for building innovation into the physical and social structures of the schools. This, of course, includes the latest equipment for aiding the teacher and the student. Centralization enhances this process, for example, by providing efficient concentration of all electronic information storage, retrieval, and console facilities. The accent should be on individualized instruction as the unifying and positive theme—a theme far more possible in the park design than in the present model of scattered "little red schoolhouses."

Many innovations made possible by the metropolitan park extend beyond the equipment realm. For instance, the teaching profession today suffers from being one of the most undifferentiated by rank of all professions, a characteristic which discourages a lifelong orientation to the field. While the medical profession has a graded rank order of roles from intern and resident to chief of a service, teachers must either enter administration and become principals or shift to more prestigious schools in order to move up the ladder. By concentrating a large number of teachers in a relatively small area, far more role differentiation becomes possible. Thus, a teacher might progress from an apprentice in a team-teaching situation, to a master teacher in a team, to a supervisor of master teachers, etc. Faculty concentration also allows more intensive across-school inservice training and the formation of departments across schools with rankings within

departments as in universities (e.g., a junior high history department consisting of all history teachers in the four or five junior highs on the campus).

Concentration of students also allows wider course offerings. Specialized classes, from playing the lute to seventeenth-century English literature, become economically possible when the students electing them are gathered from units throughout the park. Moreover, concentration makes possible some remarkable facilities that can be shared by all of the park's units—e.g., an Olympic-sized swimming pool, extensive auditorium and theatrical equipment, etc. These special facilities could far surpass what is now available in all but the most affluent districts, become a source of student and community pride, and provide a competitive status advantage over private schools. They also would be used efficiently, in contrast to the minimal use that expensive facilities receive in single-site schools.

The metropolitan park offers unusual opportunities for an effective liaison with a local university or college. Nova, the extensive educational park near Fort Lauderdale, Florida, even plans to include college and graduate work right on its campus. But direct contiguity is not necessary to develop a mutually beneficial coordination.

Recall that an important cause of public school segregation in many central cities is the enrollment of large percentages of white children in parochial schools. This fact suggests closer cooperation between public and parochial schools. The metropolitan educational park could facilitate such cooperation under optimal conditions. Most parochial systems are currently in serious financial condition. Tapping into the park's superior facilities should prove attractive. Roman Catholic educators point out that those items that cost the most—the physical science laboratories, gymnasium, and stadium—tend to be least related to the "moral training" that they believe to be the distinctive feature of their schools. Scattered-site schools, public and parochial, make "shared time" and other cooperative arrangements awkward at best. And when parochial students come to take their public school class as a group, such segregation often reaps its usual harvest of intergroup tension and hostility.

A recent idea from Vermont introduces a more promising possibility. At the time of planning a large educational park, Roman Catholic educators are provided the opportunity of buying an adjoining plot of land and constructing a new facility of their own. As long as the land price is consistent with its true value, no constitutional infringements appear to be involved. The new parochial facility need only concentrate on housing courses directly needed for "moral training." Parochial pupils would be free as individuals, not as separated groups, to cross the park's grass, not urban streets, and attend physical education, science, and other public school courses when they fit their particular schedules. The Vermont Plan offers construction and operating savings to hard-pressed parochial systems; and it offers a greater race and class student balance to hard-pressed public systems.

Cost efficiency, educational innovations, more individualized instruction, wider course offerings, special facilities, and coordination with universities and parochial schools—all of these advantages of the well-designed metropolitan park are features that parents, white and Negro, would welcome in the schools of tomorrow. This is politically critical, for desegregation efforts of the past have seldom come as intrinsic parts of a larger package promising an across-the-board improvement in education for *all* children.

In addition to the natural resistance to change, four major objections have been raised to the park concept: (1) excessive capital costs; (2) the phasing-out of existing schools; (3) the problem of impersonalization in the large complexes; and (4) the loss of neighborhood interest and involvement in the school. Each is a serious objection and deserves comment.

The park *is* expensive, and major federal funding is necessary. Furthermore, mistakes in design and location could be disastrous. A park is an enormous commitment of resources, and, if poorly conceived, it could stand for years as a major mistake in planning. This is precisely what would happen if parks were operated totally within central city systems, for demographic projections prove the folly of building parks for a single central city system as a desegregation device. It is for this reason that the parks of the future must be *metropolitan* in character.

Present schools were expensive, too, and raise the problem of phasing out existing facilities. For many urban districts this is not a problem; they already have overutilized schools with double shifts and rising enrollments or old schools long past their usefulness. But some urban districts have many new schools and would be hesitant to join a park consortium. The program, however, is a long-term one. Hopefully, by the early 1970's most of the nation's leading metropolitan areas would boast one or more parks; these in turn could serve as models for completing the park rings in the decade. Moreover, elementary and secondary student enrollments will rise rapidly: from 48.4 million in 1964 to a projected 54.9 million in 1974 and 66 million in the fateful year of 1984. Metropolitan parks,

then, could be phased-in as older facilities are phased-out and enrollments swiftly rise.

Such a process would be ideal nationally, but there will be special problems in localities with "planned *de facto* school segregation." If racial progress is to be made in these cities, recent structures will have to be converted to new uses—perhaps to much-needed community centers.

The third objection to parks centers upon the impersonalization of organizational bigness—"the Kafka problem." Indeed, much of the park's description—15,000 students, a staff approaching 1,000, the latest electronic equipment—has a frightening Kafka ring; and one can easily imagine how an ill-designed park could justify these fears. But such a prospect is not inherent in the park plan; nor is bigness a park problem alone, for many of today's huge urban high schools accommodate many thousands of students in a single unit and arouse the same uneasiness. In fact, imaginatively designed parks could act to counter the urban trend toward ever-larger public school units. *Smaller* schools at each level can be economically built as units within the park; and careful planning can afford a reasonable degree of privacy for each unit while still providing access to the shared facilities of the park.

Some critics are particularly concerned about the park's loss of neighborhood interest and involvement. The criticism assumes that most urban public schools today are neighborhood-based, and that they generate considerable neighborhood involvement. Serious doubts can be raised about both assumptions; we may well be worrying about the loss of something already lost. In any event, there is no evidence to indicate that only a neighborhood-based school can generate parental concern, or that a metropolitan park could not duplicate this feat, or that there is a close and negative association between the size of the attendance area and involvement.

The criticism does raise an important planning issue: How can the park be initiated and planned to heighten parental and community interest? Certainly, the special facilities, the university liaison, and cooperation with parochial schools could help generate community pride and interest. So could smaller schools and a park school board of parents with wide authority short of taxing power. Furthermore, widespread use of the park for adult education, community affairs, etc., would also contribute to public involvement; indeed, the special facilities of the park lend themselves to such adult use more readily than does the typical school today.

Finally, one might ask how such a metropolitan educational park plan fits with other such widely discussed possibilities as "decentralization" and "community schools." First, it should be noted that decentralization and community control are typically advanced either apart from integration considerations or as outright alternatives to integration. "The Bundy Report" for New York City, for instance, could well lead to racially homogeneous districts that would institutionalize racial segregation for generations to come. Yet there is an obvious need in such large and unwieldy systems as New York and Chicago to decentralize authority, as well as a general need to increase parental and community involvement in public education.

Similar to compensatory education, however, these possibilities acquire force and meaning when they *accompany* the drive for integration rather than substitute for it. Thus, effective decentralization need not take the form of isolated social class or racial islands, but should assume the metropolitan pie-slice shapes described earlier as ideal attendance areas for educational parks. New York City's schools *could* be organized along the lines suggested by "The Bundy Report" in such a way as to help rather than hinder integration.

In summary, then, those who say there is nothing we can do about the educational segregation of our major cities are fortunately wrong. This is not to say that desegregation progress will be easy, or even that we will do what is necessary to achieve such progress. But it is to say that it potentially *can* be done for a significant number of urban Americans, white and Negro.

79

Learning and Thinking [1]

Jerome S. Bruner

At this point in the book, the reader needs no further introduction to Jerome S. Bruner. The following short passages were taken from a paper Bruner presented in 1958. Unfortunately, his discussion of problems that he saw at that time is still relevant today.

. . .

I should like to consider now some conditions in our schools today that promote and inhibit progress across the barrier from learning to thinking. I should point out in advance that I am not very cheerful on this subject.

The Passivity of Knowledge-Getting

I have been struck during the past year or so, sitting in classrooms as an observer, by the passivity of the process we call education. The emphasis is upon gaining and storing information, gaining it and storing it in the form in which it is presented. We carry the remainder in long division so, peaches are grown in Georgia, transportation is vital to cities, New York is our largest port, and so on. Can the facts or the methods presented be mimicked? If

¹ Paper presented to Massachusetts Council on Teacher Education, February 13, 1958.

so, the unit is at an end. There is little effort indeed which goes into the process of putting the information together, finding out what is generic about it. Long division is a skill, like threading a needle. The excitement of it as a method of partitioning things that relates it to such matters as subtraction is rarely stressed. One of the great inventions of man—elementary number theory— is presented as a cookbook. I have yet to see a teacher present one way of doing division and then put it squarely to the class to suggest six other ways of doing it—for there are at least six other ways of doing it than any one that might be taught in a school. So too with algebra. Algebra is not a set of rules for manipulating numbers and letters except in a trivial sense. It is a way of thinking, a way of coping with the drama of the unknown. Lincoln Steffens, in his *Autobiography,* complains upon his graduation from the University of California that his teachers had taught him only of the known, how to commit it to mind, and had done little to instruct him in the art of approaching the unknown, the art of posing questions. How does one ask questions about the unknown? Well, algebra is one technique, the technique for arranging the known in such a way that one is enabled to discern the value of an unknown quantity. It is an enriching strategy, algebra, but only if it is grasped as an extended instance of common sense.

Once I did see a teacher specifically encourage a class to organize and use minimal information to draw a maximum number of inferences. The teacher modeled his technique, I suppose, on the tried method of the storyteller. He presented the beginnings of the Whisky Rebellion and said to his pupils, much in the manner of Ellery Queen speaking of his readers, "You now have enough to reconstruct the rest of the story. Let's see if we can do it." He was urging them to cross the barrier from learning into thinking. It is unhappily true that this is a rare exception in our schools.

So knowledge-getting becomes passive. Thinking is the reward for learning, and we may be systematically depriving our students of this reward as far as school learning is concerned.

One experiment which I can report provides encouragement. It was devised and carried out by the research group with which I am associated at Harvard in collaboration with teachers in the fifth grade of a good public school. It is on the unpromising topic of the geography of the North Central States and is currently in progress so that I cannot give all of the results. We hit upon the happy idea of presenting this chunk of geography not as a set

Jerome S. Bruner, "Learning and thinking," *Harvard Educational Review,* 29, 1959, 184–192. Copyright © 1959 by President and Fellows of Harvard College. Reprinted with abridgement by permission.

of knowns, but as a set of unknowns. One class was presented blank maps, containing only tracings of the rivers and lakes of the area as well as the natural resources. They were asked as a first exercise to indicate where the principal cities would be located, where the railroads, and where the main highways. Books and maps were not permitted and "looking up the facts" was cast in a sinful light. Upon completing this exercise, a class discussion was begun in which the children attempted to justify why the major city would be here, a large city there, a railroad on this line, etc.

The discussion was a hot one. After an hour, and much pleading, permission was given to consult the rolled up wall map. I will never forget one young student, as he pointed his finger at the foot of Lake Michigan, shouting, "Yipee, *Chicago* is at the end of the pointing-down lake." And another replying, "Well, OK: but Chicago's no good for the rivers and it should be here where there is a big city (St. Louis)." These children were thinking, and learning was an instrument for checking and improving the process. To at least a half dozen children in the class it is not a matter of indifference that no big city is to be found at the junction of Lake Huron, Lake Michigan, and Lake Ontario. They were slightly shaken up transportation theorists when the facts were in.

The children in another class taught conventionally, got their facts all right, sitting down, bench-bound. And that was that. We will see in six months which group remembers more. But whichever does, one thing I will predict. One group learned geography as a set of rational acts of induction—that cities spring up where there is water, where there are natural resources, where there are things to be processed and shipped. The other group learned passively that there were arbitrary cities at arbitrary places by arbitrary bodies of water and arbitrary sources of supply. One learned geography as a form of activity. The other stored some names and positions as a passive form of registration.

· · ·

The Embarrassment of Passion

I should like to consider now the guiding myth. Let me begin with a summary of the young Christopher Columbus as he is presented in a popular social studies textbook. Young Chris is walking along the water front in his home town and gets to wondering where all those ships go. Eventually he comes back to his brother's cobbler shop and exclaims, "Gee, Bart, I wonder where all those ships go, whether maybe if they just kept going they wouldn't come back because the world is round." Bart replies with pleasant brotherly encouragement. Chris is

a well-adjusted kid. Bart is a nice big brother. And where is the passion that drove this obsessed man across uncharted oceans? What impelled this Columbus with such force that he finally enlisted the aid of Ferdinand and Isabella over the protest of their advisors? Everything is there in the story except the essential truth—the fanatical urge to explore in an age of exploration, the sense of an expanding world. Columbus did not have a schoolboy's whim, nor was he the well-adjusted grownup of this account. He was a man driven to explore, to control. The justification for the pablum that makes up such textbooks is that such accounts as these touch more directly on the life of the child.

What is the "life of the child" as seen by text writers and publishers? It is an image created out of an ideal of adjustment. The ideal of adjustment has little place for the driven man, the mythic hero, the idiosyncratic style. Its ideal is mediocentrism, reasonableness above all, being nice. Such an ideal does not touch closely the deeper life of the child. It does not appeal to the dark but energizing forces that lie close beneath the surface. The Old Testament, the Greek Myths, the Norse legends—these are the embarrassing chronicles of men of passion. They were devised to catch and preserve the power and tragedy of the human condition—and its ambiguity, too. In their place, we have substituted the noncontroversial and the banal.

Here a special word is needed about the concept of "expressing yourself," which is our conception of how one may engage the deeper inpulses of the child. I have seen a book review class in a public school in which the children had the choice of reporting on any book they wished to choose, in or out of the school library, and where the discussion by the other children had to do entirely with the manner in which the reciting child presented his material. Nothing was said about the book in the discussion. The emphasis was on nice presentation, and whether the book sounded interesting. I have no quarrel with rewarding self-expression. I wonder simply whether it is not perhaps desirable, too, to make known the canons of excellence. The children in this class were learning to be seductive in their recounting; they were not concerned with an honest accounting of the human condition. The books they had read were cute, there was no excitement in them, none to be extracted. Increasingly the children in American elementary schools grow out of touch with the guiding myths. Self-expression is not a substitute. Adjustment is a worthy ideal, if not an ennobling one. But when we strive to attain it by shutting our eyes to the turmoils of human life, we will not get adjustment, but a niggling fear of the unusual and the excellent.

· · ·

80

The Changing World of Mental Measurement and Its Social Significance [1]

Wayne H. Holtzman

Recent criticism of normative testing for college admission and grading in courses is discussed in Wayne Holtzman's article, along with current attempts at educational reform. Holtzman is director of the Hogg Foundation for Mental Health, University of Texas, and is editor of the Journal of Educational Psychology.

One of the great success stories of modern psychology is the development of objective tests for measuring human abilities that are of importance to society. During the past half century, the standardized mental test with nationally based norms has proven to be a highly effective instrument for selection and classification of men in the armed forces; for evaluation of educational progress within our school systems; for selective admission of college students; for selection of employees within government, business, and industry; and for clinical assessment of individuals in need of psychological services. It is estimated that within American schools alone, over 250 million standardized tests of ability are administered each year (Brim, Glass, Neulinger, Firestone, & Lerner, 1969). It is a rare individual indeed, especially among children and young adults, who has not been evaluated by a standardized mental test, a test that has played a significant role in determining his place in society.

From World War I until the late 1950s, the testing movement enjoyed a degree of public acceptance it is unlikely to see again. Judging each person on the basis of his measured performance rather than on his family background, social status, or political connections has been a powerful agent of social change. Assuming unbiased, reliable measurement, what could be more just within the American concept of an egalitarian society than recognizing merit by objective tests of ability? Even today, college entrance examinations have made it possible for able but financially poor students to obtain scholarships in the best private colleges.

CRITICISMS OF TESTING

By the late 1950s, it became generally apparent that the large-scale normative use of objective tests for rewarding selected individuals among many in competition has serious social consequences of debatable value. The testing movement has always had its critics, but they failed to gain a foothold until the impact of adverse decisions based on tests had been felt by millions of individuals. In the post-Sputnik period, a growing number of critics have claimed that mental tests are unfair to the bright but unorthodox person, to the culturally disadvantaged, and to the naïve individual who lacks experience in taking standardized tests (Anastasi, 1967; Commission on Tests, 1970).

The growing controversies surrounding mental tests have become especially acute within educational institutions. It is generally recognized that the educated person enjoys the riches of society as well as enhanced self-esteem and personal development, while the person who prematurely drops out of school is cast into an inferior role. It is not surprising that the angry cries of black students are directed at normative tests that deprive them of entrance to the better colleges, jobs, and social positions.

A major dilemma arises in attempting to meet these criticisms. The traditional academic curricula of our schools and colleges are becoming increasingly dependent on verbal communication, verbal memory, and the same kind of abstract reasoning as measured by scholastic aptitude tests. Therefore, sufficiently high correlations arise between standardized multiple-choice aptitude tests

[1] Presidential Address of Division 5, presented at the annual meeting of the American Psychological Association, Miami Beach, Florida, September 1970.

and course examinations to justify the use of tests for prediction of academic achievement and selective admissions. The rapid growth of higher education and the greatly increased number of students per course have forced more and more instructors to employ multiple-choice objective examinations for grading students. As a result, the relevance of scholastic aptitude tests for prediction of academic grades has increased, rather than decreased, in recent years. The compelling economics of mass education and objective normative testing are exceedingly difficult to resist in a rapidly expanding system of higher education. Tests that are designed for normative use, whether for college admissions or course examinations, discriminate against those who are culturally different from the majority.

Such incidental discrimination might be more justifiable if there were a close correspondence between success in school and subsequent occupational success. But for a number of reasons, the correlation between grades and later success is too low to argue generally that measured performance in the traditional academic curriculum is that critical. The issue is made more complex by the fact that entry to many occupations is denied an individual who fails to complete the prescribed academic program, regardless of the program's relevance. The growing meritocracy built around traditional curricula that are uniformly prescribed, normative tests that are competitively graded, and restrictive credentials for job entry may be efficient means of building a technological society, but it does so by exacting a heavy toll on those members of society who fail to conform to the majority. The more tightly the meritocracy is drawn, the more self-fulfilling the prophecies.

EDUCATIONAL REFORM AND THE NEW TECHNOLOGIES

A way out of this dilemma may be closer at hand than many realize. The number of pressures within American society and new developments in measurement and instruction are moving in the same general direction. Led by students, spokesmen for minority rights, and concerned academicians, the general public is becoming increasingly aware of serious inequities within our educational system. As higher education becomes more essential to vocational advancement and personal fulfillment, the fruits of education cannot be denied to anyone who is motivated and capable of profiting from it.

The growing attacks on normative testing for college admission and course grading are having an impact as more and more individuals call for less emphasis on scholastic aptitude measures and more

on other abilities and new forms of instruction. The kinds and variety of curricula recognized as appropriate for various forms of education are increasing markedly. Courses aimed at social problems and individual self-development are eroding the traditional, discipline-oriented curricula in many colleges. This new thrust may involve individual competencies in such things as social leadership, self-awareness, regard for human rights and social responsibilities, or other aspects of behavior that typically have not been important in traditional academic pursuits. As the curriculum moves through reform, there will be opportunities for new kinds of measurement as well.

Emphasis is being given in many circles to the idea of individualized instruction in which the learner moves at his own pace and at a time and place that is appropriate for him as an individual. The units of instruction emphasize self-paced learning with regular social reinforcement to maintain a high degree of motivation and relevance, coupled with the concept of continuous progress from one unit to the next. These "microcurriculum units" or modules have fairly well-defined behavioral objectives or performance criteria by which mastery can be recognized. The curriculum itself is viewed in a more global manner as consisting of strings of modules arranged according to an explicit hierarchy of values that are in harmony with the future goals of individual development. In many fields of learning, these specific modules involve training objectives where criterion testing for standardized mastery is employed rather than normative testing for measuring individual differences. Much of what goes on in education is susceptible to treatment in this form. The broader educational objectives differ considerably from one individual to the next in order to maximize potentiality for individual development.

A major force for social change in educational reform is the emergence of new educational technology and related techniques of measurement. Keeping track of a person moving at his own pace in a continuous progress environment, where the particular branching of the curriculum is tailor-made for the student's own learning aptitudes and level, requires a computer to manage the curriculum and assist with the instruction (Holtzman, 1970). In a traditional setting, the instructor keeps a record of how well each student does on each achievement test for the course, while the periodically collected scores from standardized normative tests are stored centrally. When instruction is individualized, testing must be done more frequently and at different times for each student. In many cases, performance testing and instruction are so closely interwoven that they appear as one integrated learning activity. Except for periodic testing at a later date to determine how much a person has retained, even the conceptual nature of measurement shifts from a normative basis, where each person is compared with a general population, to a criterion-referenced basis, where the only decision made is whether or not the student has achieved the desired objective for a specific instructional module. Not only are more short tests given, but many more have to be constructed, again requiring a computer for generating tests from item pools as well as scoring and storing them for each student.

Several large-scale programs of individualized instruction are sufficiently advanced to demonstrate the feasibility and power of this approach to educational reform. Now in its fourth year of operation under the leadership of John Flanagan, and jointly developed by the American Institutes for Research and Westinghouse Learning Corporation, Project PLAN consists of over 1,000 modules divided across nine operating grades and four subject-matter areas (Dunn, 1969). Each teaching unit is coded as to reading difficulty, required teacher supervision, media richness, required social involvement, and a number of other characteristics. A profile is prepared for each student containing measures of abilities, interests, aspirations, and background data for use by the computer in matching the curriculum to the student. The combination of normative measurement on nationality standardized tests for initial guidance and placement of the student and criterion-referenced tests for assessing progress in mastering the curriculum modules is especially noteworthy. Experience to date with over 10,000 students indicates that most individuals like the new freedom provided by PLAN, and that learning proceeds at a faster pace.

A still more detailed form of individualized instruction can be found in the program of individually prescribed instruction developed by Glaser and associates at the University of Pittsburgh's Learning Research and Development Center (Cooley & Glaser, 1969). A specific lesson plan is prescribed individually for each child every day, depending on his performance and desires of the previous day. Thousands of curriculum modules are stored and retrieved manually by clerks at the end of each day until the experimental system can be perfected and stored electronically in computers. Interwoven with each module is a criterion-referenced achievement test that provides a basis for decision making in selecting the next module.

A recent study by Ferguson (1969) serves to illustrate computer-assisted branched testing with elementary arithmetic materials in the Pittsburgh individually prescribed instruction program. A model was developed and tested in which items are selected on the basis of previous responses and are thus tailored to the competencies of the student. A learning hierarchy of prerequisite relationships among 18 objectives in addition and subtraction was formulated on the basis of previous studies. Two major sequences emerged as dominant in the hierarchy, one involving only addition skills and the other exclusively concerned with subtraction. A third sequence integrated both addition and subtraction. Initially, an examinee was presented with a randomly generated item for the specific objective being tested. The computer scored his response as correct or incorrect and generated another item. The process continued until a sufficient number of items had been answered for the computer to make a decision regarding the individual's proficiency on the objective. The decision model involved assigning a priori probability values to the two types of error constituting incorrect decisions and applying Wald's sequential probability ratio test to terminate the testing on the objective in question. Selection of the next objective to be tested depended on the examinee's proficiency on the first objective as well as the proposed learning hierarchy. When given to 74 students in Grades 1–6 at the Oakleaf Elementary School, Pittsburgh, Pennsylvania, the sequential branched testing method proved to be three times as efficient as a fixed-length conventional test, requiring, on the average, only 52 items instead of 150.

A sequential branched testing procedure proves far superior to conventional testing when one has a computer for generating and scoring items, a suitable communication terminal for interaction of computer and examinee, and a good basis for arranging the skills to be tested in a learning hierarchy. The procedure is ideally suited to criterion-referenced testing but is of questionable value where normative testing is employed. As Lord (1970) has demonstrated, little is to be gained by the use of tailored testing with conventional items for normative measurement except in the case of best and worst students.

Integrating the elements of programmed learning and sequential branched testing into a single curriculum requires a computer for electronic storage and retrieval of the material to be learned, the test items for measuring mastery, and the instructional branching strategy for both the curriculum and the tests. Suitable multimedia teaching terminals with visual display devices, light pens, audio units, and typewriters under either student or computer control, depending on the nature of the curriculum and purpose of the student, must be provided in large numbers at reasonable cost before computer-assisted instruction, testing, and guidance can become operational. Several major companies are now designing hardware configurations that will soon have the required functional capabilities for fully implementing computer-assisted instruction. It is now fairly certain that the cost of such a system can be sharply reduced by mass production to the point where it is economically feasible to think of large-scale implementation (Alpert & Bitzer, 1970). Psychological laboratories for computer-assisted instruction at Stanford University, the University of Texas, the University of Illinois, Florida State University, System Development Corporation, the Mitre Corporation, and a dozen other universities and research institutes have already demonstrated the feasibility of this new technology as well as its dramatic impact on individual learning in many areas.

Such new technologies as Project PLAN, individually prescribed instruction, and computer-assisted instruction are highly promising in their eventual impact on educational practices and the concomitant measurement of standardized mastery using criterion-referenced tests instead of normative testing for competitive selection. Successful prototypes have been developed, but these represent only a small beginning compared to what must be done in the way of research and development before individualized instruction in the true sense of the term can be properly implemented on a large scale.

NATIONAL ASSESSMENT OF EDUCATIONAL CHANGE

Still another important departure from standardized normative measurement of individual differences in mental abilities grows out of the increased concern for developing a national system of social indicators, measures that reflect the quality of life, the rate of educational progress, and the value of human resources for the nation as a whole as well as for different regional, ethnic, and socioeconomic groups. A recent report of the Behavioral and Social Sciences Survey Committee (1969) has recommended the establishment of a system of social indicators by the federal government that would lead to an annual social report for measuring changes in many aspects of society. A step in this direction has already been taken by the National Assessment of Educational Progress, a project of the Education Commission of the States (Womer, 1970).

Under the leadership of Ralph Tyler and support from the Carnegie Corporation, the Exploratory Committee on Assessing the Progress of Education

began in 1964 to collect information about the knowledge and skills held by 9-year-olds, 13-year-olds, and 17-year-olds and of young adults in 10 subject areas taught in schools. After five years of planning and public debate as to the merits of the project, National Assessment launched its first annual survey for all four age levels in three subject areas—citizenship, science, and writing. The national sample contained a total of approximately 100,000 persons carefully chosen on a stratified random basis involving 52 sampling units from each of four geographic regions.

The first step in preparing materials for National Assessment was to determine a list of educational objectives for each subject. Using these objectives as guides, various measurement research organizations took responsibility for preparing exercises designed to assess what young people actually know. A variety of approaches—questionnaires, interviews, observations, and performance tasks—were employed in addition to traditional multiple-choice and short-answer questions similar to those used in standardized mental tests.

Five important distinctions can be made between the National Assessment exercises and multiple-choice items employed in normative tests. First, the assessment exercises are designed to discover what defined segments of the nation's population can do or what they know, rather than to distribute people normatively according to measured individual differences. For example, what percentage of the 9-year-olds in the country know that most plants get most of their water directly from the soil? Or know how to report a fire? Or report that they had ever taken part in some organized civic project to help other people? Does this percentage shift significantly across different segments of the population or over time?

Second, while items in a test are summed to give a score for each individual, exercises in National Assessment are each analyzed in their own right by pooling data across individuals. For this reason, it is particularly important that the exercises be meaningful to specialist and layman alike, that they be directly related to the stated objectives, and that they have high content validity. Extensive review sessions involving a variety of judges were held for every exercise retained for National Assessment.

Third, the exercises are designed for a broad range of difficulty in order to report to the American public examples of knowledges, skills, and understandings that are common to almost all American youth of a given age, examples that are common to a typical or average American youth, and examples that are common to only the most knowledgeable youth. Ideally, one-third of the exercises should be passed by most of the population, one-third by about half, and one-third by only a small percentage. By contrast, item difficulty level in the typical normative test is likely to hover near the 50% level or to be evenly distributed throughout the range.

Fourth, all exercises, except those in reading, are presented aurally as well as visually, so that no one is severely penalized in responding, say, to citizenship or science questions.

And fifth, the exercises are assembled in heterogeneous packages with different sets of exercises given to different individuals on a sampling basis. A package for 17-year-olds last year, for example, contained seven multiple-choice science exercises, three free-response citizenship exercises, and one essay exercise for writing. Exercises are packaged in any convenient fashion that adds up to no more than 50 minutes of assessment time for each person. Items in a normative test, on the other hand, are assembled in relatively homogeneous scales so that they can be added together to give a reliable score.

Unlike most measurement applications in psychology and education, in National Assessment a person is never asked to record his name. Responses are clustered and analyzed by sex, age, race, region, community, and family characteristics in order to obtain censuslike information about the educational progress of various segments of the population. Repeated applications in the years ahead will provide a wealth of data dealing with change over time—data that should be useful in national planning, particularly when examined together with other social indicators.

Individuals and schools approached by National Assessment were given the option of declining to participate in order to respect their rights to privacy. Exceedingly few refused to participate under these permissive conditions, testifying to the wisdom of this policy. My own experience in soliciting the cooperation of 13,000 high school students in a probability statewide sample (Moore & Holtzman, 1965) and in asking for the continued participation of 420 families in a longitudinal study of personality development (Holtzman, Diaz-Guerrero, Swartz, & Lara Tapia, 1968) has been similarly favorable. Unbiased samples can be obtained in most measurement studies without coercion of even a mild sort. National Assessment provides an exemplary model of how one should proceed in order to protect the privacy of individual participants and their freedom to decline.

Preserving the confidentiality of data is a related problem that continues to worry many thoughtful individuals. As we move into large-scale programs with extensive, centralized data banks stored in computers, the possibility of harm to an individual cannot yet be completely eliminated. The files that may do greatest damage to the individual are those that are kept secret from him but not from those who can take action affecting him. While much of the national concern expressed in recent congressional hearings deals with personal information that psychologists are unlikely to find interesting, specific attention has been directed at potential abuses of individual privacy involving psychological test data, biographical information, and social attitudinal data typically employed in psychological research. The proper balance between protecting the individual against the misuse of information about himself and collating data to help solve major social, economic, and educational problems has not yet been achieved. On the other hand, continuation of the present highly decentralized systems will not cure present abuses of individual privacy, although it will prevent the integration of information required for future social development. As Ruggles (1969) has pointed out, the key to the problem of protecting privacy is not to depend blindly on the inefficiency that accompanies the present situation. Properly developed centralized data banks can eventually assure greater protection for the individual while also providing essential information for basic research as well as future national planning.

One interesting solution to the problem of protecting the confidentiality of data from individual respondents is the Link system that has been devised for the national study of college student characteristics by the American Council on Education's Cooperation Institutional Research Program (Astin & Boruch, 1970). Measurement data and biographical information on several hundred thousand college freshmen are collected each year as part of an ongoing educational data bank. Initially, a more or less traditional system was instituted. Two physically separate tape files were created, one containing the student's answers to research questions together with an arbitrary identification number, and a second containing only the student's name and address and the same arbitrary number. The first tape with the research data file was openly accessible for analysis. The second tape with the name and address file was locked in a vault and used only to print labels for follow-up mailings. The original questionnaires and punched cards were then destroyed.

Good as it may seem, this system still did not offer complete protection against government subpoena or unauthorized disclosure by staff members with access to both files. A third file, the Link file, was created which contained two sets of numbers—

the original arbitrary identification numbers from the research data file, and a completely new set of random numbers which were substituted for the original identification numbers in the second file. The final step in establishing the new system was to deposit the new Link file at a computer facility in a foreign country with a firm agreement that the foreign facility would never release it to anyone, including the American Council on Education. Follow-up mailing tapes now have to be prepared by the foreign facility. There is no way that anyone can identify individual responses in the research file.

Such elaborate steps to guarantee the complete confidentiality of personal information in research files may seem far too expensive. Why go to this extreme when the chances are exceedingly remote that any harm could be done to an individual by using a more traditional system? The reason for foolproof data files is that the public demands it. However unlikely, there does exist the possibility of court subpoena or improper invasion of privacy when the data files and decoding files are under the control of the same organization.

RECOGNITION OF SOCIAL, CULTURAL, AND LINGUISTIC VARIABILITY

One of the most important changes of the past decade in the field of mental measurement as well as in society as a whole is the greatly increased respect for social, cultural, and linguistic variability among different kinds of people. Until recently, the "American way of life" was defined almost entirely by middle-class values of white, English-speaking people of largely western-European origin. In general, school curricula, symbols of social status and privilege, occupations, the more highly valued life styles, and to some extent even suggested definitions of intelligence, all conformed to the dominant values of which most Americans were proud. The forgotten minorities were expected to adjust to these values if they were to enjoy the fruits of the nation. As recently as 10 years ago, school principals in the Southwest often pointed proudly to the fact that the speaking of Spanish by Mexican-American children was prohibited on their school grounds, English being the only permissible language in which to receive an education.

The emergence of black culture, the Chicano movement, and the stirring of the American Indian as well as other forgotten groups in the wake of desegregation and civil rights legislation have forced white America to reexamine its soul. The result in the field of mental measurement has been a recognition and acceptance of cultural variability,

a search for new kinds of cognitive, perceptual, and affective measures by which to gauge mental development, and a renewed determination to contribute significantly to the task of overcoming educational and intellectual deprivation.

A generation ago, the typical study involving mental measurement and social variability consisted of giving tests, standardized largely on middle-class whites, to people of other ethnic, linguistic, and socioeconomic backgrounds. Countless individual and group differences were observed and classified in a descriptive manner. Today, more attention is given to devising procedures for measurement and evaluation which are indigenous to the culture under study. Illustrative of this new approach is the work of Freeberg (1970), who developed a test battery specifically tailored in content, format, and administration to disadvantaged adolescents drawn largely from the black and Puerto Rican ghettos of New York. The extensive six-year longitudinal study of 2,000 Headstart children undertaken last year by the Educational Testing Service also contains a large variety of new measures that are specifically designed for culturally disadvantaged children (Anderson, 1969). The problem with most such tailored procedures is that they may be just as ill-suited for use with other markedly different individuals as are tests standardized on middle-class whites when employed for assessing educationally disadvantaged children.

The most difficult methodological problems arise in cross-cultural research where two or more distinctly different cultures are compared systematically (Holtzman, 1968). The translation, calibration, and administration of psychological measures across cultures require close and continual collaboration of specialists from each culture who have learned to trust each other fully. In a similar manner, measurement across subcultures within a given nation requires the full participation of representatives from each subculture, a condition that is met by all too few investigators thus far. In spite of such problems, studies dealing systematically with cultural, social, and linguistic variability are growing rapidly in number while also increasing greatly in the power of their research designs. Is it too much to hope that by the end of the coming decade the lingering ethnocentrism of the testing movement will disappear?

. . .

In the short span of this article, it has been possible to highlight only selected topics within the broad field of mental measurement. It should be obvious to even the casual observer of trends in the field that other areas also deserve attention. It is worth noting that every one of the new advances reviewed is heavily dependent on the modern electronic computer for its implementation. Fundamental to the changing world of mental measurement is the rapid growth in power, versatility, and accessibility of high-speed computers. Large-scale testing; new educational technology such as individually prescribed instruction, sequential branched testing within the curriculum, Project PLAN, and computer-assisted instruction; national assessment of educational change and the development of a system of social indicators; new techniques for preserving the confidentiality of personal data; and even new programs for assessing the mental development of culturally different people—all require a computer for implementation.

In focusing primarily on the social implications of new advances, it is easy to overlook the numerous theoretical and methodological contributions to the field of measurement and evaluation that have been made in the past few years. New techniques of scaling, test theory, factor analysis, and multivariate experimental designs are being produced and extended in a lively manner. The immediate social significance of these developments may not be readily apparent because of their indirect, long-range nature as basic research contributions. And yet, without the continued, vigorous support of such theoretical and methodological advances, the truly great potentiality of the changing world of measurement would fail to materialize. Each of the promising new developments surveyed above is heavily dependent on the solution of difficult basic research problems before it can be fully realized to the benefit of society. There is every reason to be optimistic about the next 10 years in the field of mental measurement, given the recognized social significance of new developments and the rapid rate at which basic work is advancing.

REFERENCES

ALPERT, D., & BITZER, D. L. Advances in computer-based education. *Science,* 1970, *167,* 1582–1590.

ANASTASI, A. Psychology, psychologists, and psychological testing. *American Psychologist,* 1967, *22,* 297–306.

ANDERSON, S. B. The ETS–OEO longitudinal study of disadvantaged children. In, *Untangling the tangled web of education.* Princeton, N. J.: Educational Testing Service, 1969.

ASTIN, A. W., & BORUCH, R. E. A "Link" system for assuring confidentiality of research data in longitudinal studies. *ACE Research Reports,* 1969, *5*(3).

BEHAVIORAL AND SOCIAL SCIENCES SURVEY COMMITTEE. *The behavioral and social sciences: Outlook and needs.* Washington, D. C.; National Academy of Sciences, 1969.

BRIM, O. G., JR., GLASS, D. C., NEULINGER, J., FIRESTONE, I. J., & LERNER, S. C. *American beliefs and attitudes about intelligence.* New York: Russell Sage Foundation, 1969.

COMMISSION ON TESTS. *Report of Commission on Tests: I. Righting the balance.* New York: College Entrance Examination Board, 1970.

COOLEY, W. W., & GLASER, R. The computer and individualized instruction. *Science,* 1969, *166,* 574–582.

DUNN, J. A. The accommodation of individual differences in the development of personal programs of study. In J. C. Flanagan (Chm.), Project PLAN: A computer-supported individualized education program, Symposium presented at the meeting of the American Psychological Association, Washington, D. C., September 1969.

FERGUSON, R. L. Computer-assisted criterion-referenced testing. Working Paper No. 49, Learning Research and Development Center, University of Pittsburgh, 1969.

FREEBERG, N. E. Assessment of disadvantaged adolescents: A different approach to research and evaluation measures. *Journal of Educational Psychology,* 1970, *61,* 229–240.

HOLTZMAN, W. H. Cross-cultural studies in psychology. *International Journal of Psychology,* 1968, *3,* 83–91.

HOLTZMAN, W. H. Computers in education. In W. H. Holtzman (Ed.), *Computer-assisted instruction, testing, and guidance.* New York: Harper & Row, 1970.

HOLTZMAN, W. H., DIAZ-GUERRERO, R., SWARTZ, J. D., & LARA TAPIA, L. Cross-cultural longitudinal research on child development: Studies of American and Mexican school children. In J. P. Hill (Ed.), *Minnesota Symposia on Child Psychology.* Vol. 2. Minneapolis: University of Minnesota Press, 1968.

LORD, F. Some test theory for tailored testing. In W. H. Holtzman (Ed.), *Computer-assisted instruction, testing, and guidance.* New York: Harper & Row, 1970.

MOORE, B. M., & HOLTZMAN, W. H. *Tomorrow's parents.* Austin: University of Texas Press, 1965.

RUGGLES, R. How a data bank might operate. *Think,* 1969, *35*(3), 22–23.

WOMER, F. G. *What is National Assessment?* Denver, Colo.: Education Commission of the States, 1970.

XII

TEACHERS AND TEACHING

We have devoted a section of this book specifically to the teacher in order to emphasize the enormous importance of the role. The teacher is undoubtedly the most crucial factor in the classroom. Whatever the method, whatever the materials, the teacher's own knowledge and sensitivity count most heavily. Does he know his field? Is he able to structure lessons and explanations in an effective way? How closely is he attuned to the student's responses, and how well can he provide appropriate rewards contingent on the desired output? Does he know his students? In what ways should he attempt to arouse and sustain motivation? The article by Child, Potter, and Levine in Section VIII, for example, indicates that lessons in motivation and social development are hidden within materials designed primarily to help a child gain skills. What content may the teacher choose for that purpose that will not compromise the development of desired values and attitudes?

Despite the acknowledged importance of the teacher—and despite widespread criticism of teachers today—there has been a dearth of research into the psychology of teaching. As Miriam Goldberg points out in the first selection of this section, we do not really know what teaching is all about; what the teacher actually says and does in the classroom; how effective his teaching is, etc.

There have recently been some attempts to develop objective methods for studying the behavior of teachers. Interaction analysis, for example, developed by Ned A. Flanders, is a technique of systematic classroom observation, in which verbal statements during spontaneous classroom communication are coded and analyzed and the frequencies of different types of coded statements are related to students' achievement and attitudes. Flanders' most recent book, for those interested in learning more about his interaction analysis, is *Analyzing Teaching Behavior* (Reading, Mass.: Addison-Wesley, 1970). A similar type of analysis was used in the study by Brophy and Good presented in this section.

The Center for Research and Development in Teaching at Stanford University has worked for several years in this problem area. N. L. Gage, in his book *Teacher Education and Teacher Effectiveness: The Search for a Scientific Basis* (Palo Alto, Calif.: Pacific Books, 1970), has presented the Stanford group's point of view. They reject the idea that we must find *the* criterion of "teacher effectiveness" before we can select and train good teachers. Such an overall criterion is much too gross for scientific investigation, as well as for use in teacher-education. Rather, they use criteria of effectiveness in limited, specifically defined aspects of the role (micro-criteria). They analyze the teaching process into small, discrete components—technical skills—which can be taught, practiced, and evaluated (micro-teaching) in a teacher education program. Gage's approach is most promising, but concrete work in these areas has a long way to go.

81

Adapting Teacher Style to Pupil Differences: Teachers for Disadvantaged Children[1]

Miriam L. Goldberg

The following article is addressed to a topic of tremendous concern today, the teaching of disadvantaged children. At the same time, it makes some keen observations about teaching in general. The article by Grimes and Allinsmith in Section X showed that children's school performance depended on the match between their personality characteristics and the type of teaching method used, thus rejecting the idea of a universally "good" method. The present article similarly rejects the notion of the universally "good" instructional approach. In addition, it assumes that culturally disadvantaged children, though highly variable, are a describable pupil population in need of teachers uniquely "good" for them. The author, Miriam L. Goldberg, is at Teachers College, Columbia University.

It has become a cliché to state that the major effects on pupil learning result from what goes on in the classroom. We recognize that what the teacher and the pupils do during the five or six hours a day when they are in direct contact with each other is the "compass of learning." And yet, until recently, little of our research has addressed

itself to the teaching process. We have studied the achievement of pupils under various methods of instruction, we have described and theorized about the personality characteristics of teachers, we have explored various theoretical formulations about the nature of learning, and the effects of varying the administrative deployment of pupils and more recently of teachers have been investigated. We have examined the effects of class size, the functions of the administrator, the guidance counselor and other adjunct personnel of the school. But we still could not describe with any degree of accuracy what teaching is all about, what the teacher actually says and does in the process of teaching, and what effect this has on pupil learning.

Although little may be known about the teaching process in general, even less information is available on the "fit" between particular styles of teaching and the learning of particular pupil populations. This question looms especially large as one considers the problems of teaching children from depressed or disadvantaged areas; pupils who, thus far, have not been effectively "reached" by the teaching procedures to which they have generally been exposed. That various teaching procedures now in use are more or less effective with pupils from more affluent or academically motivating environments is undoubtedly true. But these same procedures, typically learned in teacher education programs, have rarely proved effective with disadvantaged youngsters.

Three assumptions underlie this paper: The first maintains that a pupil's learning is, in large measure, a function of the kind of teaching to which he is exposed. Thus, the extent to which a pupil masters a given set of academic tasks reflects not only his aptitudes and attitudes, but also the appropriateness of the particular approach by which he is taught.

The second assumption, implied by the title, rejects the notion of the universally "good" teacher, equally able to adapt his style to varying pupil populations, and substitutes a conception of a variety of "good" teachers, differentially suited (by temperament and training) to teaching differing groups of students.

The third assumption proposes that children from culturally disadvantaged backgrounds, though highly variable, nevertheless represent a describable pupil population in need of teachers who are uniquely "good" for them.

The first portion of this paper presents some of the evidence in support of the first two assumptions, citing studies which point up the variety of teaching styles and their effects on pupil achievement in

[1] A revision of a lecture presented at The Merrill-Palmer Institute, March, 1963.

Miriam L. Goldberg, "Adapting teacher style to pupil differences: teachers for disadvantaged children," *Merrill-Palmer Quarterly of Behavior and Development*, 1964, *10*, 161–178. Reprinted by permission.

general and on the achievement of specific categories of pupils in particular. The remainder of the paper proposes a hypothetical model of the successful teacher of disadvantaged pupils and suggests how such a model may be approached.

STUDIES OF TEACHER PERFORMANCE

The last decade has witnessed a number of efforts to study the processes of teaching. The first consideration of most of the studies has been to describe and classify what the teacher and the pupils say and do during a class session. Some of the investigations have gone beyond the descriptive material into a study of the relationships between the teacher's style of performance and the learning patterns of children.

CATEGORIZING TEACHER STYLE

A variety of more and less structured classroom observations have yielded various classifications of teacher style. For example, Flanders (1960) classified teachers as those who more often exert "direct influence," through lecturing, giving directions or criticizing students' work, and those who more often exert "indirect influence" through clarifying feelings, providing praise and encouragement, developing and making use of student ideas and asking questions.

Medley (1962) divided the teacher's performance into three broad categories: (1) his means of controlling the class, (2) his approach to the content, and (3) the interpersonal climate he creates. In the "control" category fell such behaviors as eliciting large amounts of pupil response, maintaining a high degree of order or permitting a high degree of pupil initiative. "Approach to content" included such procedures as emphasizing individualization or using interesting, original devices and materials. The "class climate" category included the teacher's consideration for pupils' problems and feelings, the degree of support given to pupil statements and responses, and the frequency with which reproof and criticism were used.

More clearly defined, perhaps, are the three dimensions of teacher style suggested by Ryans (1963). The first is a personal dimension ranging from "friendly-warm-understanding to aloof-restricted." The second is a task dimension, ranging from "responsible-organized-businesslike to unplanned-slipshod." The third describes the dynamic quality of the teacher's performance from "stimulating-informative to dull-routine." These categories are similar to those suggested by Warrener (1962), who drew his observations from social behavior in nonteaching leadership situations. His

categories were: (1) "objective" work orientation, (2) "social relations" orientation, and (3) "subjective" personal, expressive orientation.

The dimensions suggested by Ryans are sufficiently independent of each other so that a teacher may be at a different point along that scale on each one. For example, one teacher may be characterized as warm, business-like, and stimulating; another as warm, business-like but dull; or one might even be seen as aloof, business-like and stimulating. Each dimension represents a continuum, and for most teachers there will be a characteristic point along its baseline.

CATEGORIZING VERBAL BEHAVIOR

The studies mentioned above have concentrated on the teacher's stance, his characteristic mode of behavior, the flavor of his performance, and his attitudes toward his task. Little attention was paid to the handling of content, the skill of questioning, the organization of material, and the like. For aspects of the teacher's work which relate to the processes of handling content, one must turn to the work of B. Othanel Smith and his associates (1963). Here, the concern has been with the "logical operations" of teaching; with discovering "... how concepts, norms, laws, etc., are introduced, analyzed and manipulated in the course of instruction" (Smith et al., 1963, p. 2). Using large samples of electrically taped classroom sessions, the verbal behavior of both teachers and pupils was categorized into 13 "major acts"—such as defining, stating, reporting, opining, explaining, comparing and contrasting, classifying, etc. Such analyses made possible the description of a teacher's characteristic performance through quantifying the frequency with which his verbal behavior falls into one or another of the various categories. Eventually, it should become possible to discover to what extent the differential frequencies are a function of a pervasive style of teaching, a response to the inherent logic of a particular subject or phase of it or a reflection of the particular group of pupils being taught.

RELATING TEACHER STYLE TO PUPIL ACHIEVEMENT

But the analyses of teaching styles and logical operations, significant though they may be in supplying needed systematic information on the teaching process, have only just begun to shed light on two crucial questions: (1) What difference do these ways of teaching make? Do pupils, in general, come out with different kinds or amounts of learning when taught by teachers using one or another approach to teaching? (2) Does a particular teacher's style have more or less the same effect on all pupils under his tutelage? If not, are there ways of determining the characteristics of pupils who would fare better under one teaching style than under another?

Working with junior high school classes in mathematics and social studies, Flanders (1960) related teaching style to pupil achievement and degree of dependence. He reported that when learning goals were unclear, as in a new task, lecturing and giving directions increased the dependence of students on the teacher and tended to lower achievement. In general, he found that patterns of "indirect influence" resulted in greater content mastery and in more positive attitudes toward school than did the "direct influence" procedures. However, in classes designated as superior—where pupils' achievement was greatest and attitudes toward the teacher were most favorable—there was an element of flexibility in the teacher's influence patterns not found in below-average classrooms. In superior classes, teacher behavior was less predictable, "shifting from domination and close supervision" on some occasions, to "indirect participation" at other times. These studies also suggest that for pupils who tend to be dependent upon teacher direction and unable to pursue work on their own, a high level of "direct influence"—lecturing, criticizing, giving directions—tends to be associated with lower achievement than is apparent when more independent pupils are exposed to similar "direct" teaching procedures.

In their study of "The Language of Teaching," Bellack and Davitz (1963) analyzed tape-scripts of high school social studies classes studying a unit in economics. They identified four basic Pedagogical Moves: structuring, soliciting, responding, and reacting which "describe the verbal maneuvers of students and teachers . . . and set the framework for the analysis of meaning communicated in the classroom." Although the first phase of this research is largely descriptive, as are most of the other analyses of the verbal behavior of teaching, the data analysis will be used not only to categorize and describe but also to relate the linguistic variables to student learning and attitude change. In subsequent phases, Bellack plans to address himself more intensively to studying the functions of the various Pedagogical Moves—the recurring patterns or "cycles" of moves characteristic of a given teacher, and the relation between patterns of teacher verbal behavior and student performance.

Of special interest to the major concern of this paper is the work of Heil and his associates (1960). They hypothesized that "in a particular class, the teacher's behavior will evoke a certain amount of

achievement with children of a given set of feelings and level of intelligence." On the basis of assessment instruments, 5th and 6th grade pupils in a New York City school were divided into four personality categories: (1) *Conformers*—characterized by incorporation of adult standards, high social orientation, control over impulses and emphasis on mature behavior; (2) *Opposers*—showing disturbed authority relationships, oppositional trends, pessimistic tone, intolerance of ambiguity and disappointment and frustration as central dynamics; (3) *Waverers*—described as anxious, ambivalent, fearful, floundering and indecisive, and (4) *Strivers*—showing marked drive for recognition, especially in school achievement, and exhibitionistic needs. The teachers were divided into three personality types—the *Turbulent*, the *Self-controlling*, and the *Fearful*.

Pupil achievement was contrasted for each pupil category under each teacher type. In general, when achievement was controlled for I.Q., the "strivers" achieved most, followed by the "conformers," then the "opposers" and showing least gains, the "waverers." Neither the "strivers" nor the "conformers" were significantly affected by teacher personality; but for the "opposers" and the "waverers," teaching style made a significant difference. For the last two groups, the "self-controlling" teachers, who maintained an orderly, workmanlike class, focused on structure and planning—but, at the same time, showed a sensitivity to children's feelings and emphasized interpersonal relations in the classroom—were most effective. The "turbulent" teachers—characterized by greater concern for ideas than for people, freedom of expression of strong feelings and attitudes, little patience with routine tasks, "sloppiness," and inconsistency—were more successful than either of the other types in teaching math and science. In the other subjects their success was limited to "strivers" and "conformers." The "turbulent" teachers were least successful with the "opposers" who evidenced the highest intolerance of ambiguity. The "fearful" teachers—anxious, dependent on the approval of supervisors and of the children, unable to bring structure and order to the teaching task, and highly variable in their behavior—were uniformly ineffective with all kinds of children except "strivers," who fared well regardless of the teacher.

TEACHABLE GROUPS

A quite different approach to the study of the relationship between teacher style and pupil learning is found in Thelen's (1961) recent work on the formation of "teachable" groups. Since the 1930's repeated efforts at assessing the effects of "homogeneous" versus "heterogeneous" grouping or, in more modern parlance, broad and narrow ability range groups, have produced meager results. The findings, though apparently inconclusive, are consistent in reporting that in the absence of deliberate curricular modifications, grouping, on the basis of ability, has no significant effects on pupil achievement. But all of the grouping efforts were predicated on the assumption that if the class group is "homogeneous" with respect to intelligence or reading level or achievement in a particular subject, then, *ipso facto*, such a group becomes more "teachable." A teacher in such a group would accomplish more with the pupils than would be the case where the range of ability was wide. What was left out of the equation of "teachability" was the teacher's style of working and his perception of the kinds of pupils with whom he tends to be most successful. From Thelen's (1961) work it would appear that I.Q. or achievement status are by no means the most significant determinants of the teacher's perception of "teachability." Thelen states that, in general ". . . teachers recognize four kinds of students: the good, the bad, the indifferent, and the sick. But the problem is that each teacher places different students in these categories, so that whatever is being judged is not primarily some characteristic of the student" (p. 226). He urges that ". . . the teachable students for one teacher may be quite different than for another, that the fit between teacher and teachable students primarily results in better meeting the teacher's most dominant needs . . . he is able with the teachable class to do more fully what he tries to do with his other classes . . . that successful grouping must take the teacher himself into account" (p. 220). Despite finding few differences in achievement between "teachable" and random groups, Thelen states: "We remain convinced that any grouping which does not in some way attempt to 'fit' students and teachers together can have only accidental success" (p. 221).

A significant implication of the studies of teacher characteristics, teaching process, and teachable groups is the recognition that variations in pupil attainment in the classroom are related to variations in teacher performance, and that a particular teacher affects different pupils differently. We are forced to question the stereotype of the "good teacher" and the "poor teacher," although there may be some few who would prove excellent for all pupils and many more who would be inadequate no matter what the assignment. Most teachers, however, vary in their effectiveness depending upon the characteristics of the pupils they confront, the opportunity to fulfill their expectations for themselves and for their class, the content of what they teach, and the extent to which the school provides them with what they perceive to be necessary facilitations.

TEACHERS FOR DISADVANTAGED CHILDREN

In discussing the problem of "teachable groups" Thelen (1961) points out that despite great individual differences in teachers' perception of who is teachable, there are some pupils—from 10 to 25 percent of the average school—whom *no* teacher includes among the teachable. His description of this group is reminiscent of what we know about the school behavior of children from disadvantaged areas, from city slums, and rural backwoods. Similarly, Heil's "opposers" and to some extent his "waverers" remind one of typical behaviors of disadvantaged children. In the great cities these children represent an increasing proportion of the total pupil population, far more than the 10 to 25 percent suggested by Thelen. And it is expected that by 1970 one out of every two pupils in large city schools will be "culturally disadvantaged."

The approach to the problem of staffing schools in depressed areas requires several sequential efforts. The first step is to gain broad public acceptance of the assumption that disadvantaged pupils, though widely variable in their abilities and personal characteristics, nonetheless represent a describable group. That is, they represent a group which, although it overlaps other groups in many ways, has unique characteristics, stemming from common backgrounds, values and experiences. The second step is to characterize the teacher who is successful with culturally disadvantaged pupils—successful because the pupils in his classes achieve better than similar pupils in other teachers' classes and have more accepting attitudes toward school, toward the teacher, and toward learning. The third step involves re-examinations of teacher selection and education for staffing disadvantaged area schools.

Since there are no systematic data on what such teachers do, it may be worth while to create a hypothetical model of the "successful teacher of disadvantaged children." Our model can be constructed of implications from available research on teacher behavior, insights from impressionistic observations, and inferences from investigations of the characteristics of disadvantaged pupils and their social world. It may well be that several models of successful teachers will be needed to account for the great variety of pupils within the disadvantaged population. What is suggested here is a general outline which may have to be refined and subdivided to achieve optimum "fit" between pupils and teacher.

HYPOTHETICAL MODEL OF THE SUCCESSFUL TEACHER OF DISADVANTAGED PUPILS

The teacher who is successful with any group of pupils is the one who respects the children in his classes and they, in turn, respect him. As teachers in slum schools look at their pupils, they see many children who are discouraged and defeated, even in the early grades, children who express their alienation from the school and the society it represents by aggressive acting-out behavior or by a kind of tuned-out lethargy and listlessness. There are frequent transgressions against the ethical, moral, and legal codes of society. Pupils seem to be making little effort to learn, show no desire to better themselves, to break out of the limits imposed upon them by their ignorance. The teacher may feel sorry for them, realizing the limiting circumstances of their lives. Or, he may be angered by their laziness, their lack of effort, believing that they could if they would, but they won't. Or, he may write them off as hopeless, too dumb to learn, taking up time and resources that could be better utilized by pupils with more ability and greater motivation.

But the successful teacher of disadvantaged children does respect his pupils—and not because he sees them through the rose-colored lenses of the romantic—finding "beauty" and "strength" where others see poverty and cultural emptiness. On the contrary, he sees them quite realistically as different from his children and his neighbors' children, yet like all children coping in their own way with the trials and frustrations of growing up. And he sees them, unlike middle-class children, struggling to survive in the ruthless world of their peers, confused by the conflicting demands of the two cultures in which they live—the one of the home and the street and the neighborhood, the other of the school and the society that maintains it.

Like the anthropologist, the successful teacher views the alien culture of his pupils not as a judge, but as a student. He understands the backgrounds from which the children come, the values placed on various achievements, the kind of work and life to which they aspire. He recognizes and understands the reasons for their unwillingness to strive toward future goals, where such efforts provide little reward in the present.

He knows that many of the children bear the scars of intellectual understimulation in their early years. Familiar with the home life of the children, he knows how rarely they are helped to name the things they see and feel and bear, to recognize similarities and differences, to categorize and classify perceptions, to learn the word for the object, and the phrases through which to express an idea or a feeling.

The successful teacher is aware of the various family structures from which the children come: The matriarchal family in which no father is present; the home where there are two parents, but both working; where one or both parents are able-bodied but out of work, recipients of relief; where the father is disabled and stays home while the mother works; where an extended family—grandparents, aunts, uncles, and other relatives—live together. This teacher has seen the physical conditions in which the children live: their lack of privacy, the poor facilities, the absence of basic amenities. He knows the kinds of jobs the parents have, their aspirations for themselves and for their children, and what role they attribute to the school in shaping their child's future.

The teacher is aware of the ethnic group membership of his pupils and how such membership shapes the child's image of himself and of his world. He knows something about the history, traditions and social structures of the various ethnic groups, their unique culture patterns, their status in American society, the blocks and frustrations which they confront and their perceptions of what life has in store for them.

He knows that the language of his pupils is closely tied to the life they lead. While it may represent a complete lack or a distortion of acceptable English, he recognizes its functional qualities for the pupils. Though this language is not "the coin of the realm," it often represents the only known and acceptable medium of exchange in the child's home or neighborhood.

In addition to his knowledge about the child in his environment, the successful teacher has a sophisticated understanding of how a child's abilities are assessed and therefore a realistic perception of what these measurements describe and predict. He knows that native potential intelligence is, at least thus far, unmeasurable; that what tests measure is learned behavior, and that the learning results not only from the child's native ability but also from his total experience. Yet he realizes that many intellectual abilities, like some of those which enter into creative functioning are not measured by existing intelligence tests.

He is also aware that the tests provide a fairly accurate description of the child's present ability to handle academic material and, unless there is a significant expansion and reorganization of his experience, the tests will predict with fair reliability how the child will function academically in the future. The successful teacher accepts the test scores as a fair and valid measure of the child's present academic ability, while rejecting them as a measure of native intelligence.

These and many other anthropological and psychological data affect the style of the successful teacher of disadvantaged pupils. But while the anthropologist's task is to describe and compare behavior of various cultures, and the psychologist's to understand individual behavior, the teacher's job is to modify it. Therefore, he must use his knowledge about his pupils and the world in which they live to guide him as he attempts to open more and more doors for them, and to help them acquire the skills and knowledge with which to enter the new and open spaces which lie beyond. The successful teacher sees his task as preparing his pupils to make competent choices among potentially available alternatives. He is aware that with every passing year the rapidly automating economy affords fewer and fewer opportunities to the minimally educated, and more and more to the academically and technically trained, and he communicates this understanding to his pupils.

The successful teacher meets the disadvantaged child on equal terms, as person to person, individual to individual. But while he accepts, he doesn't condone. He sets clearly defined limits for his pupils and will brook few transgressions. He is aware that, unlike middle-class children, they rarely respond to exhortations intended to control behavior through invoking feelings of guilt and shame. He, therefore, sets the rules, fixes the boundaries, and establishes the routines with a minimum of discussion. Here he is impersonal, undeviating, strict, but never punitive. Within these boundaries the successful teacher is businesslike and orderly, knowing that he is there to do a job. But he is also warm and outgoing, adapting his behavior to the individual pupils in his class. He shows his respect and liking for his pupils and makes known his belief in their latent abilities.

He realizes the danger of the "self-fulfilling prophecy" of expecting, and consequently finding, a low level of achievement. He, therefore, lets each pupil know that he expects more than the pupil thinks he can produce—but his standards are not so high as to become too remote to strive toward, and the attempt fraught with frustration. He rewards each tiny upward step, alert to every opportunity for honest praise, and, as much as possible, withholds harsh criticism and censure when progress is slow or entirely lacking. Above all, he is honest. He doesn't sentimentalize, doesn't pretend that a pupil's work is good when it isn't, doesn't condone unacceptable behavior.

The successful teacher is also something of a showman, coming to his task with an extensive repertory of carefully constructed scripts and props into which he breathes a sense of drama and high interest to capture the imagination of his pupils and hold their attention.

His repertory is not only extensive, providing a great variety of materials and teaching procedures tailored to the learning patterns of his pupils, it is also carefully catalogued to allow him to find what he needs quickly and efficiently.

As do other successful teachers, our model teacher has extensive knowledge of the content of the subjects he teaches. In fact, he knows it so well, that he has no need to rely on study guides. Like the knowledgeable native, he guides his pupils through his country without a Baedeker, relying rather on his own familiarity with its terrain to take them to the important sights by paths and highways not often known to the less sophisticated.

Like all composite portraits, this hypothetical model presents an idealized version of reality. The hypothetical teacher is described as a mature, well-integrated person who respects his difficult, unmotivated, and apparently unteachable pupils. He communicates his respect by setting high but reachable expectations, by his impartial and consistent firmness and honesty, and by his warm personal regard for each individual. He combines the detached but completely accepting stance of the anthropologist observing cultural differences, with the active involvement and manipulative approach of the determined reformer, the educator, in the sense of one who *leads* his pupils *out* into the wider world. Though not a specialist in any one of the behavioral or social sciences, he gleans from each of them knowledge which helps him understand the behavior of his pupils, the meaning of their scores on tests of intelligence and aptitude, the realities of their present and future world, the demands which various social and vocational alternatives will make upon them. In addition, the model requires the teacher to have a wide repertoire of materials and procedures, the ability to devise new ways, to deviate from accepted procedures and courses of study—but always to be aware of the knowledges and skills the pupils must eventually acquire. If the hypothetical "successful teacher" were to be characterized in a single phrase it would be *ordered flexibility*.

EXAMINING THE HYPOTHETICAL MODEL

The sketch presented here needs to be examined on two counts. First, it represents a hypothetical model, derived from inference and deduced from theoretical concepts. Before it is accepted, it must be verified through systematic observation, classification, and comparison of successful and unsuccessful teachers in "slums and suburbs."

But if the model in whole or in part does fit reality, if the characteristics described in the portrait do in fact approximate the characteristics which distinguish the successful teacher of disadvantaged pupils, then we must ask: How are we to get such teachers? Although the ideal presumably represented by this characterization can act only as a remote goal, how can it be approached?

It is simple nonsense to suppose that, even if the entire pool of existing teachers were screened, one would find enough people who resemble the hypothetical model to staff even a small proportion of the depressed-area schools. We must, therefore, look to teacher education to produce new teachers more nearly in the image of the model and to reshape the styles of those already in service. We return to the question of teachability, but this time with reference to the teacher as a student.

APPROACHING THE MODEL THROUGH EDUCATION

To what extent are the attributes of the model teachable? At least three of the aspects are of a cognitive nature and, for the reasonably bright and motivated student, can probably be approached through instruction: (1) mastery of subject matter; (2) the acquisition of an understanding of the major concepts from the behavioral and social sciences and their relevance to teaching disadvantaged children; and (3) the development of a repertoire of teaching strategies which hold promise for working with disadvantaged pupils. But to accomplish these three purposes alone would require a considerable reorganization and revision of undergraduate and graduate programs of teacher education, both pre-service and in-service.

Developing New Courses. The development of appropriate courses would require the intensive collaboration of social and behavioral scientists, faculties of education, and successful classroom teachers. Out of such collaboration can grow not only curricula which would lead to a better understanding of the child in his environment, but also new strategies, new methods, new materials based on the empirical evidence provided by the social scientist and the practical wisdom of the teachers and educators. This has been successfully done in the development of some of the new curricula for the secondary and elementary schools.

Laboratory Experiences. Given increased understanding and a repertory of appropriate teaching methods, the teacher can approach his task with

greater openness, with less prejudice, and above all, with less fear. But every young teacher needs a bridge by which to cross the chasm which separates "knowing about" from actually doing something. For the teacher confronted by a class of poorly motivated, often discouraged and difficult pupils, continuous assistance and reinforcement in the teaching situation are essential. In *Teachers for the Schools in Our Big Cities*, Harry Rivlin, Dean of Teacher Education of the City University of New York, outlined a variety of desired modifications in existing modes of teacher preparation for large city schools (Rivlin, 1962). He placed major stress on the importance of laboratory experiences, starting with observation, leading to limited participation, then to student teaching, and finally, to independent responsibility for instruction. At every stage, the future teacher, and then the newly appointed teacher to the difficult school, must work under close supervision, receiving both psychological and practical support from the college staff and from the master teachers in the schools.

Hunter College (Haubrick, 1962), in an effort to improve the preparation of teachers for depressed area schools, selected a group of students who expressed a willingness to remain as regularly appointed teachers in the same "most difficult" junior high schools in which they had accepted appointments as student teachers. As part of their training, they were seen more often than was customary by a member of the college faculty and worked closely with carefully selected cooperating teachers. They spent the last 10 weeks of their student teaching in full command of the class, under constant supervision. A number of these young men and women, in due course, took and passed the required examinations and were appointed as regularly licensed teachers to the same school in which they had taught as students. But the supervision and assistance continued, reinforcing their earlier learning and providing the needed support and encouragement.

Selection of Candidates. But so far, the discussion has not taken account of those less tangible, but perhaps most significant characteristics of our model: openness to and acceptance of differences in people, firmness and consistency, warmth and respect and, above all, flexibility. Can courses, laboratory experiences, or field work assignments be devised which will develop these characteristics? The descriptive material on teacher characteristics and teaching style referred to earlier sheds little light on the antecedents of the observed behavior. Do some teachers use more and others less "direct influence," for example, because they are, by nature, more or less directive as people? Were they ever so, from childhood on? Or, does their classroom behavior reflect their teacher training and education? Are some teachers relatively "unplanned" in their approach to teaching because they believe that too much planning restricts the participation of the pupils, and given evidence to the contrary, would become more organized and business-like? Or is their unplanned, "slipshod" approach to the classroom just one case of an unplanned and inconsistent approach to most life situations, a behavioral pattern unamenable to easy change through training?

There are no simple answers to this crucial question. Perhaps, the training of teachers for the several areas of special education may be a case in point. In each area of exceptionality, teachers are exposed to technical knowledge of the medical, social, and psychological aspects of the disability with which they will work. Further, the teachers are instructed in ways of changing the general curriculum and adjusting both content and method to their special groups (Mackie and Williams, 1959). Such training has prepared large numbers of teachers who are successful in working with pupils normally viewed as difficult or unteachable.

But teachers who enter special education do so voluntarily. In fact, they select the special area in preference to teaching normal children. Their own natural styles may thus be suited to the work they select and the training falls on fertile ground. It is probably beyond common sense to expect any training to make of the potential secondary school teacher with a passion for communicating the ideas of the physical sciences, a fine teacher of retarded adolescents. To attempt to retrain the elementary school teacher who thrives on the rapid progress, the quick wit, the deep probing, and ingenious responses of his gifted pupils into a successful teacher of the dull and lethargic would be equally foolhardy.

Consider also: (1) The man or woman threatened by ambiguity, unable to adapt readily to unexpected circumstances, who functions adequately only in a meticulously ordered world; or (2) the basically weak, dominated person who seeks in the classroom, perhaps unconsciously, the opportunity to prove his power by bending others to his will; or, further (3) the bigot who clothes his prejudices in psychological theories of ethnic or class inferiority and is convinced, before he enters a classroom, that for all but a few disadvantaged children, schooling beyond the very minimum is a waste of the taxpayers' money. Such prospective teachers may or may not be adequate for other teaching assignments—the compulsive character may well make a fine college professor somewhere—but they are

probably not the kind of people who can be trained to fit the hypothetical model.

But then there are those prospective or practicing teachers who, although not completely free of prejudice, are yet not so bigoted as to resist attitudinal change in the face of new experiences. And some who may not be overly flexible in their approach are yet not immobilized by rigidity. Although somewhat at variance with the hypothetical model, the personalities, attitudes and values of some teachers would not be antithetical to those required by the model. For them we must assume, at least until proven wrong, that teacher education can produce greater consonance, better "fit" between what the pupils need in order to learn and what the teacher does in the act of teaching.

Developing Emotional Closeness. Since a considerable portion of teaching style derives from attitudes and values, teachers of disadvantaged children would need, in addition to cognitive learnings, experiences through which to come emotionally close to the feelings, the anxieties, the aspirations of slum children and through which to examine their own feelings and reactions. Such efforts might include role-playing in situations where the teacher alternately takes the part of the child as he copes with various school and out-of-school problems, and of the teacher responding to life-like classroom situations.

Teachers' feelings and values might also be involved and reshaped through the study of literary works. The novel and the short story which, at their best, provide a penetrating and illuminating exposition of life's fundamental conflicts, often have the power to transport the reader into the lives of people unlike himself but who, nonetheless, share with him many aspects of the human predicament. Books which deal with changing attitudes across generations, with the transition of immigrant groups from their original ghettos to the broader American Society, with adaptations to bicultural life, with the effects of early disability or severe deprivation on the behavior of the adult, with the universal problems of the adolescent as well as with those unique to a given time or place— these and many other literary themes might be used effectively. For the literary art is often able to create acceptance where direct contact may engender rejection or contempt. The "safe remove" of literature enables the individual to view the problems of others with greater openness, especially if his reading is geared toward exploring his own feelings as they become enmeshed with the feelings and strivings of others.

Such special efforts, though desirable for all teachers, are especially needed for teachers of the disadvantaged, since they most often come from backgrounds which provide little familiarity or personal involvement with the life which their pupils live.

In short, it is proposed that if the hypothetical model stands up under rigorous examination as embodying the characteristics, the "style" of the successful teacher of disadvantaged children, then the idealized model can be approached (though rarely reached) through deliberate preselection, and by an expanded and reconstructed approach to pre-service and in-service teacher education. Given the relatively bright student or young teacher, not completely blocked by deeply rooted attitudes and personality structures antithetical to the desired characteristics, education may help shape him in the image of the model.

ATTRACTING TEACHERS TO DIFFICULT SCHOOLS

But even assuming that there are ways to prepare successful teachers for depressed area schools, why should bright young people want to enter such a vocation? The realities are against such a choice. Teachers today are in a seller's market. There are many more vacancies than candidates, especially at the elementary level and in the sciences and mathematics, and teachers can choose the district in which they want to work. Suburban schools, for example, afford amenities which urban schools so often lack. But above all, because of their size and organization, the suburban schools more often give the teacher a sense that he is a professional, that he is respected in his job and can successfully carry out what he has set out to do. He can teach children and, in most instances, they learn.

What inducement does the slum school offer? The children are difficult, in the perceptions of many teachers now in these schools they are "unteachable." The supervision is inadequate and often hostile. Principals and their assistants are constantly harassed by continuous teacher turn-over, uncovered classes, disciplinary problems in the school, involvement with the police and the courts, lack of appropriate or even adequate books and materials. They have little time and less energy to give their teaching staffs the needed help and support. Teachers, frustrated by their inability to induce learning in their pupils, often having no place to turn for help, resort to discipline-maintaining rather than teaching activities. In this process, the teacher loses all sense of professional commitment. Many feel as did a very young woman when asked how long she had taught before leaving the field. She said, "I haven't taught a day in my life, but I served a three-year sentence in junior high school X."

What awaits them in depressed area schools is well known to prospective teachers. In fact, in 1962 better than a third of the new teachers appointed to Manhattan schools declined the appointment. Although they had prepared to teach, they apparently preferred almost any other kind of employment or none at all, to teaching in a slum school.

No matter how excellent the preparation of teachers of disadvantaged children may become, no matter how much assistance is given both to pre-service students and to beginning teachers, teaching in slum schools will remain a difficult, often frustrating and very taxing job—far more so than teaching in the unruffled surrounding of tree-lined suburbia. What, then, will induce young people to become candidates for a hard life, deliberately to choose the slum over the suburb?

Perhaps the answer to this question requires the addition of still another characteristic to our hypothetical model, one that is most difficult to teach —idealism, dedication to a cause, the desire to help the have-nots, to render service. That openness to commitment exists in many young people is confirmed by the large numbers who apply for the Peace Corps, prepare for missionary work, or choose to work in settlements, in hospital schools, and in special schools for disturbed or retarded or otherwise handicapped children. These young people feel that they are answering a call, and they rise to its demands. We have also witnessed such behavior (perhaps too often) in times of revolution and war, when young men and women have willingly gone into hardship and danger for what they believed in. How can this spirit be harnessed for teaching in difficult schools, in the "underdeveloped" areas of our own great cities? Is there, to paraphrase William James, an "educational equivalent of war"?

Perhaps each city needs to designate, as some have already begun to do, one or two schools in each depressed area which become service centers, open to view, for which teachers are carefully selected and in which they feel privileged to teach. Such schools could help to counteract the negative image now in the minds of prospective teachers. Those who are idealistic, who would like to perform a service, will see that there is hope; that the task, though difficult, can be done.

Helping the Teacher in Service. But even when colleges and universities have evolved the needed curricula and made them part of the total education of prospective teachers, when bright young people are motivated to enroll, even if the graduate programs incorporate the new developments into their courses for experienced teachers, the problem of staffing schools in depressed urban areas will be only slightly alleviated. Assistance must be given to the hundreds of thousands of teachers now serving in depressed-area schools. Obviously, no program of study can reach all teachers now in our schools through direct contact. But they could be reached and helped and encouraged by changing supervisory patterns, by reeducating existing supervisors where they may be amenable to such re-education, or by selecting from each school one teacher who comes closest to the model and exposing him to a special program. Such teachers could return to their schools as supervisors, master teachers, or team leaders. From them could be formed the corps of cooperating teachers responsible for training students.

Problems of School Organization. The problem of staffing disadvantaged-area schools must be attacked simultaneously on many fronts. We must confront the fact that teachers for difficult schools need special training. We must reshape the program of teacher preparation, attract capable young people to such programs and help them as they move through their apprenticeship into full professional status. And we must also provide a corps of trained master teachers and supervisors who will bring skills and hope to the hundreds of thousands of teachers now in service.

But there is still another front upon which the attack must be launched—making changes in the amenities and management of the schools. Some of these are easy changes to make, because they do not require devising new courses or reshaping attitudes and values. All that they require is some additional money—simple things like providing a safe parking place, a comfortable lunch and rest room; of giving the teacher, especially at the elementary level, some relief during the day. Each school must make provisions for removing the one or two most difficult children from regular classrooms so that classes may become more teachable, lessening the teacher's sense of frustration and enhancing his sense of fulfilling his professional responsibility.

Somewhat less simple are the needed changes in supervision. Additional supervisory personnel, both in the school and from affiliated teacher education institutions, need to be provided. The presence in each school of staff members—eventually trained in the new approaches—whose sole responsibility would be to help teachers, unburdened by administrative or disciplinary matters, might prove especially helpful. Perhaps if the supervisory load is spread, principals will be less harassed, less afraid of trouble, less apt to reward the teacher who maintains a quiet classroom, and

more respectful of the teachers as people and as professionals.

The solution of any problem requires first, a clear recognition and description of the problem; secondly, a concerted research and experimental effort; and thirdly, the implementation of what is already known or what is learned through systematic study. To approach a solution to the problem of staffing schools in disadvantaged areas and providing competent teachers to work with disadvantaged children requires the following steps: (1) Open recognition that slum schools and disadvantaged children need uniquely prepared teachers. (2) Systematic study of the personal qualities, knowledge, and skills needed for successful teaching in these situations. (3) Development and experimental testing of reconstructed teacher education programs, both on campus and in the field. (4) Screening of candidates to eliminate those students or young teachers now in service whose values and personality characteristics are in conflict with the desired teaching style. (5) Raising the status of the disadvantaged-area teacher to that of a high calling, by invoking all available reward systems. (6) Initiating systematic changes to make the schools more livable for the teacher, the teaching experience less frustrating, and the supervision more professional. Such efforts can go a long way toward raising the morale and the effectiveness of those presently teaching, and toward bringing into the teaching force many able young people who will not only come but will stay.

It is, of course, a romantic notion to suppose that even the best qualified teachers will, through their efforts alone, solve all the social problems which shape the lives of disadvantaged children. The work of other agencies in the community needs to be integrated with the work of the school. The more effective the school becomes, the more help both the child and the family will need to understand and accept his changed behaviors and increased academic success and aspirations. But if the presently disadvantaged child is not to be fettered by his ignorance, not to be relegated to the ranks of the unemployable in a society which provides increasing opportunities to the academically competent and has less and less room for the functional illiterate, then the school has a central role to play. And central to the school, to the development and achievement of the child is the teacher.

REFERENCES

BELLACK, A. A. The language of teaching: Relationships of the linguistic behavior of students and teachers in high school classrooms to student learning. Project proposal: Teachers College, Columbia Univer., 1963. (Dittoed)

FLANDERS, N. A. Teacher and classroom influences on individual learning. In A. H. Passow (Ed.), *Nurturing individual potential.* Washington: Ass. Supervis. & Curriclm. Develpm., NEA, 1964. Pp. 57–65.

HAUBRICK, V. F. Teachers for big-city schools. In A. H. Passow (Ed.), *Education in depressed areas.* New York: Bur. Publ., Teach. Coll., Columbia Univer., 1963. Pp. 243–261.

HEIL, L. M., POWELL, M., & FEIFER, I. Characteristics of teacher behavior related to the achievement of children in several elementary grades. New York: Author, May, 1960. (Mimeo)

MACKIE, R. P., & WILLIAMS, H. M. Teachers of exceptional children. *Rev. educ. Res.,* 1959, *29,* 395–407.

MEDLEY, D. M. The development of classroom behavior dimension for teachers and pupils. Paper presented at the Amer. Ass. Advnmnt. Sci., 1962. (Mimeo)

RIVLIN, H. N. Teachers for the schools in our big cities. New York: Div. Teach. Educ., City Univer. New York, 1962.

RYANS, D. C. Characteristics of teachers: An informative systems approach to theory of instruction with special reference to the teacher. Paper presented at Amer. Educ. Res. Ass. symposium on *Theories of teaching,* February, 1963.

SMITH, B. O., MEUX, M., et al. *A study of the logic of teaching.* III. Urbana, Ill.: Bur. Educ. Res., 1963.

THELEN, H. A. Teachability grouping. Dept. Educ., Univer. Chicago, August, 1961. (Mimeo)

WARRENER, C. K. A classification of social achievement. Paper presented at Amer. Sociol. Ass., August, 1962. (Mimeo)

82

Teachers' Communication of Differential Expectations for Children's Classroom Performance: Some Behavioral Data

JERE E. BROPHY AND THOMAS L. GOOD [1]

Pygmalion in the Classroom, by Robert Rosenthal and Lenore Jacobson (New York: Holt, Rinehart, and Winston), appeared in 1968. The authors of that book assert that a teacher's differential expectations about his students' performances will lead to differential treatment and that their performance will indeed be modified—improved or depressed—in the direction of the teacher's expectations (the self-fulfilling prophecy). These conclusions were not entirely justified on the basis of the data presented: see Robert L. Thorndike's review in the American Educational Research Journal *(volume 5, 1968, pages 708–711). However, the book made a huge impact, and a large number of similar studies have since been done.*

Jere E. Brophy and Thomas L. Good's paper, which focuses on four first-grade classrooms in Texas, supports the self-fulfilling prophecy hypothesis. Note the method: they used an observation system in which specific interactions between the teacher and an individual child were coded and analyzed. Brophy and Good are both in the Department of Educational Psychology at the University of Texas, Austin.

[1] The authors wish to thank Vern Jones for his assistance in collection of data and Jean Romigh and Betty Johnson for their help in manuscript preparation.

Rosenthal and Jacobson (1968) assert on the basis of controversial research presented in *Pygmalion in the Classroom* that teachers' expectations for student performance function as self-fulfilling prophecies. The "expectancy effects" in the Oak School experiment described in *Pygmalion* are not as consistent as the authors' interpretations of them would suggest, however, and even the support that they do provide is questionable on methodological grounds (Barber & Silver, 1968; Snow, 1969; Thorndike, 1968). Even if the data and their interpretation are accepted, the Rosenthal and Jacobson work remains only a demonstration of the *existence* of expectancy effects; their study did not address itself to any of the events intervening between the inducement of teacher expectations and the administration of the criterion achievement test. The present study focuses on these intervening processes, applying the method of classroom interaction analysis to identify and document differential teacher behavior communicating different teacher expectations to individual children.

The lack of data concerning the causal mechanisms at work in the Rosenthal and Jacobson study, combined with the tendency in most secondary sources to oversimplify or exaggerate their findings, has cast an aura of magic or mystery around expectation effects. Consequently, it is important to conceptualize such phenomena as outcomes of observable sequences of behavior. The explicit model assumed in the present research may be described as follows: (a) The teacher forms differential expectations for student performance; (b) He then begins to treat children differently in accordance with his differential expectations; (c) The children respond differentially to the teacher because they are being treated differently by him; (d) In responding to the teacher, each child tends to exhibit behavior which complements and reinforces the teacher's particular expectations for him; (e) As a result, the general academic performance of some children will be enhanced while that of others will be depressed, with changes being in the direction of teacher expectations; (f) These effects will show up in the achievement tests given at the end of the year, providing support for the "self-fulfilling prophecy" notion.

A series of interrelated studies will be required to investigate systematically the full model from beginning (how do teachers form differential expectations in the first place?) to end (how do children change so as to begin to conform more closely to teacher expectations?). The present study deals with the second step: given differential teacher expectations, how are they communicated to the children in ways that would tend to cause the children to produce reciprocal behavior? To begin to answer this question, the present study approached the problem through classroom interaction analysis. In contrast to the usual classroom interaction study, however, the present research focused on dyadic interaction between the teacher and individual children.[2]

METHOD

SUBJECTS

The research was carried out in four first-grade classrooms in a small Texas school district which serves a generally rural and lower-class population. However, a large military base located within the district contributes about 45% of the students in the school in which observations were taken. Children from the base tend to be from more urban backgrounds and of a somewhat higher socioeconomic status than the local children. The ethnic composition of the school is about 75% Anglo-American, 15% Mexican-American, and 10% Afro-American, which is representative of the general population of the area.

Research was carried out in four of the nine first-grade classrooms in the school, chosen because there were no assistant teachers present to complicate the picture (the other five classrooms had preservice teacher interns assisting the head teacher). The four teachers involved were asked to rank the children in their class in the order of their achievement. These instructions were deliberately kept vague to encourage the teachers to use complex, subjective criteria in making their judgments. The rankings were then used as the measure of the teachers' expectations for classroom performance for the children in their classes. In each class, three boys and three girls high on the teacher's list (highs) and three boys and three girls low on the teacher's list (lows) were selected for observational study. The highs were simply the first six eligible children on the list. This was generally true also for the lows, although a few children low on the lists were excluded from the study because they could not speak English fluently or because of suspected emotional or biological disturbance. Substitutes for each type of child (high boys, high girls, low boys, low girls) were also identified and these were individually observed on days when children in the designated sample were absent.

The teachers had been told that the study was concerned with the classroom behavior of children of various levels of achievement. They were not informed that their own behavior as well as that of the children was being specifically observed. Furthermore, the teachers thought that observations were being taken on everyone in the class and did not know that specific subgroups had been selected for study. By selecting subjects from the extremes of the distributions of teachers' rankings, the chances of discovering differential teacher treatment of the students were maximized. However, the school practiced tracking, achieving homogeneity within the nine classrooms by grouping the children according to readiness and achievement scores. Thus, at least in terms of test scores, objective differences among the children (and, therefore, objective support for the validity of teacher expectations) was minimized.

OBSERVATION SYSTEM

Since the object of the research was to focus on differential treatment of different children, the observation system developed was addressed only to dyadic contacts between the teacher and an individual child, with lecture-demonstration and other teacher behavior directed to the class as a group being ignored. Although the types of interactions coded were partly dictated by the range of situations seen in pilot studies, certain features of the coding system were built in for their specific relevance to the study of communication of differential teacher expectations. One major and consistent feature was that the source of the interaction was always coded, so that it could be determined later whether the interaction was initiated by the teacher or by the child. The types of dyadic interactions coded included teacher-afforded response opportunities and other types of interactions initiated by the children. The teacher-afforded response opportunities included recitations and reading turns in the reading groups and answers to teacher questions (coded separately as to whether they were *open* questions directed to the class as a whole or *direct* questions aimed at a particular child). Response opportunities were important events for studying teacher expectations, since at these times the children were attempting to deal with problems relevant to academic subject matter. Consequently, the sequential nature of the initiation and reaction cycles involved in them was retained in the coding system. In addition to coding response opportunities separately by type (as listed above), coders also noted the quality of the child's response (correct, incomplete or partially correct, incorrect or no response) and the type of feedback given by the teacher (praise, criticism, supplying the answer, repeating the question, rephrasing the question or giving a clue, or giving no feedback at all). This retention of sequential relationships allowed later analysis of the relative as well as the absolute differences between the groups.

All dyadic contacts other than response opportunities as defined above were coded as either teacher-afforded communications (individual feedback regarding seat work or homework, requests that the child perform procedural or caretaking functions, and disciplinary action or evaluative comment about the child's behavior) or interactions initiated by the child (calling out answers, showing work to the teacher or asking questions about it, and seeking permission or other procedural contact).

---

[2] In the study of dyadic interaction the individual child (or teacher-child dyad) becomes the unit of analysis, rather than the class as a group. For a discussion of the advantages of this method for studying traditional teacher-effectiveness variables and of applications of the method to problems that cannot be approached through ordinary interaction analysis methods, see Good and Brophy (1971).

Sequential data were also built into the coding of these interactions. In addition to coding the type (academic, procedural, or disciplinary) and initiator (teacher or child) of the interaction, coders also kept track of the evaluative nature of the teacher's feedback (praise, criticism, or impersonal feedback). The terms "praise" and "criticism" referred to teacher reactions which went beyond the level of simple affirmation or negation or corrective feedback by complimenting or criticizing the child personally. Simple affirmation ("yes," "OK," "that's right") was not considered "praise" unless accompanied by obvious expression or gesture connoting excitement or warmth. The latter reactions were considered "praise," as were the words "good" and "fine," as well as other, more obvious forms of verbal praise. Similarly, simple negation ("no," "that's not it") was not considered "criticism," unless accompanied by expressions or gestures communicating anger or disgust. In addition to the latter responses, verbal statements such as "that's a stupid answer," or "what's the matter with you?" were coded as "criticism." Most teacher feedback involved simple affirmation or negation and/or communication of information and was coded as "impersonal feedback" to distinguish it from praise and criticism. The fourth category, "no feedback," was coded if the teacher did not react in any way to the child's response and simply moved on to something else.

In addition to the coding of dyadic interactions as described above, the hand-raising behavior of the children was tallied as a measure of their tendency to seek response opportunities. This was coded after open questions, when the children raised their hands seeking to be called on to answer the question, and after some direct questions, when children raised their hands if the child called upon to answer the question gave a wrong answer or was unable to respond.

After several pilot applications in which the system was perfected and satisfactory intercoder reliability was established, observations were made on 4 separate days in each of the four classes. To equalize the time spent in each classroom and insure that the full range of classroom activities was included, the observation period extended for an entire morning or an entire afternoon (two of each for each class). Data were recorded for all periods of academic activity during the observation period, using one data sheet for the reading group and another for all other situations. No data were recorded when the class was out of the room for recess or washroom breaks. During nonacademic procedural activities (clean-up, getting in line, pledge to the flag, etc.), only disciplinary actions and behavioral evaluations were coded.

Data were recorded by two observers seated at the rear of the classroom. The observers were thus in front of the teacher but behind or to the side of the majority of the children, who were seated at small tables of six or eight. During each observation, one observer coded the interactions involving the six highs and the other coded the six lows. It had originally been intended that assignment of children to observers would be determined by seating location, since coding could be done more conveniently when the target children are seated close together. However, in three of the four classrooms the children were seated in order of achievement level (a fact which is itself a correlate of expectancy effects, as will be pointed out below), so that observations were made on intact high or low groups. Each observer's assignments were balanced between the high and low groups to eliminate the possibility that any obtained differences between expectancy groups could be attributed to observer differences.

DATA ANALYSIS

A variety of measures were derived from the raw coding sheets through simple arithmetic procedures, and scores were assigned to each of the 48 individual subjects. Analyses of variance then were performed to assess the effects of teacher expectancy, sex, and classroom (teacher) and their respective interactions on the obtained scores. Two types of measures were identified. The first, subsuming most of the simple frequency counts, involved group differences which are attributable to objective differences in the groups of children themselves. Consequently, any significant group differences discovered in these variables, while important in themselves, could not be taken as evidence of expectancy effects. The second set of measures, mostly percentage figures in which absolute frequency differences are statistically controlled in order to allow a comparison of relative differences between the groups, are interpreted as measures of expectancy effects. Teacher behavior tapped by these measures is more proactive or teacher initiated, going beyond simple reaction by the teacher to stimulation by the child. The distinction between these two types of measures is exemplified in the Results section below, in which the two types of findings are separately presented.

RESULTS

The results are presented in three tables, each giving mean values for the four classes, two sexes, and two expectancy groups and the *p* values for Group Effects in Class × Sex × Expectancy analyses of variance. Although no predictions were made concerning differences by class, the data are presented to show the degree to which the teachers varied on the measures taken. In addition, any interactions of class variation with expectancy effects would affect the interpretation of the latter, and need to be investigated whenever they occur. Inspection of all three tables reveals that a significant class effect was obtained for the great majority of the variables. The greatest class variation occurs on the simple frequency columns, especially in Table 1, although class effects still usually reach significance even in the ratio measures related to teacher expectations presented in Table 3. Because of this large variation across classes and the frequent significant interaction of class with expectancy, the nature of the interaction was specifically investigated for each variable to determine the consistency of expectancy effects. This information is integrated into the discussion of expectancy effects below.

Tables 1 and 2 contain the data from variables measuring objective differences among the children or aspects of teacher-child interaction which cannot be unambiguously interpreted as due either to teacher expectation effects or to objective differences among the children. Data from variables which do appear to be independent of differences among the children and, therefore, interpretable as indexes of expectation effects are presented in Table 3.

Measures of the quantity and type of teacher-child contacts are shown in Table 1. Other than the large class differences, the data are most notable for the consistency of expectancy group differences on variables measuring the tendency to seek out the teacher and initiate contact with her. Children for whom the teacher held high expectations (highs) raised their hands more frequently and initiated more procedural and especially more work-related interactions than did children for whom the teachers

held low expectations (lows). . . . The only exception to the pattern of significant differences between highs and lows in child-initiated interactions occurred in the measure of calling out answers in the reading groups. The mean difference is in favor of the highs, but it is not a significant difference and the effect occurred in only one of the four classes. The data for child-initiated contacts may be summarized, then, in the statement that, outside the reading group at least, the highs seek out the teacher and initiate interactions with her more frequently than the lows. The difference is especially notable in work-related interactions: the highs much more frequently show their work to the teacher or ask her questions about it, and they initiate many more response opportunities.

The data for contacts initiated or controlled by the teacher are less clear than for those initiated by the children. The highs were called on more frequently to answer open questions, but the teachers initiated more procedural and work-related interactions with the lows and afforded them slightly more response opportunities. None of

TABLE 1
GROUP DIFFERENCES IN QUANTITY AND TYPE OF CONTACTS WITH TEACHERS

| Variable | Group Ms | | | | | | | | p values for group effects | | | | | | |
| | Class | | | | Sex | | Expectancy | | Class | Sex | Ex-pect-ancy | Class × Sex | Class × Ex-pect-ancy | Sex × Ex-pect-ancy | Class × Sex × Ex-pect-ancy |
	1	2	3	4	Boys	Girls	Lows	Highs							
Number of times child raises hand	.00[a]	4.00	25.75	21.33	12.00	13.54	8.88	16.67	.001	ns	.01	ns	.01	.05	.10
Number of times child is called on to answer a question	.00[a]	.67	4.08	2.58	2.13	1.54	1.71	1.96	.001	ns	ns	ns	ns	.05	ns
Procedural interaction initiated by child	5.00	1.58	7.08	2.92	4.92	3.38	3.17	5.13	.001	.05	.05	.05	ns	ns	.01
Work-related interactions initiated by child	4.17	1.67	9.58	2.92	5.29	3.88	1.79	7.38	.05	ns	.01	ns	.05	ns	ns
Teacher-initiated procedural interactions	4.58	2.75	1.25	.67	2.50	2.13	2.58	2.04	.001	ns	ns	ns	.05	ns	ns
Teacher-initiated work-related interactions	9.83	4.50	4.58	.67	6.42	3.38	6.00	3.79	.001	.05	ns	.05	.05	ns	ns
Teacher-afforded behavioral criticisms	3.25	1.58	5.92	3.17	5.25	1.71	4.92	2.04	.05	.01	.01	ns	ns	.01	ns
Teacher-afforded questions during reading groups	4.50	2.58	3.75	5.33	4.63	3.46	4.79	3.29	ns	ns	.10	ns	.01	ns	ns
Calling out answers during reading groups	8.08	1.58	2.83	.50	3.58	2.92	2.96	3.54	.001	ns	ns	ns	ns	ns	ns
Total teacher-afforded response opportunities	10.33	6.00	12.17	14.00	11.75	9.50	10.96	10.29	.001	.05	ns	ns	ns	ns	ns
Total child-initiated response opportunities	17.25	4.83	19.50	6.33	13.79	10.17	7.92	16.04	.001	ns	.01	ns	.05	ns	ns
Total dyadic contacts	46.17	20.08	45.75	25.67	41.33	27.50	33.67	35.17	.001	.01	ns	ns	ns	ns	ns

[a] There were no open questions in Class 1.

TABLE 2
GROUP DIFFERENCES IN ACADEMIC PERFORMANCE AND TEACHER EVALUATIONS

Variable	Group Ms								p values for group effects						
	Class				Sex		Expectancy		Class	Sex	Expectancy	Class × Sex	Class × Expectancy	Sex × Expectancy	Class × Sex × Expectancy
	1	2	3	4	Boys	Girls	Lows	Highs							
Total correct answers	8.67	4.75	9.33	8.42	9.13	6.46	6.67	8.92	.05	.05	.10	ns	ns	ns	ns
Total part-correct, incorrect, or "don't know" responses	4.33	2.08	3.58	4.00	3.88	3.13	4.63	2.38	ns	ns	.01	ns	ns	ns	ns
Total problems in reading during reading group	16.75	1.46	11.75	6.83	9.38	9.02	13.04	5.35	.001	ns	.001	ns	.05	ns	ns
Average number of reading problems per turn during reading group	3.00	1.38	6.03	3.39	3.83	3.06	4.67	2.23	.01	ns	.01	ns	ns	ns	ns
Total number of times praised by teacher/total dyadic contacts	9.17	7.33	10.00	3.25	7.71	7.17	3.88	11.00	.05	ns	.001	ns	.10	ns	ns
Total number of times criticized by teacher/ total dyadic contacts	16.58	13.42	23.75	16.42	22.88	12.21	24.33	10.75	.10	.001	.001	ns	.05	.05	ns
Criticism/Praise + Criticism	61.92	68.83	63.33	82.38	73.00	65.23	85.04	53.19	ns	ns	.001	ns	ns	ns	ns
Average SAT score (grade level equivalent)	1.79	1.57	1.39	1.73	1.58	1.66	1.42	1.82	.001	ns	.001	ns	ns	ns	ns

these differences reach significance, however. The only significant difference occurred with teacher-afforded behavioral criticisms, which more frequently went to the lows than the highs. This effect showed an important interaction with sex, due to the high frequency of teacher criticisms directed at boys in the low group. . . .

The data regarding interactions initiated or controlled by the teacher may be summarized as follows: there is a tendency for the teachers to initiate more contacts with the lows than with the highs, but the teachers cannot be said to have been compensating for the superiority of the highs in child-initiated contacts because the trend is not completely consistent and because the only significant differences occur with teacher criticisms rather than with work-related contacts or provision of response opportunities. While the data for child-initiated contacts showed strong expectancy group differences, the measures of teacher-initiated interactions were much more closely related to sex than to expectancy. Boys were higher than girls on all measures of teacher-initiated contacts, significantly so for work-related interactions, behavioral criticisms, and total teacher-afforded response opportunities. When teacher-child dyadic contacts of all types are totaled, a clear difference favoring boys is evident; there is no difference between ex-

pectancy groups. Differences between the highs and the lows are in quality rather than quantity of interaction with the teacher.

Group differences in quality of academic performance and in frequencies of teacher praise and criticism are presented in Table 2. Consistent expectancy group differences appear for all the variables in this table. The highs produced more correct answers and fewer incorrect answers than the lows, had fewer problems in the reading groups, and achieved higher average scores on the Stanford Achievement Test given at the end of the year. They also were given more praise and less criticism than the lows by the teachers. The direction of difference follows this pattern in all four classes for every variable in Table 2 except for the total correct answers, where the group means were equal in one class. Thus the Class × Expectancy interactions affected the degree but not the direction of expectation effects.

Sex effects also appeared, with boys producing more correct answers and receiving more criticism than girls. The other, nonsignificant differences in favor of boys are consistent with the finding noted above that boys tend to have more interactions with the teacher than girls.

In summary, the data of Table 2 show that teacher expectancy consistently predicts objective measures of classroom performance, objective achievement test scores, and rates of teacher praise and criticism. Hypotheses about the role of expectation effects in producing these relationships cannot be evaluated from the data in Table 2, however, since the type and direction of causal mechanisms at work remain unknown.

Group differences on variables interpretable as indexes of teacher expectation effects are presented in Table 3. Significant group differences on these measures suggest that the teachers were systematically, although not necessarily deliberately or consciously, treating one group more favorably than the other. The first two measures concern provision of response opportunities to the children, and may be considered in combination with the data previously discussed in Table 1. Since the highs create more response opportunities for themselves than the lows, do the teachers compensate for this by calling on the lows more frequently? The data suggest only a slight tendency in this direction at best.

The one teacher measure which does suggest some compensation concerns the teacher's behavior in calling on children to answer open questions. When the number of times the child is called on is weighted by the number of times he raised his hand to seek a response opportunity, the resulting recognition rates showed a significant difference in favor of the lows. However, this difference seemed more due to the large difference in hand-raising rate between the two groups of children rather than to any systematic compensation efforts by the teachers. . . .

In summary, the data on quantity of contacts in Table 1 and Table 3 are neutral with regard to expectation effects. The highs initiate more work-related contacts and create more response opportunities for themselves than do the lows, but there is no unequivocal evidence to suggest that the teachers are systematically either exaggerating or compensating for these differences among the children.

The data for the last five variables in Table 3

TABLE 3
GROUP DIFFERENCES ON VARIABLES RELATED TO THE COMMUNICATION OF TEACHER EXPECTATIONS

| Variable | Group Ms | | | | | | | | p values for group effects | | | | | | |
| | Class | | | | Sex | | Expectancy | | | | | | Class × Ex-pect-ancy | Sex × Ex-pect-ancy | Class × Sex × Ex-pect-ancy |
	1	2	3	4	Boys	Girls	Lows	Highs	Class	Sex	Ex-pect-ancy	Class × Sex			
Number of direct questions from teacher	.42	2.00	2.25	4.00	2.67	1.67	1.83	2.50	.01	.10	ns	ns	ns	ns	ns
Number of times called on to answer open questions/number of times child raises hand	[a]	.17	.16	.12	.18	.14	.20	.12	ns	ns	.05	ns	ns	ns	ns
Percentage of correct answers followed by teacher praise	6.25	7.17	19.25	3.25	12.83	5.13	5.88	12.08	.01	.01	.05	ns	ns	ns	ns
Percentage of wrong answers followed by teacher criticism	34.08	12.46	2.08	1.83	15.50	9.73	18.77	6.46	.001	ns	.01	.001	.05	ns	ns
Percentage of wrong answers followed by repetition or rephrasing of the question	9.75	18.71	14.79	33.88	23.88	14.69	11.52	27.04	ns	ns	.10	ns	ns	ns	ns
Percentage of reading problems followed by repetition or rephrasing of the question or by giving a clue	75.08	45.75	38.91	44.64	52.10	53.39	38.37	67.05	.05	ns	.01	ns	.01	ns	ns
Percentage of answers (correct or incorrect) not followed by any feedback from the teacher	2.50	8.92	10.58	14.17	8.00	10.08	14.75	3.33	.10	ns	.001	ns	.05	ns	ns

[a] There were no open questions in Class 1.

comprise the major findings of the study, since they provide direct evidence that the teachers' differential expectations for performance were being communicated in their classroom behavior. The measures involved are all concerned with the teachers' reactions to the children's attempts to answer questions and read in the reading group. All are percentage or ratio measures which take into account absolute differences in the frequencies of the various behaviors involved so as to enable a direct comparison to be made between the teachers' behavior toward the two groups when faced with equivalent situations. The data show that the teachers consistently favored the highs over the lows in demanding and reinforcing quality performance. Despite the fact that the highs gave more correct answers and fewer incorrect answers than did the lows, they were more frequently praised when correct and less frequently criticized when incorrect or unable to respond. Furthermore, the teachers were more persistent in eliciting responses from the highs than they were with the lows. When the highs responded incorrectly or were unable to respond, the teachers were more likely to provide a second response opportunity by repeating or rephrasing the question or giving a clue than they were in similar situations with the lows. Conversely, they were more likely to supply the answer or call on another child when reacting to the lows than the highs. This group difference was observed both for difficulties in answering questions and for problems in reading during reading group. Finally, the teachers failed to give any feedback whatever only 3.33% of the time when reacting to highs, while the corresponding figure for lows is 14.75%, a highly significant difference.

. . .

DISCUSSION

The data of Tables 1 and 2, which show objective differences among the children related to their sex and achievement levels, are quite consistent with previous findings. The finding that high-achieving students receive more teacher praise and support (deGroat & Thompson, 1949; Good, 1970; Hoehn, 1954) was confirmed in the present study. Hoehn's suggestion that the differences between high- and low-achieving students in the interaction with their teachers were in quality rather than quantity of interaction is also compatible with present findings. The finding that teachers have more disapproval contacts with boys than girls has also been frequently reported (Meyer & Thompson, 1956; Jackson & Lahaderne, 1966; Lippitt & Gold, 1959). Meyer and Thompson (1956) also reported greater praise toward boys, as was found in the present

study in work-related interactions. Taken together, the findings on sex differences in the present study may be summarized as follows: boys have more interactions with the teacher than girls and appear to be generally more salient in the teacher's perceptual field. Teachers direct more evaluative comments toward boys, both absolutely and relatively. The largest and most obvious absolute differences in evaluative comments occur with teacher criticism and disapproval, which are directed far more frequently at boys. However, much of this difference appears to come in the form of behavioral criticisms and disciplinary contacts rather than criticisms of academic performance in work-related contacts. The difference appears attributable to more frequent disruptive behavior among boys which brings criticism upon themselves rather than to a consistent teacher set or bias toward being more critical toward boys than girls in equivalent situations. The latter statement agrees closely with the conclusion of Davis and Slobodian (1967), who studied teacher provision of response opportunities and evaluation of children's performance in reading groups.

While sex differences are attributable to objective differences in the classroom behavior of the children, the data in Table 3 show that differences related to teacher expectancy are only partly attributable to the children themselves. When the latter differences are statistically controlled through the use of percentage measures, it is seen that the teachers systematically discriminate in favor of the highs over the lows in demanding and reinforcing quality performance. Teachers do, in fact, communicate differential performance expectations to different children through their classroom behavior, and the nature of this differential treatment is such as to encourage the children to begin to respond in ways which would confirm teacher expectancies. In short, the data confirm the hypothesis that teachers' expectations function as self-fulfilling prophecies, and they indicate some of the intervening behavioral mechanisms involved in the process. Despite large differences in the frequencies of the various behaviors observed in the four classrooms, expectancy effects were consistent across the four teachers (two of the teachers favored the highs on four of the last five measures in Table 3, while the other two favored the highs on all five measures).

Although the direction of difference in treatment of highs and lows was constant across teachers, there were observable differences in degree. In particular one teacher stood out as extreme in this regard, while one other showed relatively small differences, even though the direction of difference was constant. It is of interest that the latter teacher who showed the least discrimination between highs and lows was the teacher who did not group the children by achievement in her classroom seating pattern. It is also worthy of note that although the teachers' expectations were highly related to the children's achievement test scores within classes, the achievement scores are not so closely related to the previous readiness and achievement data which were used as the basis of tracking into classrooms. That is, the class achievement of some classes was higher than expected, while that of others was lower. While not enough classes were included to allow a statistical test, the data suggest that the achievement levels of the classes were related to the teachers' performance demands and expectations.

While this research has demonstrated the applicability of classroom interaction analysis methods to the study of the communication of teacher expectations and has yielded data which are consistent and interpretable as far as they go, it dealt with only a few of the events intervening between the formation of teacher expectations and the initiation of reciprocal behavior by the children. Several related studies are needed to complete the picture. . . . Can teachers be made aware of their discriminatory classroom behavior? Can they learn to compensate, not only for their own differential expectations but also for objective differences in the classroom behavior of the children? Will experimentally induced expectations produce the same differences in classroom behavior as expectations formed "naturally" by the teachers themselves? These and related questions will be taken up in future research.

Additional indexes of the ways in which teachers discriminate in their classroom behavior are also needed to add to our understanding of the processes involved and to increase the effectiveness of teacher education and classroom intervention in preventing or reducing the problem. Anecdotal observations taken during the present research suggest that other useful indexes of teacher communication of differential performance expectations may be possible. Possibilities being presently explored include differences in the type of feedback given to the children (inquiry into the processes underlying the response product rather than simple negation or provision of the right answer) and differential enforcement of teaching expectations (discouraging initiative in some children by doing things for them while requiring other children to do the same things themselves). Teachers are frequently unaware of the subtle differences in their behavior in such situations, yet it is in such situations that teachers systematically communicate differential expectations to different students. Although subtle, such teacher behavior is observable and measurable, and therefore at least potentially subject to modification and control.

REFERENCES

BARBER, T. X., & SILVER, M. J. Fact, fiction, and the experimenter bias effect. *Psychological Bulletin Monograph,* 1968, *70* (6, Pt. 2).

DAVIS, O. L., JR., & SLOBODIAN, J. J. Teacher behavior toward boys and girls during first grade reading instruction. *American Educational Research Journal,* 1967, *4,* 261–269.

DEGROAT, A. F., & THOMPSON, G. G. A study of the distribution of teacher approval and disapproval among sixth grade pupils. *Journal of Experimental Education,* 1949, *18,* 57–75.

GOOD, T. L. Which pupils do teachers call on? *Elementary School Journal,* 1970, 70, 190–198.

GOOD, T. L., & BROPHY, J. Analyzing classroom interaction: A more powerful alternative. *Educational Technology,* 1971, in press.

HOEHN, A. J. A study of social status differentiation in the classroom behavior of nineteen third-grade teachers. *Journal of Social Psychology,* 1954, *39,* 269–292.

JACKSON, P. W., & LAHADERNE, H. M. Inequalities of teacher-pupil contacts. Expanded version of a paper delivered at the meeting of the American Psychological Association, New York City, September 1966.

LIPPITT, R., & GOLD, M. Classroom social structure as a mental health problem. *Journal of Social Issues,* 1959, *15,* 40–49.

MEYER, W. J., & THOMPSON, G. G. Sex differences in the distribution of teacher approval and disapproval among sixth-grade children. *Journal of Educational Psychology,* 1956, *47,* 385–396.

ROSENTHAL, R., & JACOBSON, L. *Pygmalion in the classroom: Teacher expectation and pupils' intellectual development.* New York: Holt, Rinehart & Winston, 1968.

SNOW, R. E. Unfinished pygmalion. *Contemporary Psychology,* 1969, *14,* 197–199.

THORNDIKE, R. L. Review of R. Rosenthal and L. Jacobson, "Pygmalion in the classroom." *American Educational Research Journal,* 1968, *5,* 708–711.

83

Teachers' Ratings of Student Personality Traits as They Relate to IQ and Social Desirability [1]

JAMES W. BARNARD,
PHILIP G. ZIMBARDO,
AND SEYMOUR B. SARASON

Teachers are expected to be able to evaluate their pupils in terms of personality traits as well as academic abilities, and these assessments often weigh heavily in educational decision making. How good are teachers at this task?

This article indicates that elementary school teachers' ratings on a wide variety of personality characteristics are related to IQ: desirable characteristics are more frequently attributed to the high-IQ child. The authors suggest that these evaluations may to some extent reflect the teachers' own biases.

James W. Barnard is a member of the faculty at George Peabody College; Philip G. Zimbardo is professor of psychology at Stanford University; and Seymour B. Sarason is professor of psychology at Yale University.

In most educational systems it is expected that a teacher be aware of psychological differences that exist among his students. In some instances the process of evaluation of nonacademic behavioral traits has grown to the point where the modern elementary school teacher must be as attentive to a student's entire personality development as he is to his intellectual growth. Thus, a student's permanent school record now often contains teachers' assessments which, when dressed in the psychologist's jargon, appear under such headings as "extent of peer group dependence," "control of aggression," "introversion," "anxiety," and so forth. These assessments are used not only in predicting a student's performance within the elementary school setting, but as part of his permanent record play an important role even in the screening of applicants for high school and college awards and fellowships, as well as for admission to graduate and professional schools.

Moreover, it should be recognized that the formal categorization of student personality traits by teachers can exert not only a controlling influence on how that particular teacher then perceives, organizes, and interprets later behavior, but as part of the student's record, it may also establish the frames of reference through which subsequent teachers view the student. The question of how well teachers can perform such an evaluative function is obviously of first-rate importance.

The present study represents an attempt to investigate the ability of elementary school teachers to discriminate among their students on relevant and important personality variables. Further, an attempt was made to investigate the relationship between teachers' ratings of their students on these personality variables and the students' IQ test scores.

METHOD

SUBJECT SELECTION

All of the second- and third-grade school children of Hamden, Connecticut, were administered the Test Anxiety Scale for Children (TASC) and the Lorge-Thorndike intelligence test as a part of a longitudinal study being carried out at Yale University (Sarason, Hill, & Zimbardo, 1965). From this population, those children scoring in the upper and lower fifteenth percentile of the anxiety distribution ($N = 320$) were selected to form the high-anxiety (HA) and low-anxiety (LA) groups, respectively. Within each of these groups subjects (Ss) were matched on IQ score as closely as possible in order to obtain subgroups of relatively high IQ (HIQ) and low IQ (LIQ). The effectiveness of this matching is evident from the group mean IQ of 115 for the HA–HIQ group and 116 for the LA–HIQ, as well as from the means of 99 for the HA–LIQ and 97 for the LA–LIQ groups. A total of 96 Ss were thus finally chosen, 24 in each of these four experimental groups.

[1] This study was financed by a grant to Yale University (Seymour B. Sarason, principal investigator) from the National Institute of Mental Health.

TEACHERS' RATINGS

These 96 students were rated by their classroom teachers ($N = 54$) on 24 personality and school performance characteristics. These characteristics were presented in pairs of contrasting trait names, along with a working definition of each of the terms in the pair. Each teacher had to decide first which of the two terms most accurately described the child, then she had to determine by use of a 5-point scale the degree to which the child approached the extreme description given for that trait. Each teacher was given a chance to discuss this rating task with an experimenter to insure that she understood what was being asked of her. After this discussion, each teacher worked on the task privately on her own time. The complete list of traits is given in Table 1.

The obtained ratings were then summed across Ss within each group for each of the 24 traits separately, and then subjected to simple between-Ss analyses of variance with test anxiety level and IQ group as main effects.

DESIRABILITY OF TRAIT SCORING

A second group of judges was used to provide additional information about the social desirability of each of the traits used in the teacher rating schedule. These data were necessary to test an hypothesis which emerged after preliminary analysis of the ratings. Fifteen teachers in the Yale Master of Arts in Teaching program (M.A.T.), all of whom had some teaching experience, were asked to judge how desirable it was for an elementary school child to exhibit each one of the bipolar traits which defined the 24 trait dimensions.

These judgments were made on 10-point scales and were computed in such a way that high scores for a given item would indicate agreement among the judges as to its desirability, while low scores would indicate disagreement or lack of clarity about the desirableness of that item. The items were presented to the judges using the same format as was used in the presentation to the teachers when they rated their own students.

The relationship between how conceptually clear the desirability of a trait was and how well it discriminated on the teacher ratings between IQ groups was established by means of correlation. The correlation coefficient obtained was between the mean desirability score of a trait as determined by the M.A.T. judges, and the difference in the total teacher rating score between high- and low-IQ groups on that trait. Thus, a high positive correlation would indicate that the better a trait differentiated between high- and low-IQ Ss, the greater the agreement among judges as to its desirability.

TABLE 1

TEACHERS' RATING SCALE OF STUDENT CHARACTERISTICS

Trait No.

1. Anxious: Unanxious
2. (Dependent: Independent)
3. Shows or expresses emotions: Hides or suppresses emotions
4. (Communicates easily: Difficulty communicating)
5. Aggressive: Submissive
6. Impulsive: Cautious
7. Sensitive: Not sensitive
8. Tense: Relaxed
9. (Ambitious: Unambitious)
10. (Adapts to changes: Set in ways)
11. (Well-liked: not well-liked)
12. (Mature psychologically or emotionally: Immature psychologically or emotionally)
13. Withdraws: Sociable
14. Daydreams: Does not daydream
15. Active: Inactive
16. Overachievers: Underachievers
17. (Learns slowly (new material): Learns quickly (new material))
18. (Retains material: Forgets material)
19. Fears failure: Does not fear failure
20. (Pays attention: Does not pay attention)
21. (Strong conscience: Weak conscience)
22. (Feminine: Masculine)
23. (Pessimistic: Optimistic)
24. (Responsible: Not responsible)

Note.—Trait numbers in parentheses have highest agreement as to the desirability of that trait, while those not in parentheses have least agreement, and thus are least clearly positive or negative.

RESULTS

The teachers did not differentiate in their ratings between LA and HA children on any of the 24 traits. The nonsignificant differences between anxiety groups can be seen from the F values presented in Table 2.

On the other hand, it is obvious from the rest of the evidence presented in this table that the teachers did discriminate on the basis of IQ. On 14 of 24 traits, students with high IQ were characterized differently from those with low IQ at beyond the .05 level of confidence. Over the combined teacher ratings the difference between HIQ and LIQ Ss was highly significant ($F = 20.03$, $p < .001$).

Although none of the second-order effects was significant, nevertheless, in most instances the differences in teacher ratings between Ss of the two IQ groups were greater among HA Ss than among LA ones. Thus, LA children tended to be rated more similarly, whether their IQ was high or low, than were HA children. To substantiate this observation, a difference score for each trait was generated by subtracting the scores of the high-IQ Ss from the low-IQ Ss within each of the anxiety groups. The analysis of these difference scores, using a t test with nonindependent observations, demonstrated that difference scores on these 24 traits between IQ subgroups within the HA group were significantly greater than those difference

TABLE 2
F-VALUES OF ANXIETY AND IQ SOURCES OF
VARIANCE FOR EACH TRAIT

Trait	Anxiety	IQ
1	.84	1.30
2	.07	16.39**
3	.00	1.98
4	.43	.77
5	1.00	5.70*
6	3.25	2.97
7	1.29	6.34*
8	.21	.75
9	.25	10.97**
10	.98	2.43
11	.23	4.87*
12	.49	7.86**
13	1.83	12.28**
14	.03	4.74*
15	.73	8.20**
16	2.12	5.43*
17	.07	28.38**
18	.03	13.84**
19	.01	1.73
20	.67	7.20**
21	2.27	2.79
22	.08	.45
23	.37	3.36
24	.01	7.34**

Note.—Trait numbers correspond to traits listed in Table 1.
* $p < .05$.
** $p < .01$.

scores of the IQ subgroups within the LA group ($t = 2.45$, $p < .05$).

A further examination of the data revealed that there were marked differences in how well various traits differentiated high- from low-IQ Ss. It appeared that those items that showed the largest differences in scores between the two IQ groups were the items that were most clearly desirable traits for an elementary school child to have. Apparently, then, this inconsistency in the ability of items to differentiate between high and low Ss was related to a tendency on the part of the teachers to assign more favorable ratings to high-IQ Ss to the extent that it was clear to them what a favorable rating would be. To investigate this notion a correlation was computed between IQ group differences on each trait and the desirability score of that trait as judged by the M.A.T. teachers.

The traits in parentheses in Table 1 are those that demonstrated the highest clarity of desirability (i.e., above the median), while for the others there was a lack of agreement among judges as to whether one of the bipolar traits was desirable and the other one undesirable for a child to exhibit in school. The product-moment correlation between item discriminability and desirability was .60 ($p < .01$).

DISCUSSION

The results of this study can be interpreted in such a way as to cast some doubt on the validity of ratings by elementary school teachers of student personality traits. The present teachers were unable to distinguish reliably between students who were extremely different, by their own self report, in test anxiety, on traits that have been found in past research to be related to the variable of test anxiety. Although other interpretations are possible, these data are consistent with the earlier conclusion drawn from the research of Sarason.

In none of our studies using teachers' ratings of anxiety in relation to a test performance or a child's self-report criterion is there evidence that teachers can recognize the anxious child to a degree which would be of practical significance [Sarason, Davidson, Lighthall, Waite, & Ruebush, 1960, p. 265].

It does appear from our data, however, that teachers are sensitive to differences in IQ level. This sensitivity is reflected in their differential rating of children with high- and low-IQ scores on a wide variety of academic and personality traits. The child with a high IQ tends to be perceived, relative to a child with a low IQ, as one who learns quickly, pays attention, retains material, overachieves, and is ambitious. Such traits are the obvious correlates of high IQ for the adequately motivated student. However, even on traits which bear little correspondence to academic performance and intellectual functioning, teachers discriminate between children of different intelligence levels. The bright child tends to be seen by the teachers as being less dependent and daydreamy and more aggressive, while at the same time being more sensitive, mature, sociable, popular, and active.

The issue which becomes immediately apparent is whether these evaluations are reflecting actually occurring behavioral differences, or whether they are distortions of social reality. Without an independent criterion analysis of each of these traits, there cannot be an unequivocal answer to such a problem. However, several lines of converging evidence lead us to believe that a major source of variance in these ratings is accounted for by teacher bias in perception as a consequence of overly positive evaluations of bright children. First, it was demonstrated that these teachers distinguished most clearly between IQ levels on those traits which could be most easily categorized as desirable or undesirable for a child to possess or exhibit in school. Second, it was learned (after completion of our data collection) that all teachers in the sample had access to, and were familiar with, information pertaining to the results of the IQ and achievement testing which were routinely conducted in this school system. Finally, a biasing in terms of a halo effect appears to be a tenable explanation for this data, since teachers evaluated anxious children who were bright differently from anxious children who were not, and did so on traits shown by previous research *not* to be characteristic of the bright, anxious child. Thus, for example, while these teachers characterized the bright, anxious child with the desirable traits of "independence" and "adaptability," it has been demonstrated that the bright but anxious child is extremely dependent upon task and instruction factors as well as upon the approval of authority figures, all of which inhibit spontaneity, independence, personal expression, and flexibility in school settings (Sarason et al., 1960).

It is also interesting to note that teachers do not consistently differentiate in their ratings of the bright and the nonbright children when these students have low levels of test anxiety. In some way then, the bright, anxious child is perceived as special and possessing traits of which teachers approve. In short, teachers are most positive about such children.

It is likely, however, that this favorable attitude is engendered in large part by the child's dependent need for approval by the teacher and by his attempts to secure it. By not recognizing that such a child is frequently experiencing anxiety in relation to school and the resultant evaluation of his abilities (the definition implicit in the test anxiety construct), teachers are unable to provide the help necessary to improve the child's self-conception, and in fact may even reinforce these test anxiety attitudes. In turn, these attitudes may generalize to influence many kinds of behavior (e.g., speech, as shown by Zimbardo, Barnard, & Berkowitz, 1963) and become the core of an enduring per-

sonality syndrome. Such a pattern of attitudes may cause many of the bright but anxious students who do get into college to lower their levels of aspiration, and become satisfied with minimal standards of learning which do not require utilization of their full intellectual and creative capacity (Mandler & Sarason, 1952).

The results of this study are consistent with a recent plea for teacher training in the knowledge and use of psychological variables, as well as in detection of subtle stimulus cues necessary for the understanding, modification, and control of behavior (Sarason, Davidson, & Blatt, 1962). The questions raised for future research are the extent to which knowledge of a child's IQ or anxiety level influences the overt classroom behavior of teachers in their handling of their students, and to what extent is this recognition perceived and reacted to by the students.

REFERENCES

MANDLER, G., & SARASON, S. B. A study of anxiety and learning. *Journal of Abnormal and Social Psychology,* 1952, *47,* 166–173.

SARASON, S. B., DAVIDSON, K. S., LIGHTHALL, F. F., WAITE, R. R., & RUEBUSH, B. K. *Anxiety in elementary school children.* New York: Wiley, 1960.

SARASON, S. B., DAVIDSON, K. S., & BLATT, B. *The preparation of teachers.* New York: Wiley, 1962.

SARASON, S. B., HILL, K., & ZIMBARDO, P. G. A longitudinal study of the relation of test anxiety to performance on intelligence and achievement tests. *Monographs of the Society for Research in Child Development,* 1965, *29*(7, Whole No. 98).

ZIMBARDO, P. G., BARNARD, J. W., & BERKOWITZ, L. The role of anxiety and defensiveness in children's verbal behavior. *Journal of Personality,* 1963, *31,* 79–96.

84

Teachers' Attitudes Toward Children's Behavior Revisited

Alexander Tolor,
William L. Scarpetti,
and Paul A. Lane

How sensitive are teachers to the behavior problems of their pupils? Wickman's classic study in 1928 indicated an enormous difference between the views of teachers and clinicians. In 1959, Harry Beilin updated that study and found that there had been some rapprochement between the two groups. Beilin's article, "Teachers' and Clinicians' Attitudes Toward Behavior Problems of Children: A Reappraisal," was published in Child Development, *volume 30, pages 9–25, and was reprinted in the second edition of* The Causes of Behavior. *The following article is a very recent study on the topic. It points out that while the gap has closed to some extent, there are still large differences between teachers and clinicians. It examines the reasons for the discrepancy. Alexander Tolor is associate professor of psychology and director of the Institute of Human Development at Fairfield University; William L. Scarpetti is in the Division of Psychology, Northwestern University Medical School; and Paul A. Lane is associate professor of psychology at the University of Bridgeport.*

A classic study by E. K. Wickman (1928) found a great discrepancy between the views of teachers and mental health workers toward the behavior problems of children. Although this study has been criticized on methodological grounds, its influence on American education has been profound. Several more recent investigations (Griffiths, 1952; Schrupp & Gjerde, 1953; Stouffer, 1952) suggest that while there has been considerable change in the attitudes of teachers to make them more congruent with those of clinicians, marked differences between the two groups continue to exist. These differences are still in the direction of teachers being more concerned with management, sexual adjustment, and adherence to authority problems whereas the mental health professionals are more sensitive to withdrawal behavior and behavior not directly related to the school routine but suggesting a deterioration of social or emotional patterns.

The purpose of this study was to explore further the relationship between the evaluations by teachers and psychologists of a wide range of child behavior patterns. More specifically, it was anticipated that by employing a comprehensive scale of unambiguous behavioral items, which can be grouped on an empirical or theoretical basis to focus on patterns of functioning, it would be possible to identify the types of behavioral patterns that teachers and psychologists perceive most differently. The effect that the teachers' experience level has on the ratings was also to be determined.

Method

The teacher respondents consisted of 90 female and 28 male elementary public school teachers randomly selected from a large urban school system. They were drawn from all grades ranging from the kindergarten to the seventh grade level, inclusively. There were 9 teachers at the kindergarten level, 13 at Grade 1, 16 at Grade 2, 15 at Grade 3, 17 at Grade 4, 16 at Grade 5, 15 at Grade 6, and 17 at Grade 7. The professional experience of the teachers encompassed the range of less than 1 year to 44 years (mean 11.9 years).

The psychologist respondents consisted of 17 males and 6 females, all of whom were functioning in clinical settings in the same state as the teachers. The highest degree held by the psychologists was the Ph.D. for 15 and the M.A. or M.S. by eight. In experience the psychologists ranged from under one year to over 30 years (mean 10.7 years).

The measuring device was the Staten Island Behavior Scale (Mandell & Silberstein, 1965) which consists of 295 items descriptive of children's behavior. The items were originally selected from published and unpublished scales used to evaluate children's adjustment and from an analysis of a large number of case records in the files of a child guidance clinic.

The items were classified for the purposes of the present study by six raters (5 advanced students and 1

Alexander Tolor, William L. Scarpetti, and Paul A. Lane, "Teachers' attitudes toward children's behavior revisited," *Journal of Educational Psychology, 58,* 1967, 175–180. Copyright 1967 by the American Psychological Association, and reproduced by permission.

Diplomate in Clinical Psychology), making independent judgments, into the following classifications: psychosomatic and physical disturbance (71 items); phobias (18 items); aggressiveness (56 items); affect expression (58 items); communication disturbance (21 items); regressive behavior (15 items); inefficiency indicators (25 items); and fantasy involvement or withdrawal (31 items).

Each item was placed into the category that represented the rating of the majority of the judges. An indication of the high degree of interrater agreement is provided by the fact that on 203 of the 295 items (69%) at least five of the raters were in complete agreement in regard to the classification of an item.

Illustrations of the different types of items are the following: For the psychosomatic and physical disturbance classification—"Is slow in his movements"; for the phobic classification—"Is afraid of being alone in a wide open space"; for aggressiveness—"Hits or attacks other child"; for affect expression—"Shows inappropriate feeling"; for communication disturbance—"Talks and talks"; for regressive behavior—"Carries blanket"; for inefficiency indicators—"Does not complete his chores"; and for fantasy involvement or withdrawal—"Doesn't join in competitive games."

The written instructions accompanying the administration of the scale are presented below:

> For each of the following items please indicate whether the behavior in question, in your opinion, indicates normal or abnormal behavior in a child falling in the age range from 1 to 16 inclusive.
>
> Please answer all items without omitting any, and try to check either the "Normal" or "Abnormal" category. In the event that you really cannot decide whether the behavior is normal or abnormal, you may check the "Unknown" line. However, you will probably be able to arrive at a definite decision in all or nearly all instances.

The respondents were not given any time limit, but were cautioned against collaborating with anyone else in completing the scale.

The very broad age range was quite deliberately employed in the instructions since our intent was not so much to obtain reactions to a child's behavior at a specific point in time—even though we recognized that the appropriateness of behavior is age related—but more to distill from a less structured frame of reference behavior patterns that most frequently tend to be regarded as being normal or abnormal, even in the absence of a specific anchoring point.

RESULTS AND DISCUSSION

The main findings indicated that teachers and psychologists, when their responses for each item on the questionnaire are compared by chi-square, differ significantly ($p < .05$) on 66 of the 295 items, that is, on 22.4% of the items, in regard to whether they rated the behavior to be normal or abnormal. This number of differentiating items is significantly greater than would be expected on a chance basis alone. Of the 66 critical descriptions of behavior, 7, or 11%, are in the psychosomatic and physical disturbance category, 1, or 2%, in the phobias category, 21, or 32%, in the aggressiveness category, 19, or 29%, in the affect expression category, 3, or 5%, in the communication disturbance category, 6, or 9%, in the regressive behavior category, 3, or 5%, in the inefficiency indicators category, and 6, or 9%, in the fantasy involvement or withdrawal category.

Since the categories consisted originally of unequal numbers of scale items, the percentages reported above may be somewhat misleading. Another way of analyzing the same data is to determine the proportion of items within each category that differentiates the teachers' judgments from the psychologists' ratings. Employing this approach, we note from Table 1 that the greatest disagreement occurs in the areas of regressive behavior, aggressiveness, and affect expression. Next in order are fantasy involvement or withdrawal, communication disturbance, and inefficiency indicators in which areas the two groups are in relatively close agreement. In regard to phobias and psychosomatic and physical disturbance, the judgments of psychologists and teachers are very much in accord, as can be seen by the negligible item disagreement.

These results indicate, therefore, that elementary school teachers in general tend to evaluate behavior that may be described as regressive, aggressive, and emotional quite differently than do psychologists. In view of the fact that nearly all of the differentiating items, that is, 61 of 66, or 92.4%, were rated predominantly normal by psychologists and abnormal by teachers, it is obvious that elementary school teachers perceive regressive, aggressive, and emotional behavior to be considerably more pathological than do mental health professionals.

Two subgroups of teachers were selected based on amounts of teaching experience. The Highs consisted of the top third in experience of the over-

TABLE 1

DEGREE OF DISAGREEMENT BETWEEN TEACHERS AND PSYCHOLOGISTS IN SPECIFIC SCALE CATEGORIES

Category	Items in scale	Percentage of items disagreed upon
Physical-psychosomatic	71	10
Phobic	18	6
Aggressive	56	38
Affect	58	33
Communication	21	14
Regressive	15	40
Inefficiency	25	12
Fantasy-withdrawal	31	19

all group of teachers. The Lows consisted of the lowest third in teaching experience. The 39 teachers in the High subgroup ranged in professional experience from 14 to 44 years with a median of 24.5 years; the 39 teachers in the Low subgroup ranged in experience from less than 1 year to 6 years with a median of 3 years.

When the attitudes toward child behavior of the Lows are compared with those of the psychologists, 83 items were rated significantly differently by the two groups. Eighty of the 83 items, or 96%, were rated normal more often by psychologists than by teachers with relatively little experience. There was disagreement primarily in regard to the significance of aggressive behavior (57% of the items in that category were rated differently), regressive behavior (33% of the items here were differently rated), and affect expressions (31% of the items were judged differently). There was no difference in the ratings of the 18 phobic items, and relatively little disparity in judgments for inefficient behavior (16%) and fantasy-withdrawal behavior (16%). Communication problems and physical-psychosomatic disturbances produced only moderate disagreements (19% and 21%).

A similar chi-square analysis was done comparing the attitudes of teachers high in experience with psychologists on each of the scale items. In this comparison only 45 behavioral descriptions significantly differentiated the groups. Moreover, the patterns of disagreements between highly experienced teachers and psychologists, on the one hand, and less experienced teachers and psychologists, on the other hand, is very different. For one thing, the more experienced teachers did not nearly as often differ from psychologists in the direction of ascribing abnormality to a description of child behavior as did the less experienced teachers. As a matter of fact, the differences between the more experienced teachers and psychologists were likely to be as often in the direction of teachers considering the behavior to be benign when psychologists regarded it as being pathological as it was to be considered pathological when the psychologists rated it as being normal. (Only 52% of the differentiating items were rated normal by psychologists more often than by highly experienced teachers.) Second, the area in which the differences become manifest for the highly experienced teachers is very different from the Lows. More specifically, the Highs do not differ from the psychologists particularly in regard to aggressive, regressive, and affect behavior as do the Lows. The least disparity (0%), as a matter of fact, occurs in relation to regressive behavior; the greatest discrepancy (28% of the items in the category), occurs with the ratings of phobic behavior.

Finally, chi-square analyses of the item ratings

for teachers high and teachers low in experience yielded the largest degree of discrepancy of all comparisons. Ninety-six, or 32.5% of the total number of behavioral descriptions, were rated significantly differently by these two subgroups. Interestingly, all 96 critical items were perceived to be normal more often by the highly experienced teachers as compared with the less experienced teachers.

Table 2 presents the percentage of items within each of the scale categories rated differently by highly experienced and relatively inexperienced teaching personnel. It will be noted that phobic behavior tends most often to be viewed differently by teachers of varying degrees of experience, and that there is considerable disagreement about behavior involving communication facility and efficiency.

Illustrative of the specific differences in ratings between the more experienced and the relatively less experienced teachers are the following items, all of which were regarded to be normal by the more experienced teachers and abnormal by the less experienced teachers:

> Cries or whimpers
> Plays with or fingers his mouth
> Headache
> At the slightest upset, coordination becomes poor
> Is frightened in crowds
> Is afraid of being alone in a wide open space
> Child's thoughts are hard to understand
> Lying

Lewis (1965), in reviewing the literature bearing on the "Continuity hypothesis," which states that ". . . emotional disturbance in a child is symptomatic of a continuing psychological process that may lead to adult mental illness [p. 465]," concluded that the acting-out child is more likely to become seriously disturbed as an adult than the

TABLE 2

DEGREE OF DISAGREEMENT BETWEEN HIGHLY EXPERIENCED AND RELATIVELY INEXPERIENCED TEACHERS IN SPECIFIC SCALE CATEGORIES

Category	Items in scale	Percentage of items disagreed upon
Physical-psychosomatic	71	28
Phobic	18	67
Aggressive	56	32
Affect	58	28
Communication	21	48
Regressive	15	13
Inefficiency	25	40
Fantasy-withdrawal	31	26

timid, withdrawn child. He suggested that perhaps the judgments of teachers, as derived from the Wickman (1928) study, represented a more accurate appraisal of the pathology of children than the evaluations of clinicians, at least when adult psychiatric status is taken as the criterion. Irregardless of the validity of the perceptions of each of these groups, the study of the nature of the attitudes remains an important research problem since attitudes will influence markedly the interactions between the child and his teachers.

Beilin (1959) pointed out cogently that the attitudinal patterns of teachers and clinicians toward adjustment difficulties reflect in part their different roles, and that their roles, in turn, "influence the organization of their respective experiences [p. 22]." Since Beilin regards teachers to be essentially task-oriented, that is, concerned with the imparting of information and skills, and since mental health professionals are more concerned with preventing poor adjustment and promoting good adjustment, it is not surprising that these two groups will continue to perceive child behavior differently.

The present findings suggest that psychologists tend to be more accepting, or at least more tolerant, of a greater variety of child behavior than teachers, and tend to regard a wider range of behavior as being normal. Teachers, especially those who are relatively inexperienced, label much more behavior as being abnormal. Teachers are especially critical of categories of behavior that may be referred to as aggressive, regressive, and emotionally expressive. The fact that the greatest degree of disagreement is found between experienced and inexperienced teachers reinforces the impression that actual exposure to child behavior is an important determinant of attitudes toward pathology.

The present study also bears on the frequently voiced criticism of clinicians as being overly sensitive to the pathological aspects of others and not sufficiently sensitive to their assets. The findings indicate that this criticism is probably unjustified since the clinicians were in fact much less prone to interpret behavior as being abnormal than the teachers.

Brief reference should be made to several methodological limitations. First, a number of teachers and psychologists who were given the Staten Island Scale either did not complete the form or failed to follow instructions and had to be eliminated for that reason. Thus, of the original sample of 145 teachers, only 118 could be employed for the analysis. Whether the respondents who cooperated differ in any essential respect from those who did not is not known. Second, although some precautions were taken against the

respondents being influenced by others in making their ratings, the possibility still remains that some judgments were not made entirely independently.

Perhaps a more important problem is related to the ambiguous instructions provided the subjects. Many respondents found the task to be extremely difficult. A number took great pains to comment that since what is considered normal and abnormal is so closely related to the age level of the child, they could not arrive at a decision. Moreover, some stated that since the degree, severity, frequency, nature of onset, duration, and circumstances surrounding the appearance of the symptom remained unspecified, their confidence level in arriving at a decision was extremely low. Nevertheless, it should be noted that since both the professionals and the teachers were faced with the same need to impose structure on the scale items, there is little likelihood that the ratings reflect systematic response biases that differ for the two groups.

It is suggested that the question of whether anchoring the concept of normality versus abnormality to specific age levels affects the ratings of groups of experts and teachers merits further research attention. Also, it might be possible to investigate the effect of increased structure in the description of each item, in terms of such characteristics as frequency of the symptom, on the judgments. Other extensions of this project would concern themselves with the variance contributed to teacher ratings of such variables as their age, teaching competence, and socioeconomic status.

References

BEILIN, H. Teachers' and clinicians' attitudes toward the behavior problems of children: A reappraisal. *Child Development*, 1959, *30*, 9–25.

GRIFFITHS, W. *Behavioral difficulties of children as perceived and judged by parents, teachers and children themselves.* Minneapolis: University of Minnesota Press, 1952.

LEWIS, W. W. Continuity and intervention in emotional disturbance: A review. *Exceptional Children*, 1965, *31*, 465–475.

MANDELL, W., & SILBERSTEIN, R. M. Children's psychopathology behavior rating scale. Paper presented at the meeting of the Eastern Psychological Association, Atlantic City, April 1965.

SCHRUPP, M. H., & GJERDE, C. M. Teacher growth in attitudes toward behavior problems of children. *Journal of Educational Psychology*, 1953, *44*, 203–214.

STOUFFER, G. A. W., JR. Behavior problems of children as viewed by teachers and mental hygienists. *Mental Hygiene*, 1952, *36*, 271–285.

WICKMAN, E. K. *Children's behavior and teachers' attitudes.* New York: Commonwealth Fund, 1928.

85

Reach, Touch, and Teach

Terry Borton

Curriculum projects in the post-Sputnik years stressed cognitive development. The new math, for example, introduced elementary school pupils to mathematical concepts previously taught to high school and college students. While these curriculum projects in subject-matter fields are continuing, a different type of curriculum reform has sprung up. Schools are beginning to educate students about their feelings, their values, and their own psychological growth. Terry Borton, director of the Affective Education Research Project in the Philadelphia public schools, has written an excellent report of this new trend.

There are two sections to almost every school's statement of educational objectives—one for real, and one for show. The first, the real one, talks about academic excellence, subject mastery, and getting into college or a job. The other discusses the human purpose of school—values, feelings, personal growth, the full and happy life. It is included because everyone knows that it is important, and that it ought to be central to the life of every school. But it is only for show. Everyone knows how little schools have done about it.

In spite of this, the human objectives describe the things all of us cite when we try to remember what "made a difference" in our school careers:

the teacher who touched us as persons, or the one who ground out our lives to polish our intellects; the class that moved with the strength and grace of an Olympic team, or the dozens of lessons when each of us slogged separately toward the freedom of 3 o'clock. What we learned, and what we became, depended to a significant degree on how we felt about ourselves, our classmates, and our teachers. The schools were right—the human purposes *were* important. But with the exception of those teachers who were so rare we never forgot them, the schools did little to put their philosophy into practice.

Recently, however, a variety of programs have begun to build curricula and teaching methodology that speak directly to the human objectives. These programs, stemming both from within the schools and from various branches of psychology, point the way to a school practice which not only recognizes the power of feelings, but also combines academic training with an education directly aimed at the student's most important concerns. Schools may soon be explicitly teaching students such things as how to sort out and guide their own psychological growth, or increase their desire to achieve, or handle their aggressive instincts in nonviolent forms.

The new impetus has a variety of names: "psychological education," "affective," "humanistic," "personological," "eupsychian," "synoetic." Some of these names are a bit bizarre, and none has yet gained wide acceptance. But taken together their presence indicates a growing recognition that in the world's present state of social and moral turmoil, the schools' traditional second objective can no longer be for show. Riots, poverty, war, student rebellion, swollen mental hospitals, and soaring crime rates have involved an enormous number of people. They have generated a broadening conviction that society is as responsible for the psychological well-being of each of its members as is each individual. And that conviction has created a receptive audience for new kinds of educational critics.

The new critics do not simply attack the schools for their academic incompetence, as did the Rickovers of a decade ago. They are equally concerned with the schools' basic lack of understanding that students are human beings with feelings as well as intellects. Jonathan Kozol has given a gripping sense of the "destruction of the hearts and minds of Negro children" in his *Death at an Early Age*. In *How Children Fail* John Holt has shown that even in the best "progressive" schools, children live in constant fear which inhibits their learning, and Paul

Goodman's *Compulsory Mis-Education* has made a powerful case for his contention that "the present school system is leading straight to 1984." The intuitive warnings of these "romantic critics" have been backed up by statistical evidence from the largest survey of education ever conducted, James Coleman's *Equality of Educational Opportunity*. This survey correlates academic achievement with attitudes such as a student's self concept, sense of control over his fate, and interest in school. The study concludes that these attitudes and feelings are more highly correlated with how well a student achieves academically than a combination of many of the factors which educators have usually thought were crucial, such as class size, salary of teachers, facilities, curriculum.

The pressure to deal more directly with student feelings (increasingly a pressure from students as well as critics) has given rise to dozens of different projects. None of the three examples which I will discuss here has yet reached the size or influence of the giant curriculum centers (such as the Educational Development Corporation) which grew up as a result of the post-Sputnik criticism. But in the long run they may be much more important. For the post-Sputnik curriculum reforms were essentially attempts to find better ways to teach the traditional disciplines of math, science, or social studies—often with the effect of moving the college curriculum into elementary and secondary schools. The programs I am describing not only operate with different techniques, but also begin to define and develop new curriculum subjects and a new school orientation toward practical and applied psychology. If expanded, they will make a profound change in American education—hopefully a change toward a more humane educational process, and a more human student.

The project which I co-directed with Norman Newberg, the Philadelphia School Board's specialist in "affective education," is an example of such a curriculum. It is being developed from within the schools—in this case by a group of urban teachers trying to find a philosophy and method which would work with the students they were asked to teach. The program is based on the assumption that every person handles massive amounts of information, and needs to be taught both logical and psychological processes for handling it. Two semester-long courses, one in communications, and one in urban affairs, isolate such processes as symbolization, simulation, dreaming, and de-escalating pressure, and teach them in an explicit fashion. At the same time the classes are designed to tie these processes to the amorphous undercurrent of student concerns for self-identity, power, and relationship.

I dropped into a high school communications class one hot day during last summer's field testing, when the teacher was working on "taxonomy of process," or a way of looking at what, why, and how behavior occurs and changes. The purpose of the class was to show the students a simple technique for analyzing their own habitual forms of processing the world around them, and then to show them how they could develop new responses if they wanted to. The class was working in groups of twos, filling in "What Wheels" for each other. One boy in the back was without a partner, so I joined him, and we agreed that I would make a What Wheel for him, and he would make one for me. I drew a circle, filled in the spokes, and wrote down my first impressions of him: "strong, quick, Afro, shy, bright."

The teacher asked us to read each other our What Wheels, select one adjective which interested us most, and ask our partner to draw a "Why Wheel" to explain *why* that adjective was meaningful to him.

Charlie read me his What Wheel—he was perceptive, as students usually are about teachers. Then I read him mine.

"Why'd you write 'shy'? I ain't shy."

"Well, I just met you, so I can't fill out a whole Why Wheel about it. But when I first sat there, I noticed you looked down at your desk instead of up at me. So I just guessed you were shy with strangers—maybe just with strange teachers."

Charlie took his What Wheel from me and looked at it. "You know, that's the truth. I thought nobody, except maybe my mother, knew that about me, but well, it's the truth anyhow."

The murmur of the class's conversation quieted while the teacher told us how to make up "How Wheels" with our partners. We were supposed to write down the range of actions which would either increase or decrease the trait we had been discussing.

"Aw, man, it would be easy to increase being shy," laughed Charlie. "I just wouldn't look at nobody."

"And decreasing it?"

"I'd look at you like I'm looking at you right now," he said, looking me straight in the eye. "And more than that, I'd look at you like that when you first came in here. Teacher, or white man, I wasn't afraid of you; no reason why I should act like I was."

We talked for a while—about my wheels, about the effectiveness of the what, why, how process questions for looking at behavior, and about school. When the bell rang, we shook hands. "See ya around," he said.

"See ya around," I said.

While many teachers have been experimenting

with techniques similar to ours, research psychologists usually have been rather disdainful of the messy problems in the schools. Increasingly, however, psychologists such as David McClelland of Harvard are beginning to work on problems of motivation and attitude in schools. The progression of McClelland's study is a good example of how basic research may be applied to problems in education. McClelland began working on problems of measuring the motivation of rats deprived of food, performed a series of experiments to measure hunger motivation in humans, and then devised a system for measuring "achievement motivation" in men by counting the frequency of its appearance in fantasy images. He defined the need for achievement (n-Ach) as a pattern of thought and fantasy about doing things well, and discovered that those people who had such a pattern were characterized by a preference for moderate risk goals, a desire for immediate feedback on their performance, and a liking for personal responsibility. McClelland reasoned that if a society had a great number of such individuals, the society itself should show outstanding achievement. Twenty years were spent in a mammoth research effort to substantiate his claim that achievement research provided a "factual basis for evaluating theories that explain the rise and fall of civilizations." The next step was to devise educational methods for increasing the achievement motive in people who did not have much of it, and to test out these methods in this country and abroad.

Dr. Alfred Alschuler, director of the Harvard Achievement Motivation Development Project, which is one result of McClelland's research, is in charge of a federally funded five-year research project to assess what factors lead to effective achievement training. The project has devised many classroom techniques for increasing achievement motivation in students, most of them involving experiential learning that takes place in a game situation. I visited one training program for teachers in a nearby city, and sat in on a session that used a contest in making paper airplanes to demonstrate to the teachers how achievement motivation affects their students.

There was a lot of joking around the table, as everyone was a little nervous.

"Now they're going to use the old carrot on us," cracked a little physics teacher sitting on my right.

The head of the math department, an enormous man, smiled broadly, first at the physics teacher, and then at me. "Feeling cut-throat?" he asked.

I didn't say so, but I was, and he knew it. My "n-Ach" was way up. We eyed each other while we set our own quotas for the number of planes we would make.

Dr. Alschuler gave us the start sign. I was making planes feverishly; out of the corner of my eye, I could see the math department head moving more slowly, but doing a better job—the quality control check at the end of the game might go in his favor. The physics teacher was using mass production techniques, making one fold at a time.

At the end of five minutes the game was up, and we were all laughing at the tension it had produced. The physics teacher had more planes than any of us, but his mass production assembly had failed—all the planes were missing one wing. I had the second largest number of planes, but several had sloppy folds and were disqualified.

"Nuts to this," said the physics teacher. "I'm not going to get another heart attack over a bunch of paper airplanes. Next time I'm dropping my quota in half. I'm only going to make six."

I was swearing at myself—I should have been more careful. Next time through the game I would set a slightly lower quota and do a better job.

The math teacher was smiling broadly. He had won.

Later we all talked about our experience in the game and how our own behavior did or did not reflect the characteristics of a high achiever. Did we set moderate risk goals? Did we utilize information on our success or failure? Then we began to dig into the more fundamental value issues that were involved. Suppose that we could use games like the paper plane construction to teach students the characteristics of a high achiever, and through a variety of such exercises could actually train him to think and act as one. Was that a good thing? Did we want to subject our students to the pressure that we had felt? Could we decide that achievement training was good for some students who were not achieving up to our standards, and bad for those who were too competitive? On what basis?

Just as researchers are becoming involved in the practical questions of education, so clinical psychotherapy is getting up off its couch and finding ways to add its skill to solving school problems. Dr. Carl Rogers, founder of client-centered therapy, is presently working with Western Behavioral Sciences Institute and a group of Catholic schools to devise ways to use "sensitivity groups" in the schools. (A "sensitivity group" or "T-group" is composed of about a dozen people who meet for the purpose of giving feedback on how each person's behavior affects the other people in the group.) The National Training Laboratory, an associate of the National Education Association, is now running a year-round series of T-groups and related experiences for teachers and administrators. And in San Diego, child psychiatrist Dr. Harold Bissell and educator Dr. Uvaldo Palomares have set up the Human Development

Training Institute which has written a two-year sequence of lesson plans to improve a primary school child's self-confidence and awareness, and has trained 1,000 teachers to use it.

One of the most eclectic approaches in the clinical tradition is the project run by Dr. George Brown of the University of California at Santa Barbara. Brown's project, sponsored by the Ford Foundation through the ebullient Esalen Institute, utilizes many different approaches, but particularly the theories of Gestalt therapy which attempt to get youth in touch with how they are feeling in the "here and now." With such theoretical orientations in their background, the teachers in Brown's project are encouraged to devise their own techniques to integrate academic with affective or emotional learning in order to achieve a more "humanistic education."

I joined the teachers at one of the monthly meetings where they learn about new ideas, and share with each other the techniques they have developed. Gloria Siemons, a pretty first-grade teacher, was describing an exercise that she had first conducted with the entire class, and then used when one child became angry at another. She lined the class up in two rows on the playground, had them find a partner, put their hands up facing each other, and push.

Push they did, laughing all over the field, especially at their teacher, who was being pushed around in a circle by several of the bigger kids.

Later, when two kids got into an argument at recess, Mrs. Siemons simply asked them: "Are you angry now? Would you like to push?"

"Yes, I'm angry. I'm angry at him."

Both agreed to the contest, pushed for a minute as hard as they could, and then collapsed into each other's arms giggling. Their anger was worked out, but without hurting each other.

"What would happen," I asked Mrs. Siemons, "if one kid pushed another hard enough to hurt him?"

"We have a rule about that. 'It's OK to be angry with someone, and it's OK to push, but it's *not* OK to push him into the rosebush.'"

Good teachers, particularly good first-grade teachers such as Mrs. Siemons, have always responded to the emotional side of their students' lives, and it is precisely this intuitive gift which Dr. Brown is capitalizing on. By systematizing such techniques and relating them to a general theoretical framework, he and the teachers of his staff have begun to generate hundreds of ways to integrate the feelings of students with the regular curriculum taught from kindergarten to high school.

The techniques being developed, the dozens of programs, and the various theories differ in many

respects, but they have several features in common. First, and most important, all of them deal in a very explicit and direct way with the student's feelings, interpersonal relations, or values. It is the fact that they are so explicit and direct which sets them apart from the vague protestations that schools have usually made about this area. While schools were concentrating on math, science, or English, they often ignored or actively suppressed feelings. The new programs make what was covert behavior the subject of overt discussion; they make the implicit explicit. They legitimize feelings, clarify them for the student, and suggest a variety of behaviors which he can use to express them. They do so on the assumption that these feelings exert a powerful effect on a student's behavior, both in the present and in the future. If schools want to influence behavior, then it makes sense to deal directly with its major sources, not just with the binomial theorem, the gerund, or the Seventeenth Amendment.

A factor in the new field which often causes misunderstanding is that most of the programs use non-verbal experiences, either through physical expression and involvement, or through art, sculpture, or music. For the most part, this involvement with the *non*-verbal is not *anti*-verbal or *anti*-intellectual. Non-verbal educational techniques are based on the obvious but little-utilized fact that a child learns most of his emotional response patterns at a very young age—before he can talk. His knowledge of love, rejection, anger, and need does not come through words, but through his physical senses— touch, a flushed face, a gnawing in his stomach. Even later, when he begins to talk, the words he learns are "Mama," "doggie," "see"—words for things and actions, not feelings. Indeed, many children seem entirely unable to give a name to their current feelings—they have been taught how to say "I am bad," but not "I feel bad." Education that deals with feelings is often facilitated by skipping over the verbal labels which have been learned relatively late in life, regaining the other senses, and then reintegrating them with verbal thought and new behaviors.

Another common technique which causes confusion is the reliance of many of the programs on games, dramatic improvisations, and role-playing. Again, though those utilizing the techniques believe in fun and use games, few of them are simply advocating "fun and games." Their interest stems from an insight into the learning process of small children. By playing games—house, fireman, office, war —little children learn what it will be like to be an adult, and begin to develop their own style in that role. But our culture provides few such opportunities for older children or adolescents, even though the society is changing so fast that many of the response patterns they learned as a three-year-old may be no longer relevant, or even dangerous. Games and improvisation allow a simulation of the self. While they are real and produce real emotions, their tightly defined limits provide a way to try out new behavior without taking the full consequences which might occur if the same action were performed in ordinary relationships.

There are answers for questions about non-verbal and gaming emphasis, but there are many other questions which the programs raise for which there are no answers. At best, solutions will come slowly, and that is bound to produce tremendous strain in a time when events wait for no one. Many of these problems are already developing. Though Dr. Alschuler at Harvard and Dr. Willis Harmon at the Stanford Research Institute are both engaged in large surveys to find out what techniques and philosophies are presently being employed in the field, there is still no common theoretical base for the programs, and very little research on their effectiveness. The Achievement Motivation Development Project has by far the most extensive research program, and Dr. Alschuler's experience with it has made him feel strongly about the need for additional evidence before program expansion:

We have very little hard evidence that programs in this new field accomplish much more than natural maturation. We have claims, promises, and fascinating anecdotes. But we should not institute these programs without first using the most sophisticated research techniques we have to improve them and explore their consequences.

In addition to unanswered questions about effectiveness, there are practical limitations to all of the programs. Few have done an adequate job of integrating their material with the usual skills and knowledge that everyone recognizes the schools must continue to teach. No attempt has yet been made to work together with the free-flowing academic programs (such as the Leicestershire movement) which seem natural complements. Though all of the projects I have discussed here stress their responsiveness to student concerns, it is not yet clear how they can do that and yet not be heavily dependent on the skills and personalities of a few teachers like Mrs. Siemons who can both legitimize anger and make the rosebush out of bounds.

Politically, programs with both the potential and the liabilities of these are obvious hot potatoes. It is unclear as yet how projects designed by psychologists will fit in with current efforts toward more community control and what seems to be the resulting concentration on "teaching the basics." Even a mode of politics that is in consonance with the ideals and methods of the new programs is unknown, for the vision they present is often as utopian as that in George Leonard's exciting new book, *Education and Ecstasy*. How to get from here to there without waiting until 2001 is a complex political problem. Suppose, for instance, that a school district decided to adopt an entirely new curriculum and school organization based on the concepts I have been discussing. Would the teachers be able to change? Great care would have to be taken with their feelings and concerns, for not only are they as human as the children, but—as recent events in New York have indicated—they will strike if they feel they are being treated unfairly.

The most fundamental problem, and the one which is likely to get people the most upset, is the ethical question caused by changing the expectations of what schools are for. At present, students go to school to "learn stuff," and though they may expect schools to provide information, they do not expect schools to change them in any fundamental way, or even to offer that opportunity. As long as schools continue to have relatively little explicitly acknowledged impact on the students' values, attitudes, and behaviors, no one is likely to worry much about ethical issues. If schools consciously begin to make important changes in students' lives, people will suddenly become very concerned about what is happening to immature minds that are forced to accept this kind of education for twelve years. They will begin to ask whether there should be compulsory education, or whether students should be free to accept or reject schooling. And they will begin to ask hard questions about what should be taught, and how it should be presented.

If, for instance, all children should be motivated, should they also be "achievement motivated"? At what age? Who decides? And who teaches? What is to stop teachers from working out of their own needs rather than for those of their pupils? Should teachers who share an important confidence have the same legal privilege which a lawyer or a minister has? How can parents and children be assured of the privacy which is their right?

The ethical problems are likely to be compounded by the reporting of the mass media. The new field is peculiarly open to parody ("HARVARD PROF TEACHES PAPER AIRPLANE CONSTRUCTION") and to easy association with the exotic and erotic. (*Life* recently stuck a single misleading paragraph on Brown's project into a long article on Esalen Institute. By far the most arresting thing in the article was a two-page picture spread on a nude sensitivity group that had nothing to do with either Brown's project or Esalen.) Sensational publicity is not what the new field needs. It does need the time, the careful research and planning, and the critical reporting which will allow it to grow or decline on its merits. The alternative is a series of fads, created by ignorance and publicity, and death—after a short and enthusiastic life—in disillusionment.

The new programs are too important to allow that to happen. They are delicate, and they are moving into an area which is fundamentally new, so they can be expected to suffer from the attention they attract, to make mistakes, and to run into blind alleys. If it takes the big curriculum development corporations a million dollars and three years to build a single course in science or social studies, it will be even more difficult to build a fully developed curriculum in a new field. But the effort should be encouraged. For while it may not be novel to assert that a man's feelings are a crucial determinant of his public behavior and private well-being, there is no question about the novelty and significance of school programs that explicitly educate both the feelings and the intellect. Such programs raise many of society's basic questions about purpose and meaning—tough questions which will not be easy to answer. But they also offer a possibility for building a saner world—a world where people are more open about their feelings, careful in their thinking, and responsible in their actions.

Index

Huston, A. C., 176, 180, 183, 187, 197, 487
Huttenlocher, J., 533
Hyman, R., 393

Iconic signs, 267
Id, in adolescence, 319–322
Identification, 123, 128
    developmental, 507–508, 510
    kinds of, 176–177, 190
    study of, 177–180
    with teacher, 497
    theories of learning by, 181–182
Identity, sense of, 295–297 (see also Self-concepts)
    crisis in, 324
Imitation (see also Identification)
    categories of, 189
    mechanisms behind, 197
    of teacher, 497
    tests for, 183–184
Imprinting, 71 (see also Primary socialization)
Improvisation, 592–593
Impulses, defense against, 322
Incidental learning, 114, 115, 118
Incomes, of whites and nonwhites, 275
Individual differences, 60
    in children's learning, 112
    implications for teaching, 515
    in reacting to instruction, 446
Indoor settings, interpersonal spacing in, 260, 262–263
Indulgence in rearing, 81–82
Industry, sense of, 294–295, 305, 307
Infants (see also Newborn infants)
    egocentrism in, 404–405
    first year of, 312–314
    mobiles for reinforcement in, 313–314
    and psychological environment, 246
    sucking and visual stimulation of, 314
Infavoidance in children's texts, 373, 377
Information, nongenetic transmission of, 83–85
Ingle, D. J., 271
In-groups, prohibition on fighting in, 157
Inhelder, B., 406, 421
Inhibition:
    caused by failure, 459
    and guilt, 457–459
    and other threats, 459–460
    peripheral, 15
Inhibitory training of dogs, 76–80
Inhorn, S. L., 57
Initiative, sense of, 293–294
Inoculation, related to infantile stress, 87–88
Instigations, 213
Integrity, sense of, 298–299
Intelligence, 1
    correlates of, 148
    heritability of, 52
    measurement of, 432, 436
    and performance on learning tasks, 116, 117
    and personality factors, 452–464
    race vs. SES as determiner of, 274–276
Intelligence quotient (IQ):
    characteristics leading to change in, 424, 427–428
    genetic determination of, 52
    of the gifted child, 432
    and personality traits, 583
    stability of, 37
Interaction, child-teacher:
    affective, 491–493
    cognitive, 493–495
    evaluative, 493
Interaction analysis, 561, 573
Interethnic differences, 248
    in interpersonal spacing, 260–264

measured by perceptual articulation, 250–252
Internalization, 220
Interpersonal relationships, 127–212
    in the classroom, 229
    as determinants of behavior, 119
    Erikson's use of, 304
    succeeding Freud's prototypes, 301
Interpersonal spacing, 259
    anxiety aroused by, 264
    in various ethnic groups, 260–264
Interviews, with children, 398, 400
Intimacy, sense of, 297
Involvement of mothers of first-borns, 207, 208–209, 211
Irrationalism and existentialism, 33–34
Irwin, O. C., 308, 311
Iscoe, I., 222, 223, 224
Isolation, effects of, 71–73
Israel, subcultures of, 248
It Scale for Children (ITSC), 356–361
Itard, J. M. G., 384
Ivey, S. L., 277

Jackson, D. N., 250
Jackson, P. W., 579
Jackson Laboratory, 69
Jacobsen, C. F., 388
Jacobson, L., 269, 573
Jakobson, R., 21
James, W., 33, 336, 570
Janis, I. L., 540
Japanese, 254–256
Jay, P., 351
Jaynes, J., 166
Jefferson, T., 440
Jeffrey, W. E., 535, 537
Jenkins, D. H., 235
Jenkins, J. J., 91
Jensen, A. R., 52, 268
Jews, spacing patterns of, 260
Joffe, J. M., 166
Johansson, C., 55
Johnson, R., 507
Johnston, M. K., 100, 103
Jones, E., 318, 461, 500
Jones, H. E., 62, 148
Jones, S., 540
Jones, T. M., 86
Jones, V., 370
Joos, M., 420
Jouvet, M., 15, 20
Jung, C. G., 32
Justice, idea of, 144

Kagan, J., 87, 152, 153, 168
    on cognitive style, 393, 396
    on concept of rejection, 15, 16, 18
    on continuity, 36, 37, 39
    correlational analysis used by, 63
    on dependency, 496
    on identification, 176, 181
    on IQ change, 424
    on maternal hostility, 172
    on meaning of behavior, 346, 347, 350, 351
    on prematurity, 275
    on psychological development, 62
    on relativism in psychology, 14
Kahl, J. A., 489
Kalafat, J., 350
Kalhorn, J., 15
Kamenstkaya, A. G., 312
Kanner, L., 384, 385
Kaplan, E., 388
Karas, G. G., 85
Karp, S. A., 37, 248
Kass, E. H., 275
Kästner, E., 467
Katan, A., 319, 321
Katz, D., 52, 378

Katz, R. L., 267
Kaye, H., 309, 312
Keen, R., 172, 312
Keith, R. A., 357
Kelley, C. S., 100, 103
Kelly, W., 469n
Kelson, P., 139
Kendall, J. G., 364
Kennedy, W. A., 272
Kennel dog syndrome, 76–77, 80
Kent, N., 154
Kessen, W., 164, 347
Keys, N., 435
Kibbutz, 248–250
Kinch, J., 44
King, J. A., 70
Klein, E., 456, 458, 461, 462
Klein, M., 181, 458
Klein, R. E., 113
Kleinsasser, A. J., 388
Klineberg, S. L., 499
Klinefelter's syndrome, 57
Klinger, E., 253
Klopfer, P. H., 20
Kluckhohn, C., 523
Knapp, R. H., 436, 437
Knights, R. M., 172
Knobloch, H., 171
Kobasigawa, A., 198
Koch, H. L., 205
Koch, S., 331
Kohlberg, L., 405, 507
Kohler, W., 519
Kohls, M., 249
Kohn, L. G., 142
Koran, M. L., 445n, 446n
Korchin, S. J., 475
Korn, S. J., 386, 387
Kounin, J. S., 387, 491
Kozol, J., 589
Krech, D., 85, 148
Kris, E., 306, 492
Krueski, J., 447
Krushinski, I. V., 73
Kruskal-Wallis technique, 193
Kubany, E. S., 253
Kubie, L. S., 242, 492
Kuhn, T., 10
Kunst, M. S., 458
Kupers, C. J., 198

Labels, self-descriptive, 16–17
Labor:
    psychological variation in, 244–245
    setting of, 245–246
    speed of, 245
Labov, W., 280, 418
Lacey, B., 350
Lacey, J. L., 350
Lahaderne, H. M., 579
Landauer, T. K., 86, 87, 458, 461, 462
Landreth, C., 99
Landy, F., 137, 138
Lane, P. A., 585
Lange-Eichbaum, W., 438
Language, 383
    competence in use of, 420–421
    and mental development, 387
    nature of, 420
    performance characteristics of, 421
    public vs. formal, 418, 421
Language development:
    of preoperational child, 405
    and SES, 266
Lansky, L. M., 356, 357, 358, 360
Lantos, B., 469n
Lasater, T. M., 539, 540, 542
Lashley, K., 387–388
Lasko, J. K., 165, 171, 205
Latané, B., 263
Latency period, 66, 300, 303, 307